New Perspectives on

Microsoft® Access 7 for Windows® 95

COMPREHENSIVE

The New Perspectives Series

The New Perspectives Series consists of texts and technology that teach computer concepts and the programs listed below. Both Windows 3.1 and Windows 95 versions of these programs are available. You can order these New Perspectives texts in many different lengths, software releases, custom-bound combinations, CourseKits™ and Custom Editions® Contact your CTI sales representative or customer service representative for the most up-to-date details.

The New Perspectives Series

Computer Concepts

dBASE®

Internet Using Netscape Navigator™ Software

Lotus® 1-2-3®

Microsoft® Access

Microsoft® Excel

Microsoft® Office Professional

Microsoft® PowerPoint®

Microsoft® Windows® 3.1

Microsoft® Windows® 95

Microsoft® Word

Microsoft® Works

Corel Perfect Office™

Paradox®

Presentations™

Quattro Pro®

WordPerfect®

New Perspectives on Microsoft® Access 7 for Windows® 95

COMPREHENSIVE

Joseph J. Adamski
Grand Valley State University

A DIVISION OF COURSE TECHNOLOGY
ONE MAIN STREET, CAMBRIDGE, MA 02142

an International Thomson Publishing company I(T)P®

Cambridge • Albany • Bonn • Boston • Cincinnati • London • Madrid • Melbourne • Mexico City
New York • Paris • San Francisco • Singapore • Tokyo • Toronto • Washington

New Perspectives on Microsoft Access 7 for Windows 95—Comprehensive is published by CTI.

Managing Editor	Mac Mendelsohn
Series Consulting Editor	Susan Solomon
Senior Editor	Kristen Duerr
Senior Product Manager	Barbara Clemens
Product Manager/Developmental Editor	Rachel Biheller Bunin
Production Editor	Roxanne Alexander
Text and Cover Designer	Ella Hanna
Cover Illustrator	Nancy Nash

For more information contact:

Course Technology
One Main Street
Cambridge, MA 02142

International Thomson Publishing Europe
Berkshire House 168-173
High Holborn
London WCIV 7AA
England

Thomas Nelson Australia
102 Dodds Street
South Melbourne, 3205
Victoria, Australia

Nelson Canada
1120 Birchmount Road
Scarborough, Ontario
Canada M1K 5G4

International Thomson Editores
Campos Eliseos 385, Piso 7
Col. Polanco
11560 Mexico D.F. Mexico

International Thomson Publishing GmbH
Königswinterer Strasse 418
53227 Bonn
Germany

International Thomson Publishing Asia
211 Henderson Road
#05-10 Henderson Building
Singapore 0315

International Thomson Publishing Japan
Hirakawacho Kyowa Building, 3F
2-2-1 Hirakawacho
Chiyoda-ku, Tokyo 102
Japan

ISBN 0-7600-3543-1

Printed in the United States of America

10 9 8 7 6 5 4 3

New Perspectives on

Microsoft® Access 7 for Windows® 95

COMPREHENSIVE

Joseph J. Adamski
Grand Valley State University

A DIVISION OF COURSE TECHNOLOGY
ONE MAIN STREET, CAMBRIDGE, MA 02142

an International Thomson Publishing company I(T)P®

Cambridge • Albany • Bonn • Boston • Cincinnati • London • Madrid • Melbourne • Mexico City
New York • Paris • San Francisco • Singapore • Tokyo • Toronto • Washington

New Perspectives on Microsoft Access 7 for Windows 95—Comprehensive is published by CTI.

Managing Editor	Mac Mendelsohn
Series Consulting Editor	Susan Solomon
Senior Editor	Kristen Duerr
Senior Product Manager	Barbara Clemens
Product Manager/Developmental Editor	Rachel Biheller Bunin
Production Editor	Roxanne Alexander
Text and Cover Designer	Ella Hanna
Cover Illustrator	Nancy Nash

For more information contact:

Course Technology
One Main Street
Cambridge, MA 02142

International Thomson Publishing Europe
Berkshire House 168-173
High Holborn
London WCIV 7AA
England

Thomas Nelson Australia
102 Dodds Street
South Melbourne, 3205
Victoria, Australia

Nelson Canada
1120 Birchmount Road
Scarborough, Ontario
Canada M1K 5G4

International Thomson Editores
Campos Eliseos 385, Piso 7
Col. Polanco
11560 Mexico D.F. Mexico

International Thomson Publishing GmbH
Königswinterer Strasse 418
53227 Bonn
Germany

International Thomson Publishing Asia
211 Henderson Road
#05-10 Henderson Building
Singapore 0315

International Thomson Publishing Japan
Hirakawacho Kyowa Building, 3F
2-2-1 Hirakawacho
Chiyoda-ku, Tokyo 102
Japan

ISBN 0-7600-3543-1

Printed in the United States of America

10 9 8 7 6 5 4 3

From the New Perspectives Series Team

At Course Technology, we have one foot in education and the other in technology. We believe that technology is transforming the way people teach and learn, and we are excited about providing instructors and students with materials that use technology to teach about technology.

Our development process is unparalleled in the higher education publishing industry. Every product we create goes through an exacting process of design, development, review, and testing.

Reviewers give us direction and insight that shape our manuscripts and bring them up to the latest standards. Every manuscript is quality tested. Students whose backgrounds match the intended audience work through every keystroke, carefully checking for clarity and pointing out errors in logic and sequence. Together with our own technical reviewers, these testers help us ensure that everything that carries our name is error-free and easy to use.

We show both *how* and *why* technology is critical to solving problems in college and in whatever field you choose to teach or pursue. Our time-tested, step-by-step instructions provide unparalleled clarity. Examples and applications are chosen and crafted to motivate students.

As the New Perspectives Series team at Course Technology, our goal is to produce the most timely, accurate, creative, and technologically sound product in the entire college publishing industry. We strive for consistent high quality. This takes a lot of communication, coordination, and hard work. But we love what we do. We are determined to be the best. Write us and let us know what you think. You can also e-mail us at NewPerspectives@course.com.

The New Perspectives Series Team

Joseph J. Adamski
Judy Adamski
Roy Ageloff
David Auer
Rachel Bunin
Joan Carey
Patrick Carey
Barbara Clemens
Kim Crowley
Kristen Duerr
Jessica Evans
Kathy Finnegan
Robin Geller
Roger Hayen
Charles Hommel
Chris Kelly
Mary Kemper
Terry Ann Kremer
Melissa Lima
Nancy Ludlow
Mac Mendelsohn
Jennifer Normandin
Dan Oja
June Parsons
Sandra Poindexter
Mark Reimold
Ann Shaffer
Susan Solomon
Christine Spillett
Susanne Walker
John Zeanchock
Beverly Zimmerman
Scott Zimmerman

Preface The New Perspectives Series

What is the New Perspectives Series?

CTI's **New Perspectives Series** is an integrated system of instruction that combines text and technology products to teach computer concepts and microcomputer applications. Users consistently praise this series for innovative pedagogy, creativity, supportive and engaging style, accuracy, and use of interactive technology. The first New Perspectives text was published in January of 1993. Since then, the series has grown to more than 40 titles and has become the best-selling series on computer concepts and microcomputer applications. Others have imitated the New Perspectives features, design, and technologies, but none have replicated its quality and its ability to consistently anticipate and meet the needs of instructors and students.

What is the Integrated System of Instruction?

You hold in your hands a textbook that is one component of an Integrated System of Instruction: text, graphics, video, sound, animation, and simulations that are linked and that provide a flexible, unified, and interactive system to help you teach and help your students learn. Specifically, the *New Perspectives Integrated System of Instruction* consists of five components: a CTI textbook, Course Labs, Course Online, Course Presenter, and Course Test Manager. These components—shown in the graphic on the back cover of this book—have been developed to work together to provide a complete, integrative teaching and learning experience.

How is the New Perspectives Series different from other microcomputer concepts and applications series?

The **New Perspectives Series** distinguishes itself from other series in at least four substantial ways: sound instructional design, consistent quality, innovative technology, and proven pedagogy. The applications texts in this series consist of two or more tutorials, which are based on sound instructional design. Each tutorial is motivated by a realistic case that is meaningful to students. Rather than learn a laundry list of features, students learn the features in the context of solving a problem. This process motivates all concepts and skills by demonstrating to students *why* they would want to know them.

Instructors and students have come to rely on the high quality of the **New Perspectives Series** and to consistently praise its accuracy. This accuracy is a result of CTI's unique multi-step quality assurance process that incorporates student testing at three stages of development, using hardware and software configurations appropriate to the product. All solutions, test questions, and other CourseTools (discussed later in this Preface) are tested using similar procedures. Instructors who adopt this series report that students can work through the tutorials independently, with a minimum of intervention or "damage control" by instructors or staff. This consistent quality has meant that if instructors are pleased with one product from the series, they can rely on the same quality with any other New Perspectives product.

The **New Perspectives Series** also distinguishes itself by its innovative technology. This series innovated Course Labs, truly *interactive* learning applications. These have set the standard for interactive learning.

How do I know that the New Perspectives Series will work?

Some instructors who use this series report a significant difference between how much their students learn and retain with this series as compared to other series. With other series, instructors often find that students can work through the book and do well on homework and tests, but still not demonstrate competency when asked to perform particular tasks outside the context of the text's sample case or project. With the **New Perspectives Series**, however, instructors report that students have a complete, integrative learning experience that stays with them. They credit this high retention and competency to the fact that this series incorporates critical thinking and problem solving with computer skills mastery.

How does this book I'm holding fit into the New Perspectives Series?

New Perspectives microcomputer concepts and applications books are available in the following categories:

Brief books are about 100 pages long and are intended to teach only the essentials. They contain 2 to 4 chapters or tutorials.

Introductory books are about 300 pages long and consist of 6 or 7 chapters or tutorials. An Introductory book is designed for a short course or for a one-term course, used in combination with other Introductory books.

Comprehensive books are about 600 pages long and consist of all of the chapters or tutorials in the Introductory book, plus 3 or 4 more Intermediate chapters or tutorials covering higher-level topics. Comprehensive applications texts include Brief Windows tutorials, the Introductory and Intermediate tutorials, 3 or 4 Additional Cases, and a Reference Section. The book you are holding is a Comprehensive book.

Advanced applications books cover topics similar to those in the Comprehensive books, but in more depth. Advanced books present the most high-level coverage in the series.

Custom Books The New Perspectives Series offers you two ways to customize a New Perspectives text to fit your course exactly: *CourseKits*™, 2 or more texts packaged together in a box, and *Custom Editions*®, your choice of books bound together. Custom Editions offer you unparalleled flexibility in designing your concepts and applications courses. You can build your own book by ordering a combination of titles bound together to cover only the topics you want. Your students save because they buy only the materials they need. There is no minimum order, and books are spiral bound. Both CourseKits and Custom Editions offer significant price discounts. Contact your CTI sales representative for more information.

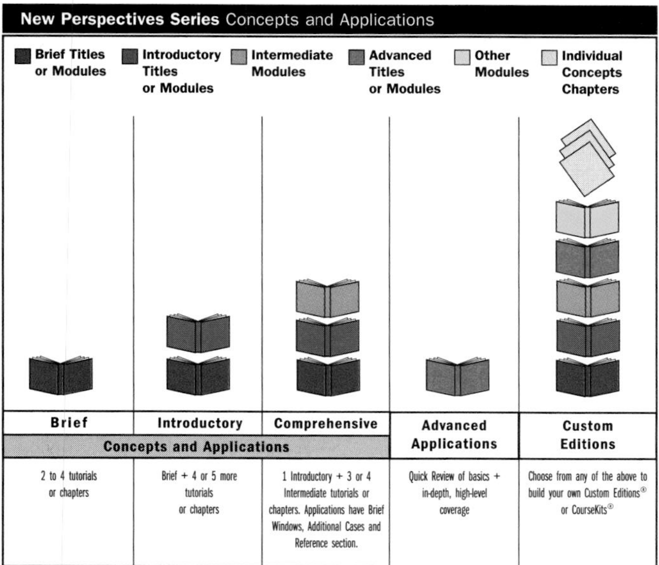

New Perspectives Series Concepts and Applications
Brief Titles or Modules
Introductory Titles or Modules
Intermediate Modules
Advanced Titles or Modules
Other Modules
Individual Concepts Chapters
Brief
Introductory
Comprehensive
Concepts and Applications
Advanced Applications
Custom Editions
2 to 4 tutorials or chapters
Brief + 4 or 5 more tutorials or chapters
1 Introductory + 3 or 4 Intermediate tutorials or chapters. Applications have Brief Windows, Additional Cases and Reference section.
Quick Review of basics + in-depth, high-level coverage
Choose from any of the above to build your own Custom Editions® or CourseKits®

In what kind of course could I use this book?

This book can be used in any course in which you want students to learn all the most important topics of Microsoft Access 7 for Windows 95, including planning, creating, and maintaining Access databases. Students learn how to retrieve information using queries and develop professional-looking reports, as well as create customized forms to access and enter data in a database. Students also learn how to

How do the Windows 95 editions differ from the Windows 3.1 editions?

Larger Page Size If you've used a New Perspectives text before, you'll immediately notice that the book you're holding is larger than the Windows 3.1 series books. We've responded to user requests for a larger page with larger screen shots and associated labels. Look on page AC 12 for an example of how we've made the screen shots easier to read.

Sessions We've divided the tutorials into sessions. Each session is designed to be completed in about 45 minutes to an hour (depending, of course, upon student needs and the speed of your lab equipment). With sessions, learning is broken up into more easily-assimilated chunks. You can more accurately allocate time in your syllabus. Students can better manage the available lab time. Each session begins with a "session box," which quickly describes the skills students will learn in the session. Furthermore, each session is numbered, which makes it easier for you and your students to navigate and communicate about the tutorial. Look on page AC 5 for the session box that opens Session 1.1.

Quick Checks Each session concludes with Quick Checks, meaningful, conceptual questions that test students' understanding of what they learned in the session. Answers to all of the Quick Check questions are at the back of the book preceding the Index. You can find examples of Quick Checks on pages AC 30, AC 48, and AC 115.

New Design We have retained the best of the old design to help students differentiate between what they are to *do* and what they are to *read*. The steps are clearly identified by their shaded background and numbered steps. Furthermore, this new design presents steps and screen shots in a larger, easier to read format. Some good examples of our new design are pages AC 18 and AC 19, and AC 46 and AC 47.

What features are retained in the Windows 95 editions of the New Perspectives Series?

"Read This Before You Begin" Pages These pages are consistent with CTI's unequaled commitment to helping instructors introduce technology into the classroom. Technical considerations and assumptions about software are listed to help instructors save time and eliminate unnecessary aggravation. This book contains two Read This Before You Begin pages, one before the Introductory tutorials on page AC 2, and one before the Intermediate tutorials on page IAC 2.

CASE

Tutorial Case Each tutorial begins with a problem presented in a case that is meaningful to students. The problem turns the task of learning how to use an application into a problem-solving process. The problems increase in complexity with each tutorial. These cases touch on multicultural, international, and ethical issues—so important to today's business curriculum. See page AC 3 for the case that begins Tutorial 1.

1.
2.
3.

Step-by-Step Methodology This unique CTI methodology keeps students on track. They enter data, click buttons, or press keys always within the context of solving the problem posed in the tutorial case. The text constantly guides students, letting them know where they are in the course of solving the problem. In addition, the numerous screen shots include labels that direct students' attention to what they should look at on the screen. On almost every page in this book, you can find an example of how steps, screen shots, and labels work together.

TROUBLE?

TROUBLE? Paragraphs These paragraphs anticipate the mistakes or problems that students are likely to have and help them recover and continue with the tutorial. By putting these paragraphs in the book, rather than in the Instructor's Manual, we facilitate independent learning and free the instructor to focus on substantive conceptual issues rather than on common procedural errors. Two representative examples of Trouble? are on pages AC 9 and AC 12.

Reference Windows Reference Windows appear throughout the text. They are succinct summaries of the most important tasks covered in the tutorials. Reference Windows are specially designed and written so students can refer to them when doing the Tutorial Assignments and Case Problems, and after completing the course. Page AC 10 contains the Reference Window for Exiting Access.

Task Reference The Task Reference is a summary of how to perform common tasks using the most efficient method, as well as references to pages where the task is discussed in more detail. It appears as a table at the end of the book.

Tutorial Assignments, Case Problems, and Lab Assignments Each tutorial concludes with Tutorial Assignments, which provide students with additional hands-on practice of the skills they learned in the tutorial. The Tutorial Assignments are followed by four Case Problems that have approximately the same scope as the tutorial case. In the Windows 95 applications texts, there is always one Case Problem in the book and one in the Instructor's Manual that require students to solve the problem independently, either "from scratch" or with minimum guidance. Finally, if a Course Lab (see next page) accompanies the tutorial, Lab Assignments are included. Look on page AC 30 for the Tutorial Assignments for Tutorial 1. See pages AC 70 through AC 74 for examples of Case Problems. The Lab Assignment for Tutorial 1 is on page AC 31.

Exploration Exercises The Windows environment allows students to learn by exploring and discovering what they can do. Exploration Exercises can be Tutorial Assignments or Case Problems that challenge students, encourage them to explore the capabilities of the program they are using, and extend their knowledge using the online Help facility and other reference materials. Pages AC 157–AC 160 contain Exploration Exercises for Tutorial 4.

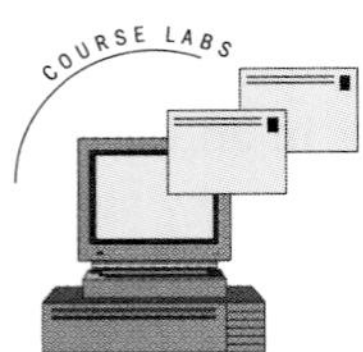

The New Perspectives Series is known for using technology to help instructors teach and administer, and to help students learn. What CourseTools are available with CTI textbooks?

All of the teaching and learning materials available with the New Perspectives Series are known as CourseTools.

Course Labs: Now, Concepts Come to Life Computer skills and concepts come to life with the New Perspectives Course Labs—highly interactive tutorials that combine illustrations, animation, digital images, and simulations. The Labs guide students step-by-step, present them with Quick Check questions, let them explore on their own, test their comprehension, and provide printed feedback. Lab Assignments are included at the end of each relevant chapter or tutorial in the text book. The Lab available with this book and the tutorial in which it appears is:

Databases
Tutorial 1

Course Online: A Website Dedicated to Keeping You and Your Students Up-To-Date When you use a New Perspectives product, you can access CTI's faculty and student sites on the World Wide Web. You can browse the password-protected Faculty Online Companion to obtain all the materials you need to prepare for class, including online Instructors Manuals, Solutions Files, and Student Files. Please see your Instructor's Manual or call your CTI customer service representative for more information. Students may access their Online Companion in the Student Center using the URL **http://coursetools.com**.

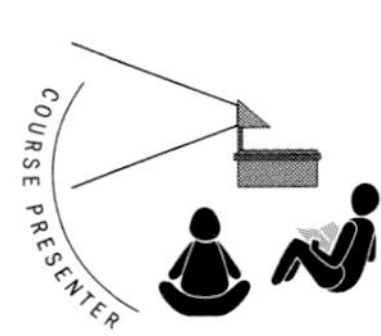

Course Presenter: Ready-Made or Customized Dynamic Presentations
Course Presenter is a CD-ROM-based presentation tool that provides instructors with a wealth of resources for use in the classroom, replacing traditional overhead transparencies with computer-generated screenshows. Course Presenter includes a structured presentation for each tutorial or chapter of the book, and also gives instructors the flexibility to create custom presentations, complete with matching student notes and lecture notes pages. Instructors can also use Course Presenter to create traditional overhead transparencies. Call your CTI Customer Service representative to obtain your copy of Course Presenter.

Course Test Manager: Testing and Practice at the Computer or on Paper
Course Test Manager is cutting-edge Windows-based testing software that helps instructors design and administer pretests, practice tests, and actual examinations. This full-featured program allows students to randomly generate practice tests that provide immediate on-screen feedback and detailed study guides for questions incorrectly answered. On-screen pretests help instructors assess student skills and plan instruction. Instructors can also use Course Test Manager to produce printed tests. Also, students can take tests at the computer that can be automatically graded and can generate statistical information on students' individual and group performance.

What other supplements are available with CTI textbooks?

Instructor's Manual New Perspectives Series Instructor's Manuals are available in printed form and through the CTI Faculty Online Companion on the World Wide Web. (Call your customer service representative for the URL and your password.) Each Instructor's Manual contains the following items:

- Instructor's Notes containing an overview, an outline, technical notes, lecture notes, and an extra case problem for each tutorial.
- *Printed solutions* to all of the Tutorial Assignments, Case Problems, Additional Cases and Lab Assignments.

Solutions Files Solution Files contain every file students are asked to create or modify in the tutorials, Tutorial Assignments, Case Problems and Additional Cases.

Student Files Student Files, containing all of the data that students will use for the tutorials, Tutorial Assignments, Case Problems and Additional Cases, are provided through CTI's online companions, as well as on disk. A Readme file includes technical tips for lab management. See the inside covers of this book and the "Read This Before You Begin" page before Tutorial 1 for more information on Student Files.

Most of the CourseTools and supplements are supplied in a package called an Instructor's Resource Kit. Which CourseTools and supplements are included in the Instructor's Resource Kit for this text book?

You will receive the following items in the Instructor's Resource Kit:

- Instructor's Manual
- Solution Files
- Student Files
- Course Labs
- Course Test Manager Engine and Test Bank

To obtain a copy of the Course Presenter for this textbook, contact your CTI Customer Service Representative.

Acknowledgments

I want to thank Charles Hommel, University of Puget Sound, for his perceptive ideas on Access 7 and database design, devotion to excellence, good humor, and steadfast work in revising this book to meet the Windows 95 standards. Thanks to Nancy Acree for her thorough work on the References section and to Anna Hommel for her help with icons and backups. Thanks to Terry Ann Kremer for her literary contributions and her thoroughness. Special thanks to Rachel Bunin for her tireless editorial work, her guidance in difficult times, and her dedication to bringing out the best book possible.

I also thank the dedicated and enthusiastic Course Technology staff, including Mac Mendelsohn, Managing Editor; Susan Solomon, Series Consulting Editor; Kristen Duerr, Editor; Barbara Clemens, Senior Product Manager; Mark Reimold, Product Manager; and Melissa Lima, Editorial Assistant, for their support. Special thanks to the Course Technology Production staff, including Roxanne Alexander, Production Editor; all the staff at Gex. Thanks go to Jim Valente, Manuscript QA Coordinator, U Jin Wong, Associate QA Manuscript Coordinator, and the student testers Patrick Reilly, Tia McCarthy Alex Turoczi, and Brian McCooey.

Joseph J. Adamski

Table of Contents

INTERMEDIATE TUTORIAL 4

Visual Basic

New Perspectives on

Microsoft® Windows® 95

BRIEF

TUTORIALS

Read This **Before You Begin**

TO THE STUDENT

STUDENT DISKS

To complete the tutorials and Tutorial Assignments, you need a Student Disk. Your instructor will either provide you with a Student Disk or ask you to make your own.

If you are supposed to make your own Student Disk, you will need a blank, formatted high-density disk. Follow the instructions in the section called "Creating Your Student Disk" in Tutorial 2 to use the Make Student Disk program to create your own Student Disk. See the inside front or inside back cover of this book for more information on Student Disk files, or ask your instructor or technical support person for assistance.

COURSE LABS

This book features three interactive Course Labs to help you understand Windows concepts. There are Lab Assignments at the end of each tutorial that relate to these Labs. To start a Lab, click the Start button on the Windows 95 taskbar, point to Programs, point to CTI Windows 95 Applications, point to Windows 95 New Perspectives Brief, and click the name of the Lab you want to use.

USING YOUR OWN COMPUTER

If you are going to work through this book using your own computer, you need:

- **Computer System** Windows 95 must be installed on your computer. This book assumes a complete installation of Windows 95.
- **Student Disk** Ask your instructor or lab manager for details on how to get the Student Disk. You will not be able to complete the tutorials or exercises in this book using your own computer until you have the Student Disk. The student files may also be obtained electronically over the Internet. See the inside front or inside back cover of this book for more details.
- **Course Labs** See your instructor or technical support person to obtain the Course Lab software for use on your own computer.

TO THE INSTRUCTOR

To complete the tutorials and Tutorial Assignments in this book, your students must use a set of files on a Student Disk. The Instructor's Resource Kit for this book includes either two Student Files Setup Disks or a CD-ROM containing the student disk setup program. Follow the instructions on the disk label or in the Readme file to install the Make Student Disk program onto your server or standalone computers. Your students can then use the Windows 95 Start menu to run the program that will create their Student Disk. Tutorial 2 contains steps that instruct your students on how to generate student disks.

If you prefer to provide Student Disks rather than letting students generate them, you can run the Make Student Disk program yourself following the instructions in Tutorial 2.

COURSE LAB SOFTWARE

This book features three online, interactive Course Labs that introduce basic Windows concepts. The Instructor's Resource Kit for this book contains the Lab software either on four Course Labs Setup Disks or on a CD-ROM. Follow the instructions on the disk label or in the Readme file to install the Lab software on your server or standalone computers. Refer also to the Readme file for essential technical notes related to running the labs in a multiuser environment.
Once you have installed the Course Lab software, your students can start the Labs from the Windows 95 desktop by clicking the Start button on the Windows 95 taskbar, pointing to Programs, pointing to CTI Windows 95 Applications, pointing to Windows 95 New Perspectives Brief, and then clicking the name of the Lab they want to use.

CT LAB SOFTWARE AND STUDENT FILES

You are granted a license to copy the Student Files and Course Labs to any computer or computer network used by students who have purchased this book.

TUTORIAL 1

Exploring the Basics

Investigating the Windows 95 Operating System in the Computer Lab

OBJECTIVES

In this tutorial you will learn to:

- Identify the controls on the Windows 95 desktop
- Use the Windows 95 Start button to run software programs
- Identify and use the controls in a window
- Switch between programs using the taskbar
- Use Windows 95 controls such as menus, toolbars, list boxes, scroll bars, radio buttons, tabs, and check boxes

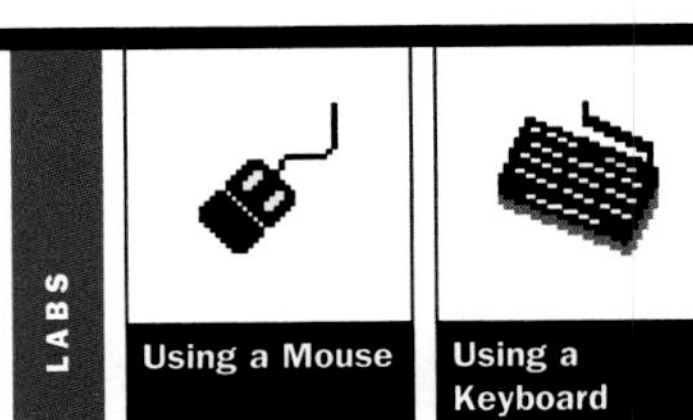

CASE

Your First Day in the Lab

You walk into the computer lab and sit down at a desk. There's a computer in front of you, and you find yourself staring dubiously at the stack of software manuals. Where to start? As if in answer to your question, your friend Steve Laslow appears.

Gesturing to the stack of manuals, you tell Steve that you were just wondering where to start.

"You start with the operating system," says Steve. Noticing your slightly puzzled look, Steve explains that the **operating system** is software that helps the computer carry out basic operating tasks such as displaying information on the computer screen and saving data on your disks. Your computer uses the **Microsoft Windows 95** operating system—Windows 95, for short.

Steve tells you that Windows 95 has a "gooey" or **graphical user interface (GUI)**, which uses pictures of familiar objects, such as file folders and documents, to represent a desktop on your screen. Microsoft Windows 95 gets its name from the rectangular-shaped work areas, called "windows," that appear on your screen.

Steve continues to talk as he sorts through the stack of manuals on your desk. He says there are two things he really likes about Windows 95. First, lots of software is available for computers that have the Windows 95 operating system and all this software has a standard graphical user interface. That means once you have learned how to use one Windows software package, such as word-processing software, you are well on your way to understanding how to use other Windows software. Second, Windows 95 lets you use more than one software package at a time, so you can easily switch between your word-processing software and your appointment book software, for example. All in all, Windows 95 makes your computer an effective and easy-to-use productivity tool.

Steve recommends that you get started right away by using some tutorials that will teach you the skills essential for using Microsoft Windows 95. He hands you a book and assures you that everything on your computer system is set up and ready to go.

You mention that last summer you worked in an advertising agency where the employees used something called Windows 3.1. Steve explains that Windows 3.1 is an earlier version of the Windows operating system. Windows 95 and Windows 3.1 are similar, but Windows 95 is more powerful and easier to use. Steve says that as you work through the tutorials you will see notes that point out the important differences between Windows 95 and Windows 3.1.

Steve has a class, but he says he'll check back later to see how you are doing.

Using the Tutorials Effectively

These tutorials will help you learn about Windows 95. The tutorials are designed to be used at a computer. Each tutorial is divided into sessions. Watch for the session headings, such as Session 1.1 and Session 1.2. Each session is designed to be completed in about 45 minutes, but take as much time as you need. It's also a good idea to take a break between sessions.

Before you begin, read the following questions and answers. They are designed to help you use the tutorials effectively.

Where do I start?

Each tutorial begins with a case, which sets the scene for the tutorial and gives you background information to help you understand what you will be doing in the tutorial. Read the case before you go to the lab. In the lab, begin with the first session of the tutorial.

How do I know what to do on the computer?

Each session contains steps that you will perform on the computer to learn how to use Windows 95. Read the text that introduces each series of steps. The steps you need to do at a computer are numbered and are set against a color background. Read each step carefully and completely before you try it.

How do I know if I did the step correctly?

As you work, compare your computer screen with the corresponding figure in the tutorial. Don't worry if your screen display is somewhat different from the figure. The important parts of the screen display are labeled in each figure. Check to make sure these parts are on your screen.

What if I make a mistake?

Don't worry about making mistakes—they are part of the learning process. Paragraphs labeled "TROUBLE?" identify common problems and explain how to get back on track. Follow the steps in a TROUBLE? paragraph *only* if you are having the problem described. If you run into other problems:

- Carefully consider the current state of your system, the position of the pointer, and any messages on the screen.
- Complete the sentence, "Now I want to...." Be specific, because you are identifying your goal.
- Develop a plan for accomplishing your goal, and put your plan into action.

How do I use the Reference Windows?

Reference Windows summarize the procedures you learn in the tutorial steps. Do not complete the actions in the Reference Windows when you are working through the tutorial. Instead, refer to the Reference Windows while you are working on the assignments at the end of the tutorial.

How can I test my understanding of the material I learned in the tutorial?

At the end of each session, you can answer the Quick Check questions. The answers for the Quick Checks are at the end of the book.

After you have completed the entire tutorial, you should complete the Tutorial Assignments. The Tutorial Assignments are carefully structured so you will review what you have learned and then apply your knowledge to new situations.

What if I can't remember how to do something?

You should refer to the Task Reference at the end of the book; it summarizes how to accomplish commonly performed tasks.

What are the 3.1 Notes?
The 3.1 Notes are helpful if you have used Windows 3.1. The notes point out the key similarities and differences between Windows 3.1 and Windows 95.

What are the Interactive Labs, and how should I use them?
Interactive Labs help you review concepts and practice skills that you learn in the tutorial. Lab icons at the beginning of each tutorial and in the margins of the tutorials indicate topics that have corresponding Labs. The Lab Assignments section includes instructions for how to use each Lab.

Now that you understand how to use the tutorials effectively, you are ready to begin.

SESSION 1.1

In this session, in addition to learning basic Windows terminology, you will learn how to use a mouse, to start and stop a program, and to use more than one program at a time. With the skills you learn in this session, you will be able to use Windows 95 to start software programs.

Starting Windows 95

Windows 95 automatically starts when you turn on the computer. Depending on the way your computer is set up, you might be asked to enter your user name and password. If prompted to do so, type your assigned user name and press the Enter key. Then type your password and press the Enter key to continue.

To start Windows 95:

1. Turn on your computer.

TROUBLE? If the Welcome to Windows 95 box appears on your screen, press the Enter key to close it.

The Windows 95 Desktop

In Windows terminology, the screen represents a **desktop**—a workspace for projects and the tools needed to manipulate those projects. Look at your screen display and locate the objects labeled in Figure 1-1 on the following page.

Because it is easy to customize the Windows environment, your screen might not look exactly the same as Figure 1-1. You should, however, be able to locate objects on your screen similar to those in Figure 1-1.

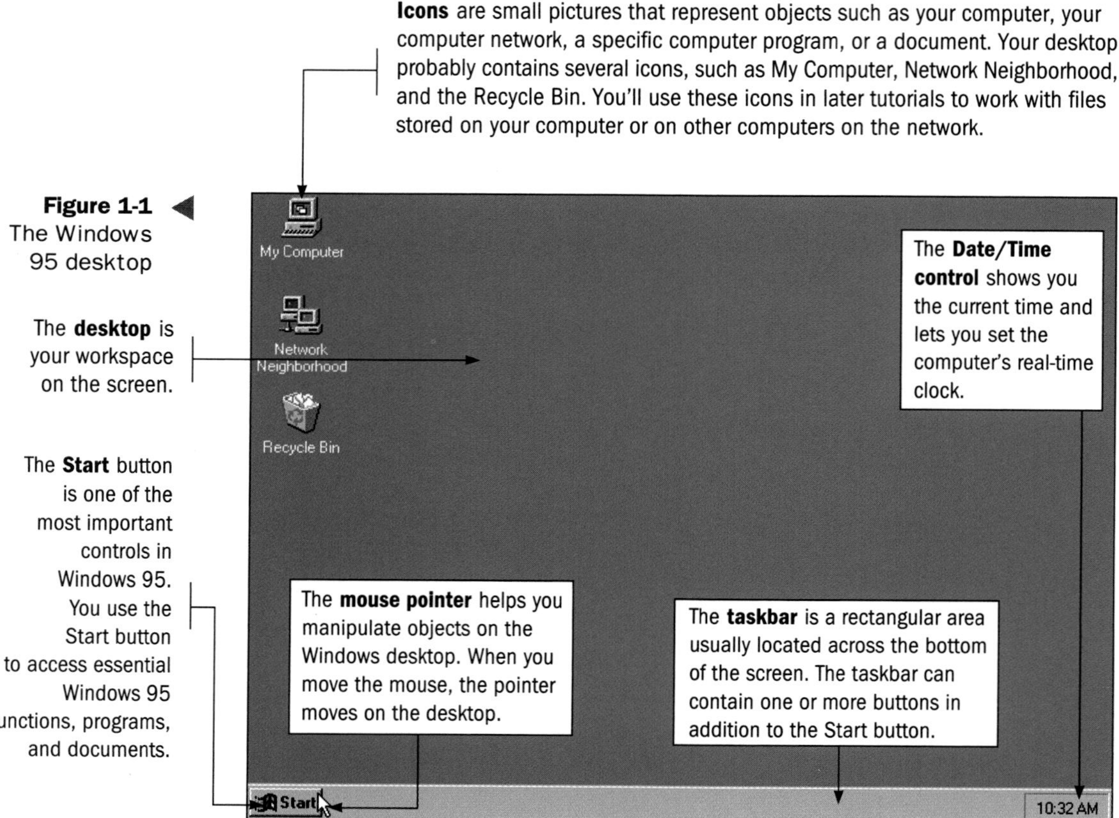

Icons are small pictures that represent objects such as your computer, your computer network, a specific computer program, or a document. Your desktop probably contains several icons, such as My Computer, Network Neighborhood, and the Recycle Bin. You'll use these icons in later tutorials to work with files stored on your computer or on other computers on the network.
The **desktop** is your workspace on the screen.
The **Start** button is one of the most important controls in Windows 95. You use the Start button to access essential Windows 95 functions, programs, and documents.
My Computer
Network Neighborhood
Recycle Bin
The **Date/Time control** shows you the current time and lets you set the computer's real-time clock.
The **mouse pointer** helps you manipulate objects on the Windows desktop. When you move the mouse, the pointer moves on the desktop.
The **taskbar** is a rectangular area usually located across the bottom of the screen. The taskbar can contain one or more buttons in addition to the Start button.
Start
10:32 AM

Figure 1-1 The Windows 95 desktop

TROUBLE? If the screen goes blank or starts to display a moving design, press any key to restore the image.

Using the Mouse

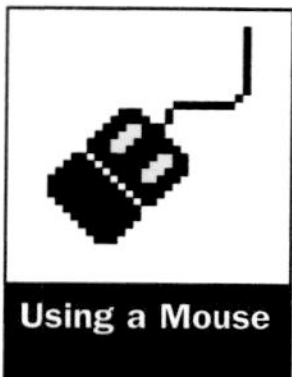

A **mouse**, like those shown in Figure 1-2, is a pointing device that helps you interact with objects on the screen. In Windows 95 you need to know how to use the mouse to point, click, and drag. In this session you will learn about pointing and clicking. In Session 1.2 you will learn how to use the mouse to drag objects.

You can also interact with objects by using the keyboard; however, the mouse is much more convenient for most tasks, so the tutorials in this book assume you are using one.

Pointing

The **pointer**, or **mouse pointer**, is a small object that moves on the screen when you move the mouse. The pointer is usually shaped like an arrow. As you move the mouse on a flat surface, the pointer on the screen moves in the direction corresponding to the movement of the mouse. The pointer sometimes changes shape depending on where it is on the screen or the action the computer is completing.

Find the arrow-shaped pointer on your screen. If you do not see the pointer, move your mouse until the pointer comes into view.

Figure 1-2 The mouse

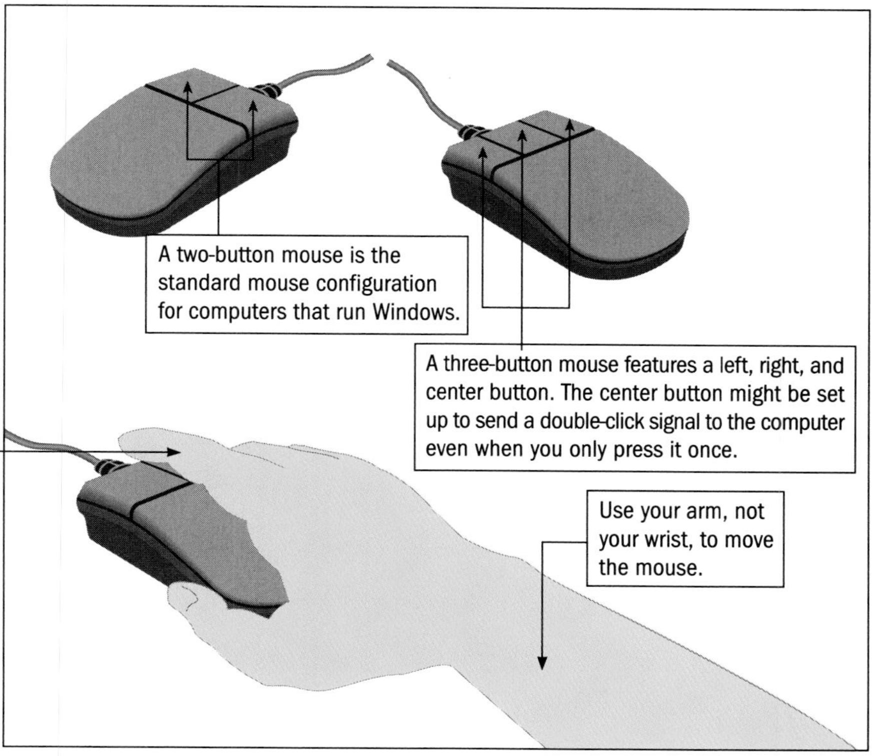

To hold the mouse, place your forefinger over the left mouse button. Place your thumb on the left side of the mouse. Your ring and small fingers should be on the right side of the mouse.

A two-button mouse is the standard mouse configuration for computers that run Windows.
A three-button mouse features a left, right, and center button. The center button might be set up to send a double-click signal to the computer even when you only press it once.
Use your arm, not your wrist, to move the mouse.

Basic "mousing" skills depend on your ability to position the pointer. You begin most Windows operations by positioning the pointer over a specific part of the screen. This is called **pointing**.

To move the pointer:

1. Position your right index finger over the left mouse button, as shown in Figure 1-2. Lightly grasp the sides of the mouse with your thumb and little finger.

   TROUBLE? If you want to use the mouse with your left hand, ask your instructor or technical support person to help you use the Control Panel to change the mouse settings to swap the left and right mouse buttons. Be sure you find out how to change back to the right-handed mouse setting, so you can reset the mouse each time you are finished in the lab.

2. Locate the arrow-shaped pointer on the screen.
3. Move the mouse and watch the movement of the pointer.

If you run out of room to move your mouse, lift the mouse and move it to a clear area on your desk, then place the mouse back on the desk. Notice that the pointer does not move when the mouse is not in contact with the desk.

When you position the mouse pointer over certain objects, such as the objects on the taskbar, a "tip" appears. These "tips" are called **ToolTips**, and they tell you the purpose or function of an object.

To view ToolTips:

1. Use the mouse to point to the **Start** button Start. After a few seconds, you see the tip "Click here to begin" as shown in Figure 1-3 on the following page.

Figure 1-3
Viewing ToolTips

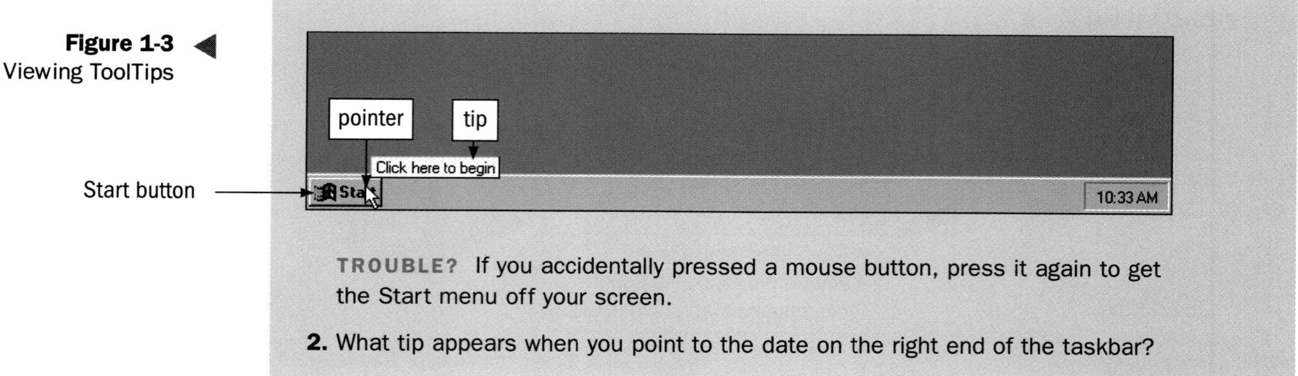

TROUBLE? If you accidentally pressed a mouse button, press it again to get the Start menu off your screen.

2. What tip appears when you point to the date on the right end of the taskbar?

Clicking

3.1 NOTE

Windows 3.1 users frequently double-click the mouse to accomplish tasks. Double-clicking means pressing the mouse button twice in rapid succession. Many people had trouble learning how to double-click, so Windows 95 does not require double-clicking.

When you press a mouse button and immediately release it, it is called **clicking**. Clicking the mouse selects an object on the desktop. *You usually click the left mouse button, so* unless the instructions tell you otherwise, always click the left mouse button.

Windows 95 shows you which object is selected by highlighting it, usually by changing the object's color, putting a box around it, or making the object appear to be pushed in, as shown in Figure 1-4.

Figure 1-4
Selected objects

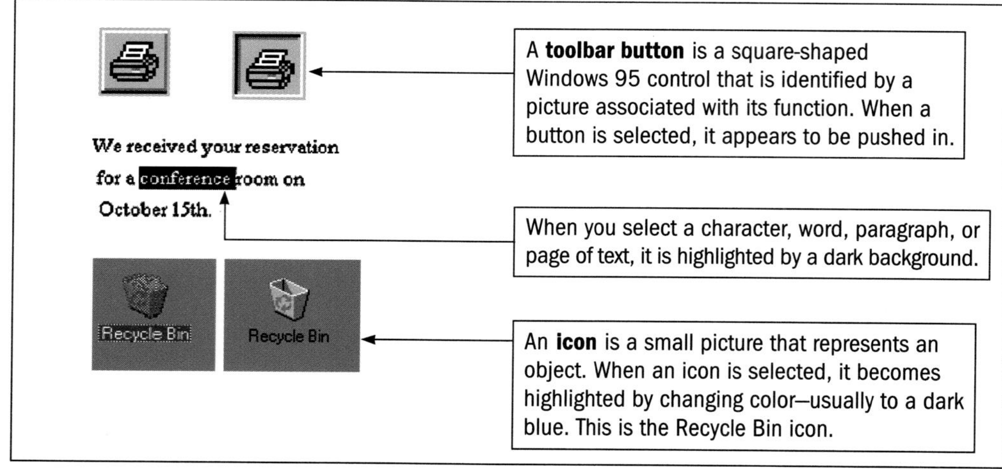

A **toolbar button** is a square-shaped Windows 95 control that is identified by a picture associated with its function. When a button is selected, it appears to be pushed in.
We received your reservation for a conference room on October 15th.
When you select a character, word, paragraph, or page of text, it is highlighted by a dark background.
Recycle Bin
Recycle Bin
An **icon** is a small picture that represents an object. When an icon is selected, it becomes highlighted by changing color—usually to a dark blue. This is the Recycle Bin icon.

To select the Recycle Bin icon:

1. Position the pointer over the **Recycle Bin** icon.
2. Click the mouse button and notice how the color of the icon changes to show that it is selected.

Starting and Closing a Program

The software you use is sometimes referred to as a program or an application. To use a program, such as a word-processing program, you must first start it. With Windows 95 you start a program by clicking the Start button. The Start button displays a menu.

A **menu** is a list of options. Windows 95 has a **Start menu** that provides you with access to programs, data, and configuration options. One of the Start menu's most important functions is to let you start a program.

The Reference Window below explains how to start a program. Don't do the steps in the Reference Window now; they are for your later reference.

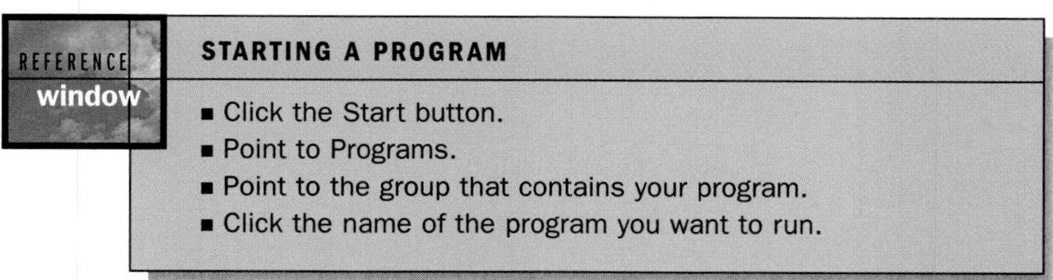
REFERENCE window

STARTING A PROGRAM

- Click the Start button.
- Point to Programs.
- Point to the group that contains your program.
- Click the name of the program you want to run.

3.1 NOTE

WordPad is similar to Write in Windows 3.1.

Windows 95 includes an easy-to-use word-processing program called WordPad. Suppose you want to start the WordPad program and use it to write a letter or report.

To start the WordPad program from the Start menu:

1. Click the **Start** button [Start] as shown in Figure 1-5. A menu appears.

Figure 1-5 ◀ Starting the WordPad program

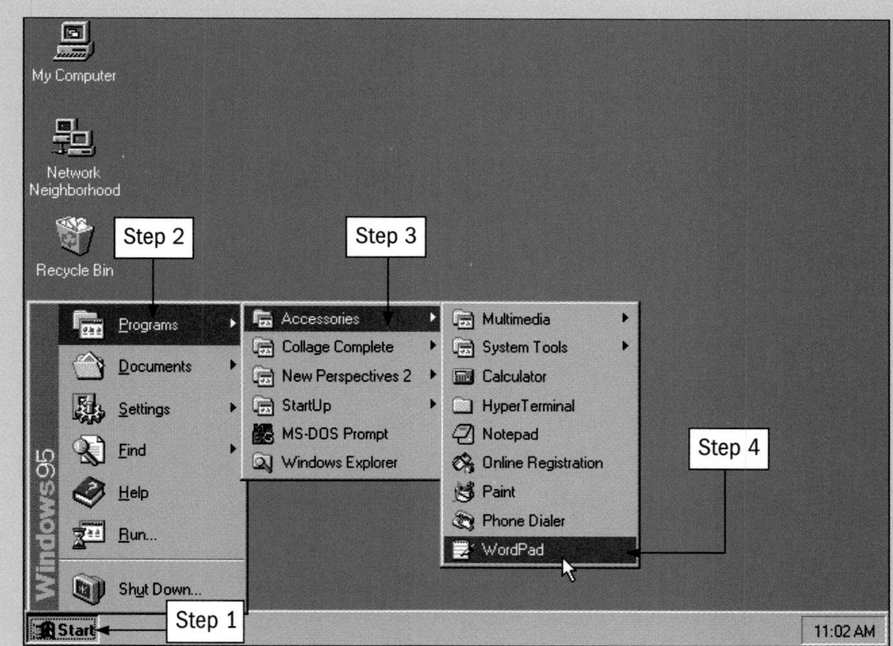

2. Point to **Programs**. After a short pause, the next menu appears.

   TROUBLE? If you don't get the correct menu, go back and point to the correct menu option.

3. Point to **Accessories**. Another menu appears.

4. Click **WordPad**. Make sure you can see the WordPad program as shown in Figure 1-6 on the following page.

Figure 1-6 The WordPad program

WordPad program window

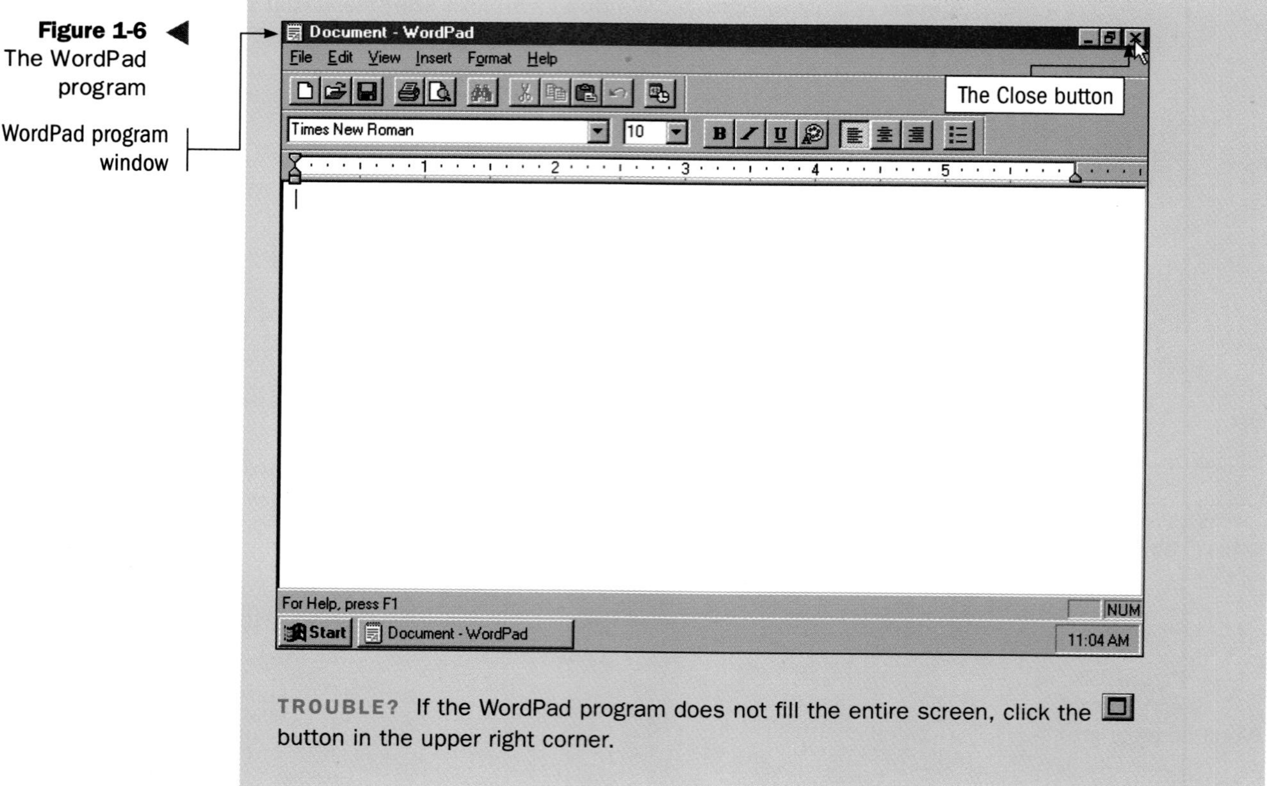

TROUBLE? If the WordPad program does not fill the entire screen, click the [maximize] button in the upper right corner.

3.1 NOTE

As with Windows 3.1, in Windows 95 you can also exit a program using the Exit option from the File menu.

When you are finished using a program, the easiest way to return to the Windows 95 desktop is to click the Close button [X].

To exit the WordPad program:

1. Click the **Close** button [X]. See Figure 1-6. You will be returned to the Windows 95 desktop.

Running More than One Program at the Same Time

3.1 NOTE

Paint in Windows 95 is similar to Paintbrush in WIndows 3.1.

One of the most useful features of Windows 95 is its ability to run multiple programs at the same time. This feature, known as **multi-tasking**, allows you to work on more than one task at a time and to quickly switch between tasks. For example, you can start WordPad and leave it running while you then start the Paint program.

To run WordPad and Paint at the same time:

1. Start WordPad.

   TROUBLE? You learned how to start WordPad earlier in the tutorial: Click the Start button, point to Programs, point to Accessories, and then click WordPad.

2. Now you can start the Paint program. Click the **Start** button [Start] again.
3. Point to **Programs**.
4. Point to **Accessories**.
5. Click **Paint**. The Paint program appears as shown in Figure 1-7. Now two programs are running at the same time.

TROUBLE? If the Paint program does not fill the entire screen, click the button in the upper right corner.

Figure 1-7 The Paint Program

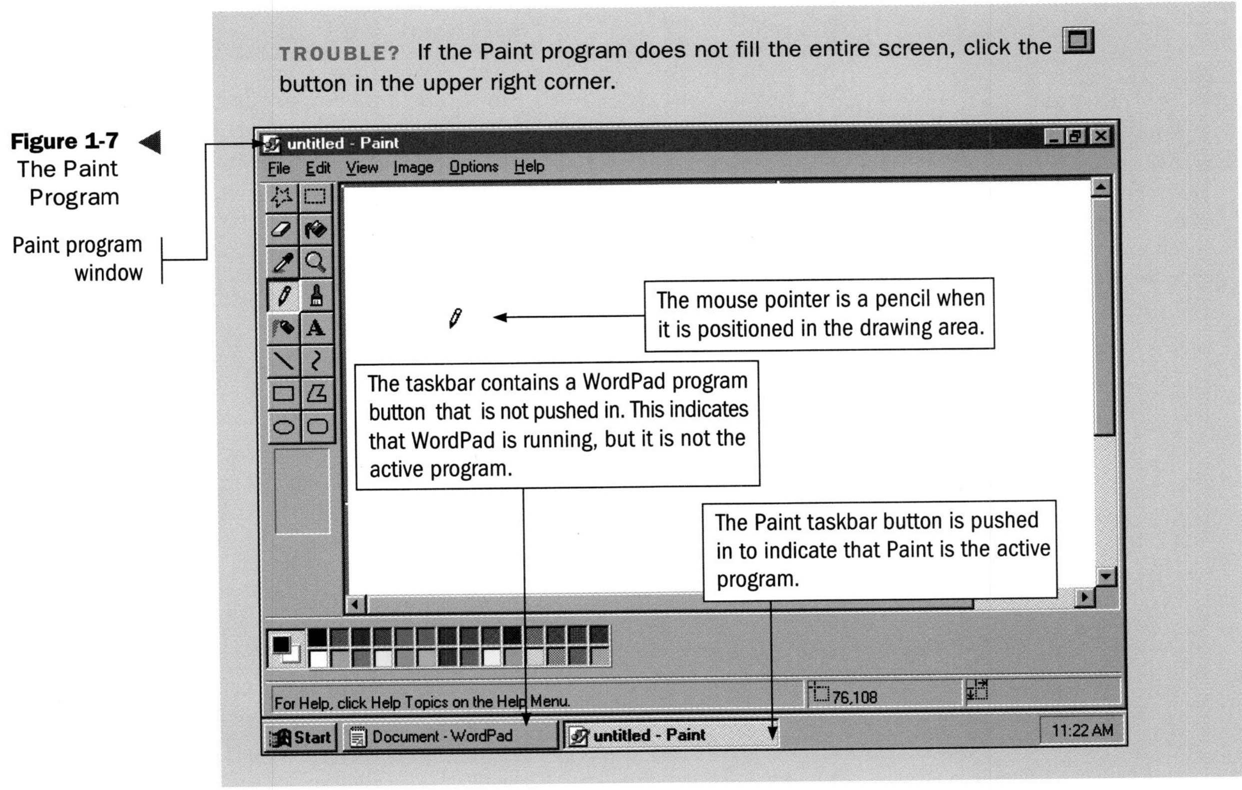

The mouse pointer is a pencil when it is positioned in the drawing area.

3.1 NOTE

With Windows 3.1, some users had difficulty finding program windows on the desktop. The buttons on the Windows 95 taskbar make it much easier to keep track of which programs are running.

What happened to WordPad? The WordPad button is still on the taskbar, so even if you can't see it, WordPad is still running. You can imagine that it is stacked behind the Paint program, as shown in Figure 1-8.

Figure 1-8 Programs stacked on top of a desk

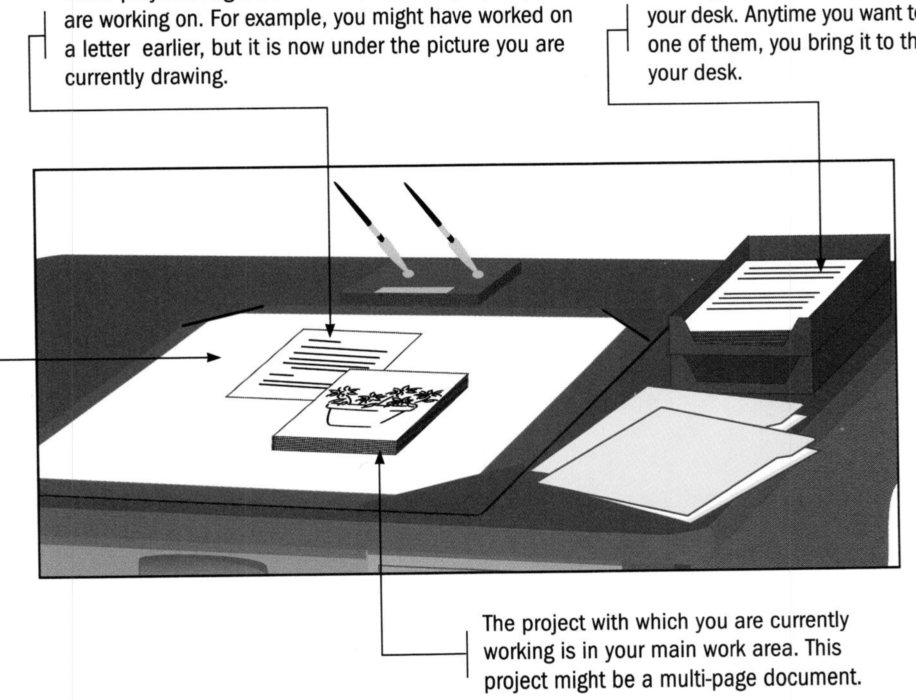

Other projects might be hidden under the project you are working on. For example, you might have worked on a letter earlier, but it is now under the picture you are currently drawing.
You might keep other projects handy on your desk. Anytime you want to work with one of them, you bring it to the center of your desk.
Think of your screen as the main work area of your desk.
The project with which you are currently working is in your main work area. This project might be a multi-page document.

Switching Between Programs

3.1 NOTE

In Windows 95, you can still use Alt-Tab to switch between programs. You can also click any open window to switch to it.

Although Windows 95 allows you to run more than one program, only one program at a time is active. The **active** program is the program with which you are currently working. The easiest way to switch between programs is to use the buttons on the taskbar.

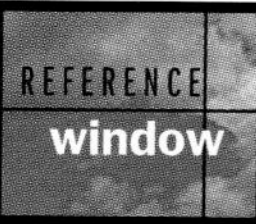

SWITCHING BETWEEN PROGRAMS

- Click the taskbar button that contains the name of the program to which you want to switch.

To switch between WordPad and Paint:

1. Click the button labeled **Document - WordPad** on the taskbar. The Document - WordPad button now looks like it has been pushed in to indicate it is the active program.
2. Next, click the button labeled **untitled - Paint** on the taskbar to switch to the Paint program.

Closing WordPad and Paint

It is good practice to close each program when you are finished using it. Each program uses computer resources such as memory, so Windows 95 works more efficiently when only the programs you need are open.

To close WordPad and Paint:

1. Click the **Close** button for the Paint program. The button labeled "untitled - Paint" disappears from the taskbar.
2. Click the **Close** button for the WordPad program. The WordPad button disappears from the taskbar, and you return to the Windows 95 desktop.

Shutting Down Windows 95

It is very important to shut down Windows 95 before you turn off the computer. If you turn off your computer without correctly shutting down, you might lose data and damage your files.

To shut down Windows 95:

1. Click the **Start** button on the taskbar to display the Start menu.
2. Click the **Shut Down** menu option to display the Shut Down Windows dialog box.
3. Make sure the **Shut down the computer?** option is selected.
4. Click the **Yes** button.
5. Wait until you see a message indicating it is safe to turn off your computer, then switch off your computer.

You should typically use the option "Shut down the computer?" when you want to turn off your computer. However, other shut-down options are available. For example, your school might prefer that you select the option to "Close all programs and log on as a different user." This option logs you out of Windows 95, leaves the computer turned on, and allows another user to log on without restarting the computer. Check with your instructor or technical support person for the preferred method for your school's computer lab.

Quick Check

1 Label the components of the Windows 95 desktop in the figure below:

Figure 1-9

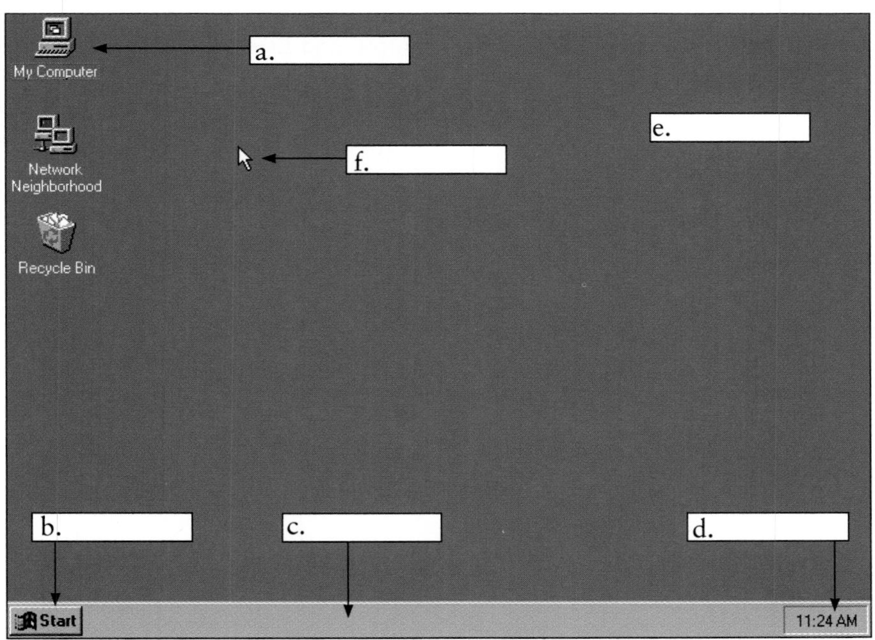

2 The ____________ feature of Windows 95 allows you to run more than one program at a time.

3 The ____________ is a list of options that provides you with access to programs, data, and configuration options.

4 What should you do if you are trying to move the pointer to the left edge of your screen, but your mouse runs into the keyboard?

5 Windows 95 shows you that an icon is selected by ____________ it.

6 Even if you can't see a program, it might be running. How can you tell if a program is running?

7 Why is it good practice to close each program when you are finished using it?

8 Why do you need to shut down Windows 95 before you turn off your computer?

SESSION 1.2

In this session you will learn how to use many of the Windows 95 controls to manipulate windows and programs. You will learn how to change the size and shape of a window and to move a window so that you can customize your screen-based workspace. You will also learn how to use menus, dialog boxes, tabs, buttons, and lists to specify how you want a program to carry out a task.

Anatomy of a Window

When you run a program in Windows 95, it appears in a window. A **window** is a rectangular area of the screen that contains a program or data. A window also contains controls for manipulating the window and using the program. WordPad is a good example of how a window works.

Windows, spelled with an uppercase "W," is the name of the Microsoft operating system. The word "window" with a lowercase "w" refers to one of the rectangular windows on the screen.

To look at window controls:

1. Make sure Windows 95 is running and you are at the Windows 95 desktop screen.
2. Start WordPad.

   TROUBLE? To start WordPad, click the Start button, point to Programs, point to Accessories, and then click WordPad.
3. Make sure WordPad takes up the entire screen.

   TROUBLE? If WordPad does not take up the entire screen, click the button in the upper right corner.
4. On your screen, identify the controls labeled in Figure 1-10.

Figure 1-10 Window controls

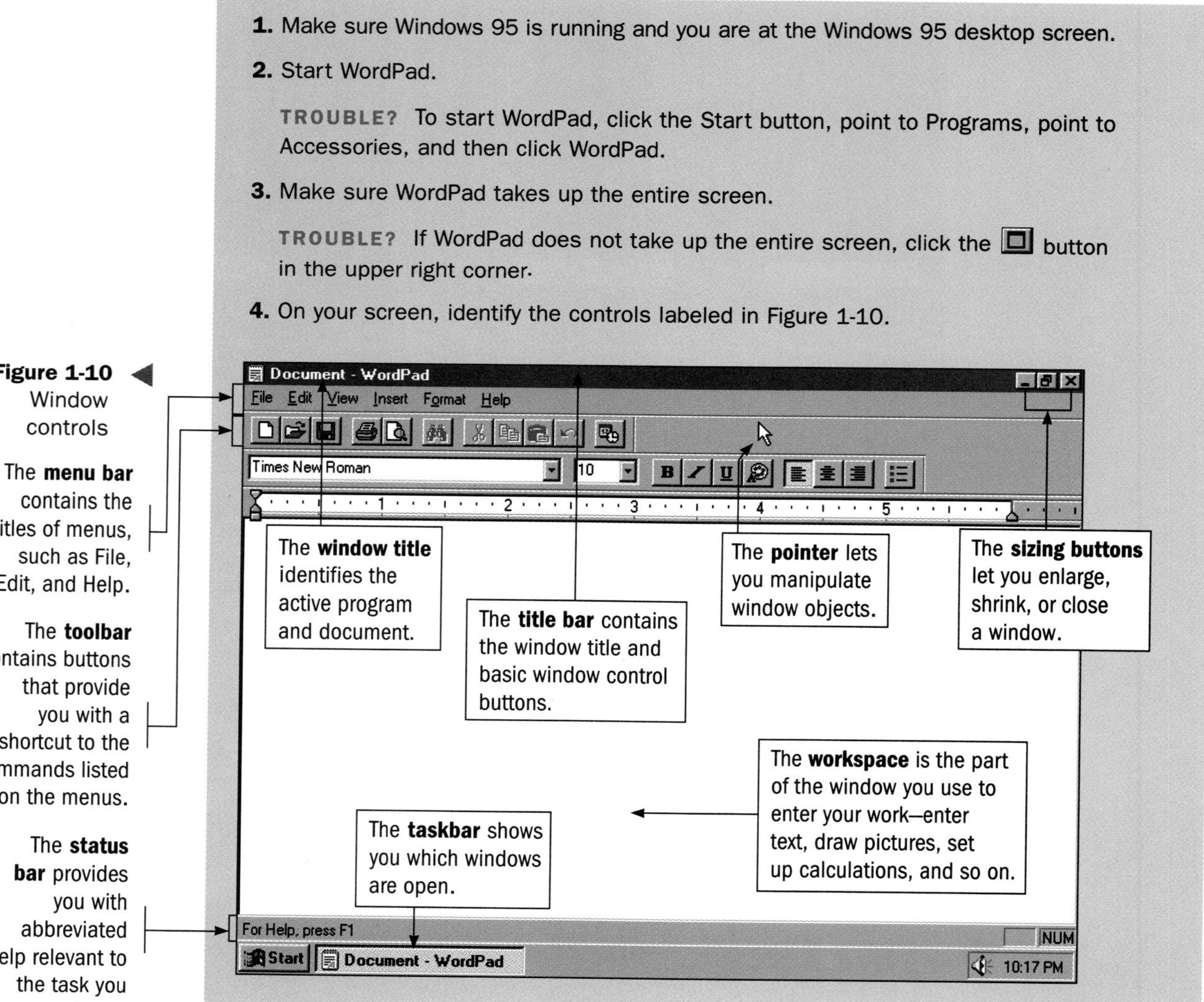

Document - WordPad
File Edit View Insert Format Help
Times New Roman
10
For Help, press F1
NUM
Start
Document - WordPad
10:17 PM
The **window title** identifies the active program and document.
The **title bar** contains the window title and basic window control buttons.
The **pointer** lets you manipulate window objects.
The **sizing buttons** let you enlarge, shrink, or close a window.
The **workspace** is the part of the window you use to enter your work—enter text, draw pictures, set up calculations, and so on.
The **taskbar** shows you which windows are open.
The **menu bar** contains the titles of menus, such as File, Edit, and Help.
The **toolbar** contains buttons that provide you with a shortcut to the commands listed on the menus.
The **status bar** provides you with abbreviated help relevant to the task you are doing.

Manipulating a Window

There are three buttons located on the right side of the title bar. You are already familiar with the Close button. The Minimize button hides the window. The other button either maximizes the window or restores it to a predefined size. Figure 1-11 shows how these buttons work.

Figure 1-11 Minimize, Maximize and Restore buttons

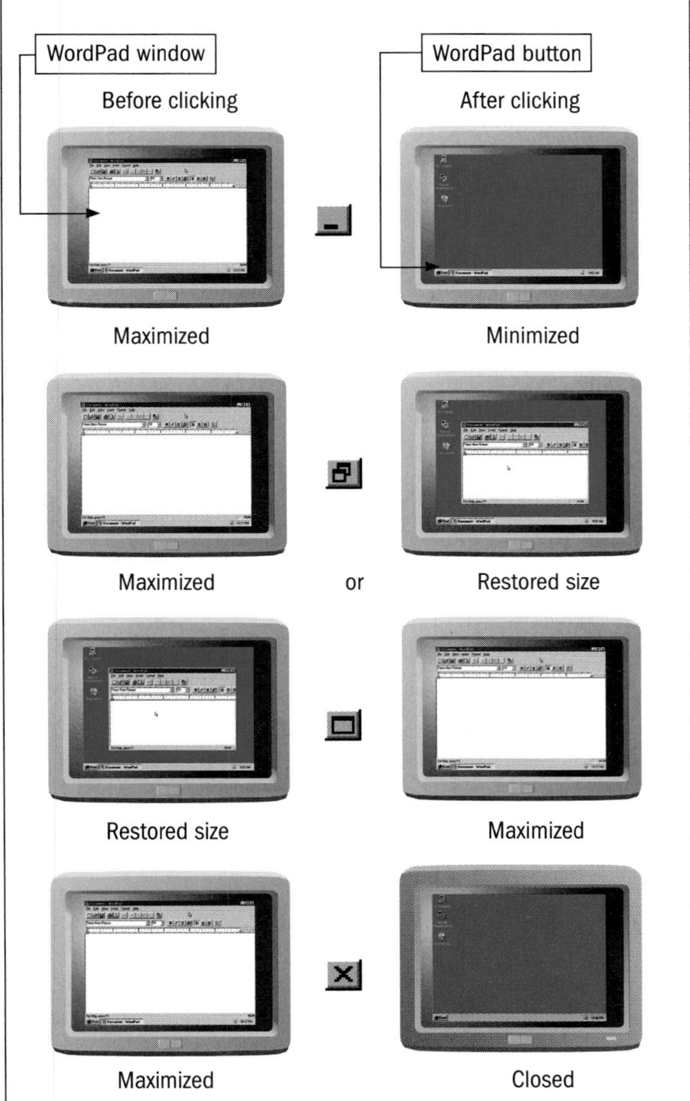

The **Minimize button** shrinks the window, so you only see its button on the taskbar.

The middle button appears as a **Restore button** or a **Maximize button.** When the window is maximized, the Restore button appears. It can be used to reduce the size of the window to a predetermined or "normal" size. When the window does not fill the entire screen, the Maximize button appears. Clicking the Maximize button enlarges the window to fill the screen.

The **Close button** closes the window and removes its button from the taskbar at the bottom of the screen.

Minimizing a Window

The **Minimize button** shrinks the current window so that only the button on the taskbar remains visible. You can use the Minimize button when you want to temporarily hide a window but keep the program running.

To minimize the WordPad window:

1. Click the **Minimize** button. The WordPad window shrinks so only the Document - WordPad button on the taskbar is visible.

   TROUBLE? If you accidentally clicked the Close button and closed the window, use the Start button to start WordPad again.

Redisplaying a Window

You can redisplay a minimized window by clicking the program's button on the taskbar. When you redisplay a window, it becomes the active window.

To redisplay the WordPad window:

1. Click the **Document - WordPad** button on the taskbar. The WordPad window is restored to its previous size. The Document - WordPad button looks pushed in as a visual clue that it is now the active window.

Restoring a Window

The **Restore** button reduces the window so it is smaller than the entire screen. This is useful if you want to see more than one window at a time. Also, because of its small size, you can drag the window to another location on the screen or change its dimensions.

To restore a window:

1. Click the **Restore** button on the WordPad title bar. The WordPad window will look similar to Figure 1-12, but the exact size of the window on your screen might be slightly different.

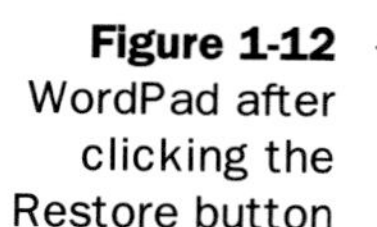

Figure 1-12 WordPad after clicking the Restore button

The WordPad window no longer fills the entire screen.

Moving a Window

You can use the mouse to **move** a window to a new position on the screen. When you hold down the mouse button while moving the mouse, it is called **dragging**. You can move objects on the screen by dragging them to a new location. If you want to move a window, you drag its title bar.

To drag the WordPad window to a new location:

1. Position the mouse pointer on the WordPad window title bar.
2. While you hold down the left mouse button, move the mouse to drag the window. A rectangle representing the window moves as you move the mouse.
3. Position the rectangle anywhere on the screen, then release the left mouse button. The WordPad window appears in the new location.
4. Now drag the WordPad window to the upper-left corner of the screen.

Changing the Size of a Window

3.1 NOTE

You can also change the size of a window by dragging the top, bottom, sides, and corners of the window, as you did in Windows 3.1.

You can also use the mouse to change the size of a window. Notice the sizing handle at the lower right corner of the window. The **sizing handle** provides a visible control for changing the size of a current window.

To change the size of the WordPad window:

1. Position the pointer over the sizing handle. The pointer changes to a diagonal arrow.
2. While holding down the mouse button, drag the sizing handle down and to the right.
3. Release the mouse button. Now the window is larger.
4. Practice using the sizing handle to make the WordPad window larger or smaller.

Maximizing a Window

The **Maximize button** enlarges a window so that it fills the entire screen. You will probably do most of your work using maximized windows because you can see more of your program and data.

To maximize the WordPad window:

1. Click the **Maximize** button on the WordPad title bar.

Using Program Menus

Most Windows programs use menus to provide an easy way for you to select program commands. The **menu bar** is typically located at the top of the program window and shows the titles of menus such as File, Edit, and Help.

Windows menus are relatively standardized—most Windows programs include similar menu options. It's easy to learn new programs, because you can make a pretty good guess about which menu contains the command you want.

Selecting Commands from a Menu

When you click any menu title, choices for that menu appear below the menu bar. These choices are referred to as **menu options**. To select a menu option, you click it. For example, the File menu is a standard feature in most Windows programs and contains the options related to working with a file: creating, opening, saving, and printing a file or document.

To select Print Preview from the File menu:

1. Click **File** in the WordPad menu bar to display the File menu.

   TROUBLE? If you open a menu but decide not to select any of the menu options, you can close the menu by clicking its title again.

2. Click **Print Preview** to open the preview screen and view your document as it will appear when printed. This document is blank because you didn't enter any text.

3. After examining the screen, click the button labeled "Close" to return to your document.

Not all menu options immediately carry out an action—some show submenus or ask you for more information about what you want to do. The menu gives you hints about what to expect when you select an option. These hints are sometimes referred to as **menu conventions**. Study Figures 1-13a and 1-13b so you will recognize the Windows 95 menu conventions.

Figure 1-13a Menu Conventions

View Image Options
Tool Box Ctrl+T
Color Box Ctrl+A
Status Bar
Zoom
View Bitmap Ctrl+F
Text Toolbar
Normal Size Ctrl+PgUp
Large Size Ctrl+PgDn
Custom...
Show Grid Ctrl+G
Show Thumbnail

Some menu options are toggle switches that can be either "on" or "off." When a feature is turned on, a **check mark** appears next to the menu option. When the feature is turned off, there is no check mark.

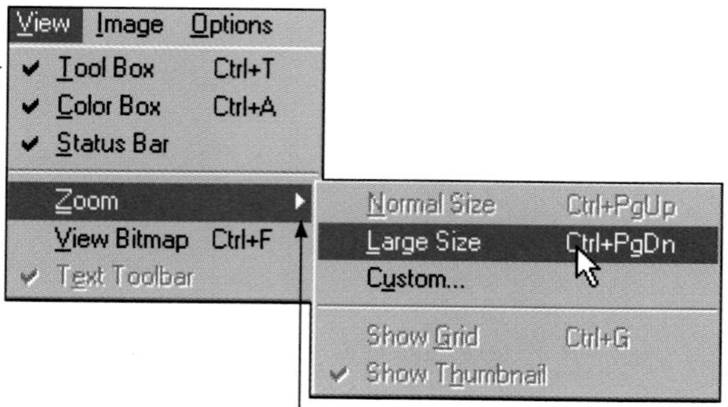

Certain menu selections lead you to an additional menu, called a **submenu**. A triangle on the right side of the menu choice indicates menu options that lead to submenus. When you move the pointer to a menu option with a triangle next to it, the submenu automatically appears.

Figure 1-13b Menu conventions (continued)

Edit View Insert Format Help
Undo Ctrl+Z
Cut Ctrl+X
Copy Ctrl+C
Paste Ctrl+V
Paste Special...

Paste Special
Source: Bitmap Image
As:
Paste
Paste Link
Bitmap Image
Picture (Metafile)
Device Independent Bitmap
OK
Cancel
Display As Icon
Result
Inserts the contents of the clipboard into your document so that you may activate it using Paint.

Sometimes certain menu options are unavailable. For example, a word-processing program might prevent you from trying to delete text if a document is blank. When a menu option is not available, it is usually **"grayed-out"** to provide you with a visual cue that the function is not available.

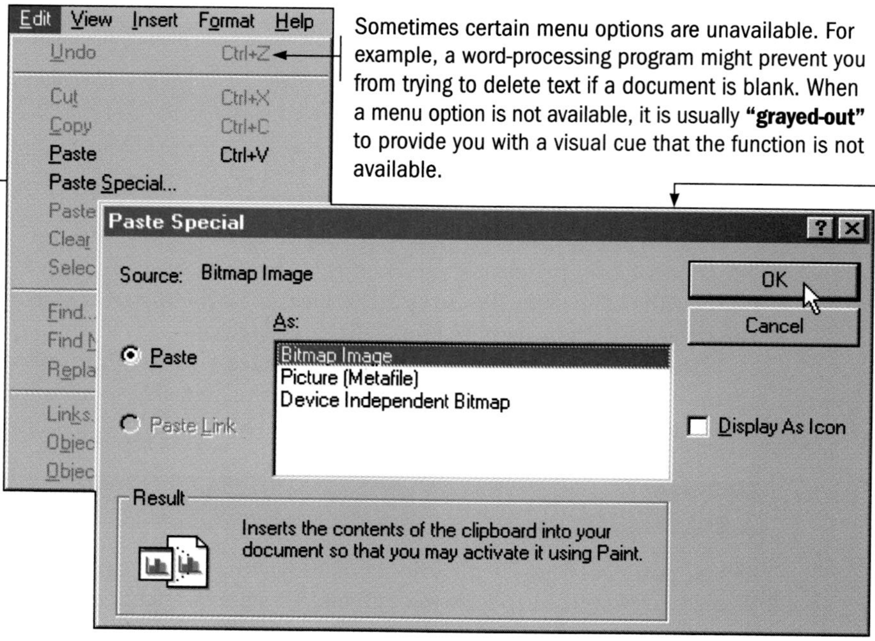

Some menu options are followed by a series of three dots, called an **ellipsis**. The dots indicate that you must make additional selections from a dialog box after you select that option. Options without dots do not require additional choices—they take effect as soon as you click them.

A **dialog box** lets you enter specification for how you want a task carried out.

Using Toolbars

A **toolbar** contains buttons that provide quick access to important program commands. Although you can usually perform all program commands using the menus, the toolbar provides convenient one-click access to frequently-used commands. For most Windows 95 functions, there is usually more than one way to accomplish a task. To simplify your introduction to Windows 95 in this tutorial, you will learn only one method for performing a task. As you become more accomplished using Windows 95, you can explore alternative methods.

In Session 1.1 you learned that Windows 95 programs include ToolTips that indicate the purpose and function of a tool. Now is a good time to explore the WordPad toolbar buttons by looking at their ToolTips.

To find out a toolbar button's function:

1. Position the pointer over any button on the toolbar, such as the Print Preview icon. After a short pause, the name of the button appears in a box and a description of the button appears in the status bar just above the Start button.
2. Move the pointer to each button on the toolbar to see its name and purpose.

You select a toolbar button by clicking it.

To select the Print Preview toolbar button:

1. Click the **Print Preview** button. The Print Preview dialog box appears. This is the same dialog box that appeared when you selected File, Print Preview from the menu bar.
2. Click Close to close the Print Preview dialog box.

Using List Boxes and Scroll Bars

As you might guess from the name, a **list box** displays a list of choices. In WordPad, date and time formats are shown in the Date/Time list box. List box controls include arrow buttons, a scroll bar, and a scroll box, as shown in Figure 1-14.

Figure 1-14 List box

Date and Time dialog box

The list box shows the available date fomats.

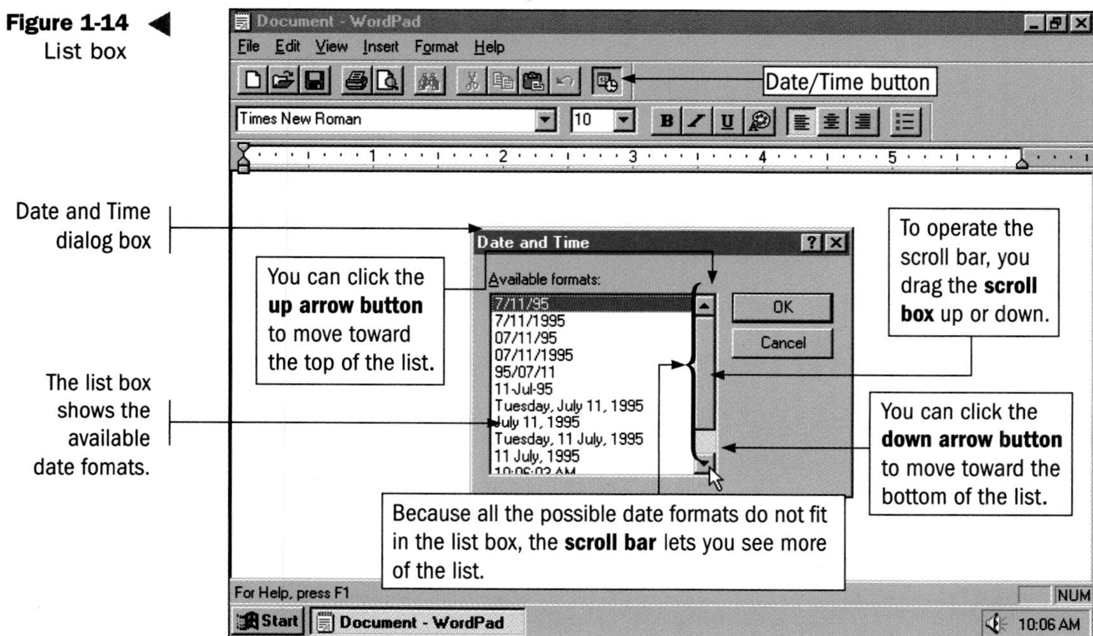

To use the Date/Time list box:

1. Click the **Date/Time** button to display the Date and Time dialog box. See Figure 1-14.
2. To scroll down the list, click the **down arrow** button. See Figure 1-14.
3. Find the scroll box on your screen. See Figure 1-14.
4. Drag the **scroll box** to the top of the scroll bar. Notice how the list scrolls back to the beginning.
5. Find a date format similar to "October 2, 1997." Click that date format to select it.
6. Click the **OK** button to close the Date and Time list box. This inserts the current date in your document.

A variation of the list box, called a **drop-down list box**, usually shows only one choice, but can expand down to display additional choices on the list.

To use the Font Size drop-down list:

1. Click the **down arrow** button shown in Figure 1-15.

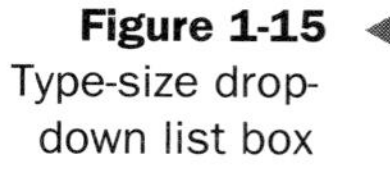

Figure 1-15 Type-size drop-down list box

2. Click **18**. The drop-down list disappears and the font size you selected appears at the top of the pull-down list.
3. Type a few characters to test the new font size.
4. Click the **down arrow** button in the Font Size drop-down list box again.
5. Click **12**.
6. Type a few characters to test this type size.
7. Click the **Close** button to close WordPad.
8. When you see the message "Save changes to Document?" click the **No** button.

Using Tab Controls, Radio Buttons, and Check Boxes

Dialog boxes often use tabs, radio buttons, or check boxes to collect information about how you want a program to perform a task. A **tab control** is patterned after the tabs on file folders. You click the appropriate tab to view different pages of information or choices. Tab controls are often used as containers for other Windows 95 controls such as list boxes, radio buttons, and check boxes.

Radio buttons, also called **option buttons**, allow you to select a single option from among one or more options. **Check boxes** allow you to select many options at the same time. Figure 1-16 explains how to use these controls.

Figure 1-16 Tabs, radio buttons, and check boxes

A **tab** indicates an "index card" that contains information or a group of controls, usually with related functions. To look at the functions on an index card, click the tab.

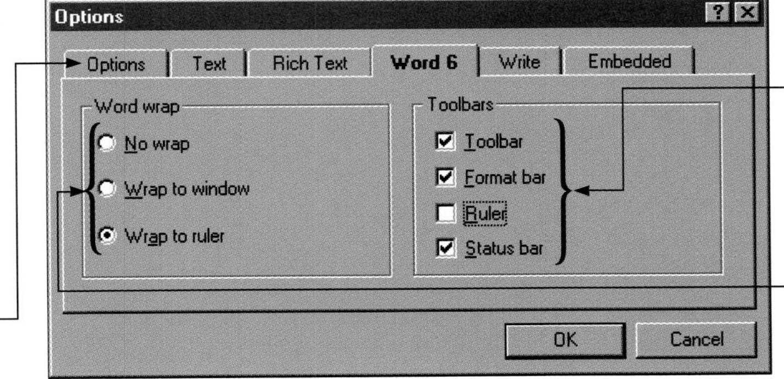

Check boxes allow you to select one or more options from a group. When you click a check box, a check mark appears in it. To remove a check mark from a box, click it again.

Radio buttons are round and usually come in groups of two or more. You can select only one radio button from a group. Your selection is indicated by a black dot.

Using Help

Windows 95 **Help** provides on-screen information about the program you are using. Help for the Windows 95 operating system is available by clicking the Start button on the taskbar, then selecting Help from the Start menu. If you want Help for a program, such as WordPad, you must first start the program, then use the Help menu at the top of the screen.

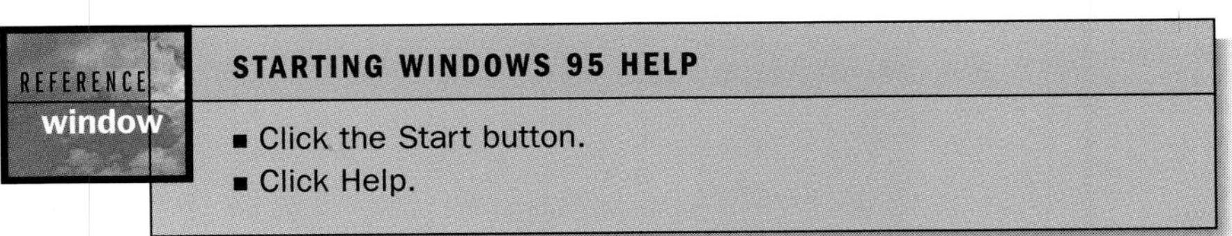

REFERENCE window

STARTING WINDOWS 95 HELP

- Click the Start button.
- Click Help.

To start Windows 95 Help:

1. Click the **Start** button.
2. Click **Help.**

Help uses tabs for each section of Help. Windows 95 Help tabs include Contents, Index, and Find as shown in Figure 1-17 on the following page.

Figure 1-17 ◀ Windows 95 Help

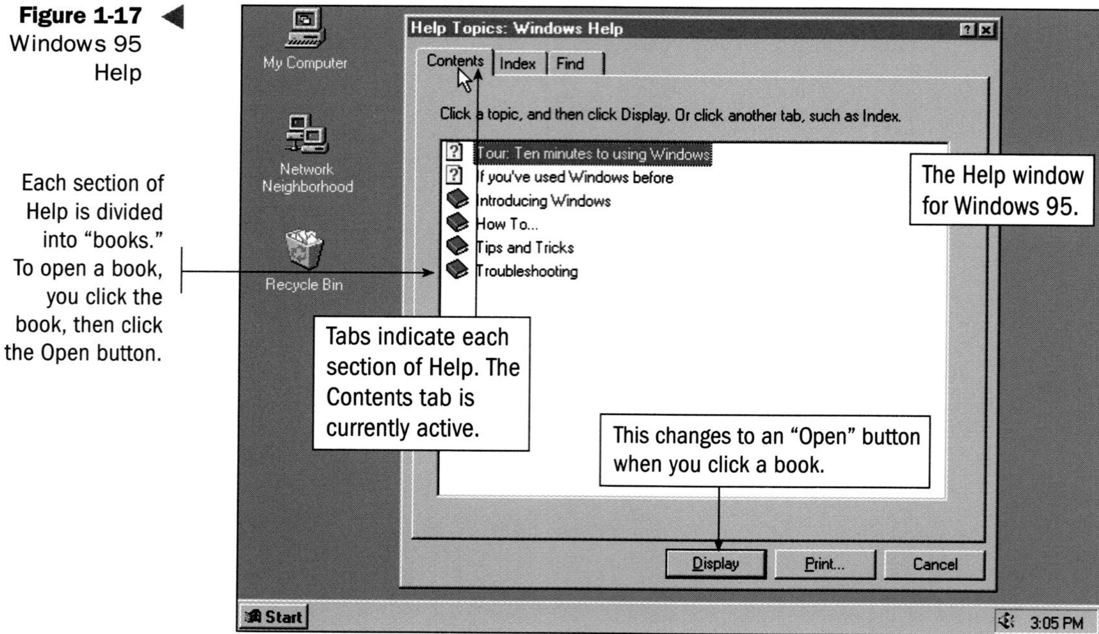

Each section of Help is divided into "books." To open a book, you click the book, then click the Open button.

The **Contents tab** groups Help topics into a series of books. You select a book, which then provides you with a list of related topics from which you can choose. The **Index tab** displays an alphabetical list of all the Help topics from which you can choose. The **Find tab** lets you search for any word or phrase in Help.

Suppose you're wondering if there is an alternative way to start programs. You can use the Contents tab to find the answer to your question.

3.1 NOTE

You can also double-click to select and open a topic in a single step.

To use the Contents tab:

1. Click the **Contents** tab to display the Contents window.
2. Click the **How To...** book title, then click the **Open** button. A list of related books appears below the book title. See. Figure 1-18.

Figure 1-18 ◀ Help window

Click this book, then click the Open button to display a list of related books.

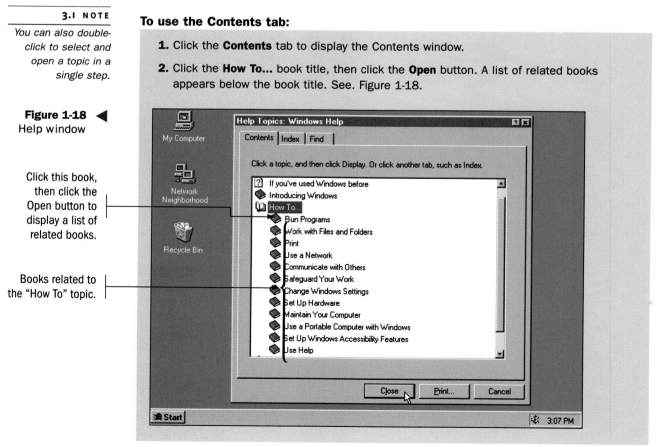

Books related to the "How To" topic.

My Computer
Network Neighborhood
Recycle Bin
Help Topics: Windows Help
Contents | Index | Find
Click a topic, and then click Display. Or click another tab, such as Index.
If you've used Windows before
Introducing Windows
How To...
Run Programs
Work with Files and Folders
Print
Use a Network
Communicate with Others
Safeguard Your Work
Change Windows Settings
Set Up Hardware
Maintain Your Computer
Use a Portable Computer with Windows
Set Up Windows Accessibility Features
Use Help
Close | Print... | Cancel
Start
3:07 PM

3. Click the **Run Programs** book, then click the **Open** button. The table of contents for this Help book is displayed.

4. Click the topic **Starting a Program**, then click the **Display** button. A Help window appears and explains how to start a program.

Help also provides you with definitions of technical terms. You can click any underlined term to see its definition.

To see a definition of the term "taskbar":

1. Point to the underlined term, taskbar until the pointer changes to a hand. Then click.

2. After you have read the definition, click the definition to deselect it.

3. Click the **Close** button on the Help window.

The **Index tab** allows you to jump to a Help topic by selecting a topic from an indexed list. For example, you can use the Index tab to learn how to arrange the open windows on your desktop.

To find a Help topic using the Index tab:

1. Click the **Start** button.

2. Click **Help**.

3. Click the **Index** tab.

4. A long list of indexed Help topics appears. Drag the scroll box down to view additional topics.

5. You can quickly jump to any part of the list by typing the first few characters of a word or phrase in the line above the Index list. Type **desktop** to display topics related to the Windows 95 desktop.

6. Click the topic **arranging open windows on** in the bottom window.

7. Click the **Display** button as shown in Figure 1-19.

Figure 1-19
Displaying a Help Topic

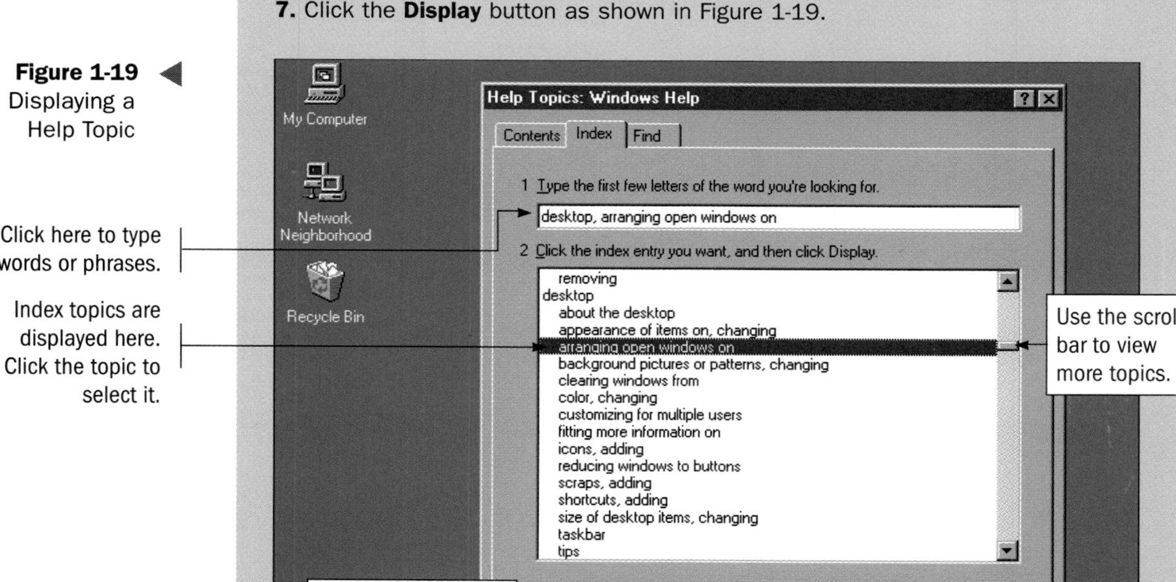

8. Click the **Close** button [X] to close the Windows Help window.

The **Find tab** contains an index of all words in Windows 95 Help. You can use it to search for Help pages that contain a particular word or phrase. For example, suppose you heard that a screen saver blanks out your screen when you are not using it. You could use the Find tab to find out more about screen savers.

To find a Help topic using the Find tab:

1. Click the **Start** button [Start].
2. Click **Help**.
3. Click the **Find** tab.

   TROUBLE? If the Find index has not yet been created on your computer, the computer will prompt you through several steps to create the index. Continue with Step 4 below after the Find index is created.

4. Type **screen** to display a list of all topics that start with the letters "screen."
5. Click **screen-saver** in the middle window to display the topics that contain the word "screen-saver."
6. Click **Having your monitor automatically turn off**, then click the **Display** button.
7. Click the **Help window** button shown in Figure 1-20. The screen saver is shown on a simulated monitor.

   TROUBLE? If you see an error message, your lab does not allow students to modify screen savers. Click the OK button and go to Step 9.

Figure 1-20 Clicking a Button in Help

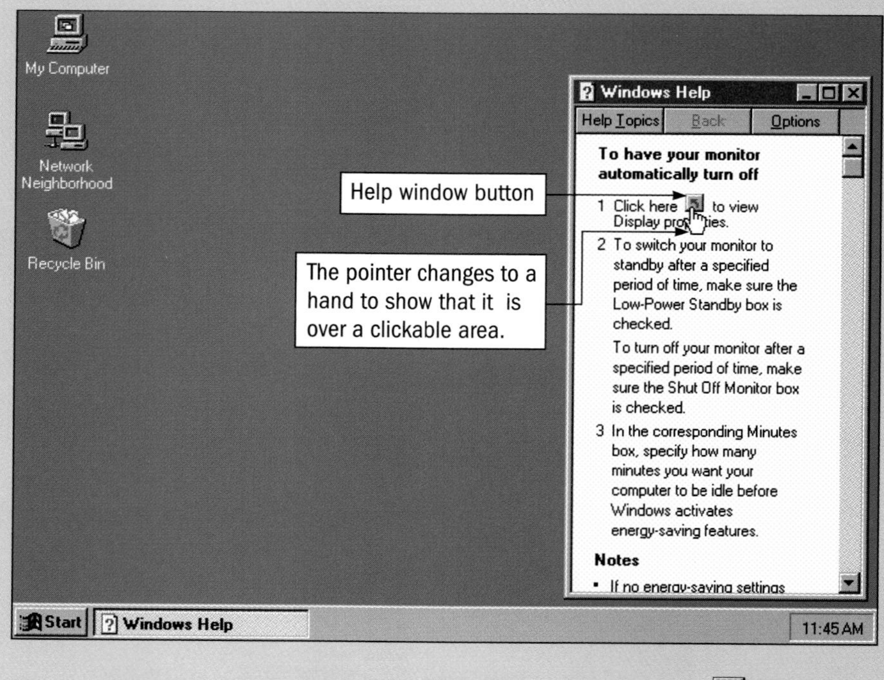

8. To close the Display properties window, click the **Close** button [X] in the Display Properties window.
9. Click the **Close** button [X] to close the Help window.

Now that you know how Windows 95 Help works, don't forget to use it! Use Help when you need to perform a new task or when you forget how to complete a procedure.

Quick Check

1 Label the parts of the window shown in Figure 1-21.

Figure 1-21

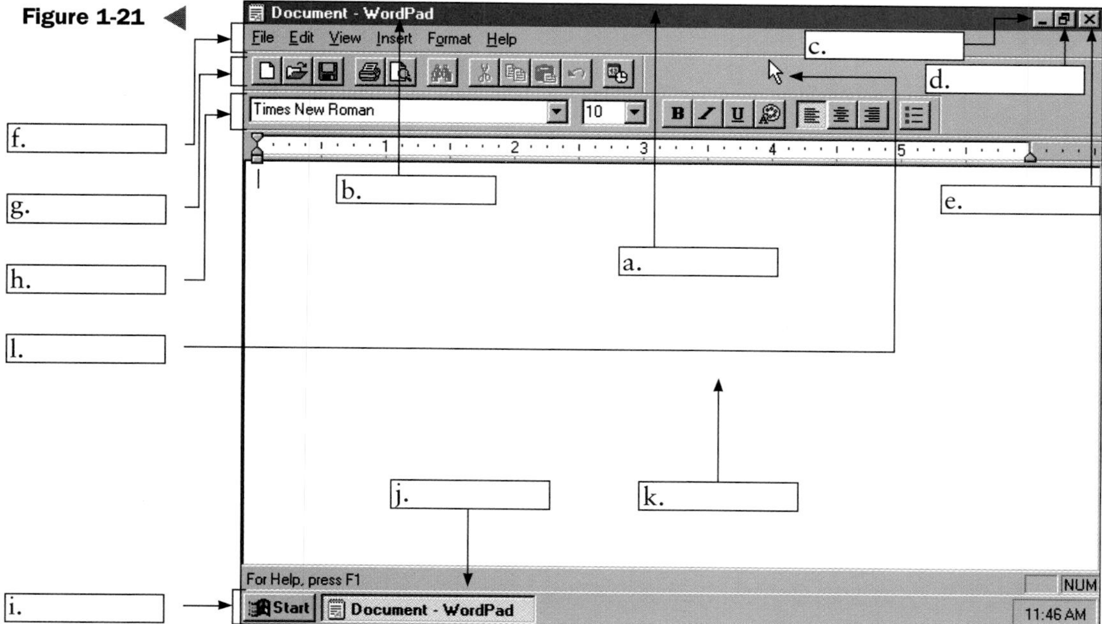

2 Provide the name and purpose of each button:
a.
b.
c.
d.

3 Explain each of the following menu conventions:
a. Ellipsis...
b. Grayed out
c. ▶
d. ✔

4 A(n) ____________ consists of a group of buttons, each of which provides one-click access to important program functions.

5 Label each part of the dialog box below:

Figure 1-22

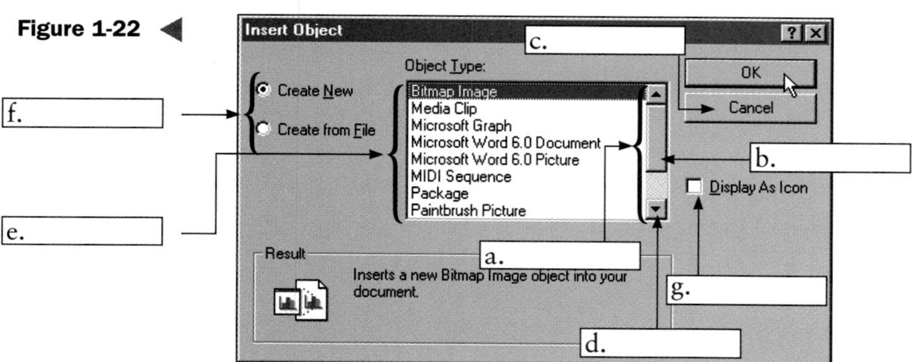

6 Radio buttons allow you to select __________ option(s) at a time, but __________ allow you to select one or more options.

7 It is a good idea to use __________ when you need to learn how to perform new tasks, simplify tedious procedures, and correct actions that did not turn out as you expected.

End Note

You've finished the tutorial, but Steve Laslow still hasn't returned. Take a moment to review what you have learned. You now know how to start a program using the Start button. You can run more than one program at a time and switch between programs using the buttons on the taskbar. You have learned the names and functions of window controls and Windows 95 menu conventions. You can now use toolbar buttons, list boxes, drop-down lists, radio buttons, check boxes, and scroll bars. Finally, you can use the Contents, Index, and Find tabs in Help to extend your knowledge of how to use Windows 95.

Tutorial Assignments

1. Running Two Programs and Switching Between Them In this tutorial you learned how to run more than one program at a time using WordPad and Paint. You can run other programs at the same time, too. Complete the following steps and write out your answers to questions b through f:

a. Start the computer. Enter your user name and password if prompted to do so.
b. Click the Start button. How many menu options are on the Start menu?
c. Run the program Calculator program located on the Programs, Accessories menu. How many buttons are now on the taskbar?
d. Run the Paint program and maximize the Paint window. How many application programs are running now?
e. Switch to Calculator. What are the two visual clues that tell you that Calculator is the active program?
f. Multiply 576 by 1457. What is the result?
g. Close Calculator, then close Paint.

2. WordPad Help In Tutorial 1 you learned how to use Windows 95 Help. Just about every Windows 95 program has a help feature. Many computer users can learn to use a program just by using Help. To use Help, you would start the program, then click the Help menu at the top of the screen. Try using WordPad Help:

a. Start WordPad.
b. Click Help on the WordPad menu bar, then click Help Topics.
c. Using WordPad help, write out your answers to questions 1 through 3.
    1. How do you create a bulleted list?
    2. How do you set the margins in a document?
    3. What happens if you hold down the Alt key and press the Print Screen key?
d. Close WordPad.

3. Using Help to Explore Paint In this assignment, you will use the Paint Help to learn how to use the Paint program. Your goal is to create and print a picture that looks like the one in Figure 1-23.

Figure 1-23

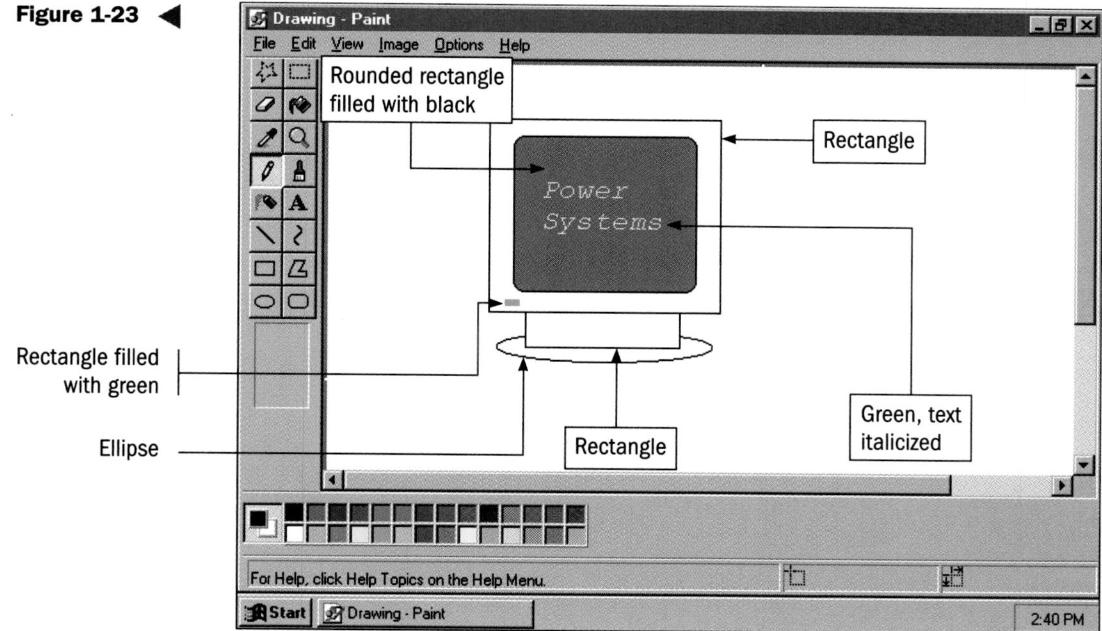

a. Start Paint.
b. Click Help, then click Help Topics.
c. Use Paint Help to learn how to put text in a picture and how to draw rectangles and circles.
d. Draw a picture of a monitor using rectangles, circles, and text as shown in Figure 1-23.
e. Print your picture.
f. Close Paint.

4. The Windows 95 Tutorial Windows 95 includes a five part on-line tutorial. In Tutorial 1 you learned about starting programs, switching windows, and using Help. You can use the on-line Windows 95 Tutorial to review what you learned and pick up some new tips for using Windows 95. Complete the following steps and write out your answers to questions f, g, and h:

a. Click the Start button to display the Start menu.
b. Click Help to display Windows help.
c. Click the Contents tab.
d. From the Contents screen, click Tour: Ten minutes to using Windows.
e. Click the Display button. If an error message appears, the Tour is probably not loaded on your computer. You will not be able to complete this assignment. Click Cancel, then click OK to cancel and check with your instructor or technical support person.
f. Click Starting a Program and complete the tutorial. What are the names of the seven programs on the Accessories menu in the tutorial?
g. Click Switching Windows and complete the on-line tutorial. What does the Minimize button do?
h. Click Using Help and complete the tutorial. What is the purpose of the ? button?
i. Click the Exit button to close the Tour window.
j. Click the Exit Tour button to exit the Tour and return to the Windows 95 desktop.

Lab Assignments

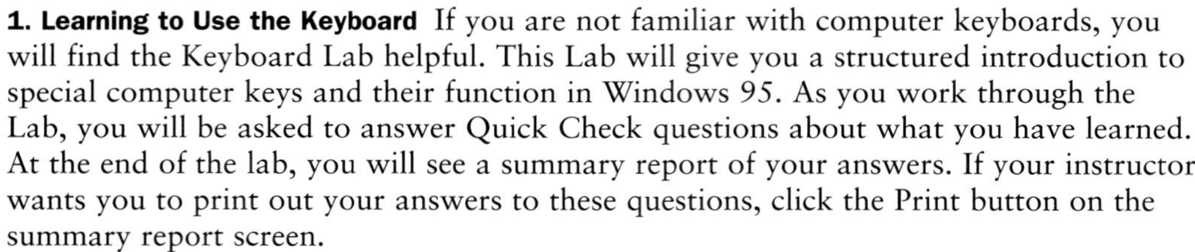

1. Learning to Use the Keyboard If you are not familiar with computer keyboards, you will find the Keyboard Lab helpful. This Lab will give you a structured introduction to special computer keys and their function in Windows 95. As you work through the Lab, you will be asked to answer Quick Check questions about what you have learned. At the end of the lab, you will see a summary report of your answers. If your instructor wants you to print out your answers to these questions, click the Print button on the summary report screen.

a. Click the Start button.
b. Point to Programs, then point to CTI Windows 95 Applications.
c. Click Windows 95 New Perspectives Brief.
d. Click Using a Keyboard. If you cannot find Windows 95 New Perspectives Brief or Using a Keyboard, ask for help from your instructor or technical support person.

2. Mouse Practice If you would like more practice using a mouse, you can complete the Mouse Lab. As you work through the Lab, you will be asked to answer Quick Check questions about what you have learned. At the end of the lab, the Quick Check Report shows you how you did. If your instructor wants you to print out your answers to these questions, click the Print button on the summary report screen.

a. Click the Start button.
b. Point to Programs, then point to CTI Windows 95.
c. Point to Windows 95 New Perspectives Brief.
d. Click Using a Mouse. If you cannot find Windows 95 New Perspectives Brief or Using a Mouse, ask for help from your instructor or technical support person.

TUTORIAL 2

Working with Files

OBJECTIVES

In this tutorial you will learn to:

- Format a disk
- Enter, select, insert, and delete text
- Create and save a file
- Open and edit a file
- Print a file
- Create a Student Disk
- View the list of files on your disk
- Move, copy, delete, and rename a file
- Make a backup of your floppy disk

LABS

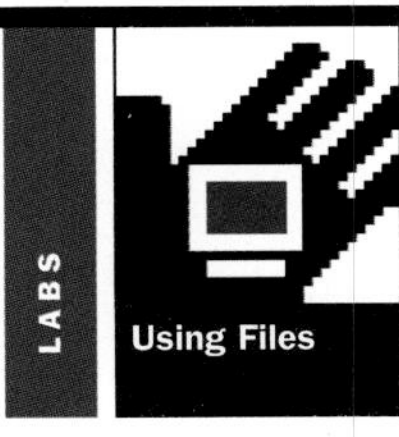

CASE

Your First Day in the Lab—Continued

Steve Laslow is back from class, grinning. "I see you're making progress!"

"That's right," you reply. "I know how to run programs, control windows, and use Help. I guess I'm ready to work with my word-processing and spreadsheet software now."

Steve hesitates before he continues, "You could, but there are a few more things about Windows 95 that you should learn first."

Steve explains that most of the software you have on your computer—your word-processing, spreadsheet, scheduling, and graphing software—was created especially for the Windows 95 operating system. This software is referred to as **Windows 95 applications** or **Windows 95 programs**. You can also use software designed for Windows 3.1, but Windows 95 applications give you more flexibility. For example, when you name a document in a Windows 95 application, you can use descriptive filenames with up to 255 characters, whereas in Windows 3.1 you are limited to eight-character names.

You typically use Windows 95 applications to create files. A **file** is a collection of data that has a name and is stored in a computer. You typically create files that contain documents, pictures, and graphs when you use software packages. For example, you might use word-processing software to create a file containing a document. Once you create a file, you can open it, edit its contents, print it, and save it again—usually using the same application program you used to create it.

Another advantage of Windows 95 is that once you know how to save, open, and print files with one Windows 95 application, you can perform those same functions in *any* Windows 95 application. This is because Windows 95 applications have similar controls. For example, your word-processing and spreadsheet software will have identical menu commands to save, open, and print documents. Steve suggests that it would be worth a few minutes of your time to become familiar with these menus in Windows 95 applications.

You agree, but before you can get to work, Steve gives you one final suggestion: you should also learn how to keep track of the files on your disk. For instance, you might need to find a file you have not used for a while or you might want to delete a file if your disk is getting full. You will definitely want to make a backup copy of your disk in case something happens to the original. Steve's advice seems practical, and you're eager to explore these functions so you can get to work!

Tutorial 2 will help you learn how to work with Windows 95 applications and keep track of the files on your disk. When you've completed this tutorial, you'll be ready to tackle all kinds of Windows 95 software!

SESSION 2.1

In Session 2.1 you will learn how to format a disk so it can store files. You will create, save, open, and print a file. You will find out how the insertion point is different from the mouse pointer, and you will learn the basic skills for Windows 95 text entry, such as inserting, deleting, and selecting.

For this tutorial you will need two blank 3 ½-inch disks.

Formatting a Disk

Before you can save files on a disk, the disk must be formatted. When the computer **formats** a disk, the magnetic particles on the disk surface are arranged so data can be stored on the disk. Today, many disks are sold preformatted and can be used right out of the box. However, if you purchase an unformatted disk, or if you have an old disk that you want to completely erase and reuse, you can format the disk using the Windows 95 Format command.

The following steps tell you how to format a 3 ½-inch high-density disk using drive A. Your instructor will tell you how to revise the instructions given in these steps if the procedure is different for your lab equipment.

All data on the disk you format will be erased, so don't perform these steps using a disk that contains important files.

To format a disk:

1. Start Windows 95, if necessary.
2. Write your name on the label of a 3 ½-inch disk.
3. Insert your disk in drive A. See Figure 2-1.

Figure 2-1 Inserting a disk into the disk drive

TROUBLE? If your disk does not fit in drive A, put it in drive B and substitute drive B for drive A in all of the steps for the rest of the tutorial.

4. Click the **My Computer** icon to select it, then press the **Enter** key. Make sure you can see the My Computer window. See Figure 2-2.

TROUBLE? If you see a list instead of icons like those in Figure 2-2, click View. Then click Large Icon.

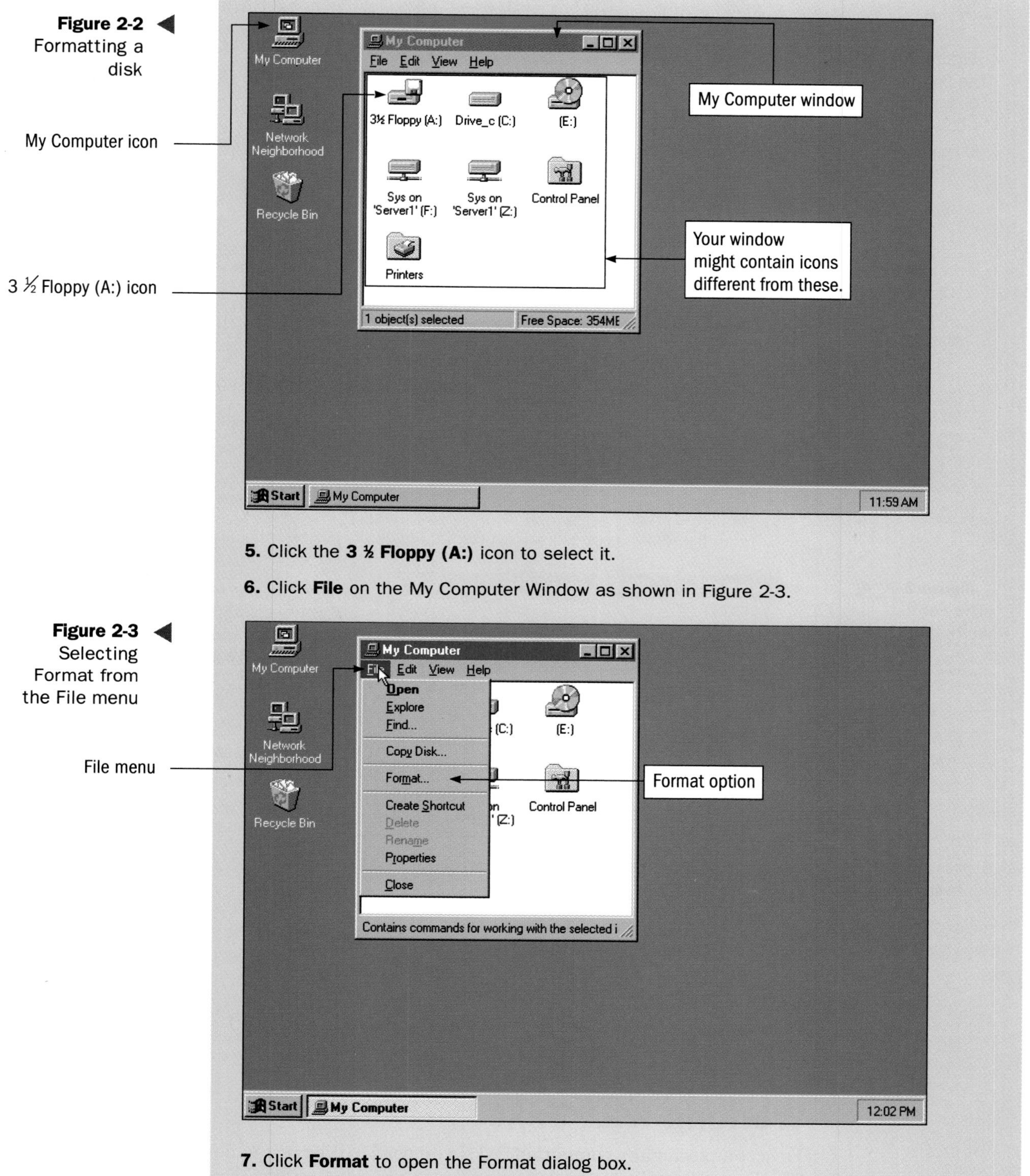

Figure 2-2 Formatting a disk

5. Click the **3 ½ Floppy (A:)** icon to select it.
6. Click **File** on the My Computer Window as shown in Figure 2-3.

Figure 2-3 Selecting Format from the File menu

7. Click **Format** to open the Format dialog box.

8. Make sure the dialog box settings on your screen match those in Figure 2-4.

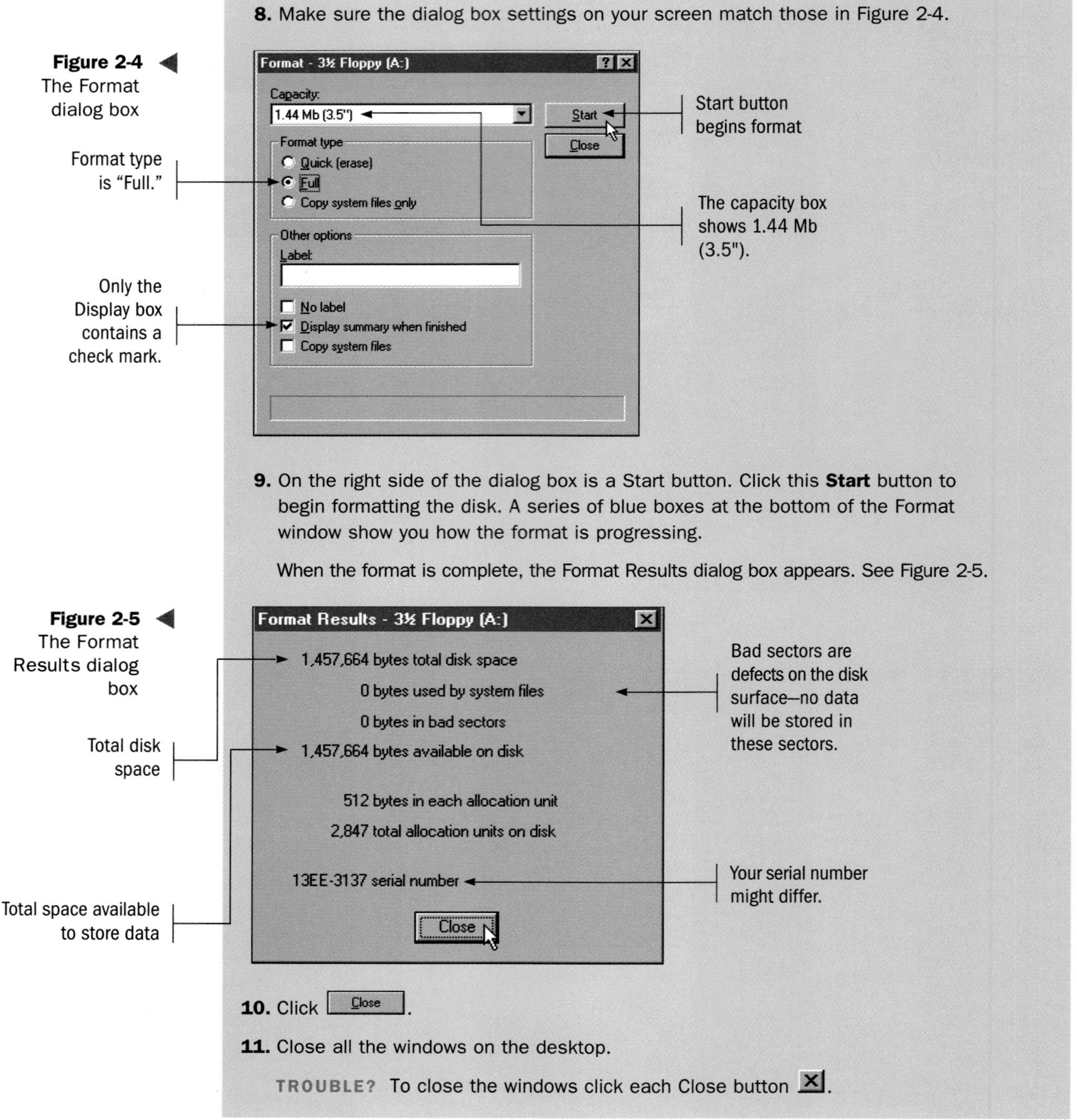

Figure 2-4 The Format dialog box

9. On the right side of the dialog box is a Start button. Click this **Start** button to begin formatting the disk. A series of blue boxes at the bottom of the Format window show you how the format is progressing.

When the format is complete, the Format Results dialog box appears. See Figure 2-5.

Figure 2-5 The Format Results dialog box

10. Click Close.

11. Close all the windows on the desktop.

TROUBLE? To close the windows click each Close button ☒.

Working with Text

To accomplish many computing tasks, you need to type text in documents and text boxes. Windows 95 facilitates basic text entry by providing a text-entry area, by showing you where your text will appear on the screen, by helping you move around on the screen, and by providing insert and delete functions.

When you type sentences and paragraphs of text, do *not* press the Enter key when you reach the right margin. The software contains a feature called **word wrap** that automatically continues your text on the next line. Therefore, you should press Enter only when you have completed a paragraph.

If you type the wrong character, press the Backspace key to backup and delete the character. You can also use the Delete key. What's the difference between the Backspace and the Delete keys? The Backspace key deletes the character to left. The Delete key deletes the character to the right.

Now you will type some text using WordPad to learn about text entry.

To type text in WordPad:

1. Start WordPad.

   TROUBLE? If the WordPad window does not fill the screen, click the Maximize button.

2. Notice the flashing vertical bar, called the **insertion point**, in the upper-left corner of the document window. The insertion point indicates where the characters you type will appear.

3. Type your name, using the Shift key to type uppercase letters and using the spacebar to type spaces, just like on a typewriter.

4. Press the **Enter** key to end the current paragraph and move the insertion point down to the next line.

5. As you type the following sentences, watch what happens when the insertion point reaches the right edge of the screen:

   This is a sample typed in WordPad. See what happens when the insertion point reaches the right edge of the screen.

   TROUBLE? If you make a mistake, delete the incorrect character(s) by pressing the Backspace key on your keyboard. Then type the correct character(s).

The Insertion Point versus the Pointer

The insertion point is not the same as the mouse pointer. When the mouse pointer is in the text-entry area, it is called the **I-beam pointer** and looks like I. Figure 2-6 explains the difference between the insertion point and the I-beam pointer.

Figure 2-6 The insertion point vs. the pointer

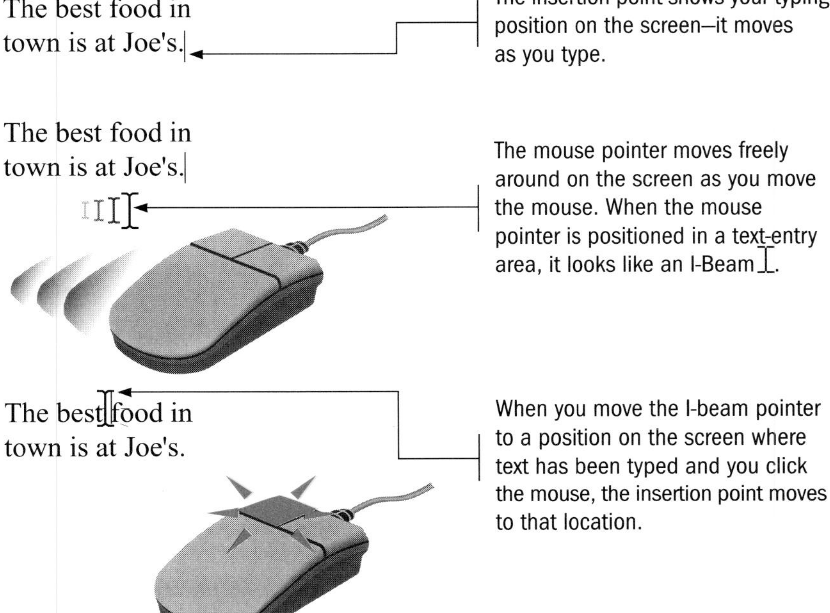

The best food in town is at Joe's.
The insertion point shows your typing position on the screen—it moves as you type.
The best food in town is at Joe's.
The mouse pointer moves freely around on the screen as you move the mouse. When the mouse pointer is positioned in a text-entry area, it looks like an I-Beam.
The best food in town is at Joe's.
When you move the I-beam pointer to a position on the screen where text has been typed and you click the mouse, the insertion point moves to that location.

To move the insertion point:

1. Check the location of the insertion point and the I-beam pointer. The insertion point should be at the end of the sentence you typed in the last set of steps.

   TROUBLE? If you don't see the I-beam pointer, move your mouse until you see it.

2. Use the mouse to move the I-beam pointer to the word "sample," then click the left mouse button. The insertion point jumps to the location of the I-beam pointer.
3. Move the I-beam pointer to a blank area near the bottom of the work space and click the left mouse button. *Notice that the insertion point does not jump to the location of the I-beam pointer.* Instead the insertion point jumps to the end of the last sentence. The insertion point can move only within existing text. It cannot be moved out of the existing text area.

Selecting Text

Many text operations are performed on a **block** of text, which is one or more consecutive words, sentences, or paragraphs. Once you select a block of text, you can delete it, move it, replace it, underline it, and so on. As you select a block of text, the computer highlights it. If you want to remove the highlighting, just click in the margin of your document.

Suppose you want to replace the phrase "See what happens" with "You can watch word wrap in action." You do not have to delete the text one character at a time. Instead you can highlight the entire phrase and begin to type the replacement text.

To select and replace a block of text:

1. Move the I-beam pointer just to the left of the word "See."
2. While holding down the left mouse button, drag the I-beam pointer over the text to the end of the word "happens." The phrase "See what happens" should now be highlighted. See Figure 2-7.

Figure 2-7 Highlighting text

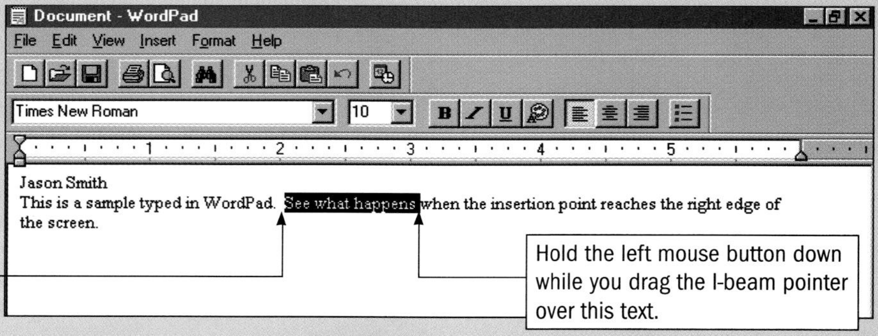

3. Release the left mouse button.

   TROUBLE? If the phrase is not highlighted correctly, repeat Steps 1 through 3.

4. Type: **You can watch word wrap in action**

   The text you typed replaces the highlighted text. Notice that you did not need to delete the highlighted text before you typed the replacement text.

Inserting a Character

Windows 95 programs usually operate in **insert mode**—when you type a new character, all characters to the right of the cursor are pushed over to make room.

Suppose you want to insert the word "sentence" before the word "typed."

To insert characters:

1. Position the I-beam pointer just before the word "typed," then click.
2. Type: **sentence**.
3. Press the **spacebar**.

Notice how the letters in the first line are pushed to the right to make room for the new characters. When a word gets pushed past the right margin, the word-wrap feature pushes it down to the beginning of the next line.

3.1 NOTE

When you save a file with a long filename, Windows 95 also creates an eight-character filename that can be used by Windows 3.1 applications. The eight-character filename is created by using the first six non-space characters from the long filename, then adding a tilde (~) and a number. For example, the filename Car Sales for 1997 would be converted to Carsal~1.

Saving a File

As you type text, it is held temporarily in the computer's memory. For permanent storage, you need to save your work on a disk. In the computer lab, you will probably save your work on a floppy disk in drive A.

When you save a file, you must give it a name. Windows 95 allows you to use filenames containing up to 255 characters, and you may use spaces and punctuation symbols. You cannot use the symbols \ ? : * " < > | in a filename, but other symbols such as &, -, and $ are allowed.

Most filenames have an extension. An **extension** is a suffix of up to three characters that is separated from the filename by a period, as shown in Figure 2-8.

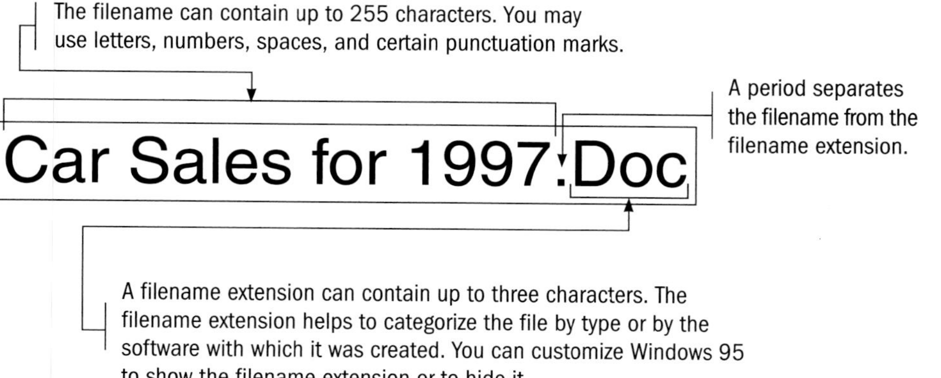
The filename can contain up to 255 characters. You may use letters, numbers, spaces, and certain punctuation marks.
A period separates the filename from the filename extension.
Car Sales for 1997.Doc
A filename extension can contain up to three characters. The filename extension helps to categorize the file by type or by the software with which it was created. You can customize Windows 95 to show the filename extension or to hide it.

Figure 2-8 Filename and extension

The file extension indicates which application you used to create the file. For example, files created with Microsoft Word software have a .Doc extension. In general, you will not add an extension to your filenames, because the application software automatically does this for you.

Windows 95 keeps track of file extensions, but does not always display them. The steps in these tutorials refer to files using the filename, but not its extension. So if you see the filename Sample Text in the steps, but "Sample Text.Doc" on your screen, don't worry—these are the same files.

Now you can save the document you typed.

To save a document:

1. Click the **Save** button on the toolbar. Figure 2-9 shows the location of this button and the Save As dialog box that appears after you click it.

Figure 2-9
The Save button

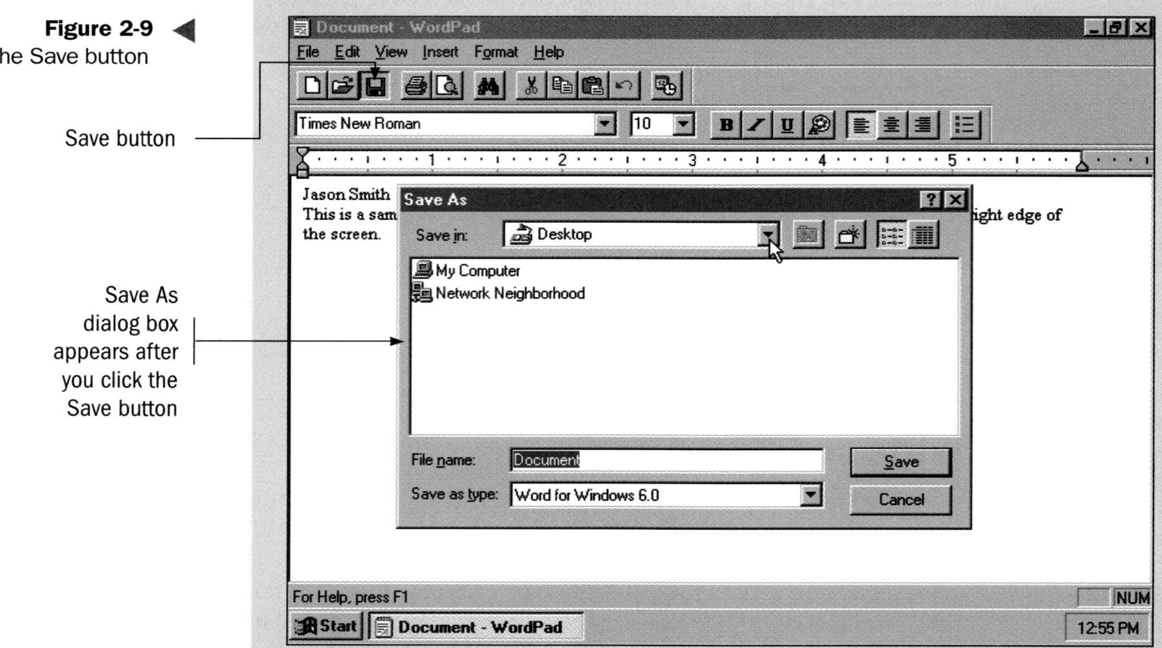

2. Click on the side of the Save in: box to display a list of drives. See Figure 2-10.

Figure 2-10
Selecting the drive

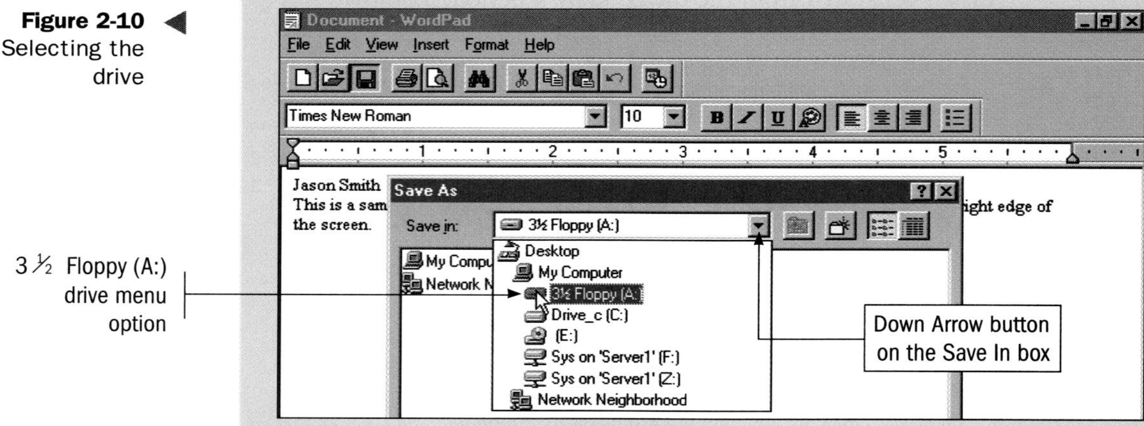

3. Click **3½ Floppy (A:)**.
4. Select the text in the File Name box.

   TROUBLE? To select the text, position the I-beam pointer at the beginning of the word "Document." While you hold down the mouse button, drag the I-beam pointer to the end of the word.

5. Type **Sample Text** in the File Name box.
6. Click the **Save** button. Your file is saved on your Student Disk and the document title, "Sample Text," appears on the WordPad title bar.

What if you tried to close WordPad *before* you saved your file? Windows 95 would display a message—"Save changes to Document?" If you answer "Yes," Windows displays the Save As dialog box so you can give the document a name. If you answer "No," Windows 95 closes WordPad without saving the document.

After you save a file, you can work on another document or close WordPad. Since you have already saved your Sample Text document, you should continue this tutorial by closing WordPad.

To close WordPad:

1. Click the **Close** button [X] to close the WordPad window.

Opening a File

Suppose you save and close the Sample Text file, then later you want to revise it. To revise a file you must first open it. When you **open** a file, its contents are copied into the computer's memory. If you revise the file, you need to save the changes before you close the application or work on a different file. If you close a revised file without saving your changes, you will lose the revisions.

Typically, you would use one of two methods to open a file. You could select the file from the Documents list or the My Computer window, or you could start an application program and then use the Open button to open the file. Each method has advantages and disadvantages. You will have an opportunity to try both methods.

3.1 NOTE

Document-centric features are advertised as an advantage of Windows 95. But you can still successfully use the application-centric approach you used with Windows 3.1 by opening your application, then opening your document.

The first method for opening the Sample Text file simply requires you to select the file from the Documents list or the My Computer window. With this method the document, not the application program, is central to the task; hence this method is sometimes referred to as *document-centric*. You only need to remember the name of your document or file—you do not need to remember which application you used to create the document.

The Documents list contains the names of the last 15 documents used. You access this list from the Start menu. When you have your own computer, the Documents list is very handy. In a computer lab, however, the files other students use quickly replace yours on the list.

If your file is not in the Documents list, you can open the file by selecting it from the My Computer window. Windows 95 starts an application program that you can use to revise the file, then automatically opens the file. The advantage of this method is its simplicity. The disadvantage is that Windows 95 might not start the application you expect. For example, when you select Sample Text, you might expect Windows 95 to start WordPad because you used WordPad to type the text of the document. Depending on the software installed on your computer system, however, Windows 95 might start the Microsoft Word application instead. Usually this is not a problem. Although the application might not be the one you expect, you can still use it to revise your file.

To open the Sample Text file by selecting it from My Computer:

1. Click the **My Computer** icon. Press the **Enter** key. The My Computer window opens.
2. Click the **3½ Floppy (A:)** icon, then press the **Enter** key. The 3½ Floppy (A:) window opens.

   TROUBLE? If the My Computer window disappears when you open the 3½ floppy (A:) window, click View, click Options, then click the Folder tab, if necessary. Click the radio button labelled "Browse Folders using a separate window for each folder." Then click the OK button.

3. Click the **Sample Text** file icon, then press the **Enter** key. Windows 95 starts an application program, then automatically opens the Sample Text file.

   TROUBLE? If Windows 95 starts Microsoft Word instead of WordPad, don't worry. You can use Microsoft Word to revise the Sample Text document.

Now that Windows 95 has started an application and opened the Sample Text file, you could make revisions to the document. Instead, you should close all the windows on your desktop so you can try the other method for opening files.

To close all the windows on the desktop:

1. Click [X] on each of the windows.

   TROUBLE? If you see a message, "Save changes to Document?" click the No button.

The second method for opening the Sample Text file requires you to open WordPad, then use the Open button to select the Sample Text file. The advantage of this method is that you can specify the application program you want to use—WordPad in this case. This method, however, involves more steps than the method you tried previously.

To start WordPad and open the Sample Text file using the Open button:

1. Start WordPad.
2. Click the **Open** button on the toolbar. Figure 2-11 shows the location of this button and the dialog box that appears after you click it.

Figure 2-11 The Open button and dialog box

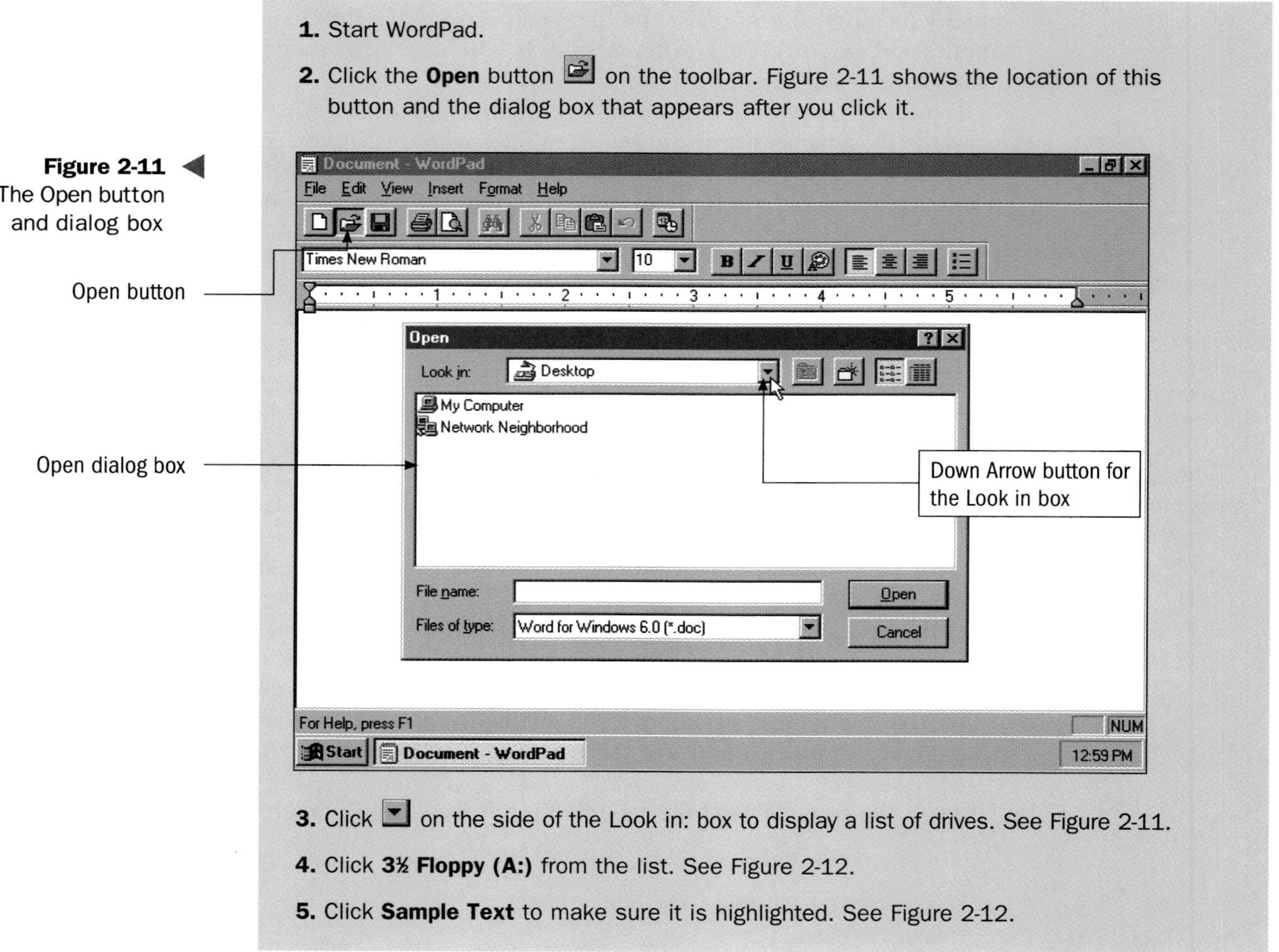

3. Click the down arrow on the side of the Look in: box to display a list of drives. See Figure 2-11.
4. Click **3½ Floppy (A:)** from the list. See Figure 2-12.
5. Click **Sample Text** to make sure it is highlighted. See Figure 2-12.

Figure 2-12 ◀ Opening the Sample Text file

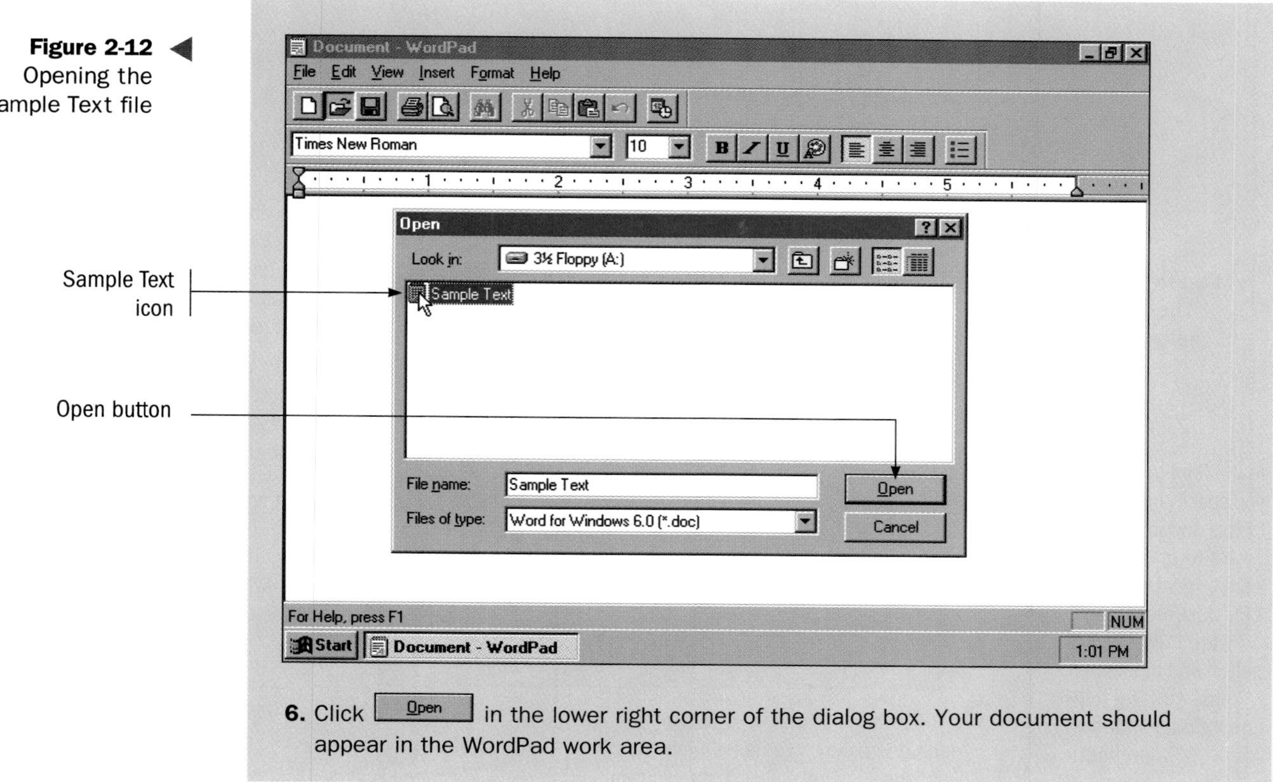

6. Click Open in the lower right corner of the dialog box. Your document should appear in the WordPad work area.

Printing a File

Now that the Sample Text file is open, you can print it. It is a good idea to use Print Preview before you send your document to the printer. **Print Preview** shows on screen exactly how your document will appear on paper. You can check your page layout so you don't waste paper printing a document that is not quite the way you want it. Your instructor or technical support person might supply you with additional instructions for printing in your school's computer lab.

To preview, then print the Sample Text file:

1. Click the **Print Preview** button on the toolbar.
2. Look at your print preview. Before you print the document and use paper, you should make sure that the font, margins, and other document features look the way you want them to.

   TROUBLE? If you can't read the document text on screen, click the Zoom In button.
3. Click the **Print** button. A Print dialog box appears.

4. Study Figure 2-13 to familiarize yourself with the controls in the Print dialog box.

Figure 2-13 The Print dialog box

This is the name of the printer that Windows 95 will use for this printout. If you are using a network, you might have a choice of printers. If you need to select a different printer, ask your instructor or your technical support person for help.

The Properties button lets you modify the way your printer is set up. Do not change any of the settings on your school printer without the consent of your instructor or technical support person.

When you click this check box, your printout will go on your disk instead of to the printer.

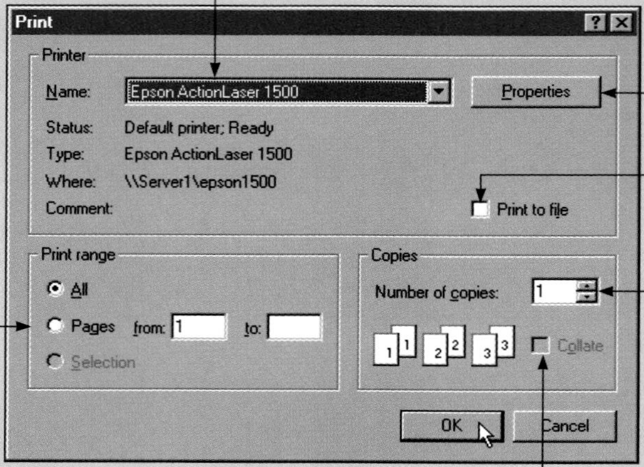

You can specify how many copies you want by typing the number in this box. Alternatively, you can use the arrow buttons to increase or decrease the number in the box.

In the Print range box, you specify how much of the document you want to print. If you want to print only part of a document, click the Pages radio button and then enter the starting and ending pages for the printout.

If you print more than one copy of a multi-page document, you can specify that you want the printout collated, so you don't have to collate the pages manually.

5. Make sure your screen shows the Print range set to “All” and the number of copies set to “1.”

6. Click the **OK** button to print your document. If a message appears telling you printing is complete, click the **OK** button.

   TROUBLE? If your document does not print, make sure the printer has paper and the printer on-line light is on. If your document still doesn't print, ask your instructor or technical support person for help.

7. Close WordPad.

   TROUBLE? If you see the message “Save changes to Document?” click the “No” button.

Quick Check

1. A(n) ____________ is a collection of data that has a name and is stored on a disk or other storage medium.

2. ____________ erases all the data on a disk and arranges the magnetic particles on the disk surface so the disk can store data.

3. When you are working in a text box, the pointer shape changes to a(n) ____________.

4. The ____________ shows you where each character you type will appear.

5. ____________ automatically moves text down to the beginning of the next line when you reach the right margin.

6. Explain how you select a block of text: ____________.

7. Which of these characters are not allowed in Windows 95 file names: \ ? : * “ < > | ! @ # $ % ^ & ; + - ( ) /

8 In the filename New Equipment.Doc, .Doc is a(n) ____________.

9 Suppose you created a graph using the Harvard Graphics software and then you stored the graph on your floppy disk under the name Projected 1997 Sales - Graph. The next day, you use Harvard Graphics to open the file and change the graph. If you want the new version of the file on your disk, you need to ____________.

10 You can save ____________ by using the Print Preview feature.

SESSION 2.2

In this session, you will learn how to manage the files on your disk—a skill that can prevent you from losing important documents. You will learn how to list information about the files on your disk; organize the files into folders; and move, delete, copy, and rename files.

Creating Your Student Disk

For this session of the tutorial, you must create a Student Disk that contains some sample files. *You can use the disk you formatted in the previous session.*

If you are using your own computer, the CTI Windows 95 Applications menu selection will not be available. Before you proceed, you must go to your school's computer lab and find a computer that has the CTI Windows 95 Applications installed. Once you have made your own Student Disk, you can use it to complete this tutorial on any computer you choose.

To add the sample files to your Student Disk:

1. Write "Windows 95 Student Disk" on the label of your formatted disk.
2. Place the disk in Drive A.

   TROUBLE? If your 3½-inch disk drive is B, place your formatted disk in that drive instead, and for the rest of this session substitute Drive B where ever you see Drive A.

3. Click the **Start** button Start. See Figure 2-14.

Figure 2-14 Making your Student Disk

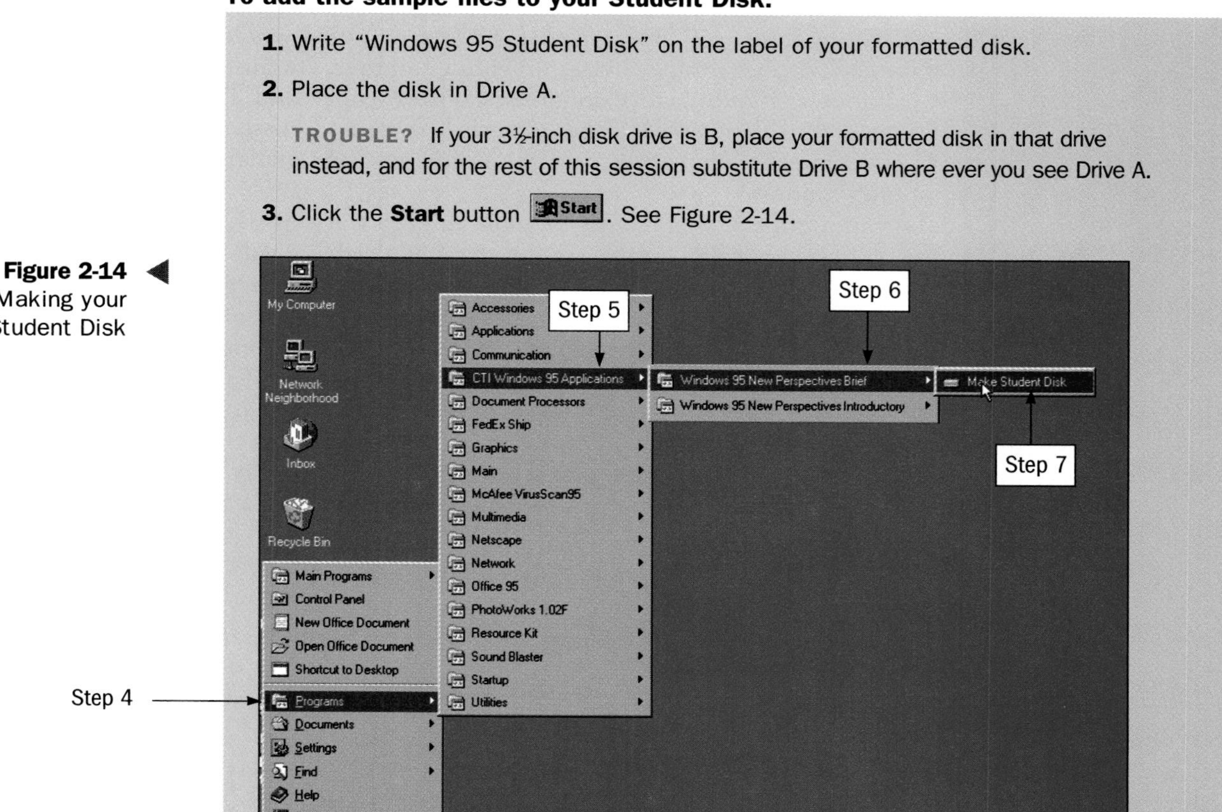

4. Point to **Programs.**
5. Point to **CTI Windows 95 Applications.**

   TROUBLE? If CTI Windows 95 Applications is not listed, contact your instructor or technical support person.
6. Point to **Windows 95 New Perspectives Brief.**
7. Select **Make Student Disk.**

   A dialog box opens, asking you to indicate the drive that contains your formatted disk.
8. If it is not already selected, click the Drive radio button that corresponds to the drive containing your student disk.
9. Click the **OK** button.

   The sample files are copied to your formatted disk. A message tells you when all the files have been copied.
10. Click **OK.**
11. If necessary, close all the open windows on your screen.

Your Student Disk now contains sample files that you will use throughout the rest of this tutorial.

My Computer

The **My Computer** icon represents your computer, its storage devices, and its printers. The My Computer icon opens into the My Computer window, which contains an icon for each of the storage devices on your computer. On most computer systems the My Computer window also contains Control Panel and Printers folders, which help you add printers, control peripheral devices, and customize your Windows 95 work environment. Figure 2-15 on the following page explains more about the My Computer window.

You can use the My Computer window to keep track of where your files are stored and to organize your files. In this section of the tutorial you will move and delete files on your Student Disk in drive A. If you use your own computer at home or computer at work, you would probably store your files on drive C, instead of drive A. However, in a school lab environment you usually don't know which computer you will use, so you need to carry your files with you on a floppy disk that you use in drive A. In this session, therefore, you will learn how to work with the files on drive A. Most of what you learn will also work on your home or work computer when you use drive C.

In this session you will work with several icons, including My Computer. As a general procedure, when you want to open an icon, you click it and then press the Enter key.

Figure 2-15 Information about My Computer

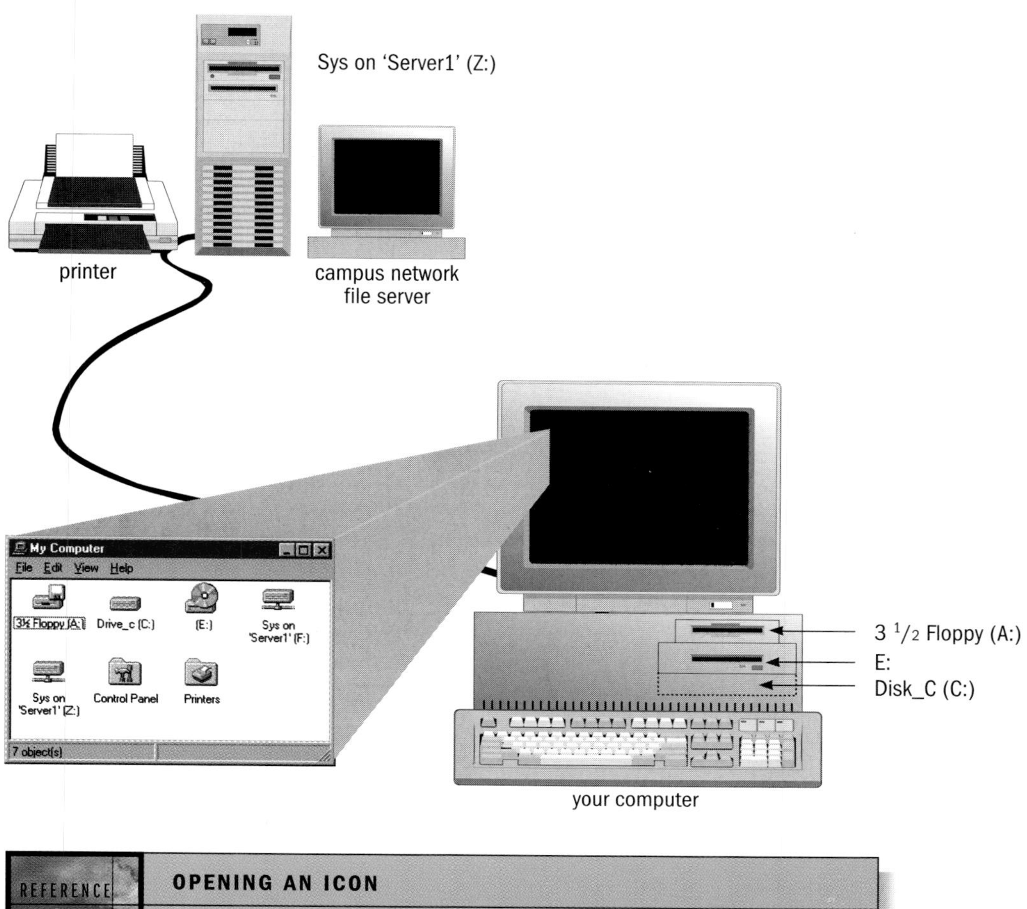

REFERENCE window

OPENING AN ICON

- Click the icon you want to open.
- Press the Enter key.

Now you should open the My Computer icon.

To open the My Computer icon:

1. Click the **My Computer** icon to select it.
2. Press the **Enter** key. The My Computer window opens.

Now that you have opened the My Computer window, you can find out what is on your Student Disk in drive A.

To find out what is on your Student Disk:

1. Open the **3½ Floppy (A:)** icon by clicking it, then pressing the **Enter** key. A window appears showing the contents of drive A:. See Figure 2-16.

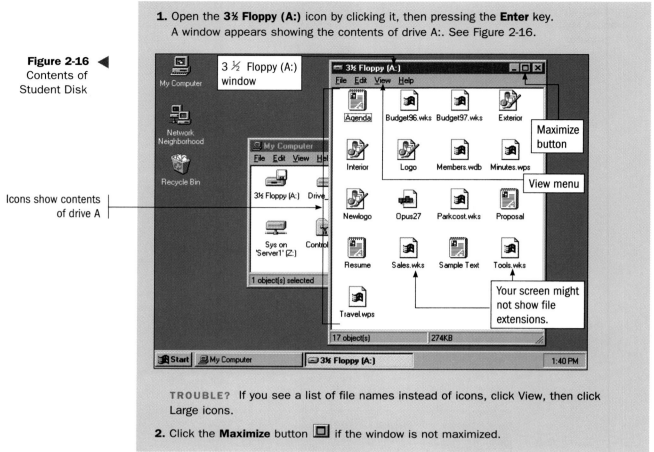

Figure 2-16 Contents of Student Disk

3 ½ Floppy (A:) window

Maximize button

View menu

Icons show contents of drive A

Your screen might not show file extensions.

TROUBLE? If you see a list of file names instead of icons, click View, then click Large icons.

2. Click the **Maximize** button if the window is not maximized.

Windows 95 provides four ways to view the contents of a disk—large icons, small icons, list, or details. The standard view, shown on your screen, displays a large icon and title for each file. The icon provides a visual cue to the type and contents of the file, as Figure 2-17 illustrates.

Figure 2-17 Program and file icons

Text files that you can open and read using the WordPad or NotePad software are represented by notepad icons.

The icons for Windows programs usually depict an object related to the function of the program. For example, an icon that looks like a calculator signifies the Windows Calc program; an icon that looks like a computer signifies the Windows Explorer program.

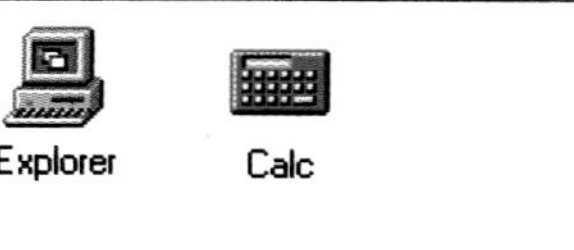

Many of the files you create are represented by page icons. Here the page icon for the Circles file shows some graphics tools to indicate the file contains a graphic. The Page icon for the Access file contains the Windows logo, indicating that Windows does not know if the file contains a document, graphics, or data base.

Folders provide a way to group and organize files. A folder icon contains other icons for folders and files. Here, the System folder contains files used by the Windows operating system.

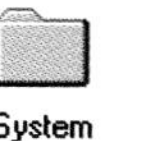

Non-Windows programs are represented by this icon of a blank window.

The **Details** view shows more information than the large icon, small icon, and list views. Details view shows the file icon, the filename, the file size, the application you used to create the file, and the date/time the file was created or last modified.

To view a detailed list of files:

1. Click **View** then click **Details** to display details for the files on your disk as shown in Figure 2-18.

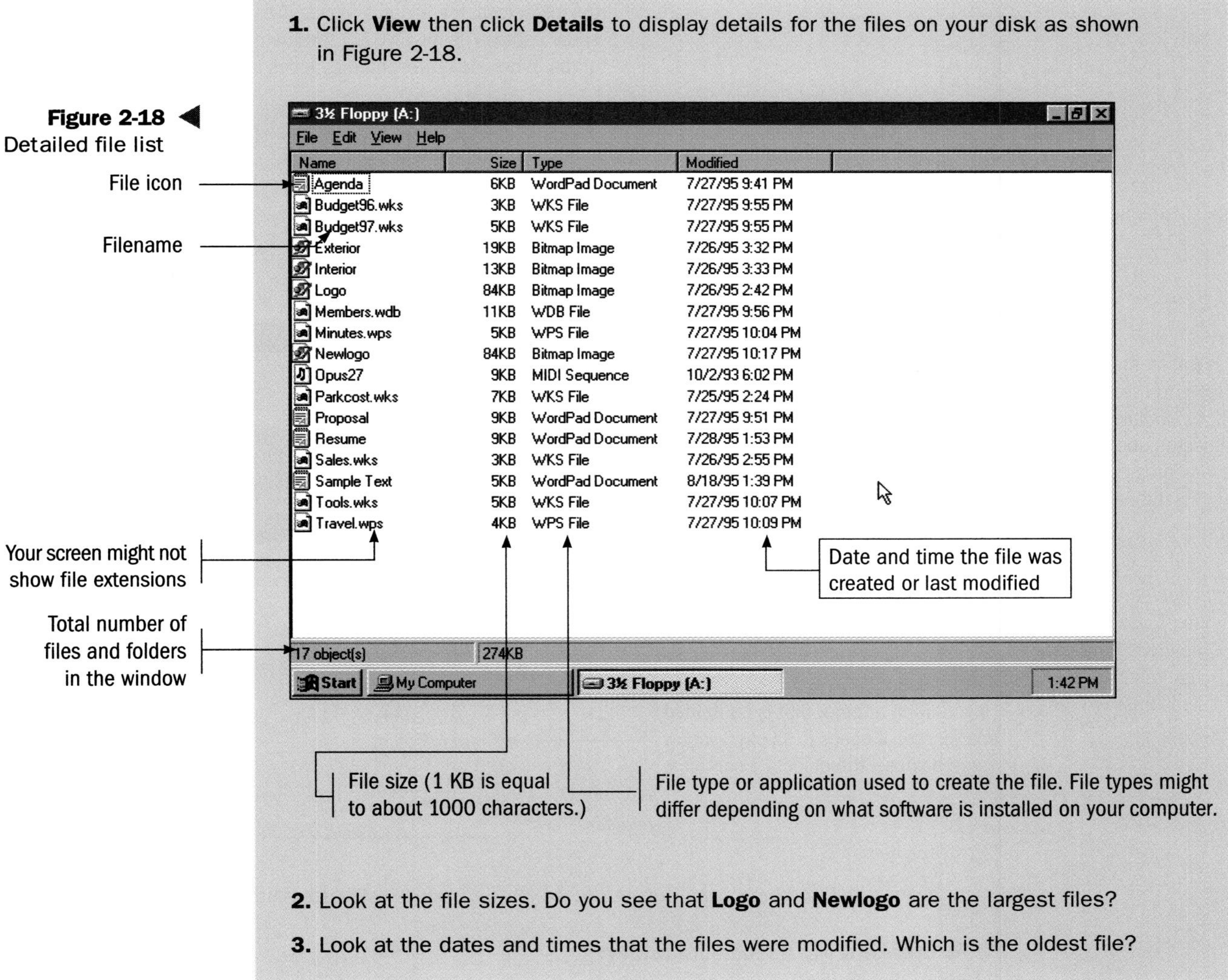

Figure 2-18 Detailed file list

2. Look at the file sizes. Do you see that **Logo** and **Newlogo** are the largest files?
3. Look at the dates and times that the files were modified. Which is the oldest file?

Now that you have looked at the file details, switch back to the large icon view.

To switch to the large icon view:

1. Click **View** then click **Large Icons** to return to the large icon display.

Folders and Directories

A list of files is referred to as a **directory**. The main directory of a disk is sometimes called the **root directory**. The root directory is created when you format a disk and is shown in parentheses at the top of the window. For example, at the top of your screen you should see "3 ½ Floppy (A:)." The root directory is A:. In some situations, the root directory is indicated by a backslash after the drive letter and colon, such as A:\. All of the files on your Student Disk are currently in the root directory.

If too many files are stored in a directory, the directory list becomes very long and difficult to manage. A directory can be divided into **folders** (also called **subdirectories**), into which you group similar files. The directory of files for each folder then becomes much shorter and easier to manage. For example, you might create a folder for all the papers you write for an English 111 class as shown in Figure 2-19.

Figure 2-19 Folders and directories

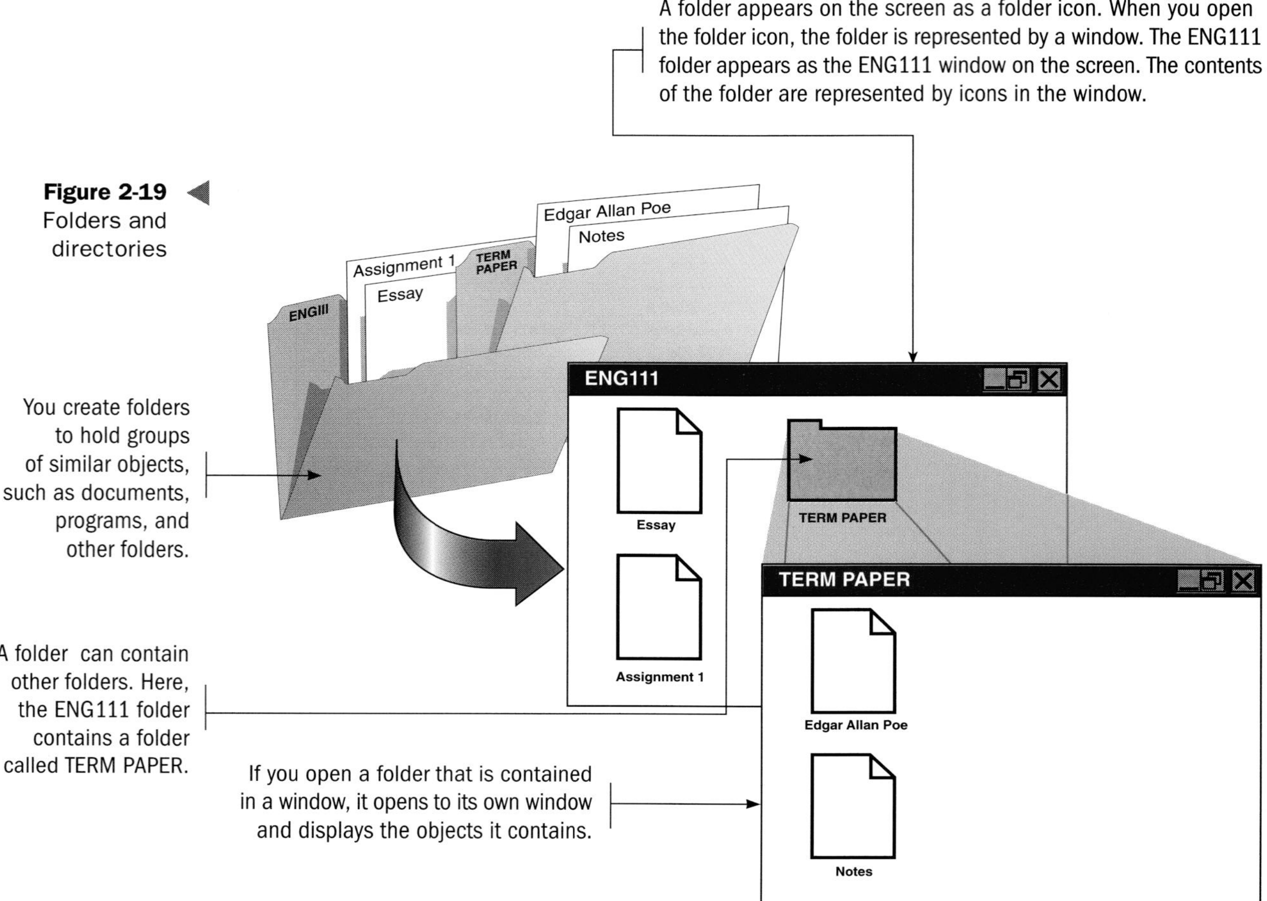

A folder appears on the screen as a folder icon. When you open the folder icon, the folder is represented by a window. The ENG111 folder appears as the ENG111 window on the screen. The contents of the folder are represented by icons in the window.
Edgar Allan Poe
Notes
Assignment 1
TERM PAPER
Essay
ENGIII
ENG111
Essay
TERM PAPER
Assignment 1
TERM PAPER
Edgar Allan Poe
Notes
You create folders to hold groups of similar objects, such as documents, programs, and other folders.
A folder can contain other folders. Here, the ENG111 folder contains a folder called TERM PAPER.
If you open a folder that is contained in a window, it opens to its own window and displays the objects it contains.

Now, you'll create a folder called My Documents to hold your document files.

To create a My Documents folder:

1. Click **File** then point to **New** to display the submenu.
2. Click **Folder**. A folder icon with the label "New Folder" appears.
3. Type **My Documents** as the name of the folder.
4. Press the **Enter** key.

When you first create a folder, it doesn't contain any files. In the next set of steps you will move a file from the root directory to the My Documents folder.

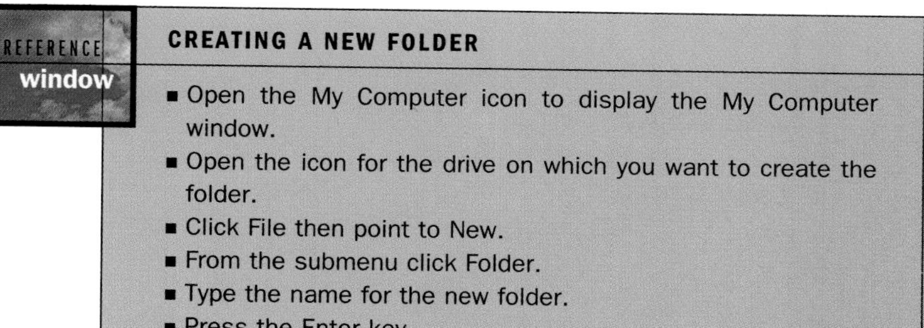
REFERENCE window

CREATING A NEW FOLDER

- Open the My Computer icon to display the My Computer window.
- Open the icon for the drive on which you want to create the folder.
- Click File then point to New.
- From the submenu click Folder.
- Type the name for the new folder.
- Press the Enter key.

Moving and Copying a File

You can move a file from one directory to another or from one disk to another. When you move a file it is copied to the new location you specify, then the version in the old location is erased. The move feature is handy for organizing or reorganizing the files on your disk by moving them into appropriate folders. The easiest way to move a file is to hold down the *right* mouse button and drag the file from the old location to the new location. A menu appears and you select Move Here.

You can also copy a file from one directory to another, or from one disk to another. When you copy a file, you create an exact duplicate of an existing file in whatever disk or folder you specify. To copy a file from one folder to another on your floppy disk, you use the same procedure as for moving a file, except that you select Copy Here from the menu.

Suppose you want to move the Minutes file from the root directory to the My Documents folder. Depending on the software applications installed on your computer, this file is either called Minutes or Minutes.wps. In the steps it is referred to simply as Minutes.

To move the Minutes file to the My Documents folder:

1. Click the **Minutes** icon to select it.
2. Press and hold the right mouse button while you drag the **Minutes** icon to the My Documents folder. See Figure 2-20.

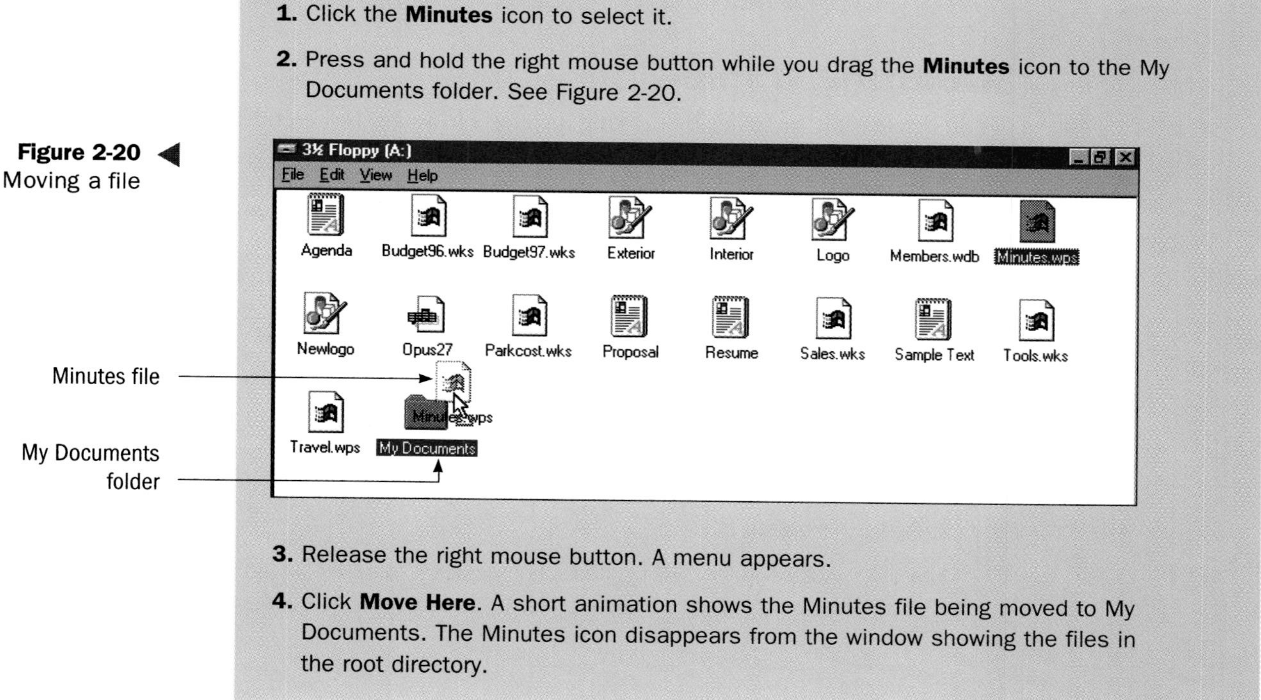

Figure 2-20 Moving a file

3. Release the right mouse button. A menu appears.
4. Click **Move Here**. A short animation shows the Minutes file being moved to My Documents. The Minutes icon disappears from the window showing the files in the root directory.

MOVING A FILE

- Open the My Computer icon to display the My Computer window.
- If the document you want to move is in a folder, open the folder.
- Hold down the *right* mouse button while you drag the file icon to its new folder or disk location.
- Click Move Here.
- If you want to move more than one file at a time, hold down the Ctrl key while you click the icons for all the files you want to move.

3.1 NOTE

Windows 3.1 users be careful! When you delete or move an icon in the Windows 95 My Computer window you are actually deleting or moving the file. This is quite different from the way the Windows 3.1 Program Manager worked.

Anything you do to an icon in the My Computer window is actually done to the file represented by that icon. If you move an icon, the file is moved; if you delete an icon, the file is deleted.

After you move a file, it is a good idea to make sure it was moved to the correct location. You can easily verify that a file is in its new folder by displaying the folder contents.

To verify that the Minutes file was moved to My Documents:

1. Click the **My Documents** folder, then press **Enter**. The My Documents window appears and it contains one file—Minutes.
2. Click the My Documents window **Close** button ☒.

   TROUBLE? If the My Computer window is no longer visible, click the My Computer icon, then press Enter. You might also need to open the 3 ½ Floppy (A:) icon.

Deleting a File

You delete a file or folder by deleting its icon. However, be careful when you delete a *folder*, because you also delete all the files it contains! When you delete a file from the hard drive, the filename is deleted from the directory but the file contents are held in the Recycle Bin. If you change your mind and want to retrieve the deleted file, you can recover it by clicking the Recycle Bin.

When you delete a file from a floppy disk, it does not go into the Recycle Bin. Instead it is deleted as soon as its icon disappears. Try deleting the file named Agenda from your Student Disk. Because this file is on the floppy disk and not on the hard disk, it will not go into the Recycle Bin.

To delete the file Agenda:

1. Click the icon for the file **Agenda**.
2. Press the **Delete** key.
3. If a message appears asking, "Are sure you want to delete Agenda?", click **Yes**. An animation, which might play too quickly to be seen, shows the file being deleted.

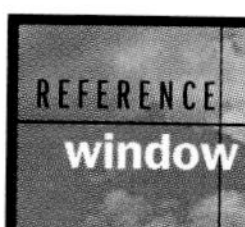

DELETING A FILE

- Click the icon for the file you want to delete.
- Press the Delete key.

Renaming a File

You can easily change the name of a file using the Rename option on the File menu or by using the file's label. Remember that when you choose a filename it can contain up to 255 characters, including spaces, but it cannot contain \ ? : " < > | characters.

Practice using this feature by renaming the Sales file to give it a more descriptive filename.

To rename Sales:

1. Click the **Sales** file to select it.
2. Click the label "Sales". After a short pause a solid box outlines the label and an insertion point appears.
3. Type **Preliminary Sales Summary** as the new filename.
4. Press the **Enter key**.
5. Click the **Close** button ☒ to close the 3 ½-inch Floppy (A:) window.

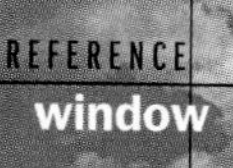

RENAMING A FILE

- Click the icon for the file you want to rename.
- Click the label of the icon.
- Type the new name for the file.
- Press the Enter key.

Copying an Entire Floppy Disk

You can have trouble accessing the data on your floppy disk if the disk gets damaged, exposed to magnetic fields, or picks up a computer virus. If the damaged disk contains important files, you will have to spend many hours to try to reconstruct those files. To avoid losing all your data, it is a good idea to make a copy of your floppy disk. This copy is called a **backup** copy.

If you wanted to make a copy of an audio cassette, your cassette player would need two cassette drives. You might wonder, therefore, how your computer can make a copy of your disk if you have only one disk drive. Figure 2-21 illustrates how the computer uses only one disk drive to make a copy of a disk.

Figure 2-21 Using one disk drive to make a copy of a disk

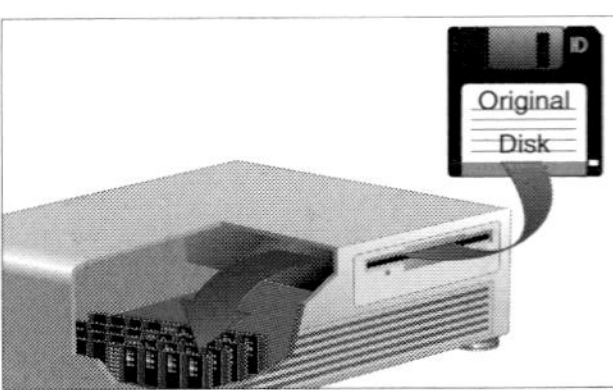

1. First, the computer copies the data from your original disk into memory.

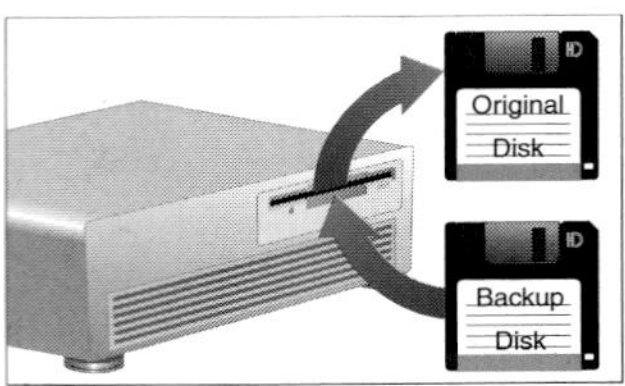

2. Once the data is in memory, you remove your original disk from the drive and replace it with your backup disk.

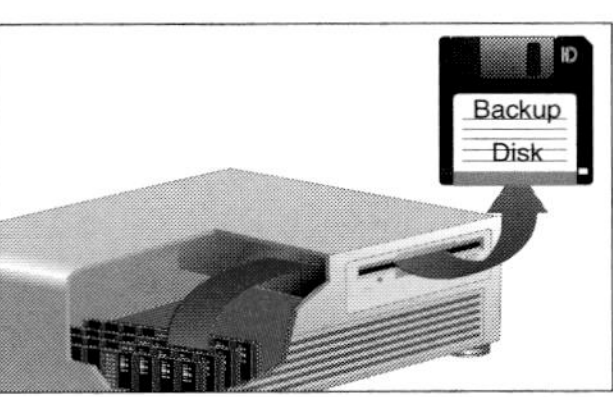

3. The computer moves the data from memory onto your backup disk.

REFERENCE window

MAKING A BACKUP OF YOUR FLOPPY DISK

- Click My Computer then press the Enter key.
- Insert the disk you want to copy in drive A.
- Click the 3 ½ Floppy (A:) icon 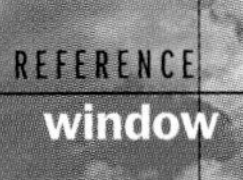 to select it.
- Click File then click Copy Disk to display the Copy Disk dialog box.
- Click Start to begin the copy process.
- When prompted, remove the disk you want to copy. Place your backup disk in drive A.
- Click OK.
- When the copy is complete, close the Copy Disk dialog box.
- Close the My Computer dialog box.

If you have two floppy disks, you can make a backup of your Student Disk now. Make sure you periodically follow the backup procedure, so your backup is up-to-date.

To back up your Student Disk:

1. Write your name and "Backup" on the label of your second disk. This will be your backup disk.
2. Make sure your Student Disk is in drive A.
3. Make sure the My Computer window is open. See Figure 2-22.

Figure 2-22 ◀ The My Computer window

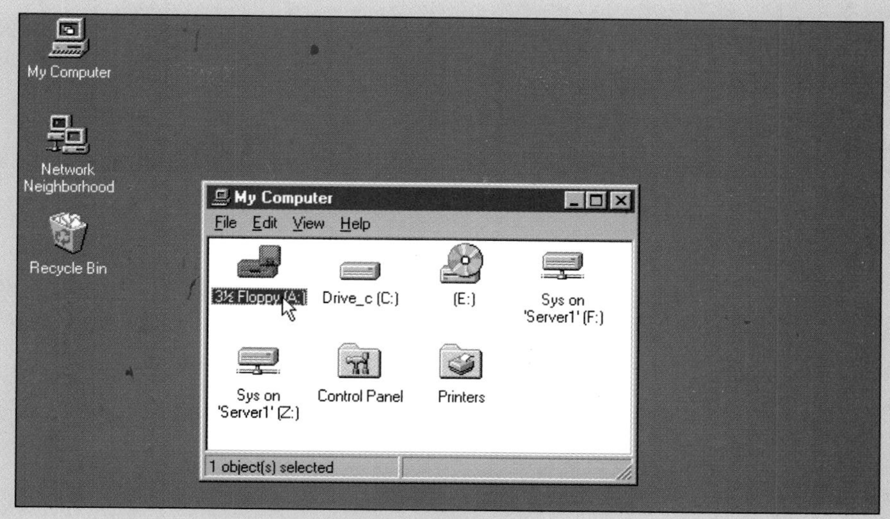

4. Click the **3 ½ Floppy (A:)** icon (3½ Floppy (A:)) to select it.

TROUBLE? If you mistakenly open the 3½ Floppy (A:) *window*, click ☒.

5. Click **File**.
6. Click **Copy Disk** to display the Copy Disk dialog box as shown in Figure 2-23.

Figure 2-23 ◀ The Copy Disk dialog box

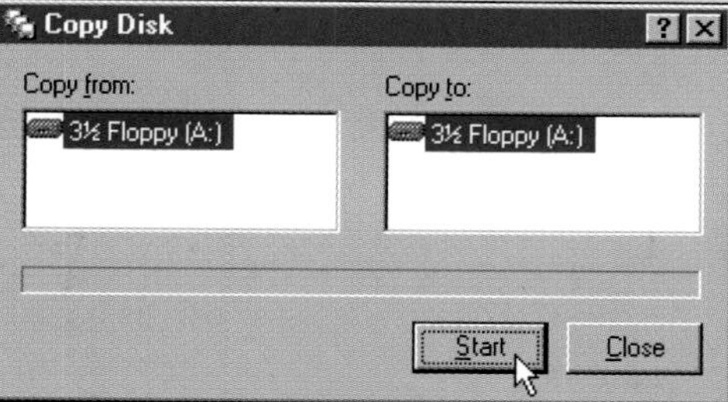

7. On the lower right side of the dialog box, you'll see a Start button. Click this **Start** button to begin the copy process.
8. When the message, "Insert the disk you want to copy from (source disk)..." appears, click the **OK** button.
9. When the message, "Insert the disk you want to copy to (destination disk)..." appears, insert your backup disk in drive A.
10. Click the **OK** button. When the copy is complete, you will see the message "Copy completed successfully."
11. After the data is copied to your backup disk, click ☒ on the blue title bar of the Copy Disk dialog box.
12. Click ☒ on the My Computer window to close the My Computer window.
13. Remove your disk from the drive.

Each time you make a backup, the data on your backup disk is erased, and replaced with the data from your updated Student Disk. Now that you know how to copy an entire disk, make a backup whenever you have completed a tutorial or you have spent a long time working on a file.

Quick Check

1. If you want to find out about the storage devices and printers connected to your computer, click the ____________ icon.
2. If you have only one floppy disk drive on your computer, it is identified by the letter ____________.
3. The letter C: is typically used for the ____________ drive of a computer.
4. What are the five pieces of information that the Details view supplies about each of your files?
5. The main directory of a disk is referred to as the ____________ directory.
6. You can divide a directory into ____________.
7. If you delete the icon for a file, what happens to the file?
8. If you have one floppy disk drive, but you have two disks, can you copy a file from one floppy disk to another?

End Note

Just as you complete the Quick Check for Session 2.2, Steve appears. He asks how you are doing. You summarize what you remember from the tutorial, telling him that you learned how to insert, delete, and select text. You also learned how to work with files using Windows 95 software—you now know how to save, open, revise, and print a document. You tell him that you like the idea that these file operations are the same for almost all Windows 95 software. Steve agrees that this makes work a lot easier.

When Steve asks you if you have a supply of disks, you tell him you do, and that you just learned how to format a disk and view a list of files on your disk. Steve wants you to remember that you can use the Details view to see the filename, size, date, and time. You assure him that you remember that feature—and also how to move, delete, and rename a file.

Steve seems pleased with your progress and agrees that you're now ready to use software applications. But he can't resist giving you one last warning—don't forget to back up your files frequently!

Tutorial Assignments

1. Opening, Editing, and Printing a Document In this tutorial you learned how to create a document using WordPad. You also learned how to save, open, and print a document. Practice these skills by opening the document on your Student Disk called Resume, which is a résumé for Jamie Woods. Make the changes shown in Figure 2-24, and then print the document. After you print, save your revisions.

Figure 2-24

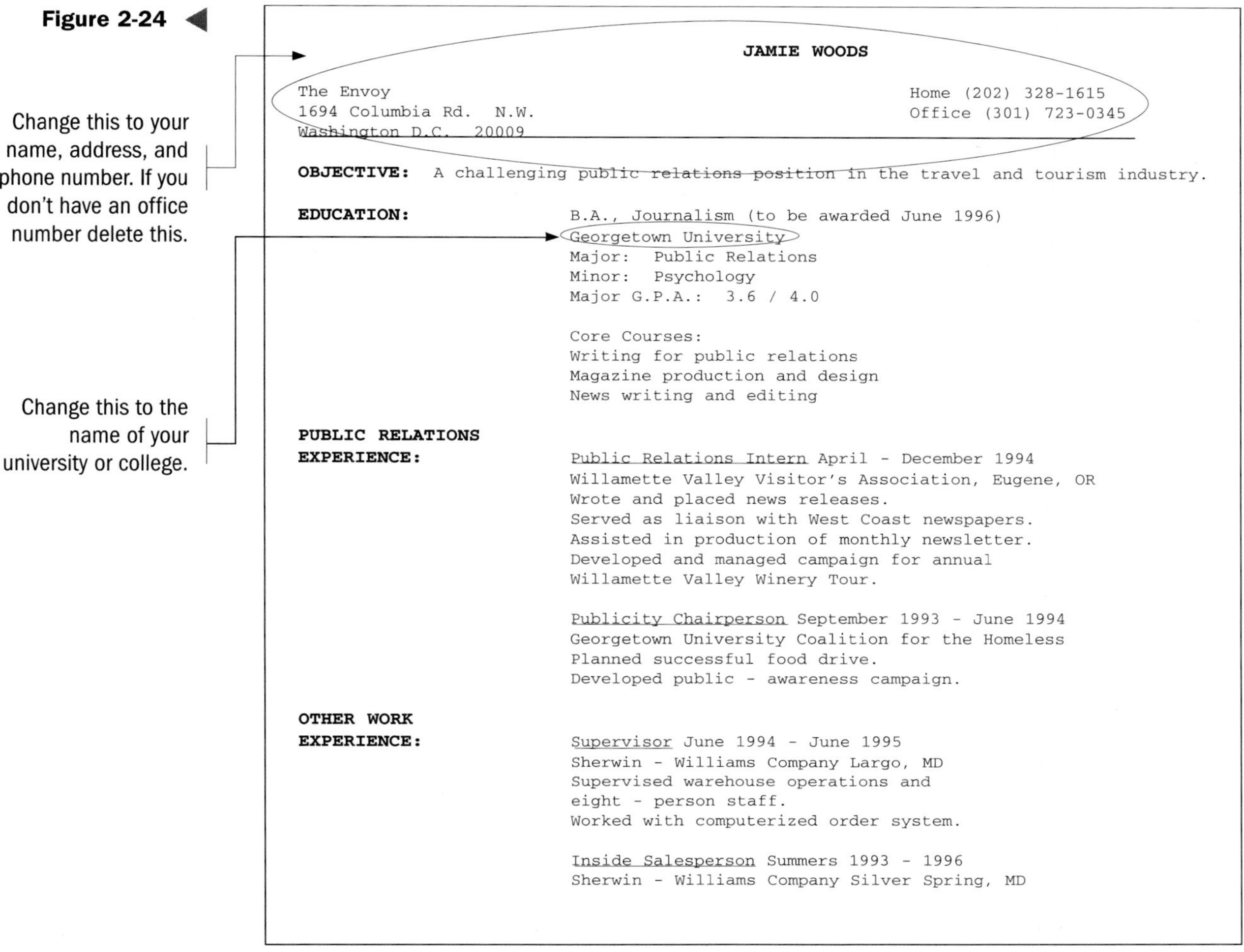
Change this to your name, address, and phone number. If you don't have an office number delete this.
Change this to the name of your university or college.

JAMIE WOODS

The Envoy
1694 Columbia Rd. N.W.
Washington D.C. 20009

Home (202) 328-1615
Office (301) 723-0345

OBJECTIVE: A challenging public relations position in the travel and tourism industry.

EDUCATION:
B.A., Journalism (to be awarded June 1996)
Georgetown University
Major: Public Relations
Minor: Psychology
Major G.P.A.: 3.6 / 4.0

Core Courses:
Writing for public relations
Magazine production and design
News writing and editing

PUBLIC RELATIONS EXPERIENCE:
Public Relations Intern April - December 1994
Willamette Valley Visitor's Association, Eugene, OR
Wrote and placed news releases.
Served as liaison with West Coast newspapers.
Assisted in production of monthly newsletter.
Developed and managed campaign for annual
Willamette Valley Winery Tour.

Publicity Chairperson September 1993 - June 1994
Georgetown University Coalition for the Homeless
Planned successful food drive.
Developed public - awareness campaign.

OTHER WORK EXPERIENCE:
Supervisor June 1994 - June 1995
Sherwin - Williams Company Largo, MD
Supervised warehouse operations and
eight - person staff.
Worked with computerized order system.

Inside Salesperson Summers 1993 - 1996
Sherwin - Williams Company Silver Spring, MD

2. Creating, Saving, and Printing a Letter Use WordPad to write a one-page letter to a relative or a friend. Save the document in the My Documents folder with the name "Letter." Use the Print Preview feature to look at the format of your finished letter, then print it, and be sure you sign it.

3. Managing Files and Folders Earlier in this tutorial you created a folder and moved the file called Minutes into it. Now complete a through g below to practice your file management skills.

a. Create a folder called Spreadsheets on your Student Disk.
b. Move the files ParkCost, Budget96, Budget97, and Sales into the Spreadsheets folder.
c. Create a folder called Park Project.
d. Move the files Proposal, Members, Tools, Logo, and Newlogo into the Park Project folder.
e. Move the ParkCost file from the Spreadsheets folder to the Park Project folder.
f. Delete the file called Travel.
g. Switch to the Details view and answer the following questions:

Write out your answers to questions a through e.

a. What is the largest file in the Park Project folder?
b. What is the newest file in the Spreadsheets folder?
c. How many files are in the root directory?
d. How are the Members and Resume icons different?
e. What is the file with the most recent date on the entire disk?

4. More Practice with Files and Folders For this assignment, you will format your disk again and put a fresh version of the Student Disk files on it. Complete a through h below to practice your file management skills.

a. Format a disk.
b. Create a Student Disk. Refer to the section "Creating Your Student Disk" in Session 2.2.
c. Create three folders on your new Student Disk: Documents, Budgets, and Graphics.
d. Move the files Interior, Exterior, Logo, and Newlogo to the Graphics folder.
e. Move the files Travel, Members and Minutes to the Documents folder.
f. Move Budget96 and Budget97 to the Budgets folder.
g. Switch to the Details view.

Answer questions a through f.

a. What is the largest file in the Graphics folder?
b. How many WordPad documents are in the root directory?
c. What is the newest file in the root directory?
d. How many files in all folders are 5KB in size?
e. How many files in the Documents folder are WKS files?
f. Do all the files in the Graphics folder have the same icon?

5. Finding a File Microsoft Windows 95 contains an on-line Tour that explains how to find files on a disk without looking through all the folders. Start the Windows 95 Tour (if you don't remember how, look at the instructions for Tutorial Assignment 1 in Tutorial 1), then click Finding a File, and answer the following questions:

a. To display the Find dialog box, you must click the __________ button, then select __________ from the menu, and finally click __________ from the submenu.
b. Do you need to type in the entire filename to find the file?
c. When the computer has found your file, what are the steps you have to follow if you want to display the contents of the file?

6. Help with Files and Folders In Tutorial 2 you learned how to work with Windows 95 files and folders. What additional information on this topic does Windows 95 Help provide? Use the Start button to access Help. Use the Index tab to locate topics related to files and folders. Find at least two tips or procedures for working with files and folders that were not covered in the tutorial. Write out the tip in your own words and indicate the title of the Help screen that contains the information.

Lab Assignments

1. Using Files Lab In Tutorial 2 you learned how to create, save, open, and print files. The Using Files Lab will help you review what happens in the computer when you perform these file tasks. To start the Lab, follow these steps:

a. Click the Start button.
b. Point to Programs, then point to CTI Windows 95 Applications.
c. Point to Windows 95 New Perspectives Brief.
d. Click Using Files. If you can't find Windows 95 New Perspectives Brief or Using Files, ask for help from your instructor or technical support person.

Answer the Quick Check questions that appear as you work through the Lab. You can print your answers at the end of the Lab.

Answers to Quick Check Questions

SESSION 1.1

1 a. icon b. Start button c. taskbar d. Date/Time control e. desktop f. pointer

2 Multitasking

3 Start menu

4 Lift up the mouse, move it to the right, then put it down, and slide it left until the pointer reaches the left edge of the screen.

5 Highlighting

6 If a program is running, its button is displayed on the taskbar.

7 Each program that is running uses system resources, so Windows 95 runs more efficiently when only the programs you are using are open.

8 Answer: If you do not perform the shut down procedure, you might lose data.

SESSION 1.2

1 a. title bar b. program title c. Minimize button d. Restore button e. Close button f. menu bar g. toolbar h. formatting bar i. status bar j. taskbar k. workspace l. pointer

2 a. Minimize button—hides the program so only its button is showing on the taskbar.
b. Maximize button—enlarges the program to fill the entire screen.
c. Restore button—sets the program to a pre-defined size.
d. Close button—stops the program and removes its button from the taskbar.

3 a. Ellipses—indicate a dialog box will appear.
b. Grayed out—the menu option is not currently available.
c. Submenu—indicates a submenu will appear.
d. Check mark—indicates a menu option is currently in effect.

4 Toolbar

5 a. scroll bar b. scroll box c. Cancel button d. down arrow button e. list box f. radio button g. check box

6 one, check boxes

7 On-line Help

SESSION 2.1

1 file

2 formatting

3 I-beam

4 insertion point

5 word wrap

6 You drag the I-beam pointer over the text to highlight it.

7 \ ? : * < > | “

8 extension

9 save the file again

10 paper

SESSION 2.2

1 My Computer

2 A (or A:)

3 Hard (or hard disk)

4 Filename, file type, file size, date, time

5 Root

6 Folders (or subdirectories)

7 It is deleted from the disk.

8 Yes

Windows 95 Brief Tutorials **Index**

W

Windows 95 Brief **Task Reference**

TASK	PAGE #	RECOMMENDED METHOD	NOTES
Character, delete	33	Press Backspace	
Check box, de-select	21	Click the check box again	Tab to option, press Spacebar
Check box, select	21	Click the checkbox	Tab to option, press Spacebar
Detailed file list, view	45	From My Computer, click View, Details	
Disk, copy your	50	Place disk in drive A:, from My Computer click 3½ Floppy (A:), click File, Copy Disk, Start	See "Making a Backup of Your Floppy Disk."
Disk, format	30	Click My Computer, click 3½ Floppy (A:), press Enter, click File click Format, click Start	
Drop-down list, display	20	Click	
File, copy		From My Computer, right-click the file, drag to the new location, press C	
File, delete	49	From My Computer, click the file, press Delete, click Yes	See "Deleting a File."
File, move	48	From My Computer, use the left mouse button to drag the file to the desired folder or drive	See "Moving a File."
File, open	37	Click	
File, print	39	Click	
File, print preview	39	Click	
File, rename	49	From My Computer, click the file, click File, click Rename, type new name, press Enter	See "Renaming a File."
File, save	35	Click	
Folder, create	46	From My Computer, click File, New, Folder	See "Creating a New Folder."
Help topic, display	23	From the Help Contents window, click the topic, then click Open	
Help topic, open	23	From the Help Contents window, click the book, then click Display	
Help, start	21	Click Start, then click Help	F1, See "Starting Windows 95 Help."
Icon, open	43	Click the icon, then press Enter or double-click the icon	See "Opening an Icon."

Windows 95 Brief **Task Reference**

TASK	PAGE #	RECOMMENDED METHOD	NOTES
Icons, view large	45	From My Computer, click View, Large Icons	
Insertion point, move	34	Click the desired location in the document Use arrow keys	
List box, scroll	20	Click ▲ or ▼, or drag the scroll box	
Menu option, select	17	Click the menu option	
Menu, open		Click the menu option	Alt-underlined letter
Program, quit	10	Click ✕	Alt-F4
Program, start	9	Click the Start button, point to Programs, point to the program option, click the program	See "Starting a Program."
Radio button, de-select	21	Click a different radio button	Tab to option, press Spacebar
Radio button, select	21	Click the radio button	Tab to option, press Spacebar
Start menu, display			Ctrl-Esc
Student data disk, create	41	Click Start, click Programs, CTI Win95, Windows 95 Brief, Make Windows 95 Student Disk, press Enter	
Text, select	34	Drag the pointer over the text	
Tooltip, display	19	Position pointer over the tool	
Window, change size	17	Drag	
Window, close	10	Click ✕	Ctrl-F4
Window, maximize	17	Click □	
Window, minimize	15	Click _	
Window, move	17	Drag the title bar	
Window, redisplay	16	Click the taskbar button	
Window, restore	16	Click 🗗	
Window, switch	12	Click the taskbar button of the program	Alt-Tab, See "Switching Between Programs."
Windows 95, shut down	12	Click Start, click Shut Down, Click Yes	
Windows 95, start	5	Turn on the computer	

New Perspectives on

Microsoft® Access 7 for Windows® 95

INTRODUCTORY

TUTORIALS

Read This **Before You Begin**

TO THE STUDENT

STUDENT DISKS

To complete the tutorials, Tutorial Assignments, and Case Problems in this book, you need three Student Disks. Your instructor will either provide you with Student Disks or ask you to make your own.

If you are supposed to make your own Student Disks, you will need three blank, formatted high-density disks. You will need to copy a set of folders from a file server or standalone computer onto your disks. Your instructor will tell you which computer, drive letter, and folders contain the folders you need. The following table shows you which folders go on each of your disks, so that you will have enough disk space to complete all the tutorials, Tutorial Assignments, and Case Problems:

Student Disk	Write this on the disk label	Put these folders on the disk
1	Tutorials 1-6, Tutorials and Tutorial Assignments	Tutorial from Disk 1 folder
2	Case Problems 1 and 2	Cases from Disk 2 folder
3	Case Problems 3 and 4	Cases from Disk 3 folder

When you begin each tutorial, be sure you are using the correct Student Disk. See the inside front or inside back cover of this book for more information on Student Disk files, or ask your instructor or technical support person for assistance.

COURSE LABS

Database

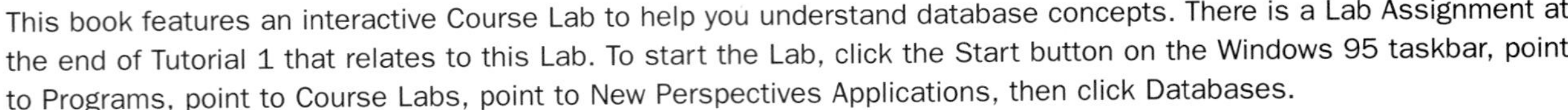

This book features an interactive Course Lab to help you understand database concepts. There is a Lab Assignment at the end of Tutorial 1 that relates to this Lab. To start the Lab, click the Start button on the Windows 95 taskbar, point to Programs, point to Course Labs, point to New Perspectives Applications, then click Databases.

USING YOUR OWN COMPUTER

If you are going to work through this book using your own computer, you need:

- **Computer System** Microsoft Windows 95 and Microsoft Access 7 for Windows 95 must be installed on your computer. This book assumes a full installation of Access.
- **Student Disks** Ask your instructor or lab manager for details on how to get the Student Disks. You will not be able to complete the tutorials or exercises in this book using your own computer until you have Student Disks. The student files may also be obtained electronically over the Internet. See the inside front or inside back cover of this book for more details.
- **Course Lab** See your instructor or technical support person to obtain the Course Lab for use on your own computer.

VISIT OUR WORLD WIDE WEB SITE

Additional materials designed especially for you are available on the World Wide Web. Go to **http://www.vmedia.com/cti/**.

TO THE INSTRUCTOR

To complete the tutorials in this book, your students must use a set of Student Files. These files are stored on the Student Files Disk(s) included in the Instructor's Resource Kit. Follow the instructions on the disk label(s) and the Readme.doc file to copy them to your server or standalone computer. You can view the Readme.doc file using WordPad.

Once the files are copied, you can make Student Disks for the students yourself, or tell students where to find the files so they can make their own Student Disks. Make sure the files get correctly copied onto the Students Disks by following the instructions in the Student Disks section above, which will ensure that students have enough disk space to complete all the tutorials, Tutorial Assignments, and Case Problems.

COURSE LAB SOFTWARE

Tutorial 1 features an online, interactive Course Lab that introduces basic database concepts. This software is distributed on the Course Labs Setup Disk(s), included in the Instructor's Resource Kit. To install the Lab software, follow the setup instructions on the disk label(s) and in the Readme.doc file. Once you have installed the Course Lab software, your students can start the Lab from the Windows 95 desktop by clicking Start, pointing to Programs/Course Labs/New Perspectives Applications, and clicking Databases.

CTI SOFTWARE AND STUDENT FILES

You are granted a license to copy the Student Files and Course Lab to any computer or computer network used by students who have purchased this book. The Student Files are included in the Instructor's Resource Kit and may also be obtained electronically over the Internet. See the inside front or inside back cover of this book for more details.

TUTORIAL 1

Introduction to Database Concepts and Access 7 for Windows 95

Planning a Special Magazine Issue

OBJECTIVES

In this tutorial you will:

- Learn terms used with databases
- Start and exit Access
- Identify the components of Access windows
- Open and close an Access database
- Open and close Access objects
- Print an Access table
- View an Access table using a datasheet and a form
- Use the Access Help system and shortcut menus

CASE

Vision Publishers

Brian Murphy is the president of Vision Publishers, which produces five specialized monthly magazines from its Chicago headquarters. Brian founded the company in March 1973 when he began publishing *Business Perspective*, a magazine featuring articles, editorials, interviews, and investigative reports that are widely respected in the financial and business communities. Using the concept, format, style, and strong writing of *Business Perspective* as a model, Brian began *Total Sports* in 1975, *Media Scene* in 1978, *Science Outlook* in 1984, and *Travel Vista* in 1987. All five magazines are leaders in their fields and have experienced consistent annual increases in circulation and advertising revenue.

Brian decides to do something special to commemorate the upcoming 25th anniversary of *Business Perspective* and schedules a meeting with three key employees of the magazine. At the meeting are Judith Rossi, managing editor; Harold Larson, marketing director; and Elena Sanchez, special projects editor. After reviewing alternatives, they agree that they will create a special 25th-anniversary issue of *Business Perspective*. The issue will include several articles reviewing the past 25 years of the magazine as well as the business and financial worlds during those years. Most of the special issue, however, will consist of articles from previous issues, a top article from each year of the magazine's existence. The *Business Perspective* team expects to sign up many advertisers for the issue and to use it as an incentive bonus gift for new and renewing subscribers.

Brian instructs Judith to select past articles and Elena to plan for the special issue. Brian will decide on the concept for the new articles and will communicate assignments to the writers.

Judith begins her assignment by using the Vision Publishers database that contains all articles published in the five magazines. From this Microsoft Access 7 for Windows 95 database, Judith will review the articles from *Business Perspective* and select the top articles.

Elena will also use Access for her assignment. Once Judith and Brian determine which articles will be in the special issue, Elena will use Access to store information about the selected business articles and their writers.

In this tutorial, you will work with Judith to complete her task. You will also learn about databases and how to use the features of Access to view and print your data.

Using the Tutorials Effectively

These tutorials will help you learn about Microsoft Access 7 for Windows 95. The tutorials are designed to be used at a computer. Each tutorial is divided into sessions, such as Session 1.1 and Session 1.2. The headings identify the tutorial and session number; for example, Tutorial 2 will have Session 2.1 and 2.2. Each session is designed to be completed in about 45 minutes, but you can take as much time as you need. It's also a good idea to take a break between sessions.

Before you begin, read the following questions and answers. They are designed to help you use the tutorials effectively.

Where do I start?

Each tutorial begins with a case, which sets the scene for the tutorial and gives you background information to help you understand what you will be doing in the tutorial. Ideally, you should read the case before you go to the lab.

How do I know what to do on the computer?

Each session contains steps that you will perform on the computer to learn how to use Access. Read the text that introduces each series of steps. The steps you need to do at a computer are numbered and are set against a colored background. Read each step carefully and completely before you try it.

How do I know if I did the step correctly?

As you work, compare your computer screen with the corresponding figure in the tutorial. Don't worry if your screen display is somewhat different from the corresponding figures. The important parts of the screen display are labeled in each figure. Check to make sure these parts are on your screen.

What if I make a mistake?

Don't worry about making mistakes—they are part of the learning process. Paragraphs labeled "TROUBLE?" identify common problems and explain how to get back on track. Follow the steps in a TROUBLE? paragraph *only* if you are having the problem described. If you run into other problems:

- Carefully consider the current state of your system, the position of the pointer, and any messages on the screen.
- Complete the sentence, "Now I want to...." Be specific, because you are identifying your goal.
- Develop a plan for accomplishing your goal, and put your plan into action.

How do I use the Reference Windows?

Reference Windows summarize the procedures you learn in the tutorial steps. Do not complete the actions in the Reference Windows when you are working through the tutorial. Instead, refer to the Reference Windows while you are working on the assignments at the end of the tutorial.

How can I test my understanding of the material I learned in the tutorial?

At the end of each session, you can answer the Quick Check questions. The answers for the Quick Checks are at the end of the tutorials.

After you have completed the entire tutorial, you should complete the Tutorial Assignments. The Tutorial Assignments are carefully structured so you will review what you have learned and then apply your knowledge to new situations.

What if I can't remember how to do something?

You should refer to the Task Reference at the end of the tutorials; it summarizes how to accomplish commonly performed tasks.

To follow the tutorials, you need to know how to use menus, dialog boxes, the Help facility, and My Computer in Microsoft Windows 95. Course Technology, Inc. publishes two excellent texts for learning Windows 95: *New Perspectives on Microsoft Windows 95—Brief* and *New Perspectives on Microsoft Windows 95—Introductory.*

Now that you've read how to use the tutorials effectively, you are ready to begin.

SESSION 1.1

In this session, you will learn how to start and exit Access. You will also learn how to open a database, view and print a table, and close an object window. With these skills, you will be able to open, view, and print tables in Access databases.

Introduction to Database Concepts

Before you work along with Judith on her Vision Publishers assignment, you need to understand a few key terms and concepts associated with databases.

Organizing Data

Data is a valuable resource to companies. At Vision Publishers, for example, writers' names, payments, past magazine article titles, and publication dates are data of great value. Organizing, creating, maintaining, retrieving, and sorting such data are important activities that lead to the display and printing of information useful to a company.

When you plan to create and store new types of data, either manually or on a computer, you follow a general three-step procedure:

1. Identify the individual fields.
2. Group fields for each entity in a table.
3. Store the field values for each record.

You first identify the individual fields. A **field** is a single characteristic of an entity and is also called a data element, data item, or attribute. An **entity** is a person, place, object, event, or idea. For example, Vision Publishers uses one entity, magazine articles (which includes several fields, such as Article Title and Article Length) to store data about its published articles. It uses another entity, writers (which includes the fields Writer Name and Writer Phone) to maintain information about the writers who have contributed to its magazines. Descriptive **field names**, such as Article Title and Writer Name, are used to label the fields.

Next, you group together all fields for a specific entity into a **table.** Corresponding to the entities discussed above, Vision Publishers has a MAGAZINE ARTICLES table and a WRITERS table, as shown in Figure 1-1. The MAGAZINE ARTICLES table has fields named Article Title, Magazine Issue, Magazine Name, and Article Length (number of words). The WRITERS table includes fields named Writer ID, Writer Name, and Writer Phone. By identifying the fields for each entity and then organizing them into tables, you have created the physical structure for your data.

Figure 1-1 Fields organized in two tables

MAGAZINE ARTICLES table

Article Title	Magazine Issue	Magazine Name	Article Length

WRITERS table

Writer ID	Writer Name	Writer Phone

magazine articles entity

fields

writers entity

Your final step is to store specific values for the fields of each table. The specific value, or content, of a field is called the **field value**. In the MAGAZINE ARTICLES table shown in Figure 1-2, for example, the first set of field values for Article Title, Magazine Issue, Magazine Name, and Article Length are, respectively, Trans-Alaskan Oil Pipeline Opening, 1977 JUL, Business Perspective, and 803. This set of field values is called a **record**. Each magazine article that appears in the MAGAZINE ARTICLES table is a separate record. In Figure 1-2, nine records are shown, corresponding to the nine rows of field values.

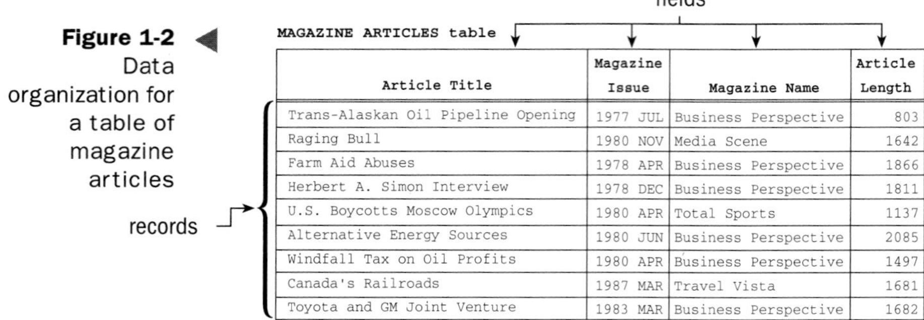
MAGAZINE ARTICLES table

Article Title	Magazine Issue	Magazine Name	Article Length
Trans-Alaskan Oil Pipeline Opening	1977 JUL	Business Perspective	803
Raging Bull	1980 NOV	Media Scene	1642
Farm Aid Abuses	1978 APR	Business Perspective	1866
Herbert A. Simon Interview	1978 DEC	Business Perspective	1811
U.S. Boycotts Moscow Olympics	1980 APR	Total Sports	1137
Alternative Energy Sources	1980 JUN	Business Perspective	2085
Windfall Tax on Oil Profits	1980 APR	Business Perspective	1497
Canada's Railroads	1987 MAR	Travel Vista	1681
Toyota and GM Joint Venture	1983 MAR	Business Perspective	1682

Figure 1-2 Data organization for a table of magazine articles

Databases and Relationships

Organizing information in tables helps database users obtain information easily. However, what if you need information that is stored in more than one table? For example, suppose Judith wants information about a specific writer, Leroy W. Johnson, and the articles he wrote. To be able to access this information, the WRITERS table would have to be related to the MAGAZINE ARTICLES table. A collection of related tables is called a **database**, or a **relational database**.

To have a relational database, records must be connected from the separate tables through a **common field** that appears in all tables. For the WRITERS table and the MAGAZINE ARTICLES table, that common field is named Writer ID (Figure 1-3). For example, Leroy W. Johnson is the third writer in the WRITERS table and has a Writer ID field value of J525. This same Writer ID field value, J525, appears in the first and third records of the MAGAZINE ARTICLES table. Using these related tables, Judith can now find out specific information about Leroy W. Johnson and the articles he wrote.

Figure 1-3 Database relationships between tables for magazine articles and writers

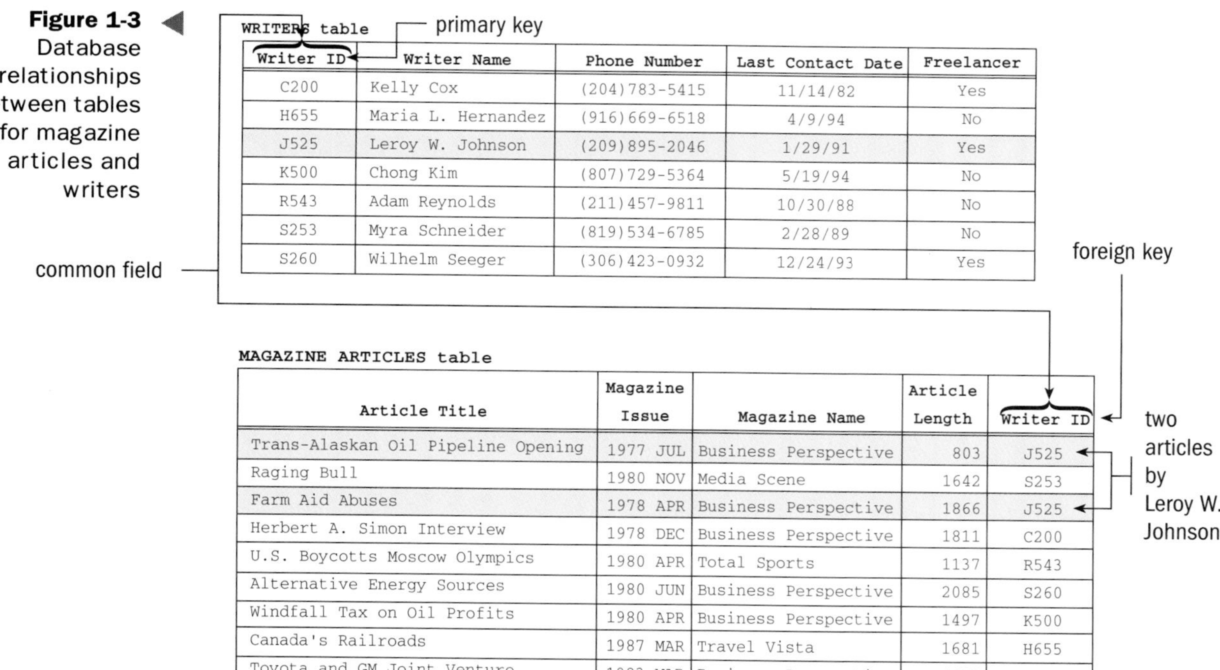

WRITERS table

Writer ID	Writer Name	Phone Number	Last Contact Date	Freelancer
C200	Kelly Cox	(204)783-5415	11/14/82	Yes
H655	Maria L. Hernandez	(916)669-6518	4/9/94	No
J525	Leroy W. Johnson	(209)895-2046	1/29/91	Yes
K500	Chong Kim	(807)729-5364	5/19/94	No
R543	Adam Reynolds	(211)457-9811	10/30/88	No
S253	Myra Schneider	(819)534-6785	2/28/89	No
S260	Wilhelm Seeger	(306)423-0932	12/24/93	Yes

MAGAZINE ARTICLES table

Article Title	Magazine Issue	Magazine Name	Article Length	Writer ID
Trans-Alaskan Oil Pipeline Opening	1977 JUL	Business Perspective	803	J525
Raging Bull	1980 NOV	Media Scene	1642	S253
Farm Aid Abuses	1978 APR	Business Perspective	1866	J525
Herbert A. Simon Interview	1978 DEC	Business Perspective	1811	C200
U.S. Boycotts Moscow Olympics	1980 APR	Total Sports	1137	R543
Alternative Energy Sources	1980 JUN	Business Perspective	2085	S260
Windfall Tax on Oil Profits	1980 APR	Business Perspective	1497	K500
Canada's Railroads	1987 MAR	Travel Vista	1681	H655
Toyota and GM Joint Venture	1983 MAR	Business Perspective	1682	S260

Notice that each Writer ID value in the WRITERS table is unique, so that we can distinguish one writer from another and identify the writer of specific articles in the MAGAZINE ARTICLES table. We call the Writer ID field the **primary key** of the WRITERS table. A primary key is a field or a collection of fields, whose values uniquely identify each record in a table.

When we include a primary key from one table in a second table to form a relationship between the two tables, we call it a **foreign key** in the second table. For example, Writer ID is the primary key in the WRITERS table and is a foreign key in the MAGAZINE ARTICLES table. Although the primary key Writer ID has unique values in the WRITERS table, the same field as a foreign key in the MAGAZINE ARTICLES table does not. The Writer ID values J525 and S260, for example, each appear twice in the MAGAZINE ARTICLES table. Each foreign key value, however, must match one of the field values for the primary key in the other table. Each Writer ID value in the MAGAZINE ARTICLES table, for instance, appears as a Writer ID value in the WRITERS table.

Relational Database Management Systems

As you might imagine, a company relies on numerous databases to store its data. To manage its databases, a company uses **database management system (DBMS)** software to let its employees create databases and then manipulate data in the databases. Most of today's database management systems, including Access, are called relational database management systems. In a **relational database management system**, data is organized as a collection of tables. These tables are formally called relations, which is how the term relational databases originated.

A relationship between two tables in a relational DBMS is formed through the common field. A relational DBMS (Figure 1-4) controls the physical databases on disk storage by carrying out data creation and manipulation requests. Specifically, a relational DBMS allows you to:

- create database structures containing fields, tables, and table relationships
- add new records, change field values in existing records, and delete records
- obtain immediate answers to the questions you ask about your data through its built-in query language
- produce professional-looking, formatted, hardcopy reports from your data through its built-in report generator
- protect databases through its security, control, and recovery facilities

Figure 1-4
A relational database management system

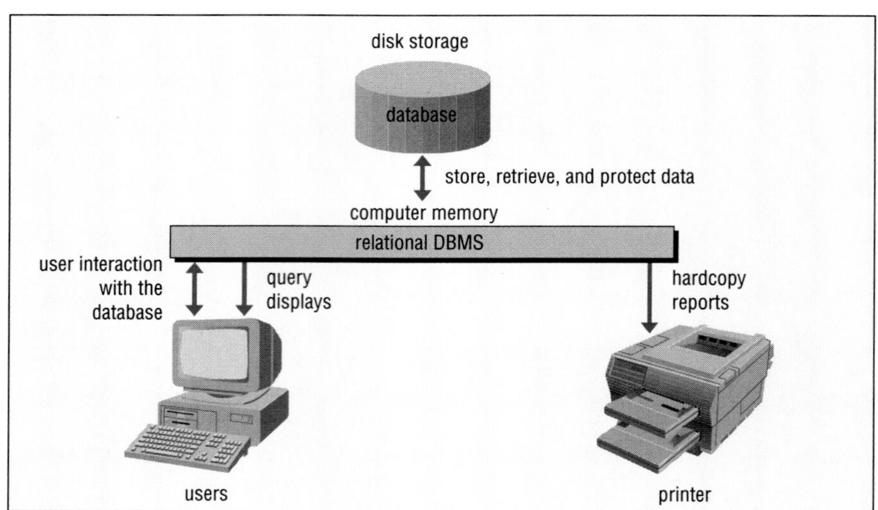

A company like Vision Publishers additionally benefits from a relational DBMS because it allows several people working in different departments to share the same data. More than one person can enter data into a database, and more than one person can retrieve and analyze data that was entered by others. For example, Vision Publishers keeps only one copy of the WRITERS table, and all employees use it to meet their specific needs for writer information.

A DBMS can handle massive amounts of data and can easily form relationships among multiple tables. Each Access database, for example, can be up to 1 gigabyte in size and can contain up to 32,768 tables.

Starting and Exiting Access

Access is rapidly becoming one of the most popular relational DBMSs in the Windows 95 environment. For the rest of this tutorial, you will learn to use Access as you work with Judith and Elena on their project.

You first need to learn how to start Access, so let's do that now.

To start Access:

1. Make sure you have created your copy of the Access Student Disk and that you have started Windows 95.

   TROUBLE? If you don't have a Student Disk, then you need to get one before you can proceed. Your instructor will either give you one or ask you to make your own. See your instructor for information.

2. Click the **Start** button.
3. Point to **Programs** to display the programs list.
4. Point to **Microsoft Office**. See Figure 1-5.

Figure 1-5 Starting Microsoft Access

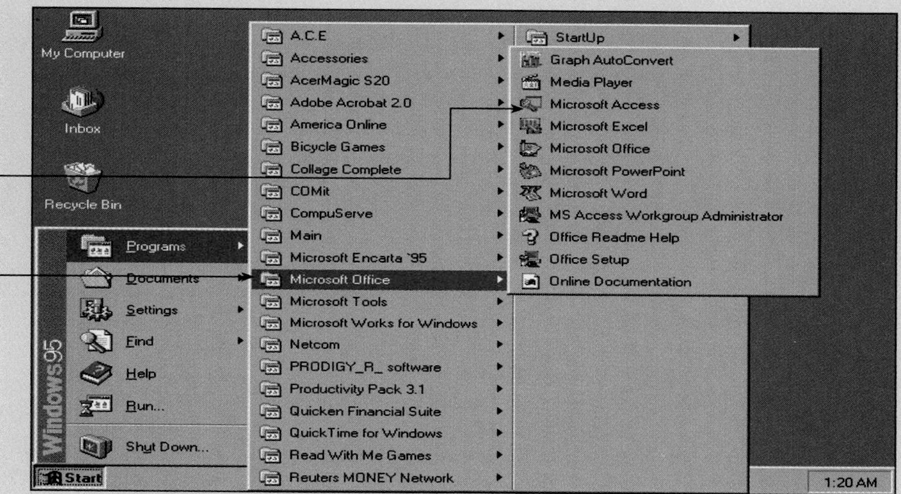

   TROUBLE? If you don't see a Microsoft Office in the program list, then look for a program labeled Microsoft Access and use it instead. If you do not have either of these, ask your technical support person or instructor for help finding Microsoft Access. Perhaps Access has not been installed on the computer you are using. If you are using your own computer, make sure you have installed the Access software.

5. Click **Microsoft Access** to start Access. After a short pause, the Access copyright information appears in a message box and remains on the screen until Access displays the Microsoft Access window. See Figure 1-6.

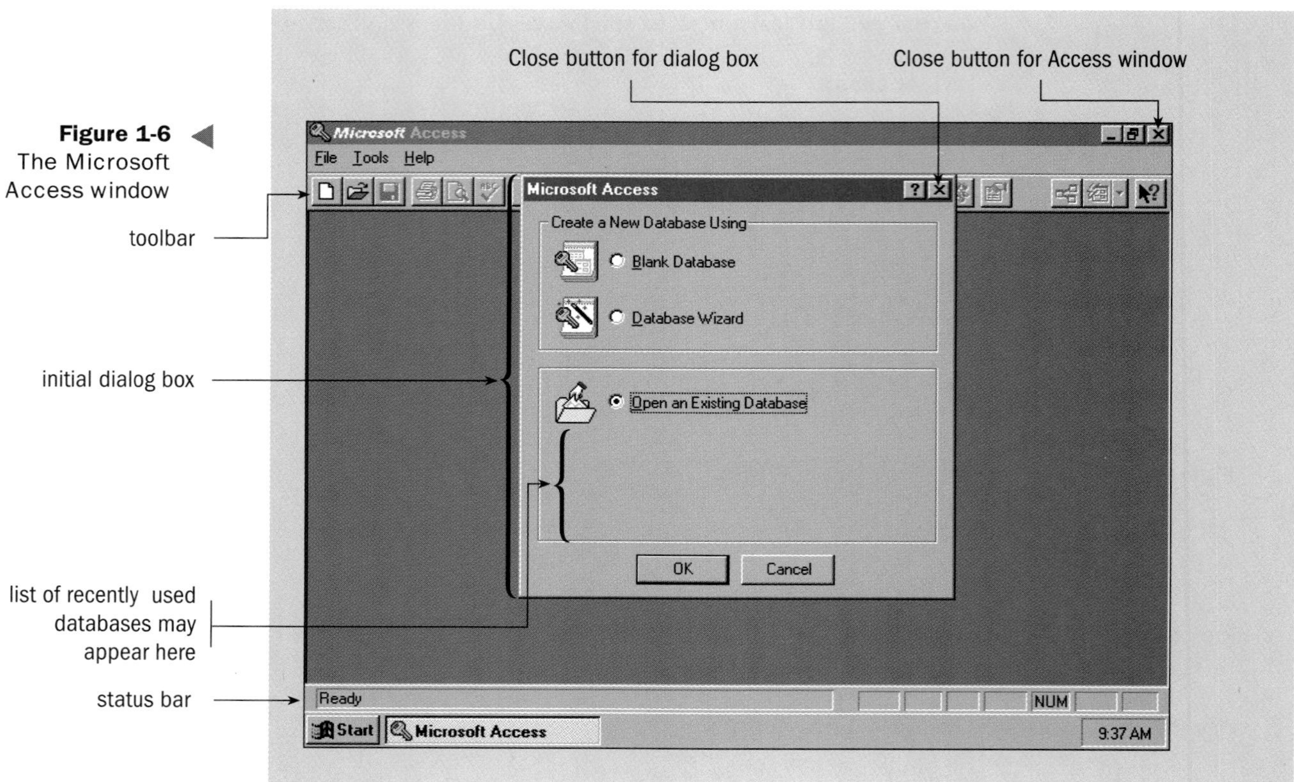

Figure 1-6 The Microsoft Access window

Access is now loaded into your computer's memory. When you start Access, the Access window contains a dialog box that allows you to create a new database or open an existing database. Although Judith wants to work with an existing database, it's always a good idea to know how to exit a software application when you first start working with it.

The Reference Window called "Exiting Access" lists the general steps for exiting Access. Don't try the steps in the Reference Window now. Instead, just read the information in the Reference Window to get a general idea of what you are going to do. Specific instructions that you will follow are provided in the next section of numbered steps.

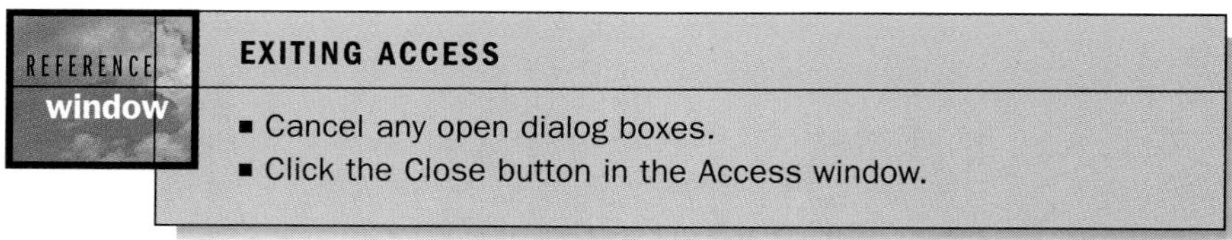

EXITING ACCESS

- Cancel any open dialog boxes.
- Click the Close button in the Access window.

By completing the following set of steps, you can exit Access at almost any time, no matter what you are doing. If you ever try to exit Access and find you cannot, your active window is likely to be an open dialog box. An open dialog box will prevent you from immediately exiting Access. Simply cancel the dialog box, and you will then be able to exit Access.

To exit Access:

1. Click the **Close** button ☒ to close the dialog box.
2. Click the **Close** button ☒ in the upper-right corner of the Access window.

You have now exited Access. In the next section of the tutorial, as the first step in helping Judith complete her assignment, you'll learn how to open a database.

Opening a Database

To select the articles for the 25th anniversary issue, Judith will work with an existing database, so her first step is to open that database. When you want to use a database that was previously created, you must first open it. When you open a database, a copy of the database file is transferred into the random access memory (often referred to as RAM) of your computer and becomes available for your use. You can then view, print, modify, or save it on your disk.

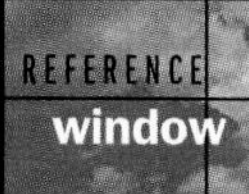

OPENING A DATABASE

- Click the radio button next to "Open an Existing Database," then click the OK button to display the Open dialog box.
  or
  Click the Open Database button on the toolbar in the Access window to display the Open dialog box.
- Change the drive and directory information, if necessary, to the disk location of the database.
- Scroll through the File name list box until the database name appears and then click it.
- Click the Open button to open the database.

Judith opens the database for Vision Publishers now.

To open an existing database:

1. Start Access by following the steps described earlier. The Access window appears with the initial dialog box.
2. Make sure your Access Student Disk is in the appropriate drive—either drive A or drive B.

   You may see a list of databases in a list box below the Open an Existing Database radio button. This is a list of databases recently used on your machine. The first entry in the list, More Files, gives you access to databases not shown in the list. If this list box is visible, make sure that More Files is highlighted.
3. Make sure the radio button next to "Open an Existing Database" is selected. Click the **OK** button to display the Open dialog box. See Figure 1-7.

Figure 1-7 Open dialog box

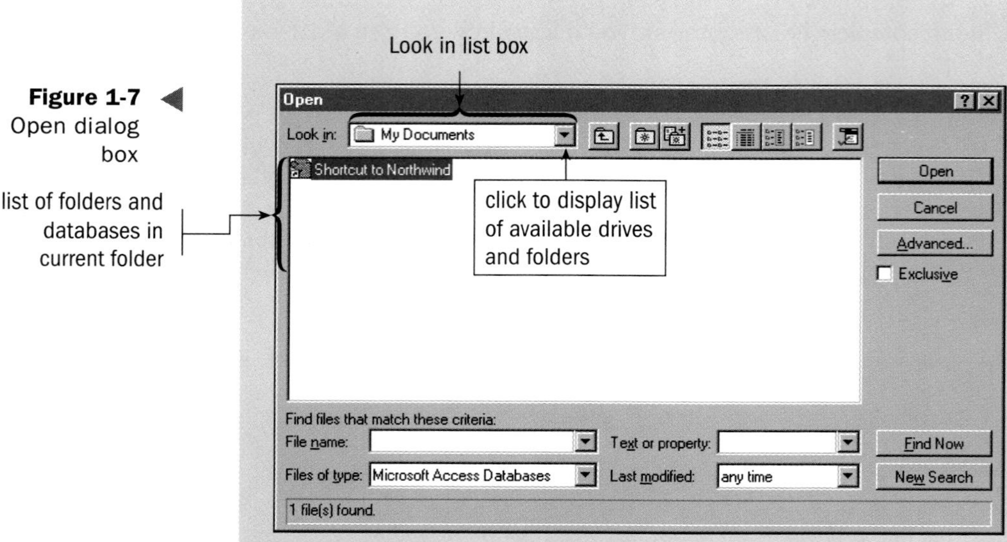

4. Click the **Look in** list arrow. A list of available drives drops down. Click the icon of the drive in which you put your Student Disk. The panel below the Look in list box now displays a list of folders and databases on your disk.
5. Click **Tutorial** in the folders list to select it, then click the **Open** button.
6. Click **Vision** in the database list to select it. See Figure 1-8.

Figure 1-8 Completed Open dialog box

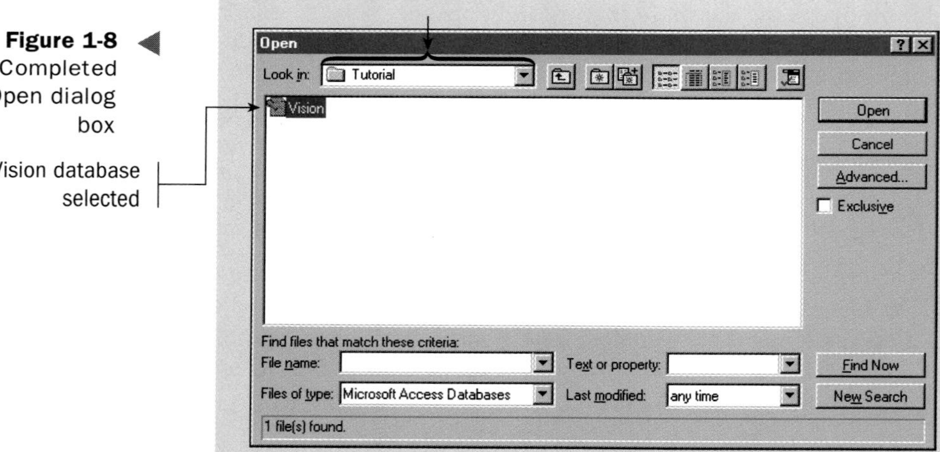

TROUBLE? Depending on your computer configuration, your screen may show the database name with the extension name. In that case, click Vision.mdb to select the database.

TROUBLE? If you can't find a file named Vision, check that the Look in list box indicates the Tutorial folder of your Student Disk. If the Look in list box shows the correct folder, perhaps you are using the wrong disk in the drive. Check your disk to be sure it's your Student Disk. If it is the correct disk, check with your technical support person or instructor. If it is not the correct disk, place the correct Student Disk in the drive and resume your work from Step 4.

7. Click the **Open** button to let Access know you have completed the Open Database dialog box. Access opens the Vision database and displays the Database window in the Access window.

Before beginning her assignment for Brian, Judith checks the window on the screen to familiarize herself with her options. You should also.

Access Windows

Access windows, like other Windows software such as Word and Excel, contain toolbars and menu bars that vary depending on the window you are viewing. As in other Windows programs, the toolbar buttons represent common operations you perform with the software you are using—in this case, databases.

When you first view the toolbar, you might be unsure of the function associated with each toolbar button. Fortunately, when you stop the mouse pointer on a toolbar button, Access displays a ToolTip under the button and a description of the button in the status bar at the bottom of the screen. A **ToolTip** is a boxed caption showing the name of the indicated toolbar button.

Judith displays the ToolTip for the Print button.

To display a ToolTip:

1. Move the mouse pointer to the toolbar and stop the pointer on the Print button. It is the fourth button from the left. After a short pause, Access displays a ToolTip under the button and the button's description in the status bar. See Figure 1-9.

Figure 1-9 The Print ToolTip in the Access window

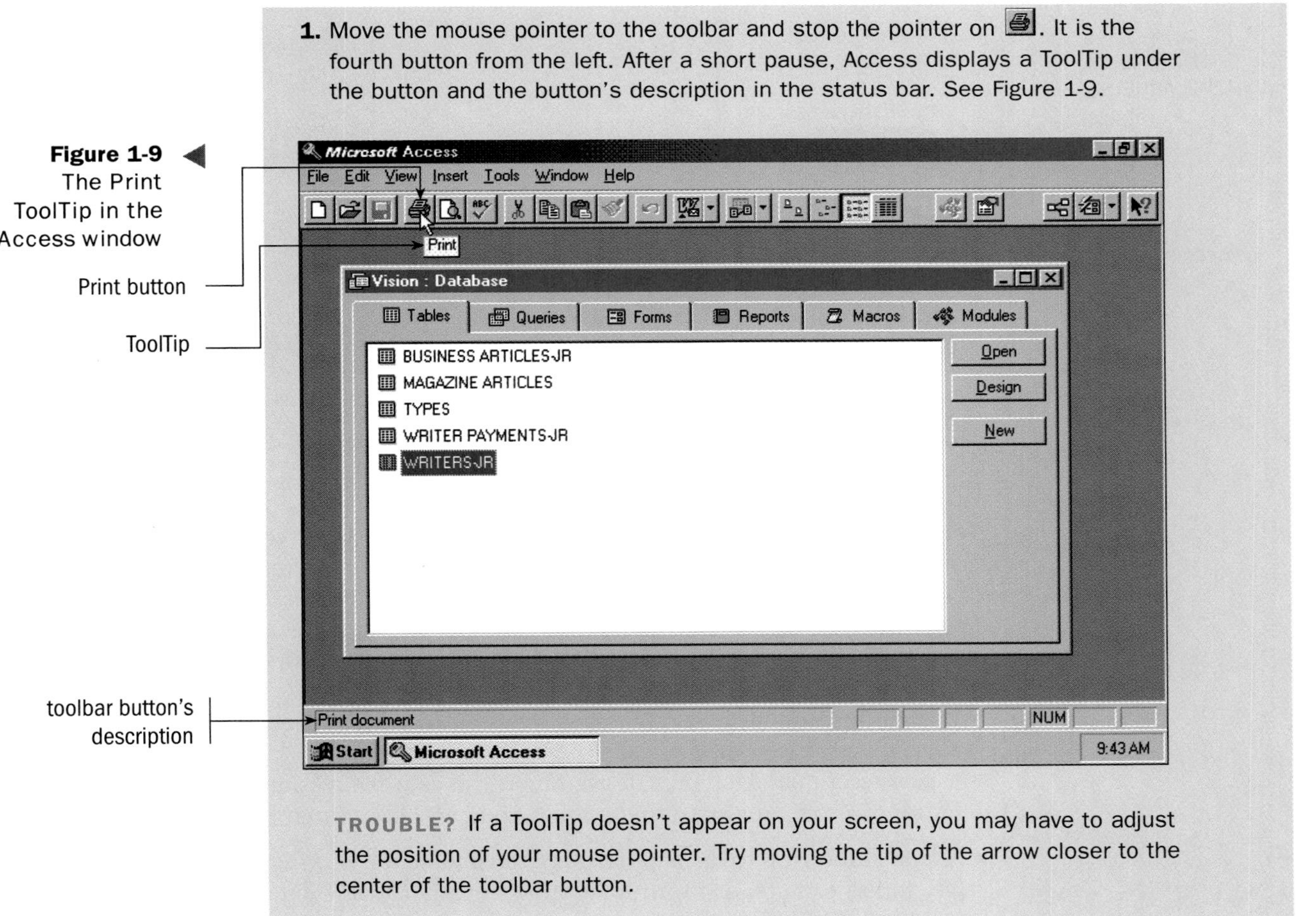

TROUBLE? If a ToolTip doesn't appear on your screen, you may have to adjust the position of your mouse pointer. Try moving the tip of the arrow closer to the center of the toolbar button.

Some toolbar buttons, such as the Format Painter button, appear dimmed because they are not active now. They will become active later, after you have opened a database or taken some other action. Spend a few moments now stopping at active toolbar buttons to view their ToolTip and status bar descriptions.

The Database Window

After a database is opened, Access displays the Database window, shown in Figure 1-10. Because you already have experience with the Windows 95 graphical user interface (GUI), you will recognize the following components of the Database window: the Access window title bar, the Access window sizing buttons, the menu bar, the toolbar, the toolbar buttons, the Database window sizing buttons, and the status bar.

Figure 1-10 The Database window

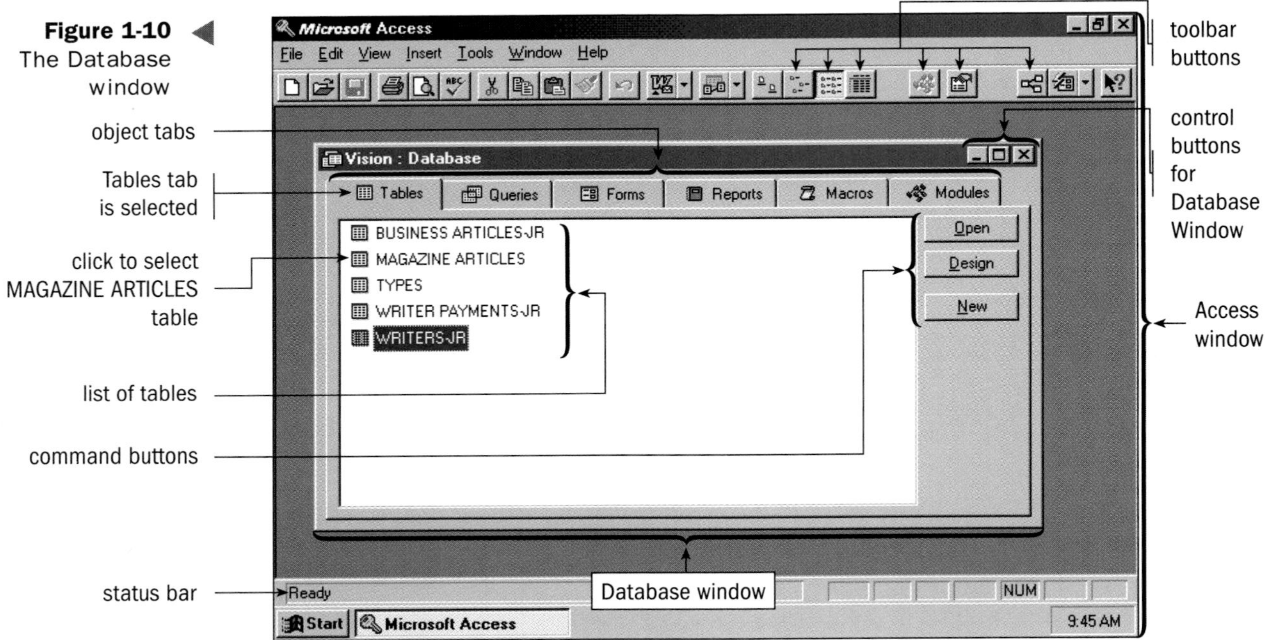

You might not be familiar with the six object tabs and the three command buttons. The object tabs represent the six types of objects you can create for an Access database. Unlike most other DBMSs, Access stores each database, which includes all of its defined tables, queries, forms, reports, macros, and modules, in a single file. Each object is handled separately so that if Vision Publishers has three tables, five queries, and four reports in a database, Access treats them as 12 separate objects.

You already know what a table is, so let's consider the other five objects:

- A **query** is a question you can ask about the data from your tables. For example, Judith can use a query to find all magazine articles written by a particular writer.
- A **form** allows you to display records from a table for viewing or editing. For example, Judith can create a form that allows others to view data one record at a time from the WRITERS table.

- A **report** is a customized format for printing the data from tables. If Brian needs to review all writer information, a report can be generated to display this data in a readable format.
- A **macro** is a saved list of operations to be performed on data. Judith can use a macro, for example, to open a special form automatically whenever someone opens the company database.
- A **module** is a set of one or more Visual Basic procedures (Visual Basic is Access's built-in programming language). At Vision Publishers, for example, a module is used to calculate payments to writers.

The three command buttons in the Database window represent the major operations performed on tables. You can create a new table by clicking the New button. For an existing table, click the Open button to view table records or click the Design button to change the table structure.

The Tables tab is automatically selected when you first open a database, and a list of available tables for the database appears. When you click one of the other object tabs to select it, a list of available objects of that type appears.

Viewing and Printing a Table

Now that you have opened a database and familiarized yourself with the components of the Database window, you are ready to view and print an existing Access table. If you want to look up information contained in just a few records in a table, you usually view the table on the screen. If you need information from a large number of records or need to present the information to other people, however, you usually print a hardcopy of the table.

Datasheet View

The Vision Publishers table named MAGAZINE ARTICLES contains data about all the magazine articles published by the company. Judith opens this table to start her selection of top past articles from *Business Perspective* magazine for use in the special issue.

OPENING THE DATASHEET VIEW WINDOW FOR A TABLE

- Scroll through the Tables list until the table name appears and then click it.
- Click the Open button.

Judith opens the MAGAZINE ARTICLES table for Vision Publishers.

To open the Datasheet View window for the MAGAZINE ARTICLES table:

1. If necessary, click **MAGAZINE ARTICLES** to select it, then click the **Open** button. The Datasheet View window for the MAGAZINE ARTICLES table appears on top of the previous windows. See Figure 1-11.

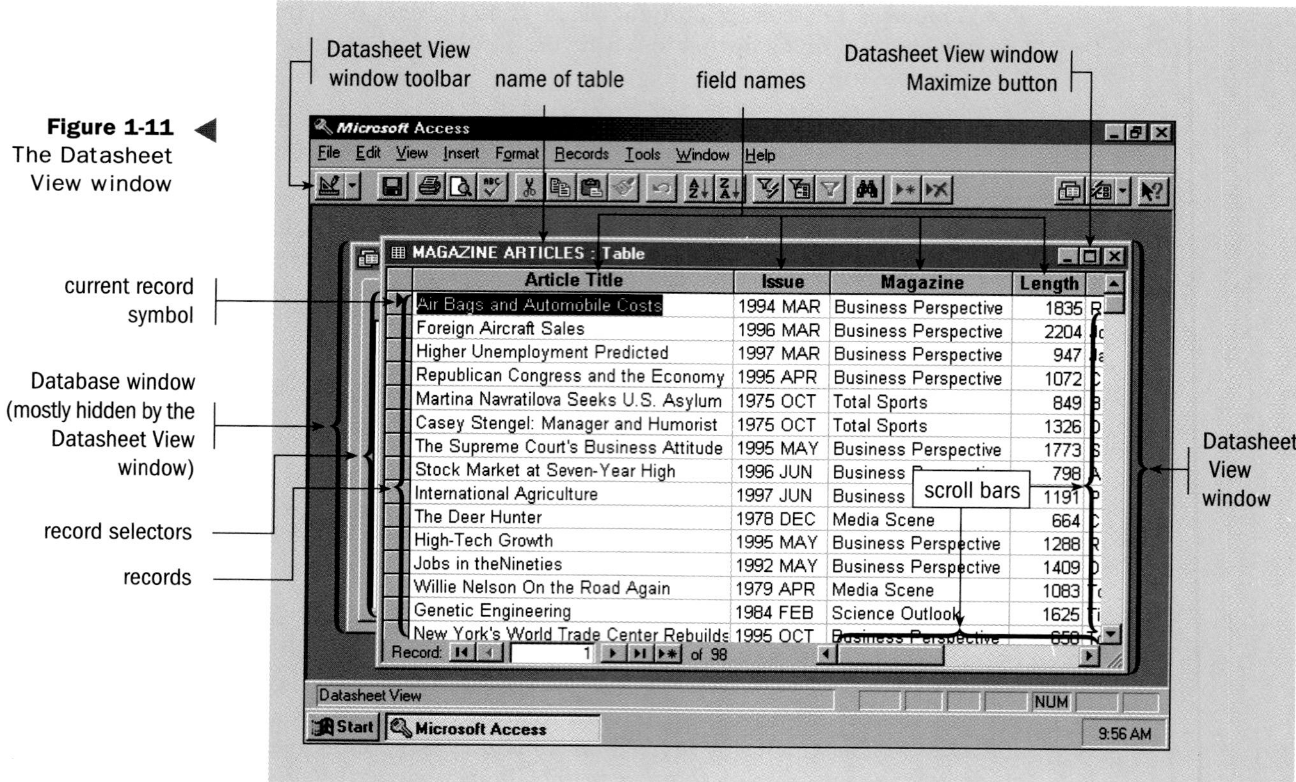

Figure 1-11 The Datasheet View window

The **Datasheet View** window shows a table's contents in rows and columns, the way a spreadsheet does. Each row is a separate record in the table, and each column contains the field values for one field from the table. When you first open a datasheet, Access automatically selects the first field value in the first record for processing. This field is highlighted and a darkened triangle symbol, called the **current record symbol**, appears in the record selector to the left of the first record. If you move your mouse pointer over any field value, the pointer shape changes to I. If you then click the I on a field value in another row, that field value becomes the currently selected field and the current record symbol moves to that row. Although the entire field value is not highlighted, the insertion point stays where you clicked, and the new record becomes the current record. Practice clicking the I on different fields and records and notice the changes that occur in the datasheet.

Even though the MAGAZINE ARTICLES table has only five fields, depending on your computer system the Datasheet View window may not be large enough to display all the fields across the screen. You may only see only the first group of records from the table. To see more of the table on the screen, you can maximize the Datasheet View window in the Access window.

To maximize the Datasheet View window:

1. Click the **Maximize** button for the Datasheet View window. Notice that a Restore button replaces the Maximize button and that the table title appears in the Access title bar.

   TROUBLE? If your datasheet is not maximized, you probably clicked the Datasheet View window Minimize button or one of the Microsoft Access window sizing buttons instead. Use the appropriate sizing button to restore your screen to its previous condition, and then refer to Figure 1-11 for the location of the Datasheet View window Maximize button.

Even though the Datasheet View window is maximized, depending on your computer system, the fields in the MAGAZINE ARTICLES table may still be too wide to fit on the screen and there might be too many records to see them all on the screen at one time. One way to see different parts of a table is to use the vertical and horizontal scroll bars and arrows on the right and bottom of the datasheet. Practice clicking these scroll bars and arrows to become comfortable with their use. Use the vertical scroll bar (also called the elevator) to move vertically through the table to display different records. Use the horizontal scroll bar to scroll right and left to display different fields.

Using the lower-left navigation buttons, shown in Figure 1-12, is another way to move vertically through the records. From left to right, respectively, the four **navigation buttons** select the first record, the previous record, the next record, and the last record in the table. The last button ▶* creates a blank (new) record. The current record number appears between the two sets of navigation buttons. The total number of records in the table appears to the right of the navigation buttons. Practice clicking the four navigation buttons (but not the blank record button) and notice the changes that occur in the datasheet, in the current record number, and in the placement of the current record symbol.

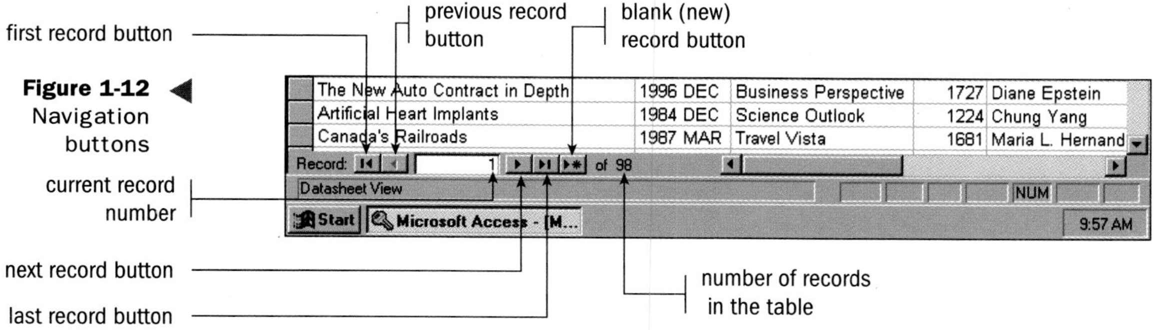

Figure 1-12 Navigation buttons

The Datasheet View window displays the table records on the screen. To obtain a hardcopy of the records, you can print them on your printer. Because the table contains several datasheet pages, Judith decides to print only the records from the first datasheet page to study their contents more closely. Remember, a datasheet page allows you to view the actual records.

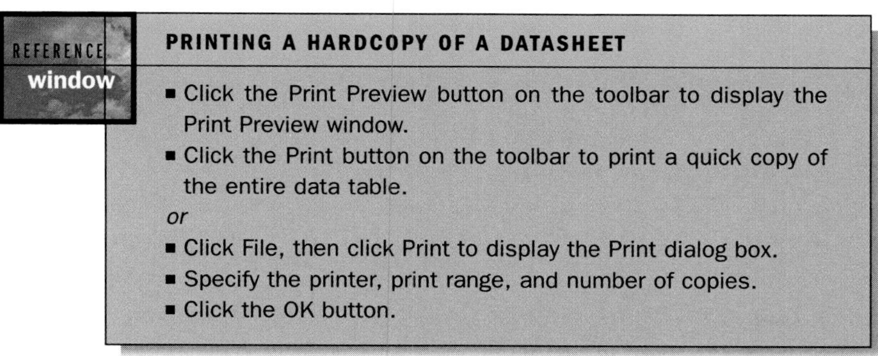

PRINTING A HARDCOPY OF A DATASHEET

- Click the Print Preview button on the toolbar to display the Print Preview window.
- Click the Print button on the toolbar to print a quick copy of the entire data table.

or

- Click File, then click Print to display the Print dialog box.
- Specify the printer, print range, and number of copies.
- Click the OK button.

Before you actually print the records, it is sometimes useful to preview them on the Print Preview screen. The Print Preview screen displays the records as they will appear on the hardcopy.

Judith previews the datasheet and then print its first page.

To preview and print a datasheet:

1. Click the **Print Preview** button on the toolbar. The Print Preview window opens. See Figure 1-13.

Figure 1-13 The Print Preview window

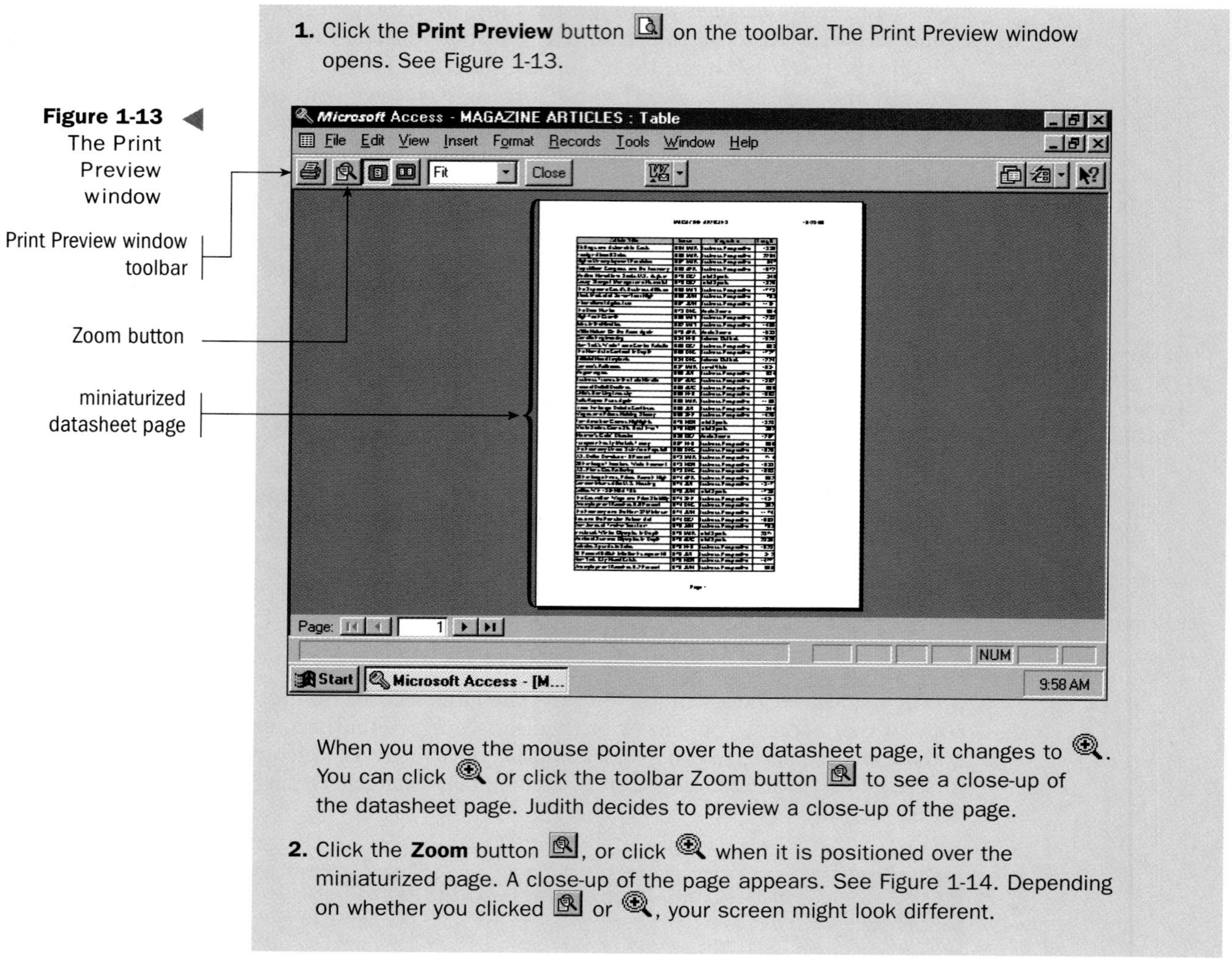

When you move the mouse pointer over the datasheet page, it changes to . You can click or click the toolbar Zoom button to see a close-up of the datasheet page. Judith decides to preview a close-up of the page.

2. Click the **Zoom** button , or click when it is positioned over the miniaturized page. A close-up of the page appears. See Figure 1-14. Depending on whether you clicked or , your screen might look different.

Figure 1-14
Zoomed Print Preview window

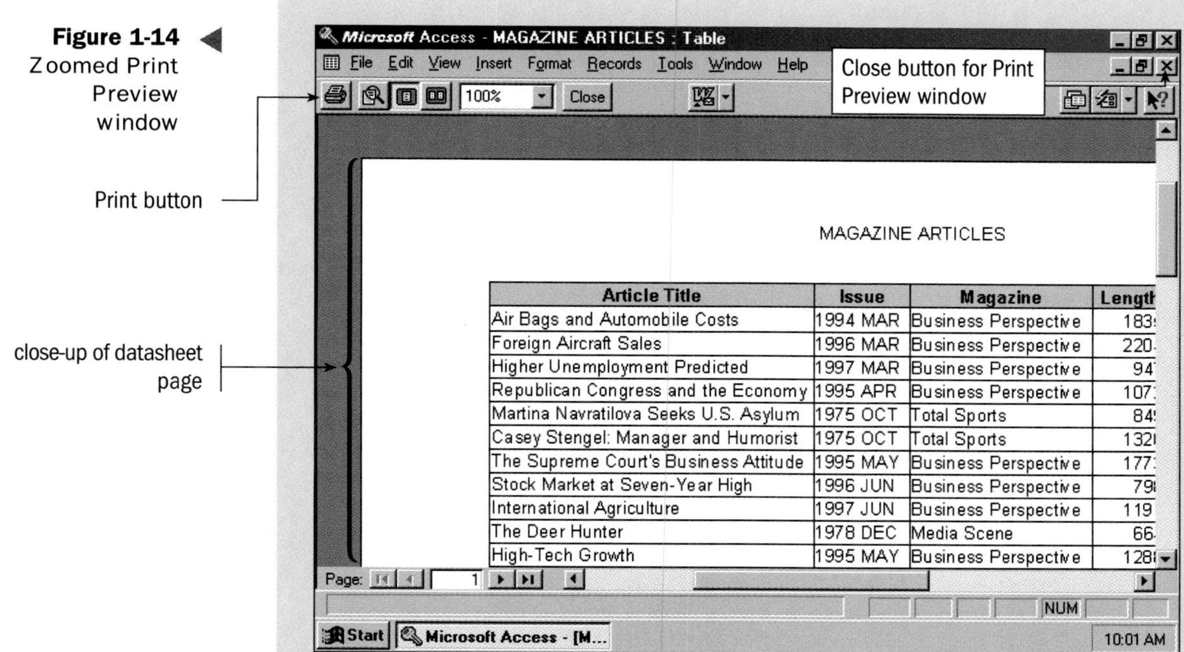

Article Title	Issue	Magazine	Lengtl
Air Bags and Automobile Costs	1994 MAR	Business Perspective	183
Foreign Aircraft Sales	1996 MAR	Business Perspective	220
Higher Unemployment Predicted	1997 MAR	Business Perspective	94
Republican Congress and the Economy	1995 APR	Business Perspective	107
Martina Navratilova Seeks U.S. Asylum	1975 OCT	Total Sports	84
Casey Stengel: Manager and Humorist	1975 OCT	Total Sports	132
The Supreme Court's Business Attitude	1995 MAY	Business Perspective	177
Stock Market at Seven-Year High	1996 JUN	Business Perspective	79
International Agriculture	1997 JUN	Business Perspective	119
The Deer Hunter	1978 DEC	Media Scene	66
High-Tech Growth	1995 MAY	Business Perspective	128

When you move the mouse pointer over the datasheet page, it changes to [icon]. If you click [icon] or [icon], the page returns to its original miniaturized view. Practice clicking [icon], [icon], [icon], and the navigation buttons. When you are done practicing, you are ready to print the datasheet page.

Microsoft Access offers two ways to print a datasheet. If you click the Print button [icon] on the toolbar, Access will immediately print the entire datasheet. If you want to print only selected pages or selected records, you can specify this in the Print dialog box that appears when you choose the Print option from the File menu.

3. Make sure your printer is on-line and ready to print. Because you want to print just the first datasheet page, click **File**, then click **Print**. The Print dialog box opens. Check the Printer section of the dialog box to make sure your printer is selected.

   TROUBLE? If the correct printer is not selected, click the list arrow in the Name text box and select the correct printer from the printer list.

4. Click the radio button next to "**Pages**" in the Print Range panel, then type **1**, press the **Tab** key, type **1** to print just the first page of the datasheet, then click the **OK** button. A dialog box informs you that your datasheet page is being sent to the printer.

5. After the dialog box closes, click the Print Preview window **Close** button [icon] to return to the Database window.

   TROUBLE? If Access displays a message box asking if you want to save changes, click the No button. You accidentally changed the datasheet and do not want to save the modified version in your table.

   TROUBLE? If your document hasn't printed yet, check the print status in the print queue for your printer. Remove your document from the print queue before returning to your datasheet and then print the first datasheet page again. If it still doesn't print, see your technical support person or instructor.

Quick Check

1. What three steps should you generally follow to create and store a new type of data?
2. What are fields and entities, and how are they related?
3. What are the differences between a primary key and a foreign key?
4. Describe what a DBMS is designed to do.
5. Describe the six different objects you can create for an Access database.
6. What do the columns and rows of a datasheet represent?

Use the data in Figure 1-15 to answer Question 7.

Figure 1-15

CHECKING ACCOUNTS table

Account Number	Name	Balance
2173	Theodore Lamont	842.27
4519	Beatrice Whalley	2071.92
8005	t Zambrano	1132.00

CHECKS table

Account Number	Check Number	Date	Amount
4519	1371	10/22/98	45.00
4519	1372	10/23/98	115.00
2173	1370	10/24/98	50.00
4519	1377	10/27/98	60.00
2173	1371	10/29/98	20.00

7. Name the fields in the CHECKS table. How many records are in the CHECKS table? What is the primary key of the CHECKING ACCOUNTS table?

Now that you've completed Session 1.1, you can exit the program or continue on to the next session. If you want to take a break and resume the tutorial at a later time, you can exit Access by clicking the Access window Close button in the upper-right corner of the screen. When you resume the tutorial, place your Student Disk in the appropriate drive and start Access. Open the database Vision, maximize the Database window, and then continue working on the next session of the tutorial.

SESSION 1.2

In this session, you will learn to view table records in a form, close a database, and use Access Help and shortcut menus.

Form View

Judith now opens an existing form to view the records from the MAGAZINE ARTICLES table. As we discussed earlier, a form gives you a customized view of data from a database. You use a form, for example, to view one record at a time from a table, to view data in a more readable format, or to view related data from two or more tables. The way you open a form is similar to the way you opened a datasheet.

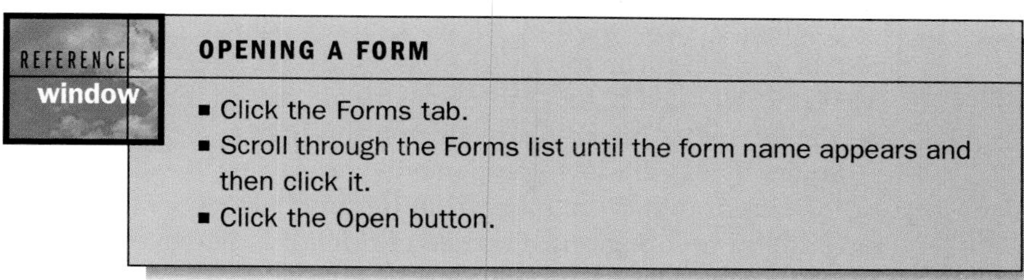

REFERENCE window

OPENING A FORM

- Click the Forms tab.
- Scroll through the Forms list until the form name appears and then click it.
- Click the Open button.

Judith now opens the form named Magazine Articles.

To open a form:

1. Make sure that the Database window is open and maximized, then click the **Forms** tab. A list of available forms appears in the Forms list. See Figure 1-16.

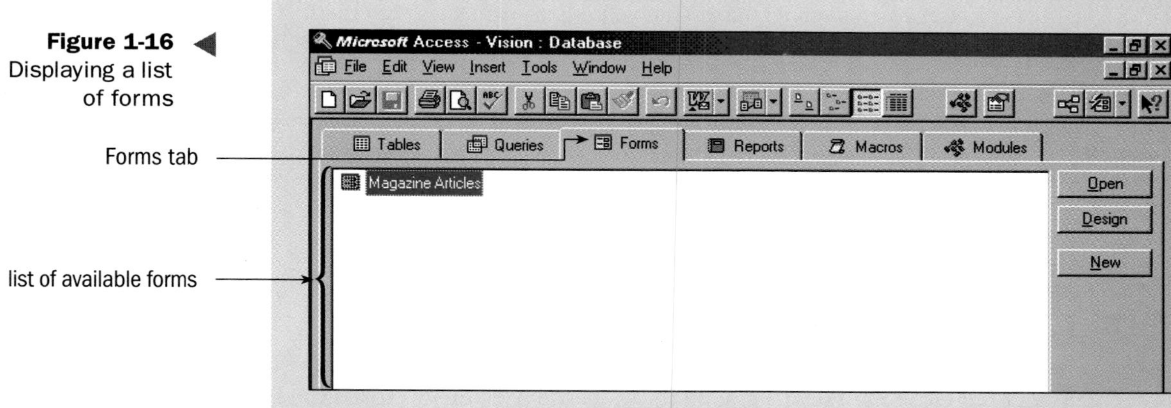

Figure 1-16 Displaying a list of forms

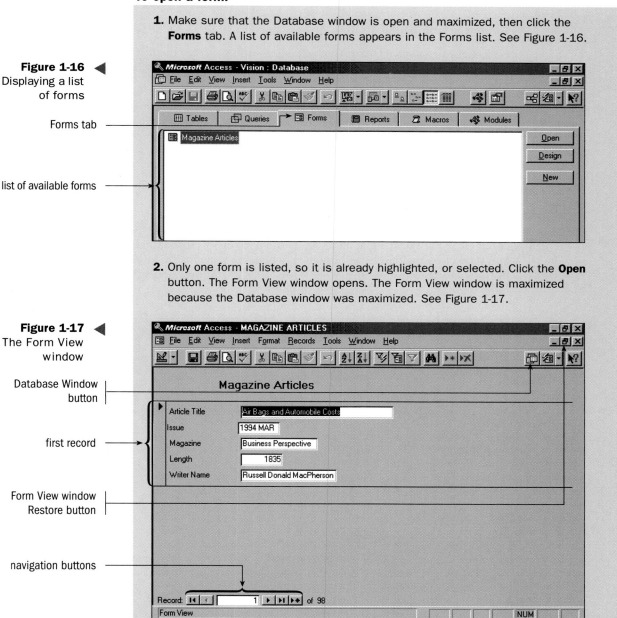

2. Only one form is listed, so it is already highlighted, or selected. Click the **Open** button. The Form View window opens. The Form View window is maximized because the Database window was maximized. See Figure 1-17.

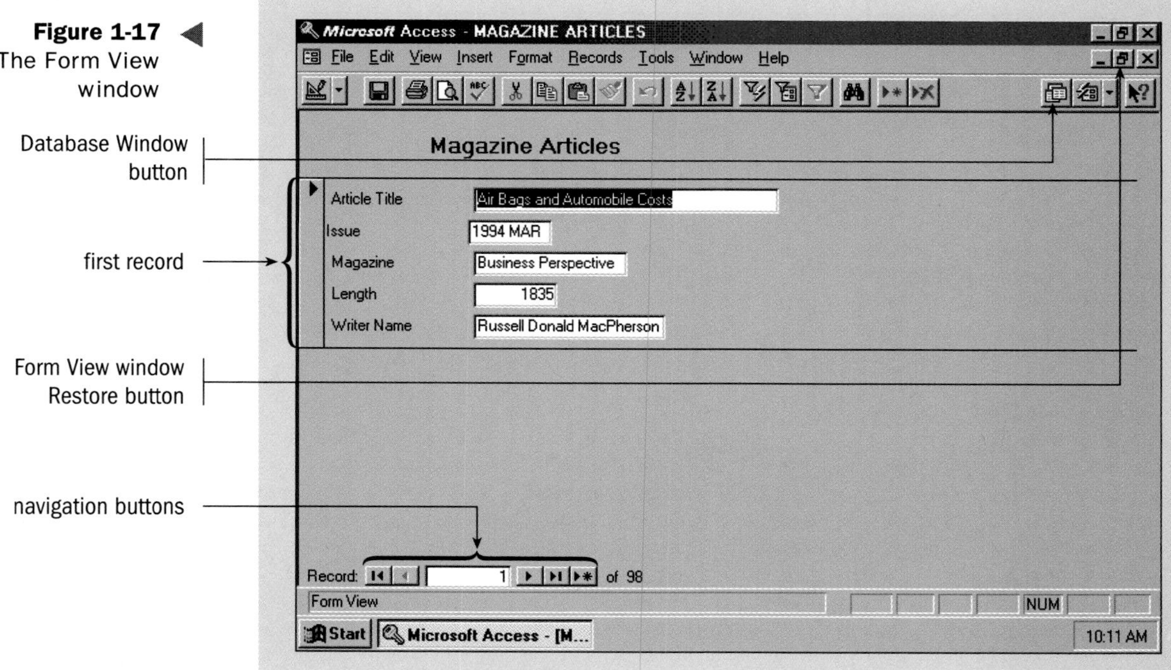

Figure 1-17 The Form View window

The Form View window shows a table's contents in a customized format, usually one record at a time. The form shown in Figure 1-17 vertically displays all five fields from the MAGAZINE ARTICLES table for a single record. Each field has a label (the field name) on the left and a boxed field value on the right.

Some of the window components you saw in the Datasheet View window (e.g., the Restore button and the navigation buttons) also appear in the Form View window and have the same functions. Practice clicking the navigation buttons and clicking different field values. Notice the changes that occur in the form.

Judith decides to print the first page of records from Form View. Access prints as many form records as can fit on a printed page. Judith decides not to use the Print Preview option. The steps you follow to print from Form View are similar to those used to print in Datasheet View.

To print a form page:

1. Before continuing, make sure you are in Form View with the first record displayed in a maximized window. Click **File**, then click **Print**. The Print dialog box opens.
2. Make sure your printer is on-line and ready to print. Check the Printer panel of the dialog box to make sure the correct printer is selected. Click the radio button next to "**Pages**" in the Print Range panel, type **1**, press the **Tab** key, type **1**, and then click the **OK** button. A dialog box informs you that your form page is being sent to the printer. After the dialog box closes, Access returns you to Form View.

Closing a Database

Judith is done viewing both the form and the database, so she closes the database. She could close the Form View window, as she previously closed the Datasheet View window, and then close the database. However, whenever you close a database without closing the Form View window or any other open object window, Access automatically closes all open windows before closing the database.

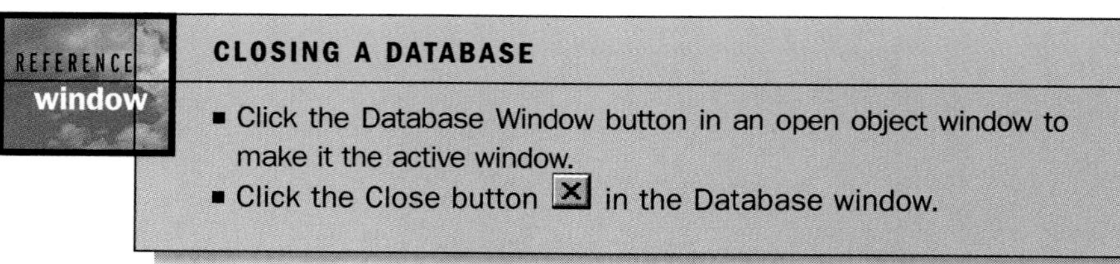

REFERENCE
window
CLOSING A DATABASE
■ Click the Database Window button in an open object window to make it the active window.
■ Click the Close button in the Database window.

Judith closes the Vision Publishers database.

To close the Vision database:

1. Click the **Database Window** button on the toolbar to activate the Database window. See Figure 1-18.

Figure 1-18 Activating the Database window

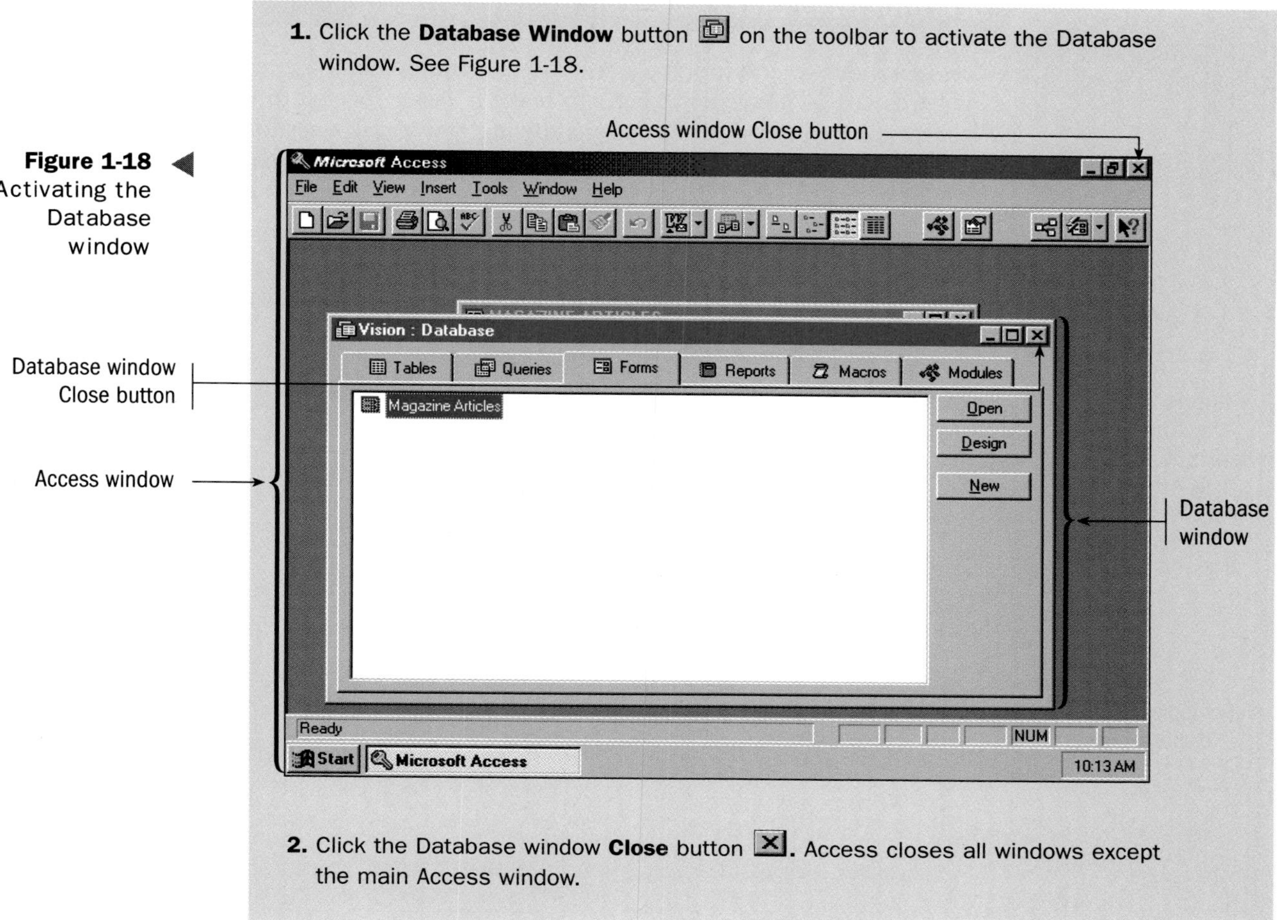

2. Click the Database window **Close** button. Access closes all windows except the main Access window.

Getting Help

While you are using Access on your computer, there might be times when you are puzzled about how to complete a task—or, you might need to clarify a definition or Access feature or investigate more advanced Access capabilities. You can use Access's Help system to give you on-line information about your specific questions. Access offers you five ways to get on-line help as you work: the Answer Wizard, the Help Contents, the Help Index, the Find feature, and the context-sensitive Help system. Let's practice using Answer Wizard, the Help Index, and the context-sensitive Help system, the three methods you will find most useful as you work through the tutorials.

Starting Help and Using the Answer Wizard

Access provides several tools to assist you in common database tasks. These tools, known as wizards, act as guides or experts to make it easier for you to use Access. The Answer Wizard assists you in using Help by allowing you to ask questions in ordinary language and finding a list of useful help topics for you to read. Judith has some questions about moving the toolbar on the screen and uses the Answer Wizard to find the answer.

To use the Answer Wizard to get help on moving the toolbar:

1. Click **Help** and then click **Answer Wizard**. The Access Help window opens and the Answer Wizard page is visible. See Figure 1-19.

Figure 1-19 The Answer Wizard page of the Access Help window

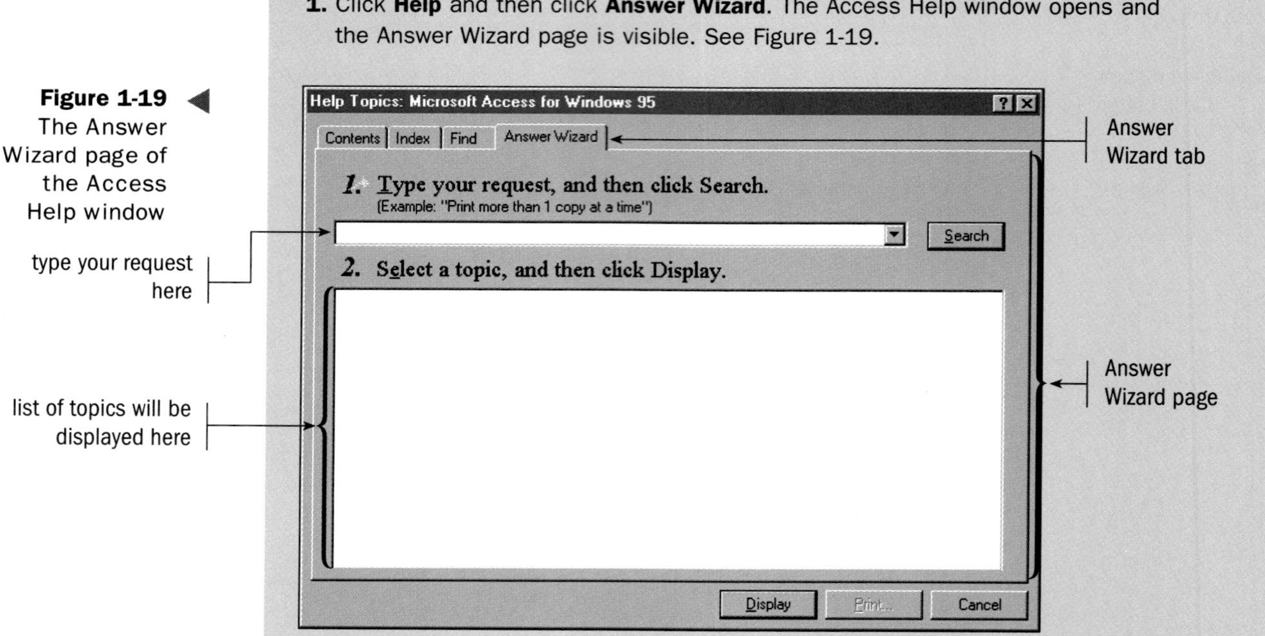

The Answer Wizard page is one of four pages available in the Access Help window. The other pages include the **Contents** page, which, like the table of contents in a book, displays a list of major topics available in Access Help; the **Index** page, which allows you to enter a key word or phrase and displays a topic (or topics) that matches that key word or phrase; and the **Find** page, which allows you to search the entire help file for the occurrence of a particular word.

The Answer Wizard page has two boxes, labeled 1 and 2. In the first box, you enter the request for the Answer Wizard. When you click the Search button, the Answer Wizard searches through the help files and presents you with a list of relevant help topics in the second box. Because Judith wants to know how to move a toolbar, you'll enter that question in the first box now.

2. In the first box, type **How do I move the toolbar?** then click the **Search** button. The Answer Wizard displays a list of relevant topics in the second box. See Figure 1-20.

Figure 1-20 Help topics found by the Answer Wizard

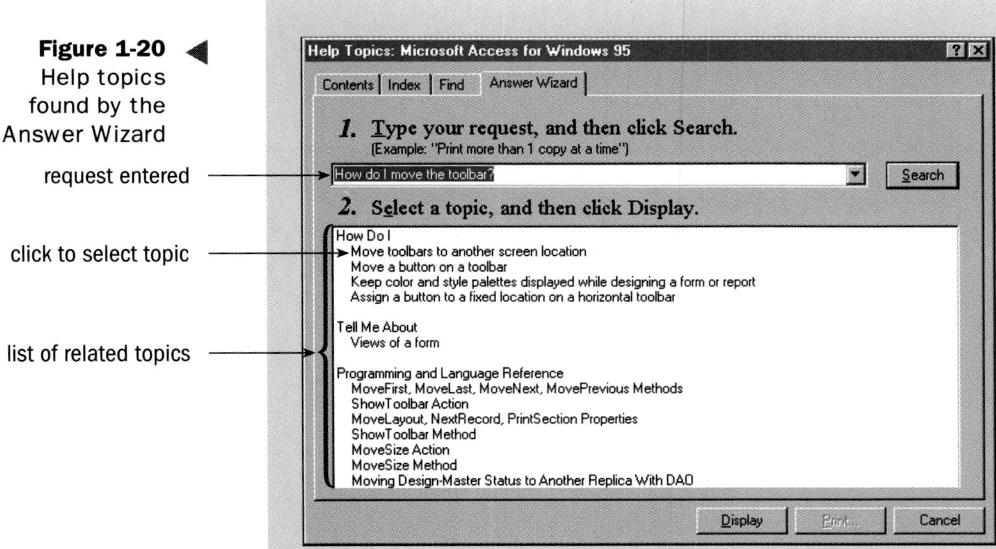

The list box displays several different topics. The second line in the box lists a topic that should provide Judith with the answer to her question. Let's look at that Help topic.

3. Click **Move toolbars to another screen location** to select that topic.

4. Click the **Display** button. The Answer Wizard finds the help text for you and displays it in the Help window. See Figure 1-21.

Figure 1-21 Help on moving the toolbars

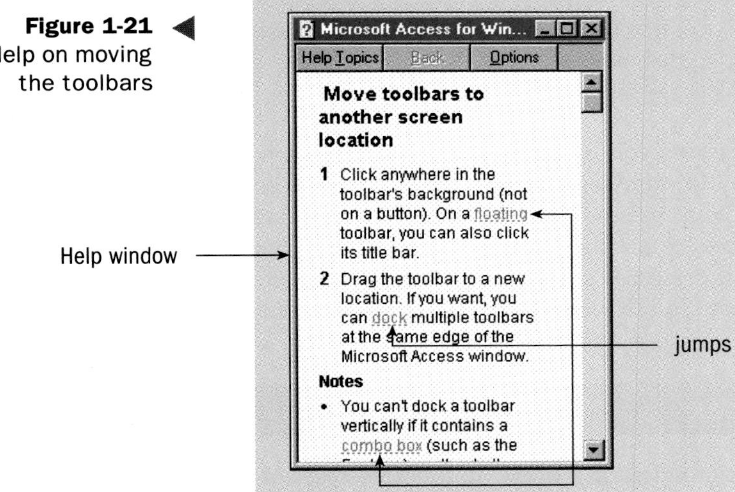

Help window
jumps
Microsoft Access for Win...
Help Topics
Back
Options
Move toolbars to another screen location
1 Click anywhere in the toolbar's background (not on a button). On a floating toolbar, you can also click its title bar.
2 Drag the toolbar to a new location. If you want, you can dock multiple toolbars at the same edge of the Microsoft Access window.
Notes
• You can't dock a toolbar vertically if it contains a combo box (such as the

TROUBLE? If you see the message "Help topic does not exist," you might not have the complete Access Help system installed on your system. Ask your technical support person or instructor for assistance.

The Help window displays the answer to Judith's question. Notice that some words in the Help window are in color and underlined and that the mouse pointer changes to 👆 when you move it over these words. These underlined words or topics in the Help window are called **jumps**. A jump provides a link to other Help topics or to more information or a definition of the current word or topic. Judith wants to view the definition of a floating toolbar.

5. Move the pointer over the word **floating** and click the left mouse button when the pointer changes to 👆. Access Help displays a definition of the term. See Figure 1-22.

Figure 1-22 Definition of "floating"

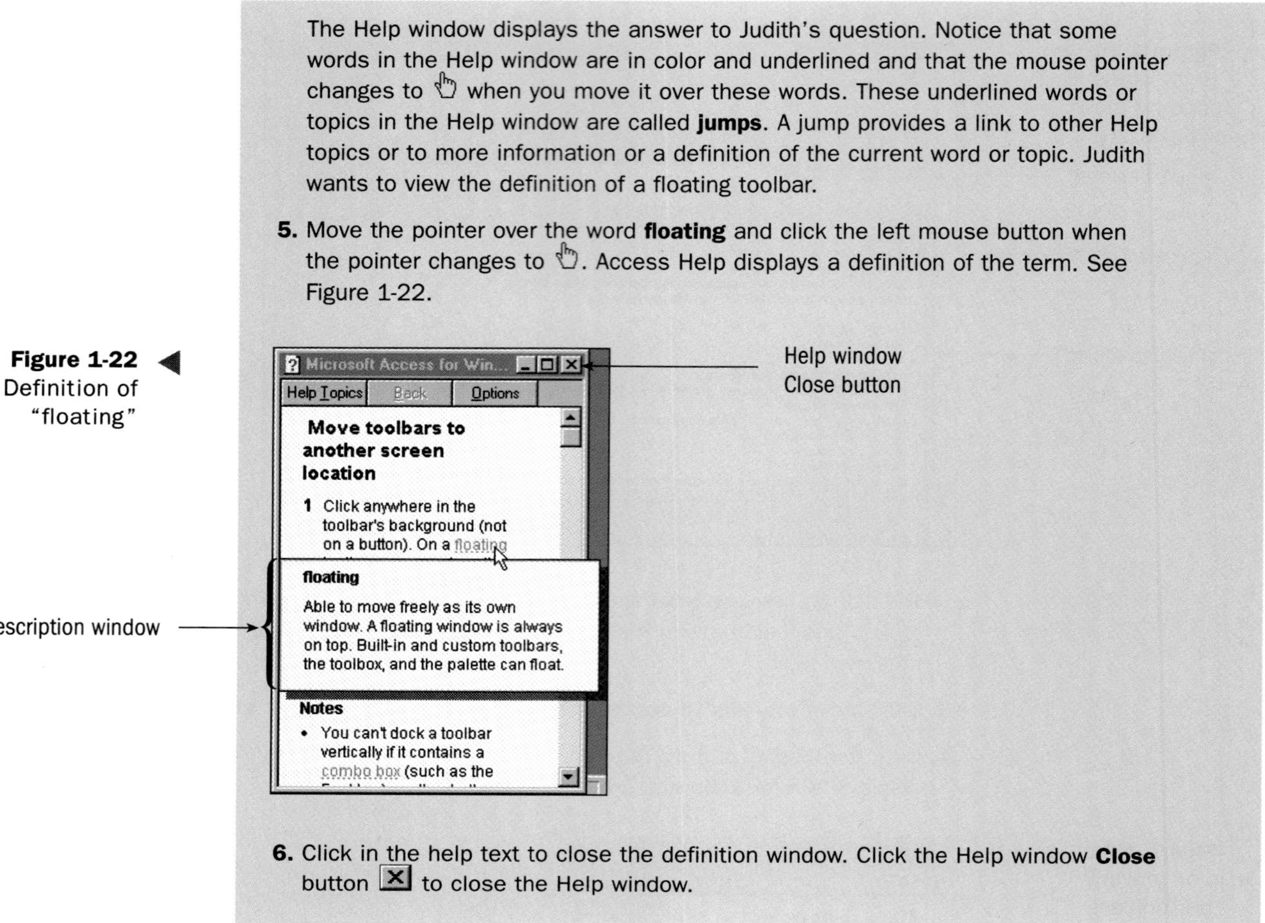

6. Click in the help text to close the definition window. Click the Help window **Close** button ☒ to close the Help window.

The Answer Wizard assists you by interpreting your question and suggesting possible help topics. Another way to use Access Help is to search for a key word or phrase in the Help Index. Judith decides to use the Help Index to find information about some printing options. By default, Access prints the datasheet across the narrow dimension of a page, called **portrait orientation**. Printing "sideways," across the longer dimension of a page, is called **landscape orientation**. Judith wants to find out how to change the default orientation for a page.

Using the Help Index

The Help Index is like the index of a book. It contains a list of key words and phrases that describe Help topics. Judith uses the Help Index to find information about page orientation.

To use the Help Index in Access Help:

1. Click **Help**, then click **Microsoft Access Help Topics**. The Access Help window is displayed. Notice that the Answer Wizard page is visible, since that was the last page you used in Help.
2. Click the **Index** tab to display the Index page. See Figure 1-23.

Figure 1-23
Index page in the Help window

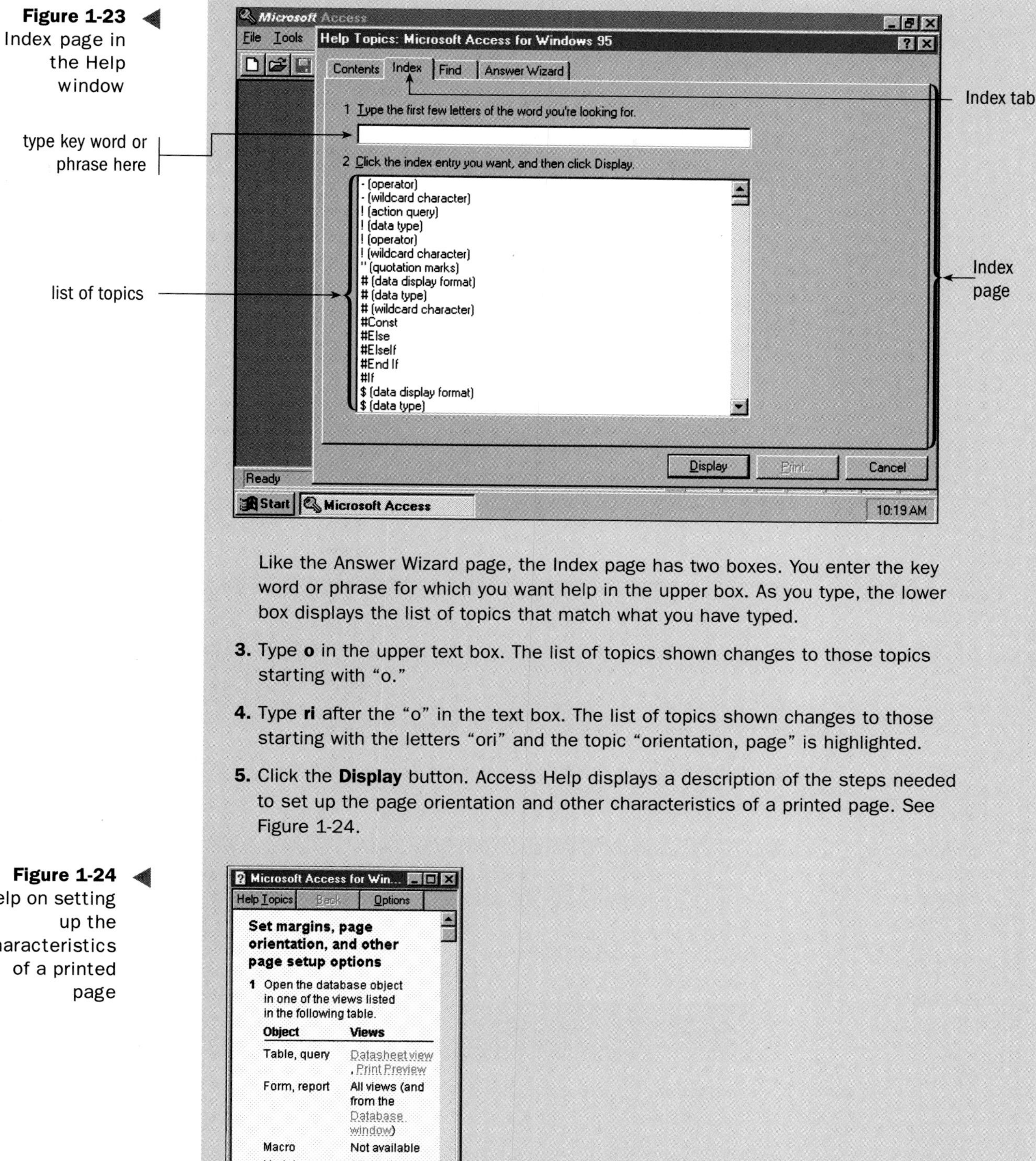

Like the Answer Wizard page, the Index page has two boxes. You enter the key word or phrase for which you want help in the upper box. As you type, the lower box displays the list of topics that match what you have typed.

3. Type **o** in the upper text box. The list of topics shown changes to those topics starting with "o."
4. Type **ri** after the "o" in the text box. The list of topics shown changes to those starting with the letters "ori" and the topic "orientation, page" is highlighted.
5. Click the **Display** button. Access Help displays a description of the steps needed to set up the page orientation and other characteristics of a printed page. See Figure 1-24.

Figure 1-24
Help on setting up the characteristics of a printed page

7. Read the information about setting up the page orientation, using the scroll bar to view the entire topic.

8. Click the **Close** button on the help topic window. The Help window closes.

Using Context-Sensitive Help

In addition to the Help menu, Access provides a Help button on the toolbar. This Help button is context-sensitive, which means that it displays information that is relevant to the window or operation that is currently active. If you want Help information about a particular component of an Access window, click the Help button on the toolbar. The mouse pointer changes to , which is the Help pointer. You then click the on the window component about which you want information, and Help opens a window specific to that component.

Judith is interested in learning more about the purpose of the on the Access toolbar by clicking the Help button.

To use context-sensitive Help on a specific window component:

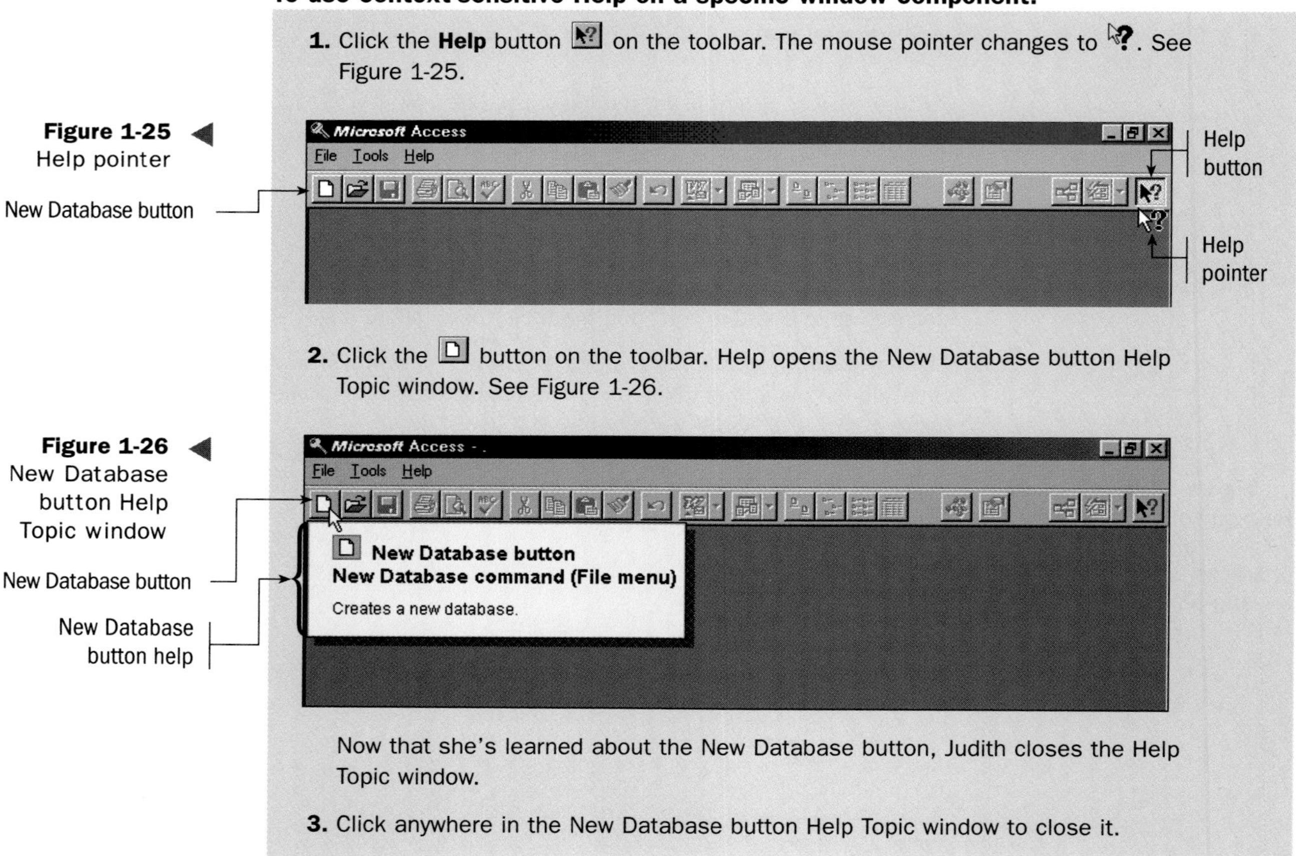

1. Click the **Help** button on the toolbar. The mouse pointer changes to . See Figure 1-25.

Figure 1-25 Help pointer

2. Click the button on the toolbar. Help opens the New Database button Help Topic window. See Figure 1-26.

Figure 1-26 New Database button Help Topic window

Now that she's learned about the New Database button, Judith closes the Help Topic window.

3. Click anywhere in the New Database button Help Topic window to close it.

Judith now feels comfortable about using Access's Help system when she needs it. But before she does any more work on her assignment, she decides that learning about shortcuts will save her valuable time.

Shortcut Menus

As you work with Access objects, you may find it helpful to use a shortcut menu. A shortcut menu contains a list of commands that relate to the object you click. To display a shortcut menu, you position the mouse pointer on a specific object or area and click the right mouse button. Using a shortcut menu is often faster than using a menu option or toolbar button.

Judith opens the Vision database, and then displays a shortcut menu.

To open a database:

1. From the main Access window, click the **Open Database** button to display the Open dialog box.
2. Click **Vision** to select it, then click the **Open** button.

Judith now opens the shortcut menu for the table objects.

To display a shortcut menu:

1. Click the **Tables** tab to display the list of tables.
2. Move the mouse pointer into the Database window and position it on the last table listed.
3. Click the right mouse button. Access displays the shortcut menu. See Figure 1-27.

Figure 1-27 The shortcut menu

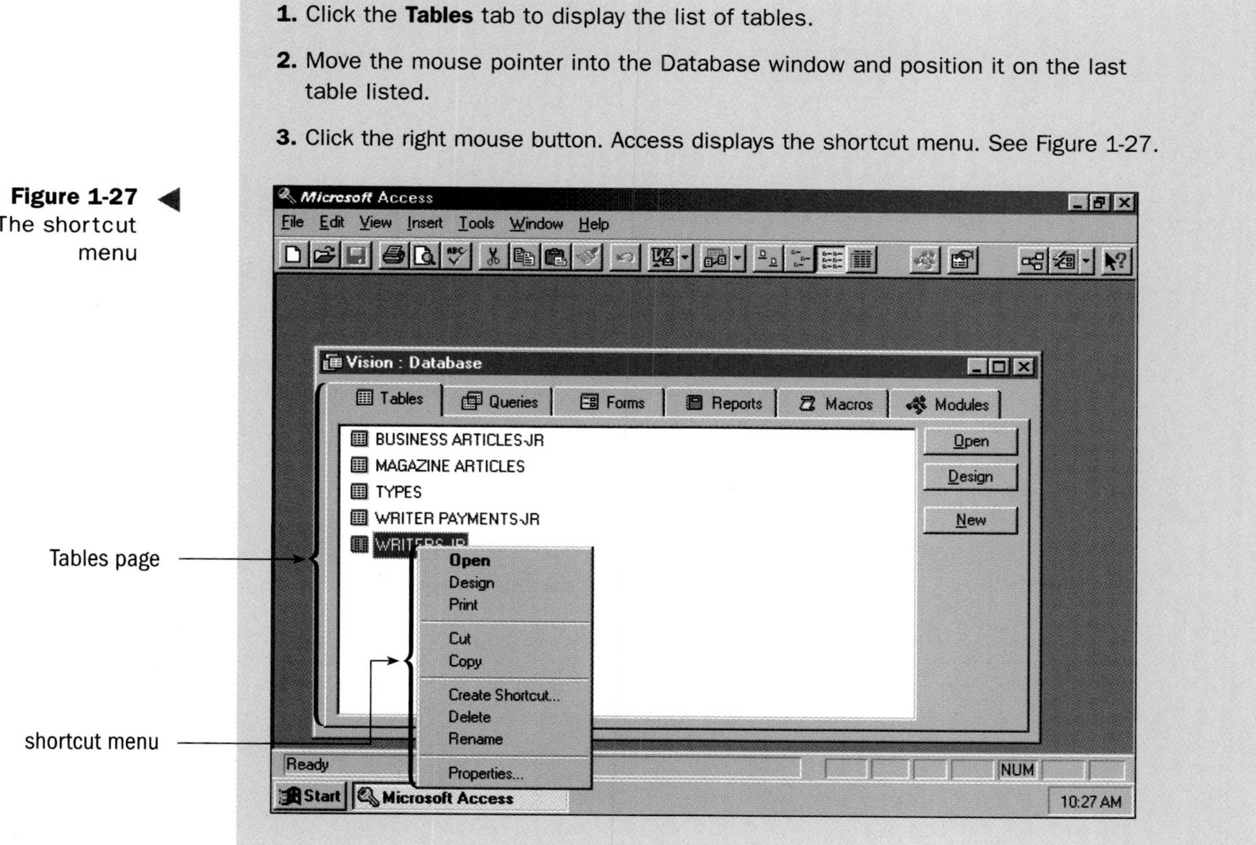

If you select a shortcut menu command, it applies to the highlighted table. Judith does not want to select a command, so she closes the shortcut menu.

To close a shortcut menu:

1. Move the pointer off the shortcut menu and click the left mouse button to close the shortcut menu.

Judith feels confident that she can use Access effectively to complete her assignment and exits Access.

To exit Access:

1. Click the **Close** button [X] to close the main Access window and return to the Windows 95 desktop.

Now Judith knows how to use the Vision database to select articles for the special issue. In the next tutorial you will assist Elena, who will create a specific database for the 25th anniversary issue.

Quick Check

1 What does the Form View window show?

2 Name the five ways you can use Access's Help system to get on-line information.

3 How does the Help Index differ from the Answer Wizard?

4 How would you find out the meaning of the [button] button?

5 What is the purpose of a shortcut menu, and why would you use it?

6 How do you open and close a shortcut menu?

Tutorial Assignments

Start Access, open the Vision database in the Tutorial folder on your Student Disk, and do the following:

1. Open the MAGAZINE ARTICLES table in Datasheet View.
2. Preview the datasheet for printing.
3. Print the first page of the datasheet.
4. Close the Print Preview window and then the Datasheet View window.
5. Open the Magazine Articles form.
6. Preview the form for printing. What is the page number of the last page?
7. Print the last two pages of the form.

8. Look at the toolbars that are available in the following active windows: the Database window, the Datasheet View window, and the Print Preview window. Describe the differences you see from toolbar to toolbar. Use the context-sensitive Help button to learn about the different toolbar buttons available.

Lab Assignment

This Lab Assignment is designed to accompany the interactive Course Lab called Database. To start the Database Lab, click the Start button on the Windows 95 taskbar, point to Programs, point to Course Labs, point to New Perspectives Applications, and click Database. If you do not see Course Labs on your Programs menu, see your instructor or lab manager.

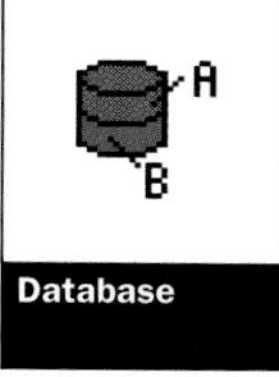

Database This Database Lab demonstrates the essential concepts of file and database management systems. You will use the Lab to search, sort, and report the data contained in a file of classic books.

1. Click the Steps button to review basic database terminology and to learn how to manipulate the classic books database. As you proceed through the Steps, answer the Quick Check questions that appear. After you complete the Steps, you will see a Quick Check Report. Follow the instructions on the screen to print this report.

2. Click the Explore button. Make sure you can apply basic database terminology to describe the classic books database by answering the following questions:
   a. How many records does the file contain?
   b. How many fields does each record contain?
   c. What is the contents of the Catalog # field for the book written by Margaret Mitchell?
   d. What is the contents of the Title field for the record with Thoreau in the Author field?
   e. Which field has been used to sort the records?

3. Manipulate the database as necessary to answer the following questions:
   a. When the books are sorted by title, what is the first record in the file?
   b. Use the Search button to search for all the books in the West location. How many do you find?
   c. Use the Search button to search for all the books in the Main location that are checked in. What do you find?

4. Use the Report button to print out a report that groups the books by Status and sorted by title. On you report, circle the four field names. Put a box around the summary statistics showing which books are currently checked in and which books are currently checked out.

TUTORIAL 2

Creating Access Tables

Creating the WRITERS Table at Vision Publishers

OBJECTIVES

In this tutorial you will:

- Design a database
- Create a database
- Create tables using the Design View window and the Table Wizard
- Define the fields for a table
- Change field properties
- Modify a table's structure
- Create and delete an index

Vision Publishers

Vision Publishers' Brian Murphy, Judith Rossi, and Elena Sanchez meet to exchange ideas about the cover design and article layout for the 25th-anniversary issue of *Business Perspective*. Now that Judith has selected the articles to be included in the special issue, Elena needs to create a database to store information about the articles and writers so that she can coordinate production of the issue. Her first task will be to contact the writers of these past articles.

Elena will also record information about reprint payments that Vision Publishers will make to the writers. Elena realizes, therefore, that the database she will create for the special issue will contain several tables: a table each for writers, past articles, and reprint payments. She decides to concentrate first on creating a table of all the writers. After that she will create a table in which to record the reprint payments. Elena knows from her previous work with databases that—before she can create any of her database tables on the computer—she must first design the database.

Designing a Database

A database management system can be a useful tool, but only if you first carefully design your database to represent your data requirements accurately. In database design, you determine the fields, tables, and relationships needed to satisfy your data and processing requirements. Some database designs can be complicated because the underlying data requirements are complex. Most data requirements and their resulting database designs are much simpler, however, and these are the ones we will consider in the tutorials.

When you design a database, you should follow these guidelines:

- *Identify all fields needed to produce the required information.* Because, for example, Vision Publishers has a policy that only freelancers will be paid for reprints of their articles, Elena needs to know if a writer is a freelancer and, if so, what the reprint payment amount is. After looking over the list of past articles chosen for the special issue, Elena notes that the 25 articles were written by only 13 writers and Chong Kim wrote four of them. Brian points out that the writer of "Cola Advertising Wars" is a different Chong Kim, so Elena realizes that a writer name is not unique. She will need to identify the writer of each article with a unique Writer ID. Only after carefully considering her requirements is Elena able to determine the fields that will produce the information she needs (Figure 2-1).

Figure 2-1 Elena's data requirements

article title	writer phone number
issue of Business Perspective	is the writer a freelancer?
length of article	freelancer reprint payment amount
writer name	writer ID
writer age	check number
reprint check amount	check date

- *Determine the entities involved in the data requirements.* Recall that an entity is a person, place, object, event, or idea for which you want to store and process data. Elena's data requirements, for example, involve entities for articles, writers, and payments. The type of entity in a table usually suggests the name for the table in a database.
- *Group the identified fields by entity to form tables.* Elena groups the fields in her list under each entity name, as shown in Figure 2-2. So far, Elena's database design has three tables: BUSINESS ARTICLES, WRITERS, and WRITER PAYMENTS. Elena's design and using more than one table eliminates unnecessarily redundant information in the database. When Elena enters the data for a new payment in the WRITER PAYMENTS table, for example, she needs to enter only the Writer ID to identify the writer to whom the payment is made. It is not necessary for her to enter the writer's name, phone number, etc., since that information is kept in the WRITERS table. Information about each writer is stored as a single record in the WRITERS table, and each payment can be linked to the writer through the Writer ID field.

Figure 2-2 Elena's fields describing each entity

Business Articles	Writers	Writer Payments
article title	writer ID	check number
issue of Business Perspective	writer name	check amount
length of article	writer phone number	check date
	is the writer a freelancer?	
	freelancer reprint payment amount	
	writer age	

- *Designate each table's primary key.* A primary key uniquely identifies each record in a table. Although not mandatory, it's usually a good idea to have a primary key for each table to help you select records accurately. For example, Elena has decided to include a Writer ID field in the WRITERS table to identify each writer uniquely because she needs to distinguish between the two writers named Chong Kim. The primary key for the WRITER PAYMENTS table will be Check Number. At this point, however, Elena does not have a primary key for the BUSINESS ARTICLES table because no field in this table is guaranteed to have unique field values. Elena delays a final decision on a primary key for this table until later in the database design process.

- *Include a common field in related tables.* You use a common field to link two tables. In the BUSINESS ARTICLES and WRITER PAYMENTS tables, Elena includes the Writer ID field, the primary key for the WRITERS table, to serve as a foreign key. Doing so will allow Elena quick access to information in the WRITERS and BUSINESS ARTICLES tables, telling her who wrote which article.

- *Avoid data redundancy.* **Data redundancy**, which occurs when you store the same data in more than one place, can cause inconsistencies. For example, Figure 2-3 shows an example of what might happen if Elena designs her database incorrectly. Here, the BUSINESS ARTICLES table has a redundant field (Writer Name), which results in inconsistent spellings of the same name (Leroy Johnson vs. Leroy W. Johnson vs. Leroy W. Jonson; Kellie Kox vs. Kelly Cox). In contrast, Figure 2-4 shows a correct database design for the BUSINESS ARTICLES and WRITERS tables, where the only data redundancy is the Writer ID field, which serves as the common field to link the two tables.

Figure 2-3 Incorrect database design with redundancy

BUSINESS ARTICLES table

Article Title	Issue of Business Perspective	Length of Article	Writer ID	Writer Name
Trans-Alaskan Oil Pipeline Opening	1977 JUL	803	J525	Leroy Johnson
Farm Aid Abuses	1978 APR	1866	J525	Leroy W. Jonson
Herbert A. Simon Interview	1978 DEC	1811	C200	Kellie Kox
Alternative Energy Sources	1980 JUN	2085	S260	Wilhelm Seeger
Windfall Tax on Oil Profits	1980 APR	1497	K500	Chong Kim
Toyota and GM Join Venture	1983 MAR	1682	S260	Wilhelm Seeger

WRITERS table

Writer ID	Writer Name	Writer Phone Number	Freelancer	Freelancer Reprint Payment Amount
C200	Kelly Cox	(204)783-5415	Yes	$100
J525	Leroy W. Johnson	(209)895-2046	Yes	$125
K500	Chong Kim	(807)729-5364	No	$0
S260	Wilhelm Seeger	(306)423-0932	Yes	$250

inconsistent data

Writer Name redundant in BUSINESS ARTICLES table

Figure 2-4 Correct database design without redundancy

BUSINESS ARTICLES table

Article Title	Issue of Business Perspective	Length of Article	Writer ID
Trans-Alaskan Oil Pipeline Opening	1977 JUL	803	J525
Farm Aid Abuses	1978 APR	1866	J525
Herbert A. Simon Interview	1978 DEC	1811	C200
Alternative Energy Sources	1980 JUN	2085	S260
Windfall Tax on Oil Profits	1980 APR	1497	K500
Toyota and GM Joint Venture	1983 MAR	1682	S260

WRITERS table

Writer ID	Writer Name	Writer Phone Number	Freelancer	Freelancer Reprint Payment Amount
C200	Kelly Cox	(204)783-5415	Yes	$100
J525	Leroy W. Johnson	(209)895-2046	Yes	$125
K500	Chong Kim	(807)729-5364	No	$0
S260	Wilhelm Seeger	(306)423-0932	Yes	$250

- *Determine the properties of each field.* The **properties**, or characteristics, of each field determine how the DBMS will store, display, and process the field. These properties include the field name, the field's maximum number of characters or digits, the field's description or explanation, and other field characteristics. Because this is Elena's first time designing and creating a database, she will plan her field properties later.

With these guidelines in mind, Elena completes her initial database design (shown in Figure 2-5) and begins to create her database. Notice that the WRITERS table contains a field for Freelancer Reprint Payment Amount — the amount the writer is paid for each reprint. The WRITER PAYMENTS table contains a field for the Check Amount, which is the amount actually paid to a writer. Because a writer might be paid for more than one reprint, these fields are not redundant.

Figure 2-5 Elena's initial database design

BUSINESS ARTICLES table
Article Title
Issue of Business Perspective
Length of Article
Writer ID — foreign key

WRITERS table
Writer ID — primary key
Writer Name
Writer Phone
Freelancer
Freelancer Reprint Payment Amount
Writer Age

WRITER PAYMENTS table
Check Number — primary key
Writer ID — foreign key
Check Amount
Check Date

SESSION 2.1

In this session, you will learn how to create an Access database, create an Access table, save a table, and switch between Design View and Datasheet View.

Creating a Database

You must first name each database you create. Choose a descriptive name that will remind you of the database's purpose or contents. Elena chooses for her new database the name Issue25, as it will contain all the information necessary to produce the 25th-anniversary issue of *Business Perspective*. Windows 95 and Access allow you to name your database anything you want. When you create a database, Access saves all of the database's tables, forms, queries, and other information in a single disk file identified with the database name.

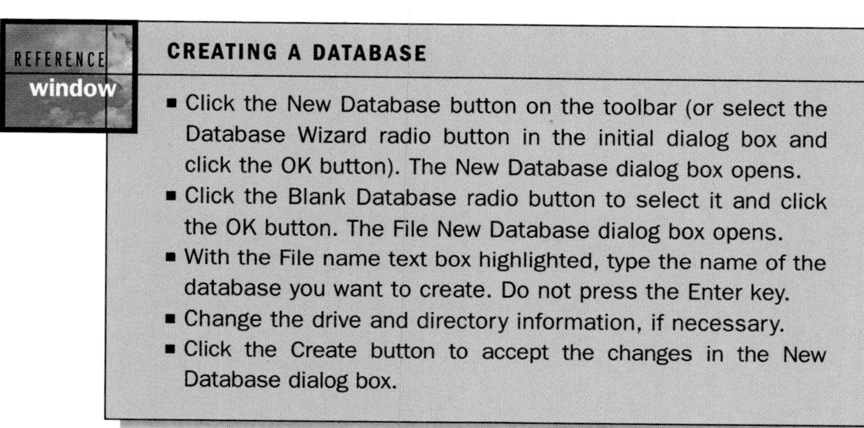

REFERENCE window

CREATING A DATABASE

- Click the New Database button on the toolbar (or select the Database Wizard radio button in the initial dialog box and click the OK button). The New Database dialog box opens.
- Click the Blank Database radio button to select it and click the OK button. The File New Database dialog box opens.
- With the File name text box highlighted, type the name of the database you want to create. Do not press the Enter key.
- Change the drive and directory information, if necessary.
- Click the Create button to accept the changes in the New Database dialog box.

Elena creates the Issue25 database.

To create a database:

1. Start Access. The Access window appears with the initial dialog box. See Figure 2-6.

Figure 2-6 Initial dialog box

click to select Blank Database

The initial dialog box provides two ways to create a new database. The Blank Database option creates a new database having no defined tables or other objects. The Database Wizard option allows you to create a blank database or to use one of several predefined databases as models for creating your own. Here Elena will define the database herself. (You will explore using a predefined database model in the Tutorial Assignments for this tutorial.)

TROUBLE? If Access is already running, return to the main Access window, click File, click New Database, select Blank Database, then click the OK button. Then continue with Step 3.

2. Click the **Blank Database** radio button to select it, then click the **OK** button. Access displays the File New Database dialog box. See Figure 2-7. The File name text box contains the highlighted default name, db1.

Figure 2-7 The File New Database dialog box

click to display list of drives and folders

enter database file name here

File New Database

Save in: My Documents

Shortcut to Northwind

Create

Cancel

Exclusive

File name: db1

Save as type: Microsoft Access Databases

TROUBLE? Depending on your computer's configuration, your screen may show filenames with the .mdb extension.

3. Type **Issue25** in the File name text box.

TROUBLE? If the contents of the File name text box do not show Issue25, the text box might not have been highlighted when you began typing. If this is the case, highlight the contents of the text box and retype Issue25.

4. Click the **Save in** list arrow, then click the drive in which you put your Student Disk. Double-click the **Tutorial** folder to open it. See Figure 2-8.

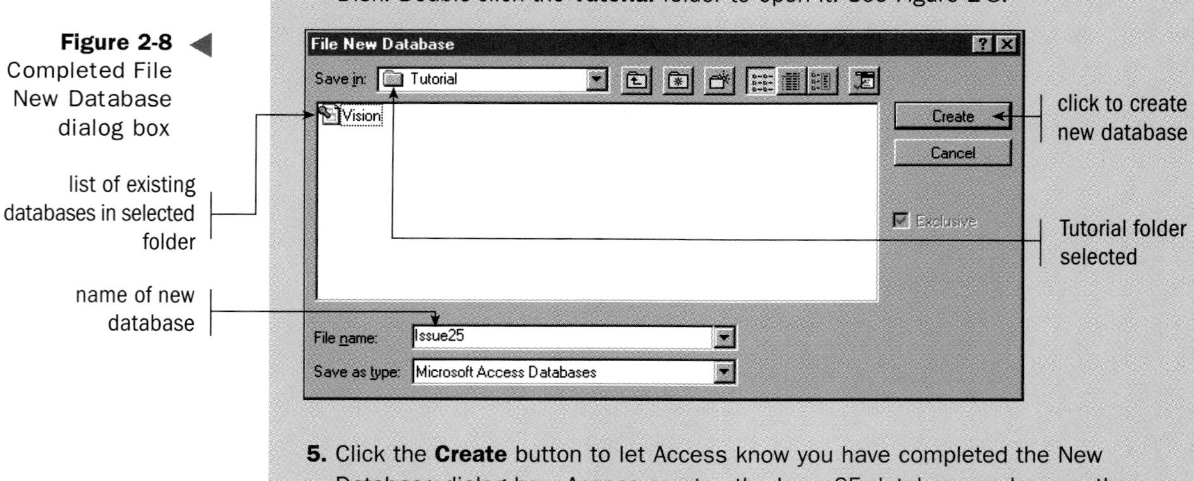

Figure 2-8 Completed File New Database dialog box

5. Click the **Create** button to let Access know you have completed the New Database dialog box. Access creates the Issue25 database and opens the Database window.

Now that she has created her new database, Elena's next step is to create the WRITERS table structure.

Creating a Table

Creating a table entails defining the table's fields. To create the structure of the WRITERS table, Elena looks at her plan again and notes that the fields that should be included are Writer ID, Writer Name, Writer Phone, Freelancer, Freelancer Reprint Payment Amount, and Writer Age. In Access, you can define a table from the keyboard or use the Table Wizard to automate the table creation process. A **wizard** is an Access tool that asks you questions and creates an object according to your answers. When you use the Table Wizard, for example, you will be asked questions about your table. Access then automatically creates the table based on your answers. Since Elena has already given careful thought to her WRITERS table, she realizes it will be much quicker and easier to define it from the keyboard.

You use the Design View window to define or modify a table structure or the properties for the fields in a table. If you create a table without using the Table Wizard, you enter the fields and their properties for your table directly in this window.

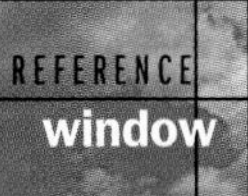

CREATING A TABLE IN DESIGN VIEW

- In the Tables list of the Database window, click the New button.
- Click Design View, then click the OK button to open the Design View window.
- Enter field names, data types, and field descriptions in the grid in the upper panel of the Design View window.
- If the table has a primary key field, click in the primary key field definition, then click the Primary Key button to designate the field as the primary key.
- Specify field properties in the lower panel of the Design View window.

To define a table using Design View:

1. If necessary, click the **Tables** tab to display the Tables list, then click the **New** button. Access displays the New Table dialog box. See Figure 2-9.

Figure 2-9 The New Table dialog box

New Table

Create a new table in Datasheet view.

Datasheet View
Design View
Table Wizard
Import Table Wizard
Link Table Wizard

OK Cancel

click to select Design View

click to open Design View

2. Click **Design View**, then click the **OK** button. The Design View window opens. See Figure 2-10.

Figure 2-10 The Design View window

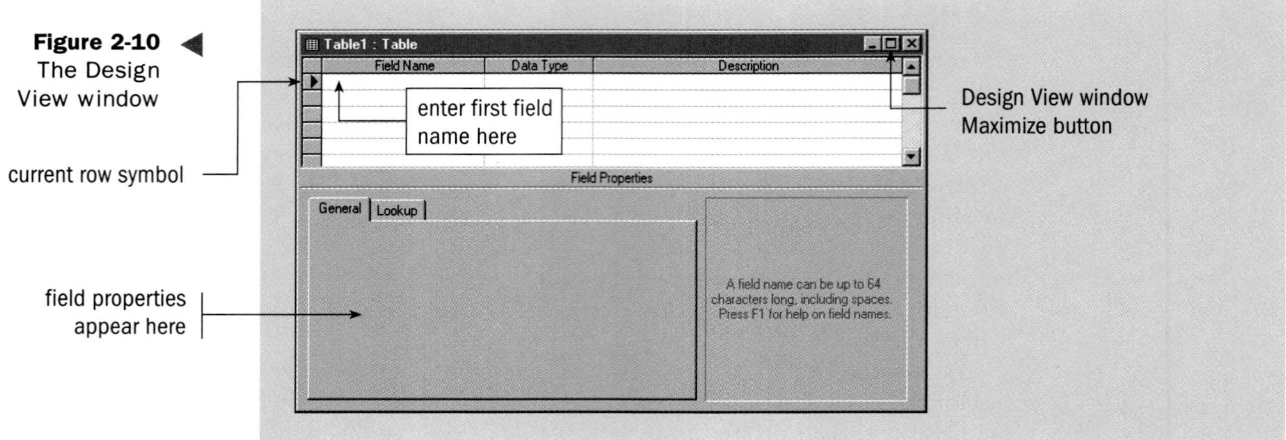

The upper panel of the Design View window contains a grid in which you define each field in the table. The lower-left panel of the window displays the properties associated with the currently selected field. The panel in the lower right displays a short Help message to assist you in defining fields. Note that the title bar will identify the table as Table1 until Elena saves the table as WRITERS (which she'll do later in this tutorial). The cursor is now in the first row of the Field Name column and the row selector is in the first row. Access is ready for you to enter the name for the first field.

Elena can now enter information about the first field in the WRITERS table.

Naming Fields and Objects

You must name each object in a database so that Access can save and retrieve information about the object. For the Issue25 database, Elena will name her tables WRITERS, BUSINESS ARTICLES, and WRITER PAYMENTS, because these names suggest the contents of the tables. For the same reason, she chooses Writer ID, Writer Name, Writer Phone, and Writer Age as some of the field names in the WRITERS table. To differentiate between table and field names, Elena decides to use all uppercase letters for table names, and uppercase and lowercase letters for field names and other database objects.

In Access, although users can choose whether or not to capitalize names of fields and objects, there are some basic conventions that all users must follow regarding names:

- They can be up to 64 characters long.
- They can contain letters, numbers, spaces, and special characters except period (.), exclamation mark (!), square brackets ([]), and accent grave (`).
- They must not start with a space.

Elena is now ready to enter the first field name, Writer ID, into the WRITERS table.

To enter the Writer ID field name:

1. Type **Writer ID**, then press the **Tab** key to move the cursor to the Data Type column of the first row. The Field Properties list displays the default properties for the new field.

Looking at the screen, Elena notes that her next step is to enter a data type for the Writer ID field.

Assigning Field Data Types

You must assign a **data type** for each field. The data type determines what field values you can enter for that field and what other properties the field will have. In Access, you assign one of the following nine data types to each field:

- **Text** allows field values containing letters, digits, spaces, and special characters. Text fields can be up to 255 characters long. You should assign the text data type to fields in which you will store names, addresses, and descriptions, and to fields containing digits that are not used in calculations. Elena assigns the Text data type to the Writer ID field, the Writer Name field, the Writer Age field, and the Writer Phone field. Note that three of these fields contain digits not used in calculations.

- **Memo**, like the Text data type, allows field values containing letters, digits, spaces, and special characters. Memo fields, however, can be up to 64,000 characters long and are used for long comments or explanations. Elena does not have any fields like this, so she does not assign the Memo data type to any of her fields.

- **Number** limits field values to digits. It allows an optional leading sign to indicate a positive or negative value (i.e., + or -) and an optional decimal point. Use the Number data type for fields that you will use in calculations—except those involving money for which there is a special data type. Elena will assign this type to the Writer Age fields.

- **Date/Time** allows field values containing valid dates and times only. Usually you enter dates in mm/dd/yy format, for example, 12/02/98 (December 2, 1998). This data type also permits other date formats and a variety of time formats. With the Date/Time data type, you can perform calculations on dates and times and you can sort them. The number of days between two dates, for example, can be determined. Elena does not have any dates in the table and does not assign the Date/Time data type to any of the WRITERS table fields.

- **Currency** allows field values similar to those for the Number data type. Unlike calculations with Number data type decimal values, however, calculations performed using the Currency data type will not be subject to round-off error. Elena assigns the Currency data type to the Freelancer Reprint Payment Amount field in the WRITERS table.

- **AutoNumber** consists of integers with values that are automatically inserted in the field as each new record is created. You can specify sequential numbering or random numbering. This guarantees a unique field value, so that such a field can serve as a table's primary key. Because the Writer ID field already contains unique field values, Elena does not assign the AutoNumber data type to any of the WRITERS table fields.

- **Yes/No** limits field values to yes and no entries. Use this data type for fields that indicate the presence or absence of a condition, such as whether an order has been filled, or if an employee is eligible for the company dental plan. Elena assigns the Yes/No data type to the Freelancer field in the WRITERS table.

- **OLE Object** allows field values that are created in other software applications as objects, such as photographs, video images, graphics, drawings, sound recordings, voice-mail messages, spreadsheets, and word processing documents. OLE is an acronym for object linking and embedding. You can either import or link to the object, but you cannot modify it in Access. Elena does not assign the OLE Object data type to any of the WRITERS table fields.

- **Lookup Wizard** creates a field that lets you select a value from another table or from a predefined list of values. You'll have a chance to use the Lookup Wizard in Tutorial 3.

Now that Elena is familiar with the data types, she can enter the appropriate type for the Writer ID field. By default, Access assigns the Text data type to each field that is defined. Since Elena wants the Writer ID field to have the Text data type, she does not need to change the default type. She could easily select a different type, however, by clicking on the Data Type text box and then clicking the list arrow that appears. She could then select a different data type. Elena accepts the default Text data type and moves the cursor to the Description column.

To accept the default Text data type and move the cursor to the Description column:

1. Press the **Tab** key. The cursor moves to the Description column.

Assigning Field Descriptions

When you define a field, you can assign an optional description for the field (up to 255 characters long). Later, when you view the field values in the table records, the description will appear on the status bar to explain the purpose or usage of the field. Even if you choose a descriptive field name, you may want to enter a description. For example, Elena decides it will be helpful to enter the description "primary key" for the Writer ID field.

To enter a description for the Writer ID field:

1. Type **primary key**.

Elena has included the description of the Writer ID field, but she still needs to designate the Writer ID field as the primary key.

Selecting the Primary Key

Although Access does not require that tables have a primary key, choosing a primary key has several advantages.

- Based on its definition, a primary key serves to identify uniquely each record in a table. Elena uses Writer ID, for example, to distinguish one writer from another when both have the same name.
- Access does not allow duplicate values in the primary key field. If Elena has a record with N425 as the field value for Writer ID, she will not be allowed to add another record with this same field value in the Writer ID field. Preventing duplicate values ensures the uniqueness of the primary key field.
- Access enforces entity integrity on the primary key field. **Entity integrity** means that every record's primary key field must have a value. If you do not enter a value for a field, you have actually given the field what is known as a **null value**. You cannot give a null value to the primary key field; Access will not store the record for you unless you've entered a field value in the primary key field.
- Access displays records in primary key sequence when you view a table in the Datasheet View window or the Form View window. Even if you enter records in no specific order, you are ensured that you will later be able to work with them in a more meaningful, primary key sequence.
- Access responds faster to your requests for specific records based on the primary key.

To designate the primary key:

1. If necessary, click in the row for the **Writer ID** field, and then click the **Primary Key** button on the toolbar. An icon now appears to the left of the Writer ID field name. See Figure 2-11.

Figure 2-11 Designating a primary key

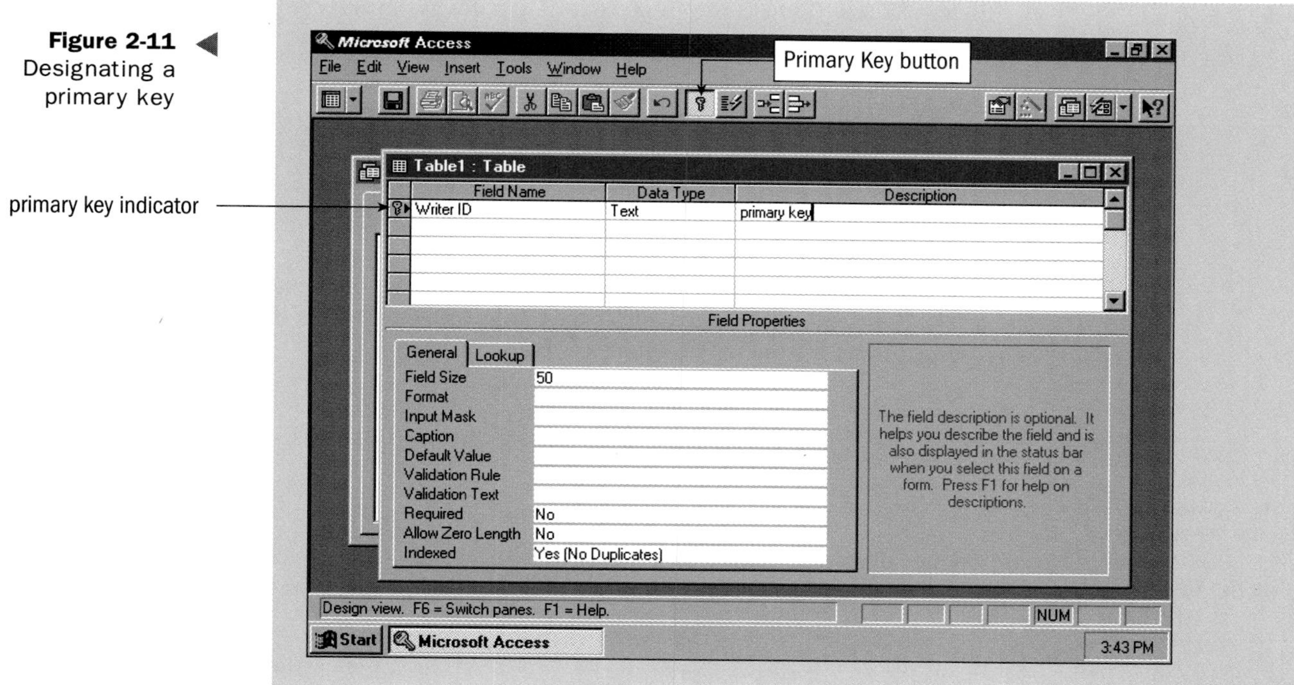

After designating the primary key, Elena moves to the first field property, Field Size.

Assigning Field Sizes

The Field Size property determines a field value's maximum storage size for Text and Number fields. The other data types have no field size property, either because their storage size is a predetermined fixed size (e.g., 8 bytes for a Date/Time field) or because the size is dependent on the actual value stored (e.g., a Memo field). You should document every Text field's maximum size so that you allow enough room for it on entry screens and on reports and other outputs, without wasting space.

A Text field, like Writer ID, has a default field size of 50 characters. You can change its field size by entering a number in the range of 1 to 255 in the text box for the Field Size property in the Field Properties panel. For a Number field, you select the field size from five choices: byte, integer, long integer, double, and single, as shown in Figure 2-12. Double is the default field size for a Number field.

Figure 2-12 Number data type field size options

Field Size	Storage Size (Bytes)	Number Type	Field Values Allowed
Byte	1	Integer	0 to 255
Integer	2	Integer	–32,768 to 32,767
Long Integer	4	Integer	–2,147,483,648 to 2,147,483,647
Double	8	Decimal	15 significant digits
Single	4	Decimal	7 significant digits

Elena's Writer ID field is a Text field that is always exactly four characters long, so she enters 4 as its field size.

To change a field size:

1. Double-click in the **Field Size** property text box to highlight the current value.
2. Type **4**.

Now that Elena has entered all the information for the first field in the WRITERS table, she returns to her original database design and determines the field data types, sizes, and descriptions for the other fields, as shown in Figure 2-13.

Figure 2-13 Elena's database design for the WRITERS, BUSINESS ARTICLES, and WRITER PAYMENTS tables

	Data Type	Field Size	Description
WRITERS table			
Writer ID	Text	4	primary key
Writer Name	Text	25	
Writer Phone	Text	14	(999) 999-9999 format
Freelancer	Yes/No		
Freelancer Reprint Payment Amount	Currency		$250 maximum
Writer Age	Number	4	byte field size
BUSINESS ARTICLES table			
Article Title	Text	44	
Issue of Business Perspective	Text	8	
Length of Article	Number	4	integer field size
Writer ID	Text	4	foreign key
WRITER PAYMENTS table			
Check Number	Number	16	primary key, double field size
Writer ID	Text	4	foreign key
Check Amount	Currency		
Check Date	Date/Time		

Elena is now ready to define the rest of the fields in the WRITERS table.

To define the remaining fields in the WRITERS table:

1. Click in the **Field Name** column for the second row. Type **Writer Name**, then press the **Tab** key to move to the Data Type column. Press the **Tab** key again to accept the default Text data type. Double-click in the **Field Size** property text box to highlight the current value, then type **25.**
2. Click in the **Field Name** column for the third row. Type **Writer Phone**, then press the **Tab** key to move to the Data Type column. Press the **Tab** key to accept the default Text data type and move to the Description column. Type **(999) 999-9999**.

3. Double-click in the **Field Size** property text box to highlight the current value, then type **14.**

4. Click in the **Field Name** column for the fourth row. Type **Freelancer** and then press the **Tab** key to move to the Data Type column. The Freelancer field is a Yes/No field. You can use the drop-down Data Type list box to select the correct data type.

5. Click the **Data Type** list arrow to display the list of available data types. See Figure 2-14. Click **Yes/No**.

Figure 2-14 Selecting the data type

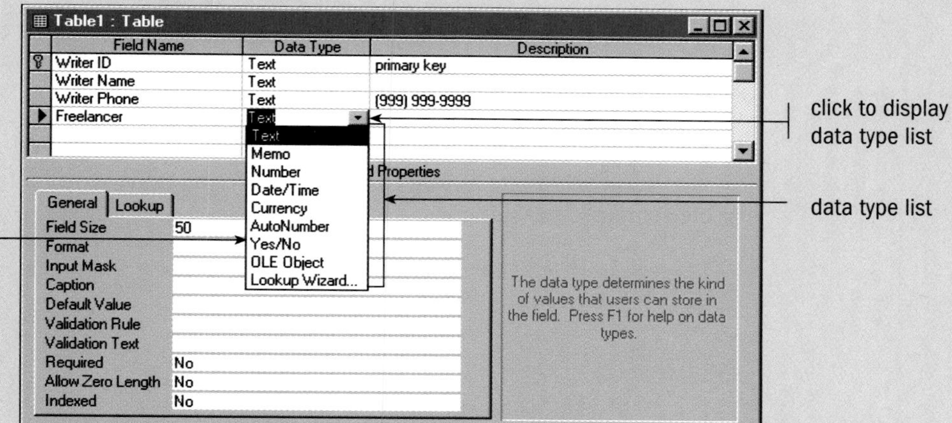

Note that instead of selecting a field's data type by clicking one of the choices in the Data Type list box, you can type the entire data type name in the field's Data Type text box. Alternatively, type just the first character of the data type name to select that data type. You will use this technique in the next step.

6. Click in the **Field Name** column for the fifth row. Type **Freelancer Reprint Payment Amount**, then press the **Tab** key to move to the Data Type column. Since this field is a currency field, type **C**. Access automatically changes the data type to Currency.

7. Click in the **Field Name** column for the sixth row. Type **Writer Age**, then press the **Tab** key to move to the Data Type column. Notice that the field list scrolls so that you can see the Writer Age row.

8. Type **N** to select the Number data type, then press the **Tab** key.

   The Writer Age field will contain the ages of writers. Since these will be integers, probably less than 100, the byte field size is appropriate. The byte field size can store integers from 0 to 256. Using the byte field size rather than the default double field size will save space in the database.

9. Click in the **Field Size** text box, then click the **Field Size** list arrow, then click **Byte**. The list closes and the Field Size property value is changed to Byte.

Elena has now finished defining the fields for the WRITERS table. The final screen is shown in Figure 2-15. Elena wants to save the table structure before proceeding.

Figure 2-15 Field definitions for the WRITERS table

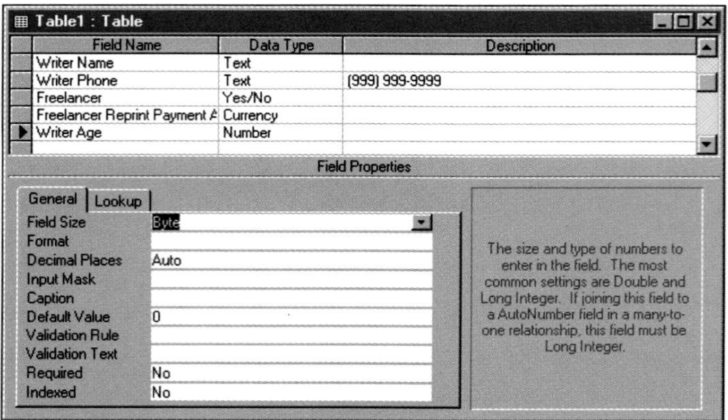

Saving a Table Structure

When you first create a table, you must save the table with its field definitions to add the table structure permanently to your database.

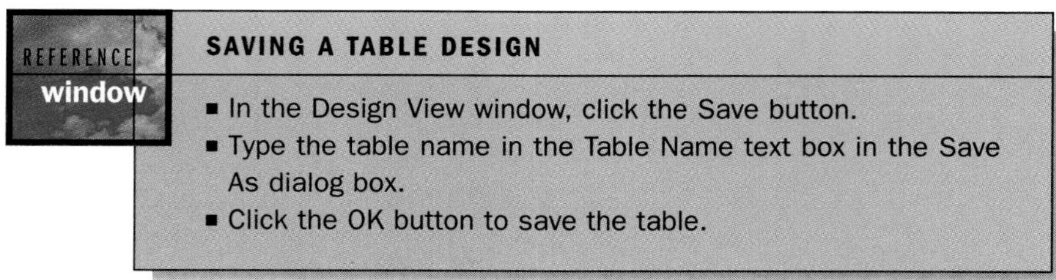
REFERENCE window

SAVING A TABLE DESIGN

- In the Design View window, click the Save button.
- Type the table name in the Table Name text box in the Save As dialog box.
- Click the OK button to save the table.

To save the WRITERS table:

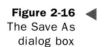

1. Click the **Save** button on the toolbar. Access displays the Save As dialog box. See Figure 2-16.

Figure 2-16 The Save As dialog box

2. Type **WRITERS** in the Table Name text box, then click the **OK** button. The dialog box closes and Access saves the WRITERS table on your Student Disk.

Switching to the Datasheet View Window

Once you have defined a table, you can view the table in either Design View or Datasheet View. You use Design View to view or change a table's field definitions and properties, and Datasheet View to view or change the field values and records stored in a table. Even though she has not yet entered any of the field values and records in the WRITERS table, Elena displays the WRITERS table in Datasheet View. She can study the datasheet to determine if she needs to make any changes to the table fields.

To switch to a different view of a table, you use Table View button, which is the left-most button on the toolbar. The appearance of the this button changes, depending on which view is current. The button is currently the icon for Datasheet View and looks like . Clicking the button switches you to Datasheet View, and the button changes to . Clicking again switches you to Design View. If you have more than two views open (such as Datasheet View, Design View, and Form View), clicking the list arrow will display a list of views from which you can choose.

To switch from Design View to Datasheet View:

1. Click the **Table View** button on the toolbar. Access displays the Datasheet View window for the WRITERS table.

2. Click the **Maximize** button for the Datasheet View window to maximize the window. See Figure 2-17.

field names

Figure 2-17 Maximized Datasheet View window for a new table

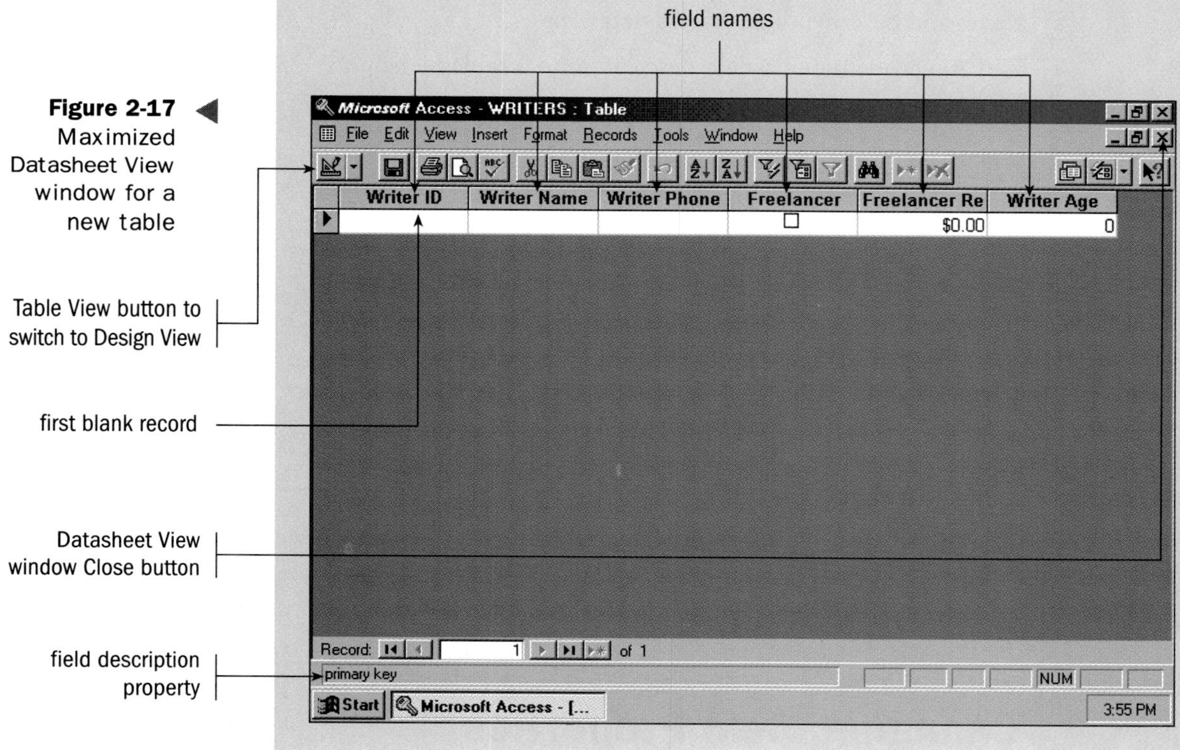

Table View button to switch to Design View

first blank record

Datasheet View window Close button

field description property

Microsoft Access - WRITERS : Table

File Edit View Insert Format Records Tools Window Help

Writer ID	Writer Name	Writer Phone	Freelancer	Freelancer Re	Writer Age
			☐	$0.00	0

Record: 1 of 1

primary key

NUM

Start Microsoft Access - [...

3:55 PM

At first glance, Elena is pleased with her table. She notices that all the information for the Writer ID field appears accurate and that its description appears in the status bar. Looking closer, however, Elena sees several problems that she wants to correct. First, some field names, such as Freelancer Reprint Payment Amount, are only partially displayed, and their field value boxes are wider than they need to be to accommodate the field values that will be entered. Second, the Writer Name field value box is too narrow to display the entire field value. Before making these changes, though, Elena prints the datasheet for the WRITERS table so that she can refer to it as she corrects the problems she discovered.

Printing a Datasheet

To print the datasheet:

1. Click the **Print** button on the toolbar. After the message box closes, Access returns you to the Datasheet View window.

Elena switches back to Design View to make her field property changes.

To switch from Datasheet View to Design View:

1. Click the **Table View** button on the toolbar. Access displays the Design View window for the WRITERS table.

Elena is now ready to make her changes, which she'll do in the next session.

Quick Check

1. What two types of keys represent a common field when you form a relationship between tables?
2. What is data redundancy?
3. Name and describe three Access data types.
4. Why might including a field description in a table be helpful?
5. What is one advantage of designating a primary key?
6. Which data types need to have field sizes determined?
7. Describe two different ways to select a field's data type.
8. How do you switch from one view window to another?

If you want to take a break and resume the tutorial at a later time, exit Access. When you resume the tutorial, place your Student Disk in the appropriate drive and start Access. Open the Issue25 database, click the Design button to open the Design View window for the WRITERS table, and maximize the Design View window.

SESSION 2.2

In this session, you will learn to change field properties and change the appearance of the columns in the Datasheet View Window. You will also modify the structure of an Access table, create another table by using the Table Wizard, and create and delete indexes.

Changing Field Properties

Elena has noted several changes she would like to make in the design of her table. She wants to add a caption to the Freelancer Reprint Payment Amount field since that field name is too wide to be displayed. To make data entry easier, she wants to define the default value Yes for the Freelancer field. Elena has heard about the benefit of using input masks. **Input masks** restrict data entry to the appropriate type and format required for the field. She wants to create an input mask for the Writer Phone field that will automatically add the parentheses and hyphen to the phone number. Since the Freelancer Reprint Payment Amount will always be in whole dollars, she wants the values to appear without the two zeros after the decimal. These changes to the field properties can be done i48n the Design View window. Elena also wants to adjust the column widths in the Datasheet View to improve the readability of the table datasheet.

Elena is now ready to change the Caption property for the Freelancer Reprint Payment Amount field.

Entering a Caption

Even though the field name Freelancer Reprint Payment Amount is too wide to fit in the datasheet column heading box, Elena does not want to change it because it is descriptive. Instead, Elena will use the Caption field property. It will replace the field name in the datasheet column heading box and in the label on a form, without changing the actual field name. You can use the Caption property to display a shorter version of a long, more descriptive table field name.

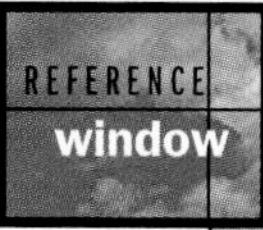

ENTERING A CAPTION

- In the Design View window, click in the Field Name text box that has the field name you want to change.
- Click in the Caption text box in the Field Properties panel of the Design View window.
- Enter the caption for the field.

To enter a caption for the Freelancer Reprint Payment Amount field:

1. Click anywhere in the **Field Name** text box containing Freelancer Reprint Payment Amount. The current row symbol moves to the Freelancer Reprint Payment Amount row and the Field Properties options for this field appear below. Click the **Caption** text box and then type **Amount**. See Figure 2-18.

Figure 2-18 Entering a Caption property for a field

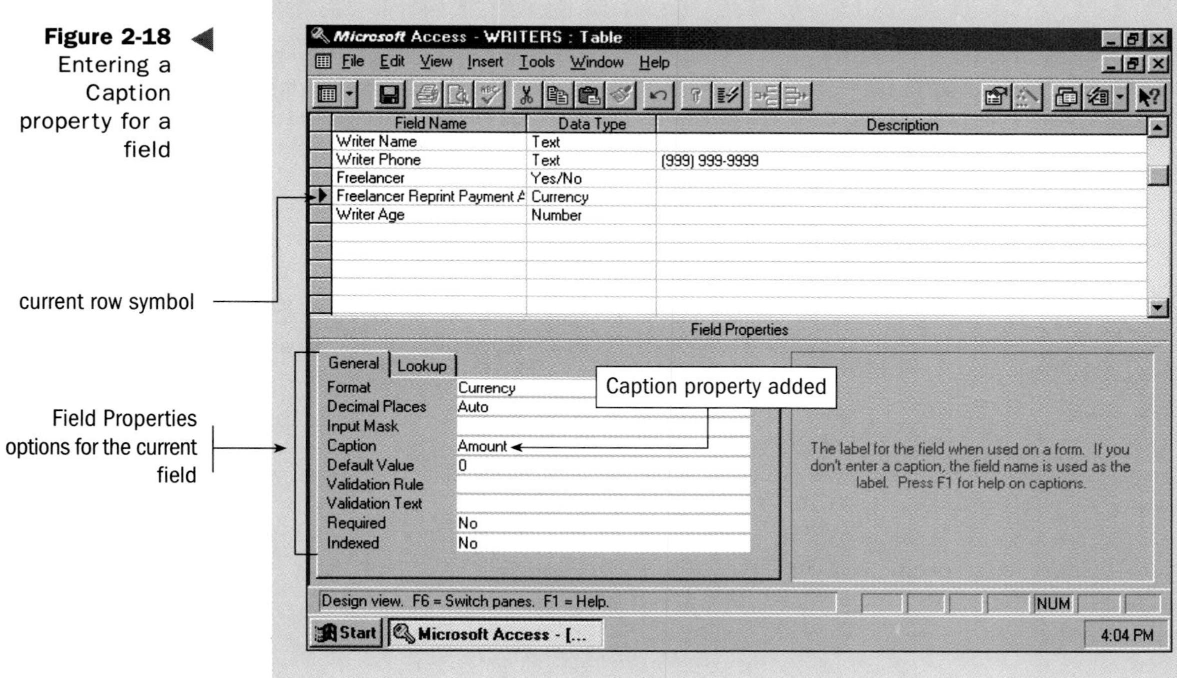

Elena switches to Datasheet View to review her change.

To switch to Datasheet View:

1. Click the **Table View** button on the toolbar. Access displays the Save now? dialog box.

   Access makes your table structure changes permanent only when you take action to save the changes or when you close the Design View window. Switching to Datasheet View first involves closing the Design View window, so Access displays the dialog box to ask you about saving your table changes.

2. Click the **Yes** button. (Note that if you wanted to keep the Design View window open and continue making table structure changes, you would click the No button instead.) Access saves your table structure changes, closes the Design View window, and opens the Datasheet View window. See Figure 2-19.

Figure 2-19 Reviewing a change in the Datasheet View window

Caption property added

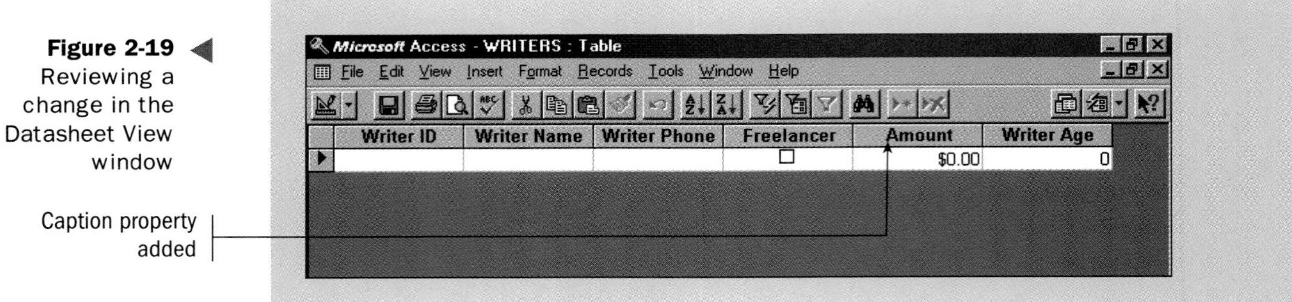

Elena is pleased with the caption she has created. Now she wants to change the column widths in some of the fields in the datasheet.

Resizing Columns in a Datasheet

As with all software programs, there are often several ways to accomplish a task in Access. In these tutorials, we will show you the simplest and fastest method to accomplish tasks. Because you may not have resized datasheet columns before, however, we'll practice three of the different techniques available: using the Format menu, using the mouse pointer, and the best-fit column width method.

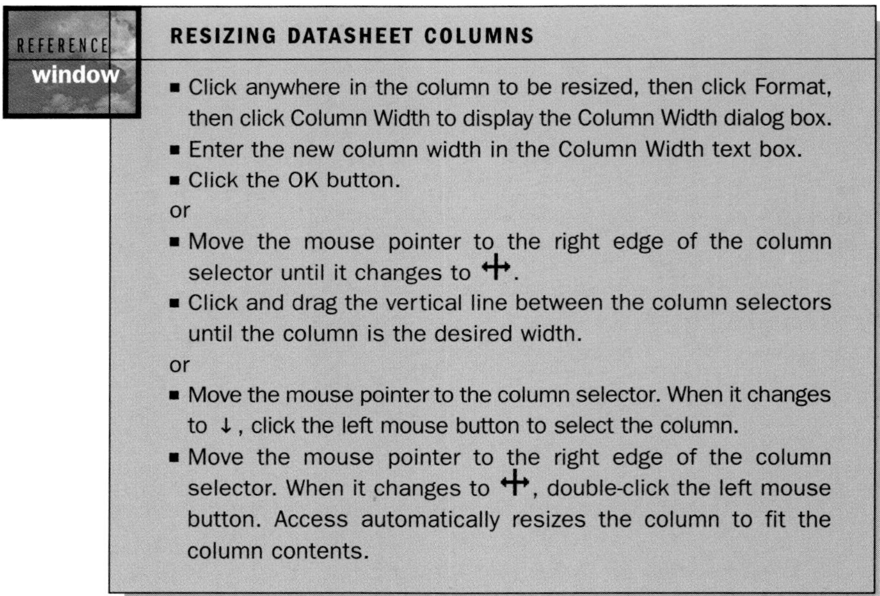

RESIZING DATASHEET COLUMNS

- Click anywhere in the column to be resized, then click Format, then click Column Width to display the Column Width dialog box.
- Enter the new column width in the Column Width text box.
- Click the OK button.

or

- Move the mouse pointer to the right edge of the column selector until it changes to ↔.
- Click and drag the vertical line between the column selectors until the column is the desired width.

or

- Move the mouse pointer to the column selector. When it changes to ↓, click the left mouse button to select the column.
- Move the mouse pointer to the right edge of the column selector. When it changes to ↔, double-click the left mouse button. Access automatically resizes the column to fit the column contents.

First, Elena will resize a datasheet column using the Format menu.

To resize a datasheet column using the Format menu:

1. Click anywhere in the **Writer ID** column, click **Format**, and then click **Column Width**. Access opens the Column Width dialog box. See Figure 2-20. Access has automatically selected the default, standard column width of 15.6667 positions and has checked the Standard Width check box.

Figure 2-20 The Column Width dialog box

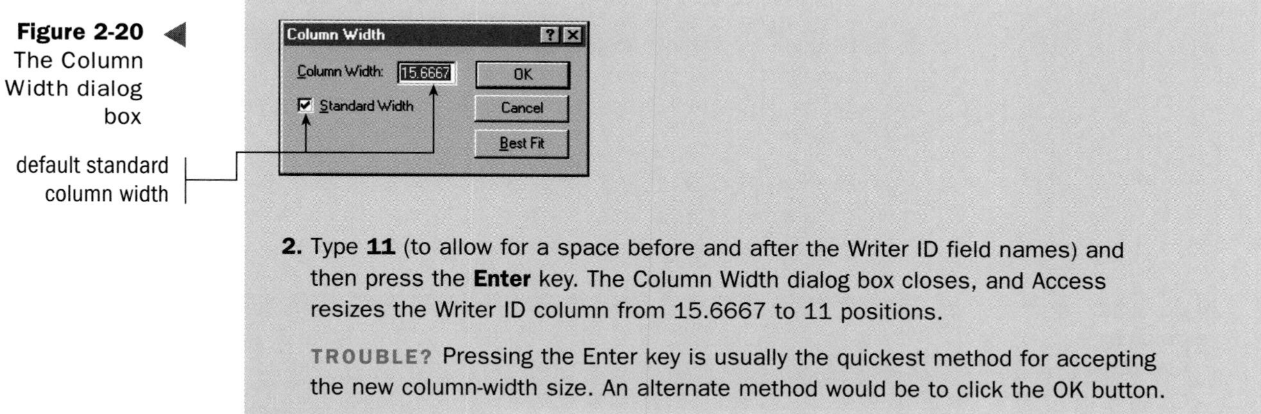

2. Type **11** (to allow for a space before and after the Writer ID field names) and then press the **Enter** key. The Column Width dialog box closes, and Access resizes the Writer ID column from 15.6667 to 11 positions.

TROUBLE? Pressing the Enter key is usually the quickest method for accepting the new column-width size. An alternate method would be to click the OK button.

Elena resizes the Writer Name field using the second method—dragging the column's right edge with the mouse pointer. To resize this way, you must first position the mouse pointer in the field's **column selector,** which is the gray box that contains the field name at the top of the column. A column selector is also called a **field selector**.

To resize a datasheet column using the mouse pointer to drag the column's right edge:

1. Move the mouse pointer to the right edge of the Writer Name column selector until it changes to ✛. See Figure 2-21.

Figure 2-21 Resizing columns using the resizing pointer

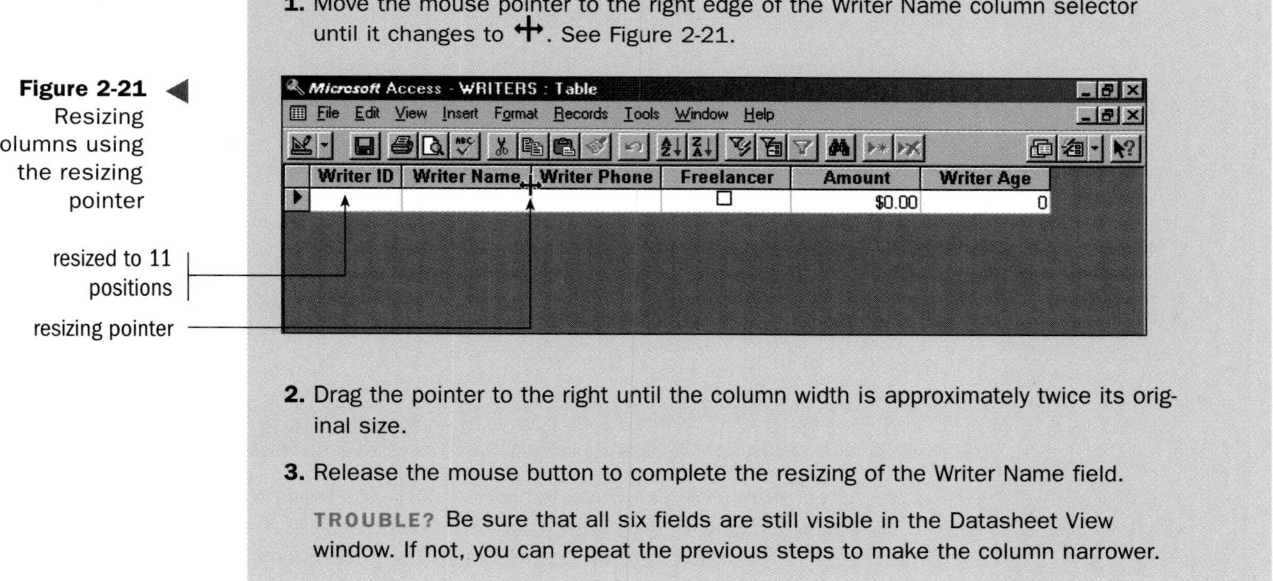

2. Drag the pointer to the right until the column width is approximately twice its original size.
3. Release the mouse button to complete the resizing of the Writer Name field.

TROUBLE? Be sure that all six fields are still visible in the Datasheet View window. If not, you can repeat the previous steps to make the column narrower.

Elena tries a third technique, the best-fit column width method, to resize the Freelancer, Amount, and Writer Age columns. When you use the best-fit column width method, Access automatically resizes the column to accommodate its largest value, including the field name at the top of the column. To use this method, you position the mouse pointer at the right edge of the column selector for the field and, when the mouse pointer changes to ✛, double-click the left mouse button. Access then automatically resizes the column.

For the best-fit method, you can resize two or more adjacent columns at the same time. Simply move the mouse pointer to the column selector of the leftmost of the fields. When the pointer changes to ↓, drag it to the column selector of the rightmost field and then release the mouse button. You then double-click the ✛ at the right edge of the column selector for any field in the group.

To resize datasheet columns using the best-fit column width method:

1. Move the mouse pointer to the Freelancer column selector. When it changes to ↓, click the left mouse button, drag the pointer to the right to the Writer Age column selector, and then release the mouse button. The last three columns are now highlighted.

2. Move the mouse pointer to the right edge of the Freelancer column selector. When it changes to ✛, double-click the left mouse button. Access automatically resizes the three columns to their best fits. See Figure 2-22.

Figure 2-22 Five columns resized

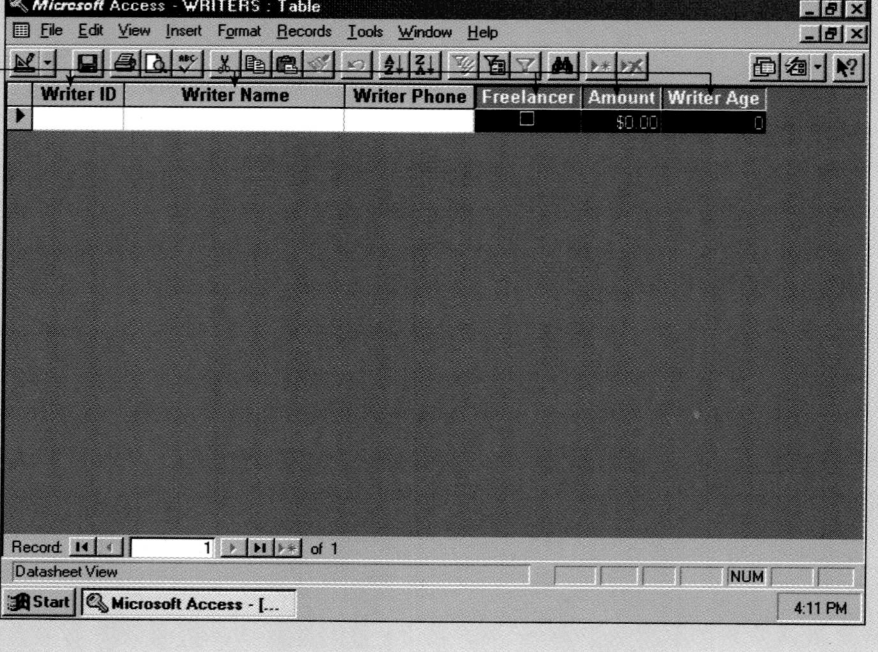

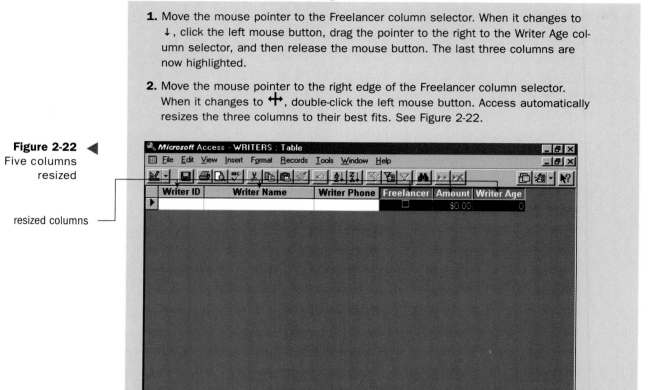

For her final set of field property changes, Elena will assign a default value to the Freelancer field, eliminate the decimal places in the Freelancer Reprint Payment Amount field, and add an input mask to the Writer Phone field.

Assigning a Default Value

With a few exceptions, Elena knows which writers are freelancers and which are staff writers. To be safe, Elena will assume that the exceptions are freelancers until she finds out for sure. She assigns the default value Yes to the Freelancer field, which means each writer will have the value Yes in the Freelancer field unless it is specifically changed to No. A default value must be assigned in the Design View window, so Elena first switches from the Datasheet View window.

To assign a default value:

1. Click the **Table View** button on the toolbar to switch to the Design View window.

2. Click anywhere in the **Freelancer** field row to make it the current field, click the **Default Value** property text box, and then type **Yes**. See Figure 2-23.

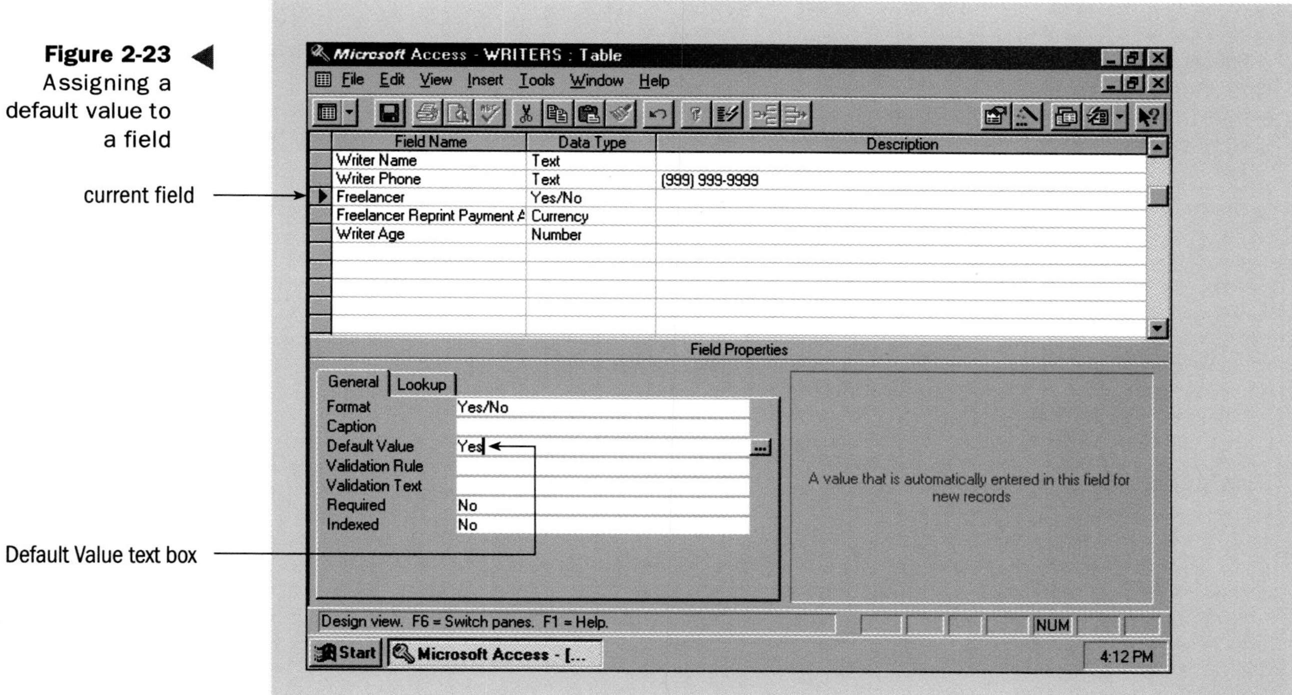

Figure 2-23 Assigning a default value to a field

Elena's next change is to eliminate the decimal places in the Freelancer Reprint Payment Amount field.

Changing Decimal Places

Elena knows that the amount that Vision Publishers pays its freelancers is always a whole dollar figure. She therefore changes the Freelancer Reprint Payment Amount field to show only whole dollar amounts. To do this, she modifies the Decimal Places property for the field.

To change the number of decimal places displayed:

1. Click anywhere in the Freelancer Reprint Payment Amount field row to make it the current field and to display its Field Properties options.
2. Click in the **Decimal Places** text box, then click **list arrow** that appears. Access displays the Decimal Places list box. See Figure 2-24.

Figure 2-24 Changing the Decimal Places field property

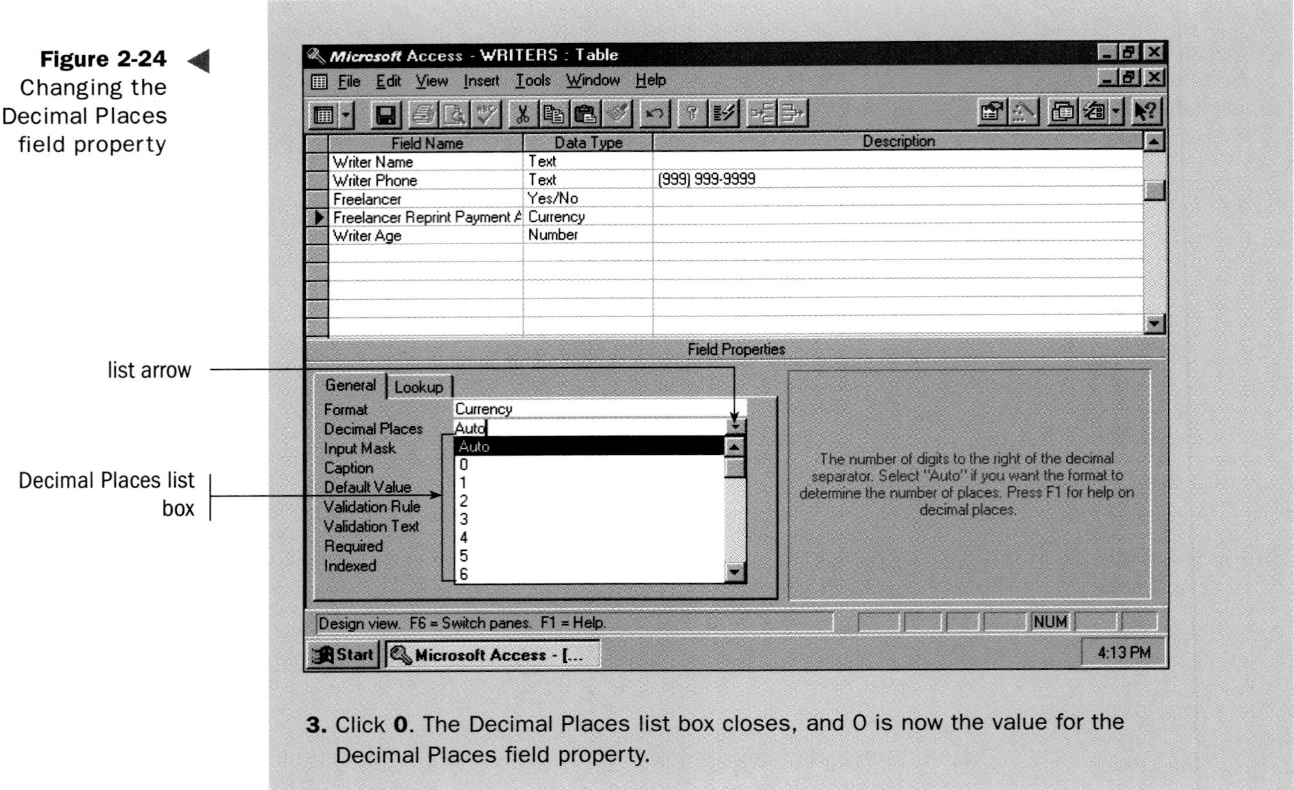

3. Click **0**. The Decimal Places list box closes, and 0 is now the value for the Decimal Places field property.

Elena is now ready to make her final change. She will use the Input Mask Wizard to create an input mask for the Writer Phone field.

Input Masks

One standard way to format a telephone number is with parentheses, a space, and a hyphen as in (917) 555-5364. If you want these special formatting characters to appear whenever Writer Phone field values are entered, you need to create an input mask. Remember that an input mask dictates the format for data entered in a particular field. With an input mask described above for the Writer Phone field, users simply enter the numbers; the parentheses, space, and hyphen are added by Access. An input mask helps to make the data more readable, more consistent, and reduces the chance of error when data is entered.

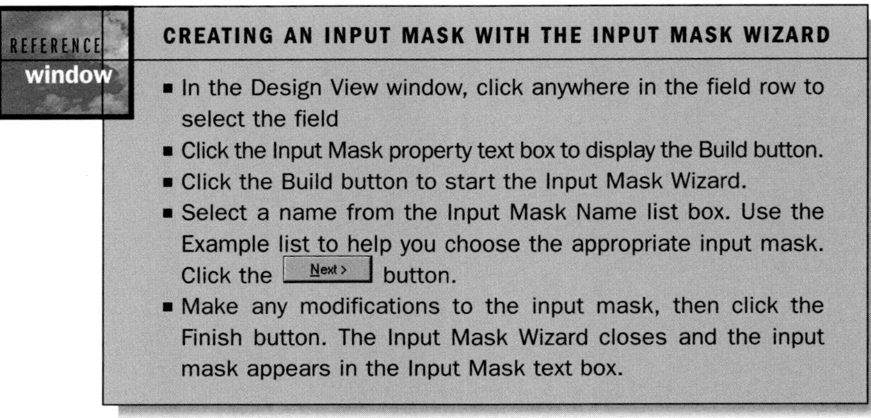

CREATING AN INPUT MASK WITH THE INPUT MASK WIZARD

- In the Design View window, click anywhere in the field row to select the field
- Click the Input Mask property text box to display the Build button.
- Click the Build button to start the Input Mask Wizard.
- Select a name from the Input Mask Name list box. Use the Example list to help you choose the appropriate input mask. Click the Next > button.
- Make any modifications to the input mask, then click the Finish button. The Input Mask Wizard closes and the input mask appears in the Input Mask text box.

Elena creates an input mask for the Writer Phone field.

To create an input mask:

1. Click anywhere in the **Writer Phone** field row to make it the current field and to display its Field Properties options.
2. Click in the Input Mask text box to display the Build button. See Figure 2-25.

Figure 2-25 Defining an Input Mask property

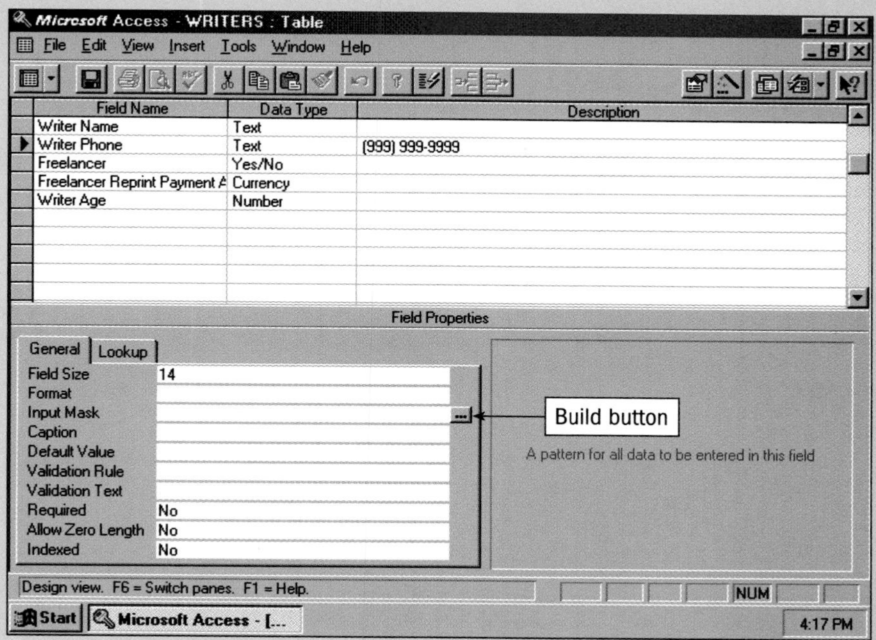

For most common formats it is not necessary to create input masks from scratch. When you click in the Input Mask property text box, Access displays the Build button at the right of the text box. When you click the Build button, Access starts the Input Mask Wizard to assist you in creating an input mask.

3. Click the **Build** button to start the Input Mask Wizard. The Input Mask Wizard lets you select from a list of common input masks, such as masks for social security numbers, zip codes, etc. Before starting the Input Mask Wizard, Access displays the Save now? dialog box. This allows you to save any changes you have made up to this point.
4. Click the **Yes** button to save the changes and close the dialog box. Access saves the WRITERS table and displays the first Input Mask Wizard dialog box. See Figure 2-26.

Figure 2-26 The first Input Mask Wizard dialog box

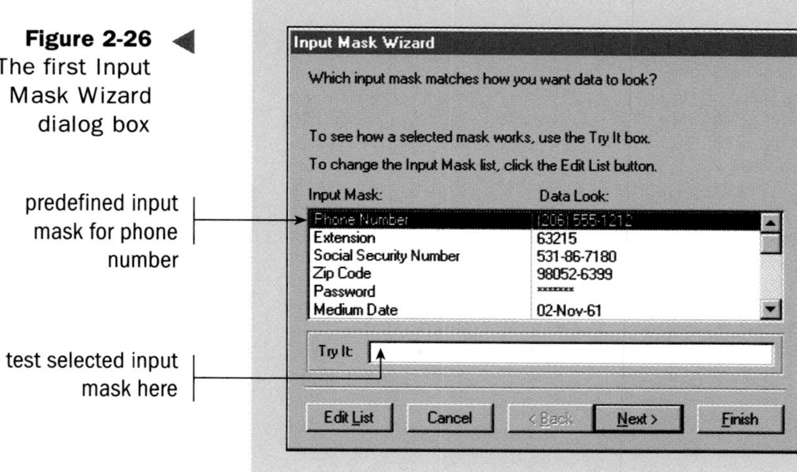

5. If necessary, click **Phone Number** in the Input Mask list box to highlight it.
6. Click in the **Try it** text box. Access displays (___) ___-____ in the text box. The underscores are placeholder characters that are replaced with numbers as you type.
7. Click to the right of the first parenthesis, then type **9876543210** to enter a sample phone number.
8. Click the Next > button. Access displays the next Input Mask Wizard dialog box. See Figure 2-27.

Figure 2-27 The next Input Mask Wizard dialog box

Input Mask Wizard

Do you want to change the input mask?

Input Mask Name: Phone Number

Input Mask: !(999) 000-0000

What placeholder character do you want the field to display?

Placeholders are replaced as you enter data into the field.

Placeholder character: _

Try It:

Cancel | < Back | Next > | Finish

make any changes here

specify placeholder character here

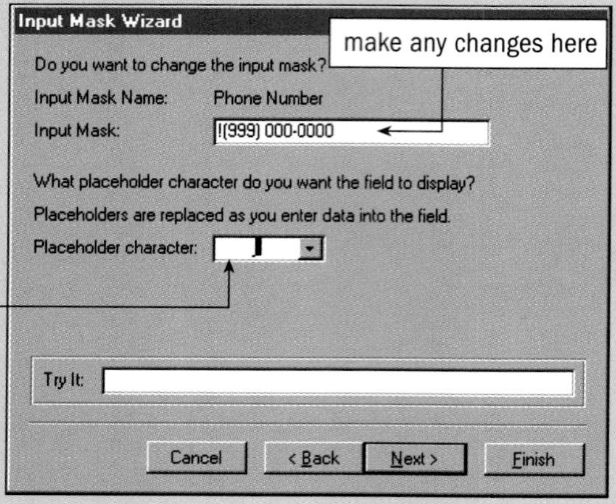

The Input Mask Wizard allows you to modify, or customize, the input mask. You can change the default underscore placeholder character, for example, to a space or one of the following special characters: # @ ! $ % or *. For now, Elena accepts the predefined input mask and continues through the remaining Input Mask Wizard dialog boxes.

To finish an input mask:

1. Click the Next > button. Access displays the next Input Mask Wizard dialog box.
2. Click the top radio button so that you store the data "With the symbols in the mask, like this: (206) 555-1212." Then click the Next > button. Access displays the next Input Mask Wizard dialog box.
3. Click the **Finish** button. Access closes Input Mask Wizard and displays the newly created input mask for the Writer Phone field. See Figure 2-28.

Figure 2-28 The newly created input mask

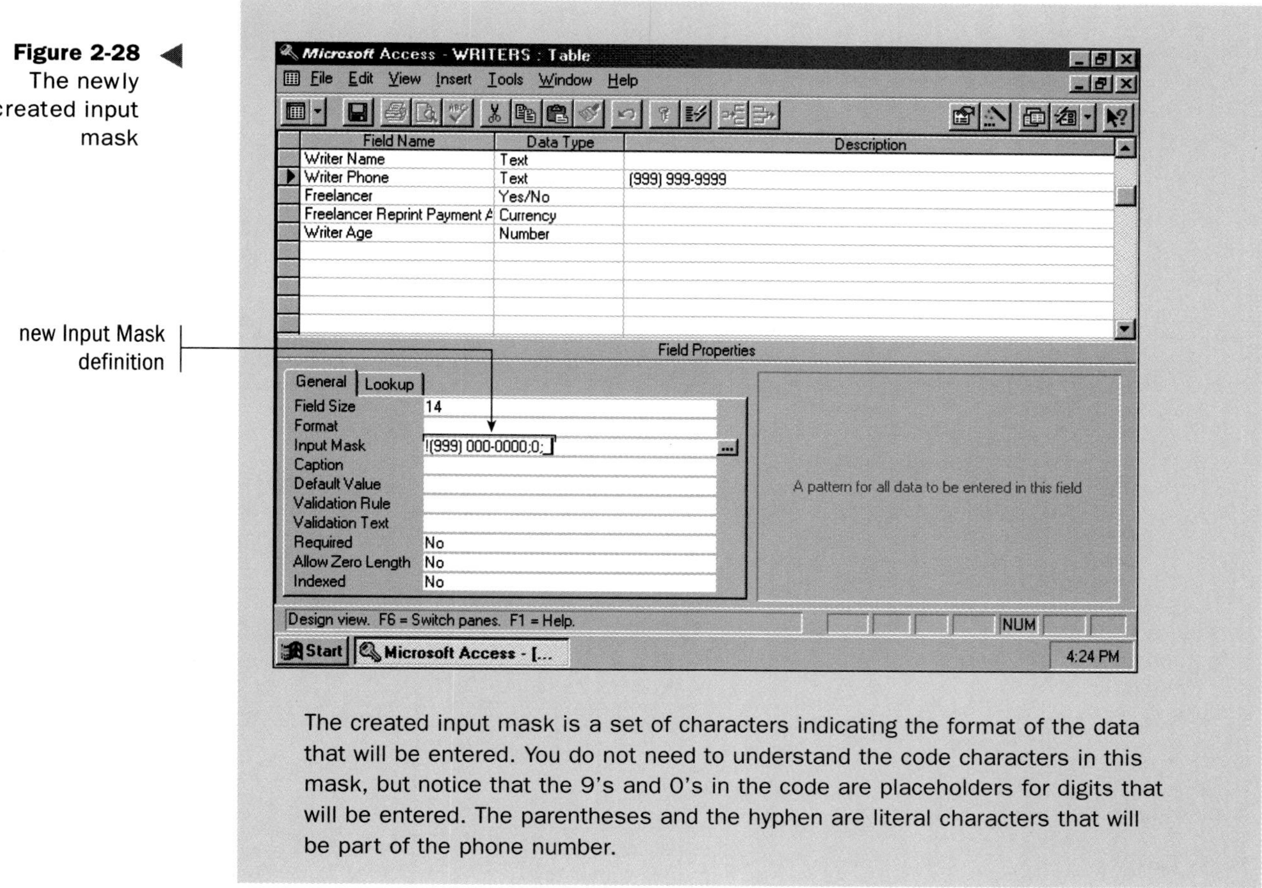

The created input mask is a set of characters indicating the format of the data that will be entered. You do not need to understand the code characters in this mask, but notice that the 9's and 0's in the code are placeholders for digits that will be entered. The parentheses and the hyphen are literal characters that will be part of the phone number.

Elena has finished making her modifications to the field properties and decides to show her table design to Brian for his comments.

Modifying the Structure of an Access Table

When Elena shows Brian her modified WRITERS table, he tells her she has made a good start and then suggests the following structural changes that will improve the table.

- The Writer Age field is unnecessary and could even lead to potential legal problems for Vision Publishers in the future. Brian suggests that Elena delete that information from the table.
- For magazine indexing purposes, Brian needs a list of all the WRITERS table information arranged alphabetically by writer last name. Elena had been planning to enter names in the Writer Name field in the regular order of first, middle, and last name, and now realizes that she needs to change the WRITERS table structure by renaming the Writer Name field Last Name, and then adding a field for First Name, which will include the middle initial, to allow for Brian's list.
- Because Vision Publishers has not contacted some writers for years, Elena needs to add a field named Last Contact Date. That way, she can contact those writers who have a reasonably current contact date first.

While the changes Elena made previously involved changes to individual fields, the changes that Brian wants Elena to make will modify the actual structure of the table.

Deleting a Field

Elena's first priority is to delete the Writer Age field.

DELETING A FIELD FROM A TABLE STRUCTURE

- In the Design View window, click the right mouse button anywhere in the row for the field you want to delete. Access displays the shortcut menu.
- Click Delete Field in the shortcut menu. Access closes the shortcut menu and deletes the field from the table structure.

To delete a field:

1. Make sure you are in Design View, then move the mouse pointer to the row for the Writer Age field and click the right mouse button. Access displays the shortcut menu. See Figure 2-29.

Figure 2-29 The shortcut menu for Writer Age

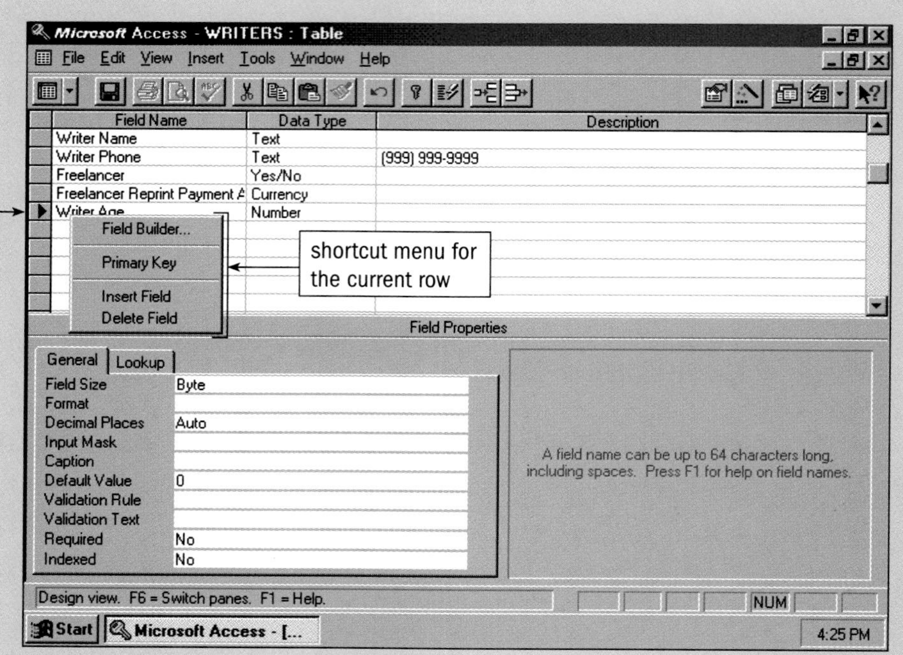

2. Click **Delete Field** in the shortcut menu. Access deletes the Writer Age field from the WRITERS table structure. The row where Writer Age had been positioned is also deleted.

   TROUBLE? If you deleted the wrong field, immediately click the Undo button. The field you deleted is inserted again. (Note that not all changes can be undone, in which case the Undo button will be dimmed). Repeat the deletion steps for the correct field starting with Step 1.

Adding a Field

The order in which the fields are listed in the Design View window determines the order of the fields in the Datasheet View window. Elena wants the new field, First Name, to be positioned right after the Writer Name row, which she will rename Last Name. Then she will position the other new field, Last Contact Date, between the Writer Phone and Freelancer rows.

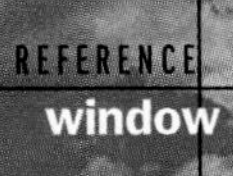

ADDING A FIELD TO A TABLE STRUCTURE

- In the Design View window, open the shortcut menu by clicking the right mouse button anywhere in the row that will fall below the field you are adding.
- Click Insert Field in the shortcut menu. Access inserts a blank row.
- Define the new field by entering a field name, data type, and optional description in the new row.

or

- If the new field is to be added to the end of the table, click the Field Name column for the first blank row. Then enter the field name, data type, and optional description.

Before Elena adds any fields, she wants to change the Writer Name field to Last Name.

To change a field name:

1. Click in the **Field Name** text box for the Writer Name field, then press the **F2** key to highlight the field name.
2. Type **Last Name** to make it the new field name.

Elena is now ready to add two new fields to the WRITERS table.

To add a field to a table structure:

1. Click the right mouse button anywhere in the Writer Phone row. You want to insert the new First Name field above it. Access displays the shortcut menu.
2. Click **Insert Field** in the shortcut menu. Access adds a blank row between the Last Name and Writer Phone rows and closes the shortcut menu. The insertion point is in the Field Name box of the new row. See Figure 2-30.

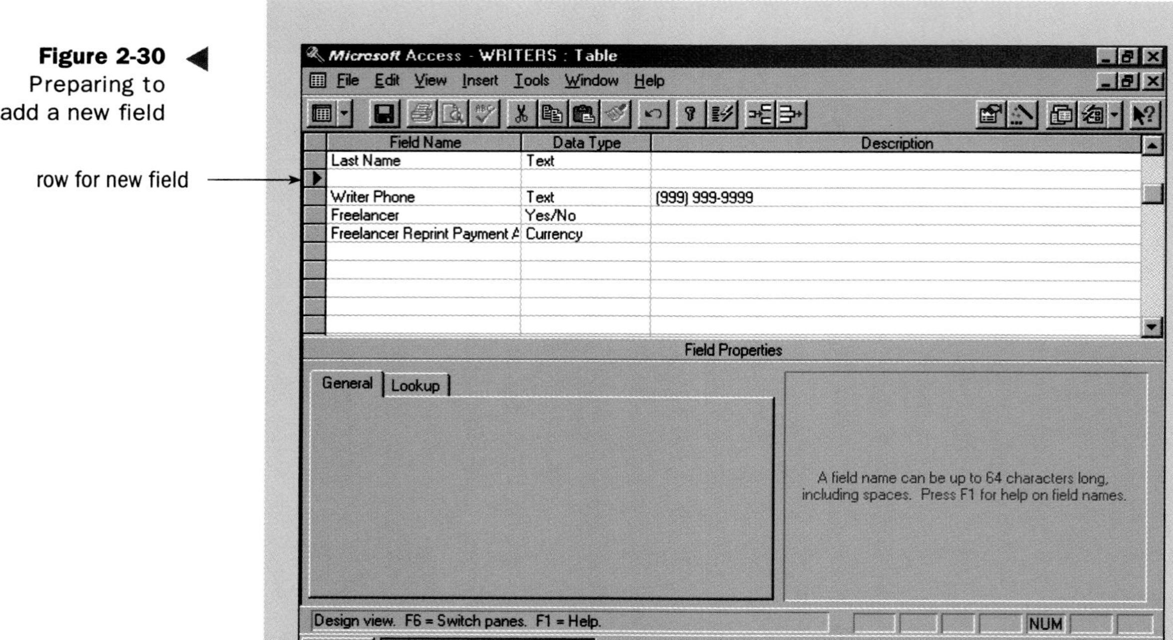

Figure 2-30 Preparing to add a new field

3. Type **First Name** to type in the new field name, then press the **Tab** key.

   Elena estimates that first names and initials should require a field size of 15, and therefore needs to change the field size accordingly.

4. Double-click the **50** in the Field Size box, then type **15**.

   After adding the First Name field, Elena adds the Last Contact Date field to the WRITERS table.

5. Click the right mouse button anywhere in the Freelancer row and then click **Insert Field** in the shortcut menu to insert a row between the Writer Phone and Freelancer rows.

6. Type **Last Contact Date**, press the **Tab** key, type **D** (because it is a Date/Time field), and then press the **Tab** key. See Figure 2-31.

Figure 2-31 Last Contact Date field added

Last Contact Date row

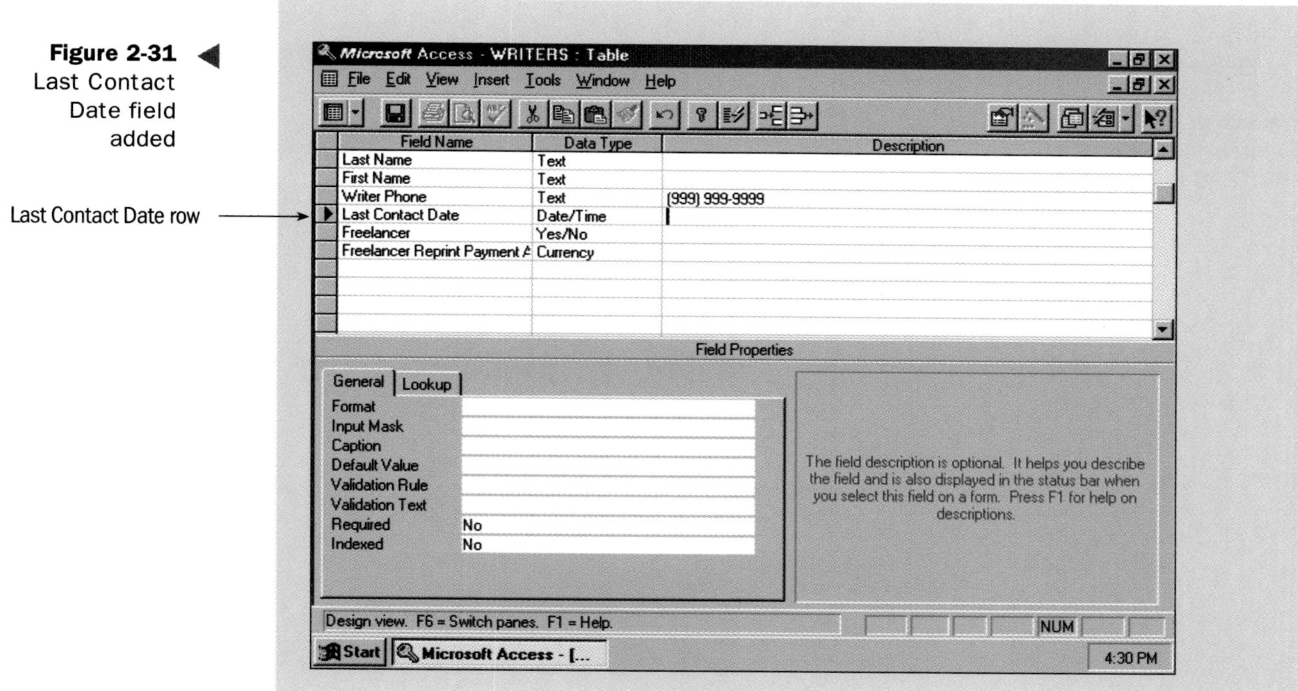

Elena has now modified the WRITERS table structure. Once again, however, she wants to review the appearance of the WRITERS table to see if further modifications are needed.

To review and modify a datasheet:

1. Click the **Table View** button . The Save now? dialog box opens.
2. Click the **Yes** button. Access displays the Datasheet View window. The Last Name and First Name fields appear to the right of the Writer ID field, and Last Contact Date is to the right of the Writer Phone field. The one change that needs to be made is to widen the column for Last Contact Date so the whole field name will be visible.
3. Using the procedure discussed earlier, resize the column for Last Contact Date for best fit so that the entire record is visible. See Figure 2-32.

Figure 2-32 The final Datasheet View window for the WRITERS table

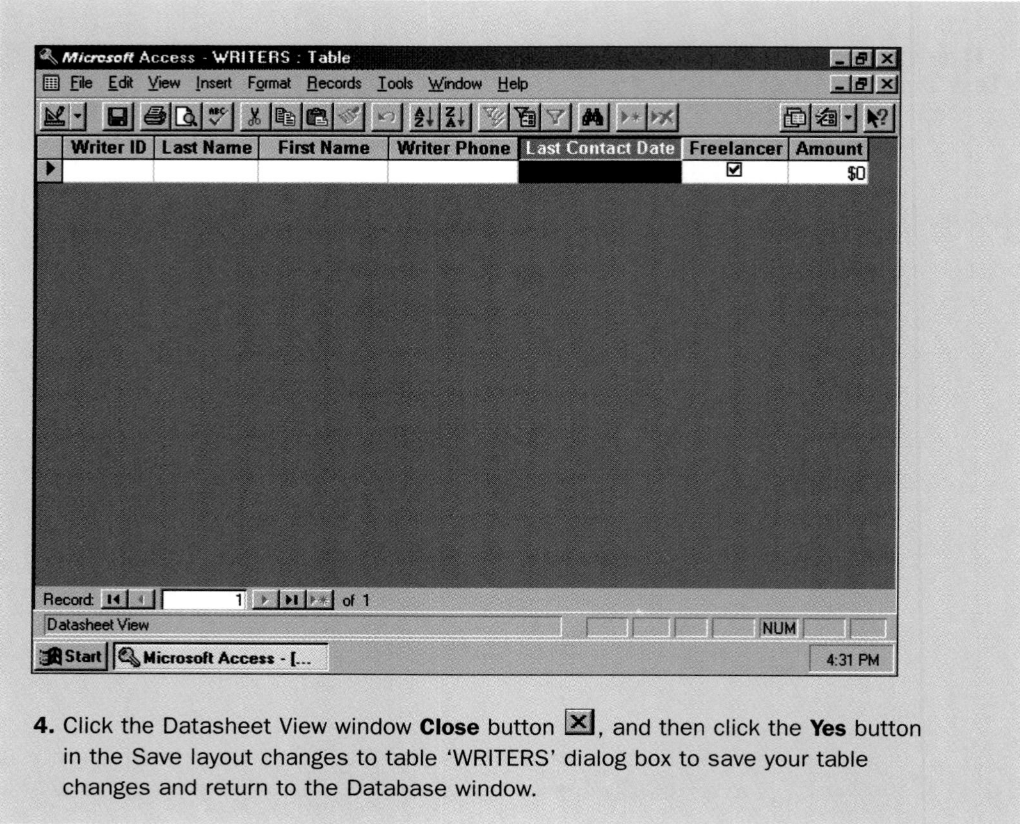

4. Click the Datasheet View window **Close** button, and then click the **Yes** button in the Save layout changes to table 'WRITERS' dialog box to save your table changes and return to the Database window.

Elena has defined the WRITERS table structure and refined the table's datasheet. In the next tutorial Elena will add data to the WRITERS table, but for now she turns her attention to creating a new table for her Issue25 database that will allow her to record reprint payments to writers easily.

Creating a Table with the Table Wizard

As discussed previously, in Access you can define a table from the Design View window—as Elena did with the WRITERS table—or you can use the Table Wizard to automate the table creation process. (In a third method, creating tables from entered data, Access creates a table structure by analyzing data as you enter it in a blank Datasheet View window. In general, it is a good idea to plan and define your table structures carefully before you enter any data.) Because her new table will contain standard fields, Elena will use the Table Wizard to create this table more quickly and efficiently than she could using the keyboard.

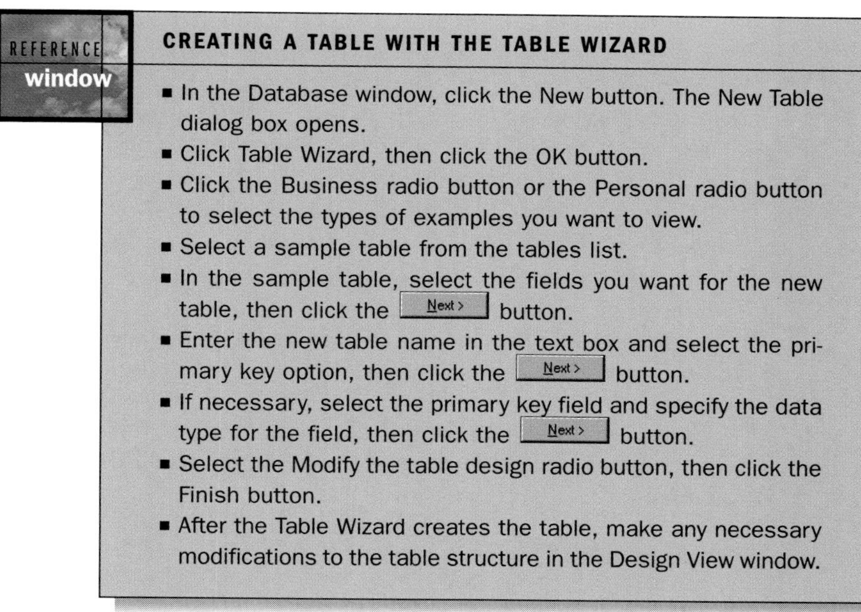

REFERENCE window

CREATING A TABLE WITH THE TABLE WIZARD

- In the Database window, click the New button. The New Table dialog box opens.
- Click Table Wizard, then click the OK button.
- Click the Business radio button or the Personal radio button to select the types of examples you want to view.
- Select a sample table from the tables list.
- In the sample table, select the fields you want for the new table, then click the Next > button.
- Enter the new table name in the text box and select the primary key option, then click the Next > button.
- If necessary, select the primary key field and specify the data type for the field, then click the Next > button.
- Select the Modify the table design radio button, then click the Finish button.
- After the Table Wizard creates the table, make any necessary modifications to the table structure in the Design View window.

Elena uses the Table Wizard now.

To use the Table Wizard:

1. Make sure you are in the Database window, then click the **New** button. The New Table dialog box opens.
2. Click **Table Wizard**, then click the **OK** button. The first Table Wizard dialog box opens. See Figure 2-33.

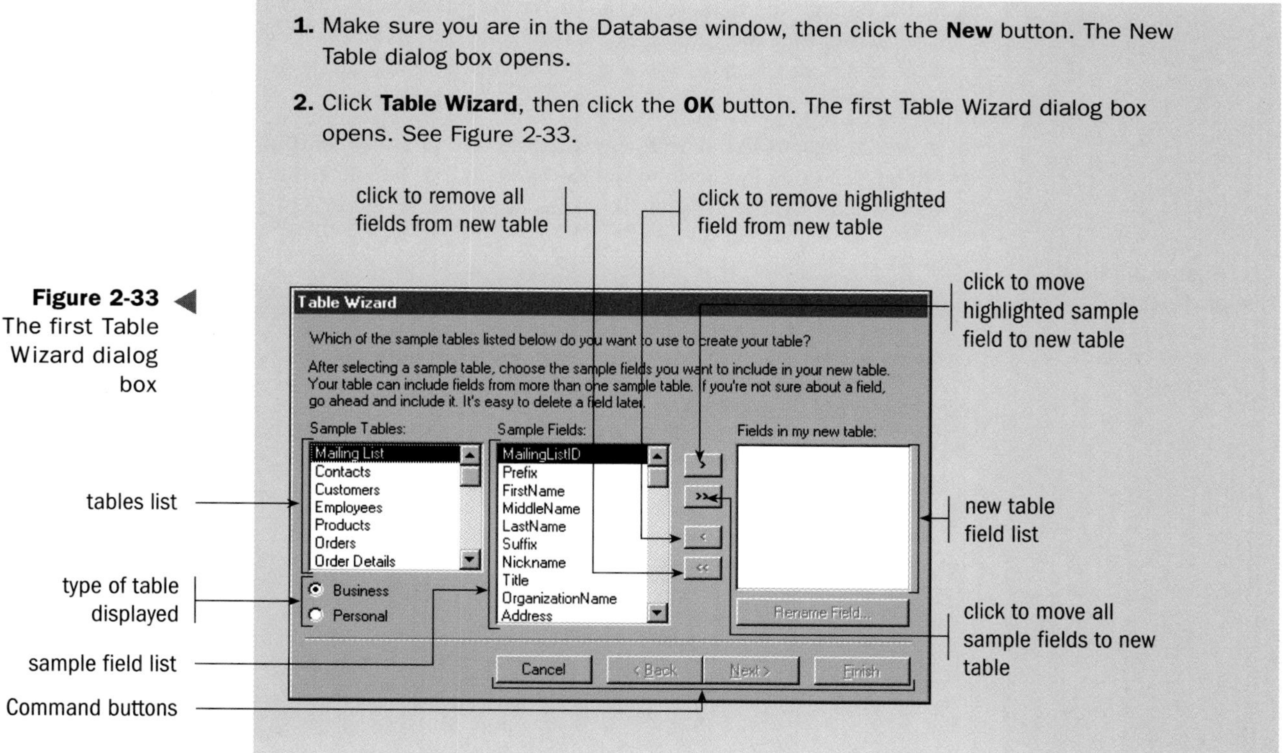

Figure 2-33 The first Table Wizard dialog box

In the first Table Wizard dialog box, you select the fields for your table from sample fields in dozens of sample tables. Two types of sample tables are available: Business and Personal. Simply click the Business or Personal radio button to display the corresponding list of sample tables. Scroll through the Sample Tables list until you find an appropriate table and then select fields to add to your table from the Sample Fields list. If necessary, you can select fields from more than one table. Do not be concerned about selecting field names that exactly match the ones you need—you can change the names later. Instead, select fields that seem like they have the general properties you need for your fields. If a field's properties do not exactly match, you can change the properties later.

You select fields in the order you want them to appear in your table. If you want to select fields one at a time, highlight a field by clicking it, and then click the > button. If you want to select all the fields, click the >> button. The fields appear in the list box on the right as you select them. If you make a mistake, click the < button to remove all the fields from the list box on the right or highlight a field and click the << button to remove one field at a time.

At the bottom of each Table Wizard dialog box is a set of buttons. These buttons allow you to move quickly to other Table Wizard dialog boxes or to cancel the table creation process.

Elena scrolls through the Business sample tables and decides that the Payments sample table contains fields that she will need. She selects fields from the Payments sample table to create the WRITER PAYMENTS table.

To select fields for a new table:

1. Make sure that the Business radio button is selected, and then scroll through the Sample Tables list to find the Payments table.
2. Click **Payments** to select it. Access displays a list of fields available for the Payments table.
3. Scroll through the Sample Fields list box until it displays the CheckNumber field. Click **CheckNumber** in the Sample Fields list box and then click the **>** button. Access places CheckNumber into the list box on the right as the first field in the new table.
4. In order, select **CustomerID**, **PaymentAmount,** and **PaymentDate** for the WRITER PAYMENTS table by clicking the field name in the Sample Fields list box, scrolling as needed, and then clicking the > button. See Figure 2-34.

Figure 2-34 Fields selected for the WRITER PAYMENTS table

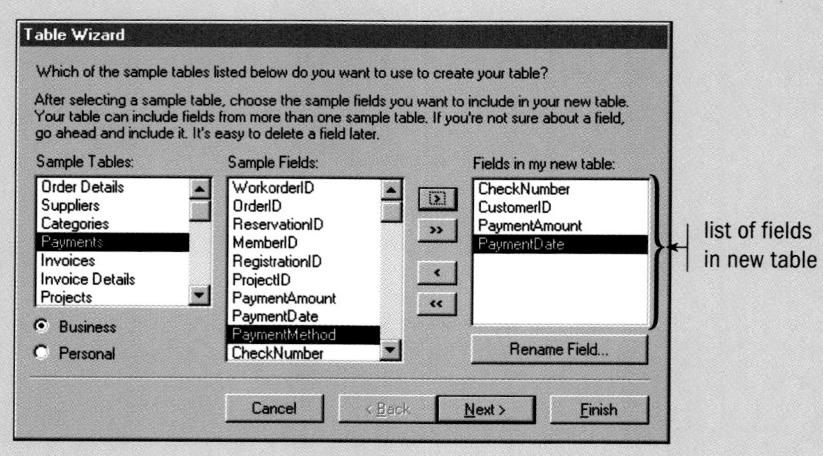

Elena has selected all the fields she needs for her table, so she continues through the remaining Table Wizard dialog boxes to finish creating the WRITER PAYMENTS table.

To finish creating a table using Table Wizard:

1. Click the Next > button. Access displays the next Table Wizard dialog box.
2. Type **WRITER PAYMENTS** in the text box and then click the radio button beside 'No, I'll set the primary key.' See Figure 2-35.

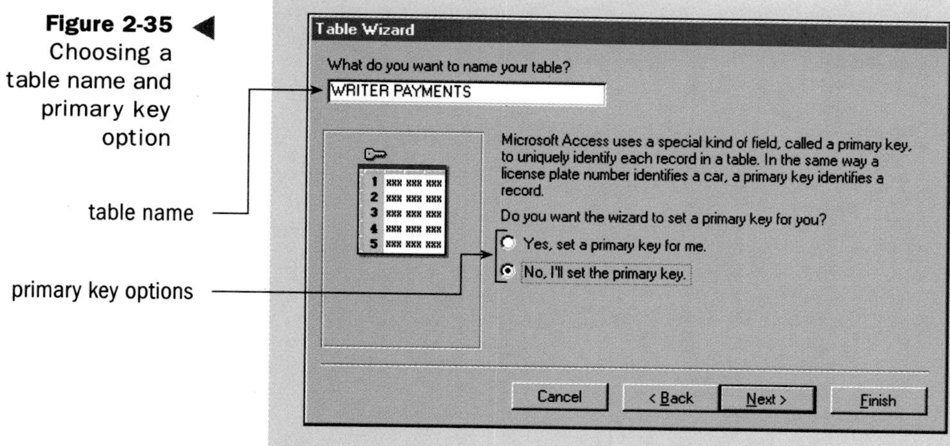

Figure 2-35 Choosing a table name and primary key option

3. Click the Next > button. Access displays the next Table Wizard dialog box.

4. Click the **list arrow** in the text box to display the list of fields, then click **CheckNumber**. If necessary, click the middle radio button for the option that reads "Numbers I enter when I add new records." You have now selected the CheckNumber field as the primary key for the table. See Figure 2-36.

Figure 2-36 Choosing the primary key

Table Wizard
What field will hold data that is unique for each record?
CheckNumber
primary key options
What type of data do you want the primary key field to contain?
Consecutive numbers Microsoft Access assigns automatically to new records.
Numbers I enter when I add new records.
Numbers and/or letters I enter when I add new records.
Cancel
< Back
Next >
Finish
primary key field

5. Click the Next > button to display the next Table Wizard dialog box.

   Since there is another table in the database (the WRITERS table), Access asks if the WRITER PAYMENTS table is related to it. Defining a relation between two tables is an important tool in building a powerful and useful database. You will investigate defining relations in a later tutorial.

6. Click the Next > button. Access displays the next Table Wizard dialog box.

   Elena needs to change the field names and field properties for the sample fields inserted into the WRITER PAYMENTS table by the Table Wizard so that they agree with her table design. To make these changes she must modify the table design. First, she closes the Table Wizard.

7. If necessary, click the first radio button to select "Modify the table design." Make sure that the box next to Display Help on working with the table at the bottom is unchecked. See Figure 2-37.

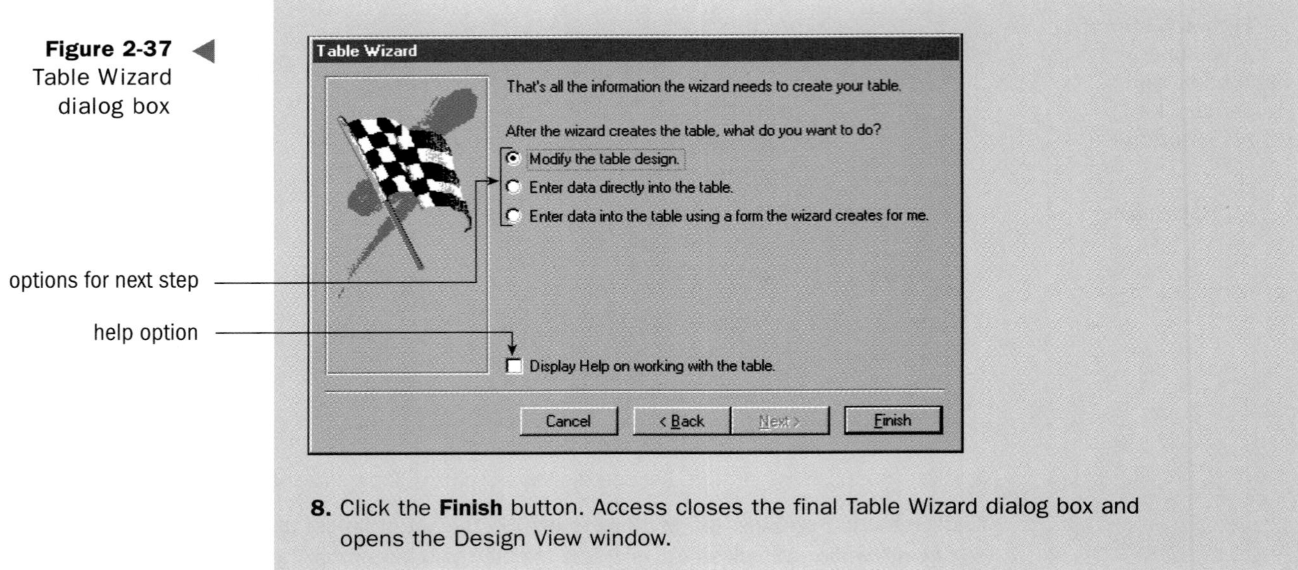

Figure 2-37 Table Wizard dialog box

8. Click the **Finish** button. Access closes the final Table Wizard dialog box and opens the Design View window.

Now that she has created a table using the Table Wizard, Elena realizes that she should view all the fields to make sure the sample field properties are accurate.

Changing the Sample Field Properties

For the first field, CheckNumber, Elena decides to change the field name to Check Number to make it more consistent with the other field names (i.e., by adding a space between the words). She also wants to add "primary key" as a description, and to set the Required property to Yes.

To change the first field's properties:

1. Double-click in the **Field Name** text box for the CheckNumber field to select the name, then type **Check Number**.
2. Click in the Description text box for the Check Number field and type **primary key**.

Elena wants to set the Required property for this field to Yes. Setting the Required property to Yes for a field means you must enter a value in the field for every record in the table. Every primary key field should have the Required property set to Yes, so that each record has a value entered for the primary key field. Fields other than a primary key should have the Required property set to Yes if it is important that a value be entered for each record. Elena decides that the Writer ID, PaymentDate, and PaymentAmount fields also must have data entered for each payment record, so she sets the Required property to Yes for each field.

For the second field, she changes the field name to Writer ID, the data type to Text, the Field Size property to 4, the Required property to Yes. She changes the names of the other fields to check Amount and check Date and sets the Required property to Yes for each of them.

To change the remaining fields' properties:

1. Click in the **Required** property text box, then click the **list arrow** that appears. Click **Yes** to choose that as the property value.
2. Double-click **CustomerID** to highlight it, then type **Writer ID** and press the **Tab** key to move to the Data Type column.

3. Type **T** to select the Text data type, then press the **Tab** key.

4. Double-click the **Field Size** property text box and type **4.**

5. Click in the **Required** property text box and then click the **list arrow** that appears. Click **Yes** to choose that as the property value.

6. Click the **Caption** property text box, press the **F2** key, then press the **Delete** key to delete the caption.

7. Double-click in the **Field Name** text box for the PaymentAmount field to select it, then type **Amount**.

8. Click in the **Required** property text box and then click the **check list arrow** that appears. Click **Yes** to choose that as the property value.

9. Double-click in the **Field Name** text box for the PaymentDate field to select it, then type **Date**.

10. Click in the **Required** property text box and then click the **check list arrow** that appears. Click **Yes** to choose that as the property value.

Elena realizes that she's almost finished creating the WRITER PAYMENTS table; she's defined all the fields, established each field's properties, and designated a primary key. Along with designating a primary key, however, Elena needs to create an index for her table. She does that next.

Creating Indexes

Access automatically creates and maintains an index for the primary key field. An **index** for a field is a list of the field values (in this case, primary key values) and their corresponding record numbers. Indexes serve several functions. First, an index allows Access to sort a table quickly in order by the indexed field. Access uses the primary key index to display the records in primary key order at all times. When you add a new record in the Datasheet View window, Access automatically inserts the new record in its correct place. Second, an index makes searching for a particular field value much more efficient. In large tables, this efficiency greatly increases the speed with which Access can locate the records you want to find. Indexes are also important when you define a relationship between two tables. Access uses the index to match records in the two related tables.

Although it may seem like a good idea to index every field in a table, indexes add to the database disk storage requirements, and they require extra time for Access to maintain them as you add, delete, and modify records. You should, therefore, create indexes only for fields that you will be using frequently for searching and sorting, or for a field you will use as a linking field when you define a relation between two tables.

Elena views the indexes that currently exist for the WRITER PAYMENTS table by using the Indexes button on the toolbar.

To display the indexes for a table:

1. Click the **Indexes** button on the toolbar. Access displays the Indexes window. See Figure 2-38.

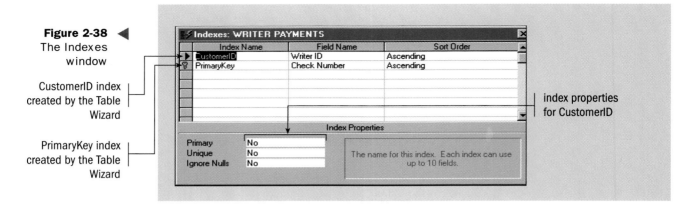

Figure 2-38 The Indexes window

CustomerID index created by the Table Wizard

PrimaryKey index created by the Table Wizard

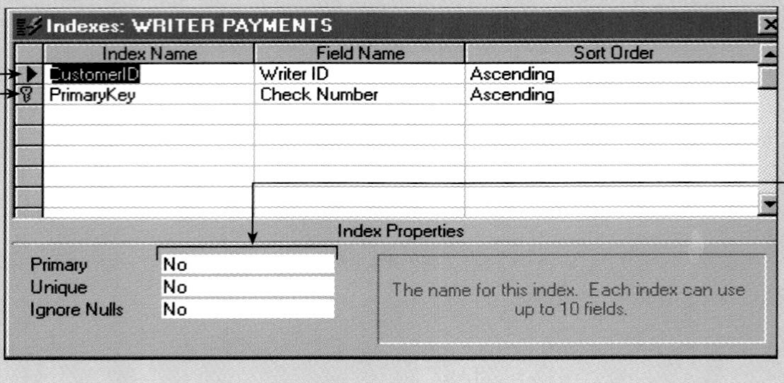

index properties for CustomerID

Index Name	Field Name	Sort Order
CustomerID	Writer ID	Ascending
PrimaryKey	Check Number	Ascending

Index Properties

Primary	No
Unique	No
Ignore Nulls	No

The name for this index. Each index can use up to 10 fields.

Two indexes appear in the Indexes window: one for the primary key field, Check Number, and a second for the Writer ID field. How was the Writer ID index created? Recall that you used the Table Wizard to create the WRITER PAYMENTS table. When you select Table Wizard fields, you also select all their predefined properties. The original sample table had an index associated with the CustomerID field. When you changed CustomerID to Writer ID, the index for the CustomerID field was retained.

Elena notices that the Writer ID index is still named CustomerID, and that the Check Number index is called PrimaryKey, so she decides to rename them. She does not want to create indexes for the other two fields, but if she ever needs an index for another field in the future, she can create it by using the Indexes window or the Indexed property for the field.

Elena renames the index then saves the changes and exits Access.

To rename an index:

1. If necessary, position the mouse pointer in the first row of the Indexes window under Index Name. Double-click **CustomerID** to highlight it.
2. Type **Writer ID** to rename the index.
3. Position the mouse pointer in the second row of the Indexes window under Index Name. Double-click **PrimaryKey** to highlight it.
4. Type **Check Number** to rename the index.
5. Click the Indexes window **Close** button [X] to close the Indexes window.
6. Click the Design View window **Close** button [X]. Access displays the Save changes dialog box. Click the **Yes** button to save the changes to the table design.
7. Click the Access window **Close** button [X] to exit Access.

Elena has now created two of the three tables for her Issue25 database: WRITERS and WRITER PAYMENTS. The tables will allow her to store information about the writers and record reprint payments made to them. In the next tutorial, she will add data to the WRITERS table.

1. What is a caption?
2. Describe three different ways to resize a datasheet column.
3. Why would you assign a default value to a field?
4. What are the steps for changing decimal places?
5. What is an input mask?
6. Describe two recommended ways to create an Access table.
7. What is an index and why is it useful?

Tutorial Assignments

Elena creates the BUSINESS ARTICLES table structure, as shown in Figure 2-39.

Figure 2-39

BUSINESS ARTICLES table	Data Type	Input/Display Field Size	Description
Article Title	Text	44	
Issue of Business Perspective	Text	8	yyyy mmm format
Length of Article	Number	4	Integer field size
Writer Name	Text	25	

Start Access, open the Issue25 database in the Tutorial folder on your Student Disk, and do the following:

1. Create a new table without using the Table Wizard. Define the fields directly in the Design View window. Use Figure 2-39 to define properties, as appropriate, for each of the four fields in the table. For the Number data type field, use the Description column in Figure 2-39 to set its Field Size property.
2. Save the table and the name it BUSINESS ARTICLES. Do not select a primary key.
3. Switch to the Datasheet View window and resize columns so that the entire field name can be read in the column heading for every field.
4. Print the datasheet for the table.
5. In the Design View window, change the field name Length of Article to Article Length. For the field Issue of Business Perspective, add the Caption property Issue. Resize the columns, if necessary, for these two fields in the Datasheet View window.
6. Print the datasheet for the table.
7. Delete the field Writer Name from the table structure.
8. Add a four-character Text field named Writer ID to the end of the table. For a description, enter "foreign key."
9. Change the data type of the field Issue of Business Perspective to Date/Time.
10. Add a three-character Text field named Type between the Article Length and Writer ID fields. For this new field, enter the description "article type" and the Default Value BUS, which represents a business article.
11. Resize columns, as necessary, in the Datasheet View window.
12. Print the datasheet for the table.

13. Switch the order of the Article Length and Type columns in the datasheet. (Use the Help Index to find help on moving columns.) Do not switch their order in the table structure. Print the datasheet for the table.

14. Using Access Help for guidance, move the field named Type in the Design View window so that it follows the field named Article Title. Save and print the datasheet for the table and then close the Issue25 database.

15. (This exercise requires approximately 600KB of free disk space. You might want to use a blank formatted disk.) Use the Database Wizard to create a new database called MyMusic. Use the Music Collection model database as a template. Use the default choices in setting up the database.
    a. What tables are in the MyMusic database?
    b. What other database objects were created (forms, queries, etc.)?
    c. Describe the structure of each database table (field names, types, sizes, etc.).
    d. Open the ALBUMS table. What is the primary key field?
    e. What input mask is used for the DatePurchased field?
    f. What indexes are used in the ALBUMS table?

Case Problems

1. Walkton Daily Press Carriers Grant Sherman, circulation manager of the *Walkton Daily Press*, wants a better way to supervise the carriers who deliver the newspaper. Grant meets with Robin Witkop, one of the newspaper's computer experts, to discuss what can be done to improve his current tracking system.

After reviewing Grant's information needs, Robin offers to design a database to keep track of carriers and their outstanding balances. Grant agrees, and Robin designs a database that has two tables: CARRIERS and BILLINGS. Robin first creates the CARRIERS table structure, as shown in Figure 2-40.

Figure 2-40 

CARRIERS table

Field Name	Data Type	Input/Display Field Size	Description
Carrier ID	AutoNumber		primary key; unique carrier identification number
Carrier First Name	Text	14	
Carrier Last Name	Text	15	
Carrier Phone	Text	8	
Carrier Birthdate	Date/time		

Do the following:

1. Start Access and create a new database in the Cases folder on your Student Disk. Name the database Press.
2. Create a new table using the Design View window. Use Figure 2-40 to define properties, as appropriate, for each of the five fields in the table.
3. Select Carrier ID as the table's primary key.
4. Save the table with the name CARRIERS.
5. Switch to Datasheet View and resize columns so that the entire field name can be read in the column heading for every field.
6. In Design View, change the field name Carrier Birthdate to Birthdate. Add the Caption property First Name for the field Carrier First Name. Add the Caption property Last Name for the field Carrier Last Name. Resize the columns, if necessary, for the fields in the Datasheet View window.

7. Using Access Help for guidance, move the field named Carrier Last Name in the Design View window so that it follows the field named Carrier ID. Print the datasheet for the table.
8. Save your changes and then close the datasheet.

2. Lopez Lexus Dealerships Maria and Hector Lopez own a chain of Lexus dealerships throughout Texas. They have used a computer in their business for several years to handle payroll and normal accounting functions. Their phenomenal expansion, both in the number of car locations and the number of cars handled, forces them to develop a database to track their car inventory. They design a database that has two tables: CARS and LOCATIONS. They first create the CARS table structure, as shown in Figure 2-41.

Figure 2-41

CARS table

Field Name	Data Type	Input/Display Field Size	Description
Vehicle ID	Text	5	primary key
Manufacturer	Text	13	
Model	Text	15	
Class Type	Text	2	code for type of vehicle; foreign key
Transmission Type	Text	3	code for type of transmission; foreign key
Year	Number	4	Integer field size
Cost	Currency		
Selling Price	Currency		
Location Code	Text	2	lot location within the state; foreign key

Do the following:

1. Create a new database in the Cases folder on your Student Disk. Name the database Lexus.
2. Create a new table using Design View. Using Figure 2-41 as a guide, change the sample field names and properties appropriately.
3. Select Vehicle ID as the table's primary key.
4. Switch to Datasheet View and resize columns using the Column Width dialog box. You want to see all column headings on the screen at one time.

5. Switch to Design View, then move the Location Code field so that it follows the Year field.
6. Save your changes and print the datasheet for the table.

Hector and Maria next create the LOCATIONS table structure, as shown in Figure 2-42.

Figure 2-42

LOCATIONS table

Field Name	Data Type	Input/Display Field Size	Description
Location Code	Text	2	primary key
Location Name	Text	15	
Manager Name	Text	25	

Make sure you are in Database View and do the following:

7. Create a new table without using the Table Wizard. Using Figure 2-42 as a guide, define properties as appropriate.
8. Select Location Code as the primary key and then save the table with the name LOCATIONS.

9. Switch to Datasheet View and resize columns so that the entire field name can be read in the column heading for every field.
10. Save your changes and then print the datasheet for the table.

3. Tophill University Student Employment Olivia Tyler is an administrative assistant in the financial aid department at Tophill University. She is responsible for tracking the companies that have announced part-time jobs for students. She keeps track of each available job and the person to contact at each company. Olivia had previously relied on student workers to do the paperwork, but reductions in the university budget have forced her department to reduce the number of part-time student workers. As a result, Olivia's backlog of work is increasing. After discussing the problem with her supervisor, Olivia meets with Lee Chang, a database analyst on the staff of the university computer center.

Lee questions Olivia in detail about her requirements and then develops a database to reduce her workload. Lee designs a database that has two tables: JOBS and EMPLOYERS. Lee first creates the JOBS table structure, as shown in Figure 2-43.

Figure 2-43

JOBS table

Field Name	Data Type	Input/Display Field Size	Description
Job Order	AutoNumber		primary key; unique number assigned to the job position
Employer ID	Text	4	foreign key
Job Title	Text	30	
Wage	Currency		rate per hour
Hours	Number	2	Integer field size; hours per week

Do the following:

1. Create a new database in the Cases folder on your Student Disk. Name the database Parttime.
2. Create a new table using the Table Wizard. (*Hint:* Select the Time Billed sample table listed in the Business sample tables list.) Using Figure 2-43 as a guide, change the sample field names and properties as appropriate.
3. Select Job Order as the table's primary key.
4. Save the table with the name JOBS.
5. Switch to Datasheet View and resize columns so that the entire field name can be read in the column heading for every field.
6. In the Design View window, remove the caption for the all fields, change the field name Hours to Hours/Week. Add the Caption property Job# for the field Job Order and the Caption property Wages for the field Wage. In the Datasheet View window, resize the columns, if necessary.
7. Move the field named Hours/Week in the Design View window so that it follows the field named Job Order.
8. Save your changes, print the datasheet for the table, and then close the Datasheet View window.

Lee next creates the EMPLOYERS table structure, as shown in Figure 2-44.

Figure 2-44

EMPLOYERS table

Field Name	Data Type	Input/Display Field Size	Description
Employer ID	Text	4	primary key
Employer Name	Text	40	
Contact Name	Text	25	
Contact Phone	Text	14	(999) 999-9999 format

Make sure you are in Database Window and do the following:

9. Open the database named Parttime in the Cases folder on your Student Disk.
10. Create a new table without using the Table Wizard. Using Figure 2-44 as a guide, define properties, as appropriate, for each of the four fields in the table.
11. Select Employer ID as the primary key and then save the table with the name EMPLOYERS.
12. Switch to Datasheet View and resize columns so that the entire field name can be read in the column heading for every field.
13. Save your changes and then print the datasheet for the table.

4. Rexville Business Licenses Chester Pearce works as a clerk in the town hall in Rexville, North Dakota. He has just been assigned responsibility for maintaining the licenses issued to businesses in the town. He learns that the town issues over 30 different types of licenses to over 1,500 businesses, and that most licenses must be annually renewed by March 1.

The clerk formerly responsible for the processing gave Chester the license information in two full boxes of file folders. Chester has been using a computer to help him with his other work, so he designs a database to keep track of the town's business licenses. When he completes his database design, he has two tables to create: LICENSES, which will contain data about the different types of business licenses the town issues, and BUSINESSES, which will store data about all the businesses in town. Chester first creates the LICENSES table structure, as shown in Figure 2-45.

Figure 2-45

LICENSES table

Field Name	Data Type	Input/Display Field Size	Description
License Type	Text	2	primary key
License Name	Text	60	license description
Basic Cost	Currency		cost of the license

Do the following:

1. Create a new database in the Cases folder on your Student Disk. Name the database Buslic.
2. Create a new table without using the Table Wizard. Using Figure 2-45 as a guide, define properties, as appropriate, for each of the three fields in the table.
3. Select License Type as the table's primary key.
4. Save the table with the name LICENSES.
5. Switch to Datasheet View and resize columns so that the entire field name can be read in the column heading for every field.
6. In Design View, change the field name License Name to License Description. Add the Caption property License Code for the field License Type. Change the Decimal Places property of the field Basic Cost to 0. In the Datasheet View window, resize the columns, if necessary.

7. Save your changes, print the datasheet for the table, and then close the Datasheet View window.

Chester next creates the BUSINESSES table structure, as shown in Figure 2-46.

Figure 2-46

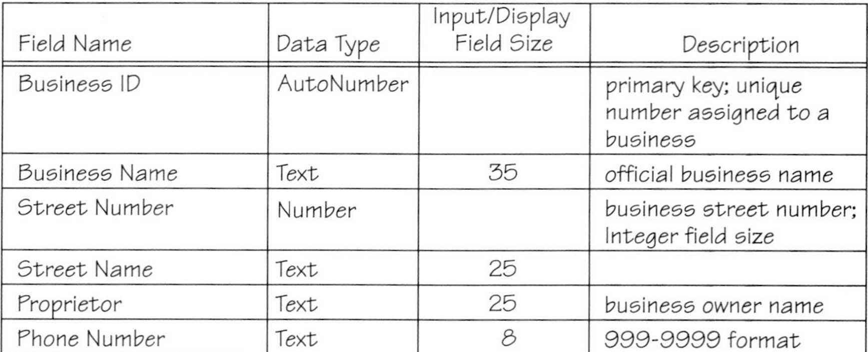

BUSINESSES table

Field Name	Data Type	Input/Display Field Size	Description
Business ID	AutoNumber		primary key; unique number assigned to a business
Business Name	Text	35	official business name
Street Number	Number		business street number; Integer field size
Street Name	Text	25	
Proprietor	Text	25	business owner name
Phone Number	Text	8	999-9999 format

Make sure you are in Database View and do the following:

8. Create a new table without using the Table Wizard. Using Figure 2-46 as a guide, define properties, as appropriate, for each of the six fields in the table.
9. Select Business ID as the primary key and then save the table with the name BUSINESSES.
10. Switch to Datasheet View and resize columns so that the entire field name can be read in the column heading for every field.
11. In Design View, add the Caption property Street# for the field Street Number. In the Datasheet View window, resize the columns, if necessary.

12. Move the field named Phone Number in the Design View window so that it follows the field named Street Name.
13. Save your changes and then print the datasheet for the table.

TUTORIAL 3

Maintaining Database Tables

Maintaining the WRITERS Table at Vision Publishers

OBJECTIVES

In this tutorial you will:

- Add data to a table using Datasheet View
- Change table field values
- Delete records from a table
- Import a table to a database and use the Table Analyzer Wizard
- Delete and rename tables in a database
- Change datasheet properties
- Find and replace field values in a table
- Sort records in a datasheet
- Use Access's Spelling feature and Lookup Wizard
- Back up and compact a database

CASE

Vision Publishers

Vision Publishers' special projects editor Elena Sanchez meets with the production staff to set the schedule for the special 25th-anniversary issue of *Business Perspective*. After the meeting, she plans the work she needs to do with the WRITERS table. Because Elena has already created the WRITERS table structure, she is now ready to enter data.

Elena decides to begin by entering only three records into the WRITERS table. Then she will review the table structure and the datasheet and make any necessary changes. Elena will then confirm her WRITERS table with president Brian Murphy and managing editor Judith Rossi before entering the remaining records. Finally, Elena will examine the WRITERS table records and correct any errors she finds. Elena takes her written plan, as shown in Figure 3-1, to her computer and begins work.

Figure 3-1 Elena's task list for the WRITERS table

WRITERS table task list:
- Enter complete information for three writers
- Change the table structure and datasheet, if necessary
- Confirm the WRITERS table data
- Enter complete information for remaining writers
- Correct errors

SESSION 3.1

In this session, you will learn to update an Access table by adding records, changing field values, and deleting records. You will also learn to navigate through a table using the mouse, import a table, delete and rename a table, and change datasheet properties.

Adding Records

Elena created the WRITERS table by defining the table's fields and the fields' properties. Before the Issue25 database can provide useful information, however, Elena must **update**, or **maintain**, the database. That is, she must add, change, and delete records in the database tables to keep them current and accurate. When you initially create a database, adding records to the tables is the first step in updating a database. You also add records to an existing database whenever you encounter new occurrences of the entities represented by the tables. For example, an editorial assistant adds a record to the MAGAZINE ARTICLES table in the Vision database for each new article that is published.

Using the Datasheet to Enter Data

In Tutorial 1 you used Datasheet View to look at a table's records. You can also use Datasheet View to update a table. As her first step in updating the Issue25 database, Elena adds the three records to the WRITERS table shown in Figure 3-2. She uses the WRITERS table datasheet to enter these records.

	Writer ID	Last Name	First Name	Writer Phone	Last Contact Date	Freelancer	Amount
Record 1:	N425	Nilsson	Tonya	(909) 702-4082	7/9/97	No	$0
Record 2:	S260	Seeger	Wilhelm	(706) 423-0932	12/24/93	Yes	$350
Record 3:	S365	Sterns	Steven B.	(710) 669-6518	12/13/84	No	$0

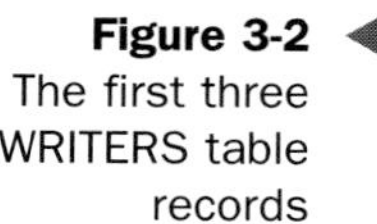

Figure 3-2 The first three WRITERS table records

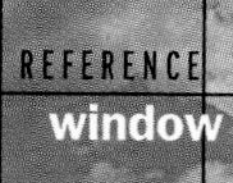

ADDING A RECORD TO A TABLE

- Open the table in Datasheet View.
- If necessary, click the New Record button to position the insertion point in the first field of a new record.
- Type the value for the first field, then press the Tab key. The insertion point moves to the next field.
- Enter the values for the remaining fields in the same way.
- When you press the Tab key after entering the value in the last field, Access saves the record.

To add records to a table's datasheet:

1. If necessary, place your Student Disk in the appropriate drive, start Access, double-click **Issue25** to open the database, maximize the Database window, click **WRITERS**, and then click the **Open** button. The Datasheet View window opens, and the insertion point is at the beginning of the Writer ID field for the first record.
2. Type **N425**, which is the first record's Writer ID field value, and press the **Tab** key. Each time you press the Tab key, the insertion point moves to the right, to the next field in the record.

   Notice that two new symbols appear in the record selectors for rows one and two. The pencil symbol in the first row indicates that you have made changes to the current record and have not yet saved the changes. The asterisk symbol in the second row shows you the next available row for entering a new record.
3. Continue to enter the field values for all three records shown in Figure 3-2. For the Writer Phone field values, type the numbers only. Access automatically supplies the parentheses, spaces, and hyphens from the field's input mask. Notice that the Freelancer field contains a check box. The box contains a check indicating a Yes value—the default value for the Freelancer field. If the value for the Freelancer field is Yes, simply press the Tab key to accept the displayed value and move to the next field. If the value for the Freelancer field is No, place the mouse pointer on the check box and click the left mouse button to remove the check mark. Note that, because the Amount field is defined as a currency field, a dollar sign ($) already appears in the field; you simply enter the numbers. When you've entered the value for the Amount field, press the Tab key to move to the start of the next record. Do not, however, press the Tab key after typing the Amount field for the third record. After entering the three records, your screen should look like Figure 3-3.

Figure 3-3 The WRITERS table datasheet with the first three records entered

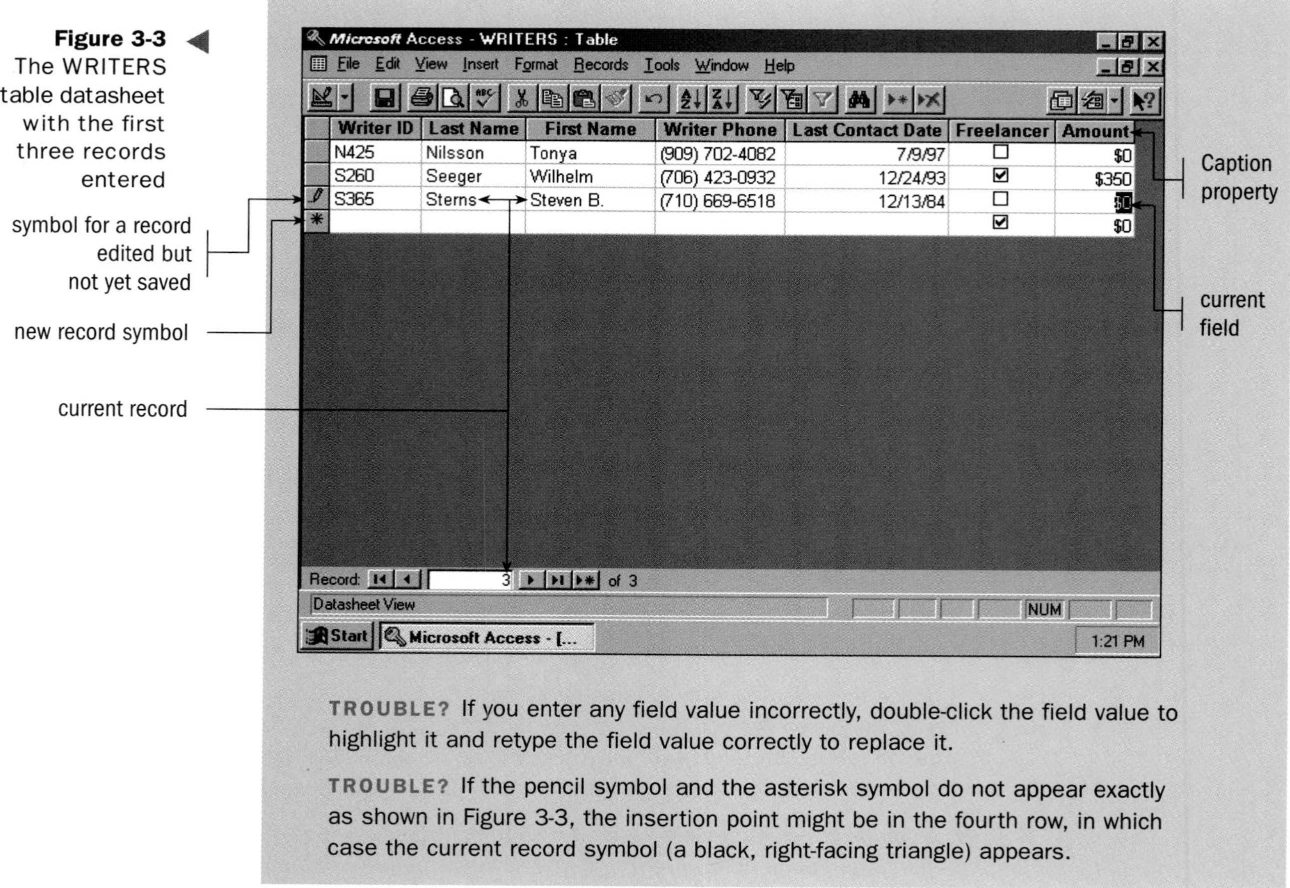

TROUBLE? If you enter any field value incorrectly, double-click the field value to highlight it and retype the field value correctly to replace it.

TROUBLE? If the pencil symbol and the asterisk symbol do not appear exactly as shown in Figure 3-3, the insertion point might be in the fourth row, in which case the current record symbol (a black, right-facing triangle) appears.

Elena has completed her first task, so she continues with the next task on her list: reviewing the table structure and datasheet for any problems.

Changing Records

As Elena looks over the first three records, she realizes that the information she entered is from the preliminary list of writers for the special issue. Upon comparing the preliminary list with the final list that she received at her last meeting with Brian and Judith, Elena notices some differences. First, Tonya Nilsson, who is one of the three writers she just added to the WRITERS table, is a freelancer and will be paid $450 for each of her two reprinted articles. Elena entered Nilsson as a staff writer, so she needs to change both the Freelancer and Amount fields for Nilsson. Also, because Steven B. Sterns does not appear in the final list of writers, Elena needs to delete his record from her WRITERS table.

Before Elena makes any of these changes, however, she decides that she first needs to learn how to select and change a specific record quickly. She investigates different techniques for using the mouse to move through a datasheet.

Using the Mouse to Navigate in a Table

You are probably already familiar with how to use the mouse to move through fields and records in a datasheet or to make changes to field values. The specific mouse techniques you use for movement, selection, and placement are listed in Figure 3-4.

Figure 3-4 Using the Mouse to navigate in a table

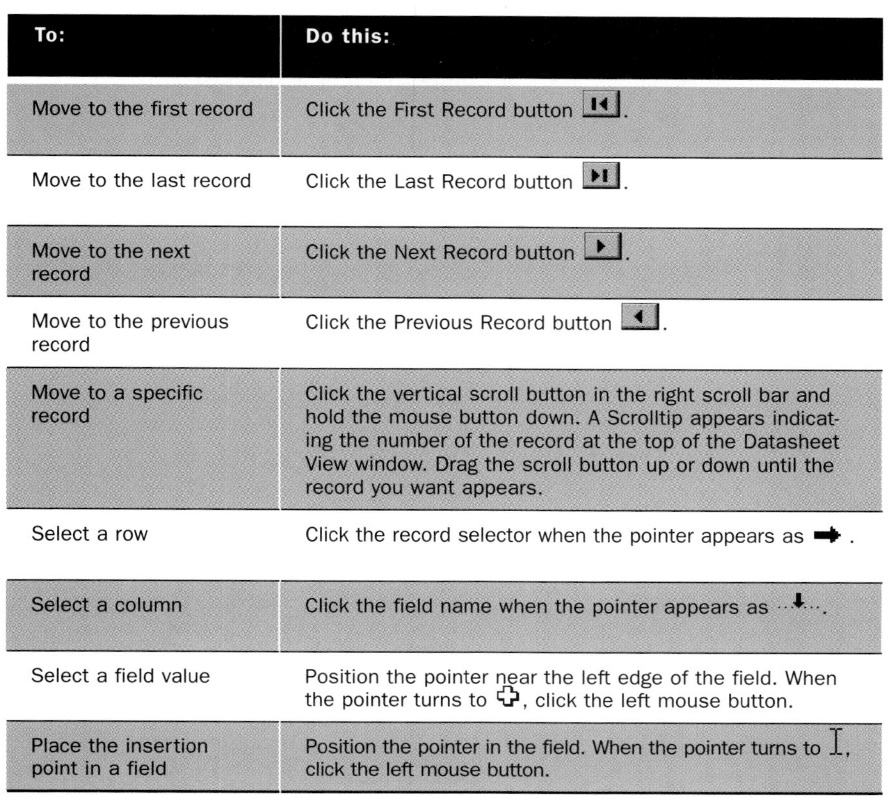

To:	Do this:
Move to the first record	Click the First Record button.
Move to the last record	Click the Last Record button.
Move to the next record	Click the Next Record button.
Move to the previous record	Click the Previous Record button.
Move to a specific record	Click the vertical scroll button in the right scroll bar and hold the mouse button down. A Scrolltip appears indicating the number of the record at the top of the Datasheet View window. Drag the scroll button up or down until the record you want appears.
Select a row	Click the record selector when the pointer appears as ➡.
Select a column	Click the field name when the pointer appears as ⬇.
Select a field value	Position the pointer near the left edge of the field. When the pointer turns to ✥, click the left mouse button.
Place the insertion point in a field	Position the pointer in the field. When the pointer turns to I, click the left mouse button.

Now that Elena is familiar with using the mouse for moving to and modifying records, she is ready to change the field values for Tonya Nilsson in the WRITERS table.

Changing Field Values

Elena's task is to change the field values for Freelancer and for Amount to Yes and $450, respectively.

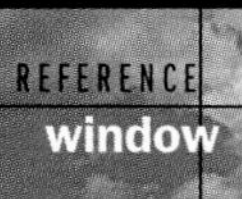

CHANGING A FIELD VALUE IN A RECORD

- Open the table that contains the record to be changed in Datasheet View.
- For a Yes/No field displayed as a check box, click the check box to change the value.
- For any other field, double-click the field value and enter the new value.
- Press the Tab key to move to the next field. Access saves the new value.

To change field values in a datasheet:

1. Click the **check box** in the Freelancer column for the first record, press the **Tab** key, and then type **450**. Both field values in the first record are now correctly changed. See Figure 3-5.

Figure 3-5 The WRITERS table datasheet after field value change

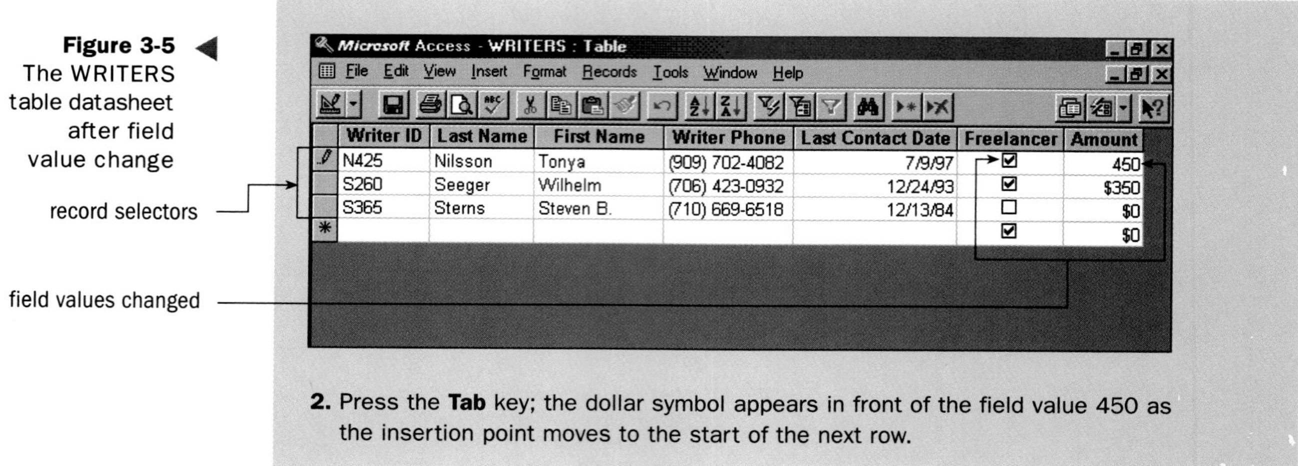

2. Press the **Tab** key; the dollar symbol appears in front of the field value 450 as the insertion point moves to the start of the next row.

Access saves the changes you make to the current record whenever you move to a different record. Your data is kept current as you make changes, and you do not need to worry about losing your changes if a hardware or software problem occurs.

Deleting Records

Elena is now ready to delete Steven B. Sterns from her WRITERS table. After she makes this last change to her initial table, she will print her work and have Brian and Judith confirm the table's structure.

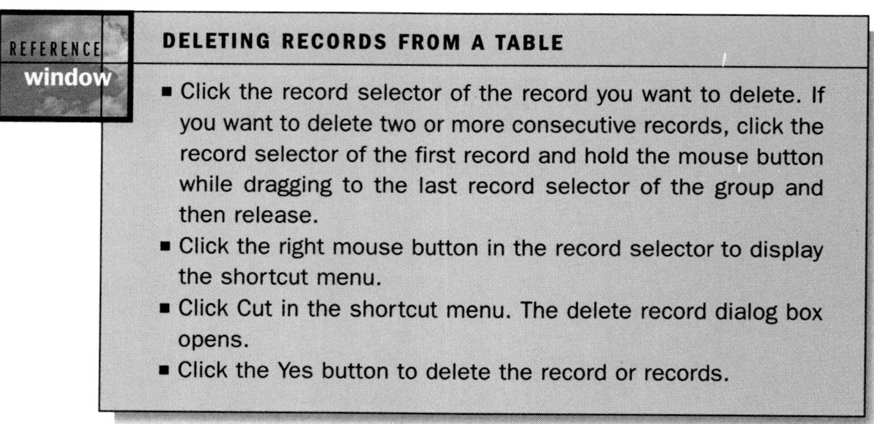
REFERENCE window

DELETING RECORDS FROM A TABLE

- Click the record selector of the record you want to delete. If you want to delete two or more consecutive records, click the record selector of the first record and hold the mouse button while dragging to the last record selector of the group and then release.
- Click the right mouse button in the record selector to display the shortcut menu.
- Click Cut in the shortcut menu. The delete record dialog box opens.
- Click the Yes button to delete the record or records.

Elena deletes the third record from the WRITERS datasheet.

To delete a datasheet record:

1. Click the record selector for the third record. Access highlights the entire third row.
2. Click the right mouse button in the record selector for the third record. Access displays the shortcut menu.
3. Click **Cut** in the shortcut menu. Access displays the delete record dialog box. See Figure 3-6. The current record indicator is positioned in the third row's record selector, and all field values (except default values) in the third record are deleted.

   TROUBLE? If you selected the wrong record for deletion, click the No button. Access ends the deletion process and redisplays the deleted record. Repeat Steps 1–3 to delete the third record.

Figure 3-6 The delete record dialog box

deleted record

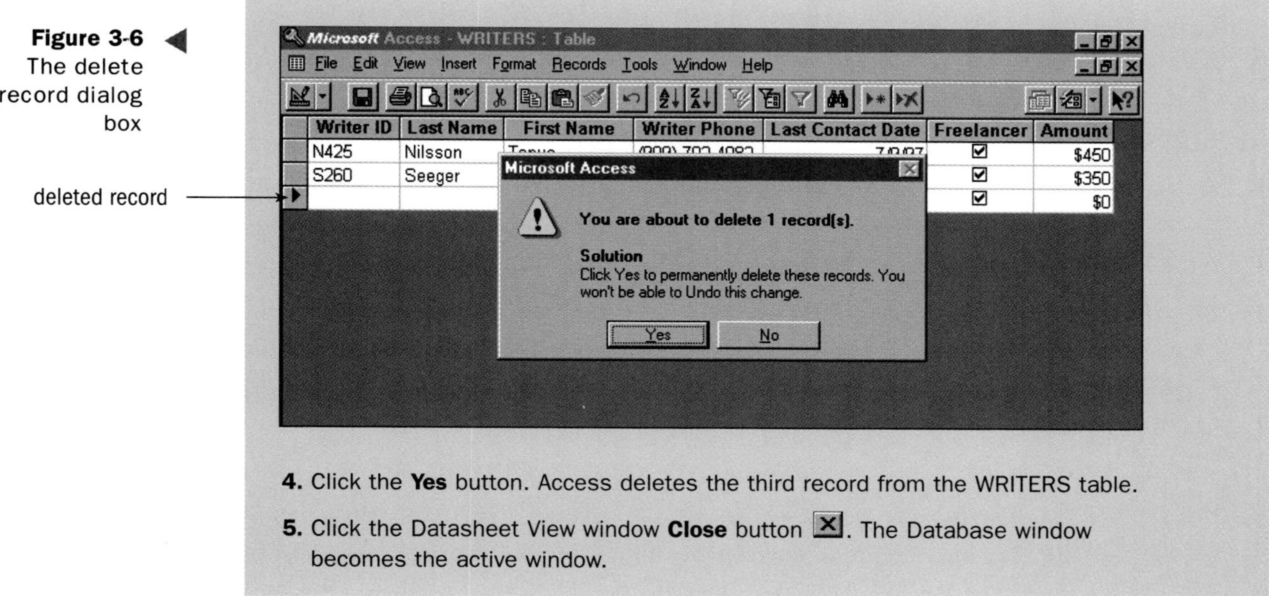

4. Click the **Yes** button. Access deletes the third record from the WRITERS table.
5. Click the Datasheet View window **Close** button ☒. The Database window becomes the active window.

Elena prints the datasheet so that Judith and Brian can confirm the structure of her WRITERS table.

Importing Data

When Elena meets with Brian and Judith, she learns that Judith is also maintaining a table in the company's main database (the Vision database), containing information about the writers selected for the 25th-anniversary issue. Judith and Elena realize that Elena does not need to enter all that information in her Issue25 database. She can simply import the data from Judith's database to Elena's database. This will not only save time but will also reduce the possibility of introducing typing errors.

Importing data involves copying data from a text file, spreadsheet, or database table into a new Access table. You can import objects from an existing Access database, as well as data from Access tables. You can also import from spreadsheets, such as Excel and Lotus 1-2-3; from other database management systems, such as Paradox, dBASE, and FoxPro; and from certain text files. Importing existing data, as shown in Figure 3-7, saves you time and eliminates potential data-entry errors.

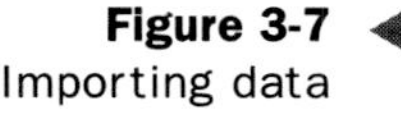

Figure 3-7 Importing data

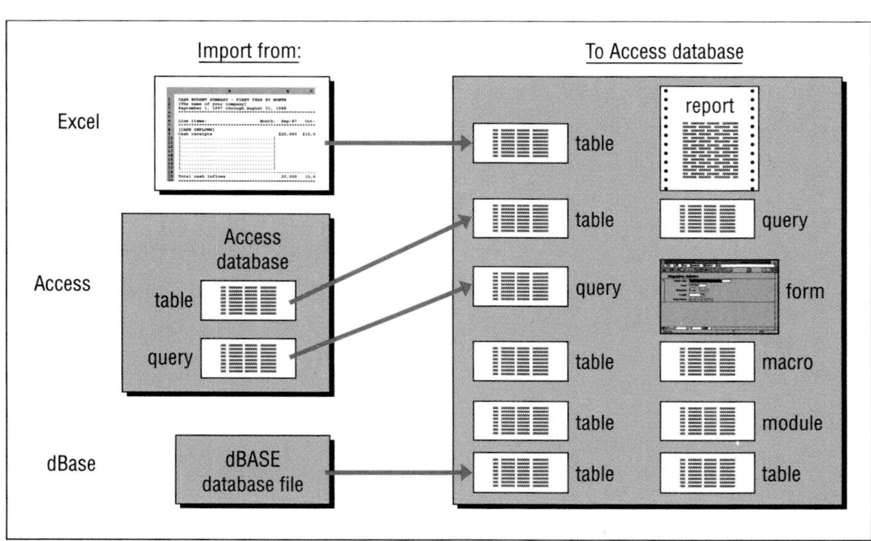

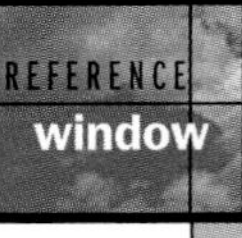

IMPORTING AN ACCESS TABLE

- Click File, then point to Get External Data to highlight it, then click Import. The Import dialog box opens.
- In the Look in text box, select the disk drive and directory that contains the database from which you want to import.
- Select the database that contains the table you want to import, then click Import. Access displays the Import Objects dialog box.
- Select the table that you want to import, then click the OK button.
- Access imports the table. The Import Objects dialog box closes and the table name now appears in the Database window.

After Judith verifies that her table has the same fields that Elena needs for her WRITERS table, Elena is ready to import Judith's table (the WRITERS-JR table) to the Issue25 database. Judith includes her initials on all her table names for easy identification.

To import an Access table:

1. Make sure that the Issue25 database is open and the active Database window is maximized, then click **File,** point to **Get External Data** to highlight it, then click **Import**. Access displays the Import dialog box.
2. If necessary, use the Look in text box to select the Tutorial folder on the drive that contains your Student Disk. Click **Vision** in the file list. Click **Import** to display the Import Objects dialog box. See Figure 3-8.

Figure 3-8 The Import Objects dialog box

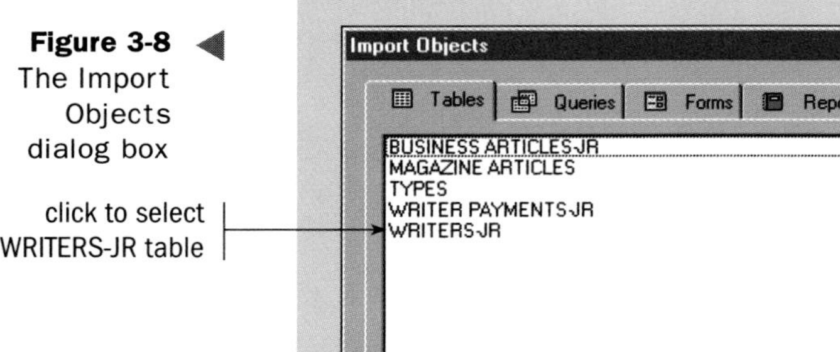

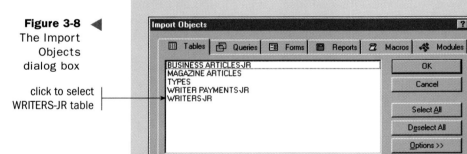

3. Click **WRITERS-JR** in the Tables list, then click the **OK** button. Access imports the table and closes the Import Objects dialog. The Database window now displays the new table in the Tables list. Open this new table to view its 14 records, but do not update any of them. When you are done viewing the records, close the table by clicking the Datasheet View window **Close** button ☒.

Elena quickly views the records of the WRITERS-JR table to confirm that they contain the information she needs. She believes that the table is correctly designed, since it is identical in design to her WRITERS table, but to be sure, she uses the Table Analyzer Wizard to help identify problems.

Using the Table Analyzer Wizard

The **Table Analyzer Wizard** analyzes the table for repeated data and, if necessary, suggests ways to split a table into two or more tables to eliminate data redundancy.

REFERENCE window

USING THE TABLE ANALYZER WIZARD

- In the Database window, click the Analyze button.
- Click the Next > button twice to move past the first two informational windows.
- Click to select the table to be analyzed, then click the Next > button.
- Click the Yes button to ask the wizard to make suggestions for splitting the table, then click the Next > button. The Table Analyzer Wizard analyzes the table and makes any necessary suggestions for splitting the table.

If the Table Analyzer Wizard suggests splitting the table, do the following:

- Review the suggested changes. Click the Cancel button to ignore the changes or move fields to different tables if desired, name the newly created tables, and then click the Next > button.
- If you desire, specify primary key fields for the tables, then click the Next > button.
- If you want Access to create a query that has the same structure as the original table, select that option, then click the Finish button. Access creates any new tables and the new query. The original table is renamed with its original name followed by the word OLD. Access then opens the new query in Datasheet View. Click the OK button in the dialog box to view the tables or query.

If the Table Analyzer Wizard recommends not splitting the table, click the Cancel button in the dialog box. Access returns to the Database window.

Elena uses the Table Analyzer Wizard to check the design of the WRITERS-JR table.

To use the Table Analyzer Wizard to analyze a table:

1. If necessary, click the **Tables** tab to view the Tables list in the Database window.
2. Click the **Analyze** button on the toolbar. Access starts the Table Analyzer Wizard and displays the first Table Analyzer Wizard dialog box. This dialog box contains examples of the kinds of problems the Table Analyzer Wizard can identify and correct.
3. Click the Next > button to display the next Table Analyzer Wizard dialog box. This dialog box describes how the Table Analyzer Wizard will correct any problems it identifies.
4. Click the Next > button to display the next Table Analyzer Wizard dialog box. In this dialog box, you select the table you want to analyze. See Figure 3-9.

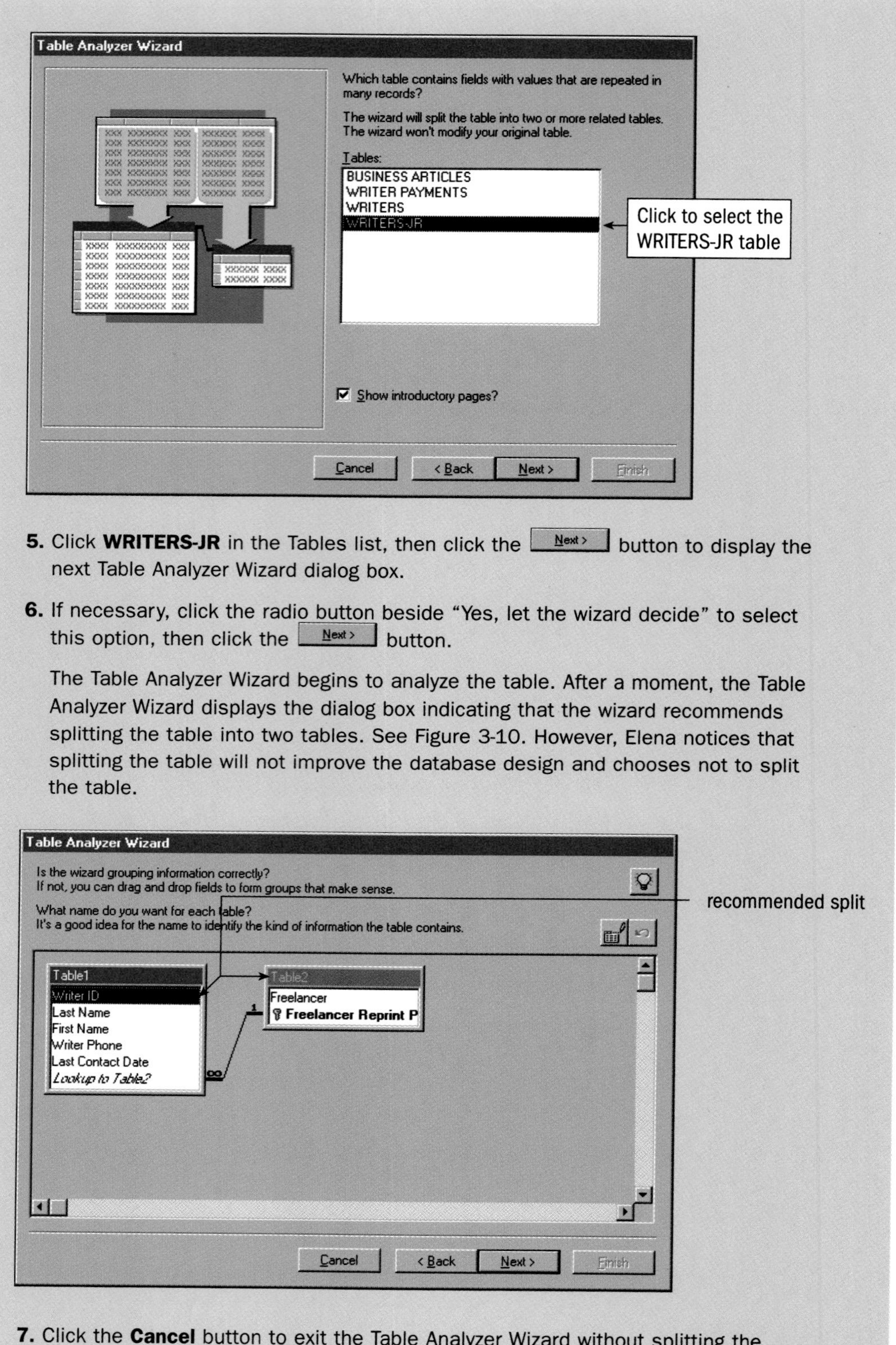

Figure 3-9 Choosing the table to analyze

5. Click **WRITERS-JR** in the Tables list, then click the Next > button to display the next Table Analyzer Wizard dialog box.

6. If necessary, click the radio button beside "Yes, let the wizard decide" to select this option, then click the Next > button.

   The Table Analyzer Wizard begins to analyze the table. After a moment, the Table Analyzer Wizard displays the dialog box indicating that the wizard recommends splitting the table into two tables. See Figure 3-10. However, Elena notices that splitting the table will not improve the database design and chooses not to split the table.

Figure 3-10 The Table Analyzer Wizard recommends splitting the table

7. Click the **Cancel** button to exit the Table Analyzer Wizard without splitting the table.

Deleting a Table

Because the WRITERS-JR table contains the information she needs, and because it appears to be designed correctly, Elena no longer needs the WRITERS table that she initially created. Elena deletes this table from her database to avoid any future confusion.

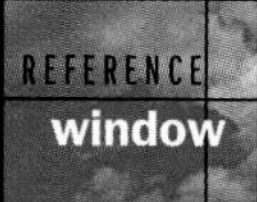

DELETING A TABLE

- In the Database window, click the table you want to delete.
- Click the right mouse button to open the shortcut menu.
- Click Delete. The Delete Table dialog box opens.
- Click the Yes button. The Delete Table dialog box closes, and Access deletes the table. When the active Database window appears, it does not list the table you just deleted.

To delete the WRITERS table:

1. In the Tables list of the Database window, click the **WRITERS** table to select it.
2. Click the right mouse button to display the shortcut menu. Click **Delete**. Access displays a dialog box that asks, "Do you want to delete the table WRITERS?".
3. Click the **Yes** button. The dialog box closes, and the WRITERS table no longer appears in the Tables list.

Renaming a Table

Elena decides that the name for the current writers table, WRITERS-JR, is no longer appropriate. This table will no longer be used only by Judith, but by others at Vision Publishers as well. Because she's already deleted her initial table, Elena is free to rename the WRITERS-JR table WRITERS.

To rename a table:

1. Move the pointer to the WRITERS-JR table in the Tables list and click **WRITERS-JR** with the right mouse button. Access displays the shortcut menu. See Figure 3-11.

Figure 3-11 The shortcut menu for a table

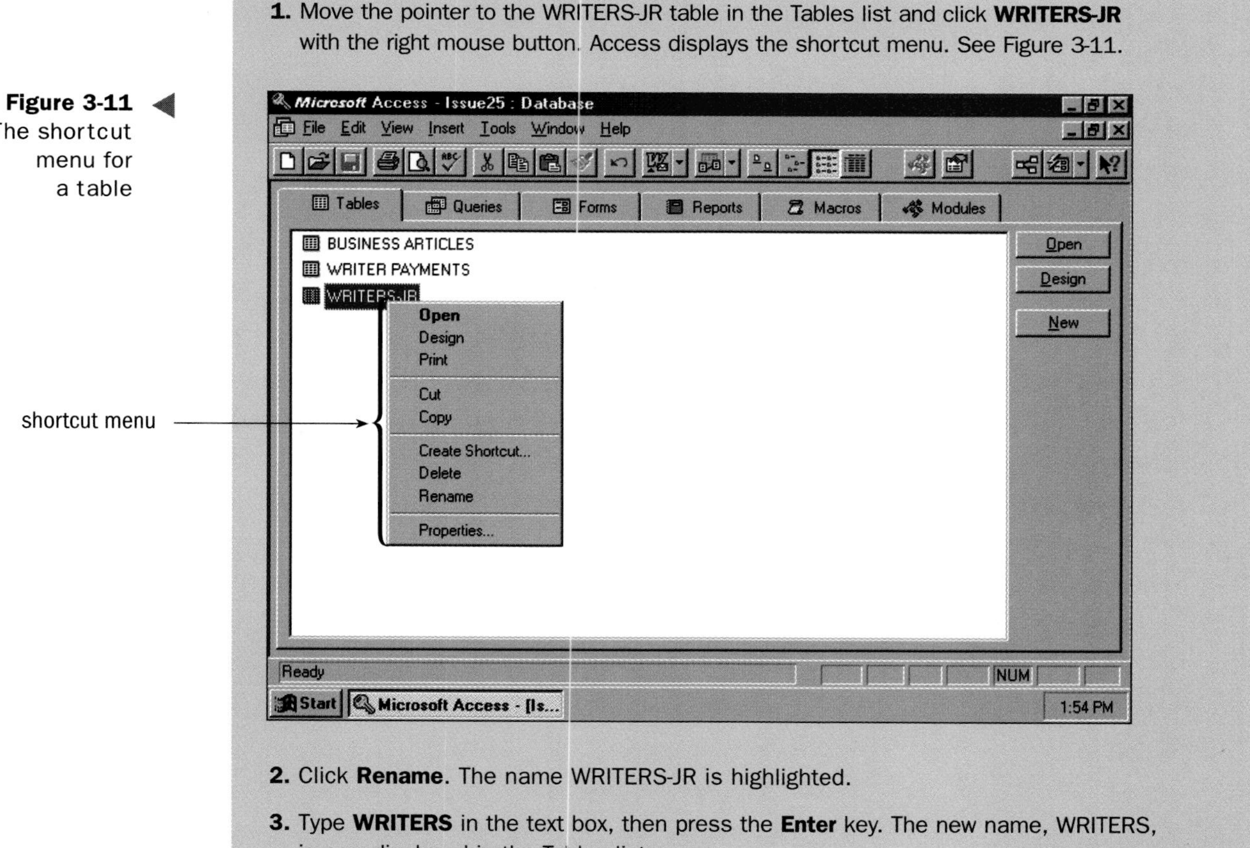

2. Click **Rename**. The name WRITERS-JR is highlighted.
3. Type **WRITERS** in the text box, then press the **Enter** key. The new name, WRITERS, is now displayed in the Tables list.

Although Elena already looked briefly at the imported table records, she now needs to review them more closely for any possible errors. She begins by opening the datasheet. You already know how to open a table's datasheet from the Database window by clicking the table name and then clicking the Open button. You can also open a datasheet by double-clicking the table name. Because this second method is faster, we'll use it from now on.

To open the WRITERS table datasheet:

1. Double-click **WRITERS** in the Tables list. The Datasheet window opens, and the records appear arranged in order by Writer ID, which is the primary key. See Figure 3-12.

Figure 3-12 The WRITERS datasheet with newly imported records

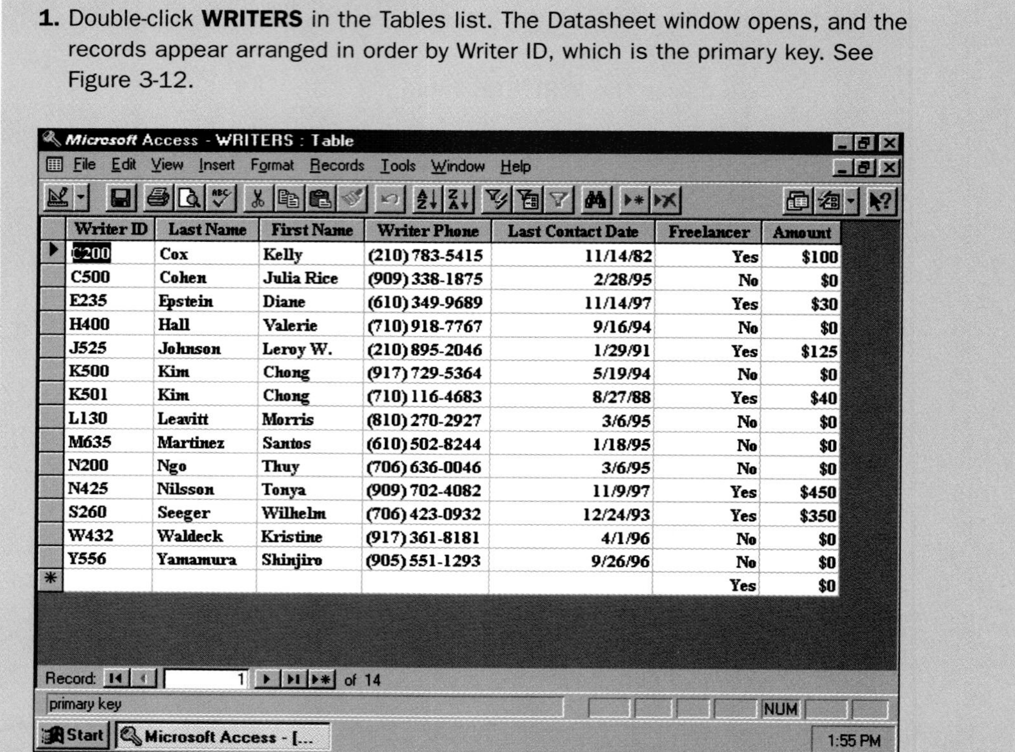

Writer ID	Last Name	First Name	Writer Phone	Last Contact Date	Freelancer	Amount
C200	Cox	Kelly	(210) 783-5415	11/14/82	Yes	$100
C500	Cohen	Julia Rice	(909) 338-1875	2/28/95	No	$0
E235	Epstein	Diane	(610) 349-9689	11/14/97	Yes	$30
H400	Hall	Valerie	(710) 918-7767	9/16/94	No	$0
J525	Johnson	Leroy W.	(210) 895-2046	1/29/91	Yes	$125
K500	Kim	Chong	(917) 729-5364	5/19/94	No	$0
K501	Kim	Chong	(710) 116-4683	8/27/88	Yes	$40
L130	Leavitt	Morris	(810) 270-2927	3/6/95	No	$0
M635	Martinez	Santos	(610) 502-8244	1/18/95	No	$0
N200	Ngo	Thuy	(706) 636-0046	3/6/95	No	$0
N425	Nilsson	Tonya	(909) 702-4082	11/9/97	Yes	$450
S260	Seeger	Wilhelm	(706) 423-0932	12/24/93	Yes	$350
W432	Waldeck	Kristine	(917) 361-8181	4/1/96	No	$0
Y556	Yamamura	Shinjiro	(905) 551-1293	9/26/96	No	$0
*					Yes	$0

With the WRITERS datasheet open, Elena is ready to make any necessary changes to the table. First, she decides to change the font of the table records to make the information easier to read.

Changing Datasheet Properties

When Judith created her version of the WRITERS table, she changed the font to Times New Roman and the font style to bold. Elena believes that Access's default setting (Arial, font size 10) with the normal font style is easier to read. She decides to change the font to improve readability.

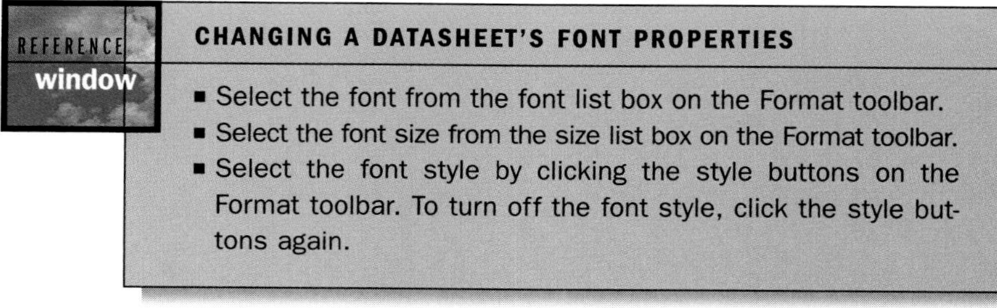

CHANGING A DATASHEET'S FONT PROPERTIES

- Select the font from the font list box on the Format toolbar.
- Select the font size from the size list box on the Format toolbar.
- Select the font style by clicking the style buttons on the Format toolbar. To turn off the font style, click the style buttons again.

To change the datasheet font:

1. If necessary, click **View**, click **Toolbars**, then click **Formatting (Datasheet)** to display the Format toolbar on the screen. Then click the **font name** list arrow. The list of available fonts appears in alphabetical order. See Figure 3-13.

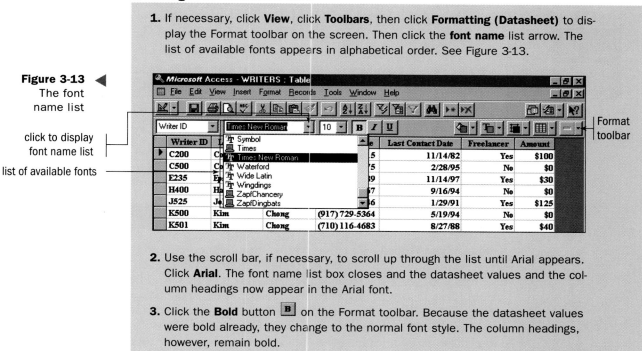

Figure 3-13 The font name list

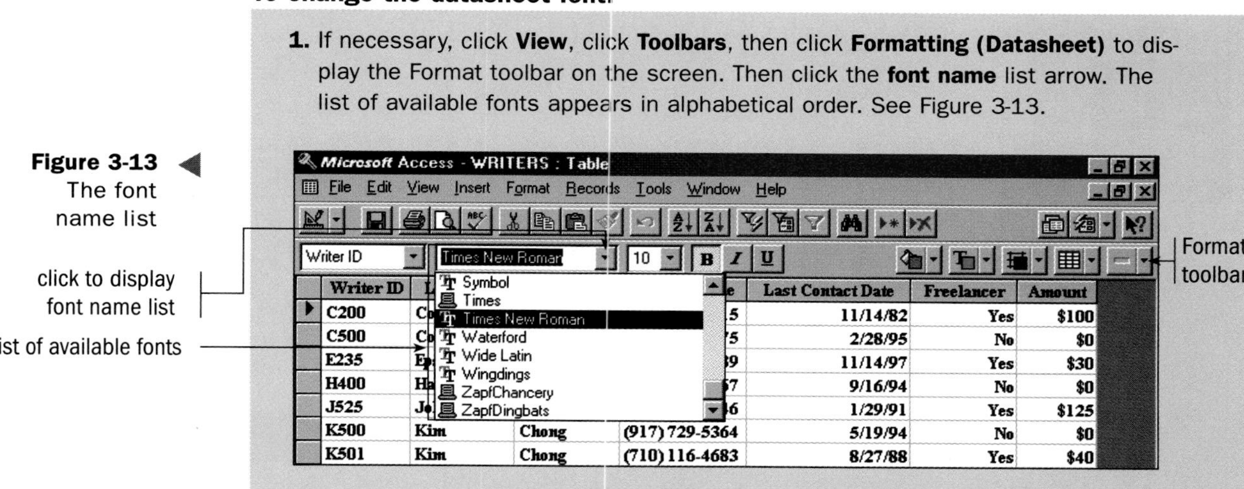

2. Use the scroll bar, if necessary, to scroll up through the list until Arial appears. Click **Arial**. The font name list box closes and the datasheet values and the column headings now appear in the Arial font.

3. Click the **Bold** button **B** on the Format toolbar. Because the datasheet values were bold already, they change to the normal font style. The column headings, however, remain bold.

When you change datasheet fonts, you may need to change the column widths to make some fields fully visible. Access automatically adjusts row heights to accommodate font changes. In this case, Elena realizes that changing the column widths won't be necessary.

The WRITERS table now contains the data Elena needs, in the format she wants. Her next task is to look at the table more closely for any possible errors.

If you want to take a break and resume the tutorial at a later time, exit Access. When you resume the tutorial, place your Student Disk in the appropriate drive, start Access, open the Issue25 database on your Student Disk, maximize the Database window, and open the WRITERS table in Datasheet View.

Quick Check

1. What operations are performed when you update a database?
2. What does a pencil symbol signify in a record selector? An asterisk symbol?
3. Which button do you use to move to the last record in the table?
4. If you change field values in a table, what do you have to do to save your changes?
5. If you delete a record from a table, do all field values disappear? Which field values, if any, remain?
6. What are some advantages of importing data?
7. When would you use the Table Analyzer Wizard?
8. How do you change a datasheet's font?

SESSION 3.2

In this session you will learn how to find data and replace data in a datasheet and how to sort records using a single sort key field and multiple sort key fields. You will also learn to use Access's Spelling feature and link tables by defining a Lookup Wizard field as a foreign key. Finally, you will learn to back up and compact a database.

Finding and Replacing Data in a Datasheet

Even though records are physically stored on disk in the order in which you add them to a table, Access displays them in primary key sequence in the datasheet. Finding a record in the WRITERS table based on a specific Writer ID value, therefore, is a simple process.

Finding Data

Finding records based on a specific value for a field other than the primary key is not so simple, especially when you are working with larger tables. You can spend considerable time trying to locate the records and can easily miss one or more of them in your visual search. Elena discovers this when she learns that the area codes for some writers' phone numbers have changed from 909 to 910. If she quickly reviews the WRITERS table records, she might overlook some of the phone numbers that need to be changed. In situations like this, you can use the Find button on the toolbar to help your search.

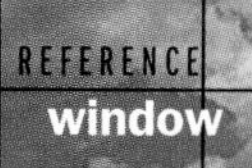

FINDING DATA IN A TABLE

- Click anywhere in the field column you want to search.
- Click the Find button on the toolbar. This opens the Find in field dialog box.
- In the Find What box, type the field value you want to find.
- To find field values that entirely match a value, select Whole Field in the Match box.
- To find a match between a value and any part of a field's value, select Any Part of Field in the Match box; to find a match between a value and the start of a field's value, select Start of Field in the Match box.
- To find all fields that contain the search value, remove the check mark from the Search Only Current Field check box.
- To find matches with a specific pattern of lowercase and uppercase letters, click the Match Case check box.
- To search all records, select All in the Search box.
- To search from the current record to earlier records, select Up in the Search box; to later records, select Down in the Search box.
- Click the Find First button to have Access begin the search at the top of the table, or click the Find Next button to begin the search at the current record as well as to continue the search for the next match. If a match is found, Access scrolls the table and highlights the field value.
- Click the Close button to stop the search operation.

Elena searches the WRITERS table for phone numbers that have a 909 area code.

To find data in a table:

1. Click anywhere in the **Writer Phone** text box for the first record.
2. Click the **Find** button on the toolbar. Access displays the Find in field dialog box. See Figure 3-14.

Figure 3-14
The Find in field dialog box

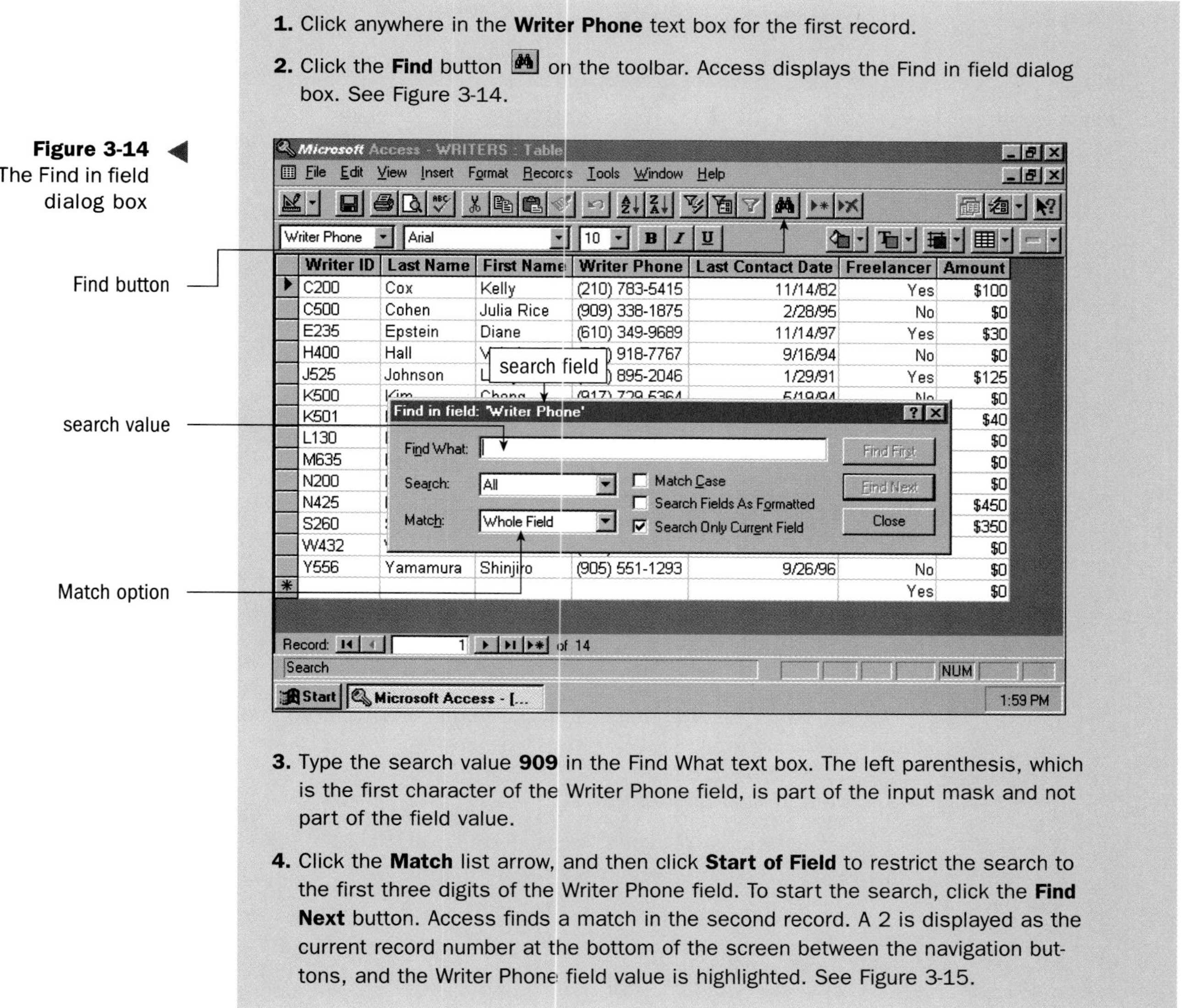

3. Type the search value **909** in the Find What text box. The left parenthesis, which is the first character of the Writer Phone field, is part of the input mask and not part of the field value.
4. Click the **Match** list arrow, and then click **Start of Field** to restrict the search to the first three digits of the Writer Phone field. To start the search, click the **Find Next** button. Access finds a match in the second record. A 2 is displayed as the current record number at the bottom of the screen between the navigation buttons, and the Writer Phone field value is highlighted. See Figure 3-15.

Figure 3-15 Completed Find in field dialog box

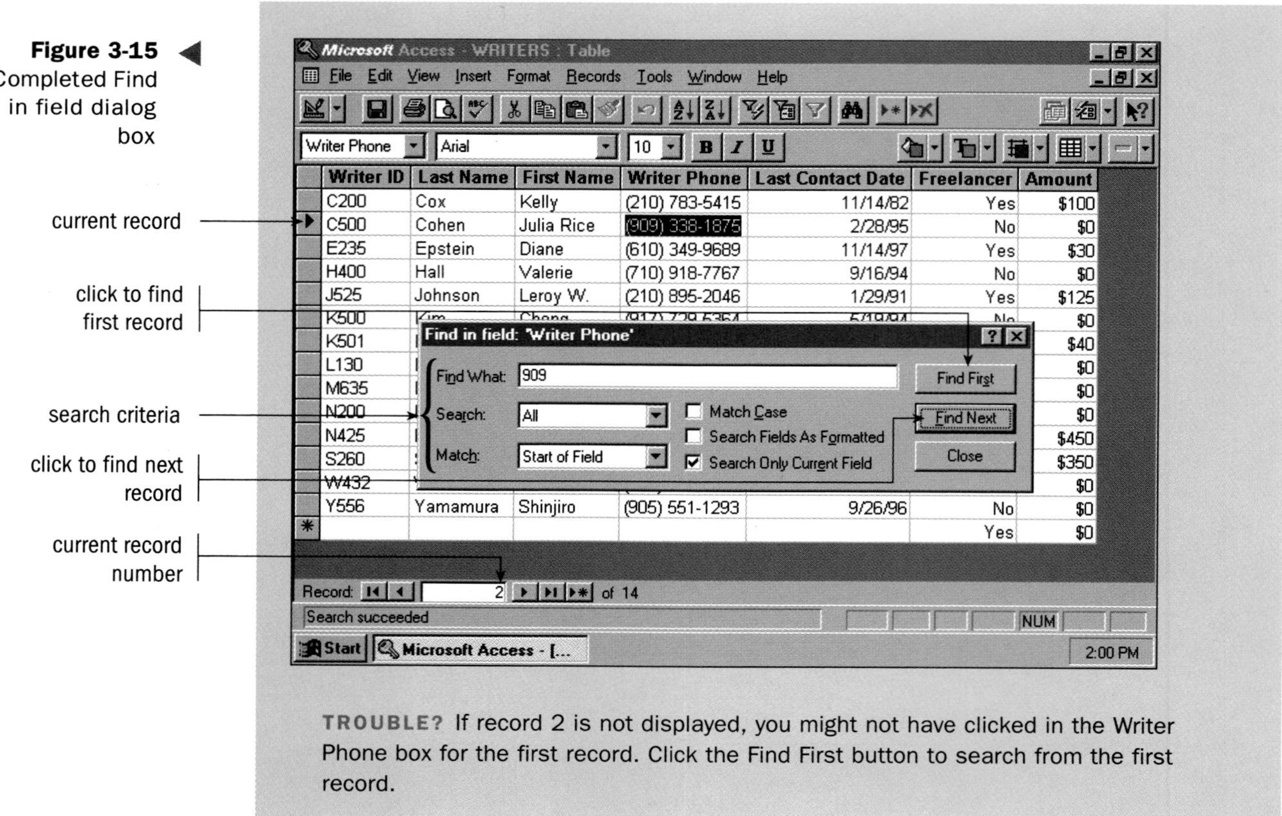

TROUBLE? If record 2 is not displayed, you might not have clicked in the Writer Phone box for the first record. Click the Find First button to search from the first record.

To find other records that match the search criterion, you continue by again clicking the Find Next button.

To continue a Find operation:

1. Click the **Find Next** button. Access finds a match in the 11th record and highlights the entire Writer Phone field value.

   TROUBLE? If the Find in field dialog box obscures the datasheet, drag the dialog box to the lower-right corner of the screen so that it covers less critical parts of the datasheet.

2. Click the **Close** button in the Find in field dialog box. The Find in field dialog box closes.

If you are unsure of the exact text or value you are trying to locate, you can use "wildcard" characters in the Find What text box. Use an asterisk (*) to represent any sequence of characters, a question mark (?) to represent any single character, and the number symbol (#) to represent any single digit. If Elena did not know whether she was looking for 909 or 919 area codes, for example, she would search for "9#9" in her WRITERS table.

You can use the wildcard characters in Find operations, but not for replacing data. Elena will replace data in the WRITERS table next.

Replacing Data

Elena does not want simply to find those area code phone numbers that need to be changed; she wants to replace the value with the new area code, 910. Elena corrects these values by using the Replace option on the Edit menu. You use the Replace option to find a specific value in your records and replace that value with another value.

REFERENCE window

REPLACING DATA IN A TABLE

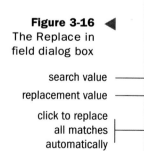

- Click anywhere in the field column in which you want to replace data.
- Click Edit and then click Replace. This opens the Replace in field dialog box.
- In the Find What box, type the field value you want to find.
- Type the replacement value in the Replace With box.
- To search all fields for the search value, remove the check mark from the Search Only Current Field check box.
- To find and change field values that entirely match a value, click the Match Whole Field check box.
- To find and change matches with a specific pattern of lowercase and uppercase letters, click the Match Case check box.
- Click the Find Next button to begin the search at the current record. If a match is found, Access scrolls the table and highlights the field value.
- Click the Replace button to substitute the replacement value for the search value, or click the Find Next button to leave the highlighted value unchanged and to continue the search for the next match.
- Click the Replace All button to perform the find and replace operations without stopping for confirmation of each replacement.
- Click the Close button to stop the replacement operation.

Elena searches the WRITERS table to replace the 909 phone number area codes with 910.

To replace data in a table:

1. Click in the **Writer Phone** text box for the first record.
2. Click **Edit**, and then click **Replace** to open the Replace in field dialog box. See Figure 3-16. Note that if you previously repositioned the Find in field dialog box, the Replace in field dialog box is similarly positioned. Your previous search value, 909, appears in the new Find What box.

Figure 3-16
The Replace in field dialog box

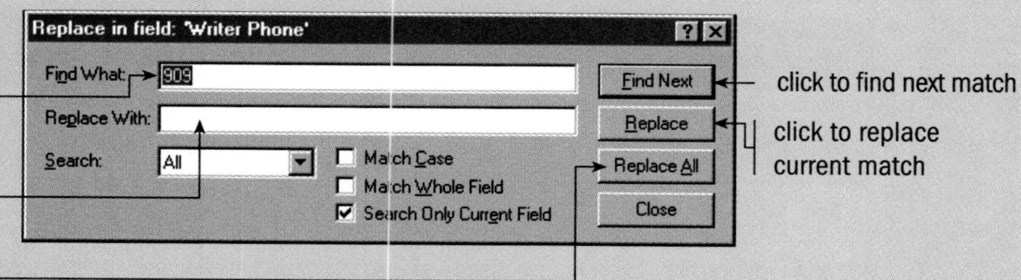

3. Press the **Tab** key and type **910** in the Replace With text box.
4. If necessary, click the **Match Whole Field** check box to remove the check mark.
5. To start the replacement process, click the **Replace All** button.
6. Access displays a dialog box that states, "You won't be able to undo this Replace operation. Do you want to continue?". Access displays this message when more than one replacement occurs, because it cannot undo all the replacements it makes. When this message box appears, click the **Yes** button to complete the replacement operation. Access finds all 909 area codes in the table (in records 2 and 11) and replaces them with 910 area codes.

7. Click the **Close** button in the Replace in field dialog box.
8. Preview and print a copy of the datasheet, using the Print Preview button as you have done before.

   TROUBLE? If a field in the printed datasheet, such as Writer Phone, does not display the whole field value, return to Datasheet View and resize the column. Also, if the printed datasheet takes up two pages, return to Datasheet View and resize the columns to make them narrower without hiding any of the field and names or field values.

Now that Elena has changed the 909 area codes so that all the phone numbers are accurate, she can use the WRITERS table to contact the writers. She feels she will be most successful reaching those writers having a recent contact date. To view the datasheet records arranged by the Last Contact Date field, Elena sorts the records.

Sorting Records in a Datasheet

Sorting is the process of temporarily arranging records in a specified order or sequence. Most companies sort their data before they display or print it because staff use the information differently according to their needs. Brian might want to review writer information arranged by the Amount field, for example, because he is interested in knowing which freelancers will be paid the most for each reprinted article. On the other hand, Elena wants her information arranged by date of last contact because she will be calling the writers. She feels she'll have a better chance of reaching those writers who were contacted most recently.

To sort a table's records, you select the **sort key**—the field used to determine the order of the records in the datasheet. Elena wants to sort the WRITERS data by last contact date, so the Last Contact Date field will be the sort key.

The data type of sort keys can be Text, Number, Date/Time, Currency, AutoNumber, or Yes/No fields, but not Memo or OLE Object. Sort options by data type are shown in Figure 3-17. You sort records in either ascending (increasing) or descending (decreasing) order. Sorting the WRITERS data in descending order by the Last Contact Date field means that the record with the most recent date will be the first record in the datasheet. The record with the earliest date will be the last record in the datasheet.

Figure 3-17 Sorting options for the different data types

Data Type	Ascending order	Descending order
Number, Currency, AutoNumber	numerical, lowest to highest	numerical, highest to lowest
Text	alphabetical, A-Z	alphabetical, Z-A
Yes/No	yes precedes no	no precedes yes
Date	chronological, earliest dates first	chronological, latest dates first

Sort keys can be unique or nonunique. Sort keys are **unique** if the value of the sort key field for each record is different. The Writer ID field in the WRITERS table is an example of a unique sort key, because each writer has a different value in the Writer ID field. Sort keys are **nonunique** if more than one record can have the same value for the sort key field. The Freelancer field in the WRITERS table is a nonunique sort key because more than one record has the same value (either yes or no).

When the sort key is nonunique, records with the same sort key value are grouped together, but they are not arranged in a specific order within the group. If Elena wanted to contact staff writers before freelancers, for example, she could sort by the Freelancer field, which would result in the arrangement shown in Figure 3-18. Notice that the last contact dates are not arranged in a useful order.

Figure 3-18 Sorting by Freelancer field

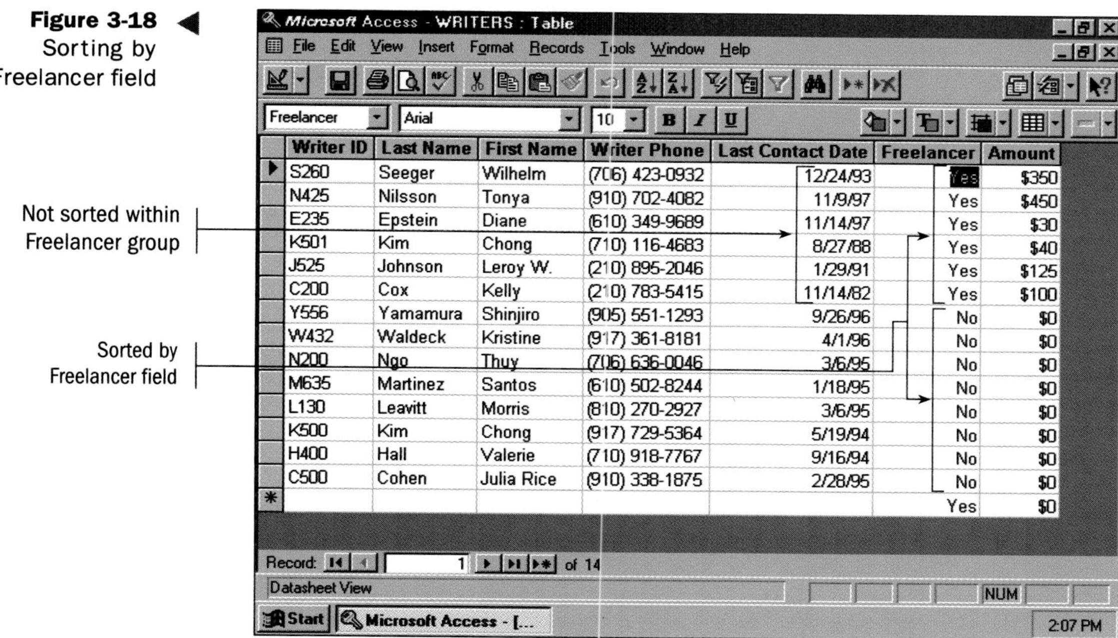

	Writer ID	Last Name	First Name	Writer Phone	Last Contact Date	Freelancer	Amount
▶	S260	Seeger	Wilhelm	(706) 423-0932	12/24/93	Yes	$350
	N425	Nilsson	Tonya	(910) 702-4082	11/9/97	Yes	$450
	E235	Epstein	Diane	(610) 349-9689	11/14/97	Yes	$30
	K501	Kim	Chong	(710) 116-4683	8/27/88	Yes	$40
	J525	Johnson	Leroy W.	(210) 895-2046	1/29/91	Yes	$125
	C200	Cox	Kelly	(210) 783-5415	11/14/82	Yes	$100
	Y556	Yamamura	Shinjiro	(905) 551-1293	9/26/96	No	$0
	W432	Waldeck	Kristine	(917) 361-8181	4/1/96	No	$0
	N200	Ngo	Thuy	(706) 636-0046	3/6/95	No	$0
	M635	Martinez	Santos	(610) 502-8244	1/18/95	No	$0
	L130	Leavitt	Morris	(810) 270-2927	3/6/95	No	$0
	K500	Kim	Chong	(917) 729-5364	5/19/94	No	$0
	H400	Hall	Valerie	(710) 918-7767	9/16/94	No	$0
	C500	Cohen	Julia Rice	(910) 338-1875	2/28/95	No	$0
*						Yes	$0

To arrange these grouped records in a useful order, you can specify a **secondary sort key**, which is a second sort key field. The first sort key field is called the **primary sort key**. In the example in Figure 3-18, the primary sort key is the Freelancer field, and the secondary sort key can be the Last Contact Date field. Records would then be sorted by last contact date within each group, freelancers and staff writers. Note that the primary sort key is not the same as the table's primary key field. For sorting a table's records, any field in a table can serve as a primary sort key.

Sorting a Single Field Quickly

The **Sort Ascending** button and the **Sort Descending** button on the toolbar are called quick-sort buttons. **Quick-sort buttons** allow you to sort records immediately, based on the selected field. You first select the column on which you want to base the sort and then click the appropriate quick-sort button on the toolbar to rearrange the records in either ascending or descending order.

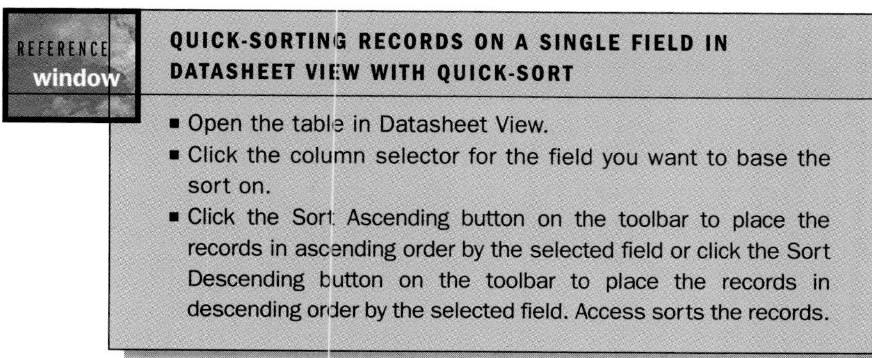

REFERENCE window

QUICK-SORTING RECORDS ON A SINGLE FIELD IN DATASHEET VIEW WITH QUICK-SORT

- Open the table in Datasheet View.
- Click the column selector for the field you want to base the sort on.
- Click the Sort Ascending button on the toolbar to place the records in ascending order by the selected field or click the Sort Descending button on the toolbar to place the records in descending order by the selected field. Access sorts the records.

Elena uses the Sort Descending button to rearrange the records in descending order by the Last Contact Date field.

To sort records in a datasheet with quick-sort buttons:

1. Click anywhere in the **Last Contact Date** column to establish that field as the current field.
2. Click the **Sort Descending** button on the toolbar. Access rearranges the records in descending order by last contact date. See Figure 3-19.

Figure 3-19 Quick-sorting records in a datasheet

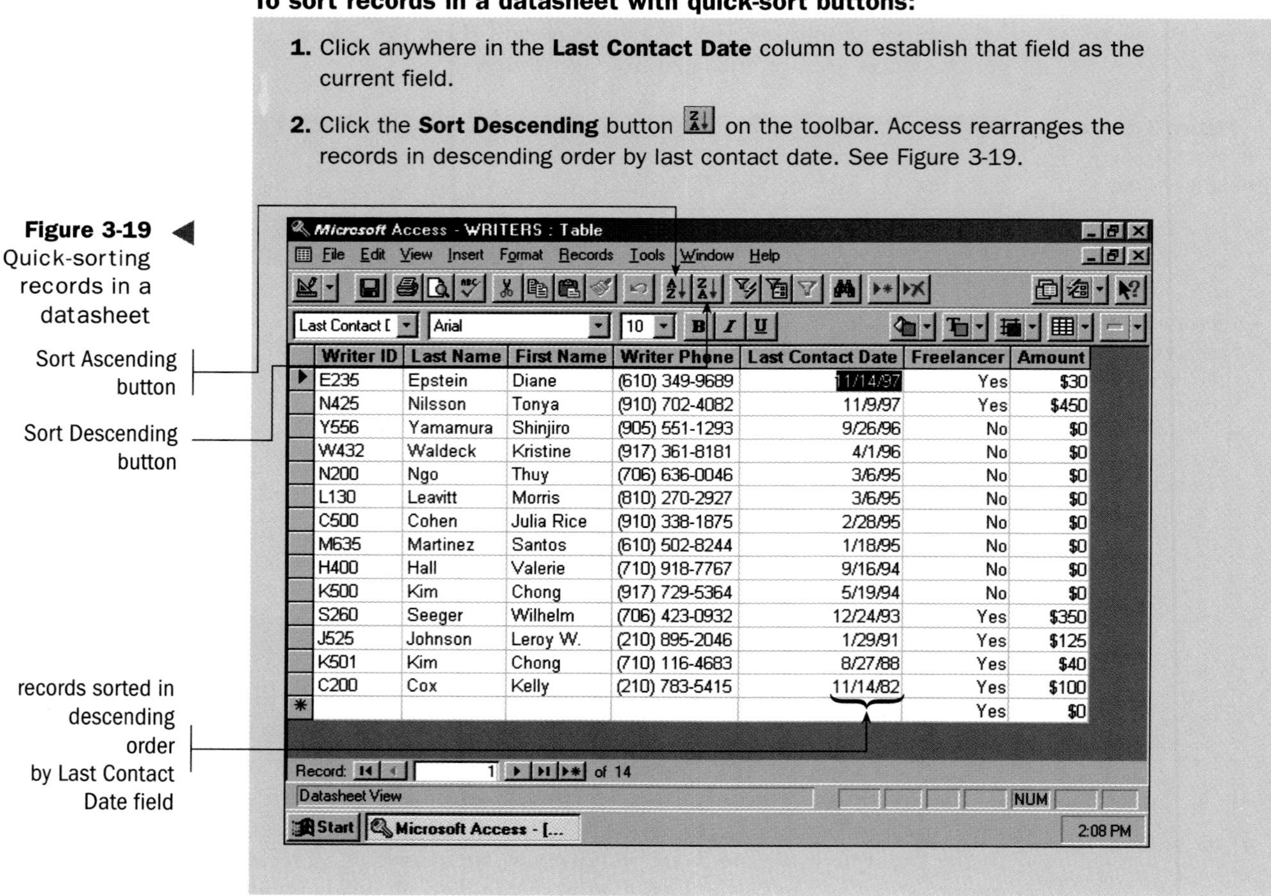

Writer ID	Last Name	First Name	Writer Phone	Last Contact Date	Freelancer	Amount
E235	Epstein	Diane	(610) 349-9689	11/14/97	Yes	$30
N425	Nilsson	Tonya	(910) 702-4082	11/9/97	Yes	$450
Y556	Yamamura	Shinjiro	(905) 551-1293	9/26/96	No	$0
W432	Waldeck	Kristine	(917) 361-8181	4/1/96	No	$0
N200	Ngo	Thuy	(706) 636-0046	3/6/95	No	$0
L130	Leavitt	Morris	(810) 270-2927	3/6/95	No	$0
C500	Cohen	Julia Rice	(910) 338-1875	2/28/95	No	$0
M635	Martinez	Santos	(610) 502-8244	1/18/95	No	$0
H400	Hall	Valerie	(710) 918-7767	9/16/94	No	$0
K500	Kim	Chong	(917) 729-5364	5/19/94	No	$0
S260	Seeger	Wilhelm	(706) 423-0932	12/24/93	Yes	$350
J525	Johnson	Leroy W.	(210) 895-2046	1/29/91	Yes	$125
K501	Kim	Chong	(710) 116-4683	8/27/88	Yes	$40
C200	Cox	Kelly	(210) 783-5415	11/14/82	Yes	$100
*					Yes	$0

You can use this same method to restore the records quickly to their original order by clicking in the Writer ID column and then clicking the Sort Ascending button.

To restore records to their original order:

1. Click anywhere in the **Writer ID** column.
2. Click the **Sort Ascending** button on the toolbar. Access rearranges the records in ascending order by Writer ID (the primary key).

Quick-Sorting Multiple Fields

Access allows you to sort a datasheet quickly using two or more sort keys. The sort key fields must be in adjacent columns in the datasheet. You highlight the columns, and Access sorts first by the first highlighted column and then by any other highlighted column, in order from left to right. Because you click either the Sort Ascending or the Sort Descending button to perform a quick-sort, all of the highlighted fields are sorted in either ascending or descending sort order.

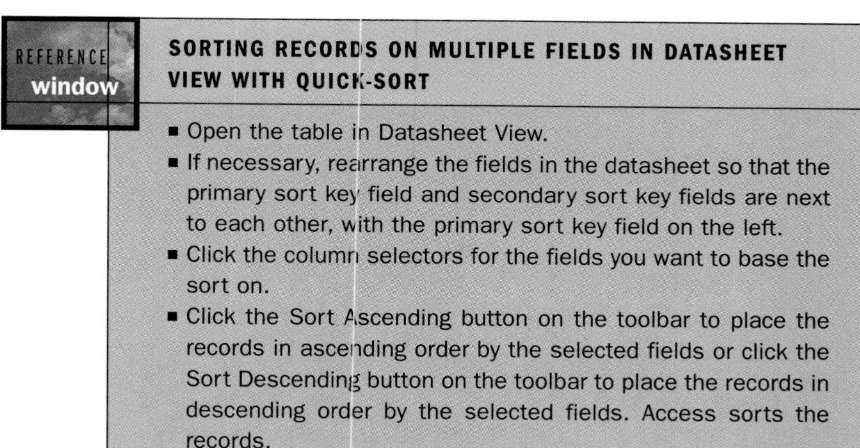

REFERENCE window

SORTING RECORDS ON MULTIPLE FIELDS IN DATASHEET VIEW WITH QUICK-SORT

- Open the table in Datasheet View.
- If necessary, rearrange the fields in the datasheet so that the primary sort key field and secondary sort key fields are next to each other, with the primary sort key field on the left.
- Click the column selectors for the fields you want to base the sort on.
- Click the Sort Ascending button on the toolbar to place the records in ascending order by the selected fields or click the Sort Descending button on the toolbar to place the records in descending order by the selected fields. Access sorts the records.

Elena selects the adjacent fields Freelancer and Amount and performs an ascending-order quick-sort.

To use multiple sort keys to sort records in a datasheet using quick-sort:

1. Click the **Freelancer** field selector. (The field selector, remember, is the gray box containing the field name at the top of the column.) While holding down the mouse button, drag the ↓ to the right until both the Freelancer and Amount columns are highlighted. Then release the mouse button.
2. Click the **Sort Ascending** button on the toolbar. Access rearranges the records, placing them in ascending order by Freelancer and—when the Freelancer field values are the same—in ascending order by Amount. See Figure 3-20.

Figure 3-20 Datasheet sorted on two adjacent fields with quick–sort

Microsoft Access - WRITERS : Table

Writer ID	Last Name	First Name	Writer Phone	Last Contact Date	Freelancer	Amount
E235	Epstein	Diane	(610) 349-9689	11/14/97	Yes	$30
K501	Kim	Chong	(710) 116-4683	8/27/88	Yes	$40
C200	Cox	Kelly	(210) 783-5415	11/14/82	Yes	$100
J525	Johnson	Leroy W.	(210) 895-2046	1/29/91	Yes	$125
S260	Seeger	Wilhelm	(706) 423-0932	12/24/93	Yes	$350
N425	Nilsson	Tonya	(910) 702-4082	11/9/97	Yes	$450
Y556	Yamamura	Shinjiro	(905) 551-1293	9/26/96	No	$0
W432	Waldeck	Kristine	(917) 361-8181	4/1/96	No	$0
N200	Ngo	Thuy	(706) 636-0046	3/6/95	No	$0
M635	Martinez	Santos	(610) 502-8244	1/18/95	No	$0
L130	Leavitt	Morris	(810) 270-2927	3/6/95	No	$0
K500	Kim	Chong	(917) 729-5364	5/19/94	No	$0
H400	Hall	Valerie	(710) 918-7767	9/16/94	No	$0
C500	Cohen	Julia Rice	(910) 338-1875	2/28/95	No	$0
					Yes	$0

Record: 1 of 14

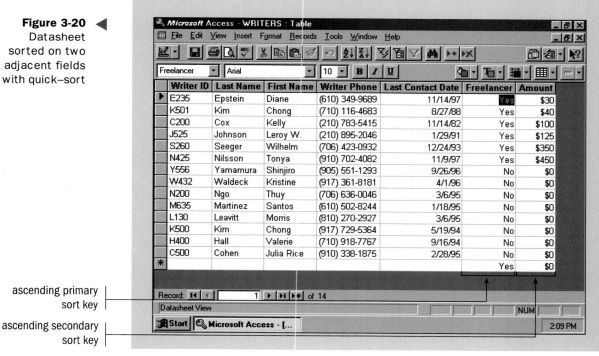

ascending primary sort key

ascending secondary sort key

Elena prints the results of her sort to use in contacting the writers, then does a final review of the data in the WRITERS table and determines that she is finished with her updates. She closes the WRITERS table Datasheet View window.

To close the Datasheet View window:

1. Click the **Close** button [X] in the Datasheet View window. Access displays the Save changes? dialog box.
2. Click the **Yes** button to save the changes to the WRITERS table and return to the Database window.

Access closes the Datasheet View window and saves the formatting changes made earlier to the table. Access also saves the sort order. Access will display the records in the last sorted order when you open the table again.

Elena next uses Access to work on the other table in her Issue25 database, BUSINESS ARTICLES.

Using Access's Spelling Feature

Judith not only created a WRITERS table, she also maintains a table in the Vision database containing information about the selected business articles for the 25th-anniversary issue. Instead of entering all that information herself, Elena decides to import Judith's database table (BUSINESS ARTICLES-JR) into her Issue25 database. After she confirms that Judith's table contains all the correct information, Elena can delete the BUSINESS ARTICLES table that she initially created.

To import the BUSINESS ARTICLES-JR table:

1. Click **File,** then point to **Get External Data,** then click **Import**. Access displays the Import dialog box.
2. If necessary, use the Look in text box to select the Tutorial folder on the drive that contains your Student Disk. Click **Vision** in the file list. Click the **Import** button to close the Import dialog box
3. Click **BUSINESS ARTICLES-JR** in the Tables list, then click the **OK** button. Access imports the table and closes the Import Objects dialog box. The Database window now displays the BUSINESS ARTICLES-JR table in the Tables list.

   After viewing the table and confirming its contents, Elena decides to use Judith's table instead of her own.
4. Using the procedure for deleting a table described earlier in the tutorial, delete the current BUSINESS ARTICLES table and rename the BUSINESS ARTICLES-JR table BUSINESS ARTICLES.

Elena wants to make sure that the data in the BUSINESS ARTICLES table is accurate. She uses Access's Spelling feature to help her with this. Access's Spelling feature will check the contents of any text field. Each word is checked against Access's internal dictionary. If a word is not found, Access displays a dialog box with a suggested replacement for the word. You can then accept the suggested replacement, select from a list of alternate spellings, or choose to make no changes.

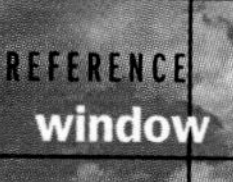

USING ACCESS'S SPELLING FEATURE TO CHECK SPELLING OF FIELD VALUES

- Open the table in Datasheet View.
- Click the column selector to select the column or columns you want checked.
- Click the Spelling button on the toolbar.
- For each suggested change, choose to use one of the suggested alternative spellings or to ignore the change.
- When the spelling check is complete, click the OK button to close the "Spell Checking is complete" dialog box.

Elena decides to check the article titles in the BUSINESS ARTICLES table to make sure that they are spelled correctly. She does not check the Type or Writer ID fields because the correct values will not appear in Access's internal dictionary. The Issue field values are dates and are checked for validity by Access when the values are entered. The Article Length field contains numeric values and cannot be checked for spelling.

To check the spelling in the article titles:

1. Double-click **BUSINESS ARTICLES** in the Tables list. Access opens the Datasheet View window of the BUSINESS ARTICLES table.

2. Click the **Article Title** column selector to select the column, then click the **Spelling** button on the toolbar. Access begins checking the spelling of each word in the Article Title column. Access finds a word not in the dictionary and displays the Spelling dialog box. See Figure 3-21.

Figure 3-21 The Spelling dialog box

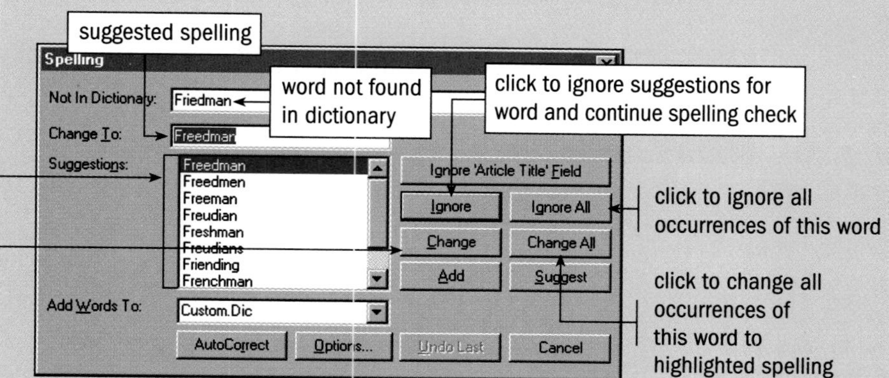

Access does not find the word "Friedman" in the dictionary and suggests changing it to "Freedman." Elena doesn't want to make this change since this is a correctly spelled name.

3. Click the **Ignore All** button to bypass this suggested change and continue with the spelling check. Clicking the Ignore All button tells Access to ignore any other occurrences of this word in the table. Access next displays the Spelling dialog box for the word "Reagan's."

4. Click the **Ignore All** button to ignore this suggested change and continue with the spelling check. Access next displays the Spelling dialog box for the word "Trans-Alaskan." Although this does not match any entry in the dictionary, Access does not have any suggested alternatives.

5. Click the **Ignore All** button to continue the spelling check. Access next displays the Spelling dialog box for "Pipline" and suggests changing it to "Pipeline." Elena wants to change this to its correct spelling.
6. Click the **Change** button to change "Pipline" to "Pipeline." Access continues the spelling check.
7. Click the **Ignore All** button when Access displays the Spelling dialog box for "Chrysler" and for "Bingham." Access finishes checking the rest of the article titles and displays the "Spell checking is complete" dialog box.
8. Click the **OK** button to close the dialog box.

Access's Spelling feature is useful, but it will not find all misspellings. It only finds words that are not in its dictionary. For example, the word "beast" (as a misspelling of "best") will not be identified as incorrect because "beast" is a correctly spelled word that is found in the dictionary.

Defining a Lookup Wizard Field

In the BUSINESS ARTICLES table, each record has a field for Writer ID, which identifies the writer of the article. If she needs to enter a new article into the table, Elena enters the Writer ID that corresponds to the record for the writer in the WRITERS table. So that she can locate that information more quickly, Elena redefines the Writer ID field in the BUSINESS ARTICLES table to make it a Lookup Wizard field. Then, whenever she enters a new record in the table, Access will display the list of writers from the WRITERS table. Elena can select from the list, and Access will automatically enter the correct Writer ID value. This makes it much easier to enter Writer ID field values for the BUSINESS ARTICLES table and reduces the chance of making an error.

DEFINING A LOOKUP WIZARD FIELD

- Open the table in Design View.
- Click in the Data Type text box of the field for which you want to give the Lookup Wizard data type.
- Click the Data Type text list arrow to display the list of available data types.
- Click Lookup Wizard to start the Lookup Wizard and display the first dialog box.
- Make sure that the radio button for "I want the lookup column to look up values in a table or query" is checked, then click the Next > button. The next Lookup Wizard dialog box opens.
- Click to select the table for the lookup, then click the Next > button to display the next Lookup Wizard dialog box.
- Select the fields you want to appear in the lookup list, then click the Next > button.
- Adjust the width of the columns that will appear in the lookup list, then click the Next > button.
- Select the field that will provide the value for the Lookup Wizard field, then click the Next > button.
- Enter the name you want for the field in the original table. Then click the Finish button to close the Lookup Wizard and return to the Design View window.

To add a new record to the table with a defined Lookup Wizard field:

1. Click the **Table View** button on the toolbar.
2. Click the **New Record** button to move the current record pointer to a new record at the end of the table, then type **Toyota and GM Joint Venture**, and then press the **Tab** key to move to the Type field.
3. Type **INT** to replace the default value BUS for Type, then press the **Tab** key to move to the Issue column.

   Here, the type INT refers to an article about international business. Other types listed in the BUSINESS ARTICLES table include BUS (general business), ITV (interview), LAW (legal article), and POL (politics).
4. Type **1983 Mar**, then press the **Tab** key to move to the Article Length column. Remember that article length refers to the number of words.
5. Type **1682**, then press the **Tab** key to move to the Writer ID column.

   Because the Writer ID field is a Lookup Wizard field, Access displays a list arrow at the right side of the Writer ID field. When you click the arrow, Access displays a list of Writer ID, Last Name, and First Name values from the WRITERS table. To select a writer from the WRITERS table, simply scroll as needed and click on a value from the list. Access automatically inserts the corresponding Writer ID in the data entry field.
6. Click the **Writer ID** list arrow. Access displays a list of Writer ID, Last Name, and First Name values from the WRITERS table. See Figure 3-26.

Figure 3-26 List of Writer ID, Last Name, and First Name values from the WRITERS table

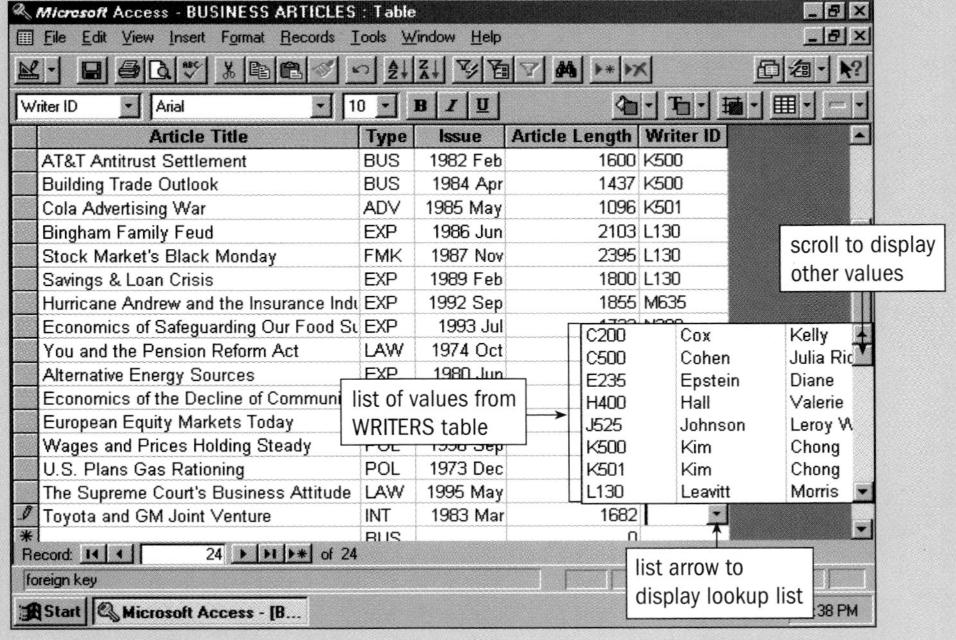

7. Scroll down the list until the name Seeger (Writer ID S260) appears. Click **Seeger**. Access places S260 in the data entry field for the Writer ID. See Figure 3-27.

Figure 3-27 ◀ Writer ID for Wilhelm Seeger entered

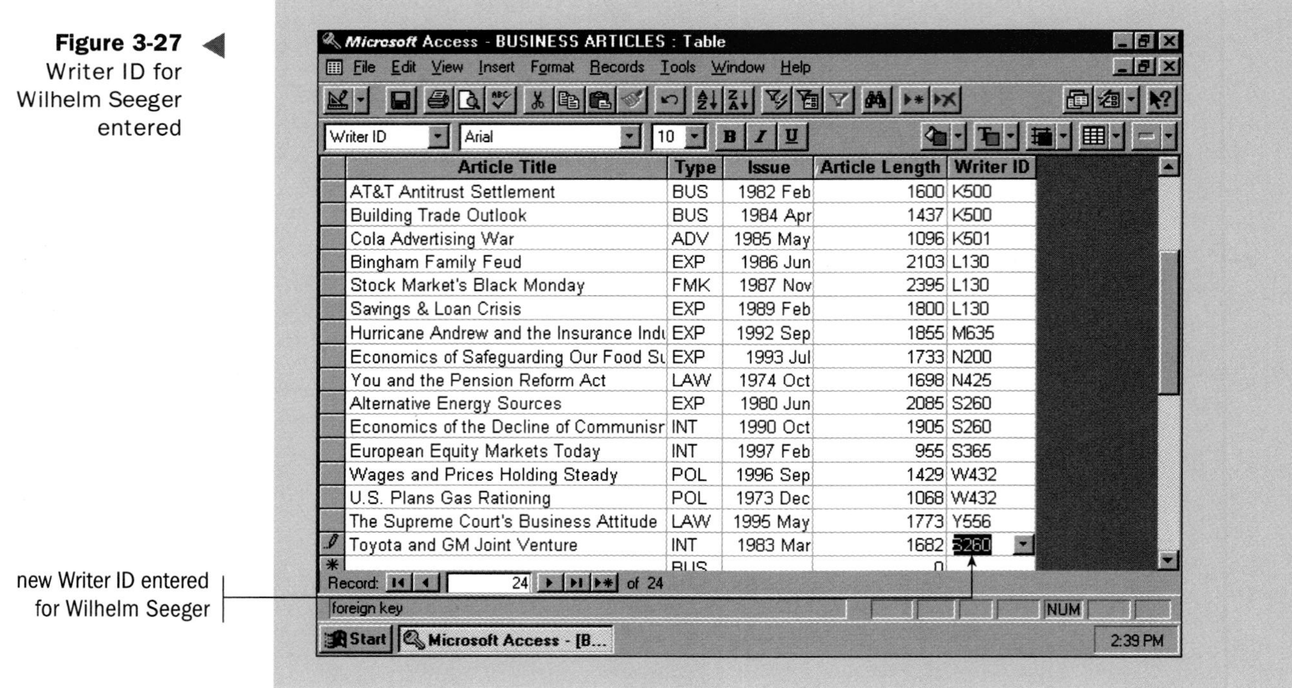

	Article Title	Type	Issue	Article Length	Writer ID
	AT&T Antitrust Settlement	BUS	1982 Feb	1600	K500
	Building Trade Outlook	BUS	1984 Apr	1437	K500
	Cola Advertising War	ADV	1985 May	1096	K501
	Bingham Family Feud	EXP	1986 Jun	2103	L130
	Stock Market's Black Monday	FMK	1987 Nov	2395	L130
	Savings & Loan Crisis	EXP	1989 Feb	1800	L130
	Hurricane Andrew and the Insurance Indu	EXP	1992 Sep	1855	M635
	Economics of Safeguarding Our Food Su	EXP	1993 Jul	1733	N200
	You and the Pension Reform Act	LAW	1974 Oct	1698	N425
	Alternative Energy Sources	EXP	1980 Jun	2085	S260
	Economics of the Decline of Communisr	INT	1990 Oct	1905	S260
	European Equity Markets Today	INT	1997 Feb	955	S365
	Wages and Prices Holding Steady	POL	1996 Sep	1429	W432
	U.S. Plans Gas Rationing	POL	1973 Dec	1068	W432
	The Supreme Court's Business Attitude	LAW	1995 May	1773	Y556
✎	Toyota and GM Joint Venture	INT	1983 Mar	1682	S260
*		BUS		0	

new Writer ID entered for Wilhelm Seeger

Elena has now finished entering the new record into the BUSINESS ARTICLES table. She closes the table.

To close the table:

1. Click the **Close** button ☒ for the Datasheet View window. Access returns you to the Database window.

Backing Up a Database

Elena is done with her work on the WRITERS and BUSINESS ARTICLES tables. Before exiting Access, however, Elena backs up the Issue25 database. **Backing up** is the process of making a duplicate copy of a database on a separate disk. In Access, remember that a database and all its objects are contained a single file. Elena does this to protect against loss of, or damage to, the original database. If problems occur, she can simply use the backup database.

Access does not have its own backup command. Instead you use Windows' My Computer. (Before backing up a database file, therefore, you must close the database in Access.) The database file icon contains the gray image of a datasheet.

If you have both a drive A and a drive B, copy the Issue25 database file from the drive containing your Student Disk to the other drive. If you have only a drive A, however, you need to copy the Issue25 database file from your Student Disk to the hard disk. Then you place another disk, the backup disk, in drive A and move the database to it from the hard disk.

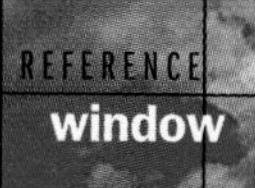

BACKING UP AN ACCESS DATABASE

- Minimize the Access window by clicking the Minimize button in the Access window.
- Open My Computer and copy a database file from one disk to a backup disk, using the procedure appropriate for the disk and hardware configuration.
- Close the My Computer window.
- Be sure that the original disk is in the same drive you've been using for your Access work.
- Switch back to Access. The Access window is the active window.

To back up a database:

1. Click the Database window **Close** button to close the Issue25 database.
2. Minimize the Access window by clicking the **Minimize** button in the Access window.
3. Open My Computer and copy the Issue25 file from your Student Disk to a backup disk, using the procedure appropriate for your disk and hardware configuration.
4. Close the My Computer window.
5. Be sure that your Student Disk is in the same drive you've been using for your Access work.
6. Switch back to Access. The Access window is the active window.

Compacting a Database

Elena deleted a record from the WRITERS table while updating the Issue25 database. She knows that when records are deleted in Access, the space occupied by the deleted records does not automatically become available for other records. The same is true if an object, such as a form or report, is deleted. To make the space available, you must compact the database. When you compact a database, Access removes deleted records and objects and creates a smaller version of the database. Unlike backing up a database, which you do to protect your database against loss or damage, you compact a database to make it smaller, thereby making more space available on your disk. Before compacting a database, you must close it.

COMPACTING A DATABASE

- Close any database you are using, so that the Access window is active.
- Click Tools, point to Database Utilities, and then click Compact Database to open the Database to Compact From dialog box.
- In the Look in box, select the drive and directory that contain the database you want to compact.
- In the File name list box, select the database you want to compact.
- Click the Compact button. Access closes the Database to Compact From dialog box and opens the Compact Database Into dialog box.
- In the Save in box, select the drive and directory for the location of the compacted form of the database.
- In the File name text box, type the name you want to assign to the compacted form of the database.
- Click the Save button. The Compact Database Into dialog box closes, and Access starts compacting the database.
- If you use the same name for both the original and compacted database, Access displays the message "Replace existing file?" Click the Yes button to continue compacting the database.
- After the database compacting is complete, Access returns you to the Access window.

Elena compacts her Issue25 database before exiting Access. Because she has just made a backup copy, she uses Issue25 as the compacted database name. You can use the same name, or a different name, for your original and compacted databases. If you use the same name, you should back up the original database first in case a hardware or software malfunction occurs in the middle of the compacting process.

To compact a database and exit Access:

1. Click **Tools**, point to **Database Utilities**, and then click **Compact Database**. Access displays the Database to Compact From dialog box. See Figure 3-28.

Figure 3-28 The Database to Compact From dialog box

2. If necessary, use the Look in list box to select the drive and directory that contain the database to compact.

3. Click **Issue25** in the File name list box.

4. Click the **Compact** button. The Database to Compact From dialog box closes and Access displays the Compact Database Into dialog box. See Figure 3-29.

Figure 3-29 The Compact Into dialog box

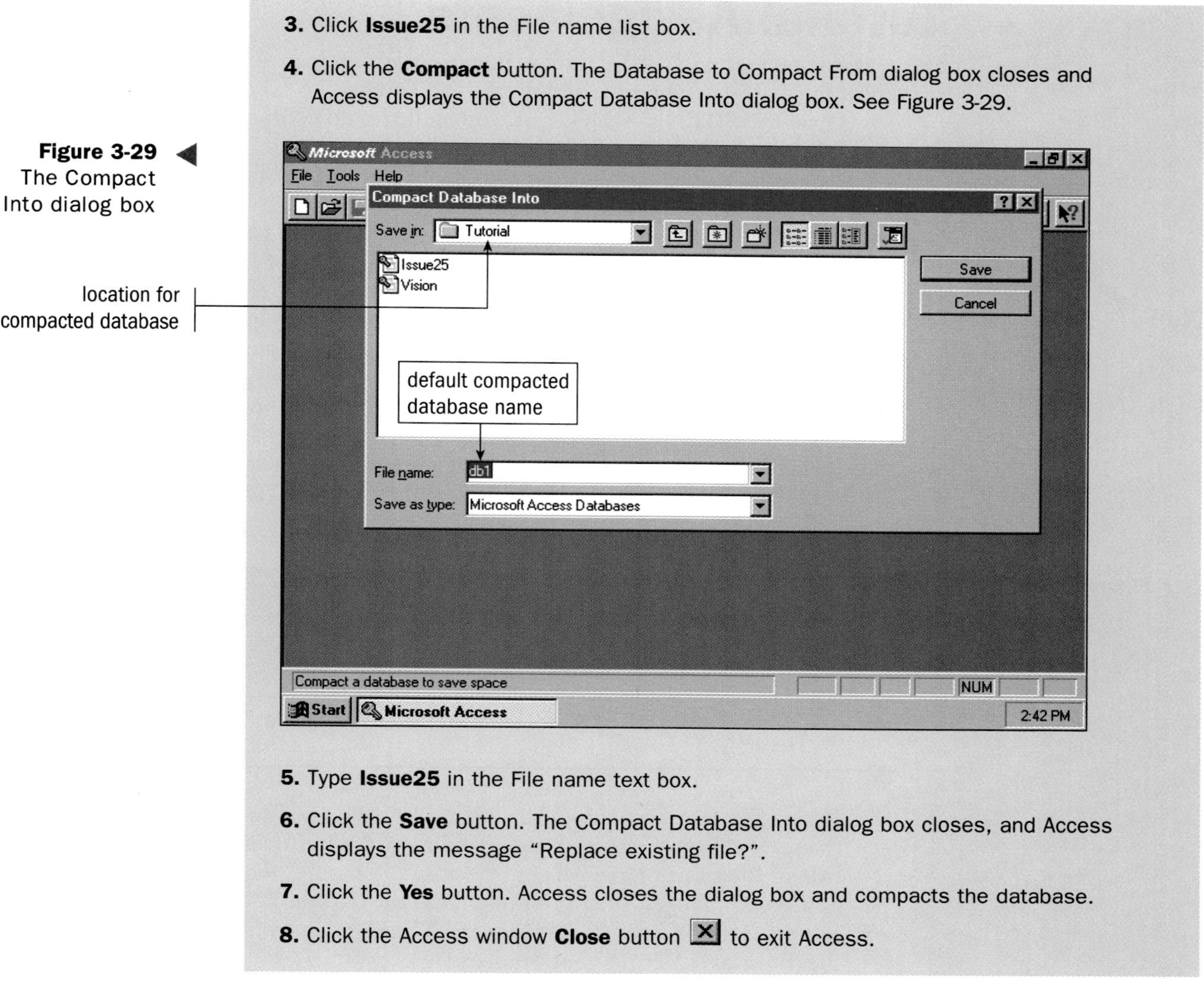

5. Type **Issue25** in the File name text box.

6. Click the **Save** button. The Compact Database Into dialog box closes, and Access displays the message "Replace existing file?".

7. Click the **Yes** button. Access closes the dialog box and compacts the database.

8. Click the Access window **Close** button [X] to exit Access.

Elena has finished updating the WRITERS and BUSINESS ARTICLES tables. In the next tutorial, she will use the Access query feature to answer questions and obtain information from the data in the WRITERS and BUSINESS ARTICLES tables.

Quick Check

1. How can you find a specific field value in a table?
2. Why do you need to be cautious about using the Replace All option when replacing table field values?
3. What are the advantages of sorting a datasheet's records?
4. When might you consider using a secondary sort key?
5. What are some advantages of using Access's Spelling feature?
6. What is the purpose of the Lookup Wizard?
7. How many different files do you copy when you back up one Access database that includes three tables?
8. What is the purpose of compacting a database?

Tutorial Assignments

Start Access, open the Issue25 database in the Tutorial folder on your Student Disk, maximize the Database window, and do the following:

1. Open the BUSINESS ARTICLES table. It should contain 24 records.
2. Print the BUSINESS ARTICLES datasheet.
3. Delete the record for the article entitled "European Equity Markets Today," which is an article that appeared in a 1997 issue.
4. In the Type field, change the type of the 1988 article from LAW to POL.

5. Switch to Design View. Make the row for the Issue of Business Perspectives field the current field, click in its Format property box, and start the Access Help system. Click Index, type date/time, click the Display button, click the jump for Date/Time display formats, and read the discussion of Custom Formats. Explain the meaning of the date/time format yyyy mmm. Exit the Access Help system, switch back to Datasheet View, and observe the format of the field values in the Issue column.
6. Add the two new records shown in Figure 3-30 to the end of the BUSINESS ARTICLES table. Notice the format of the Issue field and enter the two new Issue field values in the exact same format.

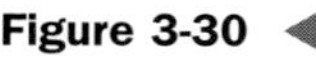
Figure 3-30

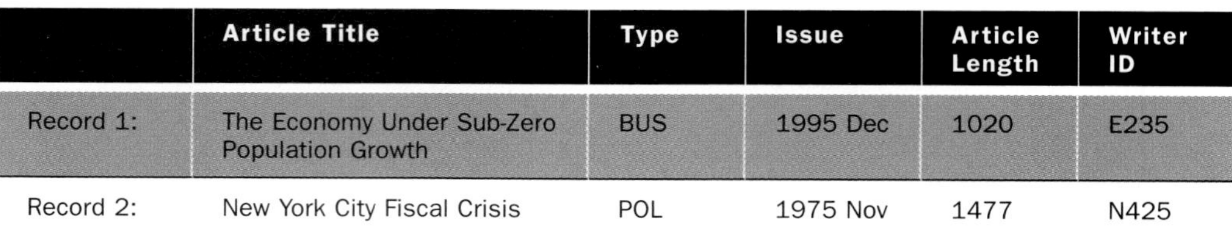

	Article Title	Type	Issue	Article Length	Writer ID
Record 1:	The Economy Under Sub-Zero Population Growth	BUS	1995 Dec	1020	E235
Record 2:	New York City Fiscal Crisis	POL	1975 Nov	1477	N425

7. Resize the datasheet columns so that all field names and field values appear on the screen. Sort the records in ascending order by Article Length. What is the title of the shortest article?
8. Save your changes, then print and close the datasheet.
9. Import into the Issue25 database the TYPES table from the Vision database in the Tutorial folder on your Student Disk.
10. Use Access's Spelling feature to correct the spelling of values in the Description column of the TYPES table.
11. Back up the Issue25 database from your Student Disk to your backup disk.
12. Compact the Issue25 database using Issue25 as the filename in the Compact Database Into dialog box.

Case Problems

1. Walkton Daily Press Carriers Robin Witkop has created a database to help Grant Sherman track newspaper carriers and their outstanding balances. Grant starts his maintenance of the CARRIERS table. He imports data to his database and then adds, changes, and deletes data to update the CARRIERS table.

Start Access and do the following:

1. Open the Press database in the Cases folder on your Student Disk and maximize the Database window.
2. Delete the CARRIERS table.
3. Import the CARRIERS-RW table from the Walkton database on your Student Disk.
4. Change the table name CARRIERS-RW to CARRIERS.
5. Open the CARRIERS table, which should contain 19 records.
6. Delete the record that has a value of 10 in the Carrier ID field. This is the record for Joe Carrasco.

7. In the Last Name field of the record having a Carrier ID value of 11, change Thompson to Thomson.
8. Make the following changes to the record that has a Carrier ID value of 17—the record for Bradley Slachter. Change the First Name field value to Sean; change the Birthdate field value 3/4/79 to 3/14/79.
9. Add the two new records shown in Figure 3-31 to the end of the CARRIERS table. Because Access automatically controls fields that are assigned an autonumber data type, press the Tab key instead of typing a field value in the Carrier ID field. Notice that Access assigns a unique number for the Carrier ID field value.

Figure 3-31

	Carrier ID	Last Name	First Name	Carrier Phone	Birthdate
Record 1:	AutoNumber	Rivera	Nelia	281-3787	6/3/80
Record 2:	AutoNumber	Hansen	Gunnar	949-6745	4/30/81

10. Sort the records in descending order by Last Name. Whose name appears last alphabetically? Put the records back in original order by sorting the Carrier ID field in ascending order.
11. Import the BILLINGS table from the Walkton database on your Student Disk. Use the Lookup Wizard to change the data type of the Carrier ID field to look up the Carrier ID in the CARRIERS table. Tell the Lookup Wizard to display the Carrier ID, Carrier Last Name and Carrier First Name fields when the Carrier ID field is selected.
12. Change the font and type style of the Billings table to settings of your choosing.
13. Save your changes, then print and close the datasheet.
14. Back up the Press database from your Student Disk to your backup disk.
15. Compact the Press database using Press as the filename in the Database to Compact Database Into dialog box.

2. Lopez Lexus Dealerships Maria and Hector Lopez have created a database to track their car inventory in the lots they own throughout Texas. They start their maintenance of the CARS table. They import data and then add, change, and delete data to update the CARS table.

Start Access and do the following:

1. Open the Lexus database in the Cases folder on your Student Disk and maximize the Database window.
2. Delete the CARS and LOCATIONS tables.
3. Import the CARS-LL table from the Lopez database on your Student Disk.
4. Change the table name CARS-LL to CARS.
5. Open the CARS table. It should contain 25 records.
6. Delete the record that has the value JT4AA in the Vehicle ID field. The record is for a Lexus GS300.
7. In the record having the Vehicle ID QQRT6, which is a Lexus LS400, change the value of the Cost field from $36,700 to $36,900. Change the value of the Class field from S1 to S5. You might need to scroll the datasheet to see these values.
8. Make the following changes to the record that has the Vehicle ID value AB7J8, which is a Lexus SC300. Change the Model field from SC300 to SC400; change the Cost field value from $41,300 to $42,300.
9. Add the two new records shown in Figure 3-32 to the end of the CARS table.

	Vehicle ID	Manufacturer	Model	Class	Transmission Type	Year	Location Code	Cost	Selling Price
Record 1:	MX8M4	Lexus	ES300	S4	A4	1996	P1	31,700	37,600
Record 2:	BY7BZ	Lexus	LS400	S5	M5	1996	H1	47,900	55,150

Figure 3-32

10. Resize the datasheet columns so that all field names and field values appear on the screen. Sort the records in descending order by Selling Price. What is the most expensive car?
11. Print the datasheet. If any columns are too narrow to print all field names and values, or if more than one page is needed to print the datasheet, resize the datasheet columns and reprint the datasheet.
12. Import the CLASSES, LOCATIONS, and TRANSMISSIONS tables from the Lopez database on your Student Disk. (*Hint*: Press the Control key to highlight and import all three tables together.)
13. Open the TRANSMISSIONS table and use Access's Spelling feature to check the spelling of values in the Transmission Desc field. Correct any misspelled words.
14. Change the font in the TRANSMISSIONS table to Arial, the size to 10, and the style to normal. Close the TRANSMISSIONS table.
15. Open the CARS table. Use the Lookup Wizard to change the data type for the Class, Transmission Type, and Location Code fields to Lookup Wizard. Define the following lookups:

    Class—look up the Class Type field in the CLASSES table. Display Class Type and Class Description.

    Transmission Type—look up the Transmission Type in the TRANSMISSIONS table. Display the Transmission Type and Transmission Desc fields.

    Location Code—look up the Location Code in the LOCATIONS table. Display the Location Code and Location Name fields.

    Close the CARS table, saving changes.
16. Back up the Lexus database from your Student Disk to your backup disk.
17. Compact the Lexus database using Lexus as the filename in the Compact Database Into dialog box.

3. Tophill University Student Employment Lee Chang has created a database to help Olivia Tyler track employers and their advertised part-time jobs for students. Olivia starts her maintenance of the JOBS table. She imports data to her database and then adds, changes, and deletes data to update the JOBS table.

Start Access and do the following:

1. Open the Parttime database in the Cases folder on your Student Disk and maximize the Database window.
2. Delete the JOBS table.
3. Import the JOBS-LC table from the Tophill database on your Student Disk.
4. Change the table name JOBS-LC to JOBS.
5. Open the JOBS table. It should contain 17 records.
6. Delete the record that has a value of 16 in the Job# field. This record describes a position for a night stock clerk.
7. In the Job Title field of the record having a Job# value of 3, change Computer Analyst to Computer Lab Associate.
8. Make the following changes to the record that has a Job# value of 13–the record describing a position for an actuarial aide. Change the Employer ID field to BJ93; change the Wage field value $8.40 to $9.25.

9. Add the two new records shown in Figure 3-33 to the end of the JOBS table. Because Access automatically controls fields that are assigned an autonumber data type, press the Tab key instead of typing a field value in the Job Order field. Notice that Access assigns a unique number for the Job Order field value. This number is not necessarily the next in sequence.

Figure 3-33

	Job Order	Hours/ Week	Employer ID	Job Title	Wages
Record 1:	AutoNumber	21	ME86	Lab Technician	5.30
Record 2:	AutoNumber	18	BJ92	Desktop Publishing Aide	5.80

10. Print the datasheet. If any columns are too narrow to print all field names and values, or if more than one page is needed to print the datasheet, resize the datasheet columns and reprint the datasheet.
11. Delete the EMPLOYERS table. Import the EMPLOYERS table from the Tophill database on your Student Disk. Redefine the data type of the Employer ID field in the JOBS table to Lookup Wizard. Link the Employer ID field in the JOBS table to the Employer ID field in the EMPLOYERS table. Display the Employer ID and Employer Name fields.
12. Sort the records in the JOBS table in descending order by Wages. Which Job Title earns the most? Return the records to their original order by sorting the Job# field in ascending order.
13. Use Access's Spelling feature to check the spelling of values in the Job Title field. Correct any spelling errors.
14. Open the EMPLOYERS table and change the font in the Employers table to one of your choosing. Print the datasheet, then close the datasheet, saving changes.
15. Back up the Parttime database from your Student Disk to your backup disk.
16. Compact the Parttime database using Parttime as the filename in the Compact Database Into dialog box.

4. Rexville Business Licenses Chester Pearce has created a database to help him track the licenses issued to businesses in the town of Rexville. Chester starts his maintenance of the BUSINESSES table. He imports data to his database and then adds, changes, and deletes data to update the BUSINESSES table.

Start Access and do the following:

1. Open the Buslic database in the Cases folder on your Student Disk and maximize the Database window.
2. Delete the BUSINESSES table.
3. Import the BUSINESSES-CP table from the Rexville database on your Student Disk.
4. Change the table name BUSINESSES-CP to BUSINESSES.
5. Open the BUSINESSES table. It should contain 12 records.
6. Switch to Design View. Enter the Caption property value Bus ID for the Business ID field and the Caption property value Phone# for the Phone Number field.
7. Use the best-fit method to resize the datasheet columns.
8. Delete the record that has a value of 3 in the Business ID field. The content of the Business Name field for this record is Take a Chance.
9. In the Street Name field of the record having a Business ID value of 9, change West Emerald Street to East Emerald Street.
10. Make the following changes to the record that has a Business ID value of 8. The Business Name for this field reads Lakeview House. Change the Business Name field to Rexville Billiards; change the Street# field value 2425 to 4252.

11. Add the two new records shown in Figure 3-34 to the end of the BUSINESSES table. Because Access automatically controls fields that are assigned an autonumber data type, press the Tab key instead of typing a field value in the Business ID field.

	Business ID	Business Name	Street Number	Street Name	Phone Number	Proprietor
Record 1:	AutoNumber	Kyle Manufacturing, Inc.	4818	West Paris Road	942-9239	Myron Kyle
Record 2:	AutoNumber	Merlin Auto Body	2922	Riverview Drive	243-5525	Lester Tiahrt

Figure 3-34

12. Sort the records in the BUSINESSES table in ascending order by Business Name. Print the datasheet. If any columns are too narrow to print all field names and values, or if more than one page is needed to print the datasheet, resize the datasheet columns and reprint the datasheet.
13. Restore the BUSINESSES table records to their original order by sorting the Business ID field in ascending order.
14. Import the ISSUED LICENSES table from the Rexville database on your Student Disk. Redefine the Business ID field to Lookup Wizard. Link the Business ID field in the ISSUED LICENSES table to the Business ID field in the BUSINESSES table. Display the Business ID and Business Name fields.
15. Delete the LICENSES table and then import the LICENSES table from the Rexville database in the Cases folder on your Student Disk. Use Access's Spelling feature to check the spelling of the values in the License Description field. Correct any misspelled words.
16. Redefine the data type of the License Type field in the ISSUED LICENSES table to Lookup Wizard. Link the License Type field in the ISSUED LICENSES table to the License Type field in the LICENSES table. Display the License Description and License Type fields.
17. Change the font in the LICENSES table to one of your choosing. Print the datasheet, then close the Datasheet window, saving changes.
18. Back up the Buslic database from your Student Disk to your backup disk.
19. Compact the Buslic database using Buslic as the filename in the Compact Database Into dialog box.

TUTORIAL 4

Querying Database Tables

Querying the Issue25 Database at Vision Publishers

OBJECTIVES

In this tutorial you will:

- Create and modify a query
- Run a query and view the results
- Save and open a query
- Define record selection criteria
- Sort records in a query
- Print selected query results
- Perform query calculations
- Add relationships between tables
- Create a parameter query

CASE

Vision Publishers

At the next progress meeting on the special 25th-anniversary issue of *Business Perspective*, Brian Murphy, Elena Sanchez, Judith Rossi, and Harold Larson discuss the information each needs to obtain from the database. Brian asks for a list of the freelancers, their phone numbers, and the amounts owed to them.

Judith and Elena decide to develop two writer contact lists, one based on specific area codes and the other based on the last dates the writers were contacted. Because Elena is starting the magazine layout process, she also wants to see the article titles and lengths.

Harold plans to highlight the diversity of articles in his marketing campaign, so he needs a list of writers and article titles, arranged by article type. Harold also wants to spotlight one or two writers in the marketing campaign, and the group decides that Valerie Hall and Wilhelm Seeger should be featured. Elena agrees to get Harold the contact information for these two writers.

Elena will use Access' query capability to obtain the answers to the preliminary list of questions shown in Figure 4-1.

Figure 4-1 Elena's questions about the Issue25 database

Answer these questions:

1. What are the names and phone numbers of and amounts owed to the freelancers?
2. What is the contact information for writers with specific area codes?
3. What is the contact information for Valerie Hall and Wilhelm Seeger?
4. What is the contact information for writers, arranged in order by last contact date?
5. What are the article titles, types, and lengths for each writer, arranged by article type?
6. What are the article titles and writer names, in order by article type?

Using a Query

A **query** is a question you ask about the data stored in a database in order to retrieve specific records. It means you don't have to scan through an entire database to find the information you need. Elena's list of questions about the Issue25 database are examples of queries. You create a query based on the specific information you need to extract from the database. A **criterion** is a rule that determines which records are selected. The query will tell Access which fields you need and what criterion (or criteria) Access should use to obtain the necessary information for you.

Access has a powerful query capability that can do the following:

- display selected fields and records from a table
- sort records
- perform calculations
- generate data for forms, reports, and other queries
- access data from two or more tables

The specific type of Access query that Elena will use to answer her questions is called a select query. A **select query** asks a question about the data stored in a database and returns an answer in a datasheet format. When you create a select query, you specify the conditions that the fields must meet in order for the records to be selected. The select query conditions are stored in the Query Design grid and can be stored as a file for later use. A second type of query, called a **filter**, is used with forms and is often created for one-time use. (You will work with filters in the next tutorial.) In the remainder of this tutorial, a select query will simply be called a query.

To create a query, you can use the Query Wizards, the Query Design window, or Structured Query Language (SQL). SQL (pronounced *sequel* or *ess cue ell*) is a powerful computer language used in querying, updating, and managing relational databases. In this tutorial, you will create queries using the Simple Query Wizard and the Query Design window. You will not use SQL here, as it is a more advanced Access capability.

SESSION 4.1

In this session, you will create a query using the Simple Query Wizard, run a query, view the query results, save a query design, and open a saved query design. You will also define selection criteria for a query and exclude a query field from the query results.

Creating a Query with the Simple Query Wizard

Query Wizards can be used for simple queries or for more complex queries. A simple query allows you to select records and fields and perform calculations and summaries. A complex query allows you to find duplicate records in a table, copy table records to a new table, or update groups of records. Because Elena has not created queries before, she decides first to practice by using the Simple Query Wizard. She begins by creating a query that will use all the records in the WRITERS table to answer the question: What are the names and phone numbers of and amounts owed to all writers?

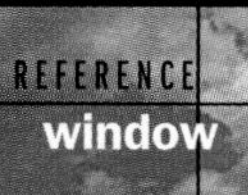

CREATING A QUERY WITH THE SIMPLE QUERY WIZARD

- Click the Queries tab in the Database window to display the Queries list.
- Click the New button.
- In the New Query dialog box, select the Simple Query Wizard, then click the OK button.
- Select the table to be used in the query.
- Select the fields to be used in the query, then click the Next > button.
- Enter a name for the query.
- Click the Finish button.

To create a new query using the Simple Query Wizard:

1. If you have not done so, place your Student Disk in the appropriate drive, start Access, open the Issue25 database in the Tutorial folder on your Student Disk, maximize the Database window, then click the **Queries** tab in the Database window to display the Queries list. The Queries list box is empty because you haven't defined any queries yet.
2. Click the **New** button to open the New Query dialog box.
3. Click **Simple Query Wizard** to select it, then click the **OK** button. Access starts the Simple Query Wizard. See Figure 4-2.

   Clicking the Tables/Queries list arrow allows you to choose the table (or previous query) from which you will select fields. The Available Fields list box displays the fields from the chosen table. You click a field to highlight it, then click [>] to move the field to the Selected Fields list box. Clicking [>>] moves all available fields to the Selected Fields list box. Clicking [<] moves the highlighted field from the Selected Fields list box to the Available Fields list box and clicking [<<] moves all fields in the Selected Fields list box to the Available Fields list box.

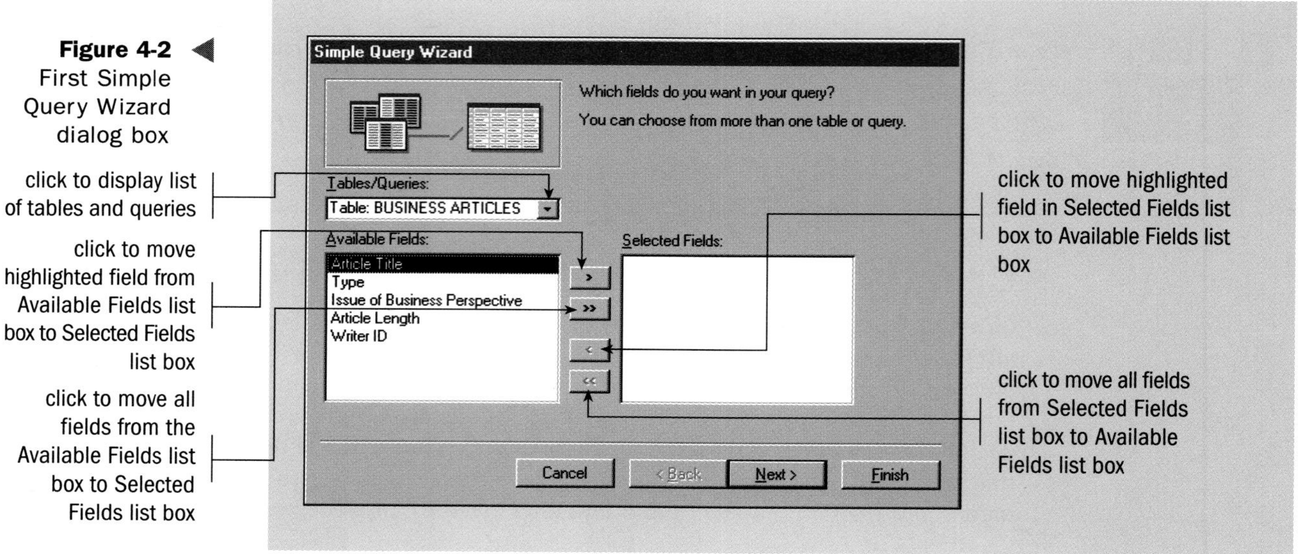

Figure 4-2 First Simple Query Wizard dialog box

Elena needs the Last Name, First Name, Writer Phone, and Freelancer Reprint Payment Amount fields from the WRITERS table.

To select fields for a query:

1. Click the **Tables/Queries** list arrow, then click **Table:WRITERS** to select the WRITERS table.
2. Click **Last Name** in the Available Fields list box, then click [>] to move it to the Selected Fields list box.
3. Using the same procedure, move the First Name, Writer Phone, and Freelancer Reprint Payment Amount fields to the Selected Fields list box, then click the [Next >] button to display the next Simple Query Wizard dialog box.

   This dialog box asks you to choose between a detail or a summary query. A detail query shows every field of every record that answers the query.
4. Make sure the Detail radio button is selected, then click the [Next >] button to display the next Simple Query Wizard dialog box.

   This dialog box asks you to enter the name you will use for this query. The name will appear in the list of queries in the Database window.
5. Type **Practice List Query**. Make sure the radio button is selected next to "Open the query to view information", then click the **Finish** button. See Figure 4-3.

Figure 4-3 ◀ Naming the query design

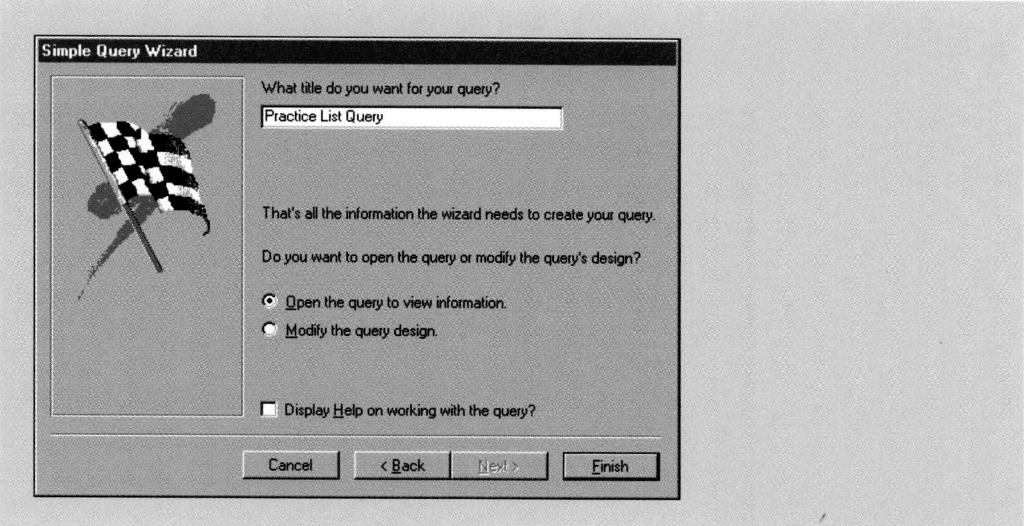

Access saves the query design and then runs the query. The query results are displayed in the Datasheet View window for the query.

Viewing the Query Results

The Datasheet View of the query results contains only the fields that you selected for the Practice List Query. These fields are displayed for each record in the WRITERS table. Although the query results look just like a table's datasheet and appear in the same Datasheet View window, the results are temporary and are not stored as a table on the disk. Instead, the query design is stored on the disk; you can re-create the query results at any time by running the query again.

In the Datasheet View of the query results, if you change a field value in a record, the change will be recorded in the underlying table. Records deleted from the query results will be deleted from the underlying table as well. In this case, however, you cannot add a record to the Practice List Query results, because each new record must have a value for the primary key field (Writer ID), which is not a field selected by the query. In general, to avoid any inconsistencies or errors, any changes to the data should be made directly to the underlying table.

Elena views the results of running the Practice List Query and decides that she would like to make some changes to the query design. She switches to the Query Design window to make the changes.

To switch to the Query Design window:

1. Click the **Query View** button on the toolbar. Access opens the Query Design window.

The Query Design Window

The Query Design window contains a standard title bar, menu bar, toolbar, and status bar. As shown in Figure 4-4, the title bar displays the query type, Select Query, and the query name, Practice List Query. You can use the Query Design window to make changes to existing queries. In addition to the standard window components, the Query Design window contains a field list and the Query Design grid. The field list, which appears in the upper-left part of the window, states the table name and contains all the fields from the table you are querying. The primary key is shown in bold. If your query needs fields from two or more tables, each table's field list appears in this upper portion of the Query Design window.

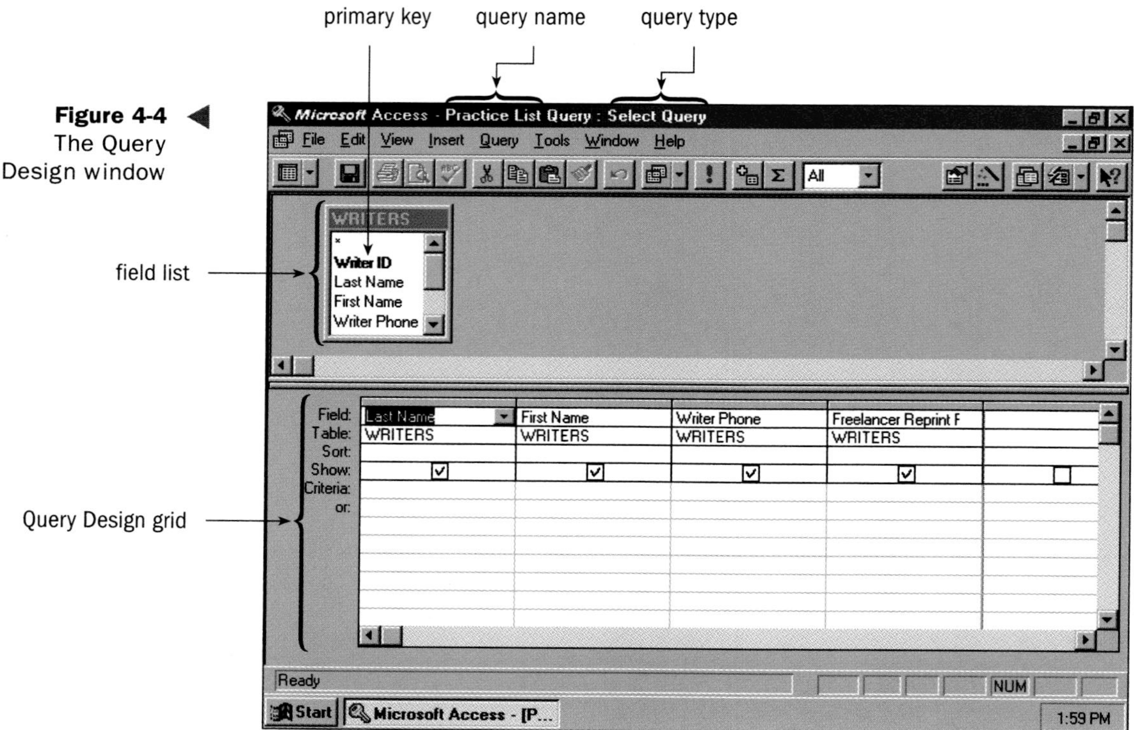

Figure 4-4 The Query Design window

In the Query Design window, you can specify the data you want to see by constructing a query by example. When you create a **query by example (QBE)**, you give Access an example of the information you are requesting. Access then retrieves the information that precisely matches your example. In the Query Design grid, you include the fields and record selection criteria for the information you want to obtain. Each column in the Query Design grid contains specifications about a field you will use in the query. If the Query Design grid contains many fields depending upon your computer system you may need to use the horizontal scroll bar to view all of them.

Elena thinks reading the Practice List Query results will be easier if the First Name field precedes the Last Name field. She uses the Query Design grid in the Query Design window to make this change.

Moving a Field

The Query Design grid displays the fields in the order in which they appear in the query results. Elena moves the First Name field to the left of the Last Name field so that it will appear first in the query results.

To move a field in the Query Design grid:

1. Click the **First Name** field selector to highlight the entire column. (The field selectors are the gray bars above the Field row.) Click the **First Name** field selector again and drag the pointer, which appears as ⇱, to the left. When the pointer is anywhere in the Last Name column, release the mouse button. Access moves the First Name field to the left of the Last Name field. See Figure 4-5.

Figure 4-5 The Query Design grid showing moved fields

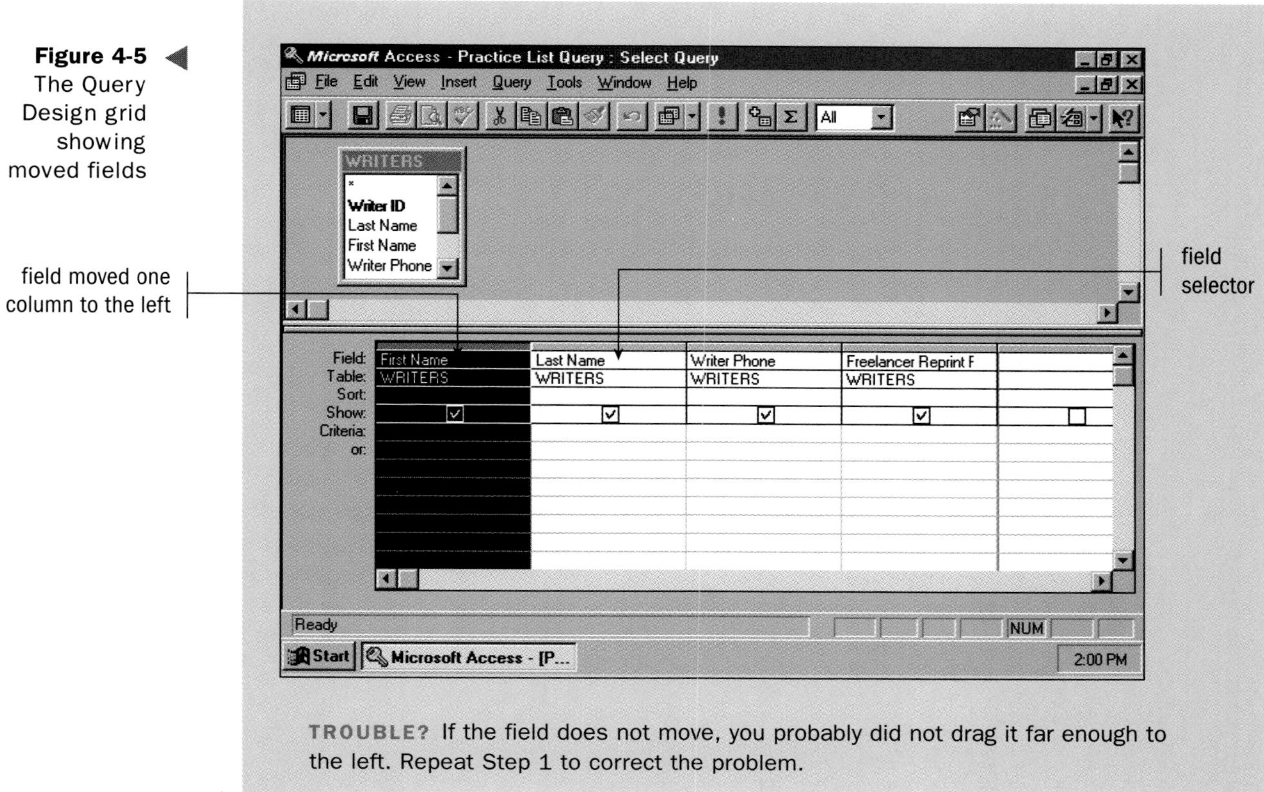

TROUBLE? If the field does not move, you probably did not drag it far enough to the left. Repeat Step 1 to correct the problem.

Elena now runs the query results for the modified query design.

To run a query:

1. Click the **Run** button on the toolbar. Access displays the query results in Datasheet View. See Figure 4-6. The First Name field now appears to the left of the Last Name field.

Figure 4-6 Query results with fields rearranged

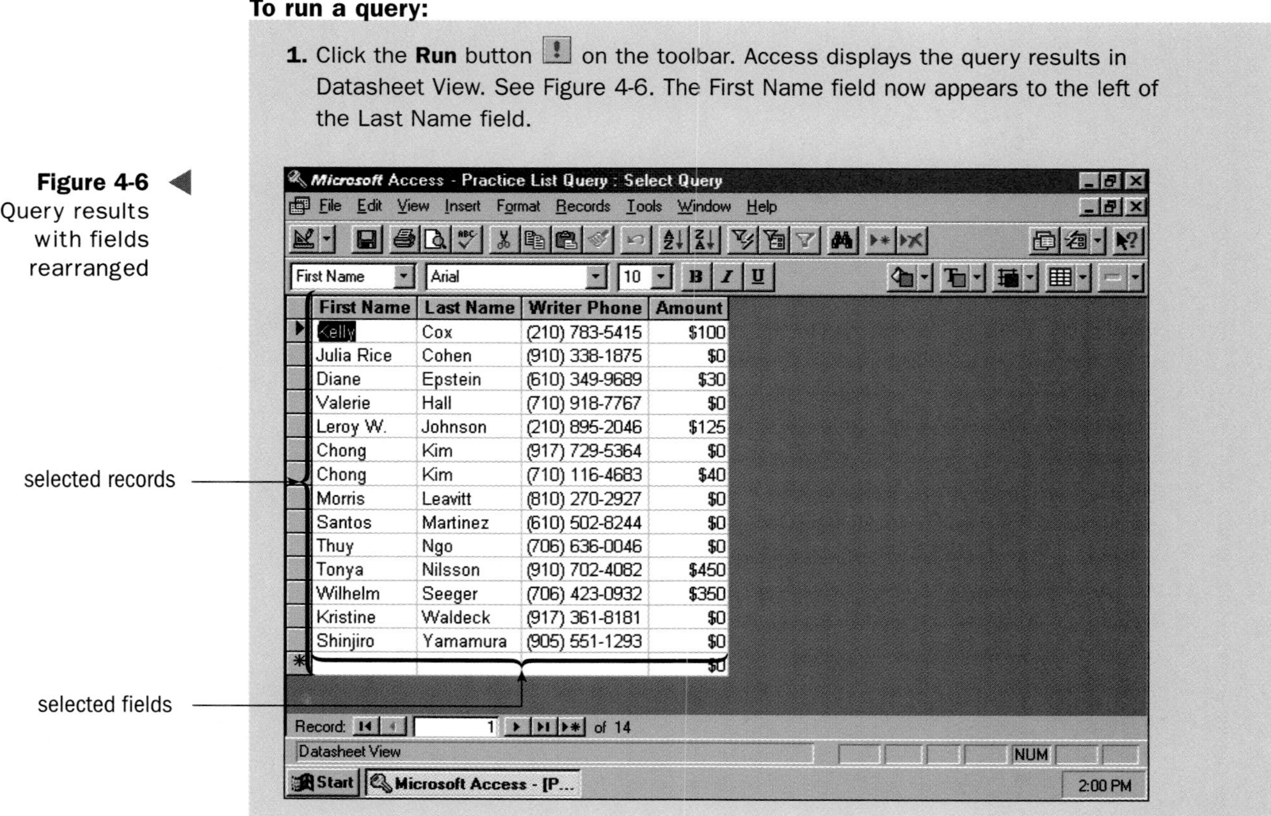

Moving fields in the query has no effect on the underlying WRITERS table. All fields remain in the table in the order you specified in the table structure design. With queries, you can view information any way you want without being restricted by the table structure.

Elena is satisfied with the appearance of the query and saves this modified query design.

To save the query design:

1. Click the **Save** button on the toolbar. Access saves the modified query design.

Remember that when Access saves the query design, the query results are not saved. You can view the query results any time by opening and rerunning the query.

Adding a Field to a Query

Elena is ready to consider the first question she needs to answer from the WRITERS table: What are the names and phone numbers of and amounts owed to all freelancers? Because this is similar to Elena's practice query, she decides to modify the Practice List Query to answer this question. She begins by adding the Freelancer field to the query design. She decides to add the Freelancer field between the Writer Phone and the Freelancer Reprint Payment Amount fields in the Query Design grid.

ADDING A FIELD TO A QUERY DESIGN

- Drag the field name from the field list to the Query Design grid or double-click the field name in the field list. Use the first method if you want to position the new field between other fields in the Query Design grid. When you use the second method, the new field becomes the last field in the Query Design grid.

To add a field to the query design:

1. Click the **Query View** button on the toolbar to switch to the Query Design window.
2. Scroll the field list in the upper panel until the Freelancer field is visible. Drag the **Freelancer** field to the Query Design grid. When the pointer moves over the Query Design grid, it changes to . Position the anywhere in the column for the Freelancer Reprint Payment Amount and release the mouse button.

   The Freelancer field is now inserted between the Writer Phone and the Freelancer Reprint Payment Amount fields in the Query Design grid. See Figure 4-7.

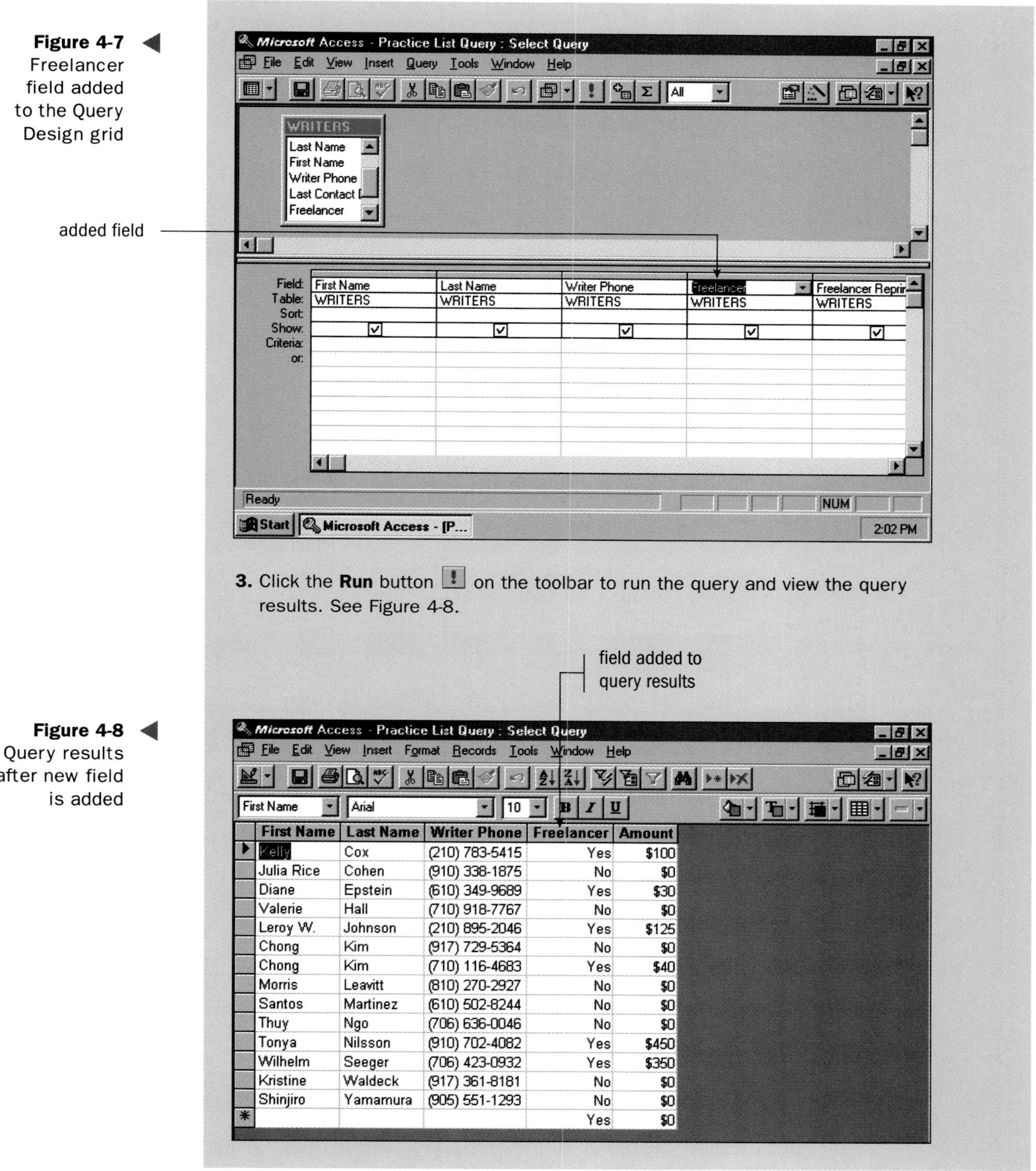

Figure 4-7 Freelancer field added to the Query Design grid

3. Click the **Run** button on the toolbar to run the query and view the query results. See Figure 4-8.

Figure 4-8 Query results after new field is added

First Name	Last Name	Writer Phone	Freelancer	Amount
Kelly	Cox	(210) 783-5415	Yes	$100
Julia Rice	Cohen	(910) 338-1875	No	$0
Diane	Epstein	(610) 349-9689	Yes	$30
Valerie	Hall	(710) 918-7767	No	$0
Leroy W.	Johnson	(210) 895-2046	Yes	$125
Chong	Kim	(917) 729-5364	No	$0
Chong	Kim	(710) 116-4683	Yes	$40
Morris	Leavitt	(810) 270-2927	No	$0
Santos	Martinez	(610) 502-8244	No	$0
Thuy	Ngo	(706) 636-0046	No	$0
Tonya	Nilsson	(910) 702-4082	Yes	$450
Wilhelm	Seeger	(706) 423-0932	Yes	$350
Kristine	Waldeck	(917) 361-8181	No	$0
Shinjiro	Yamamura	(905) 551-1293	No	$0
			Yes	$0

Elena has completed the basic design of the freelancer list query for Brian, although she still needs to modify it. Before making any further changes, however, Elena decides to save the query design under a different name.

Elena saves the query, so that she and others can open and run it again in the future. Since she has modified the Practice List Query, Access will use that name for this query if Elena uses the Save button to save it now. Instead, Elena wants to save this query under a new name: Freelancer List for Brian Query.

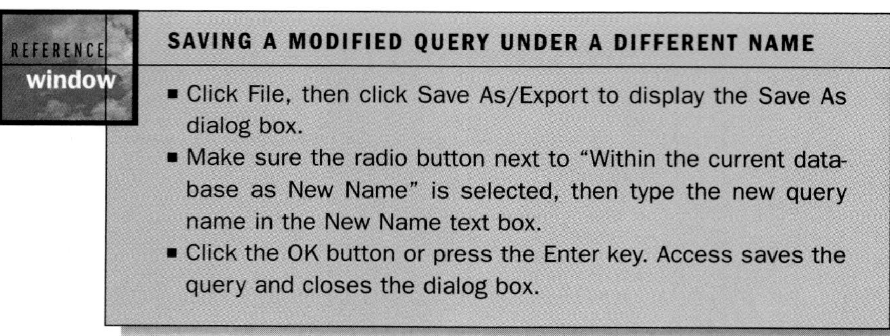

REFERENCE window

SAVING A MODIFIED QUERY UNDER A DIFFERENT NAME

- Click File, then click Save As/Export to display the Save As dialog box.
- Make sure the radio button next to "Within the current database as New Name" is selected, then type the new query name in the New Name text box.
- Click the OK button or press the Enter key. Access saves the query and closes the dialog box.

To save a query with a new name:

1. Click **File**, then click **Save As/Export**. The Save As dialog box opens, with the current query name highlighted.
2. Type **Freelancer List for Brian Query** in the New Name text box.
3. Click the **OK** button. Access saves the query, and the Save As dialog box closes.
4. Click the **Close** button ☒ for the Query Design window. The Database window is now the active window.
5. If necessary, click the **Queries** tab to display the Queries list. Access displays both queries (Practice List Query and Freelancer List for Brian Query) in the Queries list. See Figure 4-9.

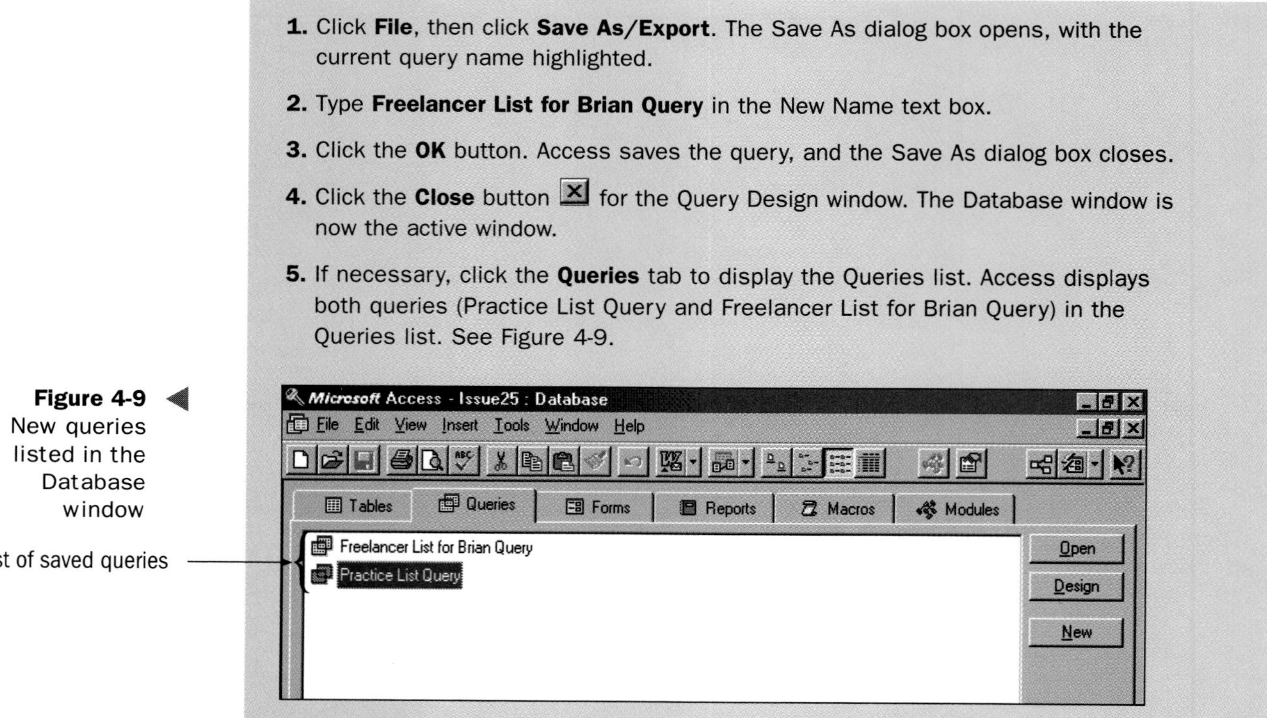

Figure 4-9 New queries listed in the Database window

You can use the same procedure to save a query from the Design View window. If you try to close either the Design View window or the Datasheet View window without saving the query, Access displays a dialog box asking if you want to save the query. If you click the Yes button, Access saves the query under its current name.

Opening a Saved Query

Elena reviews the design of the Freelancer List for Brian Query. She already knows that the query results should display only the records for writers who are freelancers. Elena realizes there will then be no need to display the Freelancer column in the query results. She opens the Freelancer List for Brian Query to make these changes.

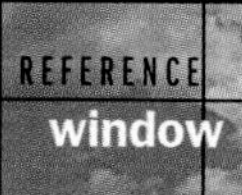

OPENING A SAVED QUERY

- Click the Query tab to display the Queries list in the Database window.
- To view the query results, click the query name and then click the Open button.
- To view the query design, click the query name and then click the Design View button.

To open a saved query to change its design:

1. If necessary, click the **Queries** tab to display the Queries list.
2. If necessary, click **Freelancer List for Brian Query** in the Queries list to select it, then click the **Design** button. The Query Design window appears with the saved query on the screen.

Defining Record Selection Criteria

Elena wants to modify the query design to include information on freelancers only. Some of the other questions in her list include finding contact information on Valerie Hall and Wilhelm Seeger and locating writers who have specific area codes. Unlike her Practice List Query, which selected some fields but all records from the WRITERS table, these questions ask Access to select specific records based on a criterion. Remember that a criterion determines which records are selected, based on conditions set for a field value.

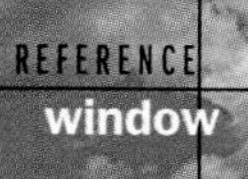

DEFINING RECORD SELECTION CRITERIA

- In the Query Design grid, click the Criteria text box for the field for which you want to define a selection criterion.
- Enter the selection criterion. Use an exact match, pattern match, list-of-values match, range-of-values match, or non-matching value criterion.
- Click the Run button on the toolbar. Access executes the query, selects the records that match the selection criterion, and displays the selected records in the Datasheet View window.

To define a condition for a field, you place the condition in the Query Design grid Criteria text box for the field. When you select records based on one criterion (for a single field), you are using a simple condition. To form a simple condition, you enter a comparison operator and a value. A **comparison operator** asks Access to compare the relationship between the criterion value and the field value and to select the record if the relationship is true. For example, because Elena wants records selected if they meet the condition that a writer is a freelancer, the simple condition =Yes for the Freelancer field selects all records having Freelancer field values equal to Yes. The Access comparison operators are shown in Figure 4-10.

Figure 4-10 Access comparison operators

Operator	Meaning	Example
=	equal to (optional, default operator)	="Hall"
<	less than	<#1/1/94#
<=	less than or equal to	<=100
>	greater than	>"C400"
>=	greater than or equal to	>=18.75
<>	not equal to	<>"Hall"
Between ... And...	between two values (inclusive)	Between 50 And 325
In ()	in a list of values	In ("Hall", "Seeger")
Like	matches a pattern that includes wildcards	Like "706*"

When you specify a comparison value for a Text field, the value should be enclosed in quotation marks. The quotation marks are optional for text that contains no spaces or punctuation, but it is usually a good idea to use them whenever you specify a text value. Similarly, when entering a date or time value in a Date/Time field, enclose the value with the # character.

Simple conditions fit into the following categories, you'll have an opportunity to use them in this tutorial:

- exact match
- pattern match
- list-of-values match
- non-matching value
- range-of-values match

Using an Exact Match

An **exact match** selects records that have a value for the selected field exactly matching the simple condition value. Elena modifies the Freelancer List for Brian Query to select only the records for freelancers. She enters the simple condition =Yes in the Criteria text box for the Freelancer field. When Elena runs the query, Access selects records that have the exact value Yes in the Freelancer field.

To select records that match a specific value:

1. Click the **Criteria** text box in the Query Design grid for the Freelancer field and then type **=Yes**. See Figure 4-11. Access will select a record only if the Freelancer field value is Yes. (You can also omit the equals symbol and just type Yes, because the equals sign is the default comparison operator automatically inserted by Access. However, it is good practice to type the comparison operator.)

Figure 4-11 Record selection based on exact match

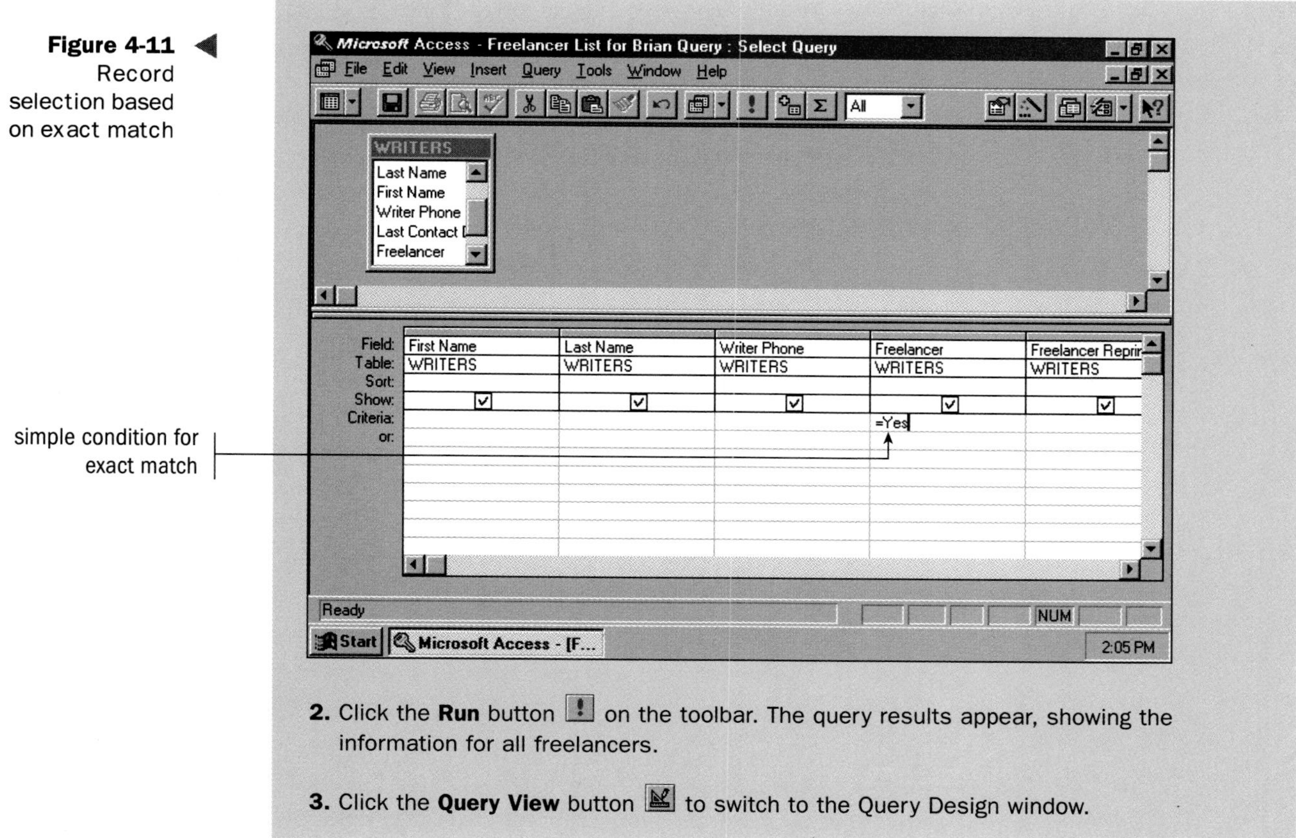

2. Click the **Run** button on the toolbar. The query results appear, showing the information for all freelancers.

3. Click the **Query View** button to switch to the Query Design window.

Now that the query design selects only the freelancer records, it is not necessary to display the Freelancer column in the query results. Elena next excludes the Freelancer column from the display.

Excluding a Field from the Query Results

Elena cannot delete the Freelancer column from the Query Design grid because it is needed to specify the selection criterion. Instead, she can click the Show box in the Query Design grid for the Freelancer column to remove the check mark from the Show box and prevent the field from appearing in the query results. Clicking the Show box again re-inserts the check mark in the Show box and includes the field in the query results.

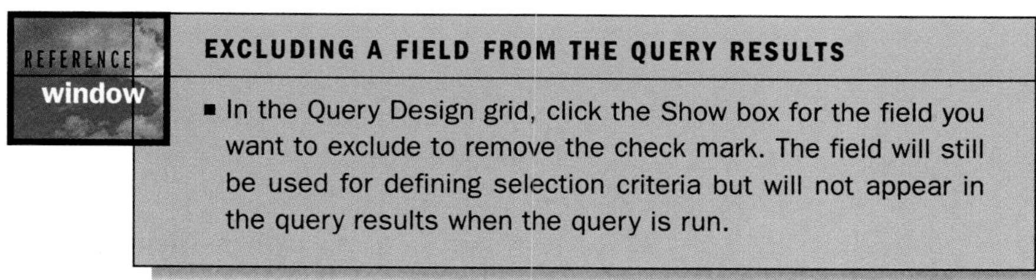

REFERENCE window

EXCLUDING A FIELD FROM THE QUERY RESULTS

- In the Query Design grid, click the Show box for the field you want to exclude to remove the check mark. The field will still be used for defining selection criteria but will not appear in the query results when the query is run.

To exclude the Freelancer field from the query results:

1. Click the **Show** box in the Freelancer column to remove the check mark. Access will no longer show the Freelancer field in the query results.
2. Click the **Run** button on the toolbar to display the query results. Only records for freelancers are selected, and the Freelancer field does not appear in the query results.

Elena is now satisfied with the design of the Freelancer List for Brian Query. She prints the query results, saves the query design, and returns to the Database window.

To print the query results and save the query design:

1. Click the **Print** button on the toolbar. Access prints the query results.
2. Click the **Save** button on the toolbar. Access saves the changes that you have made to the query design.
3. Click the **Close** button in the Datasheet View window. Access closes the window and returns to the Database window.

Using a Pattern Match

The second question on Elena's list is to find the contact information for writers with specific area codes. Elena decides to use a **pattern match**, which selects records that have a value for the selected field matching the pattern of the simple condition value, in this case, to select writers with 706 area codes. Elena does this using the Like comparison operator.

The Like comparison operator selects records by matching field values to a specific pattern that includes one or more wildcard characters—asterisk (*), question mark (?), and number symbol (#). The asterisk represents any string of characters, the question mark represents any single alphabetic character, and the number symbol represents any single digit. Using a pattern match is similar to using an exact match, except that a pattern match includes wildcard characters.

As further practice, Elena also decides to create the query design directly in the Query Design window.

REFERENCE window

CREATING A QUERY DESIGN IN THE QUERY DESIGN WINDOW

- In the Queries list in the Database window, click the New button.
- Make sure that Design View is selected, then click the OK button.
- In the Show Table dialog box, select the table(s) on which the query is based, then click the OK button.
- In the Query Design window, select the fields to appear in the query results.
- Specify selection criteria and sorting options.
- Click the Save button on the toolbar to save the query design.

To create the query design in the Query Design window:

1. In the Queries list of the Database window, click the **New** button. Access displays the New Query dialog box. Design View is highlighted in the list box.
2. Click the **OK** button. Access displays the Query Design window and the Show Table dialog box.

   The Show Table dialog box allows you to select the tables and queries to be used in the query design. Elena needs only the WRITERS table for this query.
3. Click **WRITERS**, then click the **Add** button. See Figure 4-12.

Figure 4-12 The Show Table dialog box

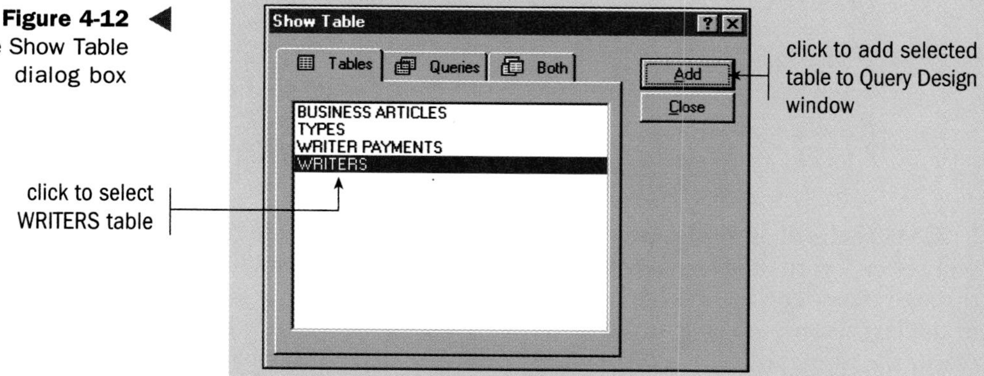

4. Click the **Close** button to close the Show Table dialog box. The WRITERS table now appears in the upper panel of the Query Design window. No fields appear in the Query Design grid because no fields have been selected yet.

Elena wants to use all the fields from the WRITERS table in the query. She could drag each field individually, but Access has two other methods for moving all of the fields at once. One method is to click the asterisk at the top of the field list. Access then places WRITERS.* in the Query Design grid, which represents all fields of the WRITERS table. The advantage of using this method over dragging each field individually is that you do not need to change the query if you add or delete fields from the underlying table structure. All changes to the table's fields will automatically appear in the query. However, this does not allow rearranging the order of the fields, sorting the records, or adding selection criteria. Elena uses a third method instead.

To include all fields in the query:

1. Double-click the **title bar** of the WRITERS field list to highlight, or select, all the fields in the table. Notice that the asterisk in the first row of the field list is not highlighted.
2. Click and hold the mouse button anywhere in the highlighted area of the WRITERS field list, then drag the pointer to the Query Design grid's first column Field box. As you near the destination Field box, the pointer changes to [pointer icon]. Release the mouse button in the Field box. Access adds each field in a separate Field box, from left to right. See Figure 4-13. If necessary, scroll right in the Query Design grid to see the fields that are off the screen.

Figure 4-13 Adding all fields to the query by the dragging method

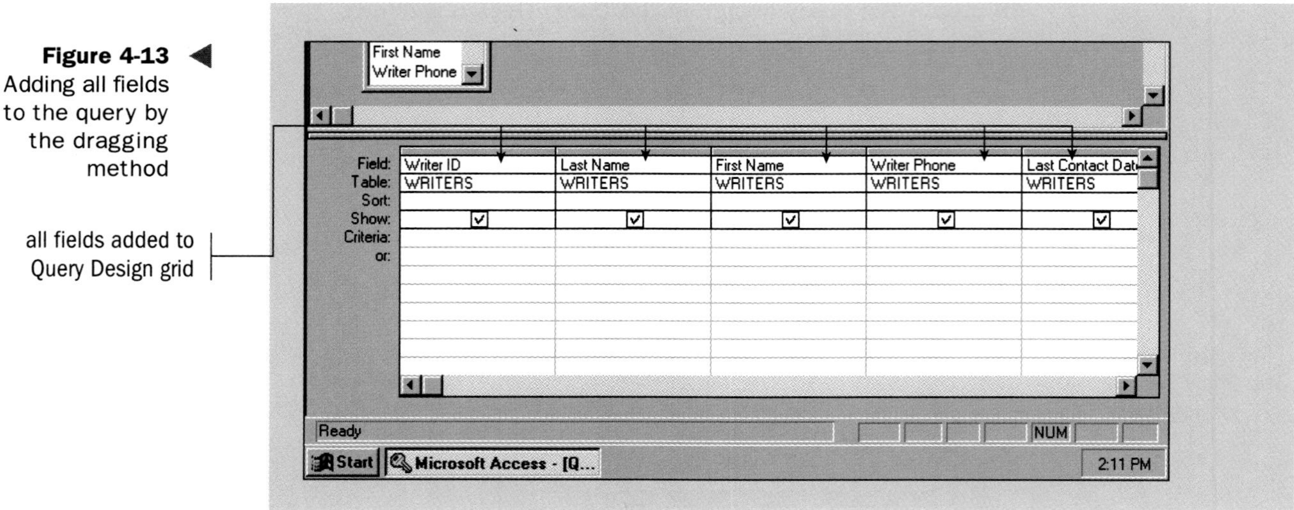

Elena enters the simple condition Like "706*" for the Writer Phone field so that Access will select records that have a Writer Phone field value containing 706 in positions one through three. The asterisk (*) wildcard character specifies that any characters can appear in the last seven positions of the field value. Because the Writer Phone field has an input mask, the displayed placeholder characters (the parentheses, space, and hyphen) are not part of the field value.

To select records that match a specific pattern:

1. Click the **Criteria** text box in the Query Design grid for the Writer Phone field and then type **Like "706*"**. See Figure 4-14. (Note that Access will automatically add Like and the quotation marks to the simple condition if you omit them.)

Figure 4-14 Record selection based on matching a specific pattern

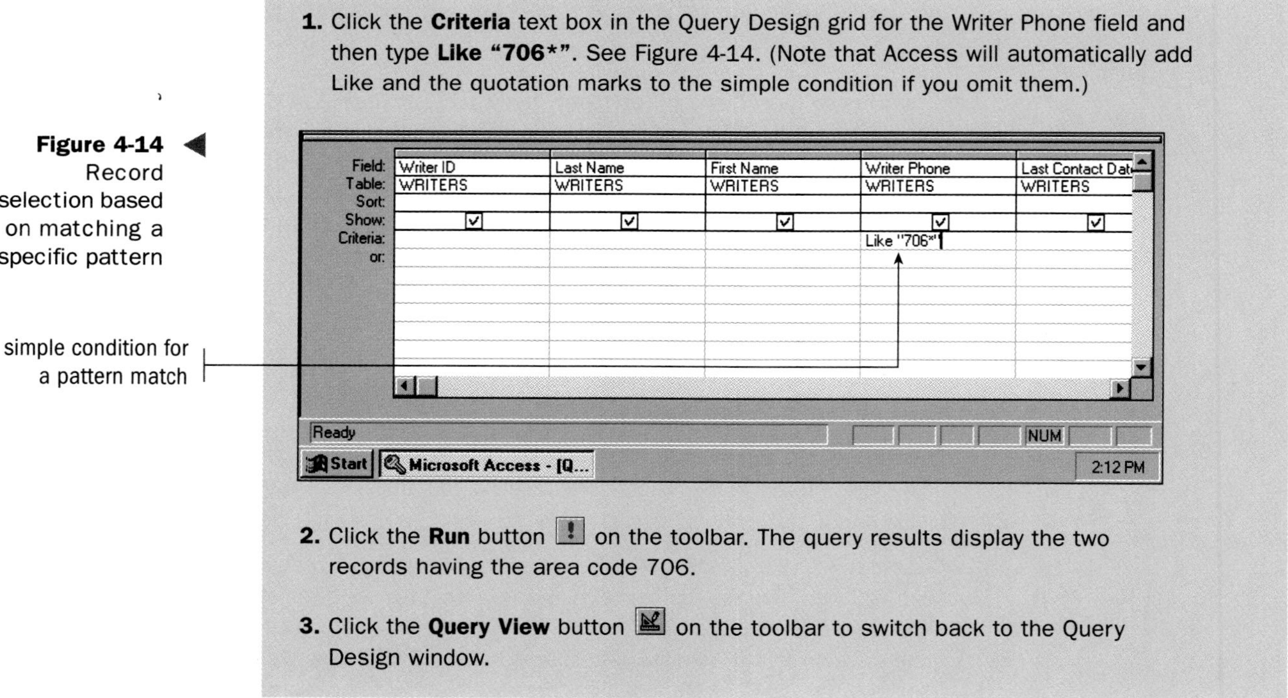

2. Click the **Run** button on the toolbar. The query results display the two records having the area code 706.

3. Click the **Query View** button on the toolbar to switch back to the Query Design window.

Elena prints her results and decides that she will next obtain the contact information for Valerie Hall and Wilhelm Seeger by using a list-of-values match.

Using a List-of-Values Match

A **list-of-values match** selects records that have a value for the selected field matching one of two or more simple condition values. Elena uses the In comparison operator to create the condition to find the contact information needed by Harold for Valerie Hall and Wilhelm Seeger. The In comparison operator allows you to define a condition with two or more values. If a record's field value matches at least one value from the list of values, Access selects that record.

Elena wants records selected if the Last Name field value is equal to Hall or to Seeger. These are the values she will use with the In comparison operator. The simple condition she enters is: In ("Hall","Seeger"). Because matching is not case-sensitive, hall and HALL and other variations will also match Hall. Notice that when you make a list of values, you place them inside parentheses.

To select records having a field value that matches a value in a list of values:

1. Click the **Criteria** text box for the Writer Phone field, press the **F2** key to highlight the entire condition, and then press the **Delete** key to remove the previous condition.
2. Scroll left in the Query Design grid if necessary to display the Last Name column. Click the **Criteria** text box for the Last Name field and then type **In ("Hall", "Seeger")**. See Figure 4-15.

Figure 4-15 Record selection based on matching field values to a list of values

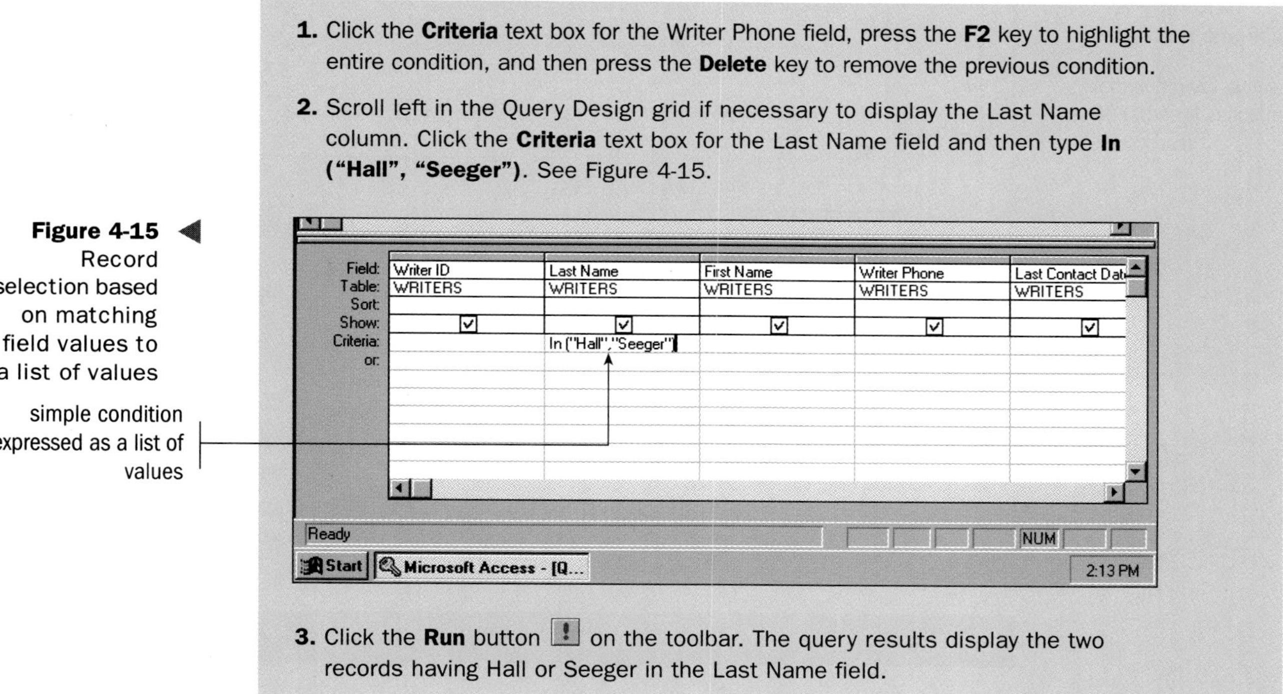

3. Click the **Run** button on the toolbar. The query results display the two records having Hall or Seeger in the Last Name field.

Elena prints the query results for Harold and proceeds to her next query.

Using a Non-Matching Value

Judith offers to help Elena with the task of contacting the writers and will call those writers with 706 area codes; Elena will contact the rest. Elena therefore needs to find all writers who do not have 706 area codes. To obtain this information, Elena uses a **non-matching value**, which selects records that have a value for the selected field that does not match the simple condition value. She will use a combination of the Like comparison operator and the Not logical operator. The Not logical operator allows you to find records that do not match a value. If Elena wants to find all records that do not have Hall in the Last Name field, for example, her condition is Not ="Hall".

Elena enters the simple condition Not Like "706*" in the Writer Phone field to select writers who do not have 706 area codes.

To select records having a field value that does not match a specific pattern:

1. Click the **Query View** button on the toolbar to switch back to the Query Design window.
2. If necessary, click the **Criteria** text box for the Last Name field, press the **F2** key to highlight the entire condition, and then press the **Delete** key to remove the previous condition.
3. Click the **Criteria** text box for the Writer Phone field and then type **Not Like "706*"**. See Figure 4-16. Access will select a record only if the Writer Phone field value does not have a 706 area code.

Figure 4-16 Record selection based on not matching a specific pattern

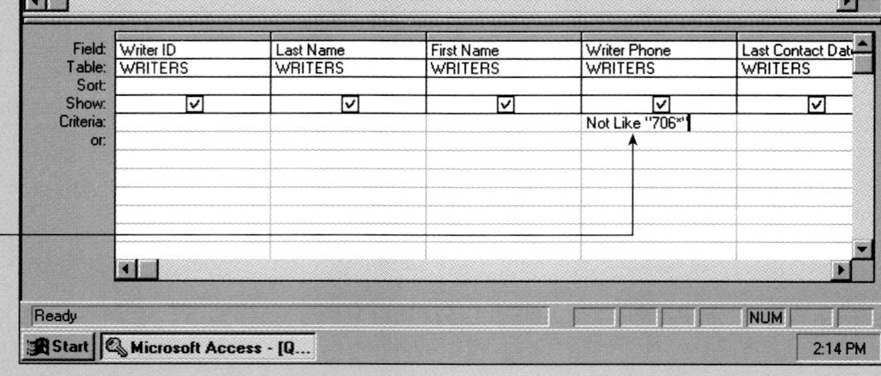

4. Click the **Run** button on the toolbar. The query results display only those records having a Writer Phone field value that does not have a 706 area code. Elena prints the results.
5. Click the **Query View** button to switch back to the Query Design window.

Elena is ready to go on to the next question on her list when Harold drops by with a new request. He needs to know all writers who were last contacted prior to 1994 for a meeting he will attend in an hour. To find this information, Elena will use a range-of-values match.

Using a Range-of-Values Match

A **range-of-values match** selects records that have a value for the selected field within a range specified in the simple condition. For Harold's request, Elena uses the less than (<) comparison operator with a date value of 1/1/94 and enters <#1/1/94# as the simple condition. Access will select records that have, in the Last Contact Date field, a date anywhere in the range of dates prior to January 1, 1994. You place date and time values inside number symbols (#). (If you omit the number symbols, Access will automatically include them, but it is good practice to include them yourself.)

To select records having a field value in a range of values:

1. Click the **Criteria** text box for the Writer Phone field, press the **F2** key to highlight the entire condition, and then press the **Delete** key to remove the previous condition.
2. Click the **Criteria** text box for the Last Contact Date field and then type **<#1/1/94#**. See Figure 4-17. Access will select a record only if the Last Contact Date field value is a date prior to January 1, 1994.

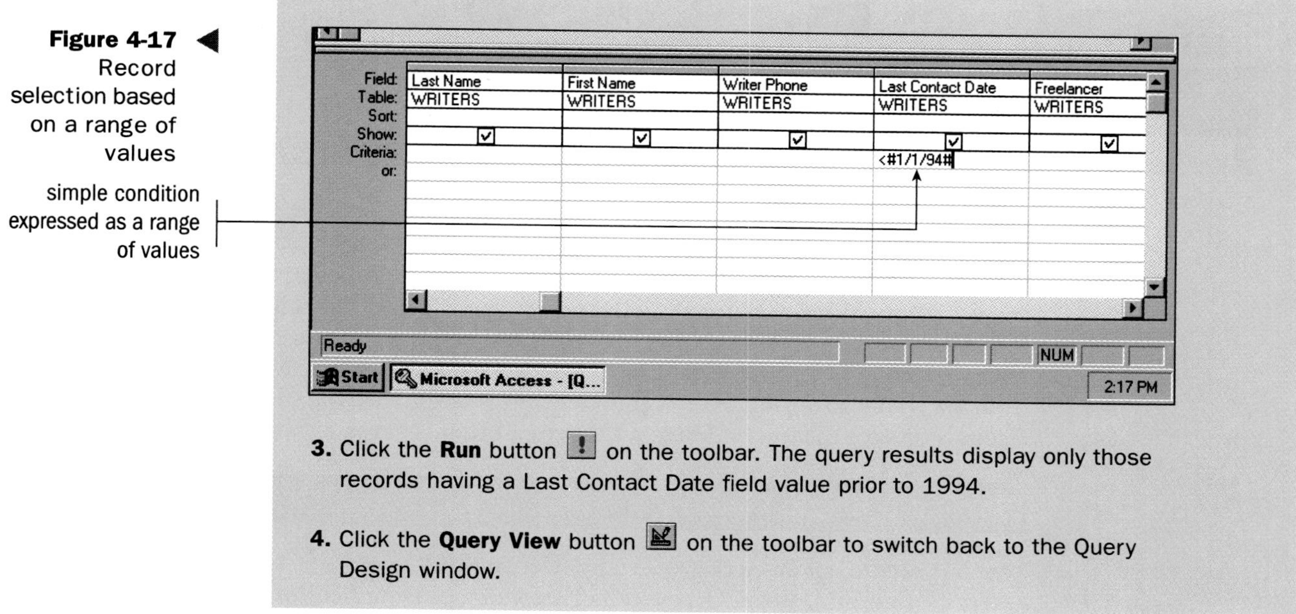

Figure 4-17 Record selection based on a range of values

3. Click the **Run** button on the toolbar. The query results display only those records having a Last Contact Date field value prior to 1994.

4. Click the **Query View** button on the toolbar to switch back to the Query Design window.

As Elena finishes and prints her query, Harold stops by to pick up the information and also reminds her that she also needs to attend the meeting. Because creating this query was easy and she wants to conserve disk space, Elena closes the Query Design window without saving the query.

To close the Query Design window without saving the query:

1. Click the Query Design window **Close** button. A dialog box asks if you want to save changes to the design of the Query1 query.

2. Click the **No** button. Access closes the Query Design window without saving the query.

If you want to take a break and resume the tutorial at a later time, exit Access. When you resume the tutorial, place your Student Disk in the appropriate drive, start Access, open the Issue25 database in the Tutorial folder on your Student Disk, click the Queries tab in the Database window to display the Queries list, and maximize the Database window.

Quick Check

1. What is the Simple Query Wizard?
2. In what format do the query results appear? What are the advantages of this format?
3. What is QBE?
4. What are two methods for adding a field from a table to the Query Design grid?
5. What are the two components of a simple condition?
6. How do you exclude a field that appears in the Query Design grid from the query results?
7. What comparison operator is used to select records based on a specific pattern?
8. When do you use the In comparison operator?

SESSION 4.2

In this session, you will learn to sort data in a query, print query results, define multiple selection criteria, and perform calculations in a query.

Sorting Data

After the meeting, Elena resumes work on the Issue25 database queries. The next item on her list of questions asks for writers arranged in order by last contact date. Because the WRITERS table displays records in Writer ID, or primary key, sequence, records in the query results will appear in Writer ID sequence as well. Elena will need to sort records from the table to produce the requested information. If you sort records in the query results and save the query design, the sorting order is saved as well.

Sorting a Single Field

You sort records in an Access query by selecting one or more fields to be sort keys in the Query Design grid. Elena chooses the Last Contact Date field to be the sort key for her next query. Because her last Access task was to return to the Database window, she first opens the Query Design window. Elena then adds all the fields from the WRITERS table to the Query Design grid.

To start a new query for a single table:

1. Make sure the Database window is open and maximized and that the Queries list is visible. Click the **New** button to open the New Query dialog box.
2. Make sure that Design View is selected, then click the **OK** button. Access opens the Query Design window.
3. Click **WRITERS** in the Show Table dialog box, then click the **Add** button. The WRITERS table appears in the upper panel of the Query Design window.
4. Click the **Close** button ☒ to close the Show Table dialog box.
5. Double-click the title bar of the WRITERS field list to highlight all the fields in the table.
6. Click and hold the mouse button anywhere in the highlighted area of the WRITERS field list, and then drag the pointer to the Query Design grid's first column Field text box and release the mouse button when the pointer changes to 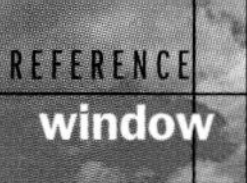. Access adds all the fields from the WRITERS table to separate boxes in the Query Design grid.

Elena now selects the Last Contact Date field to be the sort key.

REFERENCE window

SELECTING A SORT KEY IN THE QUERY DESIGN WINDOW

- Click the Sort text box in the Query Design grid for the field designated as the sort key.
- Click the Sort list arrow to display the Sort list.
- Click Ascending or Descending from the Sort list. Access displays the selected sort order in the Sort text box.

Elena decides a descending sort order for the Last Contact Date field (with most recent dates shown first) will be the best way to display the query results, and she now selects the sort key and its sort order. She does this by clicking the Sort list arrow for the Last Contact Date column in the Query Design grid.

To select a sort key and view sorted query results:

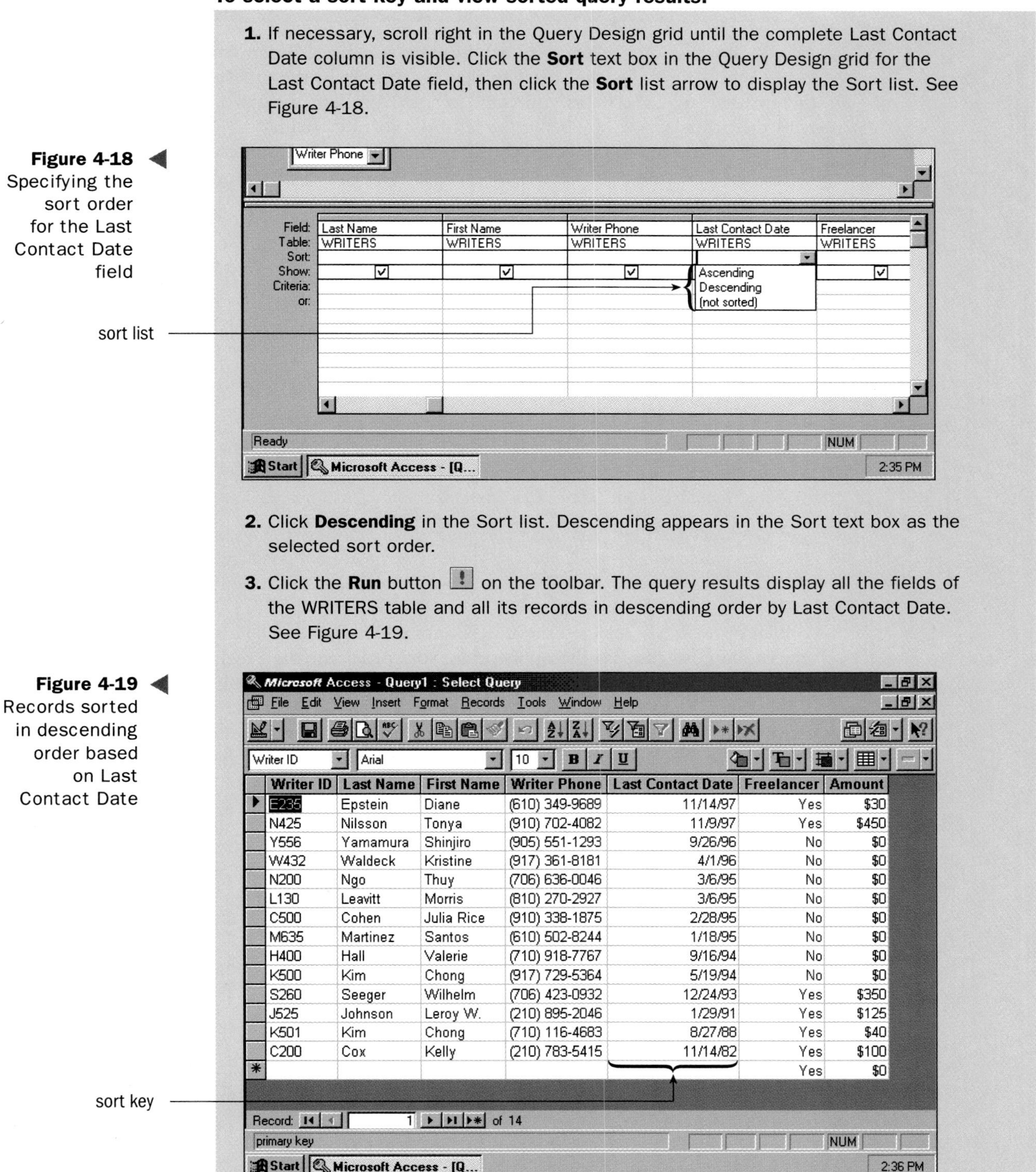

1. If necessary, scroll right in the Query Design grid until the complete Last Contact Date column is visible. Click the **Sort** text box in the Query Design grid for the Last Contact Date field, then click the **Sort** list arrow to display the Sort list. See Figure 4-18.

Figure 4-18 Specifying the sort order for the Last Contact Date field

2. Click **Descending** in the Sort list. Descending appears in the Sort text box as the selected sort order.

3. Click the **Run** button on the toolbar. The query results display all the fields of the WRITERS table and all its records in descending order by Last Contact Date. See Figure 4-19.

Figure 4-19 Records sorted in descending order based on Last Contact Date

Writer ID	Last Name	First Name	Writer Phone	Last Contact Date	Freelancer	Amount
E235	Epstein	Diane	(610) 349-9689	11/14/97	Yes	$30
N425	Nilsson	Tonya	(910) 702-4082	11/9/97	Yes	$450
Y556	Yamamura	Shinjiro	(905) 551-1293	9/26/96	No	$0
W432	Waldeck	Kristine	(917) 361-8181	4/1/96	No	$0
N200	Ngo	Thuy	(706) 636-0046	3/6/95	No	$0
L130	Leavitt	Morris	(810) 270-2927	3/6/95	No	$0
C500	Cohen	Julia Rice	(910) 338-1875	2/28/95	No	$0
M635	Martinez	Santos	(610) 502-8244	1/18/95	No	$0
H400	Hall	Valerie	(710) 918-7767	9/16/94	No	$0
K500	Kim	Chong	(917) 729-5364	5/19/94	No	$0
S260	Seeger	Wilhelm	(706) 423-0932	12/24/93	Yes	$350
J525	Johnson	Leroy W.	(210) 895-2046	1/29/91	Yes	$125
K501	Kim	Chong	(710) 116-4683	8/27/88	Yes	$40
C200	Cox	Kelly	(210) 783-5415	11/14/82	Yes	$100
					Yes	$0

Elena studies the query results and decides the information would be more helpful if it was also sorted into staff writers and freelancers. This entails using two sort keys. Elena needs to select Freelancer as the primary sort key and Last Contact Date as the secondary sort key.

Sorting Multiple Fields

Access allows you to select up to 10 different sort keys. When you have two or more sort keys, Access first uses the sort key that is leftmost in the Query Design grid. You must therefore arrange the fields you want to sort from left to right in the Query Design grid, with the primary sort key being the leftmost sort key field.

The Freelancer field appears to the right of the Last Contact Date field in the Query Design grid. Because the Freelancer field is the primary sort key, Elena must move it to the left of the Last Contact Date field.

To move a field in the Query Design grid:

1. Click the **Query View** button on the toolbar to switch back to the Query Design window.
2. Click the **right arrow** button of the Query Design grid horizontal scroll bar until the Last Contact Date and Freelancer fields are visible.
3. Click the **Freelancer** field selector to highlight the entire column.
4. Click the **Freelancer** field selector again and drag the pointer, which appears as , to the left. When the pointer is anywhere in the Last Contact Date column, release the mouse button. Access moves the Freelancer field one column to the left.

   TROUBLE? If the Freelancer column does not move to the correct place, click the Freelancer field selector and move it to the correct position.

Elena previously selected the Last Contact Date field to be a sort key, and it is still in effect. She now chooses the appropriate sort order for the Freelancer field. Elena wants staff writers, which are identified in the Freelancer field by a value of No, to appear first in the query. Elena uses a descending sort order for the Freelancer field so that all No values appear first (Yes is considered to be less than No for the purpose of sorting Yes/No values). The Freelancer field will serve as the primary sort key, and the Last Contact Date field will be the secondary sort key.

To select a sort key:

1. Click the **Sort** text box in the Query Design grid for the Freelancer field, then click the **Sort** list arrow to display the Sort list.
2. Click **Descending** in the Sort list. Descending appears in the Sort text box as the selected sort order. See Figure 4-20.

Figure 4-20 Sort orders specified for two fields

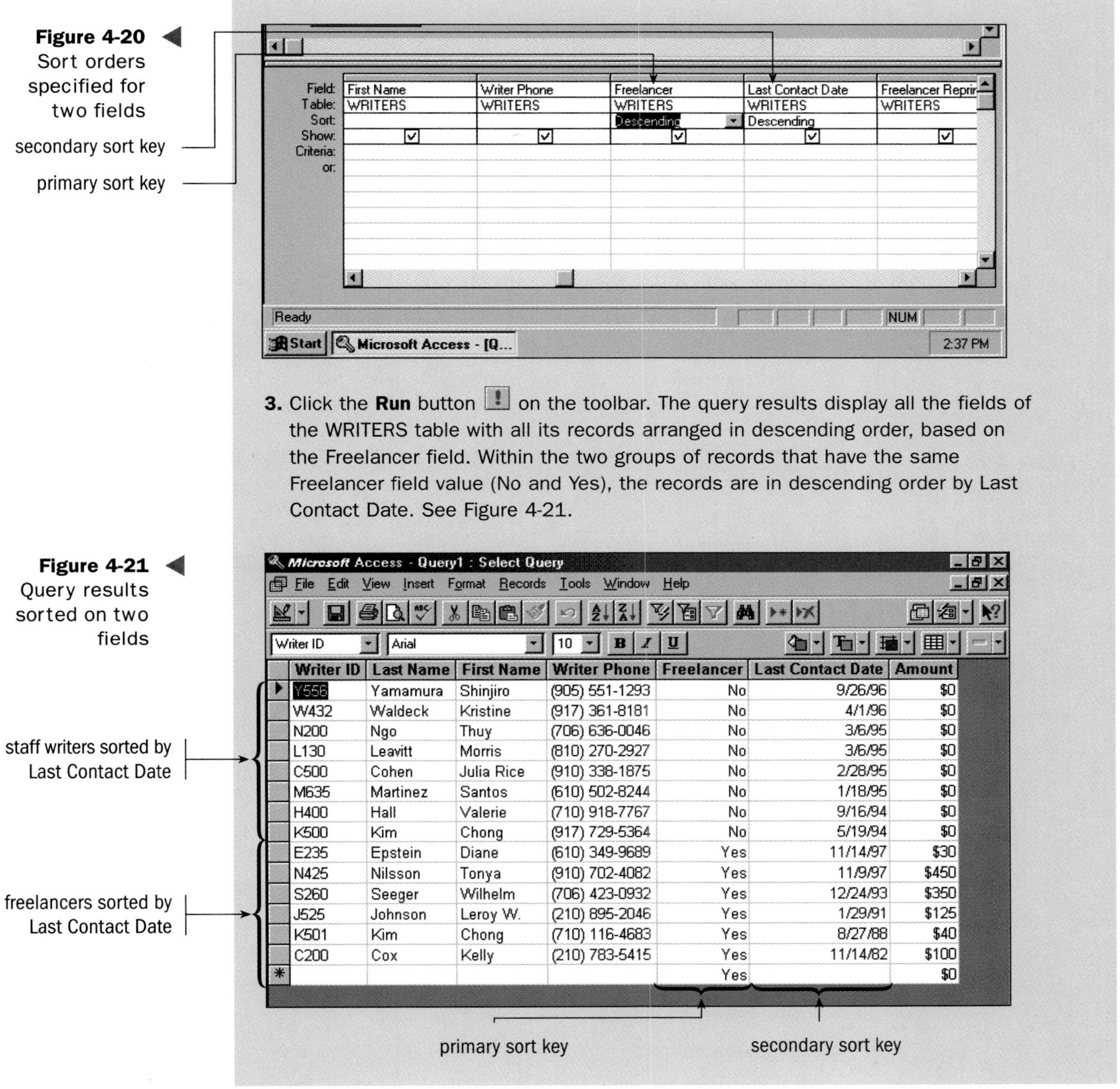

3. Click the **Run** button on the toolbar. The query results display all the fields of the WRITERS table with all its records arranged in descending order, based on the Freelancer field. Within the two groups of records that have the same Freelancer field value (No and Yes), the records are in descending order by Last Contact Date. See Figure 4-21.

Figure 4-21 Query results sorted on two fields

Writer ID	Last Name	First Name	Writer Phone	Freelancer	Last Contact Date	Amount
Y556	Yamamura	Shinjiro	(905) 551-1293	No	9/26/96	$0
W432	Waldeck	Kristine	(917) 361-8181	No	4/1/96	$0
N200	Ngo	Thuy	(706) 636-0046	No	3/6/95	$0
L130	Leavitt	Morris	(810) 270-2927	No	3/6/95	$0
C500	Cohen	Julia Rice	(910) 338-1875	No	2/28/95	$0
M635	Martinez	Santos	(610) 502-8244	No	1/18/95	$0
H400	Hall	Valerie	(710) 918-7767	No	9/16/94	$0
K500	Kim	Chong	(917) 729-5364	No	5/19/94	$0
E235	Epstein	Diane	(610) 349-9689	Yes	11/14/97	$30
N425	Nilsson	Tonya	(910) 702-4082	Yes	11/9/97	$450
S260	Seeger	Wilhelm	(706) 423-0932	Yes	12/24/93	$350
J525	Johnson	Leroy W.	(210) 895-2046	Yes	1/29/91	$125
K501	Kim	Chong	(710) 116-4683	Yes	8/27/88	$40
C200	Cox	Kelly	(210) 783-5415	Yes	11/14/82	$100
*				Yes		$0

Elena is ready to print the query results.

Printing Selected Query Results

Rather than print the staff writers and freelancers together, Elena wants to print the staff writers and the freelancers as separate lists. Elena could change the query to select one group, run the query, print the query results, and then repeat the process for the other group. Instead, she uses a quicker method by selecting one group in the query results, printing the selected query results, and then doing the same for the other group.

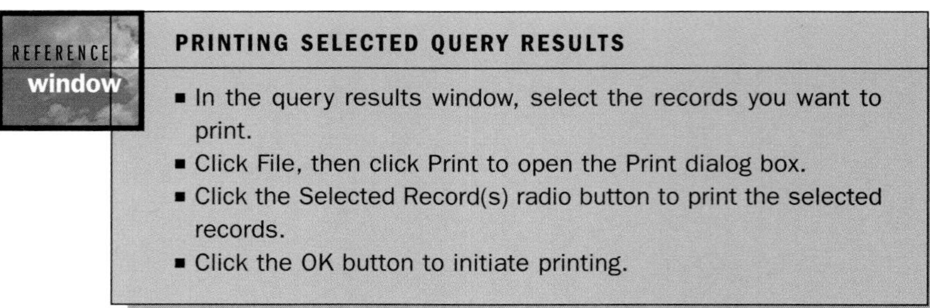

PRINTING SELECTED QUERY RESULTS

- In the query results window, select the records you want to print.
- Click File, then click Print to open the Print dialog box.
- Click the Selected Record(s) radio button to print the selected records.
- Click the OK button to initiate printing.

To print selected query results:

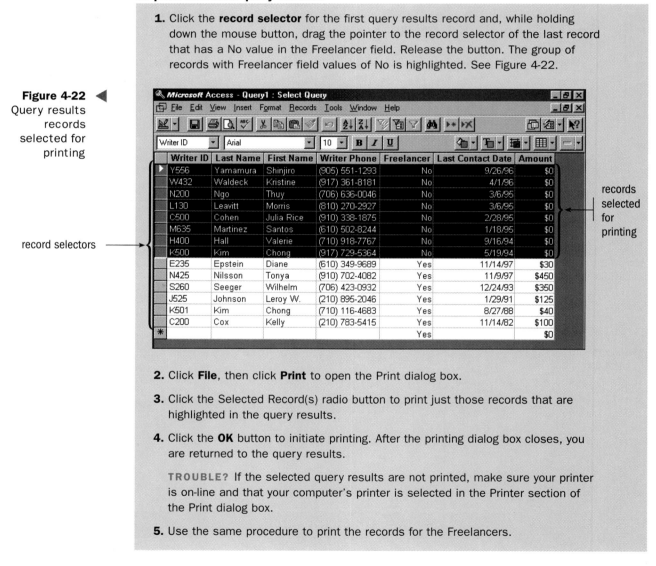

1. Click the **record selector** for the first query results record and, while holding down the mouse button, drag the pointer to the record selector of the last record that has a No value in the Freelancer field. Release the button. The group of records with Freelancer field values of No is highlighted. See Figure 4-22.

Figure 4-22 Query results records selected for printing

Microsoft Access - Query1 : Select Query

File Edit View Insert Format Records Tools Window Help

Writer ID | Arial | 10

Writer ID	Last Name	First Name	Writer Phone	Freelancer	Last Contact Date	Amount
Y556	Yamamura	Shinjiro	(905) 551-1293	No	9/26/96	$0
W432	Waldeck	Kristine	(917) 361-8181	No	4/1/96	$0
N200	Ngo	Thuy	(706) 636-0046	No	3/6/95	$0
L130	Leavitt	Morris	(810) 270-2927	No	3/6/95	$0
C500	Cohen	Julia Rice	(910) 338-1875	No	2/28/95	$0
M635	Martinez	Santos	(610) 502-8244	No	1/18/95	$0
H400	Hall	Valerie	(710) 918-7767	No	9/16/94	$0
K500	Kim	Chong	(917) 729-5364	No	5/19/94	$0
E235	Epstein	Diane	(610) 349-9689	Yes	11/14/97	$30
N425	Nilsson	Tonya	(910) 702-4082	Yes	11/9/97	$450
S260	Seeger	Wilhelm	(706) 423-0932	Yes	12/24/93	$350
J525	Johnson	Leroy W.	(210) 895-2046	Yes	1/29/91	$125
K501	Kim	Chong	(710) 116-4683	Yes	8/27/88	$40
C200	Cox	Kelly	(210) 783-5415	Yes	11/14/82	$100
*				Yes		$0

record selectors

records selected for printing

2. Click **File**, then click **Print** to open the Print dialog box.

3. Click the Selected Record(s) radio button to print just those records that are highlighted in the query results.

4. Click the **OK** button to initiate printing. After the printing dialog box closes, you are returned to the query results.

   TROUBLE? If the selected query results are not printed, make sure your printer is on-line and that your computer's printer is selected in the Printer section of the Print dialog box.

5. Use the same procedure to print the records for the Freelancers.

Defining Multiple Selection Criteria

The previous queries that Elena created involved just one condition—for example, a condition to obtain information for freelancers. What if Elena needs to find all freelancers who were last contacted prior to 1990? This query involves two conditions.

Multiple conditions require you to use logical operators to combine two or more simple conditions. When you want a record selected only if all conditions are met, then you need to use the And logical operator. To use the And logical operator, you place two or more simple conditions in the same Criteria row of the Query Design grid. If a record meets every one of the conditions in the Criteria row, then Access selects the record.

If you place multiple conditions in different Criteria rows, Access selects a record if at least one of the conditions is satisfied. If none of the conditions is satisfied, then Access does not select the record. This is known as the Or logical operator. The difference between the two logical operators is illustrated in Figure 4-23.

Figure 4-23 Logical operators And and Or for multiple selection criteia

Query Design grid using the And logical operator

Criteria: simple condition | simple condition

conditions on same line

Record is selected if:

both conditions are satisfied

Query Design grid using the Or logical operator

Criteria: simple condition

or: simple condition

conditions on separate lines

at least one condition is satisfied

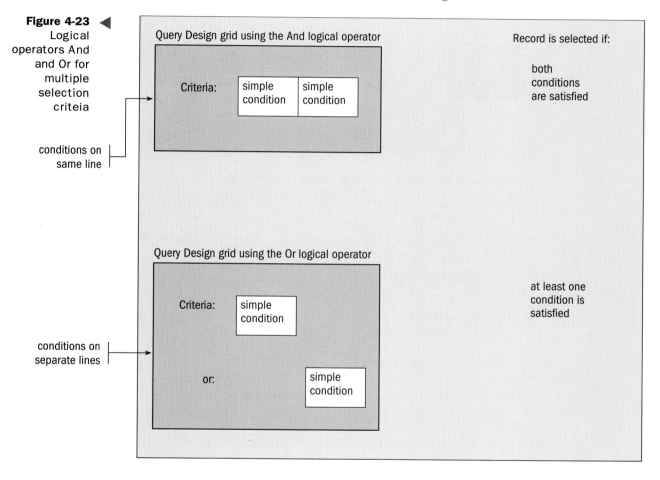

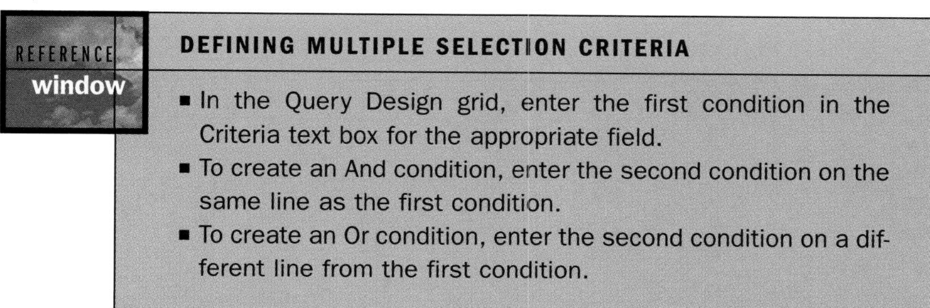
REFERENCE window

DEFINING MULTIPLE SELECTION CRITERIA

- In the Query Design grid, enter the first condition in the Criteria text box for the appropriate field.
- To create an And condition, enter the second condition on the same line as the first condition.
- To create an Or condition, enter the second condition on a different line from the first condition.

The use of the word "and" in a question is usually a clue that you should use the And logical operator. The word "or" usually means that you should use the Or logical operator. To obtain information on all writers who are freelancers *and* who were last contacted prior to 1990, Elena uses the And logical operator.

The And Logical Operator

Elena will use the And logical operator and enter conditions for the Freelancer field and the Last Contact Date field in the same Criteria row. She will enter =Yes as the condition for the Freelancer field and <#1/1/90# as the condition for the Last Contact Date field to obtain information on all writers who are freelancers and who were last contacted prior to 1990. Because the conditions appear in the same Criteria row, Access selects records only if both conditions are met.

Elena's new query does not need sort keys, so Elena first removes the sort keys for the Freelancer and Last Contact Date fields.

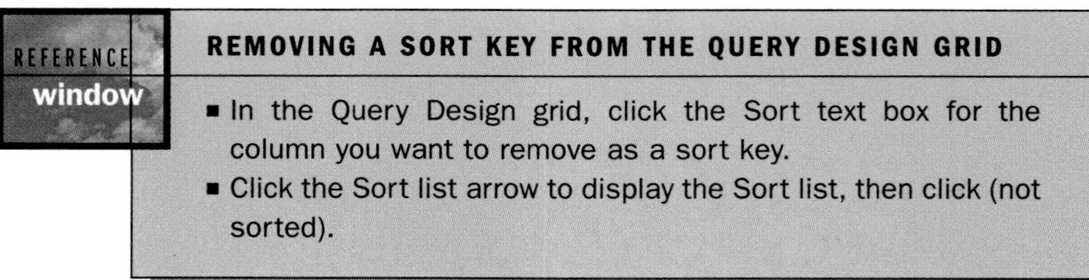

REFERENCE window

REMOVING A SORT KEY FROM THE QUERY DESIGN GRID

- In the Query Design grid, click the Sort text box for the column you want to remove as a sort key.
- Click the Sort list arrow to display the Sort list, then click (not sorted).

To remove sort keys from the Query Design grid:

1. Click the **Query View** button on the toolbar to switch back to the Query Design window.
2. Click the **Sort** text box in the Freelancer column, then click the **Sort** list arrow to display the Sort list.
3. Click **(not sorted)** in the Sort list. The Sort list closes, and Access removes the sort order from the Sort text box.
4. Repeat this procedure to remove the sort key from the Last Contact Date column.

Elena now enters the two conditions.

To select records using the And logical operator:

1. Click the **Criteria** text box for the Freelancer field and then type **=Yes**.
2. Click the **Criteria** text box for the Last Contact Date field and then type **<#1/1/90#**. See Figure 4-24. Access will select a record only if both conditions are met.

Figure 4-24 Criteria to find freelancers last contacted prior to 1990

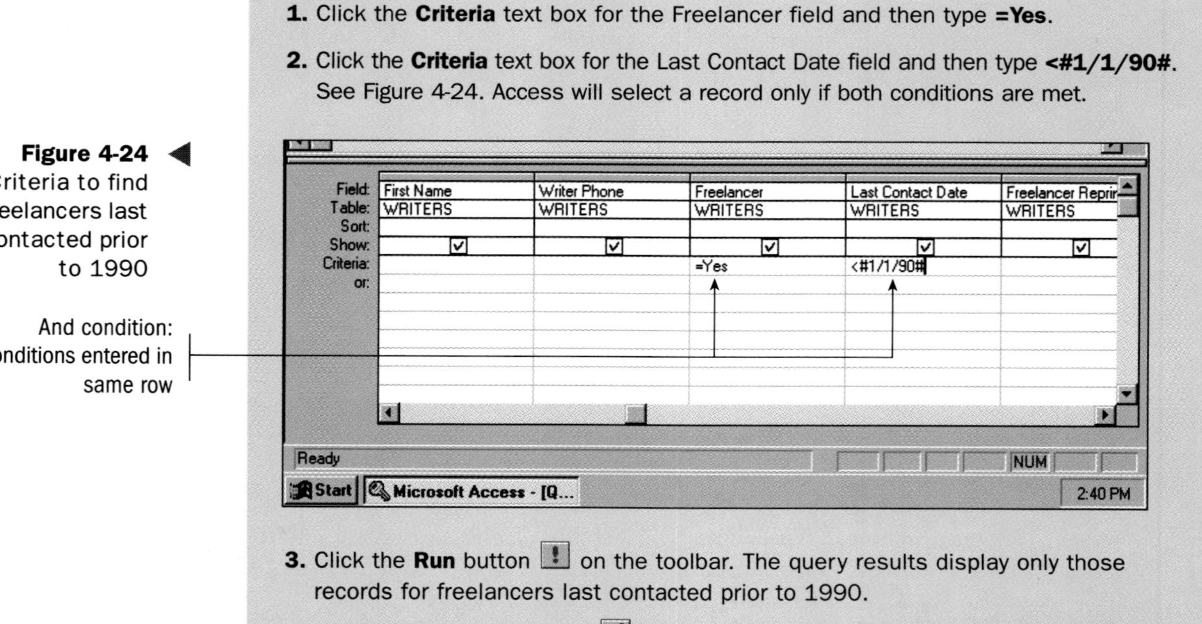

3. Click the **Run** button on the toolbar. The query results display only those records for freelancers last contacted prior to 1990.
4. Click the **Query View** button on the toolbar to switch back to the Query Design window.

Elena is pleased with how easy it is to use multiple selection criteria. She decides to try the Or logical operator next.

The Or Logical Operator

Elena practices using the Or logical operator by creating a query that asks for those writers who have 210 or 706 area codes. For this query, Elena will enter Like "210*" in one row and Like "706*" in another row. Because the conditions appear in different Criteria rows, Access selects records if either condition is satisfied.

To select records using the Or logical operator:

1. Move the pointer to the left side of the Criteria text box for the first column (Writer ID) and click when the pointer changes to ➡. Access highlights the entire Criteria row.
2. Press the **Delete** key to remove all of the previous conditions from the Query Design grid.
3. Click the **Criteria** text box in the Writer Phone column and then type **Like "210*"**.
4. Click the **or:** text box below the one you just used and type **Like "706*"**. See Figure 4-25. Access will select a record if either condition is met.

Figure 4-25 Criteria to find writers with 210 or 706 area codes

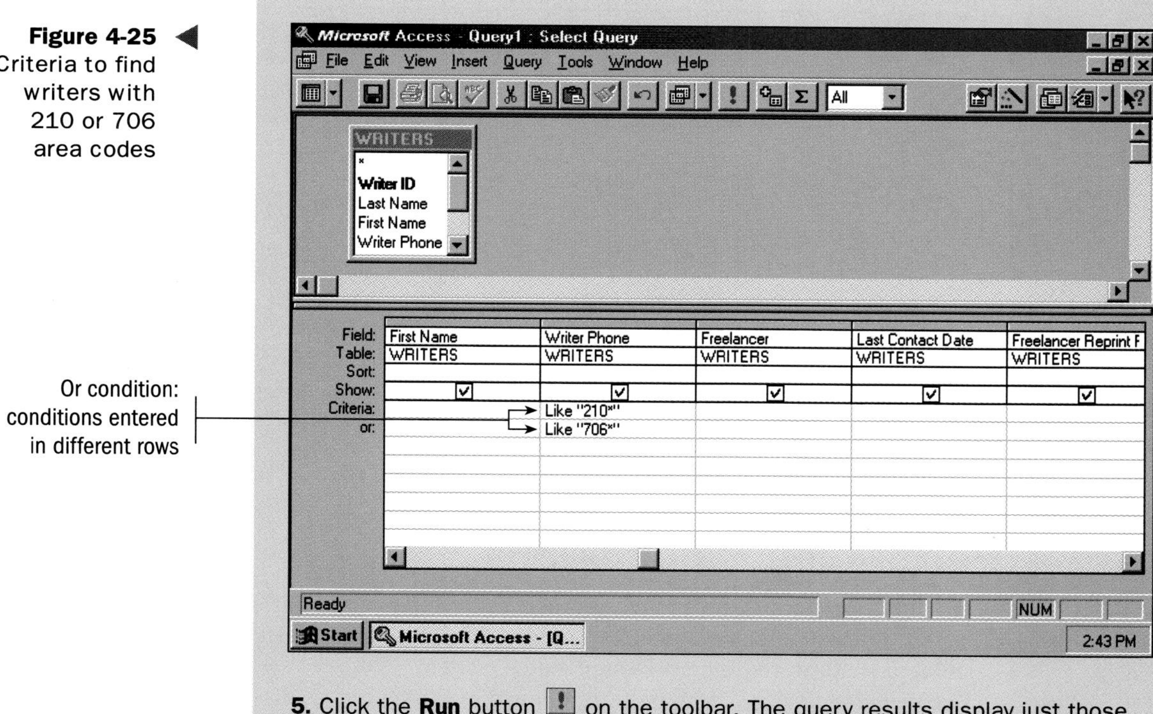

Or condition: conditions entered in different rows

5. Click the **Run** button on the toolbar. The query results display just those records for writers with 210 or 706 area codes.
6. Click the **Query View** button on the toolbar to switch back to the Query Design window.

Using And with Or

Now that Elena has used both the And and Or logical operators, she wants to know if she can combine both operators to obtain information. Can she, for example, create a query that will select only freelancers who have 210 or 706 area codes? In other words, she wants writers who are freelancers *and* have 210 area codes, *or* who are freelancers *and* have 706 area codes. To create this query, she needs to add the =Yes condition for the Freelancer field to both rows that already contain the Writer Phone conditions. Access will select a record if either And condition is met. Only freelancers will be selected, and only if their area codes are 210 or 706.

Elena needs to add the Freelancer conditions to the Query Design grid to complete her new query.

To select records using the And logical operator with the Or logical operator:

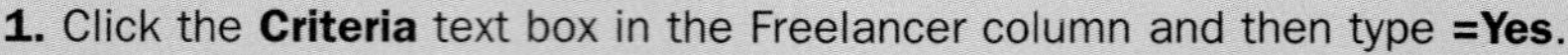

1. Click the **Criteria** text box in the Freelancer column and then type **=Yes**.
2. Press the **down arrow** button and then type **=Yes**. Access will select a record if either And condition is met.

   Because she is listing only Freelancer records, Elena removes the Freelancer field from the query results.

3. Click the **Show** box for the Freelancer field to remove the check mark. See Figure 4-26.

Figure 4-26
Criteria to find freelancers who have 210 or 706 area codes

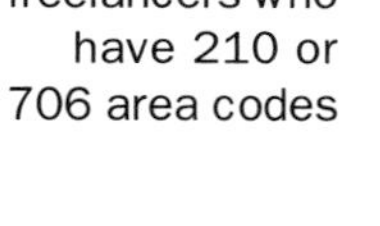

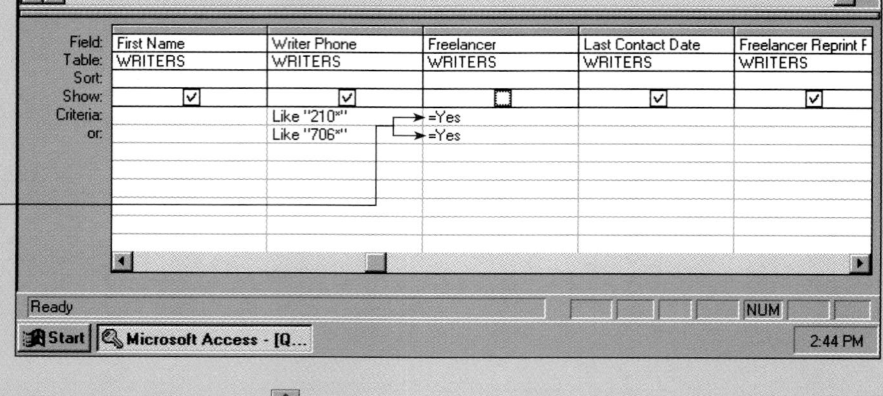

And with Or condition: two rows containing two conditions

4. Click the **Run** button on the toolbar. The query results display only those records for freelancers with 210 or 706 area codes.
5. Click the **Query View** button on the toolbar to switch back to the Query Design window.

Performing Calculations

Brian thanks Elena for the list of freelancers that she printed out for him earlier. He is now considering giving all freelancers an extra $50. This query requires a new field, called a calculated field, in the Query Design grid.

A **calculated field** is a new field that exists in the query results but does not exist in the database. When you run a query, the value of a calculated field is determined from fields that are in a database. You can perform calculations using Number, Currency, or Date/Time fields from your database. Among the arithmetic operators you can use are those for addition (+), subtraction (−), multiplication (*), and division (/).

Using Calculated Fields

Elena creates a calculated field that adds 50 to the amount stored in the Freelancer Reprint Payment Amount field. Whenever a calculation includes a field name, you place brackets around the name to tell Access that the name is a field name from your database. Elena's calculation, for example, will be expressed as [Freelancer Reprint Payment Amount]+50.

Access supplies the default name Expr1 for the first calculated field, but Elena changes the name to Add50. Because the Field text box is too small to show the entire calculated field, Elena uses the Zoom box while she enters the calculated field. The Zoom box is a large text box for entering text or other values. You can open the Zoom box by using the shortcut menu.

The new query will select all Freelancer records in the WRITERS table, so Elena must remove the unnecessary conditions in the Criteria rows. At the same time, she decides to delete the fields that are not needed for her query: Writer ID, Last Name, First Name, Writer Phone, and Last Contact Date.

To delete fields and remove conditions from the Query Design grid:

1. Scroll to make the Writer ID column visible. Click the **Writer ID** field selector to highlight the entire column. Click the right mouse button in the Writer ID field selector to display the shortcut menu and click **Cut** to delete the column.
2. Use the same procedure to delete the Last Name, First Name, Writer Phone, and Last Contact Date columns in the Query Design grid.
3. Move the pointer to the left side of the or: text box for the first column. When the pointer changes to ➡, click to highlight the entire row. Press the **Delete** key to remove the previous Or condition from the Query Design grid.

The Query Design grid now contains two fields: Freelancer and Freelancer Reprint Payment Amount. Elena next adds the calculated field.

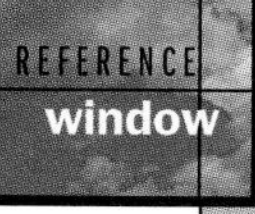

ADDING A CALCULATED FIELD TO THE QUERY DESIGN GRID

- Click the right mouse button in the Field text box for the first unused column to open the shortcut menu.
- Click Zoom to open the Zoom box.
- Enter the name for the calculated field followed by a colon and then the expression for the calculated value.
- Click the OK button. The Zoom box closes, and the new calculated field has been added to the Query Design grid.

To add a calculated field to the Query Design grid and run the query:

1. Click the right mouse button in the Field text box for the first unused column (the third column) to open the shortcut menu.
2. Click **Zoom** to open the Zoom box.
3. Type **Add50:[Freelancer Reprint Payment Amount]+50**. See Figure 4-27.

Figure 4-27 The Zoom box for entering long calculations

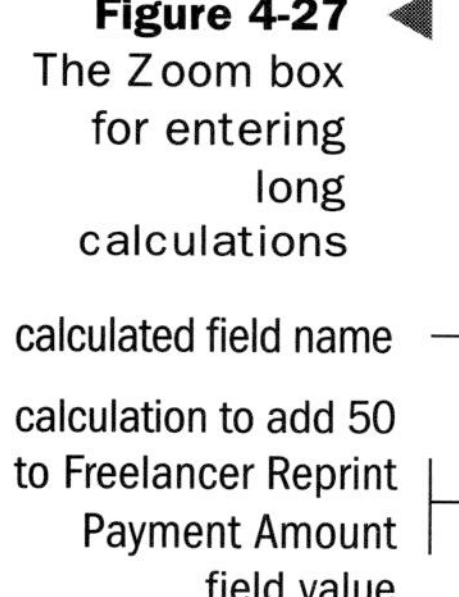

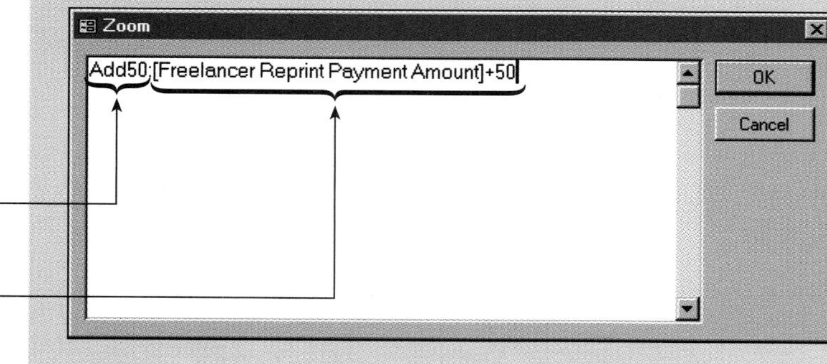

4. Click the **OK** button. The Zoom box closes, and the new calculated field appears as the third column in the Query Design grid.

5. Click the **Run** button on the toolbar. The query results display all records in the WRITERS table and include the new calculated field. See Figure 4-28.

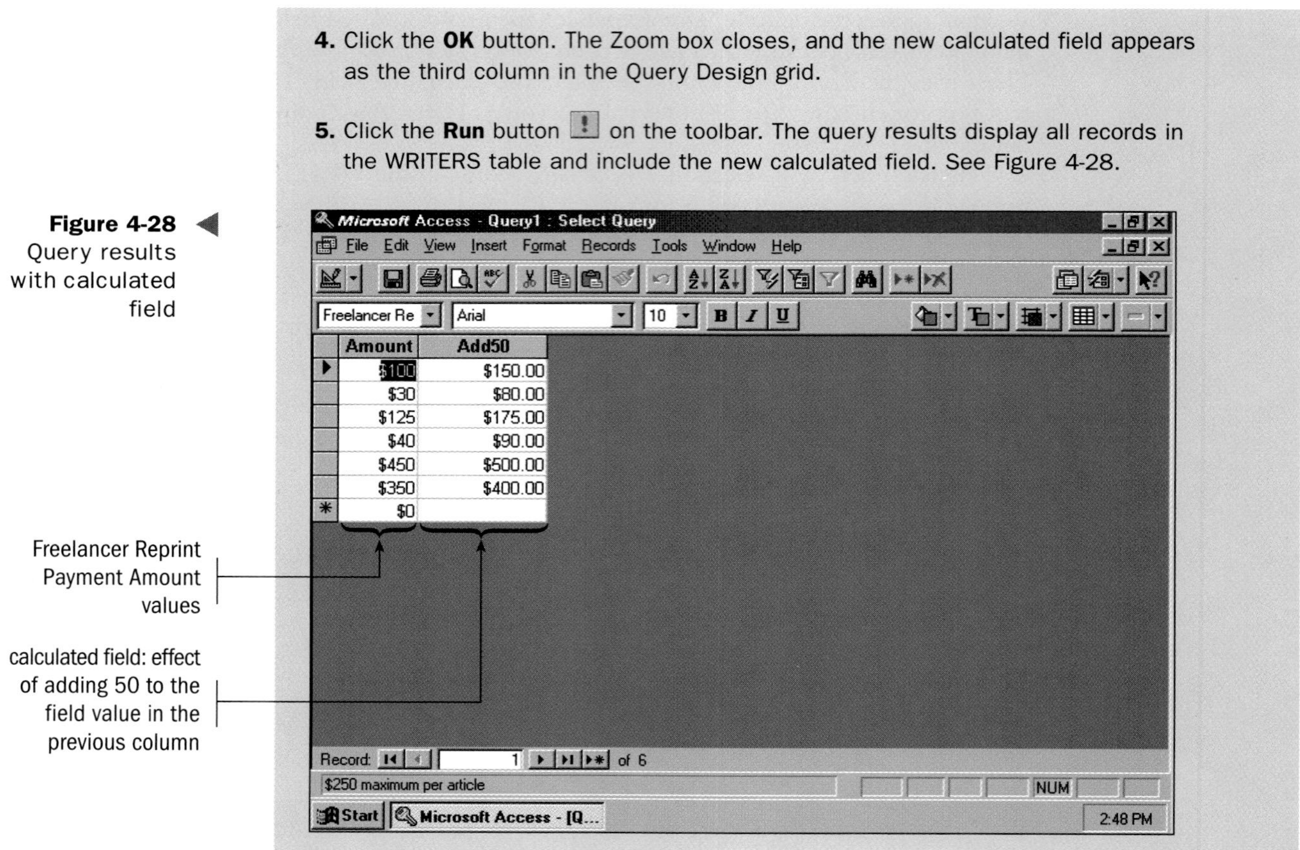

Figure 4-28 Query results with calculated field

The calculated field values in the new Add50 column are $50 more than those in the Amount column. (Remember that Amount is the Caption property for the Freelancer Reprint Payment Amount field.)

Using Aggregate Functions

Brian looks at the numbers and thinks giving the freelancers an extra $50 is possible. However, before he gives the go-ahead, he wants to know both the total cost and the average cost, with and without the extra $50. To obtain this information, Elena will create a query that uses aggregate functions. **Aggregate functions** perform arithmetic operations on the records in a database. The most frequently used aggregate functions are listed in Figure 4-29. Aggregate functions calculate the values from the fields in the records that meet a query's selection criteria. You specify an aggregate function for a specific field, and the appropriate operation applies to that field's values for the selected records.

Figure 4-29 Frequently used aggregate functions

Function	Meaning
Avg	average of the field values for the selected records
Count	number of records selected
Min	lowest field value for the selected records
Max	highest field value for the selected records
Sum	total of the field values for the selected records

REFERENCE window

USING AGGREGATE FUNCTIONS IN THE QUERY DESIGN GRID

- In the Query Design window, click the Totals button on the toolbar. Access adds a Totals row to the Query Design grid.
- Click in the Total text box for the field you want to aggregate.
- Click the Total list arrow to display the list of available aggregate functions.
- Click the function you want to select it.

Elena uses the Sum and Avg aggregate functions for both the Freelancer Reprint Payment Amount field and for the Add50 calculated field she just created in her previous query. The Sum aggregate function gives the total of the selected field values, and the Avg aggregate function gives the average of the selected field values. Elena's query results will contain one record displaying the four requested aggregate function values.

To use aggregate functions in the Query Design window, you click the toolbar Totals button. Access inserts a Total row between the Table and Sort rows in the Query Design grid. You specify the aggregate functions you want to use in the Total row. When you run the query, one record appears in the query results with your selected aggregate function values. The individual table records themselves do not appear.

Elena has three fields in the Query Design grid: the Freelancer and Freelancer Reprint Payment Amount fields, and the Add50 calculated field. She needs a column for the Sum aggregate function and a column for the Avg aggregate function for each of the Freelancer Reprint Payment Amount and Add50 fields. The columns will allow her to find the total cost and average cost for freelancers with and without the extra $50. She inserts a second copy of the Freelancer Reprint Payment Amount field in the Query Design grid. She then renames the first Freelancer Reprint Payment Amount field AmountSum and the second AmountAvg. She likewise makes a second copy of the Add50 calculated field and renames the first one Add50Sum and the second Add50Avg.

First Elena adds the copy of the Freelancer Reprint Payment Amount field to the Query Design grid and renames the four summary fields.

To add and rename fields in the Query Design grid:

1. Click the **Query View** button on the toolbar. If necessary, scroll to the left to make all fields visible in the Query Design grid. Click **Freelancer Reprint Payment Amount** in the WRITERS field list, drag it to the Add50 calculated field column in the Query Design grid, and then release the mouse button. The four fields in the Query Design grid, from left to right, are Freelancer, Freelancer Reprint Payment Amount, Freelancer Reprint Payment Amount, and Add50.

2. Click the beginning of the Field box for the first Freelancer Reprint Payment Amount field and type **AmountSum:**.

3. Click the beginning of the Field box for the second Freelancer Reprint Payment Amount field and type **AmountAvg:**.

4. Click just before the colon in the Field box for the Add50 calculated field and type **Sum**. The name of the calculated field is now Add50Sum.

Elena next selects aggregate functions for these three fields.

To select aggregate functions:

1. Click the **Totals** button Σ on the toolbar. The Total row appears in the Query Design grid.

2. Click in the **Total** text box for the AmountSum field, then click the **Total** list arrow, then click **Sum** in the Total list box. See Figure 4-30.

Figure 4-30 Aggregate function selection

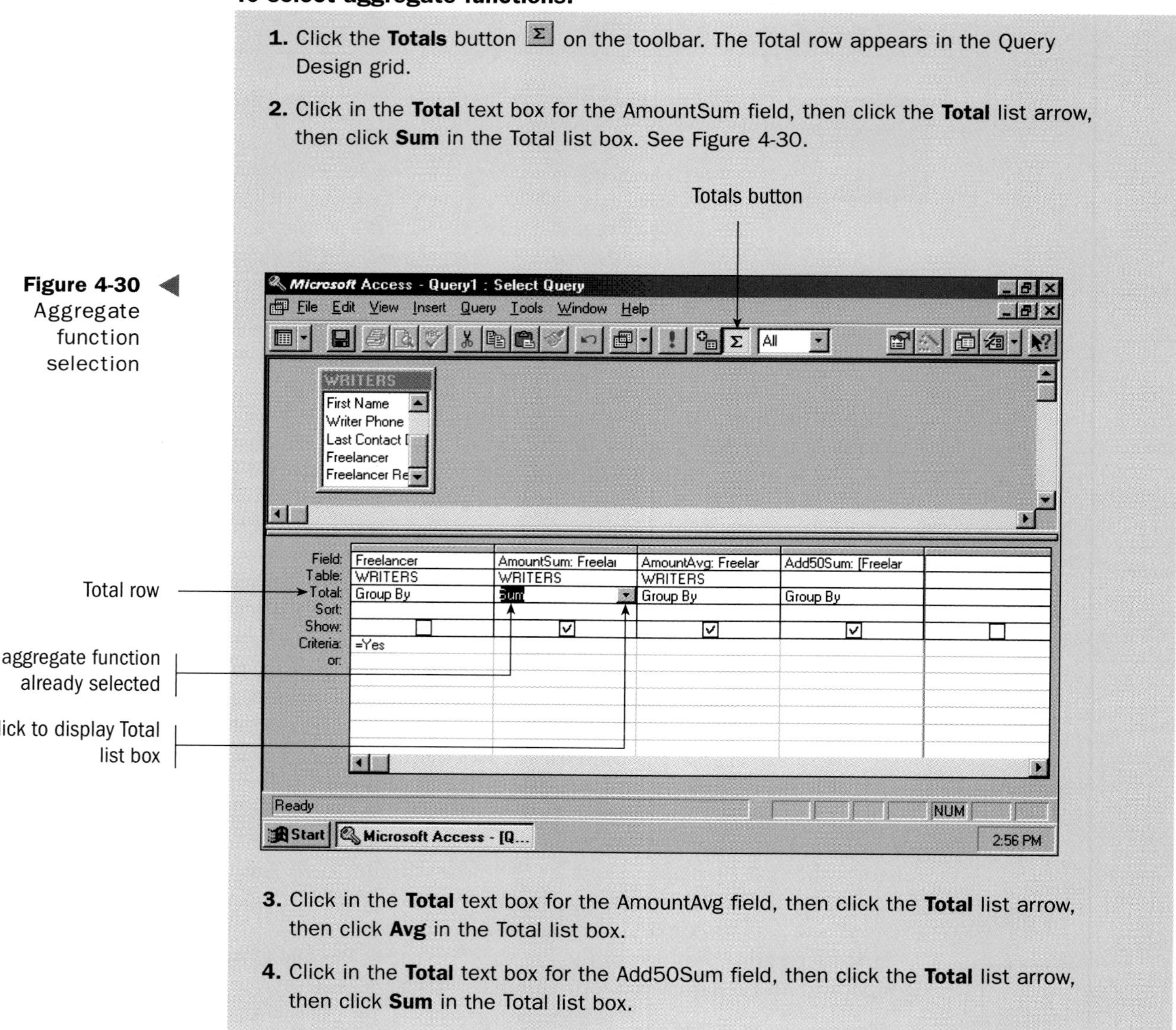

3. Click in the **Total** text box for the AmountAvg field, then click the **Total** list arrow, then click **Avg** in the Total list box.

4. Click in the **Total** text box for the Add50Sum field, then click the **Total** list arrow, then click **Sum** in the Total list box.

Elena's last steps are to copy a calculated field, paste it into the fifth column, rename the new field Add50Avg, and change its Total text box to Avg.

To copy and paste a new calculated field with an aggregate function:

1. Click the **Add50Sum** field selector to highlight the entire column.
2. Click the right mouse button in the Add50Sum field selector to display the shortcut menu and then click **Copy** to copy the column to the Clipboard.
3. Click the field selector for the fifth column to highlight the entire column. Click the right mouse button in the fifth column's field selector to display the short-cut menu and then click **Paste**. A copy of the fourth column appears in the fifth column.
4. Highlight **Sum** in the Field text box for the fifth column and type **Avg**. The renamed field name is now Add50Avg.
5. Click in the **Total** text box for the Add50Avg column, then click the **Total** list arrow, and then click **Avg** in the Total list box. See Figure 4-31.

Figure 4-31 Calculating total cost and average cost of freelancers with and without an extra $50

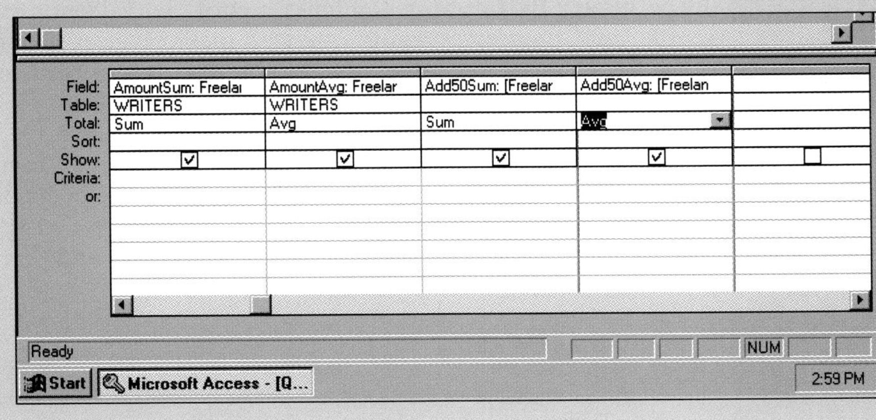

As her final step, Elena runs the query and then views the query results.

To run the query and view the query results:

1. Click the **Run** button on the toolbar. The query results display one record containing the four aggregate function values. See Figure 4-32.

Figure 4-32 Results of a query using aggregate functions

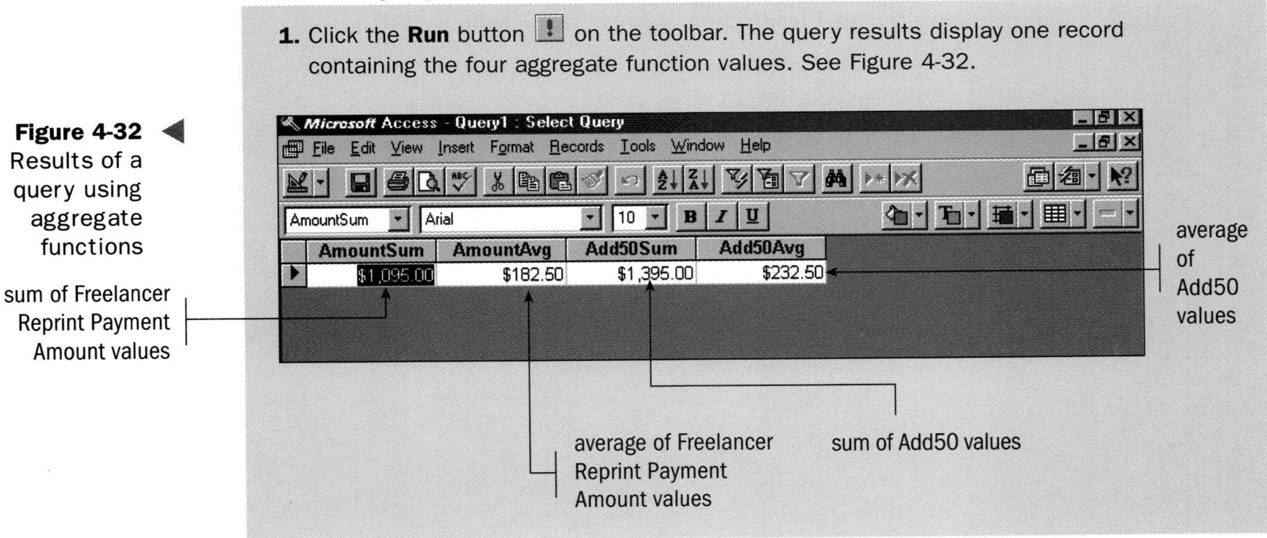

Elena prints the query results to give to Brian. Then she saves the query and closes the Datasheet window.

To save the query and close the Datasheet window:

1. Click the **Save** button on the toolbar. Access displays the Save As dialog box. Type **Freelancer Summary Query**, then click the **OK** button. Access saves the query design.
2. Click the Datasheet View window **Close** button. Access closes the Datasheet window.

Using Record Group Calculations

Elena has one more query to create requiring the use of aggregate functions. Brian wants to know how many staff writers and how many freelancers there are in the WRITERS table. To do this, Elena creates a query that uses the Group By operator and the Count function.

The Group By operator combines records with identical field values into a single record. The Group By operator used with the Freelancer field results in two records: one record for the Yes field values and another for the No field values. If you use aggregate functions, Access will calculate the value of the aggregate function for each group. The Count function counts the number of records that match the criteria. When Elena uses the Group By operator with the Freelancer field, and the Count function with the Writer ID field, Access will count the number of Writer IDs for freelancers and the number of Writer IDs for staff writers.

Elena creates a new query containing the Writer ID and Freelancer fields, and specifies the necessary operator and aggregate function.

To create the new query:

1. In the Queries list of the Database window, click the **New** button to open the New Query dialog box. Make sure that Design View is selected, then click the **OK** button. Access opens the Query Design window.
2. Click **WRITERS** in the Show Table dialog box, then click the **Add** button. The WRITERS table appears in the upper panel of the Query Design window.
3. Click the **Close** button to close the Show Table dialog box.
4. Double-click **Writer ID** in the field list to add the Writer ID field to the Query Design grid.
5. Scroll down the field list, then double-click **Freelancer** in the field list to add the Freelancer field to the Query Design grid.
6. Click the **Totals** button Σ on the toolbar. The Total row appears in the Query Design grid. By default, the Group By operator appears in the Total row for each column.
7. Click in the **Total** text box for the Writer ID field, then click the **Total** list arrow, then click **Count**. See Figure 4-33.

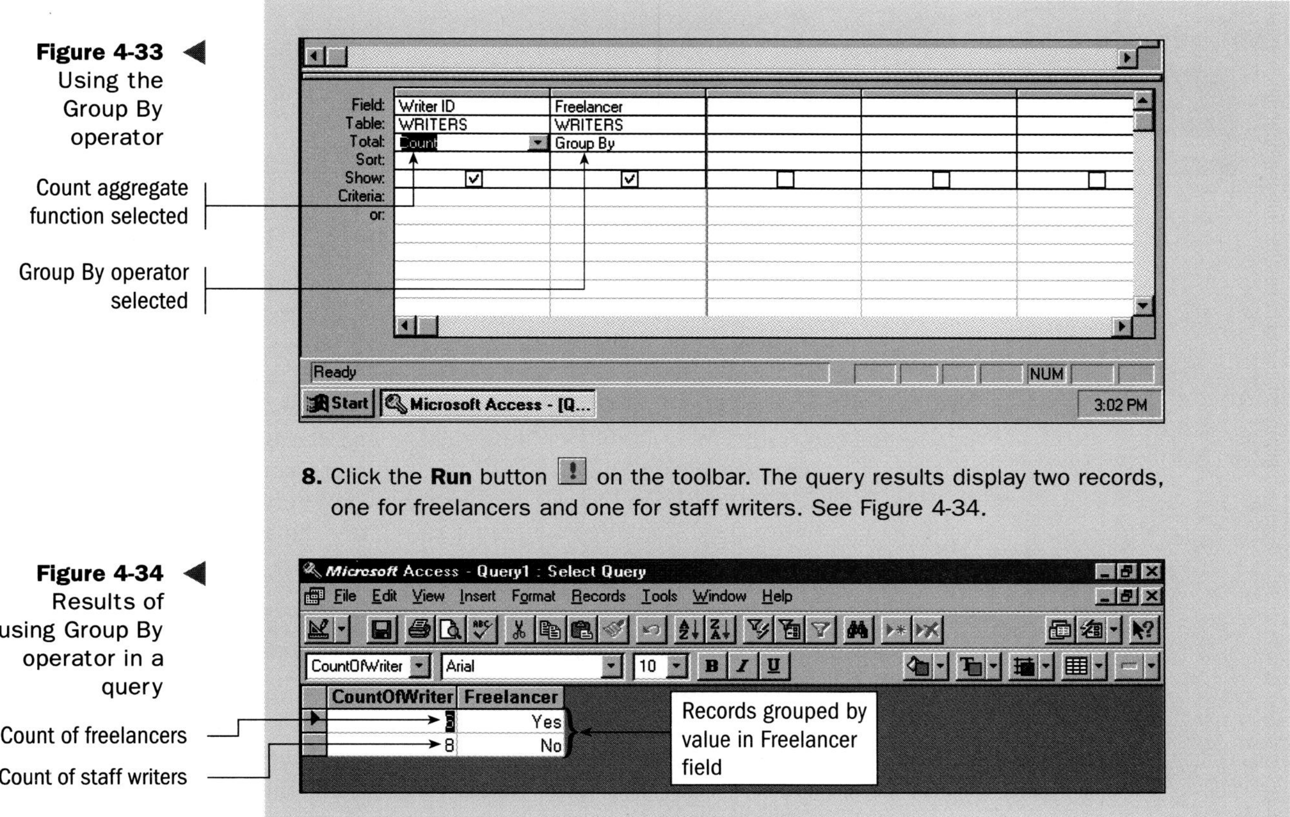

Figure 4-33 Using the Group By operator

8. Click the **Run** button on the toolbar. The query results display two records, one for freelancers and one for staff writers. See Figure 4-34.

Figure 4-34 Results of using Group By operator in a query

After printing the results to submit to Brian, Elena closes the Datasheet window. She decides not to save the latest query because she won't need to obtain this information again.

To close the Datasheet window without saving the query:

1. Click the Datasheet View window **Close** button. A dialog box asks if you want to save changes to the Query1 query.
2. Click the **No** button. Access closes the dialog box and then closes the Datasheet View window without saving the query.

If you want to take a break and resume the tutorial at a later time, exit Access. When you resume the tutorial, place your Student Disk in the appropriate drive, start Access, open the Issue25 database in the Tutorial folder on your Student Disk, and click the Queries tab to display the Queries list.

Quick Check

1. Why might you need to sort a single field?
2. How must you position the fields in the Query Design grid when you have multiple sort keys?
3. Why might you print selected query results?
4. When do you use logical operators?
5. What is a calculated field?
6. When do you use an aggregate function?
7. What does the Group By operator do?

SESSION 4.3

In this session, you will learn more about how to establish relationships between tables, design a query using related tables, and create a parameter query.

Understanding Table Relationships

One of the most powerful features of a database management system is its ability to establish relationships between tables. You've already seen how to use a common field to relate, or link, one table with another table. Linking tables (often called performing a **join**) with a common field allows you to extract data from them as if they were one larger table. For example, the WRITERS and BUSINESS ARTICLES tables are linked by using the Writer ID field in both tables as the common field. Elena can use a query to extract all the article data for each writer, even though the fields are contained in two separate tables. The WRITERS and BUSINESS ARTICLES tables have a type of relationship called a one-to-many relationship. The other two types of relationships are the one-to-one relationship and the many-to-many relationship.

Types of Relationships

A **one-to-one relationship** exists between two tables when each record in one table has exactly one matching record in the other table. Suppose, for example, Elena invites all of the writers to attend a meeting. Since most of the writers will be coming from out of town, she creates a table to keep track of airline reservations, hotel reservations, and other appropriate data. The RESERVATIONS table contains one record for each writer, with Writer ID as the primary key. In this example the WRITERS table and the RESERVATIONS table have a one-to-one relationship, as shown in Figure 4-35. Both tables have Writer ID as the primary key, which is also the common field between the two tables. Each record in the WRITERS table matches one record in the RESERVATIONS table through the common field.

Figure 4-35 One-to-one relationship

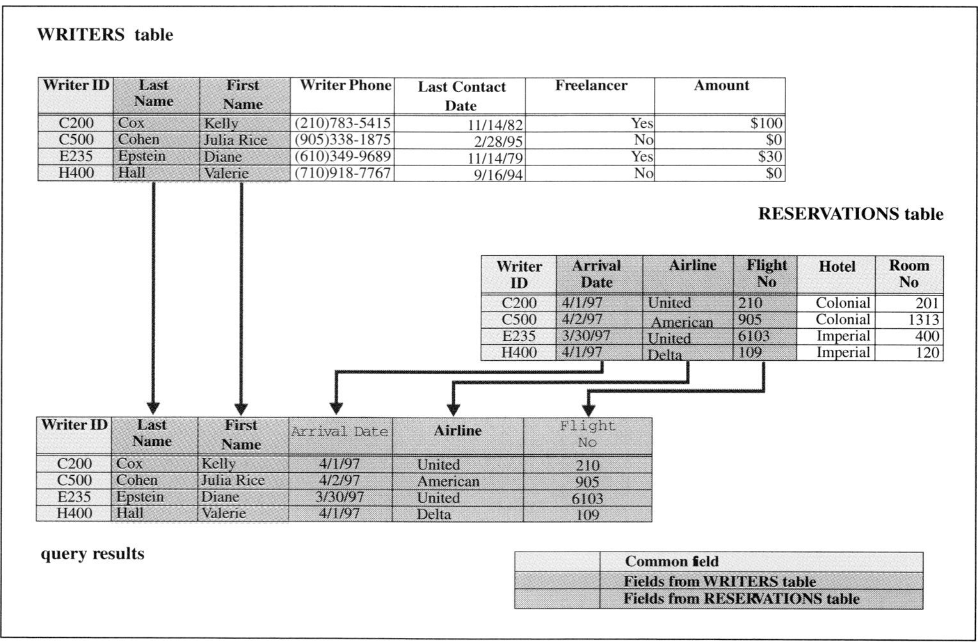

WRITERS table

Writer ID	Last Name	First Name	Writer Phone	Last Contact Date	Freelancer	Amount
C200	Cox	Kelly	(210)783-5415	11/14/82	Yes	$100
C500	Cohen	Julia Rice	(905)338-1875	2/28/95	No	$0
E235	Epstein	Diane	(610)349-9689	11/14/79	Yes	$30
H400	Hall	Valerie	(710)918-7767	9/16/94	No	$0

RESERVATIONS table

Writer ID	Arrival Date	Airline	Flight No	Hotel	Room No
C200	4/1/97	United	210	Colonial	201
C500	4/2/97	American	905	Colonial	1313
E235	3/30/97	United	6103	Imperial	400
H400	4/1/97	Delta	109	Imperial	120

query results

Writer ID	Last Name	First Name	Arrival Date	Airline	Flight No
C200	Cox	Kelly	4/1/97	United	210
C500	Cohen	Julia Rice	4/2/97	American	905
E235	Epstein	Diane	3/30/97	United	6103
H400	Hall	Valerie	4/1/97	Delta	109

A **one-to-many relationship** exists between two tables when one record in the first table matches many records in the second table, but one record in the second table matches only one record in the first table. The relationship between the WRITERS table and the BUSINESS ARTICLES table, as shown in Figure 4-36, is an example of a one-to-many relationship. Each record in the WRITERS table may match many records in the BUSINESS ARTICLES table. Valerie Hall's record in the WRITERS table with a Writer ID of H400, for example, links to three records in the BUSINESS ARTICLES table: 25% Tax Cut Bill Approved, The BCCI Scandal and Computers in the Future. Conversely, each record in the BUSINESS ARTICLES table links only to a single record in the WRITERS table, with Writer ID used as the common field.

Figure 4-36
One-to-many relationship

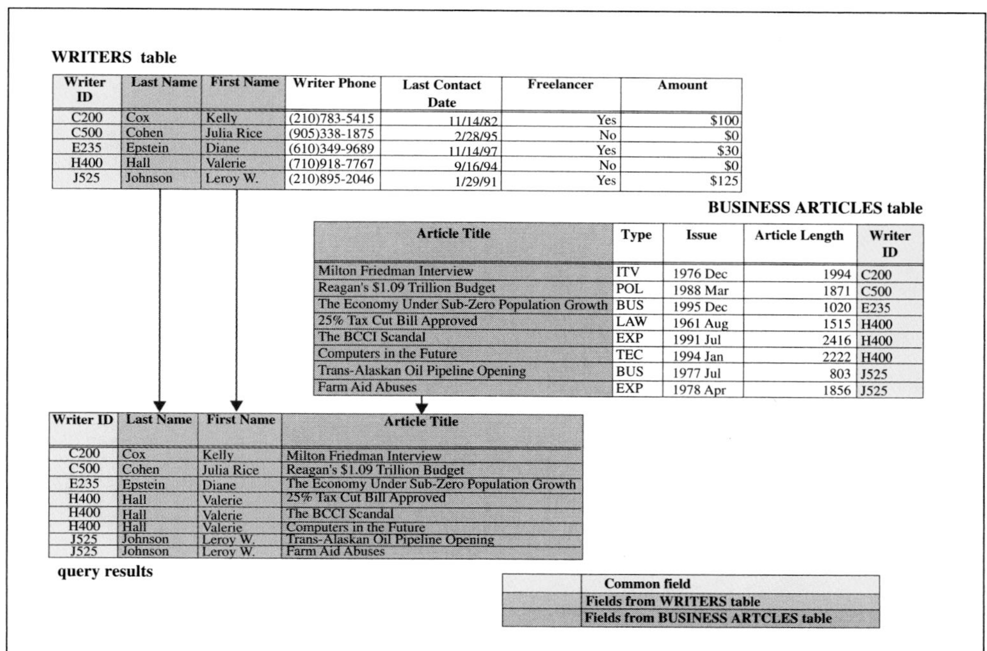

WRITERS table

Writer ID	Last Name	First Name	Writer Phone	Last Contact Date	Freelancer	Amount
C200	Cox	Kelly	(210)783-5415	11/14/82	Yes	$100
C500	Cohen	Julia Rice	(905)338-1875	2/28/95	No	$0
E235	Epstein	Diane	(610)349-9689	11/14/97	Yes	$30
H400	Hall	Valerie	(710)918-7767	9/16/94	No	$0
J525	Johnson	Leroy W.	(210)895-2046	1/29/91	Yes	$125

BUSINESS ARTICLES table

Article Title	Type	Issue	Article Length	Writer ID
Milton Friedman Interview	ITV	1976 Dec	1994	C200
Reagan's $1.09 Trillion Budget	POL	1988 Mar	1871	C500
The Economy Under Sub-Zero Population Growth	BUS	1995 Dec	1020	E235
25% Tax Cut Bill Approved	LAW	1961 Aug	1515	H400
The BCCI Scandal	EXP	1991 Jul	2416	H400
Computers in the Future	TEC	1994 Jan	2222	H400
Trans-Alaskan Oil Pipeline Opening	BUS	1977 Jul	803	J525
Farm Aid Abuses	EXP	1978 Apr	1856	J525

Writer ID	Last Name	First Name	Article Title
C200	Cox	Kelly	Milton Friedman Interview
C500	Cohen	Julia Rice	Reagan's $1.09 Trillion Budget
E235	Epstein	Diane	The Economy Under Sub-Zero Population Growth
H400	Hall	Valerie	25% Tax Cut Bill Approved
H400	Hall	Valerie	The BCCI Scandal
H400	Hall	Valerie	Computers in the Future
J525	Johnson	Leroy W.	Trans-Alaskan Oil Pipeline Opening
J525	Johnson	Leroy W.	Farm Aid Abuses

query results

A **many-to-many relationship** exists between two tables when one record in the first table may match many records in the second table, and one record in the second table may match many records in the first table. Suppose, for example, that an article has two authors. The relationship between the WRITERS and BUSINESS ARTICLES tables is then a many-to-many relationship, as shown in Figure 4-37. Access does not allow you to define a many-to-many relationship between two tables. To handle this type of relationship, you would need to create a primary key for the BUSINESS ARTICLES table. An AutoNumber-field named Article ID could be added as a primary key. Then you would create a new table with a primary key that combines the primary keys of the other two tables. The WRITERS AND BUSINESS ARTICLES table would have the combination of Article ID and Writer ID as its primary key. Each record in this new table represents one article and one of the article's writers. Even though an Article ID and Writer ID value can appear more than once, each combination of Article ID and Writer ID is unique.

Figure 4-37 Many-to-many relationship

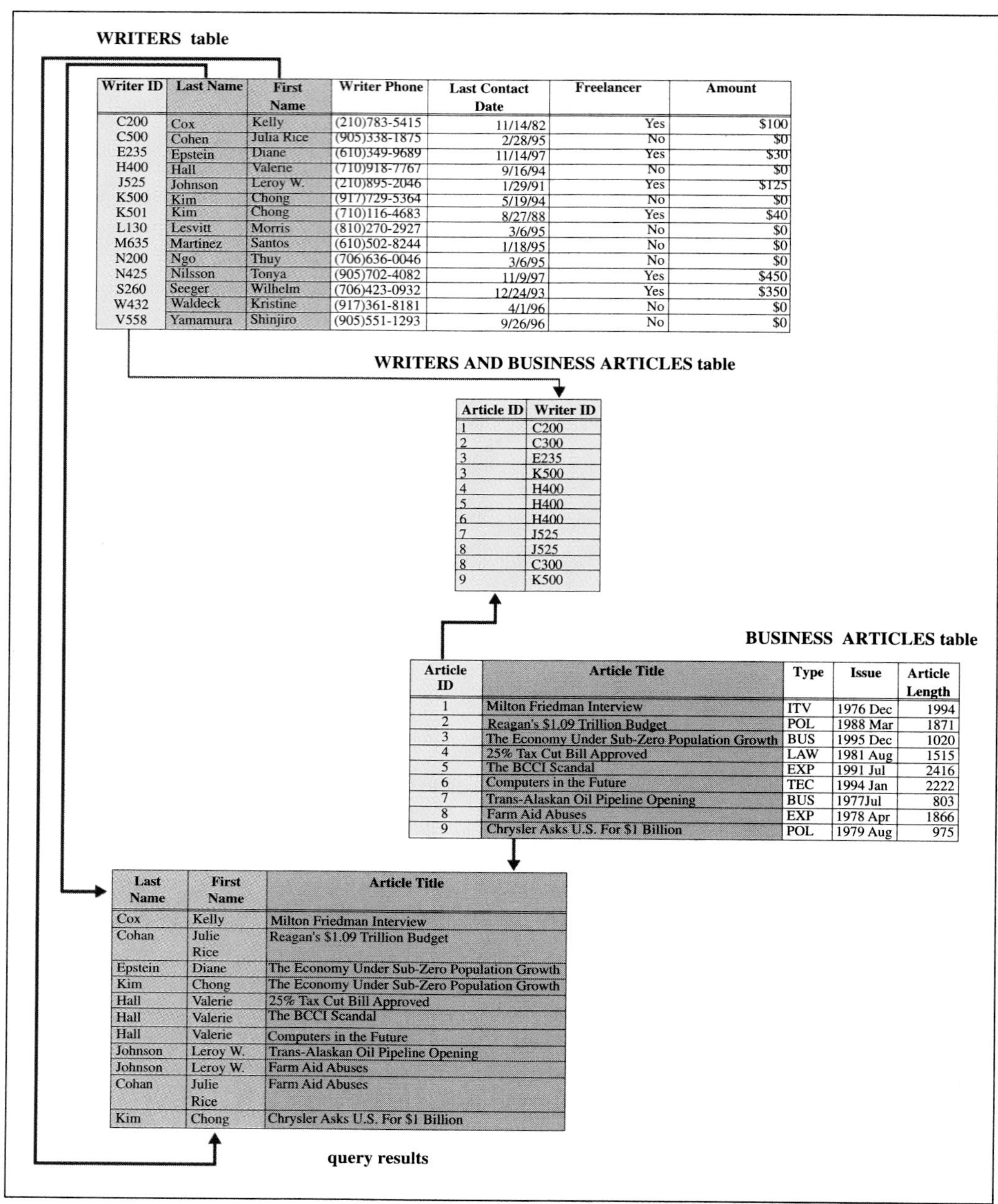

WRITERS table

Writer ID	Last Name	First Name	Writer Phone	Last Contact Date	Freelancer	Amount
C200	Cox	Kelly	(210)783-5415	11/14/82	Yes	$100
C500	Cohen	Julia Rice	(905)338-1875	2/28/95	No	$0
E235	Epstein	Diane	(610)349-9689	11/14/97	Yes	$30
H400	Hall	Valerie	(710)918-7767	9/16/94	No	$0
J525	Johnson	Leroy W.	(210)895-2046	1/29/91	Yes	$125
K500	Kim	Chong	(917)729-5364	5/19/94	No	$0
K501	Kim	Chong	(710)116-4683	8/27/88	Yes	$40
L130	Lesvitt	Morris	(810)270-2927	3/6/95	No	$0
M635	Martinez	Santos	(610)502-8244	1/18/95	No	$0
N200	Ngo	Thuy	(706)636-0046	3/6/95	No	$0
N425	Nilsson	Tonya	(905)702-4082	11/9/97	Yes	$450
S260	Seeger	Wilhelm	(706)423-0932	12/24/93	Yes	$350
W432	Waldeck	Kristine	(917)361-8181	4/1/96	No	$0
V558	Yamamura	Shinjiro	(905)551-1293	9/26/96	No	$0

WRITERS AND BUSINESS ARTICLES table

Article ID	Writer ID
1	C200
2	C300
3	E235
3	K500
4	H400
5	H400
6	H400
7	J525
8	J525
8	C300
9	K500

BUSINESS ARTICLES table

Article ID	Article Title	Type	Issue	Article Length
1	Milton Friedman Interview	ITV	1976 Dec	1994
2	Reagan's $1.09 Trillion Budget	POL	1988 Mar	1871
3	The Economy Under Sub-Zero Population Growth	BUS	1995 Dec	1020
4	25% Tax Cut Bill Approved	LAW	1981 Aug	1515
5	The BCCI Scandal	EXP	1991 Jul	2416
6	Computers in the Future	TEC	1994 Jan	2222
7	Trans-Alaskan Oil Pipeline Opening	BUS	1977Jul	803
8	Farm Aid Abuses	EXP	1978 Apr	1866
9	Chrysler Asks U.S. For $1 Billion	POL	1979 Aug	975

query results

Last Name	First Name	Article Title
Cox	Kelly	Milton Friedman Interview
Cohan	Julie Rice	Reagan's $1.09 Trillion Budget
Epstein	Diane	The Economy Under Sub-Zero Population Growth
Kim	Chong	The Economy Under Sub-Zero Population Growth
Hall	Valerie	25% Tax Cut Bill Approved
Hall	Valerie	The BCCI Scandal
Hall	Valerie	Computers in the Future
Johnson	Leroy W.	Trans-Alaskan Oil Pipeline Opening
Johnson	Leroy W.	Farm Aid Abuses
Cohan	Julie Rice	Farm Aid Abuses
Kim	Chong	Chrysler Asks U.S. For $1 Billion

By creating the WRITERS AND BUSINESS ARTICLES table, you change the many-to-many relationship between the WRITERS and BUSINESS ARTICLES tables into two one-to-many relationships. The WRITERS table has a one-to-many relationship with the WRITERS AND BUSINESS ARTICLES table, and the BUSINESS ARTICLES table has a one-to-many relationship with the WRITERS AND BUSINESS ARTICLES table.

Access refers to the two tables that form a relationship as the primary table and the related table. The **primary table** is the "one" table in a one-to-many relationship, and the **related table** is the "many" table. In a one-to-one relationship, you can choose either table as the primary table and the other table as the related table.

Elena's next step is to define relationships for the WRITERS and BUSINESS ARTICLES tables. She will then use these relationships to obtain additional information from the Issue25 database.

Adding a Relationship Between Two Tables

When two tables have a common field, you can define the relationship between them in the Relationships window. The **Relationships window** illustrates the one-to-one and one-to-many relationships among a database's tables. In this window you can view or change existing relationships, define new relationships between tables, rearrange the layout of the tables, and change the structures of the related tables.

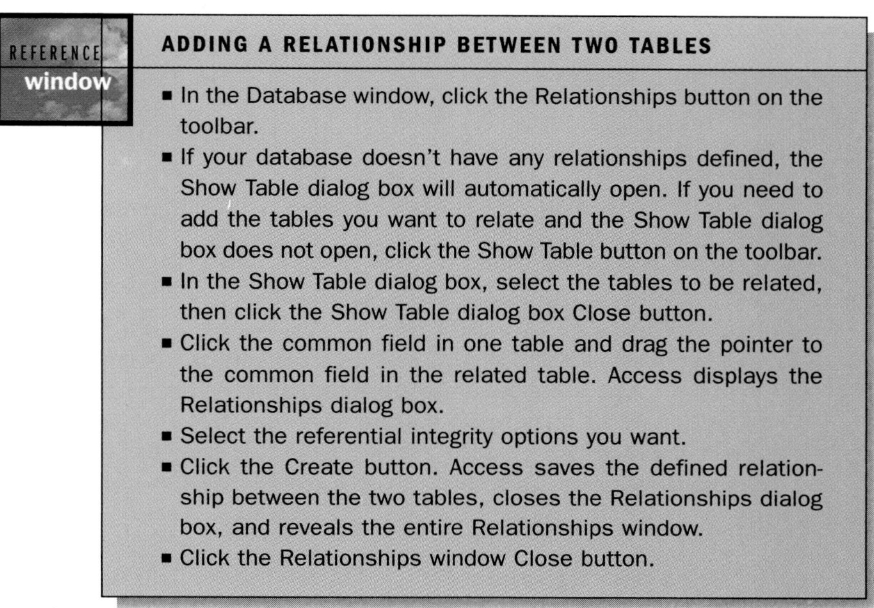

REFERENCE window

ADDING A RELATIONSHIP BETWEEN TWO TABLES

- In the Database window, click the Relationships button on the toolbar.
- If your database doesn't have any relationships defined, the Show Table dialog box will automatically open. If you need to add the tables you want to relate and the Show Table dialog box does not open, click the Show Table button on the toolbar.
- In the Show Table dialog box, select the tables to be related, then click the Show Table dialog box Close button.
- Click the common field in one table and drag the pointer to the common field in the related table. Access displays the Relationships dialog box.
- Select the referential integrity options you want.
- Click the Create button. Access saves the defined relationship between the two tables, closes the Relationships dialog box, and reveals the entire Relationships window.
- Click the Relationships window Close button.

Elena defines the one-to-many relationship between the WRITERS and BUSINESS ARTICLES tables. First, she opens the Relationships window.

To open the Relationships window:

1. Make sure the Issue25 database is open and the Queries list is displayed. Click the **Relationships** button on the toolbar. Access displays the Relationships window. See Figure 4-38.

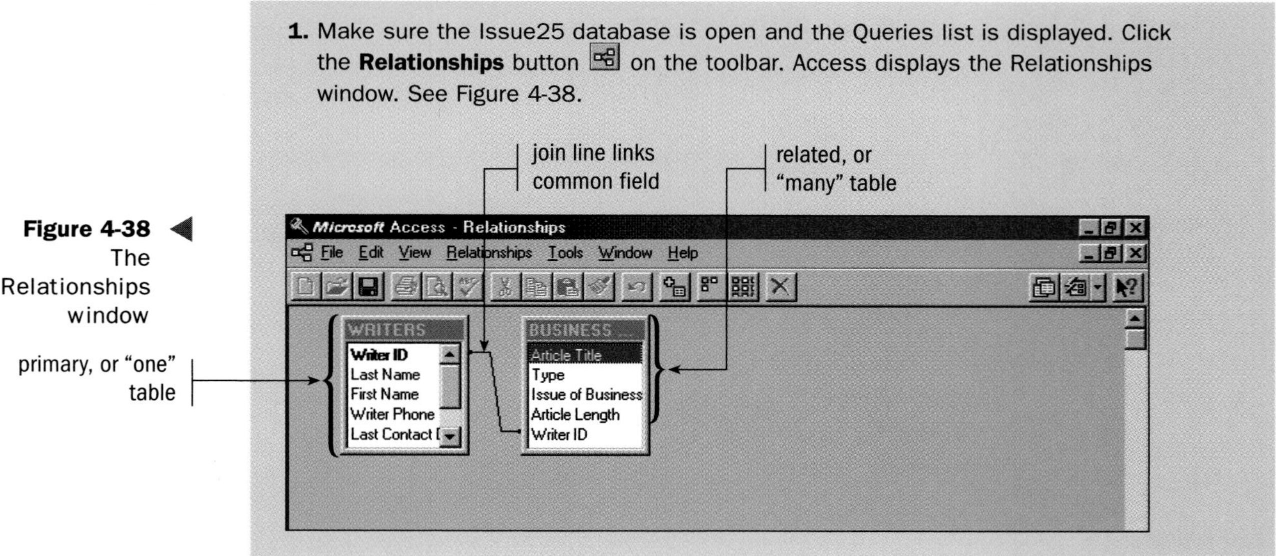

Figure 4-38 The Relationships window

The Relationships window shows the WRITERS table and the BUSINESS ARTICLES table and a line connecting them. This line is called the **join line** and identifies the common field in the two tables in the relationship. Recall that in Tutorial 3, you defined the Writer ID field in the BUSINESS ARTICLES table as a Lookup Wizard field and linked it to the Writer ID field in the WRITERS table. When you did this, Access automatically created a relationship between the WRITERS table and the BUSINESS ARTICLES table with the Writer ID field as the common field.

If you had not already defined the relationship, you could do so by adding the tables to the Relationships window using the Show Table dialog box. Then, you would drag the common field from one table to the other table to create the join line. Specifically, you would click the primary key field in the primary table and drag it to the foreign key field in the related table.

When two tables are related, you can choose to enforce referential integrity rules. The **referential integrity rules** are:

- When you add a record to a related table, a matching record must already exist in the primary table.
- You cannot delete a record from a primary table if matching records exist in the related table, unless you choose to cascade deletes.

When you delete a record with a particular primary key value from the primary table and choose to **cascade deletes**, Access automatically deletes from related tables all records having foreign key values equal to that primary key value. You can also choose to cascade updates. When you change a table's primary key value and choose to **cascade updates**, Access automatically changes all related tables' foreign-key values that equal that primary key value.

To define a relationship between two tables:

1. Click on the **join line** between the WRITERS and the BUSINESS ARTICLES table to highlight it. Click **Relationships**, then click **Edit Relationship**. Access displays the Relationships dialog box. Access analyzes the relationship and determines that it is one-to-many.
2. Click the **Enforce Referential Integrity** check box to turn on this option.
3. Click the **Cascade Update Related Fields** check box to turn on this option. See Figure 4-39. Do not turn on the Cascade Delete Related Records option.

Figure 4-39 The Relationships dialog box

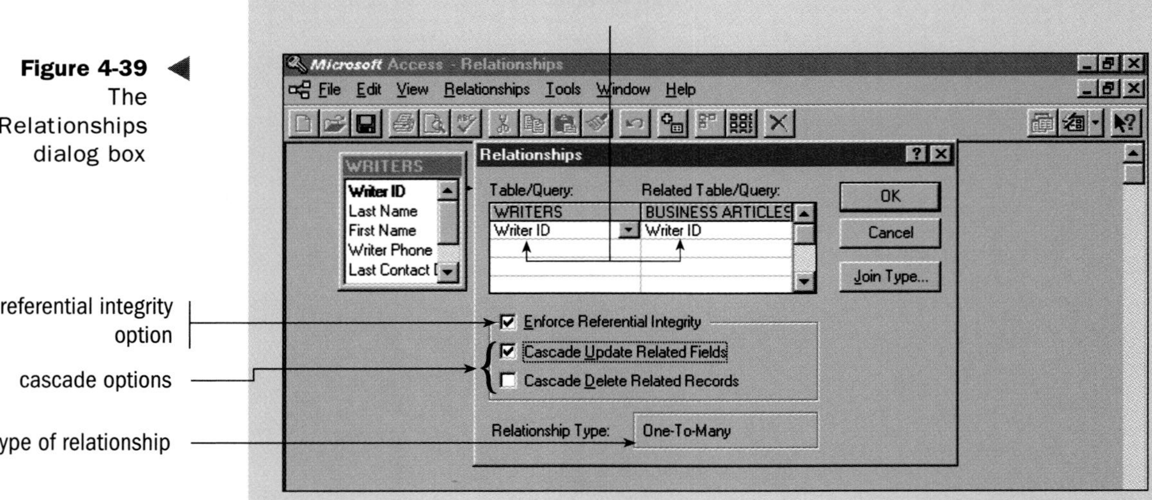

4. Click the **Create** button. Access saves the relationship defined between the two tables, closes the Relationships dialog box, and displays the entire Relationships window. See Figure 4-40.

Figure 4-40 Two tables related with a join line

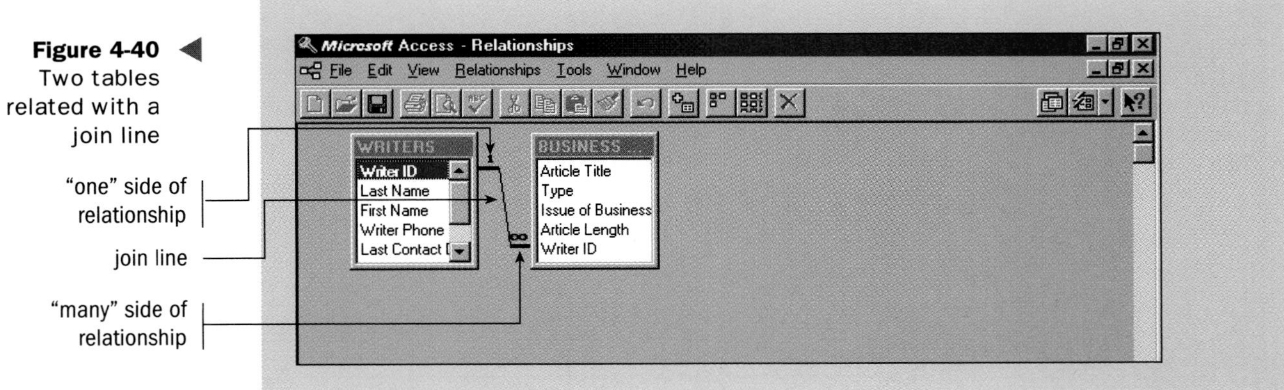

Notice the join line that connects the Writer ID fields common to the two tables. The common fields link (or join) the two tables, which have either a one-to-one or one-to-many relationship. The join line is bold at both ends; this signifies that you have chosen the option to enforce referential integrity. If you do not select this option, the join line is thin at both ends. The "one" side of the relationship has the digit 1 at its end (to indicate the primary table), and the "many" side of the relationship has the infinity symbol (∞) at its end (to indicate the related table). Although the two tables are still separate tables, you have now defined the one-to-many relationship between them.

Now that she has defined the relationship between the WRITERS and BUSINESS ARTICLES tables, Elena closes the Relationships window.

To close the Relationships window:

1. Click the Relationships window **Close** button ☒. Access closes the dialog box and the Relationships window, and returns you to the Database window.

Elena can now build her next query, which requires data from both the WRITERS and BUSINESS ARTICLES tables.

Querying More Than One Table

Elena's present task is to obtain information about the article titles, types, and lengths for each writer, arranged by article type. This query involves fields from both the WRITERS and BUSINESS ARTICLES tables and requires a sort.

Elena first opens the Query Design window and selects the two needed tables.

To start a query using two tables:

1. Make sure that the Queries tab is selected in the Database window and then click the **New** button. The New Query dialog box opens.
2. Make sure that Design View is selected, then click the **OK** button. The Show Table dialog box appears on top of the Query Design window.
3. Double-click **WRITERS** and then double-click **BUSINESS ARTICLES** in the Tables list box. In the upper panel of the Query Design window, Access displays the WRITERS and BUSINESS ARTICLES field lists and indicates their relationship.
4. Click the **Close** button. The Show Table dialog box closes. See Figure 4-41.

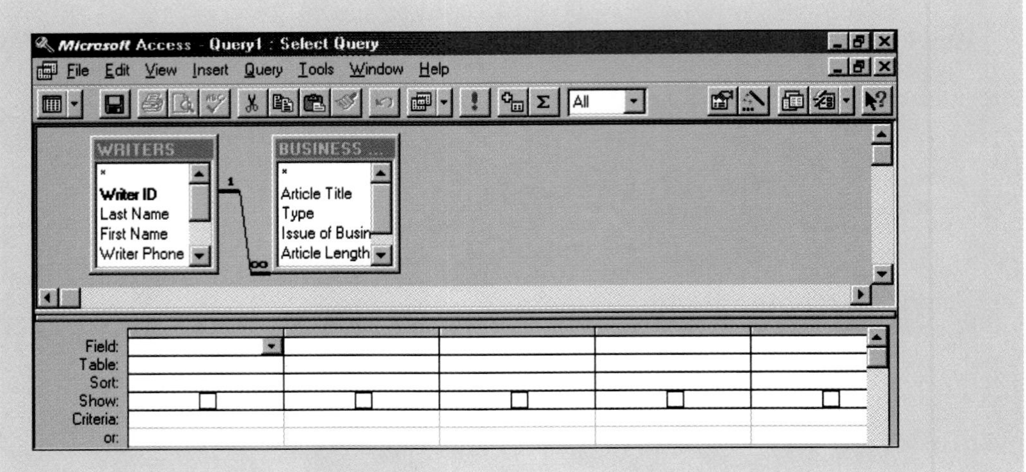

Figure 4-41 Two tables related with a join line in the Query Design window

Elena now defines the query. In the Query Design grid, she inserts the Article Title, Type, and Article Length fields from the BUSINESS ARTICLES table. She inserts the Last Name and First Name fields from the WRITERS table. She then saves the query.

To define and save a query using two tables:

1. Double-click **Article Title** in the BUSINESS ARTICLES field list. Access places this field in the first column's Field text box.
2. Using the same procedure, select Type and Article Length from the BUSINESS ARTICLES field list as the second and third columns, and Last Name and First Name from the WRITERS field list as the fourth and fifth columns. See Figure 4-42.

Figure 4-42 Query Design grid after fields are selected

fields from WRITERS table

fields from BUSINESS ARTICLES table

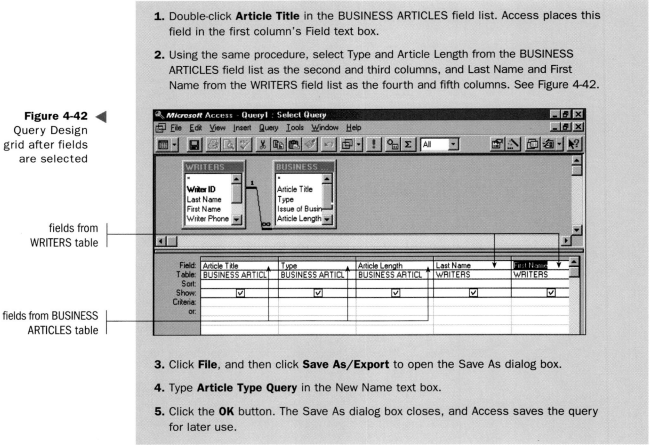

3. Click **File**, and then click **Save As/Export** to open the Save As dialog box.
4. Type **Article Type Query** in the New Name text box.
5. Click the **OK** button. The Save As dialog box closes, and Access saves the query for later use.

Elena runs the query to view the query results.

To view the query results:

1. Click the **Run** button on the toolbar. The query results display the fields from the two tables.

2. If necessary, click the Datasheet View window's **Maximize** button to see all the fields and records. See Figure 4-43.

Figure 4-43 Results of a query using fields from two tables

fields from WRITERS table

fields from BUSINESS ARTICLES table

Microsoft Access - Article Type Query : Select Query

File Edit View Insert Format Records Tools Window Help

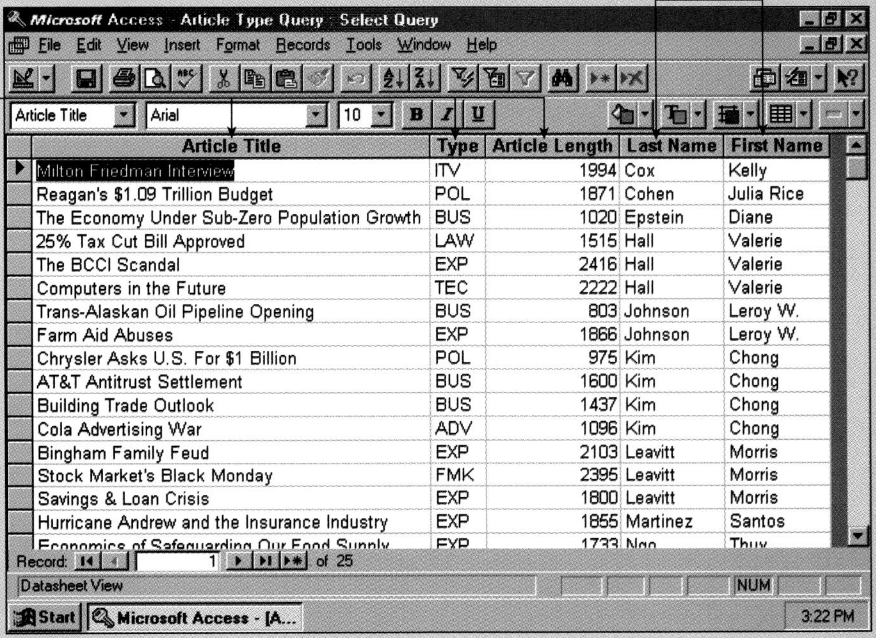

Article Title	Type	Article Length	Last Name	First Name
Milton Friedman Interview	ITV	1994	Cox	Kelly
Reagan's $1.09 Trillion Budget	POL	1871	Cohen	Julia Rice
The Economy Under Sub-Zero Population Growth	BUS	1020	Epstein	Diane
25% Tax Cut Bill Approved	LAW	1515	Hall	Valerie
The BCCI Scandal	EXP	2416	Hall	Valerie
Computers in the Future	TEC	2222	Hall	Valerie
Trans-Alaskan Oil Pipeline Opening	BUS	803	Johnson	Leroy W.
Farm Aid Abuses	EXP	1866	Johnson	Leroy W.
Chrysler Asks U.S. For $1 Billion	POL	975	Kim	Chong
AT&T Antitrust Settlement	BUS	1600	Kim	Chong
Building Trade Outlook	BUS	1437	Kim	Chong
Cola Advertising War	ADV	1096	Kim	Chong
Bingham Family Feud	EXP	2103	Leavitt	Morris
Stock Market's Black Monday	FMK	2395	Leavitt	Morris
Savings & Loan Crisis	EXP	1800	Leavitt	Morris
Hurricane Andrew and the Insurance Industry	EXP	1855	Martinez	Santos
Economics of Safeguarding Our Food Supply	EXP	1733	Ngo	Thuy

Record: 1 of 25

Datasheet View NUM

Start Microsoft Access - [A... 3:22 PM

TROUBLE? You should see 25 records in the query results. If you don't see any, then you probably did not import the BUSINESS ARTICLES table correctly with the Data and Structure option. Save the query with the name Article Type Query. Delete the table and import it again. Then try running the query. If you see more than 25 records, then you created the relationship between the two tables incorrectly. Save the query with the name Article Type Query, repeat the steps for adding the relationship between the two tables, and then try running the query again.

Elena notices that she neglected to sort the query results by Type. She can do that now in the Datasheet View window.

3. Click the field selector for the Type field to select the column.

4. Click the **Sort Ascending** button to sort the query results in ascending order by Type.

After printing the query results, Elena saves the changes to the query and then closes the Datasheet View window.

To save changes to a query and close the Datasheet View window:

1. Click the Datasheet View window **Close** button. Access displays the Save changes? dialog box.

2. Click the **Yes** button to save the changes you made to the sort order for this query. The Save changes? dialog box closes and the Database window becomes the active window.

Creating a Parameter Query

Elena's final query task is to obtain the article titles and writer names for specific article types—examples of article types are advertising (ADV), business (BUS), exposé (EXP), and political (POL). She will use the BUSINESS ARTICLES table for the Article Title and Type fields, and the WRITERS table for the Last Name and First Name fields. Article Title will be the sort key and will have an ascending sort order. Because this query is similar to her last saved query, Elena will open the Article Type Query in the Query Design window and modify its design.

To obtain the information she needs, Elena could create a simple condition using an exact match for the Type field that she would change in the Query Design window every time she runs the query. Instead, Elena creates a parameter query. A **parameter query** is a query that prompts you for information when the query runs. In this case, Elena wants to create a query that prompts her for the type of article to select from the table.

When Access runs the query, it will display a dialog box and prompt Elena to enter the article type. Access then creates the query results just as if she had changed the criteria in the Query Design window.

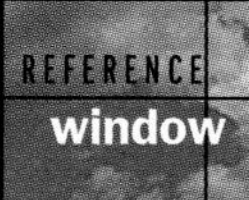

CREATING A PARAMETER QUERY

- Create a select query that includes all the fields that will appear in the query results. Also choose the sort keys and set the criteria that do not change when you run the query.
- Decide on the fields that will have prompts when you run the query. For each of them, type the prompt you want in the field's Criteria box and enclose the prompt in brackets.
- Highlight the prompt, but do not highlight the brackets. Click Edit and then click Copy to copy the prompt to the Clipboard.
- Click Query and then click Parameters to open the Query Parameters dialog box.
- Press Ctrl + V to paste the contents of the Clipboard into the Parameter text box. Press the Tab key and select the field's data type.
- Click the OK button to close the Query Parameters dialog box.

Elena opens the Article Type Query in the Query Design window and changes its design.

To open a saved query and modify its design:

1. Make sure that the Database window is active and the Queries tab is selected. Click **Article Type Query** in the Queries list and then click the **Design** button to open the Query Design window.
2. To add a sort key for the Article Title field, click the **Sort** text box, then click the **Sort** list arrow, and then click **Ascending**.

Elena has completed the changes to the select query. She now changes the query to a parameter query.

To create a parameter query:

1. Click the **Criteria** text box for the Type field and type **[Enter an Article Type:]**. See Figure 4-44.

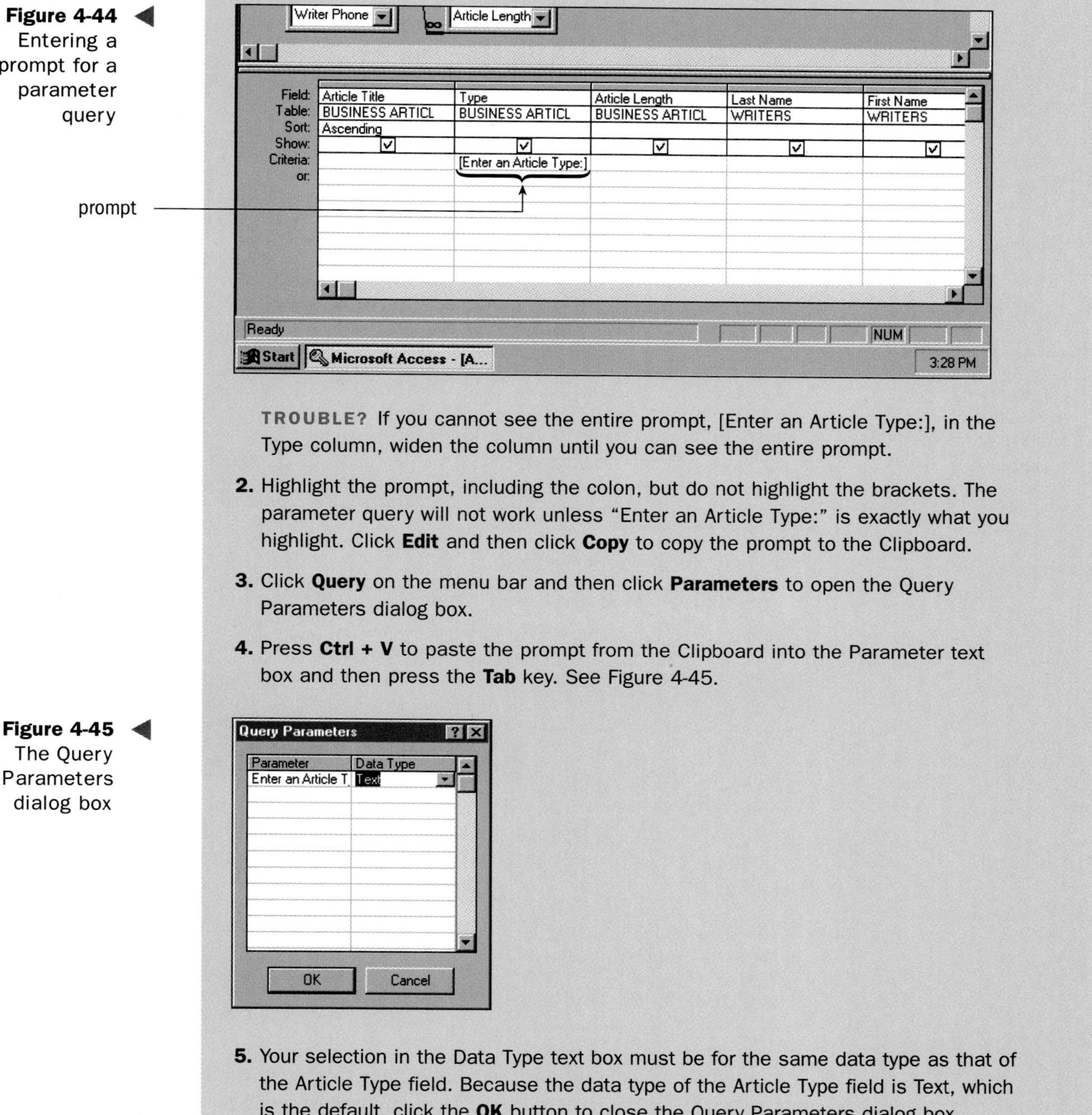

Figure 4-44 Entering a prompt for a parameter query

TROUBLE? If you cannot see the entire prompt, [Enter an Article Type:], in the Type column, widen the column until you can see the entire prompt.

2. Highlight the prompt, including the colon, but do not highlight the brackets. The parameter query will not work unless "Enter an Article Type:" is exactly what you highlight. Click **Edit** and then click **Copy** to copy the prompt to the Clipboard.

3. Click **Query** on the menu bar and then click **Parameters** to open the Query Parameters dialog box.

4. Press **Ctrl + V** to paste the prompt from the Clipboard into the Parameter text box and then press the **Tab** key. See Figure 4-45.

Figure 4-45 The Query Parameters dialog box

5. Your selection in the Data Type text box must be for the same data type as that of the Article Type field. Because the data type of the Article Type field is Text, which is the default, click the **OK** button to close the Query Parameters dialog box.

Elena runs the parameter query, saves it with the name Article Type Parameter Query, and closes the query results. She then exits Access.

To run and save a parameter query and exit Access:

1. Click the **Run** button [!] on the toolbar. The Enter Parameter Value dialog box appears with your prompt above the text box.

2. To see all the articles that are exposés, type **EXP** in the text box. See Figure 4-46.

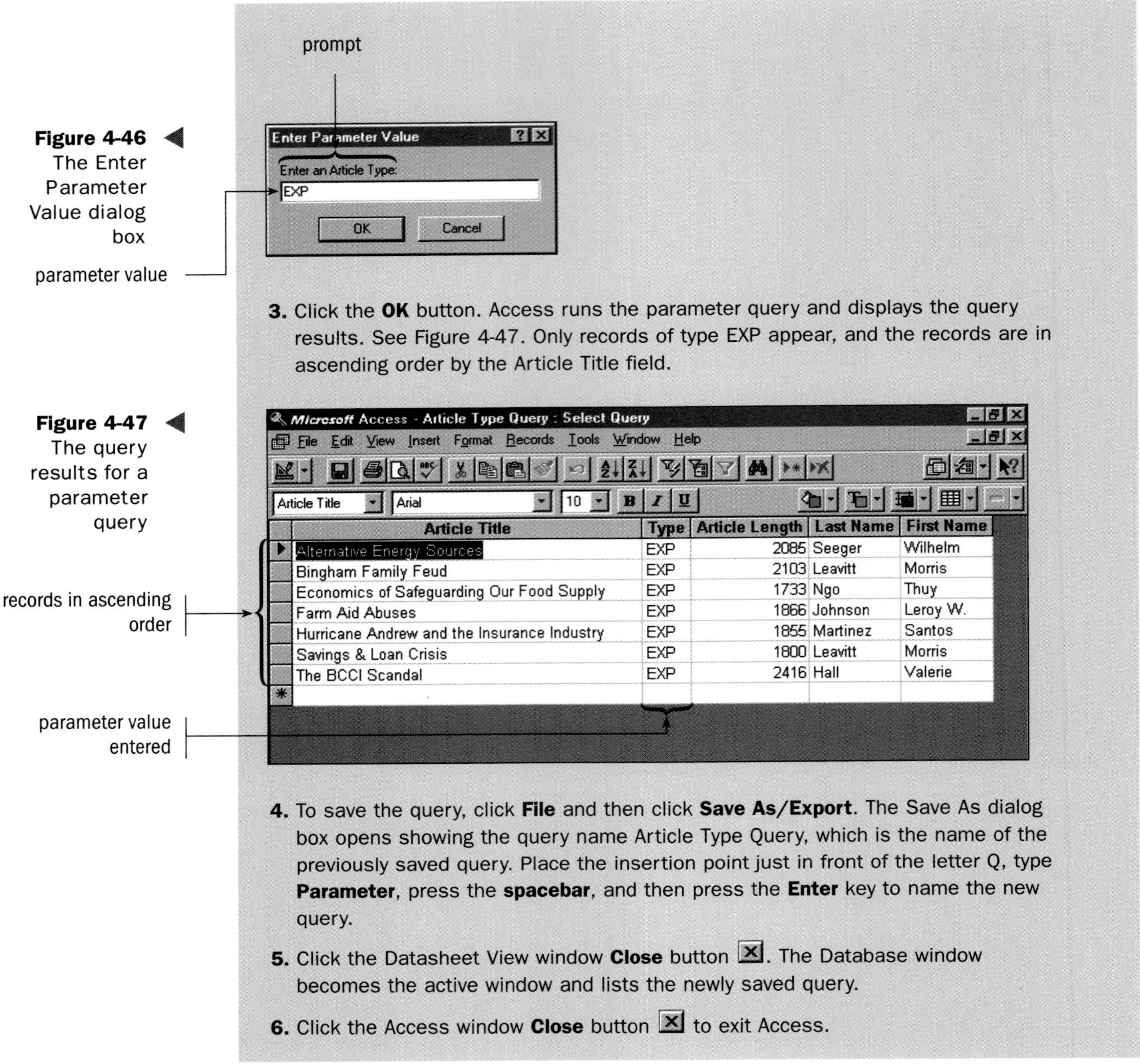

Figure 4-46 The Enter Parameter Value dialog box

3. Click the **OK** button. Access runs the parameter query and displays the query results. See Figure 4-47. Only records of type EXP appear, and the records are in ascending order by the Article Title field.

Article Title	Type	Article Length	Last Name	First Name
Alternative Energy Sources	EXP	2085	Seeger	Wilhelm
Bingham Family Feud	EXP	2103	Leavitt	Morris
Economics of Safeguarding Our Food Supply	EXP	1733	Ngo	Thuy
Farm Aid Abuses	EXP	1866	Johnson	Leroy W.
Hurricane Andrew and the Insurance Industry	EXP	1855	Martinez	Santos
Savings & Loan Crisis	EXP	1800	Leavitt	Morris
The BCCI Scandal	EXP	2416	Hall	Valerie

Figure 4-47 The query results for a parameter query

4. To save the query, click **File** and then click **Save As/Export**. The Save As dialog box opens showing the query name Article Type Query, which is the name of the previously saved query. Place the insertion point just in front of the letter Q, type **Parameter**, press the **spacebar**, and then press the **Enter** key to name the new query.

5. Click the Datasheet View window **Close** button ☒. The Database window becomes the active window and lists the newly saved query.

6. Click the Access window **Close** button ☒ to exit Access.

Elena schedules a meeting with her colleagues to review the results of her queries. In the next tutorial, she will create forms for displaying records on the screen.

Quick Check

1. What is a join?
2. Describe the difference between a one-to-many relationship and a one-to-one relationship.
3. What functions can you perform in the Relationships window?
4. What are the two referential integrity rules?
5. What does a join line signify?
6. How do you query more than one table?
7. When do you use a parameter query?

Tutorial Assignments

Elena creates several queries using the BUSINESS ARTICLES table that she imported into the Issue25 database. Start Access, open the Issue25 database in the Tutorial folder on your Student Disk, and maximize the Database window.

For each of the following questions, prepare an appropriate query in the Query Design window and print the query results.

If fields are listed in any of the questions, display the fields in the order listed. Unless the question explicitly says to save, do not save the queries.

1. Which articles are of type BUS? Print all fields for this query.
2. What are the article titles and article lengths for all articles that have a length greater than 2103?
3. What are the article titles, article lengths, and writer IDs for all articles written by writers with Writer IDs H400 or W432?
4. What are the article titles, article lengths, writer IDs, and issues for all articles published in *Business Perspective* in the 1980s?
5. What are the article lengths, article titles, writer IDs, and issues for all articles of type EXP that have a length less than 2100?
6. What are the article titles, writer IDs, and issues for all articles of type ITV or that were written by writer L130?
7. What are the article lengths, writer IDs, issues, types, and article titles for all articles that have a length less than 2000 and are of type BUS or LAW? Print in ascending order by the Article Length field.
8. What are the article lengths, writer IDs, issues, types, and article titles for all articles in descending order by the Article Length field?
9. What are the writer IDs, article titles, issues, types, and article lengths for all articles? Display the query results in ascending order, with Writer ID as the primary sort key and Article Length as the secondary sort key.
10. What are the article titles, writer IDs, issues, types, article lengths, and costs per article for all articles, based on a cost per article of three cents per word? Use the name CostPerArticle for the calculated field, assume that the Article Length field gives the number of words in the article, and use ascending sort order for the Article Length field.
11. What is the total cost, average cost, lowest cost, and highest cost for all articles? Assume that the Article Length field gives the number of words in an article and that the cost per article is three cents per word.
12. What is the total cost, average cost, lowest cost, and highest cost for all articles by type? Assume that the Article Length field gives the number of words in an article and that the cost per article is three cents per word.

13. Using the BUSINESS ARTICLES and WRITERS tables, list the article titles, article types, issues, writer last names, and writer first names in ascending order by the Article Length field for all articles of type BUS, LAW, or POL. Do not print the Article Length field in the query results. Be sure that there is no Total row in the Query Design grid. Remember to change the name of the Issue of Business Perspective field to Issue in the query results.
14. Using the BUSINESS ARTICLES and WRITERS tables, list the article titles, issues, writer last names, and writer first names in ascending order by the Article Length field for a selected article type. This query should be a parameter query. Save the query as Business Articles and Writers Parameter Query.

Case Problems

1. Walkton Daily Press Carriers Grant Sherman has created and updated his Press database and is now ready to query it. Start Access and do the following:

1. Open the Press database in the Cases folder on your Student Disk and maximize the Database window.
   Grant creates several queries using the CARRIERS table. For each of the following questions, prepare an appropriate query in the Query Design window and print its entire query results. Whenever you use one of the carrier name fields, rename it omitting the word Carrier. Whenever fields are listed in the question, display the fields in the order listed.
2. What is all the carrier information on Ashley Shaub?
3. What is all the information on those carriers whose last names begin with the letter S?
4. What are the birthdates, phone numbers, first names, and last names of carriers born in 1981 or later?
5. What are the birthdates, phone numbers, last names, and first names of carriers whose phone numbers end with the digits 4 or 7?
6. What are the birthdates, carrier IDs, first names, and last names of those carriers born prior to 1980 who have a carrier ID either less than 5 or greater than 10?
7. What are the birthdates, carrier IDs, first names, last names, and phone numbers of all carriers in descending order by birthdate?

Close the query results to return to the Database window without saving your queries. Complete the following queries using the BILLINGS table.

8. What is the total, average, lowest, and highest balance amount for all carriers? Your four calculated fields should use the Balance Amount field as is. Note that Balance Amount is the table field name and Balance is the Caption property name.

9. What is the total, average, lowest, and highest balance amount, grouped by carrier?
10. Create a parameter query to display all the fields in the BILLINGS table based on a selected Carrier ID.
11. Open the BILLINGS table. For the records with Route ID J311 and J314, change the Carrier ID to 11. Then add a one-to-many relation between the CARRIERS and BILLINGS tables using Carrier ID as the common field. Create a query to find the Route ID, Carrier ID, Carrier Last Name and Carrier First Name sorted by Carrier Last Name.

2. Lopez Lexus Dealerships Maria and Hector Lopez have created and updated their Lexus database and are now ready to query it. Start Access and do the following:

1. Open the Lexus database in the Cases folder on your Student Disk and maximize the Database window.
   Maria and Hector create several queries using the CARS table. For each of the following questions, prepare an appropriate query in the Query Design window and print its entire query results. Whenever fields are listed in the question, display the fields in the order listed. If a field has a Caption property, rename the field to match the caption in the Query Design window.
2. What are the models, years, and selling prices for all cars?
3. What are the years, costs, and selling prices for ES300 models?
4. What are the models, classes, years, costs, and selling prices for cars manufactured in 1995 and having either an S4 or an S5 class?
5. What are the models, classes, years, costs, and selling prices for all cars in descending sequence by selling price?
6. Create a field that calculates the difference (profit) between the Selling Price and the Cost and name it Diff. What are the models, classes, years, costs, selling prices, and profits for all cars?

7. What is the total cost, total selling price, total profit, and average profit for all the cars?
8. What is the total cost, total selling price, total profit, and average profit for all the cars, grouped by model?
9. What is the total cost, total selling price, total profit, and average profit grouped by year?
10. Create a parameter query to display all the fields from the CARS table based on a selected model.

Close the query results Datasheet View window to return to the Database window without saving your query, and then complete the following problem.

11. Using a one-to-many relationship between the LOCATIONS and CARS tables using Location Code as the common field. Create a query to find the models, selling prices, location names, and manager names for all cars in descending sequence by manager name.

3.Tophill University Student Employment Olivia Tyler has created and updated her Parttime database and is now ready to query it. Start Access and do the following:

1. Open the Parttime database in the Cases folder on your Student Disk and maximize the Database window.

Olivia creates several queries using the JOBS table. For each of the following questions, prepare an appropriate query in the Query Design window and print its entire query results. Whenever fields are listed in the question, display the fields in the listed order. If a field has a Caption property, rename the field to match the caption in the Query Design window.

2. What is all the job information on job order 7?
3. What is all the information on jobs having job titles that begin with the word "Computer?"
4. What are the job titles, hours per week, and wages of jobs paying wages greater than or equal to $7.05?
5. What are the job titles, hours per week, employer IDs, and wages of jobs requiring between 20 and 24 hours per week, inclusive?
6. What are the job titles, hours per week, employer IDs, and wages of jobs requiring between 20 and 24 hours per week, inclusive, and paying wages less than or equal to $6.75?
7. What are the job titles, hours per week, employer IDs, and wages of all jobs in ascending order by hours per week (the primary sort key) and in descending order by job title (the secondary sort key)?
8. Create a calculated field that is the product of hours per week and wage, and name it Weekly. What are the hours per week, wages, weekly wages, and job titles for all jobs?

9. What is the total, average, lowest, and highest weekly wage for all the jobs listed in the jobs table?
10. What is the total, average, lowest, and highest weekly wage for all jobs grouped by employer ID?
11. Create a parameter query to display all the fields in the JOBS table based on a selected employer ID.
12. Add a one-to-many relationship between the EMPLOYERS and JOBS tables using the Employer ID as the common field. Create a query to find the Employer ID, Employer Name, Job Order and Job Title, sorted by Employer Name.

4. Rexville Business Licenses Chester Pearce has created and updated his Buslic database and is now ready to query it. Start Access and do the following:

1. Open the Buslic database in the Cases folder on your Student Disk and maximize the Database window.

Chester creates several queries using the BUSINESSES table. For each of the following questions, prepare an appropriate query in the Query Design window and print its entire query results. Whenever fields are listed in the question, display the fields in the listed order. If a field has a Caption property, rename the field to match the caption in the Query Design window.

2. What is all the information for business ID 11?
3. What is all the information on those businesses that have the word "avenue" in the Street Name field?
4. What are the business names, street numbers, street names, and proprietors for businesses having street numbers greater than 5100?
5. What are the business names, street numbers, street names, proprietors, and phone numbers for businesses having phone numbers starting 243 or 942?
6. What are the proprietors, business names, street numbers, street names, and phone numbers of all businesses in ascending sequence by business name?

Close the query results to return to the Database window without saving your queries. Complete the following queries using the ISSUED LICENSES table.

7. What is the total amount, total count, and average amount for all issued licenses?

8. What is the total amount, total count, and average amount for all issued licenses grouped by license type?
9. Create a parameter query to display all the fields based on a selected business ID.

10. Add a one-to-many relationship between the BUSINESSES and the ISSUES LICENSES tables using the Business ID as the common field. Add a one-to-many relationship between the LICENSES and the ISSUES LICENSES tables using the License Type as the common field. Create a query to find the Business ID, Business Name, License Type and License Description sorted by Business Name.

TUTORIAL 5

Designing Forms

Creating Forms at Vision Publishers

OBJECTIVES

In this tutorial you will:

- Create forms using AutoForm and the Form Wizard
- Save and open a form
- View and maintain data using forms
- Use a filter to select and sort records in a form
- Design and create a custom form
- Select, move, and delete controls
- Use Control Wizards
- Add form headers and footers

CASE

Vision Publishers

At the next progress meeting on the special 25th-anniversary issue of *Business Perspective*, Brian Murphy, Judith Rossi, and Harold Larson are pleased when Elena Sanchez presents her query results from the Issue25 database. They agree that Elena should place the Issue25 database on the company network so that everyone can access and query the data. To make the selected data easier to read and understand, Elena decides to create several forms to display the information. She begins by creating a form to display information about one writer at a time on the screen. This will be easier to read than a datasheet, and Elena can also use the form to make changes to a writer's data or to add new writers to the database.

Using a Form

A **form** is an object you use to maintain, view, and print records from a database. A form is used to display records on the screen in a more attractive and readable format. In Access, you can design your own form using several different methods:

- **AutoForm** uses all of the fields in the underlying table or query, and is a quick way to create a basic form that you can use as is or customize. AutoForm creates a form in one of three standard formats: Columnar, Tabular, or Datasheet. A **columnar form** displays the fields, one on a line, vertically on the form. Field values appear in boxes. Labels, which are the table field names, appear to the left of the field values. A **tabular form** displays multiple records and field values in a row-and-column format. Field values appear in boxes with the table field names as column headings. A **datasheet form** displays records in the same format as in the Datasheet View window. Figure 5-1 shows forms created from the BUSINESS ARTICLES table in each of these three formats.

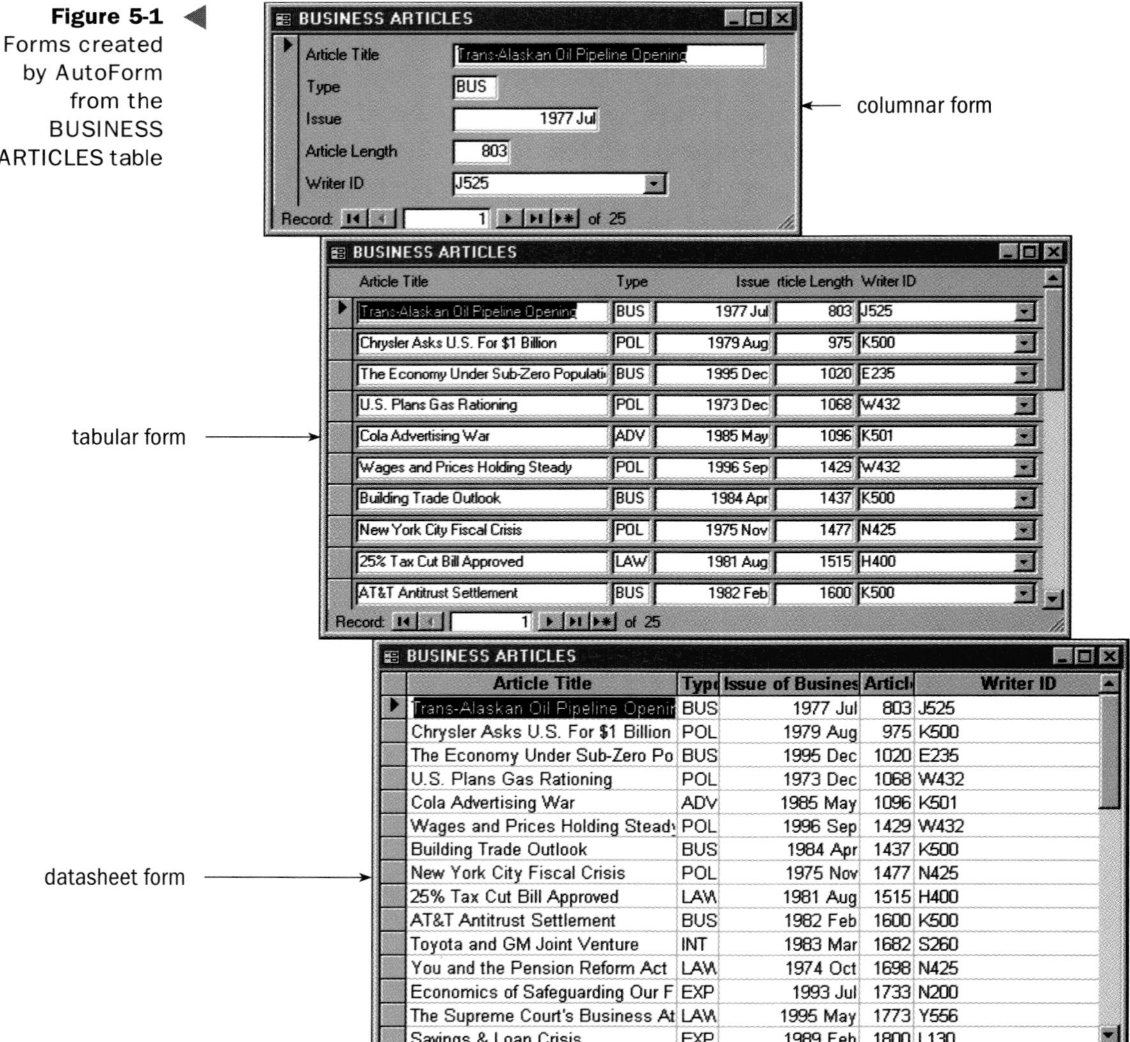

Article Title	Type	Issue	rticle Length	Writer ID
Trans-Alaskan Oil Pipeline Opening	BUS	1977 Jul	803	J525
Chrysler Asks U.S. For $1 Billion	POL	1979 Aug	975	K500
The Economy Under Sub-Zero Populati	BUS	1995 Dec	1020	E235
U.S. Plans Gas Rationing	POL	1973 Dec	1068	W432
Cola Advertising War	ADV	1985 May	1096	K501
Wages and Prices Holding Steady	POL	1996 Sep	1429	W432
Building Trade Outlook	BUS	1984 Apr	1437	K500
New York City Fiscal Crisis	POL	1975 Nov	1477	N425
25% Tax Cut Bill Approved	LAW	1981 Aug	1515	H400
AT&T Antitrust Settlement	BUS	1982 Feb	1600	K500

Article Title	Type	Issue of Busines	Articl	Writer ID
Trans-Alaskan Oil Pipeline Openin	BUS	1977 Jul	803	J525
Chrysler Asks U.S. For $1 Billion	POL	1979 Aug	975	K500
The Economy Under Sub-Zero Po	BUS	1995 Dec	1020	E235
U.S. Plans Gas Rationing	POL	1973 Dec	1068	W432
Cola Advertising War	ADV	1985 May	1096	K501
Wages and Prices Holding Stead	POL	1996 Sep	1429	W432
Building Trade Outlook	BUS	1984 Apr	1437	K500
New York City Fiscal Crisis	POL	1975 Nov	1477	N425
25% Tax Cut Bill Approved	LAW	1981 Aug	1515	H400
AT&T Antitrust Settlement	BUS	1982 Feb	1600	K500
Toyota and GM Joint Venture	INT	1983 Mar	1682	S260
You and the Pension Reform Act	LAW	1974 Oct	1698	N425
Economics of Safeguarding Our F	EXP	1993 Jul	1733	N200
The Supreme Court's Business At	LAW	1995 May	1773	Y556
Savings & Loan Crisis	EXP	1989 Feb	1800	L130

Figure 5-1 Forms created by AutoForm from the BUSINESS ARTICLES table

- The **Form Wizard** asks you a series of questions and then creates a form based on your answers. Using the Form Wizard, you can select the fields that you want to appear in the form.
- The **Form Design** window allows you to create your own customized form that you design directly on the screen.

- The **Chart Wizard** displays a graph created from your data.
- The **Pivot Table** form displays a Pivot Table created in Microsoft Excel. A Pivot Table summarizes the data in a table or query and can be based on the data in your Access table or query.

SESSION 5.1

In this session, you will create a form using AutoForm, create a main/subform form with the Form Wizard, save a form, and use a form for navigating in and updating records in a database table. You will also learn to use filter by selection and filter by form to select records in the table, and to save a filter as a query so that you can use it again at a later time.

Creating a Columnar Form with AutoForm

The quickest way to create a form is to use AutoForm. Once you select the type of form and the table or query upon which the form is based, AutoForm selects all the fields from the table or query, creates a form for these fields, and displays the form on the screen.

REFERENCE window

CREATING A FORM WITH AUTOFORM

- In the Database window, click the Forms tab to display the Forms list.
- Click the New button to display the New Form dialog box.
- In the list box, select an AutoForm design (Columnar, Tabular, or Datasheet).
- Click the "Choose the table or query where the object's data comes from" list arrow to display the list of available tables and queries.
- Click the table or query you want as the basis for the form.
- Click the OK button. AutoForm creates the form and displays the first record.

Because Elena wants to create a form to display information about one writer at a time on the screen, she chooses the AutoForm columnar design for her form and bases it on the WRITERS table.

To create a columnar form using AutoForm:

1. If you have not done so, place your Student Disk in the appropriate drive, start Access, open the Issue25 database in the Tutorial folder on your Student Disk, and maximize the Database window. Click the **Forms** tab to display the Forms list. No forms appear in the list yet.
2. Click the **New** button. Access displays the New Form dialog box.
3. Click **AutoForm: Columnar** in the list box to highlight it.
4. Click the **Choose the table or query where the object's data comes from** list arrow to display a list of available tables.
5. Click **WRITERS** to select the WRITERS table. See Figure 5-2.

Figure 5-2 ◀
Completed New Form dialog box

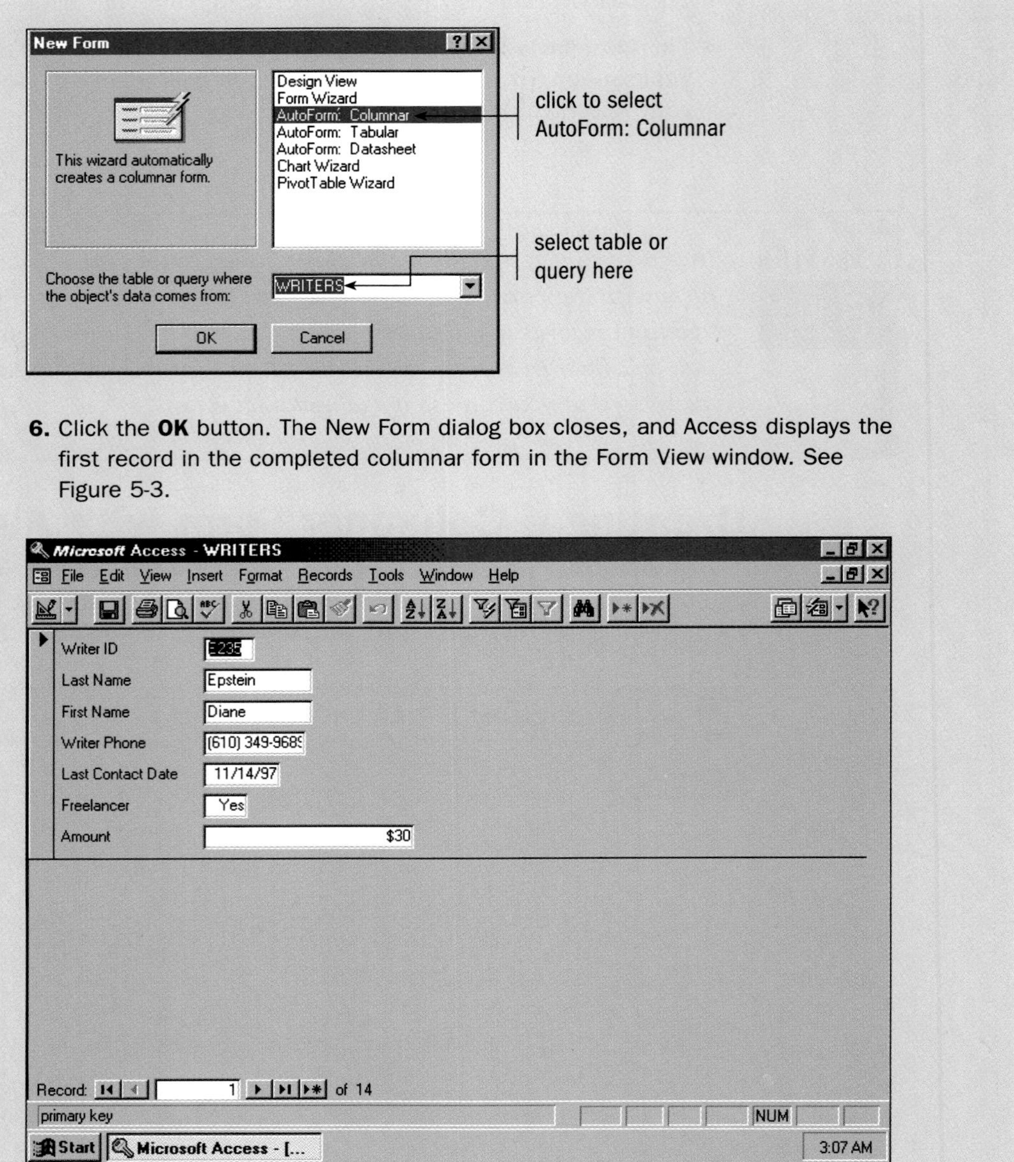

6. Click the **OK** button. The New Form dialog box closes, and Access displays the first record in the completed columnar form in the Form View window. See Figure 5-3.

Figure 5-3 ◀
First record in the completed columnar form for the WRITERS table

Access displays the first record from the WRITERS table in the new form. If you want to view other records from the WRITERS table, click the form navigation buttons. Or, if you know the specific record, type its number in the record number text box that is displayed between the form navigation buttons.

Saving a Form

Elena saves the form so that she and others can use it for future work with data from the WRITERS table. Elena saves the form with the name Writers Column Form and then closes the Form View window.

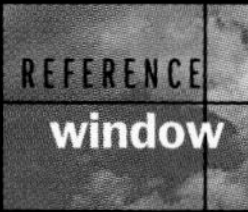

SAVING A NEW FORM

- Click the Save button on the toolbar. Access opens the Save As dialog box.
- Type the new form name in the Form Name text box.
- Click the OK button. Access saves the form and closes the dialog box.

To save and close a new form:

1. Click the **Save** button on the toolbar. Because you have not provided a name for this form yet, the Save As dialog box opens.
2. Type **Writers Column Form** in the Form Name text box.
3. Click the **OK** button. The Save As dialog box closes, and Access saves the form. The new form name will appear in the Forms list.
4. Click the Form View window **Close** button. The Form View window closes, and the Database window becomes the active window.

Next, Elena creates a form to show a specific writer, using data from the WRITERS table, and his or her articles, using data from the BUSINESS ARTICLES table. Elena will use this form to update the records in the WRITERS and BUSINESS ARTICLES tables.

Creating a Form with the Form Wizard

Because AutoForm creates forms based only on a single table or query, Elena must use a different method to create her next form. She decides to use the Form Wizard to create this new form. To base the form on two tables, Elena needs a main form and a subform. Elena will choose the WRITERS table data for the main form and the BUSINESS ARTICLES table data for the subform, so that the form will display the information for a single writer with a subform displaying all the articles by that writer. If Elena had decided to select the BUSINESS ARTICLES table data to be the main form and the WRITERS table data to be the subform instead, the form would display a single article with the information for the article's writer.

The main/subform form type uses data from two (or more) tables; therefore, the tables must be related. Elena has already defined a one-to-many relationship between the WRITERS and the BUSINESS ARTICLES tables, so she can create the form now.

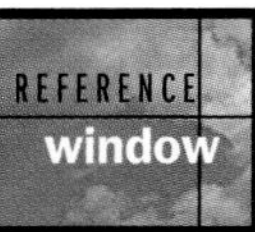

CREATING A MAIN/SUBFORM FORM WITH THE FORM WIZARD

- In the Forms list of the Database window, click the New button to display the New Form dialog box.
- Click Form Wizard, then click the OK button.
- Select the fields from tables and queries upon which the form will be based, then click the Next > button.
- Select the way in which you will view the records in the form, then click the Next > button.
- Select tabular or datasheet style for the subform, then click the Next > button.
- Select the predefined form style you want, then click the Next > button.
- Enter a name for the main form and for the subform, then click the Finish button. Access creates the form and saves the main form and the subform on the disk. Access opens the form and displays the first record in Form View.

Elena creates the form using the Form Wizard.

To create a main/subform form:

1. Click the **New** button. The New Form dialog box opens. Click **Form Wizard** to highlight it, then click the **OK** button. Access starts the Form Wizard, and the first Form Wizard dialog box is displayed. See Figure 5-4.

Figure 5-4 The first Form Wizard dialog box

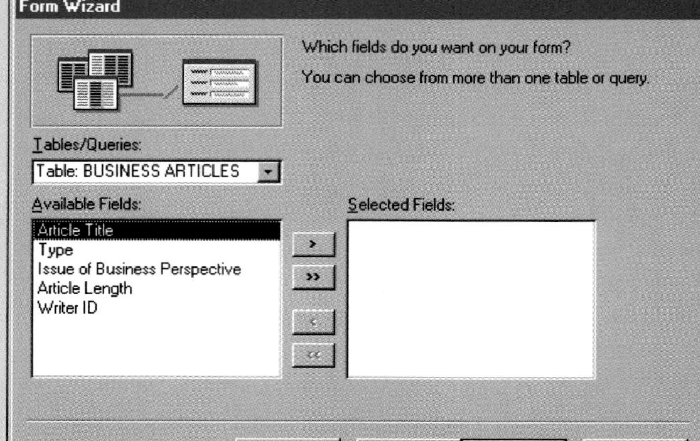

In this dialog box, you select the fields to be used in the form. The Tables/Queries list box displays Table: BUSINESS ARTICLES, the currently selected table or query, and the Available Fields list box displays the fields that are available in the selected table or query. Elena selects the WRITERS table fields first to create the main form.

2. Click the **Tables/Queries** list arrow to display the list of available tables and queries and then click **Table: WRITERS**.

3. Click the >> button to move all fields from the WRITERS table from the Available Fields list box to the Selected Fields list box.

Elena is now ready to select all the fields from the BUSINESS ARTICLES table except for the Writer ID field (which was already included with the WRITERS table).

4. Click the **Tables/Queries** list arrow to display the list of available tables and queries, then click **Table: BUSINESS ARTICLES**. Use the [>] button to move the Article Title, Type, Issue of Business Perspective, and Article Length fields to the Selected Fields list.

5. Click the [Next >] button to display the next Form Wizard dialog box.

   This dialog box allows you to choose how to view the records in this form. Elena wants to view the records by writer.

6. If necessary, click **by WRITERS** in the list box. Make sure the radio button next to "Form with subform(s)" is selected. See Figure 5-5. Click the [Next >] button to display the next Form Wizard dialog box.

Figure 5-5 The next Form Wizard dialog box

click to see WRITERS table records in main form

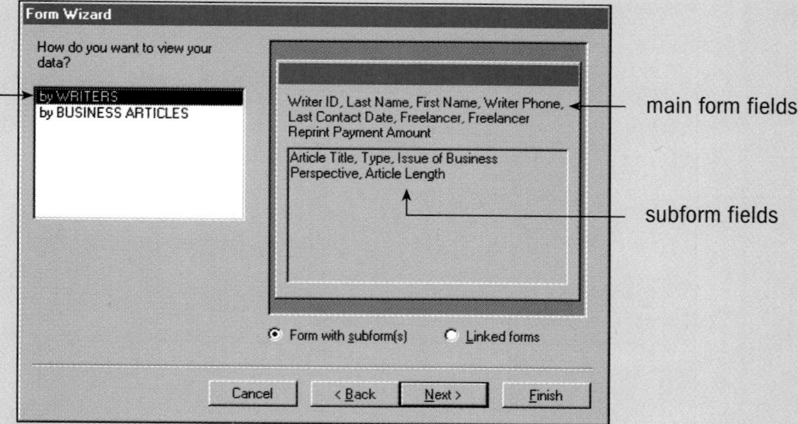

This dialog box allows you to choose between two layouts for the subform: tabular or datasheet. The main form will use a columnar layout, but you can choose tabular or datasheet layout for the subform. Elena chooses Tabular.

7. Click the **Tabular** radio button. Click the [Next >] button to display the next Form Wizard dialog box.

   This dialog box allows you to choose a style for the form. Access has several predefined styles that use various background patterns and styles for the labels and data text boxes. Elena uses the standard style.

8. If necessary, click **Standard** to select it, then click the [Next >] button to display the next Form Wizard box. See Figure 5-6.

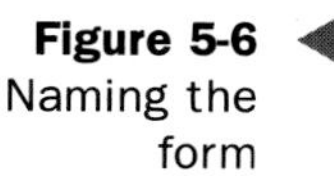

Figure 5-6 Naming the form

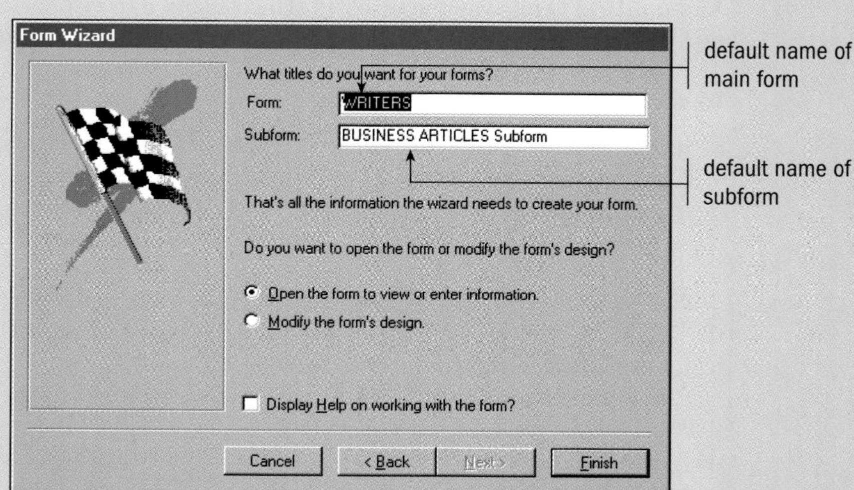

This dialog box lets you name the form. Access displays the default name WRITERS for the main form and BUSINESS ARTICLES Subform for the subform. Elena decides a more descriptive name for the main form will be helpful and that using a mix of uppercase and lowercase letters for the subform name will make it more consistent with the other form names.

9. Type **Writers and Business Articles Form** in the Form text box, press the **Tab** key, then type **Business Articles Subform** in the Subform text box. Make sure the radio button next to "Open the form to view or enter information" is selected, then click the **Finish** button. Access saves the main form and the subform and displays the first WRITERS record with the related BUSINESS ARTICLES records. See Figure 5-7.

Figure 5-7 The completed Writers and Business Articles Form

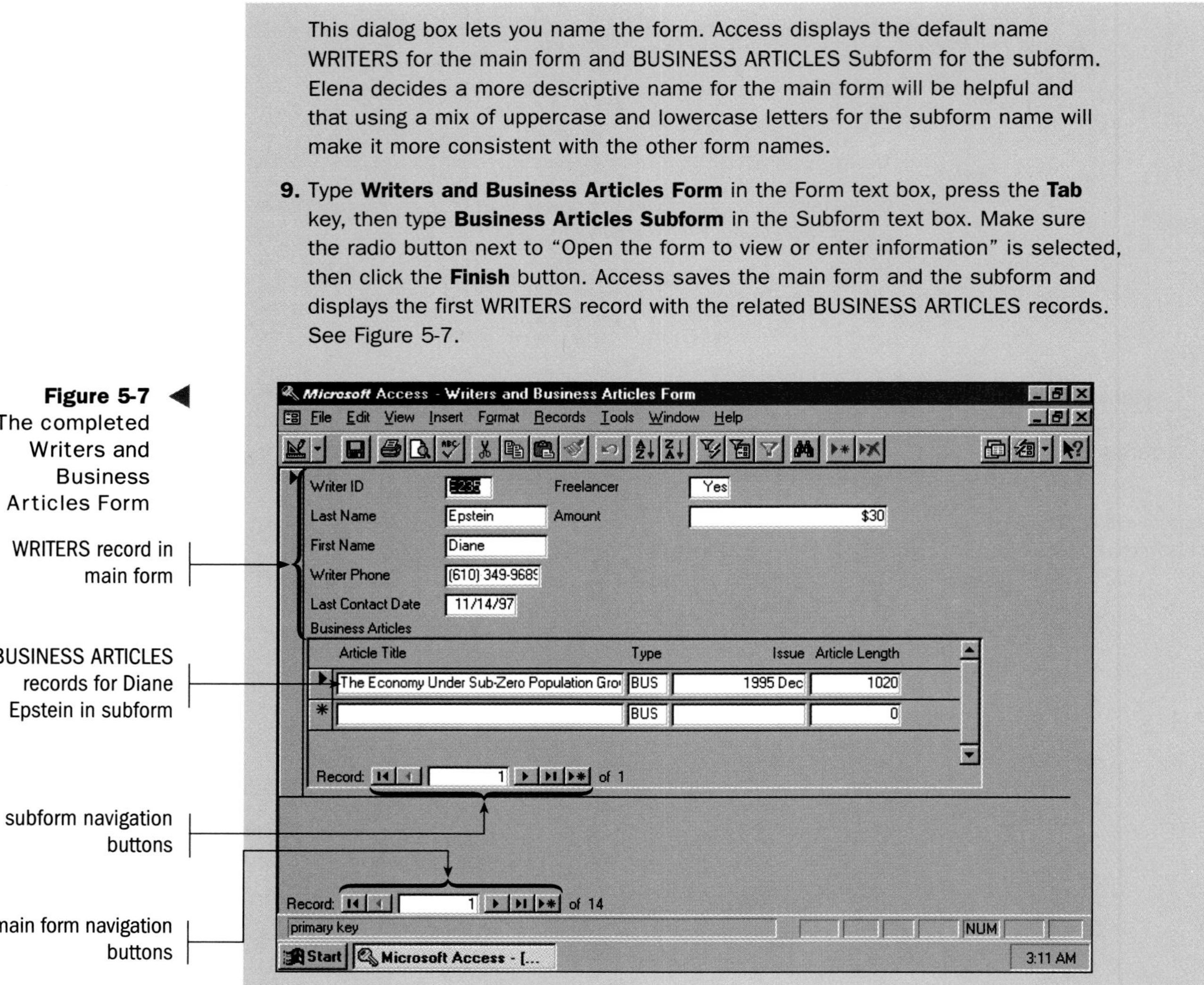

Because the Form View window is maximized, the form title is displayed in the Access title bar. Access displays the fields from the first record in the WRITERS table in the main form in a columnar format. The records in this main form appear sorted in ascending order by the Freelancer field and subsorted in ascending order by the Freelancer Reprint Payment Amount field. This was the order in which Elena had last sorted the table. She decides to sort the records in primary key sequence (by Writer ID) to view the records in the form.

To sort the records by Writer ID:

1. If necessary, click in the **Writer ID** text box to select it, then click the **Sort Ascending** button on the toolbar. Access sorts the records in ascending order by Writer ID.

The record for Kelly Cox (Writer ID C200) now appears in the form, since her Writer ID is alphabetically first. Kelly Cox has one record in the BUSINESS ARTICLES table, which is shown in the subform in tabular format.

Elena wants to view the data for a writer who has more than one record in the BUSINESS ARTICLES table. Two sets of navigation buttons appear at the bottom of the form, as shown in Figure 5-7. You use the top set of navigation buttons to select records from the related table (BUSINESS ARTICLES) in the subform and the bottom set to select records from the primary table (WRITERS) in the main form.

To navigate to different main and subform records:

1. To find a writer who has more than one record in the BUSINESS ARTICLES table, click the main form **Next Record** button three times. Access displays the record for Valerie Hall in the main form and her three articles in the subform.
2. Click the subform **Next Record** button once. Access changes the current record to the second article in the subform.
3. Click the main form **First Record** button. The main form displays the record for Kelly Cox and the subform displays the BUSINESS ARTICLES record for Kelly Cox.

   If you know which record you want to view, you can enter the record number in the text box between the navigation buttons. Elena wants to view the record for Leroy W. Johnson, the fifth record in the WRITERS table.
4. Click the record number that is displayed between the main form navigation buttons and then press the **F2** key to highlight the number. Type **5** and then press the **Enter** key. The form now displays the record for Leroy W. Johnson, record number 5 in the WRITERS table.

Now that Elena has created the Writers and Business Articles Form, she is ready to use it to update the records in the WRITERS and the BUSINESS ARTICLES tables.

Maintaining Table Data Using a Form

Elena needs to add a new article to the Issue25 database for a writer already listed in the WRITERS table, and a new writer to the WRITERS table and an article by that writer to the BUSINESS ARTICLES table. She also wants to make two changes to the record for one of Valerie Hall's articles. These database modifications involve both tables, as shown in Figure 5-8.

Figure 5-8 Changes to records in the Issue25 database

Table	Action
WRITERS	Add new writer Writer ID: L350 Last Name: Lawton FIrst Name: Pat Writer Phone: (705) 677-1991 Last Contact Date: 9/4/94 Freelancer: No Amount: 0
BUSINESS ARTICLES	Add: Article Title: Law Over the Past 25 Years (by Pat Lawton) Type: LAW Issue: 1994 Dec Article Length: 2834 Add: Article Title: Advertising Over the Past 25 Years (by Thuy Ngo) Type: ADV Issue: 1994 Dec Article Length: 3285 Change: Article Title: The BCCI Scandal (by Valerie Hall) New Issue Date: 1991 Aug New Article Length: 2779

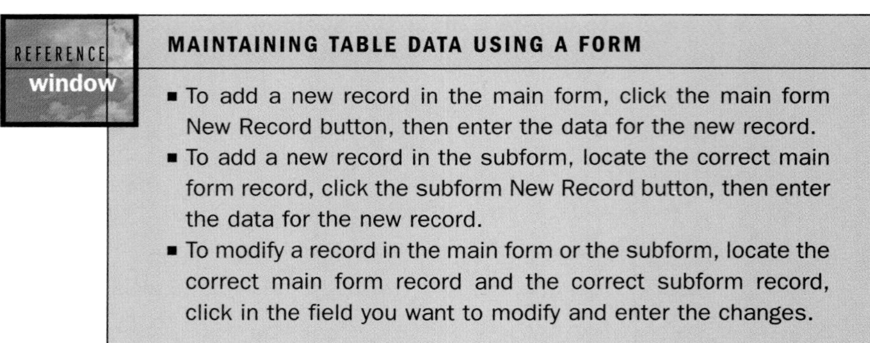

REFERENCE window

MAINTAINING TABLE DATA USING A FORM

- To add a new record in the main form, click the main form New Record button, then enter the data for the new record.
- To add a new record in the subform, locate the correct main form record, click the subform New Record button, then enter the data for the new record.
- To modify a record in the main form or the subform, locate the correct main form record and the correct subform record, click in the field you want to modify and enter the changes.

Elena begins by adding the new article for Thuy Ngo. Elena knows from her previous work with the Issue25 database that there is already a record for Thuy Ngo in the WRITERS table, record number 10.

To add a record in a subform:

1. Click the record number text box that is displayed between the main form navigation buttons and then press the **F2** key to highlight the number. Type **10** and then press the **Enter** key. Thuy Ngo's record appears, and the Writer ID field is selected in the main form.
2. Click the **New Record** button in the subform. Access displays a blank record in the Business Articles Subform.

   TROUBLE? If the entire form appears blank, you may have clicked the New Record button for the main form. Repeat Steps 1 and 2.

3. Type **Advertising Over the Past 25 Years**, press the **Tab** key, type **ADV**, press the **Tab** key, type **1994 Dec**, press the **Tab** key, type **3285**, and then press the **Tab** key. See Figure 5-9. Access has added this record not just to the Writers and Business Articles Form but also to the BUSINESS ARTICLES table.

Figure 5-9 Adding a record in a subform

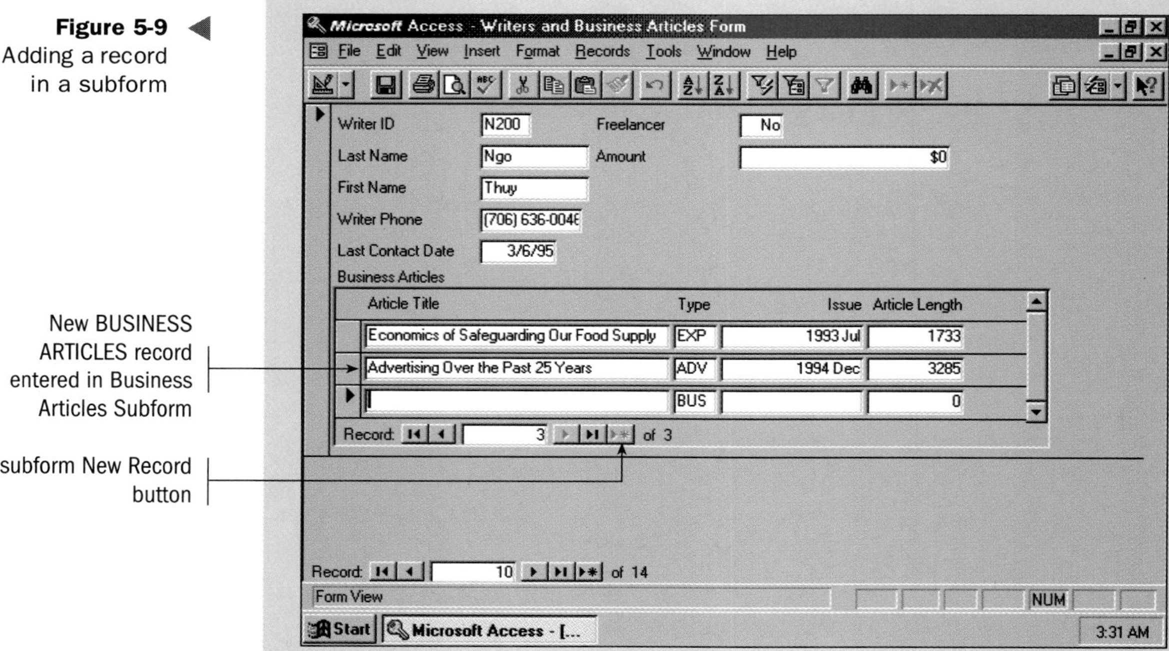

When you created the Writers and Business Articles Form, you selected all fields from the WRITERS table for the main form. However, you did not select the Writer ID field for the Business Articles Subform. Because the Writer ID field is the common field between the two tables, Access uses the Writer ID field value from the main form when it saves the subform new record in the BUSINESS ARTICLES table. Therefore, Thuy's article will be saved with his current Writer ID value.

Next, Elena adds the new writer, Pat Lawton, to the WRITERS table and then adds her article to the BUSINESS ARTICLES table.

To add a new writer and a new article using a form:

1. Click the main form's **New Record** button. Access moves to record 15 in the main form and to record 1 in the subform. These new records contain no data. Click in the main form's Writer ID field to position the pointer there.
2. To enter the first five field values, type **L350**, press the **Tab** key, type **Lawton**, press the **Tab** key, type **Pat**, press the **Tab** key, type **7056771991**, press the **Tab** key, type **9/4/94,** and then press the **Tab** key.
3. Type **No** to change the Freelancer field value to No, and then press the **Tab** key to move to the Amount field.
4. Press the **Tab** key. Access automatically enters the field value of $0, saves the new record in the WRITERS table, and then positions the insertion point in the Article Title field in the subform.
5. Type **Law Over the Past 25 Years**, press the **Tab** key, type **LAW**, press the **Tab** key, type **1994 Dec**, press the **Tab** key, and then type **2834**.
6. Press the **Tab** key. Access saves the new record in the BUSINESS ARTICLES table and positions the insertion point in the Article Title field for the next available record in the Business Articles Subform. See Figure 5-10.

Figure 5-10 Adding records in a main form and a subform

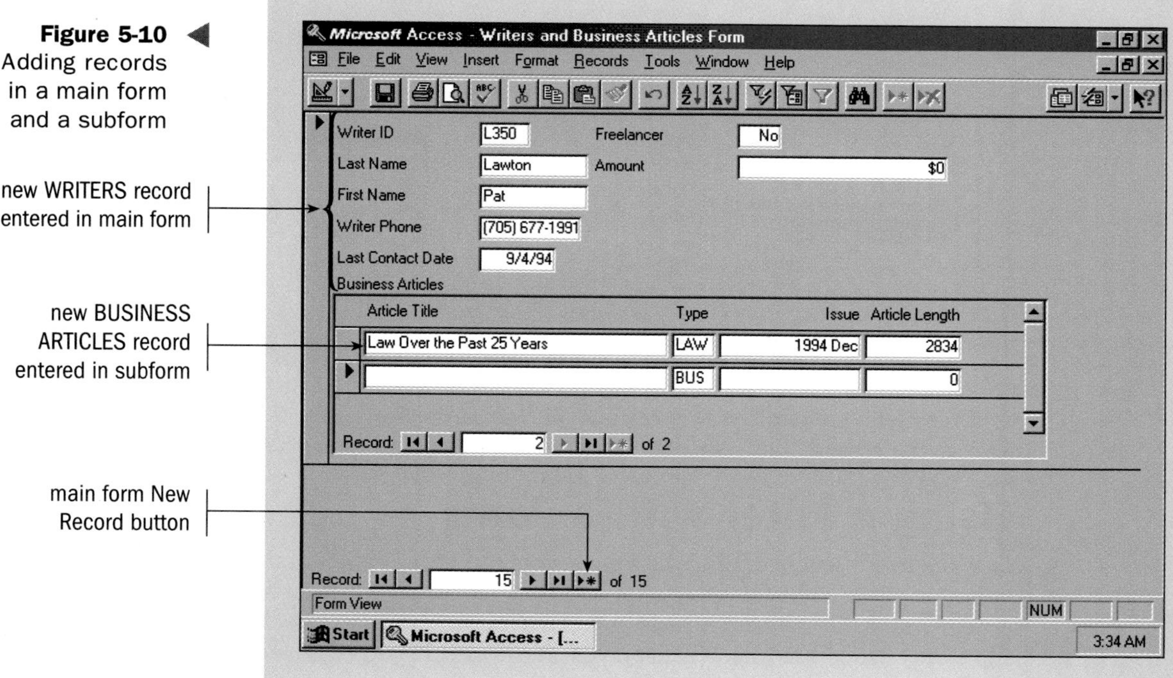

Finally, Elena finds the record for Valerie Hall and makes the two changes to one of her articles.

To find a record and change table field values using a form:

1. Click the **First Record** button in the main form. Access displays the record for Kelly Cox. Click in the Last Name text box for the record.
2. Click **Edit**, then click **Find** to display the Find in Field dialog box. Be sure that the Search Only Current field box is not selected.
3. Type **Hall** in the Find What text box, then click the **Find First** button. Access displays the record for Valerie Hall.
4. Click the Find in Field **Close** button to close the dialog box.
5. Double-click **Jul** in the Issue field for the article title The BCCI Scandal and then type **Aug** as the correct month value for the Issue field.
6. Press the **Tab** key to move to and highlight the Article Length field.
7. Type **2779** as the correct field value for the Article Length field.

Elena has completed her maintenance tasks, which have been automatically saved to the underlying tables. She closes the Form View window and returns to the Database window.

To close the Form View window:

1. Click the Form View window **Close** button. The Form View window closes and the Database window becomes the active window. Notice that both Business Articles Subform and Writers and Business Articles Form appear in the Forms list. See Figure 5-11.

Figure 5-11 The Forms list in the Database window

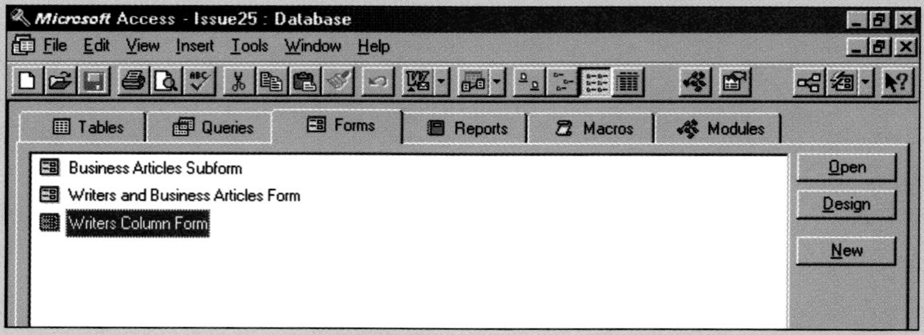

Microsoft Access - Issue25 : Database
File Edit View Insert Tools Window Help
Tables Queries Forms Reports Macros Modules
Business Articles Subform
Writers and Business Articles Form
Writers Column Form
Open
Design
New

First Elena created the Writers and Business Articles Form, then she used the form to update the records, now she can use it to select records from the table.

Using a Filter with a Form

In Datasheet View, you used the Find command to find records that match a specific field value, and you used the Quick Sort buttons to display all records in a specified order by a field or by two adjacent fields. The Find button and the Quick Sort buttons work the same way when records are displayed in a form. If you want Access to display selected records, display records sorted by two or more fields, or display selected records and sort them, you use a filter.

A **filter** is a set of criteria that describes the records you want to see in a form and specifies their sequence. A filter is similar to a query, but it applies only to the form that is currently in use. If you want to use a filter at another time, you can save the filter as a query.

Access has three filter tools that allow you to specify and apply filters: filter by selection, filter by form, and advanced filter/sort. With filter by selection and filter by form, you specify the record selection criteria directly in the form. Filter by selection finds records that match a particular field value. Filter by form finds records that match multiple selection criteria using the same Access logical And and Or comparison operators discussed in Tutorial 4. After applying a filter by selection or filter by form, you can rearrange the records using the Quick Sort buttons.

Advanced filter/sort allows you to specify multiple selection criteria and to specify a sort order for the selected records in the Advanced Filter/Sort window, in the same way you specify record selection criteria and sort order for a query in the Query Design window. Since you are already familiar with using the Query Design window to specify selection criteria and sort order, you will only use filter by selection and filter by form in this tutorial.

Using Filter by Selection

Harold asks Elena to select all the records for freelancers, as he needs their names and phone numbers. Elena uses a filter by selection to specify the criterion that only records for freelancers be selected. In filter by selection, you first display a record that contains the field value you want and then apply the filter. Access selects all records that have a matching value in the same field.

REFERENCE window

SELECTING RECORDS WITH FILTER BY SELECTION

- Open the form you want to use for selecting and viewing records.
- In the Form View window, display a record that contains a field that meets the selection criterion.
- Click in that field's text box to indicate that this is the value you want to match.
- Click the Filter By Selection button on the toolbar. Access selects all records that meet the selection criterion.

Because Elena needs information from the WRITERS table, she uses the Writers Column Form created earlier to view the records.

To find records for freelancers using filter by selection:

1. Double-click **Writers Column Form** to select and open the form. Access opens the form and displays the first record.
2. The first record displayed is for Diane Epstein, a freelancer, which matches the selection criterion. The record for Diane Epstein is the first record because the last time this table was sorted (by Freelancer field and then by Freelancer Reprint Payment Amount), her record appeared first in the sorted table. Click in the **Freelancer** text box to indicate that this is the value you want to match.
3. Click the **Filter By Selection** button on the toolbar. Access searches the WRITERS table and finds all records that have Yes as the Freelancer field value. See Figure 5-12.

Figure 5-12 Form View after filter by selection is applied

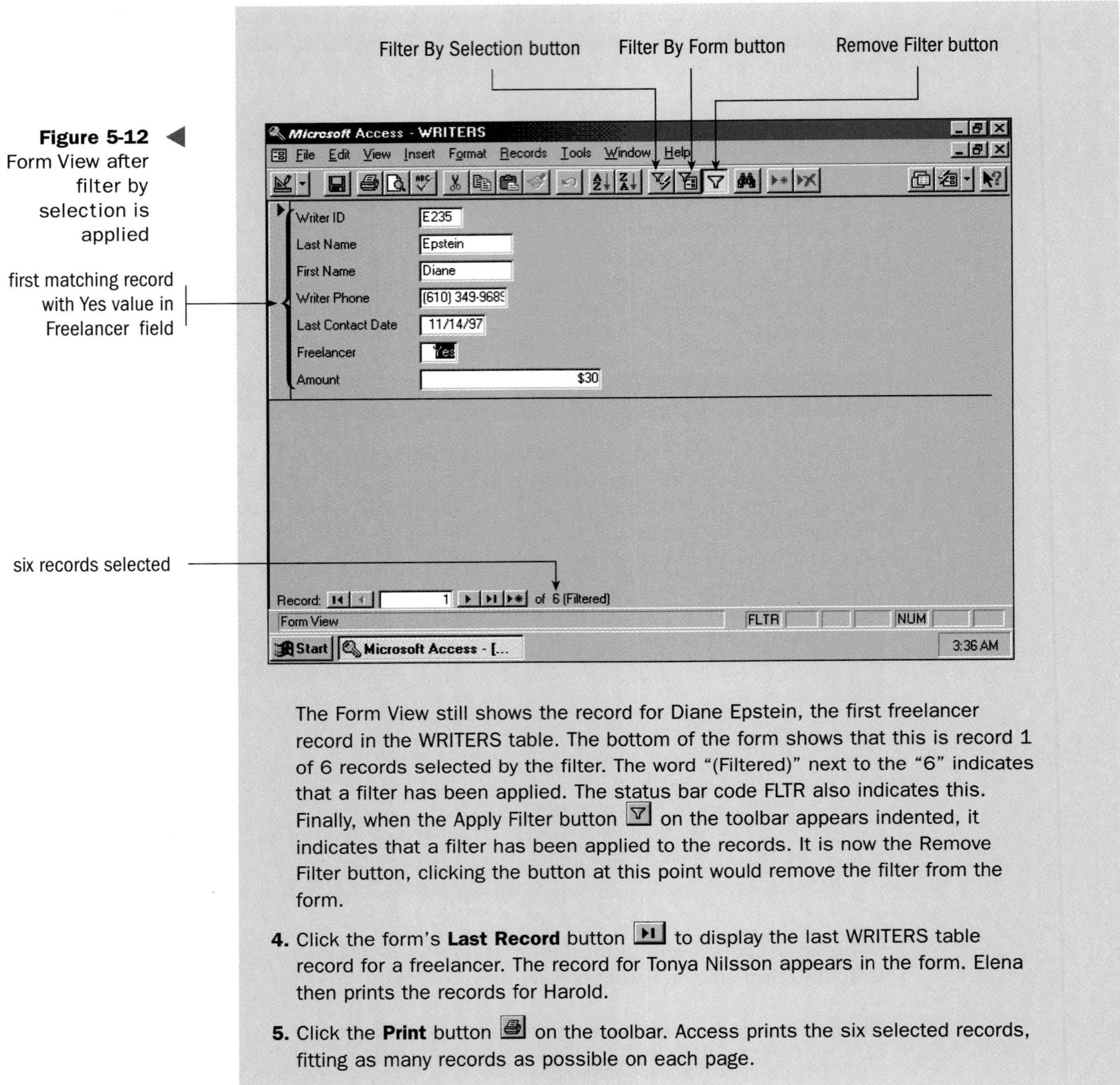

The Form View still shows the record for Diane Epstein, the first freelancer record in the WRITERS table. The bottom of the form shows that this is record 1 of 6 records selected by the filter. The word "(Filtered)" next to the "6" indicates that a filter has been applied. The status bar code FLTR also indicates this. Finally, when the Apply Filter button on the toolbar appears indented, it indicates that a filter has been applied to the records. It is now the Remove Filter button, clicking the button at this point would remove the filter from the form.

4. Click the form's **Last Record** button to display the last WRITERS table record for a freelancer. The record for Tonya Nilsson appears in the form. Elena then prints the records for Harold.

5. Click the **Print** button on the toolbar. Access prints the six selected records, fitting as many records as possible on each page.

Elena is finished finding the freelancers' names and phone numbers for Harold so she removes the filter and closes the Form View window.

To remove the filter and close the Form View window:

1. Click the **Remove Filter** button on the toolbar. The Apply Filter button appears raised, Access removes the filter, and the bottom of the screen again shows there are 15 records. The FLTR code in the status bar disappears.

2. Click the **Close** button on the Form View window. Access closes the Form View window, and the Database window becomes active.

Using Filter by Form

After she gives the list of freelancers and their phone numbers to Harold, Elena is given another task by Brian. He asks Elena to create a form that displays all recent (that is, printed after 1990) business articles of type EXP (exposé) or BUS (business). He would like the list sorted in ascending order, from earliest to the most recent publication date. Because this requires data from the BUSINESS ARTICLES table only, Elena first creates a columnar form based on the BUSINESS ARTICLES table, then uses filter by form to find the requested records, and then uses the Quick Sort buttons to sort the information.

SELECTING RECORDS WITH FILTER BY FORM

- Open the form you want to use for selecting and viewing records.
- In the Form View window, click the Filter By Form button on the toolbar.
- Enter a simple selection criterion or an And condition in the first form by entering the selection criteria in the text boxes for the appropriate fields.
- If there is an Or condition, click the Or tab and enter the second part of the Or condition in the second form. Continue to enter Or conditions on separate forms by using the Or tab.
- Click the Apply Filter button on the toolbar. Access applies the filter and displays the first record matching the selection criteria.

To create the columnar form based on the BUSINESS ARTICLES table:

1. If necessary, click the **Forms** tab to display the Forms list. Click the **New** button. Access displays the New Form dialog box.
2. Click **AutoForm: Columnar** in the list box to highlight it.
3. Click the **Choose the table or query where the object's data comes from** list arrow to display a list of available tables.
4. Click **BUSINESS ARTICLES** to select the BUSINESS ARTICLES table.
5. Click the **OK** button. The New Form dialog box closes, and Access displays the completed form.

Elena saves this form for later use.

To save a form:

1. Click the **Save** button on the toolbar. Access displays the Save As dialog box.
2. Type **Business Articles Column Form** in the Form Name text box, then click the **OK** button to save the form.

Elena is now ready to use a filter by form to select the records from the Business Articles Column Form. The multiple selection criteria Elena wants to specify are: BUS article *and* after 12/31/90 *or* EXP article *and* after 12/31/90.

To select records using filter by form:

1. Click the **Filter By Form** button on the toolbar. Access displays a blank form. See Figure 5-13.

Figure 5-13 Blank form for filter by form

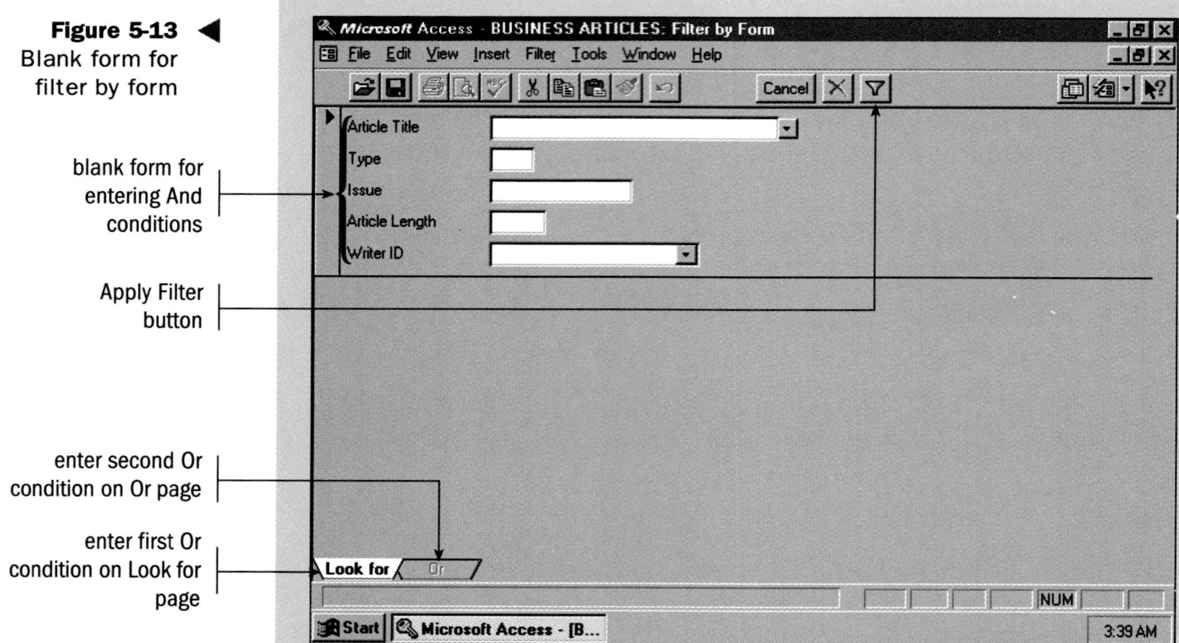

In this blank form, you specify multiple selection criteria by entering conditions in the text boxes for the fields in a record. If you enter criteria in more than one field, you create the equivalent of an And condition: Access will select any record that matches all of the criteria. To create an Or condition, you enter the criteria for the first part of the Or in the field on the first (Look for) blank form, then click the Or tab. The Or tab displays a new blank form. You enter the criteria for the second part of the Or in the same field on this new blank form. Access selects any record that matches either all criteria on the first form *or* all criteria on the second form. Elena uses the blank form to enter the criteria for the first part of the Or condition.

2. Click the **Type** text box, then click the **Type** list arrow, then click **BUS** to select the BUS type.
3. Click the **Issue** text box and type **>#12/31/90#**. You have now specified the logical operator (And) and the comparison operator (>) for the condition BUS type article *and* after 12/31/90. To add the second part of the Or condition, Elena displays the second blank form.
4. Click the **Or** tab to display a second blank form. The cursor is in the text box for the Issue field.
5. Click the **Type** text box, then click the **Type** list arrow, then click **EXP**.
6. Click the **Issue** text box and type **>#12/31/90#**. The form now contains the equivalent of the second And condition: EXP type article *and* after 12/31/90. See Figure 5-14.

Figure 5-14 Completed filter by form

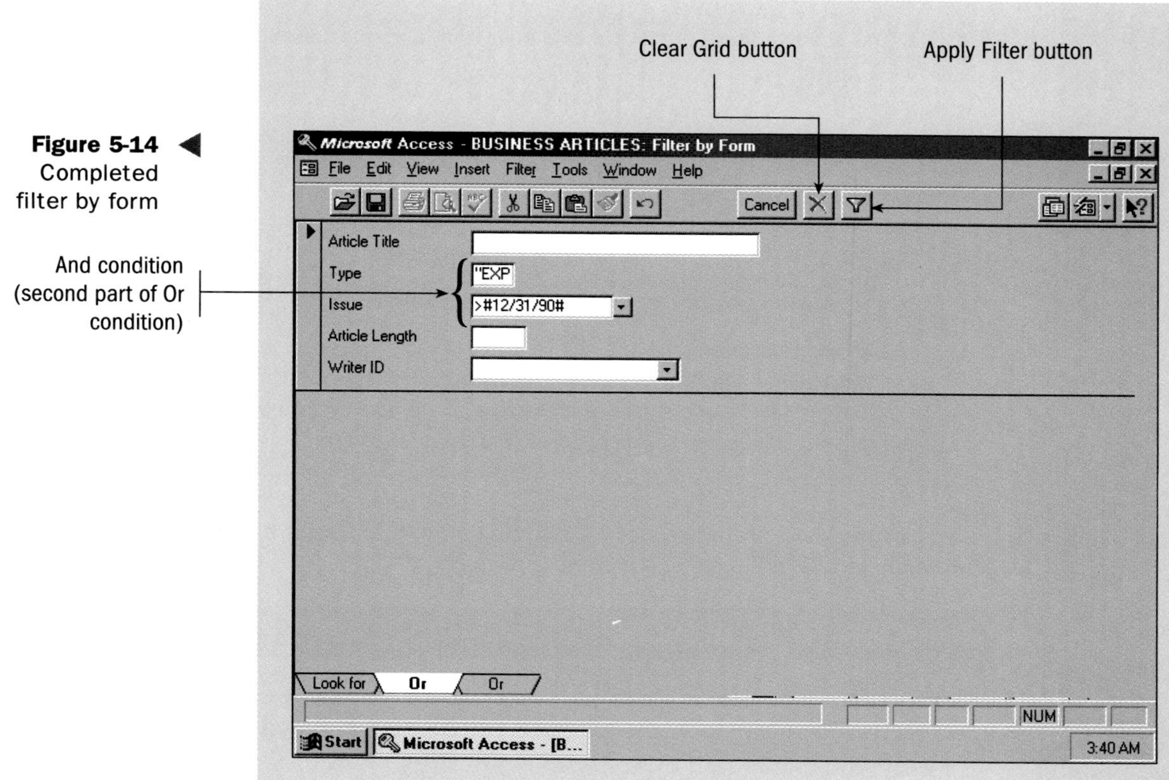

Combined with the first form, you now have the Or condition, and the filter by form conditions are complete.

7. Click the **Apply Filter** button on the toolbar to apply the filter to the records in the BUSINESS ARTICLES table. Access applies the filter and displays the first record (The Economy Under Sub-Zero Population Growth, a BUS article in the 1995 Dec issue) that matches the selection criteria. The bottom of the screen shows that four records were selected. See Figure 5-15.

Figure 5-15 First record that matches the selection criteria

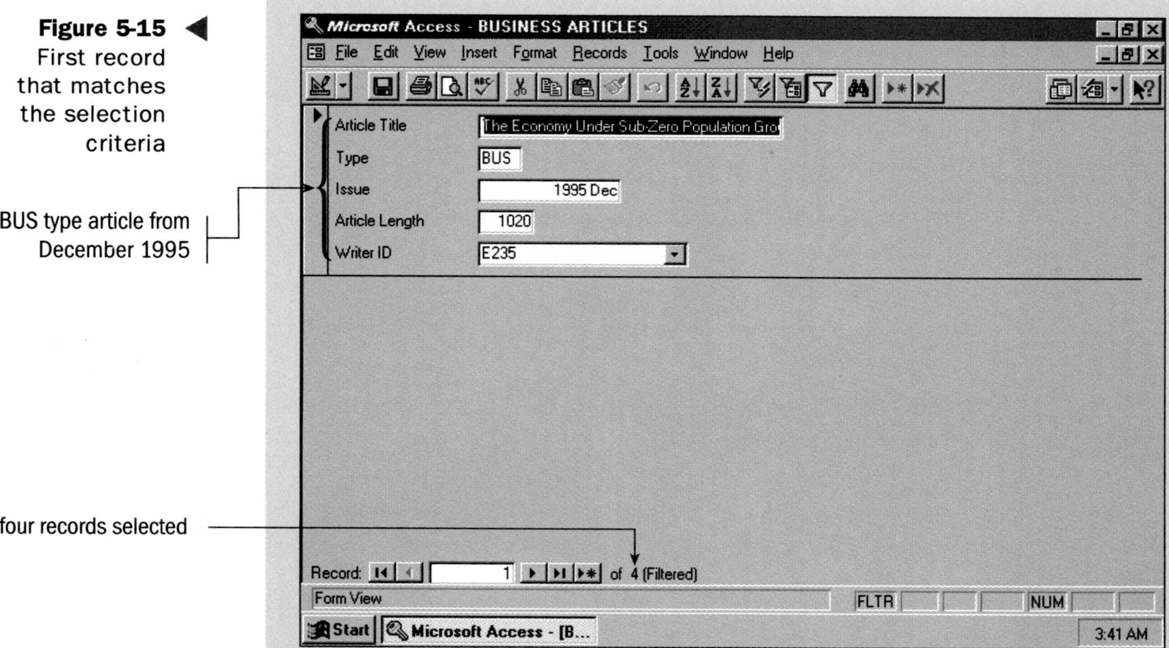

8. Click the **Last Record** button to display the last selected record (The BCCI Scandal).

Elena notices that the records are not sorted from earliest to most recent date, so she does that now.

To sort the records from earliest to most recent date:

1. Click in the **Issue** text box on the form to select that field.
2. Click the **Sort Ascending** button on the toolbar. Access sorts the selected records in ascending order by issue. The record for "The BCCI Scandal" article, the earliest of the selected records, appears in the form and the record number at the bottom of the screen shows that it is the first of the four selected records.

Elena prints the selected records for Brian. Now that Elena has defined the filter, she decides she would like to save the filter as a query.

Saving a Filter As a Query

By saving a filter as a query, Elena can reuse the filter in the future by opening the saved query. The saved query stores the selection criteria used in the filter.

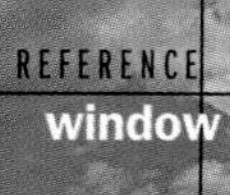

SAVING A FILTER AS A QUERY

- Create a filter by form.
- Click the Save button on the toolbar to display the Save As Query dialog box.
- Type the name for the query, then click the OK button. Access saves the query.

To save a filter as a query:

1. Click the **Filter By Form** button on the toolbar. Access displays the form with the selection criteria.
2. Click the **Save** button on the toolbar. The Save As Query dialog box opens.
3. Type **Recent BUS and EXP Articles Query** in the Query Name text box and then click the **OK** button. Access saves the filter as a query, and the Save As Query dialog box closes.

   Next, Elena clears the selection criteria, closes the filter window, and returns to the Form View window.

4. Click the Filter window Close button. The filter window closes and the Form View window becomes active.
5. Click the the **Remove Filter** button on the toolbar. The bottom of the screen shows that there are 27 records available in the BUSINESS ARTICLES table.

Elena wants to check that the filter was saved as a query, so she closes the Form View window.

To close the Form View window and view the query list:

1. Click the Form View window **Close** button. Access closes the Form View window and opens the Database window.
2. Click the **Queries** tab to display the Queries list. See Figure 5-16. Recent BUS and EXP Articles Query is now listed.

Figure 5-16 Queries list in the Database window

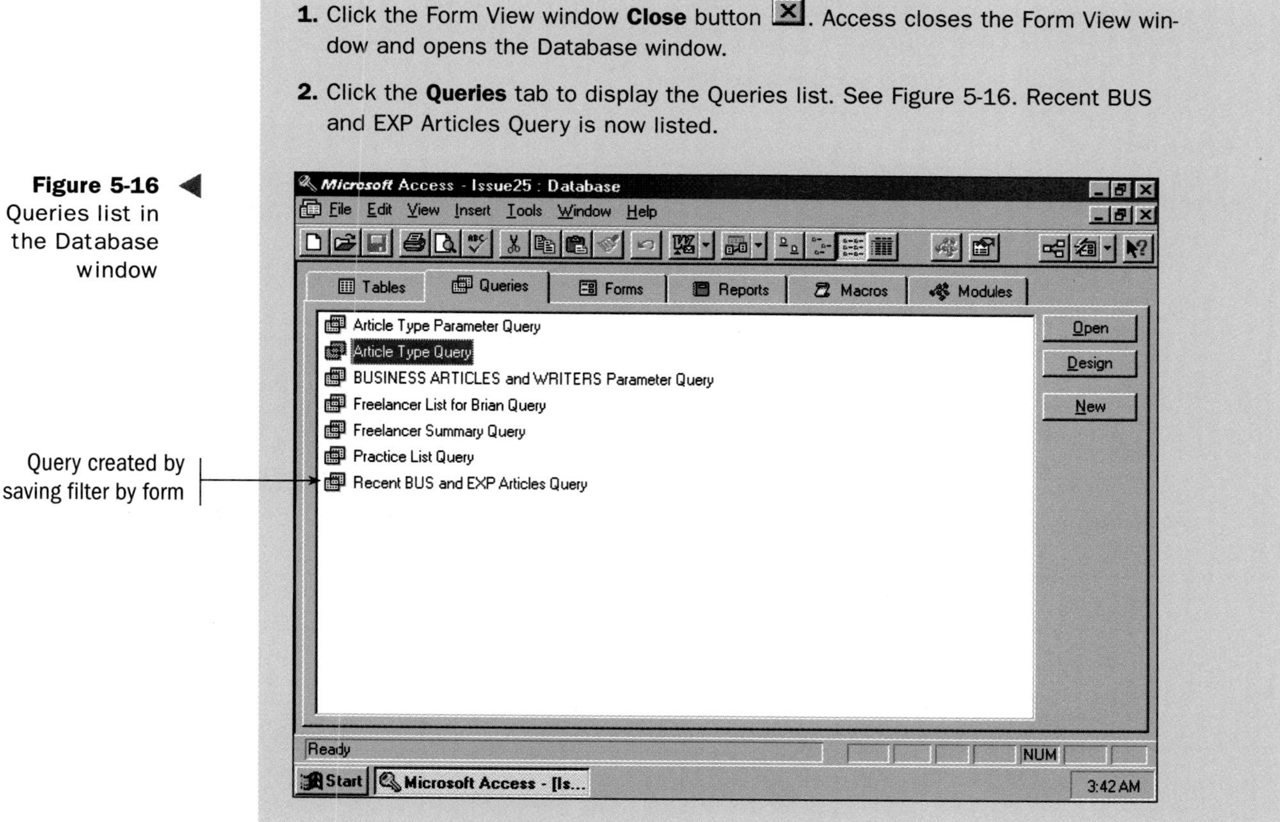

Next, Elena wants to practice applying a filter that was saved as a query.

Applying a Filter That Was Saved As a Query

Elena opens the Business Articles Column Form and applies the Recent BUS and EXP Articles Query as a filter.

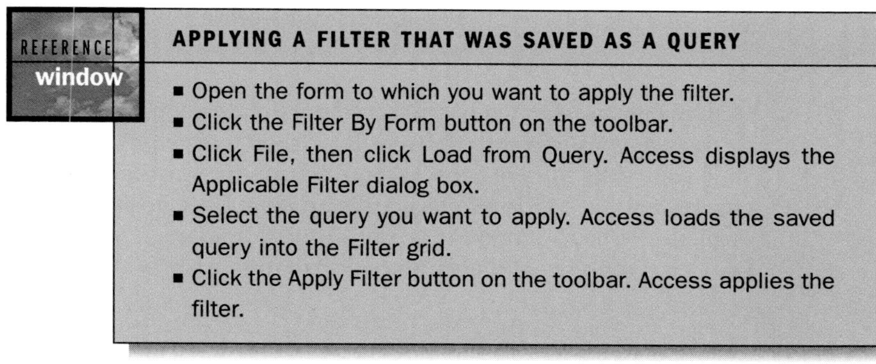

REFERENCE window

APPLYING A FILTER THAT WAS SAVED AS A QUERY

- Open the form to which you want to apply the filter.
- Click the Filter By Form button on the toolbar.
- Click File, then click Load from Query. Access displays the Applicable Filter dialog box.
- Select the query you want to apply. Access loads the saved query into the Filter grid.
- Click the Apply Filter button on the toolbar. Access applies the filter.

To apply a filter that was saved as a query:

1. Click the **Forms** tab in the Database window and double-click **Business Articles Column Form** in the Forms list. The Form View window opens.
2. Click the **Filter By Form** button on the toolbar.
3. Click **File**, then click **Load from Query**. Access displays the Applicable Filter dialog box. See Figure 5-17.

Figure 5-17 Applicable Filter dialog box

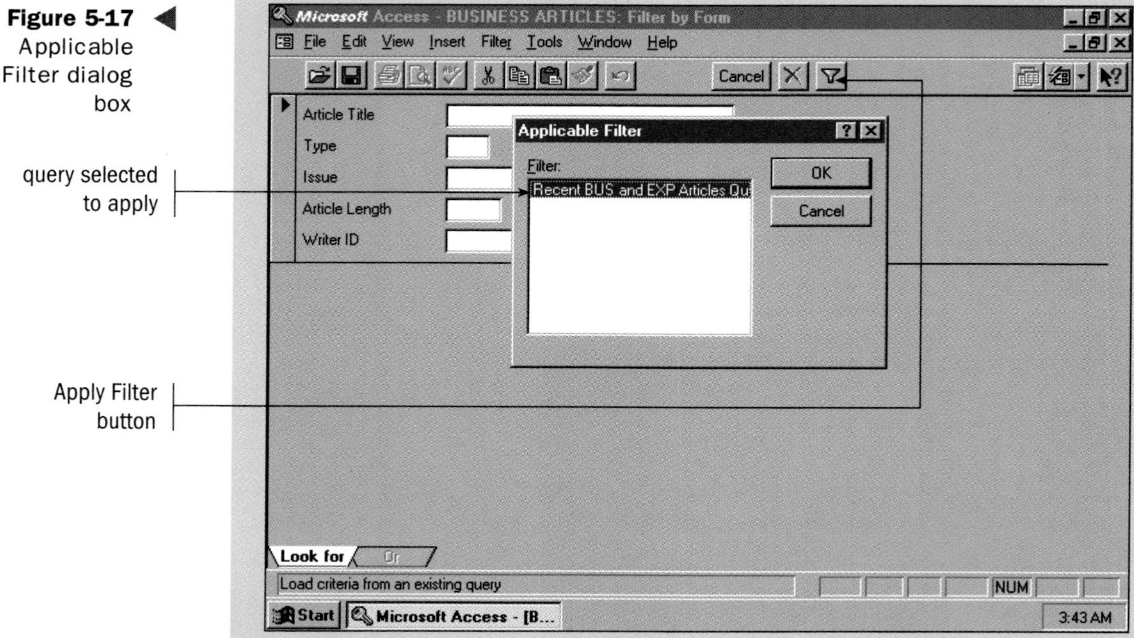

4. Double-click **Recent BUS and EXP Articles Query** in the Filter list box. The Applicable Filter dialog box closes, and Access loads the saved query into the Filter grid.
5. Click the **Apply Filter** button on the toolbar. Access applies the filter and displays the first record in the form. Notice that the first record is for the article "The Economy Under Sub-Zero Population Growth." This is not the article that appeared first when you sorted the articles by date. The saved query did not save the sort order.
6. Click the Form View window **Close** button. The Form View window closes, and the Database window becomes the active window.

In the next session, you will learn how to create a custom form. Custom forms allow you to create layouts that are different from those created by the Form Wizard and AutoForm.

If you want to take a break and resume the tutorial at later time, exit Access. When you resume the tutorial, place your Student Disk in the appropriate drive, start Access, open the Issue25 database in the Tutorial folder on your Student Disk, maximize the Database window, and click the Forms tab to display the Forms list.

Quick Check

1. What is a form?
2. What are three form designs that you can create with AutoForm?
3. What formats does the Form Wizard use to display records in a main/subform form?
4. How many sets of navigation buttons appear in a main/subform form, and what does each set control?
5. What is a filter?
6. What is the purpose of filter by selection? Filter by form?
7. How can you tell if a Form View window is displaying records to which a filter has been applied?
8. How do you reuse a filter in the future?

SESSION 5.2

In this session, you will learn to create a custom form using the Form Design window; add, delete, and modify controls on a form; add a form header; and add a graphic image to a form. You will also learn to change object colors and add special effects to form controls.

Creating a Custom Form

Elena places the Issue25 database on the company network, so others can use it to answer their questions. The most popular query proves to be the Article Type Query (created in Tutorial 4), which lists the article title, type, and length, and the writer's first and last names. Harold suggests that Elena present the same information in a more attractive layout. Elena designs a custom form based on the query to display this information.

To create a custom form, Elena can modify a form created by the Form Wizard or AutoForm, or design and create a form directly in the Form Design window. A custom form can be designed to match a paper form. It can display some fields side by side and others top to bottom; it can include color highlighting and special buttons and list boxes.

Designing a Custom Form

Elena plans to create a relatively simple custom form. Whether she creates a simple or complex custom form, she knows it is always best to plan the form's content and appearance first. Elena's sketch for her finished design is shown in Figure 5-18. The designed form displays all fields from the Article Type Query in single-column format, except for the writer's First Name and Last Name fields, which are side by side. Each field value will appear in a text box and will be preceded by a label (Access's default label name is the field name or the Caption property if there is one). Elena indicates the locations and lengths of each field value by a series of X's. The three X's that follow the Type field label indicate that the field value will be three characters wide. Elena also wants a graphic image for the 25th-anniversary issue to appear at the top of the form.

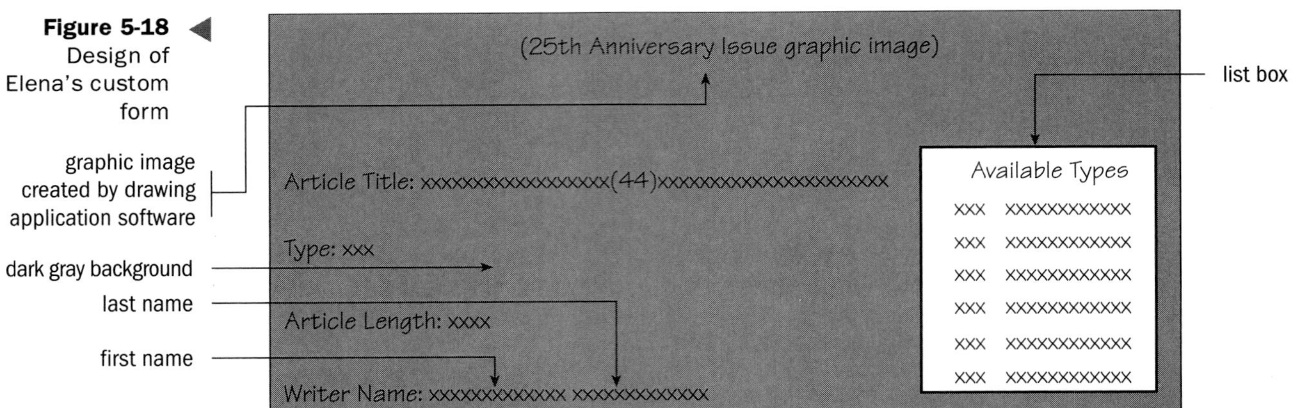

Figure 5-18 Design of Elena's custom form

Because many of her co-workers are unfamiliar with the article type codes, a list box containing the article type codes and their meaning will appear on the right. Elena also plans to add a dark gray background to improve the contrast of the form and make it easier to read.

Unlike her previous forms, which were based on tables, Elena's custom form will be based on the Article Type Query, which obtains data from both the BUSINESS ARTICLES and WRITERS tables and displays records in ascending order by the Type field. The form, which Elena plans to name Article Type Form, will likewise display records in ascending order by the Type field.

Now that she has planned her custom form, Elena is ready to create it. Elena could use AutoForm or the Form Wizard to create a basic form and then customize it in the Form Design window. Because her custom form differs from a basic form in many details, however, she decides to design the entire form directly in the Form Design window.

The Form Design Window

You use the Form Design window to create and modify forms. To create the custom form, Elena creates a blank form based on the Article Type Query in the Form Design window.

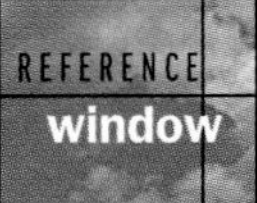

CREATING A FORM IN THE FORM DESIGN WINDOW

- In the Database window, click the Forms tab to display the Forms list.
- Click the New button to display the New Form dialog box.
- Click Design View to highlight it.
- Select the table or query on which the form will be based, then click the OK button to display the Form Design window.
- Place the necessary controls in the design. Modify the size, position, and other properties of the controls as necessary.
- To save the form, click the Save button on the toolbar and enter a name for the form.

To create a blank form in the Form Design window:

1. Make sure the Issue25 database from the Tutorial folder on your Student Disk is open, the Database window is maximized, and the Forms list is displayed in the Database window, then click the **New** button. The New Form dialog box opens.

2. If necessary, click Design View to select it, then click the **text box** list arrow. Scroll, if necessary, then click **Article Type Query**, and then click the **OK** button. The Form Design window opens. See Figure 5-19.

Figure 5-19 The Form Design window

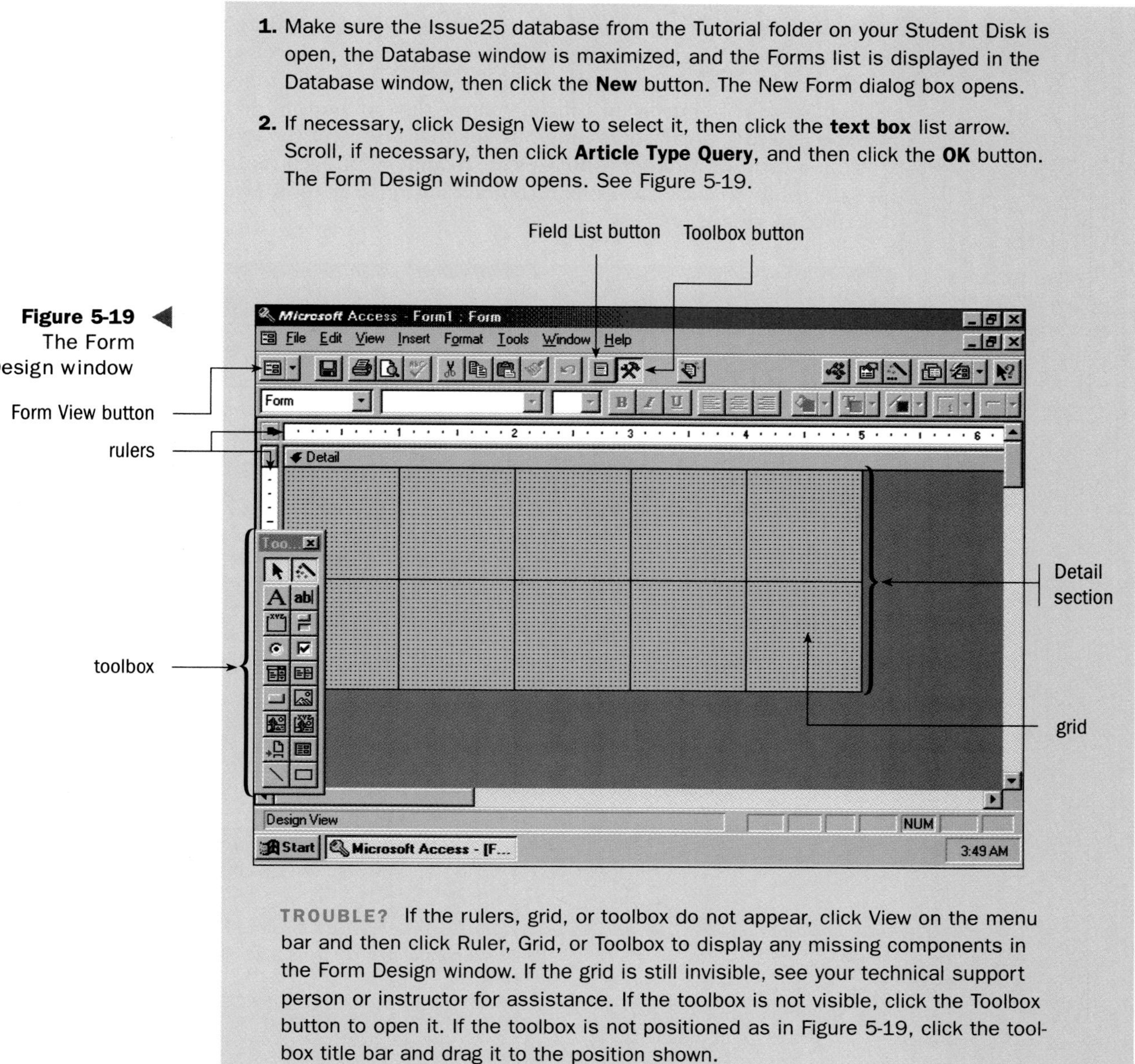

TROUBLE? If the rulers, grid, or toolbox do not appear, click View on the menu bar and then click Ruler, Grid, or Toolbox to display any missing components in the Form Design window. If the grid is still invisible, see your technical support person or instructor for assistance. If the toolbox is not visible, click the Toolbox button to open it. If the toolbox is not positioned as in Figure 5-19, click the toolbox title bar and drag it to the position shown.

The Form Design window contains the tools necessary to create a custom form. You create the form by placing objects in the blank form in the window. Each object, such as a text box, list box, rectangle, or command button, that you place in a form is called a **control**; there are three kinds of controls that you can place on the form:

- A **bound control** is linked, or bound, to a field in the underlying table or query. You use a bound control to display table field values.
- An **unbound control** is not linked to a field in the underlying table or query. You use an unbound control to display text, such as a form title or instructions, or to display graphics and pictures from other software programs. An unbound control that displays text is called a **label**.
- A **calculated control** displays a value calculated from data from one or more fields.

To create a bound control, you click the toolbar Field List button to display a list of fields available from the underlying table or query. You drag fields from the field list box to the Form Design window and place the bound controls where you want them to appear on the form. Clicking the Field List button a second time closes the field list box.

To place other controls on a form, you use the tool buttons on the toolbox. The **toolbox** is a specialized toolbar containing buttons that represent the tools you use to place controls on a form or a report. ToolTips are available for each tool. If you want to show or hide the toolbox, click the toolbar Toolbox button. The tools available in the toolbox are described in Figure 5-20.

Figure 5-20 Summary of tools available in the toolbox for a form or a report

Button	Tool Name	Control Purpose on a Form or a Report	Control Wizard
	Select Objects	Selects, moves, sizes, and edits controls	
	Control Wizards	When selected, activates Control Wizards for certain other toolbox tools	
	Label	Displays text, such as title or instructions; an unbound control	
	Text Box	Displays a label attached to a text box that contains a bound control or a calculated control	
	Option Group	Displays a group frame containing toggle buttons, option buttons, or check boxes	Yes
	Toggle Button	Displays a toggle button control bound to a Yes/No field	Yes
	Option Button	Displays a radio button control bound to a Yes/No field	Yes
	Check Box	Displays a check box control bound to a Yes/No field	Yes
	Combo Box	Displays a control that combines the features of a list box and a text box. You can type in the text box or select an entry in the list box to add a value to an underlying field	Yes
	List Box	Displays a control that contains a scrollable list of values	Yes
	Command Button	Displays a control button you can use to link to an action—for example, finding a record, printing a record, or applying a form filter	Yes
	Image	Displays a graphic image in the form or report	Yes
	Unbound Object Frame	Displays a frame for enclosing an unbound OLE object, such as a Microsoft Excel spreadsheet, on a form or report	Yes
	Bound Object Frame	Displays a frame for enclosing a bound OLE object stored in an Access database table	Yes
	Page Break	Begins a new screen on a form or a new page on a report	
	Subform/ Subreport	Displays data from more than one table on a form or report	Yes
	Line	Displays a line on a form or report	
	Rectangle	Displays a rectangle on a form or report	

The Form Design window also contains a Detail section, which appears as a light gray rectangle. You place the fields, labels, and values for your form in the Detail section. You can change the size of the Detail section by dragging the edges. The grid consists of dots that appear in the Detail section to help you to position controls precisely on a form. The rulers at the top and at the left edge of the Detail section define the horizontal and vertical dimensions of the form and serve as a guide to the placement of controls on the form.

Elena's first task in the Form Design window is to add bound controls to the form Detail section for all the fields from the Article Type Query.

Adding Fields to a Form

When you add a bound control to a form, Access adds a field-value text box and, to its left, a label. To create a bound control, you display the field list by clicking the Field List button. Then you select one or more fields from the field list box and drag them to the form. You select a single field by clicking the field. You select two or more fields by holding down the Ctrl key and clicking each field, and you select all fields by double-clicking the field list title bar.

Elena adds bound controls to the form Detail section for all the fields in the field list. To make more of the Form Design window visible, she closes the toolbox for now.

To close the toolbox and add bound controls for all the fields in the field list:

1. Click the **Close** button on the toolbox to close it.
2. Click the **Field List** button on the toolbar. The field list box opens.
3. Double-click the **field list** title bar to select all the fields in the field list. Access highlights the field list box.
4. Click anywhere in the highlighted area of the field list box and drag to the form's Detail section. Release the mouse button when the is positioned at the 1.5" mark on the horizontal ruler and the .25" mark on the vertical ruler. Access adds bound controls for the five selected fields. Each bound control consists of a text box and, to its left, an attached label. See Figure 5-21.

Figure 5-21 Text boxes and attached labels added to a form as bound controls

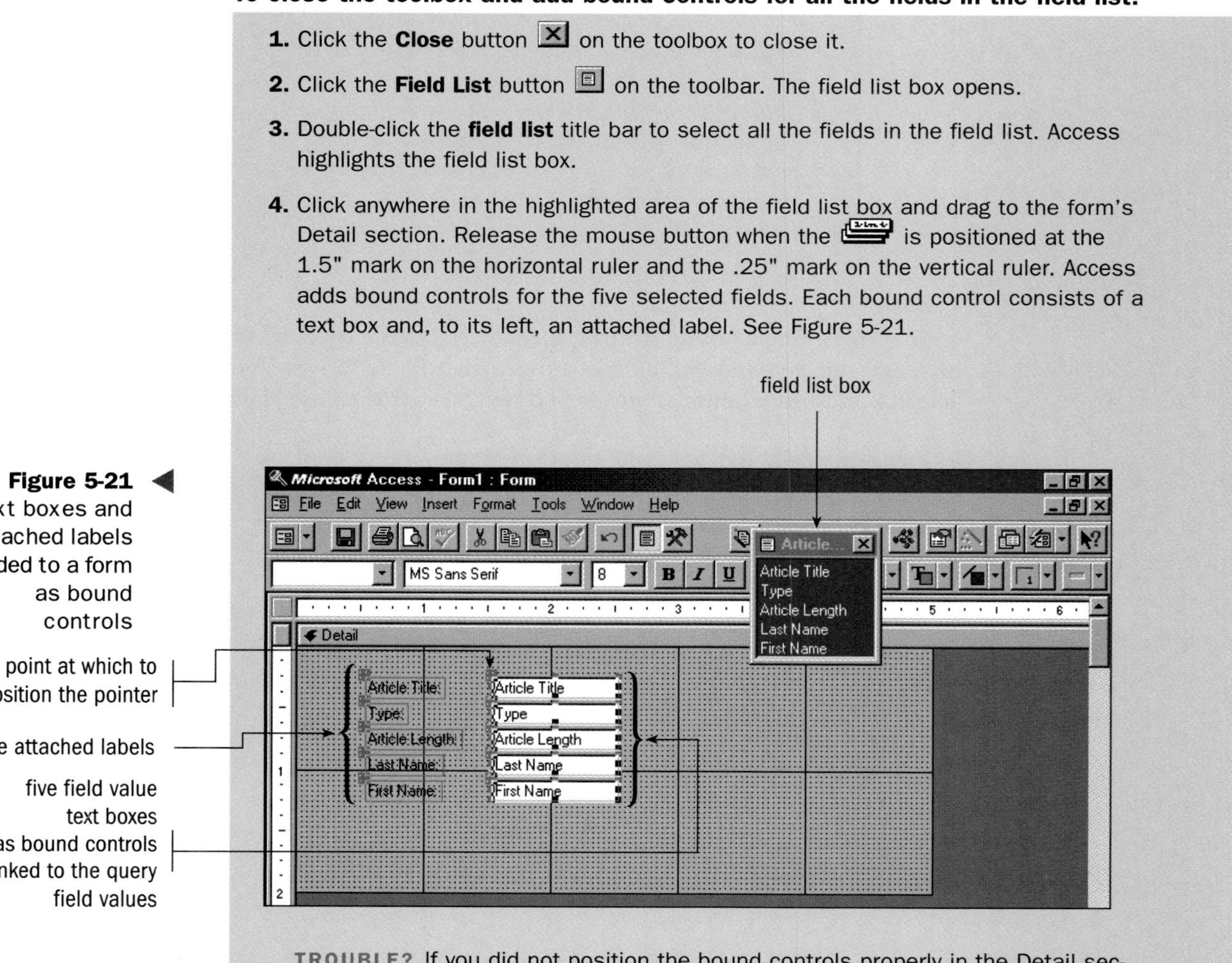

TROUBLE? If you did not position the bound controls properly in the Detail section, click the Undo button to delete the text boxes and labels from the Detail section. Repeat Step 4 to position the bound controls.

Performing operations in the Form Design window might seem awkward at first. With practice you will become comfortable with creating a custom form. Remember that you can always click the Undo button immediately after you make an undesired form adjustment.

Five text boxes now appear in a column in the form Detail section. Each text box is a bound control linked to a field in the underlying query and has an attached label box to its left. This means that if you move the text box, the label will move with it. Each text box and each label is an object on the form, and each appears with square boxes on the corners and edges. These boxes are called **handles**. Handles appear around an object when it is selected and they allow you to move or resize the control.

Selecting, Moving, and Deleting Controls

Elena is done with the field list box and closes it by clicking the Field List button. Elena next compares the form Detail section with her design. She needs to arrange the Last Name and First Name text boxes side by side to agree with her form design.

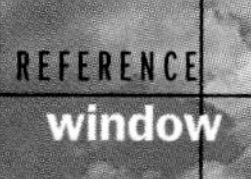

SELECTING, MOVING, AND DELETING CONTROLS

- Click on any control to select it. To select several controls at once, press the Shift key while clicking on each control. Handles appear around selected controls.
- To move a single selected control, click the control's move handle and drag it to its new position.
- To move a group of selected controls, click anywhere in a selected control (but not on its move handle) and drag the group of selected controls to its new position.
- To delete selected controls, point to any selected control, then click the right mouse button to display the shortcut menu. Click Cut to delete the selected controls.

To move a single bound control, Elena needs to select just that control. All controls are currently selected and will all move together if Elena moves any one of them. Elena first deselects all of the bound controls and then selects the Last Name control to move it.

To close the field list box and select a single bound control:

1. Click the **Field List** button on the toolbar to close the field list box.
2. Two boxes in the Detail section have Last Name inside them. The box on the left is the label box, and the box on the right is the field-value text box. Click in the gray area outside the Detail section to deselect any previous selection and then click the **Last Name** field-value text box to select it. Move handles, the larger handles, appear in the upper-left corner of the field-value text box and its attached label box. Sizing handles also appear, but only on the field-value text box. See Figure 5-22.

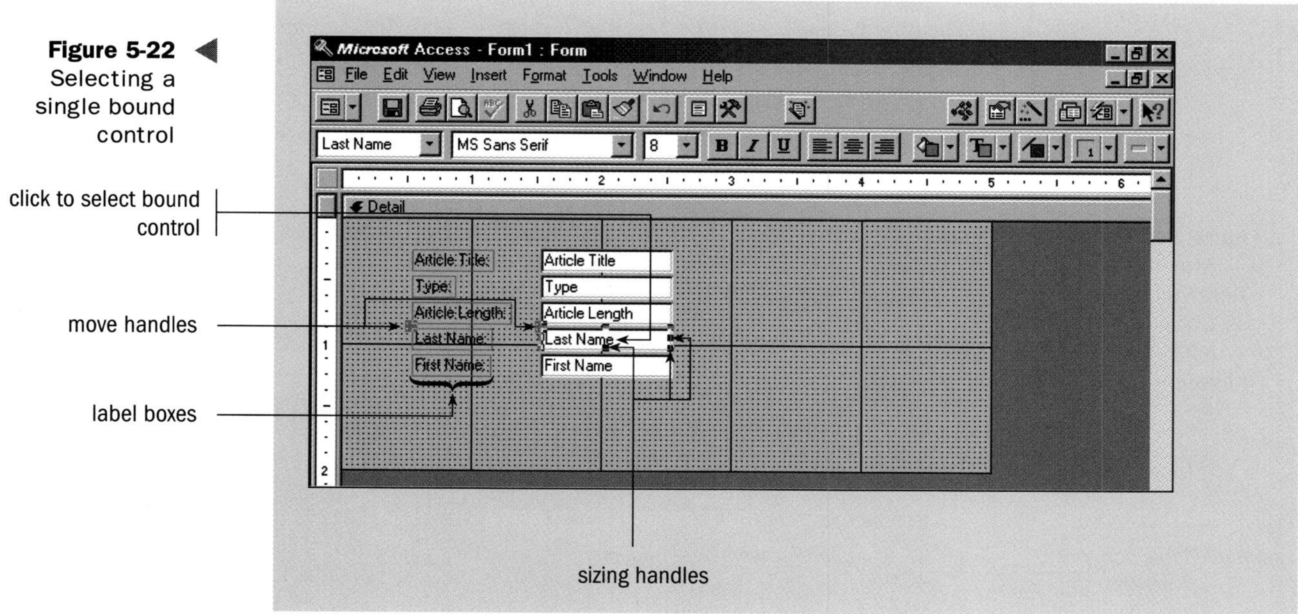

Figure 5-22 Selecting a single bound control

You can move a field-value text box and its attached label box together. To move them, place the pointer anywhere on the border of the field-value text box, but not on a move handle or a sizing handle. When the pointer changes to ✋, you can drag the field-value text box and its attached label box to the new location. As you move the boxes, their outline moves to show you the changing position.

You can also move either the field-value text box or its label box individually. If you want to move the field-value text box but not its label box, for example, place the pointer on the text box's move handle. When the pointer changes to ☝, drag the field-value text box to the new location. You use the label box's move handle to move just the label box.

You can delete a field-value text box and its attached label box or delete just the label box. To delete both boxes together, click inside the field-value text box to select both boxes, click the right mouse button inside the text box to open its shortcut menu, and then click Cut. To delete just the label box, use the same procedure but click inside the label box instead of the field-value text box.

To arrange the Last Name and First Name text boxes to agree with her design, Elena must move the Last Name field-value text box to the right without moving its label box, move the First Name field-value text box (without its label box) up beside the Last Name label box, delete the First Name label box, and then change the Last Name label box to read Writer Name. Elena first moves the field-values text boxes and deletes the First Name label box.

To move field-value text boxes and delete labels:

1. Move the pointer to the Last Name field-value text box move handle. When the mouse pointer changes to ☝, drag the text box horizontally to the right, leaving enough room for the First Name field-value text box to fit in its place. An outline of the box appears as you change its position to guide you in the move operation. Use the grid dots in the Detail section to help you position the box outline.

   TROUBLE? If you move the field-value text box incorrectly, click the Undo button and then repeat Step 1.

2. Click the **field-value** text box for the First Name field and then move the pointer to its move handle. When the mouse pointer changes to ☛, drag the box up to the position previously occupied by the Last Name field-value text box.

3. Click the **First Name** label box with the right mouse button to open the shortcut menu and then click **Cut**. The First Name label box is deleted. See Figure 5-23.

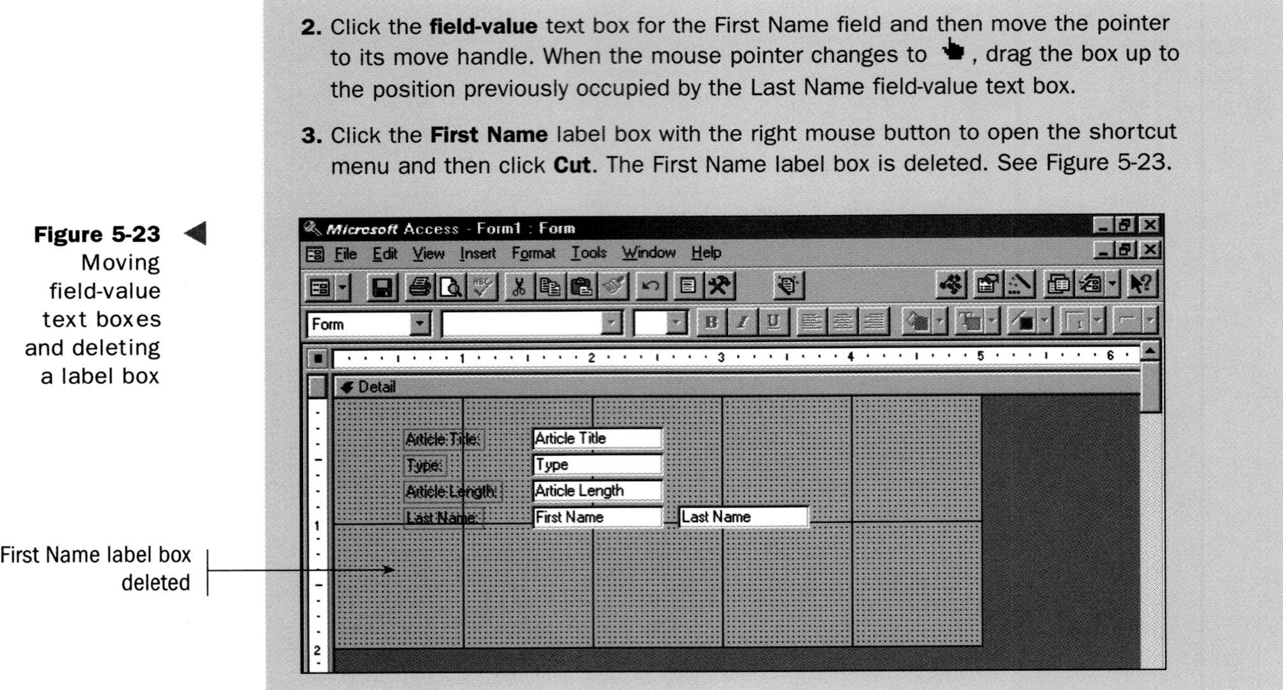

Figure 5-23 Moving field-value text boxes and deleting a label box

Next, Elena changes the text in the Last Name label box to Writer Name.

Changing a Label's Caption

The text in a label is defined by the field name or Caption property.

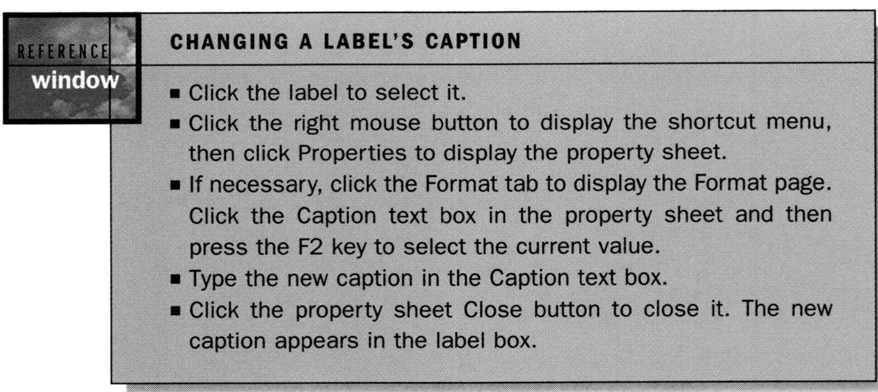

REFERENCE window

CHANGING A LABEL'S CAPTION

- Click the label to select it.
- Click the right mouse button to display the shortcut menu, then click Properties to display the property sheet.
- If necessary, click the Format tab to display the Format page. Click the Caption text box in the property sheet and then press the F2 key to select the current value.
- Type the new caption in the Caption text box.
- Click the property sheet Close button to close it. The new caption appears in the label box.

Elena uses the label's property sheet to change the Caption property value.

To change the Caption property value for a label:

1. Click the **Last Name** label box to select it.

2. Click the right mouse button to display the shortcut menu, then click **Properties**. The property sheet for the Last Name label opens.

3. If necessary, click the **Format** tab to display the Format page. Click the **Caption** text box in the property sheet and then press the **F2** key to select the entire value.

4. Type **Writer Name:**. Be sure to type a colon at the end of the caption. See Figure 5-24.

Figure 5-24 ◀ Changing a property for a label

selected control

Caption property value

property sheet

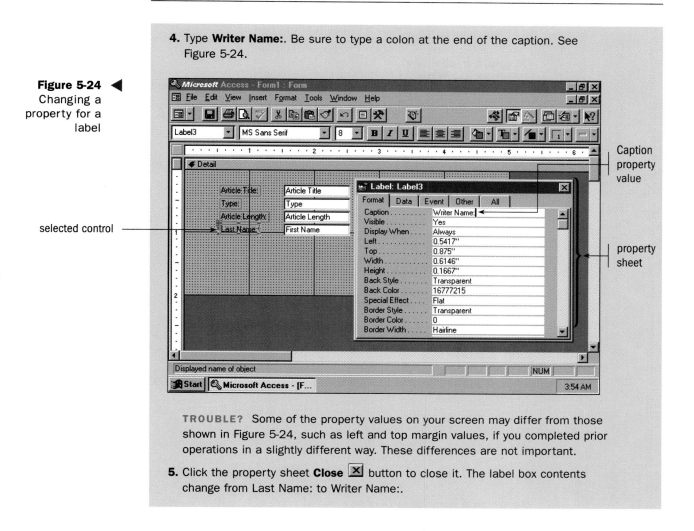

TROUBLE? Some of the property values on your screen may differ from those shown in Figure 5-24, such as left and top margin values, if you completed prior operations in a slightly different way. These differences are not important.

5. Click the property sheet **Close** ☒ button to close it. The label box contents change from Last Name: to Writer Name:.

Resizing a Control

Looking at her new Writer Name caption, Elena notices that only part of the new caption is visible in the label box. Elena must resize the label box. Elena also notices that the Article Title field-value text box is too small to contain long titles, so she must resize it as well.

A selected object displays seven sizing handles: one on each side of the object and one at each corner, except the upper-left corner. The upper-left corner displays the move handle. Moving the pointer over a sizing handle changes the pointer to a two-headed arrow; the pointer's direction indicates the direction in which you can move the sizing handle. When you drag the sizing handle, you resize the control. Thin lines appear, which guide you as you drag the control.

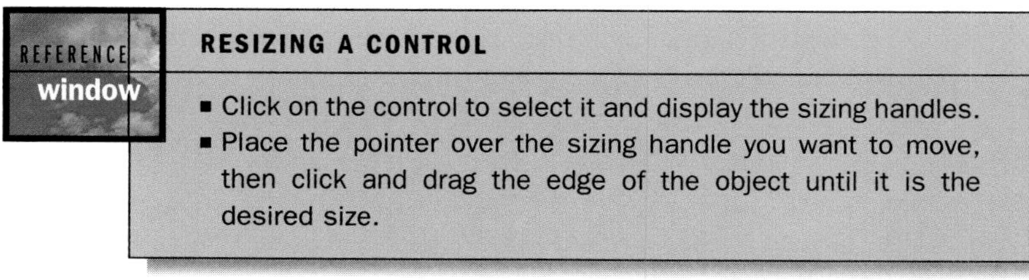
REFERENCE window

RESIZING A CONTROL

- Click on the control to select it and display the sizing handles.
- Place the pointer over the sizing handle you want to move, then click and drag the edge of the object until it is the desired size.

Elena resizes the Writer Name label box first.

To resize a label box:

1. The Writer Name label box is still the selected control, so move the pointer to the left side of the control over the middle handle. When the pointer changes to ↔ , drag the left border horizontally to the left two entire sets of grid dots. See Figure 5-25.

Figure 5-25 Resizing the Writer Name label box

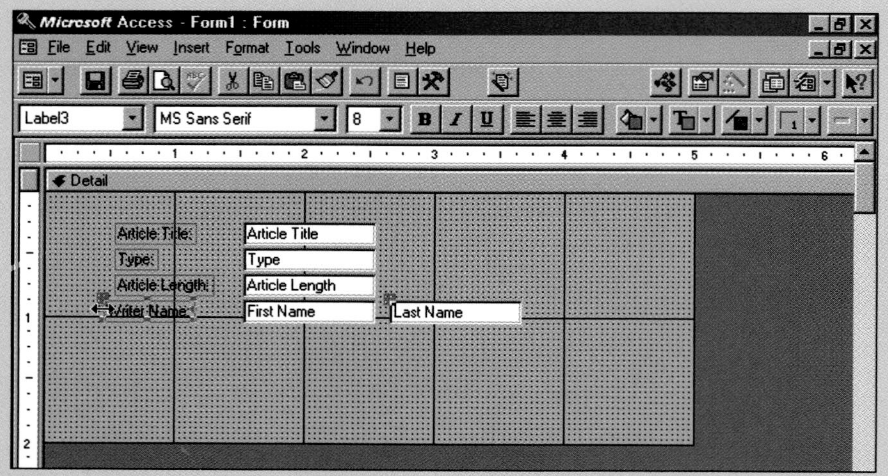

TROUBLE? If you change the vertical size of the box by mistake, just click the Undo button and try again.

Next, Elena resizes the Article Title field-value text box by stretching it to the right.

To resize a field-value text box:

1. Click the **Article Title** field-value text box to select it. Move handles and sizing handles appear.
2. Move the pointer to the right side of the box over the middle handle. The pointer changes to ↔ .
3. Drag the right border horizontally to the right until the right edge is at the 4" mark on the horizontal ruler. The text box will now accommodate longer Article Title field values.

Aligning Controls

Elena next notices that the top three label boxes are left-justified; that is, they are aligned on the left edges. She feels that the form will look better if all the labels are right-justified, or aligned on their right edges.

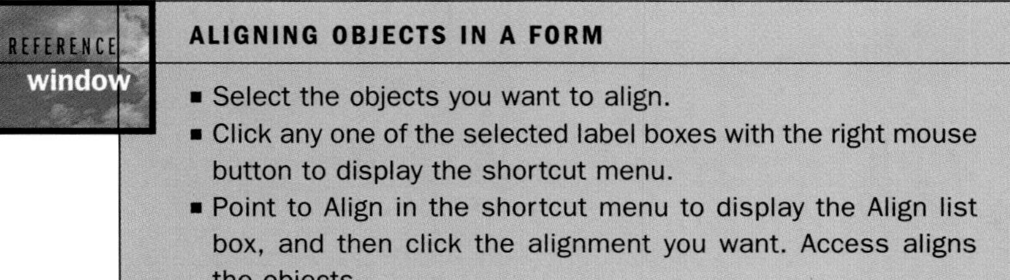

REFERENCE window

ALIGNING OBJECTS IN A FORM

- Select the objects you want to align.
- Click any one of the selected label boxes with the right mouse button to display the shortcut menu.
- Point to Align in the shortcut menu to display the Align list box, and then click the alignment you want. Access aligns the objects.

Elena selects all of the labels and uses the shortcut menu to align them.

To select and align all label boxes on the right:

1. Click in the **Article Title** label box to select it.
2. Press the **Shift** key and hold it as you click each of the remaining label boxes so that all four are selected, and then release the Shift key.
3. Click any one of the selected label boxes with the right mouse button to display the shortcut menu.
4. Point to **Align** in the shortcut menu to display the Align list box, and then click **Right**. Access aligns the label boxes on their right edges. See Figure 5-26.

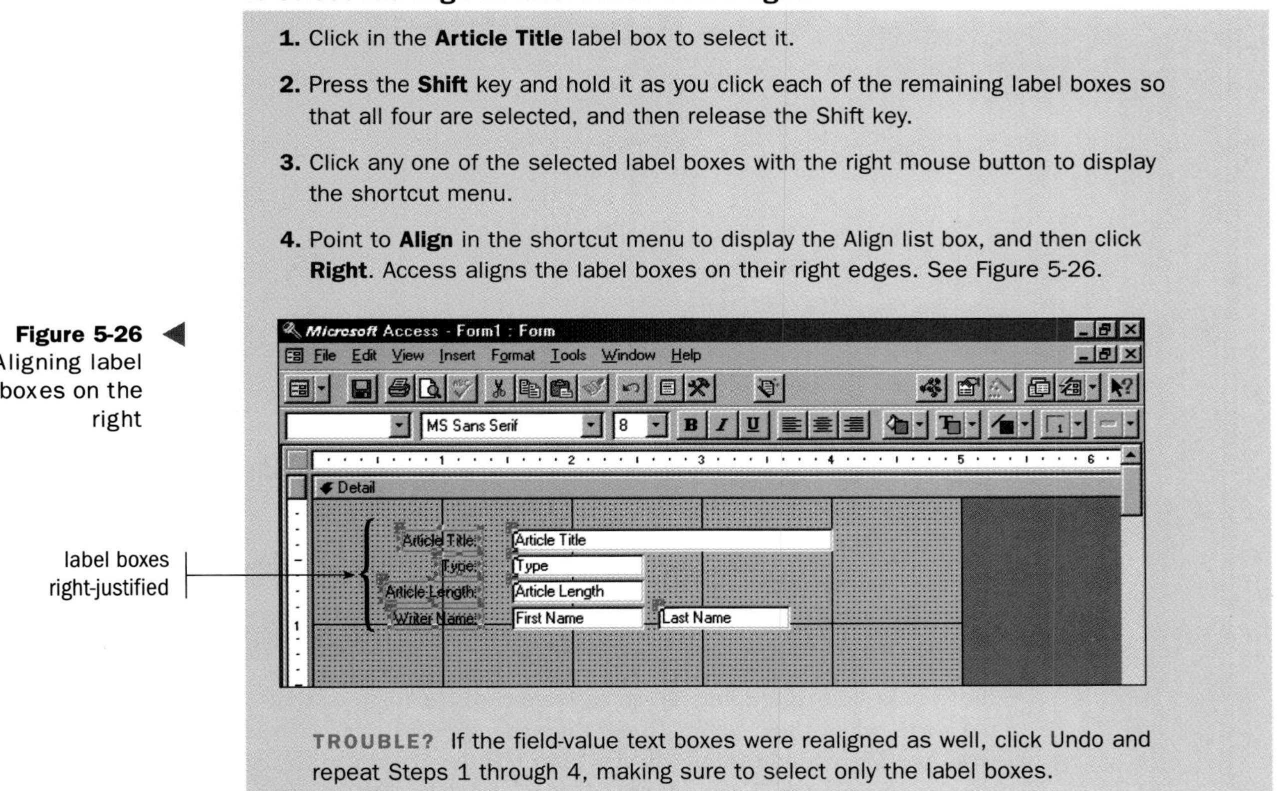

Figure 5-26 Aligning label boxes on the right

TROUBLE? If the field-value text boxes were realigned as well, click Undo and repeat Steps 1 through 4, making sure to select only the label boxes.

Before Elena makes further changes in the Form Design window, she saves her work and then switches to the Form View window to study her form.

To save the form:

1. Click the **Save** button on the toolbar. The Save As dialog box opens.
2. Type **Article Type Form** and then click the **OK** button. Access saves the custom form.

Viewing a Form in the Form View Window

When you create a form, you should periodically check your progress in the Form View window. You might see adjustments you want to make on your form in the Form Design window.

To switch to the Form View window:

1. Click the **Form View** button on the toolbar. Access closes the Form Design window and opens the Form View window. See Figure 5-27.

Figure 5-27
The Form View window

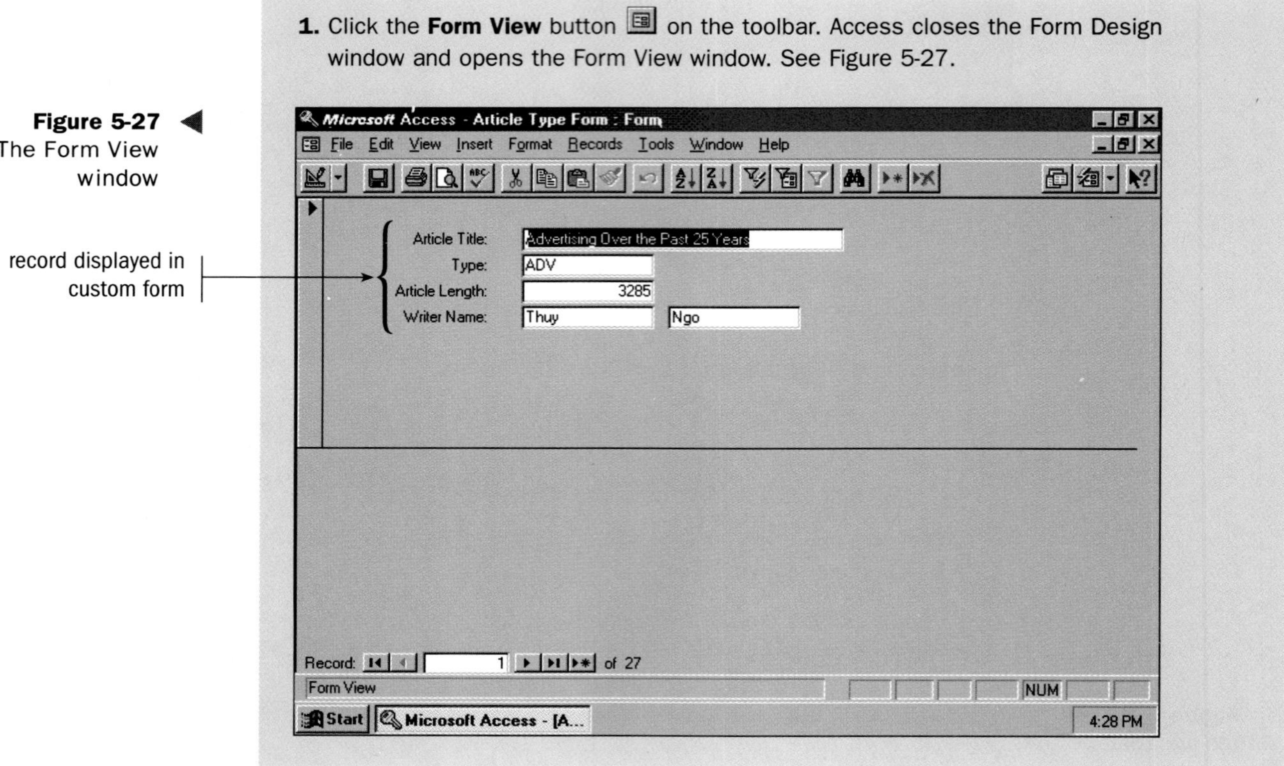

Your form uses the Article Type Query to sort the records in ascending order by the Type field. Access displays the first record in this sort order. You can use navigation buttons to view other records from the query on the form.

Elena sees some adjustments she wants to make to her design. She wants to add a form title, with a graphic, and add the list box for the article types and descriptions.

Using Form Headers and Footers

Elena next adds a graphic image to the top of the form so that others can easily identify the form when they see it. To do this, she chooses the Form Header/Footer command from the View menu to add header and footer sections to the form. She then places the graphic image in the Form Header section and deletes the Form Footer section by decreasing its height to zero.

In the Form Header and Form Footer sections you can add titles, instructions, command buttons, and other information to the top and bottom of your form. You add the Form Header and Form Footer as a pair. If your form needs one of them but not the other, you can remove the one you don't want by setting its height to zero, which is the method you would use to remove any section on a form.

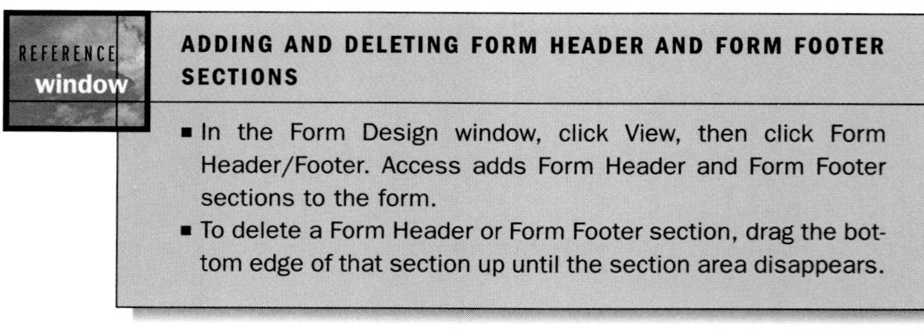

ADDING AND DELETING FORM HEADER AND FORM FOOTER SECTIONS

- In the Form Design window, click View, then click Form Header/Footer. Access adds Form Header and Form Footer sections to the form.
- To delete a Form Header or Form Footer section, drag the bottom edge of that section up until the section area disappears.

Elena adds the Form Header and Form Footer sections to the form.

To add Form Header and Form Footer sections to a form:

1. Click the **Form View** button on the toolbar. Access closes the Form View window and opens the Form Design window.
2. Click **View**, and then click **Form Header/Footer**. Access inserts a Form Header section above the Detail section and a Form Footer section below the Detail section. See Figure 5-28.

Figure 5-28 Form Header and Form Footer sections added to custom form

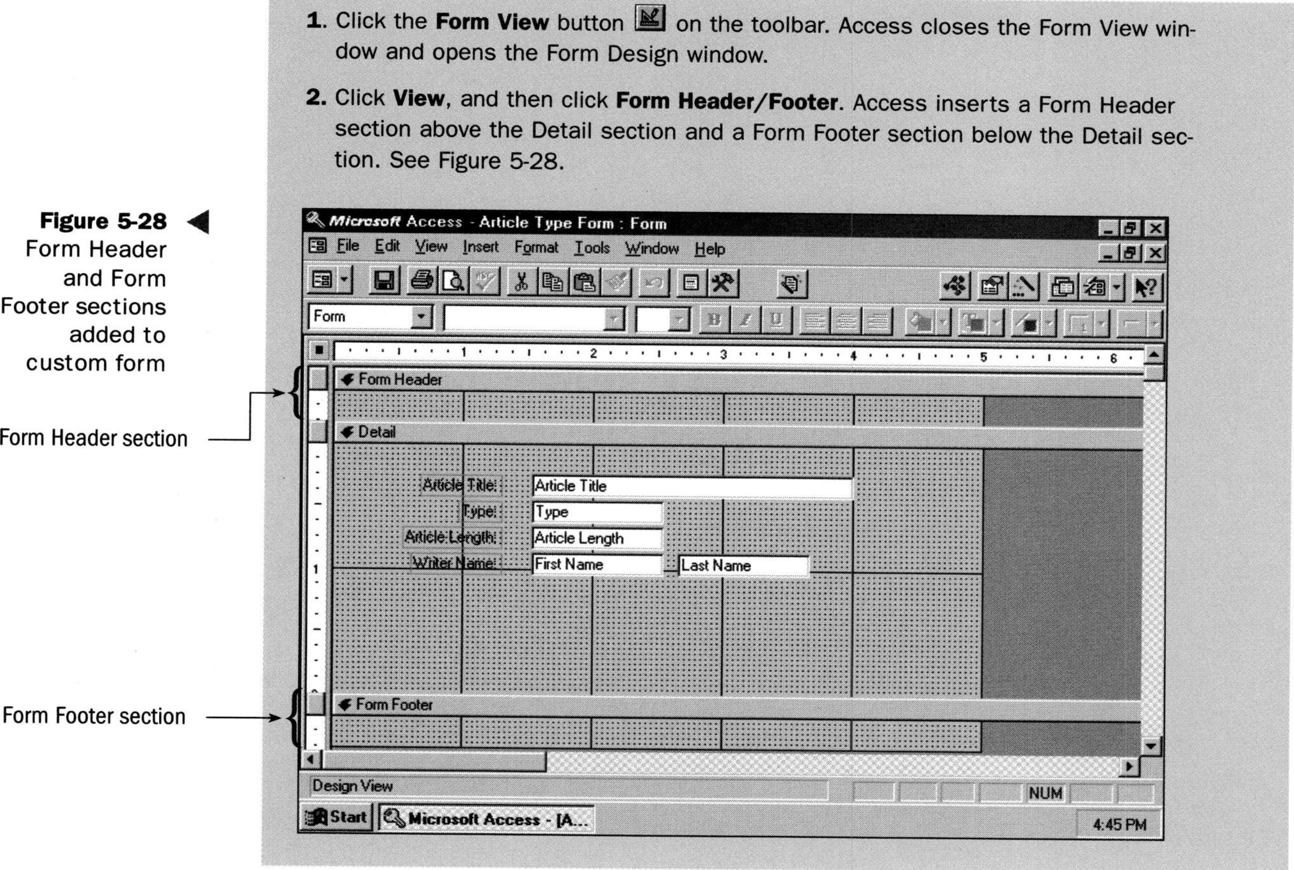

Elena does not want to use a Form Footer section in this form, so she removes it by making its height zero.

To remove the Form Footer section:

1. Move the pointer to the bottom edge of the Form Footer section. When the pointer changes to ✢, drag the bottom edge upward until it disappears. Even though the words "Form Footer" remain, the area defining the section is set to zero, and the section will not appear in the form.

Elena now adds the graphic image to the Form Header section with the toolbox Image tool.

Adding a Graphic Image to a Form

Elena has designed a small graphic image that she wants displayed in the header. Access has the ability to use files and data created by other software programs. In this case, Elena has used a drawing program and saved her image in a file named 25th. To place the image in the form header, she uses the toolbox Image tool.

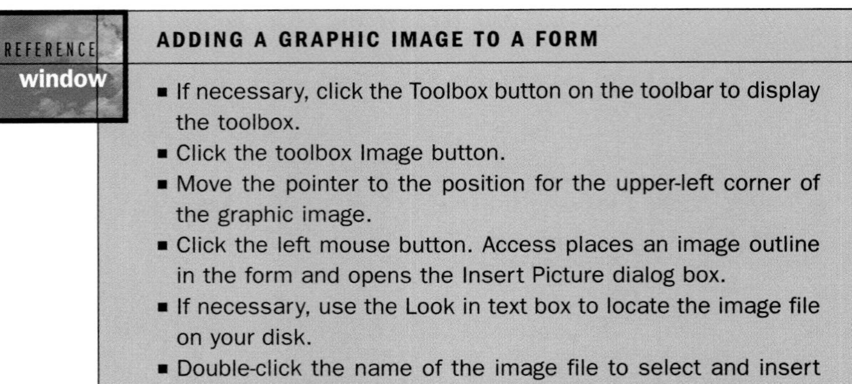

REFERENCE window

ADDING A GRAPHIC IMAGE TO A FORM

- If necessary, click the Toolbox button on the toolbar to display the toolbox.
- Click the toolbox Image button.
- Move the pointer to the position for the upper-left corner of the graphic image.
- Click the left mouse button. Access places an image outline in the form and opens the Insert Picture dialog box.
- If necessary, use the Look in text box to locate the image file on your disk.
- Double-click the name of the image file to select and insert the image file in the form. Access closes the Insert Picture dialog box and inserts the image.

To place a graphic image on the form:

1. Click the **Toolbox** button on the toolbar to display the toolbox.
2. Click the toolbox **Image** button.
3. Move the pointer to the Form Header. The pointer changes to . Use the ruler bar to place the pointer slightly below the top of the Form Header, approximately 1" from the left edge. This will be the upper-left corner of the image.
4. Click the left mouse button. Access places an image outline in the Form Header and opens the Insert Picture dialog box. See Figure 5-29.

Figure 5-29 The Insert Picture dialog box

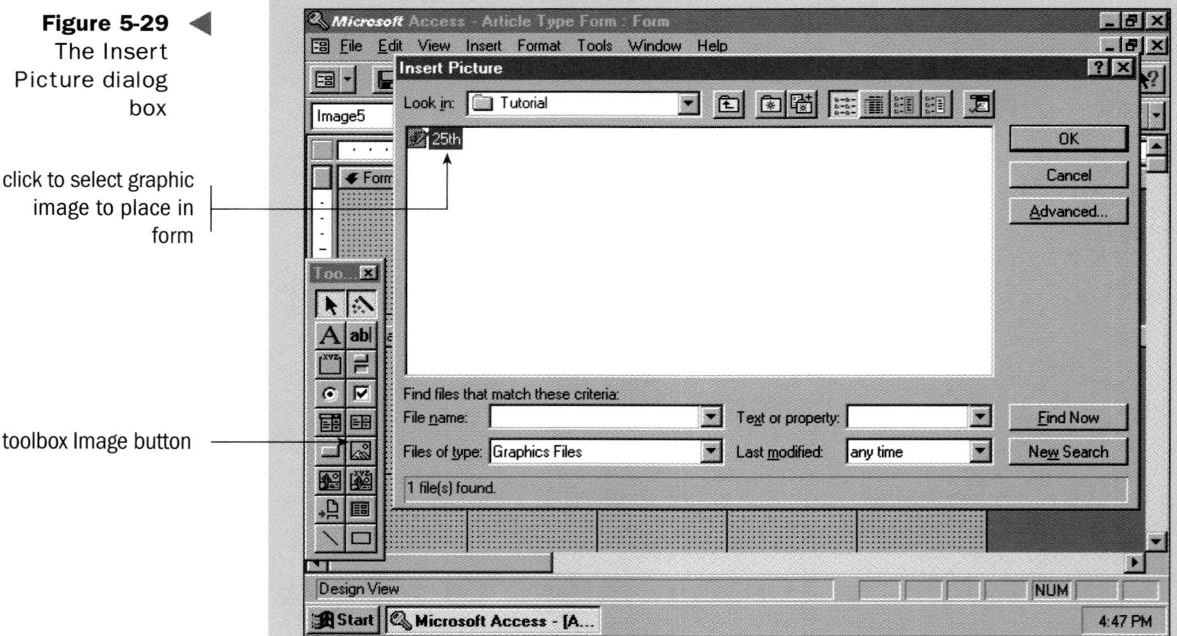

Elena is ready to insert her image. The image is saved under the name "25th" in your Tutorial folder.

5. If necessary, click the **Look in** list arrow to display the contents of the Tutorial folder on your Student Disk.
6. Double-click **25th** to select and insert the image file in the Form Header.

Access closes the Insert Picture dialog box and inserts the image. The Form Header section automatically becomes larger to accommodate the size of the image.

Elena views the form with the new header.

7. Click the **Form View** button on the toolbar to view the form. See Figure 5-30.

Figure 5-30 New header in Form View

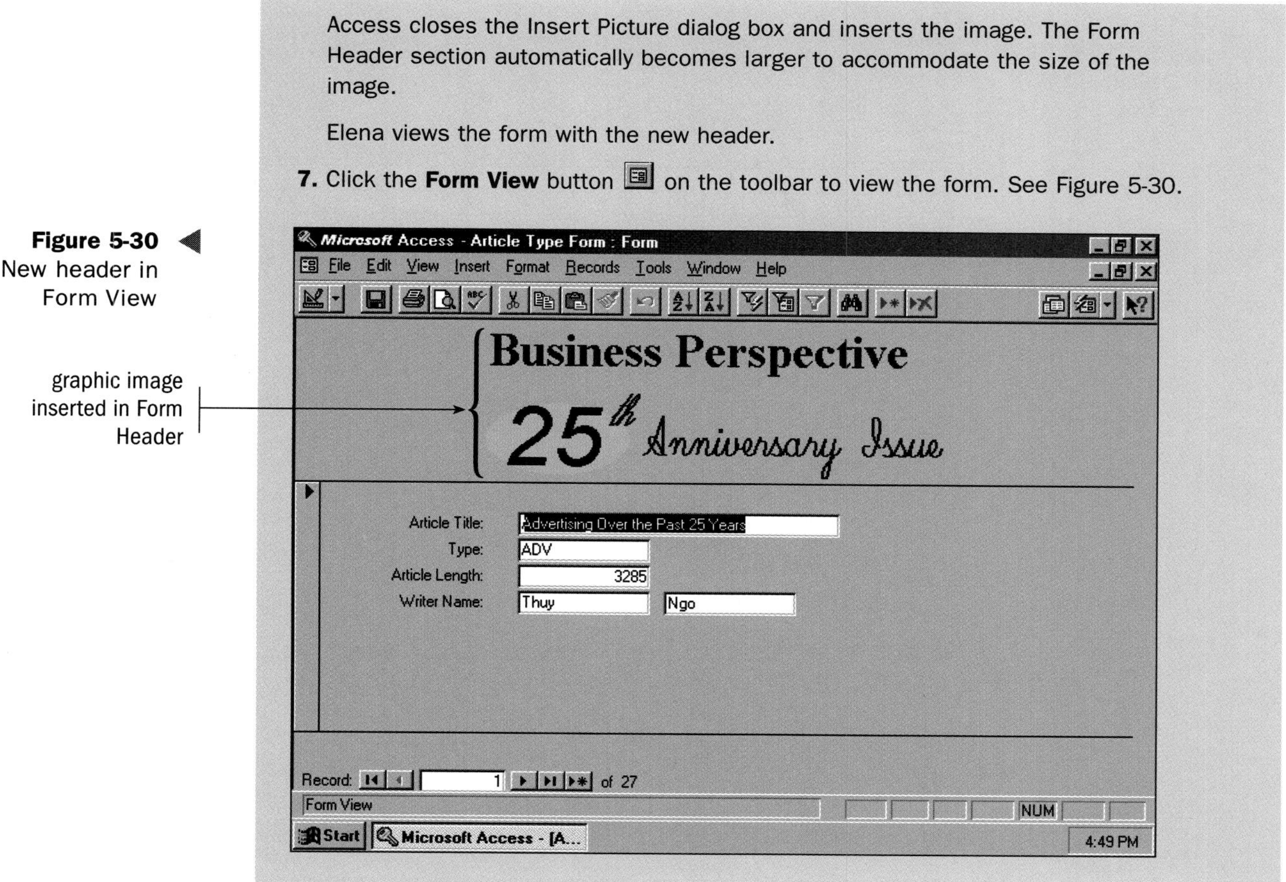

Adding a List Box with Control Wizards

Because many of her co-workers are unfamiliar with the various article type codes, Elena adds a list box to the form's Detail section. A **list box** is a control that displays a list of values. The list box in this form will display all the article types and their full descriptions from the TYPES table so that anyone using this form will not need to remember all the Type field values. Clicking one of the list box values will replace the form's Type field value with the clicked value. Thus, you can eliminate the need to enter a Type field value from the keyboard. When you add a list box to a form, by default Access adds a label box to its left.

You use the toolbox List Box tool to add a list box to a form. If you want help in defining the list box, you can first select one of Access's Control Wizards. A **Control Wizard** asks you a series of questions and then creates a control on a form or report based on your answers. Access offers Control Wizards for the toolbox Combo Box tool, List Box tool, Option Group tool, Command Button tool, and the Subform/Subreport tool, among others.

Elena will use the List Box Wizard to add the list box for the article types and descriptions. Before she adds the list box, Elena increases the width of the Detail section (and the Form Header section) to make room for the list box.

To resize the Detail section:

1. Click the **Form View** button on the toolbar to switch to the Form Design window.

2. Drag the right edge of the Detail section to the horizontal ruler's 6" mark. The Form Header section is also widened. See Figure 5-31.

Figure 5-31 ◀ Resized Detail section

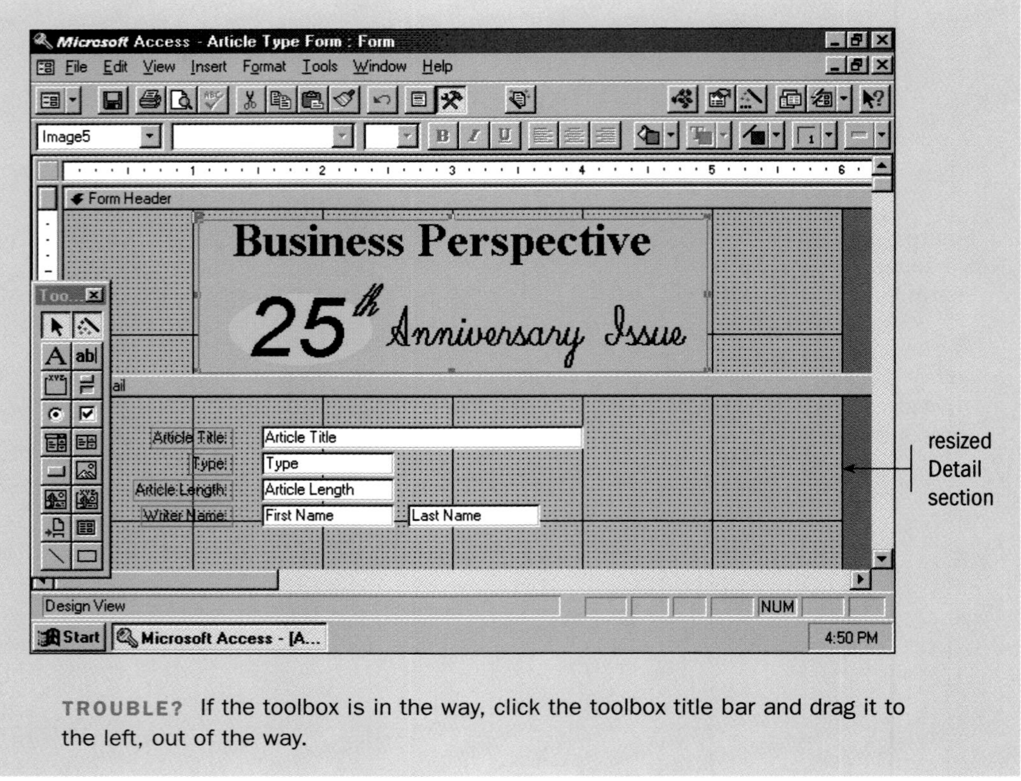

TROUBLE? If the toolbox is in the way, click the toolbox title bar and drag it to the left, out of the way.

Next, Elena adds a list box to the Detail section using the List Box Wizard.

Using the List Box Wizard

Elena will use the List Box Wizard to add the list box for the article types and descriptions.

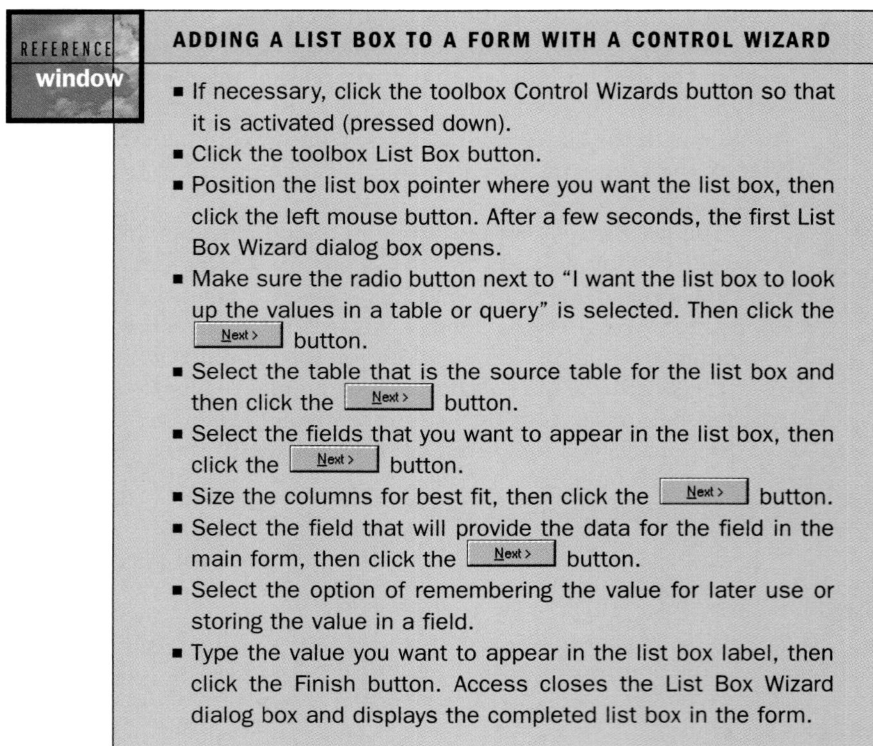

REFERENCE window

ADDING A LIST BOX TO A FORM WITH A CONTROL WIZARD

- If necessary, click the toolbox Control Wizards button so that it is activated (pressed down).
- Click the toolbox List Box button.
- Position the list box pointer where you want the list box, then click the left mouse button. After a few seconds, the first List Box Wizard dialog box opens.
- Make sure the radio button next to "I want the list box to look up the values in a table or query" is selected. Then click the Next > button.
- Select the table that is the source table for the list box and then click the Next > button.
- Select the fields that you want to appear in the list box, then click the Next > button.
- Size the columns for best fit, then click the Next > button.
- Select the field that will provide the data for the field in the main form, then click the Next > button.
- Select the option of remembering the value for later use or storing the value in a field.
- Type the value you want to appear in the list box label, then click the Finish button. Access closes the List Box Wizard dialog box and displays the completed list box in the form.

To start the List Box Wizard:

1. If necessary, click the toolbox **Control Wizards** button so that it is activated (pressed down).
2. Click the toolbox **List Box** button. As you move the pointer away from the toolbox, the pointer changes to See Figure 5-32.

Figure 5-32 Positioning a list box

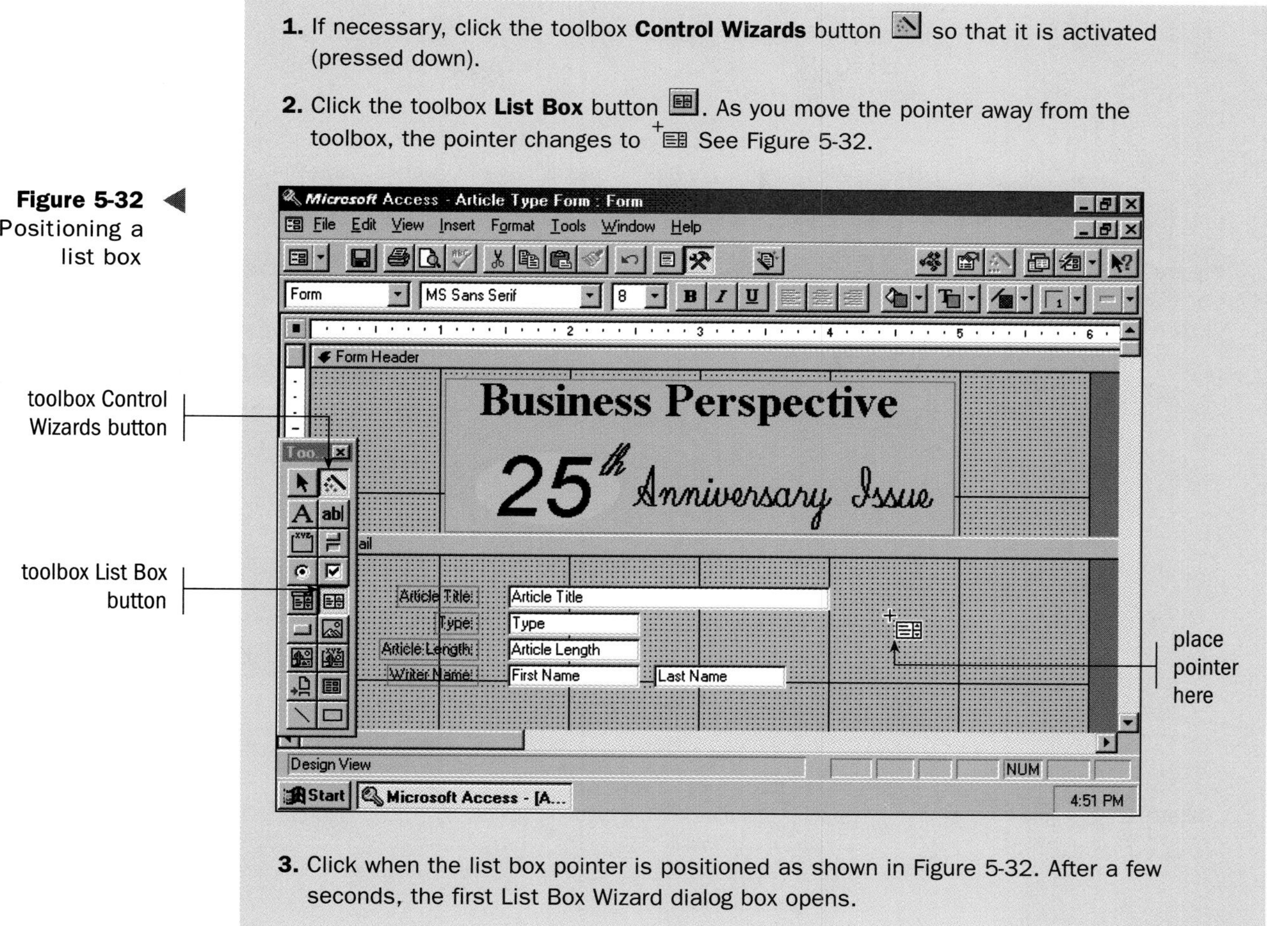

3. Click when the list box pointer is positioned as shown in Figure 5-32. After a few seconds, the first List Box Wizard dialog box opens.

Elena uses the List Box Wizard to display the two fields from the TYPES table: the Type field and the Description field. She also uses the List Box Wizard dialog box to size the two fields' column widths and to add the label Article Types.

To add a list box using the List Box Wizard:

1. The TYPES table will supply the values for the list box, so make sure the radio button next to "I want the list box to look up the values in a table or query" is selected. Then click the Next > button. The next List Box Wizard dialog box opens.
2. Click **TYPES** as the source table for the list box and then click the Next > button. The next List Box Wizard dialog box opens.
3. Because you want both the Type and Description fields to appear in the list box, click the >> button to select both fields and then click the Next > button. The next List Box Wizard dialog box opens.
4. For both columns, double-click the right edge of each column selector to get the best column fit and then click the Next > button. The next List Box Wizard dialog box opens.
5. If Type is not selected in the Available Fields list box, click it to select it. Then click the Next > button.

6. Click the radio button beside "Store that value in this field," click the **text box** list arrow, and click **Type**. Then click the Next > button. Access will store the Type value selected from the TYPES table in the Type field of the BUSINESS ARTICLES record.

7. For a label, type **Article Types:** in the text box and then click the **Finish** button. Access closes the List Box Wizard dialog box and displays the completed list box in the Detail section of the form. See Figure 5-33.

Figure 5-33 List box added to a form

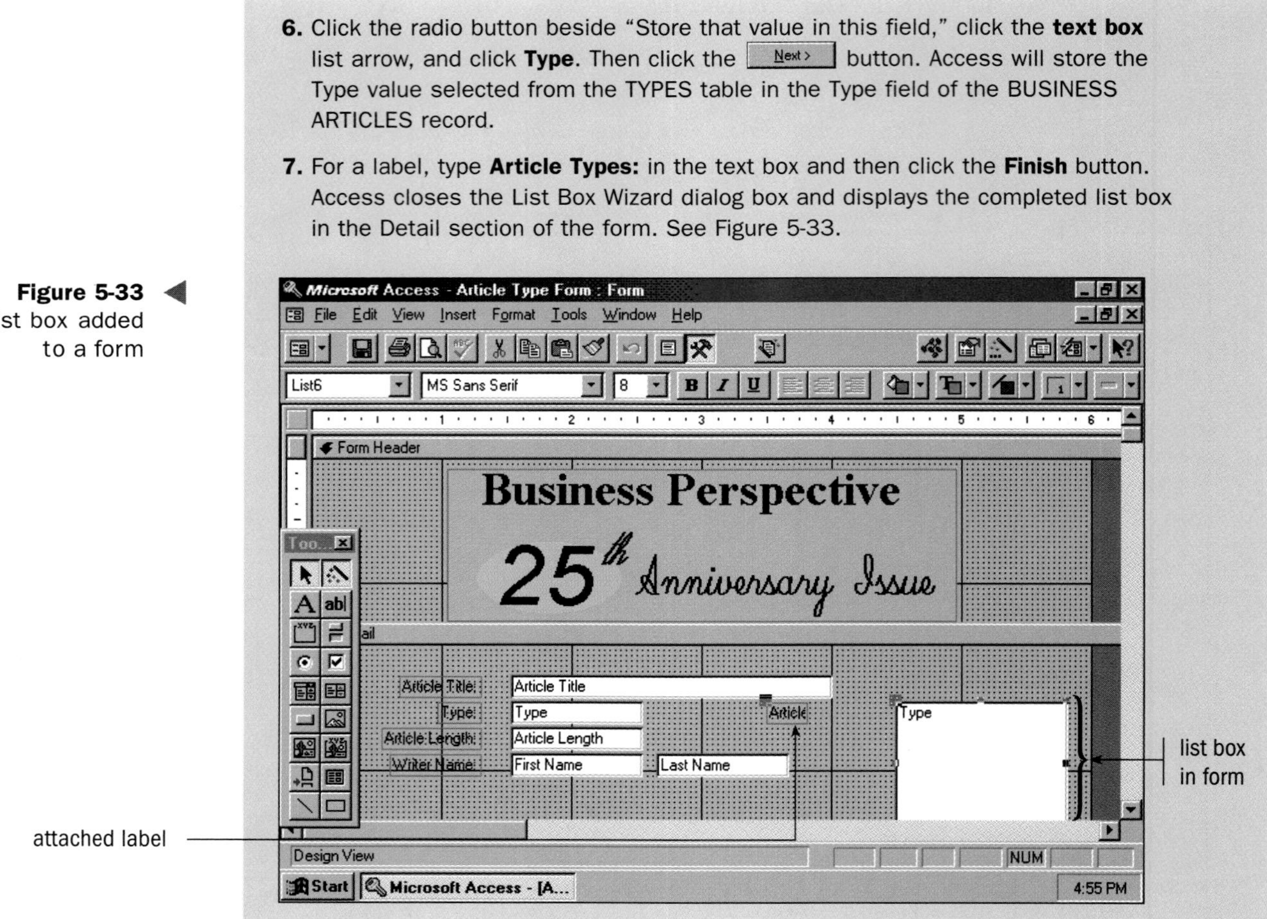

Elena notices that the attached label does not fit in the label box and also that it appears too far to the left of the list box. She resizes the label and then moves it above the list box.

To resize and move a label:

1. Click the **label box** attached to the list box to select it.

2. Click **Format**, click **Size**, and then click **to Fit**. The label's entire caption is now visible.

3. Click and drag the label box's **move handle** to position the label box above the list box. See Figure 5-34.

Figure 5-34 ◀
Resizing and moving a label

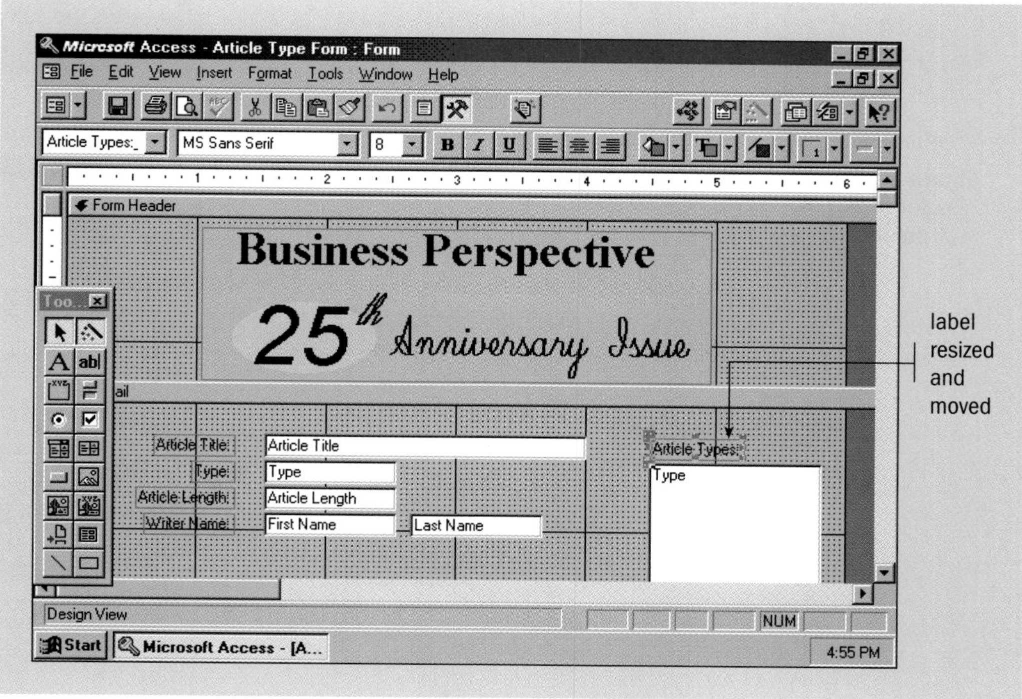

Elena's final tasks are to add background colors to the Form Header and Detail sections and to change the style of the graphic image.

Adding Background Colors and Special Effects to a Form

Elena changes the background of the Detail and Form Header sections to a darker gray and applies a special effect to the graphic image to make it stand out.

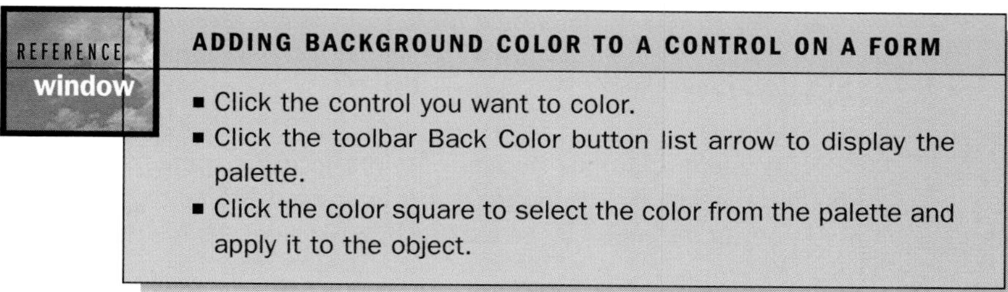
REFERENCE window

ADDING BACKGROUND COLOR TO A CONTROL ON A FORM

- Click the control you want to color.
- Click the toolbar Back Color button list arrow to display the palette.
- Click the color square to select the color from the palette and apply it to the object.

Elena changes the background colors of the two form sections.

To change the background colors of the form sections:

1. Click the **Detail** section, but do not click any of the controls in that section. This makes the Detail section the selected control.
2. Click the **Back Color** button list arrow on the toolbar. Access displays the color palette. See Figure 5-35.

Figure 5-35 Back color palette

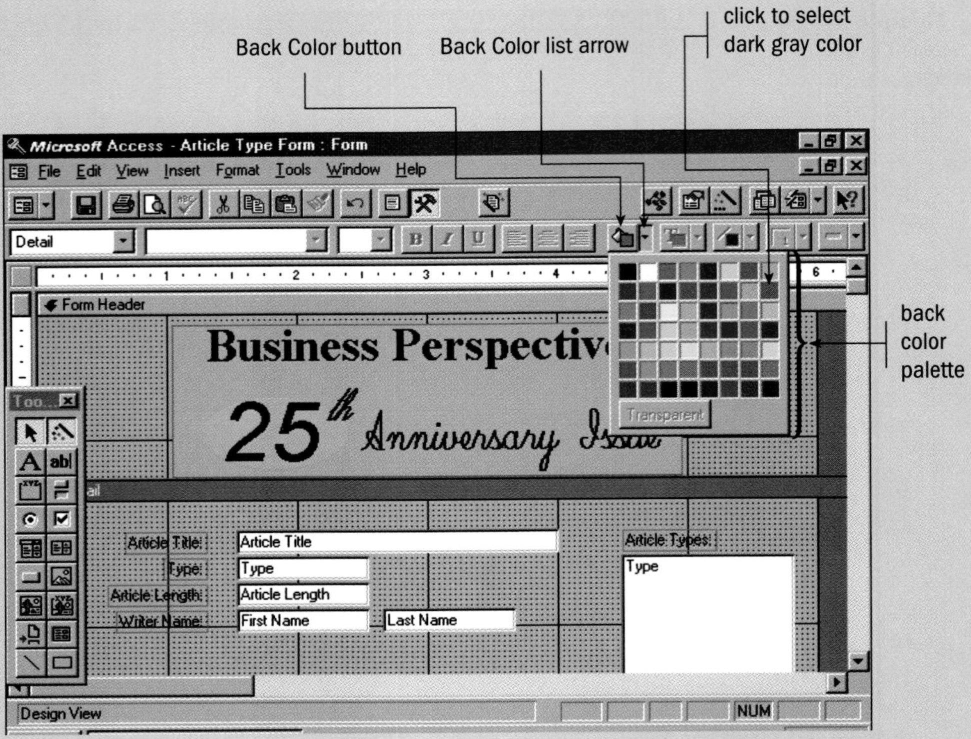

Click the **dark gray color box** in the color palette (at the right end of the second row). The Detail section displays the dark gray background.

TROUBLE? If your screen shows a different color palette, select any dark gray color of your choice.

3. Click the Form Header section, but do not click the graphic image. This makes the Form Header section the selected control.
4. Click the **Back Color** button (not the list arrow) on the toolbar. The Form Header section appears with the dark gray background.

Now Elena changes the style of the graphic image so that it stands out in the Form Header section by applying a special raised effect to the graphic image. Since she has made many changes to the form, she also saves the form again

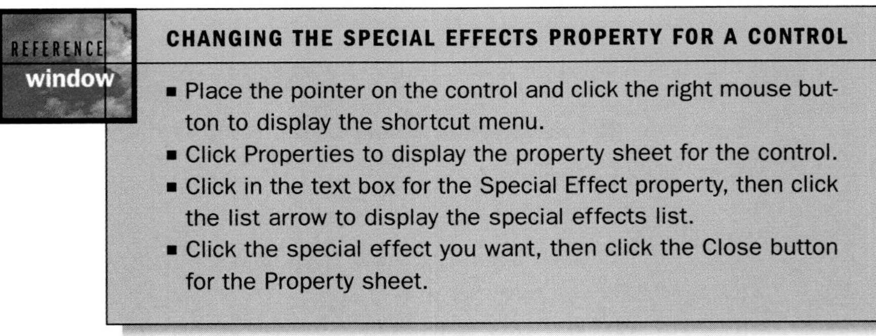

REFERENCE window

CHANGING THE SPECIAL EFFECTS PROPERTY FOR A CONTROL

- Place the pointer on the control and click the right mouse button to display the shortcut menu.
- Click Properties to display the property sheet for the control.
- Click in the text box for the Special Effect property, then click the list arrow to display the special effects list.
- Click the special effect you want, then click the Close button for the Property sheet.

To apply the special effect to the graphic image and save the form:

1. Position the pointer in the graphic image, then click the right mouse button to display the shortcut menu.
2. Click **Properties** to display the property sheet for the graphic image.
3. If necessary, click the **Format** tab to display the Format page. Then use the elevator bar in the property sheet to scroll down until the Special Effect property is visible. Click in the text box for the Special Effect property, then click the **list arrow** to display the special effects list. See Figure 5-36.

Figure 5-36 Adding a special effect to the graphic image

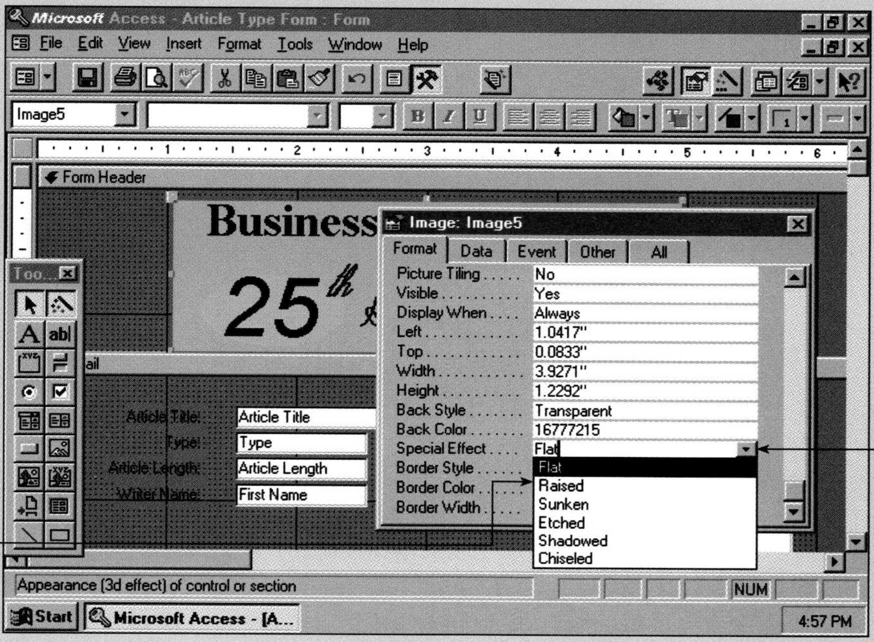

click to add Raised special effect

click to display list of special effects

4. Click **Raised** to apply the special effect, then click the property sheet **Close** button to close it.
5. Click the **Save** button on the toolbar to save the form.

Making Final Revisions to a Custom Form

Elena switches to the Form View window to review the custom form. She wants to see if there are any further changes she needs to make to the form.

To switch to the Form View window to review a custom form:

1. Click the **Form View** button on the toolbar. Access closes the Form Design window and opens the Form View window. See Figure 5-37.

Figure 5-37 Article Type Form in the Form View window

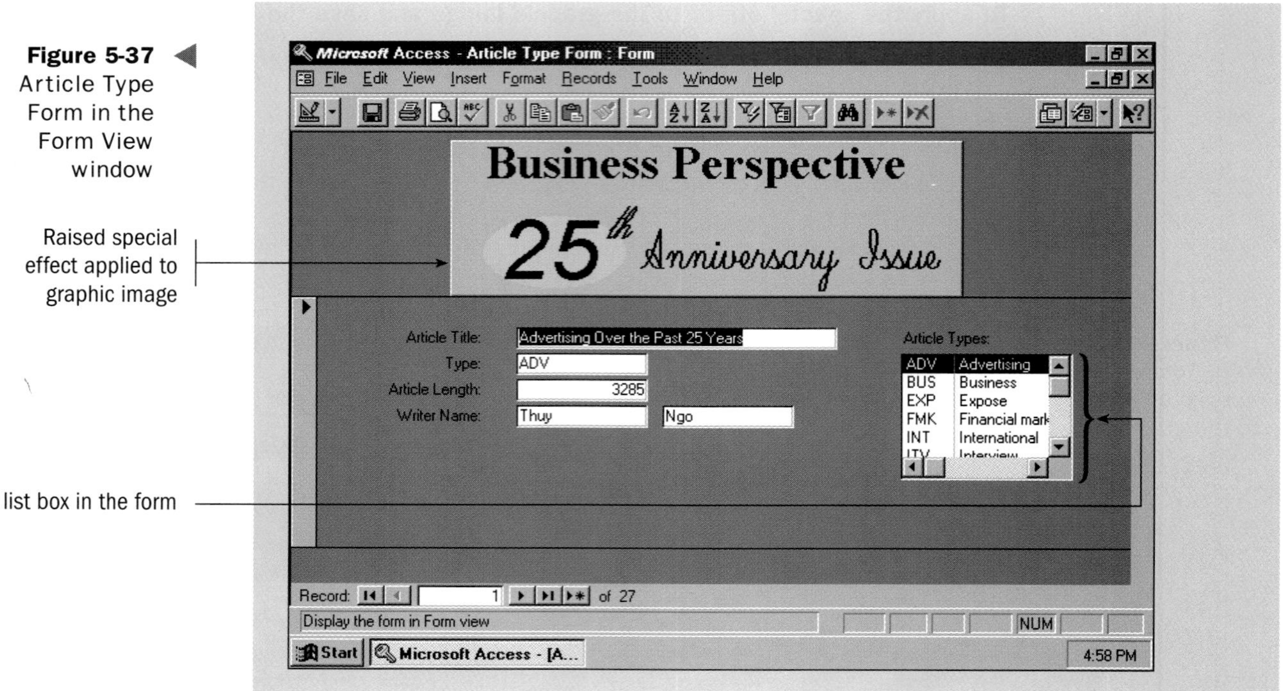

Elena sees two changes she would like to make. She doesn't like the appearance of the Article Types list box and decides to change it to a combo box control. She also sees that the graphic image extends to the bottom of the Form Header section and rests on the dividing line. She decides to increase the height of the Form Header section. She switches back to the Form Design window to change the list box control first.

As you have seen, a list box contains a field-value text box and a list displayed below. You can select any item from the list and it appears in the field-value text box. A combo box is very similar, but the list is not always displayed. A combo box contains a list arrow instead of a displayed list. When you click the list arrow, the list is displayed. When you click to select an entry in the list, the value appears in the field-value text box, and the list closes. Elena changes the control type to combo box in her custom form.

Changing the Control Type with Control Morphing

To change the control type, Elena could delete the list box control on the form and replace it with a combo box control. However, Access also allows you to change a control's type directly on the form. This is known as **control morphing**. Elena will use control morphing to change the list box control to a combo box control.

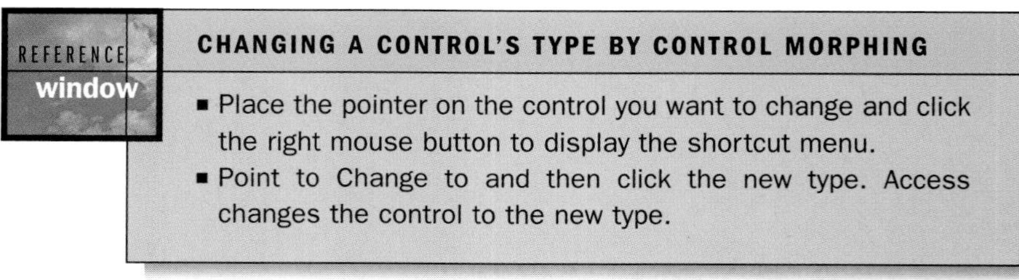

CHANGING A CONTROL'S TYPE BY CONTROL MORPHING

- Place the pointer on the control you want to change and click the right mouse button to display the shortcut menu.
- Point to Change to and then click the new type. Access changes the control to the new type.

To change the list box control to a combo box control:

1. Click the **Form View** button on the toolbar. Access closes the Form View window and opens the Form Design window.
2. Place the pointer on the list box control and click the right mouse button to display the shortcut menu.
3. Point to **Change to** and then click **Combo Box**. Access changes the control to a combo box.

As her final task to complete her custom form, Elena resizes the Form Header section.

To resize the Form Header section:

1. Position the pointer at the top edge of the bar that divides the Form Header section from the Detail section. When the pointer changes to ‡, drag the divider down approximately .25", then release the mouse button.

   TROUBLE? If you move the divider too far, drag the divider again until it is correctly positioned.

2. Switch back and forth between the Form View window and the Form Design window until the Form Header section is the correct size. See Figure 5-38.

Figure 5-38 The final version of a custom form in the Form View window

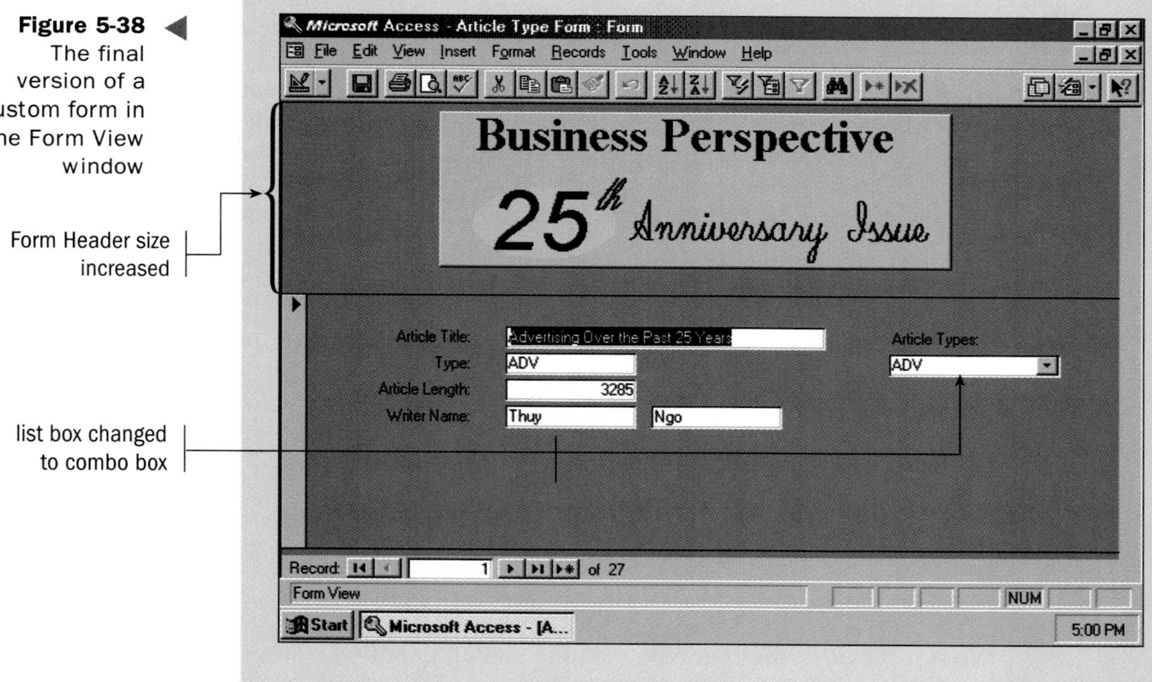

3. When you have completed the custom form, switch to the Form Design window to view the form's final design. See Figure 5-39.

Figure 5-39 The final version of a custom form in the Form Design window

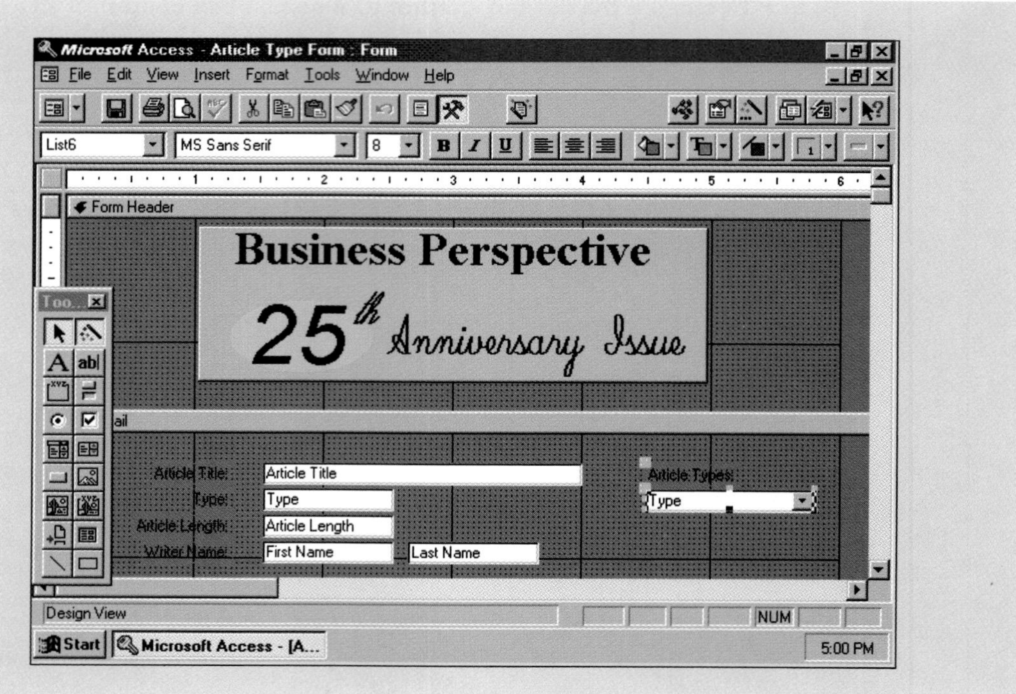

Elena prints the completed form and shows it to Harold, who tells her this format is much easier to read and use than the Article Type Query results. Elena then saves her changes to the Article Type Form, and closes the Form Design window. Having completed her work with forms for the Issue25 database, Elena also exits Access at this time.

To save changes to a form, close the Form Design window, and exit Access:

1. Click the **Save** button on the toolbar. Access saves the form.
2. Click the Form Design window **Close** button. Access closes the Form Design window and switches to the Database window.
3. Click the Access window **Close** button to exit Access.

In the next tutorial, Elena will create reports that will allow her to print table records and query results in a useful hardcopy format.

Quick Check

1 What is the difference between a bound and an unbound control?

2 How do you move a control and its label together, and how do you move each separately?

3 How do you change a label name?

4 How would you resize a control?

5 What is the Form Header section?

6 Describe how you would use a Control Wizard to add a list box to a form.

7 How do you insert into a form a graphic created with another software program?

8 What is control morphing?

Tutorial Assignments

Elena creates two new forms for the Issue25 database. Start Access, open the Issue25 database in the Tutorial Folder on your Student Disk, and do the following:

1. Use the Form Wizard to create a columnar form based on the BUSINESS ARTICLES table. Select all the fields from the table in the order in which they are stored in the table, and use the form title Business Articles Columnar Form.
2. Open the Form View window and then print the first page.
3. Change the form's design so that the Article Length text box and its attached label box are to the right of, and on the same line as, the Issue field.
4. Move the Writer ID text box and its attached label box up to the position previously occupied by the Article Length bound control.
5. Change the Caption property for the Article Length label box to Length followed by a colon.
6. Resize the Article Title text box so that the field value for each record is completely displayed.
7. Verify your design changes in the Form View window by navigating through all records.
8. Print the first page and close the Form View window.

Elena next creates a custom form and names it Business Articles by Issue and Length Form. Use the Issue25 database in the Tutorial folder on your Student Disk to do the following:

9. Create a query by selecting the BUSINESS ARTICLES and WRITERS tables and selecting the following fields in the order given here: Article Title, Type, Issue of Business Perspective, Article Length, Last Name, and First Name. Rename the Issue of Business Perspective field as Issue. Then sort the records based on Issue as the primary sort key in descending order and Article Length as the secondary sort key in ascending order. Print the entire query results for this query. Finally, save the query, naming it Articles Sorted by Issue and Length Query, and switch to the Database window.
10. Create a custom form by selecting the query Articles Sorted by Issue and Length Query, clicking the New button, and selecting Design View.
11. Add all the fields from the query Articles Sorted by Issue and Length Query to the Detail section and print the first page of the form.
12. Change the Caption property for the Article Length label box to Length, right-align all the label boxes, resize the Article Title text box so that the field-value for each record is completely displayed, and print the first page of the form.
13. Move the First Name text box to the right of, and on the same line as, the Last Name text box; delete the First Name label; change the Caption property for the Last Name label to Writer Name; resize the Writer Name label; and print the first page of the form.
14. Use the Format menu's to Fit option under the Size command for the five labels and then right-align all the labels. Print the first page of the form.
15. Change the form width to 4.5" and then move the Issue text box and its attached label to the right of, and on the same line as, the Type field. Move all the lines that follow the Type and Issue fields up to eliminate blank lines. If necessary, right-align all the labels that appear on the left of the form and then left align the field-value text boxes to their immediate right. Print the first page of the form.
16. Add Form Header and Form Footer sections; delete the Form Footer section; add to the Form Header section the form title Business Articles by Issue and Length Form. Add the graphic image 25th to the Form Header, change the height of the Detail section to accommodate the title and graphic image, and print the first page of the form.

17. Use the List Box Wizard to create a list box to display all the article types and their descriptions. Position the list box under all the fields. Use the TYPES table for the list box, and display both table fields. Use Types as the label and position it just to the left of the list box. Resize the list box to display all types and descriptions.

18. In Design View, use AutoFormat to change the style of the form (click Format, then AutoFormat). Select Colorful 2 as the style. Print the first and last pages of the form.
19. Save the form as Business Articles by Issue and Length Form.

20. Import the WRITER PAYMENTS-JR table from the Vision database in the Tutorial folder on your Student Disk. Delete the WRITER PAYMENTS table you created in Tutorial 2 and rename WRITER PAYMENTS-JR as WRITER PAYMENTS. Create a custom form using the WRITER PAYMENTS table. Since this table contains records of checks, make your form resemble a check
21. Save the form with the name WRITERS PAYMENT form.

Case Problems

1. Walkton Daily Press Carriers Grant Sherman uses the Form Wizard to create a form for his Press database. Start Access, open the Press database in the Cases folder on your Student Disk, and do the following:

1. Use AutoForm to create a columnar form based on the CARRIERS table.
2. Open the Form View window and then print the second page.
3. Save the form with the name Carriers Form and close the Form View window on your screen.

Grant creates a custom form named Carriers by Name and Route ID Form. Use the Press database in the Cases folder on your Student Disk to do the following:

4. Create a query by selecting the BILLINGS and CARRIERS tables. If necessary, create a join line for the Carrier ID fields and select fields in the order given here: Carrier Last Name, Carrier First Name, Carrier Phone, Route ID, and Balance Amount. Rename the Balance Amount field simply Balance, and then sort the records based on Carrier Last Name as the primary sort key in ascending order and on Route ID as the secondary sort key in ascending order. Print the entire query results for this query. Finally, save the query, naming it Carriers Sorted by Name and Route ID Query. Switch to the Database window.
5. Create a custom form based on the Carriers Sorted by Name and Route ID Query.
6. To the Detail section of the form, add all the fields from the Carriers Sorted by Name and Route ID Query. Print the first page of the form.
7. Move the Carrier Last Name text box without its attached label to the right on the same line, leaving room to move the Carrier First Name text box from the line below up in front of it. Then move the Carrier First Name text box without its attached label up between the Carrier Last Name label box and the Carrier Last Name text box. Delete the Carrier First Name label box, change the Caption property for the Last Name label box to Carrier Name: (include the colon), resize the Carrier Name label box to accommodate the caption, and print the first page of the form.
8. Move the Carrier Phone text box and its attached label up one line, and move the Route ID text box and its attached label up one line. Move the Balance text box and its attached label to the right of, and on the same line as, the Route ID bound control. Print the first page of the form.
9. Move the Balance label to the right, so that it is closer to its attached text box.
10. Right-align all the labels on the left side of the form.
11. Change the Detail section background color to blue-green (third color from the right in the second row of the palette).

12. Add Form Header and Form Footer sections. Add to the Form Header section the form title Carriers by Name and Route ID. (*Hint:* use the toolbox Label tool.) Add to the Form Footer section the label Press Database, and print the first page of the form.
13. Save the form as Carriers by Name and Route ID Form.

2. Lopez Lexus Dealerships Hector Lopez uses the Form Wizard to create a form for his Lexus database. Start Access, open the Lexus database in the Cases folder on your Student Disk, and do the following:

1. Use the Form Wizard to create a columnar form type with the Colorful 1 style based on the CARS table. Select all the fields from the table in the order in which they are stored in the table. Use the form title Cars Data.
2. Open the Form View window, print the first two pages, then close the Form View window.

Maria Lopez creates a custom form, naming it Cars by Model and Year Form. Use the Lexus database on your Student Disk to do the following:

3. Create a query by selecting the CLASSES, LOCATIONS, CARS, and TRANSMISSIONS tables. You need join lines between the two Transmission Type fields, between the two Location Code fields, and between Class Type and Class. If any of these join lines are not shown, then create them. Select fields in the order given here: Manufacturer, Model, Class Description, Transmission Desc, Year, Location Name, Manager Name, Cost, and Selling Price. Sort the records based on Model as the primary sort key in ascending order and on Year as the secondary sort key in ascending order. Print the entire query results for this query. Finally, save the query, naming it Cars by Model and Year Query.
4. Create a custom form based on the Cars by Model and Year Query.
5. Add to the Detail section all the fields from the Cars by Model and Year Query. Place the fields at the left edge of the Design View. Print the fourth page of the form.
6. Resize the field-value text boxes, as necessary, so that, in the Form View window, all the field values for each record are completely displayed without unnecessary extra space. Navigate through the records in the Form View window to be sure the box sizes are correct. The Class Description and Transmission Desc text boxes should be widened, for example, and the Year, Cost, and Selling Price text boxes should be narrowed.
7. Change the width of the Detail section to 5.75" and its height to 2.75".
8. Move the Model text box and its attached label to the right of, and on the same line as, the Manufacturer bound control. Then move the Model text box to the left to be one grid dot away from its related label.
9. Move the Year text box and its attached label to the right of, and on the same line as, the Model bound control. Then move the Year label to the right to be one grid dot away from its related text box.
10. Move the Manager Name text box and its attached label to the right of, and on the same line as, the Location Name bound control. Move the Selling Price text box and its attached label to the right of, and on the same line as, the Cost bound control.
11. Eliminate blank lines by moving text boxes and their attached labels up, and then print the fourth page of the form.
12. Change the Caption properties for these labels: Class Description to Class, Transmission Desc to Trans, and Location Name to Location.
13. Apply the Format menu's to Fit option under the Size command for the labels on the left side of the form, right-align these labels, and then print the fourth page of the form.

14. Use the List Box Wizard to add two list boxes to the form—one for class types and descriptions and one for location codes and names. Position the list boxes side by side below all the control boxes in the Detail section, placing the one containing class types and descriptions on the left. For the class list box, use the CLASSES table, display both table fields, and enter Classes for the label. For the location list box, use the LOCATIONS table, display the Location Code and Location Name fields, and enter Locations as the label. Resize and move the labels and list boxes to display as much of each record as possible.
15. Use control morphing to change the location list box to a combo box.
16. Print the fourth page of the form.
17. Save the form as Cars by Model and Year Form.

3. Tophill University Student Employment Olivia Tyler uses the Form Wizard to create a form for her Parttime database. Start Access, open the Parttime database in the Cases folder on your Student Disk, and do the following:

1. If you have not already defined a one-to-many relation from the EMPLOYERS table to the JOBS table, use the Relationships window to do so now.
2. Use the Form Wizard to create a tabular main/subform form type based on the EMPLOYERS table as the primary table for the main form and the JOBS table as the related table for the subform. Choose your own style for the form. Select all the fields from the EMPLOYERS table in the order in which they are stored in the table. Select all the fields from the JOBS table, except for the Employer ID field, in the order in which they are stored in the table. Save the form with the name Employers and Jobs Form, save the subform with the name Jobs Subform.
3. Open the Form View window and print the first page, then close the Form View window.

Olivia creates a custom form named Jobs by Employer and Job Title Form. Use the Parttime database on your Student Disk to do the following:

4. Create a query by selecting the EMPLOYERS and JOBS tables and, if necessary, create a join line for the Employer ID fields. Select all the fields from the EMPLOYERS table in the order in which they are stored in the table, and then select fields from the JOBS table in the order given here: Hours/Week, Job Title, and Wage. Sort the records based on Employer Name as the primary sort key in ascending order and on Job Title as the secondary sort key in ascending order. Print the query results for this query. Finally, save the query, naming it Jobs Sorted by Employer and Job Title Query.
5. Create a custom form based on the query Jobs Sorted by Employer and Job Title Query.
6. Add all the fields from Jobs Sorted by Employer and Job Title Query to the Detail section and then print the first page of the form.
7. Resize the Employer Name and Job Title text boxes and print the first page of the form.
8. Right-align all the labels.
9. Add Form Header and Form Footer sections, add to the Form Header section the form title Jobs by Employer and Job Title, add to the Form Footer section the Tophill University logo graphic image TU from the Cases folder on your student disk, and print the first page of the form.
10. Save the form as Jobs by Employer and Job Title Form.

4. Rexville Business Licenses Chester Pearce uses AutoForm to create a form for his Buslic database. Start Access, open the Buslic database in the Cases folder on your Student Disk, and do the following:

1. Use AutoForm to create a columnar form based on the BUSINESSES table.
2. Open the Form View window and then print the first two pages.
3. Save the form as Businesses Form and close the Form View window.

Chester creates a custom form, naming it Businesses by License Type and Business Name Form. Use the Buslic database on your Student Disk to do the following:

4. Create a query by selecting the BUSINESSES, ISSUED LICENSES, and LICENSES tables and, if necessary, create join lines for the Business ID fields and the License Type fields. Select all the fields, except the Business ID field, from the BUSINESSES table in the order in which they are stored in the table; select the License Number, License Type, Amount, and Date Issued fields (in the order given here) from the ISSUED LICENSES table; and then select the License Description and Basic Cost fields from the LICENSES table. Rename the License Description field simply License. Sort the records based on License Type as the primary sort key in ascending order and on Business Name as the secondary sort key in ascending order, but do not show the License Type field in the query results. Print the entire query results for this query. Finally, save the query, naming it Businesses Sorted by License Type and Business Name Query.
5. Create a custom form by selecting the Businesses Sorted by License Type and Business Name Query.
6. Add all the fields from Businesses Sorted by License Type and Business Name Query to the Detail section and then print the first page of the form.
7. Resize the Business Name and License text boxes, and print the first page of the form.
8. Right-align all the labels.
9. Change the Detail section background color to blue-green (third color from the right in the second row on the palette), and then print the first page of the form.
10. Add Form Header and Form Footer sections, add to the Form Header section the form title Businesses by License Type and Business Name, add to the Form Footer section the label Buslic Database, and print the first page of the form.
11. Save the form as Businesses by License Type and Business Name Form.

TUTORIAL 6

Creating Reports

Creating a Marketing Report at Vision Publishers

OBJECTIVES

In this tutorial you will:

- Create a report using AutoReport and the Report Wizard
- Save and print a report
- Design and create a custom report
- Modify report controls and properties
- Sort and group data
- Calculate group and overall totals
- Hide duplicate values
- Embed and link objects in a report

CASE

Vision Publishers

At the next progress meeting on the special 25th-anniversary issue of *Business Perspective*, Harold Larson mentions to Elena Sanchez that the forms she created from the Issue25 database certainly provided information in a more attractive, readable format than query results. Now he needs information from the Issue25 database presented even more professionally, for an upcoming meeting with several advertisers in New York for the special 25th-anniversary issue of *Business Perspective*. He asks Elena to produce a report that includes information about the articles and authors to help him discuss the special issue with potential advertisers.

Using a Report

A **report** is a formatted hardcopy of the contents of one or more tables from a database. Although you can format and print data using datasheets, queries, and forms, reports allow you greater flexibility and provide a more professional, custom appearance. Reports can be used, for example, to print billing statements and mailing labels.

An Access report is divided into sections. Each report can have seven different sections, which are described in Figure 6-1. You do not need to use all seven report sections in a report. When you design your report, you determine which sections to use and what information to place in each section. Figure 6-2 shows a sample report produced from the Issue25 database.

Figure 6-1
Access report sections

Report Section	Description
Report Header	Appears once at the beginning of a report. Use it for report titles, company logos, report introductions, and cover pages.
Page Header	Appears at the top of each page of a report. Use it for column headings, report titles, page numbers, and report dates. If your report has a Report Header section, it precedes the first Page Header section.
Group Header	Appears once at the beginning of a new group of records. Use it to print the group name and the field value that all records in the group have in common. A report can have up to 10 grouping levels.
Detail	Appears once for each record in the underlying table or query. Use it to print selected fields from the table or query and to print calculated values.
Group Footer	Appears once at the end of a group of records. Use it to print totals for the group.
Report Footer	Appears once at the end of the report. Use it for report totals and other summary information.
Page Footer	Appears at the bottom of each page of a report. Use it for page numbers and brief explanations of symbols or abbreviations. If your report has a Report Footer section, it precedes the Page Footer section on the last page of the report.

Figure 6-2 A sample report showing the seven sections of a report

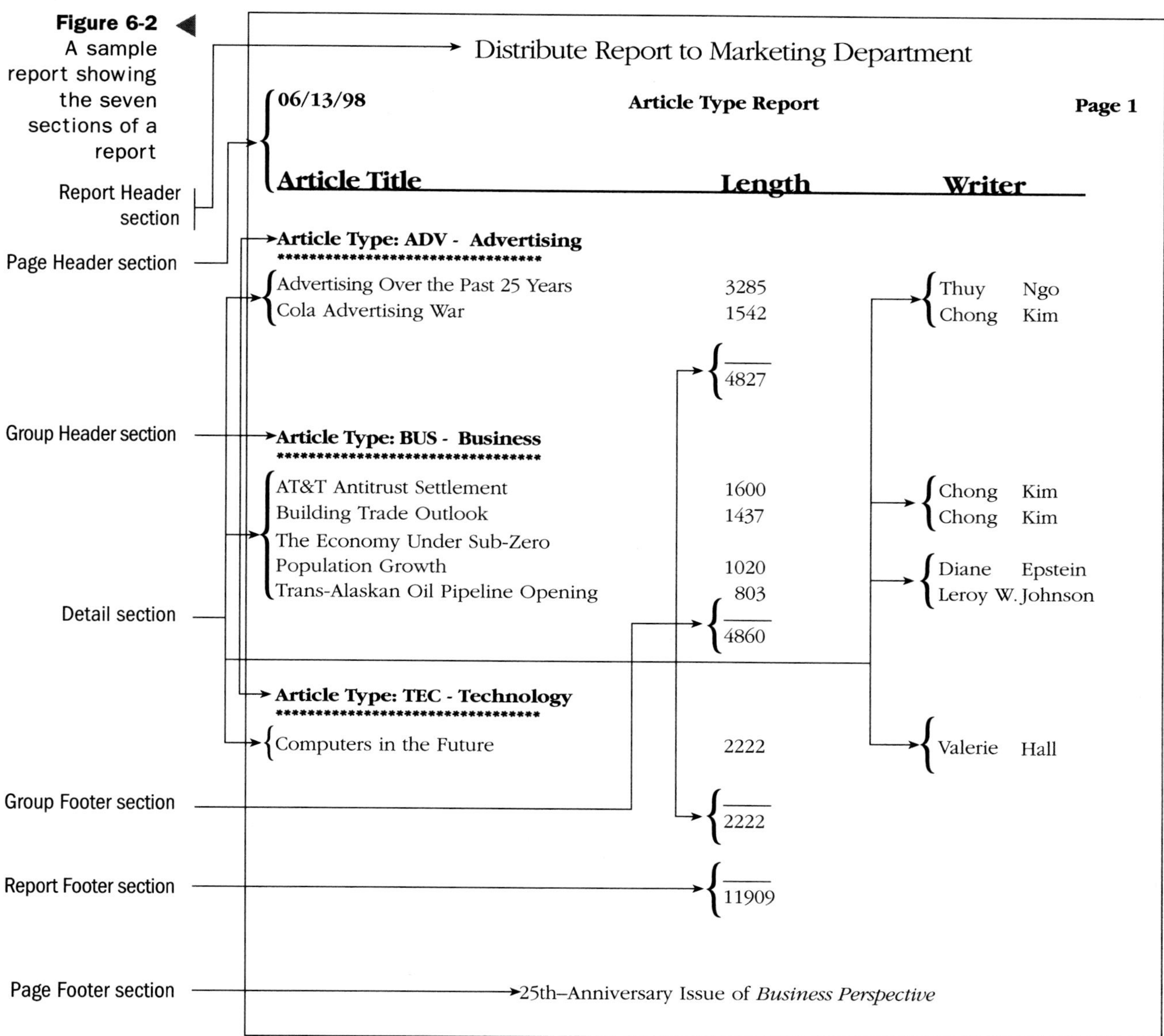

Report Header section
Page Header section
Group Header section
Detail section
Group Footer section
Report Footer section
Page Footer section
Distribute Report to Marketing Department
06/13/98
Article Type Report
Page 1
Article Title
Length
Writer
Article Type: ADV - Advertising
Advertising Over the Past 25 Years 3285 Thuy Ngo
Cola Advertising War 1542 Chong Kim
4827
Article Type: BUS - Business
AT&T Antitrust Settlement 1600 Chong Kim
Building Trade Outlook 1437 Chong Kim
The Economy Under Sub-Zero
Population Growth 1020 Diane Epstein
Trans-Alaskan Oil Pipeline Opening 803 Leroy W. Johnson
4860
Article Type: TEC - Technology
Computers in the Future 2222 Valerie Hall
2222
11909
25th–Anniversary Issue of Business Perspective

Creating a Report

In Access, there is more than one way to create your own report:

- **AutoReport** creates a report in one of two standard formats, columnar or tabular; it uses all of the fields in the underlying table or query. This is a quick way to create a basic report that you can use without modification or that you can customize later. Figure 6-3 shows columnar and tabular reports created from the WRITERS table with AutoReport. In Figure 6-3, notice that the report created by AutoReport would have to be modified to include the entire Writer Phone field values.

Figure 6-3A The AutoReport Columnar

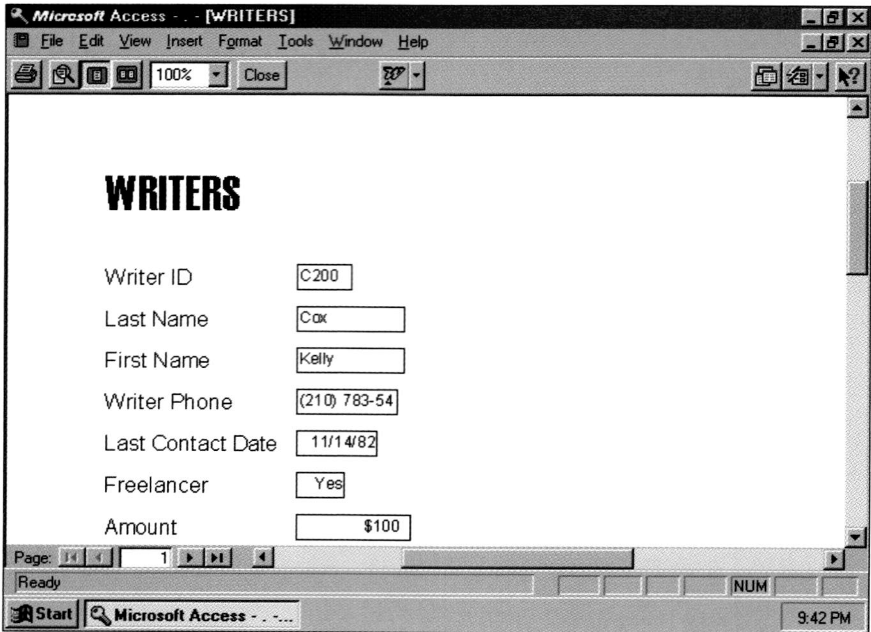

Figure 6-3B The AutoReport Tabular

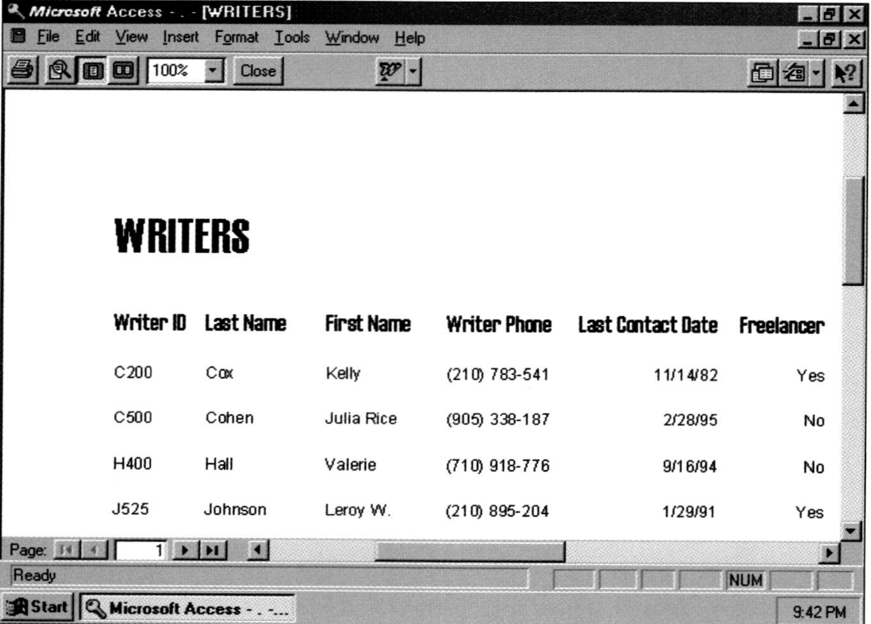

- The **Report Wizard** asks you a series of questions and then creates a report based on your answers. Using the Report Wizard, you can select fields that you want to appear in the report.
- The **Report Design** window allows you to create your own customized report that you design directly on the screen.
- The **Chart Wizard** designs a graph based on your data.
- The **Label Wizard** designs labels (such as mailing labels) based on your data.

Elena has never created an Access report, so she first familiarizes herself with AutoReport.

SESSION 6.1

In this session, you will create reports using AutoReport and the Report Wizard, save a report, and print a report. You will also create a blank report and then begin to customize it by adding and modifying fields.

Creating a Report with AutoReport

The quickest way to create a report is to use AutoReport. AutoReport uses all the fields from the selected table or query, creates a columnar or tabular report for these fields, and displays the report on the screen in the Print Preview window.

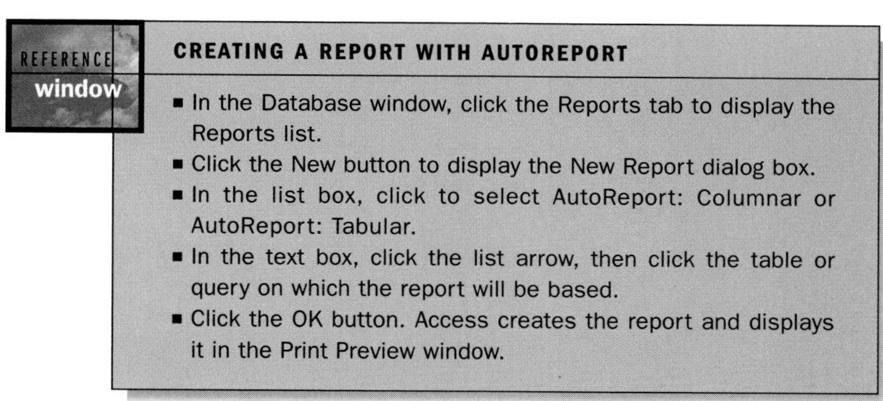

REFERENCE window

CREATING A REPORT WITH AUTOREPORT

- In the Database window, click the Reports tab to display the Reports list.
- Click the New button to display the New Report dialog box.
- In the list box, click to select AutoReport: Columnar or AutoReport: Tabular.
- In the text box, click the list arrow, then click the table or query on which the report will be based.
- Click the OK button. Access creates the report and displays it in the Print Preview window.

In order to become familiar with AutoReport, Elena uses AutoReport: Columnar to create a report containing all the fields from the WRITERS table.

To create a columnar report using AutoReport:

1. If you have not done so, place your Student Disk in the appropriate drive, start Access, and open the Issue25 database in the Tutorial folder on your Student Disk. Click the **Reports** tab to display the Reports list. No reports appear in the list yet.
2. Click the **New** button. Access displays the New Report dialog box.
3. Click **AutoReport: Columnar** in the list box to highlight it.
4. Click the **list arrow** in the text box to display a list of available tables and queries.
5. If necessary, scroll the list until WRITERS is visible. Click **WRITERS** to select the WRITERS table. See Figure 6-4.

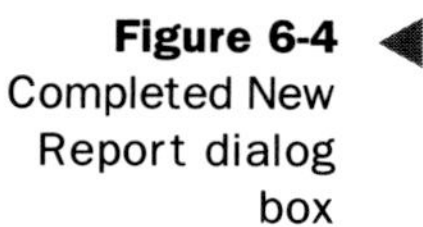

Figure 6-4 Completed New Report dialog box

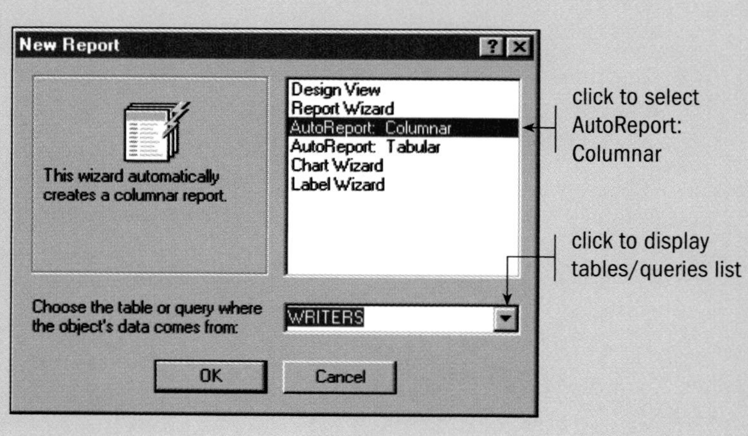

6. Click the **OK** button. The New Report dialog box closes, and Access displays the completed columnar report in the Print Preview window. Click the Print Preview window **Maximize** button. See Figure 6-5. You can use the elevator bar to scroll down and display all the fields of the report.

Figure 6-5 The completed columnar report in the Print Preview window

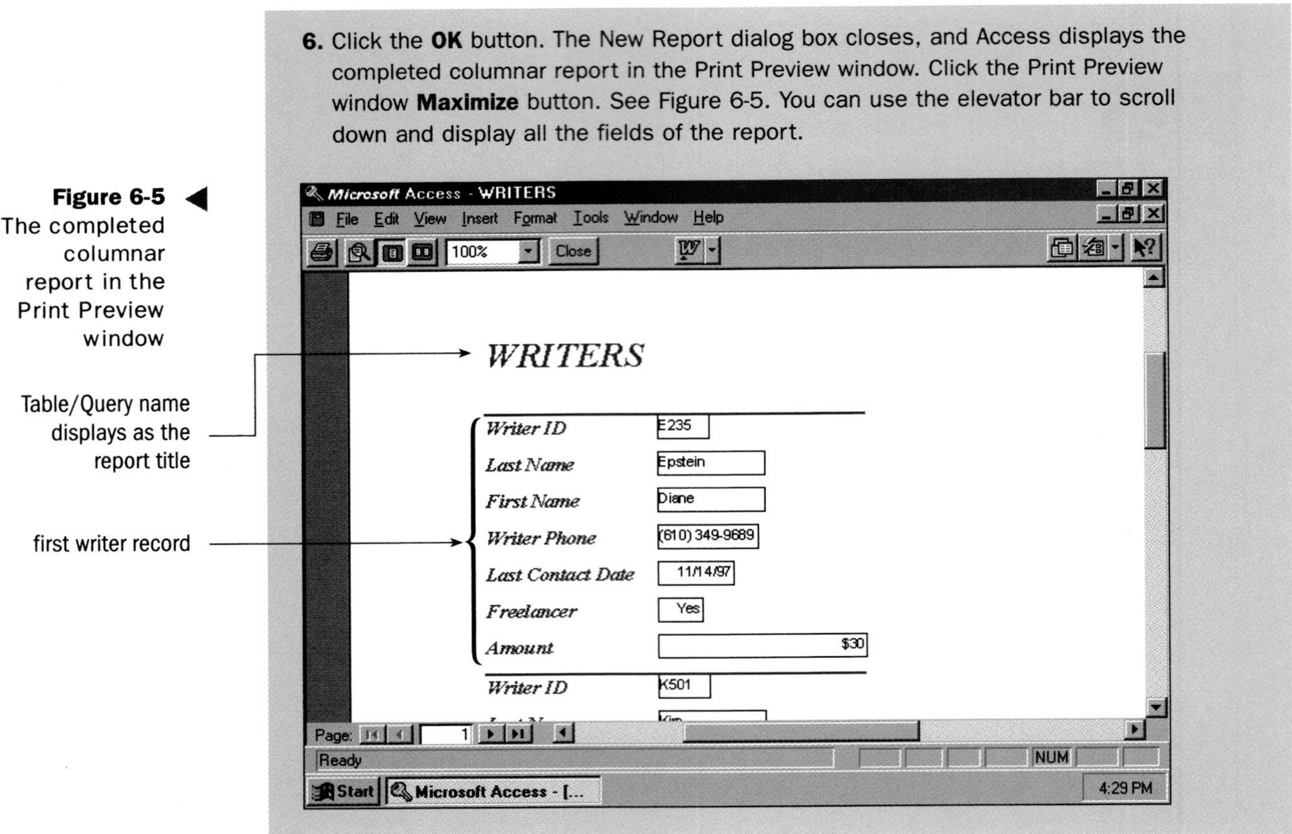

After viewing the report, Elena saves it.

Saving a Report

Elena saves her report so that she and others can print it whenever they need an updated copy. When you save a report, you actually save the report design. When you preview or print the report later, Access uses the current data from the underlying table or query to create the report.

Elena saves the report using the name Writers Columnar Report and then closes the Print Preview window.

To save and close a new report:

1. Click **File** and then click **Save As/Export** to display the Save As dialog box.
2. Type **Writers Columnar Report** in the New Name text box and then click the **OK** button. The Save As dialog box closes, and Access saves the report.
3. Click the Print Preview window **Close** button ☒ (in the upper-right corner) to close the report and return to the Database window. Notice that Writers Columnar Report appears in the Reports list.

   TROUBLE? If Access switches to the Report Design window instead of the Database window, you clicked the Close button on the Print Preview toolbar. Click the Report Design window Close button to return to the Database window.

Creating a Report with the Report Wizard

After viewing the columnar report created by AutoReport, Elena decides that she would like to create a report listing selected fields from the WRITERS table in a tabular format. She wants to use a different title and style for the report and to print the staff writers and freelancers in separate groups. Since AutoReport uses all of the fields in the selected table and creates a standard title and layout, Elena would have to make many modifications to a report created by AutoReport. Instead, Elena uses the Report Wizard to create her report.

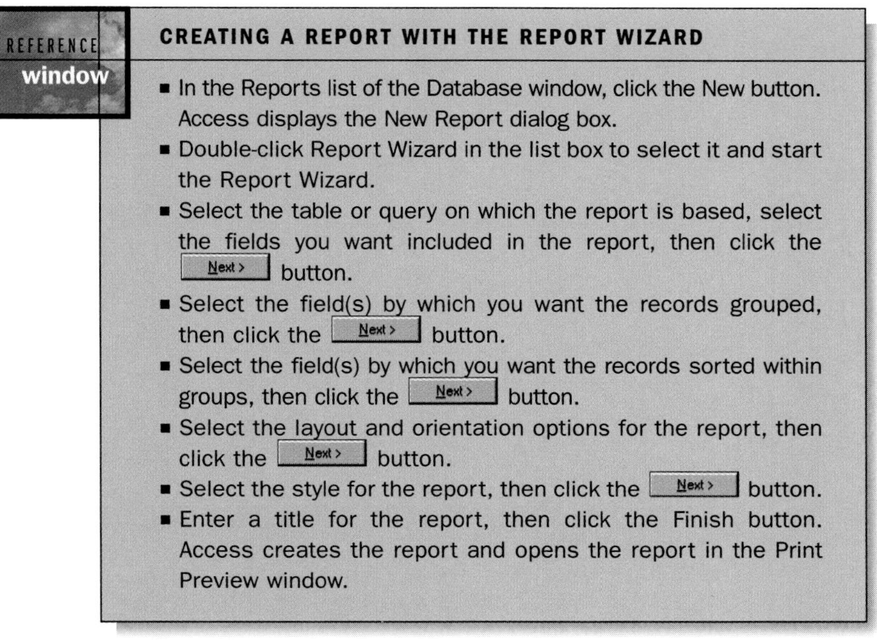

REFERENCE window

CREATING A REPORT WITH THE REPORT WIZARD

- In the Reports list of the Database window, click the New button. Access displays the New Report dialog box.
- Double-click Report Wizard in the list box to select it and start the Report Wizard.
- Select the table or query on which the report is based, select the fields you want included in the report, then click the Next > button.
- Select the field(s) by which you want the records grouped, then click the Next > button.
- Select the field(s) by which you want the records sorted within groups, then click the Next > button.
- Select the layout and orientation options for the report, then click the Next > button.
- Select the style for the report, then click the Next > button.
- Enter a title for the report, then click the Finish button. Access creates the report and opens the report in the Print Preview window.

Elena creates a report with the Report Wizard.

To start the Report Wizard and select a report type:

1. In the Reports list of the Database window, click the **New** button. Access displays the New Report dialog box. Double-click **Report Wizard** in the list box to select it and start the Report Wizard. The first Report Wizard dialog box appears.

2. If necessary, click the **Tables/Queries** list arrow and then click **Table: WRITERS** to select the WRITERS table.

   Elena wants to include the Last Name, First Name, Writer ID, Last Contact Date, and Freelancer fields from the WRITERS table.

3. Click **Last Name** to select it, then click the > button to move the Last Name field from the Available Fields list box to the Selected Fields list box. Use the same procedure to move the First Name, Writer ID, Last Contact Date, and Freelancer fields from the Available Fields list box to the Selected Fields list box.

4. Click the Next > button to display the next Report Wizard dialog box. This dialog box allows you to select the grouping for the records in the report. To print the staff writers and freelancers in separate groups, click **Freelancer**, then click the > button to select grouping by the value in the Freelancer field. The sample panel on the right changes to show grouping by the Freelancer field. See Figure 6-6.

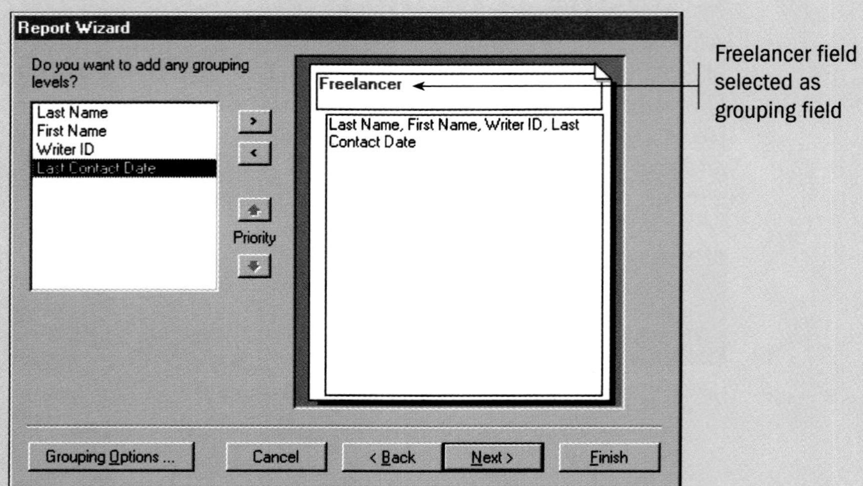

Figure 6-6 Selecting the grouping field

Click the Next > button to display the next Report Wizard dialog box.

This dialog box allows you to select the sort order for records within groups. Elena decides to sort the records by the Last Name field.

5. Click the first **sort order** list arrow to display the field list, then click **Last Name** to select sorting by the Last Name field. See Figure 6-7.

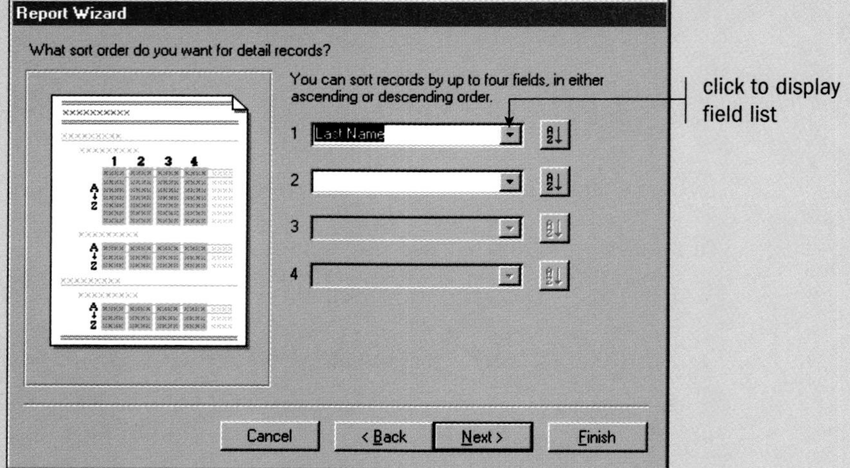

Figure 6-7 Selecting the sort order

6. Click the Next > button to display the next Report Wizard dialog box. This dialog box allows you to select from several predefined layouts for the report. "Layout" refers to the physical placement of fields, titles, page numbers, and other objects on the report page. The sample box on the left displays the selected layout. Elena clicks different layout radio buttons to view the samples and decides on the layout called Outline 1.

7. If necessary, click the **Outline 1** radio button to select this layout. Make sure that the Portrait orientation radio button is selected and that the check box next to "Adjust field width so all fields fit on a page" is checked, then click the Next > button to display the next Report Wizard dialog box.

This dialog box allows you to select a predefined style for the report. "Style" refers to the use of color, fonts, and other formatting options applied to objects on the report page.

8. If necessary, click **Corporate** to select the Corporate style, then click the Next > button to display the next Report Wizard dialog box.

   This dialog box allows you to specify a title for the report. This title will appear at the top of the printed report and will also appear as the name of the report in the Reports list in the Database window.

9. Type **Freelancer/Staff Writer Report** in the text box. Make sure the radio button next to "Preview the report" is selected, then click the **Finish** button. The Report Wizard closes and the report is displayed in the Print Preview window. See Figure 6-8.

Figure 6-8 The completed report in the Print Preview window

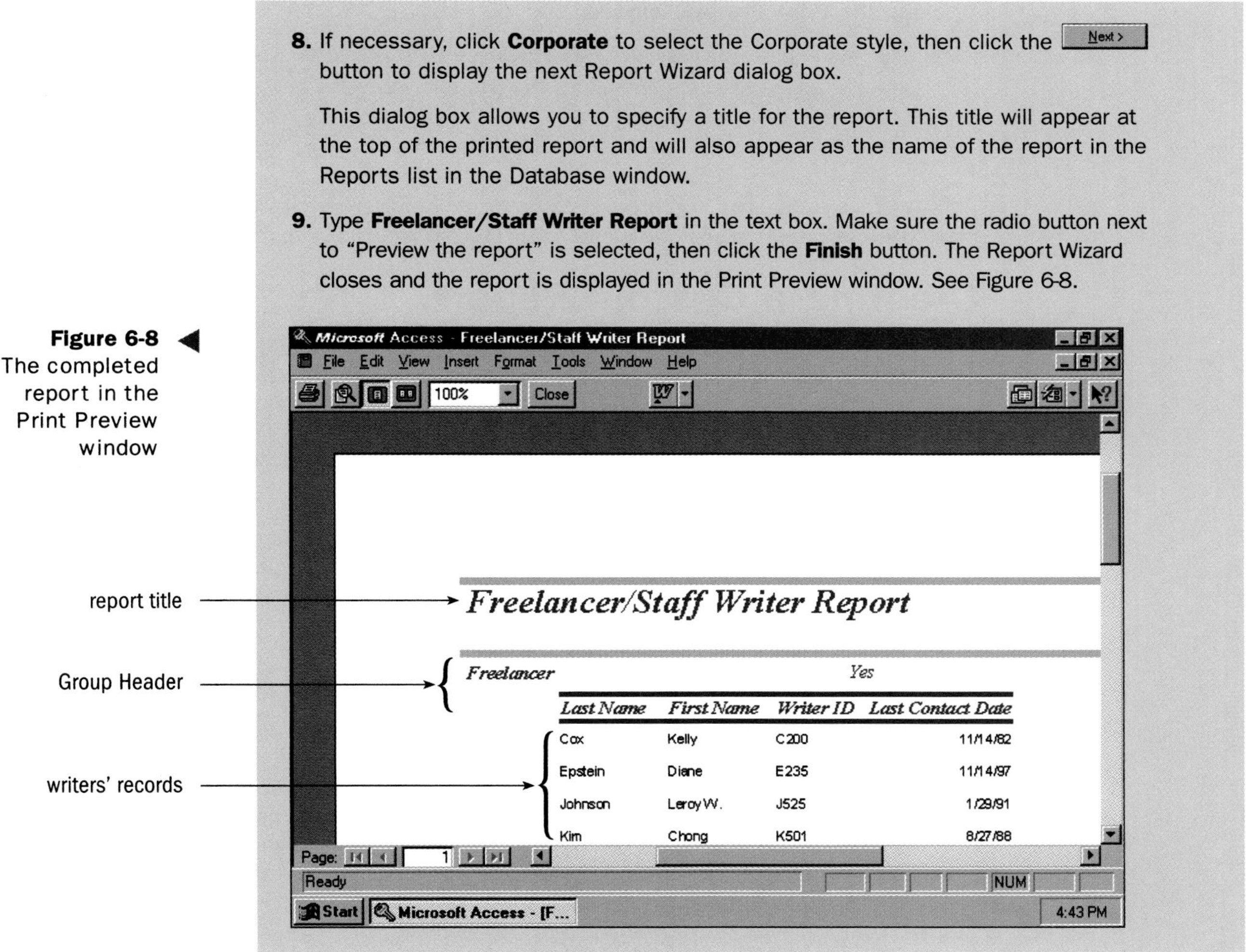

Access displays the report title at the top of the report page. Lines are used to separate the title from the rest of the report page. Since the records are grouped by the value in the Freelancer field, there is a Group Header for each group. The header consists of the label Freelancer and the value of the Freelancer field (Yes or No) for the group. The Group Header also includes labels for the columns in the Detail section. Remember that the default label is the field name or Caption property for that field.

Below each Group Header are column headings and the detail records for that group, in ascending order by the Last Name field. You can use the elevator bar and horizontal scroll bar to view the other records in the report. At the bottom of the page is the Page Footer, which contains the date of the report and page number for each page. Since all of the WRITERS records fit on one page, there is only one page for this report.

Printing a Report

Next, Elena prints the report from the Print Preview window.

To print the report from the Print Preview window:

1. Make sure your printer is on-line and ready to print. Click the **Print** button on the toolbar. Access prints the report.

Elena closes the Print Preview window. Since this report was created by the Report Wizard, Access has already saved the report, using the report title as the report name.

To close the Print Preview window:

1. Click the Print Preview window **Close** button [X]. The Print Preview window closes and the Database window becomes the active window. The new report appears in the Reports list.

Now that Elena has some practice creating reports, she is ready to begin work on Harold's requested report. She meets with Harold to discuss his requirements.

Creating a Custom Report

Elena and Harold discuss his report requirements and decide that the report for his meeting with the advertisers should contain the following four different report sections:

- A Page Header section that shows the current date, report title, page number, and column headings for each field.
- A Detail section that lists the title, type, and length of each article, and the name of the writer. Records should be grouped by the Type field value and the groups printed in ascending order. Within each group, records should appear in descending order based on the Article Length field.
- A Group Footer section that prints subtotals of the Article Length field for each Type group.
- A Report Footer section that prints the overall total of the Article Length field.

The report will not include Report Header, Group Header, or Page Footer sections.

From her work with AutoReport and the Report Wizard, Elena knows that, by default, Access places the report title in the Report Header section and the date and page number in the Page Footer section. Harold prefers all three items at the top of each page, so Elena needs to place that information in the Page Header section.

Elena could use the Report Wizard to create the report, and then modify the report to match her report design. The Report Wizard would construct the majority of the report, so Elena would save time and reduce the possibility for errors. However, Elena decides to create a custom report using the Report Design window so that she can control the precise placement of fields and labels and become more skilled at constructing reports.

If you modify a report created by AutoReport or the Report Wizard, or if you design and create your own report, you produce a **custom report**. You should create a custom report whenever AutoReport or the Report Wizard cannot automatically create the specific report you need.

Designing a Custom Report

Before she creates the custom report, Elena first plans the report's contents and appearance. Elena's completed design is shown in Figure 6-9. The Page Header section contains the report title, Article Type Report, and below that, descriptive column heads. The Page Header section also contains the current date and page number on the same line as the report title.

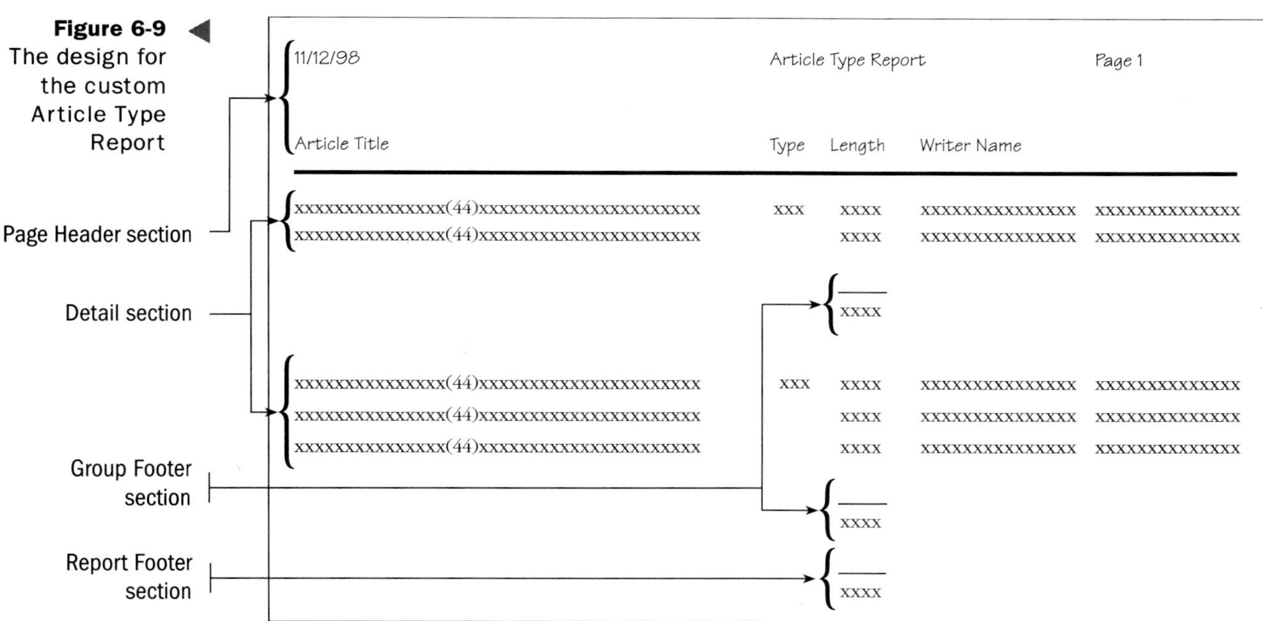

Figure 6-9 The design for the custom Article Type Report

In the Detail section, Elena indicates the locations and lengths of the field values by a series of X's. The three X's under the Type field label indicate that the field value will be three characters wide. The Type field value will appear only with the first record of a group.

The subtotals for each group will appear in the Group Footer section, and an overall total will appear in the Report Footer section. Article Length is the only field for which totals will appear.

The data for a report can come either from a single table or from a query based on one or more tables. Elena's report will contain data from the WRITERS and BUSINESS ARTICLES tables; therefore, she must use a query for this report. She will use the Article Type Query she created earlier because it contains the fields she needs from the two tables.

The Report Design Window

Elena's first step is to create a blank report in the Report Design window. You use the Report Design window to create and modify reports.

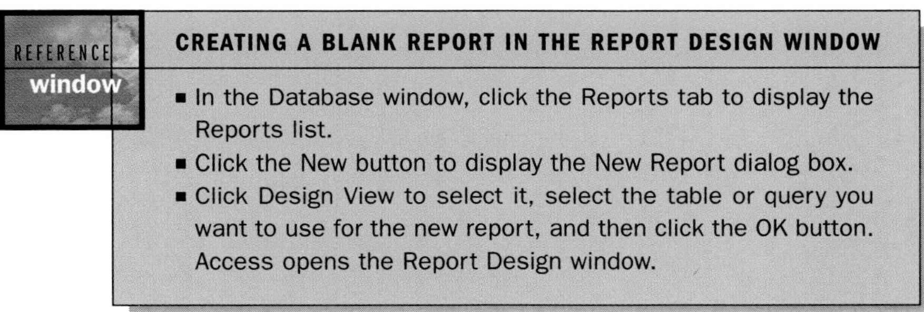

CREATING A BLANK REPORT IN THE REPORT DESIGN WINDOW

- In the Database window, click the Reports tab to display the Reports list.
- Click the New button to display the New Report dialog box.
- Click Design View to select it, select the table or query you want to use for the new report, and then click the OK button. Access opens the Report Design window.

Elena creates a blank report.

To create a blank report in the Report Design window:

1. If necessary, click the **Reports** tab to display the Reports list then click the **New** button to open the New Report dialog box.
2. If necessary, click **Design View** to select it, then click the **text box** list arrow to display the list of Issue25 database tables and queries.
3. Click **Article Type Query** to select it, then click the **OK** button. The Report Design window opens.

The Report Design window has several components in common with the Form Design window. The toolbar for both windows has a Properties button, a Field List button, and a Toolbox button. Both windows also have horizontal and vertical rulers, a grid, and a format toolbar.

The Report Design window displays one new toolbar button, the Sorting and Grouping button. Recall that to display records in a specific order for a form, you use a filter. In reports, you use the **Sorting and Grouping button** to establish sort keys and grouping fields. A maximum of 10 fields can serve as sort keys, and any number of these can be grouping fields.

Unlike the Form Design window, which initially displays only the Detail section on a blank form, the Report Design window also displays a Page Header section and a Page Footer section. Reports often contain these sections, so Access automatically includes them in a blank report.

Adding Fields to a Report

Elena's first task is to add bound controls to the report Detail section for all the fields from the Article Type Query. You use bound controls to print field values from a table or query on a report, and add them to a report the same way you added them to a form. In fact, every task that you accomplished in the Form Design window is done in a similar way in the Report Design window.

REFERENCE window

ADDING FIELDS TO A REPORT

- In the Report Design window, click the Field List button on the toolbar to display the field list.
- To place all fields in the report, double-click the field list title bar to highlight all the fields in the field list. Then click anywhere in the highlighted area of the field list and drag to the report. Release the mouse button when the pointer is correctly positioned. Access places all the field in the report.
- To place a single field in the report, place the pointer on the field name in the field list, then click and drag the field name to the report. Release the mouse button when the pointer is correctly positioned. Access places the field in the report.

Elena begins her custom report.

To open the field list box and add bound controls for all the fields in the field list:

1. Click the **Field List** button on the toolbar. The field list box opens. See Figure 6-10.

Figure 6-10 The blank Report Design window

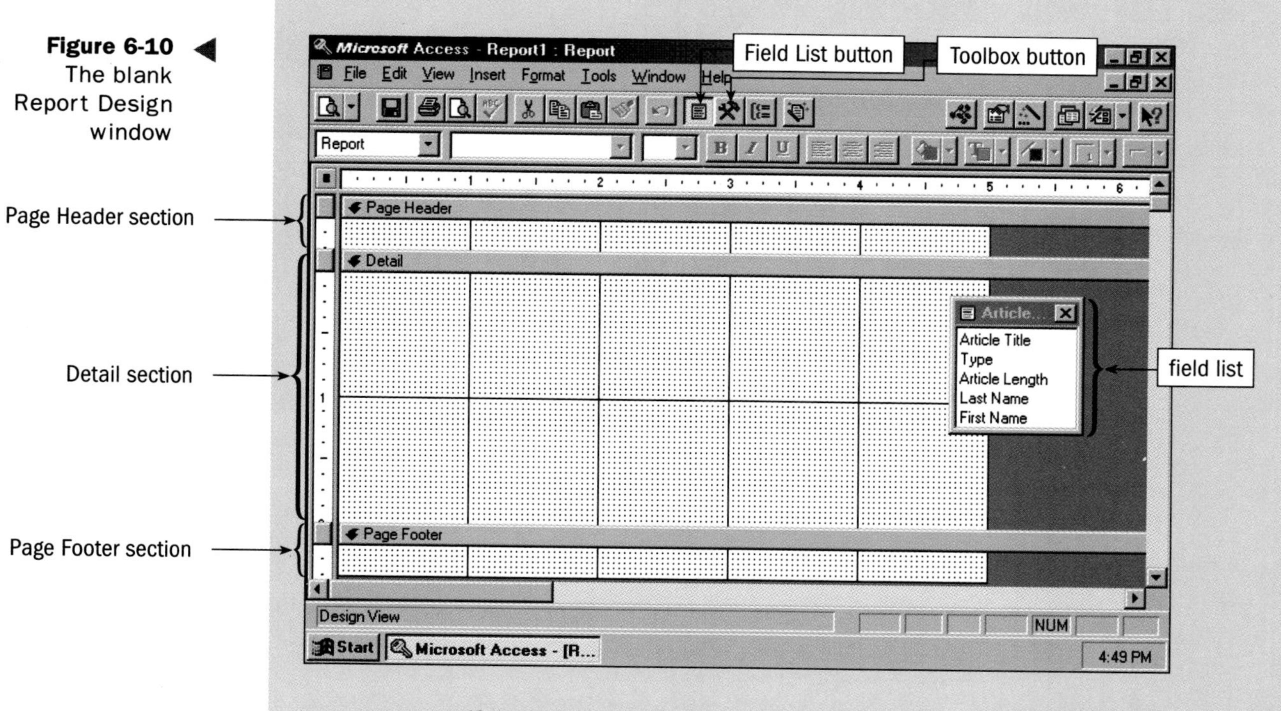

TROUBLE? If the rulers or grid do not appear, click View on the menu bar and then click Ruler or Grid to display the missing component in the Report Design window. A check mark appears in front of these components when they are displayed in the Report Design window. If the grid is still invisible, see your technical support person or instructor for assistance.

If the toolbox is visible, click the Close button for the toolbox to hide it.

2. Double-click the **field list** title bar to highlight all the fields in the Article Type Query field list.

3. Click anywhere in the highlighted area of the field list and drag to the report Detail section. Release the mouse button when the is positioned at the top of the Detail section and at the 1.25" mark on the horizontal ruler. Access resizes the Detail Section and adds bound controls for the five selected fields. Each bound control consists of a text box and, to its left, an attached label. See Figure 6-11. Notice that the text boxes align at the 1.25" mark.

Figure 6-11
Bound controls added to a report

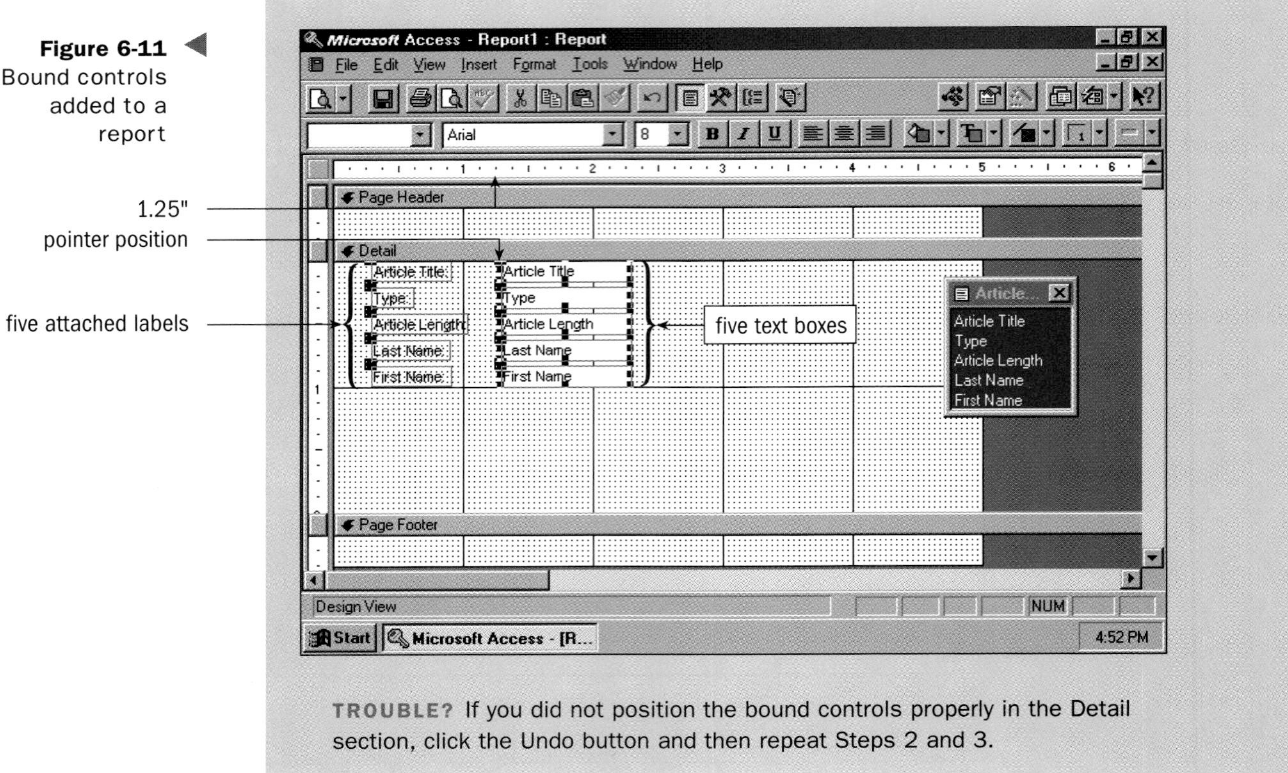

TROUBLE? If you did not position the bound controls properly in the Detail section, click the Undo button and then repeat Steps 2 and 3.

Performing operations in the Report Design window will become easier with practice. Remember, you can always click the Undo button immediately after you make a report design change that has undesired results. You can also click the toolbar Print Preview button at any time to view your progress on the report. Recall that you return to the Report Design window by clicking the Print Preview window Close button on the toolbar.

Using Controls

Five text boxes now appear in a column in the Detail section. Each text box is a bound control linked to a field in the underlying query and has, to its left, an attached label box. Because she is done with the field list box, Elena closes it by clicking the Close button on the field list box. Elena next compares the report Detail section with her design. She needs to move all the label boxes to the Page Header section, and then reposition the label boxes and text boxes so that they agree with her report design.

To close the field list and move all label boxes to the Page Header section:

1. Click the **Close** button ☒ on the field list box to close the field list.
2. Click anywhere in the Page Footer section to deselect the five text boxes and their attached label boxes. While pressing and holding the **Shift** key, click each of the five label boxes in the Detail section, then release the Shift key. This action selects all the label boxes in preparation for cutting them from the Detail section and pasting them in the Page Header section.
3. Position the pointer in any one of the selected label boxes. The pointer turns to ✋. Click the right mouse button to display the shortcut menu.
4. Click **Cut** in the shortcut menu to delete the label boxes from the Detail section and place them in the Windows Clipboard. See Figure 6-12.

Figure 6-12 ◀
Label boxes cut from the Detail section

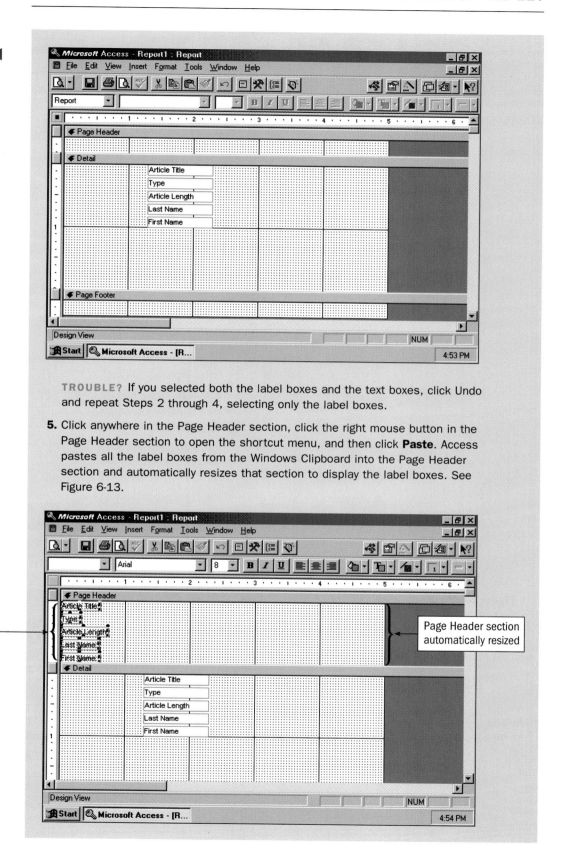

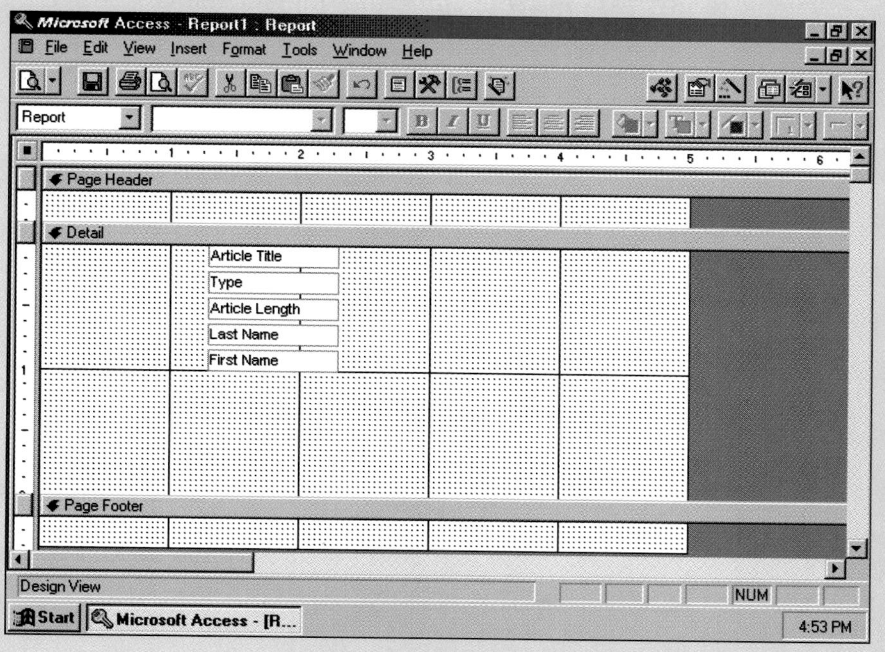

TROUBLE? If you selected both the label boxes and the text boxes, click Undo and repeat Steps 2 through 4, selecting only the label boxes.

5. Click anywhere in the Page Header section, click the right mouse button in the Page Header section to open the shortcut menu, and then click **Paste**. Access pastes all the label boxes from the Windows Clipboard into the Page Header section and automatically resizes that section to display the label boxes. See Figure 6-13.

Figure 6-13 ◀
Label boxes pasted in the Page Header section

pasted labels

Page Header section automatically resized

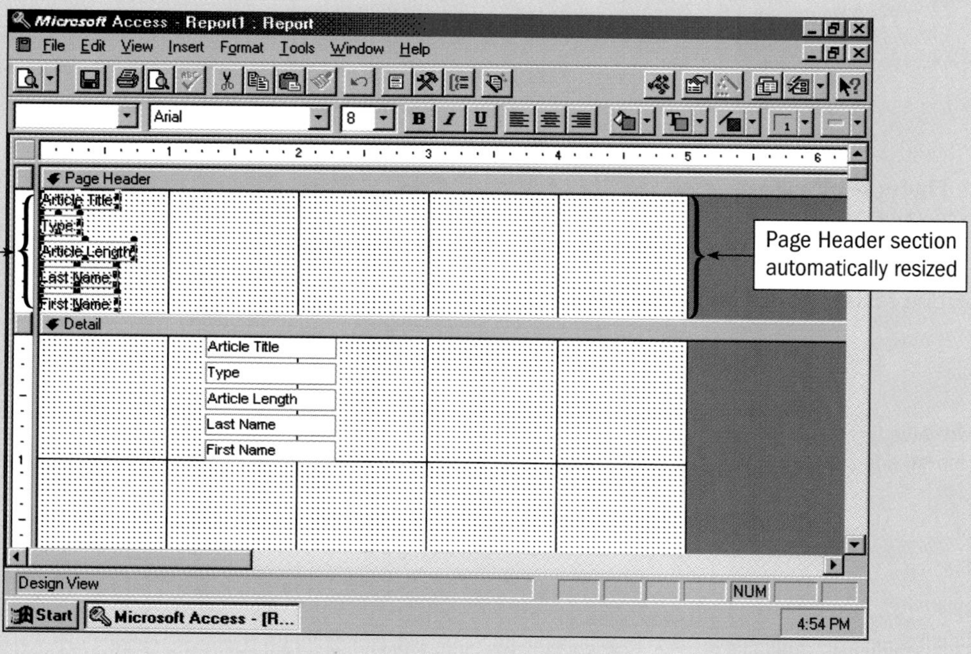

Moving the label boxes has unlinked them from their attached text boxes. You can now select and move either a label box or a text box, but not both at once.

Moving and Resizing Controls

Elena needs to reposition the text boxes and label boxes. She first drags the Article Title text box to the left into the corner of the Detail section and resizes it. She then moves and resizes the other four text boxes and resizes the Detail section.

REFERENCE window

MOVING AND RESIZING CONTROLS

- In the Report Design window, click the control to select it.
- To move a control, place the pointer on the control's move handle. Click and drag the control to its new position, then release the mouse button.
- To resize a control, place the pointer on one of the control's sizing handles. Click and drag the sizing handle until the control is the proper size, then release the mouse button.

To move and resize text boxes and resize the Detail section:

1. Click the **Article Title** field-value text box in the Detail section, move the pointer to the move handle in the upper-left corner of the field-value text box, and drag to the upper-left corner of the Detail section.
2. Next, move the pointer to the middle sizing handle on the right side of the Article Title field-value text box. When the pointer changes to ↔, drag the right border horizontally to the right, to the 2.5" mark on the horizontal ruler.
3. Use the same procedure to move and resize each of the other four field-value text boxes in the Detail section, using the sketch of the report design (See Figure 6-9) as a guide.
4. If necessary, scroll down to display the bottom edge of the Detail section. Move the pointer to the bottom edge of the Detail section. When the pointer changes to ╪, drag the bottom edge upward to align with the bottom of the field-value text boxes. If necessary, scroll up to display the top of the report. See Figure 6-14. When the Detail section height is the same as the text-box height, the lines in the Detail section of the report will be single spaced.

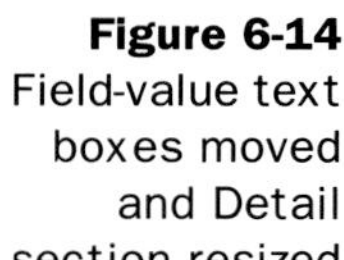

Figure 6-14 Field-value text boxes moved and Detail section resized

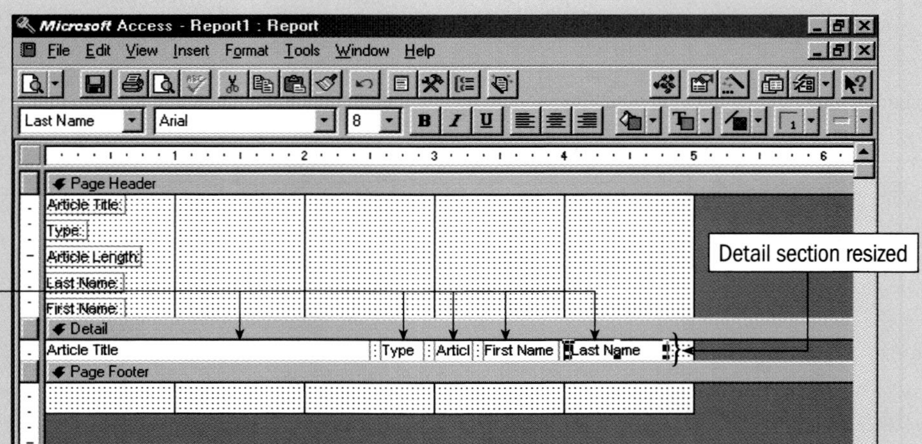

TROUBLE? If Access widens the report too much while you are moving and resizing the text boxes, wait until you are finished with these operations and then reduce the width of the report. To reduce the width of the report, start by moving the pointer to the right edge of the Detail section. When the pointer changes to ✛, drag the right edge to the left to narrow the report's width to 5".

Next, Elena deletes the First Name label and changes the Caption property for all other labels in the Page Header section.

Deleting Controls

To match her report design, Elena must change the Last Name Caption property to Writer Name and the Article Length Caption property to Length. She also deletes the colons in the Caption properties for the Article Title label and the Type label.

DELETING CONTROLS

- In the Report Design window, click the control to select it.
- With the pointer on the control, click the right mouse button to display the shortcut menu.
- Click Cut to delete the control.

Elena makes these changes now.

To delete a label and change label Caption properties:

1. Move the pointer to the First Name label box, then click the right mouse button to open the shortcut menu, and then click **Cut** to delete the First Name label box.
2. Move the pointer to the Last Name label box, then click the right mouse button to display the shortcut menu, and then click **Properties** to display the property sheet for the Last Name label. If necessary, click the **Format** tab to display the Format page of the property sheet. The Caption property value is selected.
3. Type **Writer Name** to replace the Caption property value.
4. Click the **Article Length** label box to select it. The property sheet changes to show the properties for the Article Length field. Click the **Caption** text box in the property sheet, press the **F2** key to select the caption property value, and then type **Length**.
5. Click the **Type** label box to select it. Click near the end of the Caption text box in the property sheet and press the **Backspace** key to remove the colon from the caption.
6. Use the same procedure to remove the colon from the caption in the Article Title label box.
7. Click the property sheet **Close** button ☒ to close the property sheet.

After checking her report design, Elena realizes she needs to resize the Length and Writer Name label boxes and rearrange the label boxes in the Page Header section.

To resize and move labels:

1. Click in an unoccupied area of the grid to deselect the Article Title label box. While holding down the **Shift** key, click the **Length** label box and then click the **Writer Name** label box to select both of them.
2. Click **Format**, point to **Size**, and then click **to Fit**. Access resizes the two label boxes to fit around the captions.
3. Individually select and move each of the label boxes in the Page Header section, following the sketched report design. See Figure 6-15.

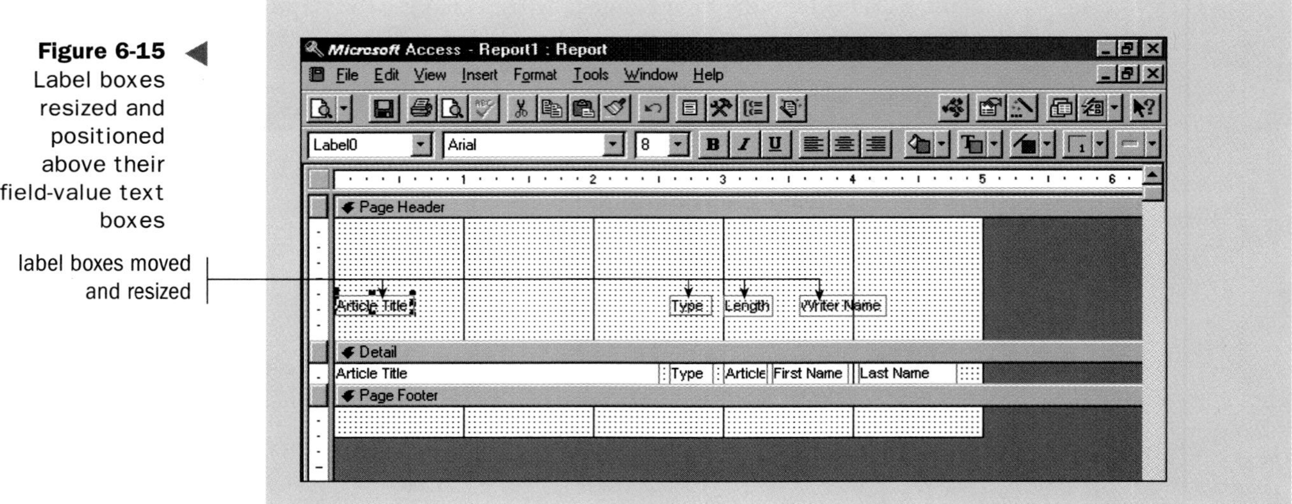

Figure 6-15 Label boxes resized and positioned above their field-value text boxes

Elena has made many modifications to the report design, so she saves the report before proceeding.

To save the report design:

1. Click the **Save** button on the toolbar. Access displays the Save As dialog box.
2. Type **Article Type Report** in the Report Name text box, then click the **OK** button. The dialog box closes and Access saves the report.

If you want to take a break and resume the tutorial at a later time, exit Access by clicking the Access window Close button. When you resume the tutorial, open the Issue25 database, and select Article Type Report in the Reports list. Click the Design button to open the Report Design window and maximize the window.

Quick Check

1. What are the seven Access report sections?
2. What types of reports can AutoReport create and what is the difference between them?
3. What is a group?
4. Why is it not necessary to save manually a report created by the Report Wizard?
5. What is a custom report?
6. What does the Report Design window have in common with the Form Design window? What is different?
7. In the Report Design window, how is adding, moving, resizing, and deleting controls different from accomplishing these tasks in the Form Design window?

SESSION 6.2

In this session, you will add a title, a page number and date, and a Report Footer. You will also sort and group records, add a Group Footer, calculate group and overall totals, and hide duplicate values in a report.

Adding a Title, Date, and Page Number to a Report

To match her design, Elena must also include a report title, date, and page number in the Page Header section. She does these tasks next.

Adding a Title to a Report

Elena's report design includes the title Article Type Report. She places this report title in the Page Header section using the toolbox Label tool. To make the report title stand out, Elena will increase the report title font size from 8, the default, to 10 (the default typeface is Arial).

ADDING A LABEL TO THE REPORT

- In the Report Design window, click the toolbox Label tool.
- Move the pointer to the position in the report where you want to place the label, then click to place the label.
- Type the label text, then press the Enter key.

To add a report title to the Page Header section and change the font size:

1. Click the **Toolbox** button on the toolbar to display the toolbox.
2. Click the **toolbox Label** button .
3. Move the pointer into the Page Header section. As you move the pointer into the report, the pointer changes to +A. Click the left mouse button when the pointer's plus symbol (+) is positioned at the top of the Page Header section at the 2" mark on the horizontal ruler. Access places a narrow text box in the Page Header section.
4. Type **Article Type Report** and then press the **Enter** key. See Figure 6-16.

Figure 6-16 Report title label added to Page Header section

default font

report title

Label tool

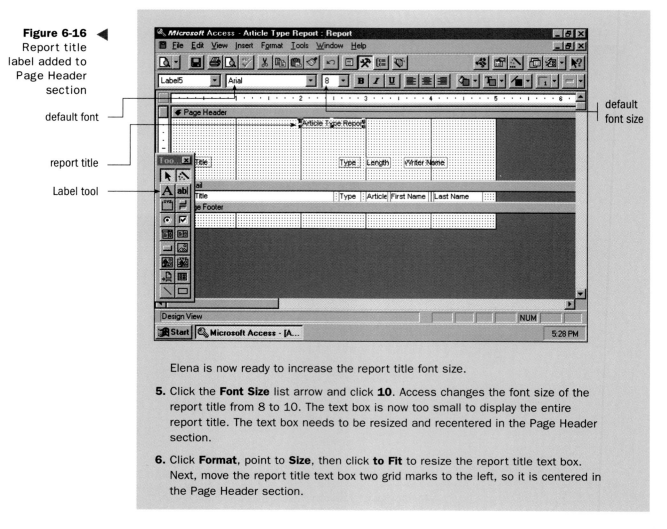

default font size

Elena is now ready to increase the report title font size.

5. Click the **Font Size** list arrow and click **10**. Access changes the font size of the report title from 8 to 10. The text box is now too small to display the entire report title. The text box needs to be resized and recentered in the Page Header section.

6. Click **Format**, point to **Size**, then click **to Fit** to resize the report title text box. Next, move the report title text box two grid marks to the left, so it is centered in the Page Header section.

Next, Elena adds a text box to the Page Header section in which she will insert the Date function.

Adding a Date to a Report

You use the toolbox Text Box tool to add a text box with an attached label to a report or form. Text boxes are most often used to contain bound controls or calculated controls. In this case, the text box will contain the Date function, which is a type of calculated control. It will print the current date each time the report is generated.

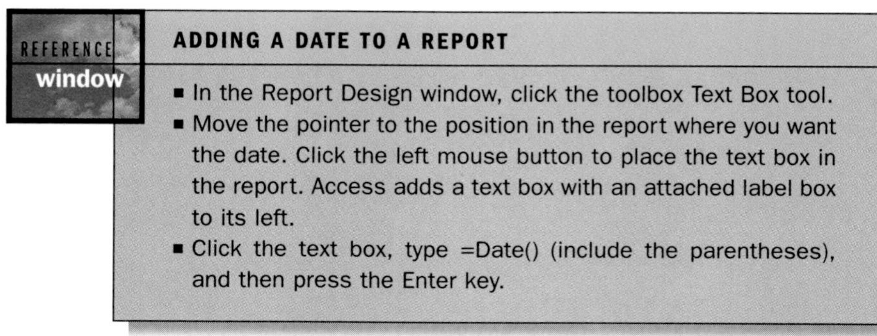

REFERENCE window

ADDING A DATE TO A REPORT

- In the Report Design window, click the toolbox Text Box tool.
- Move the pointer to the position in the report where you want the date. Click the left mouse button to place the text box in the report. Access adds a text box with an attached label box to its left.
- Click the text box, type =Date() (include the parentheses), and then press the Enter key.

Elena adds the date to the Page Header section.

To use the Text Box tool to add the Date function:

1. Click the **toolbox Text Box** button. Move the pointer into the Page Header section. As you move the pointer into the report, the pointer changes to. Click the left mouse button when the pointer's plus (+) symbol is positioned at the top of the Page Header section just to the right of the .75" mark on the horizontal ruler. Access adds a text box with an attached label box to its left. Inside the text box is the description Unbound.
2. Click the **Unbound** text box, type **=Date()** (type the left and right parentheses), and then press the **Enter** key. See Figure 6-17.

Figure 6-17 Current date added to a report

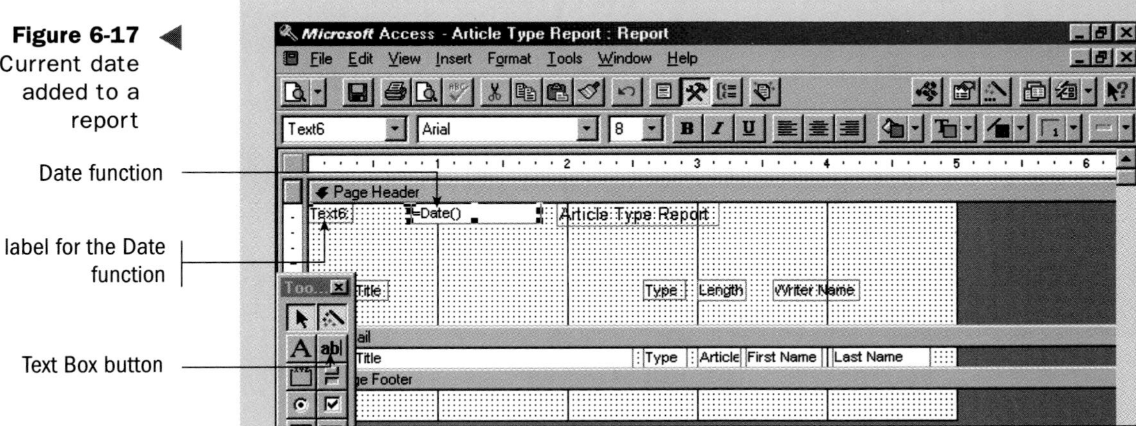

TROUBLE? If your text box and attached label box are too close together, resize and reposition the text box using Figure 6-17 as a guide. The attached label box on your screen might have a Caption other than the one shown (such as "Text7"), depending on the exact way you completed previous steps. This causes no problem.

When Access prints your report, the current date replaces the Date function you entered in the Unbound text box. Because a current date in a Page Header section does not usually need a label, Elena deletes the label box. She then changes the Date text box to font size 10 and moves it to the upper-left corner of the Page Header section.

3. Position the pointer on the Date label box, which is located in the upper-left corner of the Page Header section. Click the right mouse button to open the shortcut menu and then click **Cut** to delete the label.
4. Click the **Date** text box and then drag its move handle to the upper-left corner of the Page Header section.
5. Click the **Font Size** list arrow and click **10** to change the font size of the Date text box.

Elena is now ready to complete her report's Page Header section by adding page numbers.

Adding Page Numbers to a Report

Elena adds the page number to the upper-right corner of the Page Header section. The page number function automatically prints the correct page number on each page of a report.

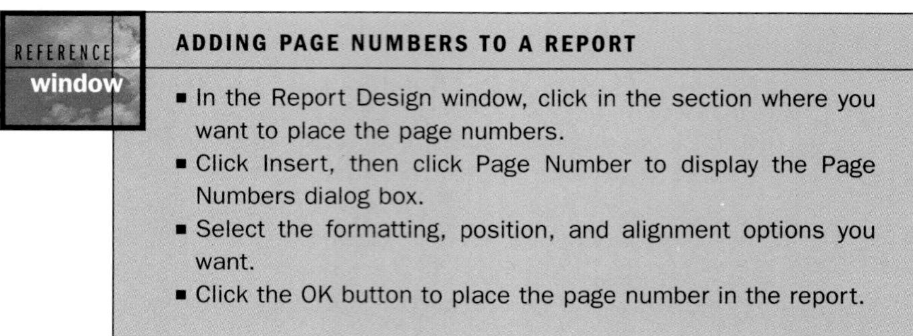

REFERENCE window

ADDING PAGE NUMBERS TO A REPORT

- In the Report Design window, click in the section where you want to place the page numbers.
- Click Insert, then click Page Number to display the Page Numbers dialog box.
- Select the formatting, position, and alignment options you want.
- Click the OK button to place the page number in the report.

To add a page number in the Page Header section:

1. Click **Insert**, then click **Page Number** to display the Page Numbers dialog box. Make sure that the Page N radio button is selected in the Format panel and that the Top of Page [Header] radio button is selected in the Position panel.

2. Click the **Alignment** list arrow to display the list of alignment options, then click **Right**. Make sure that the Show Number on First Page check box is checked. See Figure 6-18.

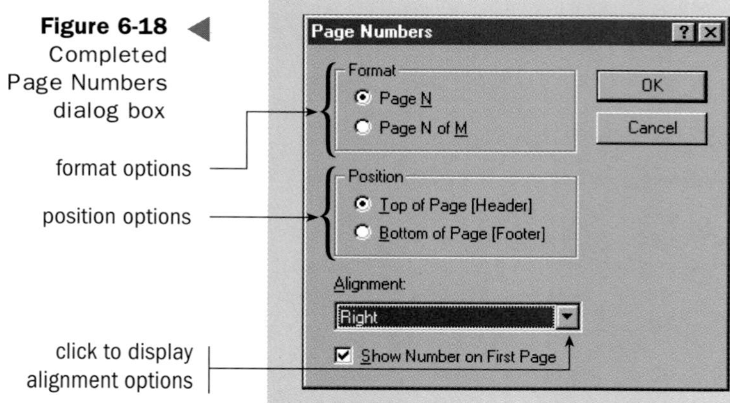

Figure 6-18 Completed Page Numbers dialog box

3. Click the **OK** button to place the page number in the report. Access adds a text box to the upper-right corner of the Page Header section. See Figure 6-19. The value ="Page" & [Page] means that, when it is printed, the report will show the word "Page" followed by the page number.

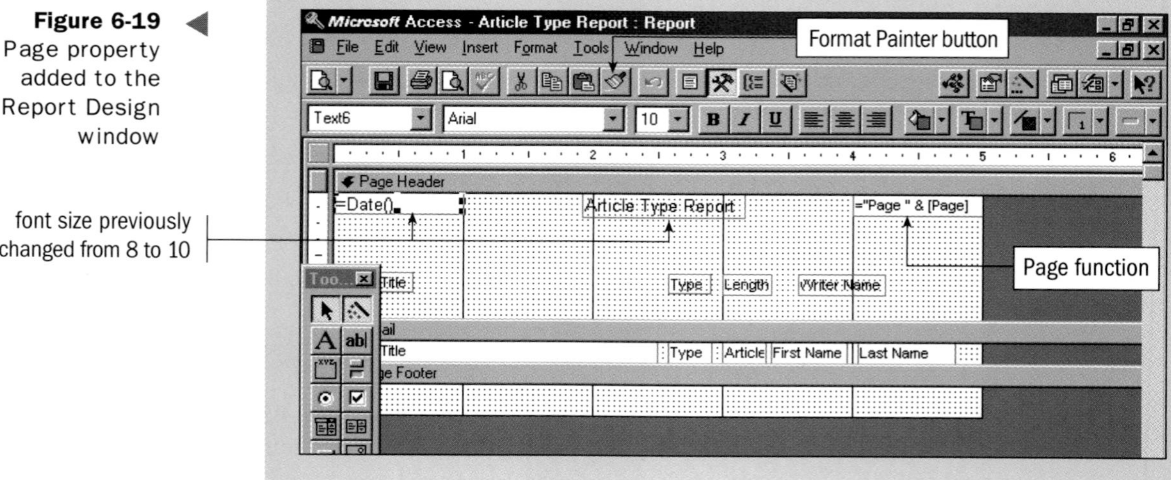

Figure 6-19 Page property added to the Report Design window

Elena wants to change the Page Number text box to font size 10 to match the date and report title. To duplicate the formatting of the Date text box, she can use the Format Painter. The Format Painter allows you to copy the format of an object to other objects in the report. This makes it easy to create several objects having the same font style and size, the same color, and the same special effect.

To use the Format Painter to format the Page Number text box:

1. If necessary, click the **Date** text box to select it.
2. Click the **Format Painter** button on the toolbar. The Format Painter button appears indented.
3. Click the **Page Number** text box. The Format Painter automatically formats the Page Number text box like the Date text box (with a font size of 10) and resizes the text box to fit. The label ="Page" & [Page] is now larger than the text box, but the actual page number will fit when the report is printed. Notice that after you use the Format Painter, the Format Painter button is no longer indented, meaning it is inactive.

Now that Elena has completed the Page Header section of her report, she switches to the Print Preview window to check the appearance of the report against her design.

To view a report in the Print Preview window:

1. Click the **Print Preview** button on the toolbar to open the Print Preview window. See Figure 6-20.

Figure 6-20 A custom report in the Print Preview window

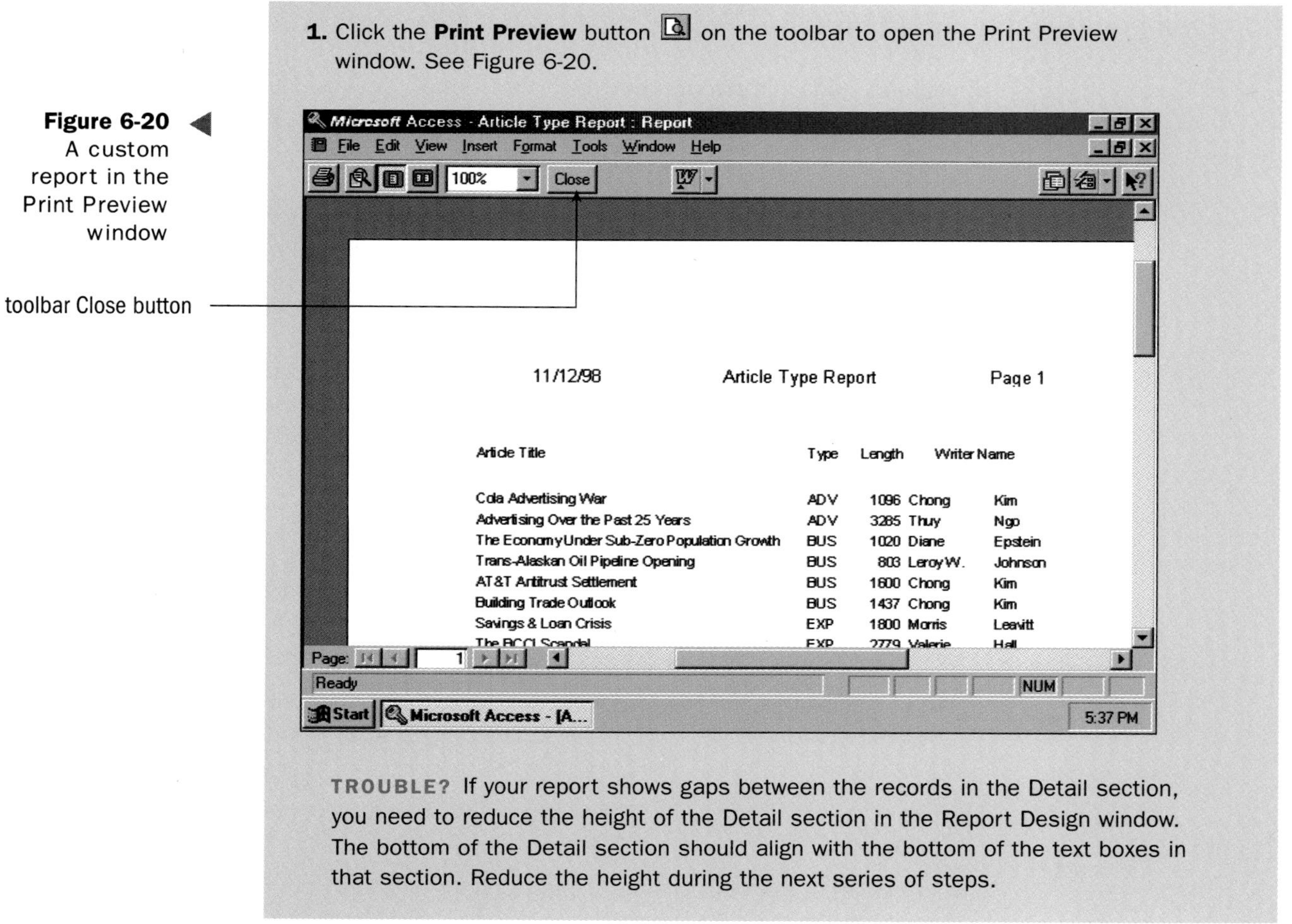

TROUBLE? If your report shows gaps between the records in the Detail section, you need to reduce the height of the Detail section in the Report Design window. The bottom of the Detail section should align with the bottom of the text boxes in that section. Reduce the height during the next series of steps.

Adding Lines to a Report

Looking at her report, Elena decides to reposition the column heading labels just below the report title line and decrease the height of the Page Header section. She also decides to add a horizontal line to the Page Header section below the column heads.

To move labels and decrease the Page Header section height:

1. Click the toolbar **Close** button to close the Print Preview window and return to the Report Design window.
2. Click in the Page Header section, but not on any object, to deselect the Date text box. While pressing and holding down the **Shift** key, click each of the four label boxes in the Page Header section to select them. When the pointer changes to ✋, drag the label boxes up so they are positioned just below the report title. Position the labels so that the top of each label box is at the .25" mark on the vertical ruler.

   TROUBLE? If the label boxes do not move, the Page Number text box is probably selected along with the label boxes. Click in any unoccupied portion of the Page Header section to deselect all boxes, then repeat Step 2.
3. Move the pointer to the bottom edge of the Page Header section. When the pointer changes to ✣, drag the bottom edge upward to reduce the height of the Page Header section. Align the bottom edge with the grid marks that are just below the .5" mark on the vertical ruler.

Elena now adds a horizontal line to the bottom of the Page Header section to separate it visually from the Detail section when the report is printed. You use the toolbox Line tool to add a line to a report or form.

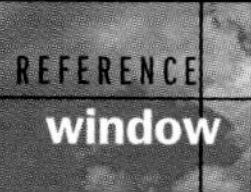

ADDING A LINE TO A REPORT

- In the Report Design window, click the toolbox Line button on the toolbox.
- Move the pointer to position one end of the line.
- Click and hold the left mouse button, drag the pointer to the position of the other end of the line, and then release the mouse button.

To add a line to a report:

1. Click the **toolbox Line** button ⧅. Move the pointer into the Page Header section; the pointer changes to ⁺╲. Position the pointer's plus (+) symbol at the left edge of the Page Header section just below the column headings.
2. Click and hold the left mouse button, drag a horizontal line from left to right, ending just after the 4.25" mark on the horizontal ruler, and then release the mouse button.

   Elena views the line and decides to increase its thickness to make it stand out more.
3. To increase the thickness of the line, position the pointer on the line, click the right mouse button to display the shortcut menu, then click **Properties** to display the property sheet. The Border Width property controls width, or thickness, of lines.

4. Click the **Border Width** text box in the property sheet, then click the **Border Width** list arrow that appears, and then click **3 pt**. The line's width increases to 3 points. See Figure 6-21.

Figure 6-21 Changing the width of a line

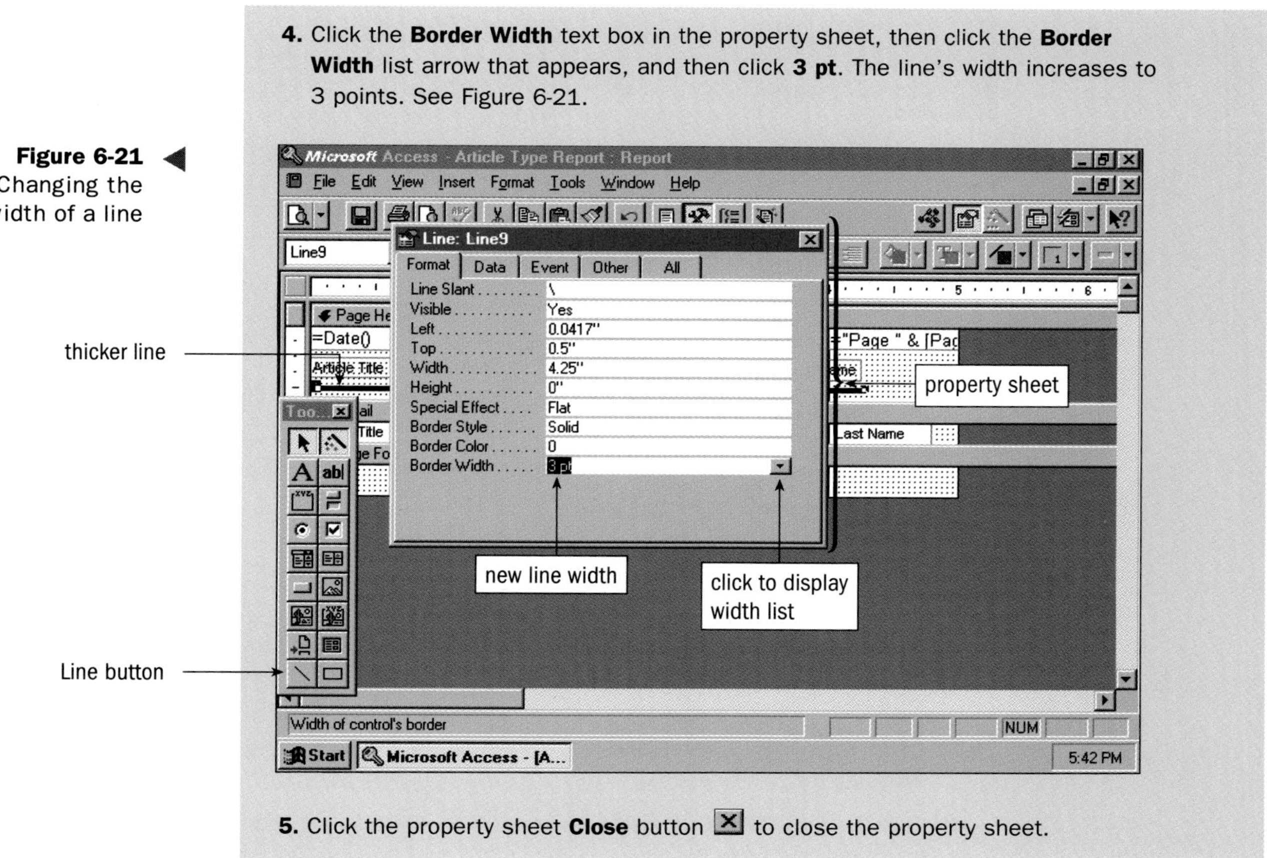

5. Click the property sheet **Close** button to close the property sheet.

Elena has finished formatting the Page Header section. She decides to save her report before she chooses the sort fields and the grouping field for the report.

To save the report:

1. Click the **Save** button on the toolbar. Access saves the report design.

Sorting and Grouping Data in a Report

Elena wants Access to print records in ascending order based on the Type field and to print subtotals for each set of Type field values. The Type field is both the primary sort key and the grouping field. Elena wants the records within a Type to be printed in descending order based on the Article Length field. This makes Article Length the secondary sort key.

You use the Sorting and Grouping button on the toolbar to select sort keys and grouping fields. Each report can have up to 10 sort fields, and any of the sort fields can also be grouping fields.

REFERENCE window

SORTING AND GROUPING DATA IN A REPORT

- In the Report Design window, click the Sorting and Grouping button on the toolbar. The Sorting and Grouping dialog box opens.
- Click the first Field/Expression list arrow in the Sorting and Grouping dialog box and select the field to be used as the primary sort key. In the Sort Order text box, select the sort order.
- Repeat the previous step to select subsorting keys and their sort orders.
- To group data, click the field in the Field/Expression text box by which you want to group records. In the Group Properties panel, select the grouping option for this field.
- Click the Close button on the Sorting and Grouping dialog box to close it.

Elena selects the sort keys and grouping fields now.

To select sort keys and grouping fields:

1. If you haven't done so already, click the **toolbox title bar** and drag the toolbox to the right side of the Report Design window. This will make it easier to see the report sections.
2. Click the **Sorting and Grouping** button on the toolbar. The Sorting and Grouping dialog box opens.
3. Click the first **Field/Expression** list arrow in the Sorting and Grouping dialog box and then click **Type**. Ascending is the default sort order in the Sort Order text box.
4. Click anywhere in the second Field/Expression text box in the Sorting and Grouping dialog box, click the **list arrow** that appears, and then click **Article Length**. Ascending, the default sort order, needs to be changed to Descending in the Sort Order text box.
5. Click anywhere in the second Sort Order text box, click the **list arrow** that appears, and then click **Descending**. See Figure 6-22.

Figure 6-22 The Sorting and Grouping dialog box

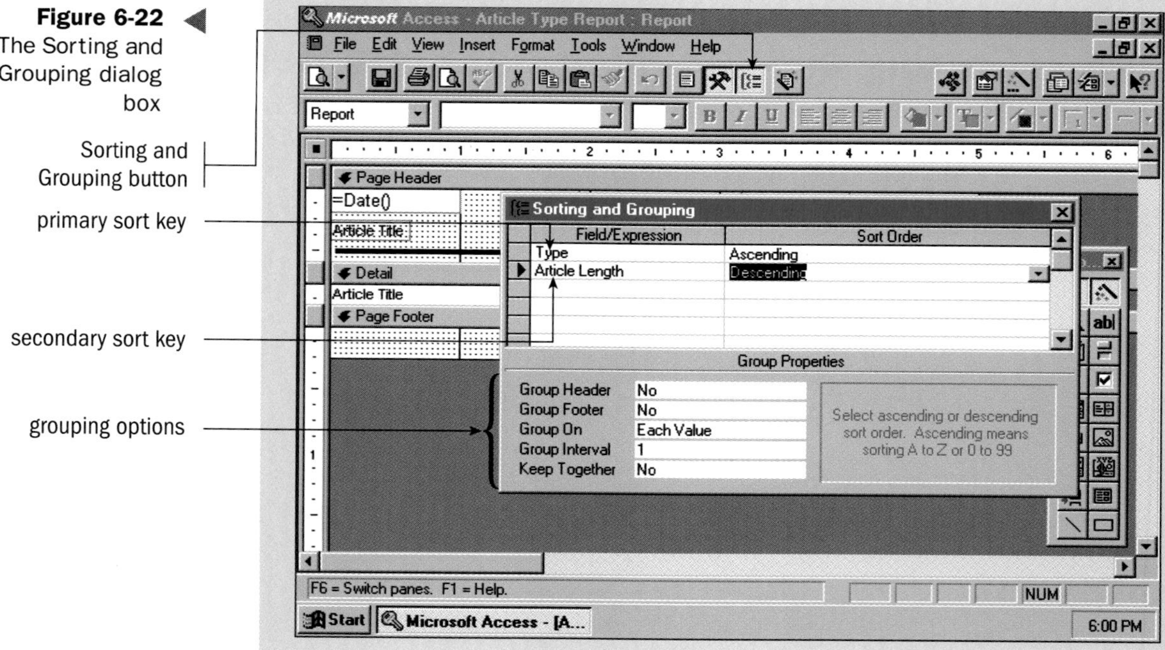

Elena uses the Group Properties panel to add a Group Footer to the report. To add a Group Footer, she must choose the Group Footer option for the Type field in the Sorting and Grouping dialog box.

To add a Group Footer to a report:

1. Click the **Field/Expression** text box for the Type field in the Sorting and Grouping dialog box, click the **Group Footer** text box, click the **list arrow** that appears, and then click **Yes**. Access adds a Group Footer section called Type Footer to the Report Design window. See Figure 6-23.

Figure 6-23 Adding a Group Footer section

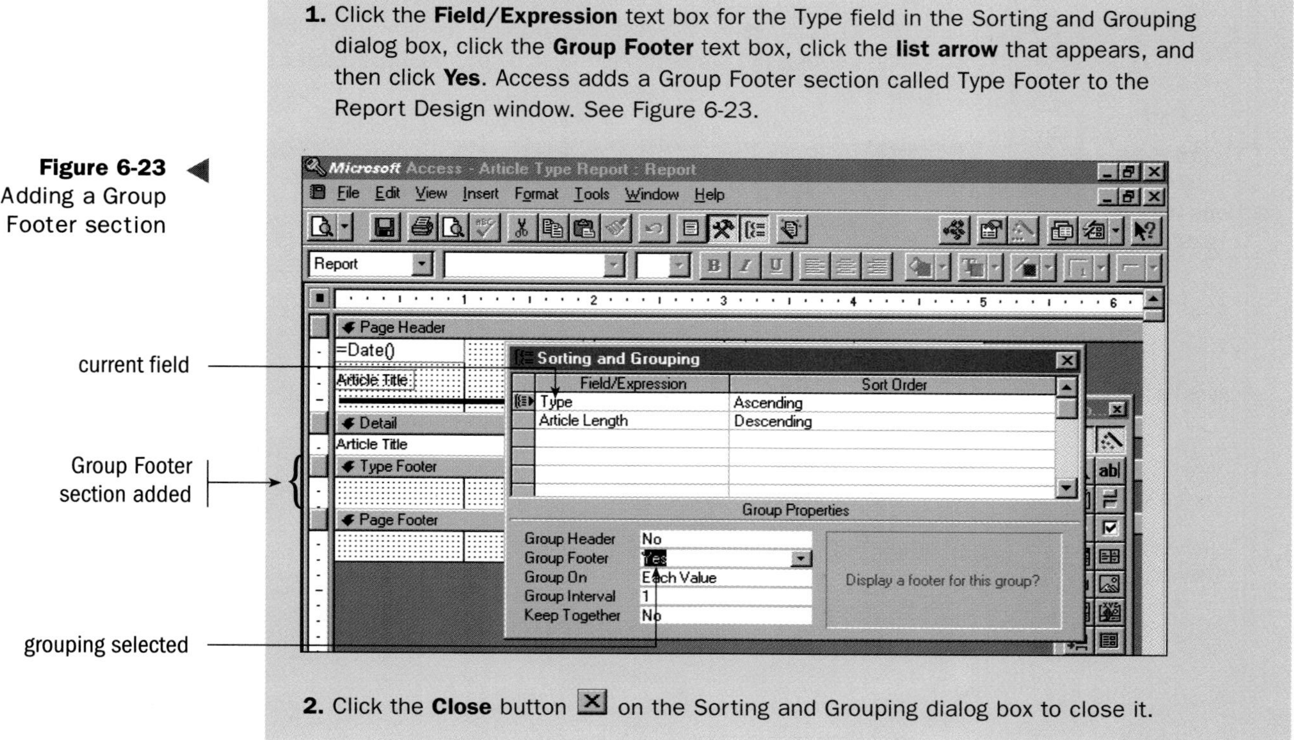

2. Click the **Close** button on the Sorting and Grouping dialog box to close it.

Adding and Deleting a Report Header and Footer

Elena compares her progress against her report design again and sees that she is almost done. Next she adds a Report Footer section to her report. To add this new section, Elena must add both the Report Header and Report Footer sections to the report together. She does not need the Report Header section, so she then deletes it. She also deletes the Page Footer section that was automatically included when the Report Design window was opened.

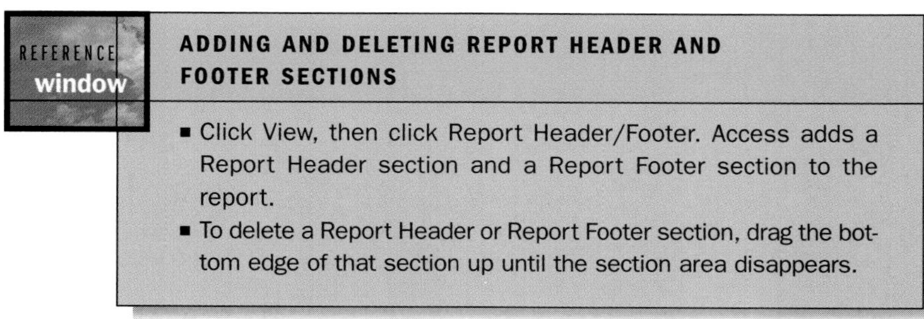

ADDING AND DELETING REPORT HEADER AND FOOTER SECTIONS

- Click View, then click Report Header/Footer. Access adds a Report Header section and a Report Footer section to the report.
- To delete a Report Header or Report Footer section, drag the bottom edge of that section up until the section area disappears.

To add and delete sections from a report:

1. Click **View** and then click **Report Header/Footer**. Access creates a Report Header section at the top of the report and a Report Footer section at the bottom of the report.
2. Move the pointer to the bottom edge of the Report Header section. When the pointer changes to ✝, drag the bottom edge upward until the section disappears. Use the same procedure to delete the Page Footer section. See Figure 6-24.

Figure 6-24 Report sections added and deleted

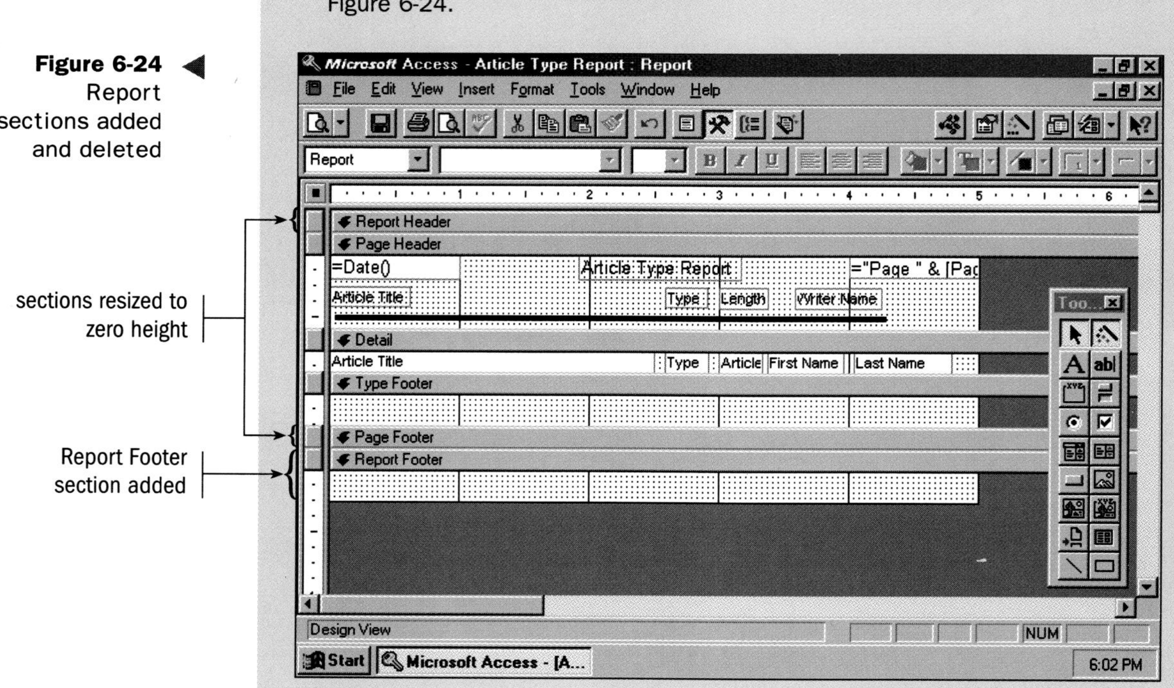

Calculating Group Totals and Overall Totals

Elena wants the report to print subtotals for each Type group, as well as an overall total, based on the Article Length field. To calculate these totals for the Article Length field, Elena uses the **Sum function**. She places the Sum function in a Group Footer section to print each group total and in the Report Footer section to print the overall total. The format for the Sum function is =Sum([*field name*]). You use the toolbar Text Box tool to create appropriate text boxes in the footer sections.

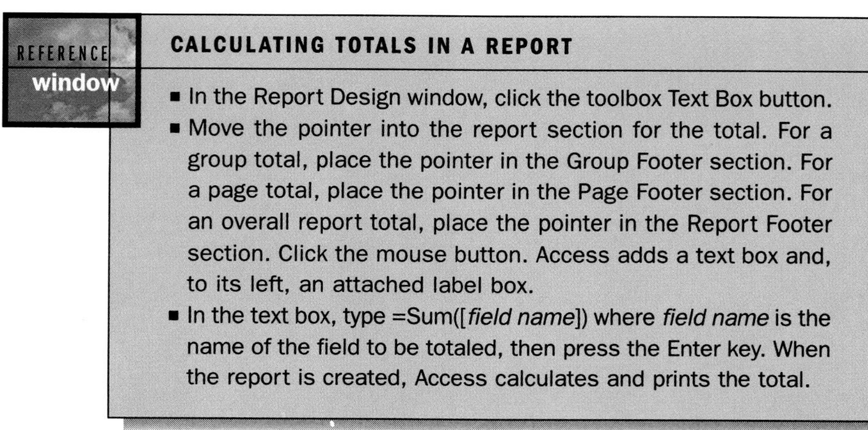

REFERENCE window

CALCULATING TOTALS IN A REPORT

- In the Report Design window, click the toolbox Text Box button.
- Move the pointer into the report section for the total. For a group total, place the pointer in the Group Footer section. For a page total, place the pointer in the Page Footer section. For an overall report total, place the pointer in the Report Footer section. Click the mouse button. Access adds a text box and, to its left, an attached label box.
- In the text box, type =Sum([*field name*]) where *field name* is the name of the field to be totaled, then press the Enter key. When the report is created, Access calculates and prints the total.

In the Type Footer (the Group Footer for Type) and Report Footer sections, Elena adds text boxes, deletes the attached labels for both, and adds the Sum function to each text box. She also draws lines above each Sum function so that the totals will be separated visually from the Detail section field values.

To add text boxes to footer sections and to delete labels:

1. Increase the height of the Type Footer section to .5" and increase the height of the Report Footer section to .5". These heights will allow sufficient room for the totals in these sections.
2. Click the **toolbox Text Box** button abl. Move the pointer into the Type Footer section. Click the mouse button when the pointer's plus (+) symbol is positioned in the second row of grid lines and vertically aligned with the right edge of the Type field-value text box. Access adds a text box and, to its left, an attached label box.
3. Click the **toolbox Text Box** button abl. Move the pointer into the Report Footer section. Click the mouse button when the pointer's plus (+) symbol is positioned in the fourth row of grid lines and vertically aligned with the right edge of the Type field-value text box. Access adds a text box, and, to its left, an attached label box. See Figure 6-25.

Figure 6-25 Text boxes added to footer sections

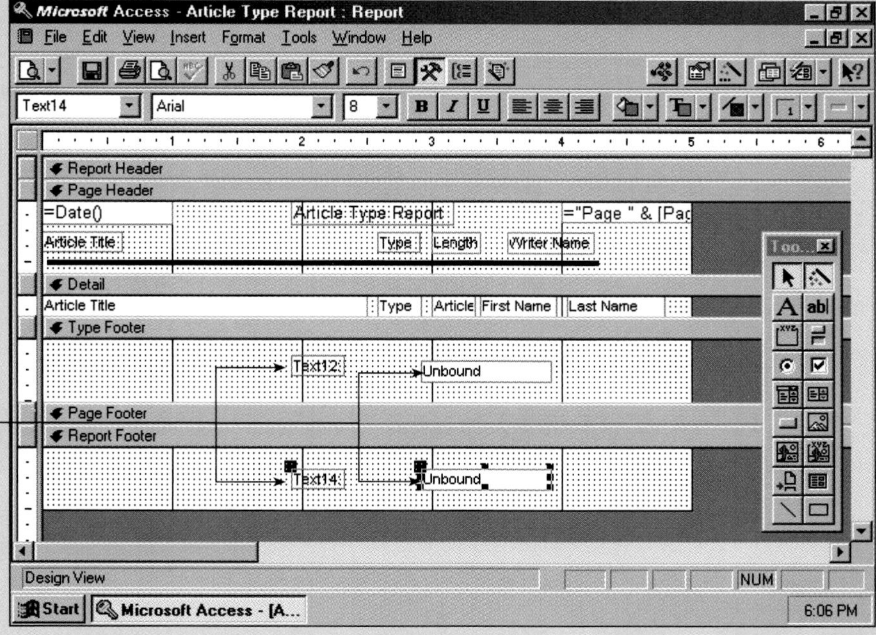

4. Click anywhere in the Type Footer section, outside both boxes, to deselect all boxes.
5. While you press and hold the **Shift** key, click the **label box** in the Type Footer section, and then click the **label box** in the Report Footer section. You have selected both boxes.
6. Click either label box with the right mouse button to open the shortcut menu and then click **Cut** to delete both label boxes.

Elena now adds the Sum function to the two footer section text boxes.

To add the Sum function to calculate group and overall totals:

1. Click the **text box** in the Type Footer section, type **=Sum([Article Length])**, and then press the **Enter** key. The text box in the Type Footer section needs to be narrower to align with the Article Length field in the Detail section.

   TROUBLE? Be sure that you enter the field name Article Length correctly. If you misspell Article Length, you will receive an error message later, when you preview or print the report.

2. Click the **middle sizing handle** on the right side of the text box and drag it to the left until the right edge of the box lines up with the right edge of the Article Length field-value text box in the Detail section. Although the formula doesn't fit in the text box, the calculated value will fit.

3. Click the **text box** in the Report Footer section, type **=Sum([Article Length])**, and then press the **Enter** key.

4. Resize the text box in the Report Footer section so that its right edge lines up with the right edge of the Article Length field-value text box in the Detail section. See Figure 6-26.

Figure 6-26 Group total and overall total formulas added to text boxes

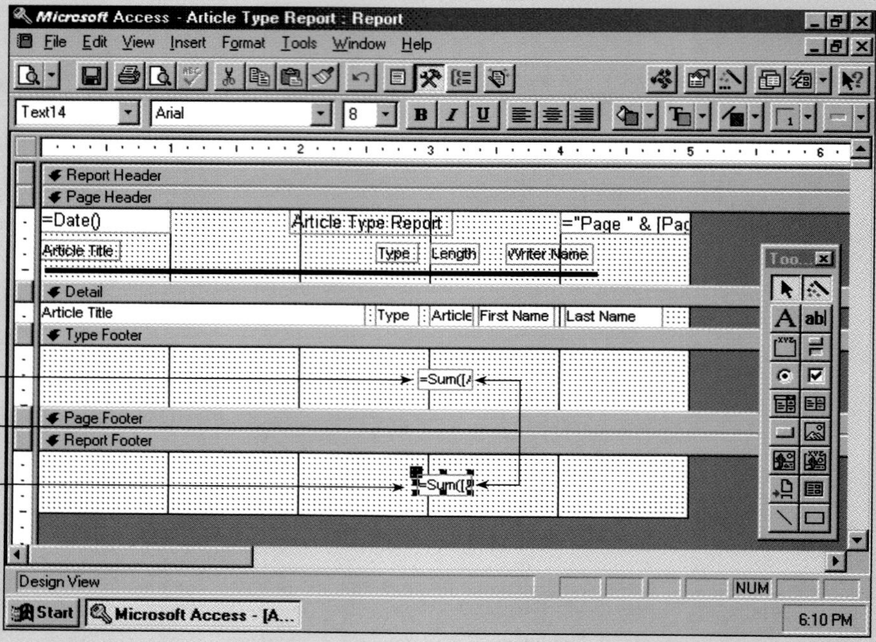

group total

Sum function

overall total

Microsoft Access - Article Type Report : Report

File Edit View Insert Format Tools Window Help

Text14 Arial 8

Report Header

Page Header

=Date() Article Type Report ="Page " & [Pa

Article Title Type Length Writer Name

Detail

Article Title Type Article First Name Last Name

Type Footer

=Sum([A

Page Footer

Report Footer

=Sum([

Design View NUM

Start Microsoft Access - [A... 6:10 PM

Elena next adds lines above each Sum function.

To add lines above totals:

1. Click the **toolbox Line** button. Move the pointer into the Type Footer section; the pointer changes to +. Position the pointer's plus (+) symbol in the second row of grid lines and align it vertically with the right edge of the Type field-value text box in the Detail section above it.

2. Click and hold the left mouse button to drag a horizontal line to the right until the right end of the line is below the right edge of the Article Length field-value text box.

3. Repeat Steps 1 and 2 for the Report Footer section. See Figure 6-27.

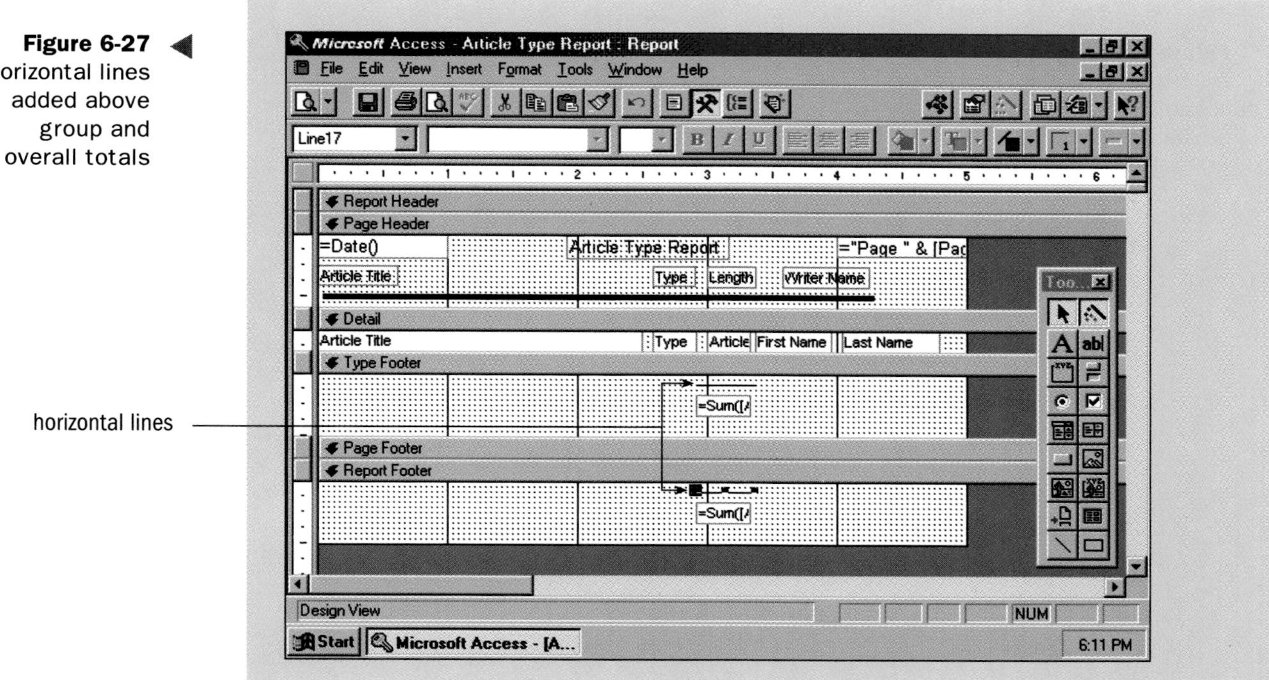

Figure 6-27 Horizontal lines added above group and overall totals

Elena's report is almost finished. There remain, however, some changes she can make to improve its appearance.

Hiding Duplicate Values in a Report

Elena's next change is to display the Type value only in the first record in a group. Within a group, all Type field values are the same, so if you display only the first one, you simplify the report and make it easier to read.

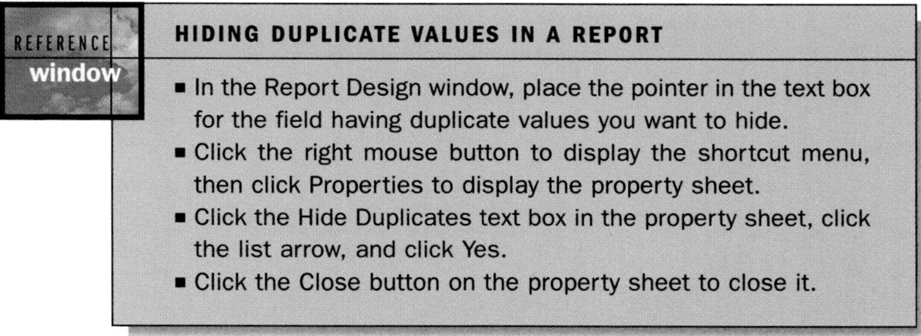
REFERENCE window

HIDING DUPLICATE VALUES IN A REPORT

- In the Report Design window, place the pointer in the text box for the field having duplicate values you want to hide.
- Click the right mouse button to display the shortcut menu, then click Properties to display the property sheet.
- Click the Hide Duplicates text box in the property sheet, click the list arrow, and click Yes.
- Click the Close button on the property sheet to close it.

Elena hides the duplicate Type values now.

To hide duplicate values:

1. Place the pointer in the Type text box in the Detail section and then click the right mouse button to display the shortcut menu, then click **Properties** to display the property sheet.

2. Click the **Hide Duplicates** text box in the property sheet, click the **list arrow**, then click **Yes**. See Figure 6-28.

Figure 6-28 ◀ Hiding duplicate field values in a group

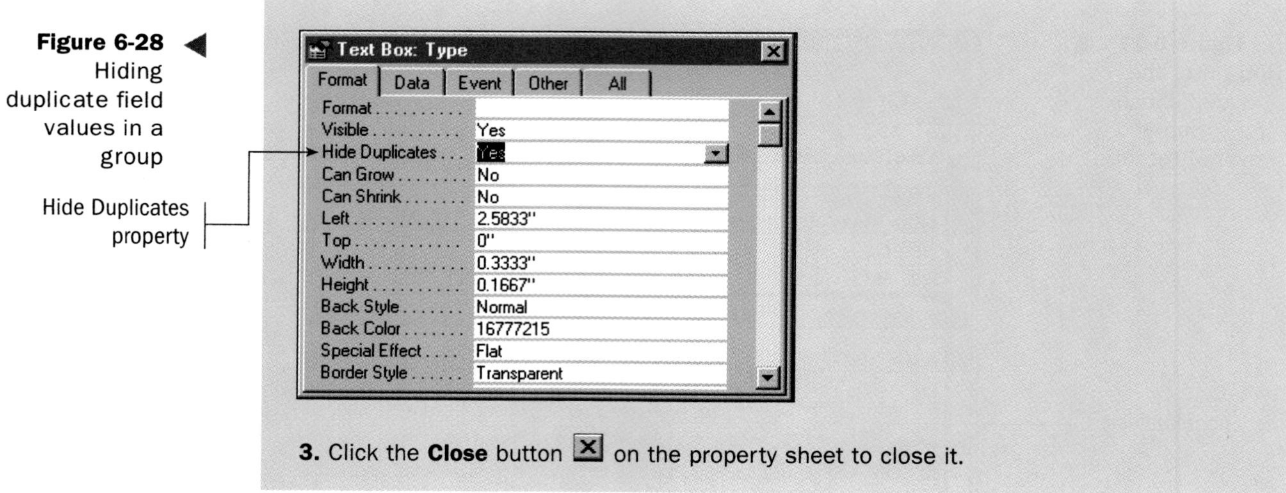

3. Click the **Close** button on the property sheet to close it.

Elena views the report in the Print Preview window, then prints and saves the report.

To view, print, and save a report:

1. Click the **Print Preview** button on the toolbar. Access displays the first page of the report. See Figure 6-29.

Figure 6-29 ◀ The beginning of the report in the Print Preview window

Page Header section

Detail section

Group Footer section

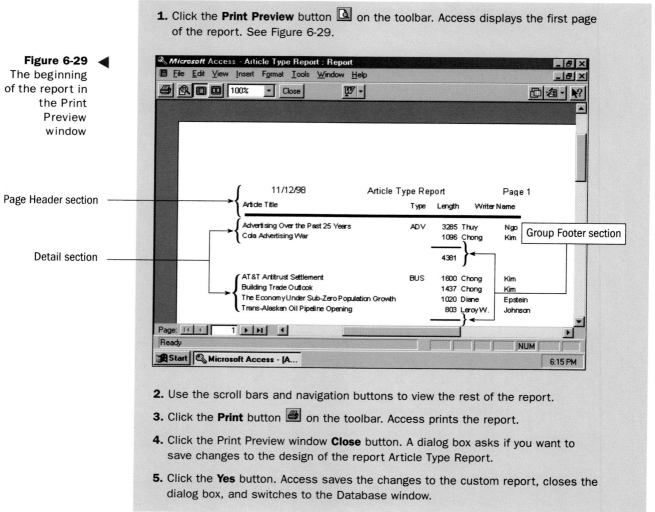

2. Use the scroll bars and navigation buttons to view the rest of the report.
3. Click the **Print** button on the toolbar. Access prints the report.
4. Click the Print Preview window **Close** button. A dialog box asks if you want to save changes to the design of the report Article Type Report.
5. Click the **Yes** button. Access saves the changes to the custom report, closes the dialog box, and switches to the Database window.

Elena brings her printed report to Harold. He is very pleased, and feels that the report will help ensure a successful meeting with the advertisers.

If you want to take a break and resume the tutorial at a later time, exit Access. When you resume the tutorial, place your Student Disk in the appropriate drive, start Access, open the Issue25 database in the Tutorial folder on your Student Disk, maximize the Database window, and click the Reports tab to display the Reports list.

Quick Check

1. When do you use the toolbox Text Box tool?
2. What do you type in a text box to tell Access to print the current date?
3. How do you insert a page number in a Page Header section?
4. What is the function of the Sorting and Grouping button?
5. How do you add a Report Footer section to a report without adding a Report Header section?
6. How do you calculate group totals and overall totals?
7. Why might you want to hide duplicate values in a group report?

SESSION 6.3

In this session, you will learn to integrate Access with other Windows 95 applications. You will create an embedded chart in a report and place a linked graphic image in a Page Header, and then edit the chart and the graphic image.

Integrating Access with Other Windows 95 Applications

Harold is so pleased with the report that Elena created for him that he immediately thinks of another report that would be helpful to include for his meeting with the advertisers. He asks Elena if she can create a report with a graph showing the number of articles of each type that are included in the 25th-anniversary issue. Elena says she will investigate creating such a report for him.

Integrating Applications

When you create a report or form in Access, you might want to include more than just the formatted listing of records. You may want to include objects such as a long text passage, a graphic image, or a graph summarizing the data. Creating long text passages is difficult with Access, and Access is also not able to create graphic images or graphs. Instead, you can create these objects with other applications and then place them in a report or form.

Access offers three ways for you to include objects created by other applications in a form or report, as shown in Figure 6-30:

- **Importing:** When you import an object, you include the contents of a file in the form or report. In Tutorial 5, for example, you imported a graphic image created by the drawing application called Microsoft Paint. Once the object is imported, it has no relation to the application that created it. It is simply an object in the form or report.

- **Embedding:** When you embed an object, you preserve its connection to the application that created it. You can edit the object by double-clicking on it. This starts the application that created it. Any changes you make in the object are reflected in the form or report in which it has been embedded. These changes affect only the copy of the object in the form or report; they do not affect the original copy of the object in the file from which it was embedded.
- **Linking:** When you link an object to a form or report, you preserve its connection to the original file from which it came. You can edit the object by double-clicking on it. This starts the application that created it, and any changes you make in the object are reflected in the form or report and in the original file from which it came. You can also start the application outside of Access and edit the object's original file. Any changes are reflected in the original file and in the linked object in the Access form or report.

Figure 6-30 Integration techniques

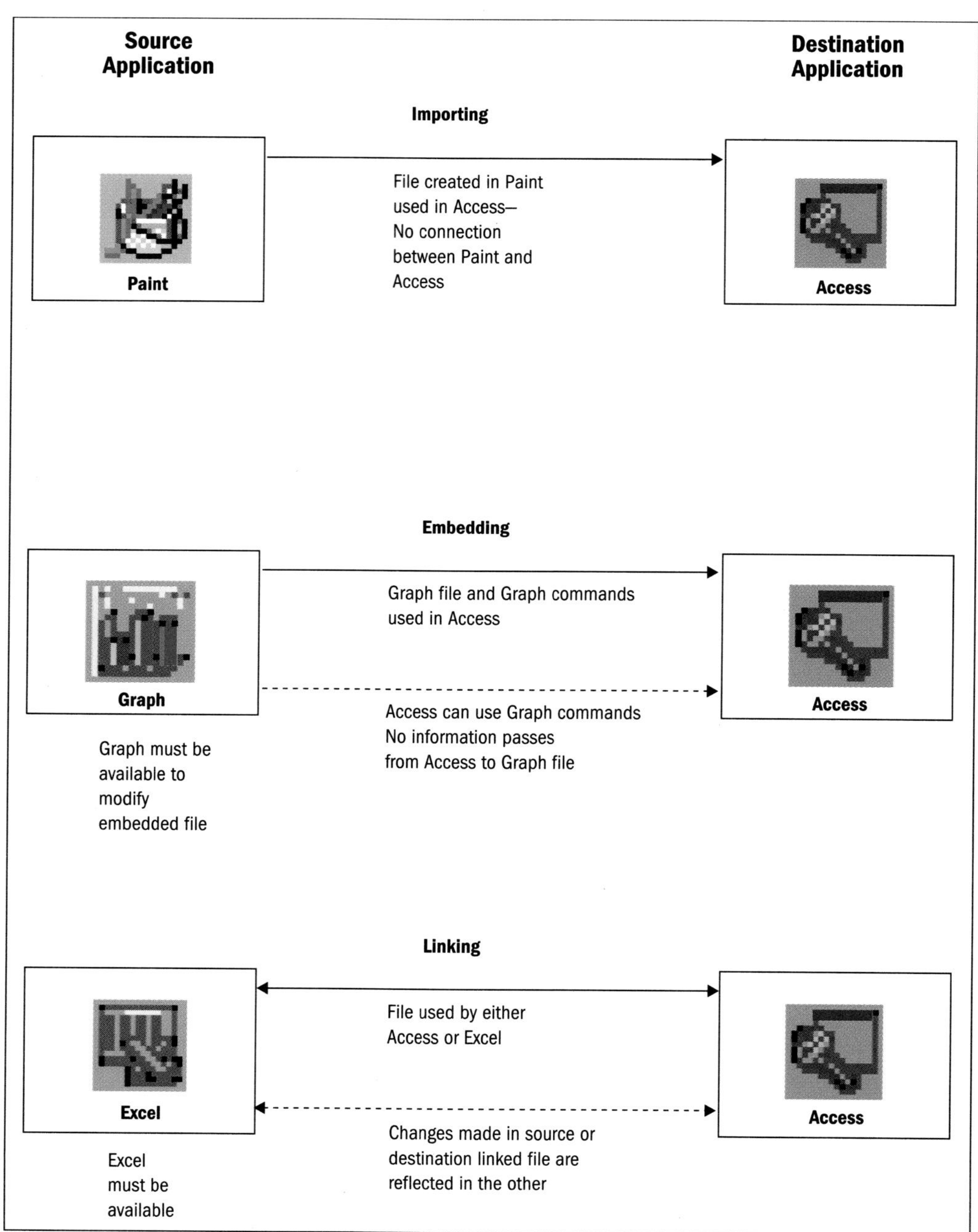

Not all applications support **Object Linking and Embedding (OLE)**, although most application software does. If you have difficulty linking or embedding objects from an application, it is possible that the application you are using does not support OLE.

Elena's design for the report requested by Harold, shown in Figure 6-31, will include an embedded chart showing the distribution of articles in the BUSINESS ARTICLES table by Type, and a linked graphic image in the Page Header.

Figure 6-31 Elena's design for Harold's chart report

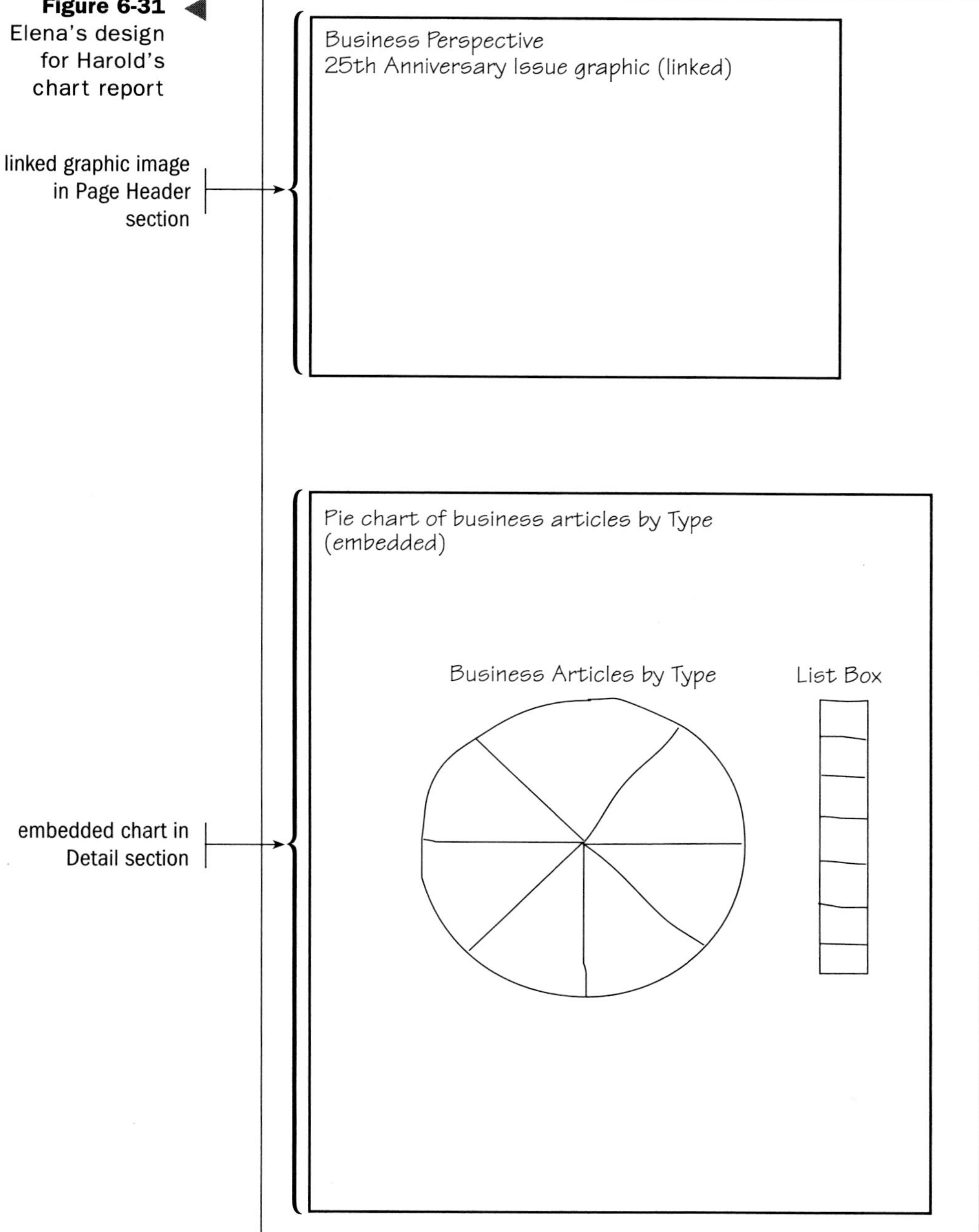

Embedding a Chart in a Report

Elena begins by creating a report with an embedded chart. Access provides the Chart Wizard to assist you in embedding the chart. The chart itself is actually created by another application, Microsoft Graph. After embedding the chart in the report, you can edit it by using the Graph program.

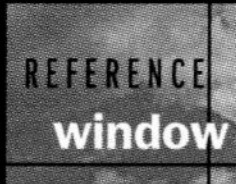

USING THE CHART WIZARD TO CREATE A REPORT WITH AN EMBEDDED CHART

- In the Database window, click the Reports tab to display the Reports list.
- Click the New button to open the New Report dialog box.
- Click Chart Wizard, select the table or query on which the report is based, then click the OK button. Access starts the Chart Wizard.
- Select the field(s) that contain the data for the chart, then click the Next > button.
- Select the type of chart you want, then click the Next > button.
- Make any modifications you want in the layout of the chart, then click the Next > button.
- Enter a title for the chart, then click the Finish button. Access places (embeds) the chart in the report. You can modify the chart by double-clicking on it and using Graph to make the modifications.

Elena creates a new report that will contain an embedded chart.

To create a report with an embedded chart:

1. In the Reports list box of the Database window, click the **New** button to display the New Report dialog box.
2. Click **Chart Wizard** to select it, click the **list arrow** in the text box, click **BUSINESS ARTICLES** to select the table, then click the **OK** button. Access starts the Chart Wizard and displays the first Chart Wizard dialog box.

   This dialog box allows you to select the fields that contain the data for the chart. Elena wants to graph the distribution of BUSINESS ARTICLES by Type, so she selects the Type field.
3. Click **Type** in the Available Fields list box to select it, then click the > button to move the Type field to the Fields for graph list. Click the Next > button. Access displays the next Chart Wizard dialog box, which allows you to select the type of graph you want.

   A pie chart is a good type of graph for showing the relative sizes of different categories (the number of articles of each type) to the whole (the total number of articles). Elena chooses it.
4. Click the **pie chart** button (first button in the third row) to select the pie chart type, then click the Next > button. See Figure 6-32.

Figure 6-32 Selecting the type of graph

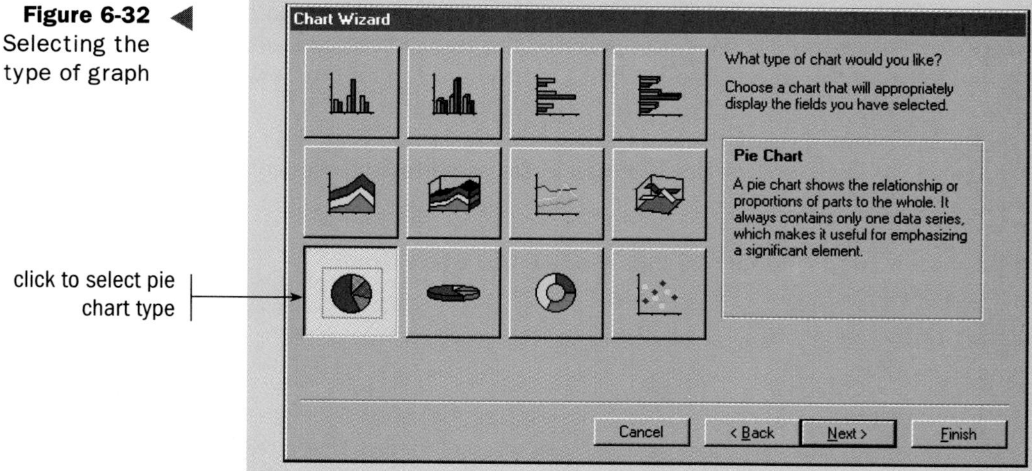

Chart Wizard

What type of chart would you like?

Choose a chart that will appropriately display the fields you have selected.

Pie Chart

A pie chart shows the relationship or proportions of parts to the whole. It always contains only one data series, which makes it useful for emphasizing a significant element.

click to select pie chart type

Cancel | < Back | Next > | Finish

Access displays the next Chart Wizard dialog box. This dialog box allows you to modify the layout of the chart. Elena decides to use the default layout and to modify it later, if necessary, once she has seen the chart in the report.

5. Click the Next > button. This dialog box allows you to enter the title that will appear at the top of the graph.

6. Type **Business Articles by Type** in the text box. Make sure the radio buttons next to the following options are selected: Yes, display a legend and Open the report with the graph displayed on it. Make sure the option, Display help showing me how to work with my chart, is not checked, then click the **Finish** button. Access creates the report and displays it, with the embedded chart, in the Print Preview window.

7. Click the Print Preview window **Maximize** button, then use the elevator bar to scroll until the entire chart is visible. See Figure 6-33.

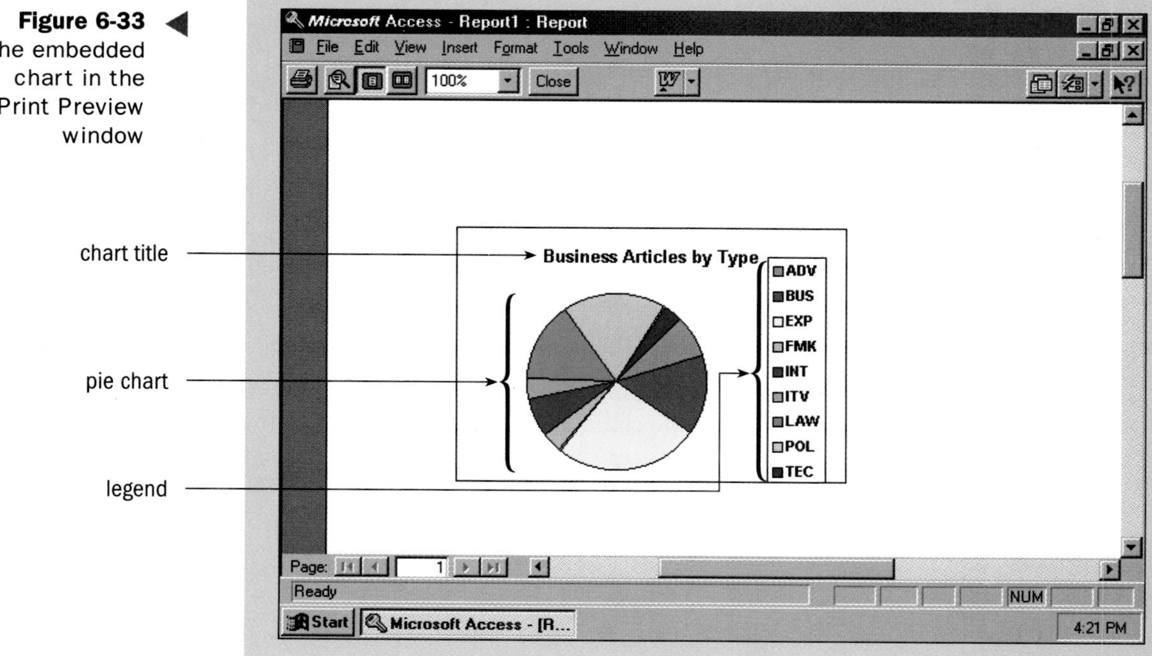

Figure 6-33 The embedded chart in the Print Preview window

Elena likes the chart, but she sees several changes she would like to make. She wants the chart to be larger and centered on the page. She notices that the wedges in the chart are color-coded and a legend appears to the right of the pie. She thinks that the colors might not reproduce well on her black-and-white printer and it will therefore be difficult to match the wedges with the article types that appear in the legend. She would prefer to have the wedges themselves marked with the article type. She prepares to make these changes by switching to the Report Design window and starting Graph so she can edit the chart.

To switch to the Report Design window and start Graph:

1. Click the **Close** button on the toolbar to close the Print Preview window and switch to the Report Design window. The chart appears in the Detail section of the report.
2. Double-click the **chart object**. Graph starts and the chart appears in the Graph window. Click the Graph window **Maximize** button. See Figure 6-34. Because Elena has not yet saved her report, it bears the default name Report1.

Figure 6-34 The chart in the Graph window

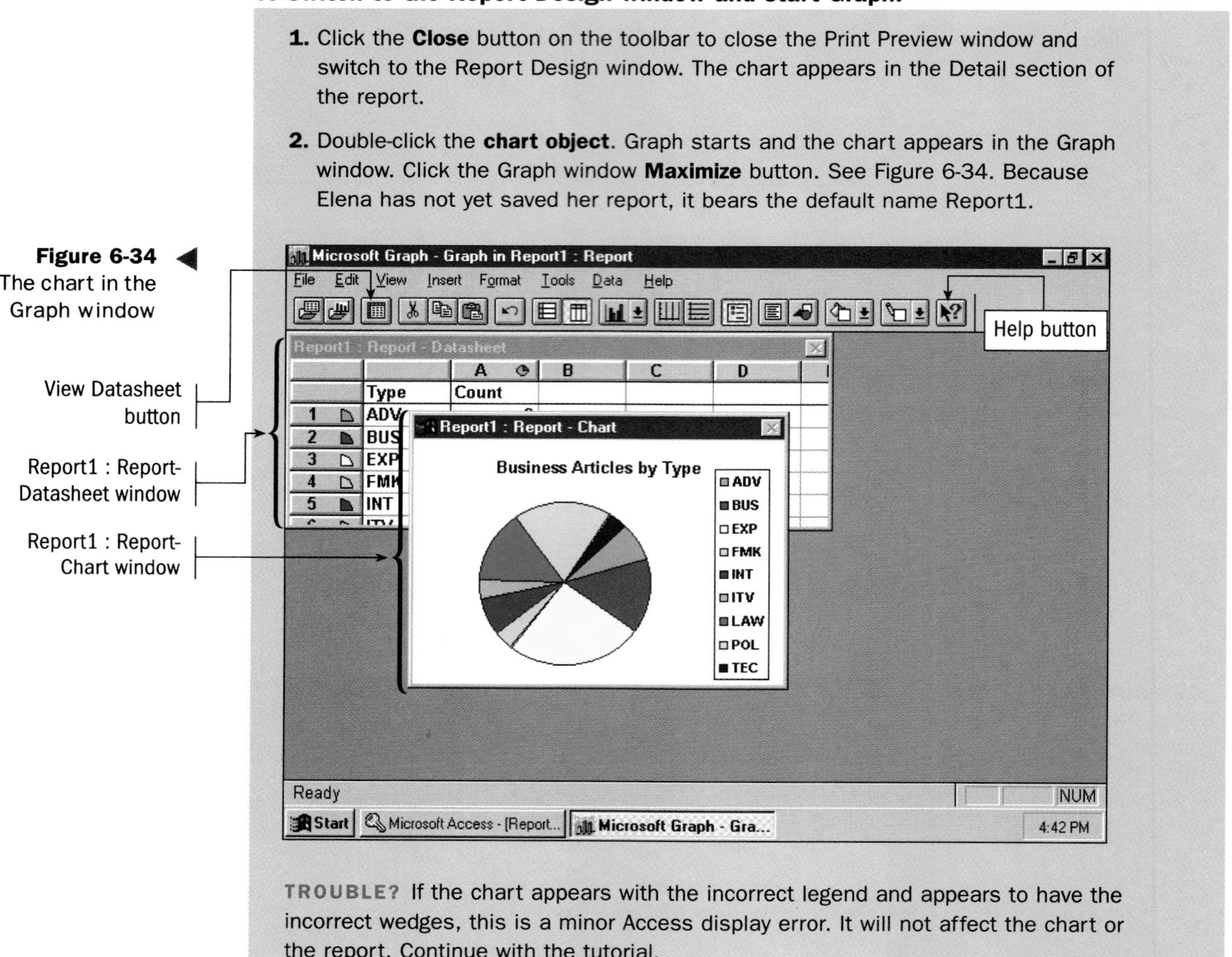

TROUBLE? If the chart appears with the incorrect legend and appears to have the incorrect wedges, this is a minor Access display error. It will not affect the chart or the report. Continue with the tutorial.

Graph is the application that created the original chart. Since the chart is embedded in the report, double-clicking the chart object starts Graph and allows you to edit the chart. The Graph window contains two smaller windows: Report1 : Report - Datasheet and Report1 : Report - Chart. The Report1 : Report - Datasheet window displays the data on which the chart is based. The Report1 : Report - Chart window displays the chart itself. All of Elena's changes will be made in the Report1 : Report - Chart window.

Elena starts by enlarging the chart.

To enlarge the chart:

1. Click in the title bar of the Report1 : Report - Chart window and drag the window up and to the left until it is directly under the toolbar and the left edge is lined up with the left edge of the View Datasheet button. Release the mouse button.
2. Position the pointer on the lower right corner of the Report1 : Report - Chart window. When the pointer turns to ↘, drag the lower right corner down and to the right until the bottom of the window is just above the status bar and the right edge is aligned with the right edge of the Help button. Release the mouse button. See Figure 6-35.

Figure 6-35 The resized chart

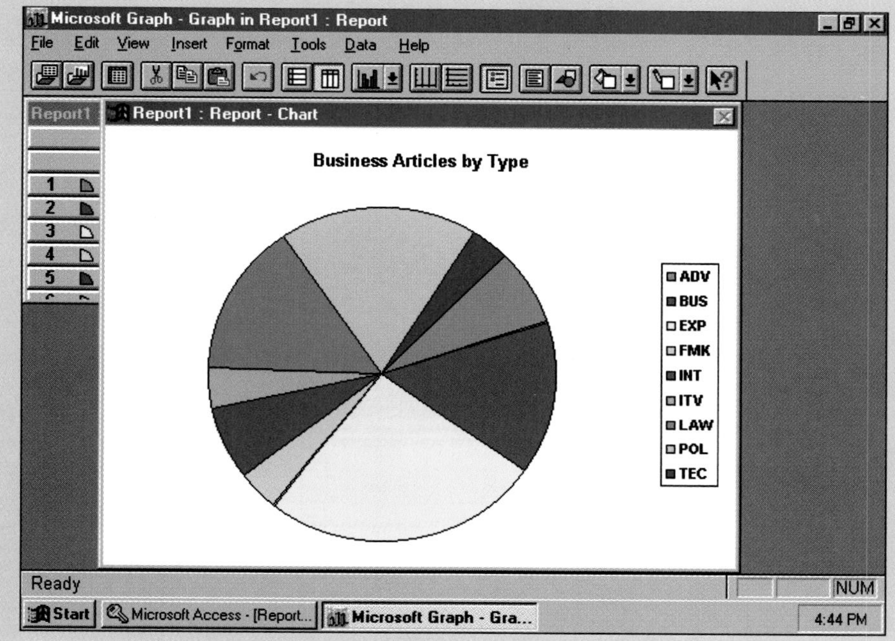

Elena now deletes the legend from the chart and creates labels for the wedges.

To delete the legend and create labels:

1. Click anywhere in the legend in the Report1 : Report - Chart window to select it. Handles appear around the edges of the legend object.
2. With the pointer inside the legend object, click the right mouse button to display the shortcut menu, then click **Clear** to remove the legend from the graph.
3. Click anywhere in the pie chart. Handles appear around the edges of the pie chart object.
4. With the pointer inside the pie chart object, click the right mouse button to display the shortcut menu, then click **Insert Data Labels** to display the Data Labels dialog box. See Figure 6-36.

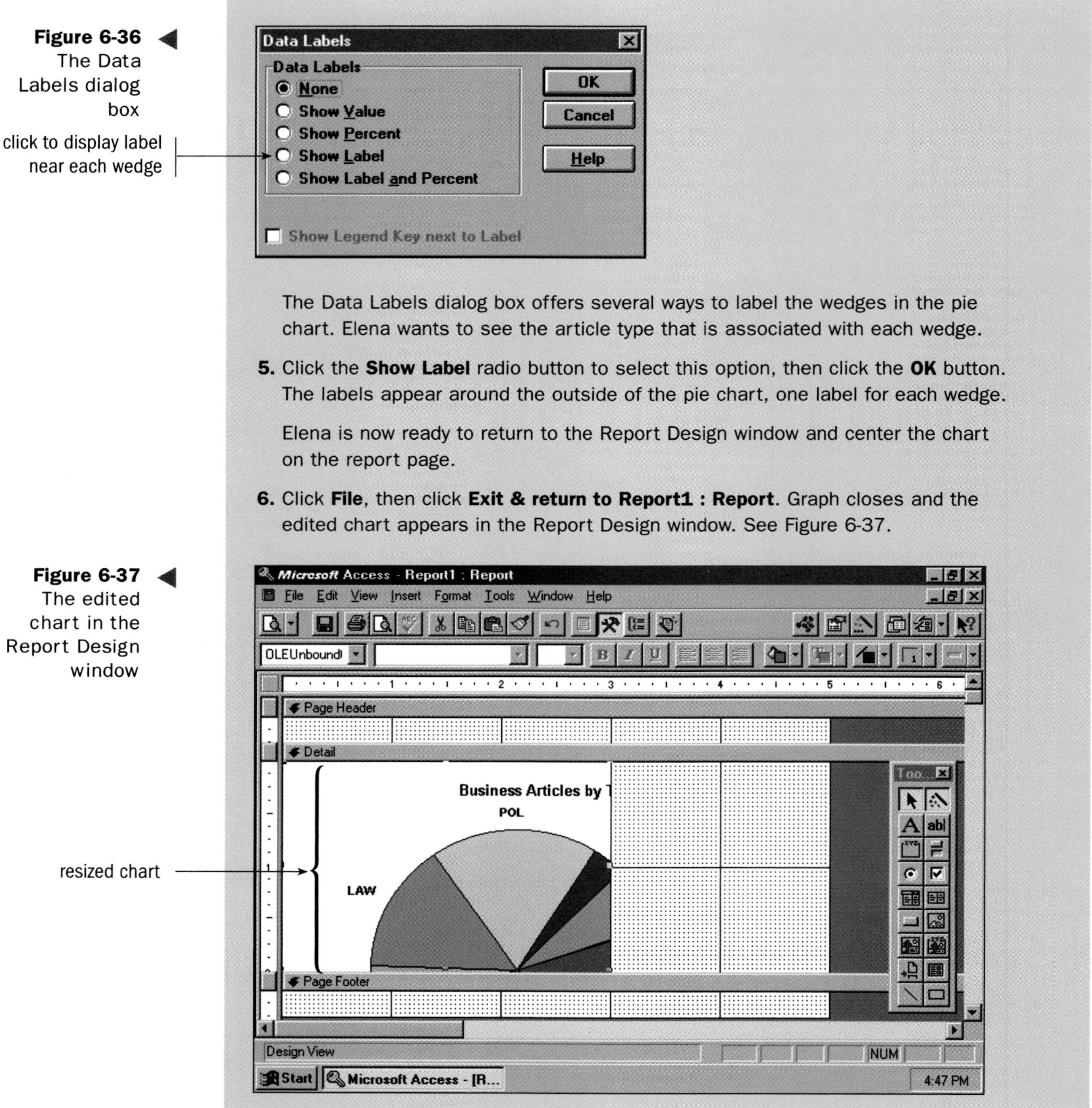

Figure 6-36 The Data Labels dialog box

click to display label near each wedge

The Data Labels dialog box offers several ways to label the wedges in the pie chart. Elena wants to see the article type that is associated with each wedge.

5. Click the **Show Label** radio button to select this option, then click the **OK** button. The labels appear around the outside of the pie chart, one label for each wedge.

   Elena is now ready to return to the Report Design window and center the chart on the report page.

6. Click **File**, then click **Exit & return to Report1 : Report**. Graph closes and the edited chart appears in the Report Design window. See Figure 6-37.

Figure 6-37 The edited chart in the Report Design window

resized chart

Although the chart is now larger, the box in which it appears in the Detail section of the report is still its original size. The box needs to be enlarged and centered in the report page.

To enlarge and center the box:

1. Click the toolbox **Close** button to hide the toolbox.
2. Position the pointer on the right edge of the report page in the Detail section. When the pointer turns to ↔, click and drag the right edge to the 6" mark on the horizontal ruler. Release the mouse button.

3. Position the pointer in the chart object. When the pointer turns to [hand pointer], click and drag the chart object to the right until the left edge of the chart object is at the 1" mark on the horizontal ruler.

4. Position the pointer on the sizing handle in the middle of the right edge of the chart object. When the pointer turns to ↔, click and drag the right edge of the chart object to the 5.5" mark on the horizontal ruler. Release the mouse button.

5. Move the pointer to the bottom of the Detail section. When the pointer changes to [resize pointer], click and drag the bottom of the Detail section to the 4" mark on the vertical ruler. Notice that the report automatically scrolls when the pointer reaches the bottom of the screen.

   TROUBLE? If you did not get the bottom of the Detail section positioned correctly, simply click and drag the bottom of the Detail section up or down as necessary. Then proceed with the following steps.

6. If necessary, scroll until the bottom of the chart object is visible, then position the pointer on the sizing handle in the middle of the bottom of the chart object. When the pointer changes to ↕, click and drag the bottom of the chart object to the bottom of the Detail section.

7. Use the elevator bar to scroll to the top of the report. See Figure 6-38.

Figure 6-38 ◀ The resized chart object

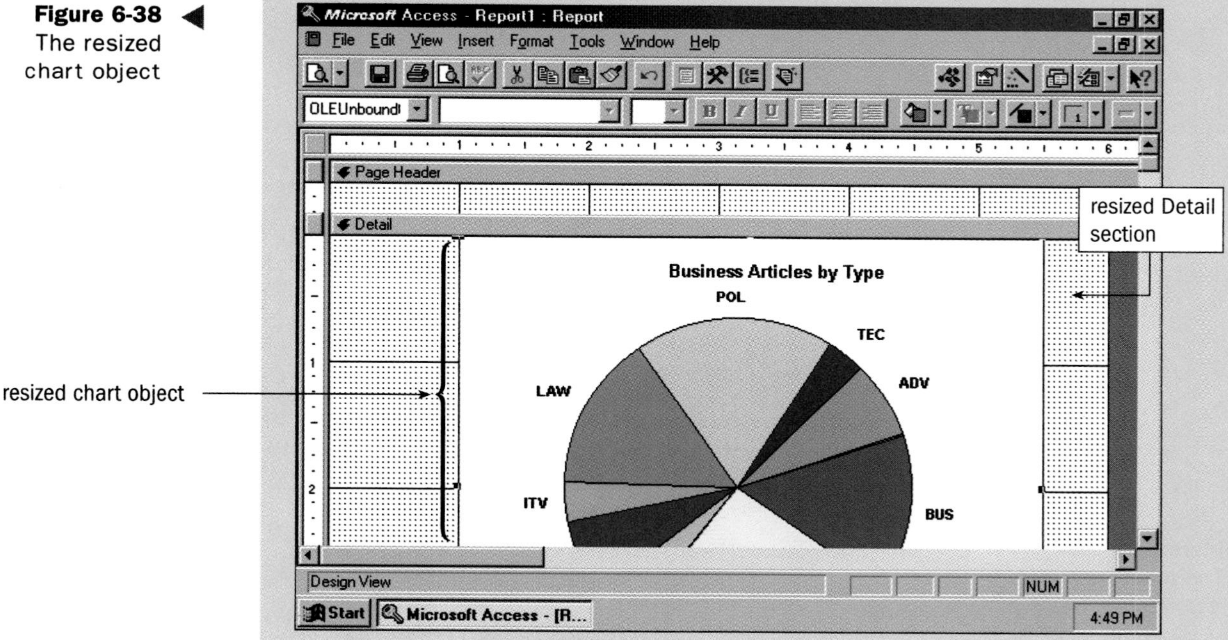

Now that the chart is properly positioned on the report page, Elena is ready to place the graphic object in the Page Header section. Since she has made many changes to the report design, she saves it before proceeding.

To save the report:

1. Click the **Save** button [Save] on the toolbar. Access displays the Save As dialog box.

2. Type **Type Pie Chart Report**, then click the **OK** button. Access saves the report.

Linking an Object in a Report

Elena decides to use the same 25th anniversary issue graphic image that she used in the Article Type Form (created in Tutorial 5). She inserts it in the Page Header, but this time, she uses linking to insert the image. That way, if she changes the graphic image later using the Microsoft Paint program, the change will also be updated in the Page Header section of the Type Pie Chart Report.

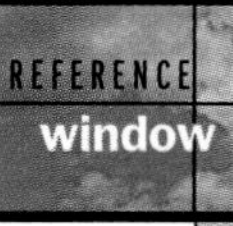

INSERTING A LINKED OBJECT IN A REPORT

- In the Report Design window, click in the report section where you want to place the linked object.
- Click Insert, then click Object to display the Insert Object dialog box.
- Click the Create from File radio button. The dialog box now displays a File Name text box.
- Enter the name of the file containing the object, or use the Browse button to display the Browse dialog box. Use the Browse dialog box to locate and select the file.
- Click the Link check box to place a check mark in it.
- Click the OK button. Access inserts the object in the report and creates a link to the original file from which the object came.

Elena first resizes the Page Header and then inserts the linked graphic image.

To resize the Page Header and insert the linked graphic image:

1. Position the pointer at the bottom of the Page Header section. When the pointer turns to ✛, click and drag the bottom of the Page Header section down until the bottom is at the 2" mark on the vertical ruler. Release the mouse button.
2. Click anywhere in the Page Header section, then click **Insert**, then click **Object** to display the Insert Object dialog box.
3. Click the **Create from File** radio button to select this option. The dialog box changes to display the File text box, the Browse button, and the Link check box. See Figure 6-39.

Figure 6-39 The Insert Object dialog box

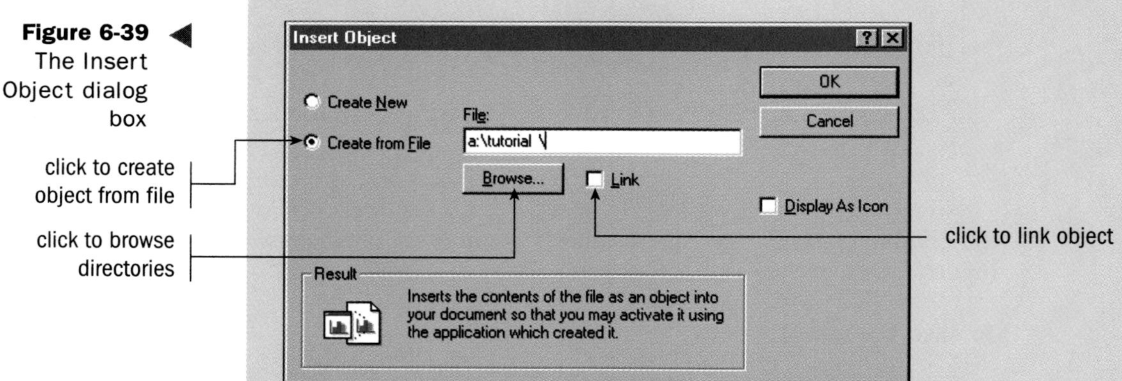

4. Click the **Browse** button to display the Browse dialog box. If necessary, use the Directories list box to display the contents of the Tutorial folder on your Student Disk.
5. In the files list box, click **25th** to select the graphic image file, then click the **OK** button. The Browse dialog box closes.

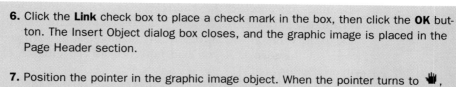

6. Click the **Link** check box to place a check mark in the box, then click the **OK** button. The Insert Object dialog box closes, and the graphic image is placed in the Page Header section.

7. Position the pointer in the graphic image object. When the pointer turns to ✋, click and drag the graphic image down and to the right until the top of the image is aligned with the fourth row of grid dots and the left edge is at the 1.25" mark on the horizontal ruler. See Figure 6-40.

Figure 6-40 The linked graphic image in the Page Header section

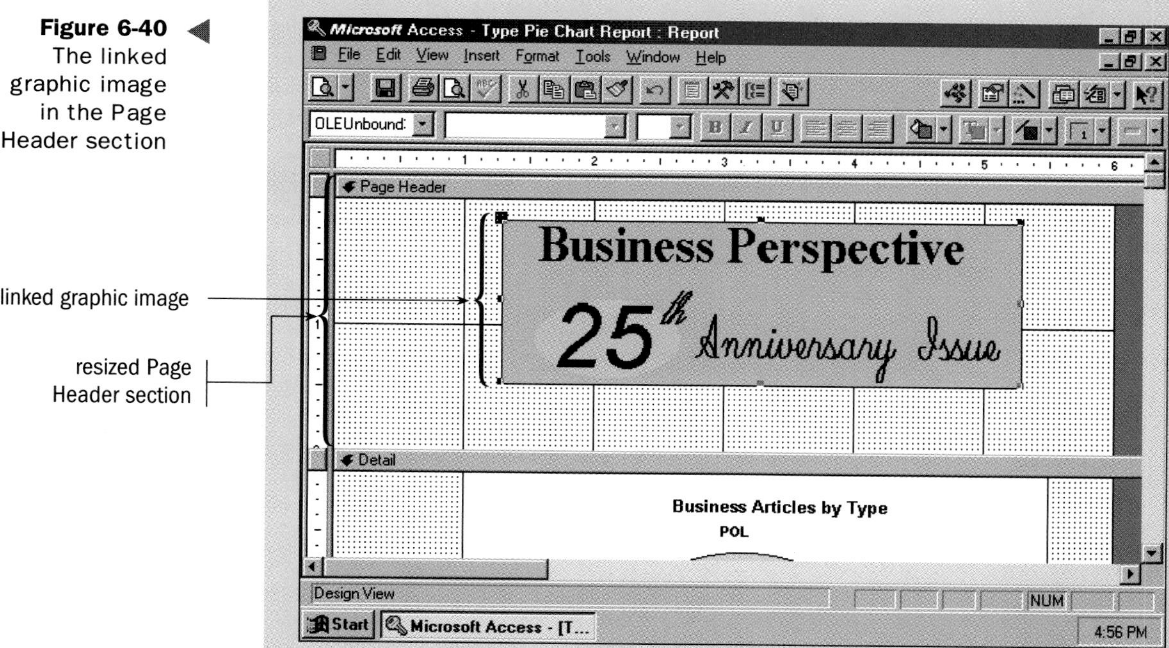

8. Click the **Print Preview** button to view the completed report. See Figure 6-41.

Figure 6-41 Completed Type Pie Chart Report

Because you checked the Link check box, the graphic image in the Page Header is *linked* to the 25th file in the Paint program that contains the original image. Any changes made to the original will automatically be included in the image that appears in the Page Header of the report. If you had not checked the Link check box, the graphic image would be *embedded*.

To see how linking works, Elena makes a change to the original graphic image using the Paint application and views the results in the Report Design window.

To make a change to the original graphic image:

1. Click the **Close** button on the toolbar to return to the Report Design window, then click the **Start** button at the bottom of the screen, point to **Programs**, point to **Accessories**, then click **Paint**. The Paint program starts and the Paint window opens. Click the Paint window **Maximize** button. See Figure 6-42.

Figure 6-42 The Paint window

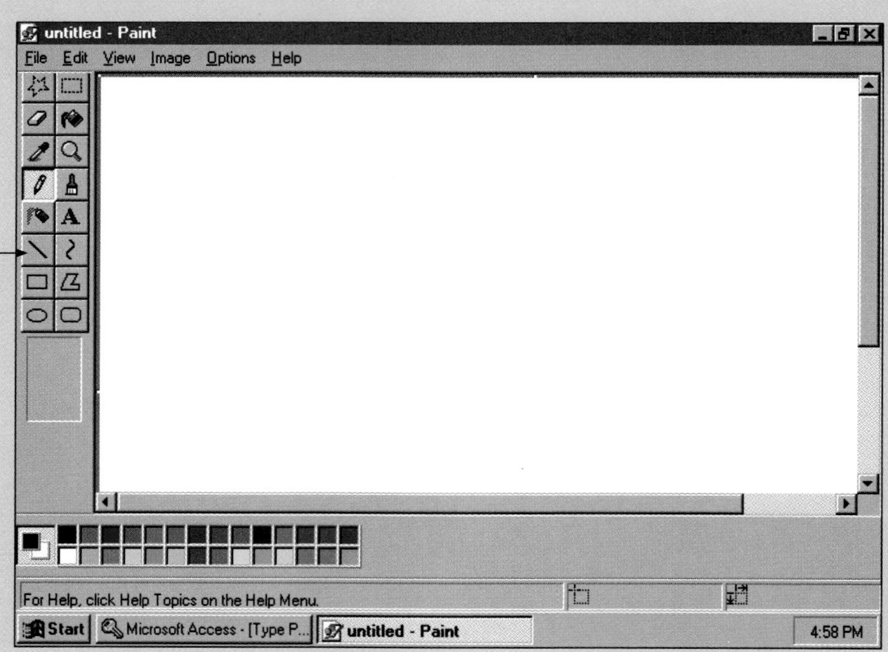

TROUBLE? If you cannot locate the Paint program in the Accessories group, it may be located in another program group on your computer. Try looking through other program groups to find it. If you cannot find it, ask your instructor or technical support person for help. If the Paint program is not installed on your computer, click in the Access window to close the Program list and skip Steps 2 through 8.

2. Click **File**, then click **Open** to display the Open dialog box. Use the Look in text box to open the Tutorial folder on your Student Disk, then double-click **25th** in the file list to open the graphic image file.

   Elena decides to place a line under the Business Perspective title in the graphic image.

3. Click the **toolbox Line** button. Move the pointer onto the image. The pointer changes shape to +.

4. Position the pointer approximately .25" under the "B" in "Business." Click and drag the pointer to the right until it is under the right edge of the final "e" in "Perspective." Paint displays a line as you move the pointer. When the pointer is in the correct position, release the mouse button. Paint places the line in the image. See Figure 6-43.

Figure 6-43
The modified graphic image

TROUBLE? If the line is not straight or is misplaced, click Edit, click Undo, and then repeat Steps 3 and 4.

5. Click **File**, then click **Save** to save the modified image, then click the Paint window **Close** button to exit Paint. The Paint window closes, and the Access Report Design window becomes active.

   The graphic image in the Page Header section does not yet reflect the change Elena made in the original file. If you close the Report Design window and then reopen the report, Access updates the link. Access automatically updates the links to linked objects whenever a form or report is opened. To see the reflected change now, you can also update the link manually.

6. Click **Edit**, then click **OLE/DDE Links** to display the Links dialog box. This dialog box allows you to select the linked objects to be updated.

7. Click **25th** in the Links list box to select it. See Figure 6-44.

Figure 6-44
Updating links

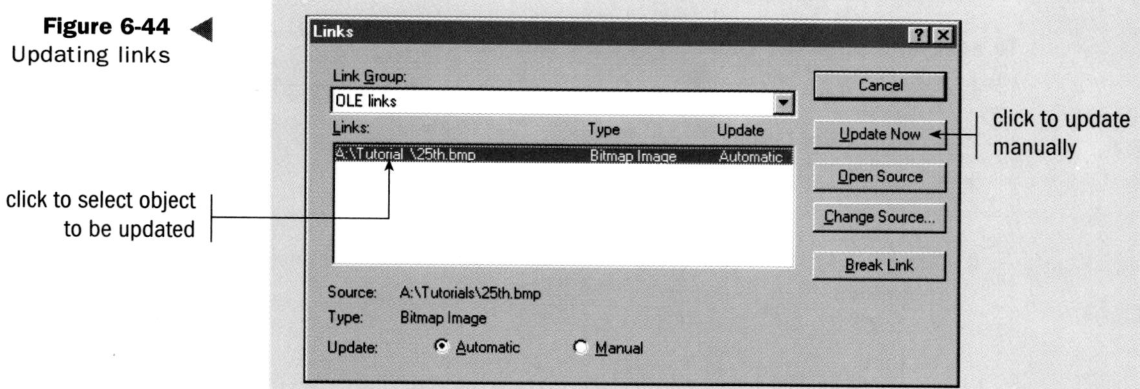

8. Click the **Update Now** button. Access opens the 25th file on your Student Disk and updates the image in the Page Header. Click the **Close** button to close the Links dialog box and view the updated graphic image. The modified graphic image appears in the Page Header. See Figure 6-45.

Figure 6-45 The report with modified graphic image in the Page Header

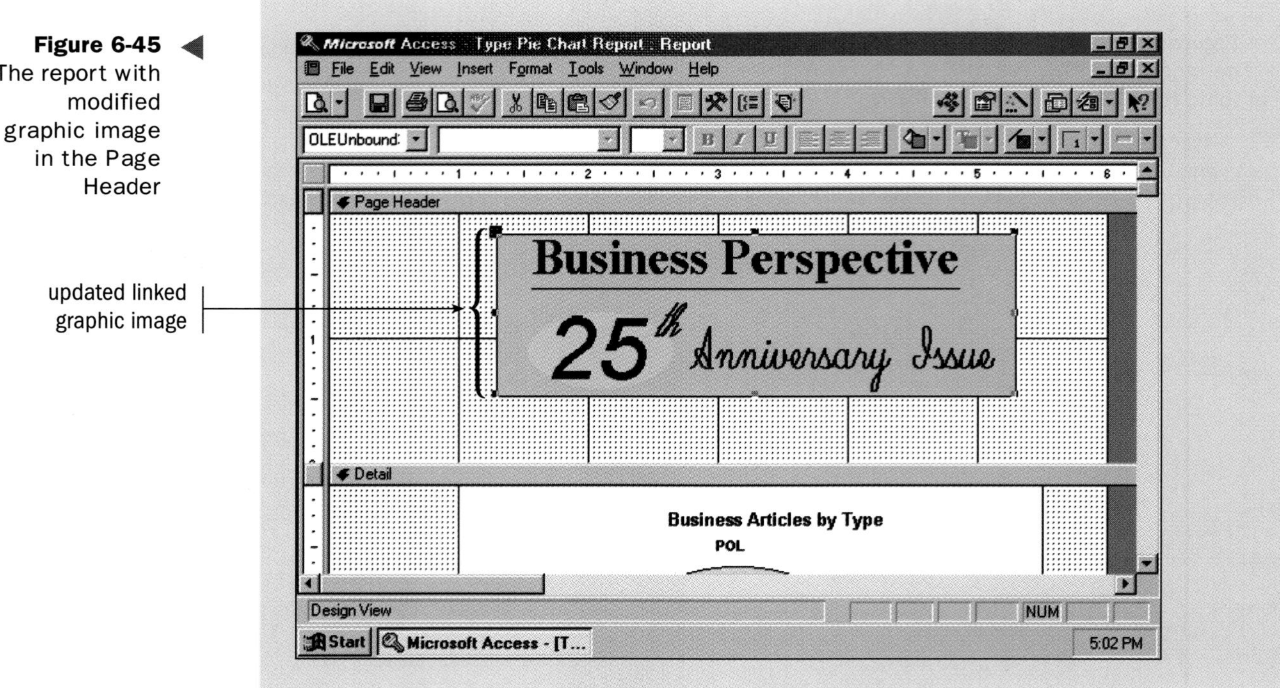

Elena is satisfied with the appearance of the report. She saves the report design, prints the report for Harold, and exits Access.

To save and print the report and then exit Access:

1. Click the **Save** button on the toolbar. Access saves the report.
2. Click the **Print** button on the toolbar to print the report.
3. Click the Report Design window **Close** button to close the Report Design window and return to the Database window.
4. Click the Access window **Close** button to exit Access and return to the Windows 95 desktop.

Elena gives Harold the printed report, which he can use in his meetings with the advertisers.

Brian, Judith, and Harold are all pleased with the Issue25 database that Elena has created. They know that Access will make it easier to keep track of the information for the 25th-anniversary issue of *Business Perspective.*

Quick Check

1. Why might you want to embed or link an object in an Access report?
2. What is the difference between embedding and linking?
3. What is OLE?
4. When you insert an object in a report or form using the Insert Object dialog box, how do you specify that the object is to be linked rather than embedded?
5. If you modify a linked object, in what application do you make the changes?
6. What are two ways to update links to linked objects in a report?

Tutorial Assignments

Elena uses the Report Wizard to create a report, named Business Articles Report, for the Issue25 database. Start Access, open the Issue25 database in the Tutorial folder on your Student Disk, and do the following:

1. Use the Report Wizard to create a report based on the BUSINESS ARTICLES table. Use the Align Left 1 layout and the Corporate style for the report. Select all the fields from the table in the order in which they are stored in the table, group the records by Writer ID, select no sort key fields, and enter Business Articles Report as the report title.
2. Display the report in the Print Preview window and then print the entire report.
3. Return to the Database window.

Elena next creates a custom report. Use the Issue25 database on your Student Disk to do the following. Use the report shown in Figure 6-2 as a model for your report design.

4. Create a blank report based on the WRITERS table.
5. Include in your report these sections: Page Header, Freelancer Header, Detail, Freelancer Footer, Page Footer, and Report Footer.
6. In the Page Header section at the beginning of the first line, enter Freelancer Group Totals as the report title. Enter the current date at the beginning of the second line. Position the labels under these lines. Add a single line below the column heads line. Do not place any lines above the column heads or above the report title.
7. Use Freelancer for the grouping field. There are no sorting fields in this report. In the Freelancer Header section, include the Freelancer field value.
8. In the Detail section, include field values for WriterID, Last Name, First Name, Writer Phone, Last Contact Date, and Freelancer Reprint Payment Amount.
9. In the Freelancer Footer section, include the group total for the Freelancer Reprint Payment Amount field.
10. In the Page Footer section, include a page number aligned with the right edge of the Freelancer Reprint Payment Amount field.
11. In the Report Footer section, include the overall total for the Freelancer Reprint Payment Amount field.
12. Embed the 25th Anniversary Issue graphic image (the file named 25th) in the Page Header.
13. When you finish creating the report, print the entire report.
14. Save the report, naming it Freelancer Group Totals Report, and then exit Access.

Case Problems

1. Walkton Daily Press Carriers Grant Sherman uses the Report Wizard to create a report for his Press database. Start Access, open the Press database in the Cases folder on your Student Disk, and do the following:

1. Use the Report Wizard to create a report based on the CARRIERS table. Select all the fields from the table in the order in which they are stored in the table. Do not select a grouping field, use the tabular format, use the compact style, and enter Carriers Report as the report title.
2. Save the report and return to the Database window.

Grant next modifies the design of this report. Open the newly created Carriers Report in the Report Design window and do the following:

3. Move the day/date (Now()) and page number text fields to the Page Header section. Change the sort order of the records to ascending order by Carrier Last Name.
4. Click the Print Preview button to display the report and then print the entire report.

5. Use Save As to save the report, naming it Carriers Report #2, and return to the Database window.

Grant next creates a custom report. Use the Press database on your Student Disk to do the following:

6. Create a blank report using the query Carriers Sorted by Name and Route ID Query.

7. Sketch a design for the report based on the requirements described in Steps 8 through 12, and then create the report following these same steps.
8. Include in your report these sections: Report Header, Page Header, Detail, Group Footer, and Report Footer.
9. In the Page Header section at the beginning of the first line, enter Carriers Sorted by Name and Route ID Report as the report title. Enter the current date at the beginning of the second line and the page number at the end of the second line. Position under these elements a row of column heads with these labels: Last Name, First Name, Carrier Phone, Route ID, and Balance. Add a single horizontal line under the column heads.
10. In the Detail section, include field values for Last Name, First Name, Carrier Phone, Route ID, and Balance. Hide duplicates for the Last Name, First Name, and Carrier Phone fields.
11. In the Group Footer section, print the group total for the Balance field. Select Last Name as the primary sort key, and use this field as a grouping field. Select Route ID as the secondary sort key, but do not use it as a grouping field. Choose ascending sort order for each sort key.
12. In the Report Footer section, print the overall total for the Balance field.

13. Insert an embedded WordPad document in the Report Header. In the document, write a short paragraph describing the contents of the report. Include your name as the creator of the report.
14. When you finish creating the report, print the entire report.
15. Save the report, and then exit Access.

2. Lopez Lexus Dealerships Maria Lopez uses the Report Wizard to create a report for her Lexus database. Start Access, open the Lexus database in the Cases folder on your Student Disk, and do the following:

1. Use the Report Wizard to create a report in the Corporate style based on the CARS table. Select all the fields from the table in the order in which they are stored in the table. Do not select a grouping field, use the tabular layout, and enter Cars by Year Report as the report title.
2. Save the report and return to the Database window.

Maria next modifies the design of this report. Open the newly created report Cars by Year Report in the Report Design window and do the following:

3. Move the day/date (Now()) and page number text fields to the Report Header section. Adjust the font size and widths in the column headings so the entire labels are visible.
4. Click the Print Preview button to display the report and then print the entire report.
5. Use Save As to save the report, naming it Cars Report #2, and return to the Database window.

Maria next creates a custom report. Use the Lexus database in the Cases folder on your Student Disk and do the following:

6. Create a blank report using the CARS table.

7. Sketch a design for the report based on the requirements described in Steps 8 through 12, and then create the report following these same steps.
8. Include in your report these sections: Page Header, Detail, Group Footer, and Report Footer.
9. In the Page Header section at the beginning of the first line, enter the report title Cars Sorted by Model and Year. Enter the current date at the beginning of the second line and the page number at the end of the second line.

Position under these elements a row of column heads with these labels: Manufacturer, Model, Year, Cost, and Selling Price. Add a single horizontal line under the column heads.

10. In the Detail section, include the field values for Manufacturer, Model, Year, Cost, and Selling Price. Hide duplicates for the Manufacturer field.
11. In the Group Footer section, print the group total for the Cost and Selling Price fields. Select Model as the primary sort key and as the grouping field. Select Year as the secondary sort key but do not use it as a grouping field. Choose ascending sort order for the sort keys.
12. In the Report Footer section, print the overall totals for the Cost and Selling Price fields.
13. When you finish creating the report, print the entire report.
14. Save the report, naming it Cars by Model and Year Report.
15. Use the Chart Wizard to create a pie chart report based on Model. Each wedge in the pie should represent the count of cars of each model. Insert percents as labels for each wedge. Save the report as Model Pie Chart Report. Print the report and exit Access.

3. Tophill University Student Employment Olivia Tyler uses the Report Wizard to create a report for her Parttime database. Start Access, open the Parttime database in the Cases folder on your Student Disk, and do the following:

1. Use the Report Wizard to create a tabular layout report based on the JOBS table. Select all the fields from the table in the order in which they are stored in the table. Do not select a grouping field and enter Jobs Report as the report title. Use the corporate style.
2. Save the report, naming it Jobs Report, and return to the Database window.

Olivia next modifies the design of this report. Open the newly created report Jobs Report in the Report Design window and do the following:

3. Adjust the size of the Detail section so that there are no blank lines between the printed records. Add double lines in the Page Footer, separating the Day/Date and Page Number text boxes from the Detail section.
4. Click the Print Preview button to display the report and then print the entire report.
5. Use Save As to save the report, naming it Jobs Report #2, and return to the Database window.

Olivia next creates a custom report. Use the Parttime database on your Student Disk to do the following:

6. Create a blank report using Jobs Sorted by Employer and Job Title Query.
7. Sketch a design for the report based on the requirements described in Steps 8 through 11, and then create the report following these same steps.
8. Include in your report a Page Header section and a Detail section.
9. In the Page Header section at the beginning of the first line, enter Jobs Sorted by Employer and Job Title as the report title. Enter the current date at the beginning of the second line and the page number at the end of the second line. Position under these elements a row of column heads with these labels: Employer Name, Hours/Week, Job Title, and Wages. Add a single horizontal line under the column heads.
10. In the Detail section, include the field values for Employer Name, Hours/Week, Job Title, and Wages. Hide duplicates for the Employer Name field.
11. Select Employer Name as the primary sort key and Job Title as the secondary sort key. Do not select a grouping field. Choose ascending sort order for each sort key.

12. Insert the graphic image file TU as a linked object in the Page Header. Edit the graphic image file in the Paint program and change the background of the TU logo to bright yellow. Save the changes to the image and view the report in the Print Preview window.
13. When you finish creating the report, print the entire report.
14. Save the report, naming it Jobs Sorted by Employer and Job Title Report and then exit Access.

4. Rexville Business Licenses Chester Pearce uses the Report Wizard to create a report for his Buslic database. Start Access, open the Buslic database in the Cases folder on your Student Disk, and do the following:

1. Use the Report Wizard to create a report in the Bold style based on the BUSINESSES table. Select all the fields from the table in the order in which they are stored in the table. Do not select a grouping field, select tabular layout, and enter Businesses Report as the report title.
2. Return to the Database window.

Chester next modifies the design of this report. Open the newly created report Businesses Report in the Report Design window and do the following:

3. In the Report Header section, center the title label.
4. Click the Print Preview button to display the report and then print the entire report.
5. Use Save As to save the report, naming it Businesses Report #2, and then return to the Database window.

Chester next creates a custom report. Use the Buslic database on your Student Disk to do the following:

6. Create a blank report using Businesses Sorted by License Type and Business Name Query.

7. Sketch a design for the report based on the requirements described in Steps 8 through 12, and then create the report following these same steps.
8. Include in your report these sections: Page Header, Detail, Group Footer, and Report Footer.
9. In the Page Header section at the beginning of the first line, enter Businesses Sorted by License Type and Business Name as the report title. Enter the current date at the beginning of the second line and the page number at the end of the second line. Position under these elements a row of column heads with these labels: License, Basic Cost, Business Name, and Amount. Add a single horizontal line under the column heads.
10. In the Detail section, include the field values for License (do not use License Number), Basic Cost, Business Name, and Amount. Hide duplicates for the License and Basic Cost fields.
11. In the Group Footer section, print the group total for the Amount field. Select License as the primary sort key and as the grouping field. Select Business Name as the secondary sort key, but do not use it as a grouping field. Choose ascending sort order for each sort key.
12. In the Report Footer section, print the overall totals for the Amount field.
13. When you finish creating the report, print the entire report.
14. Save the report, naming it Businesses Sorted by License Type and Business Name Report.

15. Use the Chart Wizard to create a 3-D column chart based on the License Type and Amount fields of the Issued Licenses table. Accept the default layout. Add a label to the X (horizontal) axis of the graph. The label should be License Types. Delete the legend. Insert an embedded WordPad document in the Detail section that explains that these numbers are license types. In the document, write a short description of the graph.
16. Print the report and save it with the name License Fee Graph Report, and then exit Access.

Answers to Quick Check Questions

SESSION 1.1

1 What three steps should you generally follow to create and store a new type of data?
When you create and store new types of data either manually or on a computer, you follow a general three-step procedure:
- Identify the individual fields.
- Group fields for each entity in a table.
- Store the field values for each record.

2 What are fields and entities, and how are they related?
An entity is a person, place, object, event, or idea that you are recording in a table. Each record in a table corresponds to an individual entity. Each entity has certain characteristics or attributes. Each attribute is represented by a field. For example, the records in a mailing list table correspond to the individual persons on the mailing list. Each person has characteristics such as Last Name, First Name, Street Address, etc. Each of these characteristics is a field in the table.

3 What are the differences between a primary key and a foreign key?
A primary key is a field, or a collection of fields, whose values uniquely identify each record in a table. When we include a primary key from one table in a second table to form a relationship between the two tables, we call it a foreign key in the second table.

4 Describe what a DBMS is designed to do.
A database management system (DBMS) is a software package that lets us create databases and then manipulate data in the databases.

5 Describe the six different objects you can create for an Access database.
A table is a structure that contains all fields for a specific entity. Records are stored in a table. A query is a question you can ask about the data from your tables. A form allows you do display records from a table for viewing or editing. A report describes a customized format for printing the data from tables. A macro is a saved list of operations to be performed on data, which Access carries out when you run the macro. Finally, Access has a built-in programming language called Visual Basic. A module is a set of one or more Visual Basic programmed procedures.

6 What do the columns and rows of a datasheet represent?
Each row is a separate record in the table, and each column, headed by a field name, contains the field values for one field from the table.

7 Name the fields in the CHECKS table. How many records are in the CHECKS table? What is the primary key of the CHECKING ACCOUNTS table?
Field names: Account Number, Check Number, Date, Amount. There are 5 records in the CHECKS table. The primary key is Account Number.

SESSION 1.2

1 What does the Form View window show?
The Form View window displays records from a table in a custom form. A custom form can be used to display records in a more readable or usable format than that used by the Datasheet View window.

2 Name the five ways you can use Access's Help system to get on-line information.
You can use Access's Help system to get on-line information through:
- Help Contents — displays a list of the major Help topics.
- Help Index — allows you to find topics related to a key word or phrase.
- Help Find — allows you to search the entire Help system for specific words.

- Answer Wizard — analyzes your typed question and suggests related Help topics.
- Context-Sensitive Help — displays short help information about objects on the current screen.

3 How does the Help Index differ from the Answer Wizard?
The Help Index searches for topics related to a specific word or phrase that you enter. The Help Index, like an index in a book, is a list of topics available in Help. When you enter a word or phrase, the Help Index searches for the word or phrase in the index and displays the relevant section of the Index. You can then ask for help on the topic displayed. The Answer Wizard analyzes a question that you enter and displays a list of topics related to your question. It is not necessary for you to enter words that exactly match the words in Help's list of topics. The Answer Wizard can use synonyms and analyze questions in various forms.

4 How would you find out the meaning of the button?
Use context-sensitive help to learn that is the Spelling button. It is used to check the spelling of text entries in Datasheet View of tables, queries, and forms. It also can be used to check the spelling of selected text in a text box in Form View.

5 What is the purpose of a shortcut menu, and why would you use it?
A shortcut menu contains a list of commands that relate to the object you click. Using a shortcut menu is often faster than using a menu or toolbar button.

6 How do you open and close a shortcut menu?
To display a shortcut menu window, you position the mouse pointer on a specific object or area and click the right mouse button. To close a shortcut menu window, you click the left mouse button outside the window.

SESSION 2.1

1 What two types of keys represent a common field when you form a relationship between tables?
A primary key and a foreign key.

2 What is data redundancy?
Data redundancy occurs when you store the same data in more than one place. With the exception of common fields to relate tables, you should avoid redundancy.

3 Name and describe three Access data types.
There are nine Access data types:

- Text allows field values containing letters, digits, spaces, and special characters. Text fields can be up to 255 characters long.
- Memo, like the Text data type, allows field values containing letters, digits, spaces, and special characters. Memo fields, however, can be up to 64,000 characters long and are used for long comments or explanations.
- Number limits field values to digits, an optional leading sign (+ or –), and an optional decimal point.
- Date/Time allows field values containing valid dates and times only.
- Currency allows field values similar to those for the Number data type. Unlike calculations with Number data type decimal values, calculations performed using the Currency data type will not be subject to round-off error.
- AutoNumber consists of integers with values automatically controlled by Access. Access automatically inserts a value in the field as each new record is created.
- Yes/No limits field values to yes and no entries.
- OLE Object allows field values that are created in other software packages as objects, such as photographs, video images, graphics, drawings, sound recordings, voice-mail messages, spreadsheets, and word processing documents.
- Lookup Wizard creates a field that lets you to select a value from another table or from a predefined list of values.

4 Why might including a field description in a table be helpful?
The field description helps the table designer identify the purpose of a field. It is an annotation to help document the table.

5 What is one advantage of designating a primary key?
Access prevents the user from entering a new record that has a primary key value identical to that of an existing record. This guarantees uniqueness of primary key values.

6 Which data types need to have field sizes determined?
You must define field sizes for Text and Number fields. Other fields have predefined sizes.

7 Describe two different ways to select a field's data type.
- Click the Data Type text box, then click the Data Type list arrow that appears, then click the data type you want.
- In the Data Type text box, type the first letter of the name of the data type. Access fills in the name of the data type in the Data Type text box.

8 How do you switch from one view window to another?
Click the Table View button to switch to a different view of the table.

SESSION 2.2

1 What is a caption?
A caption is a shorter version of a longer, more descriptive table field name.

2 Describe three different ways to resize a datasheet column.
- You can use the Format menu to display the Column Width dialog box. Specify the desired width.
- You can use the mouse pointer to drag the right edge of a selected column.
- You can use the best-fit column width method to resize a selected column Access automatically resizes the column to accommodate its largest value, including the field name at the top of the column. To use this method, you position the mouse pointer at the right edge of the column selector for the field and, when the mouse pointer changes to ✛, double-click the left mouse button. Access then automatically resizes the column.

3 Why would you assign a default value to a field?
When you assign a default value to a field, Access automatically supplies that value for each new record. This makes data entry easier and minimizes the chance of error.

4 What are the steps for changing decimal places?
In the Design View window, select the field for which you want to change decimal places. Click the text box for the Decimal places property, then click the list arrow that appears, then select the correct number of decimal places.

5 What is an input mask?
An input mask is a description of the format for data entered in a particular field. When you enter data in the field, Access requires that you enter the data according to the format specified by the input mask

6 Describe two recommended ways to create an Access table.
Create an Access Table using the Table Wizard or by designing the table directly in the Design View window.

7 What is an index and why is it useful?
An index is a list of primary key values and their corresponding record numbers. An index makes searching for and sorting records more efficient. An index also allows you to define relations between tables.

SESSION 3.1

1 What operations are performed when you update a database?
Adding records, deleting records, and modifying records are the basic operations when you update a database.

2 What does a pencil symbol signify in a record selector? An asterisk symbol?
The pencil symbol indicates a record that has been modified but not saved. The asterisk is the new record symbol.

3 Which button do you use to move to the last record in the table?
Use the Last Record button ▶|.

4 If you change field values in a table, what do you have to do to save your changes?
Once you have entered or modified data in a field, Access automatically saves the changes.

5 If you delete a record from a table, do all field values disappear? Which field values, if any, remain?
Access deletes the record from the table. The Datasheet View window will still show the default values for any blank record visible in the window.

6 What are some advantages of importing data?
Importing data saves time since you don't have to reenter the data. Importing also minimizes the chance of error in data entry.

7 When would you use the Table Analyzer Wizard?
Use the Table Analyzer Wizard to check the design of a table. The Table Analyzer Wizard makes suggestions for changes to the table design that may make the design more efficient.

8 How do you change a datasheet's font?
Use the Format toolbar to change a datasheet's font. You can change the font type, size, and style.

SESSION 3.2

1 How can you find a specific field value in a table?
Click in the field column you want to search. Click the Find button, then type the search value in the Find What text box. Select the search options, then click the Find First button to find the first occurrence of the field value.

2 Why do you need to be cautious about using the Replace All option when replacing table field values?
When you use the Replace All option, Access cannot undo the replacements after they are made.

3 What are the advantages of sorting a datasheet's records?
By sorting a datasheet's records, you can view the records in a more convenient order. You can sort the records on different fields, allowing different users to view the records in the order they need and making it easy to find and view groups of records.

4 When might you consider using a secondary sort key?
A secondary key is useful to subsort records that have matching values for the primary sort key. For example, if you wish to sort employee records by name, the Last Name would be an appropriate primary sort key and First Name would be an appropriate secondary sort key.

5 What are some advantages of using Access's Spelling feature?
Access's Spelling feature allows you to check the spelling of values entered in a Text field. This reduces the chance of error in the data and allows you to check many records quickly.

6 What is the purpose of the Lookup Wizard?
The Lookup Wizard assists you in defining a Table Lookup field. It prompts you for the necessary information to describe the source of the data and which value should be stored.

7 How many different files do you copy when you back up one Access database that includes three tables?
You only need to copy one file.

8 What is the purpose of compacting a database?
When records or objects are deleted from a database, the space does not become immediately available. Compacting a database removes deleted records and objects, creates a smaller version of the database, and releases the space for future use.

SESSION 4.1

1 What is the Simple Query Wizard?
The Simple Query Wizard assists you in creating a query design by prompting you for the tables and fields to be used in the query and by automatically saving the query design.

2 In what format do the query results appear? What are the advantages of this format?
The query results appear in the Datasheet View window. These results are temporary and are not saved as a table. Any changes you make to the data in the query results will be made in the underlying table(s).

3 What is QBE?
QBE means Query By Example. You can define a query using the Query Design grid by describing an example of the information you want. Access then retrieves the records that match you example.

4 What are two methods for adding a field from a table to the Query Design grid?
You can add a field from a table by clicking and dragging the field from the field list to the Query Design grid or by double-clicking on the field name in the field list.

5 What are the two components of a simple condition?
A simple condition is composed of a comparison operator (such as = or <) and a value.

6 How do you exclude a field that appears in the Query Design grid from the query results?
You exclude a field from the query results by removing the check mark in the Show box for that field in the Query Design grid.

7 What comparison operator is used to select records based on a specific pattern?
The Like comparison operator is used to select records based on a pattern.

8 When do you use the In comparison operator?
Use the In comparison operator to specify a list of values. A record is selected if its field value matches any value in the list.

SESSION 4.2

1 Why might you need to sort a single field?
You would sort query results for a single field in order to view the records ordered by the values in that field.

2 How must you position the fields in the Query Design grid when you have multiple sort keys?
The sort key that appears leftmost in the Query Design grid is the primary sort key. If two records match in the primary sort key field, Access uses the next leftmost sort key to subsort.

3 Why might you print selected query results?
You would print a query results selection if you want to print only some of the records in the query results.

4 When do you use logical operators?
Logical operators And and Or are used to create multiple selection criteria. For the And logical operator, Access selects all records that meet all selection criteria. For the Or logical operator, Access selects all records that meet any of the selection criteria.

5 What is a calculated field?
A calculated field is a field in the Query Design grid that is calculated from values in other fields.

6 When do you use an aggregate function?
Aggregate functions summarize data. For example, to calculate the sum of values in a field, use the SUM aggregate function.

7 What does the Group By operator do?
The Group By operator combines records with identical field values into a single record.

SESSION 4.3

1 What is a join?
A join is a relationship between two tables.

2 Describe the difference between a one-to-many relationship and a one-to-one relationship.
In a one-to-many relationship, a single record in the primary table is related to one or more records in the related table. In a one-to-one relationship, a single record in the primary table is related to only one record in the related table.

3 What functions can you perform in the Relationships window?
In the Relationships window, you can view or change existing relationships, define new relationships between tables, rearrange the layout of tables, and change the structures of related tables.

4 What are the two referential integrity rules?
The two referential integrity rules are:
- When you add a record to a related table, there must be a matching record in the primary table.
- You cannot delete a record in the primary table if matching records exist in the related table.

5 What does a join line signify?
A join line in a relationship diagram indicates the common field in the two tables, the nature of the relationship (one-to-one, one-to-many, etc.), and the enforcement of integrity rules.

6 How do you query more than one table?
You query more than one table by defining a relationship between the tables and then selecting fields from those tables in the Query Design grid.

7 When do you use a parameter query?
Use a parameter query when you want Access to prompt you for the selection criteria when you run the query.

SESSION 5.1

1 What is a form?
A form displays records from an Access database in a more attractive and readable format. You can use a form to maintain, view, and print records of data.

2 What are three form designs that you can create with AutoForm?
AutoForm creates a form in one of three standard designs: Columnar, Tabular, or Datasheet.

3 What formats does the Form Wizard use to display records in a main/subform form?
The main form is displayed in columnar format. The subform can be displayed in either tabular or datasheet format, depending on your choice when you create the subform.

4 How many sets of navigation buttons appear in a main/subform form, and what does each set control?
There are two sets of navigation buttons in a main/subform form. The bottom set controls navigation through the records displayed in the main form. The upper set controls navigation through the records displayed in the subform.

5 What is a filter?
A filter is a set of criteria that describes the records you want to see in a form and their sequence. Unlike a query, a filter applies only to the form that is currently in use. You can save the filter as a query.

6 What is the purpose of filter by selection? Filter by form?
Filter by selection allows you to specify an exact match simple selection condition by using an actual record as a model. Filter by form allows you to specify multiple selection criteria directly in a blank form. A filter by form can be saved as a query.

7 How can you tell that the Form View window is displaying records to which a filter has been applied?
The Form View window displays three indicators that a filter has been applied:
- The Apply Filter button appears pressed down.
- The word "(Filtered)" appears near the navigation buttons.
- The indicator "FLTR" appears in the status line.

8 How do you reuse a filter in the future?
After specifying a filter by form or designing a filter in the Filter Design window, you can save the filter as a query for future use. Open the form and click the Filter By Form button on the toolbar. Click File, then click Load from Query, and select the saved query. Click the Apply Filter button on the toolbar to run the query.

SESSION 5.2

1 What is the difference between a bound and an unbound control?
A bound control, such as a field-value text box, is associated with a field from a table record. The field value appears in the bound control. An unbound control, such as a label, is not associated with any field in a table.

2 How do you move a control and its label together, and how do you move each separately?
Click in the control or label to select both, then place the pointer inside either object. Click the left mouse button to change the pointer to and drag the two controls

together to their new location. To move a single selected control, click the control's move handle and drag it to its new position.

3 How do you change a label name?
Click in the label to select it, click the right mouse button to display the property sheet window. Change the Caption property value, then close the property sheet window.

4 How would you resize a control?
Click the control to select it, place the pointer on a sizing handle, and click and drag the edge of the control.

5 What is the Form Header section?
The Form Header section defines the controls that will appear at the top of each form.

6 Describe how you would use a Control Wizard to add a list box to a form.
In the toolbox, click the Control Wizards button, then click the toolbox List Box button. Place the pointer on the form and click to position the list box. Complete the Control Wizard dialog boxes to create the list box.

7 How do you insert into a form a graphic created with another software program?
In the toolbox, click the toolbox Image button. Position the pointer in the form at the position for the upper-left corner of the graphic image. Select the image from the Insert Picture dialog box.

8 What is control morphing?
Control morphing allows you to change the control type for a control without having to delete it and redefine it.

SESSION 6.1

1 What are the seven Access report sections?
- Report Header — Appears once at the beginning of a report.
- Page Header — Appears at the top of each page of a report.
- Group Header — Appears once at the beginning of a new group of records.
- Detail — Appears once for each record in the underlying table or query.
- Group Footer — Appears once at the end of a group of records.
- Report Footer — Appears once at the end of the report.
- Page Footer — Appears at the bottom of each page of a report.

2 What types of reports can AutoReport create and what is the difference between them?
AutoReport creates a report in one of two standard formats: columnar or tabular. A Columnar report lists records one field per line, vertically on the report page. A Tabular report lists one record per line, horizontally on the report page.

3 What is a group?
A group is a set of records that share a common value for one or more fields.

4 Why is it not necessary to save manually a report created by the Report Wizard?
The Report Wizard automatically saves the report before displaying it in the Print Preview window.

5 What is a custom report?
A custom report is any report you create in the Report Design window or any modified report created by AutoReport or the Report Wizard.

6 What does the Report Design window have in common with the Form Design window? What is different?
The Report Design window and the Form Design window are similar in most respects, except that the Report Design window displays a new toolbar button, the Sorting and Grouping button. By default, the Form Design window displays only a Detail section. The Report Design window displays a Page Header and Page Footer section as well as the Detail section.

7 In the Report Design window, how is adding, moving, resizing, and deleting controls different from accomplishing these tasks in the Form Design window?
Each object in the Form Design window or the Report Design window is a control. The process of adding, moving, resizing, and deleting controls is essentially the same in both windows.

SESSION 6.2

1 When do you use the toolbox Text Box tool?
The Text Box tool is used to place a bound control in the Report Design window.

2 What do you type in a text box to tell Access to print the current date?
The function =Date() will print the current date.

3 How do you insert a page number in a Page Header section?
In the Report Design window, click Insert, then click Page Number.

4 What is the function of the Sorting and Grouping button?
The Sorting and Grouping button allows you to specify how the records will be sorted when they are printed in a report. Each sort key can also be used as a grouping field for the records.

5 How do you add a Report Footer section to a report without adding a Report Header section?
Click View, then click Report Header/Footer in the Report Design window. Then reduce the height of the Report Header section to zero.

6 How do you calculate group totals and overall totals?
Place a text box in the Group Footer or Report Footer section. In the text box, enter the expression =Sum([*field name*]), where *field name* is the name of the field you want to total.

7 Why might you want to hide duplicate values in a group report?
Duplicate values clutter up the report. Hiding them makes the report easier to read.

SESSION 6.3

1 Why might you want to embed or link an object in an Access report?
You embed or link objects in an Access report to include objects created by other applications. These can be objects of a type Access cannot create (e.g., graphs).

2 What is the difference between embedding and linking?
An embedded object preserves its connection to the application that created it. You can edit the object by double-clicking on it and using the parent application. Any changes you make in the object are reflected in the Access embedded file, not in the original file. A linked object also preserves its connection to the original file from which it came. You can edit the object by double-clicking on it and using the parent application, or you can edit it outside of Access using the parent application. Any changes you make in the object are reflected in both the Access file and in the original file from which it came.

3 What is OLE?
OLE stands for Object Linking and Embedding. An application that supports OLE can create objects that can be embedded or linked in another application. Not all applications allow object linking or embedding.

4 When you insert an object in a report or form using the Insert Object dialog box, how do you specify that the object is to be linked rather than embedded?
Insert the object from a file and check the Link check box.

5 If you modify a linked object, in what application do you make the changes?
When you modify a linked object, you use the application that was originally used to create the object.

6 What are two ways to update links to linked objects in a report?
Each linked object is updated automatically when the report is opened. You can also update the links manually by clicking Edit, then clicking Update OLE/DDE links in the Report Design window.

Microsoft® **Access 7** for Windows® 95

INTERMEDIATE

TUTORIALS

Read This **Before You Begin**

TO THE STUDENT

STUDENT DISKS

To complete the Intermediate tutorials, Tutorial Assignments, Case Problems and Additional Cases in this book, you need 4 Student Disks. Your instructor will either provide you with Student Disks or will ask you to make your own.

If you are supposed to make your own Student Disks, you will need 4 blank, formatted high-density disks. You will need to copy a set of folders from a file server or standalone computer onto your disks. Your instructor will tell you which computer, drive letter, and folders contain the files you need. The following table shows you which folders go on each of your disks, so that you will have enough disk space to complete all the tutorials, Tutorial Assignments, Case Problems, and Additional Cases:

Student Disk	Write this on the disk label	Put these folders on the disk
1	Tutorials 1–4	Tutorial
2	Cases 1–2	Cases1
3	Cases 3–4	Cases2
4	Additional Cases	Addcases

When you begin each tutorial, be sure you are using the correct Student Disk. See the inside front or inside back cover of this book for more information on Student Disk files, or ask your instructor or technical support person for assistance.

USING YOUR OWN COMPUTER

If you are going to work through this book using your own computer, you need:

- **Computer System** Microsoft Access 7 for Windows 95 must be installed on your computer. This book assumes a full installation of Microsoft Access 7.
- **Student Disks** Ask your instructor or lab manager for details on how to get the Student Disks. You will not be able to complete the tutorials or exercises in this book using your own computer until you have Student Disks. The student files may also be obtained electronically over the Internet. See the inside front or inside back cover of this book for more details.

VISIT OUR WORLD WIDE WEB SITE

Additional materials designed especially for you are available on the World Wide Web. Go to **http://coursetools.com**.

TO THE INSTRUCTOR

To complete the tutorials in this book, your students must use a set of files on Student Disks. These files are included in the Instructor's Resource Kit on CD-ROM. They may also be obtained electronically over the Internet. See the inside front or inside back cover of this book for more details. Follow the instructions in the Readme file to copy the files to your server or standalone computer. You can view the Readme file using WordPad.

Once the files are copied, you can make Student Disks for the students yourself, or you can tell students where to find the files so they can make their own Student Disks. Make sure the files get correctly copied onto the Student Disks by following the instructions in the Student Disks section above, which will ensure that students have enough disk space to complete all the tutorials, Tutorial Assignments, Case Problems, and Additional Cases.

CTI STUDENT FILES

You are granted a license to copy the Student Files to any computer or computer network used by students who have purchased this book.

TUTORIAL 1

My Briefcase and Advanced Queries

Enhancing User Interaction with the Issue25 Database

OBJECTIVES

In this tutorial you will:

- Use Briefcase replication to create a Design Master and replica of a database
- Synchronize the Design Master and replica databases
- Create a crosstab query
- Create advanced select queries
- Create action queries
- Create a top value query
- Join a table using a self-join
- View SQL query statements

CASE

Vision Publishers

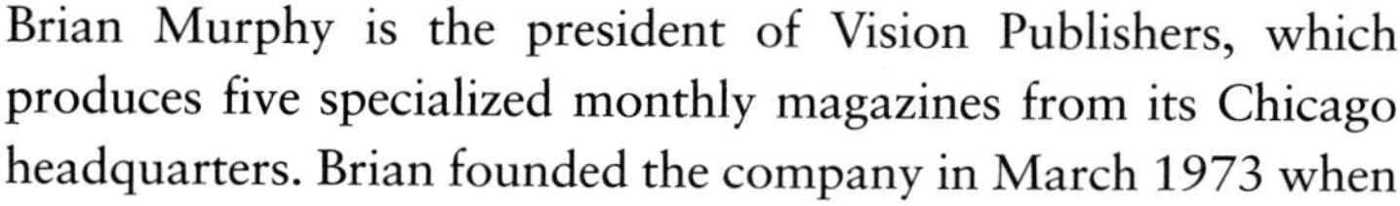

Brian Murphy is the president of Vision Publishers, which produces five specialized monthly magazines from its Chicago headquarters. Brian founded the company in March 1973 when he began publishing *Business Perspective*, a magazine featuring articles, editorials, interviews, and investigative reports that are widely respected in the financial and business communities. Using the concept, format, style, and strong writing of *Business Perspective* as a model, Brian began *Total Sports* in 1975, *Media Scene* in 1978, *Science Outlook* in 1984, and *Travel Vista* in 1987. All five magazines are leaders in their fields and have experienced consistent annual increases in circulation and advertising revenue.

In order to plan for the upcoming 25th anniversary of *Business Perspective,* Brian held a meeting with three key employees of the magazine, Judith Rossi, managing editor; Harold Larson, marketing director; and Elena Sanchez, special projects editor. After reviewing alternatives, they agreed they had to do something special to commemorate the event. They decided to create a special 25th-anniversary issue of *Business Perspective* that will include several articles reviewing the past 25 years of the magazine as well as the business and financial worlds during those years. Most of the special issue, however, will consist of articles from previous issues, a top article from each year of the magazine's existence. Brian's role will be to decide on the concept for the new articles and communicate assignments to the writers. The *Business Perspective* team expects to sign up many advertisers for the issue and to use it as an incentive bonus gift for new and renewing subscribers.

Since that meeting, Judith has been working with the Vision Publishers Microsoft Access 7 for Windows 95 database. It contains all articles published in the five magazines.

From this Vision database, Elena designed and created the Issue25 database, which includes four tables: BUSINESS ARTICLES, WRITERS, TYPES, and WRITER PAYMENTS. The BUSINESS ARTICLES table contains information about the articles chosen for the 25th-anniversary issue. The WRITERS table contains information about the writers of the articles chosen for the 25th-anniversary issue. The TYPES table is a list of the types of articles in the database. Finally, the WRITER PAYMENTS table contains records of payments made to writers for reprints of their articles.

Elena also created queries, forms, and reports that Brian, Judith, and Harold can use to select, view, and print records in the database and for Harold to use to contact advertisers and plan the marketing campaign.

Because the staff at Vision Publishers is using databases more and more in their work, Brian sends Elena to a one-week Access training seminar to learn many intermediate and advanced concepts and features of Access. The seminar will teach her about crosstab queries, advanced select queries, action queries, and SQL so that she can create more complex queries to answer important questions her team has been raising about the 25th-anniversary issue. Before leaving for the training seminar, Elena decides that she would like to take a copy of the Issue25 database with her. If she creates a copy with My Computer, her database will not include any changes made by her colleagues while she is away, nor will the changes she makes to her copy of the database be included in the original database. Therefore, Elena decides to create a Briefcase replica of the database.

SESSION 1.1

In this session, you will learn to use My Briefcase to make your database replicable, then you will create a Briefcase replica of a database. You will make changes to the data in the Briefcase replica and update the Design Master. You will then learn about advanced select queries available in Access: crosstab queries, find duplicates queries, and find unmatched queries.

Creating a Briefcase Replica Database

The My Briefcase feature of Access uses a special copy of a database called a **replica.** When you create a Briefcase replica of a database, the original copy of the database becomes the **Design Master**. The Design Master and all of its replicas are called the **replica set**. Access adds special tables and fields to the Design Master database to keep track of changes made to data and to the design of the database. Anyone using the Design Master can make changes to the design of database tables, queries, and other objects. Any changes in the data or design of database objects in the Design Master then can be automatically updated in the replica. Anyone using a replica of the database can make changes to the data in any of the database tables. A replica prevents the user from changing the structure or the design of an existing table, query, or other database object. Any changes in the data in any replicas can be automatically updated in the Design Master. The process of updating the Design Master and the replicas is called **synchronization**.

REFERENCE window

CREATING A BRIEFCASE REPLICA OF A DATABASE

- Drag the database file from the desktop into My Briefcase. Access converts the file, adding special tables, fields, and properties to create the Design Master. Access opens the Briefcase dialog box, allowing you to specify which copy of the database will become the Design Master.
- Select the copy you want to make the Design Master, then click the OK button.

Elena wants to be sure that while she is away, any changes that she or anyone else makes to the database will be updated, keeping the database accurate and current. Elena creates a replica of the Issue25 database. In the following steps, you will create a Briefcase replica of the Issue25 database, make changes to the data in the replica and then synchronize the Design Master with the replica. Because the Design Master is significantly larger than the original database, you should make a backup copy of your Student Disk containing the Tutorial folder and the Issue25 database on a blank formatted disk and use this backup copy for the Design Master. After you have learned how to create a Briefcase replica and synchronize the Design Master with the replica, you should not use the Design Master in the remainder of the tutorial—the Issue25 database will become too large for your disk. When you begin the section "Advanced Queries," follow the tutorial steps directing you to use your original Student Disk.

To create a replica of the Issue25 database:

1. Use My Computer to make a backup copy of the Student Disk containing the Tutorial folder and the Issue25 database. Use a separate disk for this backup copy. When you are finished, label the backup disk Design Master, and then place it in the disk drive.
2. On the Windows 95 desktop, use My Computer to open the Tutorial folder on your backup copy of the Student Disk.
3. Drag the Issue25 database file from the Tutorial folder to My Briefcase. Access begins making a replica copy of the Issue25 database and opens a dialog box asking if you want to continue. See Figure 1-1.

Figure 1-1 The first Briefcase dialog box

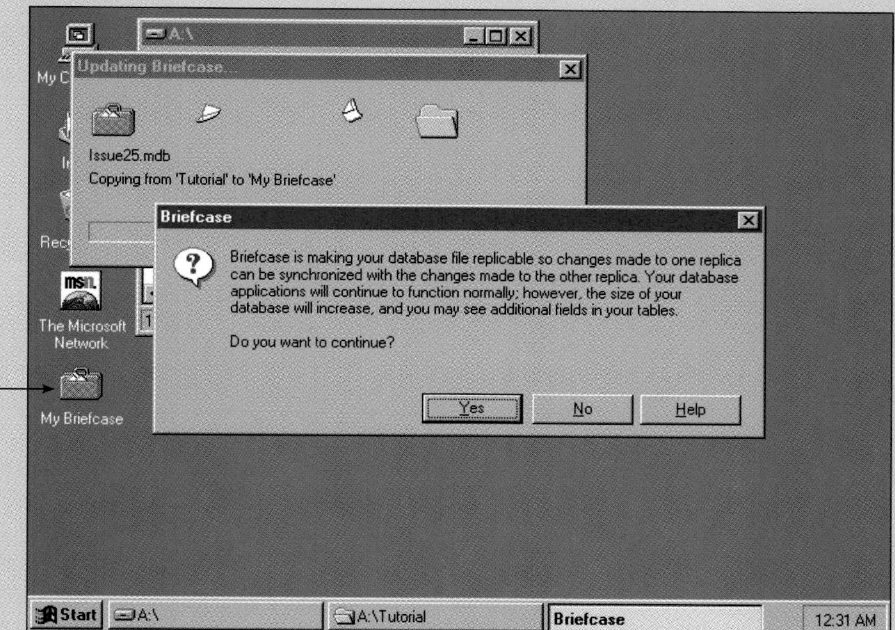

4. Click the **Yes** button. Access displays a dialog box asking if you want to make a backup copy of the Issue25 database. See Figure 1-2.

Figure 1-2 The next Briefcase dialog box

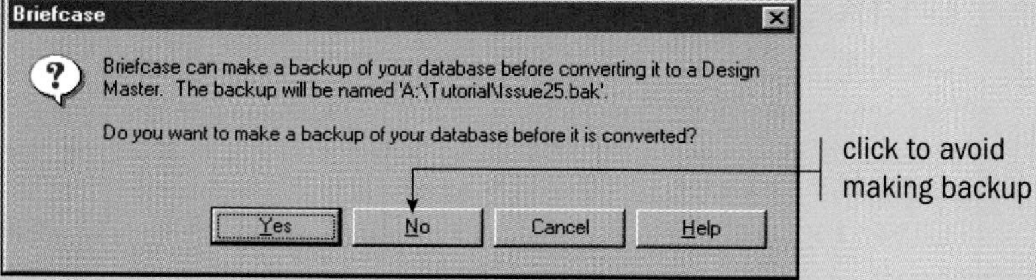

Access can make a backup copy of your database on your Student Disk. Because there is insufficient room on the Student Disk for a backup copy, however, you don't want Access to make a backup now.

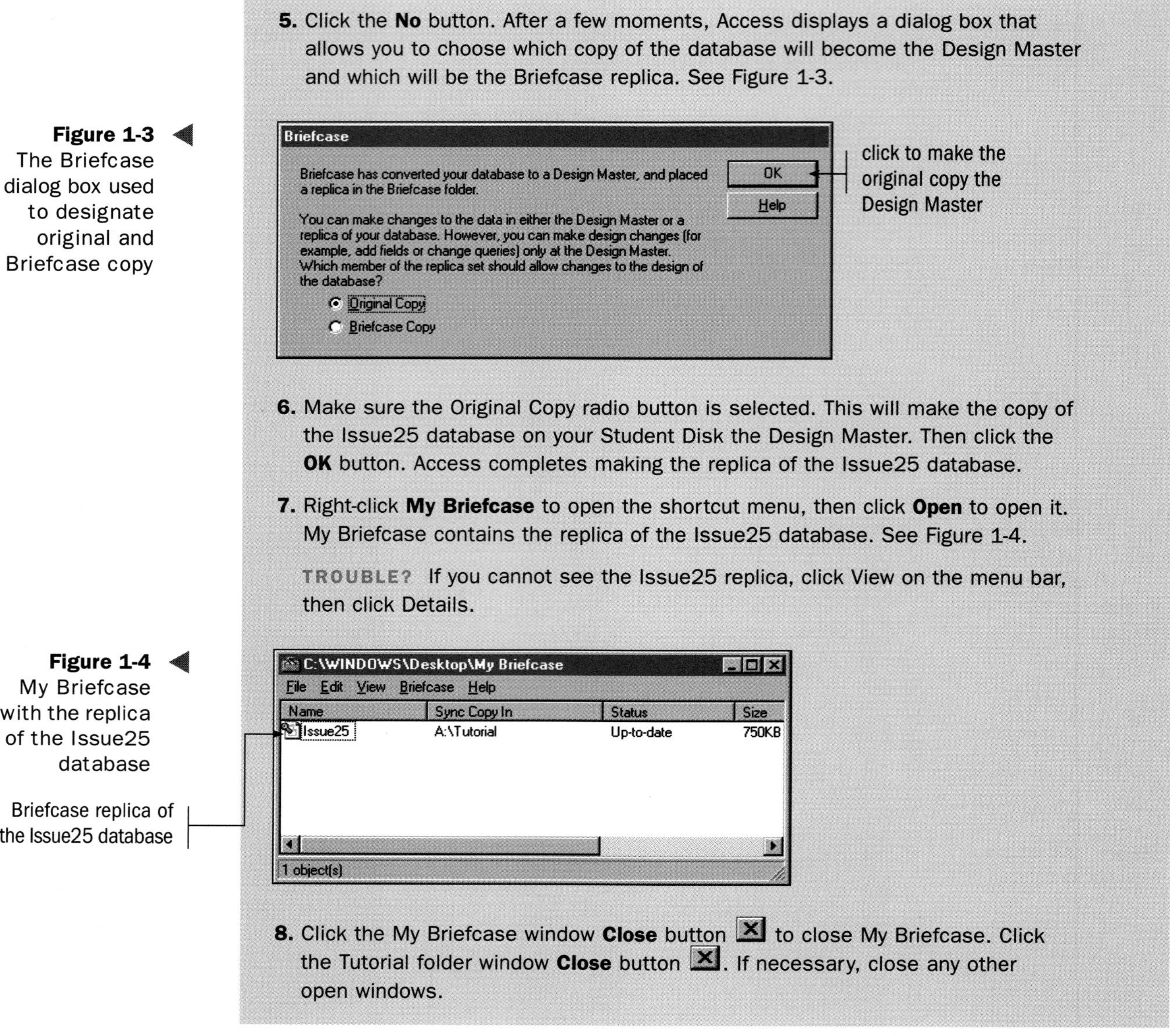

5. Click the **No** button. After a few moments, Access displays a dialog box that allows you to choose which copy of the database will become the Design Master and which will be the Briefcase replica. See Figure 1-3.

Figure 1-3 The Briefcase dialog box used to designate original and Briefcase copy

6. Make sure the Original Copy radio button is selected. This will make the copy of the Issue25 database on your Student Disk the Design Master. Then click the **OK** button. Access completes making the replica of the Issue25 database.

7. Right-click **My Briefcase** to open the shortcut menu, then click **Open** to open it. My Briefcase contains the replica of the Issue25 database. See Figure 1-4.

   TROUBLE? If you cannot see the Issue25 replica, click View on the menu bar, then click Details.

Figure 1-4 My Briefcase with the replica of the Issue25 database

8. Click the My Briefcase window **Close** button to close My Briefcase. Click the Tutorial folder window **Close** button. If necessary, close any other open windows.

Elena copies the Briefcase replica of the Issue25 database to a floppy disk and takes it with her to the training seminar.

Synchronizing the Replica and the Design Master

While she is at the training seminar, Elena receives a call from Judith who says that she has selected a new article for the 25th-anniversary issue of *Business Perspective*. It is the article Brian requested to round out the coverage of recent stock market trends.

Judith asks Elena to make sure that this new record is entered in the BUSINESS ARTICLES table. Elena replies that she can add the new record to the Briefcase replica database and then update the Design Master when she returns to the office.

To add the new record to the Briefcase replica of the Issue25 database:

1. Start Access. In the Microsoft Access dialog box, make sure that the radio button next to Open an Existing Database is selected and that More Files is highlighted, then click the **OK** button. Access displays the Open dialog box.

2. Click the **Look in** list arrow, then click **My Briefcase** to select it. Make sure Issue25 is selected in the files list, then click the **Open** button. Access opens the Issue25 database replica and displays the Database window. See Figure 1-5.

Figure 1-5 The Database window for the Issue25 database replica

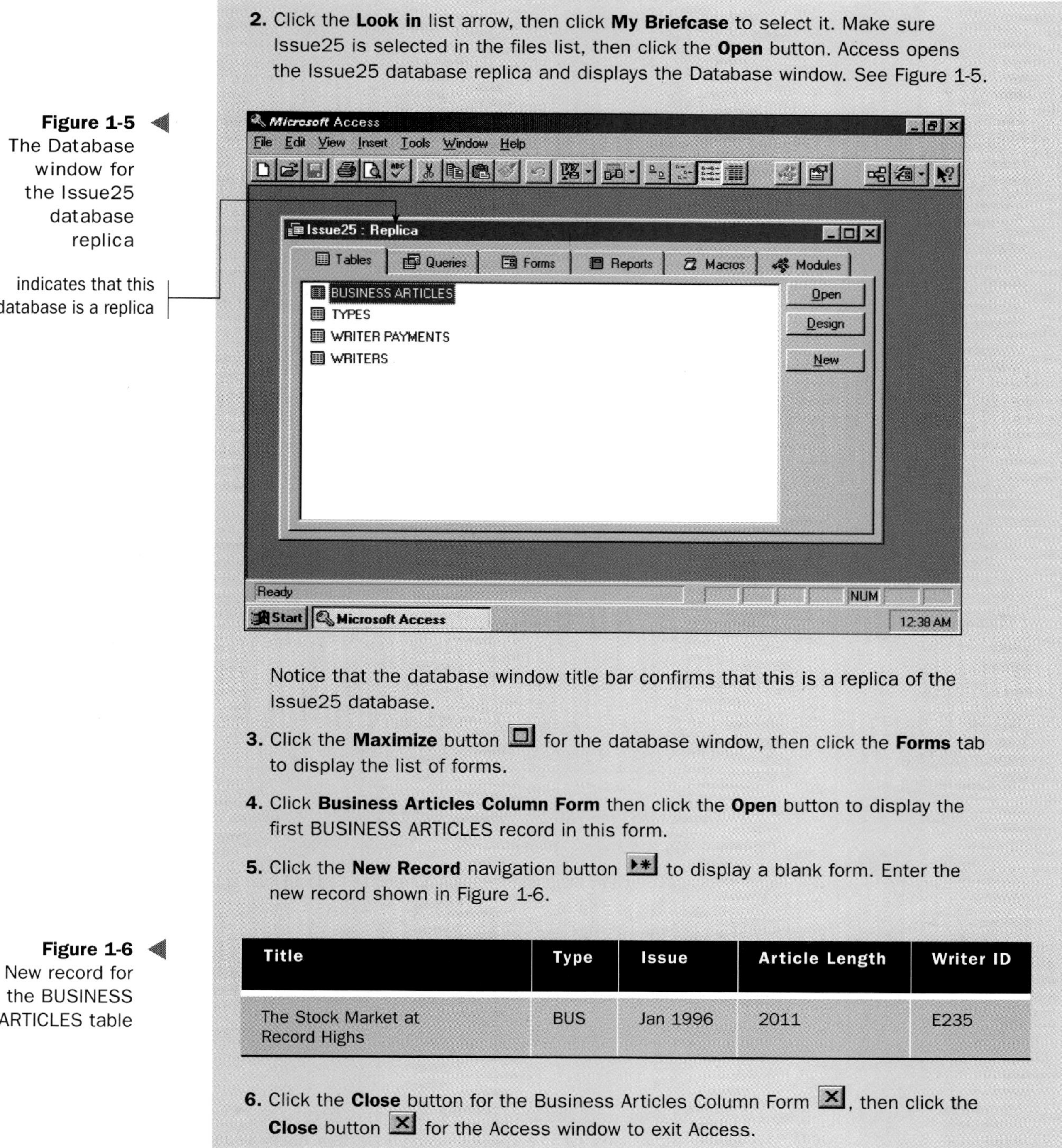

Notice that the database window title bar confirms that this is a replica of the Issue25 database.

3. Click the **Maximize** button for the database window, then click the **Forms** tab to display the list of forms.

4. Click **Business Articles Column Form** then click the **Open** button to display the first BUSINESS ARTICLES record in this form.

5. Click the **New Record** navigation button to display a blank form. Enter the new record shown in Figure 1-6.

Figure 1-6 New record for the BUSINESS ARTICLES table

Title	Type	Issue	Article Length	Writer ID
The Stock Market at Record Highs	BUS	Jan 1996	2011	E235

6. Click the **Close** button for the Business Articles Column Form, then click the **Close** button for the Access window to exit Access.

The Briefcase replica of the Issue25 database now contains a new record that is not recorded in the Design Master. When she returns from the training seminar, Elena updates the Design Master by synchronizing the Design Master and the replica. Synchronizing ensures that the Design Master and the replica are consistent. It does this by comparing the Design Master to the replica and checking for any differences. Access updates the Design Master with any changes that have been made to the data in the replica. Access updates the replica with any changes that have been made to the data or to the design of any database objects in the Design Master.

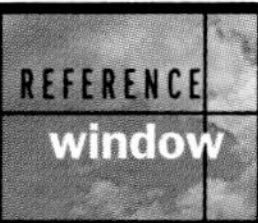

SYNCHRONIZING THE DESIGN MASTER AND A REPLICA

- Open one copy of the database (either the Design Master or the replica) that has not been updated.
- Click Tools on the menu bar, point to Replication and then click Synchronize Now. Access displays the Synchronize Database dialog box.
- In the Synchronize with text box, enter the name of the database copy that you want to synchronize with.
- Click the OK button. Access synchronizes the two databases and displays a confirming message.

To synchronize the Design Master and the replica:

1. Start Access, open the Issue25 Design Master in the Tutorial folder on your Student Disk, and maximize the Database window. Notice that the title bar of the Database window shows that this copy of the Issue25 database is the Design Master.
2. Click **Tools** on the menu bar, point to **Replication**, and then click **Synchronize Now**. Access displays the Synchronize Database 'Issue25' dialog box. See Figure 1-7.

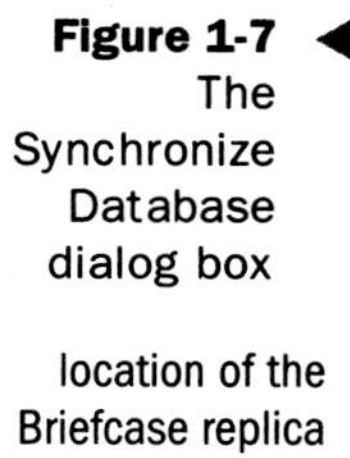
Figure 1-7 The Synchronize Database dialog box

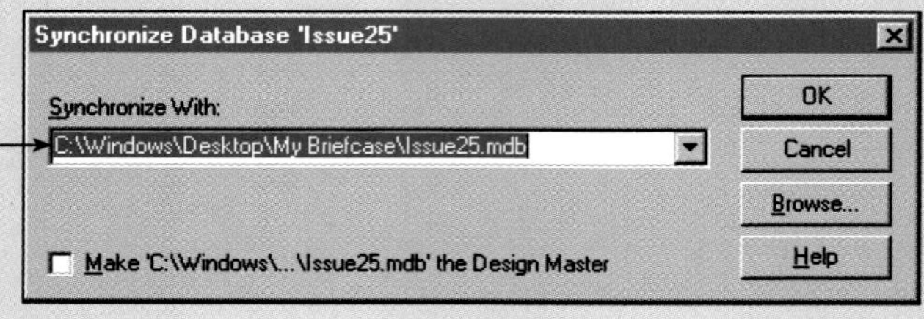

3. If the Synchronize With text box does not display the name of the Issue25 replica in the Briefcase, use the Browse button to select the Issue25 replica in the Briefcase.

   TROUBLE? The path statement in the Synchronize With text box on your screen may not match the one in the figure. Be sure that it is accurate for your system and the location of your database files.

4. Click the **OK** button. After a few seconds Access displays a dialog box indicating that the synchronization is complete.
5. Click the **Yes** button to close and reopen the Issue25 database.

The Design Master and the replica are now synchronized. The new record that Elena added to the replica copy of the Issue25 database has been added to the Design Master. Elena opens the BUSINESS ARTICLES table using the Business Articles Column Form and displays the new record in the Design Master.

To find and display the new record in the BUSINESS ARTICLES table:

1. Click the **Forms** tab to display the list of forms. Click **Business Articles Column Form**, then click the **Open** button to open the form. Access displays the first BUSINESS ARTICLES record in the form.
2. Click the **Filter by Form** button on the toolbar to display the Filter by Form window. Since the new article was written by Diane Epstein (Writer ID E235), you can use her Writer ID to locate the article.

3. Click the **Clear Grid** button to clear any existing conditions. This also clears any criteria on the OR pages. Click the **Writer ID** list arrow, and then click **E235**. See Figure 1-8.

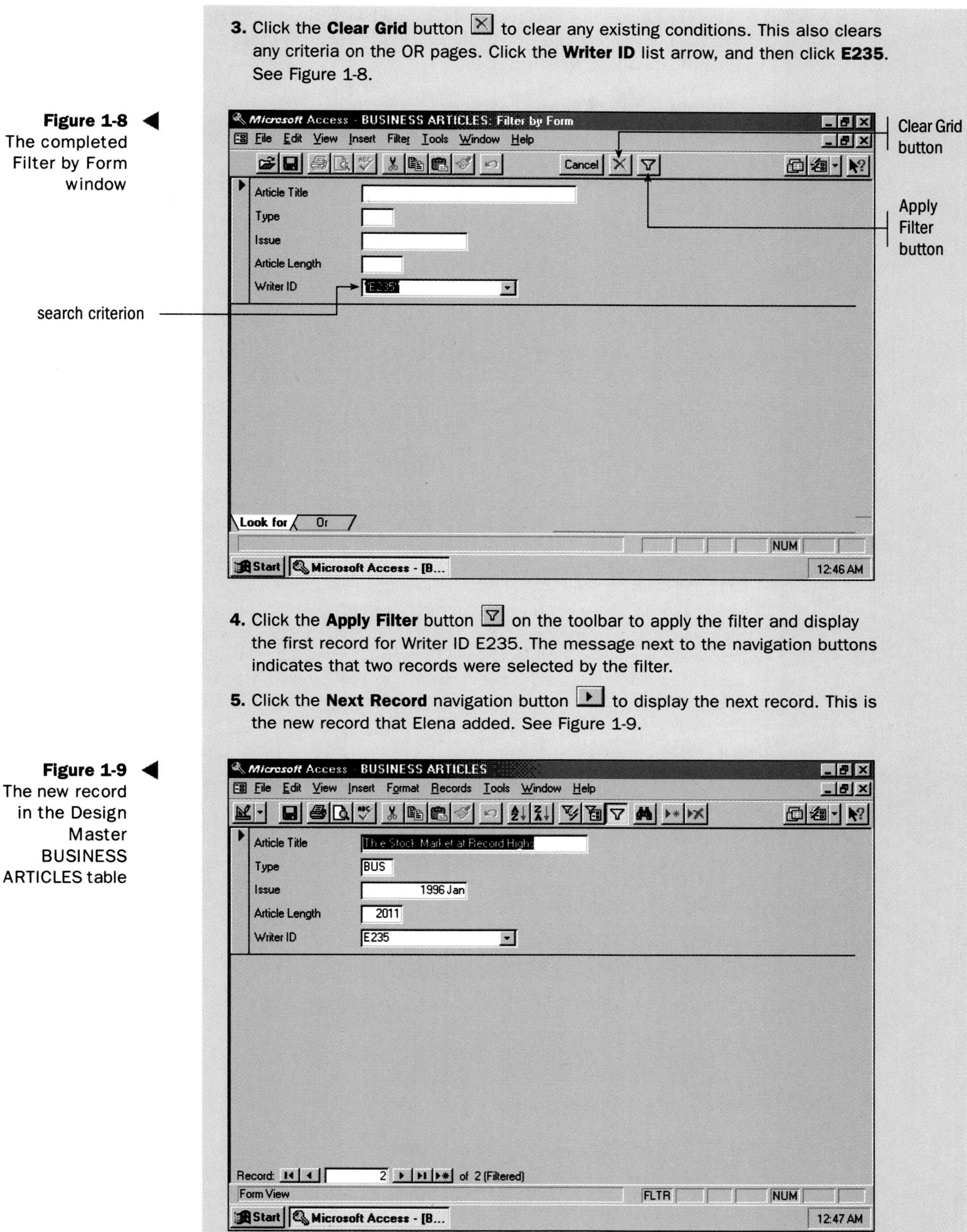

Figure 1-8 The completed Filter by Form window

4. Click the **Apply Filter** button on the toolbar to apply the filter and display the first record for Writer ID E235. The message next to the navigation buttons indicates that two records were selected by the filter.

5. Click the **Next Record** navigation button to display the next record. This is the new record that Elena added. See Figure 1-9.

Figure 1-9 The new record in the Design Master BUSINESS ARTICLES table

6. Click the **Remove Filter** button on the toolbar to remove the filter, then click the Form window **Close** button to close the form and return to the Database window.

Now that Elena has synchronized the databases, she deletes the Briefcase replica of the Issue25 database. She knows that she can easily create another replica whenever she needs to take the database with her again.

To delete the Briefcase replica of the Issue25 database:

1. Click the Access window **Close** button [X] to close Access.
2. Right-click **My Briefcase**, click **Open**, and then click the **Issue25** database to select it.
3. Click **File**, then click **Delete**. Windows 95 displays the Confirm File Delete dialog box.

   TROUBLE? If the Briefcase contains the file ISSUE25.LDB, be sure to delete it also.
4. Click the **Yes** button to delete the Briefcase replica of the Issue25 database. Windows 95 moves the Briefcase replica of the Issue25 database to the Recycle Bin.
5. Click the My Briefcase **Close** button [X] to close My Briefcase.

Elena is ready to use the new skills she learned at the training seminar. She begins by designing several advanced queries.

Advanced Queries

The Issue25 database contains select queries that use selection criteria, sorts, calculations, table joins, and parameters. These select queries were created either in the Query Design window or with the Simple Query Wizard. Elena can easily create more complicated queries that address specific needs by using the three other Access query wizards: the Crosstab Query Wizard, the Find Duplicates Query Wizard, and the Find Unmatched Query Wizard.

Figure 1-10 Aggregate functions used in crosstab queries

Aggregate Function	Meaning
Avg	Average of the field values
Count	Number of non-empty field values
First	First field value
Last	Last field value
Min	Lowest field value
Max	Highest field value
StDev	Standard deviation of the field values
Sum	Total of the field values
Var	Variance of the field values

The **Crosstab Query Wizard** guides you through the steps for creating crosstab queries. A crosstab query performs aggregate function calculations on the values of one database field and displays the results in a spreadsheet format. (Recall that aggregate functions perform arithmetic operations on the records in a database.) Figure 1-10 lists the aggregate functions you can use in a crosstab query. A crosstab query can also display one additional aggregate-function value that summarizes each row's set of values. The crosstab query uses one or more fields for the row headings on the left and one field for the column headings at the top.

Figure 1-11 shows two query results, the first from a select query and the second from a related crosstab query. The title bar indicates the type of query. Both queries use the query titled Article Type Query that joins the WRITERS and BUSINESS ARTICLES tables, but the crosstab query gives more valuable information. For each record in the BUSINESS ARTICLES table, the select query displays the Writer ID, the Last Name and First Name fields from the WRITERS table and the Type and Article Length fields from the BUSINESS ARTICLES table.

There are, for example, several rows for Wilhelm Seeger—one row for each article he wrote. Some may not be currently visible on the screen. On the other hand, the crosstab query displays just one row for Wilhelm Seeger. The Last Name and First Name fields in the leftmost columns identify each row, and the field values for the Type field identify the rightmost columns. The crosstab query uses the Sum aggregate function on the Article Length field to produce the displayed values in the remainder of the query results. The fourth column, labeled Writer Total, represents the total of the Article Length values for each row.

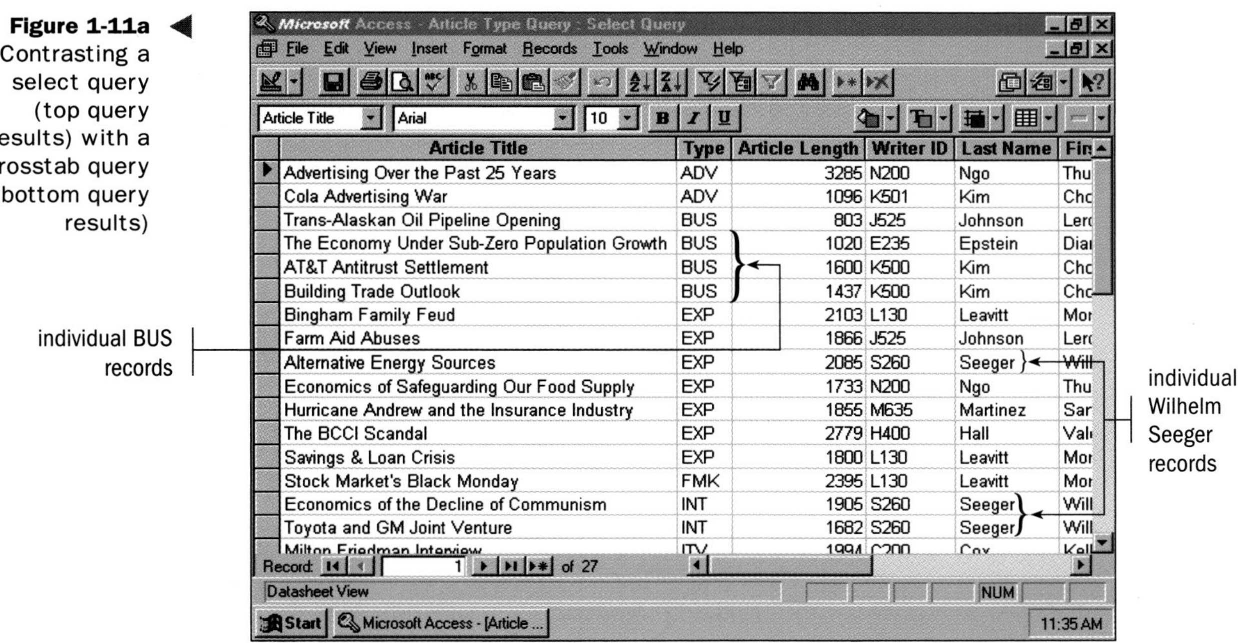

Article Title	Type	Article Length	Writer ID	Last Name	Fir
Advertising Over the Past 25 Years	ADV	3285	N200	Ngo	Thu
Cola Advertising War	ADV	1096	K501	Kim	Chc
Trans-Alaskan Oil Pipeline Opening	BUS	803	J525	Johnson	Ler
The Economy Under Sub-Zero Population Growth	BUS	1020	E235	Epstein	Dia
AT&T Antitrust Settlement	BUS	1600	K500	Kim	Chc
Building Trade Outlook	BUS	1437	K500	Kim	Chc
Bingham Family Feud	EXP	2103	L130	Leavitt	Mor
Farm Aid Abuses	EXP	1866	J525	Johnson	Ler
Alternative Energy Sources	EXP	2085	S260	Seeger	Wil
Economics of Safeguarding Our Food Supply	EXP	1733	N200	Ngo	Thu
Hurricane Andrew and the Insurance Industry	EXP	1855	M635	Martinez	Sar
The BCCI Scandal	EXP	2779	H400	Hall	Val
Savings & Loan Crisis	EXP	1800	L130	Leavitt	Mor
Stock Market's Black Monday	FMK	2395	L130	Leavitt	Mor
Economics of the Decline of Communism	INT	1905	S260	Seeger	Will
Toyota and GM Joint Venture	INT	1682	S260	Seeger	Will
Milton Friedman Interview	ITV	1994	C200	Cox	Kell

Figure 1-11a Contrasting a select query (top query results) with a crosstab query (bottom query results)

Figure 1-11b

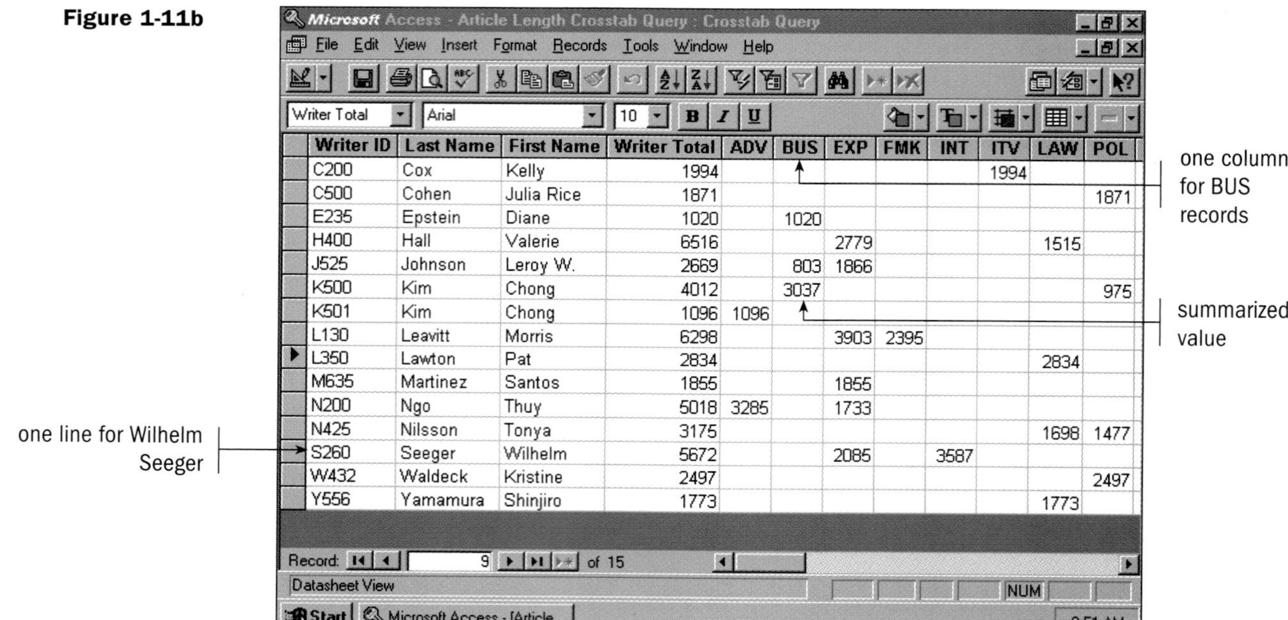

Writer ID	Last Name	First Name	Writer Total	ADV	BUS	EXP	FMK	INT	ITV	LAW	POL
C200	Cox	Kelly	1994						1994		
C500	Cohen	Julia Rice	1871								1871
E235	Epstein	Diane	1020		1020						
H400	Hall	Valerie	6516			2779				1515	
J525	Johnson	Leroy W.	2669		803	1866					
K500	Kim	Chong	4012		3037						975
K501	Kim	Chong	1096	1096							
L130	Leavitt	Morris	6298			3903	2395				
L350	Lawton	Pat	2834							2834	
M635	Martinez	Santos	1855			1855					
N200	Ngo	Thuy	5018	3285		1733					
N425	Nilsson	Tonya	3175							1698	1477
S260	Seeger	Wilhelm	5672			2085		3587			
W432	Waldeck	Kristine	2497								2497
Y556	Yamamura	Shinjiro	1773							1773	

The **Find Duplicates Query Wizard** creates a select query that locates duplicate records in a table or query. The query searches for duplicates based on the fields you choose as you answer the wizard's questions. For example, you might want to display all customers who live at the same address, all students who have the same phone number, all products that have the same description, or all writers who have the same names. Using this query, you can locate duplicates and avert potential problems (for example, you might have inadvertently assigned two different numbers to the same product), or you can eliminate duplicates that cost you money (for example, you could send just one advertising brochure to all the customers having the same address).

The **Find Unmatched Query Wizard** creates a select query that finds all the records in a table or query that have no related records in a second table or query. For example, you could display all customers who have not placed orders, all non-degree students who are not currently enrolled in classes, or all writers who have not written articles. This query might help you solicit business from the inactive customers, contact the students to find out their future educational plans, or delete the non-producing writers from your database.

Elena wants to practice the skills she learned at the seminar, so she spends the afternoon using the query wizards to create new queries that will answer questions her team has raised.

Creating a Crosstab Query

In planning for the special 25th-anniversary issue of *Business Perspective*, Elena must balance the total length of articles among the different types of articles, such as political and advertising, and among the featured writers. Elena creates a crosstab query using the Crosstab Query Wizard to provide the needed information.

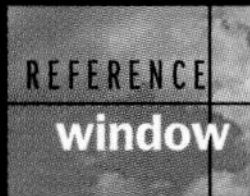

USING THE CROSSTAB QUERY WIZARD

- Click the Queries tab to display the Queries list, then click the New button. Access displays the New Query window.
- Click Crosstab Query Wizard to select it, then click the OK button to start the Crosstab Query Wizard.
- Click the Tables, Queries, or Both radio button to display the corresponding objects in the list box. In the list box click the name of the table or query that will be the basis for the crosstab query and then click the Next > button.
- Select the row heading field or fields and then click the Next > button.
- Click the column heading field and then click the Next > button.
- Click the calculation field and then click its aggregate function. Turn on the Calculate Summary for Each Row check box if you want a row-summary column or click it off if you do not. Finally, click the Next > button.
- Type the new query name in the text box and then click the Finish button to save and run the query.

The crosstab query Elena creates is similar to the one shown in Figure 1-11. Elena's crosstab query has the following characteristics:

- The Article Type Query in the Tutorial folder of your Student Disk is the basis for the new crosstab query; it includes the fields named Article Title, Type, Article Length, Last Name, and First Name. Before creating the crosstab query, Elena modifies the query Article Type Query to include the Writer ID field.
- The Writer ID, Last Name, and First Name fields from the WRITERS table are the leftmost columns and identify each crosstab-query row. If two writers have the same first and last names, as do the two Chong Kims, then they are separated into two rows so Elena can balance articles and writers.
- The field values that appear in the BUSINESS ARTICLES table for the Type field identify the rightmost columns of the crosstab query.
- The crosstab query applies the Sum aggregate function to the Article Length field from the BUSINESS ARTICLES table and displays the resulting total values in the Article Type columns of the query results. If one writer has two or more articles of the same type, then the sum of the article lengths appears in the intersecting cell of the query results.
- The Calculate Summary for Each Row check box is turned on in the Crosstab Query Wizard so that the total of the Article Length values for each row appears. The default name for this column is changed to Writer Total.

Elena begins by adding the Writer ID field to the Article Type Query.

To add the Writer ID field to the Article Type Query:

1. Place your original Student Disk containing the Tutorial folder in the disk drive. Do not use the Design Master disk you created earlier.
2. Start Access, open the Issue25 database in the Tutorial folder of your Student Disk, then maximize the Database window.

3. Click the **Queries** tab to display the Queries list. Click **Article Type Query**, then click the **Design** button. Access opens the Query Design window.
4. Click **Writer ID** in the WRITERS field list and drag it to the Last Name field column in the Query Design grid. Release the mouse button. Access places the Writer ID field before the Last Name field in the Query Design grid.
5. Click the **Save** button on the toolbar to save the query, then click the Query Design window **Close** button. Access closes the Query Design window and displays the Database window.

Elena is now ready to create the crosstab query based on the modified Article Type Query.

To create a crosstab query using the Crosstab Query Wizard:

1. Click the **New** button to open the New Query dialog box.
2. Click **Crosstab Query Wizard**, and then click the **OK** button. The first Crosstab Query Wizard dialog box opens.
3. Click the **Queries** radio button to display a list of the queries in the Issue25 database and then click **Article Type Query** in the list box. See Figure 1-12.

Figure 1-12 Choosing the table or query for a crosstab query

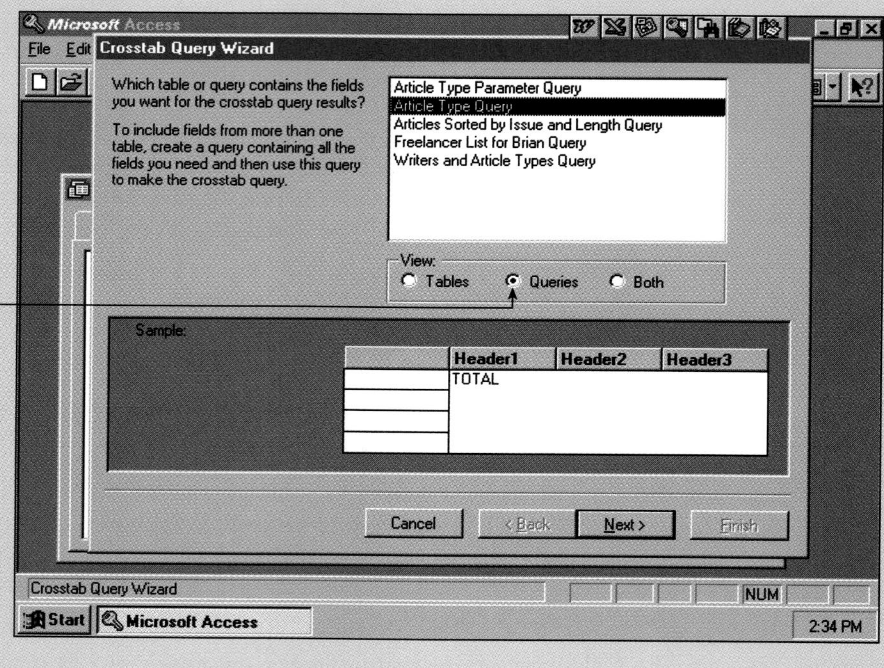

4. Click the Next > button to choose the fields for the row headings in the next Crosstab Query Wizard dialog box.
5. In the Available Fields list box, click **Writer ID**, then click the > button to move Writer ID to the Selected Fields list box. Click **Last Name**, then click the > button to move Last Name to the Selected Fields list box. Click **First Name**, then click the > button to move First Name to the Selected Fields list box. As you select a field, Access changes the sample crosstab query in the bottom of the dialog box to illustrate your choice.
6. Click the Next > button to open the next Crosstab Query Wizard dialog box, in which you select the field values that serve as column headings.

7. Click **Type** in the list box to select it as the column-headings field and then click the Next > button. In the next Crosstab Query Wizard dialog box, you choose the field that will be calculated for each row and column intersection and the function to use for the calculation. The results of the calculation will appear in the middle of the query results.

8. Click **Article Length** in the Fields list box and then click **Sum** in the Functions list box. Be sure that the check box next to Yes, include row sums is selected. See Figure 1-13.

Figure 1-13
The completed crosstab query design

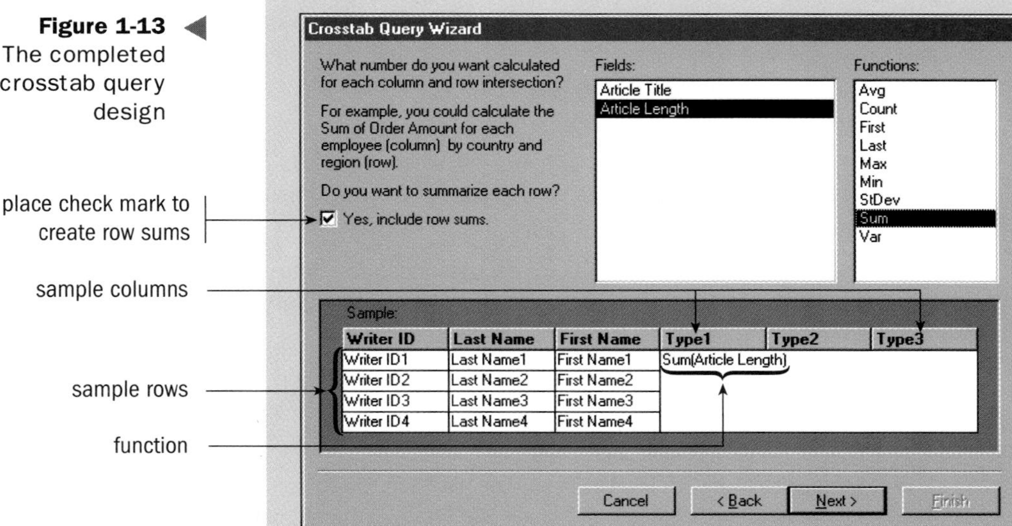

9. Click the Next > button to open the Crosstab Query Wizard dialog box in which you choose the query name. Type **Article Length Crosstab Query** in the text box, be sure the View the query radio button is selected, and then click the **Finish** button. Access saves the crosstab query and, after a short pause, displays the query results. See Figure 1-14.

Figure 1-14
The crosstab query results

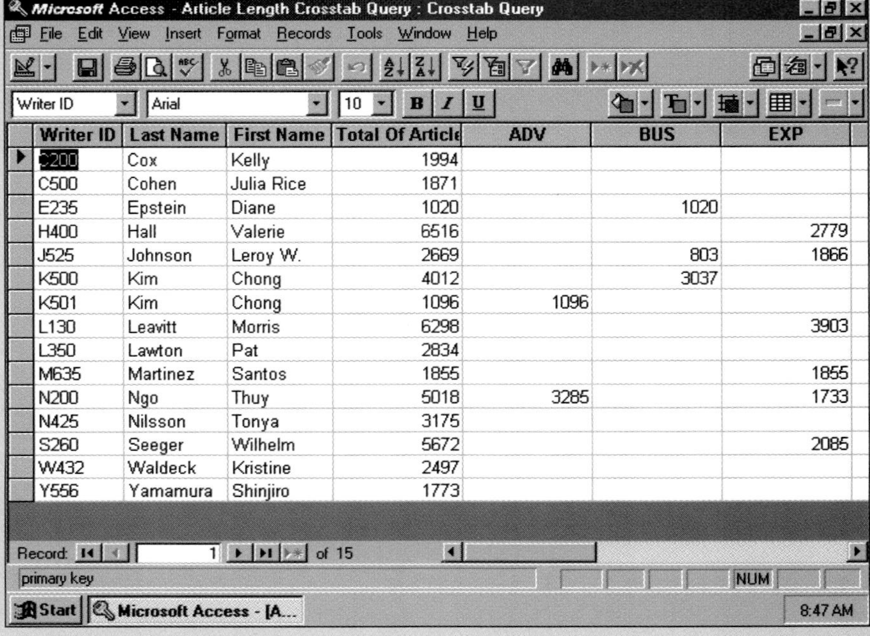

Writer ID	Last Name	First Name	Total Of Articl	ADV	BUS	EXP
S200	Cox	Kelly	1994			
C500	Cohen	Julia Rice	1871			
E235	Epstein	Diane	1020		1020	
H400	Hall	Valerie	6516			2779
J525	Johnson	Leroy W.	2669		803	1866
K500	Kim	Chong	4012		3037	
K501	Kim	Chong	1096	1096		
L130	Leavitt	Morris	6298			3903
L350	Lawton	Pat	2834			
M635	Martinez	Santos	1855			1855
N200	Ngo	Thuy	5018	3285		1733
N425	Nilsson	Tonya	3175			
S260	Seeger	Wilhelm	5672			2085
W432	Waldeck	Kristine	2497			
Y556	Yamamura	Shinjiro	1773			

Elena wants to change the fourth column heading to Writer Total. Also, many of the column widths in the query results are wider than necessary, so she wants to resize them. She will make the first change in the Query Design window and the second change in the query results window.

To rename and resize the query results columns:

1. Click the **Query View** button on the toolbar to switch to the Query Design window.

2. If necessary, scroll to the right until the sixth column is visible. Notice that the field name, Total of Article Length, is truncated. Place the pointer on the right edge of the column selector for the fifth column. When the pointer turns to ✛, click and drag the pointer to the right until the entire field name, Total of Article Length, is visible.

3. Highlight **Total of Article Length** and then type **Writer Total**. Be sure you do not delete the colon that separates the query results column name, Writer Total, from the table field name, Article Length.

4. Click the **Run** button on the toolbar. Access opens the query results and shows Writer Total instead of Total of Article Length as the query results column name.

5. Move the mouse pointer to the Writer ID column selector. When it changes to ⬇, click and drag the pointer to the right, scrolling until all columns are highlighted, and then release the mouse button.

6. Move the mouse pointer to the right edge of any highlighted column selector. When it changes to ✛, right-click to open the shortcut menu, click **Column Width**, then click the **Best Fit** button to resize all highlighted columns to their best fits. Click anywhere in the query results to remove the highlighting. See Figure 1-15.

Figure 1-15 ◀
The resized crosstab query results columns

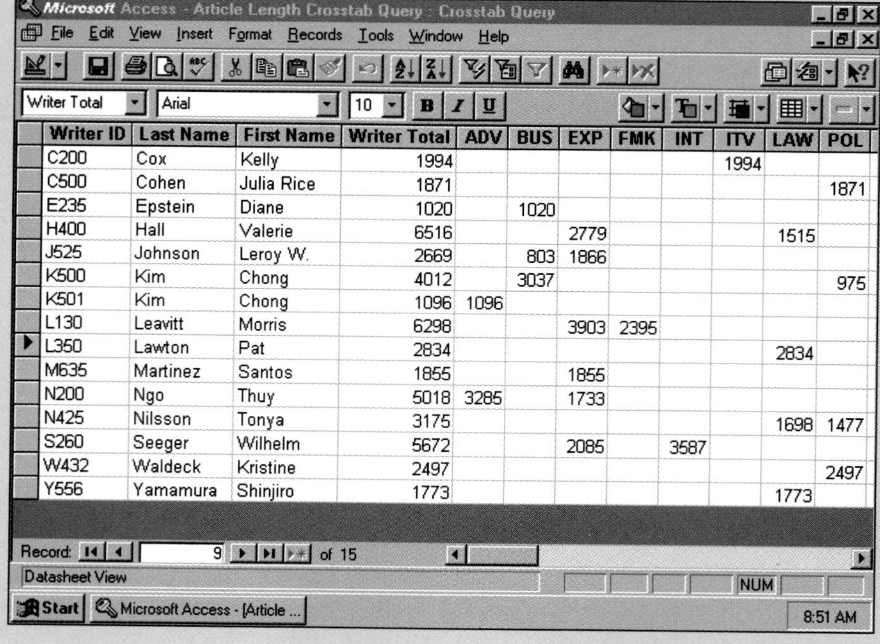

Writer ID	Last Name	First Name	Writer Total	ADV	BUS	EXP	FMK	INT	ITV	LAW	POL
C200	Cox	Kelly	1994						1994		
C500	Cohen	Julia Rice	1871								1871
E235	Epstein	Diane	1020		1020						
H400	Hall	Valerie	6516			2779				1515	
J525	Johnson	Leroy W.	2669		803	1866					
K500	Kim	Chong	4012		3037						975
K501	Kim	Chong	1096	1096							
L130	Leavitt	Morris	6298			3903	2395				
L350	Lawton	Pat	2834							2834	
M635	Martinez	Santos	1855			1855					
N200	Ngo	Thuy	5018	3285		1733					
N425	Nilsson	Tonya	3175							1698	1477
S260	Seeger	Wilhelm	5672			2085		3587			
W432	Waldeck	Kristine	2497								2497
Y556	Yamamura	Shinjiro	1773							1773	

Elena closes the completed query results. Because this query result shows the number of words for each type and each writer, Elena can use the information to balance the total length of articles among the types of articles and writers.

To close the query results:

1. Click the Article Length Query Crosstab Query window **Close** button.
2. Click the **Yes** button to close the dialog box, save the query, and return to the Database window.

Access uses unique icons to represent the select and parameter queries, the crosstab query, and each of the four action queries. The icon appearing in the Queries list box to the left of Article Length Crosstab Query is different from the icon for the select and parameter queries.

Using the Crosstab Query Wizard is the quickest way to create a crosstab query. Alternatively, you can change a select query to a crosstab query by clicking the toolbar Query Type button in the Query Design window and selecting Crosstab Query. In response, Access changes the title bar from Select Query to Crosstab Query and adds Total and Crosstab rows to the Query Design grid between the Field and the Sort rows. For more details on this more complicated method, open the Help Index, type crosstab queries, click Display, and then go to the topic: Create a crosstab query that summarizes data without using a wizard.

Creating a Find Duplicates Query

Elena wants to be sure that Chong Kim is the only duplicate writer name, so she uses the Find Duplicates Query Wizard to display writers having the same names. She uses the WRITERS table as the basis for this query, selects records that have duplicate values for both the Last Name and First Name fields, and displays all fields from the WRITERS table.

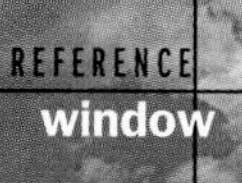

USING THE FIND DUPLICATES QUERY WIZARD

- Click the Queries tab to display the Queries list, then click the New button. Access displays the New Query window.
- Click Find Duplicates Query Wizard to select it, then click the OK button to start the Find Duplicates Query Wizard.
- Click the Tables, Queries, or Both radio button to display the corresponding objects in the list box, click the name of the table or query that will be the basis for the query, and then click the Next > button.
- Select the field or fields you want checked for duplicate values and then click the Next > button.
- Select the additional fields you want to see in the query results and then click the Next > button.
- Type the new query name in the text box and then click the Finish button to save and run the query.

Elena uses the Find Duplicates Query Wizard to create and run a new query to check for duplicate writer names.

To create a query using the Find Duplicates Query Wizard:

1. If necessary, click the **Queries** tab to display the Queries list, then click the **New** button to open the New Query dialog box.
2. Click **Find Duplicates Query Wizard**, and then click the **OK** button. The Find Duplicates Query Wizard dialog box opens.

TROUBLE? If Access notifies you that the Find Duplicates Query Wizard is not installed, see your technical support person to have it installed.

3. Click **WRITERS** in the list box to select this table as the basis for the query and then click the Next > button. Access opens the next Find Duplicates Query Wizard dialog box, in which you choose the fields you want checked for duplicate values.

4. In the Available fields list box, click **Last Name**, then click the > button, click **First Name**, then click the > button to select these fields to be checked for duplicate values.

5. Click the Next > button to open the Find Duplicates Query Wizard dialog box in which you select the additional fields you want displayed in the query results. You choose to display all the remaining fields in the WRITERS table.

6. Click the >> button to select all remaining fields from the WRITERS table. Access moves all fields listed in the Available fields list box to the Additional query fields list box.

7. Click the Next > button to open the final Find Duplicates Query Wizard dialog box in which you choose the query name.

8. Type **Duplicate Writers Name Query** in the text box, be sure the View the results radio button is selected, and then click the **Finish** button. Access saves the query and, after a short pause, displays the query results for the select query, as shown in Figure 1-16. Access displays the records with duplicate names for the two writers named Chong Kim.

Figure 1-16 The query results for the Duplicate Writers Name Query

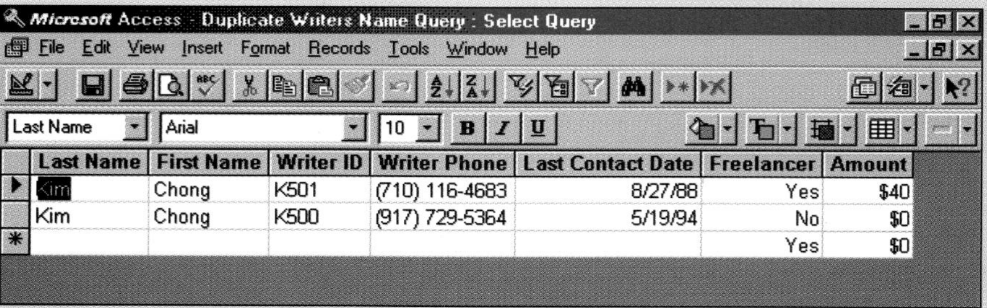

Last Name	First Name	Writer ID	Writer Phone	Last Contact Date	Freelancer	Amount
Kim	Chong	K501	(710) 116-4683	8/27/88	Yes	$40
Kim	Chong	K500	(917) 729-5364	5/19/94	No	$0
					Yes	$0

9. Click the Duplicate Writers Name Query window **Close** button to close the query results and return to the Database window.

Elena has confirmed that the two Chong Kims are the only writers in her database with the same name.

Creating a Find Unmatched Query

Elena wants to be sure that all article types are represented in the BUSINESS ARTICLES table. She uses the Find Unmatched Query Wizard to display the Type and Description fields from the TYPES table, but only when there are no records in the BUSINESS ARTICLES table having that Type field value.

USING THE FIND UNMATCHED QUERY WIZARD

- Click the Queries tab to display the Queries list, then click the New button. Access displays the New Query window.
- Click Find Unmatched Query Wizard to select it, then click the OK button to start the Find Unmatched Query Wizard.
- Click the Tables, Queries, or Both radio button to display the corresponding objects in the list box. In the list box, click the name of the table or query that contains the records you want to see in the query results and then click the Next > button.
- Click the Tables, Queries, or Both radio button to display the corresponding objects in the list box. Click the name of the table or query that contains the related records and then click the Next > button.
- Click the common field in each table or query, click the <=> button, and then click the Next > button.
- Select the fields you want to see in the query results and then click the Next > button.
- Type the new query name in the text box and then click the Finish button to save and run the query.

Elena uses the Find Unmatched Query Wizard to create and run a new query to identify the article types for which no articles have been selected for the special issue.

To create a query using the Find Unmatched Query Wizard:

1. If necessary, click the **Queries** tab to display the Queries list, then click the **New** button to open the New Query dialog box.
2. Click **Find Unmatched Query Wizard**, and then click the **OK** button. The first Find Unmatched Query Wizard dialog box opens.
3. Click **TYPES** in the list box to select this table—its records will appear in the query results. Then click the Next > button to open the Find Unmatched Query Wizard dialog box to choose the table that contains the related records.
4. Click **BUSINESS ARTICLES** in the list box and then click the Next > button to open the Find Unmatched Query Wizard dialog box in which you choose the common field for both tables.
5. Click **Type** in each list box and then click the <=> button. Access shows the Matching fields as 'Type <=> Type'.
6. Click the Next > button to open the Find Unmatched Query Wizard dialog box in which you choose the fields you want to see in the query results.
7. Click the >> button to select all fields from the TYPES table. Access moves all fields listed in the Available fields list box to the Selected fields list box.
8. Click the Next > button to open the final Find Unmatched Query Wizard dialog box in which you enter the query name.
9. Type **Types Without Matching Business Articles Query**, be sure the View the results radio button is turned on, and then click the **Finish** button. Access saves the query and, after a short pause, displays the query results. The query created by the Find Unmatched Query Wizard is a select query. See Figure 1-17. Access displays the Monetary and Statistical article type codes and descriptions in the query results.

Figure 1-17
The results for the Types Without Matching Business Articles Query

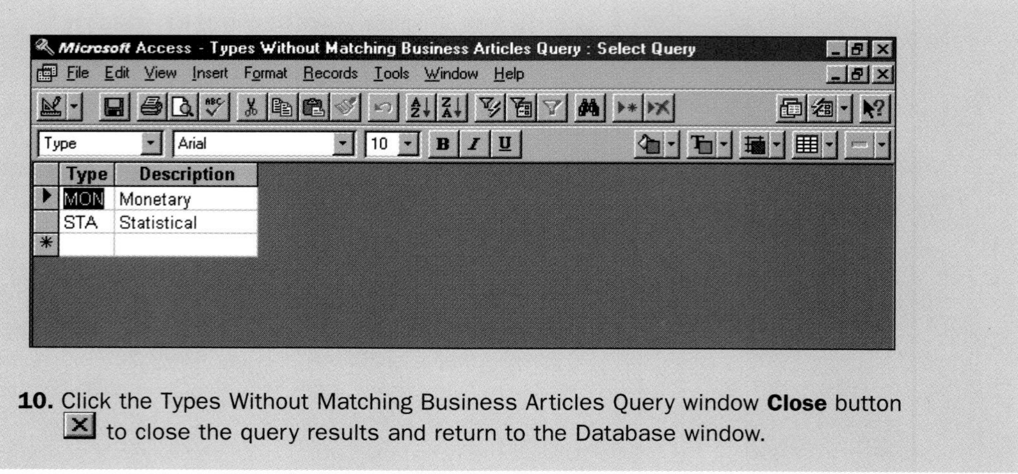

10. Click the Types Without Matching Business Articles Query window **Close** button to close the query results and return to the Database window.

Elena now knows that there are no monetary or statistical articles among those selected for the 25th-anniversary issue, because these were the only two records from the TYPES table that did not have a record with a matching Type field value in the BUSINESS ARTICLES table. Elena asks an aide to query the VISION database for several monetary and statistical articles and then give Brian Murphy a printout of the results. From these articles, Brian can choose his favorites for the 25th-anniversary issue.

Using Query Wizards is a convenient, organized way to produce queries. As you did with the crosstab query, you can change any query developed with Query Wizards, or you can develop any Access query on your own in the Query Design window, completely bypassing the Query Wizards.

Quick Check

1. What is a replica set?
2. How does a Design Master differ from a replica?
3. What does Access do when you synchronize a Design Master and a replica?
4. What is the purpose of a crosstab query?
5. What is a find duplicates query?
6. What does a find unmatched query do?

If you want to take a break and resume the tutorial at a later time, you can exit Access by clicking the Microsoft Access window Close button. When you resume the tutorial, start Access, open the Issue25 database in the Tutorial folder on your Student Disk, maximize the Database window, and click the Queries tab.

SESSION 1.2

In this session, you will learn to use four kinds of action queries: make table queries, append queries, update queries, and delete queries.

Action Queries

Queries can do more than display answers to the questions you ask; they can also perform actions on the data in your database. For example, if Elena sends a letter to all the freelance writers, she can update the Last Contact Date field for all the freelance writers in the WRITERS table with an update query. To perform this and other actions on the data in a database, you can use action queries. An **action query** is a query that adds, changes, or deletes multiple table records at one time. Because action queries modify many records in a table at a time, Access allows you to preview the query results before you actually run the query. When the query works correctly, you then save it as an action query.

Access has four types of action queries: the make table query, the append query, the update query, and the delete query.

A **make table query** creates a new table from one or more existing tables. The new table can be an exact copy of the records in an existing table, a subset of the fields and records of an existing table, or a combination of the fields and records from two or more tables. Access does not delete the selected fields and records from the existing tables. You can use make table queries, for example, to create backup copies of tables or to create customized tables for others to use. Because the new table reflects data at a point in time, you need to run the make table query periodically if you want the created table to contain reasonably current data. Notice that when you use a make table query to create the new table, the fields in the new table have the data type and field size of the fields in the query's underlying tables. The new table does not preserve the primary key designation or field properties such as input masks or lookup properties.

An **append query** adds records from an existing table or query to the end of another table. For an append query, you choose the fields you want to append from one or more tables or queries; the selected data remains in the original tables. Usually you append records to history tables. A **history table** contains data that is no longer needed for current processing but that might need to be referred to in the future. Tables containing cleared bank checks, former employees, inactive customers, and obsolete products are examples of history tables. Because the records you append to a history table are no longer needed for current processing, you delete the records from the original table.

An **update query** changes selected fields and records in one or more tables. You choose the fields and records you want to change by entering the selection criteria and the update rules. You can use update queries, for example, to increase the salaries of selected employee groups by a specified percent and to change an article type from one value to another value.

A **delete query** deletes a group of records from one or more tables. You choose which records you want to delete by entering selection criteria. Once the records are deleted, they are gone from the database. Quite often, delete queries are run after append queries have added those same records to history tables. This allows you to recapture records from the history tables if they were deleted in error from the original tables.

Creating a Make Table Query

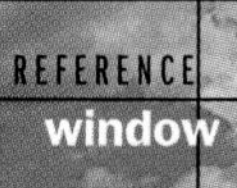

CREATING A MAKE TABLE QUERY

- In the Queries list, click the New button to open the New Query dialog box.
- Make sure that Design View is selected, then click the OK button to open the Query Design window. The Show Table dialog box opens on top of the Query Design window.
- Select the table(s) containing the fields you want to include in the query, then click the Close button to close the Show Table dialog box.
- Select the fields and specify the selection criteria you want in the query, just as you do when creating a select query.
- To preview the query results, click the Run button. Switch to the Query Design window to make any necessary changes.
- When the query is correct, make sure that you are in the Query Design window, then click the Query Type button.
- Click Make Table. Access displays the Make Table dialog box.
- In the Make New Table box, type the new table name in the Table Name text box.
- If the new table is to reside in the current database, make sure the Current Database radio button is selected. Otherwise, click the Another Database radio button and enter the database name in the File Name text box.
- To run the query and make a new table, click the Run button. Access asks you to confirm the make table operation.
- Click the Yes button to continue. Access creates the new table.

Elena wants her secretary to coordinate a conference call with all the freelance writers. Because the secretary needs to know only the freelance writers' names and phone numbers, Elena creates a new table with the name FREELANCERS. This table contains the freelance writers' Last Name, First Name, and Writer Phone fields. Although she could create a query instead of a table, Elena wants her secretary to keep notes of the phone conversations she has with the writers. Eventually, Elena will add a field to the new table; this new field will be a memo field, in which the secretary will enter notes.

Elena uses a make table query to create the FREELANCERS table.

To create a make table query:

1. If necessary, click the **Queries** tab to display the Queries list. Click the **New** button to open the New Query dialog box and then click the **OK** button. Access opens the Query Design window. The Show Table dialog box opens on top of the Query Design window.
2. Click **WRITERS** in the list box, then click the **Add** button to add the WRITERS field list to the Query Design window. Click the **Close** button to close the Show Table dialog box.
3. Scrolling the WRITERS field list as necessary, double-click **Last Name**, **First Name**, **Writer Phone**, and then **Freelancer** to add these fields to the Query Design grid.
4. Because the new table is to contain freelancers only, click the **Criteria** text box for the Freelancer field and then type **Yes**. The query is now ready to be tested.

5. Click the **Run** button on the toolbar. The query results window opens, showing the Last Name, First Name, Writer Phone, and Freelancer fields for Freelancer field values of Yes. The query is correct, except for the Freelancer field, which you want to exclude from the new table.
6. Click the **Query View** button on the toolbar to switch back to the Query Design window and then click the **Show** box in the Freelancer column to remove the check mark from it. The new table will contain only fields having checked Show boxes. You are now ready to change the query to a make table query.
7. Click the **Query Type** button on the toolbar then click **Make Table**. Access opens the Make Table dialog box, in which you enter the name of the new table. See Figure 1-18.

Figure 1-18
The Make Table dialog box

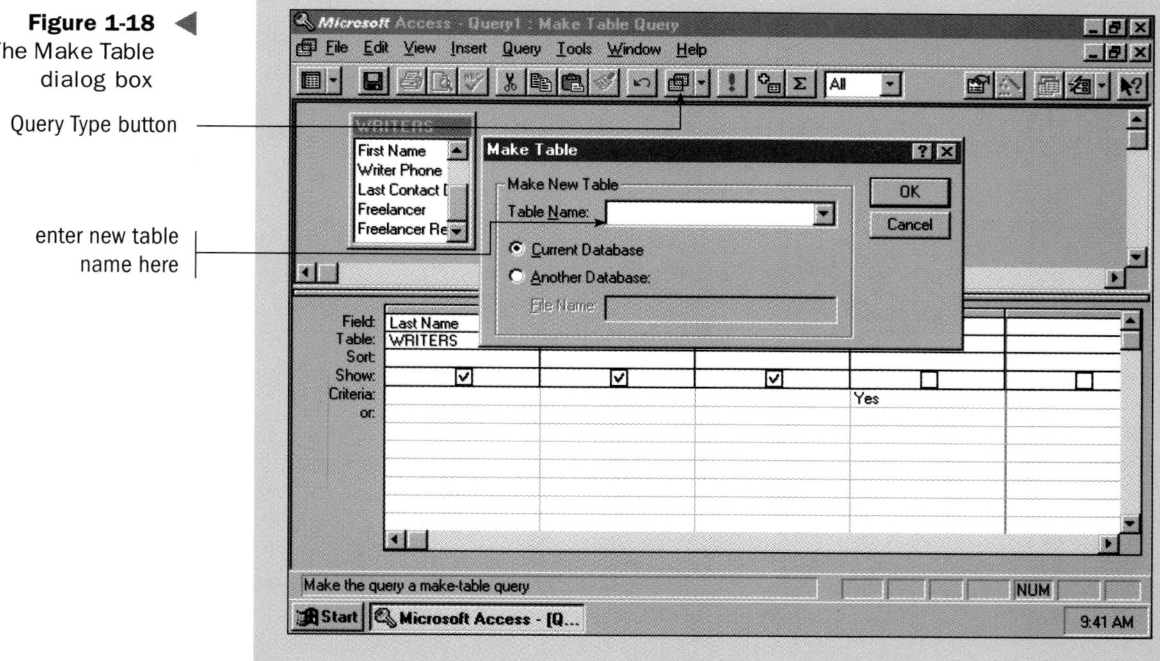

8. In the Table Name text box, type **FREELANCERS**, be sure that the Current Database radio button is selected, and then click the **OK** button.

Elena can now run and then save the make table query.

To run and save a make table query:

1. Click the **Run** button on the toolbar. Access opens a dialog box warning you about the upcoming copy operation.
2. Click the **Yes** button. Access closes the dialog box, runs the make table query to create the FREELANCERS table, and then displays the Query Design window.
3. Click the **Save** button. Access opens the Save As dialog box.
4. Type **Make Freelancers Table Query** in the Query Name text box and then click the **OK** button to name and save the query.
5. Click the Make Freelancers Table Query window **Close** button to close this window and return to the Database window.

6. Click the **Tables** tab, click **FREELANCERS** in the Tables list, and then click the **Open** button to view the new table.
7. Click the Freelancers Table window **Close** button to close this window and return to the Database window.

If you run this query again, Access will ask you if it can delete the existing FREELANCERS table before it creates a new version of the table. Click the Yes button to delete the existing table or click the No button to cancel the make table query without deleting the existing table.

Creating an Append Query

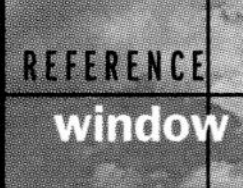

CREATING AN APPEND QUERY

- In the Queries list, click the New button to open the New Query dialog box.
- Make sure Design View is selected, then click the OK button to open the Query Design window. The Show Table dialog box opens on top of the Query Design window.
- Select the table(s) containing the fields you want to include in the query, then click the Close button to close the Show Table dialog box.
- Select the fields and specify the selection criteria you want in the query.
- To preview the query results, click the Run button. Switch to the Query Design window to make any necessary changes.
- When the query is correct, make sure that you are in the Query Design window, then click the Query Type button.
- Click Append. Access displays the Append dialog box.
- In the Table Name text box, type the name of the table to which you want to append the selected records.
- If the table to which you want to append records resides in the current database, make sure the Current Database radio button is selected. Otherwise, click the Another Database radio button and enter the database name in the File Name text box.
- To run the query and append the selected records, click the Run button. Access asks you to confirm the append operation.
- Click the Yes button to continue. Access appends the selected records to the specified table.

Elena needs a table that contains the Last Name, First Name, and Writer Phone fields for all writers for a second conference call. She could change the make table query she just created to include all the writers by deleting the Yes from the Criteria text box for the Freelancer field. This change would cause the Last Name, First Name, and Writer Phone fields for all writers, not just the freelancers, to be placed in a new table. Instead, Elena decides to create an append query to add records for the writers who are not freelancers to the FREELANCERS table she already created. She first makes a copy of the FREELANCERS table, which she created for her secretary's use, then renames the copy using the name PHONE NUMBERS for the new table. To complete the task, Elena creates and runs an append query to add records for the staff writers' Last Name, First Name, and Writer Phone fields to the PHONE NUMBERS table, which already contains these same three fields for the freelancers.

To create an append query:

1. Click the **Tables** tab to display the Tables list. Right-click **FREELANCERS** in the Tables list box to display the shortcut menu, then click **Copy**. Access copies the FREELANCERS table to the Clipboard. Right-click in the Tables list box, but not on any table name, to display the shortcut menu and then click **Paste**. Access opens the Paste Table As dialog box.
2. Type **PHONE NUMBERS** in the Table Name text box, be sure that the Structure and Data radio button is selected, and then click the **OK** button. Access creates the PHONE NUMBERS table and places a copy of the records from the FREELANCERS table into this new table.
3. Click the **Queries** tab, then click the **New** button to open the New Query dialog box.
4. Make sure that Design View is highlighted, then click the **OK** button. Access opens the Query Design window with the Show Table dialog box on top.
5. Click **WRITERS** in the Table list box, then click the **Add** button to add the WRITERS field list to the Query Design window. Click the **Close** button to close the Show Table dialog box.
6. Scrolling the WRITERS field list as necessary, double-click **Last Name**, **First Name**, **Writer Phone**, and then **Freelancer** to add these fields to the Query Design grid.
7. Because just staff writers are needed in the new table, click the **Criteria** text box for the Freelancer field, type **No**, then click the **Run** button on the toolbar. The query results window displays the Last Name, First Name, Writer Phone, and Freelancer fields for Freelancer field values of No. The query is correct, except for the Freelancer field, which you want to exclude from the new table.
8. Click the **Query View** button on the toolbar to switch back to the Query Design window and then click the **Show** box in the Freelancer column to remove the check mark from it. You can now change the query to an append query.
9. Click the **Query Type** button on the toolbar, then click **Append**. Access opens the Append dialog box in which you enter the name of the table to which you want to append the data.
10. Click the **Table Name** list arrow, click **PHONE NUMBERS**, be sure that the Current Database radio button is selected, and then click the **OK** button. Between the Sort and Criteria rows in the Query Design grid, Access replaces the Show row with the Append To row. See Figure 1-19.

Figure 1-19 The Query Design window for an append query

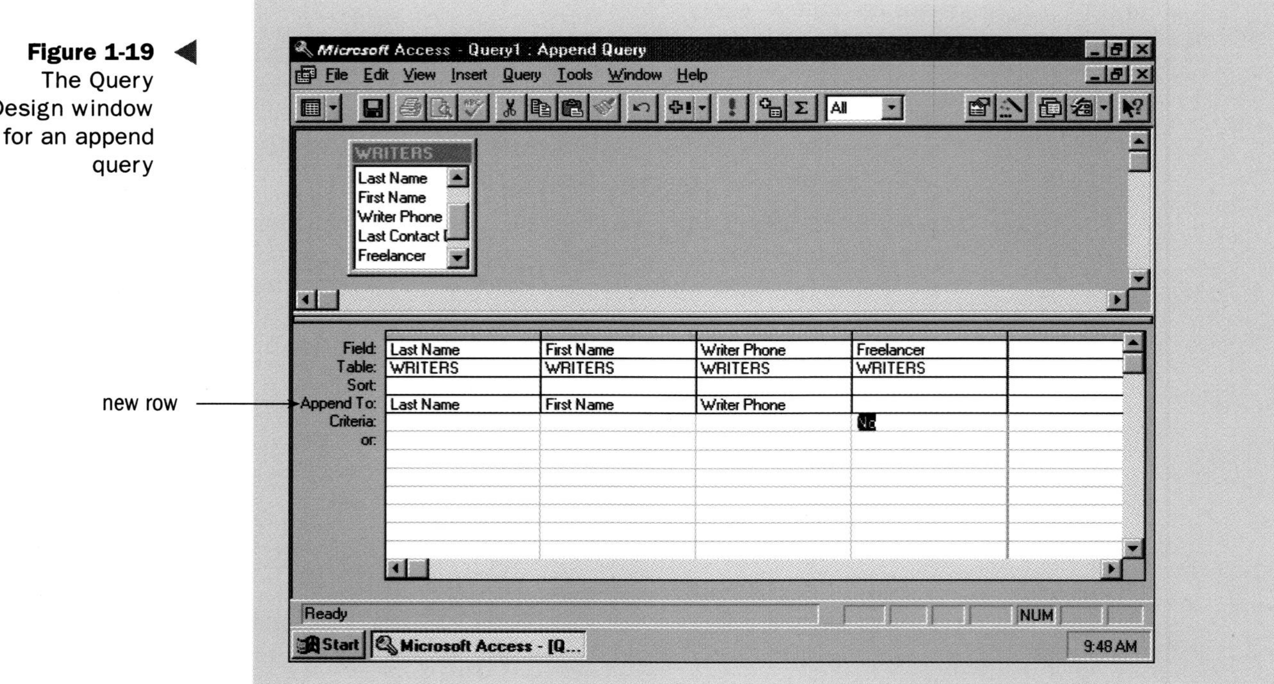

The Append To row in the Query Design grid identifies the fields that will be appended to the designated table. The Last Name, First Name, and Writer Phone fields for staff writers are to be appended to the PHONE NUMBERS table, which already contains these three fields for freelancers.

Elena can now run and then save the append query.

To run and save an append query:

1. Click the **Run** button. Access opens a dialog box warning you about the upcoming append operation.
2. Click the **Yes** button to acknowledge the warning. Access closes the dialog box, runs the append query to add records to the PHONE NUMBERS table, and leaves you in the Query Design window.
3. Click the **Save** button on the toolbar. Access opens the Save As dialog box.
4. Type **Append to PHONE NUMBERS Table Query** in the Query Name text box and then click the **OK** button. Access saves the query.
5. Click the Append to PHONE NUMBERS Table Query **Close** button to close this window and return to the Database window.

If you run the query Append to PHONE NUMBERS Table Query again, Access asks permission to append the data before it does so. Click the OK button to continue with the append query or click the Cancel button to cancel the append query.

Creating an Update Query

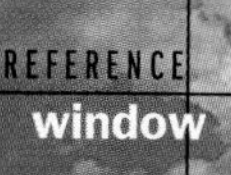

CREATING AN UPDATE QUERY

- In the Queries list, click the New button to open the New Query dialog box.
- Make sure Design View is selected, then click the OK button to open the Query Design window. The Show Table dialog box opens on top of the Query Design window.
- Select the table(s) containing the fields you want to include in the query, then click the Close button to close the Show Table dialog box.
- Select the fields and specify the selection criteria you want in the query, just as you do when creating a select query.
- To preview the query results, click the Run button. Switch to the Query Design window to make any necessary changes.
- When the query is correct, make sure that you are in the Query Design window, then click the Query Type button.
- Click Update. Access places the Update To row in the Query Design grid.
- Enter the expression for the new value for the update field in the Update To row.
- To run the query and update the selected records, click the Run button. Access asks you to confirm the update operation.
- Click the Yes button to continue. Access updates the selected records to the specified table.

Brian Murphy tells Elena that he will continue the policy of not paying staff writers for their article reprints in the 25th-anniversary issue but that he plans to pay freelancers an additional $25 for each reprinted article. Elena must update the field value for each freelancer's Freelancer Reprint Payment Amount field value in the WRITERS table but not change the field value for the staff writers. She could change each value in the table's datasheet individually, but using an update query to change all freelancers' field values at one time is faster and more accurate. As she has done before, Elena will create a query to choose the correct records, test the query, and then change the query to an update query. Several workable ways to construct the query occur to Elena before she finally decides on the best method. The query Elena creates will display just the Freelancer Reprint Payment Amount field for all writers having a Freelancer Reprint Payment Amount field value greater than zero. Only freelancer records meet this requirement, because freelancers are the only writers being paid for their reprinted articles.

To create an update query:

1. In the Queries list, click the **New** button to open the New Query dialog box. Make sure that Design View is selected, then click the **OK** button to open the Query Design window. The Show Table dialog box opens on top of the Query Design window.

2. Click **WRITERS** in the list box, then click the **Add** button to add the WRITERS field list to the Query Design window. Click the **Close** button to close the Show Table dialog box.

3. Scroll the WRITERS field list and then double-click **Freelancer Reprint Payment Amount** to add this field to the Query Design grid.

TROUBLE? If you cannot see the complete field names, resize the field list by dragging the borders of the list box.

4. Click the **Criteria** text box for the Freelancer Reprint Payment Amount field and then type **>0**. Access will select a record only if the Freelancer Reprint Payment Amount field value is greater than zero.
5. Click the **Run** button on the toolbar. The query results window displays one column, Amount, which is the caption value for the Freelancer Reprint Payment Amount field, and values for the six freelancer records. The query is correct.
6. Click the **Query View** button on the toolbar to switch back to the Query Design window.
7. Click the **Query Type** button on the toolbar and then click **Update**. In the Query Design grid, Access replaces the Sort and Show rows with the Update To row. See Figure 1-20.

Figure 1-20 The Query Design window for an update query

new row

Field: Freelancer Reprint F
Table: WRITERS
Update To:
Criteria: >0
or:
Ready
NUM
Start
Microsoft Access - [Q...
9:51 AM

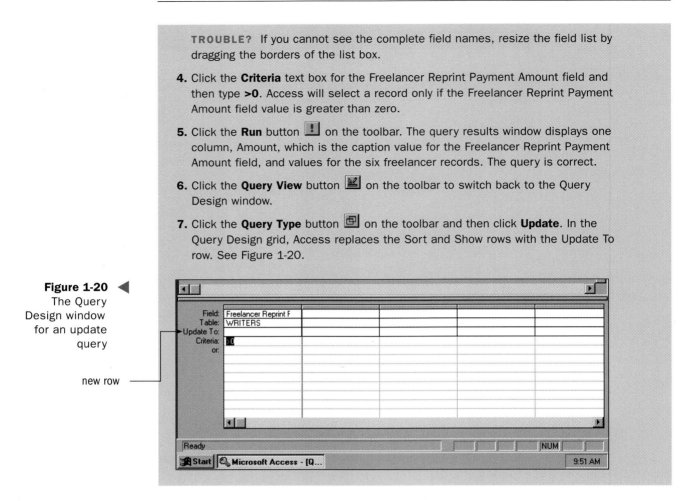

You tell Access how you want to change a field value for the selected records by entering an expression in the field's Update To text box. An **expression** is a calculation resulting in a single value. You can either type it in or generate it using the **Expression Builder**, an Access tool that contains an expression box in which the expression is entered, buttons for common operators, and one or more lists of expression elements, such as table and field names.

To use the Expression Builder to complete an update query:

1. Right-click the **Update To** text box for the Freelancer Reprint Payment Amount field, to display the shortcut menu, and then click **Build**. Access opens the Expression Builder dialog box. See Figure 1-21.

Figure 1-21 The Expression Builder dialog box

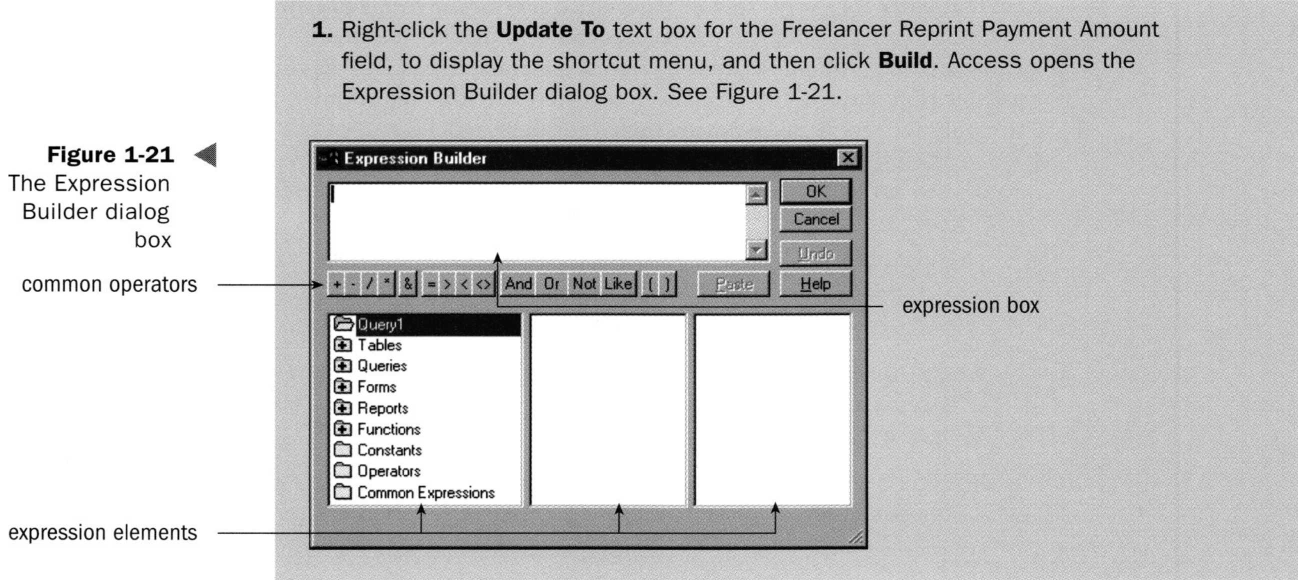

2. In the first column of expression elements, double-click **Tables** to display the Issue25 tables, then double-click **WRITERS**. Access displays the field names for the WRITERS table. See Figure 1-22.

Figure 1-22 Issue25 database tables and WRITERS table fields displayed in the Expression Builder dialog box

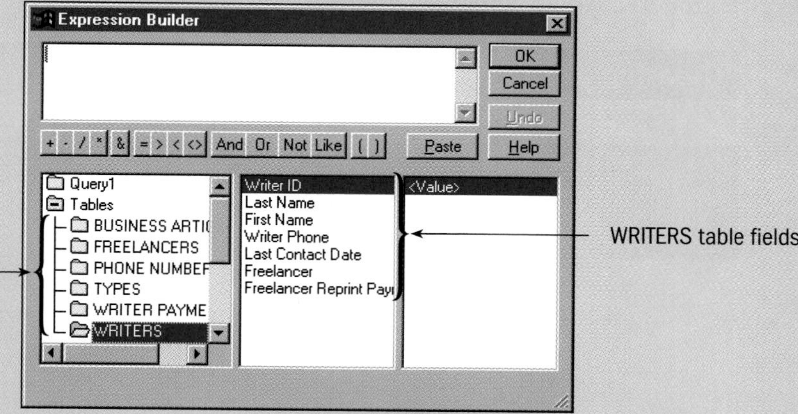

3. Double-click **Freelancer Reprint Payment Amount** in the middle column of expression elements. The expression [WRITERS]![Freelancer Reprint Payment Amount] appears in the expression box to indicate that, so far, your expression contains the Freelancer Reprint Payment Amount field, which is part of the WRITERS table.

4. Click the **+** (addition) button in the row of common operators and then type **25**. You have completed the construction of the expression. See Figure 1-23.

Figure 1-23 Completed expression for an update query

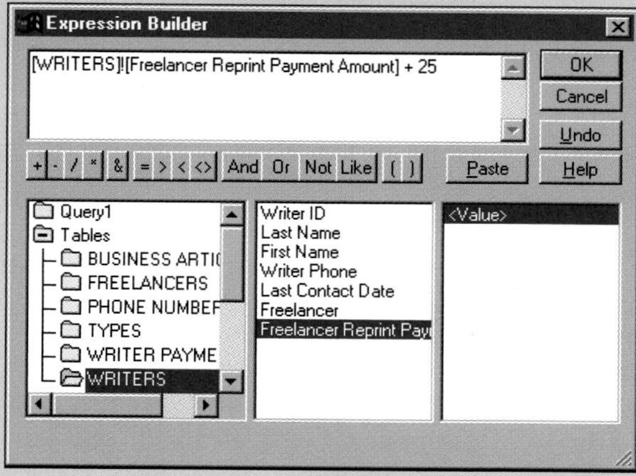

5. Click the **OK** button. Access closes the Expression Builder dialog box and adds the expression to the Update To text box for the Freelancer Reprint Payment Amount field.

6. Click the **Run** button on the toolbar. Access opens a dialog box warning you about the upcoming update operation.

7. Click the **Yes** button to close the dialog box and run the update query. Access leaves the Query Design window open.

8. Click the Query Design window **Close** button. Click the **No** button when Access asks you if you want to save the query changes.

9. Click the **Tables** tab, click **WRITERS** in the Tables list, then click the **Open** button to open the WRITERS table.

The freelancers Amount column shows $55, $65, $125, $150, $375, and $475. These figures are all $25 more than they were before the update query was run. Because you usually run an update query once, you do not need to save it. If you do happen to run a saved update query again, Access asks permission to modify the data. Click the OK button to continue with the change or click the Cancel button to cancel the update query.

Creating a Delete Query

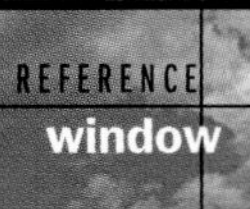

CREATING A DELETE QUERY

- In the Queries list, click the New button to open the New Query dialog box.
- Make sure that Design View is selected, then click the OK button to open the Query Design window. The Show Table dialog box opens on top of the Query Design window.
- Select the table(s) containing the fields you want to include in the query, then click the Close button to close the Show Table dialog box.
- Select the fields and specify the criteria you want in the query, just as you do when creating a select query.
- To preview the query results, click the Run button. Switch to the Query Design window to make any necessary changes.
- When you verify that the correct records are being selected and the query is correct, make sure that you are in the Query Design window, then click the Query Type button.
- Click Delete. Access replaces the Show and Sort rows with the Delete row.
- To run the query and delete the selected records, click the Run button. Access asks you to confirm the delete operation.
- Click the Yes button to continue. Access deletes the selected records.

Four writers visit the Vision Publishers offices and meet with Elena, who briefs them on the 25th-anniversary plans for *Business Perspective*. Because her secretary no longer needs to contact these four writers, Elena wants to delete their records from the PHONE NUMBERS table. She can either delete the table records individually or create a delete query to remove the four table records. Because these writers are the only ones who have 210 or 917 area codes, Elena creates a select query to choose the correct records based on the area code criteria, tests the select query, and then changes the query to a delete query.

To create a delete query:

1. Click the Writers Table window **Close** button [X] to return to the Database window. Click the **Queries** tab, then click the **New** button to open the New Query dialog box. Make sure that Design View is selected, then click the **OK** button to open the Query Design window. The Show Table dialog box opens on top of the Query Design window.
2. Click **PHONE NUMBERS** in the Tables list, then click the **Add** button to add the PHONE NUMBERS field list to the Query Design window. Click the **Close** button to close the Show Table dialog box.

3. Double-click the **title bar** of the PHONE NUMBERS field list to select all the fields in the table and then drag the pointer from the highlighted area of the PHONE NUMBERS field list to the Query Design grid's first column Field box. Access adds all the fields to the Query Design grid.

4. Click the **Criteria** text box for the Writer Phone field, type **Like "210*"**, press the **down arrow** key, and then type **Like "917*"**. Access will select a record only if the Writer Phone field value starts with either 210 or 917.

5. Click the **Run** button on the toolbar. The query results window displays four records, each one with either a 210 or 917 area code. The query is correct.

   TROUBLE? If your query did not select the correct four records, click the Query View button on the toolbar, verify that the criteria are entered correctly, then click the Run button on the toolbar.

6. Click the **Query View** button on the toolbar to switch back to the Query Design window. Click the **Query Type** button on the toolbar and then click **Delete**. In the Query Design grid, Access replaces the Sort and Show rows with the Delete row. See Figure 1-24.

Figure 1-24 The Query Design window for a delete query

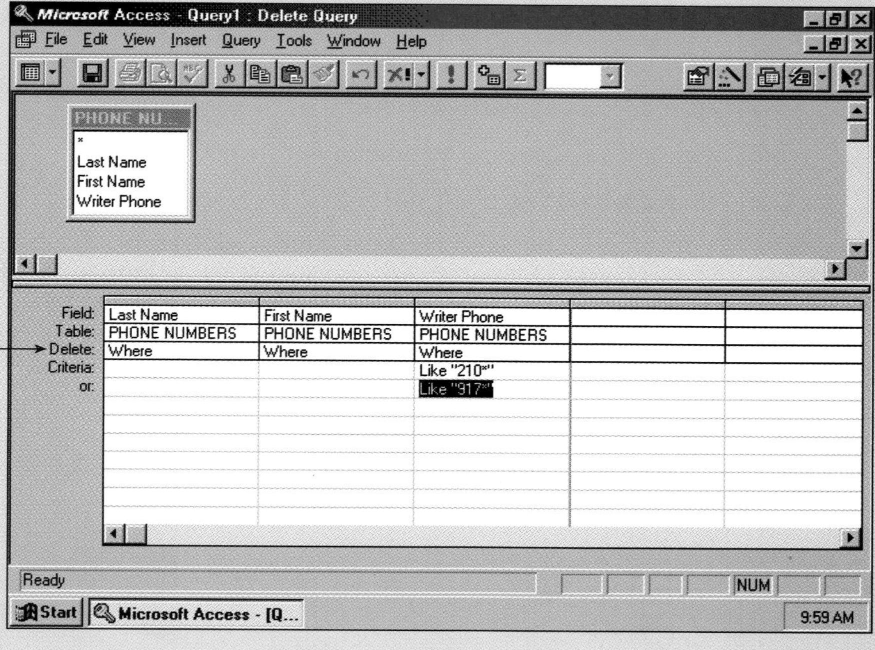

7. Click the **Run** button. Access opens a dialog box warning you about the upcoming delete operation.

8. Click the **Yes** button to close the dialog box and run the delete query. Access keeps the Query Design window open. Because this query needs to be run only once, Elena doesn't bother to save it.

9. Click the Delete Query window **Close** button, click the **No** button when Access asks if you want to save the query changes. Click the **Tables** tab, then click **PHONE NUMBERS** in the Tables list box, and click the **Open** button. Access opens the Datasheet View window for the PHONE NUMBERS table.

Access displays the 11 remaining records in the PHONE NUMBERS table; four records were correctly deleted. As is the case with update queries, you do not usually need to save delete queries. If you do happen to run a delete query again, Access asks permission to modify the data. Click the OK button to continue with the delete or click the Cancel button to cancel the delete query.

Elena returns to the Database window before taking a short break.

To return to the Database window:

1. Click the Phone Numbers Table window **Close** button ☒. Access activates the Database window.
2. Click the **Queries** tab to display the Queries list.

Quick Check

1 What is an action query?

2 What precautions should you take before running an action query?

3 How does the Query Design grid change when you create an update query?

4 What is the Expression Builder?

5 What does an update query do?

6 Why is it advisable not to save an update query?

7 What does a delete query do?

If you want to take a break and resume the tutorial at a later time, you can exit Access by clicking the Microsoft Access window Close button. When you resume the tutorial, place your Student Disk in the appropriate drive, start Access, open the Issue25 database in the Tutorial folder on your Student Disk, maximize the Database window, and click the Queries tab.

SESSION 1.3

In this session, you will learn to use top value queries. You will also learn about the different types of table joins and view the SQL statements Access creates when you design a query.

Top Value Queries

If you have a query that displays thousands of records, you might want to limit the number to a more manageable size by, for example, showing just the first 20 records. The **Top Values property** for a query lets you limit the number of records in select, append, or make table query results. For the Top Values property, you enter either an integer (like 20, to show the first 20) or percent (like 50%, to show the first half). Suppose you have a select query that displays 45 records. If you want the query results to show only the first five records, you can change the query by entering a Top Values property of either 5 or 10%. If the query contains a sort, Access displays the records sorted in order by the primary sort key. Whenever the last record that Access can choose to display is one of two or more records because they have the same value for the primary sort key, Access displays all of them.

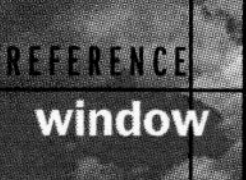

CREATING A TOP VALUE QUERY

- In the Queries list, click the New button to open the New Query dialog box.
- Make sure that Design View is selected, then click the OK button to open the Query Design window. The Show Table dialog box opens on top of the Query Design window.
- Select the table(s) containing the fields you want to include in the query, then click the Close button to close the Show Table dialog box.
- Select the fields and specify the criteria you want in the query, just as you do when creating a select query.
- Enter the number of records (or percentage of records) you want selected in the Top Values text box on the toolbar.
- Click the Run button on the toolbar to run the query.

Elena can use the Top Values property to find the longest articles by using the query named Articles Sorted by Issue and Length. She will need to remove the existing sort keys for the Issue: Issue of Business Perspectives field and change the sort from ascending to descending for the Article Length field to see the effects of the Top Values property better.

To limit records in the results of a query using the Top Values property:

1. Click **Articles Sorted by Issue and Length Query** in the Queries list, then click the Open button. Access displays 27 records in the query results. First, you will change the query sort keys.

2. Click the **Query View** button on the toolbar to switch back to the Query Design window, click the **Sort** text box for the Issue: Issue of Business Perspectives field, click the **Sort** list arrow that appears, and then click **(not sorted)**.

3. Click the **Sort** text box for the Article Length field, click the **Sort** list arrow, and then click **Descending**. The sort keys are now correct.

4. Click the **Run** button. The query results window opens, again showing 27 records. The records are in descending order sorted by the Length field.

5. Click the **Query View** button on the toolbar to switch back to the Query Design window. Double-click in the **Top Values** text box on the toolbar, then type **7**. See Figure 1-25.

Figure 1-25 Creating a top value query

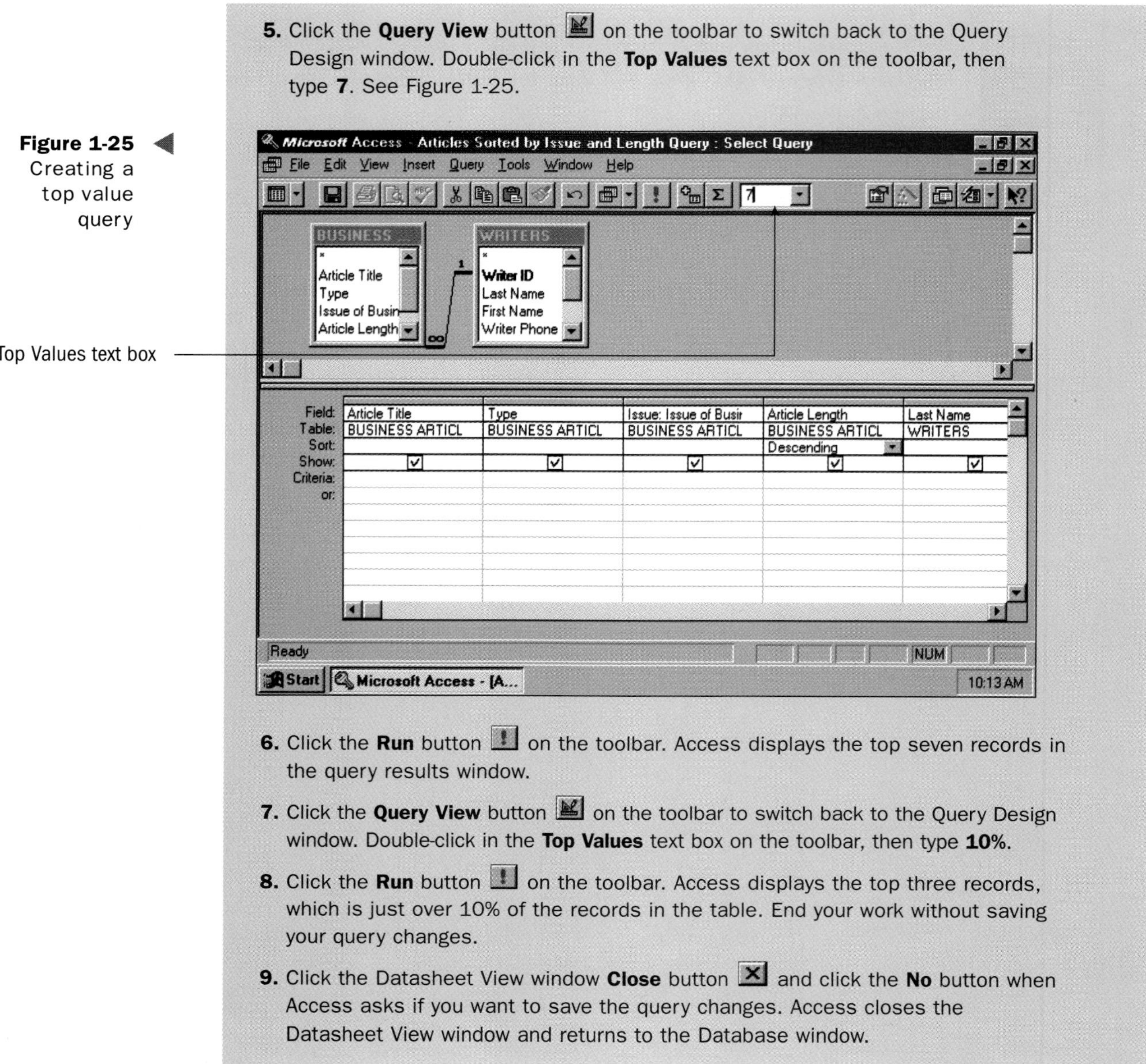

6. Click the **Run** button on the toolbar. Access displays the top seven records in the query results window.

7. Click the **Query View** button on the toolbar to switch back to the Query Design window. Double-click in the **Top Values** text box on the toolbar, then type **10%**.

8. Click the **Run** button on the toolbar. Access displays the top three records, which is just over 10% of the records in the table. End your work without saving your query changes.

9. Click the Datasheet View window **Close** button and click the **No** button when Access asks if you want to save the query changes. Access closes the Datasheet View window and returns to the Database window.

Modifying the Database Design

Freelance and staff writers have been voicing concern about not being kept informed of future writing opportunities at Vision Publishers. To correct this problem, Brian Murphy promotes Pat Lawton and Kristine Waldeck to senior writer positions. In addition, he assigns Pat the responsibility of keeping the other staff writers informed of future projects and assigns Kristine a similar responsibility with the freelancers.

Brian asks Elena to add the new contact information to the database and then to create a new query that shows which junior writers are assigned to Pat and which to Kristine. Elena first adds a field named Contact to the WRITERS table that will contain either Pat's or Kristine's Writer ID field value. Then, she creates a query that displays the writers and their senior contacts.

To add a new field to the WRITERS table:

1. Click the **Tables** tab, click **WRITERS** in the Tables list, and then click the **Design** button. Access opens the Design View window for the WRITERS table.

2. Click the **Field Name** box just below the Freelancer Reprint Payment Amount field, type **Contact**, press the **Tab** key, press the **Tab** key again, and then type **Senior Writer contact for this writer** in the new field's Description box. Finally, double-click **50** in the Field Size box and then type **4**. This completes the addition of the Contact field to the WRITERS table. See Figure 1-26.

Figure 1-26 Contact field added to the WRITERS table

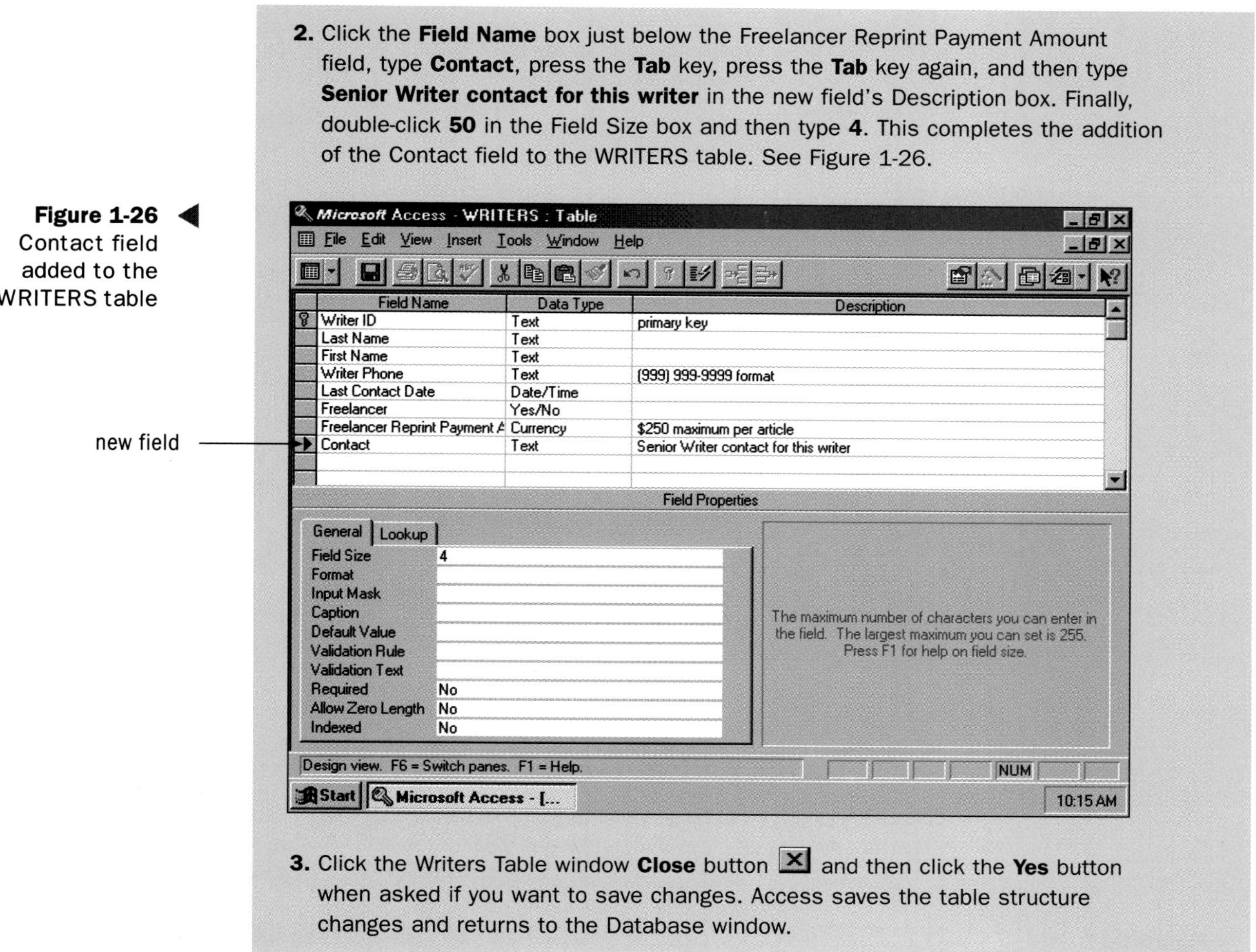

3. Click the Writers Table window **Close** button and then click the **Yes** button when asked if you want to save changes. Access saves the table structure changes and returns to the Database window.

Elena next uses an update query to update the Contact field for the records in the WRITERS table. She changes the Contact value to W432 (Writer ID for Kristine Waldeck) for each freelancer and to L350 (Writer ID for Pat Lawton) for each staff writer. She does not enter a value in the Contact field for Kristine Waldeck or Pat Lawton.

To update the Contact field for records in the WRITERS table:

1. Click the **Queries** tab to display the Queries list, then click the **New** button to open the New Query dialog box. Make sure that Design View is selected, then click the **OK** button to open the Query Design window. The Show Table dialog box opens on top of the Query Design window.

2. Click **WRITERS** in the list box, then click the **Add** button to add the WRITERS field list to the Query Design window. Then click the **Close** button to close the Show Table dialog box.

3. In the WRITERS field list, double-click the **Writer ID**, **Freelancer**, and **Contact** fields to add these fields to the Query Design grid.

4. Click the **Criteria** text box for the Freelancer field and then type **=Yes**. Access will select a record only if the Freelancer field value is Yes.

5. Click the **Criteria** text box for the Writer ID field and then type **Not In ("L350","W432")**. Access will not select the records for Pat Lawton or Kristine Waldeck.

6. Click the **Query Type** button on the toolbar and then click **Update**. In the Query Design grid, Access replaces the Sort and Show rows with the Update To row.
7. Click the **Update To** box for the Contact field and then type **W432**. This is the Writer ID field value for Kristine Waldeck.
8. Click the **Run** button on the toolbar. Access opens a dialog box, warning you about the upcoming update operation. Click the **Yes** button to close the dialog box and run the update query. Access leaves the Query Design window open.
9. Highlight the **Criteria** text box for the Freelancer field and then type **=No**. Access will select a record only if the Freelancer field value is No.
10. Highlight the **Update To** box for the Contact field and then type **L350**. This is the Writer ID field value for Pat Lawton.
11. Click the **Run** button on the toolbar. Access opens a dialog box, warning you about the upcoming update operation. Click the **Yes** button to close the dialog box and run the update query. Access leaves the Query Design window open.
12. Click the Update Query window **Close** button and click the **No** button when Access asks if you want to save the query changes. Access closes the Query Design window and returns to the Database window.

Elena now views the WRITERS table to see the results of the update operation.

To view the updated WRITERS table:

1. Click the **Tables** tab, click **WRITERS** in the Tables list, then click the **Open** button. Access displays the Datasheet View of the WRITERS table. See Figure 1-27.

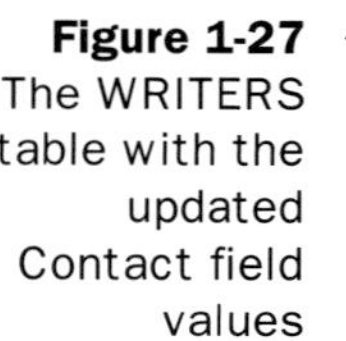
Figure 1-27 The WRITERS table with the updated Contact field values

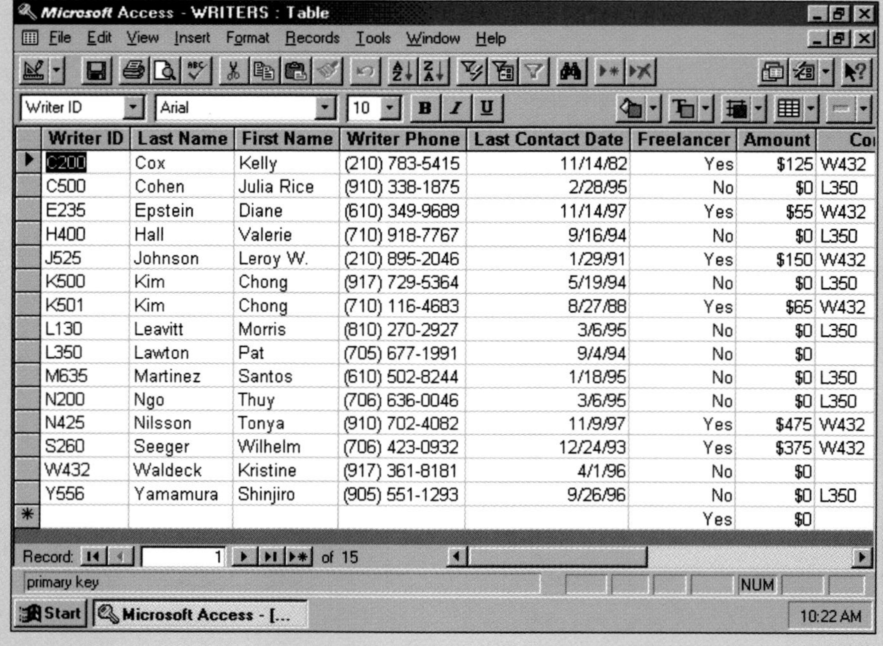

Writer ID	Last Name	First Name	Writer Phone	Last Contact Date	Freelancer	Amount	Co
C200	Cox	Kelly	(210) 783-5415	11/14/82	Yes	$125	W432
C500	Cohen	Julia Rice	(910) 338-1875	2/28/95	No	$0	L350
E235	Epstein	Diane	(610) 349-9689	11/14/97	Yes	$55	W432
H400	Hall	Valerie	(710) 918-7767	9/16/94	No	$0	L350
J525	Johnson	Leroy W.	(210) 895-2046	1/29/91	Yes	$150	W432
K500	Kim	Chong	(917) 729-5364	5/19/94	No	$0	L350
K501	Kim	Chong	(710) 116-4683	8/27/88	Yes	$65	W432
L130	Leavitt	Morris	(810) 270-2927	3/6/95	No	$0	L350
L350	Lawton	Pat	(705) 677-1991	9/4/94	No	$0	
M635	Martinez	Santos	(610) 502-8244	1/18/95	No	$0	L350
N200	Ngo	Thuy	(706) 636-0046	3/6/95	No	$0	L350
N425	Nilsson	Tonya	(910) 702-4082	11/9/97	Yes	$475	W432
S260	Seeger	Wilhelm	(706) 423-0932	12/24/93	Yes	$375	W432
W432	Waldeck	Kristine	(917) 361-8181	4/1/96	No	$0	
Y556	Yamamura	Shinjiro	(905) 551-1293	9/26/96	No	$0	L350
					Yes	$0	

2. Click the Writers Table window **Close** button. Access closes the Datasheet View window and returns to the Database window.

Now that the contact ID numbers are in place, Elena can generate the query that shows the information Brian requested: which writers are assigned to Kristen and which writers are assigned to Pat.

Joining Tables

Elena needs to create a query to display the new contact relationships in the WRITERS table. To do so, she creates a special join using the WRITERS table. When Elena designed the Issue25 database, she established a relationship between two tables using Writer ID as the common field, and then she joined the tables to run a query with data from both tables. The type of join Elena has used so far is an inner join, which is one of three available Access joins. The others are the left outer join and the right outer join.

An **inner join** is a join in which Access selects records from two tables, only when the records have the same value in the common field that links the tables. For example, Writer ID is the common field for the WRITERS and BUSINESS ARTICLES tables. As shown in Figure 1-28, an inner join of these two tables includes only those records that have a matching Writer ID value. The Writer ID W432 record in the WRITERS table and the Writer ID N425 record in the BUSINESS ARTICLES table are not included because they fail to match a record with the same Writer ID value in the other table. The inner join is the join you ordinarily use whenever you perform a query from more than one table; it is the default join you have used until now.

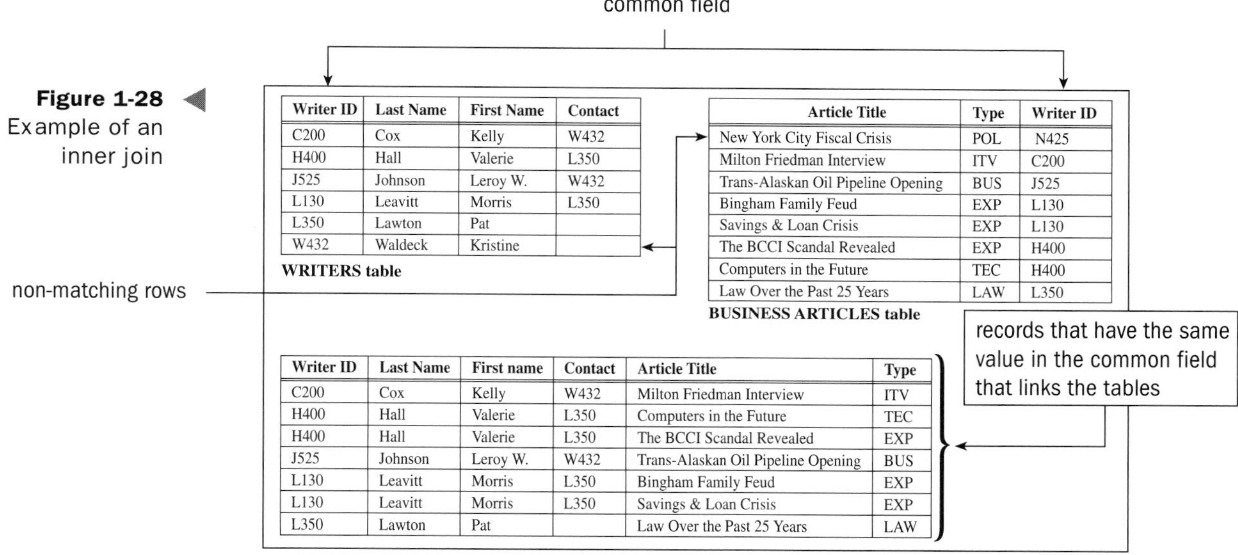

Writer ID	Last Name	First Name	Contact
C200	Cox	Kelly	W432
H400	Hall	Valerie	L350
J525	Johnson	Leroy W.	W432
L130	Leavitt	Morris	L350
L350	Lawton	Pat	
W432	Waldeck	Kristine	

WRITERS table

Article Title	Type	Writer ID
New York City Fiscal Crisis	POL	N425
Milton Friedman Interview	ITV	C200
Trans-Alaskan Oil Pipeline Opening	BUS	J525
Bingham Family Feud	EXP	L130
Savings & Loan Crisis	EXP	L130
The BCCI Scandal Revealed	EXP	H400
Computers in the Future	TEC	H400
Law Over the Past 25 Years	LAW	L350

BUSINESS ARTICLES table

Writer ID	Last Name	First name	Contact	Article Title	Type
C200	Cox	Kelly	W432	Milton Friedman Interview	ITV
H400	Hall	Valerie	L350	Computers in the Future	TEC
H400	Hall	Valerie	L350	The BCCI Scandal Revealed	EXP
J525	Johnson	Leroy W.	W432	Trans-Alaskan Oil Pipeline Opening	BUS
L130	Leavitt	Morris	L350	Bingham Family Feud	EXP
L130	Leavitt	Morris	L350	Savings & Loan Crisis	EXP
L350	Lawton	Pat		Law Over the Past 25 Years	LAW

Figure 1-28
Example of an inner join

A **left outer join** is a join in which Access selects all records from the first, or left, table and only those records from the second table that have matching common field values. Figure 1-29 shows a left outer join for the WRITERS and BUSINESS ARTICLES tables. All records from the WRITERS table, which is the left table, appear in the query results. The Writer ID W432 record appears even though it does not match a record in the BUSINESS ARTICLES table. The Writer ID N425 record in the BUSINESS ARTICLES table does not appear, however, because it does not match a record in the WRITERS table.

Figure 1-29 Example of a left outer join

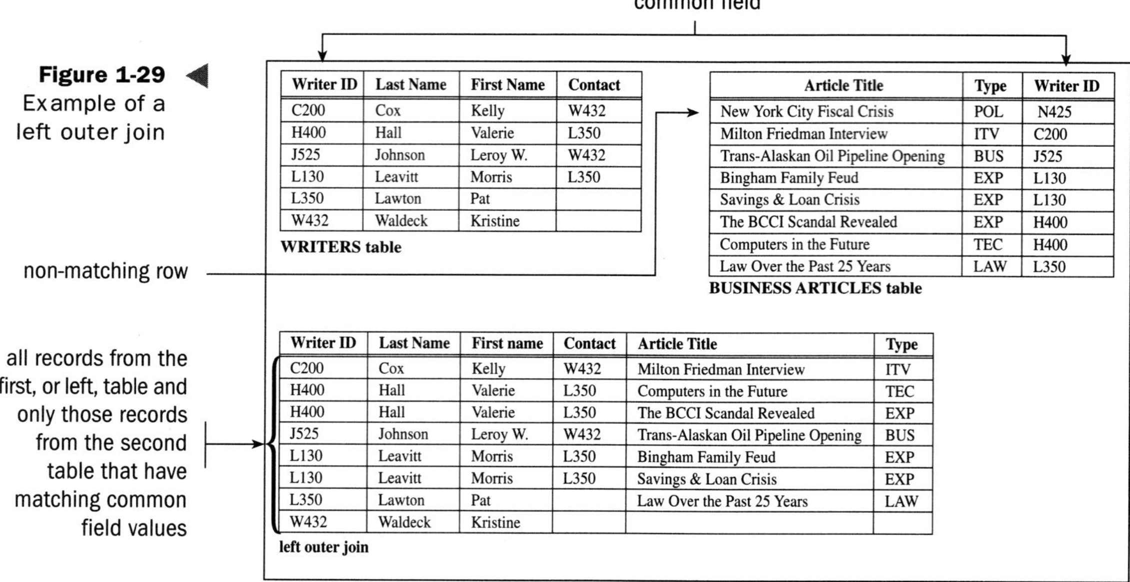

Writer ID	Last Name	First Name	Contact
C200	Cox	Kelly	W432
H400	Hall	Valerie	L350
J525	Johnson	Leroy W.	W432
L130	Leavitt	Morris	L350
L350	Lawton	Pat	
W432	Waldeck	Kristine	

WRITERS table

Article Title	Type	Writer ID
New York City Fiscal Crisis	POL	N425
Milton Friedman Interview	ITV	C200
Trans-Alaskan Oil Pipeline Opening	BUS	J525
Bingham Family Feud	EXP	L130
Savings & Loan Crisis	EXP	L130
The BCCI Scandal Revealed	EXP	H400
Computers in the Future	TEC	H400
Law Over the Past 25 Years	LAW	L350

BUSINESS ARTICLES table

Writer ID	Last Name	First name	Contact	Article Title	Type
C200	Cox	Kelly	W432	Milton Friedman Interview	ITV
H400	Hall	Valerie	L350	Computers in the Future	TEC
H400	Hall	Valerie	L350	The BCCI Scandal Revealed	EXP
J525	Johnson	Leroy W.	W432	Trans-Alaskan Oil Pipeline Opening	BUS
L130	Leavitt	Morris	L350	Bingham Family Feud	EXP
L130	Leavitt	Morris	L350	Savings & Loan Crisis	EXP
L350	Lawton	Pat		Law Over the Past 25 Years	LAW
W432	Waldeck	Kristine			

left outer join

A **right outer join** is a join in which Access selects all records from the second, or right, table and only those records from the first table that have matching common field values. Figure 1-30 shows a right outer join for the WRITERS and BUSINESS ARTICLES tables. All records from the BUSINESS ARTICLES table, which is the right table, appear in the query results. The Writer ID N425 record appears even though it does not match a record in the WRITERS table. The Writer ID W432 record in the WRITERS table does not appear, however, because it does not match a record in the BUSINESS ARTICLES table.

Figure 1-30 Example of a right outer join

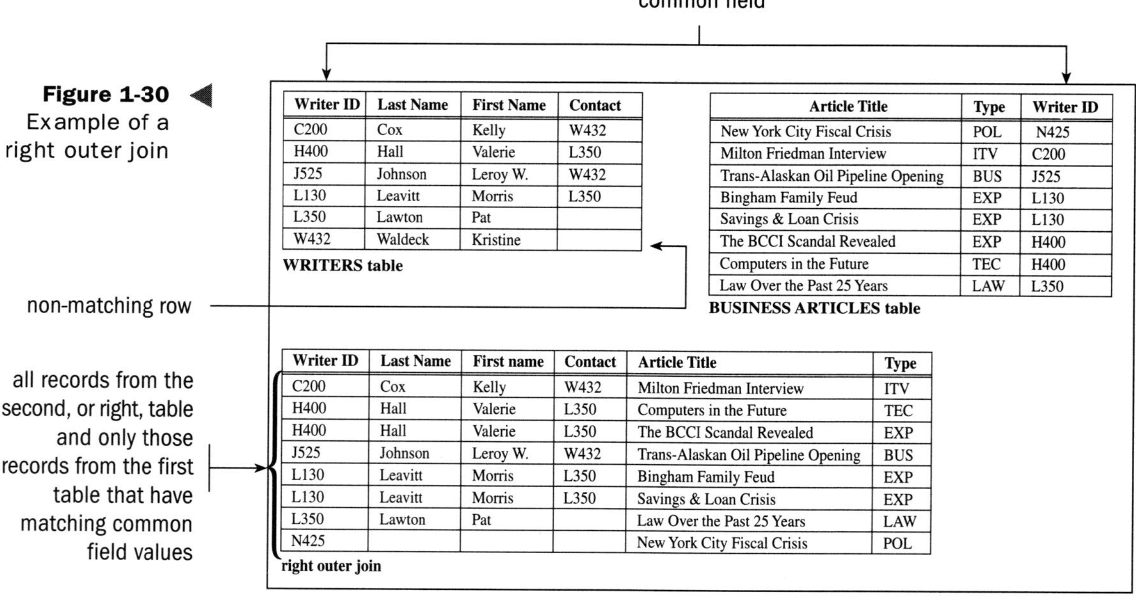

Writer ID	Last Name	First Name	Contact
C200	Cox	Kelly	W432
H400	Hall	Valerie	L350
J525	Johnson	Leroy W.	W432
L130	Leavitt	Morris	L350
L350	Lawton	Pat	
W432	Waldeck	Kristine	

WRITERS table

Article Title	Type	Writer ID
New York City Fiscal Crisis	POL	N425
Milton Friedman Interview	ITV	C200
Trans-Alaskan Oil Pipeline Opening	BUS	J525
Bingham Family Feud	EXP	L130
Savings & Loan Crisis	EXP	L130
The BCCI Scandal Revealed	EXP	H400
Computers in the Future	TEC	H400
Law Over the Past 25 Years	LAW	L350

BUSINESS ARTICLES table

Writer ID	Last Name	First name	Contact	Article Title	Type
C200	Cox	Kelly	W432	Milton Friedman Interview	ITV
H400	Hall	Valerie	L350	Computers in the Future	TEC
H400	Hall	Valerie	L350	The BCCI Scandal Revealed	EXP
J525	Johnson	Leroy W.	W432	Trans-Alaskan Oil Pipeline Opening	BUS
L130	Leavitt	Morris	L350	Bingham Family Feud	EXP
L130	Leavitt	Morris	L350	Savings & Loan Crisis	EXP
L350	Lawton	Pat		Law Over the Past 25 Years	LAW
N425				New York City Fiscal Crisis	POL

right outer join

When a table is joined with itself, the join is called a **self join**. A self join can be either an inner or outer join. Figure 1-31 shows a self-join for the WRITERS table. In this case, the self-join is an inner join because records appear in the query results only if the Contact field value matches a Writer ID field value. If you use Access to create this self join, you add two copies of the WRITERS table to the Query Design window and link the Contact field of one WRITER table to the Writer ID field of the other WRITER table.

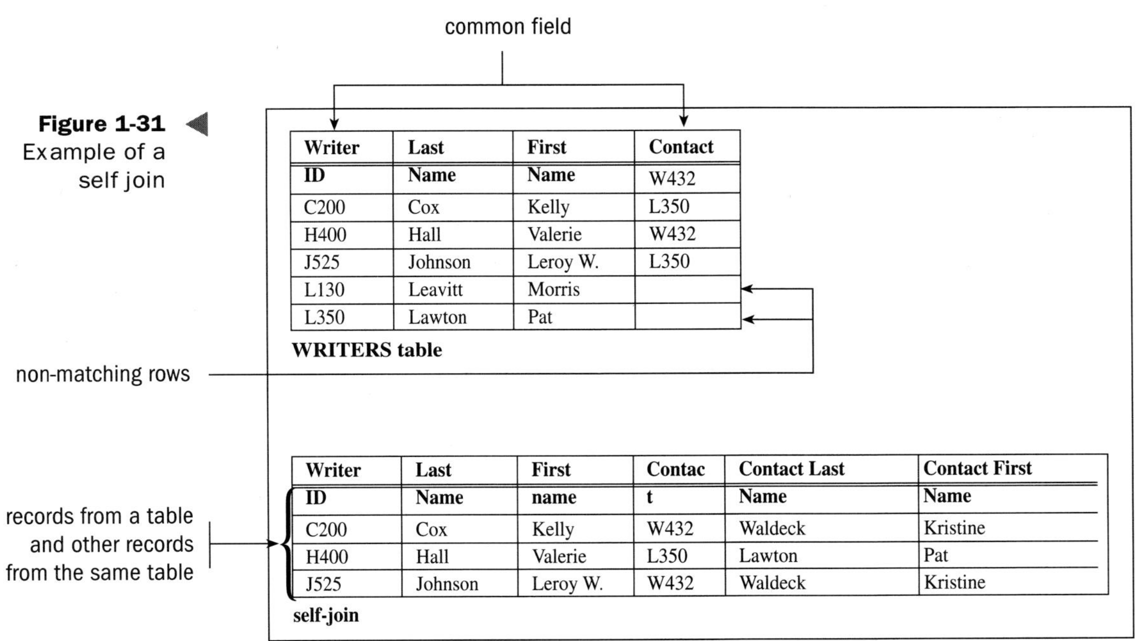

Writer ID	Last Name	First Name	Contact
			W432
C200	Cox	Kelly	L350
H400	Hall	Valerie	W432
J525	Johnson	Leroy W.	L350
L130	Leavitt	Morris	
L350	Lawton	Pat	

WRITERS table

Writer ID	Last Name	First name	Contact	Contact Last Name	Contact First Name
C200	Cox	Kelly	W432	Waldeck	Kristine
H400	Hall	Valerie	L350	Lawton	Pat
J525	Johnson	Leroy W.	W432	Waldeck	Kristine

self-join

Figure 1-31
Example of a self join

Creating a Self Join

Elena creates a query to display the new contact relationships in the WRITERS table. This query requires a self join. Elena adds two copies of the WRITERS field list to the Query Design window. Next, Elena adds a join line from the Writer ID field in the right field list to the Contact field in the left field list to establish a relationship between the WRITERS table and itself; the Contact field is a foreign key that matches the primary key field Writer ID. Finally, Elena adds the Writer ID, Last Name, First Name, and Contact fields from the left field list, adds the Last Name and First Name fields from the right field list, and then chooses an ascending sort on the Writer ID field. The query results display, in increasing order by Writer ID, all writers and their contacts, except for the two senior writers, who have null Contact field values.

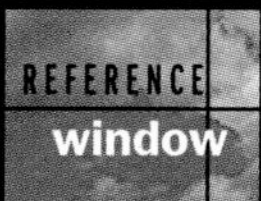

CREATING A SELF JOIN

- In the Queries list, click the New button to open the New Query dialog box. Select Design View, then click the OK button to open the Query Design window. The Show Table dialog box opens on top of the Query Design window.
- Click the table for the self join, then click the Add button to add the table's field list to the Query Design window. Click the table for the self join again, then click the Add button to add a second copy of the table's field list to the Query Design window. Click the Close button to close the Show table dialog box. Access identifies the left field list with the original table name and the right field list with the original table name followed by _1 to distinguish the two copies of the table.
- Click and drag a field from one field list to the related field in the other field list. Access adds a join line between the two fields.
- Double-click the join line between the two tables to open the Join Properties dialog box. Select the type of join by clicking the radio button for an inner join, a right outer join, or a left outer join. Click the OK button to close the Join Properties dialog box.
- Select the fields and define the selection criteria and sort options you want for the query.

To create a self join query:

1. Click the **Queries** tab to display the Queries list, then click the New button to open the New Query dialog box. Make sure that Design View is selected, then click the **OK** button to open the Query Design window. The Show Table dialog box opens on top of the Query Design window.
2. Click **WRITERS** in the Show Table dialog box, then click the **Add** button. Click the **Add** button again to add a second copy of the WRITERS field list, then click the **Close** button. Access identifies the left field list as WRITERS and the right field list as WRITERS_1 to distinguish the two copies of the table.
3. Scroll the left field list until the Contact field is visible. Then click and drag the **Writer ID** field from the right field list to the Contact field in the left field list. Access adds a join line between the two fields. You can verify that this is an inner join query by displaying the Join Properties dialog box.
4. Double-click the **join line** between the two tables to open the Join Properties dialog box. See Figure 1-32.

Figure 1-32 ◀ The Join Properties dialog box

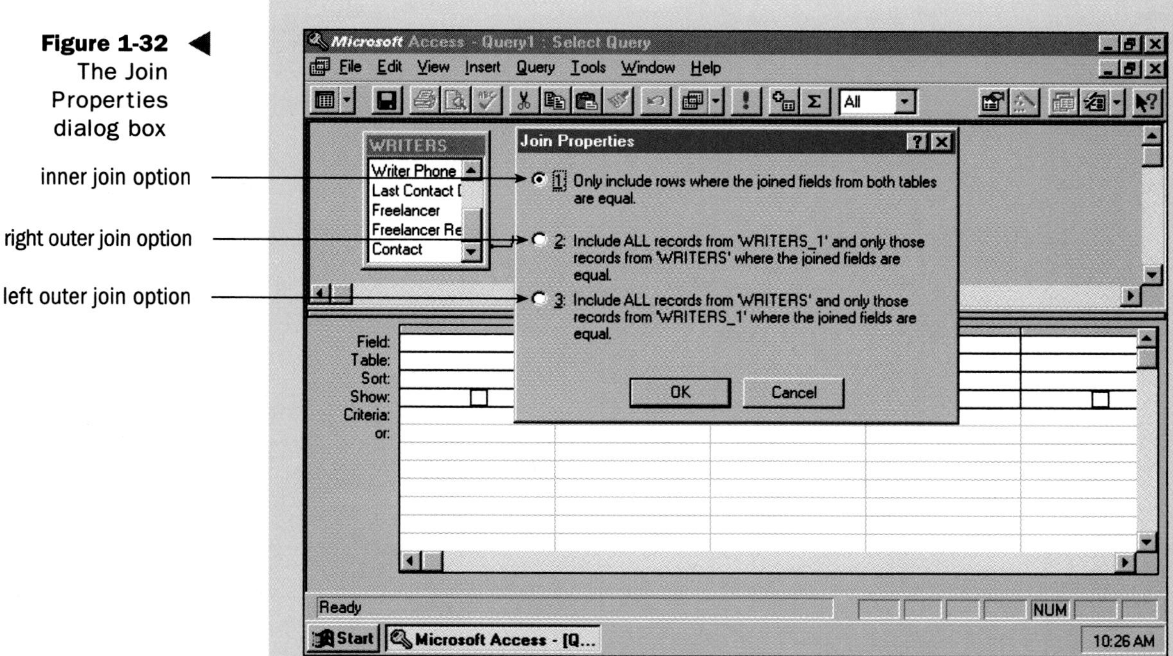

TROUBLE? If double-clicking the join line does not work, click View and then click Join Properties to open the Join Properties dialog box.

The top radio button is selected, indicating that this is an inner join. You would click the middle radio button for a right outer join or the bottom radio button for a left outer join. Because the inner join is correct, cancel the dialog box and then add fields to the Query Design grid.

5. Click the **Cancel** button and then, scrolling as necessary, double-click, in order from the left field list, the **Writer ID**, **Last Name**, **First Name**, and **Contact** fields to add them to the Query Design grid. Then double-click, in order from the right field list, the **Last Name** and **First Name** fields to add them to the Query Design grid.
6. Click the **Sort** text box for the Writer ID field, click the **Sort** list arrow, and then click **Ascending** to establish the sort order for the query results.
7. Click the **Run** button [!] on the toolbar. The query results display the records in increasing Writer ID order and show six fields and 13 records. See Figure 1-33.

Figure 1-33 The initial self join on the WRITERS table

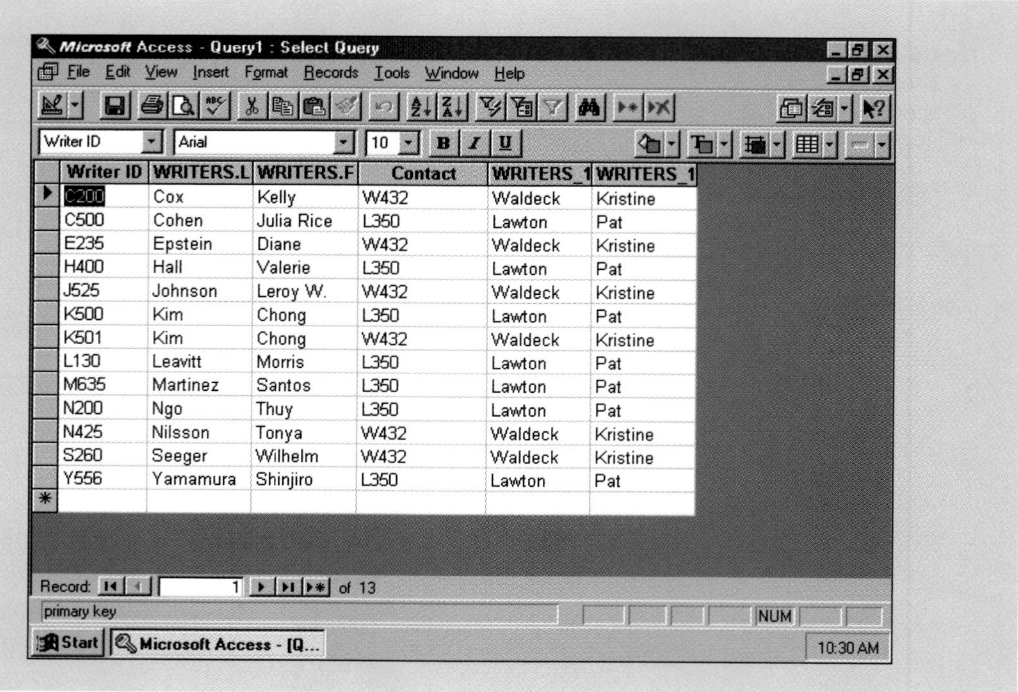

Writer ID	WRITERS.L	WRITERS.F	Contact	WRITERS_1	WRITERS_1
C200	Cox	Kelly	W432	Waldeck	Kristine
C500	Cohen	Julia Rice	L350	Lawton	Pat
E235	Epstein	Diane	W432	Waldeck	Kristine
H400	Hall	Valerie	L350	Lawton	Pat
J525	Johnson	Leroy W.	W432	Waldeck	Kristine
K500	Kim	Chong	L350	Lawton	Pat
K501	Kim	Chong	W432	Waldeck	Kristine
L130	Leavitt	Morris	L350	Lawton	Pat
M635	Martinez	Santos	L350	Lawton	Pat
N200	Ngo	Thuy	L350	Lawton	Pat
N425	Nilsson	Tonya	W432	Waldeck	Kristine
S260	Seeger	Wilhelm	W432	Waldeck	Kristine
Y556	Yamamura	Shinjiro	L350	Lawton	Pat

Access displays 13 of the 15 records from the WRITERS table; the records for Pat Lawton and Kristine Waldeck, senior writers having a null Contact field value, are not displayed. Four field names at the top of the query results columns now have prefixes indicating either WRITERS or WRITERS_1 to distinguish fields in one table from fields in the other table.

Elena decides to rename the four fields that have the table name prefixed to the field name to make the query results easier to read. When they are renamed, the field names, from left to right, will be Writer ID, Last Name, First Name, Contact, Contact Last Name, and Contact First Name.

To rename fields in a self join query:

1. Resize the rightmost query results column to its best fit column width either by using the shortcut menu or by double-clicking. The full name displayed is WRITERS_1.First Name, which means the First Name field from the WRITERS_1 table.
2. Click the **Query View** button on the toolbar to switch back to the Query Design window.
3. Place the insertion point in front of the first character in the second column's Field box, which displays Last Name, and then type **Last Name:**. Be sure the colon is the last character you type.
4. Repeat step 3 for the third column. Type **First Name:** before the field name for that column. Repeat step 3 for the fifth column, typing **Contact Last Name:** before the field name for that column. Finally, repeat step 3 for the sixth column, typing **Contact First Name:** before the field name for that column.
5. Click the **Run** button on the toolbar. The query results display the new names for each column.
6. Resize all columns to their best-fit column widths. See Figure 1-34.

Figure 1-34 ◀ The final self join on the WRITERS table

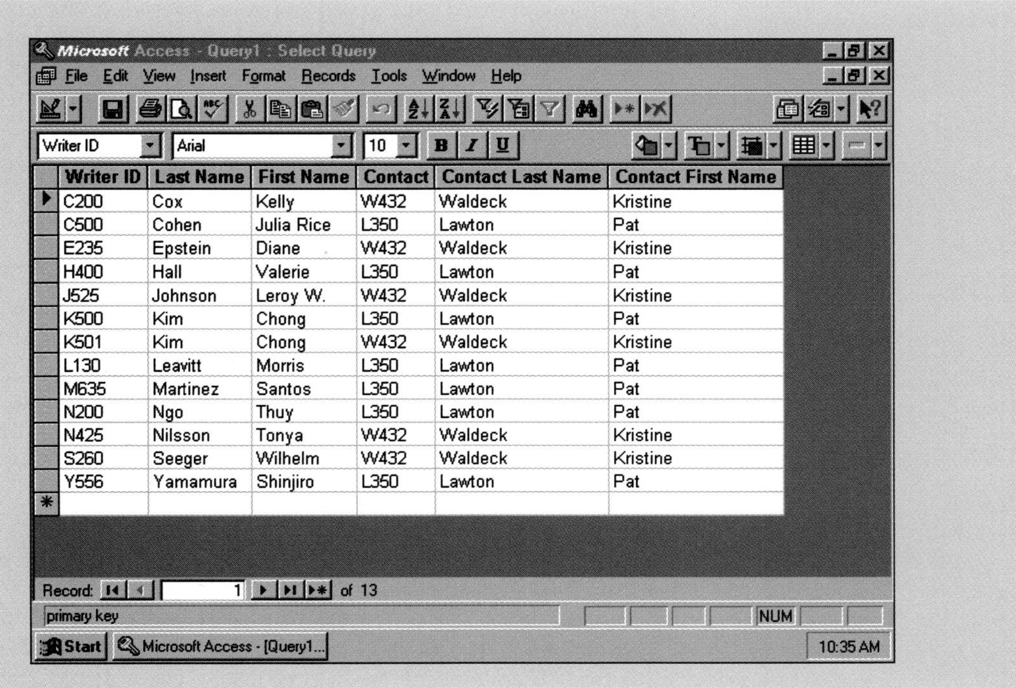

Writer ID	Last Name	First Name	Contact	Contact Last Name	Contact First Name
C200	Cox	Kelly	W432	Waldeck	Kristine
C500	Cohen	Julia Rice	L350	Lawton	Pat
E235	Epstein	Diane	W432	Waldeck	Kristine
H400	Hall	Valerie	L350	Lawton	Pat
J525	Johnson	Leroy W.	W432	Waldeck	Kristine
K500	Kim	Chong	L350	Lawton	Pat
K501	Kim	Chong	W432	Waldeck	Kristine
L130	Leavitt	Morris	L350	Lawton	Pat
M635	Martinez	Santos	L350	Lawton	Pat
N200	Ngo	Thuy	L350	Lawton	Pat
N425	Nilsson	Tonya	W432	Waldeck	Kristine
S260	Seeger	Wilhelm	W432	Waldeck	Kristine
Y556	Yamamura	Shinjiro	L350	Lawton	Pat

Elena can now give Brian a list of writers and their contacts for future article opportunities. She saves the query with the name Writers Contact Query and returns to the Database window.

To save and close a query:

1. Click **File**, click **Save As/Export**, type **Writers Contact Query** in the Save As dialog box, and then click the **OK** button. Access saves the new self join query.
2. Click the Writers Contact Query window **Close** button to close the window and return to the Database window. See Figure 1-35.

Figure 1-35 ◀ Queries saved in the Issue25 database

Append to PHONE NUMBERS Table Query
Article Length Crosstab Query
Article Type Parameter Query
Article Type Query
Articles Sorted by Issue and Length Query
Duplicate Writers Name Query
Freelancer List for Brian Query
Make Freelancers Table Query
Types Without Matching Business Articles Query
Writers Contact Query

Elena has now created and saved many queries that she and others can use to help plan the special issue of *Business Perspective*. The training seminar taught her many new and useful Access skills. One segment of the course covered the SQL language that Access uses behind the scenes when performing many of its operations. Elena knows that if she ever wants to take full advantage of Access's query abilities, she'll need to take the time to master SQL. For now, she decides simply to familiarize herself with SQL statements by looking them over after she creates queries.

SQL

SQL (Structured Query Language) is a standard language used in querying, updating, and managing relational databases. Every full-featured relational DBMS has its version of the current standard SQL, which is called SQL-92. If you learn SQL for one relational DBMS, it's a relatively easy task to begin using SQL for other relational DBMSs. This is particularly important when you work with two or more relational DBMSs, which is the case in most companies.

Much of what Access accomplishes behind the scenes is done with SQL. Whenever you create a query in the Query Design window, for example, Access automatically constructs an equivalent SQL statement. When you save a query, Access saves the SQL-statement version of the query.

When you are in the Query Design window or are viewing a query results, you can see the SQL statement that is equivalent to your query if you click the SQL View button or select SQL from the View menu. In response, Access displays the SQL statement in the SQL View window.

REFERENCE window

VIEWING THE SQL WINDOW

- In the Query Design window or the query results window, click View, then click SQL. Access opens the SQL window.
- To return to the Query Design window, click View, then click Query Design.
- To return to the query results window, click View, then click Datasheet.

Elena examines the SQL statements that are equivalent to two existing queries: Freelancer List for Brian Query and Articles Sorted by Issue and Length Query.

To view the SQL statement for the query named Freelancer List for Brian Query:

1. Click **Freelancer List for Brian Query** in the Queries list box, then click the **Open** button. Access opens the query results window and displays the six freelancer records from the WRITERS table. The fields displayed are First Name, Last Name, Writer Phone, and Amount.
2. Click the **Query View** button . Access opens the Query Design window for this saved query.
3. Click **View**, then click **SQL** to open the SQL View window. See Figure 1-36.

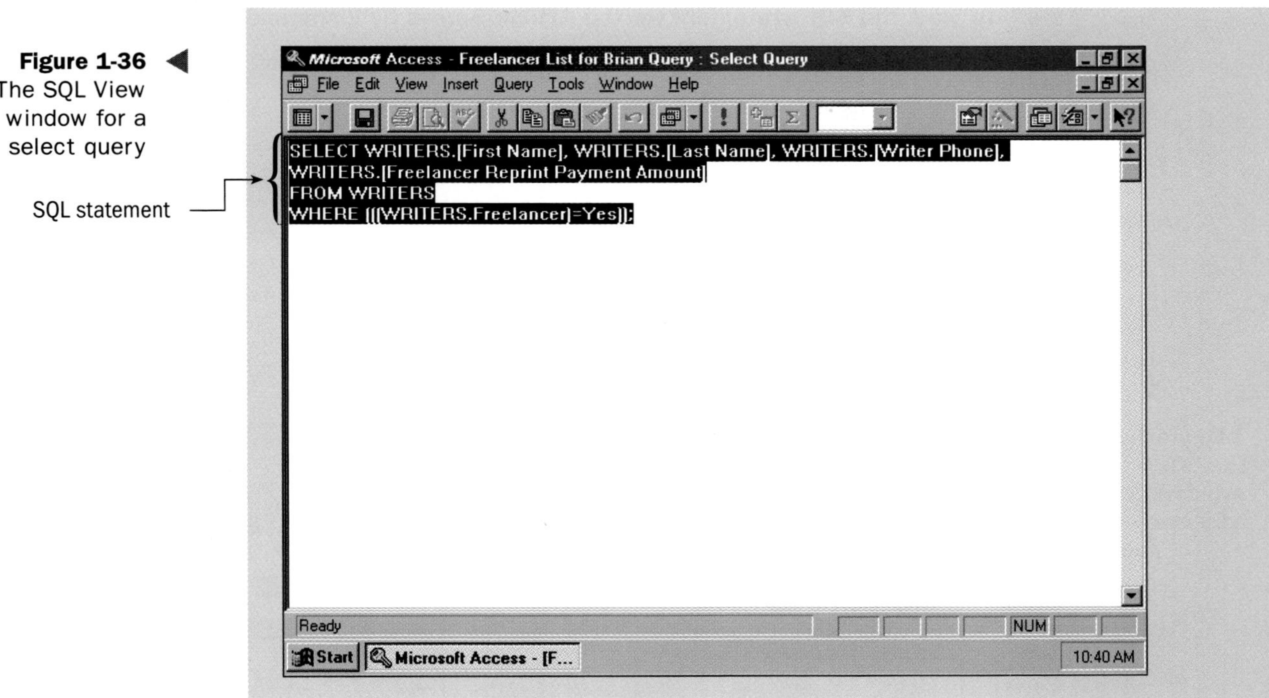

Figure 1-36 The SQL View window for a select query

SQL uses the SELECT statement to define what data it retrieves from a database and how it presents the data. For the work you've done so far, the Access menu commands and dialog box options have sufficed. If you learn SQL to the point where you can use it efficiently, you will be able to enter your own SELECT and other SQL statements in the SQL View window. You might find if you work with more complicated databases that you need the extra power of the SQL language to implement your database strategies fully.

The rules that SQL uses to construct an SQL statement, similar to the SELECT statement shown in Figure 1-36, are summarized as follows:

- The basic form of an SQL statement is: SELECT-FROM-WHERE-ORDER BY. After SELECT, list the fields you want to display. After FROM, list the tables used in the query. After WHERE, list the selection criteria. After ORDER BY, list the sort keys.
- If a field name includes a space, enclose the field name in brackets.
- Precede a field name with the name of its table. Connect the table name to the field name with a period. For example, enter Writer ID as 'WRITERS.[Writer ID].'
- Separate field names and table names by commas, and end a statement with a semicolon.

The SQL statement shown in Figure 1-36 selects the fields WRITERS.[First Name], WRITERS.[Last Name], WRITERS.[Writer Phone], WRITERS.[Freelancer Reprint Payment Amount] from the WRITERS table. The WHERE clause limits the query results to freelancer records. The SQL statement does not contain an ORDER BY clause, so the records are listed in the default order: ascending order by primary key.

You can enter or change SQL statements directly in the SQL View window. If you enter an SQL statement and then switch to the Query Design window, you will see its equivalent in the query design grid.

Elena examines the SQL statement for the Articles Sorted by Issue and Length Query.

To view the SQL statement for the Article Sorted by Issue and Length Query:

1. Click the SQL View window **Close** button. Access closes the SQL View window and displays the Queries list in the Database window.
2. Click **Articles Sorted by Issue and Length Query** in the Queries list, then click the **Open** button. Access opens the query results for this saved query and shows 27 records from the BUSINESS ARTICLES table in descending order by the Issue field as the primary sort key and in ascending order by the Article Length field as the secondary sort key. The fields displayed are Article Title, Type, Issue, and Article Length from the BUSINESS ARTICLES table and Last Name and First Name from the WRITERS table.
3. Click **View**, then click **SQL** to open the SQL View window. See Figure 1-37.

Figure 1-37 The SQL View window for a more complex query

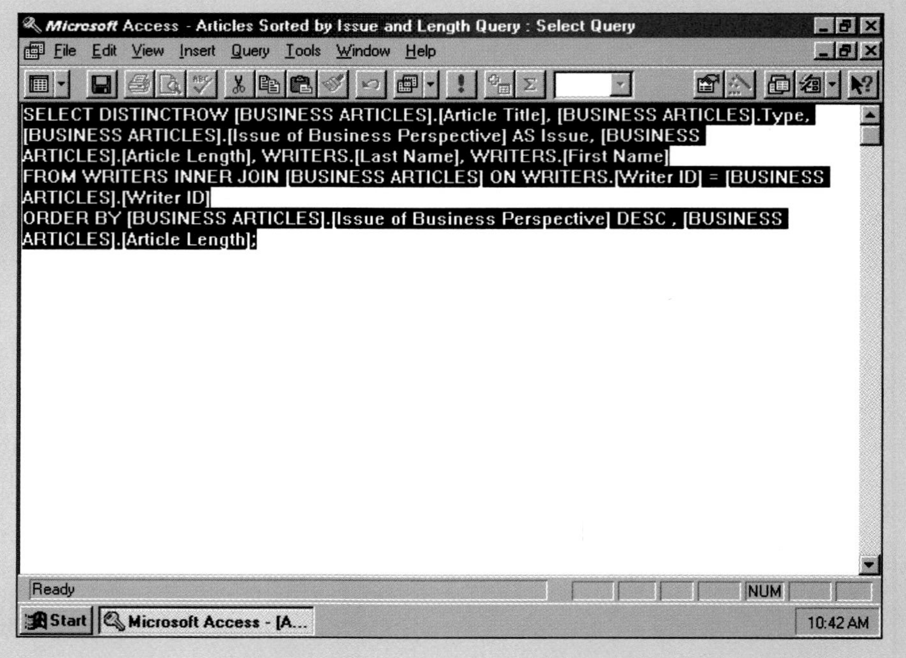

The SELECT statement for this second query is similar to the previous one, except for the following added features:

- Use DISTINCTROW to omit records that are entirely duplicates of other records in a table.
- Use DESC to indicate a descending sort order. If DESC does not follow a sort key field, then SQL uses ascending sort order.
- Use AS to rename a field. For example, the Issue of Business Perspective field in the BUSINESS ARTICLES table is renamed Issue.
- To link two tables with an inner join, use INNER JOIN between the two file names, followed by ON, and then followed by the names of the fields serving as the common field, connected by an equal sign.

Elena can see how the SQL SELECT statements mirror the options she selected in the Query Design window. In effect, every choice she made there is reflected as an SQL SELECT statement. She realizes that looking over SQL statements generated from queries that she designs really is an effective way to learn the SQL language, and she resolves to continue doing so.

To close the SQL View window and exit Access:

1. Click the SQL View window **Close** button to return to the Queries list in the Database window.
2. Click the Access window **Close** button to exit Access.

Elena is ready to present her information to Brian. If you want to pursue SQL further, you can also use the Access Help system and search on SQL.

Quick Check

1 What happens if you enter 23 for the Top Values property for a table that has only 20 records? Give an example of an alternative entry for this property.

2 What is the difference between an inner join and an outer join?

3 In what form does Access save a query?

4 What is the basic form of an SQL statement?

5 Figure 1-38 lists the field names from two tables: Telephones and Phone Calls.

Figure 1-38

Telephones	Phone Calls
Telephone Number	Calling Telephone Number
Billing Name	Called Telephone Number
Billing Address	Call Date Call Start Time Call End Time Billed Telephone Number

a. What is the primary key for each table?
b. What type of relationship exists between the two tables?
c. Is an inner join possible between the two tables? If so, give one example of an inner join.
d. Is either type of outer join possible between the two tables? Is so, give one example of an outer join.
e. Is a self join possible for one of the tables? If so, give one example of a self join.

Tutorial Assignments

Start Access and open the Issue25 database in the Tutorial folder on your Student Disk.

1. Create a query that displays the Freelancer field from the WRITERS table and the Article Title and Type fields from the BUSINESS ARTICLES table. Print the query results. Save the query with the name Writers and Article Types Query.
2. Create a crosstab query based on the Writers and Article Types Query. Use the Freelancer field values for the row headings and the Type field values for the column headings. Use the count of the Article Title field as the summarized value. Resize the query results columns and print the query results. Save the query with the name Summary of Article Types by Writer Class Crosstab Query.

3. Create a make table query based on the BUSINESS ARTICLES table. Select all fields for articles published since January 1990. Run the query, saving the results as BUSINESS ARTICLES SINCE 1990. Close the Query Design window and do not save the make table query. Open the BUSINESS ARTICLES SINCE 1990 table and print the table records.
4. Create a delete query that deletes all articles from the BUSINESS ARTICLES SINCE 1990 table except articles of type EXP. Run the query. Close the Query Design window and do not save the delete query. Rename the BUSINESS ARTICLES SINCE 1990 table EXP ARTICLES SINCE 1990. Open the table and print the table records.
5. Create an outer join between the TYPES table and the Types Without Matching Business Articles Query, printing all the Type and Description fields from the table and only those Type field values from the query that have matching records. Print the query results and save the query with the name Types Outer Join Query.

Case Problems

1. Walkton Daily Press Carriers Robin Witkop, one of the computer experts at the Walkton Daily Press newspaper, has designed a database to keep track of carriers and their outstanding balances. The database, named Press, has two tables: CARRIERS and BILLINGS. Robin has also designed queries, forms, and reports to make the database easy to use. You may want to review the tables, queries, forms, and reports in the Press database in the Cases folder on your Student Disk before completing the following.

Start Access and open the Press database in the Cases1 folder on your Student Disk.

1. Create a crosstab query based on the Carrier Sorted by Name and Route ID Query. Use the Carrier First Name and Carrier Last Name values as the row headings and the Route ID values as the column headings. Use the sum of the balance as the summarized value. Do not include a row total. Save the query with the name Carriers Sorted by Name and Route ID Crosstab Query. Run the query and resize all the datasheet columns for best fit. Print the query results.
2. Create an outer join between the CARRIERS and BILLINGS tables, printing the Carrier Last Name, Carrier First Name, Carrier ID, and Birthdate fields from the CARRIERS table and only those Route ID field values from the BILLINGS table that have matching records. Print the query results and save the query with the name Carriers Outer Join to Billings Query.
3. Create an update query to update the BILLINGS table. The query should add $50.00 to the Balance amount for each route with Carrier ID 16. Run the query. Close the Query Design window without saving the query. Open the BILLINGS table and print the table records.
4. Make a backup of the Press database on a new disk and use your backup for this exercise.
   a. Place your backup disk in drive A and use My Briefcase to create a Briefcase replica of the Press database. Make your backup the Design Master and make the Briefcase copy the replica.
   b. Open the BILLINGS table in the replica copy of the database. Delete all records for Carrier ID 21.
   c. Update the Design Master by synchronizing it with the replica.
   d. Open the Design Master database, open the BILLINGS table and print the table records.
   e. Close the Design Master database and delete the replica copy from My Briefcase.

2. Lopez Lexus Dealerships Maria and Hector Lopez own a chain of Lexus dealerships throughout Texas. They have used a computer in their business for several years to handle their payroll and normal accounting functions. To keep track of their car inventory, they have developed the Lexus database. The database has four tables: CARS, CLASSES, LOCATIONS, and TRANSMISSIONS. The CARS table contains data about each car in the inventory. The CLASSES table contains data about the different types of cars. The LOCATIONS table contains data about each of the Lopez's dealership lots. The TRANSMISSIONS table contains data about the available transmission types. They have also created queries, forms, and reports to make the database easy to use. You may want to review the tables, query, form, and report in the Lexus database in the Cases folder on your Student Disk before completing the following.

Start Access and open the Lexus database in the Cases1 folder on your Student Disk.

1. Create a query using the CARS and LOCATIONS tables. Select the Model and Cost fields from the CARS table. Select the Location Name field from the LOCATIONS table. Save the query with the name Models by Location Query.
2. Create a crosstab query (save it with the name Car Inventory Crosstab Query) that uses the Models by Location Query. Row headings are based on the Location Name field, column headings are based on the Model field, and the numbers in the middle are based on the sum of the Cost field. Do not calculate a summary for each row. Resize the columns in the query results for best fit and print the query results.
3. Create a query (save it with the name Transmissions Without Matching Cars Query) that displays the Transmission Type and Transmission Desc fields from the TRANSMISSIONS table for those records that do not match a record in the CARS table. Print the query results.
4. Create a top value query based on the CARS table. Select all fields in the table. The query should sort the records in descending order by Selling Price and select the 10 most expensive cars. Save the query with the name Most Expensive Cars Query. Print the query results.
5. Lopez Lexus Dealerships is having a sale on GS300 model cars. The selling price is reduced by $1000. Create an update query to reduce the Selling Price for all GS300 model cars. Run the query and print the query results. Do not save the query.

3. Tophill University Student Employment Olivia Tyler is an administrative assistant in the Financial Aid department at Tophill University. She is responsible for tracking the companies that have announced part-time jobs for students. She keeps track of each available job and the person to contact at each company. Olivia has asked Lee Chang, a database analyst on the staff of the university computer center, to design a database to track the company and job records.

Lee developed a database, called Parttime, that has two tables: JOBS and EMPLOYERS. Lee has also created queries, a main/subform form, and reports to make the database easier to use. You may want to review the tables, queries, forms, and report in the Parttime database in the Cases2 folder on your Student Disk before completing the following.

Start Access and open the Parttime database in the Cases2 folder on your Student Disk.

1. Create a query based on the JOBS table. Include the Employer ID and Hours/Week fields. Create a calculated field to calculate the weekly wages for each record. Use the Expression Builder to create an expression that multiplies the Hours/Week value times the Wage value. Name this new calculated field Weekly Wages. Save the query as Weekly Wage Query.
2. Create a crosstab query (save it with the name Jobs Crosstab Query) that uses the Weekly Wage Query. Row headings are based on the Employer ID field, column headings are based on the Hours/Week field, and the numbers in the middle are based on the sum of the Weekly Wages field. The Weekly Wages field is a calculated field equal to Hours/Week times Wages. Calculate a summary for each row. Resize the columns of the query results for best fit and print the query results.

3. Create an outer join between the EMPLOYERS and JOBS tables, printing all the Employer Name and Contact Name fields from the EMPLOYERS table and only those Job Title field values from the JOBS table that have matching records. Print the query results and save the query with the name EMPLOYERS Outer Join to JOBS Query.
4. Dynel International, Inc. (Employer ID GB68) has increased the wages it pays employees. Create an update query to increase the wages for all records in the JOBS table with Employer ID GB68. The new wage value should be 10% higher than the old wage value. Run the query and then print the table records. Do not save the query.
5. Make a backup of the Parttime database on a new disk and use your backup for this exercise.
   a. Place your backup disk in drive A and use My Briefcase to create a Briefcase replica of the Parttime database. Make your backup the Design Master and make the Briefcase copy the replica.
   b. Open the EMPLOYERS table in the replica copy of the database. Change the Employer Name for Phoenix Designs to Phoenix Graphics.
   c. Update the Design Master by synchronizing it with the replica.
   d. Open the Design Master database, open the EMPLOYERS table and print the table records.
   e. Close the Design Master database and delete the replica copy from My Briefcase.

4. Rexville Business Licenses Chester Pearce works as a clerk in the town hall in Rexville, North Dakota. He has just been assigned responsibility for maintaining the licenses issued to businesses in the town. He learns that the town issues over 30 different types of licenses to over 1,500 businesses, and that most licenses must be annually renewed by March 1. Clark designed a database to keep track of the town's business licenses. The database contains three tables: LICENSES, BUSINESSES, and ISSUED LICENSES. The LICENSES table contains data about the different types of business licenses the town issues. The BUSINESSES table stores data about all the businesses in town. The ISSUED LICENSES table contains data about the licenses which have been issued to local businesses. Chester has created queries, forms, and reports to make the database easier to use. You may want to review the tables, query, form, and reports in the Buslic database in the Cases2 folder on your Student Disk before completing the following.

Start Access and open the Buslic database in the Cases2 folder on your Student Disk.

1. Create an outer join between the LICENSES and ISSUED LICENSES tables, printing all the License Type and License Description fields from the LICENSES table and only those Amount field values from the ISSUED LICENSES table that have matching records. Print the query results and save the query with the name LICENSES Outer Join to ISSUED LICENSES Query.
2. Create a make table query based on the BUSINESSES and ISSUED LICENSES tables. Select the Business ID and Business Name fields from the BUSINESSES table and the Basic Cost (renamed Amount) field from the ISSUED LICENSES table. Add a Totals line to the Query Design grid and use the Sum operator to total the Amount field. Run the query and call the output table BUSINESS FEES. Do not save the query. Print the BUSINESS FEES table records.
3. The license fee amounts for automobile-related businesses have been increased by $20. Create an update query that selects all records in the LICENSES table in which the License Description field value begins with "Auto." The query should add $20 to the Amount field for these records. Run the query. Print the LICENSES table records. Do not save the query.

4. Create a query based on the ISSUED LICENSES and LICENSES tables. Include the Amount field from the ISSUED LICENSES table and the License Description field from the LICENSES table. Create a calculated field to calculate the month that the license was issued for each record. In the calculated field, use the expression Month ([Date Issued]). The Month function returns a value of 1 for January, 2 for February, and so on. Name this new calculated field Month Issued. Save the query as Licenses by Month Issued Query. Print the query results.

5. Create a crosstab query (save it with the name Issued Licenses Crosstab Query) based on the Licenses by Month Issued Query. Row headings are based on the License Description field, column headings are based on the Expr1 field, and the numbers in the middle are based on the sum of the Amount field. Do not calculate a summary for each row. Resize the columns in the query results for best fit and print the query results.

TUTORIAL 2

Macros

Using Macros with the Issue25 Database

OBJECTIVES

In this tutorial you will:

- Design a switchboard and dialog boxes for a graphical user interface
- Create and run macros
- Learn about actions, events, and event properties
- Create a control table and its queries
- Create dialog boxes
- Create a macro group
- Use the Switchboard Manager to create a switchboard

CASE

Vision Publishers

During the Access training seminar, the instructors demonstrated several database applications they had developed. Elena Sanchez and the other seminar participants judged the instructors' database applications to be more professional looking and easier to use than those any participant had created before the seminar. The instructors' applications used several advanced Access features to automate and control how a user interacts with Access. Elena explains these automation and control features to Brian Murphy, who asks her to develop a plan for applying what she learned at the seminar to the Issue25 database.

SESSION 2.1

In this session, you will design a graphical user interface. You will create, test, run, and save macros. You will also create a control table and its queries.

Designing the User Interface

A **user interface** is what you see and how you communicate with a computer application. A decade ago, you communicated with an application by typing in words that issued commands. You had to remember these commands, which were part of a command language. Most of the applications developed for today's popular operating environments, such as Microsoft Windows 95, use graphical user interfaces. A **graphical user interface** (GUI) (pronounced "gooey") displays windows, menu bars, pull-down menus, dialog boxes, and graphical pictures called **icons**, which you use to communicate with your application. Microsoft Windows 95 applications all use a similar visual interface, so once you learn one Windows 95 application, you can easily learn another. Overall, a GUI benefits a user by simplifying work, improving productivity, and decreasing errors.

Switchboards

Elena reviews the notes from her seminar and designs a special GUI for the Issue25 database. This interface is called a **switchboard**, a form that appears when you open a database and that provides controlled access to the database's tables, forms, queries, and reports. Elena plans that when a user opens the Issue25 database, Access will display a switchboard from which the user can choose the options he or she wants. The Issue25 switchboard is shown in Figure 2-1 as it will appear when Elena finishes creating it. When you create a switchboard, you are essentially creating a new interface, and it's up to you to decide what options you want to give the user.

Figure 2-1 The Issue25 switchboard

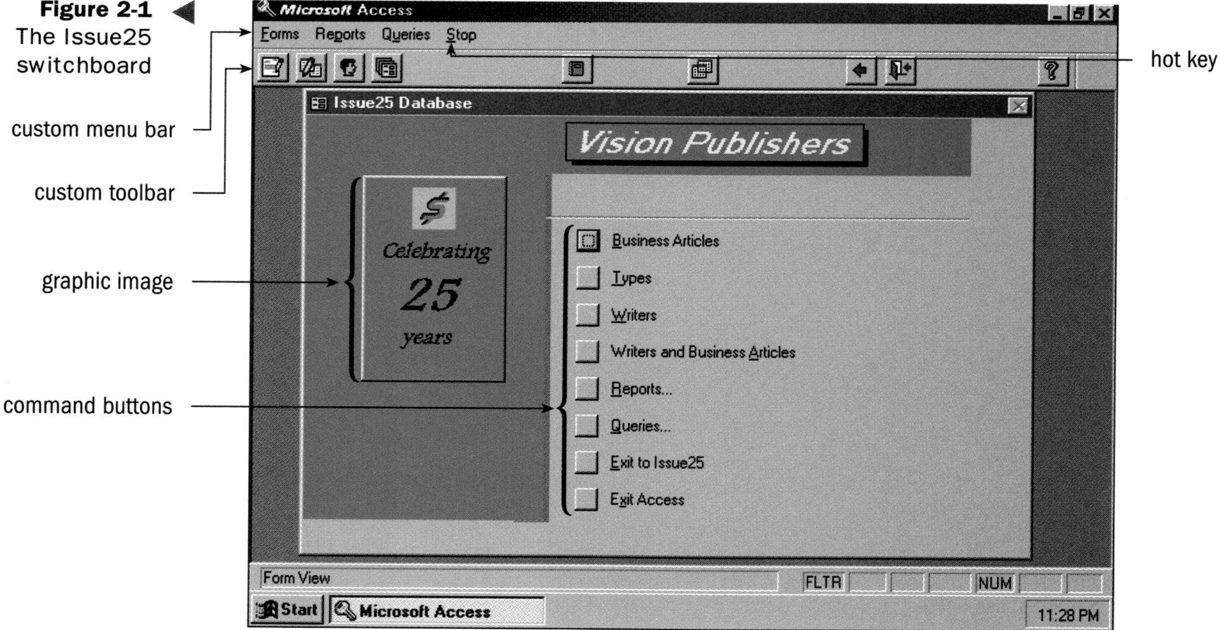

A typical switchboard has the following:

- Command buttons for all the options available to the user. In the switchboard shown in Figure 2-1, for example, a user can click command buttons to open one of four forms, to open lists of available queries or reports, to exit from the switchboard to the Database window for the Issue25 database, or to exit Access. When a selected form, query, or report list is closed, Access redisplays the switchboard, allowing the user to choose the next option. In other words, you start and end with the switchboard and navigate between options from the switchboard.
- A custom menu bar. You can choose options from the menu bar and menus or from the command buttons.
- A custom toolbar. You can use standard Access toolbar buttons or create your own buttons. You can also change the icon on the face of a button to another icon or to text.
- **Shortcut keys** or **hot keys**, underlined letters in each menu name and on each command button option. While holding down the Alt key, you press the indicated letter, to make a selection, instead of clicking a command button, menu name, or toolbar button.
- Text boxes and graphic images that provide identification and visual appeal. The display of a small number of attractively designed graphic images and text boxes can help users understand the switchboard's functions, but beware that too many can be confusing or distracting.

A switchboard gives an attractive look to your user interface, but there are two more important reasons to use a switchboard. First, a switchboard lets you customize the organization of the user interface. A second important reason to use a switchboard is to prevent users from changing the final design of your tables, forms, queries, and reports. By hiding the Database window and using a custom menu bar and toolbar, you limit users to just those database features you want them to use. If you do not include any menu, toolbar, or command-button option that lets users open a design window, users cannot inadvertently change your application design. Elena includes the Exit to Issue25 command button, which closes the switchboard and returns to the Database window for the Issue25 database, because she needs a quick and easy way to change and test the interface while she is creating it. Once she perfects the interface, she will remove the command button and, with its removal, prevent others from changing the interface.

Dialog Boxes

Two command buttons on the Issue25 switchboard, the Reports and Queries buttons, have three trailing dots. As a Windows standard, these dots signify that a dialog box containing further detailed options opens when that command button is clicked. To display the report and query names and their options, Elena will design two custom dialog boxes. Figure 2-2 shows how they will appear after they are created. A **custom dialog box** is a form that resembles a dialog box, both in appearance and function. You use a custom dialog box to ask for user input, selection, or confirmation before an action is performed, such as the opening of query results or the printing of a report.

Figure 2-2 The Reports and Queries dialog boxes

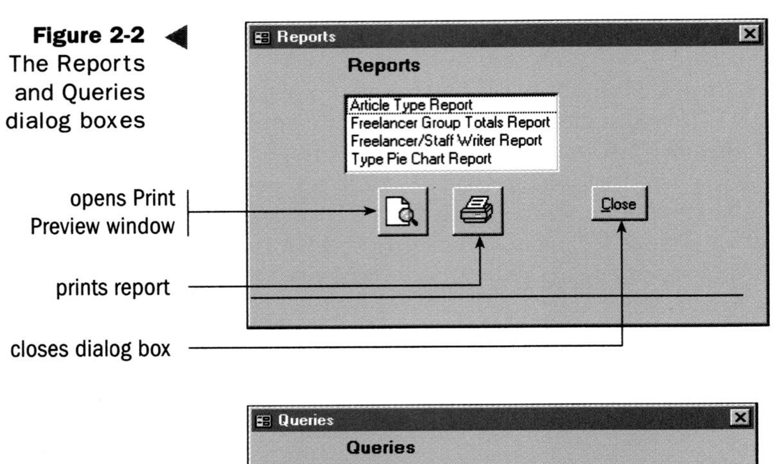

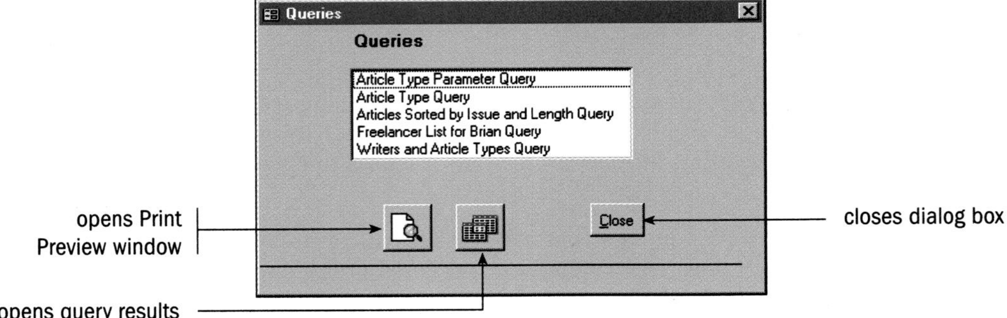

Both dialog boxes contain list boxes that display the queries and reports available for selection. Clicking the Close command buttons returns you to the switchboard. The other command buttons use graphic images to identify their functions. Each dialog box has a command button on the left with the icon of a magnifying glass over a piece of paper. This is the same graphic image Access uses on its Print Preview button. Just as the Print Preview button opens the Print Preview window, these command buttons open the Print Preview window for the selected query or report. The middle command button in the dialog boxes either prints the selected report or opens the query results for the selected query. Command buttons can contain text, standard graphic images available from Access, or graphic images you supply.

Macros

The command buttons on Elena's switchboard and custom dialog boxes gain their power from macros—and from Visual Basic code. A **macro** is a command or a series of commands you want Access to perform automatically for you. Macros automate repetitive tasks, such as opening forms, printing reports, and running queries. Each command in a macro is called an **action** or instruction. Clicking the Writers command button on Elena's switchboard, for example, causes Access to perform a macro containing the action that opens the Writers Column Form.

Access lets you automate most tasks using either macros or Visual Basic. As a beginner, you will find it easier to write macros than to program using Visual Basic. With macros, you simply select a series of actions from a list so that the macro does what you want it to do. To use Visual Basic you need to understand the Visual Basic command language well enough to be able to write your own code. Visual Basic does provide advantages over macros, including better error-handling capabilities, and it makes your application easier to change. Macros, however, are useful for small applications and for simple tasks, such as opening and closing objects. Additionally, you cannot use Visual Basic and must use macros in the following four situations.

- Assigning actions to a specific keyboard key or key combination
- Creating custom menu bars

- Opening an application in a special way, such as displaying a switchboard
- Performing actions from a toolbar button

Creating Macros

At her seminar Elena learned how to use macros by creating some simple macros and experimenting with them. To refresh her knowledge of macros, she creates a macro to open the Types Form which is stored in the Issue25 database.

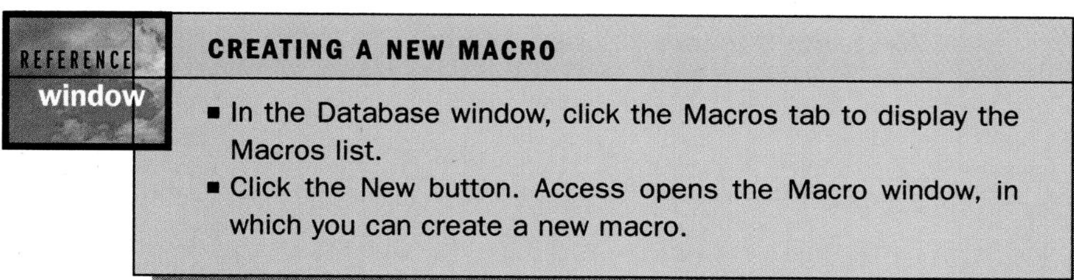
REFERENCE window

CREATING A NEW MACRO

- In the Database window, click the Macros tab to display the Macros list.
- Click the New button. Access opens the Macro window, in which you can create a new macro.

Elena opens the Issue25 database and then opens the Macro window to begin creating the new macro.

To open the Macro window:

1. Place your Student Disk in the appropriate drive, start Access, open the Issue25 database in the Tutorial folder on your Student Disk, and then maximize the Database window.
2. Click the **Macros** tab in the Database window to display the Macros list.
3. Click the **New** button. Access opens the Macro window. See Figure 2-3.

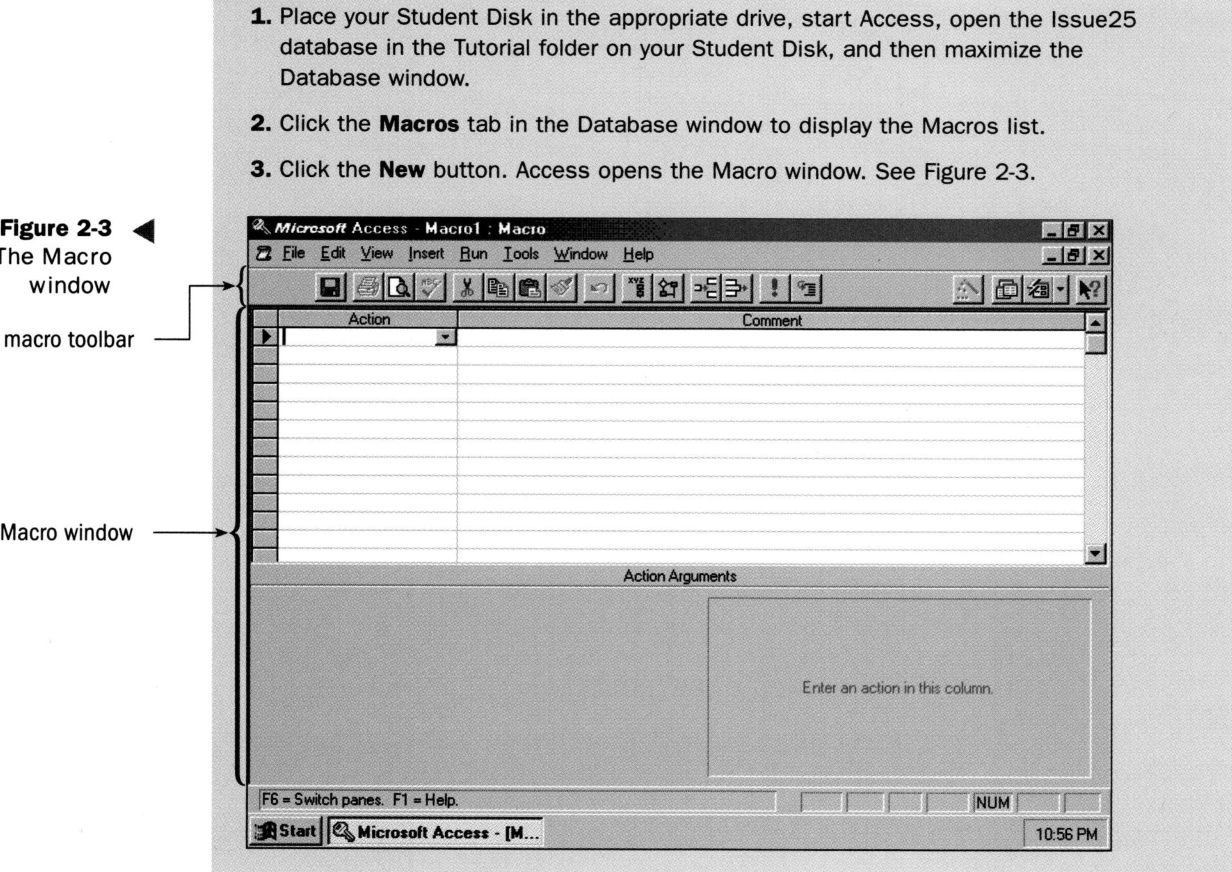

Figure 2-3 The Macro window

In the **Macro window** you create and modify macros. Both the menu bar and toolbar for the Macro window have options that are specifically related to macros. The Macro window has an **Action column**, in which you enter the action you want Access to perform, and a **Comment column**, in which you enter optional comments to document the specific action.

When you choose your first action (as you'll see in a moment), Access displays a hint for the current macro property in the lower panel of the Macro window on the right. On the left, Access lists the arguments associated with the actions you choose. Arguments are additional facts Access needs to execute an action. The action for opening a form, for example, needs the form name and the window name as arguments.

Choosing an Action

Elena creates a simple macro to open the Types Form.

To create a macro to open a form:

1. Click the first row **Action** list arrow.
2. Scroll and then click **OpenForm**. Access closes the list box, displays OpenForm as the first action, and displays six arguments for this action in the lower panel.
3. Press the **Tab** key and then type **Open the Types Form** in the Comment text box.
4. In the Action Arguments panel of the Macro Window, click the **Form Name** text box, click the **Form Name** list arrow, and then click **Types Form**. See Figure 2-4.

Figure 2-4 The OpenForm action

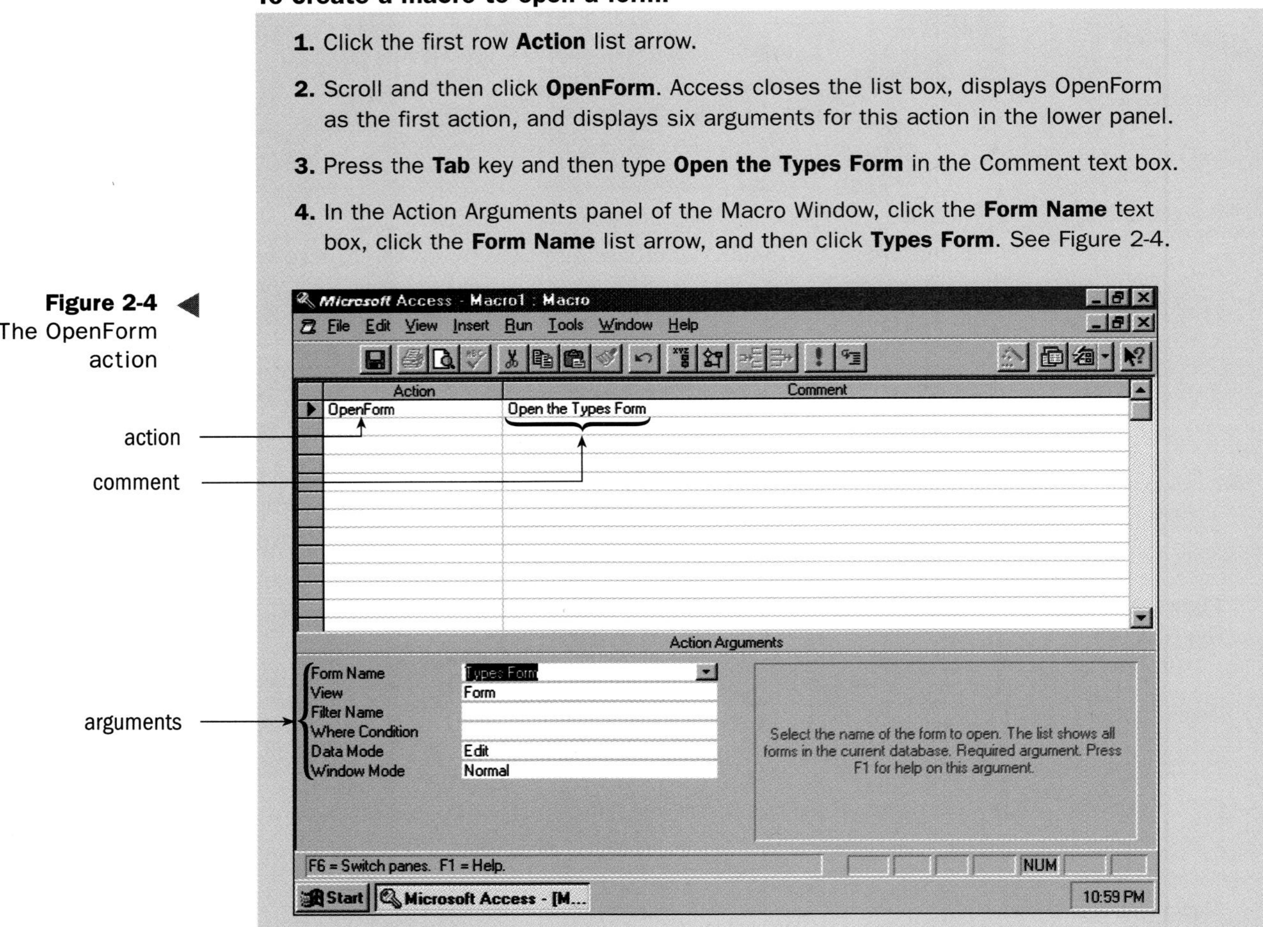

For now, do not change any other argument. When you run the macro, Access opens the Types Form in the Form View window, does not use a filter or special condition, allows edits or changes to the data, and treats the Form View window normally.

Saving a Macro

Before running the macro Elena saves it using the macro name Open Practice Macro.

To save a new macro:

1. Click the **Save** button on the toolbar.
2. Type **Open Practice Macro** in the Macro Name text box and then click the **OK** button. Access closes the dialog box and saves the macro.

Running a Macro

You can directly run a macro in three different ways:

- In the Macro window, click the Run button on the toolbar.
- Click Tools, click Macro, scroll through the Macro Name list box, click the macro name, and then click the OK button.
- In the Database window, click the Macro tab and then click the Run button.

Elena uses the first method to run the macro she just created and saved. If she had not already saved the macro, Access would tell her to save the macro before she could run it.

To run the macro that is open in the Macro window:

1. Click **Run** button on the toolbar. Access opens the form Types Form in the Form View window. See Figure 2-5.

Figure 2-5 Using a macro to open the Types Form

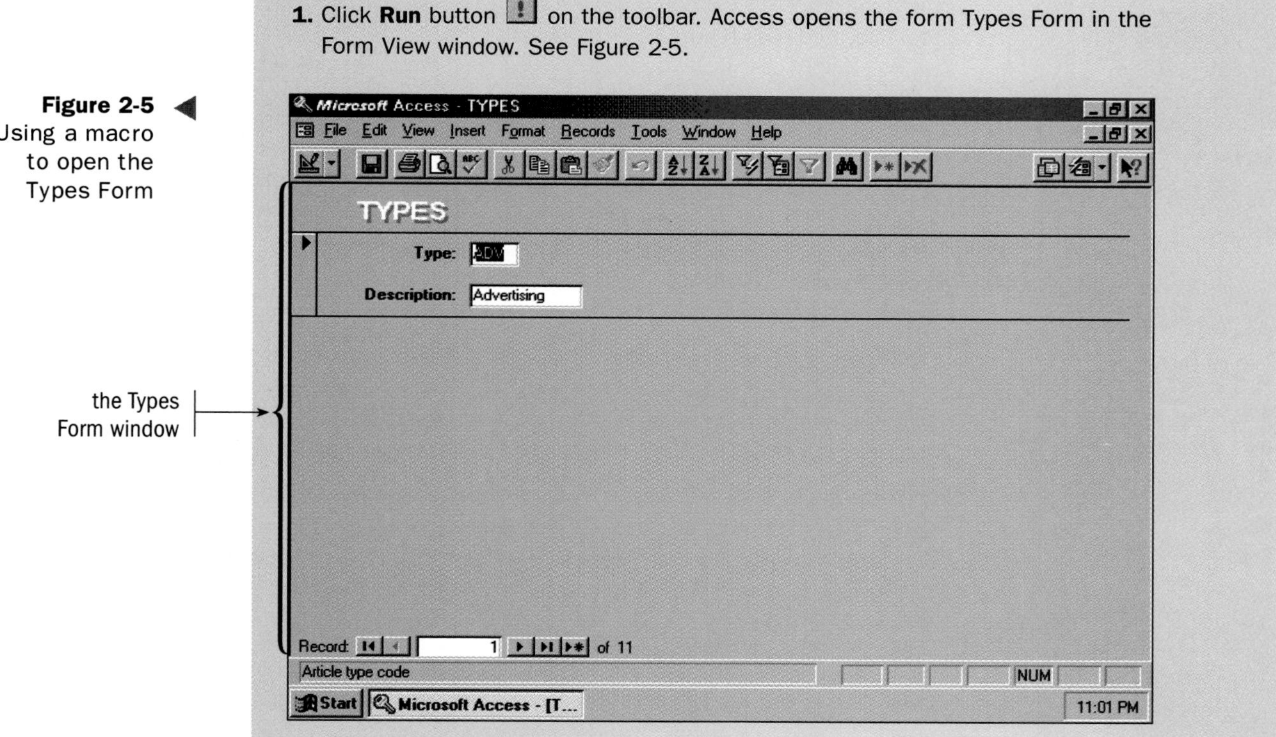

Access executes the macro by opening the Types Form in the Form View window; you can now work with the fields and records of the Types Form. Elena knows that this first macro is not very sophisticated; it involves only one action. It has, however, given her a chance to become comfortable with creating and using macros.

Adding Actions to a Macro

To practice creating a macro with more than one action, Elena adds a few actions to Open Practice Macro. Before the OpenForm action, she adds the Hourglass and Beep actions. Following the OpenForm action, she adds actions to open the Article Type Query, perform the Beep action, close the Article Type Query, close the Types Form, and then perform the Beep action. The **Hourglass action** displays an hourglass pointer while the macro is being executed, and the **Beep action** sounds a beep tone through the computer's speaker. Because the Hourglass and Beep action names are self-descriptive, Elena does not need to add comments to document them.

Once the changed macro has been executed, Elena will have heard three beep tones; two object windows will have opened and closed, and the hourglass pointer will have appeared from the start to the end of the macro's execution. Again, Elena knows that the net effect of the actions isn't very useful, but it does help her further demonstrate and understand the power of a macro with multiple actions.

To add actions to an existing macro:

1. Click the Form View window **Close** button [X] to close that window and return to the Macro window.
2. Click the **row selector** to highlight the first row in the Macro window. Right-click the row selector to open the shortcut menu and then click **Insert Row**. Access inserts a blank row above the OpenForm action. Repeat this step to insert a second blank row above the OpenForm action.
3. Click the first row's **Action** text box, click the **Action** list arrow, scroll down the list, and then click **Hourglass**. The default value for the Hourglass On argument is Yes. This is the value you want, so you are done adding the first action.
4. Click the second row's **Action** text box, click the **Action** list arrow, and then click **Beep**. The Beep action has no arguments, so you are done adding this action.
5. To add the Beep action to the fifth and eighth rows, right-click the **second row selector** and then click **Copy** in the shortcut menu. Right-click the **fifth row selector**, and then click **Paste** in the shortcut menu. Right-click the **eighth row selector**, then click **Paste** in the shortcut menu. Access adds the Beep action to the fifth and eighth rows.
6. Click the fourth row's **Action** text box, click the **Action** list arrow, scroll down the list, and then click **OpenQuery**. Press the **Tab** key and then type **Open the Article Type Query** in the Comment text box. Click the **Query Name** text box in the Action Arguments panel, click the **list arrow**, and then click **Article Type Query**.
7. Click the sixth row's **Action** text box, click the **Action** list arrow, and then click **Close**. Press the **Tab** key and then type **Close the Article Type Query** in the Comment text box. Click the **Object Type** text box, click the **list arrow**, and then click **Query**. Click the **Object Name** text box, click the **list arrow**, and then click **Article Type Query**.
8. Click the seventh row's **Action** text box, click the **list arrow**, and then click **Close**. Press the **Tab** key and then type **Close the Types Form** in the Comment text box. Click the **Object Type** text box, click the **list arrow**, and then click **Form**. Click the **Object Name** text box, click the **list arrow**, and then click **Types Form**. See Figure 2-6.

Figure 2-6
A macro with multiple actions

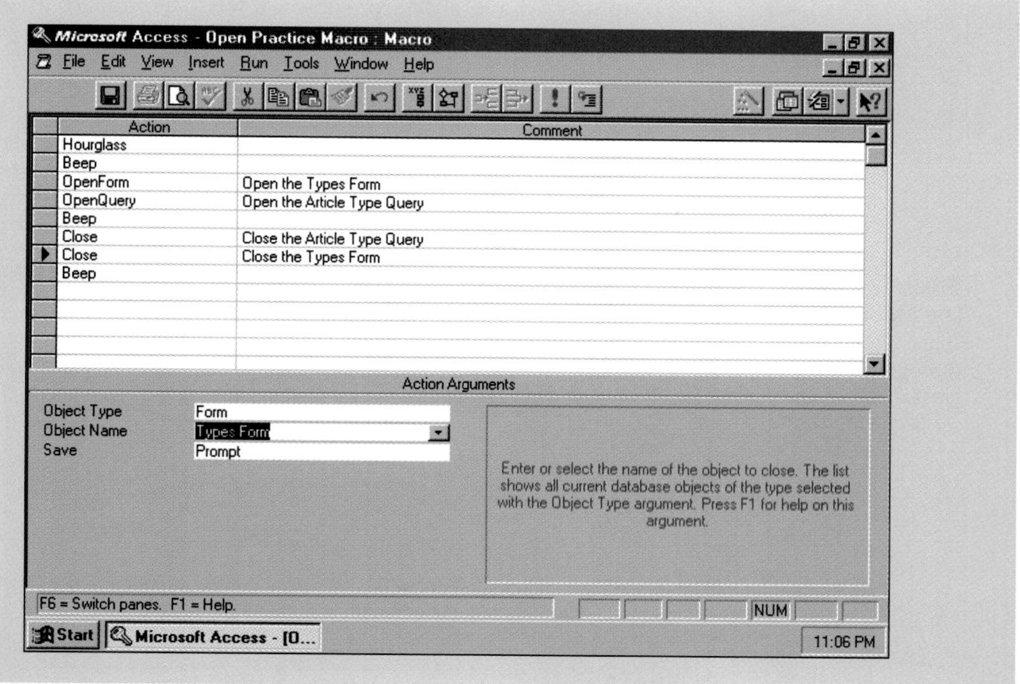

Elena executes the macro, again using the Run button on the toolbar.

To execute directly a macro having several actions:

1. Click the **Run** button on the toolbar. An Access dialog box asks, "Do you want to save the macro now?"
2. Click the **Yes** button. Access closes the dialog box, saves the macro, and executes the macro.

Depending on the speed of your computer, the form and query windows might open and close too quickly to be seen clearly, but you should be able to hear the three beeps distinctly and see the hourglass pointer. Elena runs the macro again, but this time she single-steps through it.

Single-Stepping a Macro

Single-stepping executes a macro one action at a time, pausing between actions. Use single-stepping to make sure you have placed actions in the right order and with the right arguments. If you ever have problems with a macro, use single-stepping to find the cause of the problems and to determine their proper corrections. Click the Single Step button on the toolbar to turn single-stepping on and off. Once you turn on single-stepping, it stays on for all macros until you turn it off.

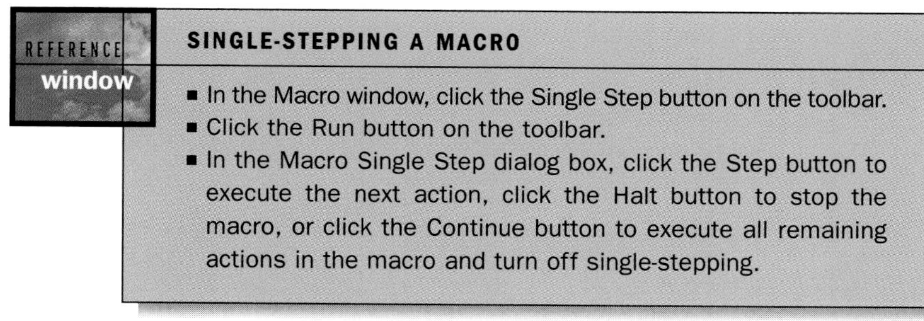

REFERENCE window

SINGLE-STEPPING A MACRO

- In the Macro window, click the Single Step button on the toolbar.
- Click the Run button on the toolbar.
- In the Macro Single Step dialog box, click the Step button to execute the next action, click the Halt button to stop the macro, or click the Continue button to execute all remaining actions in the macro and turn off single-stepping.

Elena wants to have a clearer view of what her macro is doing so she single-steps through the Open Practice Macro.

To start single-stepping through a macro:

1. Click the **Single Step** button on the toolbar to turn on single-stepping.
2. Click the **Run** button on the toolbar. Access opens the Macro Single Step dialog box. See Figure 2-7.

Figure 2-7 The Macro Single Step dialog box

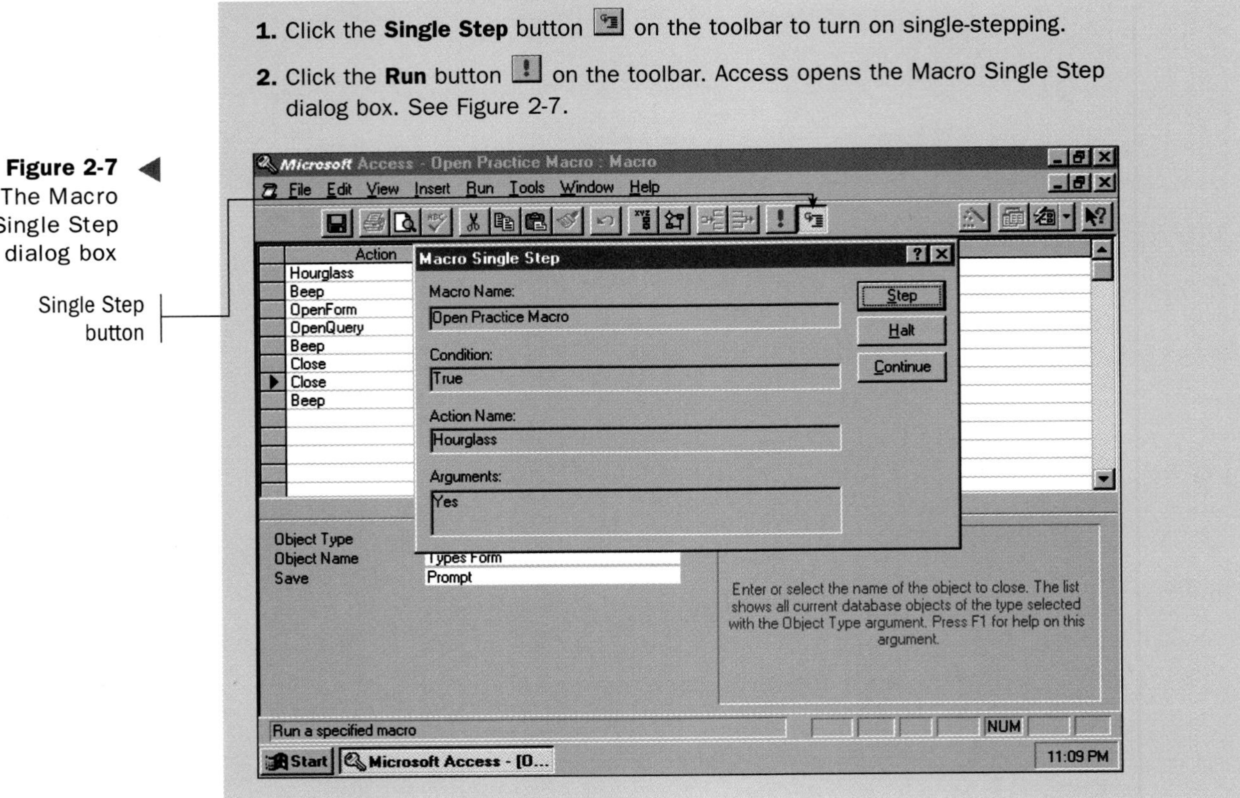

When you single-step through a macro, Access displays the Macro Single Step dialog box before performing each action. The Macro Single Step dialog box shows the macro name and the action's condition, name, and arguments. The action will be executed or not executed, depending on whether the condition is true or false. The three command buttons let you step one action at a time through the macro, halt the macro and return to the Macro window, or continue by executing all remaining actions without pause. Note that single-stepping is turned off if you click the Continue button.

Elena continues to single-step through the entire macro.

To single-step through a macro:

1. Click the **Step** button. Access runs the first action and shows the macro's second action in the Macro Single Step dialog box. Because the Hourglass action changes the pointer to an hourglass for the duration of the macro, you can see the hourglass pointer if you move the pointer outside the Macro Single Step dialog box.
2. Click the **Step** button a second time. Access runs the second action by sounding a beep and shows the macro's third action. Each remaining action is executed by a single click on the Step button.
3. Click the **Step** button six times, making sure you read the Macro Single Step dialog box carefully and observe the windows opening and closing on the screen after each click.
4. Click the Macro window **Close** button. Access closes the Macro window and returns to the Database window.

Adding Actions by Dragging

Another way to add an action to a macro is by dragging an object from the Database window to a new row in the Macro window. When you drag an object to a new row in the Macro window, Access adds the action that is appropriate and specifies default argument values for the action. Figure 2-8 describes the effect of dragging each of the six Access objects to a new row in the Macro window. For example, dragging a table creates an OpenTable action that opens the table's Datasheet View window and permits editing or updating. To use this dragging technique, be sure that the Macro and Database windows are both visible. You can move the two windows until you see all the critical components of each window, or use the Tile command on the Window menu.

Figure 2-8 Actions created by dragging objects from the Database window

Object Dragged	Action Created	Arguments and Their Default Values
Table	OpenTable	View: Datasheet Data Mode: Edit
Query	OpenQuery	View: Datasheet Data Mode: Edit
Form	OpenForm	View: Form Data Mode: Edit Filter Name: none Where Condition: none Window Mode: Normal
Report	OpenReport	View: Print Preview Filter Name: none Where Condition: none
Macro	RunMacro	Repeat Count: none Repeat Expression: none
Module	OpenModule	Procedure Name: none

REFERENCE window

CREATING AN ACTION BY DRAGGING

- Open the Macro window and the Database window.
- Drag a database object from the Database window to an Action text box in the Macro window. Access adds the action that is appropriate for the macro and sets the arguments to their default values.

Elena uses the dragging technique to add an action that opens the Article Type Form. She starts a new macro that she names More Practice Macro.

To add an action to a macro using the dragging method:

1. Click the **New** button to open the Macro window.
2. Click **Window**, then click **Tile Vertically** to tile the Macro window and the Database window. See Figure 2-9.

Figure 2-9 Macro and Database windows tiled vertically on the screen

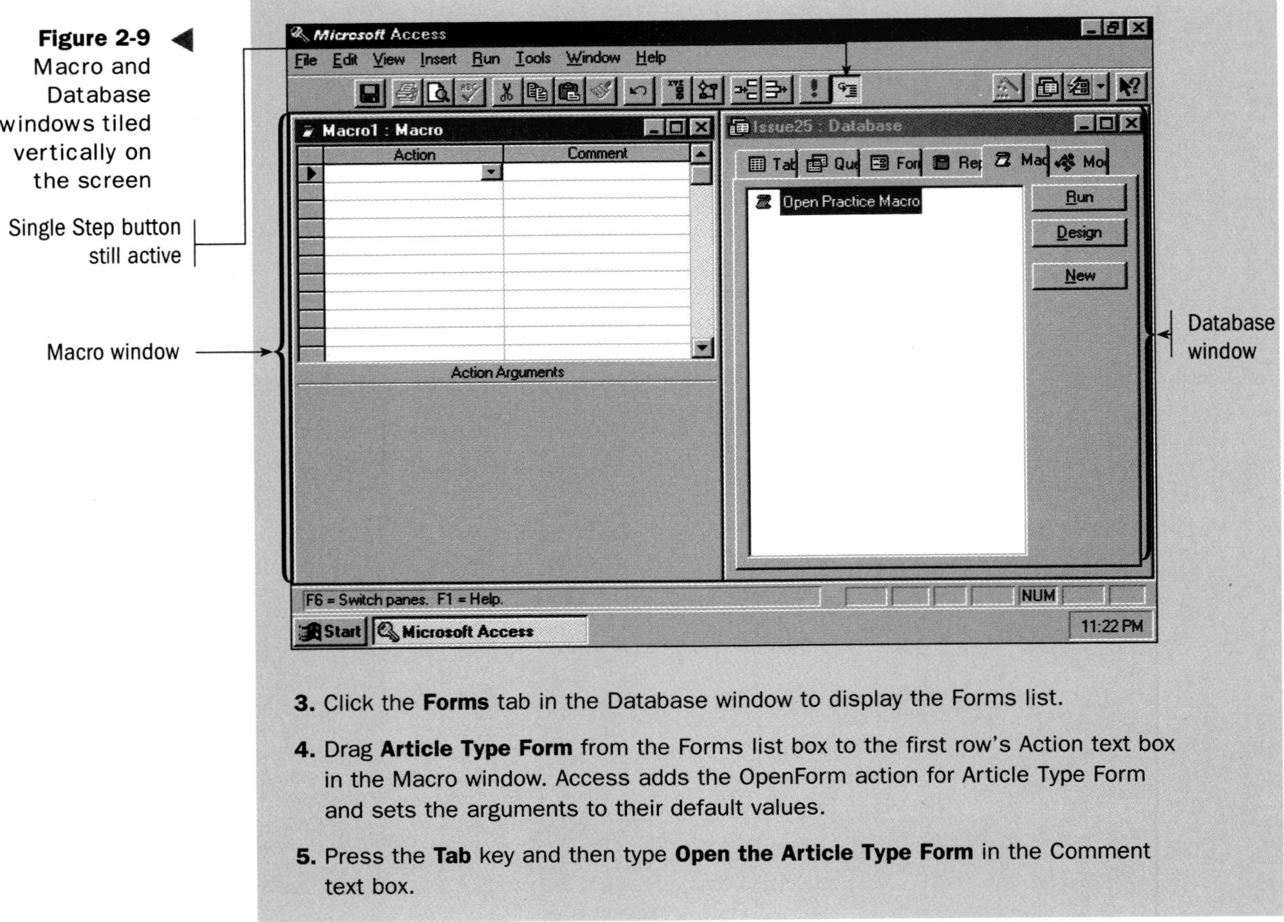

3. Click the **Forms** tab in the Database window to display the Forms list.
4. Drag **Article Type Form** from the Forms list box to the first row's Action text box in the Macro window. Access adds the OpenForm action for Article Type Form and sets the arguments to their default values.
5. Press the **Tab** key and then type **Open the Article Type Form** in the Comment text box.

Elena next adds the MsgBox action to the macro to open a dialog box containing an informational or warning message. Before adding the dialog box, Elena first uses the Access Help system to learn more about macros and actions.

Using Help to Learn About Macros and Actions

When you create Access macros, you need to know about the available actions and their arguments. Access has 49 actions for use in macros grouped under five categories. Actions in the "Data in forms and reports" category move the focus from one record to another record. **Focus** refers to the record and control that is currently active and awaiting user action. For example, a field has the focus when it is highlighted or has an I-beam pointer, and a command button has the focus when a dotted box appears around its label.

Actions in the "Import/export" category transfer data between the active database and other applications. Actions in the "Object manipulation" category open, close, size, and otherwise act upon Access objects. Actions in the "Execution" category either start or stop tasks. The "Miscellaneous" category contains actions that inform the user (Echo, Hourglass, MsgBox, SetWarnings, and ShowToolbar), emit a sound (Beep), send keystrokes (SendKeys), create a custom menu bar (AddMenu), and filter data (ApplyFilter).

Do not be concerned about learning all 49 actions. You will rarely need to use more than a dozen actions in most database applications. In this tutorial and the next two tutorials, you will gain experience with several macro actions. Since there are so many, it is difficult to remember them all. Fortunately, the Access Help system is a complete and convenient reference for macros and actions. The Access Help system contains, in a single reference source with one index, all the information you need and is available to answer your questions while you are working with Access. You can even print more complicated topics for study at your leisure away from the computer.

Elena uses the Access Help system to learn more about the available actions and to print one of the action topics. She uses the Index feature to find the specific information she wants.

To use Access Help to learn about actions:

1. Click **Help**, click **Microsoft Access Help Topics** to open the Access Help window.
2. If necessary, click the **Index** tab to display the Index page.
3. Type **actions** in the first text box. The Index page displays a list of index entries associated with actions.
4. Click **grouped by task** and then click the **Display** button. Access opens the Actions Grouped by Task topic, which is a complete list of the 49 actions. See Figure 2-10.

Figure 2-10 The Actions Grouped by Task topic in the Help system

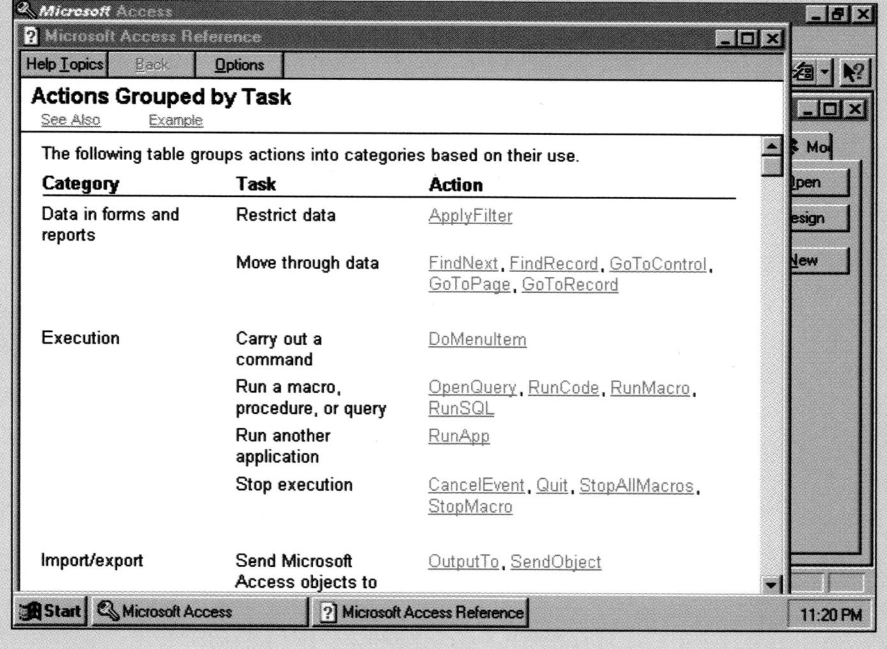

Next, Elena opens the MsgBox Action topic and prints it. She will use information from the MsgBox Action topic to complete the macro she is creating.

To open and print Help topics:

1. Scroll down the Actions Grouped by Task topic window to the Miscellaneous category and then click **MsgBox**. Access opens the MsgBox Action topic. See Figure 2-11.

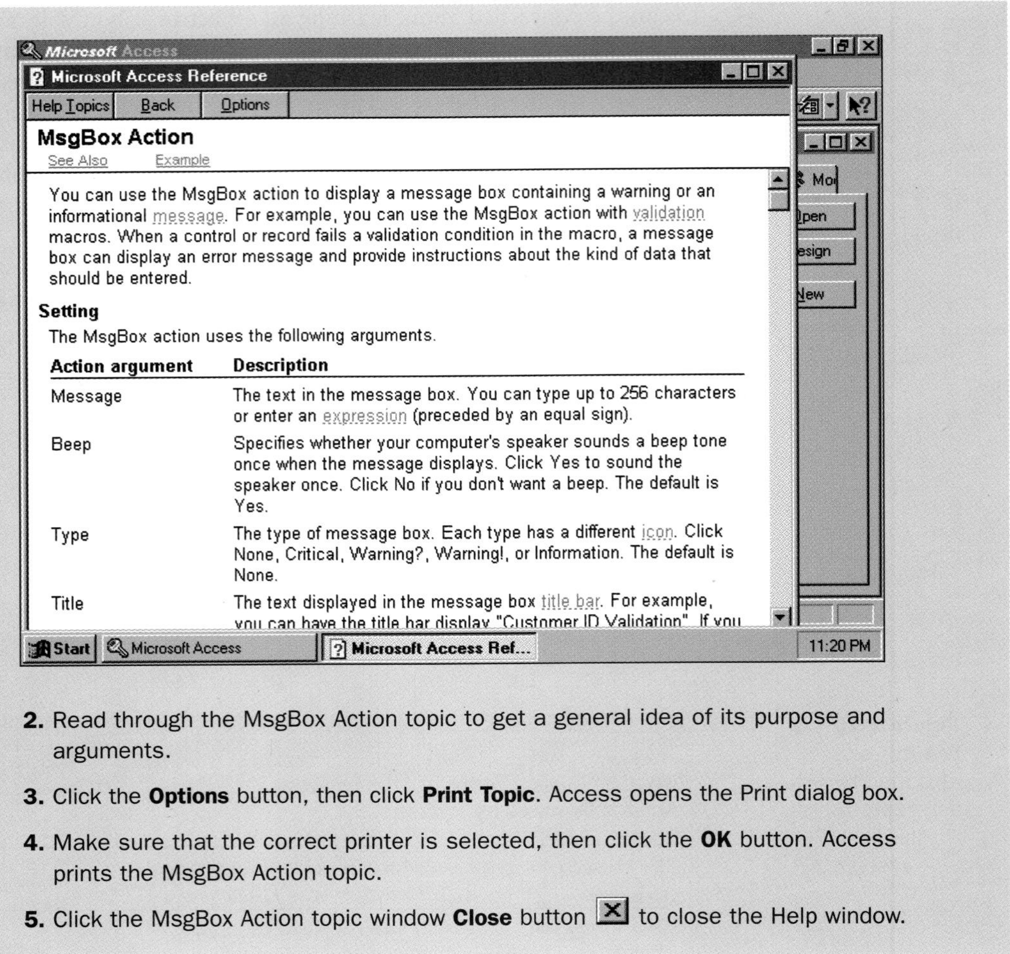

Figure 2-11 The MsgBox Action topic in the Help system

2. Read through the MsgBox Action topic to get a general idea of its purpose and arguments.
3. Click the **Options** button, then click **Print Topic**. Access opens the Print dialog box.
4. Make sure that the correct printer is selected, then click the **OK** button. Access prints the MsgBox Action topic.
5. Click the MsgBox Action topic window **Close** button [X] to close the Help window.

Adding a MsgBox Action

If you add the MsgBox action to your macro, Access will open a dialog box that remains on the screen until you click the OK button. Because the macro does not proceed to the next action until you click the OK button, you have as much time as needed to look at the opened Article Type Form.

The MsgBox action requires four arguments: Message, Beep, Type, and Title, as described in the MsgBox Action Help topic. You will provide the following action arguments for the MsgBox action:

- Message: Click OK to resume the macro
- Beep: No
- Type: Information
- Title: MsgBox Action Practice

As you move from one macro argument to the next, Access changes the description that appears to the right of the argument text boxes. The description is a brief explanation of the current macro argument. If you need a more detailed explanation, press the F1 key. When you are working with the MsgBox action in the Macro window and press the F1 key, for example, the Access Help system opens the MsgBox Action topic. This is the same topic you saw using the Access Help system.

To add a MsgBox action to a macro:

1. Click the second row's **Action** text box, click the **list arrow**, scroll down the Action list, and then click **MsgBox**. Press the **Tab** key and then type **Display a practice message box** in the Comment text box.
2. Click the **Message** text box and then type **Click OK to resume the macro**.
3. Click the **Beep** text box, click the **list arrow**, and then click **No**.
4. Click the **Type** text box, click the **list arrow**, and then click **Information**.
5. Click the **Title** text box and then type **Message Box Practice**.

The macro now has two actions: the first action opens the Article Type Form, and the second action displays a message box. To complete the macro, Elena adds the Close action for the Article Type Form. She once again drags the Article Type Form from the Database window, but this time she does it to specify the Close action's arguments.

Setting Action Arguments by Dragging

To set action arguments using the dragging method:

1. Click the third row's **Action** text box, click the **list arrow**, and then click **Close**. Press the **Tab** key and then type **Close the Article Type Form** in the Comment text box.
2. Drag **Article Type Form** from the Forms list to the Object Name text box in the Macro window. See Figure 2-12.

Figure 2-12 The Macro window with action arguments set by dragging

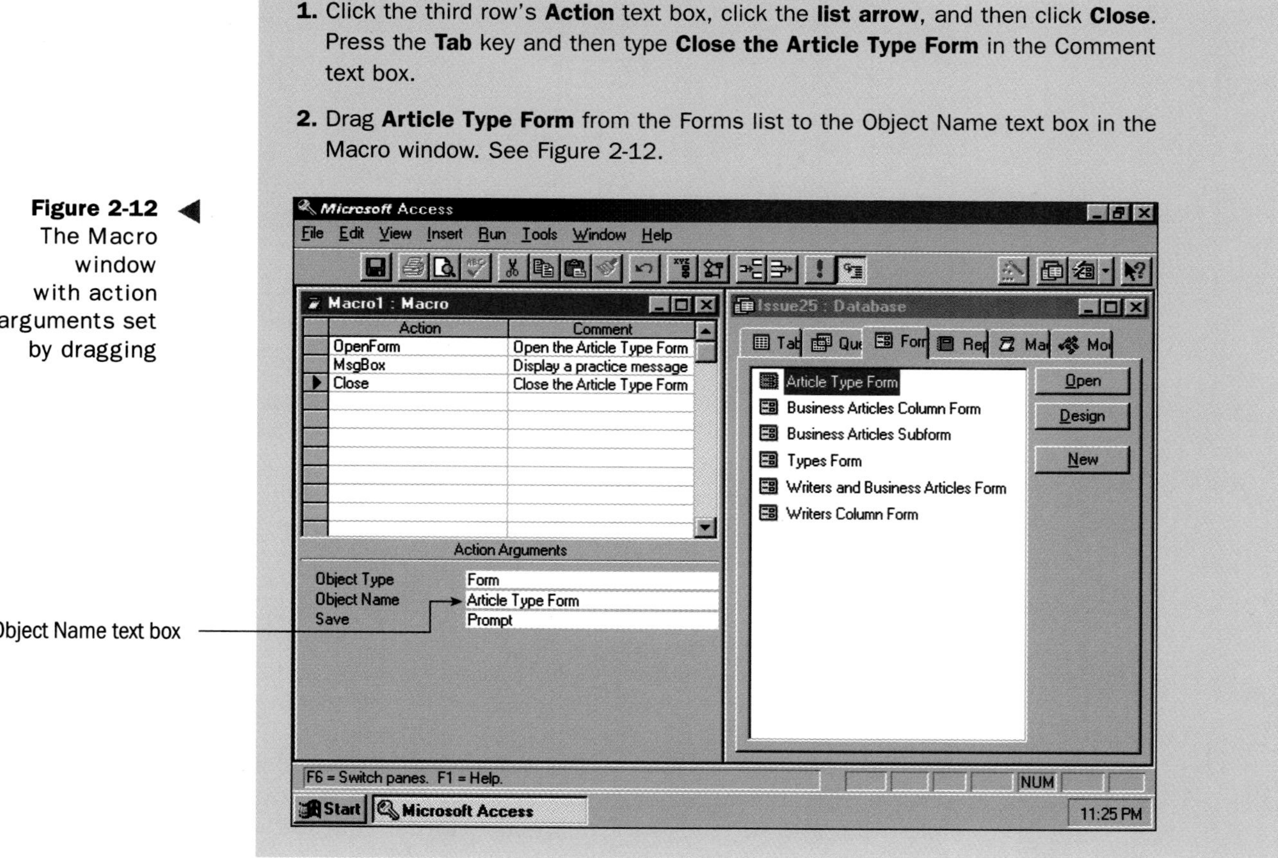

When Elena releases the mouse button in the Object Name text box, Access sets the Object Type argument to Form and the Object Name argument to Article Type Form. Because the macro is now complete, Elena runs it to be sure it is correct, saves it with the name More Practice Macro, and then exits Access.

To run and save a macro:

1. If the **Single Step** button on the toolbar is selected, click it to deselect it.
2. Click the **Run** button. An Access dialog box states "You must save the macro before you run it."
3. Click the **Yes** button to open the Save As dialog box, type **More Practice Macro** in the Macro Name text box, and then click the **OK** button. Access saves the macro and runs the first two macro actions. Access opens the message box after opening the Article Type Form. See Figure 2-13.

Figure 2-13 Running the MsgBox macro action

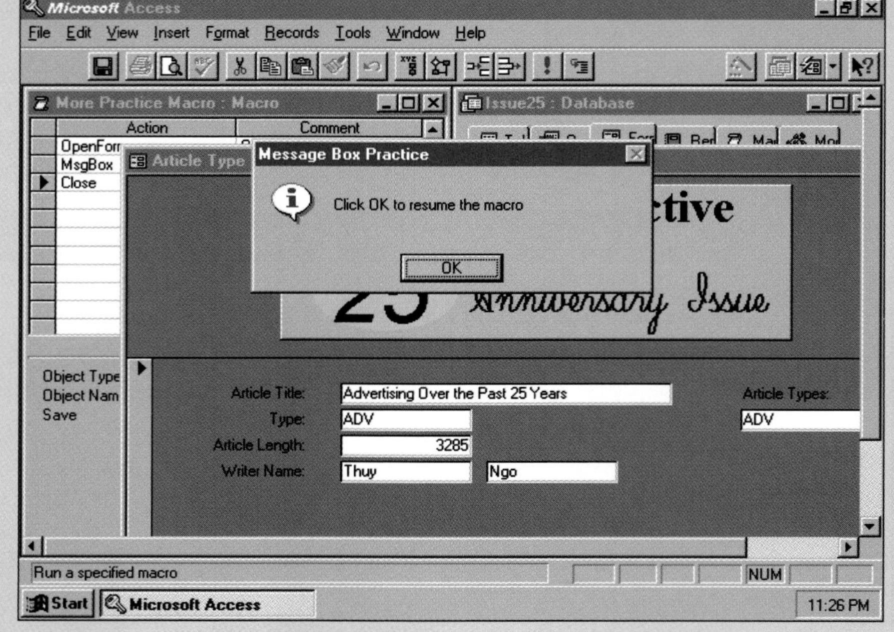

4. Click the **OK** button. Access closes the dialog box, runs the last macro action by closing the Article Type Form, and displays the Macro window.
5. Click the Macro window **Close** button to return to the Database window.

Elena has finished practicing with macros and is now confident she can create the macros she needs for the Issue25 switchboard and dialog boxes.

When to Use Macros

In reviewing her seminar notes about macros, Elena reads that, in contrast to what she did during her practice session, a macro is usually not initiated directly from the Macro window. Instead, she should design her macros to be executed in the following situations:

- When a user opens a database. If a macro with the special name **AutoExec** is created, Access automatically executes the macro when a user opens the database. A macro can also be part of an automatic startup sequence defined in the Startup dialog box.
- When a user presses a specific key combination.
- When a macro is executed from within another macro that uses the RunMacro action.
- When a user chooses a command on a custom menu bar.
- When a user clicks a toolbar button, especially a button on a custom toolbar.

- When a user clicks a command button or another special control on a form or report.
- When a user opens a form or report that has a macro attached to it.

For the last two situations, you can attach a macro to an event on a form or report.

Events

An **event** is an action to which you can define a response. Events occur, for example, when you click a button using the mouse or press a key to choose an option. In your work with Access you've initiated hundreds of events: on forms, controls, records, and reports. For example, three form events are: Open, which occurs when you open a form; Activate, which occurs when the form becomes the active window; and Close, which occurs when you close a form and it disappears from the screen. Each event has an associated event property. An **event property** is a named attribute of an object, such as a form or report, to which the object responds. For example, each form has OnOpen, OnActivate, and OnClose event properties associated with the Open, Activate, and Close events, respectively.

Event properties appear in the property sheet when you create forms and reports. Unlike most properties you've used before in property sheets, event properties do not have an initial value. If an event property contains no value, it means the event property has not been set. In this case Access takes no special action when the associated event occurs. For example, if a form's OnOpen event property is not set and you open the form, then the Open event occurs (the form opens), and no special action occurs. You can set an event property value to a macro name, and Access will execute the macro when the event occurs.

Access has 39 events and 39 associated event properties. As with actions, you do not need to learn all 39 events. You will gain experience with several event properties in these tutorials, and if you need other event properties, use the Access Help system as a reference tool. Two particularly useful Help topics are "events, list of" and "events, order of."

Elena decides to review these Help topics.

To review the "events, list of" and "events, order of" Help topics:

1. Click **Help**, then click **Microsoft Access Help Topics** to open the Access Help window.
2. If necessary, click the **Index** tab, then type **events** in the first text box.
3. Click the **list of** subtopic under events, then click **Display**. Access displays the list of events in a reference window. Scroll down the list to view the available events.
4. Click the **Help Topics** button to return to the Access Help window Index page.
5. Click **order of events**, then click Display. Access displays the Help window describing the order in which events occur. Review the contents of this window.
6. Click the Access Help window **Close** button [X] to return to the Database window.
7. Click the Access window **Close** button [X] to exit Access.

Planning the User Interface

Elena lists the work she must do to create the user interface for the Issue25 database. She will create forms for the switchboard and the two dialog boxes, build a custom menu bar, and create a custom toolbar. In addition, the dialog boxes will contain lists of available reports and queries. For these lists, Elena will create a special control table that contains the names of all the available reports and queries. Using the control table, she will then create two queries. One query will select all report names in alphabetical order, and the other query will select all query names in alphabetical order.

So far, Elena has assigned names to objects without using a specific naming convention. A **naming convention** is a consistent, standard way of naming objects in a database, making it easier to identify the type of object and its relationship to other objects. Elena will follow the naming conventions that she learned at the seminar. These are based on guidelines for the naming conventions in Visual Basic and Microsoft Access established by Stan Leszynski and Greg Reddick, specialists in custom database solutions.

- Each object name starts with a lowercase tag, or prefix, that identifies the object type. Figure 2-14 shows the tags Elena will use for Access objects and for Access controls on forms and reports.

Figure 2-14 Tags for Access objects and controls

Object or Control	Tag
Control—label	lbl
Control—other	ctl
Form	frm
Macro—custom menu	men
Macro—other	mcr
Query	qry
Report	rpt
Table	tbl
Toolbar—custom	tol
Visual Basic module	bas

- The tag is followed by a base name that describes the object contents, instead of the type of object. Examples of good base names with their tags are ctlWriterPhone, frmArticles, lblLastName, qryMagazines, rptBusinessArticles, rptTypes, and tblMagazines. Capitalize separate words in a base name and do not use spaces.

Following these naming conventions, Elena will be able to identify objects more easily in Access list boxes that display more than one type of object. Because these Access list boxes display object names in alphabetical order, the tag will group together all names for each object type. Figure 2-15 shows the objects Elena will create and their names.

Figure 2-15 Objects to be created for the Issue25 database

Object	Name
Switchboard form	frmSwitchboard
Queries dialog box	frmQueries
Reports dialog box	frmReports
Custom menu bar	menSwitchboard
Custom toolbar	tolSwitchboard
Query and report names table	tblObjectNames
Query names query	qryQueryNames
Report names query	qryReportNames

Creating a Control Table and its Queries

The switchboard command buttons run macros to do the following: display four forms, display two dialog boxes, exit the switchboard, and exit Access, as shown in Figure 2-16.

Figure 2-16 The Issue25 switchboard

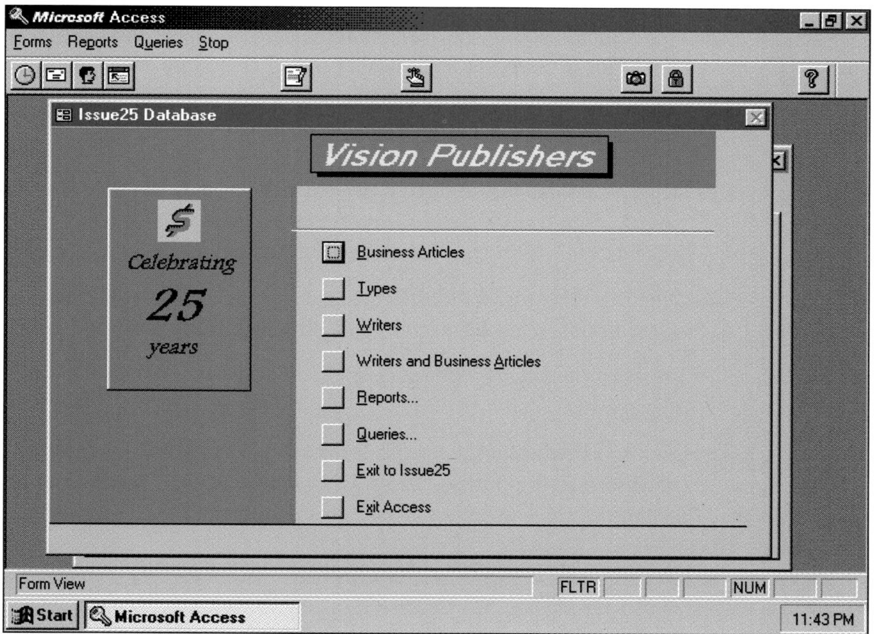

To test the switchboard design, the forms and dialog boxes must be available. Elena has some work to do before creating the switchboard. Because she has already created the four forms, her next job is to create the dialog boxes for the switchboard. In addition, each dialog box uses a query and a control table of available reports and queries, so Elena needs to create the queries and table before she can create the dialog boxes.

Creating the Control Table Structure

Elena's first step is to create the control table containing the report and query names. The table design consists of the following three fields.

- ObjectId is an AutoNumber field and is the table's primary key.
- ObjectType is a one-character Text field with two valid field values; Q for query and R for report.
- ObjectName is a 53-character Text field having the report and query names as field values.

Elena starts Access and creates the table named tblObjectNames.

To create the tblObjectNames table:

1. If necessary, place your Student Disk containing the Tutorial folder in the appropriate drive, start Access, open the Issue25 database on your Student Disk, and then maximize the Database window.
2. Click the **Tables** tab to display the Tables list, then click the **New** button. Access opens the New Table dialog box.
3. Click **Design View** to select it and then click the **OK** button. Access opens the Table Design window.

4. Type **ObjectID** in the Field Name text box, press the **Tab** key, type **a** (for Autonumber) in the Data Type text box, press the **Tab** key, type **primary key** in the Description text box, and then press the **Tab** key. The first field is now defined.

5. Type **ObjectType** in the Field Name text box, press the **[Tab]** key twice, and then type **Q for a query, R for a report** in the Description text box.

   To complete the second field's definition, you set the Field Size, Default Value, Validation Rule, and Validation Text properties.

6. Double-click **50** in the Field Size text box, type **1**, click the **Default Value** text box, type **Q**, click the Validation Rule text box, type **Q Or R**, click the Validation Text text box, and then type **Must be Q or R**. The second field is now defined.

7. Click the third row's **Field Name** text box, type **ObjectName**, press the **[Tab]** key twice, double-click **50** in the Field Size text box, and then type **53**.

   The third field is now defined, and you can now choose ObjectID to be the primary key.

8. Click the **row selector** for the ObjectID field to highlight the row and then click the **Primary Key** button on the toolbar. Access places the primary key field symbol in the row selector for the ObjectID field. See Figure 2-17.

Figure 2-17 Structure of the tblObjectNames table

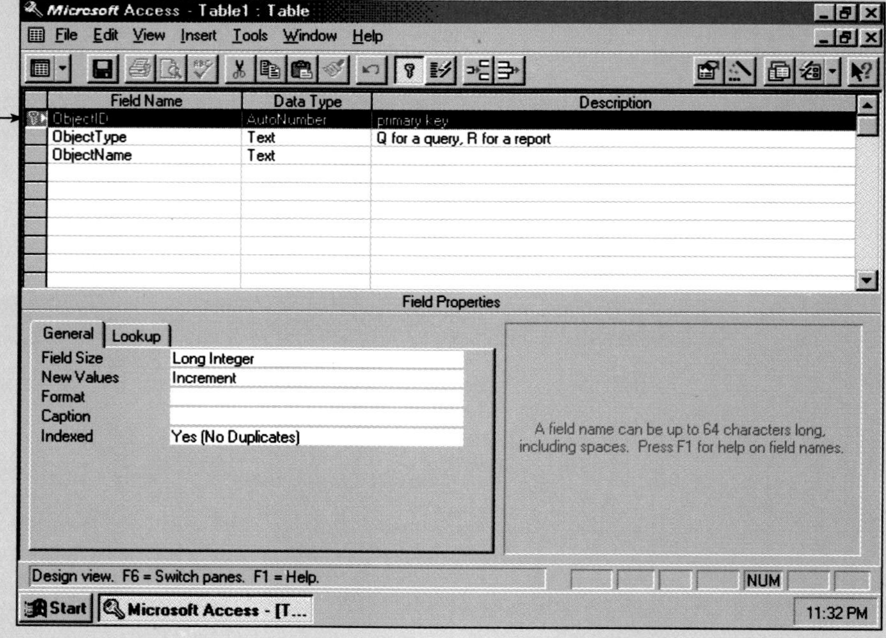

9. Click the **Table View** button on the toolbar. Access opens the dialog box to save the table.

10. Click the **Yes** button to open the Save As dialog box, type **tblObjectNames** in the Table Name text box, and then click the **OK** button. Access saves the new table structure, closes the Table Design window, and opens the datasheet.

Adding Records to the Control Table

Elena adds records to the tblObjectNames table. She first identifies the reports and queries that will be available to users of the Issue25 database and creates the list shown in Figure 2-18. The list includes the field values to be entered for the ObjectType and

ObjectName fields. You do not enter a field value for the ObjectID field, because it is an AutoNumber field that Access automatically controls.

Figure 2-18 The reports and queries for the Issue25 database

ObjectType	ObjectName
R	Type Pie Chart Report
R	Freelancer/Staff Writer Report
R	Freelancer Group Totals Report
Q	Article Type Query
Q	Article Type Parameter Query
Q	Writers and Article Types Query
R	Article Type Report
Q	Articles Sorted by Issue and Length Query
Q	Freelancer List for Brian Query

Using her list, Elena adds the records to the table.

To add records to the tblObjectNames table:

1. Press the **Tab** key, type **R**, press the **Tab** key, type **Type Pie Chart Report**, and then press the **Tab** key. The first record is added to the table.
2. Enter the remaining eight records using the field values from Figure 2-18.
3. Resize the widths of all three datasheet columns to their best fit. See Figure 2-19. Take a moment to check the values you entered and correct any that do not appear exactly as shown in Figure 2-18 and Figure 2-19. Capitalization and spelling are important since these object names will appear in the dialog boxes. Later, you will create Visual Basic event procedures that will use the ObjectName values to open the appropriate database objects.

Figure 2-19 The completed datasheet for the tblObjectNames table

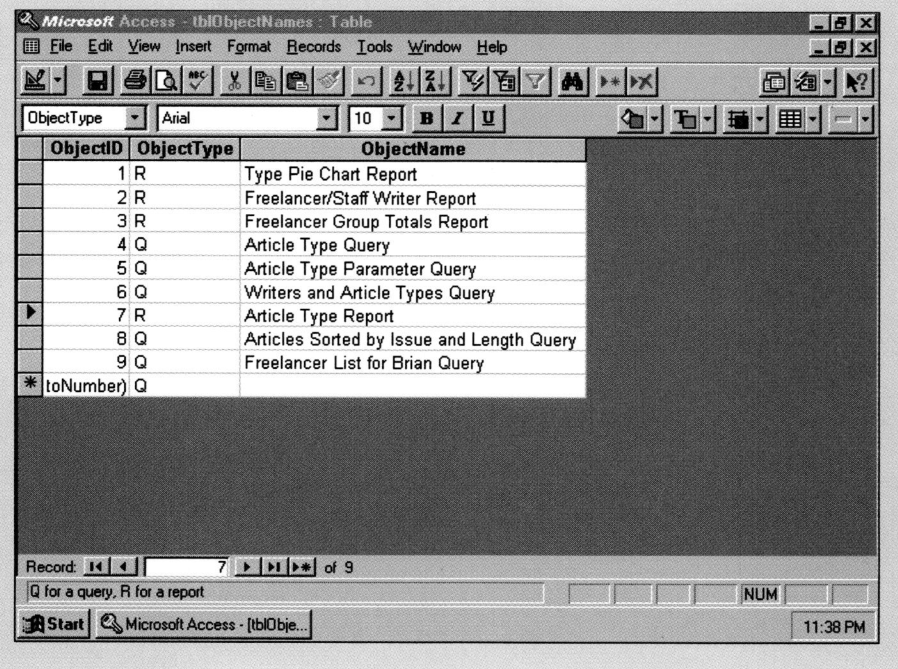

TROUBLE? Depending on how you resized the columns, your datasheet might have a field value, a column, or all columns highlighted. This is okay, as long as all the values in the ObjectType and ObjectName columns are correct.

4. Click the datasheet **Close** button [X] and then click the **Yes** button in answer to the question "Save layout changes?" Access saves the datasheet changes, closes the datasheet, and returns to the Database window.

Now that she has created and updated the control table, Elena creates the two new queries.

Creating the Queries

Both queries use the tblObjectNames table, select the ObjectID and ObjectName fields, and perform an ascending sort using the ObjectName field. One query selects only query-object records and the other query selects only report-object records.

Elena first creates the qryQueryNames query.

To create the qryQueryNames query:

1. Click the **Queries** tab to display the Queries list, then click the **New** button. Access displays the New Query dialog box.
2. Make sure that **Design View** is selected, then click the **OK** button. Access opens the Query Design window. The Show Table dialog box appears on top of the Query Design window.
3. Click **tblObjectNames** in the Tables list box, click the **Add** button to add the tblObjectNames table to the Query Design window and then click the **Close** button to close the Show Table dialog box.
4. Double-click the **title bar** of the tblObjectNames field list to highlight all the fields in the table and then drag all the fields from the highlighted area to the Query Design grid's first column Field box. Access adds all three fields to the Query Design grid.
5. Click the **Show** box in the ObjectID column to uncheck the box, so that the field does not appear in the query results, click the **Criteria** text box for the ObjectType field, and then type **Q** to select just the query-object records.
6. Click the **Sort** text box for the ObjectName field, click the **Sort** list arrow, and then click **Ascending** to produce an ascending sort based on the ObjectName field.
7. Click the **Run** button [!]. Access opens the query results. See Figure 2-20. Make sure you have spelled each query name correctly.

   TROUBLE? If you haven't spelled each name correctly, make the corrections now in the query results window.

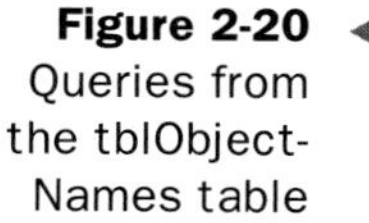

Figure 2-20 Queries from the tblObject-Names table

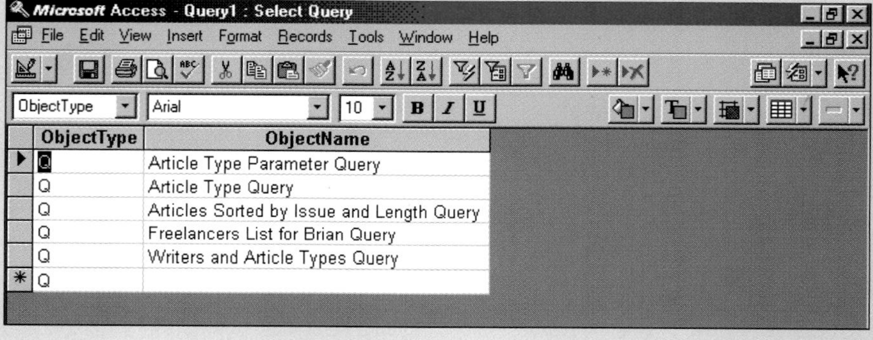

8. Click the **Query View** button to switch back to the Query Design window.

9. Click the **Save** button, type **qryQueryNames** in the Query Name text box, and then click the **OK** button. Access saves the qryQueryNames query.

Elena modifies the qryQueryNames query and saves it using the name qryReportNames. She changes the Q in the Criteria text box for the ObjectType field to an R, runs the query to test it, and then saves it as qryReportNames.

To create the qryReportNames query:

1. Double-click the **Q** in the Criteria text box for the ObjectType field and then type **R**.

2. Click the **Run** button. Access opens the query results window. See Figure 2-21. Be sure you have spelled each report name correctly.

   TROUBLE? If you haven't spelled each name correctly, make the corrections now in the query results window.

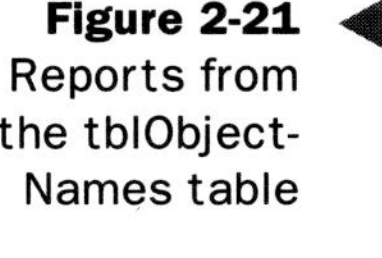

Figure 2-21 Reports from the tblObject-Names table

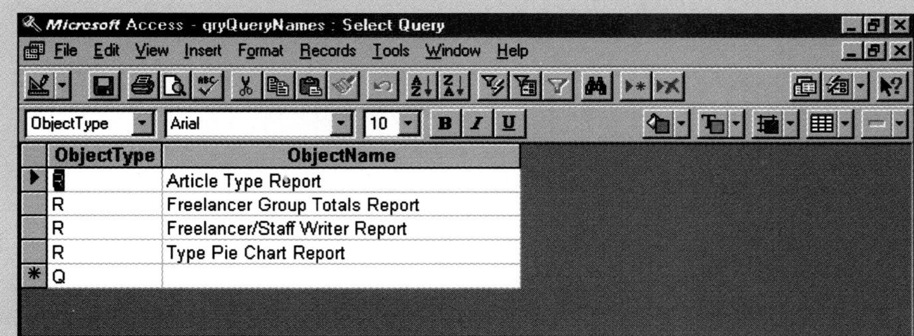

3. Click **File**, click **Save As/Export**, highlight **Query** in qryQueryNames in the New Name text box, type **Report** changing the name to qryReportNames, and then click the **OK** button. Access saves the query with the name qryReportNames.

4. Click the Datasheet window **Close** button. Access closes the query results window and returns to the Database window.

Elena has completed creating the two queries and the table for her user interface. Her next step is to create the two dialog boxes. The queries she just created will appear as the lists in the dialog boxes. Figure 2-22 shows how the lists will look in each dialog box.

Figure 2-22 The Reports (frmReports) and Queries (frmQueries) dialog boxes

list from the qryReportNames query

Reports
Reports
Article Type Report
Freelancer Group Totals Report
Freelancer/Staff Writer Report
Type Pie Chart Report
Close

list from the qryQueryNames query

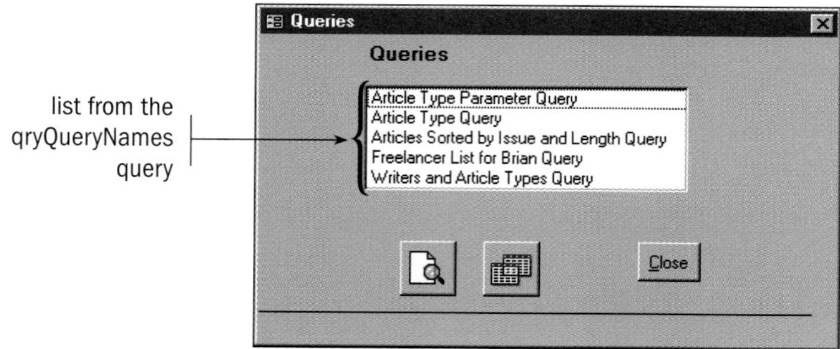

1. Give a definition of a switchboard, describe its significant features, and provide two reasons for using one.
2. What is a macro and what is the relationship between a macro and an action?
3. What is an action argument? Give an example of an action argument.
4. What are you trying to accomplish when you single-step through a macro?
5. What are two different ways to cause a macro to be executed when Access is started?

If you want to take a break and resume the tutorial at a later time, you can exit Access by clicking the Access window Close button. When you resume the tutorial, place your Student Disk containing the Tutorial folder in the appropriate drive, start Access, and open the Issue25 database on your Student Disk. Maximize the Database window.

SESSION 2.2

In this session you will create and test dialog boxes containing command buttons, and you will create a macro group that will be associated with buttons on the switchboard. You will also use the Switchboard Manager to create a switchboard form.

Creating Dialog Boxes

Elena creates the frmReports form to serve as one dialog box in the user interface. She then creates the frmQueries form by modifying the frmReports form to serve as the second dialog box. The queries based on the tblObjectNames table supply the values that appear in the list boxes in the dialog boxes.

Both dialog boxes will have similar appearances and behaviors. Neither dialog box shows scroll bars, navigation buttons, record selectors, or sizing buttons. Double-clicking a report or query name opens that report or query in the Print Preview window, as does clicking a report or query name and then clicking the command button that contains the Print Preview icon. Clicking a report name and then clicking the middle command button prints that report. Clicking a query name and then clicking the middle command button opens that query's results window. Clicking the Close button closes the dialog box and activates the switchboard.

The underlined letter C in the two Close command buttons identifies the buttons' hot key; pressing Alt + C closes the dialog box, just as clicking the Close command button does. To underline the letter C and make it the hot key, enter &Close as the Caption property value for the command button control on the form. Placing an ampersand (&) in front of a character in a caption (it doesn't need to be the first letter of a word) underlines the character on the open form and makes it that control's hot key. After a user makes a choice in the dialog box and finishes with the choice, the dialog box once again becomes the active window.

Creating the First Dialog Box

Elena creates a blank form based on the qryReportNames query to start the frmReports form.

To create the frmReports form:

1. Click the **Forms** tab to display the Forms list, then click the **New** button. Access opens the New Form dialog box.
2. Make sure that Design View is selected. Click the **list arrow**, scroll the list, click **qryReportNames**, and then click the **OK** button. Access opens the Form Design window.

Before adding any controls to the form, Elena sets the overall form properties as shown in Figure 2-23.

Figure 2-23 ◀
Form properties

Property	Setting	Function
Caption	Reports	Value appears in form's title bar
Shortcut Menu	No	Disables display of shortcut menu if right-click the form
Record Selectors	No	Disables display of record selectors
Navigation Buttons	No	Disables display of navigation buttons
Min Max Buttons	No	Disables display of Min Max buttons
Auto Resize	No	Opens a form in last saved size
Modal	Yes	Prevents users from opening the form Design View window
Border Style	Dialog	Prevents users from resizing form

Working from this list, Elena now can use the properties sheet to set the form properties.

To set properties for a form:

1. Click the **Form Selector** located at the intersection of the vertical and horizontal rules. If the property sheet is not visible, right-click the **Form Selector**, then click **Properties** to open the Form property sheet.
2. Click the **All** tab to display the All page of the property sheet.
3. If the toolbox is not visible, click the **Toolbox** button on the toolbar. If the toolbox Control Wizards tool is not selected, click the **Control Wizards** tool on the toolbox.
4. Click the property sheet's **Caption** text box and then type **Reports**.
5. Scroll down until the Record Selectors property is visible, then click the **Record Selectors** text box, click the **list arrow**, and then click **No**.
6. Continue scrolling, set the Navigation Buttons to No, set Auto Resize to No, set the Modal text box to Yes, set Min Max Buttons to None.
7. Double-click the **5** in the beginning of the Width text box and then type **3.8**.
8. Scroll down until the Shortcut Menu property is visible, and then set the Shortcut Menu to No.
9. Click the Property window **Close** button to close the property sheet.

Now that she has set all the properties for the form, Elena saves the form. She then adds the label and the list box to the form, using the Control Wizards tool for the list box. The label will identify the dialog box for the user and the list box will display the list of reports the user can choose.

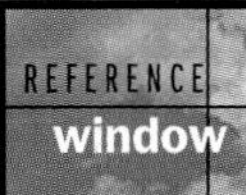

ADDING A LIST BOX TO A FORM WITH THE CONTROL WIZARD

- If necessary, click the Control Wizards tool on the toolbox so that it is activated (pressed down).
- Click the List Box tool on the toolbox.
- Position the list box pointer where you want the list box, then click the left mouse button. After a few seconds, the first List Box Wizard dialog box opens.
- Make sure to select the radio button next to "I want the list box to look up the values in a table or query." Then click the Next > button.
- Select the table that is the source table for the list box and then click the Next > button.
- Select the fields that you want to appear in the list box, then click the Next > button.
- Size the columns for best fit, then click the Next > button.
- Select the field that will provide the data for the field in the main form, then click the Next > button.
- Select the option of remembering the value for later use or storing the value in a field.
- Type the value you want to appear in the list box label, then click the Finish button. Access closes the find List Box Wizard dialog box and displays the completed list box in the form.

To save a form and add controls:

1. Click the **Save** button, type **frmReports** in the Form Name text box, and then click the **OK** button. Access saves the form and changes the title bar to frmReports : Form.
2. If necessary, click and drag the toolbox to the right side of the Form Design window, then click the **Label** tool in the toolbox, position the +A in the top line of grid dots at the ¾" mark on the horizontal ruler and then click the left mouse button. Type **Reports** and then press the **Enter** key. Next, Elena changes the label's font size from the default of 8 to 10, makes the label boldface, and then resizes the label box.
3. Click the **Font Size** list arrow on the toolbar, click **10**, click the **Bold** button on the toolbar, click **Format**, point to **Size**, and then click **to Fit**.
4. To start the List Box Wizard, click the **List Box** tool on the toolbox, position the pointer two grid dots below the left edge of the Reports text box, and then click the left mouse button. After a few seconds, Access opens the first List Box Wizard dialog box. The qryReportNames query will supply the values for the list box, so make sure the radio button next to "I want the list box to look up the values in a table or query" is selected. Then click the Next > button. The next List Box Wizard dialog box opens.
5. Click the **Queries** radio button, scroll the list box, click **qryReportNames**, and then click the Next > button. The next List Box Wizard dialog box opens.
6. Click **ObjectName** in the Available Fields list to select it, then click > to move it to the Selected Fields list. Then click the Next > button. The next List Box Wizard dialog box opens.
7. Double-click the right edge of the column selector to get the best column fit and then click the Next > button. The next List Box Wizard dialog box opens.

8. Make sure the radio button next to "Remember the value for later use" is selected, then click the Next > button. The next List Box Wizard dialog box opens. Because you will delete the label box attached to the list box, you do not need to change the label name.

9. Click the **Finish** button. Access closes the final List Box Wizard dialog box and displays the completed list box in the form's Detail section. See Figure 2-24.

Figure 2-24 Form design after a label and a list box are added

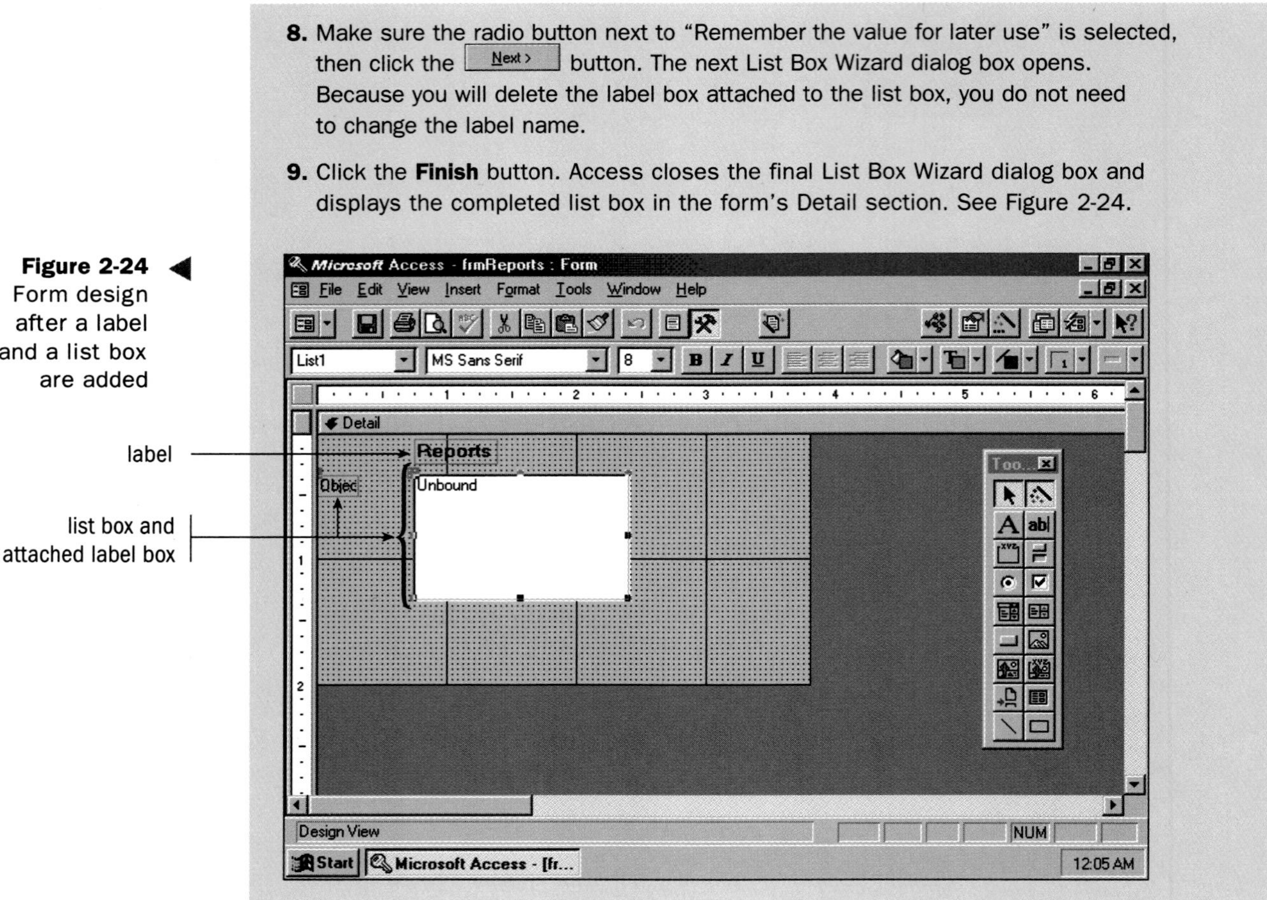

Elena saves the form and then checks her progress by switching to the Form View window.

To save a form and switch to the Form View window:

1. Click the **Save** button to save the form.

2. Click the **Form View** button. Access closes the Form Design window and opens the Form View window.

Elena makes two form changes before adding the command buttons. She needs to resize the list box so it will accommodate the list of reports better and she wants to delete the label attached to the list box.

To delete the label attached to the list box and reduce the list box height:

1. Click the **Form View** button to switch to the Form Design window.

2. Click the **label box** attached to the list box to select it.

3. Right-click in the **label box** to open the shortcut menu and then click **Cut** to delete the label box.

4. Click the **list box** to select it. Drag the bottom border upward to the row of grid dots at the 1" mark on the vertical ruler.

Elena now adds the Print Preview command button to the form. A macro cannot handle the complex interaction that is entailed in the actions of selecting a report or query in a list box and clicking a command button. This task requires Visual Basic code. Thus, the OnClick event properties for the command buttons and the OnDblClick event properties for the list-box entries are attached to Visual Basic code instead of macros.

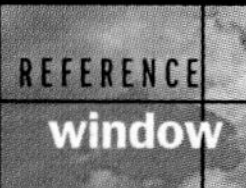

ADDING A COMMAND BUTTON TO A FORM

- Click the Command Button tool on the toolbox.
- Place the pointer in the form where you want the command button to appear, then click the left mouse button. Access places a command button on the form.
- Right-click the command button and then click Properties to display the property sheet.
- Scrolling the property sheet as necessary, click the property sheet's Picture text box and then click the Build button that appears next to the text box. Access opens the Picture Builder dialog box.
- Scroll through the Available Pictures list box and click the name of the picture you want on the command button. Access shows the picture on the command button in the Sample box.
- Click the OK button. Access places the picture on the command button.

Elena does not use the Control Wizards tool, because she will attach Visual Basic code to the OnClick event property for the command button at a later point. First, she saves the form.

To add a command button to a form:

1. Click the **Save** button to save the form.
2. Click the **Control Wizards** tool on the toolbox to deselect it.
3. Click the **Command Button** tool on the toolbox, position the just below the list box and at the 1" mark on the horizontal ruler and then click the left mouse button. Access adds a command button to the form.
4. Right-click the **command button** and then click **Properties** in the shortcut menu to open the property sheet.

   TROUBLE? If the properties sheet is covering the form, drag it out of the way.
5. Scrolling the property sheet as necessary, click the property sheet's **Picture** text box and then click the **Build** button that appears next to the text box. Access opens the Picture Builder dialog box.
6. Scroll through the Available Pictures list box and click **Preview Document**. Access shows the picture on the command button in the Sample box.
7. Click the **OK** button. Access closes the Picture Builder dialog box, resizes the command button, and places the picture on the command button.

Instead of repeating the steps to add the middle command button, Elena copies the first command button and pastes it in the Detail section. After moving the button into position, she changes the picture on the command button.

To create a command button by copying another command button:

1. Right-click the **command button** and then click **Copy** in the shortcut menu.
2. Click **Edit** and then click **Paste**. Access adds a copy of the command button to the Detail section.
3. Move the new command button into position to the right of the original command button. See Figure 2-25.

Figure 2-25 Adding a copy of a command button

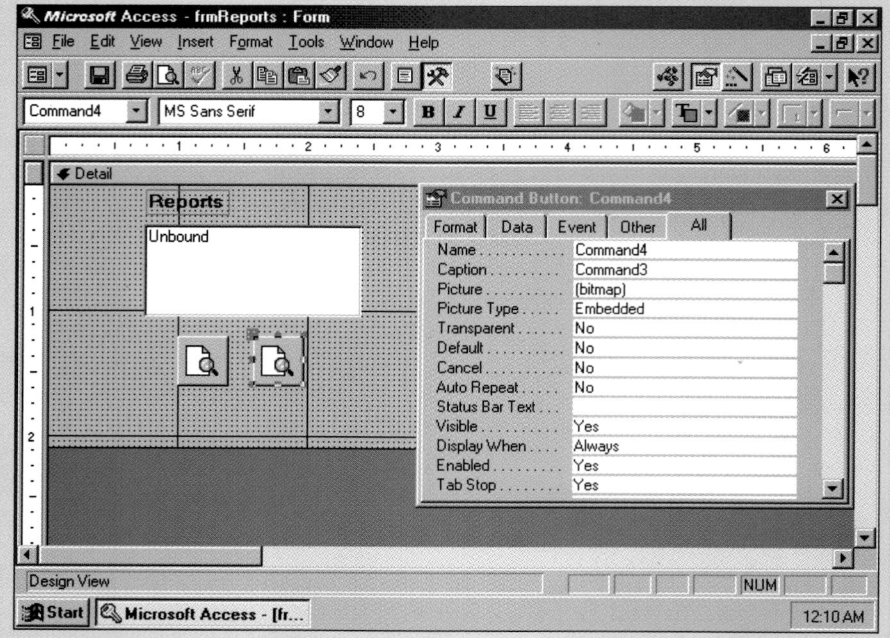

4. Click the property sheet's **Picture** text box and then click the **Build** button [...].
5. Scroll through the Available Pictures list box and click **Printer**. Access shows the picture on the command button in the Sample box.
6. Click the **OK** button. Access closes the Picture Builder dialog box and places the new picture on the command button.
7. Click the property sheet **Close** button [X] to close the property sheet.

Elena now adds the final command button. This button will close the dialog box when the user clicks it.

REFERENCE window

ADDING A COMMAND BUTTON TO A FORM USING CONTROL WIZARDS

- Click the Command Button tool on the toolbox.
- Place the pointer in the form where you want the command button to appear, then click the left mouse button. Access adds a command button to the form and, after a few seconds, opens the first Command Button Wizard dialog box.
- Select the action category and then the action for the command button, then click the [Next >] button. Access opens the next Command Button Wizard dialog box.
- In the Text box, enter the text for the command button, define a hot key and then click the [Next >] button.
- Enter a name in the text box and then click the Finish button.

She uses the Control Wizards tool because the tool automatically attaches the correct Visual Basic code to the command button that closes the dialog box. Standard operations, such as opening and closing forms, are perfect candidates for using the Control Wizards tool. Elena also sets the command button's Caption property to &Close to define the letter C as the command button's hot key. Once again, Elena saves the form before she adds the command button.

To add a command button using the Control Wizards tool:

1. Click the **Save** button to save the form.
2. Click the **Control Wizards** tool on the toolbox to select it.
3. Click the **Command Button** tool on the toolbox, position the just below the list box and just beyond the 2½"mark on the horizontal ruler, and then click the mouse button. Access adds a command button to the form and, after a few seconds, opens the first Command Button Wizard dialog box.
4. Click **Form Operations** in the Categories list box, click **Close Form** in the Actions list box, and then click the Next > button. Access opens the next Command Button Wizard dialog box.
5. Click the **Text** radio button, highlight **Close Form** in the text box, type **&Close**, and then click the Next > button. Access opens the next Command Button Wizard dialog box.
6. Type **ctlClose** in the text box to conform with the naming conventions for controls and then click the **Finish** button. Access closes the final Command Button Wizard dialog box and shows the new command button on the form.

The Visual Basic code Elena will create later in her work will need to refer to the list box control, so she enters the name ctlReportName for the list box control. She resizes and saves the form in the Form View window, then sets the form's BorderStyle property to Dialog, and saves the form again in the Form Design window.

To set properties and resize a form:

1. Right-click the **list box** to display the shortcut menu and then click **Properties** to open the properties sheet. If necessary, scroll to the top of the property sheet and double-click the **Name** text box to select it. Type **ctlReportName** and then press the **Enter** key.
2. Click the **Form View** button.

   TROUBLE? If the Form View window is maximized, click the Form View window Restore button.

3. Drag the bottom edge of the form down and then drag the right edge of the form to the left until the scroll bars are not visible. See Figure 2-26.

Figure 2-26 The resized form

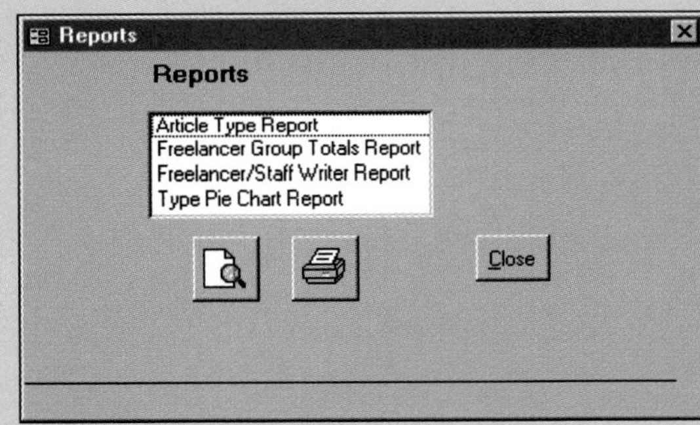

4. Click the **Save** button, and then click the **Form View** button to switch to the Form Design window.
5. In the Form Design window, right-click the **Form Selector**, click **Properties** to open the Form property sheet, and then click the **All** tab. Scroll down the Form property sheet, click the **Border Style** text box, click the **list arrow**, and then click **Dialog**.
6. Click the property sheet **Close** button to close the property sheet and then click the **Save** button.
7. Click the Form Design window **Close** button. Access closes the Form Design window and returns to the Database window.

Elena tests the form by opening it in the Form View window from the Database window. Clicking the Print Preview command button on the left, clicking the Printer command button in the middle, or double-clicking a report name in the list box should have no effect, because Elena has not yet set these event properties. However, clicking the Close button or pressing Alt + C should close the form.

To test a form's design:

1. If necessary, click the **Forms** tab. Click **frmReports** in the Forms list, then click the **Open** button. Access opens the form in the Form View window.
2. Double-click any report name in the list, click the **Print Preview** command button, and then click the **Printer** command button. Each double-click or click moves the focus but leaves the form on the screen. Recall that "focus" refers to the record and control that is currently active and awaiting user action.
3. Either click the **Close** button or press **Alt + C**. Access closes the form and returns to the Database window.

Elena has finished her initial work on the frmReports form. Her next task is to create the frmQueries form.

Creating the Second Dialog Box

Because the forms are so similar, Elena starts the frmQueries form by making a copy of the frmReports form. Then she modifies the frmQueries form to work correctly with the list of available queries.

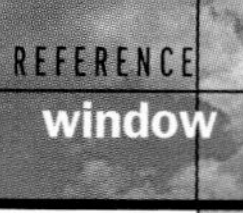

COPYING AN OBJECT IN THE SAME DATABASE

- In the Database window, click the appropriate tab, right-click the name of the object you want to copy to display the shortcut menu.
- Click Copy to copy the object to the Clipboard.
- Position the pointer in the list but not on any object, then right-click to display the shortcut menu.
- Click Paste, type the new object name, and press the Enter key.

Elena copies the frmReports form to the Clipboard and pastes it in the Forms list renaming it as frmQueries.

To copy a form in the same database:

1. Right-click **frmReports** in the Forms list of the Database window, then click **Copy**. Access copies the form to the Clipboard.
2. Position the pointer in the Forms list, but not on any object, then right-click to display the shortcut menu.
3. Click **Paste**, type **frmQueries** in the Form Name text box on the Paste As dialog box, and then click the **OK** button. Access creates a new form with the name frmQueries, which is a copy of the frmReports form.

Elena opens the frmQueries form in the Form Design window and changes the form's design so that it matches her design. Her changes include the following:

- The form's Record Source property is changed to qryQueryNames and the Caption property is changed to Queries.
- The label above the list is changed to Queries.
- The Row Source property for the list box is changed to the qryQueryNames query, and the height of the list box is increased.
- The icon on the middle command button is changed, and all command buttons are moved down to make room for the resized list box.
- The form is resized.

To change a copied form:

1. Click **frmQueries** in the Forms list, click the **Design** button. Right-click the **Form Selector** then click **Properties** to open the Form property sheet.
2. Make sure that the **Record Source** text box is selected in the property sheet, click the **Record Source** list arrow, scroll up, and then click **qryQueryNames**. Double-click the **Caption** text box and then type **Queries**.
3. Click the **label box** in the form's Detail section to open the Label:Label1 property sheet. Double-click the **Caption** text box, and then type **Queries**.

   TROUBLE? If the Label:Label1 number differs on your screen it won't affect your work.
4. Click the **list box** in the form's Detail section, double-click the **Name** text box in the property sheet, and then type **ctlQueryName**.
5. Click the **Row Source** text box. Press the → key on the keyboard until [qryReportNames] appears, highlight **Report**, type **Query** so that it now reads [qryQueryNames]; again, press the → key until [qryReportNames] appears, highlight **Report**, type **Query** so that it now reads [qryQueryNames] and then press the **Enter** key.
6. If necessary, move the property sheet window, then click the Form Design window **Maximize** button, click the **Printer** command button, the button in the middle. In the property sheet, click the **Picture** text box, and then click the **Build** button that appears to the right of the Picture text box to open the Picture Builder dialog box.
7. Scroll through the Available Pictures list, click **MS Access Query**, and then click the **OK** button. Access closes the Picture Builder dialog box and places the new picture on the command button.
8. Click the **Save** button, click the property sheet **Close** button to close the property sheet, and then click the toolbar **Form View** button. Access opens the Form View window.

Only four of the five query names appear in the list box and a scroll bar appears on the right of the list box. Elena moves the command buttons down and increases the height and width of the list box so that all five query names will be displayed.

To move controls and resize a list box:

1. Click the **Form View** button to switch back to the Form Design window.
2. Click the **Print Preview** command button, which is on the left. Press and hold the **Shift** key, click the **middle command button** and then click the **right command button**. Release the Shift key. All three buttons are selected.
3. Place the pointer over one of the selected command buttons and, when the pointer changes to ✋, drag the three command buttons straight down until the tops of the buttons are at the 1½" mark on the vertical ruler. This will make room for the list box.
4. Click the **list box**, position the pointer on the bottom middle resize handle and, when the pointer changes to ↕, drag the bottom border of the list box down to the third grid line below the 1" mark on the vertical ruler. Drag the right border of the list box right to the 3" mark on the horizontal ruler.

   TROUBLE? If you moved the list box instead of resizing it, click Edit, then click Undo Move, and then repeat step 4.

Elena now resizes the Form to accommodate the command buttons.

To resize the form:

1. Right-click the **Form Selector** ■, then click **Properties** in the shortcut menu to open the Form property sheet. Click the **Border Style** text box in the property sheet, click the **list arrow**, then click **Sizable**.
2. Click the **Form View** button. Access displays the Form View window.

   TROUBLE? If the Form View window is maximized, click the Form View window Restore button.
3. If necessary, resize the Form View window so that it is correctly proportioned. The command buttons should be visible and the scroll bars should not be visible.
4. Click the **Save** button to save the size settings.
5. Click the **Form View** button.
6. Click the **Border Style** text box in the property sheet, click the **list arrow**, then click **Dialog**.
7. Click the **Save** button to save the form design.
8. Click the Form Design window **Close** button ☒.

Elena tests the frmQueries form in the same way she tested the frmReports form.

To test a form's design:

1. If necessary, click **frmQueries** in the Forms list, then click the **Open** button. Access opens the form in the Form View window. If necessary, click the **Restore** button. See Figure 2-27.

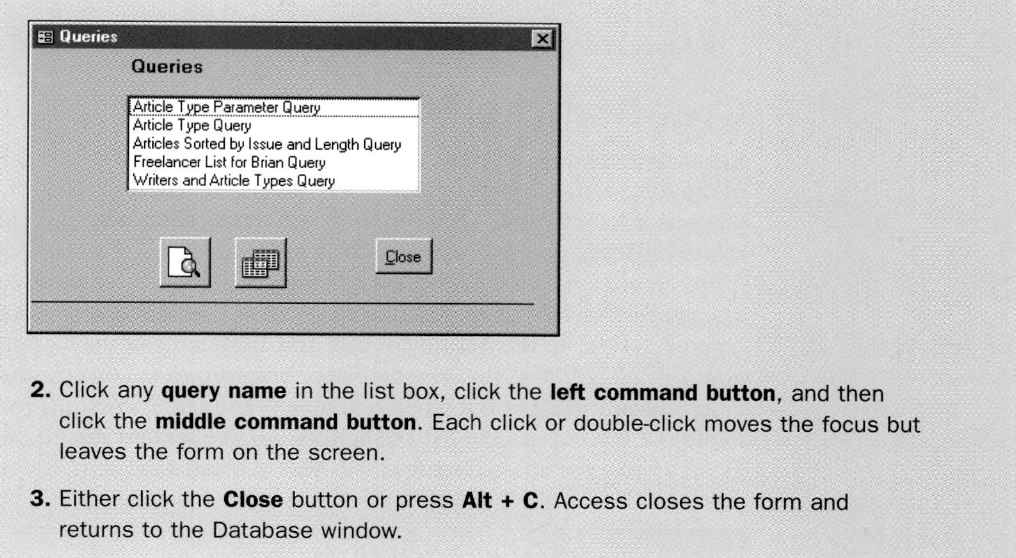

Figure 2-27 The copied form with completed changes

2. Click any **query name** in the list box, click the **left command button**, and then click the **middle command button**. Each click or double-click moves the focus but leaves the form on the screen.

3. Either click the **Close** button or press **Alt + C**. Access closes the form and returns to the Database window.

Elena has now created one table, two queries, and two forms for the Issue25 user interface. Her next task is to create the frmSwitchboard form.

Creating a Switchboard

Elena creates the frmSwitchboard form to serve as the primary user interface for the Issue25 database. Figure 2-28 shows the switchboard as it will look when it is finished.

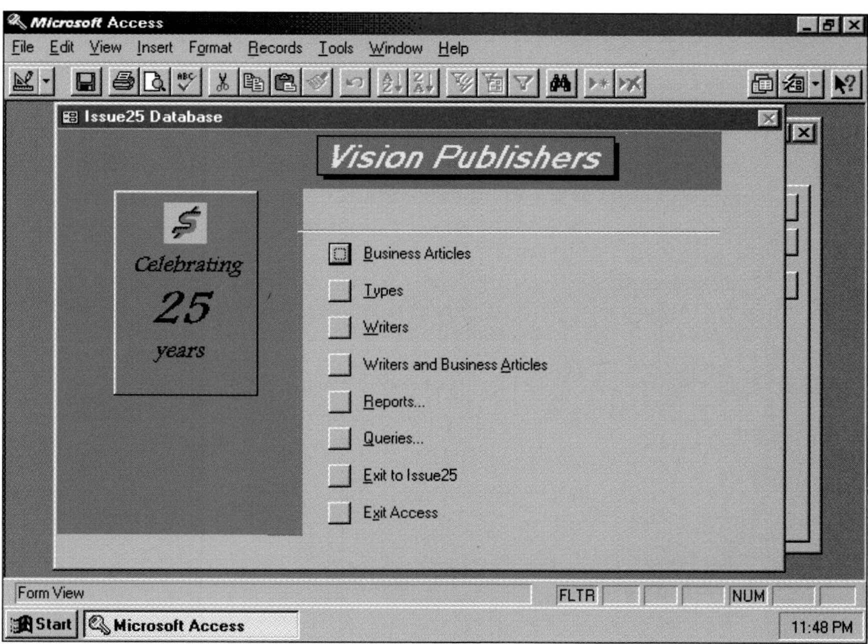

Figure 2-28 The Issue25 switchboard

Elena jots down several features she wants to include in the Issue25 frmSwitchboard form:

- The form has no Minimize, Restore, or Close buttons, scroll bars, navigation buttons, record selectors, or sizing buttons and cannot be resized.
- A graphic image appears in the left section of the form.
- The Celebrating 25 Years label is raised.

- The command buttons are all the same size.
- Macros are attached to each command button's OnClick event property.

Creating the Macro Group

Elena first creates the eight macros that she will attach to the command buttons. Instead of creating eight separate macros, she places the eight macros in a macro group. A **macro group** is a macro that contains other macros. Macro groups allow you to consolidate related macros and provide a means to manage large numbers of macros.

To create a macro group, you use the same Macro window you used to create a single macro. Recall that when you worked with the Macro window earlier in this tutorial, you entered actions in the Action column and comments in the Comment column. Now, you'll add a third column, the Macro Name column, that lets you distinguish macros in your macro group. First you'll name one macro and list the actions for that macro. Then you'll name the second macro, list the actions for the second macro, and so on. You can group as many macros as you want in the Macro window.

REFERENCE window

CREATING A MACRO GROUP

- In the Database window, click the Macros tab and then click the New button. Access opens the Macro window.
- Click the Macro Names button on the toolbar. Access adds the Macro Name column to the left of the Action column.
- Enter the macros in the macro group by entering the macro name in the Macro Name column and the action in the Action column.
- Click the Save button, enter the macro group name in the Macro Name text box, and then click the OK button.

Elena uses the name mcrSwitchboard for the macro group. Figure 2-29 shows the names and actions for the eight macros in the macro group. Elena creates the mcrSwitchboard macro group for the eight command buttons on the frmSwitchboard form. She starts a new macro, enters two of the macros, and then saves the macro group.

Figure 2-29 Macros and actions in the mcrSwitchboard macro group

Macro Name	Action	Form Name
mcrBusinessArticles	OpenForm	Business Articles Column Form
mcrTypes	OpenForm	Types Form
mcrWriters	OpenForm	Writers Column Form
mcrWritersBusinessArticles	OpenForm	Writers and Business Articles Form
mcrReports	OpenForm	frmReports
mcrQueries	OpenForm	frmQueries
mcrExitToIssue25	SendKeys Close	 frmSwitchboard
mcrExitAccess	Close Quit	frmSwitchboard

To create a macro group:

1. In the Database window, click the **Macros** tab and then click the **New** button. Access opens the Macro window. Click the Macro window **Maximize** button.
2. Click the **Macro Names** button on the toolbar. Access adds the Macro Name column to the left of the Action column. See Figure 2-30.

Figure 2-30 Macro Name column added to the Macro window

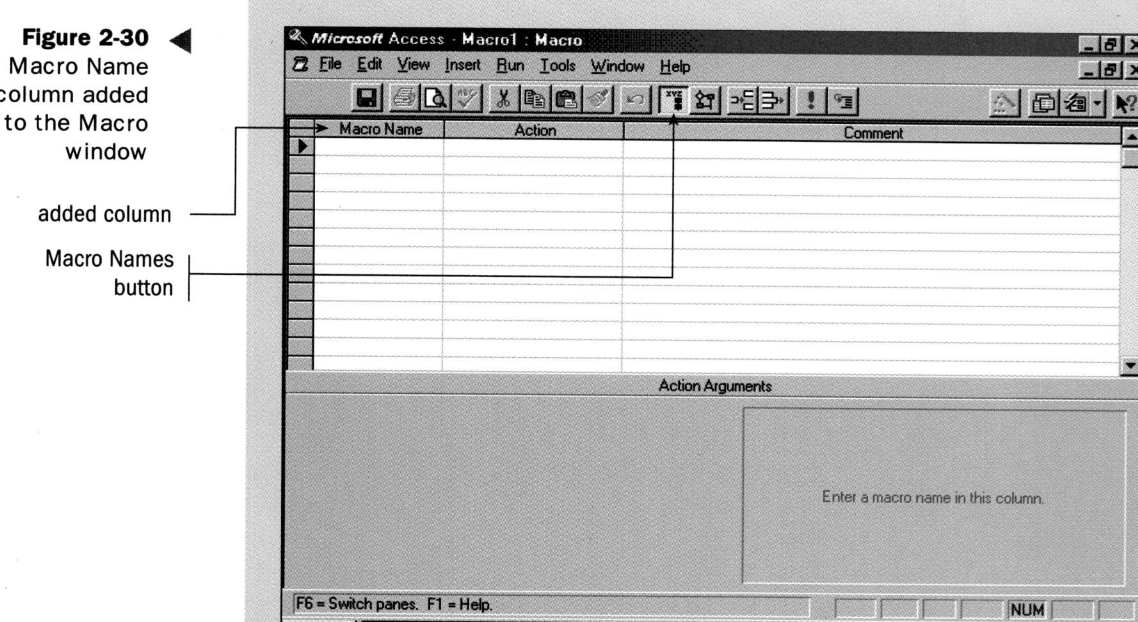

3. Type **mcrExitAccess**, press the **Tab** key, click the **Action** list arrow, click **Close**, press the **Tab** key, type **Close frmSwitchboard**.
4. Click the **Object Type** text box, click the **Object Type** list arrow, and then click **Form**. Click the **Object Name** text box, and then type **frmSwitchboard**. This completes the first action for the first macro.
5. Click the second row's **Action** text box, click the **Action** list arrow, scroll through the list, and then click **Quit**. This completes the first macro, which contains two actions.
6. Click the third row's **Macro Name** text box, type **mcrBusinessArticles**, press the **Tab** key, click the **list arrow**, scroll through the list, click **OpenForm**, press the **Tab** key, and then type **Open "Business Articles Column Form"**.
7. Click the **Form Name** text box, click the **list arrow**, and then click **Business Articles Column Form**. This completes the second macro, which contains one action.
8. Click the **Save** button, type **mcrSwitchboard** in the Macro Name text box, and then click the **OK** button. See Figure 2-31.

Figure 2-31 Two macros in a macro group

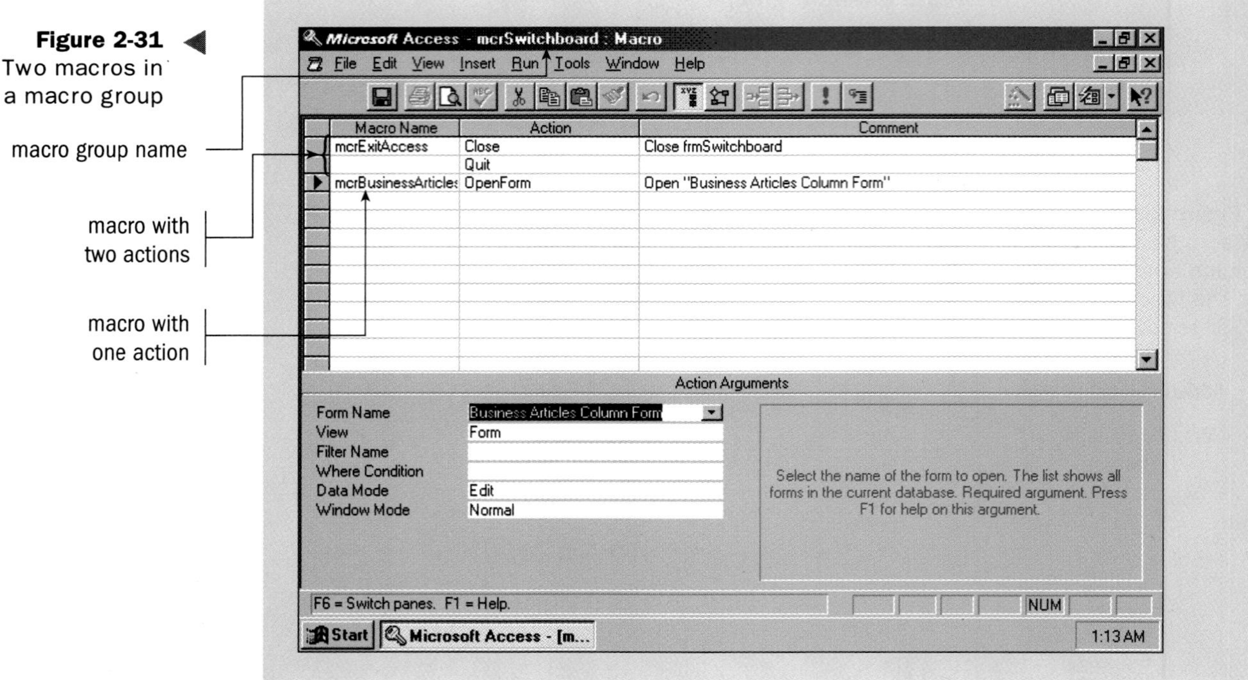

The macro name, which appears in the Macro window title bar, is mcrSwitchboard. This is also the name of the macro group, because the mcrSwitchboard macro comprises more than one macro. The first macro in the macro group is mcrExitAccess, and the second macro in the macro group is mcrBusinessArticles. A macro in a macro group starts in the row containing the macro name and continues until the row before the next macro name.

When Access executes the mcrExitAccess macro, it runs the Close action and then the Quit action and ends. The Quit action, which you have not used before, appears in the first macro and simply exits Access. The mcrBusinessArticles macro begins with the OpenForm action and then ends when it reaches the end of the macro group.

Elena completes the macro group by entering the remaining six macros.

To finish creating a macro group:

1. Click the next row's **Macro Name** text box, type **mcrTypes**, press the **Tab** key, click the **list arrow**, scroll through the list, click **OpenForm**, press the **Tab** key, type **Open "Types Form"**, click the **Form Name** text box, click the **list arrow**, and then click **Types Form**. This completes the third macro, which contains one action.

2. Click the next row's **Macro Name** text box, enter the following action: type **mcrWriters** in the Macro Name text box, click **OpenForm** to define the Action, type **Open "Writers Column Form"** as the comment, and then click **Writers Column Form** as the Form. This completes the fourth macro, which contains one action.

3. Click the next row's **Macro Name** text box, type **mcrWritersBusinessArticles** as the Macro Name, click **OpenForm** as the Action, type **Open "Writers and Business Articles Form"** to define the comment, and then click **Writers and Business Articles Form** as the form. This completes the fifth macro, which contains one action.

4. Click the next row's **Macro Name** text box, type **mcrReports** as the Macro Name, click **OpenForm** to define the Action, type **Open "frmReports"** as the comment, and then click **frmReports** as the form. This completes the sixth macro, which contains one action.

5. Click the next row's **Macro Name** text box, type **mcrQueries** as the Macro Name, click **OpenForm** to define the Action, type **Open "frmQueries"** as the comment, and then click **frmQueries** as the form. This completes the seventh macro, which contains one action.

6. Click the next row's **Macro Name** text box, type **mcrExitToIssue25**, press the **Tab** key, click the **list arrow**, scroll then click **SendKeys**, press the **Tab** key, type **Activate Database window**, click the **Keystrokes** text box, and then type **{F11}**. Be sure to type the braces but not the period. The SendKeys action sends keystrokes to an application. In this case, the Keystrokes argument value {F11} is the same as pressing the F11 key, which returns you to the Database window. This macro has a second action.

7. Click the next row's **Action** text box, click the **Action** list arrow, click **Close**, press the **Tab** key, type **Close frmSwitchboard**, click the **Object Type** text box, click the **list arrow**, click **Form**, click the **Object Name** text box, type **frmSwitchboard**, and then press the **Enter** key. This completes the second of two actions for the last macro. See Figure 2-32.

Figure 2-32 A completed macro group containing eight macros

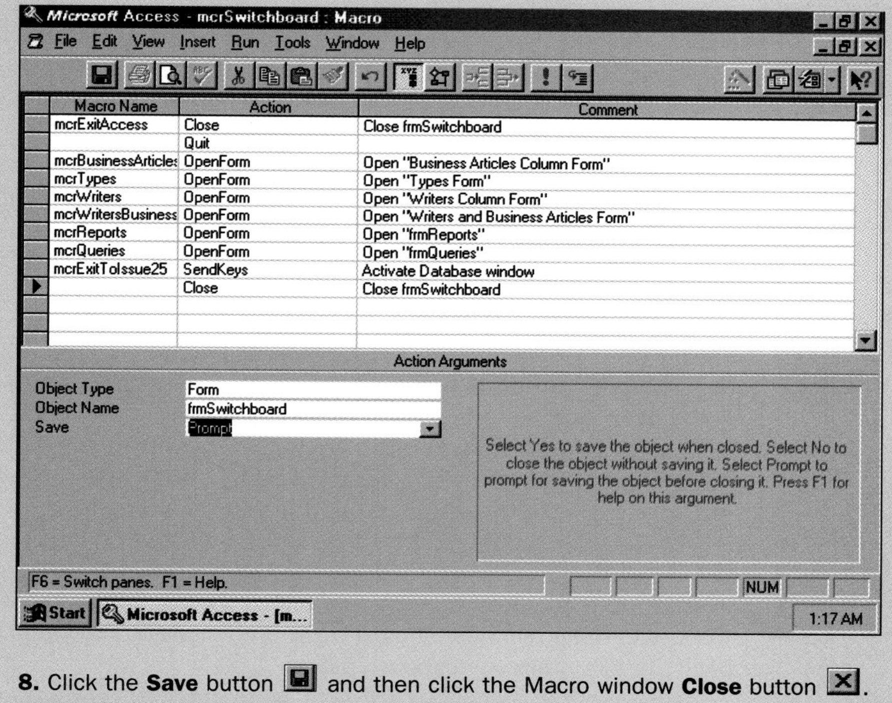

8. Click the **Save** button and then click the Macro window **Close** button. Access saves the macro group, closes the Macro window, and returns to the Database window.

Creating the Switchboard Form

Now that the switchboard macros are entered, Elena creates the switchboard by using the Access Switchboard Manager. The **Switchboard Manager** is a Microsoft Access Add-in that helps you create and customize a switchboard.

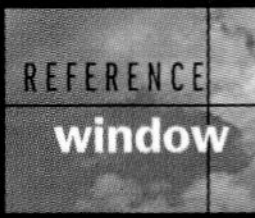

CREATING A SWITCHBOARD WITH THE SWITCHBOARD MANAGER

- Click Tools, point to Add-ins, then click Switchboard Manager to open the Switchboard Manager dialog box.
- To create a new switchboard, click the New button. Access opens the Edit Switchboard Page dialog box.
- To edit an existing switchboard, click the Edit button. Access opens the Edit Switchboard Page dialog box.
- Enter the switchboard name in the Switchboard Name text box.
- Click the New button to add a switchboard item. Access opens the Edit Switchboard Item dialog box.
- In the Text text box, enter the text that is to appear on the switchboard command button.
- In the Command text box, enter the command associated with the command button.
- In the remaining text box, select the argument(s) for the command, then click the OK button. Access returns to the Edit Switchboard Page dialog box.
- Repeat the previous four steps for each command button to appear on the switchboard. You can have as many as eight command buttons on the switchboard.
- Click the Close button to return to the Switchboard Manager dialog box.
- Click the Close button to close the Switchboard Manager dialog box.

When you use the Switchboard Manager, you specify the command buttons that are to appear on the switchboard. For each command, you identify the command to be carried out when the button is clicked. Some commands require one or more arguments, which you can specify as well. When you complete the switchboard design, the Switchboard Manager creates a form for your switchboard with the default name Switchboard. The Switchboard Manager also creates a table, called Switchboard Items, which contains records describing the command buttons on the switchboard.

The Switchboard Manager allows you to create only one switchboard for a database, but the switchboard can contain many pages. Only one of the switchboard pages can be designated as the default page. The **default page** is the switchboard page that will appear when you open the Switchboard form. You can place a command button on the default page to open other switchboard pages.

Elena uses the Switchboard Manager to create the switchboard form for the Issue25 database. She places command buttons on the switchboard and associates macros from the mcrSwitchboard macro group with the buttons.

To create the switchboard form:

1. Click **Tools**, then point to **Add-ins**, and then click **Switchboard Manager**. Access displays a dialog box asking if you want to create a switchboard.

   TROUBLE? If you do not see the Switchboard Manager in the Add-ins list, it may not have been installed on your computer. See your technical support person to have it installed.

2. Click the **Yes** button. Access opens the Switchboard Manager. See Figure 2-33.

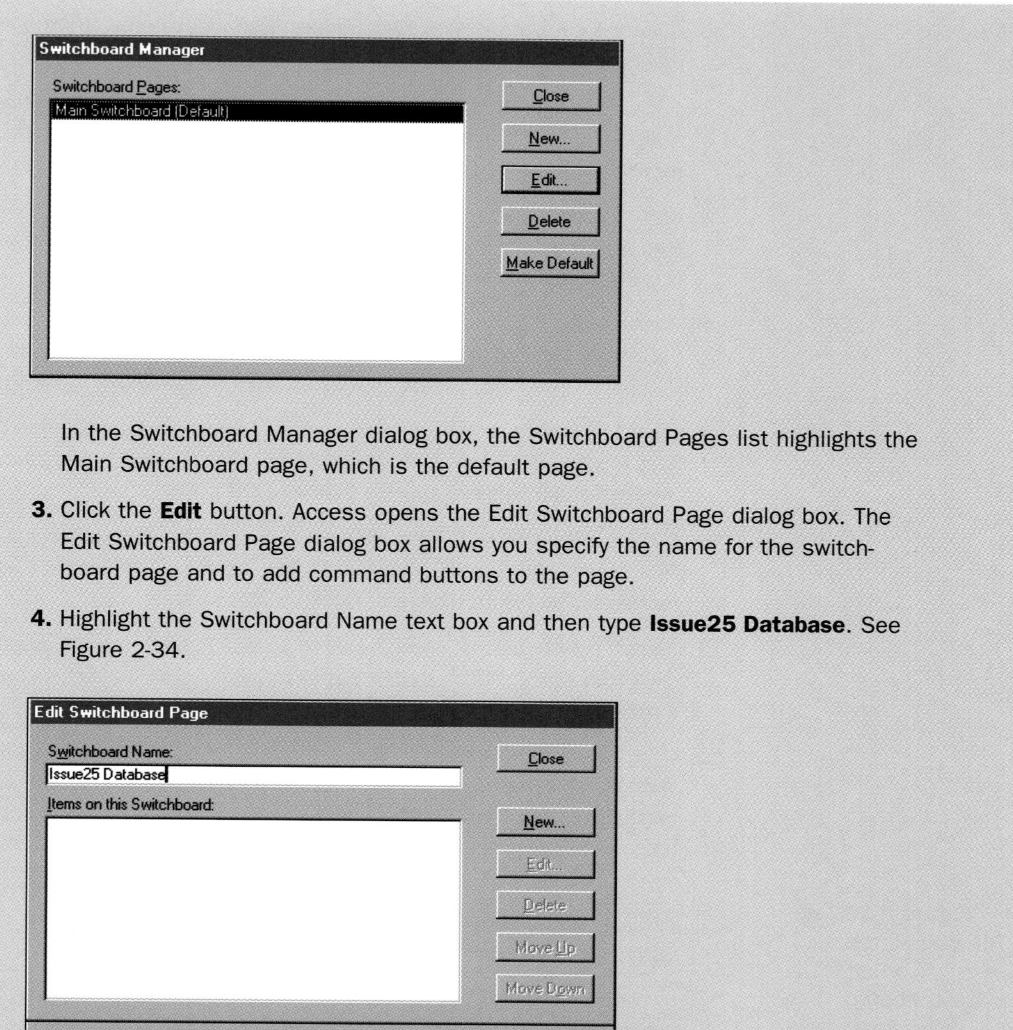

Figure 2-33 The Switchboard Manager dialog box

In the Switchboard Manager dialog box, the Switchboard Pages list highlights the Main Switchboard page, which is the default page.

3. Click the **Edit** button. Access opens the Edit Switchboard Page dialog box. The Edit Switchboard Page dialog box allows you specify the name for the switchboard page and to add command buttons to the page.

4. Highlight the Switchboard Name text box and then type **Issue25 Database**. See Figure 2-34.

Figure 2-34 The Edit Switchboard Page dialog box

Elena adds command buttons for each of the macros in the mcrSwitchboard macro group.

To add command buttons to the switchboard page:

1. Click the **New** button. The Switchboard Manager opens the Edit Switchboard Item dialog box.

2. In the Text box, type **&Business Articles**. This is the text that will appear with the command button. Recall that the ampersand (&) creates a hot key.

3. Click the **Command** list arrow then click **Run Macro**. The third text box in the Switchboard Manager dialog box now displays the label Macro.

4. Click in the Macro text box, click the **list arrow**, then click **mcrSwitchboard.mcrBusinessArticles**. The first command button definition is now complete. See Figure 2-35.

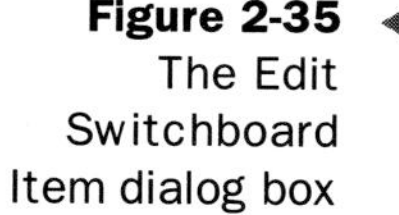

Figure 2-35 The Edit Switchboard Item dialog box

Edit Switchboard Item

Text:	&Business Articles	OK
Command:	Run Macro	Cancel
Macro:	mcrSwitchboard.mcrBusinessArticles	

5. Click the **OK** button. The Switchboard Manager returns to the Edit Switchboard Page dialog box. Now add the remaining command buttons.
6. Click the **New** button. Type **&Types**. Click the **Command** list arrow, then click **Run Macro**. Click in the Macro text box, click the **list arrow**, then click **mcrSwitchboard.mcrTypes**. Click the **OK** button.
7. Click the **New** button. Type **&Writers**. Click the **Command** list arrow, then click **Run Macro**. Click in the Macro text box, click the **list arrow**, then click **mcrSwitchboard.mcrWriters**. Click the **OK** button.
8. Click the **New** button. Type **Writers and Business &Articles**. Click the **Command** list arrow, then click **Run Macro**. Click in the Macro text box, click the **list arrow**, then click **mcrSwitchboard.mcrWritersBusinessArticles** Click the **OK** button.
9. Click the **New** button. Type **&Reports...**. Click the **Command** list arrow, then click **Run Macro**. Click in the Macro text box, click the **list arrow**, then click **mcrSwitchboard.mcrReports**. Click the **OK** button.
10. Click the **New** button. Type **&Queries...**. Click the **Command** list arrow, then click **Run Macro**. Click in the Macro text box, click the **list arrow**, then click **mcrSwitchboard.mcrQueries**. Click the **OK** button.
11. Click the **New** button. Type **&Exit to Issue25**. Click the **Command** list arrow, then click **Run Macro**. Click in the Macro text box, click the **list arrow**, then click **mcrSwitchboard.mcrExitToIssue25**. Click the **OK** button.
12. Click the **New** button. Type **E&xit Access**. Click the **Command** list arrow, then click **Run Macro**. Click in the Macro text box, click the **list arrow**, then click **mcrSwitchboard.mcrExitAccess**. Click the **OK** button. The command buttons have all been added to the switchboard design. See Figure 2-36.

Figure 2-36 The completed Edit Switchboard Page

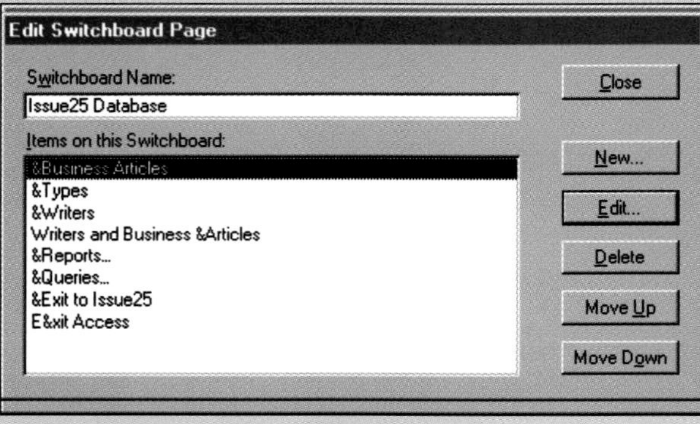

Elena is finished using the Switchboard Manager. She exits the Switchboard Manager, changes the name of the new switchboard form to frmSwitchboard and views the new switchboard.

To exit the Switchboard Manager, rename and view the switchboard form:

1. Click the **Close** button to close the Edit Switchboard Page dialog box.
2. Click the **Close** button to close the Switchboard Manager dialog box. Access closes the Switchboard Manager dialog box and returns to the Database window.
3. If necessary, position the Database window in the Access window so the database window scroll bars are not visible, then click the **Forms** tab to display the Forms list.
4. Right-click the **Switchboard** form to open the shortcut menu.

5. Click **Rename**, type **frmSwitchboard**, then press the **Enter** key.
6. Click the **Open** button. Access opens the frmSwitchboard form. If necessary, click the Form View window **Restore** button. See Figure 2-37.

Figure 2-37 The frmSwitchboard form

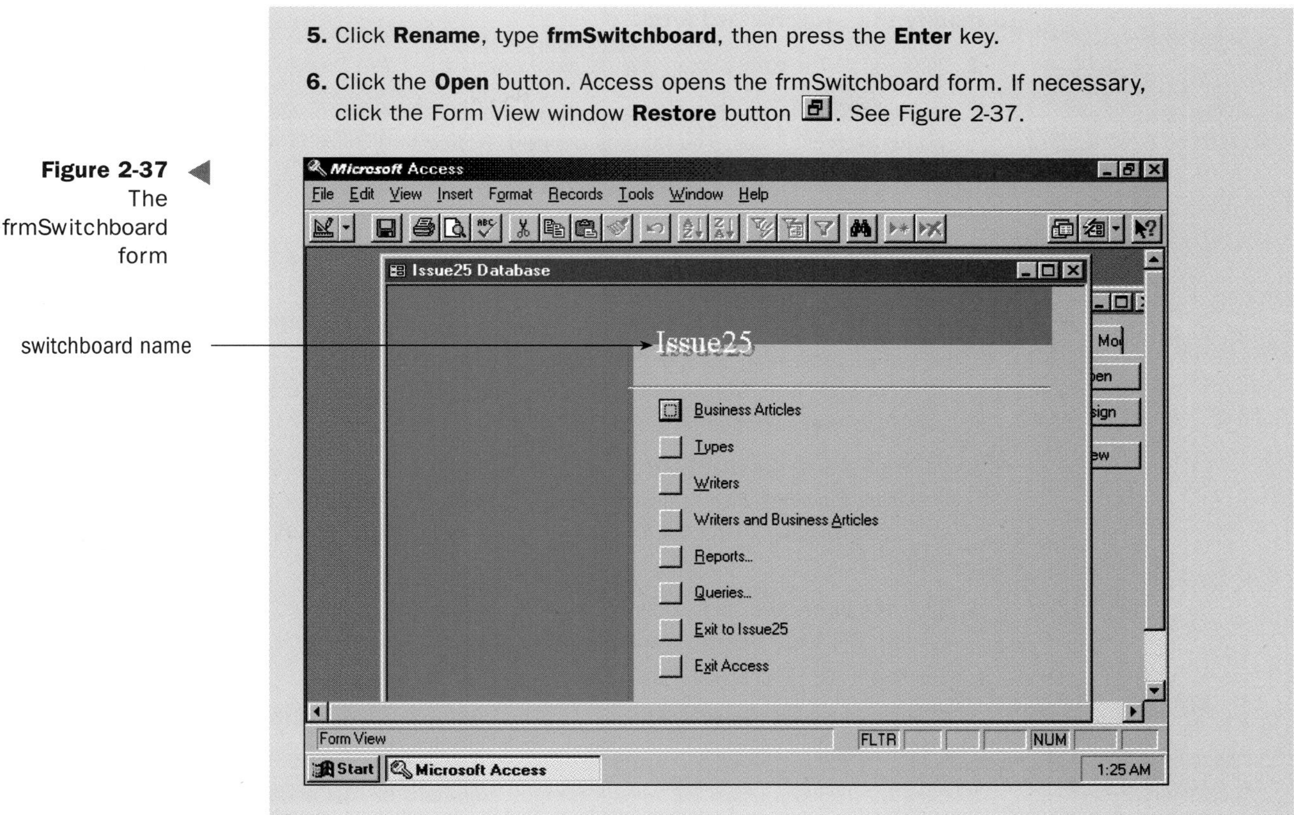

Elena is pleased with the appearance of the switchboard form, but there are some changes she would like to make. Before she changes the switchboard form, Elena tests some of the command buttons to make sure they work properly.

To test command buttons:

1. Click the **Business Articles** command button. Access displays the record for the Trans-Alaskan Oil Pipeline Opening article in the Business Articles Column Form in the Form View window. Click the Business Articles Column Form View window **Close** button to close the window and return to the switchboard form.
2. Press the **Alt** key and, while holding it down, press **T**. Access opens the Types Form and displays the first Types record. Click the Types Form View window **Close** button to close the window and return to the switchboard form.
3. Click the **Reports** command button. Access opens the mcrReports dialog box. Click the **Close** button to return to the switchboard.

Elena wants to make some changes to the design of the switchboard form. She likes the layout of the buttons, but she wants to resize the form and make sure that it always appears in the center of the screen. She also wants to remove the Issue25 label above the buttons and add a new label and a graphic image.

Because the switchboard is a form, Elena can make these changes in the Form Design window. However, she needs to be careful not to make any changes to the command buttons that would affect the actions and macros associated with them. Such changes should only be made through the Switchboard Manager. If she were to change the definitions of any of the command buttons in the Form Design window, the Switchboard Manager would not be able to make the necessary updates to the Switchboard Items table and other related objects and the switchboard would not function correctly.

Elena begins by deleting two labels and placing a new label and a graphic image on the form.

To modify the switchboard form:

1. Click the **Form View** button. Access opens the Form Design window.
2. Right-click the **Issue25 label** above the command buttons to open the shortcut menu, then click **Cut**. The label is deleted. Notice that there is a second Issue25 label now visible. This label appeared as the shadow of the first label in the switchboard form.
3. Right-click the **Issue25 label** above the command buttons to open the shortcut menu, then click **Cut**. The label is deleted.
4. If the toolbox is not visible, click the **Toolbox** button. Click the **Label** tool on the toolbox, then position the pointer at the top of the form directly at the 2" mark on the horizontal ruler, then click the mouse button to place the label box. Type **Vision Publishers** and press the **Enter** key.
5. Click the **Bold** button on the toolbar, click the **Italic** button on the toolbar, click the **Font Size** list arrow on the toolbar, and then click **18**. Click **Format**, point to **Size**, and then click **to Fit**. Access resizes the label box to display the entire label.
6. Click the **Fore Color** list arrow on the Formatting toolbar to display the palette. Click the **bright yellow** color box (the third button in the fourth row). The Vision Publishers label now appears bright yellow.
7. Click the **Special Effect** list arrow on the toolbar, then click the Shadowed button.
8. Click the **Image** button on the toolbox, position the at the ½" mark on the vertical ruler and the ½" mark on the horizontal ruler and click the mouse button to place the graphic image. Access opens the Insert Picture dialog box.
9. In the Look in text box, select the Tutorial folder on your Student Disk, click **Vis** in the file list, then click the **OK** button. Access inserts the Vis graphic image in the form.
10. Click the **Special Effect** list arrow on the toolbar, then click the **Raised** button.

Elena has made her changes to the layout of the switchboard form. She now changes the form properties so the form will be correctly sized and positioned on the screen.

To change the switchboard form properties:

1. Right-click the **Form Selector** to display the Form property sheet.
2. Click the **Format** tab. Click the **Auto Resize** text box, click the **list arrow**, then click **No**.
3. Click the **Scroll Bars** text box, click the **list arrow**, then click **Both**.
4. Click the **Auto Center** text box, click the **list arrow**, then click **No**.
5. Click the **Min Max Buttons** text box, click the **list arrow**, then click **None**.
6. Click the **Close Button** text box, click the **list arrow**, then click **No**.
7. Click the **Form View** button to display the form. Drag the switchboard's bottom border up or down, if necessary, and then drag the switchboard's right border right or left as necessary until the switchboard is properly proportioned to display all the buttons, lists, and labels and until the scroll bars are not visible.
8. Click the **Save** button to save the size of the switchboard.

9. Click the **Form View** button. In the Property sheet, click the **Border Style** text box, click the **list arrow**, then click **Dialog**.

10. Click the **Save** button to save the final switchboard design. Then click the Form Design window **Close** button to close the Form Design window and return to the Database window.

Elena opens the switchboard in the Form View window to see its final appearance.

To view the completed switchboard:

1. Click **frmSwitchboard** to select it, then click the **Open** button. The frmSwitchboard form opens. See Figure 2-38.

Figure 2-38
The completed switchboard in the Form View window

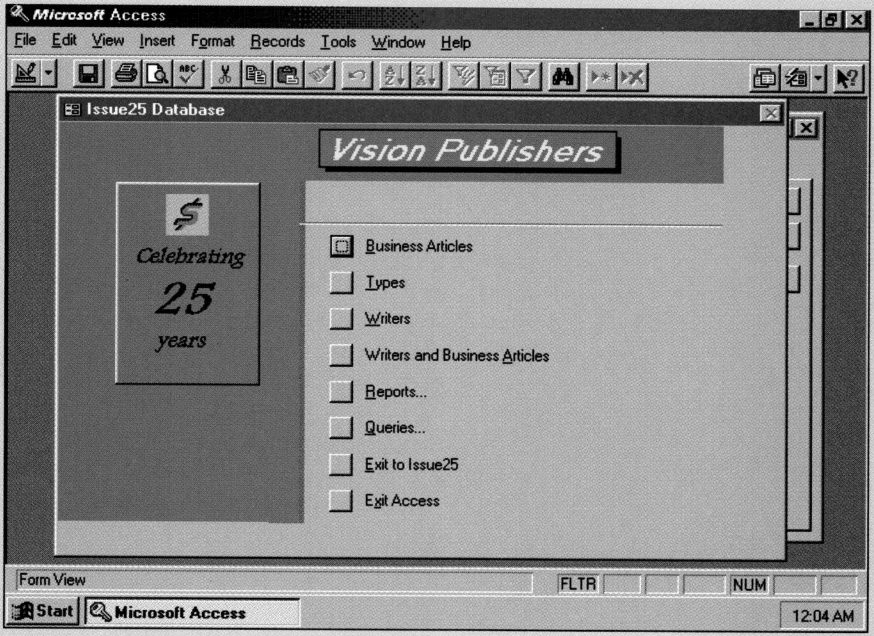

2. Click the **Exit to Issue25** button. Access closes the switchboard and returns to the Database window.

Elena has reached the end of the workday, so she exits Access.

To exit Access:

1. Click the Access window **Close** button to exit Access.

Elena's plans for the next day include adding a custom menu bar and a custom toolbar to the switchboard, as she continues her work with macros and the graphical user interface.

Quick Check

1 What is a hot key and how do you define one for a command button?

2 What is the effect of setting a form's Border Style property to Dialog?

3 How do you copy an object in the same database?

4 What is an event property?

5 What form components do not appear on a dialog box? What additional component does not appear on a switchboard?

6 What are two reasons for using macro groups?

7 What are two special effects you can use for a control?

Tutorial Assignments

Start Access and open the Issue25 database in the Tutorial folder on your Student Disk.

Elena creates a dialog box that has a list of all the Query and Report names. She adds two command buttons to this graphical interface.

1. Design and create a dialog box that has the following components and characteristics.
    a. When you save the form, use the name frmQueriesReports.
    b. The title bar contains Print Queries and Reports.
    c. A list box displays all the query and report names contained in the tblObjectNames table. The names appear in alphabetical order. (Create a new query with the name qryQueryReportNames that performs an ascending sort on the ObjectName field and has no criteria for the ObjectType field.)
    d. Queries/Reports appears as a heading above the list box.
    e. Two command buttons appear below the list box. The left command button displays the printer icon, and the right command button displays the word Close with the letter C underlined.
    f. Double-clicking a query or report name has the same effect as clicking the left command button. Both events cause Access to display the Print Preview window for the selected query or report. (You will add the Visual Basic code for the event properties in a later tutorial. For now, double-clicking or clicking should cause no action to occur.)
    g. Clicking the Close command button causes Access to close the dialog box.

Case Problems

1. Walkton Daily Press Carriers Robin Witcop decides to create a switchboard for the Press database.

Start Access and open the Press database in the Cases1 folder on your Student Disk.

1. Design and create a switchboard that has frmSwitchboard as a saved form name and that has the following components and characteristics.
    a. Provide appropriate wording for the title bar and a heading at the top center of the switchboard.
    b. Add the walk01.bmp and walk02.bmp graphic images from your Student Disk to appropriate positions on the switchboard.

c. Place five command buttons on the switchboard. The command buttons perform these actions: open the "BILLINGS" table, open the "CARRIERS Form" form, open the "CARRIERS Sorted by Name and Route ID Query" query, open the "CARRIERS Report" report, and close the switchboard and activate the Database window. Create a macro group for these command buttons.
d. Use appropriate background and foreground colors and visual effects for the switchboard and its components, and size and position the switchboard in the Form View window.

2. Lopez Lexus Dealerships Marie Lopez decides to create a switchboard for the Lexus database.

Start Access and open the Lexus database in the Cases1 folder on your Student Disk.

1. Design and create a switchboard that has frmSwitchboard as a saved form name and that has the following components and characteristics.
   a. Provide appropriate wording for the title bar and a heading at the top center of the switchboard.
   b. Add the lopez01.bmp and lopez02.bmp graphic images from your Student Disk to appropriate positions on the switchboard.
   c. Place five command buttons on the switchboard. The command buttons perform these actions: open the "LOCATIONS" table, open the "CARS Data Form" form, open the "CARS by Model and Year Query" query, open the "CARS by Year Report" report, and close the switchboard and activate the Database window. Create a macro group for these command buttons.
   d. Use appropriate background and foreground colors and visual effects for the switchboard and its components, and size and position the switchboard in the Form View window.

3. Tophill University Student Employment Olive Tyler asks Lee Chang to create a switchboard for the Parttime database.

Start Access and open the Parttime database in the Cases2 folder on your Student Disk.

1. Design and create a switchboard that has frmSwitchboard as a saved form name and that has the following components and characteristics.
   a. Provide appropriate wording for the title bar and a heading at the top center of the switchboard.
   b. Add the top01.bmp and top02.bmp graphic images from your Student Disk to appropriate positions on the switchboard.
   c. Place five command buttons on the switchboard. The command buttons perform these actions: open the "EMPLOYERS" table, open the "Employers and Jobs Form" form, open the "Jobs Sorted by Employer and Job Title Query" query, open the "JOBS Report" report, and close the switchboard and activate the Database window. Create a macro group for these command buttons.
   d. Use appropriate background and foreground colors and visual effects for the switchboard and its components, and size and position the switchboard in the Form View window.

4. Rexville Business Licenses Chester Pearce decides to create a switchboard for the Buslic database.

Start Access and open the Buslic database in the Cases2 folder on your Student Disk.

1. Design and create a switchboard that has frmSwitchboard as a saved form name and that has the following components and characteristics.
    a. Provide appropriate wording for the title bar and a heading at the top center of the switchboard.
    b. Add the rex01.bmp and rex02.bmp graphic images from your Student Disk to appropriate positions on the switchboard.
    c. Place five command buttons on the switchboard. The command buttons perform these actions: open the "LICENSES" table, open the "Businesses Form" form, open the "Businesses Sorted by License Type and Business Name Query" query, open the "Businesses Report" report, and close the switchboard and activate the Database window. Create a macro group for these command buttons.
    d. Use appropriate background and foreground colors and visual effects for the switchboard and its components, and size and position the switchboard in the Form View window.

TUTORIAL 3

Additional Macros

Completing the Macros for the Issue25 Database User Interface

OBJECTIVES

In this tutorial you will:

- Create a custom menu bar
- Use the Menu Builder
- Modify menu macro groups
- Create a custom toolbar
- Attach a custom menu bar and a custom toolbar to a form
- Test macros
- Set database startup options

Vision Publishers

Elena Sanchez has been developing a graphical user interface for the Issue25 database. She reviews her progress and plans the remaining tasks. So far, she has created the switchboard, two dialog boxes, and a macro group. She has been able to use many of the skills she learned at the Access training seminar she attended. The next tasks she undertakes are to create a custom menu bar and a custom toolbar for the switchboard. Once she creates the menu bar and toolbar, the only unfinished tasks involve adding Access Basic code to selected event properties to complete the two dialog boxes.

SESSION 3.1

In this session, you will learn to create a custom menu bar and attach the custom menu bar to a form. You will also modify menu macro groups.

Planning a Custom Menu Bar

For the Issue25 database graphical user interface, Elena designs a custom menu bar. Her plan for the menus and menu items is shown in Figure 3-1.

Figure 3-1 Elena's design for the Issue25 custom menu bar

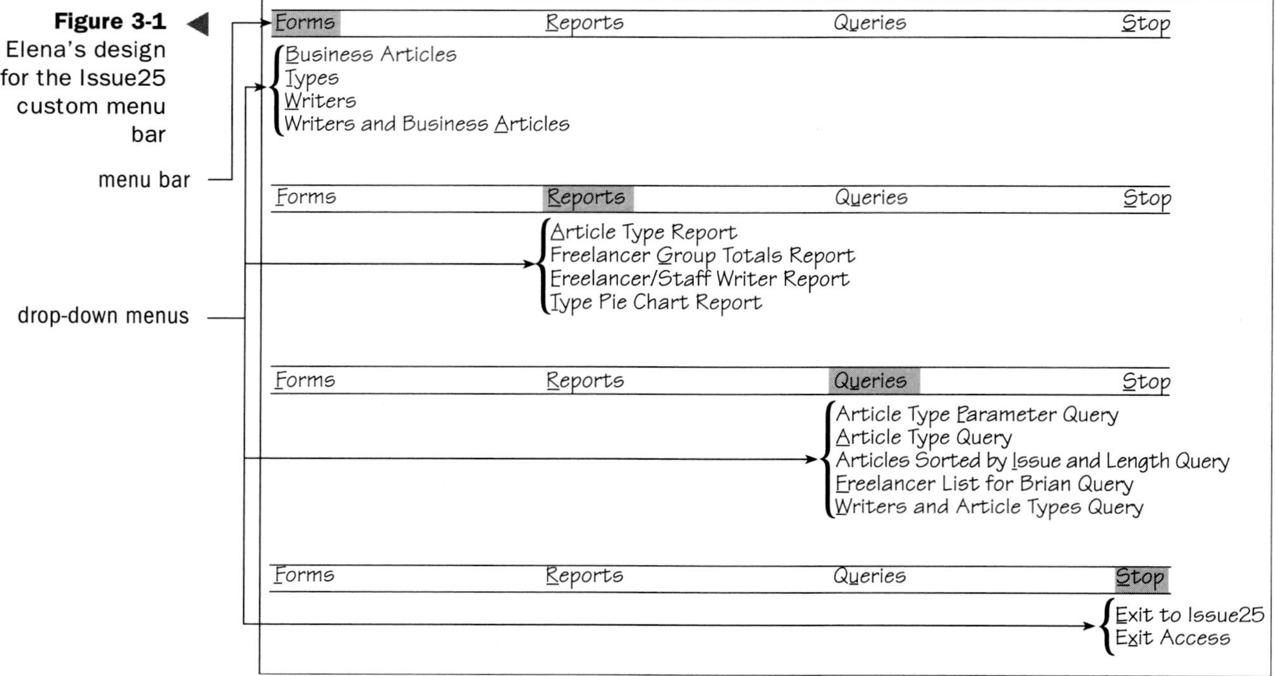

A **custom menu bar** is a menu bar you create for an application. Custom menu bars are similar to standard Access menu bars, which are called **built-in menu bars**, in the following ways.

- A custom menu bar appears immediately below the title bar, replacing the built-in menu.
- A custom menu bar contains one or more menu names. Elena's menu names are Forms, Reports, Queries, and Stop.
- A list of menu-item names, which are usually the names of commands, appears in a drop-down menu when you click a menu name on the menu bar. Elena designs the custom menu so that the menu-item names for the Forms menu are Business Articles, Types, Writers, and Writers and Business Articles.
- Each menu name has an underlined letter that identifies the hot key to the menu. Pressing Alt + F, for example, opens the Forms menu to display the four menu items.
- Each menu-item name has an underlined letter that identifies the hot key for selecting that option. Pressing the W key when Elena's Forms menu is open, for example, opens the Writers Column Form.
- A hot key can apply to only one active control or menu choice on the screen. Thus, Elena cannot assign a hot key to a custom menu bar choice if it is already used on the Switchboard or other control. When a menu is displayed, hot keys apply only to the available menu items.

Elena learned in her course that when you create a custom menu bar, you attach macros to the menu names and items. When the user clicks a menu name or item, an event occurs, and your macro responds and takes the appropriate action (for example, it opens a form). To get your custom menu bar to function, you need to create a menu bar macro and menu macro groups. A **menu bar macro** displays a custom menu bar; the macro contains a series of AddMenu actions, one action for each menu name. Each **AddMenu action** adds a drop-down menu to the custom menu bar. A **menu macro group**, also called a **menu macro**, defines the commands for a drop-down menu. The commands on the four drop-down menus in Figure 3-1 are defined by four menu macro groups.

You can attach a custom menu bar to a form or report so that Access displays the custom menu bar only when it displays the form or report. Alternatively, your custom menu bar can be **global**, so that Access displays the custom menu bar in all windows of your application. Finally, you can create all the macros for a custom menu bar or use the **Menu Builder** to help you create the macros. You start the Menu Builder from the Menu Bar event property on a form or report or from the Add-ins command in the Tools menu. An **add-in** is a Visual Basic program that adds features to the basic Access database command set. Several add-ins, such as the Menu Builder and Wizards, are included with the Access software. You can buy add-ins from third-party companies or you can create your own add-ins.

Using the Menu Builder

Elena uses the Menu Builder to create the Issue25 custom menu bar. Interacting with the Menu Builder, she enters each menu name and each menu-item name. After Elena assigns menSwitchboard as the menu bar name, Menu Builder creates a menu bar macro with the same name and four menu macro groups named menSwitchboard_Forms, menSwitchboard_Reports, menSwitchboard_Queries, and menSwitchboard_Stop.

Next, Elena adds the appropriate actions to the four menu macro groups. She then attaches menSwitchboard to the Menu Bar event property of the frmSwitchboard form. Finally, Elena tests all custom menu bar options.

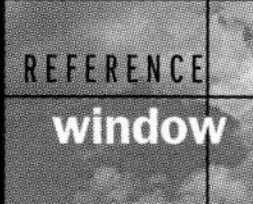

CREATING A CUSTOM MENU BAR WITH MENU BUILDER

- Click Tools, point to Add-ins, click Menu Builder, click the New button, click <Empty Menu Bar>, and then click the OK button.
- Enter a menu or menu-item name in the Caption box, type a description in the Status Bar Text text box, click an indent button to distinguish between menu names and menu-item names, and click the Next button to complete each definition.
- After entering all menu and menu-item names, click the OK button, type the custom menu bar name, and press the Enter key.

Elena starts the Menu Builder add-in to create a custom menu bar to attach to the frmSwitchboard form.

To start Menu Builder:

1. Place your Student Disk in the appropriate drive, start Access, open the Issue25 database in the Tutorial folder on your Student Disk, and then maximize the Database window.

   TROUBLE? The Issue25 database can get very large as you create new objects. We advise that you compact the database often.

2. Click **Tools**, point to **Add-ins**, and then click **Menu Builder**. Access opens the first Menu Builder dialog box. Elena begins her new menu.
3. Click the **New** button in the Menu Builder dialog box. The next dialog box opens.

4. Be sure **<Empty Menu Bar>** in the Template for New Menu Bar list box is selected, and then click the **OK** button. Access opens the Menu Builder [New Menu Bar] dialog box. See Figure 3-2.

Figure 3-2 The Menu Builder dialog box

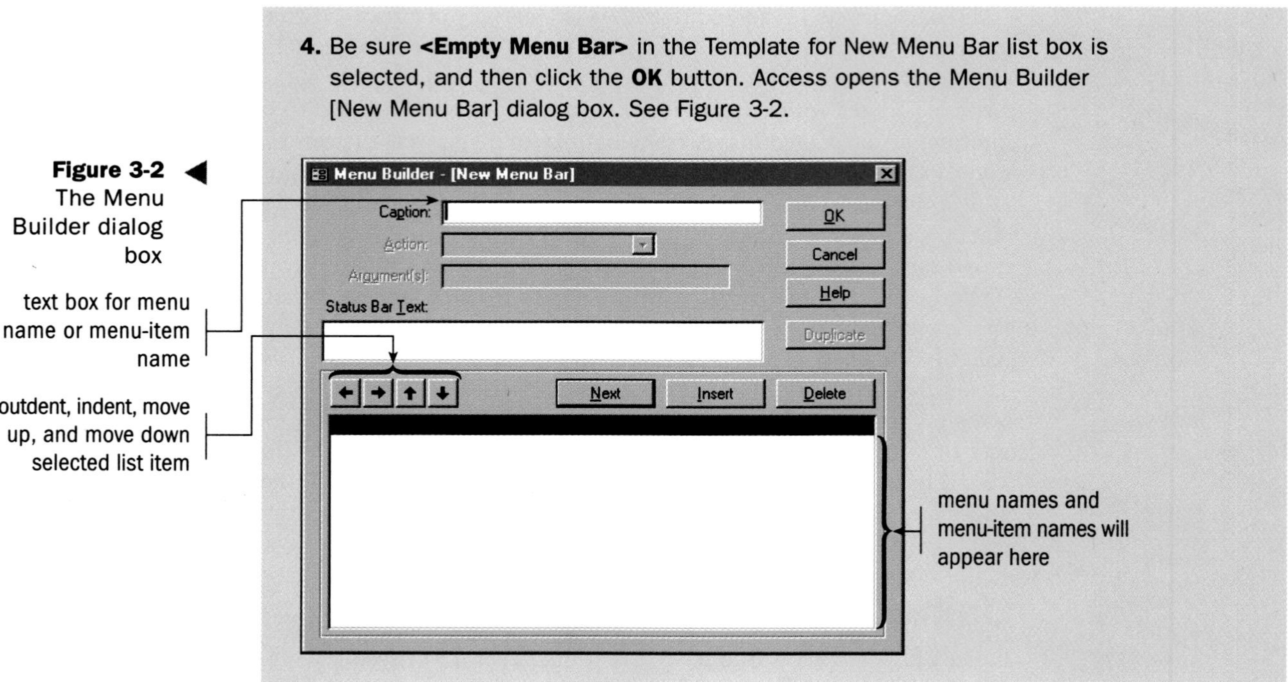

In the Caption text box, Elena enters the menu and menu-item names. In the Status Bar Text text box, she enters the comment or description she wants to be displayed in the status bar for the menu or menu item. Because she wants Menu Builder to create the menu bar macro and menu macro groups for her, Elena does not use the Action or Argument(s) text boxes.

Elena's custom menu has the following menu names: Forms, Reports, Queries, and Stop. Elena uses Stop instead of Exit on the menu in order to have unique hot keys on the switchboard. She selects the hot keys F, P, U, and S. Recall, that a letter preceded by an ampersand (&) in a menu name or menu-item name appears underlined on the custom menu bar or drop-down menu and functions as a hot key. Elena enters the first menu name.

To use Menu Builder to enter a menu name:

1. Type **&Forms** in the Caption text box, press the **Tab** key, type **Open forms** in the Status Bar Text text box, and then click the **Next** button. Access adds &Forms to the list box in the lower panel of the dialog box, moves the highlight below the &Forms entry, and places the insertion point at the start of the Caption text box.

2. Type **&Business Articles**, press the **Tab** key, type **Open Business Articles Column Form** in the Status Bar Text text box, and then click the **Indent** button →. See Figure 3-3.

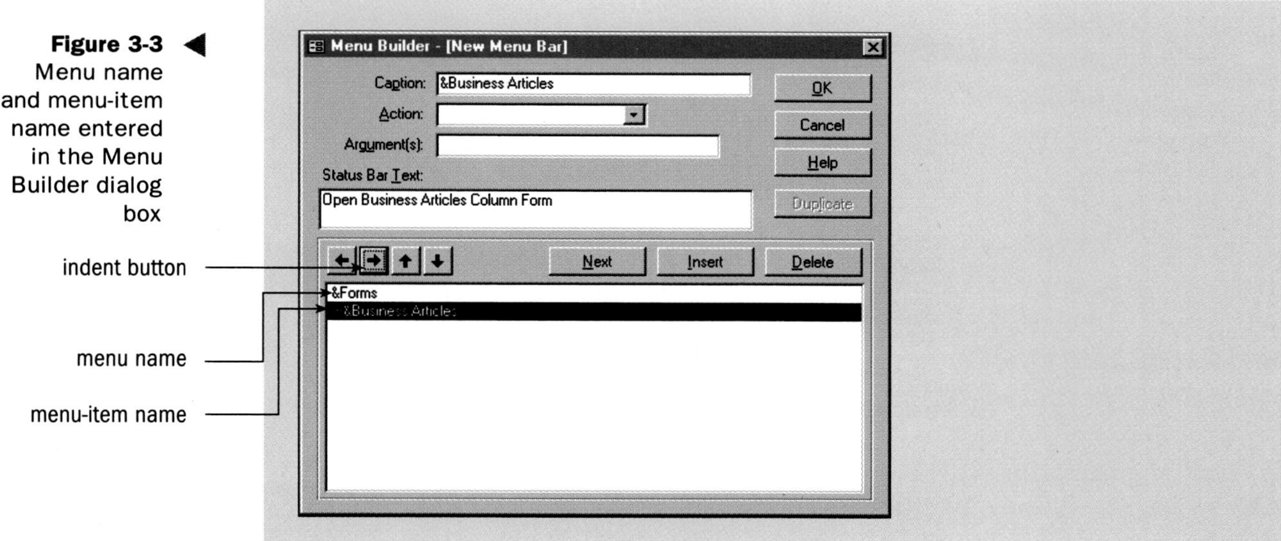

Figure 3-3 Menu name and menu-item name entered in the Menu Builder dialog box

You place menu names flush left in the list box and indent menu-item names one level. For more complicated menu bars that have submenus, you indent the submenu commands one additional level below a menu-item name. In this case, the menu-item name becomes the submenu name.

Elena continues entering menu-item names in the order she wants them to appear in the custom menu bar.

To continue entering the menu and menu-item names in a custom menu bar:

1. Click the **Next** button, type **&Types** in the Caption text box, press the **Tab** key, type **Open Types Form** in the Status Bar Text text box, and then click the **indent** button. Elena is now ready to start the third menu item for the Forms menu.

   TROUBLE? If you click the indent button an extra time, click the **outdent** button to set the menu item back one level.

2. Click the **Next** button, type **&Writers** in the Caption text box, press the **Tab** key, type **Open Writers Column Form** in the Status Bar Text text box, and then click the **indent** button.

3. Click the **Next** button, type **Writers and Business &Articles** in the Caption text box, press the **Tab** key, type **Open Writers and Business Articles Form** in the Status Bar Text text box, and then click the **indent** button. Elena has completed entering the four menu-item names for the Forms menu, so now she builds the Reports menu.

4. Click the **Next** button, type **Re&ports** in the Caption text box, press the **Tab** key, and then type **Open reports** in the Status Bar Text text box. Elena now enters the first menu-item name for the Reports menu.

5. Click the **Next** button, type **&Article Type Report** in the Caption text box, press the **Tab** key, type **Open Article Type Report** in the Status Bar Text text box, and then click the **indent** button. See Figure 3-4.

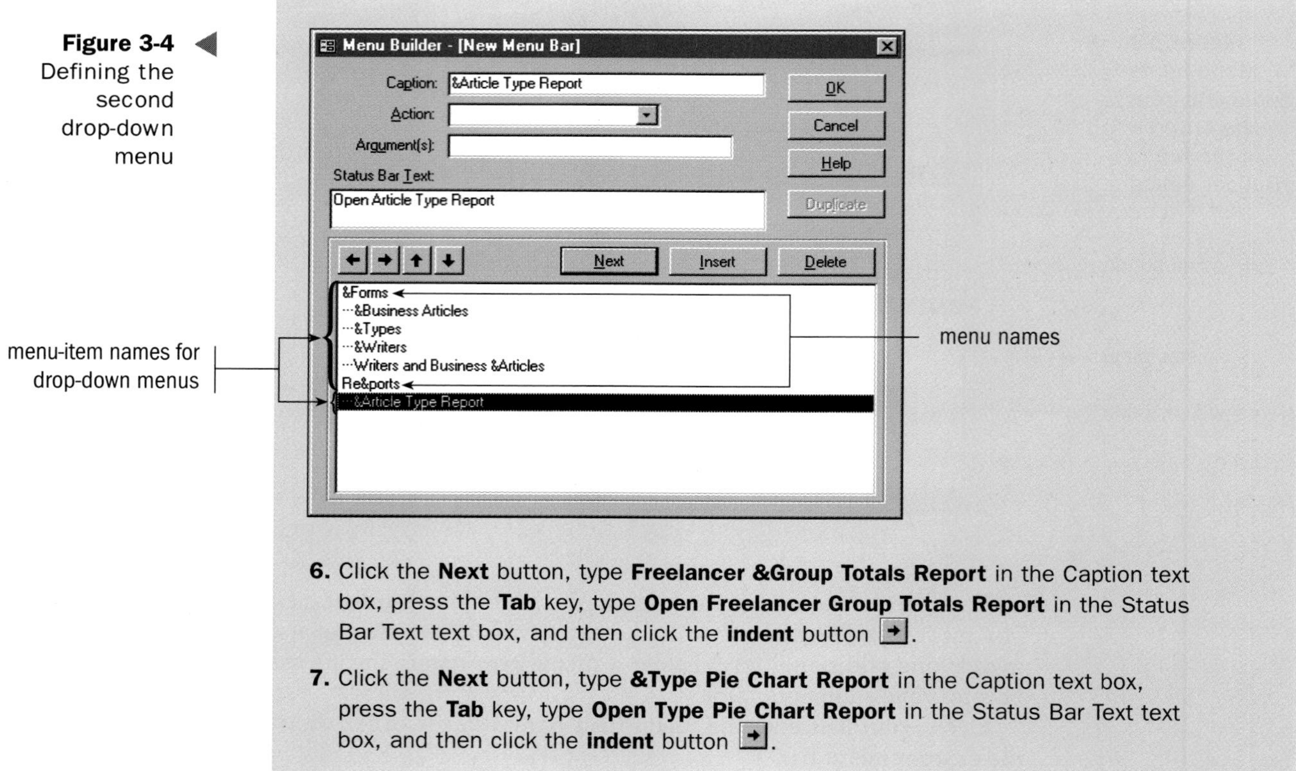

Figure 3-4 Defining the second drop-down menu

6. Click the **Next** button, type **Freelancer &Group Totals Report** in the Caption text box, press the **Tab** key, type **Open Freelancer Group Totals Report** in the Status Bar Text text box, and then click the **indent** button ➔.

7. Click the **Next** button, type **&Type Pie Chart Report** in the Caption text box, press the **Tab** key, type **Open Type Pie Chart Report** in the Status Bar Text text box, and then click the **indent** button ➔.

Elena completes the construction of the custom menu bar in the Menu Builder dialog box. She enters the Queries menu name and its five menu-item names, and then the Stop menu name and its two menu-item names.

To complete a custom menu bar using the Menu Builder:

1. Click the **Next** button, type **Q&ueries** in the Caption text box, press the **Tab** key, and then type **Open queries** in the Status Bar Text text box. See Figure 3-5.

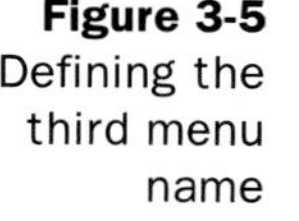

Figure 3-5 Defining the third menu name

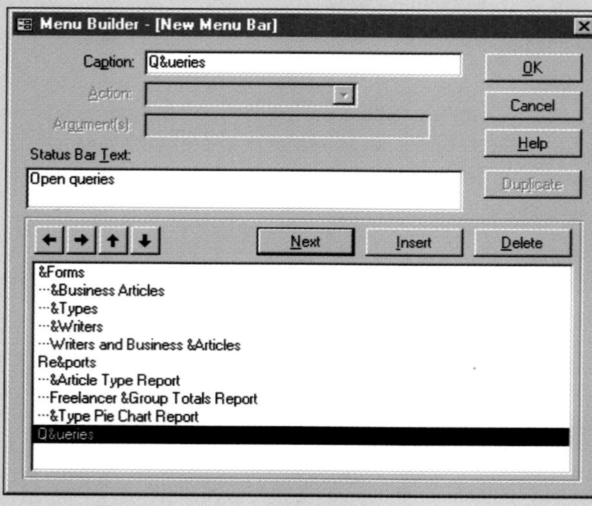

2. Click the **Next** button, type **Article Type &Parameter Query** in the Caption text box, press the **Tab** key, type **Open Article Type Parameter Query** in the Status Bar Text text box, and then click the **indent** button ➔.

3. Repeat Step 2 for the four remaining menu items for the Queries menu. Type **&Article Type Query**, **Articles Sorted by &Issue and Length Query**, **&Freelancer List for Brian Query**, and **&Writers and Article Types Query** for the four menu-item entries in the Caption text box and type corresponding entries in the Status Bar Text text box. Be sure to indent the menu item names below the Query names.
4. Click the **Next** button, type **&Stop** in the Caption text box, press the **Tab** key, and then type **Exit Switchboard** in the Status Bar Text text box.
5. Click the **Next** button, type **&Exit to Issue25** in the Caption text box, press the **Tab** key, type **Exit to Issue25 database** in the Status Bar Text text box, and then click the **indent** button.
6. Click the **Next** button, type **E&xit Access** in the Caption text box, press the **Tab** key, type **Exit Access** in the Status Bar Text text box, and then click the **indent** button.
7. Click the **OK** button, type **menSwitchboard** in the Menu Bar Name text box in the Save As dialog box, and then click the **OK** button. Access saves the custom menu bar, returns to the Database window, and opens the Macros list box. See Figure 3-6.

Figure 3-6 Macros created by the Menu Builder

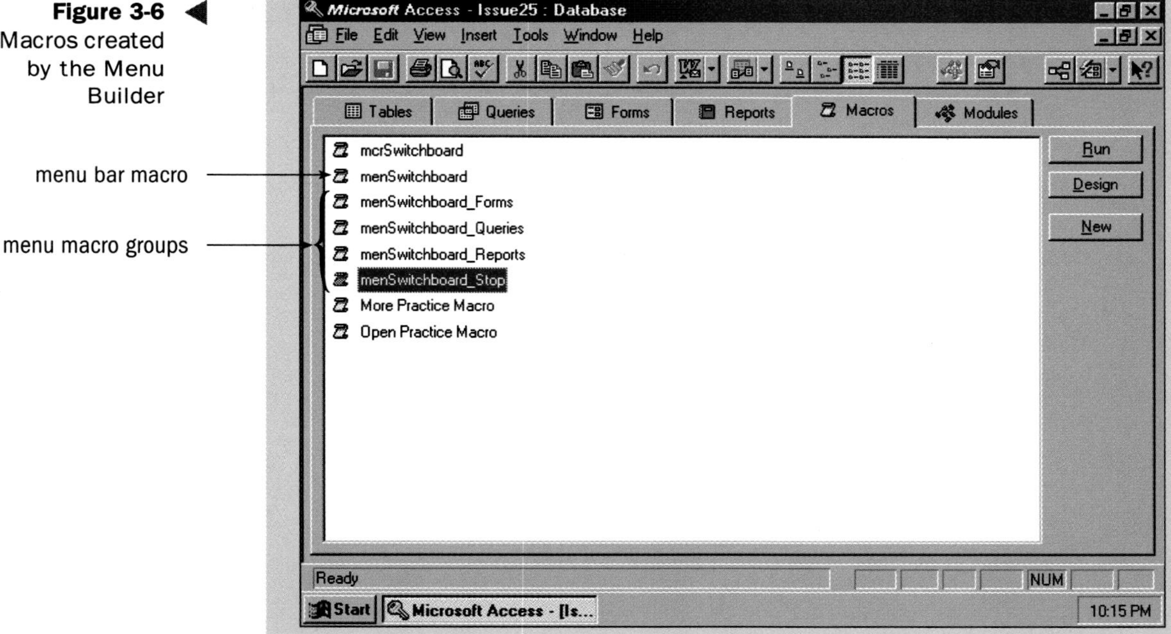

The Menu Builder created the five macros having names starting with menSwitchboard. Elena now adds the required actions to the macros that will make them open the indicated objects.

Adding Actions to Menu Macro Groups

Now that Elena has created the outline of her custom menu bar, she needs to add actions to the macros created by the Menu Builder. She doesn't need to change the menSwitchboard macro, which already contains AddMenu actions to display the custom menu bar and to define the four drop-down menus, although she does open it to be sure it's okay. The macro changes she will make fall into two categories:

- The menSwitchboard_Queries and menSwitchboard_Reports macros are menu macro groups that define the commands for the Queries and the Reports drop-down menus. For the macros in the menSwitchboard_Queries macro, Elena adds OpenQuery actions and sets the View action arguments to Print Preview. For the macros in the menSwitchboard_Reports macro, Elena adds OpenReport actions.
- The menSwitchboard_Stop and menSwitchboard_Forms macros are menu macro groups that define the commands for the Stop and Forms drop-down menus. Elena already created macros in the mcrSwitchboard macro group that perform the actions needed to exit and to open forms, so she adds RunMacro actions to the menu macro groups to run the macros she created earlier.

Elena opens the menSwitchboard macro to review its actions and to verify she does not need to make any changes.

To review a menu bar macro:

1. Click **menSwitchboard** in the Macros list box and then click the **Design** button to open the Macro window. See Figure 3-7. The first AddMenu action displays Forms on the custom menu bar, displays "Open forms" on the status bar, and runs the menSwitchboard_Forms macro. This first macro is correct. Elena reviews the three other actions.

Figure 3-7 The menSwitchboard menu bar Macro

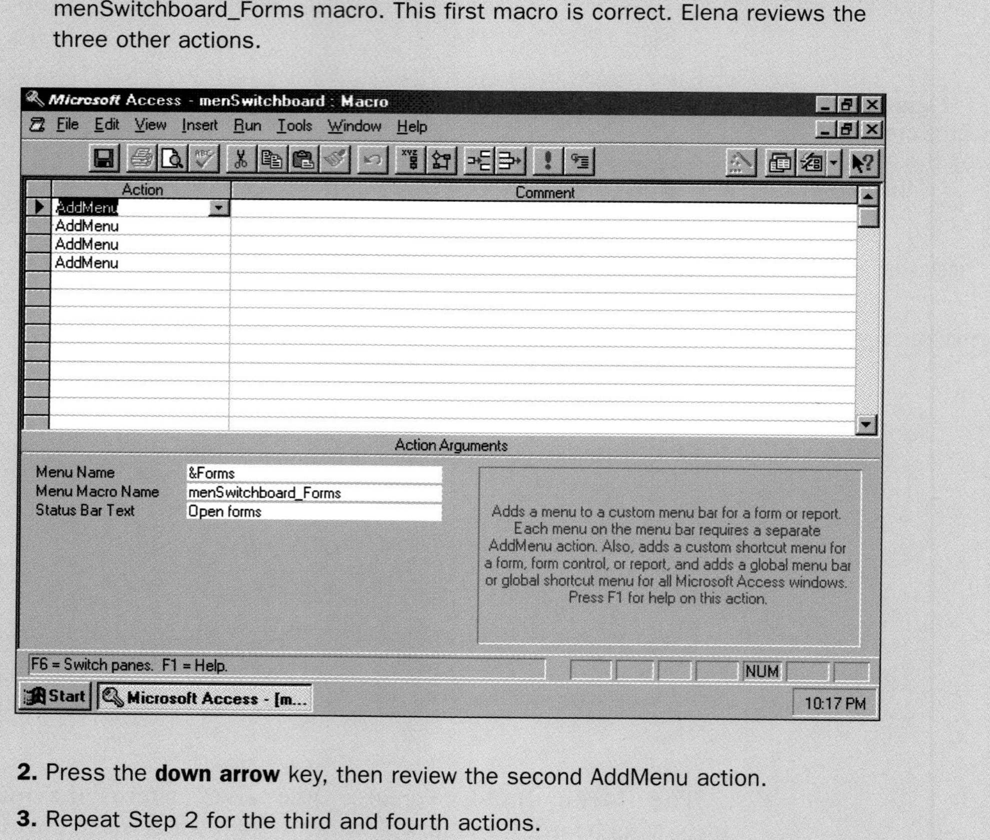

2. Press the **down arrow** key, then review the second AddMenu action.
3. Repeat Step 2 for the third and fourth actions.

Elena closes the Macro window, opens the menSwitchboard_Stop menu macro group, and adds the RunMacro action to the group's two macros. The RunMacro action runs macros Elena previously created in the mcrSwitchboard macro group.

To add actions to a menu macro group:

1. Click the Macro window **Close** button to close the Macro window.
2. Click **menSwitchboard_Stop** in the Macros list box and then click the **Design** button. Access opens the Macro window.
3. Click the **Macro Names** button on the toolbar to display the Macro Name column, then click the first row's **Action** text box, click the **list arrow**, scroll down the Action list, and then click **RunMacro**.
4. Click the **Macro Name** text box in the Action Arguments panel, click the **list arrow**, and then click **mcrSwitchboard.mcrExitToIssue25**. Access runs this macro whenever you select Exit to Issue25 on the Stop menu.
5. Click the second row's **Action** text box, click the **list arrow**, scroll down the Action list, and then click **RunMacro**.
6. Click the **Macro Name** text box in the Action Arguments panel, click the **list arrow**, scroll, and then click **mcrSwitchboard.mcrExitAccess**. Access runs this macro whenever you select Exit Access on the Stop menu. See Figure 3-8.

Figure 3-8
RunMacro macros added to a menu macro group

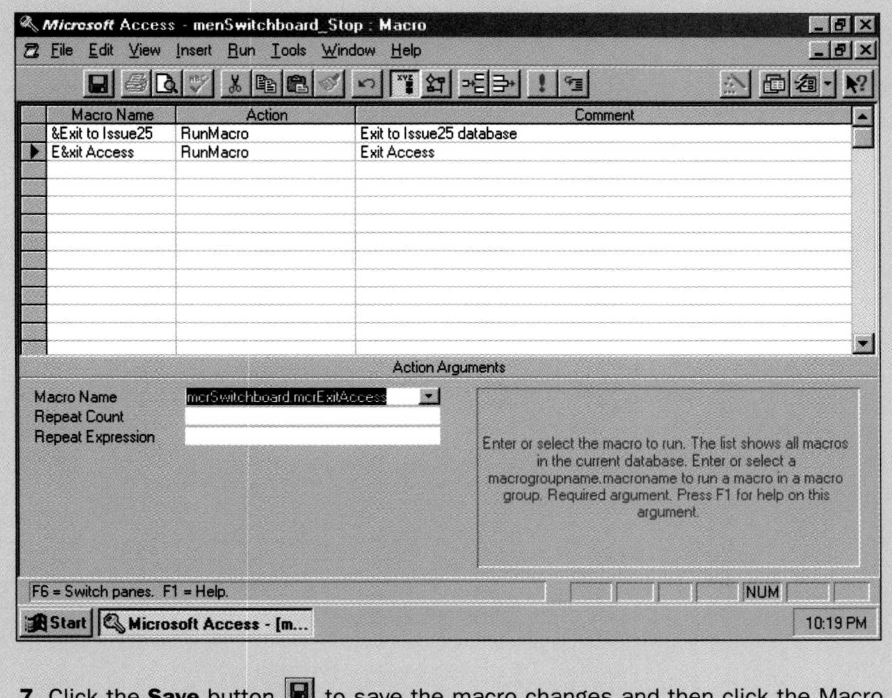

7. Click the **Save** button to save the macro changes and then click the Macro window **Close** button to close the Macro window and return to the Database window.

Next, Elena opens the Macro window for the menSwitchboard_Forms menu macro group and adds the RunMacro action to the group's four macros. The RunMacro action runs macros Elena previously created in the mcrSwitchboard macro group; these macros open the forms specified by the menu-item name.

To add RunMacro actions to a menu macro group:

1. Click **menSwitchboard_Forms** in the Macros list and then click the **Design** button. Access opens the Macro window.
2. Click the **Macro Names** button to display the Macro Name column, then click the first row's **Action** text box, click the **list arrow**, scroll down the Action list, and then click **RunMacro**.
3. Click the **Macro Name** text box in the Action Arguments panel, click the **list arrow**, and then click **mcrSwitchboard.mcrBusinessArticles**. Access runs this macro whenever you select Business Articles on the Forms menu.
4. Click the second row's **Action** text box, click the **list arrow**, scroll down the Action list, click **RunMacro**, click the **Macro Name** text box, click the **list arrow**, scroll down the list, and then click **mcrSwitchboard.mcrTypes**. Access runs this macro whenever you select Types on the Forms menu.
5. Click the third row's **Action** text box, click the **list arrow**, scroll down the Action list, click **RunMacro**, click the **Macro Name** text box, click the **list arrow**, scroll down the list, and then click **mcrSwitchboard.mcrWriters**. Access runs this macro whenever you select Writers on the Forms menu.
6. Click the fourth row's **Action** text box, click the **list arrow**, scroll down the Action list, click **RunMacro**, click the **Macro Name** text box, click the **list arrow**, scroll down the list, and then click **mcrSwitchboard.mcrWritersBusinessArticles**. Access runs this macro whenever you select Writers and Business Articles on the Forms menu. See Figure 3-9.

Figure 3-9 The completed Forms menu macro group

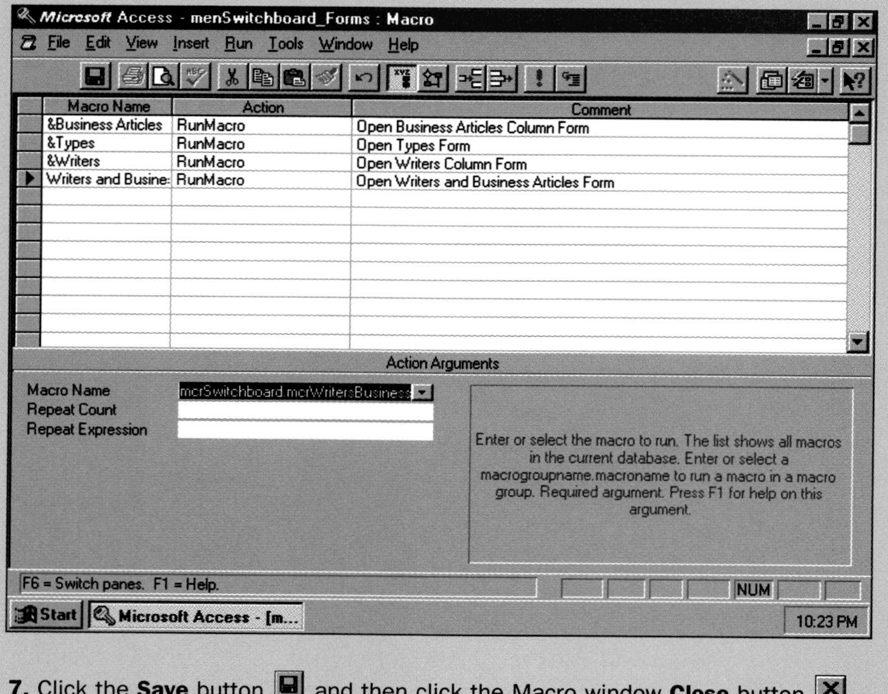

7. Click the **Save** button and then click the Macro window **Close** button.

Elena does not have existing macros for the menSwitchboard_Queries menu macro group. Therefore, instead of adding RunMacro actions, Elena adds OpenQuery actions to each macro in the group.

To add OpenQuery actions to a menu macro group:

1. Click **menSwitchboard_Queries** in the Macros list box and then click the **Design** button. Access opens the Macro window.
2. Click the **Macro Name** button to display the Macro Names column, then click the first row's **Action** text box, click the **list arrow**, scroll down the Action list, and then click **OpenQuery**.
3. Click the **Query Name** text box in the Action Arguments panel, click the **list arrow**, click **Article Type Parameter Query**, click the **View** text box, click the list arrow, and then click **Print Preview**. Access opens this query in the Print Preview window whenever you select the Article Type Parameter Query on the Queries menu.
4. Add OpenQuery Actions for the four remaining macros. Click **Article Type Query**, **Articles Sorted by Issue and Length Query**, **Freelancer List for Brian Query**, and **Writers and Article Types Query** and set the View to Print Preview for the four corresponding macros in the Query Name text box. See Figure 3-10.

Figure 3-10 The completed Queries menu macro group

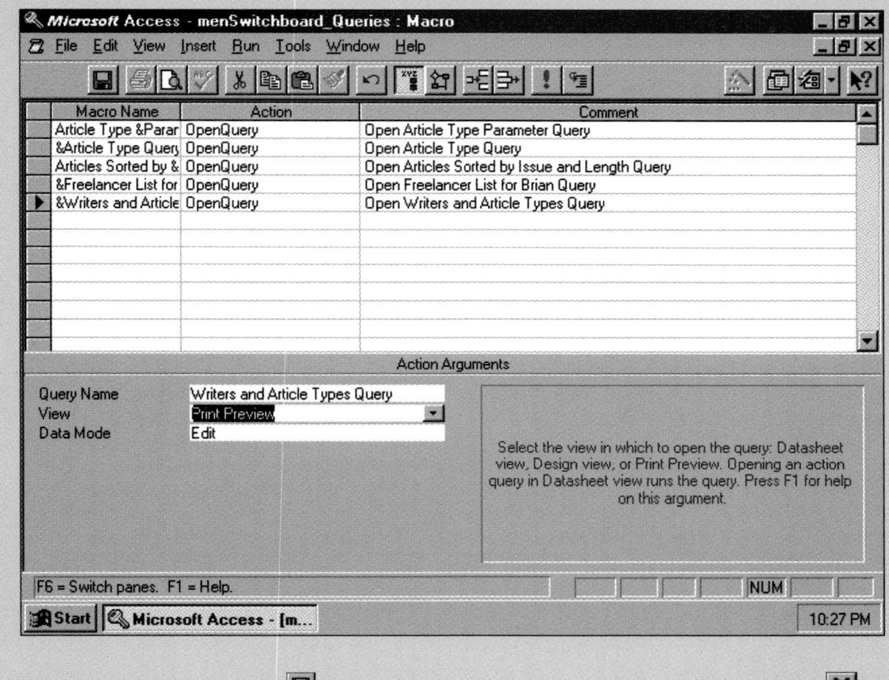

5. Click the **Save** button and then click the Macro window **Close** button.

The changes Elena will make to the menSwitchboard_Reports menu macro group are similar to those she made to the menSwitchboard_Queries menu macro group. Instead of adding OpenQuery actions, however, Elena adds OpenReport actions for each macro in the group. She also notices that the Freelancer/Staff Writer Report is missing; she must have failed to add it in the Menu Builder dialog box. For minor mistakes like this one, Elena can make corrections in the Macro window rather than reopen the Menu Builder.

To add OpenReport actions to a menu macro group:

1. Click **menSwitchboard_Reports** in the Macros list box and then click the **Design** button. Access opens the Macro window.
2. Click the **Macro Names** button on the toolbar to display the Macro Name column, then right-click the third row **selector** for the third row to open the shortcut menu, and then click **Insert Row**.

3. Click the third row's **Macro Name** text box, type **&Freelancer/Staff Writer Report**, press the **Tab** key, press the **Tab** key again, and then type **Open Freelancer/Staff Writer Report** as the comment.

4. Click the first row's **Action** text box, click the **list arrow**, scroll down the Action list, and then click **OpenReport**.

5. Click the **Report Name** text box in the Action Arguments panel, click the **list arrow**, and then click **Article Type Report**. Access opens this report in the Print Preview window whenever you select **Article Type Report** on the Reports menu.

6. Add the OpenReport actions for the three remaining macros. Click **Freelancer Group Totals Report**, **Freelancer/Staff Writer Report**, and **Type Pie Chart Report** for the three macros in the Report Name text box. See Figure 3-11.

Figure 3-11 The completed reports menu macro group

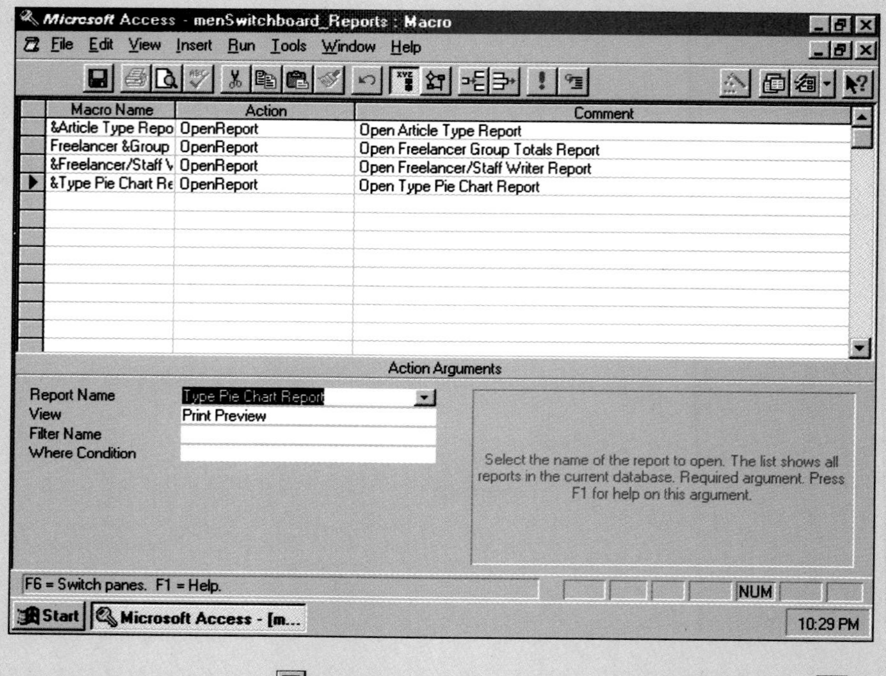

7. Click the **Save** button and then click the Macro window **Close** button.

Attaching a Custom Menu Bar to a Form

When Access displays the frmSwitchboard form, Elena wants the custom menu bar to appear instead of the built-in Form View window menu bar. For any other object in the Issue25 database, including the two dialog boxes opened from the frmSwitchboard form, Access should display the associated built-in menu bar.

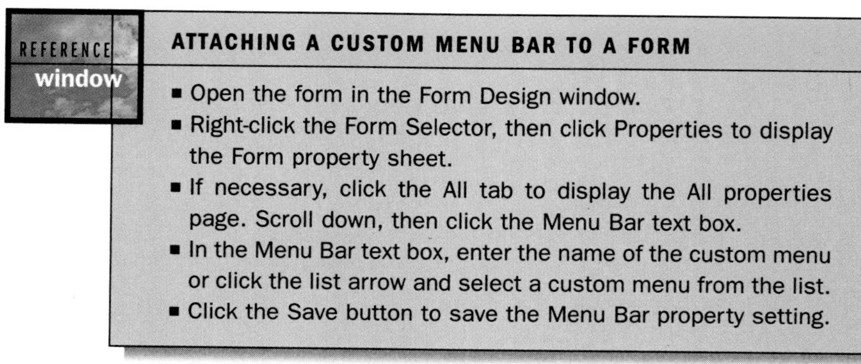

REFERENCE window

ATTACHING A CUSTOM MENU BAR TO A FORM

- Open the form in the Form Design window.
- Right-click the Form Selector, then click Properties to display the Form property sheet.
- If necessary, click the All tab to display the All properties page. Scroll down, then click the Menu Bar text box.
- In the Menu Bar text box, enter the name of the custom menu or click the list arrow and select a custom menu from the list.
- Click the Save button to save the Menu Bar property setting.

Elena attaches the custom menu bar to the frmSwitchboard form. Specifically, she sets the form's MenuBar property to the name of the custom menu bar.

To attach a custom menu bar to a form:

1. Click the **Forms** tab, click **frmSwitchboard**, and then click the **Design** button. Access opens the Form Design window for the frmSwitchboard form.
2. If the Form property sheet is not open, right-click the **Form Selector** to open the shortcut menu, then click **Properties** to open the property sheet.
3. If necessary, click the **All** tab in the property sheet, then scroll down and click the **Menu Bar** text box, click the **list arrow**, scroll down the list, and then click **menSwitchboard**.

   TROUBLE? If you can't see the complete names in the list, widen the property sheet temporarily.
4. Click the **Save** button to save the form-design changes and then click the property sheet **Close** button to close the property sheet.
5. Click the Form Design window **Close** button to close the window and return to the Database window.
6. Click the **Open** button to open the **frmSwitchboard** form in the Form View window. Click the Form View window **Restore** button to see the switchboard. See Figure 3-12.

Figure 3-12 A custom menu bar with a form

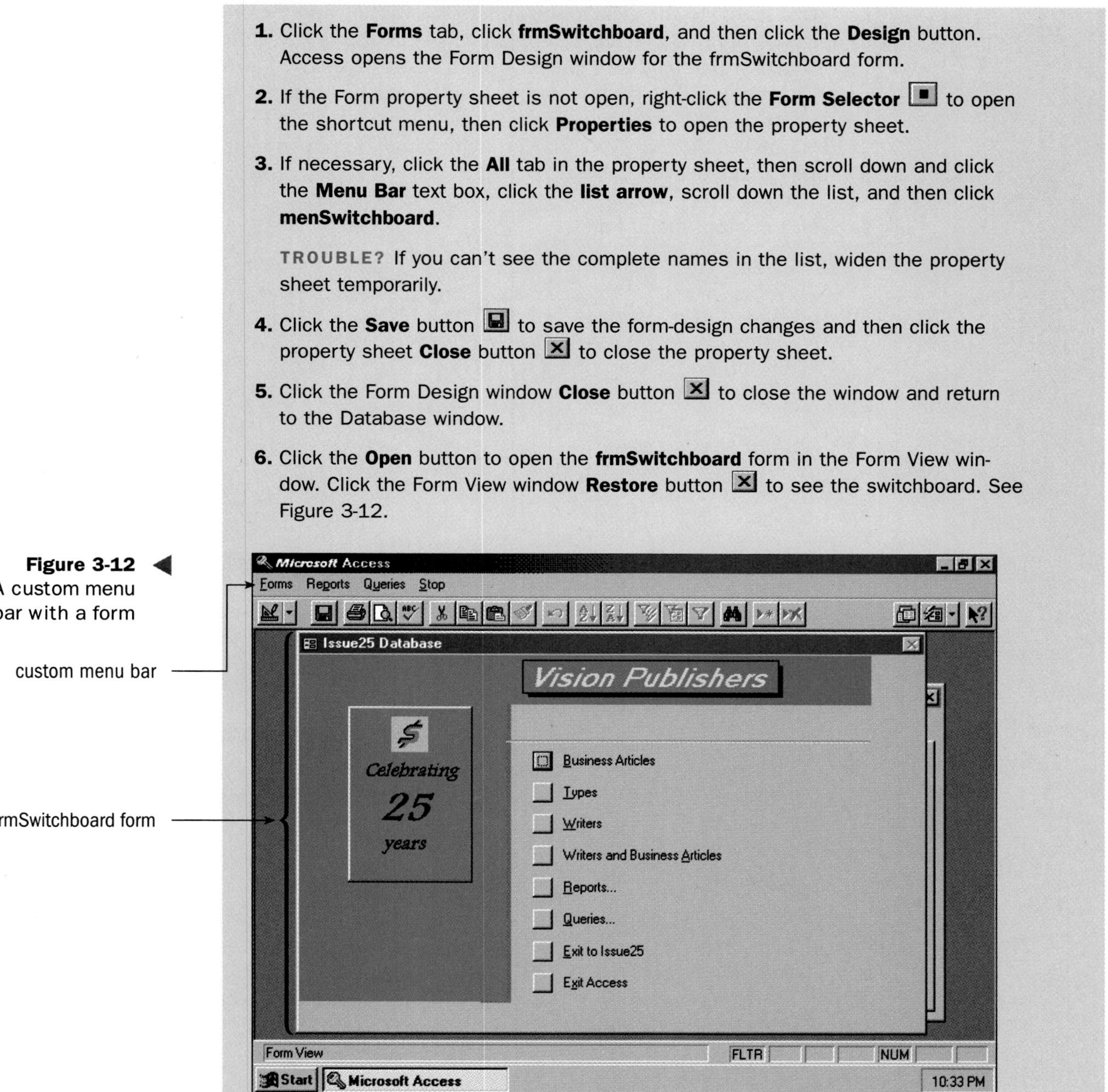

Access opens the frmSwitchboard form and displays the custom menu bar below the Microsoft Access title bar. Elena successfully attached the custom menu bar to the frmSwitchboard form.

Testing a Custom Menu Bar

Elena tests all the menus and menu items on the custom menu bar. To test each menu, Elena clicks each menu name and verifies that the drop-down menu opens in response. To test keyboard access to the menus, she presses the Alt key and the underlined menu character to open a drop-down menu, and then presses the Esc key to close that drop-down menu. In a similar way, Elena tests the mouse and keyboard access to the menu items on each drop-down menu. For keyboard access to the menu items, she simply presses the underlined character and does not use the Alt key.

Elena makes the Exit Access menu item on the Stop menu her last choice and realizes it's time to take her lunch break.

To test a custom menu bar:

1. Click each menu name, in turn, from left to right, to verify that each drop-down menu appears. Point to each menu item on each drop-down menu and verify the description in the status bar.
2. Press **Alt + F** to display the Forms drop-down menu and then press the **Esc** key to close the drop-down menu.

   TROUBLE? Whenever a menu, button, or other object provides a hot key, the hot key can be pressed either as a lowercase or uppercase letter.
3. Repeat Step 2 for the underlined character in each of the other three menu names.
4. Point to **Forms** to display its drop-down menu. Then either click **Business Articles** or press **B** to open the Business Articles Column Form. Click the Form View window **Close** box ☒ for the Business Articles Column Form to close the form. Repeat this step for each of the other three menu items on the Forms menu.

   TROUBLE? If you are tempted to skip these testing steps, remember that there are many points in the menu-building process at which things can go wrong. If other users will be using your switchboard, you should be sure to test every part of it.
5. Click **Reports** to display its drop-down menu. Then either click **Article Type Report** or press **A** to open the Article Type Report in the Print Preview window. Click the Print Preview window **Close** button ☒ to close the Print Preview window. Repeat this step for each of the other three menu items on the Reports menu.
6. Click **Queries** to display its drop-down menu. Then either click **Article Type Parameter Query** or press **P**. Type **LAW** when Access asks you for the article type and then press the **Enter** key to open the Article Type Parameter Query in the Print Preview window. Click the Print Preview window **Close** button ☒ to close the Print Preview window. Repeat this step for each of the other four menu items on the Queries menu.
7. Click **Stop** to display its drop-down menu. Then either click **Exit to Issue25** or press **E**. Access closes the form and returns to the Database window.
8. Click the **Open** button to open the frmSwitchboard form in the Form View window.
9. Click **Stop** and then either click **Exit Access** or press **X**. Access closes all windows and exits.

Elena has now completed the custom menu bar. After she breaks for lunch she will create a custom toolbar for the Issue25 graphical user interface.

If you want to take a break and resume the tutorial at a later time, now is a good point to do so. When you resume the tutorial, place your Student Disk containing the Tutorial folder in the appropriate drive.

Quick Check

1. What is the difference between a menu bar macro and a menu macro group?
2. What is a global custom menu bar?
3. When you use the Menu Builder, how do you distinguish between a menu name and a menu-item name?
4. What is the function of the text in the Status Bar Text text box in the Menu Builder?
5. What are the rules for determining hot keys in a menu?
6. What can you do if the menu you create using Menu Builder is missing a menu item?

SESSION 3.2

In this session, you will create a customize toolbar and attach it to a form. You will also set the database startup options so that Access hides the Database window and opens the switchboard form when the database is opened.

Creating a Custom Toolbar

You can customize the standard Access toolbars, called **built-in toolbars**, by replacing standard toolbar buttons with ones you choose (or create from scratch). You can position, or **float**, a toolbar anywhere on the screen. In this way, toolbars are similar to the toolbox. In any Access window you can also display two or more toolbars on the screen. Instead of customizing a built-in toolbar, Elena designs a new custom toolbar for the Issue25 database graphical user interface. A custom toolbar is a toolbar you create for an application. Your toolbar can replace one or more of the built-in Access toolbars or can appear in addition to other built-in toolbars.

Elena names her custom toolbar tolSwitchboard. When the frmSwitchboard form is open, Elena wants the custom toolbar to replace the built-in Form View window toolbar and to be the only toolbar on the screen. In all other situations the built-in Access toolbars appear. Macros control when the custom toolbar does or does not appear. The tolSwitchboard toolbar will contain nine buttons that duplicate the functions of the switchboard command buttons and the custom menu bar in the following ways.

- Four buttons on the left will be grouped together, and each will open one of the four forms that make up the user interface.
- Four more buttons will, respectively, open the Reports dialog box, open the Queries dialog box, exit to the Issue25 database, and exit Access.
- A button at the far right will open the Access Help system.

As she adds buttons to the custom toolbar, Elena changes the images that appear on the buttons. Elena will then make final adjustments to the toolbar button positions.

Placing Buttons on a Custom Toolbar

Elena creates the custom toolbar by adding a new toolbar and naming it tolSwitchboard. She adds buttons to the toolbar, changing the button images, and positions the buttons on the toolbar.

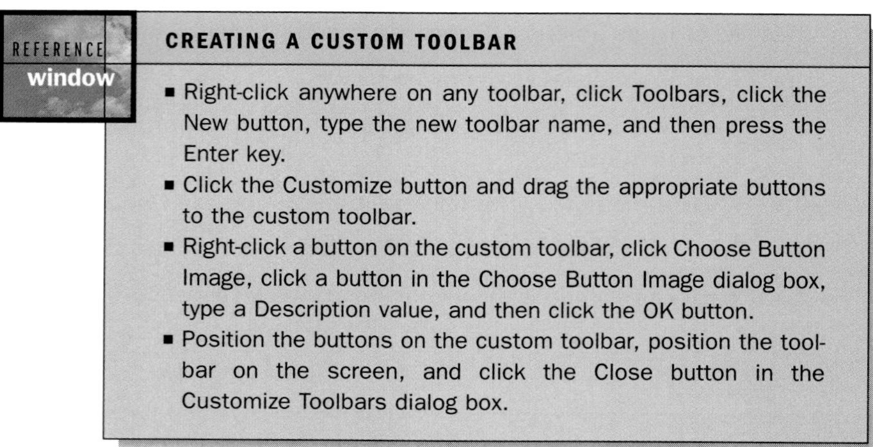

REFERENCE window

CREATING A CUSTOM TOOLBAR

- Right-click anywhere on any toolbar, click Toolbars, click the New button, type the new toolbar name, and then press the Enter key.
- Click the Customize button and drag the appropriate buttons to the custom toolbar.
- Right-click a button on the custom toolbar, click Choose Button Image, click a button in the Choose Button Image dialog box, type a Description value, and then click the OK button.
- Position the buttons on the custom toolbar, position the toolbar on the screen, and click the Close button in the Customize Toolbars dialog box.

Elena's first step is to create a new toolbar with the name tolSwitchboard.

To create a new toolbar:

1. If you have not already done so, start Access and open the Issue25 database.
2. Right-click anywhere on any toolbar to open the shortcut menu, and then click **Toolbars**. Access opens the Toolbars dialog box.
3. Click the **New** button. Access opens the New Toolbar dialog box.
4. Type **tolSwitchboard** in the Toolbar name text box and then click the **OK** button. Access closes the New Toolbar dialog box, opens the Toolbars dialog box, and then opens the tolSwitchboard custom toolbar. See Figure 3-13.

Figure 3-13 Displaying a new custom toolbar

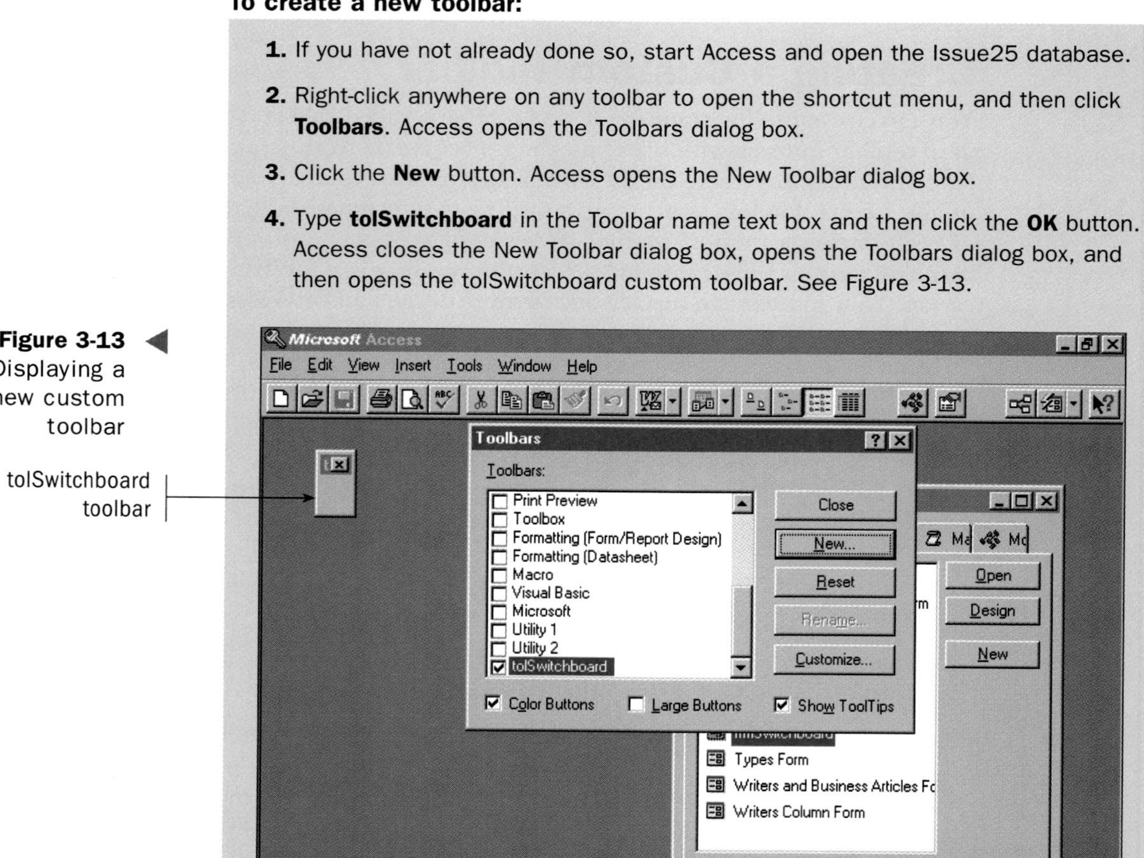

5. Click the **Customize** button. Access opens the Customize Toolbars dialog box. See Figure 3-14.

Figure 3-14 ◀ The Customize Toolbars dialog box

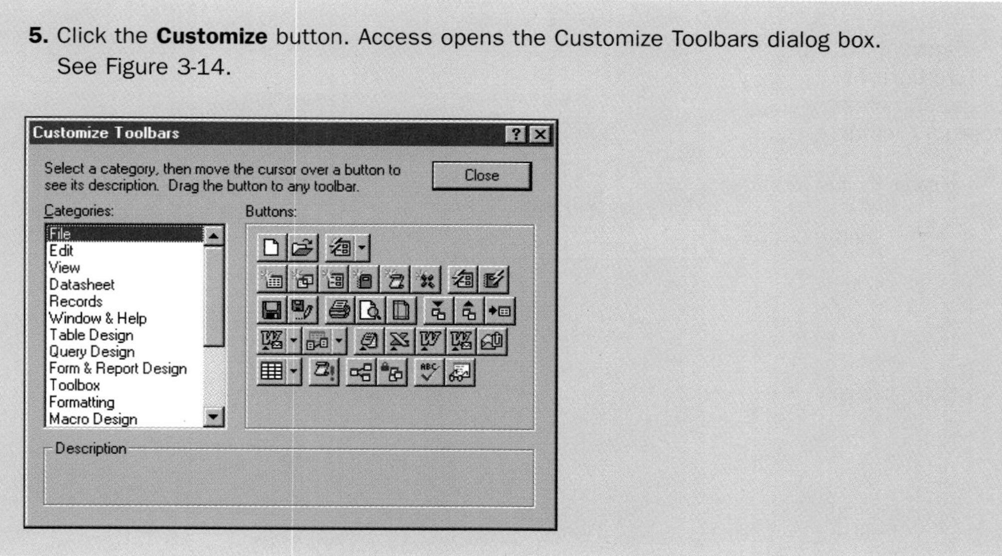

You add a button to a toolbar by dragging it from the Buttons list box in the Customize Toolbars dialog box to the custom toolbar that you are creating. As you add buttons, Access increases the toolbar size to fit around the buttons. You can add buttons to a toolbar in any order. When you drag a new button and place it on top of an already positioned button, Access positions the new button to the left of the other button. Elena positions the buttons on the new custom toolbar from right to left. The button farthest to the right is the Help button. To find the Help button, Elena selects the Window & Help category from the Categories list in the Customize Toolbars dialog box.

To place a button on the custom toolbar:

1. Click **Window & Help** in the Categories list box. Access displays buttons for the selected category in the Buttons list box.

2. Drag the **F1 Help button** from the Buttons list box to the center of the custom toolbar. Access adds to the custom toolbar.

   TROUBLE? If you place the wrong button on the custom toolbar, drag the button off the custom toolbar to any screen location except another toolbar and then repeat the drag operation for the correct button.

Now Elena drags the second button, the one that runs mcrSwitchboard.mcrExitAccess, the macro that closes the frmSwitchboard form and exits Access. It will appear immediately to the left of the Help button on the custom toolbar. Elena selects the All Macros category in the Customize Toolbars dialog box to display the relevant choices. After dragging her button choice, Elena takes a moment to stop the pointer over the new button and observes the button's ToolTip and status bar description. Then she changes the button image to a more descriptive icon and changes the button's ToolTip caption and status bar description.

To add a toolbar button and change its button image:

1. Scroll the Categories list and then click **All Macros**. Access displays the Issue25 database macros in the Objects list box.

2. Drag **mcrSwitchboard.mcrExitAccess** from the Objects list box to the custom toolbar, being sure you place the new button on top and slightly to the left of . When you release the mouse button, Access places the new button to the left of the existing button. Leave the pointer resting on the new button so that the ToolTip appears. See Figure 3-15.

Figure 3-15 Two buttons placed on a custom toolbar

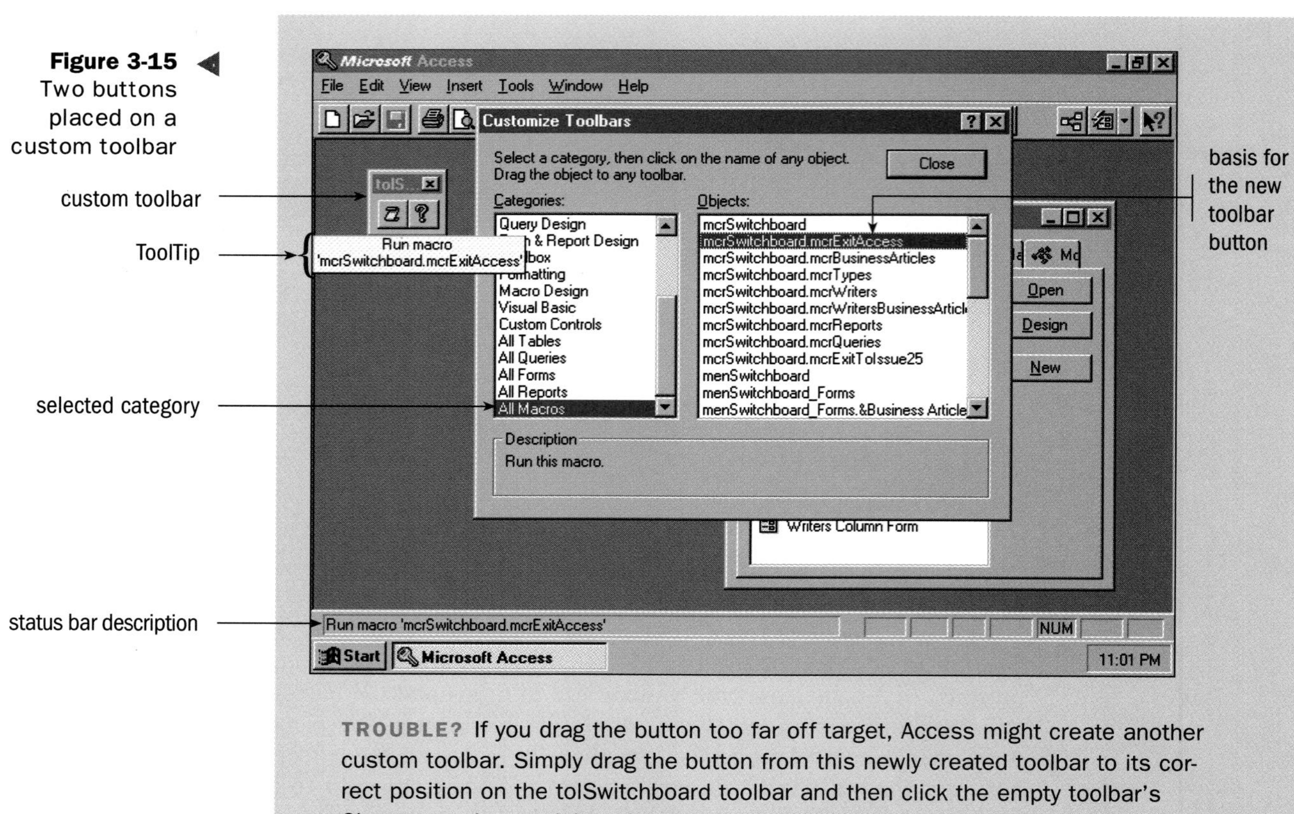

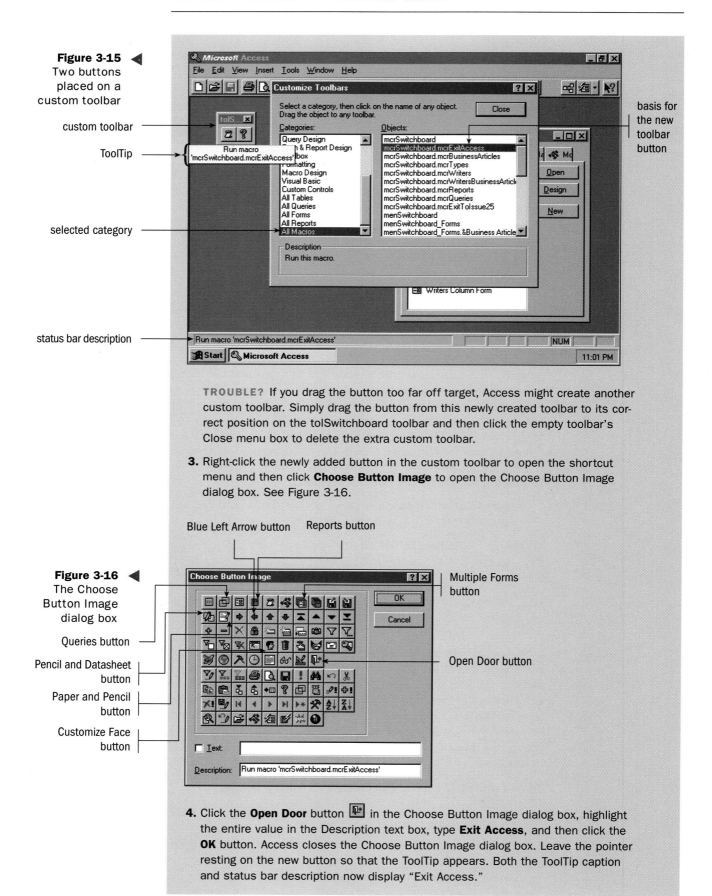

TROUBLE? If you drag the button too far off target, Access might create another custom toolbar. Simply drag the button from this newly created toolbar to its correct position on the tolSwitchboard toolbar and then click the empty toolbar's Close menu box to delete the extra custom toolbar.

3. Right-click the newly added button in the custom toolbar to open the shortcut menu and then click **Choose Button Image** to open the Choose Button Image dialog box. See Figure 3-16.

Figure 3-16 The Choose Button Image dialog box

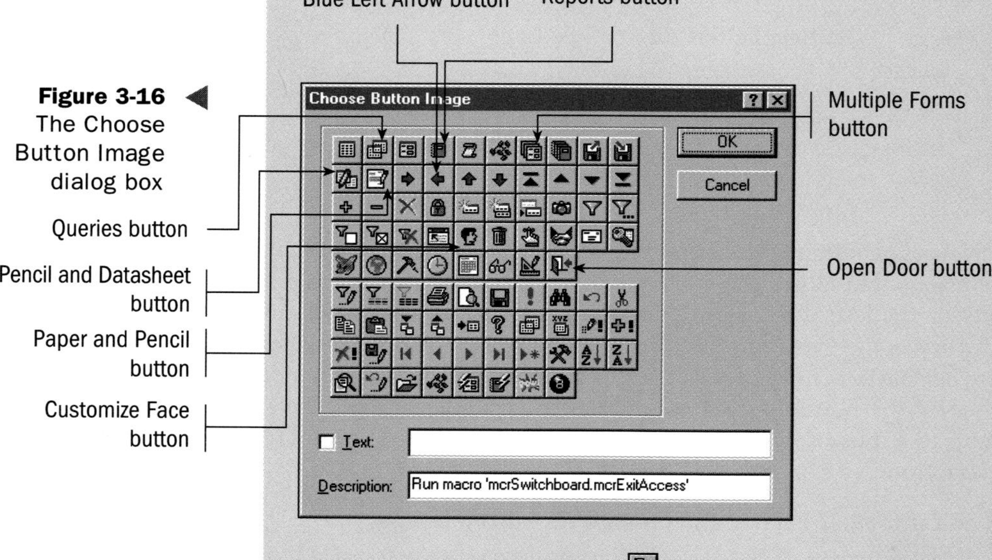

4. Click the **Open Door** button in the Choose Button Image dialog box, highlight the entire value in the Description text box, type **Exit Access**, and then click the **OK** button. Access closes the Choose Button Image dialog box. Leave the pointer resting on the new button so that the ToolTip appears. Both the ToolTip caption and status bar description now display "Exit Access."

TROUBLE? The positions of the buttons in the Choose Button Image dialog box might differ from those shown in Figure 3-16. Use Figure 3-16 to guide your selection of the button images.

Elena adds the third button to the custom toolbar and then changes its button image and description. This button runs the mcrSwitchboard.mcrExitToIssue25 macro. Elena's choice of button image is rather arbitrary, but she tries to choose a button image that will help describe the button's function.

To add the third button to the custom toolbar:

1. Drag **mcrSwitchboard.mcrExitToIssue25** from the Objects list box to the custom toolbar, being sure you place the new button on top and slightly to the left of the previously added button. When you release the mouse button, Access places the new button to the left of the existing buttons. Right-click the new button in the custom toolbar to open the shortcut menu and then click **Choose Button Image** to open the Choose Button Image dialog box.
2. Click the **Blue Left Arrow** button, highlight the entire value in the Description text box, type **Exit to Issue25**, and then click the **OK** button. Access closes the Choose Button Image dialog box. The ToolTip caption and status bar description now display "Exit to Issue25."

The custom toolbar becomes partially blocked when another window gets the focus. To keep the custom toolbar visible, Elena can drag the custom toolbar to an open area at the bottom of the screen.

To reposition the custom toolbar:

1. Drag the custom toolbar title bar down near the bottom of the screen. See Figure 3-17.

Figure 3-17 The custom toolbar positioned in open area of screen

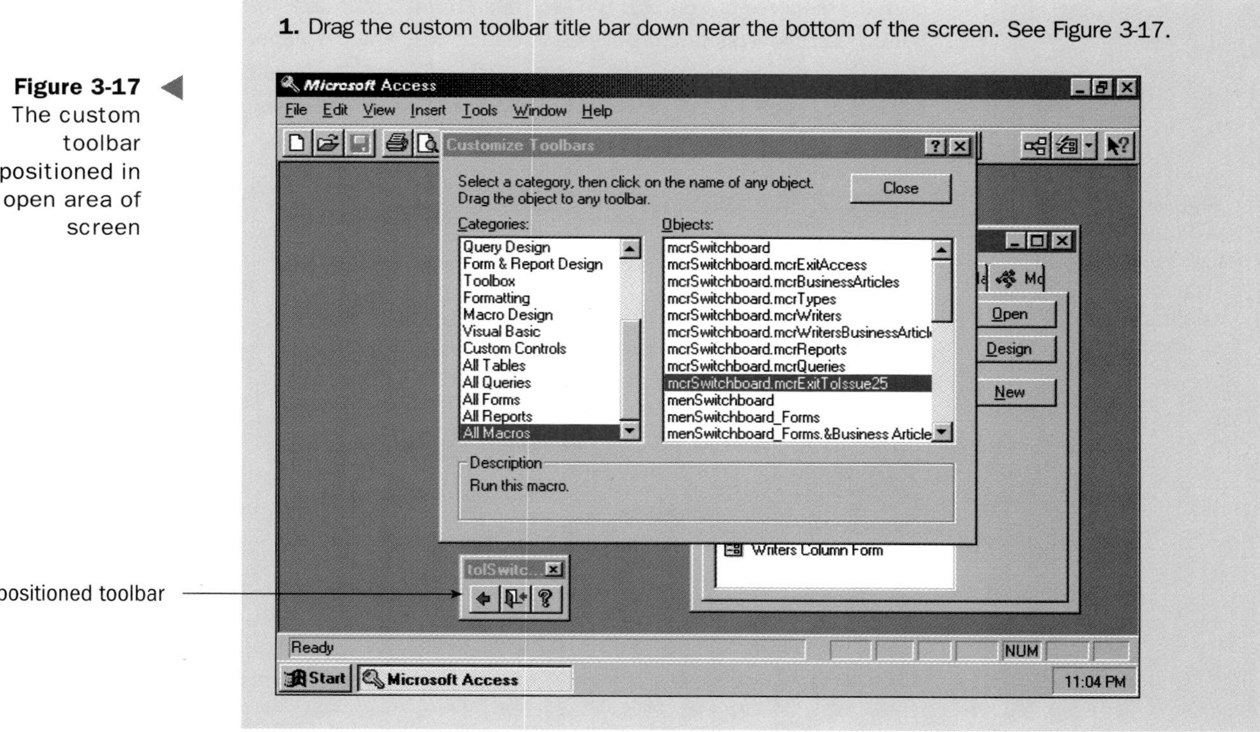

TROUBLE? Do not be concerned if your screen is different from the screen shown in Figure 3-17. Your monitor's size and resolution are among the factors that account for legitimate differences in appearance among systems. For example, the custom toolbar's title might not appear on the title bar until you add another button.

Elena drags the remaining six buttons to the custom toolbar and then changes their button images and descriptions. In right-to-left order, these buttons open the following forms: frmQueries form, frmReports form, Writers and Business Articles Form, Writers Column Form, Types Form, and Business Articles Column Form. Elena selects a unique button image for each button on the custom toolbar.

To add the remaining buttons to the custom toolbar:

1. Click **All Forms** in the Categories list box. Access displays the Issue25 database forms in the Objects list box.
2. Drag **frmQueries** from the Objects list box to the custom toolbar, being sure you place the new button on top and slightly to the left of the previously added button. When you release the mouse button, Access places the new button to the left of the existing buttons. Right-click the new button in the custom toolbar to open the shortcut menu and then click **Choose Button Image** to open the Choose Button Image dialog box.
3. Click the **Queries** button, highlight the entire value in the Description text box, type **Queries list**, and then click the **OK** button. Access closes the Choose Button Image dialog box. The ToolTip caption and status bar description now display "Queries list."
4. Repeat Steps 2 and 3 for the five remaining buttons. Drag **frmReports**, **Writers and Business Articles Form**, **Writers Column Form**, **Types Form**, and **Business Articles Column Form** for the five forms in the Objects text box. Respectively, click the **Reports** button, the **Multiple Forms** button, the **Customize Face** button, the **Pencil and Datasheet** button, and the **Paper and Pencil** button. In the Description text box, respectively enter **Reports list**, **Writers and Business Articles Form**, **Writers Column Form**, **Types Form**, and **Business Articles Column Form**. See Figure 3-18.

Figure 3-18 All custom-toolbar buttons added to toolbar and modified

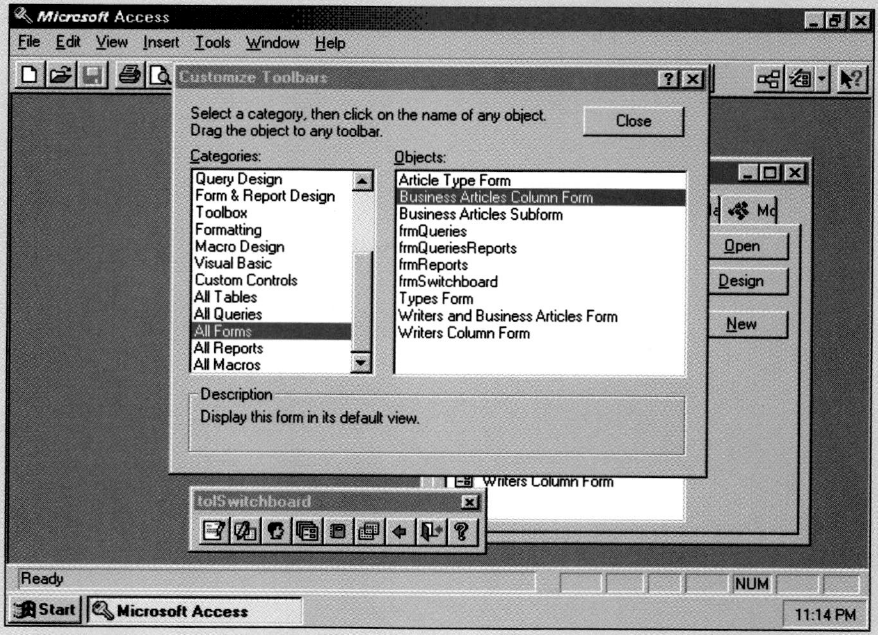

When you add a button to a toolbar, Access places the button so that it touches the button to its left. Elena further customizes the toolbar by grouping buttons and adding space between buttons and button groups. Holding down the Shift key while you drag a button to the right adds space between buttons and fixes the button's position on the toolbar. Elena now improves the appearance of the custom toolbar by adding space between the five buttons on the right, leaving the four buttons on the left grouped together. She starts with the right button and works from right to left.

Elena first docks (that is, moves to a fixed location) the custom toolbar to the bottom of the screen, so that the toolbar is just above the status bar.

To dock the toolbar and move buttons on a custom toolbar:

1. Drag the custom toolbar **title bar** down so that the toolbar's outline touches the status bar and then drag down slightly more. Access places the custom toolbar above the status bar and spreads the custom toolbar across the screen sized to fit the buttons. See Figure 3-19.

Figure 3-19 Custom toolbar docked at the bottom of the screen

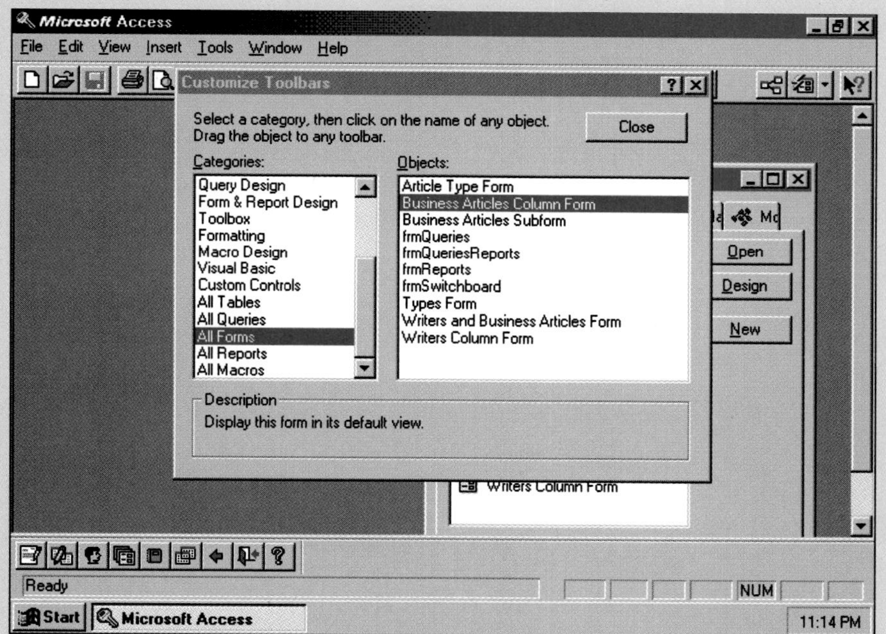

TROUBLE? If the custom toolbar retains its original shape, you dragged it too little or too much. Drag the custom toolbar title bar back to its original position and then repeat Step 1.

2. Now position the buttons by holding the Shift key and then dragging one button at a time to the right, starting with the Help button, so that your custom toolbar looks like Figure 3-20.

TROUBLE? You cannot move a button past the right edge of the toolbar (marked by the vertical bar next to the Help button). To make the bar wider, hold the Shift key down and move the button on top of the right edge, then release the mouse button. The toolbar expands to contain the button. Repeat this until the toolbar is sufficiently wide. Don't be concerned if your toolbar buttons aren't spaced identically to those in Figure 3-20.

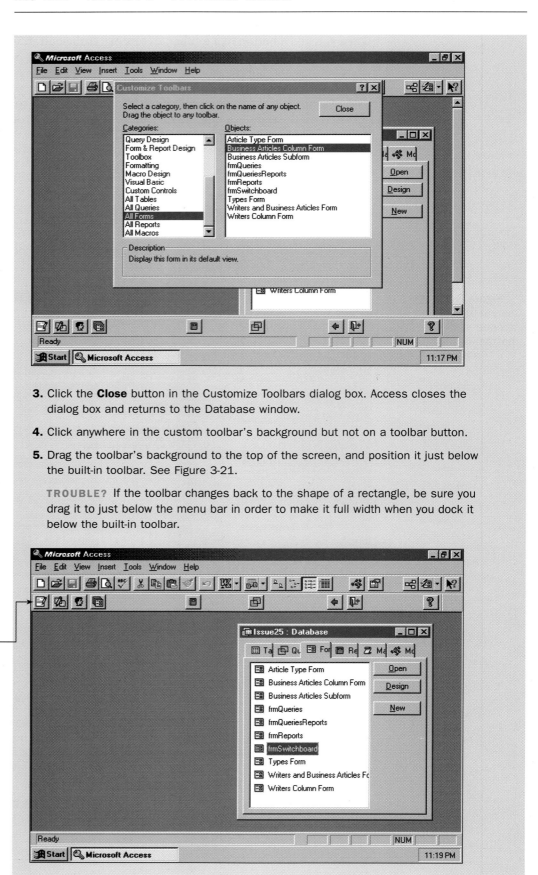

Figure 3-20 Buttons positioned on the custom toolbar

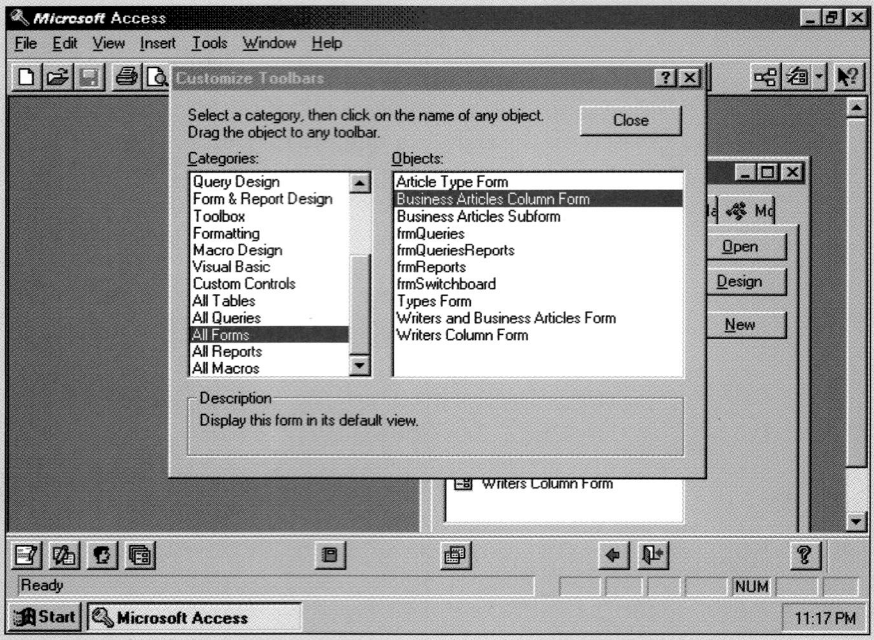

3. Click the **Close** button in the Customize Toolbars dialog box. Access closes the dialog box and returns to the Database window.
4. Click anywhere in the custom toolbar's background but not on a toolbar button.
5. Drag the toolbar's background to the top of the screen, and position it just below the built-in toolbar. See Figure 3-21.

   TROUBLE? If the toolbar changes back to the shape of a rectangle, be sure you drag it to just below the menu bar in order to make it full width when you dock it below the built-in toolbar.

Figure 3-21 Custom toolbar positioned below the built-in toolbar

custom toolbar

The custom toolbar is complete. Elena now specifies when she wants Access to show and hide the custom toolbar.

Using a Custom Toolbar with a Form

When a user opens the frmSwitchboard form, the custom toolbar should appear and the Form View toolbar should be hidden. To control the showing and hiding of these toolbars, Elena creates two macros and attaches them to the frmSwitchboard form's On Activate and On Deactivate event properties. When a form receives the focus and becomes the active window, the Activate event occurs, and Access runs the macro attached to the On Activate event property. Similarly, when a form loses the focus or is closed, the Deactivate event occurs and Access runs the macro attached to the On Deactivate event property. Elena can add ShowToolbar actions to the attached macros that hide or show, or show where appropriate, built-in and custom toolbars. To finish the custom toolbar for the Issue25 database, Elena performs four tasks:

- She hides the custom toolbar so that it no longer appears on the screen all the time.
- She adds two macros to the mcrSwitchboard macro group. The mcrActivate macro hides the Form View toolbar and shows the tolSwitchboard toolbar. The mcrDeactivate macro hides the tolSwitchboard toolbar and shows the Form View toolbar where appropriate.
- She attaches the two macros to the frmSwitchboard form—the mcrActivate macro with the On Activate event property and the mcrDeactivate macro with the On Deactivate event property.
- She opens the frmSwitchboard form and tests the tolSwitchboard toolbar.

Elena hides the tolSwitchboard toolbar, adds the two macros to the mcrSwitchboard macro group, and finally tests her work.

To hide a toolbar and add macros to a macro group:

1. Right-click the custom toolbar to open the shortcut menu, and then click **tolSwitchboard**. Access hides the tolSwitchboard toolbar.
2. Click the **Macros** tab to display the Macros list box, click **mcrSwitchboard** and then click the **Design** button. Access opens the Macro window.
3. Scroll the Macro window until several blank rows appear. Click the first blank row's **Macro Name** text box, type **mcrActivate**, press the **Tab** key, click the **list arrow**, scroll the list, click **ShowToolbar**, press the **Tab** key, and then type **Hide the Form View toolbar**. Next, click the **Toolbar Name** text box, click the **list arrow**, and then click **Form View**. Notice the Show text box is set to No, so this action tells Access not to show the Form View toolbar. This completes the first of two actions for the mcrActivate macro.
4. Click the next row's **Action** text box, click the **list arrow**, scroll the list, click **ShowToolbar**, press the **Tab** key, and then type **Show the tolSwitchboard toolbar**. Next, click the **Toolbar Name** text box, click the **list arrow**, scroll the list, click **tolSwitchboard**, click the **Show** text box, click the **list arrow**, and then click **Yes**. This completes the second of two actions for the mcrActivate macro.
5. Click the next row's **Macro Name** text box, type **mcrDeactivate**, press the **Tab** key, click the **list arrow**, scroll the list, click **ShowToolbar**, press the **Tab** key, and then type **Show the Form View toolbar where appropriate**. Next, click the **Toolbar Name** text box, click the **list arrow**, click **Form View**, click the **Show** text box, click the **list arrow**, and then click **Where Appropriate**. This completes the first of two actions for the mcrDeactivate macro.
6. Click the next row's **Action** text box, click the **list arrow**, scroll the list, click **ShowToolbar**, press the **Tab** key, and then type **Hide the tolSwitchboard toolbar**.

Next, click the **Toolbar Name** text box, click the **list arrow**, scroll the list, and then click **tolSwitchboard**. Show is set to **No**. This completes the second of two actions for the mcrDeactivate macro. See Figure 3-22.

Figure 3-22 Macros to control the frmSwitchboard form's toolbars

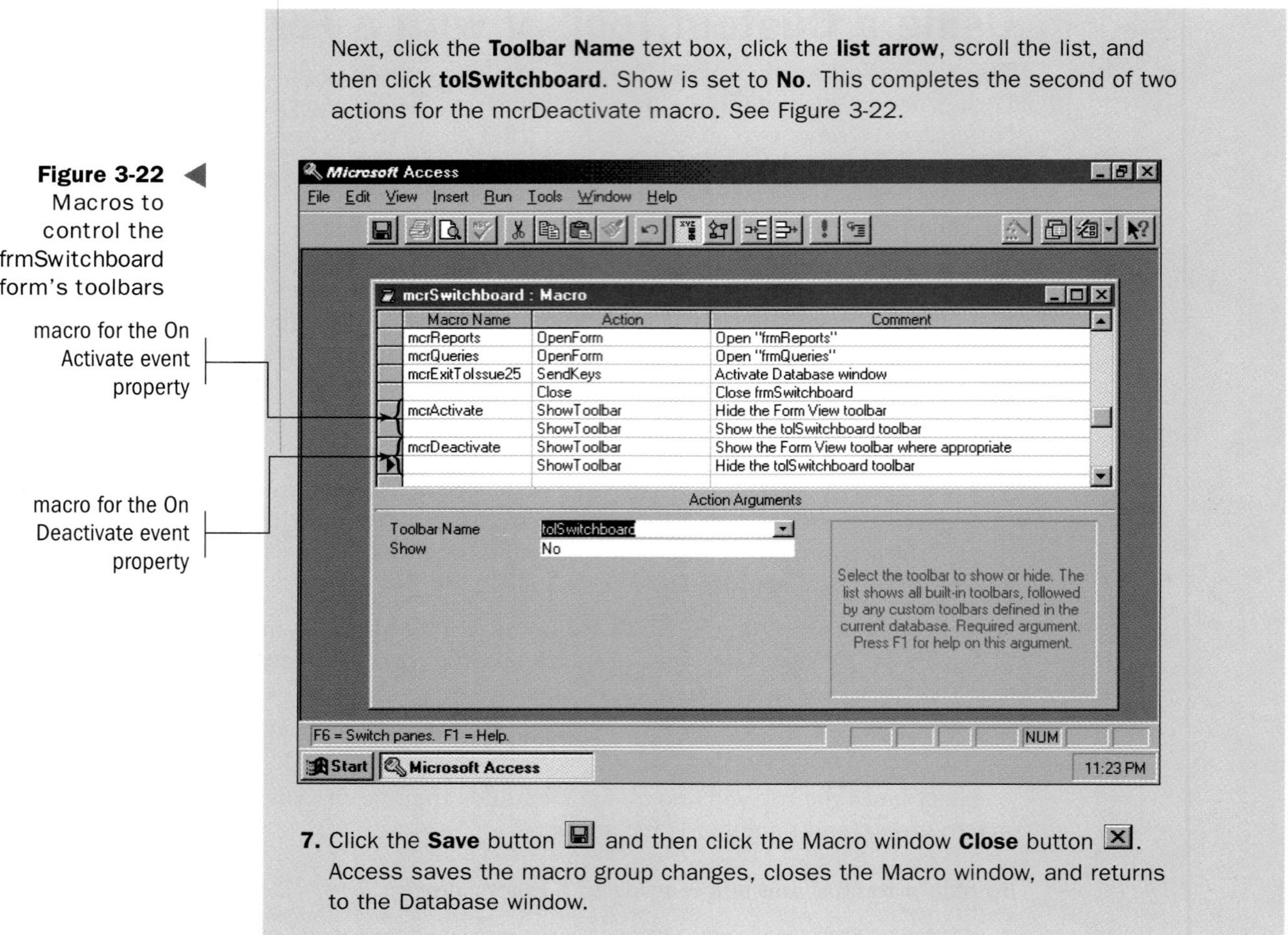

7. Click the **Save** button and then click the Macro window **Close** button. Access saves the macro group changes, closes the Macro window, and returns to the Database window.

Elena attaches the new macros to the frmSwitchboard form's On Activate and On Deactivate event properties.

To attach macros to a form's event properties:

1. Click the **Forms** tab in the Database window, if necessary, click **frmSwitchboard**, and then click the **Design** button. Access opens the Form Design window.

2. If necessary, right-click the **Form Selector**, then click **Properties** in the shortcut menu to open the Form property sheet. Scroll the property sheet, click the **On Activate** text box, click the **list arrow**, and then click **mcrSwitchboard.mcrActivate**. You might need to widen the property sheet temporarily to complete this step and the next step.

3. Click the **On Deactivate** text box, click the **list arrow**, and then click **mcrSwitchboard.mcrDeactivate**.

4. Click the **Save** button to save the form-design changes and then click the property sheet **Close** button to close the property sheet.

5. Click the Form Design window **Close** button to close the Form Design window and return to the Database window.

6. If necessary, click **frmSwitchboard** then click the **Open** button to open the form in the Form View window. See Figure 3-23.

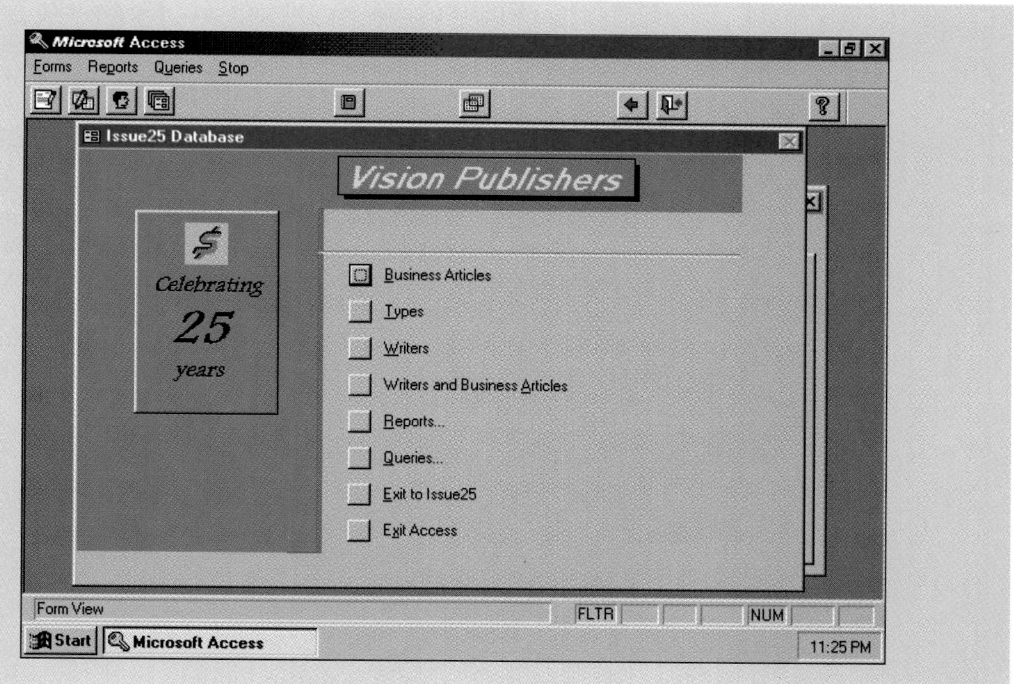

Figure 3-23 A custom toolbar displayed with its related form

Access opens the frmSwitchboard form and, below the custom menu bar, displays the custom toolbar in place of the built-in toolbar. The custom toolbar, therefore, is properly attached to the frmSwitchboard form.

Testing a Custom Toolbar

Elena tests each button on the custom toolbar. She stops the pointer on each button and verifies that its ToolTip and status bar description are correct. Then, starting with the left button and moving to the right, she clicks each button to test that the proper response occurs.

To test a custom toolbar:

1. Stop the pointer on each toolbar button and verify that the correct ToolTip and status bar description appear.
2. Click the **Business Articles Column Form** button on the toolbar to open the Business Articles Column Form. Click the Form View window **Close** button for the Business Articles Column Form to close the form. Repeat this step for the three toolbar buttons to the right of this button.
3. Click the **Reports** button on the toolbar to open the Reports dialog box. Then click the **Close** button to return to the frmSwitchboard form. Repeat this step for the **Queries** list button .
4. Click the **F1 Help** button on the toolbar to open the Access Help window and then click the Access Help **Close** button to close the window.
5. Click the **Exit to Issue25** button on the toolbar. Access closes the form and returns to the Database window.
6. Click the **Open** button to open the **frmSwitchboard** form in the Form View window.
7. Click the **Exit Access** button on the toolbar. Access closes all windows and exits.

Elena has completed the custom toolbar, and the Issue25 graphical user interface is nearing completion. She now sets the Issue25 database startup options so that Access displays the switchboard when the Issue25 database is opened.

Setting the Issue25 Database Startup Options

Access allows you to specify certain actions, called **startup options**, that take place when a database is opened. For example, you can specify the name that appears in the Access window title bar, specify a default custom menu bar to replace the standard menu bar, or specify a form that is automatically displayed. If you want to bypass the startup options, you can hold down the Shift key when you open the database. Elena wants users to be able to open the Issue25 database and have the switchboard she created appear automatically. This way, users won't need to use the Form object list to access the switchboard form.

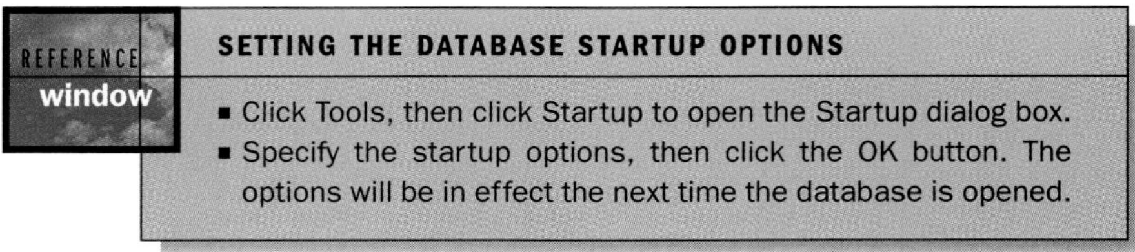

SETTING THE DATABASE STARTUP OPTIONS

- Click Tools, then click Startup to open the Startup dialog box.
- Specify the startup options, then click the OK button. The options will be in effect the next time the database is opened.

Elena sets the Issue25 database startup options so the switchboard appears automatically when the database is opened and the Database window is hidden.

To change the Issue25 database startup options:

1. Start Access and then open the Issue25 database on your Student Disk.
2. Click **Tools**, then click **Startup** to open the Startup dialog box. See Figure 3-24.

Figure 3-24 The Startup dialog box

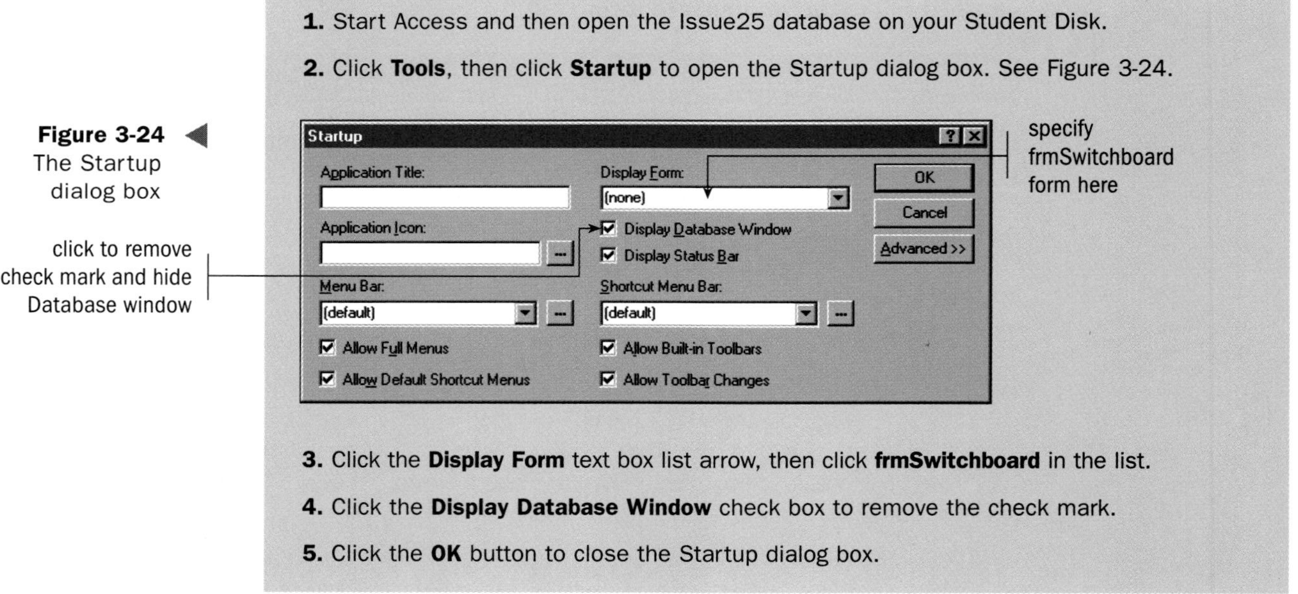

3. Click the **Display Form** text box list arrow, then click **frmSwitchboard** in the list.
4. Click the **Display Database Window** check box to remove the check mark.
5. Click the **OK** button to close the Startup dialog box.

Elena tests the startup options by closing and then opening the Issue25 database.

To test the startup options:

1. Click the Database window **Close** button to close the Issue25 database.
2. Click **File** and then click **1 A:\Tutorial\Issue25** to open the Issue25 database. See Figure 3-25.

   TROUBLE? The path may differ depending on the location of your Student Disk.

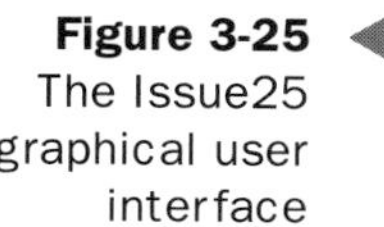

Figure 3-25 The Issue25 graphical user interface

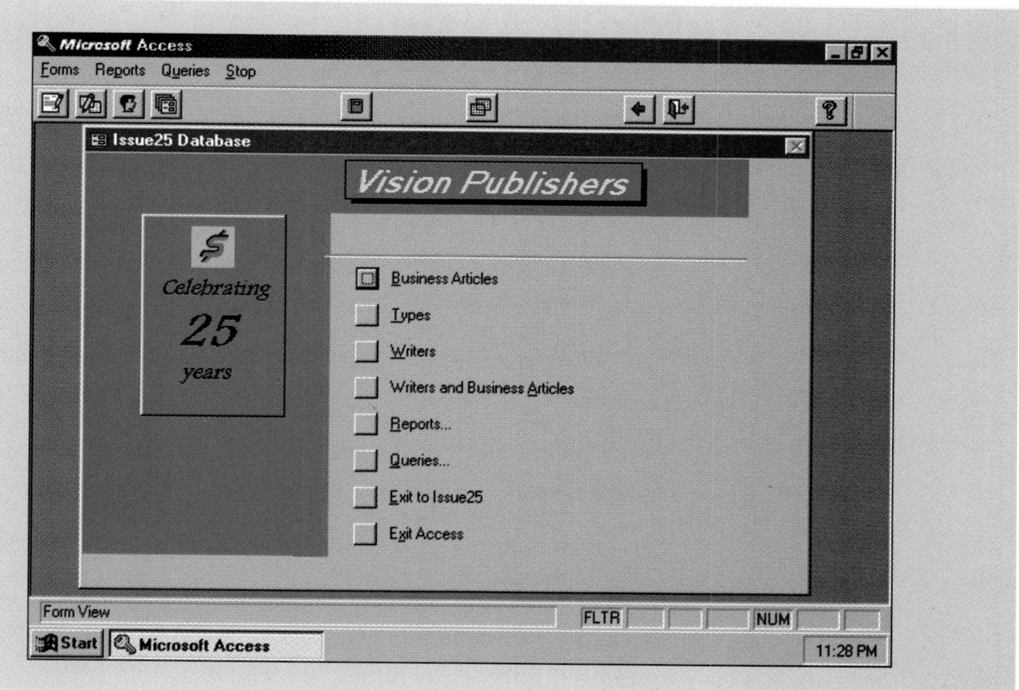

Access opens the Issue25 database, the custom toolbar replaces the built-in Form View toolbar, Access hides the Database window and displays the frmSwitchboard form. Elena's test shows that the startup options are correctly set.

Elena's development of the graphical user interface for the Issue25 database is nearly complete. Her remaining tasks are to finish the Reports and Queries dialog boxes. These dialog boxes have list boxes containing the available reports and queries, respectively. To allow a user to select a report or query and then ask Access to take the next action, Elena cannot use macros. Instead she must create procedures using Visual Basic.

Before she starts planning the Visual Basic procedures, Elena schedules a meeting to show Brian and Judith the progress she has made on the Issue25 graphical user interface. She wants to see if they have any suggestions or additional requirements for the design. When they approve the switchboard, toolbar, and menu bar design, she will begin her Visual Basic work.

To exit Access:

1. Click the **Exit Access** button to close the switchboard and exit Access.

Elena exits Access and then leaves for the meeting in Judith's office.

Quick Check

1. What two Access "tools" can you float anywhere on the screen?
2. When does the Deactivate event occur?
3. What are the three options for the ShowToolbar action?
4. What is a startup option?
5. How can you change the image on a toolbar button?
6. How do you resize and dock a toolbar?

Tutorial Assignments

Elena creates a custom menu bar and a custom toolbar for the frmQueriesReports form.

Start Access and open the Issue25 database in the Tutorial folder on your Student Disk.

1. For the frmQueriesReports form, design and create a custom menu bar and a custom toolbar that have the following characteristics.
   a. Enter the name menQueriesReports for the custom menu bar and the name tolQueriesReports for the custom toolbar.
   b. Display the custom menu bar and the custom toolbar only when the frmQueriesReports form has the focus.
   c. Add two menus to the custom menu bar: one menu named QueriesAndReports and the other named Exit. Place enough menu-item names on the QueriesAndReports menu to open each of the nine queries and reports from the tblObjectNames table in the Print Preview window. Allow both mouse and keyboard selection. Place two menu items on the Exit menu: one menu item named Close to close the form and activate the Database window, and the other menu item named Exit Access to close the form and exit Access. Make Q the hot key for the QueriesAndReports menu and E the hot key for the Exit menu.
   d. Place enough buttons on the custom toolbar to perform the same operations performed on the custom menu bar.
2. Test the custom menu bar and the custom toolbar.

Case Problems

1. Walkton Daily Press Carriers Due to company growth, new users will be working with the database so Grant Sherman decides a switchboard will make the database more user friendly. Grant decides to create a custom menu bar and a custom toolbar for the graphical user interface for his database.

Start Access and open the Press database in the Cases1 folder on your Student Disk.

1. For the frmSwitchboard form, design and create a custom menu bar and a custom toolbar that have the following characteristics.
   a. Enter the name menSwitchboard for the custom menu bar and the name tolSwitchboard for the custom toolbar.
   b. Display the custom menu bar and the custom toolbar only when the frmSwitchboard form has the focus.
   c. Add two menus to the custom menu bar: one menu named OpenObjects and the other named Exit. Place three menu items on the OpenObjects menu to open the following objects: the BILLINGS table in Datasheet View, the Carriers Form in Form View, and the Carriers Sorted by Name and Route ID Query in Datasheet View. Allow both mouse and keyboard selection. Place two menu items on the Exit menu: one menu item named Close to close the form and activate the Database window, and the other menu item named Exit Access to close the form and exit Access. Make O the hot key for the Open Objects menu and E the hot key for the Exit menu.
   d. Place enough buttons on the custom toolbar to perform the same operations performed on the custom menu bar.
2. Set the startup options to hide the Database window and open the frmSwitchboard form whenever you open the Press database.
3. Test the custom menu bar, the custom toolbar, and the startup options.

2. Lopez Lexus Dealerships Hector Lopez decides to create a custom menu bar and a custom toolbar for the graphical user interface for his database.

Start Access and open the Lexus database in the Cases1 folder on your Student Disk.

1. For the frmSwitchboard form, design and create a custom menu bar and a custom toolbar that have the following characteristics.
   a. Enter the name menSwitchboard for the custom menu bar and the name tolSwitchboard for the custom toolbar.
   b. Display the custom menu bar and the custom toolbar only when the frmSwitchboard form has the focus.
   c. Add two menus to the custom menu bar: one menu named OpenObjects and the other named Exit. Place four menu items on the OpenObjects menu to open the following objects: the LOCATIONS table in Datasheet View, the Cars Data Form in Form View, the Cars by Model and Year Query in Datasheet View, and the Cars by Year Report in Print Preview. Allow both mouse and keyboard selection. Place two menu items on the Exit menu: one menu item named Close to close the form and activate the Database window, and one menu item named Exit Access to close the form and exit Access. Make O the hot key for the Open Objects menu and E the hot key for the Exit menu.
   d. Place enough buttons on the custom toolbar to perform the same operations performed on the custom menu bar.
2. Set the startup options to hide the Database window and open the frmSwitchboard form whenever the Lexus database is opened.
3. Test the custom menu bar, the custom toolbar, and the startup options.

3. Tophill University Student Employment Olivia Tyler decides to create a custom menu bar and a custom toolbar for the graphical user interface for her database.

Start Access and open the Parttime database in the Cases2 folder on your Student Disk.

1. For the frmSwitchboard form, design and create a custom menu bar and a custom toolbar that have the following characteristics.
   a. Enter the name menSwitchboard for the custom menu bar and the name tolSwitchboard for the custom toolbar.
   b. Display the custom menu bar and the custom toolbar only when the frmSwitchboard form has the focus.
   c. Add two menus to the custom menu bar: one menu named OpenObjects and the other named Exit. Place four menu items on the OpenObjects menu to open the following objects: the EMPLOYERS table in Datasheet View, the Employers and Jobs Form in Form View, the Jobs Sorted by Employer and Job Title Query in Datasheet View, and the Jobs Report in Print Preview. Allow both mouse and keyboard selection. Place two menu items on the Exit menu: one menu item named Close to close the form and activate the Database window, and one menu item named Exit Access to close the form and exit Access. Make O the hot key for the Open Objects menu and E the hot key for the Exit menu.
   d. Place enough buttons on the custom toolbar to perform the same operations performed on the custom menu bar.
2. Set the startup options to hide the Database window and open the frmSwitchboard form whenever the Parttime database is opened.
3. Test the custom menu bar, the custom toolbar, and the startup options.

4. Rexville Business Licenses Chester Pearce decides to create a custom menu bar and a custom toolbar for the graphical user interface for his database.

Start Access and open the Buslic database in the Cases2 folder on your Student Disk.

1. For the frmSwitchboard form, design and create a custom menu bar and a custom toolbar that have the following characteristics.
   a. Enter the name menSwitchboard for the custom menu bar and the name tolSwitchboard for the custom toolbar.
   b. Display the custom menu bar and the custom toolbar only when the frmSwitchboard form has the focus.
   c. Add two menus to the custom menu bar: one menu named OpenObjects and the other named Exit. Place four menu items on the OpenObjects menu to open the following objects: the LICENSES table, the Businesses Form, the Businesses Sorted by License Type and Business Name Query, and the Businesses Report. Allow both mouse and keyboard selection. Place two menu items on the Exit menu: one menu item named Close to close the form and activate the Database window, and one menu item named Exit Access to close the form and exit Access. Make O the hot key for the Open Objects menu and E the hot key for the Exit menu.
   d. Place enough buttons on the custom toolbar to perform the same operations performed on the custom menu bar.
2. Set the startup options to hide the Database window and open the frmSwitchboard form whenever the Buslic database is opened.
3. Test the custom menu bar, the custom toolbar, and the startup options.

TUTORIAL 4

Visual Basic

Using Visual Basic with the Issue25 Database

OBJECTIVES

In this tutorial you will:

- Learn about Visual Basic functions, sub procedures, and modules
- Create functions in a standard module
- Create event procedures
- Compile and test functions, sub procedures, and event procedures
- Hide text and change display colors

Vision Publishers

Elena Sanchez is ready to finish her graphical user interface for the Issue25 database. She uses Visual Basic to control the events in the two new dialog boxes: the frmReports form and frmQueries form (you'll work on the frmReports dialog box in this tutorial and the frmQueries dialog box in the Tutorial Assignments at the end of the tutorial). Although she learned the fundamentals of Visual Basic at her Access seminar, this is the first time Elena uses Visual Basic on the job at Vision Publishers. Elena uses Visual Basic to refine her user interface further by adding two functions to help with the capitalization of data entered in forms. Then, she adds a message in color that appears only when freelancers are displayed in the Writers Column Form.

SESSION 4.1

In this session you will learn about Visual Basic functions, sub procedures, and modules. You will create and test a function in a standard module. Then you will create, compile, and test an event procedure.

Visual Basic

Visual Basic is Access's programming language. The process of writing Visual Basic statements is called **coding**. You write Visual Basic instructions, called **statements**, to respond to events that occur with the objects in a database. A language such as Visual Basic is therefore called both an **event-driven language** and an **object-oriented language**. Your experience in previous tutorials with macros, which are also event driven and object oriented, should help ease your learning of Visual Basic. You can do almost anything with Visual Basic that you can do with macros, but Visual Basic allows you to have more control over commands and objects than you can with macros. For example, with Visual Basic you can create your own functions to perform special calculations and you can change an object's properties dynamically, based on predefined conditions.

Procedures

When you work with Visual Basic, you code a group of statements in Design View and attach the group to the event property of an object. Access then executes, or **calls**, these statements every time the event occurs for that object. Each group of statements is called a **procedure**. The two types of procedures are functions and sub procedures, or subroutines.

- A **function** is a procedure that performs operations, returns a value, can accept arguments, and can be used in expressions (recall that an expression is a calculation resulting in a single value). For example, some of the Issue25 database queries use built-in functions that come with Access (Sum, Count, and Avg) to calculate a sum, a record count, and an average. Now Elena plans to create a function named CapOnlyFirst, which will accept a field value as an argument, capitalize the first character of the field value, change all other characters to lowercase, and then return the changed field value. Elena can use the CapOnlyFirst function in an expression on a form or report.
- A **sub procedure**, or **subroutine**, performs operations and can accept arguments but does not return a value and cannot be used in expressions. Elena creates a sub procedure that displays a message on the Writers Column Form that appears only when freelancers are displayed.

Modules

You store a group of related procedures together in a **module**. Figure 4-1 shows the structure of a typical module. Each module starts with a **Declarations section**, which contains statements that apply to all procedures in the module. One or more procedures, which follow the Declarations section, constitute the rest of the module. A module is either standard or it is contained in a form or report.

- A **standard module** is a separate database object that is stored in memory with other database objects when you open the database. You can use the procedures in standard modules from anywhere in a database, even from procedures in other modules, or from more than one place.

- Access automatically creates a form module for each form and a report module for each report. Also called **Code Behind Forms (CBF)** and **Code Behind Reports (CBR)**, each form or report module contains event procedures. An **event procedure** is a procedure you code to respond to an event that occurs for that specific form or report. Event procedures are **local**, or **private**, which means that they cannot be used outside the form or report. Unlike standard modules, a CBF or CBR module is stored with its form or report and is loaded into memory only when you open the form or report.

Figure 4-1
A Visual Basic module outline and its procedures

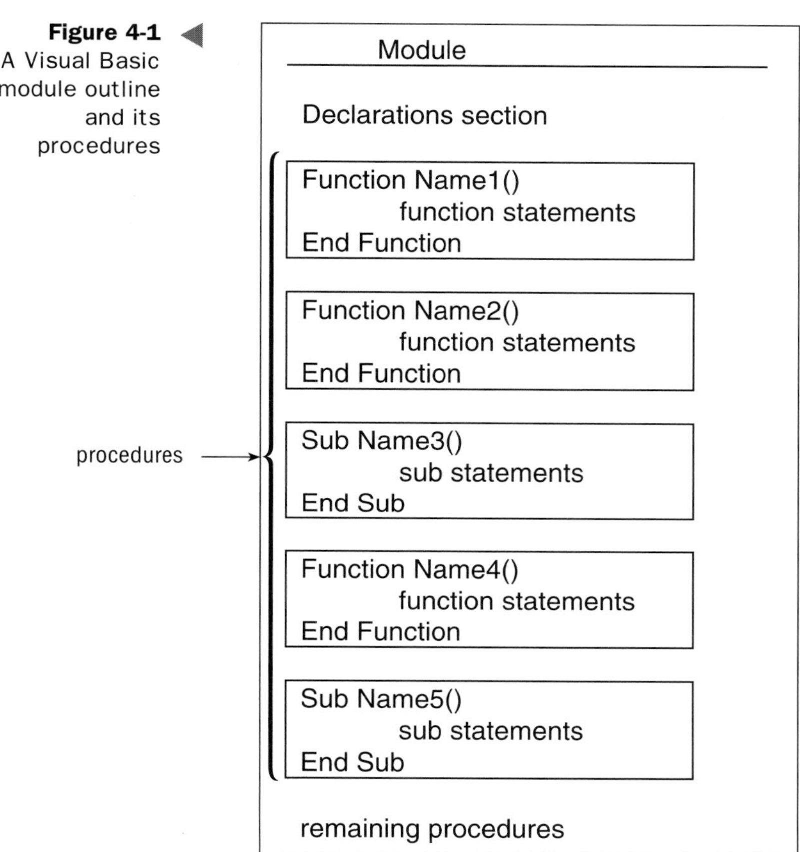

Using Help and Sample Applications

The most difficult part of becoming proficient with Access is learning how to code effective Visual Basic procedures. Visual Basic is a powerful programming language containing hundreds of statements and built-in functions, along with hundreds of event properties, object properties, and methods. Deciding when and how to use each Visual Basic feature can be intimidating to programming novices and even experts. Fortunately, you can perform many fundamental operations without using Visual Basic by setting control properties and by using macros, as you did in the previous tutorials.

When you do need to use Visual Basic, take advantage of the excellent Access Help system as a reference tool. Figure 4-2 lists several Help topics that are particularly useful when you work with Visual Basic. You can also find help for every Visual Basic statement, function, and property; most of these topics have an Example jump that displays sample Visual Basic code. If you find sample code similar to what you need, simply copy the statements to the Windows Clipboard, paste them into a procedure in your own database, and modify the statements to work for your special case.

Another source for sample Visual Basic code is the set of sample databases that comes with Access. Three databases appear in the Samples subdirectory under the Access directory: the Northwind database, the Orders database, and the Solutions database. Each

Figure 4-2 Help topics important for Visual Basic

Search Entry	Help Topic
Visual Basic	applications, creating debugging code declaring variables and constants modules, described procedures, overview troubleshooting
event properties	

database has a variety of simple and complex examples of Visual Basic procedures. You can view the effects of these procedures by using them in the sample databases. Microsoft encourages you to copy and use the proven procedures in the sample databases as a way to learn Visual Basic more quickly.

Creating Functions in a Standard Module

Elena decides to use one of the procedures she learned at the seminar: a function named CapOnlyFirst, which capitalizes the first character of a field value and changes all other characters to lowercase. In other words, if a user types the words "social Justice," the CapOnlyFirst function corrects the entry to "Social justice." Elena thinks this will be a helpful function to use in the Description field on the Types Form. Elena can program code that runs whenever a user enters or changes a value in the Description field. The data entry staff might not always be consistent about capitalizing entries in that field, and having this function running in the background will ensure consistency.

Whenever a user enters or changes a field value in a control on a form, Access automatically triggers the **AfterUpdate event**, which by default simply accepts the new or changed entry. However, Elena can set the Description field's AfterUpdate event property to [Event Procedure], and then she can code an event procedure to call the CapOnlyFirst function.

Because Elena might use the function in several other forms and reports in the Issue25 database, she places the procedure in a new standard module, which she names basIssue25Functions. This standard module name conforms to Elena's naming convention; bas is the tag for a Visual Basic module, and Issue25Functions is the base name describing the module's contents.

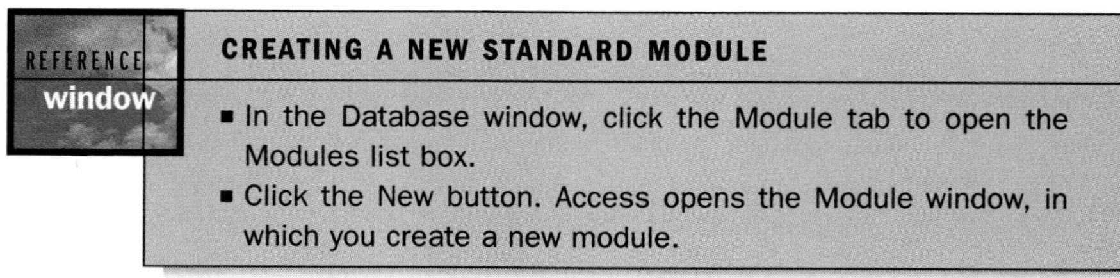

CREATING A NEW STANDARD MODULE

- In the Database window, click the Module tab to open the Modules list box.
- Click the New button. Access opens the Module window, in which you create a new module.

Elena creates the new standard module.

To create a new standard module:

1. Start Access, open the Issue25 database in the Tutorial folder on your Student Disk. Elena's macros are working well. The Issue25 switchboard opens with the custom menu bar and custom toolbar that she created in the previous tutorials.

2. Click the switchboard's **Exit to Issue25** button.

3. Click the **Modules** tab and then click the **New** button. Access opens the Module window. Click the Module window **Maximize** button. See Figure 4-3.

Figure 4-3
The Module window

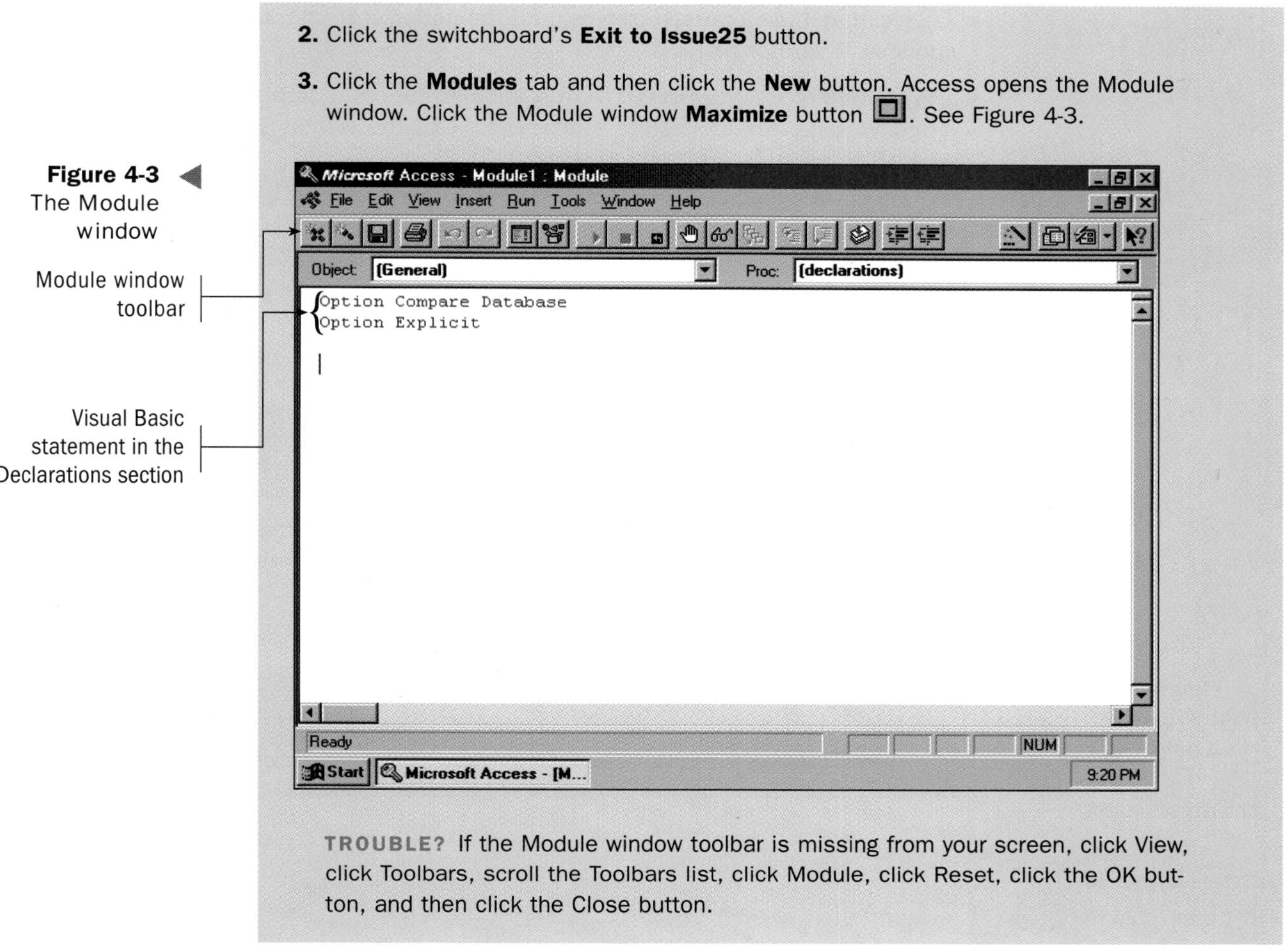

TROUBLE? If the Module window toolbar is missing from your screen, click View, click Toolbars, scroll the Toolbars list, click Module, click Reset, click the OK button, and then click the Close button.

You use the Module window to create and modify Visual Basic procedures. Access automatically includes the Option Compare statement in the Declarations section of a new module, followed by an argument specifying the technique Access uses when it executes Option Compare. The Option Compare statement designates the technique Access uses to compare and sort text data. The default argument "Database," shown in Figure 4-3, means that Access compares and sorts letters in normal alphabetical order, using the language settings specified for Access running on your computer.

The second statement, Option Explicit, states that any variable that is used in the module must be explicitly declared in the Declarations section. A **variable** is a named location in memory that can contain a value. If Elena uses a variable in the module, she must explicitly declare it in the Declarations section.

Creating a Function

Each function begins with a Function statement and ends with an End Function statement. Access places each function on a new page. You can display each page by selecting the function name from the Proc list box. Elena enters "Function CapOnlyFirst (FValue)" on the line below the Option Explicit statement. CapOnlyFirst is the function name and FValue is an argument name. In other words, the value passed to the function is assigned to the argument named FValue. All Visual Basic names you create must conform to the following rules:

- They must begin with a letter.
- They cannot exceed 200 characters.

- They can include letters, numbers, and the underscore character; other characters and spaces cannot be used.
- They cannot contain reserved words, such as Function, Sub, and Option, that the language uses for its regular statements. Use the Access Help topic "reserved words" to see a list of reserved words.
- They cannot be keywords such as If, Open, or Print. Use the Access Help topic "keywords" to see the categories of keywords.

Elena begins entering the function.

To start a new function:

1. With the insertion point on the line below the Option Explicit statement, type **Function CapOnlyFirst (FValue)** and then press the **Enter** key. Access opens a new page and places the statement at the top of the Module window. The function name CapOnlyFirst appears in the Proc text box. Access automatically adds the End Function statement and places the insertion point at the beginning of a blank line between the two statements. Access displays the reserved words Function and End Function in blue. The function name appears in black. See Figure 4-4.

Figure 4-4 Starting a new function

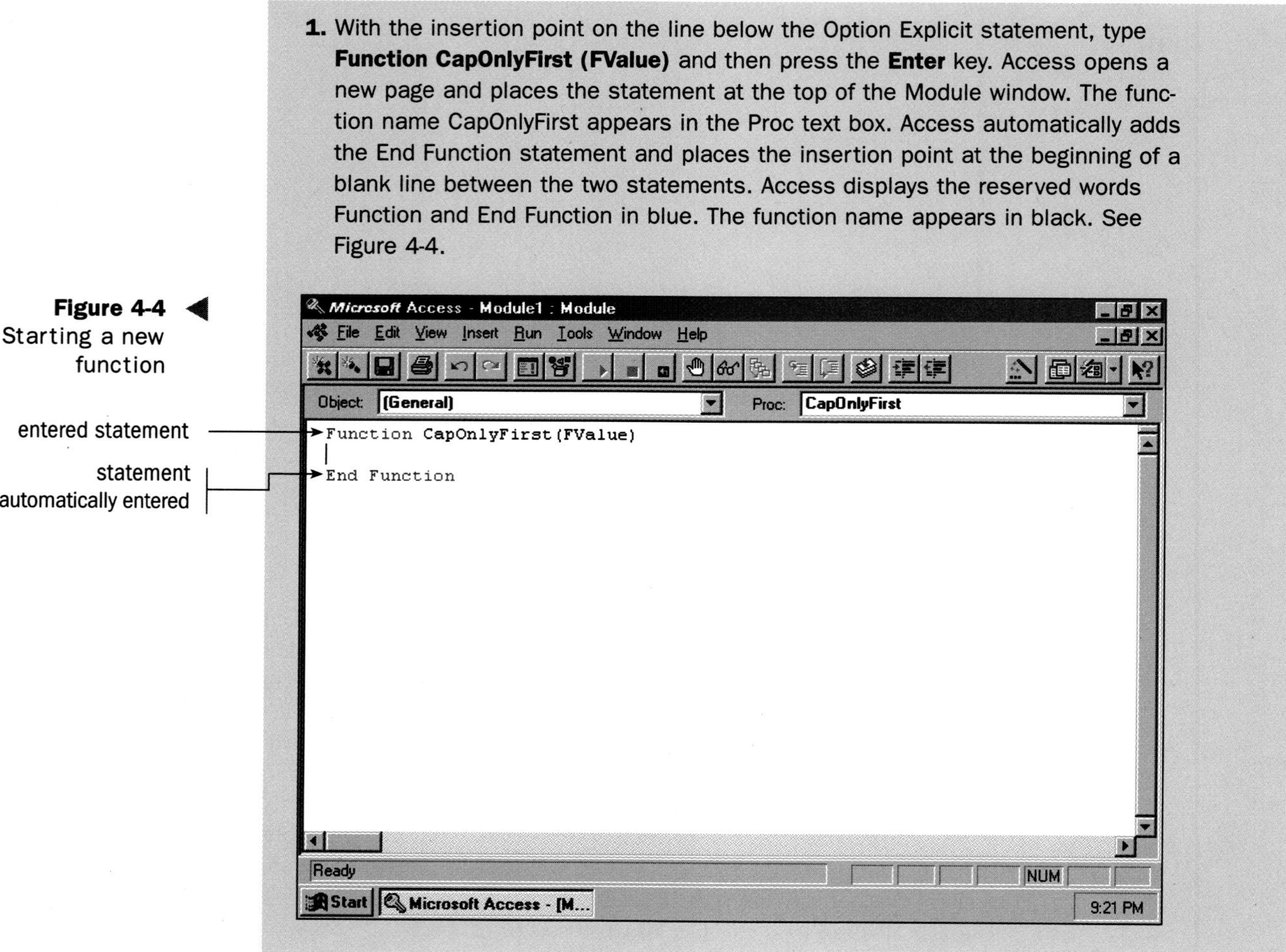

Elena's CapOnlyFirst function consists of a single executable statement, called an assignment statement, that she places between the Function and End Function statements. An **assignment statement** assigns the value of an expression to a variable. Associated with a variable is its variable name, which must follow the Visual Basic naming rules. The general format of an assignment statement is "variable name = expression." Elena needs to enter the following assignment statement: "CapOnlyFirst = UCase(Left(FValue, 1)) & LCase(Mid(FValue, 2))." CapOnlyFirst is the variable name and "UCase(Left(FValue, 1)) & LCase(Mid(FValue, 2))" is the expression. The expression in Elena's assignment statement uses four built-in Access functions (UCase, Left, LCase, and Mid) and the concatenation operator (&), which concatenates or combines two strings. Figure 4-5 describes the value returned by each function.

Figure 4-5 The built-in functions in the assignment statement

Function	Returned Value
UCase(expression)	An expression converted to uppercase letters
Left(expression, n)	The leftmost *n* characters of expression
LCase(expression)	An expression converted to lowercase letters
Mid(expression, start, [length])	Portion of an expression from character number *start*, for *length*, or to the end of the expression if *length* is omitted

Figure 4-6 shows the order in which Access evaluates the functions and shows the values each function returns, using as an example the parameter value "aDvErTiSiNg" (the parameter value appears in the expression as the argument "FValue"; this is what the expression is evaluating). After all the functions to the right of the equal sign are executed, the & operator combines the two strings and produces "Advertising," which Access assigns as a value to CapOnlyFirst.

Figure 4-6 Evaluation of the assignment statement

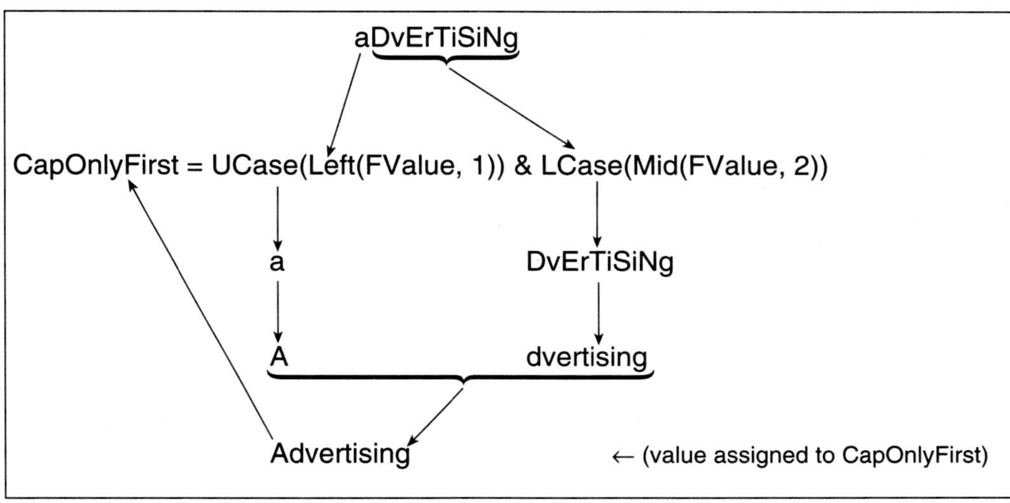

Before entering the assignment statement, Elena adds two lines of comments to explain the procedure's purpose. You can include comments to explain a Visual Basic statement. This makes it easier to remember the purpose of statements in your code. It is a good idea to include frequent comments in your code to make it easier for anyone reading it to understand it. You begin a comment with the word Rem or with a single quote mark ('). Visual Basic ignores anything following the word Rem or the single quote mark ('). Also, Elena indents these three lines; indenting statements is a common practice to make code easier to read.

To add comments and statements to a function:

1. Press the **Tab** key, type **'Capitalize only the first letter of a field value;**, press the **Enter** key, type **'Change to lowercase all other letters.**, and then press the **Enter** key. Notice that Access displays these comments in green. After entering these two comment lines, you can now enter the assignment statement.

2. Type **CapOnlyFirst = UCase(Left(FValue, 1)) & LCase(Mid(FValue, 2))**. See Figure 4-7. Access scans each statement for errors when you press the Enter key or change the focus to another statement. Because the function is complete and Elena wants Access to scan for errors, she moves the insertion point to another line.

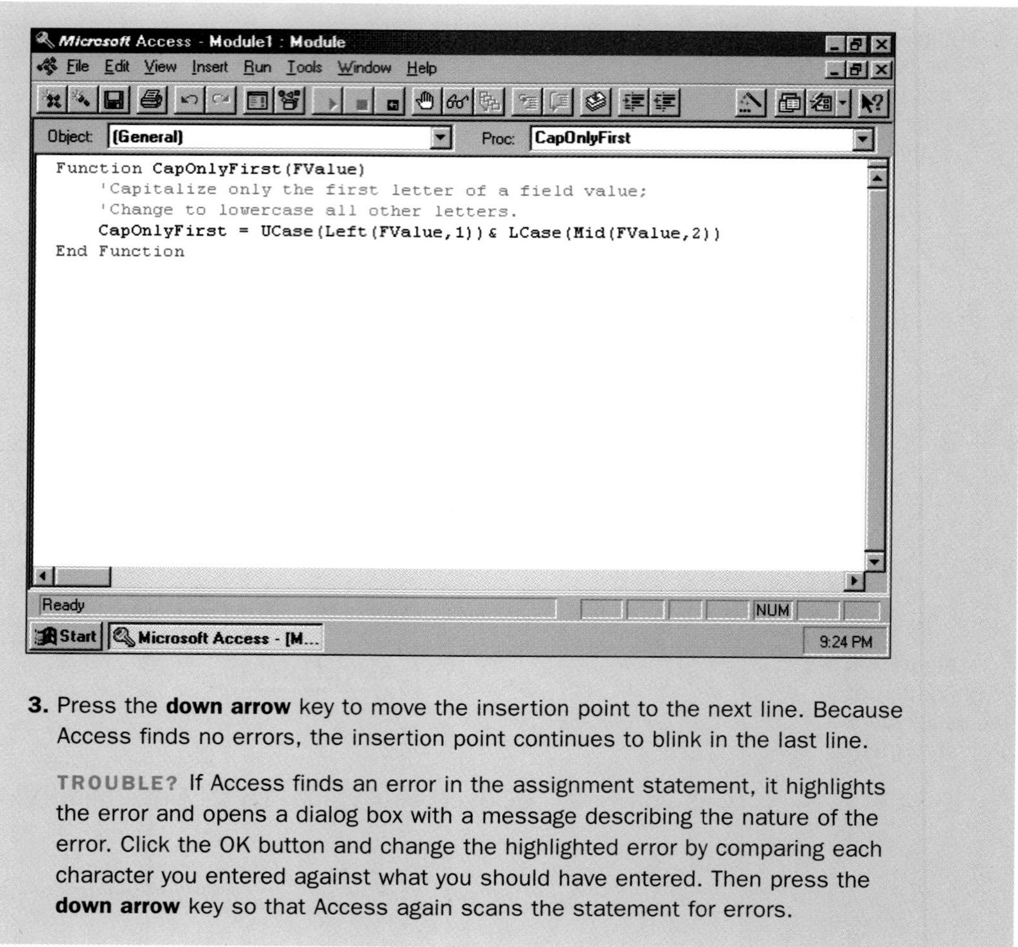

Figure 4-7 A completed function

3. Press the **down arrow** key to move the insertion point to the next line. Because Access finds no errors, the insertion point continues to blink in the last line.

   TROUBLE? If Access finds an error in the assignment statement, it highlights the error and opens a dialog box with a message describing the nature of the error. Click the OK button and change the highlighted error by comparing each character you entered against what you should have entered. Then press the **down arrow** key so that Access again scans the statement for errors.

Elena has finished entering the function, so she saves it before continuing with her work.

Saving a Module

When you click the Save button from the Module window, Access saves the module and its procedures. If you are entering a long procedure, it is a good idea to save your work periodically.

Elena saves the module with the name basIssue25Functions.

To save a module:

1. Click the **Save** button, type **basIssue25Functions** in the Module Name text box, and then click the **OK** button. Access saves the module and places the new module name in the title bar.

Before making the changes to the Types Form so that the CapOnlyFirst function automatically acts on every entry in the Description field, Elena tests the function using the Debug window.

Testing a Procedure in the Debug Window

Even the simplest procedure can have errors. Be sure to test each procedure thoroughly to ensure it does exactly what you expect it to do in all situations. When working in the Module window, use the **Debug window** to test Visual Basic procedures. Clicking the Debug Window button on the toolbar opens the Debug window on top of the Module window. In the Debug window, you can enter different parameter values to test the procedure you just entered. To test a procedure, use the key word **Print**, or question mark (?), followed by the procedure name and the parameter value you want to test in parentheses. For example, to test the CapOnlyFirst function in the Debug window using the test word "advertising," type "?CapOnlyFirst ("advertising")" and press the Enter key. Access executes the function and prints the value returned by the function (you expect it to return "Advertising"). Note that you enclose a **string** of characters with double quotes (").

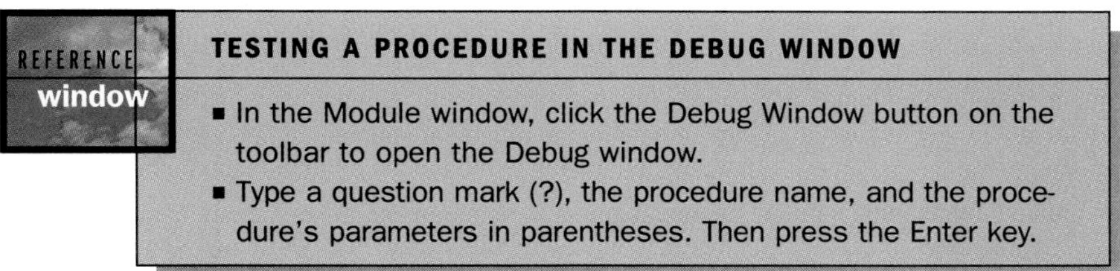

REFERENCE window

TESTING A PROCEDURE IN THE DEBUG WINDOW

- In the Module window, click the Debug Window button on the toolbar to open the Debug window.
- Type a question mark (?), the procedure name, and the procedure's parameters in parentheses. Then press the Enter key.

Elena uses the Debug window to test the CapOnlyFirst function.

To test a function in the Debug window:

1. Click the **Debug Window** button. Access opens the Debug window on top of the Module window and places the insertion point inside the window.
2. Type **?CapOnlyFirst("advertising")** and press the **Enter** key. Access executes the function and prints the function result, Advertising, on the next line. See Figure 4-8.

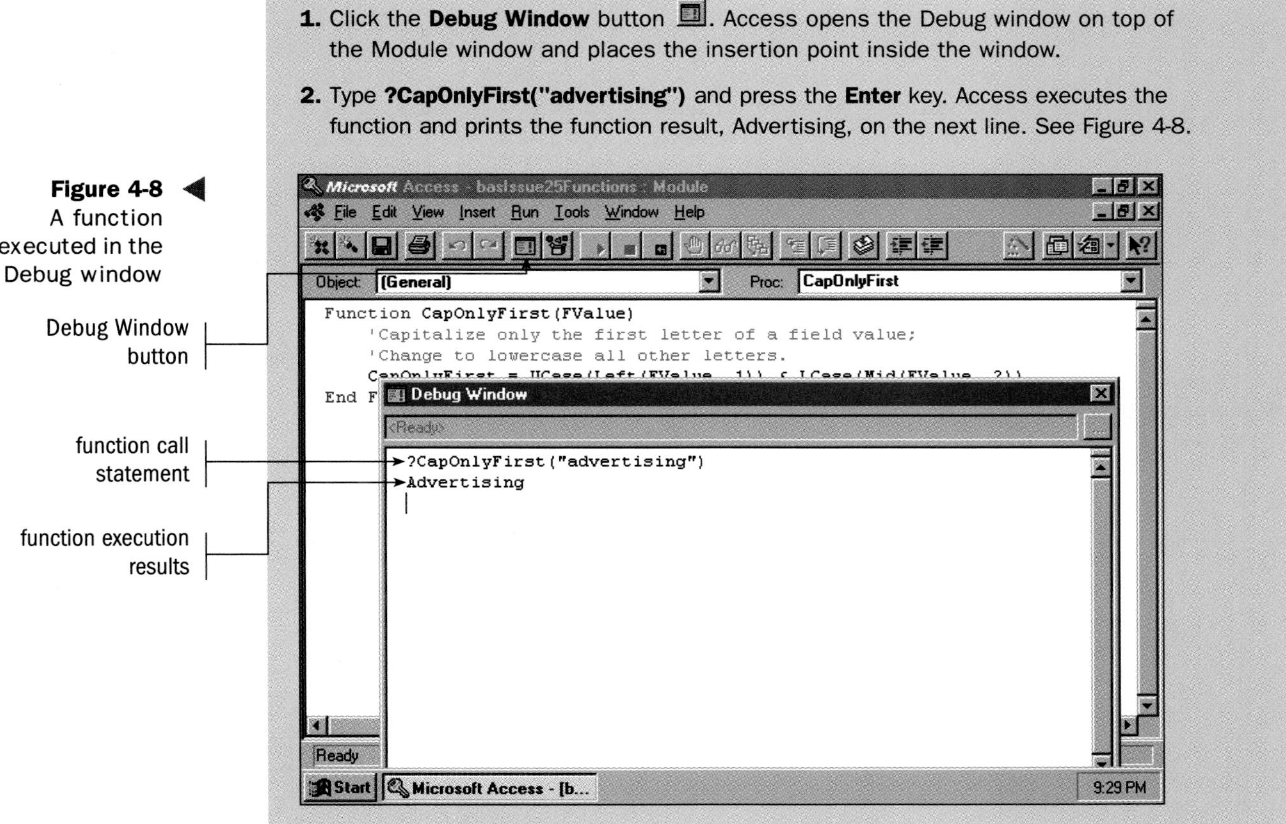

Figure 4-8 A function executed in the Debug window

To test the CapOnlyFirst function further, Elena enters several other parameter values. She could retype the entire statement each time. Instead, she highlights the parameter value, types the next parameter value, and then presses the Enter key.

To continue testing a function in the Debug window:

1. Highlight the word **advertising** in the first line of the Debug window. Type **aDVERTISING** and then press the **Enter** key. Access executes the function and prints the function result, Advertising, on the next line.
2. Repeat Step 1 two more times, using **ADVERTISING** and then **stock MARket** as parameter values. Access prints the correct values, Advertising and Stock market.
3. Click the Debug Window button **Close** button and then click the Module window **Close** button to return to the Database window. If Access opens a dialog box asking you if you want to stop running the code, click the **Yes** button.

Elena's initial test of the CapOnlyFirst function is successful. Next she modifies the Types Form to call the CapOnlyFirst function for the Description field.

Creating an Event Procedure

Recall that Access automatically creates a form module (called Code Behind Forms or CBF) for each form and a report module (called Code Behind Reports or CBR) for each report. When you add a procedure to one of these modules, Access stores the procedure with the form or report and treats the procedure as a local procedure that can be used with that form or report only. Each of these procedures is called an event procedure; Access runs a procedure when a specific event occurs.

For the Types Form, Elena codes an event procedure to call the CapOnlyFirst function for the Description field's AfterUpdate event. Whenever a user enters or changes a Description field value, the AfterUpdate event occurs and Access runs Elena's event procedure.

What exactly happens when Access calls a procedure? There is an interaction between the **calling statement** and the function statements as represented by a series of steps. Figure 4-9 shows the information for the CapOnlyFirst procedure.

Figure 4-9 The process of executing a function

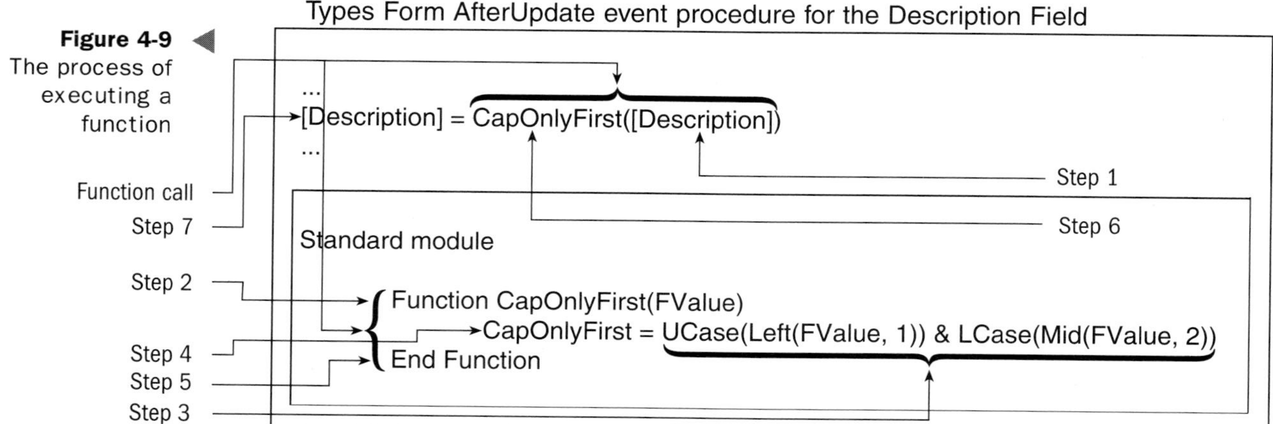

The steps in Figure 4-9 are numbered in the order in which they occur as Access processes the statement and the function. Access goes through the following steps:

- *Step 1.* Call to function CapOnlyFirst passes the value of the argument [Description]. This is the value of the Description field that is entered by the user.
- *Step 2.* Function CapOnlyFirst begins, and argument FValue receives the value of [Description].
- *Step 3.* First character of FValue is changed to uppercase; all remaining characters changed to lowercase.

- *Step 4*. Value of CapOnlyFirst set equal to the results of Step 3.
- *Step 5*. Function CapOnlyFirst ends.
- *Step 6*. Value of CapOnlyFirst is returned to the point of the call to the function.
- *Step 7*. Value of [Description] is set equal to the returned value of CapOnlyFirst.
- *Step 8*. Event procedure statement that calls the CapOnlyFirst procedure.
- *Step 9*. The CapOnlyFirst function is the basIssue25Functions standard module.

Although it looks complicated, the general function process is simple—a statement contains a function call; when the statement is executed, Access performs the function call, executes the function called, returns a single value back to the original statement, and completes that statement's execution. Study the steps in Figure 4-9 and trace their placement until you understand the complete process.

Designing an Event Procedure

Elena plans her changes to the Types Form to use the CapOnlyFirst function for the Description field. Whenever a user enters a new value or modifies an existing value in the Description field of the Types Form, Elena wants Access to execute the CapOnlyFirst function.

After a user changes a Description field value, the AfterUpdate event automatically occurs. Elena can set the AfterUpdate event property to run a macro, call a built-in Access function, or execute an event procedure. Because Elena wants to call her user-defined function from within the event procedure, she sets the AfterUpdate event property to [Event Procedure].

All event procedures are sub procedures. Access automatically adds the Sub and End Sub statements to an event procedure. All Elena needs to do is place the statements between the Sub and End Sub statements. Figure 4-10 shows her design for the event procedure. The following text describes the parts of the procedure.

Figure 4-10 AfterUpdate event procedure for the Description field

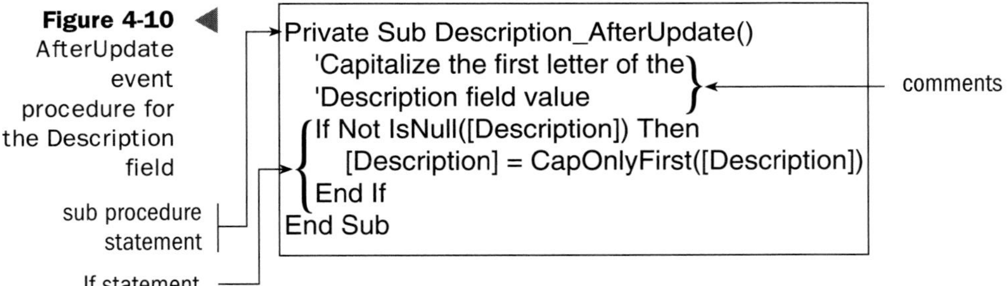

Private Sub Description_AfterUpdate()
'Capitalize the first letter of the
'Description field value
If Not IsNull([Description]) Then
[Description] = CapOnlyFirst([Description])
End If
End Sub
comments
sub procedure statement
If statement

Access names each event procedure in a standard way: name of the control, an underscore (_), and the event name. No parameters are passed to an event procedure, so Access places nothing in the parentheses following the name of the sub procedure. If the name of the control contains spaces, Access substitutes underscores for the spaces in the event procedure name.

A user might delete an existing Description field value, so that it contains no value, or becomes null. In this case, calling the function accomplishes nothing. Elena designs the procedure code to call the CapOnlyFirst function only when a user changes the Description field to a value that is not null. Elena uses the If statement to screen out the null values. In its simplest form, an **If statement** executes one of two groups of statements based on a condition, similar to common English usage. For example, consider the English statements, "If I work the night shift, then I'll earn extra spending money. Otherwise, I'll go to the movies and I'll dip into my savings." In these sentences, the two groups of statements come before and after the "otherwise," based on the condition, "if I work the night shift." The first group of statements consists of the clause "I'll earn extra spending money." This is called the **true-statement group** because it is what happens if the condition ("I work the night shift") is true. The second group of statements contains "I'll go to the movies and I'll dip into my savings." This is called the **false-statement group** because it is what happens if the condition is false. Visual Basic uses the keyword If to precede the condition. The keyword Then precedes the true-statement group and the keyword Else precedes the false-statement group. The general syntax, or valid form, of a Visual Basic If statement is:

```
If condition Then
        true-statement group
[Else
        false-statement group]
End If
```

Access executes the true-statement group when the condition is true and the false-statement group when the condition is false. Bracketed portions of a statement's syntax are optional parts of the statement. Therefore, omit the Else and its related false-statement group when you want Access to execute a group of statements only when the condition is true.

In Figure 4-10, Elena's If statement uses Access's **IsNull function**, which returns True when the Description field value is null and False when it is not null. The Not is the same logical operator you've used before to negate an expression. Thus, Access executes the statement "[Description] = CapOnlyFirst([Description])" only when the Description field value is not null.

Elena is ready to make her changes to the Types Form.

Adding an Event Procedure

Elena opens the Types Form in the Form Design window and adds an event procedure for the Description field's AfterUpdate event property.

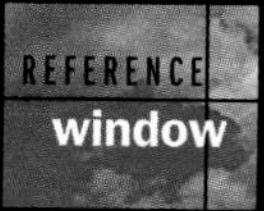

ADDING AN EVENT PROCEDURE

- Open the form or report in the Design window, open the property sheet, and click the control having the event property you want to set.
- Set the appropriate event property to [Event Procedure] and click the Build button.
- Enter the sub procedure statements in the Module window, compile the procedure, fix any statement errors, and save the event procedure.

Elena adds her event procedure to the Types Form.

To add an event procedure:

1. Click the **Forms** tab, click **Types Form**, and then click the **Design** button to open the Form Design window. Maximize the Form Design window if necessary.
2. Right-click the field-value **text box** for the Description field to display the shortcut menu, then click **Properties** to open the property sheet.
3. Click the **Event** tab. Access shows only the event properties in the property sheet.
4. Click the **After Update** text box, click the **list arrow**, click **[Event Procedure]**, and then click the **Build** button ... to the right of the AfterUpdate property. Access opens the Module window, which is maximized and contains the Private Sub and End Sub statements. See Figure 4-11.

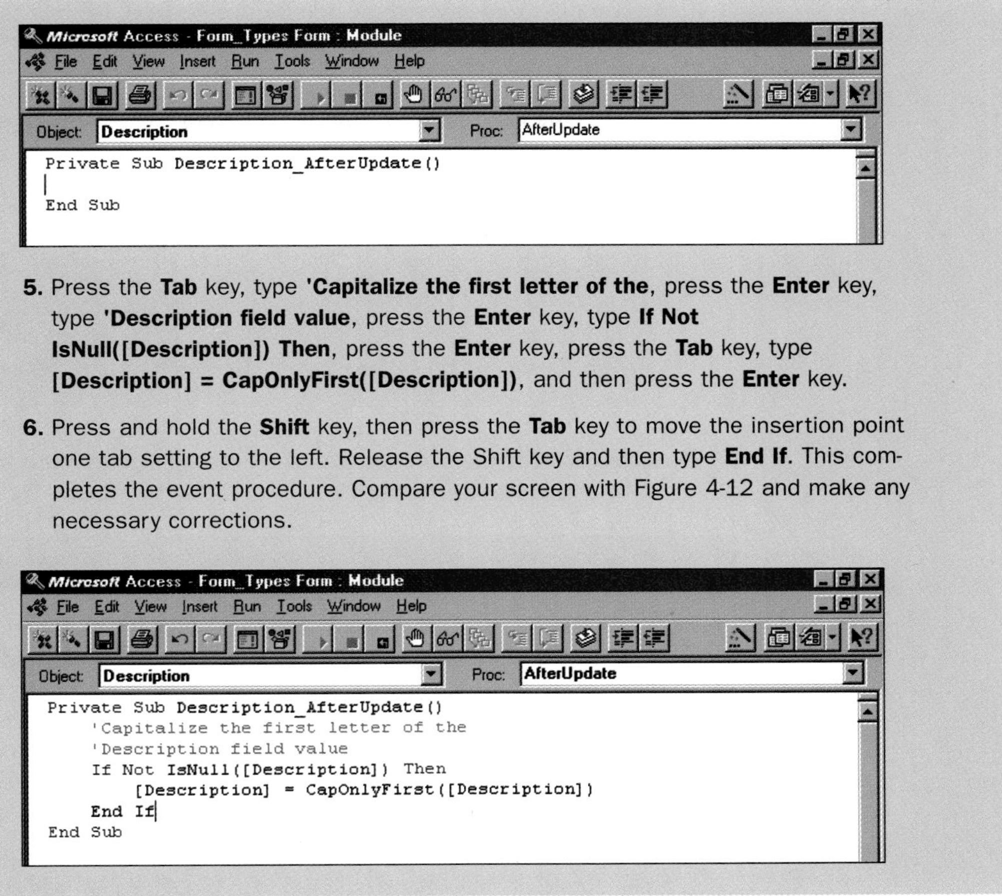

Figure 4-11 The initial event procedure in the Module window

5. Press the **Tab** key, type **'Capitalize the first letter of the**, press the **Enter** key, type **'Description field value**, press the **Enter** key, type **If Not IsNull([Description]) Then**, press the **Enter** key, press the **Tab** key, type **[Description] = CapOnlyFirst([Description])**, and then press the **Enter** key.

6. Press and hold the **Shift** key, then press the **Tab** key to move the insertion point one tab setting to the left. Release the Shift key and then type **End If**. This completes the event procedure. Compare your screen with Figure 4-12 and make any necessary corrections.

Figure 4-12 The completed event procedure

Before saving the event procedure, Elena compiles the procedure so that Access can run it.

Compiling a Procedure

Access cannot execute the Visual Basic statements you enter in a procedure without compiling them first. **Compiling** a procedure translates Visual Basic statements into a form Access can execute and checks the procedure for errors. When you run a procedure for the first time, Access compiles it for you automatically and opens a dialog box only if it finds errors in the procedure. If it finds an error, Access does not translate the procedure statements. If no errors are detected, Access translates the procedure and does not display a confirmation. You can also compile a procedure at any point as you enter it. Just click the Compile Loaded Modules button on the toolbar. In response, Access compiles the procedure and all other procedures in all modules in the database. Access does not, however, compile CBF and CBR for closed forms and reports.

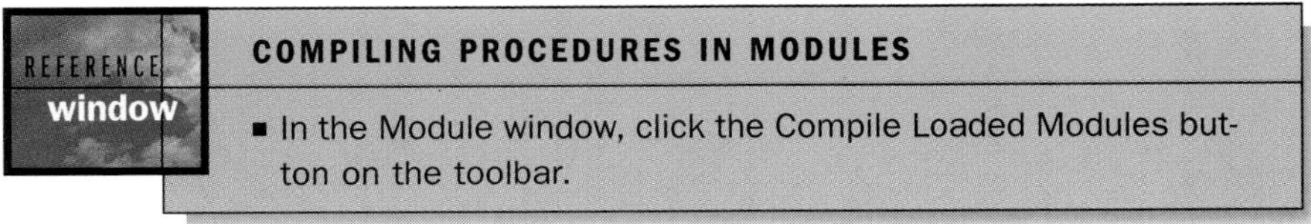
REFERENCE window

COMPILING PROCEDURES IN MODULES

- In the Module window, click the Compile Loaded Modules button on the toolbar.

Elena compiles and saves the Code Before Form (CBF) for the Types Form.

To compile and save CBF:

1. Click the **Compile Loaded Modules** button. Access compiles the CBF for the Types Form.

   TROUBLE? If Access identifies any errors in your code, correct the errors and repeat Step 1.

2. Click the **Save** button, click the Module window **Close** button to close the Module window, click the Properties window **Close** button to close the property sheet, click the Form Design window **Restore** button, and then click the Form Design window **Close** button to return to the Database window.

Elena has created the function and the event procedure and has set the event property. She now tests the event procedure.

Testing an Event Procedure

Elena opens the Form View window for the Types Form and tests the Description field's event procedure by entering a few different test Description field values in the first record of the form. Moving the focus to another control on the form or to another record triggers the AfterUpdate event for the Description field and executes the attached event procedure. After entering a value for the Description field, Elena changes the focus by clicking the first record's Type text box.

To test an event procedure:

1. Make sure that **Types Form** is selected in the Forms list box in the Database window, then click the **Open** button.

2. Press the **Tab** key, type **stock MARKET** in the Description text box, and click the **Type** text box. Access executes the AfterUpdate event procedure for the Description field and changes the Description field value to "Stock market." See Figure 4-13.

Figure 4-13 Types Form showing executed event procedure

TYPES
TYPES
Type: ADV
Description: Stock market
Record: 1

3. Repeat Step 2 three more times, entering "advertising," then "ADVERTISING," and finally "aDVERTISING" in the Description field box. Access prints the correct value, "Advertising," each time.

4. Click the Form View window **Close** button to return to the Database window.

Elena has finished her work on the CapOnlyFirst function. Next, she creates a similar, but more complicated, function for the Article Title field in the Business Articles Column Form.

If you want to take a break and resume the tutorial at a later time, you can exit Access by clicking the Access window Close button. When you resume the tutorial, place your Student Disk in the appropriate drive, start Access, open the Issue25 database in the Tutorial folder on your Student Disk, click the switchboard's Exit to Issue25 button, and click the Forms tab.

Quick Check

1. Why is Visual Basic called an event-driven, object-oriented language?
2. What are the differences between a function and a sub procedure?
3. What are the two different types of modules?
4. What is an event procedure?
5. What can you accomplish in the Debug window?
6. What does Access do when you compile a procedure?

SESSION 4.2

In this session, you will add a second function to a standard module. You will learn how to have Access hide text and change color in a form during execution of a procedure. You will also create event procedures for a dialog box.

Adding a Second Function to a Standard Module

Elena now decides to practice with a second function she learned at the seminar. This function, named CapAllFirst, capitalizes the first letter of all words in a field value and does not change any other letters in the field value. Using this function for the Article Title field in the Business Articles Column Form changes the field value "the bCCI scandal," for example, to "The BCCI Scandal." Because Elena wants to use the style convention for capitalizing article titles, she needs to be sure that the function does not capitalize the first letter of the following five words when they are not the first word of the title: and, in, of, on, the. In other words, the CapAllFirst function would change the field value "computers in the future" to "Computers in the Future."

The Design of the CapAllFirst Function

Figure 4-14 shows the CapAllFirst function that Elena learned about at the seminar she attended. You've already seen several of the statements in this function in your work with the CapOnlyFirst function. Except for the function name, the Function and End Function statements are the same. Elena enters comments on the second and third lines of the function; these comments are specific to the CapAllFirst function. An explanation of the new statements and the purpose of each group of statements are discussed in the following paragraphs.

Figure 4-14
The CapAllFirst function

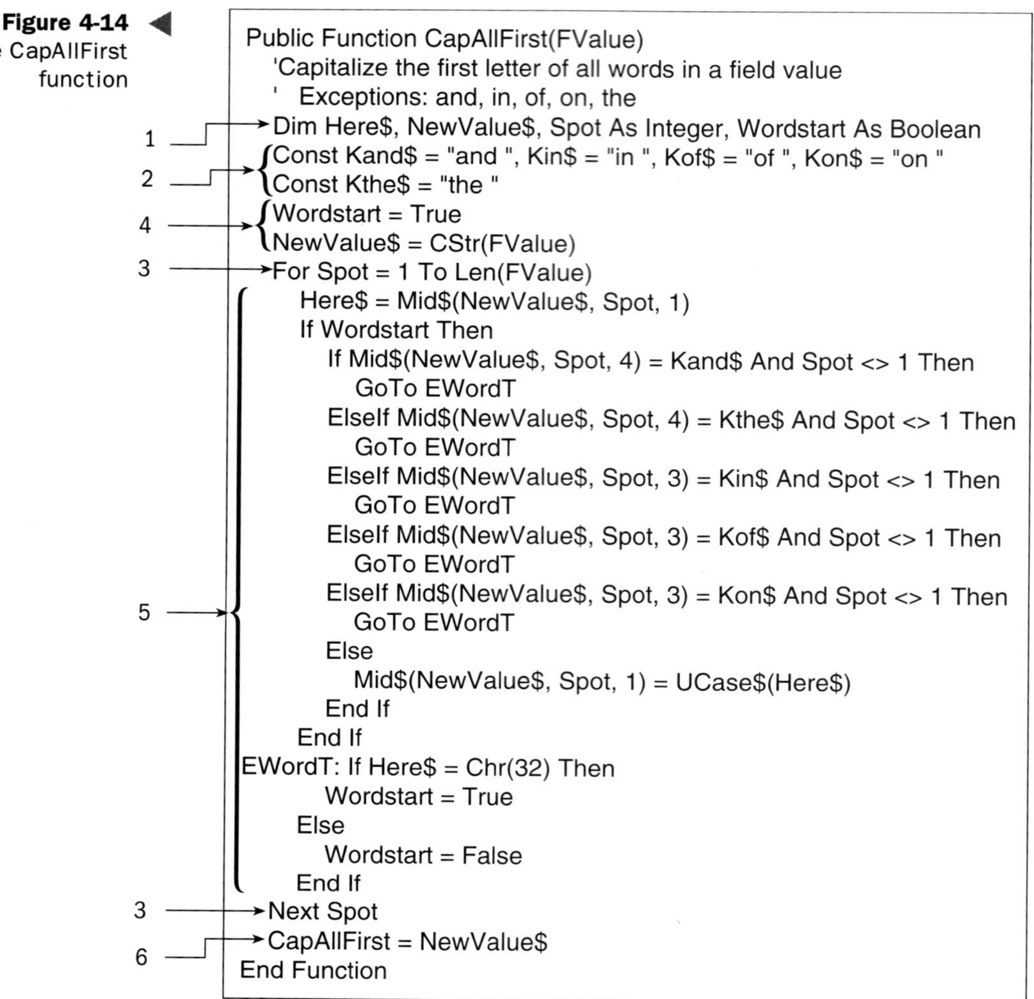


```
Public Function CapAllFirst(FValue)
  'Capitalize the first letter of all words in a field value
  '  Exceptions: and, in, of, on, the
  Dim Here$, NewValue$, Spot As Integer, Wordstart As Boolean
  Const Kand$ = "and ", Kin$ = "in ", Kof$ = "of ", Kon$ = "on "
  Const Kthe$ = "the "
  Wordstart = True
  NewValue$ = CStr(FValue)
  For Spot = 1 To Len(FValue)
    Here$ = Mid$(NewValue$, Spot, 1)
    If Wordstart Then
      If Mid$(NewValue$, Spot, 4) = Kand$ And Spot <> 1 Then
        GoTo EWordT
      ElseIf Mid$(NewValue$, Spot, 4) = Kthe$ And Spot <> 1 Then
        GoTo EWordT
      ElseIf Mid$(NewValue$, Spot, 3) = Kin$ And Spot <> 1 Then
        GoTo EWordT
      ElseIf Mid$(NewValue$, Spot, 3) = Kof$ And Spot <> 1 Then
        GoTo EWordT
      ElseIf Mid$(NewValue$, Spot, 3) = Kon$ And Spot <> 1 Then
        GoTo EWordT
      Else
        Mid$(NewValue$, Spot, 1) = UCase$(Here$)
      End If
    End If
EWordT: If Here$ = Chr(32) Then
      Wordstart = True
    Else
      Wordstart = False
    End If
  Next Spot
  CapAllFirst = NewValue$
End Function
```

The Dim Statement (Figure 4-14, Number 1) Use the **Dim statement** to define variables in a procedure. The variables in Elena's CapAllFirst function are Here$, NewValue$, Spot, and Wordstart. You'll see what these variables do in a moment. Each variable is assigned an associated data type. Figure 4-15 shows the primary data types for Visual Basic variables. Choose a data type for a variable by adding the associated suffix to the variable name or by following the variable name with As and the data type. In the CapAllFirst function, for example, the two variables Here$ and NewValue$ are string variables, Spot is an integer variable, and Wordstart is a Boolean variable. The **Boolean type** is the equivalent of the Yes/No type used to define the data type of a table record field. It can take one of two values: True or False. If you do not use the Option Explicit statement in the declarations section and you create a variable without specifying a data type, Visual Basic assigns the variant data type to the variable. The **variant data type** is the default data type, and a variant variable can store numeric, string, date/time, and null values.

Figure 4-15 Visual Basic data types

Data Type	Suffix
Boolean	none
Currency	@
Date	none
Double	#
Integer	%
Long	&
Single	!
String	$ Variant
none	

The Const Statement (Figure 4-14, Number 2) Use **Const statements** to define constants in a procedure. A **constant**, unlike a variable, is a memory location that contains a value that does not change. In a Const statement, you assign a constant name and a value to each separate constant. In the CapAllFirst function, for example, Kand$ is a constant name, has the String data type, and is assigned the string value "and". Each of the other four constants is similarly defined. The space at the end of each constant ensures that only these five words, and not just any occurrence of these characters, are not capitalized. For example, for "industry," "office," "Andrew," and other words beginning with the letters of these words, the CapAllFirst function capitalizes their first letters.

The For...Next statement (Figure 4-14, Number 3) The **For...Next statement** repeats a group of statements a fixed number of times. A group of statements repeatedly executed is called a **loop**. In the CapAllFirst function, the For statement establishes how many times to repeat the statement group, the Next statement marks the end of the For...Next statement pair, and the statements between these two statements are repeated a fixed number of times.

A For statement uses one of the variables that you've defined as a counter. You define a range that the variable will take on and tell Access, "For this range, do these steps." This tells the For statement for which values it should execute the loop. The general syntax for the For statement is "For counter = start To end [Step increment]," where increment has a default value of 1. The "For Spot = 1 To Len(FValue)" statement in the CapAllFirst function sets the starting value of Spot, which is an integer variable, to 1 and the ending value of Spot to Len(FValue). The **Len function** returns the number of characters in a string. For example, if FValue is the string "An Article Title" Len(FValue) returns 16 as the number of characters, including spaces. In this case, the statements in the loop will be executed 16 times.

Then Access executes the group of statements that follow the For statement, ending with the statement before the Next Spot statement. When execution reaches the Next Spot statement, Access adds 1 to Spot, goes back to the For statement, and compares the value of Spot to Len(FValue). If Spot is less than or equal to Len(FValue), Access executes the loop statements again, reaches the Next Spot statement, and repeats the cycle. When Spot becomes greater than Len(FValue), Access terminates the loop and executes the statement following the Next Spot statement.

Initialization (Figure 4-14, Number 4) The next steps in the CapAllFirst function initialize variables to their starting values. Access initializes the value of Wordstart to True, telling Access that when the function starts, it is at the beginning of a word. Access uses the **CStr function** to convert the value of the parameter FValue, which has the variant data type, to a string and assigns this converted value to the variable NewValue$.

The Loop Body (Figure 4-14, Number 5) The statement group between the For and the Next statements is called the **loop body**. The loop body in the CapAllFirst function finds the first character of a word and capitalizes it, when it isn't one of the exception words (that is, the words defined by the Const statements). Access changes the first character of a word to uppercase using the UCase$ function. After inspecting all characters and changing appropriate characters to uppercase, Access assigns the changed value of NewValue$ to CapAllFirst, the value of which is returned to the calling statement.

In the loop body, Access sets the variable Wordstart to a value of True whenever the current character is the first character of a word and to a value of False otherwise. (The statement "If Here$ = Chr(32)" uses the **Chr function** to convert an ANSI character code—a number assigned to a letter or other symbol—to a string character; for example, ANSI character code 32 is assigned to the space character.) The statement "If Wordstart Then" is true when Wordstart is True, and is false when Wordstart is False. This simply means that the If statement is true when the current character is the first character of a word and is false in all other cases.

After Access has evaluated a word to be sure it isn't one of the words defined in the Const statement (this evaluation takes place in the If and Else statements, as you'll see in a moment), the code tells it to go to a line beginning with the word "EWordT." This is short for EndWordTest, and all EWordT does is serve as a name for the line so Access knows what statement to execute next (for this reason its called a **line label**). The EWordT line starts a new If statement that tests whether the next character is a space or not.

Finally, for an **If...Then...ElseIf** set of statements, only one of the If or ElseIf conditions will be true. For example: If it's summer, we'll go to the beach, else if it's fall, we'll view the fall foliage, else if it's winter, we'll ski, else we'll plant our garden. In these four mutually exclusive possibilities, only one can be true. Access evaluates the very first If statement (in this case, testing to see if the word is "and"). If the statement is true, then it skips all the rest of the statements between the If and End If and jumps to the EWordT line label. If the first statement Access evaluates is not true (that is, the word is not "and") Access moves on to the next statement to see if the word is "the." The point is that Access is checking to be sure the word isn't one of the ones you don't want capitalized. The CapAllFirst function's If...Then...ElseIf statement either capitalizes the first character of a word (the assignment following the Else) or does not when the first character is for one of the exception words.

Exiting the Function (Figure 4-14, Number 6) Finally, when Access has processed all the words in NewValue$, the value of NewValue$ is assigned to CapAllFirst, the name of the function. This is the value that will be returned to the calling statement.

Elena adds the CapAllFirst function to the basIssue25Functions module.

Creating a Second Function

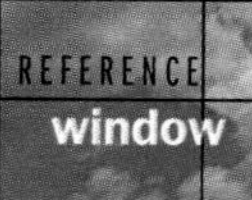

ADDING A NEW PROCEDURE TO A STANDARD MODULE

- In the Database window, click the Modules tab, click the module name, and click the Design button.
- In the Module window, click the New Procedure button, type the new procedure name, click the Sub or Function radio button, and click the OK button.
- Enter the new procedure, click the Compile Loaded Modules button, and click the Save button.

Elena opens the basIssue25Functions module in the Module window and adds the CapAllFirst function.

To add a function to an existing module:

1. Click the **Modules** tab, click the **Design** button, and then click the Module window **Maximize** button.
2. Click the **Insert Procedure** button on the toolbar to open the Insert Procedure dialog box. Type **CapAllFirst** in the Name text box, make sure the Function and Public radio buttons are selected, and then click the **OK** button. Access starts a new procedure named CapAllFirst and displays the Function and End Function statements in the Module window.
3. Click between the parentheses in the Function statement, type **FValue**, press the **down arrow** key and then press the **Tab** key.
4. Enter the statements for the CapAllFirst function exactly as listed in Figure 4-16. Be sure to use the Edit menu's Copy and Paste commands to duplicate similar statements, and use the Tab key to indent as necessary. Recall that pressing Shift + Tab moves the insertion point one tab stop to the left.

Figure 4-16 The CapAllFirst function statements

```
Public Function CapAllFirst(FValue)
  'Capitalize the first letter of all words in a field value
  '  Exceptions: and, in, of, on, the
  Dim Here$, NewValue$, Spot As Integer, Wordstart As Boolean
  Const Kand$ = "and ", Kin$ = "in ", Kof$ = "of ", Kon$ = "on "
  Const Kthe$ = "the "
  Wordstart = True
  NewValue$ = CStr(FValue)
  For Spot = 1 To Len(FValue)
    Here$ = Mid$(NewValue$, Spot, 1)
    If Wordstart Then
      If Mid$(NewValue$, Spot, 4) = Kand$ And Spot <> 1 Then
        GoTo EWordT
      ElseIf Mid$(NewValue$, Spot, 4) = Kthe$ And Spot <> 1 Then
        GoTo EWordT
      ElseIf Mid$(NewValue$, Spot, 3) = Kin$ And Spot <> 1 Then
        GoTo EWordT
      ElseIf Mid$(NewValue$, Spot, 3) = Kof$ And Spot <> 1 Then
        GoTo EWordT
      ElseIf Mid$(NewValue$, Spot, 3) = Kon$ And Spot <> 1 Then
        GoTo EWordT
      Else
        Mid$(NewValue$, Spot, 1) = UCase$(Here$)
      End If
    End If
EWordT: If Here$ = Chr(32) Then
      Wordstart = True
    Else
      Wordstart = False
    End If
  Next Spot
  CapAllFirst = NewValue$
End Function
```

5. Click the **Compile Loaded Modules** button to compile the CapAllFirst function and then click the **Save** button to save the basIssue25Functions module.

TROUBLE? If Access finds an error, it highlights the error and opens a dialog box with a message describing the nature of the error. Click the OK button and change the statement contained in the highlighted area by comparing each character you entered to what should be entered. Then repeat Step 5.

6. Click the Module window **Proc text box** list arrow, then click **CapOnlyFirst**. Access displays the CapOnlyFirst function and displays CapOnlyFirst in the Module window Proc text box. You can easily move from procedure to procedure in a module by clicking the Proc text box list arrow and selecting a procedure.
7. Click the Module window **Proc text box** list arrow, then click **(declarations)**. Access displays the module's Declarations section. Click the Module window **Proc text box** list arrow, then click **CapAllFirst** to display the top of the CapAllFirst function.
8. Click the Module window **Close** button to return to the maximized Database window.

Creating a Second Event Procedure

Elena uses the CapAllFirst function with the Article Title field in the Business Articles Column Form. She opens the Business Articles Column Form in the Form Design window and adds an event procedure for the Article Title field's AfterUpdate event property. The new event procedure looks exactly like the event procedure for the Description field in the Types Form, except for the Sub statement, the function call statement, and the sub procedure comments.

To add an event procedure for the Article Title field in the Business Articles Column Form:

1. Click the **Forms** tab, click **Business Articles Column Form**, and then click the **Design** button to open the Form Design window.
2. Right-click the **Article Title field** field-value text box to display the shortcut menu, then click **Properties** to open the Property sheet.
3. Click the **After Update** text box, click the **list arrow** that appears, click **[Event Procedure]**, and then click the **Build** button to the right of the AfterUpdate property. Access opens the Module window, which is maximized and contains the Private Sub and End Sub statements.
4. Press the **Tab** key and type the sub procedure statements exactly as listed in Figure 4-17.

Figure 4-17 The event procedure for the Article Title field

```
Private Sub Article_Title_AfterUpdate()
   'Capitalize the first letter of all words
   '  in the Article Title field value
   If Not IsNull([Article Title]) Then
      [Article Title] = CapAllFirst([Article Title])
   End If
End Sub
```

5. Click the **Compile Loaded Modules** button, click the **Save** button, click the Module window **Close** button to close the Module window, click the property sheet **Close** button to close the property sheet, click the Form Design window **Restore** button, and then click the Form Design window **Close** button to return to the Database window.

Elena has entered the function and the event procedure and has set the event property. She now tests the event procedure. Elena opens the Form View window for the Business Articles Column Form and tests the Article Title field's event procedure by entering different Article Title field values.

To test an event procedure:

1. Make sure that **Business Articles Column Form** is selected in the Forms list box in the Database window, then click the **Open** button to open the Form View window. Click the **Last record** button to display the record for the article titled "Advertising Over the Past 25 Years."
2. Type **the first of the tests on this field** in the Article Title text box and then press the **Tab** key. Access executes the AfterUpdate event procedure for the Article Title field and changes the Article Title field value to "The First of the Tests on This Field." Press the **up arrow** key to highlight the Article Title field value.
3. Repeat Step 2 two more times, entering "and the second in the field and function" (will be corrected to "And the Second in the Field and Function"), and then entering "advertising over the past 25 years" (correctly changed to "Advertising Over the Past 25 Years").
4. Click the Form View window **Close** button to return to the Database window.

Hiding Text and Changing Display Color

Elena wants to add a message to the Writers Column Form that will remind users when freelancers need to be paid. Access will display the message, in red, only when the writer is a freelancer. Also, Access will display the value in the Amount text box in red for freelancers and in black for staff writers. See Figure 4-18.

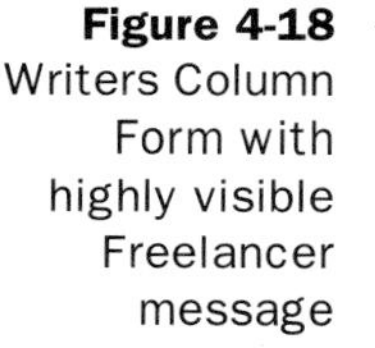

Figure 4-18 Writers Column Form with highly visible Freelancer message

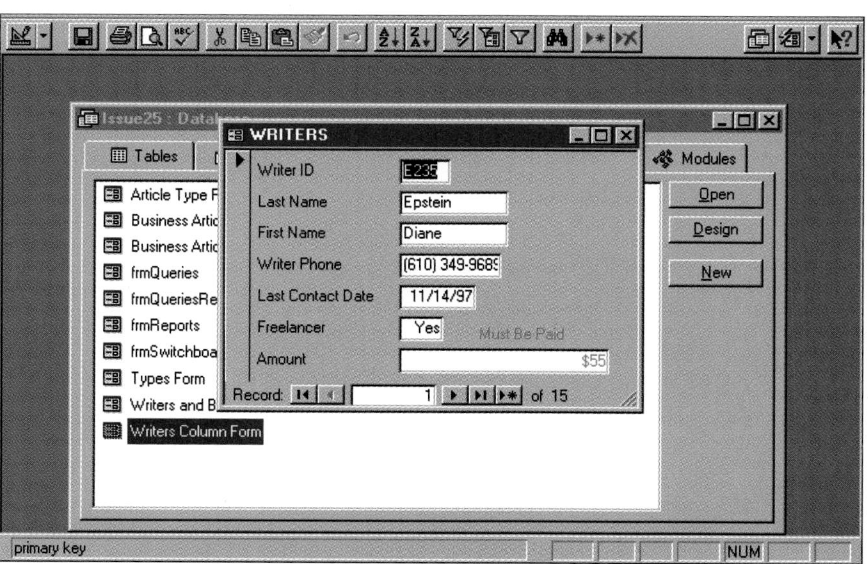

The Visible property determines when Access displays a control. Access displays a control when its Visible property is True, which is the default, and hides the control when its Visible property is False. The field's Fore Color property determines a field's foreground color. In the Writers Column Form, Elena adds a label to the right of the Freelancer check box. The text "Must Be Paid" is displayed in red letters. Because Elena wants the text to appear when the Freelancer column has the value Yes, she changes the label's Visible property during execution. Elena also changes the foreground color of the Amount field to red for freelancers and to black for staff writers.

Because the change to the Visible property takes place during execution, Elena adds code to the Current event procedure in the Writers Column Form. The Current event occurs every time Access displays a new record in a form. To set a property in a Visual Basic statement, use the object name followed by the property name, separating the two with a period. For example, if the label name for the message is FreelancerMsg, then "[FreelancerMsg].Visible = False" hides the label on the form.

To add the Current event procedure to the Writers Column Form:

1. Click the Database window **Maximize** button, click **Writers Column Form**, and then click the **Design** button to open the Form Design window.
2. If necessary, click the **Toolbox** button to open the toolbox, then click the **Label** tool. Position the $^{+}$A in the grid dots to the right of the Freelancer field value box, click the left mouse button, type **Must Be Paid**, and then press the **Enter** key. Using the move handle in the upper-left corner of the label box, drag the label box just to the right of the Freelancer field value box. See Figure 4-19.

Figure 4-19 Position of the label box

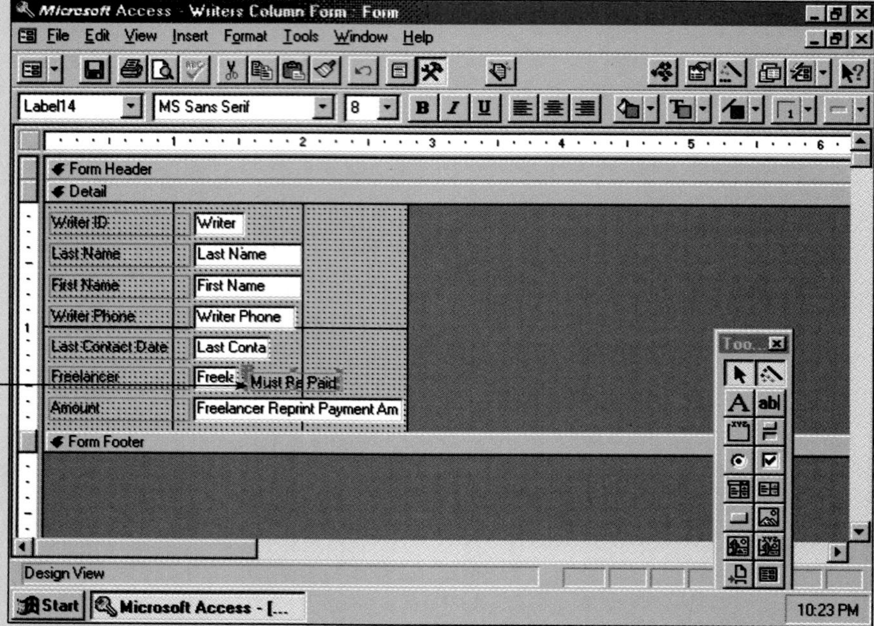

3. Right-click the **new label** to display the shortcut menu, then click **Properties** to open the property sheet. If necessary, click the **All** tab, double-click the value in the Name box, and then type **FreelancerMsg**.
4. Scroll the property sheet, click in the **Fore Color** box, then click the **Build** button. Access displays the Color dialog box. Click the **red** color box (the first color box in the second row of Basic Colors), then click the **OK** button. Access places the code for red (255) in the ForeColor property value. Access also changes the foreground color of the label box to red.
5. Click the **Form Selector**, scroll the Form property sheet, click the **On Current** box, click the **list arrow**, click **[Event Procedure]**, and then click the **Build** button. Access opens the Module window, displaying the Sub and End Sub statements.
6. Press the **Tab** key and type the sub procedure statements exactly as listed in Figure 4-20. Be sure to type the underscore character (_) between the words in the Freelancer Reprint Payment Amount field name.

Figure 4-20 The Current event procedure for the Writers Column Form

```
Private Sub Form_Current()
  'For Freelancers, display a message and the "Amount" field value in red
  'For others, display the "Amount" field value in black without a message
  If [Freelancer] = True Then
    [FreelancerMsg].Visible = True
    [Freelancer_Reprint_Payment_Amount].ForeColor = 255
  Else
    [FreelancerMsg].Visible = False
    [Freelancer_Reprint_Payment_Amount].ForeColor = 0
  End If
End Sub
```

7. Click the **Compile Loaded Modules** button, click the **Save** button, click the Module window **Close** button to close the Module window, click the property sheet **Close** button to close the property sheet, click the Form Design window **Restore** button, and then click the Form Design window **Close** button to return to the Database window.
8. Make sure that the **Writers Column Form** is selected in the Forms list, then click the **Open** button to open the Form View window. Access displays the first record for Diane Epstein, who is a freelancer. The message is in red, as is the Amount value $55.
9. Click the **Next Record** button several times to make sure each freelancer's message and Amount value appear in red and each staff writer's Amount value is in black without the message appearing.
10. Click the Form View window **Close** button to return to the Database window.

Elena has finished all work on the Current event procedure for the Writers Column Form.

Creating the Event Procedures for the frmReports Dialog Box

Elena's last task is to address the procedures for the frmReports form dialog box. When the form first opens, she wants Access to highlight the first item in the list box by placing the focus on it. Next, when a user double-clicks a report name in the list box or highlights a report name and then clicks the left command button, the action opens that report in the Print Preview window. Finally, when a user highlights a report name in the list box and clicks the middle command button, the selected report is immediately printed. Elena designs the three procedures for the dialog box to perform these functions. Figure 4-21 shows the procedure names she chooses in relation to the way they are used.

Figure 4-21 The frmReports form's procedures

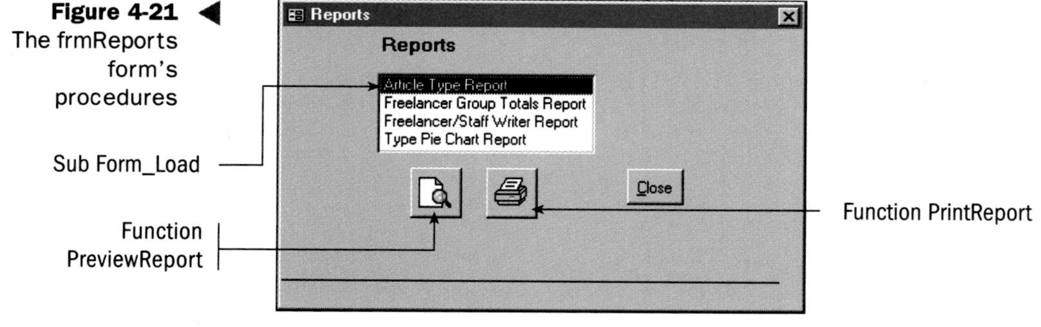

The Load Event Procedure for the Dialog Box

When a user opens the frmReports dialog box, Elena wants Access to place the focus on the top report in the list box on the form automatically. Figure 4-22 shows the code she designs for the form's Load event.

Figure 4-22 The Load event procedure for the frmReports form

```
Private Sub Form_Load()
    'Move the focus to the list box and highlight the first report
    [ctlReportName].SetFocus
    SendKeys "{Down}"
End Sub
```

The **Load event** occurs when Access opens a form. **SetFocus** is a method that moves the focus to the specified object or control. A **method** is an action that operates on specific objects or controls. The statement [ctlReportName].SetFocus moves the focus to the ctlReportName control, which is the name for the form's list box but does not set the focus to any specific report name. The SendKeys "{Down}" statement sends the down arrow keystroke to the list box; Access highlights the top report in the list box in response to this statement. The end result of these statements is that when the user opens the dialog box, the top report is highlighted and has the focus.

Elena opens the frmReports form in the Form Design window and creates the Load event procedure.

To add the Load event procedure for the frmReports form:

1. Click **frmReports** in the Forms list box, click the **Design** command button to open the Form Design window, and then click the Form Design window **Maximize** button.
2. Right-click the **Form Selector** to display the shortcut menu, then click **Properties** to open the property sheet. Scroll the property sheet, click the **On Load** box, click the **list arrow**, click **[Event Procedure]**, and then click the **Build** button. Access opens the Module window, displaying the Sub and End Sub statements.
3. Press the **Tab** key and type the sub procedure statements as listed in Figure 4-22. Make sure your final screen looks like Figure 4-23.

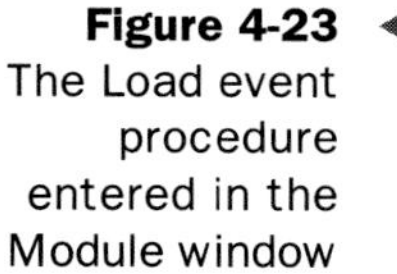

Figure 4-23 The Load event procedure entered in the Module window

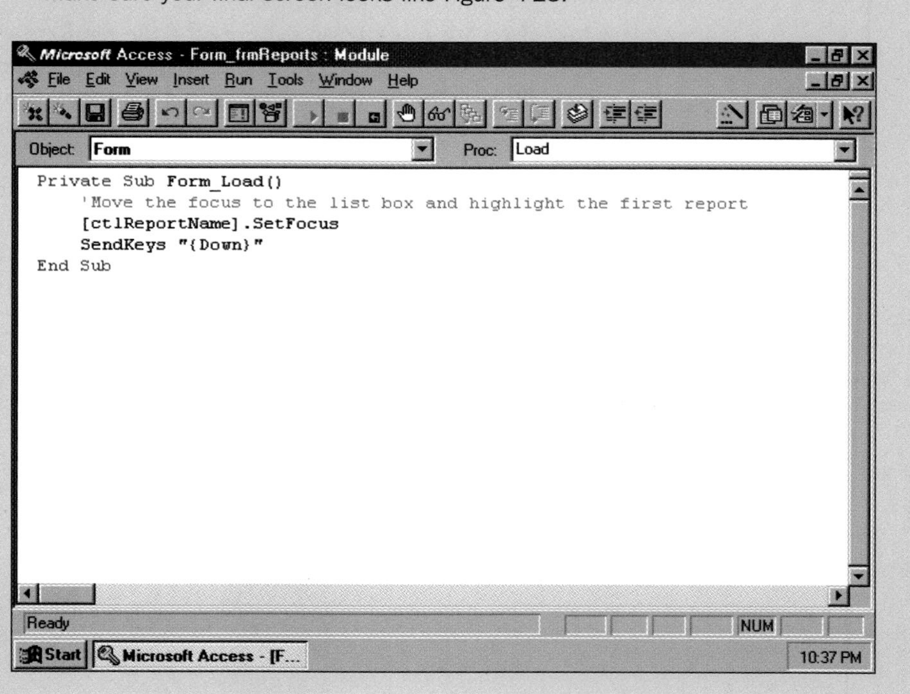

4. Click the **Compile Loaded Modules** button, click the **Save** button, click the Module window **Close** button to close the Module window, click the property sheet **Close** button to close the property sheet, click the Form Design window **Restore** button, and then click the Form Design window **Close** button to return to the Database window.
5. Make sure **frmReports** is selected in the Forms list in the Database window, then click the **Open** button to open the Form View window for the frmReports form. The top report in the list box is selected.
6. Click the **Close** button on the dialog box to close it and return to the Database window.

Elena has finished her work with the Load event procedure for the frmReports form. Next, she creates the form's PreviewReport and PrintReport functions.

The PreviewReport and PrintReport Functions for the Dialog Box

Double-clicking a report name in the list box or highlighting a report name and then clicking the left command button must open that report in the Print Preview window. Highlighting a report name in the list box and clicking the middle command button must immediately print that report. Figure 4-24 shows the code Elena designs to handle these processes.

Figure 4-24 The PreviewReport and PrintReport functions for the frmReports form

```
Public Function PreviewReport()
    'Open the selected report in the Print Preview window
    DoCmd.OpenReport [ctlReportName], A_PREVIEW
End Function
```

```
Public Function PrintReport()
    'Print the selected report
    DoCmd.OpenReport [ctlReportName], A_NORMAL
End Function
```

A Visual Basic **DoCmd statement** executes an action. Recall that you've used macros to execute actions in previous tutorials. Elena uses the DoCmd statements in her functions to run the OpenReport action. The parameter choices for the selected report of [ctlReportName] in the OpenReport action are: A_PREVIEW to open the Print Preview window, A_NORMAL to print the report, and A_DESIGN to open the Report Design window. Because the OpenReport action and its parameter values A_PREVIEW, A_NORMAL, and A_DESIGN are standard features of Access, you do not define them in a Dim statement as you do for variables you create.

Elena opens the frmReports form in the Form Design window, creates the two functions, and attaches the functions to the appropriate control properties.

To add the two functions to the frmReports form:

1. Click the **Design** button to open the Form Design window, click the **Code** button to open the Module window for the form's CBF, click the **Insert Procedure** button, type **PreviewReport** in the Name text box, be sure the Function radio button is selected, and then click the **OK** button. Access displays the Function and End Function statements for a new procedure.
2. Press the **Tab** key and type the statements for the PreviewReport function exactly as listed in Figure 4-25.

Figure 4-25 The PreviewReport function for the frmReports form

```
Public Function PreviewReport()
    'Open the selected report in the Print Preview window
    DoCmd.OpenReport [ctlReportName], A_PREVIEW
End Function
```

3. Click the **Save** button, click the **Insert Procedure** button, type **PrintReport** in the Name text box, be sure the Function radio button is selected, and then click the **OK** button.

4. Press the **Tab** key and type the statements for the PrintReport function exactly as listed in Figure 4-26.

Figure 4-26 The PrintReport function for the frmReports form

```
Public Function PrintReport()
    'Print the selected report
    DoCmd.OpenReport [ctlReportName], A_NORMAL
End Function
```

5. Click the **Compile Loaded Modules** button, click the **Save** button, click the Module window **Close** button to close the Module window, click the Form Design window **Maximize** button, right-click the form's **list box** to display the shortcut menu, then click **Properties** to open the property sheet.

6. Scrolling the property sheet as necessary, click the **On Dbl Click** box, and type **=PreviewReport().**

7. Click the form's **left command button**, click the property sheet's **On Click** text box, and then type **=PreviewReport().**

8. Click the form's **middle command button**, click the property sheet's **On Click** text box, and then type **=PrintReport().**

9. Click the **Save** button to save all form changes, click the property sheet **Close** button to close the property sheet, click the Form Design window **Restore** button, and then click the Form Design window **Close** button to return to the Database window.

Elena tests the changes made to the frmReports form.

To test the changes to the frmReports form:

1. Make sure that **frmReports** is selected in the Forms list box in the Database window, then click the **Open** button to open the form in the Form View window.

2. Double-click each of the report names, in turn, in the list box to verify that the correct report opens in the Print Preview window. From the Print Preview window, click the **Close** button each time to return to the dialog box in the Form View window.

3. Click a report name in the list box and then click the **left command button** to verify that the correct report opens in the Print Preview window. From the Print Preview window, click the **Close** button to return to the dialog box in the Form View window.

4. Repeat Step 3 for each report name in the form's list box.

5. Click a report name in the list box and then click the **middle command button** to verify that the correct report prints.

6. Repeat Step 5 for each report name in the form's list box.
7. Click the **Close** button on the dialog box to close it and return to the Database window.

Elena makes one final test of the frmSwitchboard form. She has completed all the form's features except for the options on the frmQueries form (you will add procedures in the Tutorial Assignments to finish this form), and wants to be sure everything works properly. When she finishes her final testing, Elena exits Access.

To test the features on the frmSwitchboard form:

1. Click **frmSwitchboard** in the Forms list box on the Database window, then click the **Open** button to open the form in the Form View window.
2. Make one final pass through all menu, toolbar, and command button options to verify that all features work properly on the frmSwitchboard form.
3. Click the form's **Exit Access** button as your last test to close the form, close the Issue25 database, and exit Access.

Elena's graphical user interface for the Issue25 database gives users controlled, easy access to the database's forms, queries, and reports. Brian and Judith are very happy with Elena's work and know that they will be able to use the interface to develop the 25th-anniversary issue and keep an accurate database of all writers and articles. To complete the interface, she needs to complete the frmQueries form and remove the Exit to Issue25 command button from the switchboard. Elena has a fundamental understanding of Access macros and the Visual Basic language and now can tackle more ambitious database projects for Vision Publishers.

Quick Check

1 What is the difference between a variable and a constant?

2 How many times would the following loop be executed?

```
For MyCounter = 2 To 11 Step 3
```

3 What is a method?

4 What is the Boolean data type?

5 What is the Variant data type?

Tutorial Assignments

Elena completes the modifications to the Issue25 graphical user interface.

Start Access and open the Issue25 database in the Tutorial folder on your Student Disk.

1. Elena's CapOnlyFirst function will change names like joAnn and deYoung to Joann and Deyoung. Figure 4-27 shows the CapFirstLetter function, which correctly changes names like joAnn and deYoung to JoAnn and DeYoung. Add the CapFirstLetter function to the basIssue25Functions module and create event procedures for the Last Name and First Name fields' AfterUpdate events for the Writers Column Form.

Figure 4-27

```
Public Function CapFirstLetter(FValue)
   'Capitalize only the first letter of a field value;
   'Leave unchanged all other letters.
   CapFirstLetter = UCase(Left(FValue, 1)) & Mid(FValue, 2)
End Function
```

2. Create the procedures for the frmQueries form dialog box. Highlighting a query name in the list box and clicking the left command button opens the query in the Print Preview window (use the OpenQuery action, the parameter value A_PREVIEW, and name the CBF function PreviewQuery). Double-clicking a query name in the list box or highlighting a query name and then clicking the middle command button opens the query results (use the OpenQuery action, the parameter value A_NORMAL, and name the CBF function DisplayQueryResults). Be sure to create an event procedure for the form's Load event to highlight the top query name in the list box.

3. Now that you have completed the frmSwitchboard form, remove the Exit to Issue25 command button from the form, remove the Exit to Issue25 button from the custom toolbar, and remove the Exit to Issue25 menu item from the Stop menu on the custom menu bar.
4. To retain a secured way of closing the frmSwitchboard form and activating the Database window for the Issue25 database, create an AutoKeys macro to assign to the F2 key the same actions that the Exit to Issue25 options used to have. (See the "assigning Macros" topic in Access online Help for the key assignment macro search value.) Reposition the form's controls so that the form has a professional look, and test the form.

Case Problems

1. Walkton Daily Press Carriers Robin Witkop creates a new form to help in identifying carriers who have positive balances for their routes.

Start Access and open the Press database in the Cases1 folder on your Student Disk.

1. Create a form based on the Carriers Sorted by Name and Route ID Query. Display the Carrier Last Name, Carrier First Name, Route ID, and Balance fields.
2. Add the message "Carrier Has a Positive Balance" above the Balance field. Use a Fore Color value of yellow for the message and make the message font bold. Display the message only when the Balance field value is greater than zero. Display the Balance field value in black when no message appears and in the same color as the message otherwise.
3. Save the form as frmCarriersBalance Form.

2. Lopez Lexus Dealerships Hector Lopez modifies the Cars Data form to highlight the most profitable cars in the Lopez Lexus inventory.

Start Access and open the Lexus database in the Cases1 folder on your Student Disk.

1. To the Cars Data form, add the message "BIG PROFIT" to the right of the Year field. Use a Fore Color value of red for the message and be sure the message font is bold and italic.
2. Resize the Location field-value text box so that it is just wide enough to display the location code.
3. Beneath the "BIG PROFIT" message, on the same line as Location field, display the profit amount (difference between the Selling Price and Cost field values). Use the same Fore Color and font effects for the profit amount as for the message. Display the message and the profit amount only when the profit amount is greater than $5,000. You may need to resize the form to complete this.

3. Tophill University Student Employment Olivia Tyler asks Lee Chang to create a form that highlights jobs that have a large number of hours per week or that pay a high weekly wage.

Start Access and open the Parttime database in the Cases2 folder on your Student Disk.

1. Create a form based on the Weekly Wage Query. Show all fields in the form. Add the message "High Hours" to the right of the Hours/Week field value and the message "High Wages" to the right of the Weekly Wage field value.
2. Use a Fore Color value of red for the messages and be sure the message font is bold.
3. Display the first message when the Hours/Week field value is greater than 18 and the second message when the Weekly Wage field value is greater than $140.00.
4. Save the form as frmHigh Hours/Wages.

4. Rexville Business Licenses Chester Pearce creates a new form to highlight the most expensive business licenses issued and to display a message indicating that the fees should be collected quickly.

Start Access and open the Buslic database in the Cases2 folder on your Student Disk.

1. Create a form based on the Businesses Sorted by License Type and Business Name Query. Display the message "Collect NOW!" to the right of the Basic Cost field. Use a Fore Color value of red for the message and make the message font bold. Display the message only when the Basic Cost field value is greater than or equal to $100.
2. Display the Basic Cost field value with a Fore Color value of black when no message appears and in the same color as the message otherwise.
3. Save the form as frmCollections.

ADDITIONAL CASE 1

Company Financial Information by FINSTAT Inc.

OBJECTIVES

In this case you will:

- Change field properties
- Add a table and add relationships between tables
- Create select, parameter, and crosstab queries
- Create a form using the Form Wizard
- Create custom forms
- Create custom reports
- Prepare a chart
- Design and create a switchboard
- Add macros and event procedures

CASE

FINSTAT Inc.

When Pat Mitchell graduated from a prestigious business college she had her pick of job offers. Employers could see from her internship record and her grades that she was a bright, ambitious worker who would be an asset to their company. Pat had always dreamed of being her own boss, however, so after careful market analysis and planning she founded FINSTAT Inc., an electronic information service that markets financial information to its clients. Since the time Pat started her company, competing vendors have begun to appear on the market offering similar databases of financial information.

Pat and her team of financial analysts are now realizing that to remain competitive, their products must supply current and complete data. Also their clients must be able to access the data effortlessly and with as many options as possible. Pat decides to take the current databases she has and upgrade them with ease of use in mind. Her most successful database contains recent financial statement data on several of the leading U.S. corporations. She starts her new campaign by reorganizing the financial statement information to make it more accessible, and then designing an interface that is easier for clients to use.

Pat's corporation database currently consists of two tables, tblCompany and tblFinance. Figure 1 shows the structure of the tblCompany table, which stores general data about each company. The tblCompany table contains an ID number and name for each company, a code classifying the company's industry, and a symbol that uniquely identifies the company on the stock exchange and in financial publications.

Figure 1 Structure of the tblCompany table

Field Name	Data Type	Properties
Company ID	Text	Field Size–3 Input Mask–>LOO Caption–Company ID
Company Name	Text	Field Size–30 Caption–Company Name
Industry	Text	Field Size–2 Input Mask–>LL
Symbol	Text	Field Size–6

Figure 2 shows the structure of the tblFinance table, which tracks the yearly financial data for each company. The tblFinance table contains the same ID numbers used in the tblCompany table and contains additional data on the sales, assets, and profits for each company for a given year, 1995 or later.

Figure 2 Structure of the tblFinance table

Field Name	Data Type	Properties
Company ID	Text	Field Size–3 Input Mask–>LOO Caption–Company ID
Year	Number	Field Size–Integer
Sales	Currency	Description–Rounded to the nearest million. Decimal Places–0
Assets	Currency	Description–Rounded to the nearest million. Decimal Places–0
Profits	Currency	Description–Rounded to the nearest million. Decimal Places–0

Pat wants to create a new customized version of the database so that clients can choose information more easily. She formulates the following plan: she will modify the field properties in the tblCompany and tblFinance tables, add a table for industry codes and descriptions, add relationships for the three tables, and create and save four queries. She will then create the form shown in Figure 3 using the Form Wizard. This new form makes it easier for both her own staff and her clients to add current financial data to the database.

Figure 3 ◀ The tblCompany-Finance form created by the Form Wizard

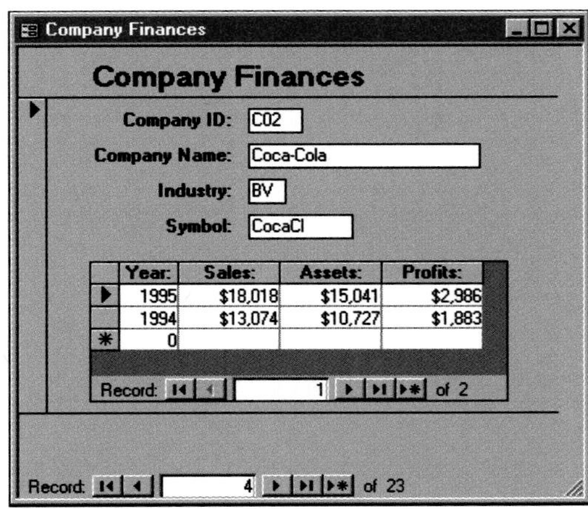

Pat plans to create a custom form, shown in Figure 4, that uses all three tables to display a company's financial information, a year at a time. Calculations are included on this form for the company's rate of return and profit margin.

Figure 4 ◀ Custom frmAnnual-Financials form

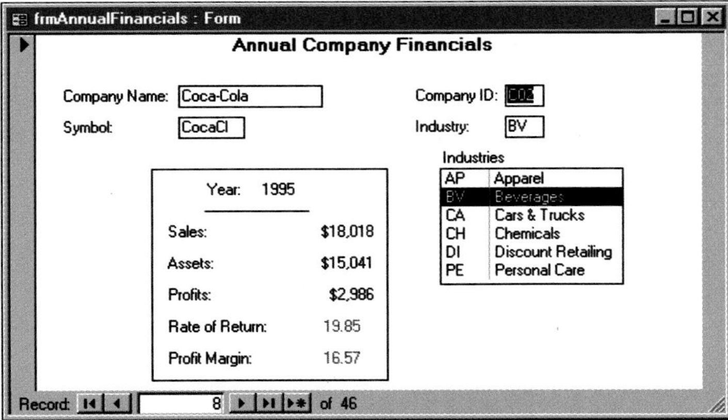

Next, Pat plans to create two reports that are easy to generate and are of presentation quality. The first report, shown in Figure 5, groups companies by industry and provides industry and overall totals. The second report, shown in Figure 6, summarizes sales, assets, and profits by industry.

Figure 5 Custom rptIndustry 1995 report

FINSTAT

Financial Analysis for 1995

Industry: Apparel

Company Name	Sales	Assets	Profits
Reebok International	$3,481	$1,669	$165
Nike	$5,594	$3,411	$492
Liz Claiborne	$2,082	$1,331	$127
Fruit of the Loom	$2,403	$2,920	($227)
Industry Total	$13,560	$9,331	$557

Industry: Beverages

Company Name	Sales	Assets	Profits
Coca-Cola	$18,018	$15,041	$2,986
PepsiCo	$30,421	$25,452	$1,606
Anheuser-Busch	$10,341	$11,535	$887
Industry Total	$58,780	$52,028	$5,479

Industry: Cars & Trucks

Company Name	Sales	Assets	Profits
Chrysler	$53,200	$53,756	$2,121
Ford Motor	$137,137	$243,300	$4,139
General Motors	$168,829	$217,100	$6,932
Industry Total	$359,166	$514,156	$13,192

Industry: Chemicals

Company Name	Sales	Assets	Profits
du Pont	$42,163	$37,312	$3,293
Monsanto	$8,962	$10,611	$739
Dow Chemical	$20,200	$23,582	$1,891
Industry Total	$71,325	$71,505	$5,923

Industry: Discount Retailing

Company Name	Sales	Assets	Profits
J.C. Penney	$21,658	$17,287	$838
Home Depot	$15,470	$7,137	$731
Wal-Mart Stores	$93,627	$37,871	$2,740
Kmart	$34,389	$17,087	($490)
Sears, Roebuck	$34,925	$33,000	$1,025
Toys "R" US	$9,022	$8,437	$464
Industry Total	$209,091	$120,819	$5,308

Industry: Personal Care

Company Name	Sales	Assets	Profits
Procter & Gamble	$34,923	$28,215	$2,835
Colgate-Palmolive	$8,358	$7,705	$172
Avon Products	$4,492	$2,053	$286
Gillette	$6,795	$6,340	$823
Industry Total	$54,568	$44,313	$4,116
Overall Total	$766,490	$812,152	$34,575

Figure 6 Custom rptIndustry 1995Summary report

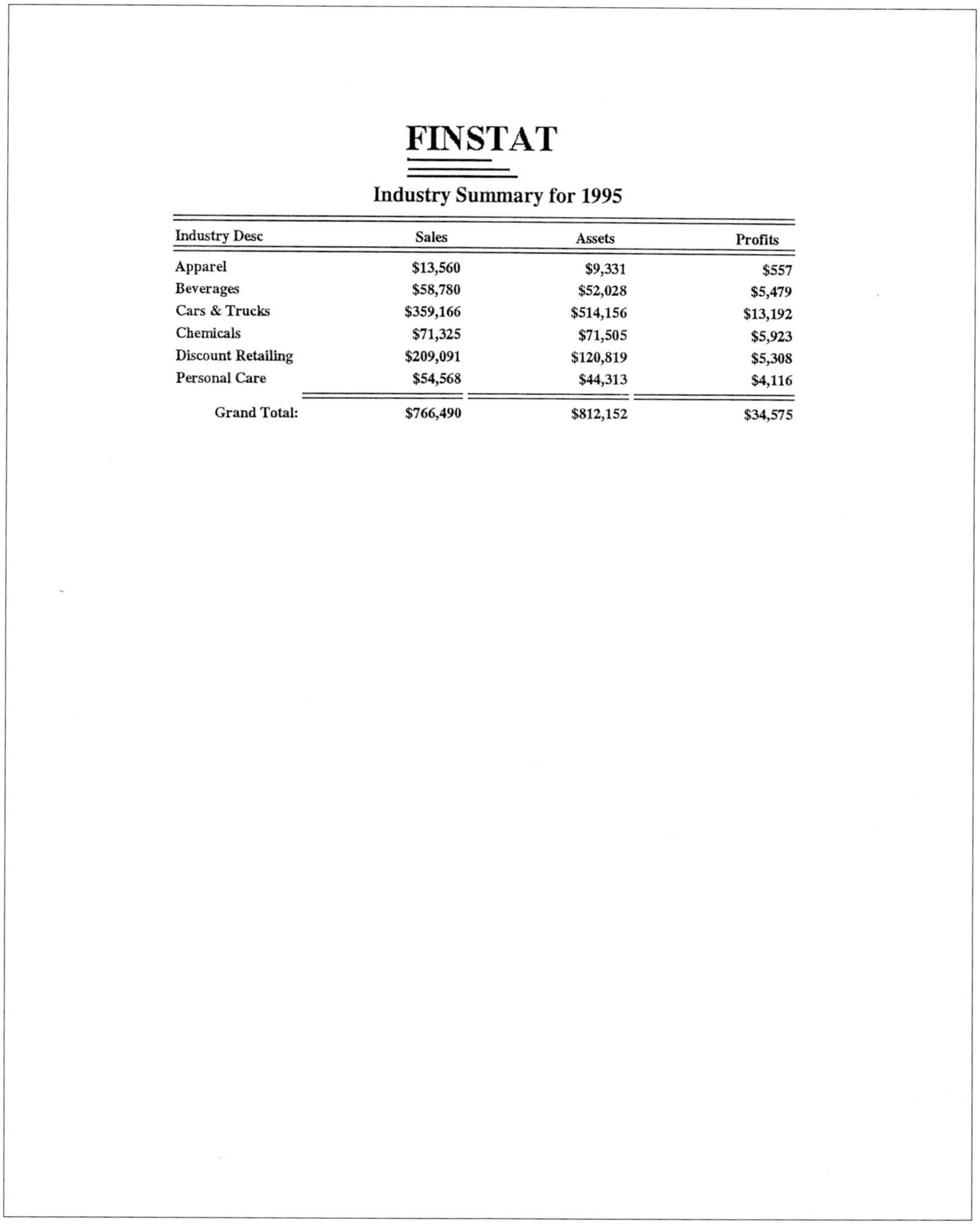

FINSTAT

Industry Summary for 1995

Industry Desc	Sales	Assets	Profits
Apparel	$13,560	$9,331	$557
Beverages	$58,780	$52,028	$5,479
Cars & Trucks	$359,166	$514,156	$13,192
Chemicals	$71,325	$71,505	$5,923
Discount Retailing	$209,091	$120,819	$5,308
Personal Care	$54,568	$44,313	$4,116
Grand Total:	$766,490	$812,152	$34,575

After creating a crosstab query showing the profits by company name and by year, and a bar chart showing average sales and average profits by year, Pat plans to design and create a switchboard, set the startup options, and create an event procedure for one of the new forms. Figure 7 shows the switchboard Pat eventually creates.

Figure 7 The FINSTAT database switchboard

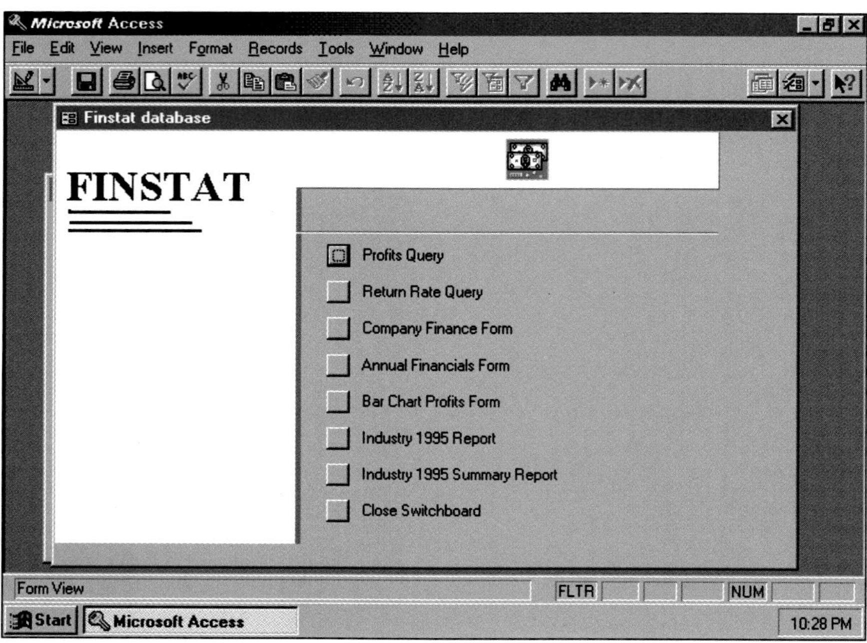

Complete the following to create the customized database:

1. Place your Student Disk in the appropriate drive, start Access, and open the Finstat database in the AddCases folder on your Student Disk.
2. Review the tblCompany and tblFinance tables to become familiar with their structures and datasheet contents. If you are unfamiliar with any property setting, use the Access Help system for an explanation of that property.
3. For the tblCompany table, make Company Name a required field and make Company ID the primary key. For the tblFinance table, add a validation rule for the Year field to allow values greater than or equal to 1994, add an appropriate validation-text message, and make the combination of Company ID and Year the primary key. Finally, add a one-to-many relationship between the primary tblCompany table and the related tblFinance table using Company ID as the common field and enforcing referential integrity.
4. The tblCompany table contains the Industry field, which stores a two-character industry code. The acceptable industry codes and associated industry descriptions are: AP (Apparel), BV (Beverages), CA (Cars & Trucks), CH (Chemicals), DI (Discount Retailing), PE (Personal Care). Design and create a new table to store the industry codes and industry descriptions, using the field names Industry and Industry Desc and making Industry the primary key. Name this table tblIndustry and add the six industry records to the table. Add a one-to-many relationship between the primary tblIndustry table and the related tblCompany table using the two-character industry code as the common field and enforcing referential integrity. Print the six records from the tblIndustry table.

5. Create and save a query with the name qryProfits that displays the Company ID, Company Name, Year, Industry Desc, Sales, and Profits fields for all companies with sales above 4000 and profits above 300. Print the query results in ascending order by profits.
6. For all companies, display Company Name, Sales, Assets, Profits, and Rate of Return for the year 1995. Calculate Rate of Return by dividing Profits by Assets (format Rate of Return as a percent with one decimal place). Print the query results in descending order by Rate of Return and save the query with the name qryReturnRate.
7. For all companies, display Company ID, Company Name, Industry, Symbol, Year, Sales, Assets, Profits, Rate of Return, and Profit Margin. Calculate Rate of Return by dividing Profits by Assets and then multiplying by 100. Calculate Profit Margin by dividing Profits by Sales and then multiplying by 100. For both Rate of Return and Profit Margin, use a fixed format with two decimal places. Print the query results in ascending order by Company Name as the primary sort key and Year as the secondary sort key and save the query with the name qryCompany.
8. Create and save a parameter query with the name qryProfitsParameter that displays the Company Name, Symbol, Sales, Assets, Profits, and Industry fields for companies during 1995 in a selected industry (use Industry as the parameter). Print the query results in ascending order by Profits using the parameter value PE.
9. Use the Form Wizard to create the form shown in Figure 3. Use the tblCompany and tblFinance tables, save the subform with the name frmSubFinance and the main/subform form with the name frmCompanyFinance, and print the first record.

10. Create the custom form shown in Figure 4 and save it with the name frmAnnualFinancials. Use the qryCompany query as the basis for the form, position label boxes and text boxes as shown in Figure 4, add a list box to display data from the tblIndustry table, and draw a rectangle around the financial information. Use the Border Style property to remove the boxes from the financial text boxes. Print the first and last records of the custom form.

11. Create a query using the tblCompany, tblFinance, and tblIndustry tables to select all the financial records for the year 1995. Refer to Figure 5 to determine which fields to include in the query and which fields to use as sort keys. Name and save the query as qryIndustry1995. Then create the custom report shown in Figure 5, using the qryIndustry1995 query as the basis for the report, save it with the name rptIndustry1995, and print the report. (Note: The FINSTAT logo at the top of the report is stored as finlogo.bmp in the AddCases folder on your Student Disk.)
12. Create the Industry Summary for 1995 report shown in Figure 6. Base the report on the qryIndustry1995 query. Save the report with the name rptIndustry1995Summary. Print the report. (*Hint:* Use the previous report as a guide, but include only summary information for this report.)
13. Create a crosstab query showing the profits by industry by year. Base the query on the qryIndustry1995 query. Save the query with the name qryProfitCrosstab, and print the query results.

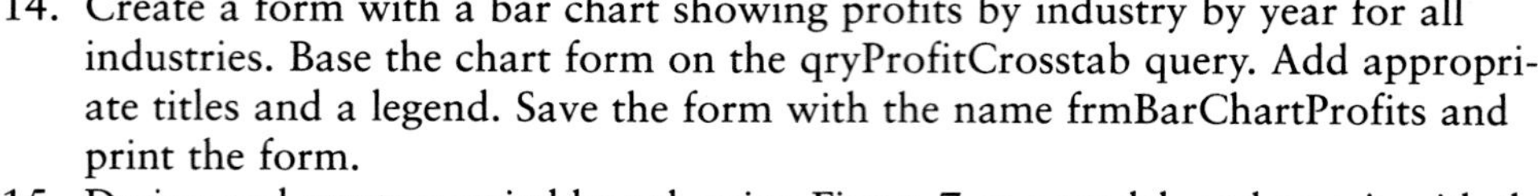

14. Create a form with a bar chart showing profits by industry by year for all industries. Base the chart form on the qryProfitCrosstab query. Add appropriate titles and a legend. Save the form with the name frmBarChartProfits and print the form.

15. Design and create a switchboard, using Figure 7 as a model, and save it with the name frmSwitchboard. Provide appropriate wording for the title bar and a heading at the top center of the switchboard. Add the finmoney.bmp graphic image from your Student Disk to an appropriate location on the switchboard. On the switchboard, place eight command buttons to perform the following actions:
    - Open the qryProfits query
    - Open the qryReturnRate query
    - Open the frmCompanyFinance form
    - Open the frmAnnualFinancials form
    - Open the frmBarChartProfits form
    - Open the rptIndustry1995 report
    - Open the rptIndustry1995Summary report
    - Close the switchboard and activate the Database window

    Create a macro group for these command buttons. Use appropriate background and foreground colors and visual effects for the switchboard and its components, and size and position the switchboard in the Form View window. Test the switchboard.

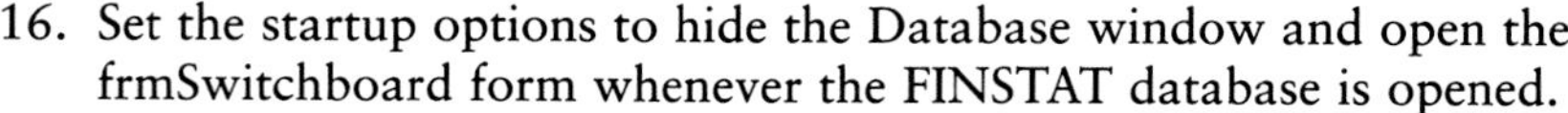

16. Set the startup options to hide the Database window and open the frmSwitchboard form whenever the FINSTAT database is opened.

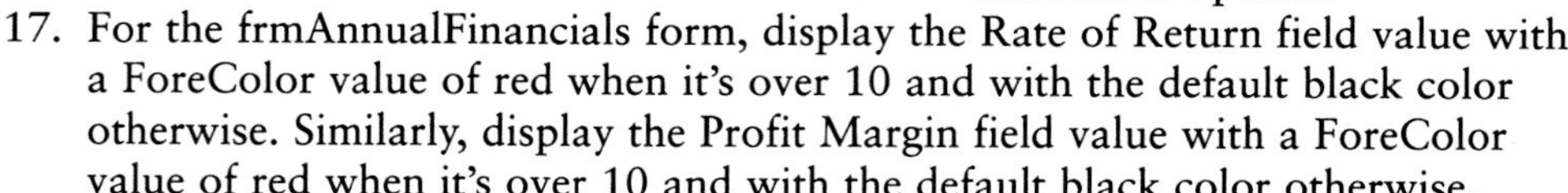

17. For the frmAnnualFinancials form, display the Rate of Return field value with a ForeColor value of red when it's over 10 and with the default black color otherwise. Similarly, display the Profit Margin field value with a ForeColor value of red when it's over 10 and with the default black color otherwise.

ADDITIONAL CASE 2

Customer Orders for Pet Provisions

OBJECTIVES

In this case you will:

- Create select queries
- Create a form using the Form Wizard
- Create custom forms
- Create custom reports
- Design and create a switchboard

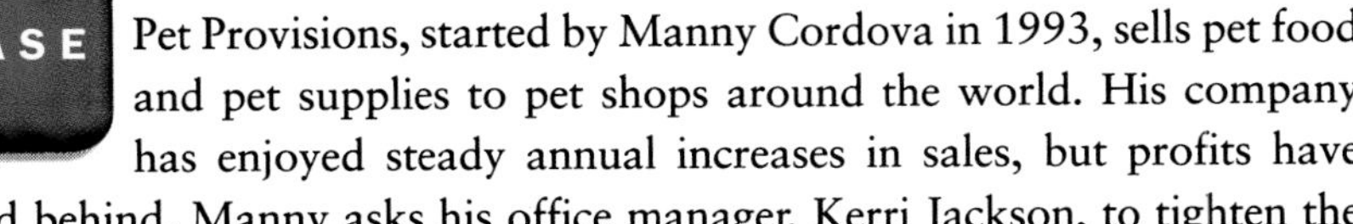

Pet Provisions

Pet Provisions, started by Manny Cordova in 1993, sells pet food and pet supplies to pet shops around the world. His company has enjoyed steady annual increases in sales, but profits have lagged behind. Manny asks his office manager, Kerri Jackson, to tighten the company's collection methods as a first step in improving profits.

Currently the office maintains an Access database that contains information on its customers. After looking over the database, Kerri realizes that there is no easy way to tell which client accounts are paid in full and which have outstanding balances. She decides to create the necessary forms, queries, and reports to automate the collection process. Her work will include creating an all-important invoice report that she can automatically generate to send to any client with an outstanding balance.

Kerri uses the Access Pet database as the starting point for her work. Among the tables in the Pet database are the tblCustomer and tblOrder tables. Figure 8 shows the structure for the tblCustomer table, which contains one record for each customer. Customer Num is the primary key for the table, which has 26 customer records. The other fields in the table are Customer Name, Street, City, State/Prov, Zip/Postal Code, Country, Phone, and First Contact.

Figure 8 Structure of the tblCustomer table

Field Name	Data Type	Properties
Customer Num	Number	Primary Key Field Size–Integer Format–Fixed Decimal Places–0 Caption–Customer Num Required–Yes
Customer Name	Text	Field Size–35 Caption–Customer Name
Street	Text	Field Size–30
City	Text	Field Size–20
State/Prov	Text	Field Size–20
Zip/Postal Code	Text	Field Size–10 Caption–Zip/Postal Code
Country	Text	Field Size–20
Phone	Text	Field Size–15
First Contact	Date/Time	Format–m/d/yy Caption–First Contact

Figure 9 shows the structure for the tblOrder table, which contains one record for each customer order. Order Num is the table's primary key. Customer Num is a foreign key in the tblOrder table, and the tblCustomer table has a one-to-many relationship with the tblOrder table.

Figure 9 ◀ Structure of the tblOrder table

Field Name	Data Type	Properties
Order Num	Number	Primary Key Field Size–Integer Format–Fixed Decimal Places–0 Caption–Order Num Required–Yes
Customer Num	Number	Field Size–Integer Format–Fixed Decimal Places–0 Caption–Customer Num Required–Yes Foreign Key
Sale Date	Date/Time	Format–m/d/yy Caption–Ship Via
Ship Via	Text	Field Size–7 Caption–Ship Via
Total Invoice	Number	Field Size–Double Format–Standard Decimal Places–2 Caption–Total Invoice
Amount Paid	Number	Field Size–Double Format–Standard Decimal Places–2 Caption–Amount Paid
Pay Method	Text	Field Size–5 Caption–Pay Method

Kerri plans to create special queries, forms, and reports to help her analyze the 144 orders in the tblOrder table. One of the special forms, shown in Figure 10, displays all orders for a customer along with totals for the customer's invoices, amount paid, and amount owed. Kerri also creates a special report, shown in Figure 11, that she can send to customers owing money to Pet Provisions.

Figure 10 The frmCustomer-WithOrders form

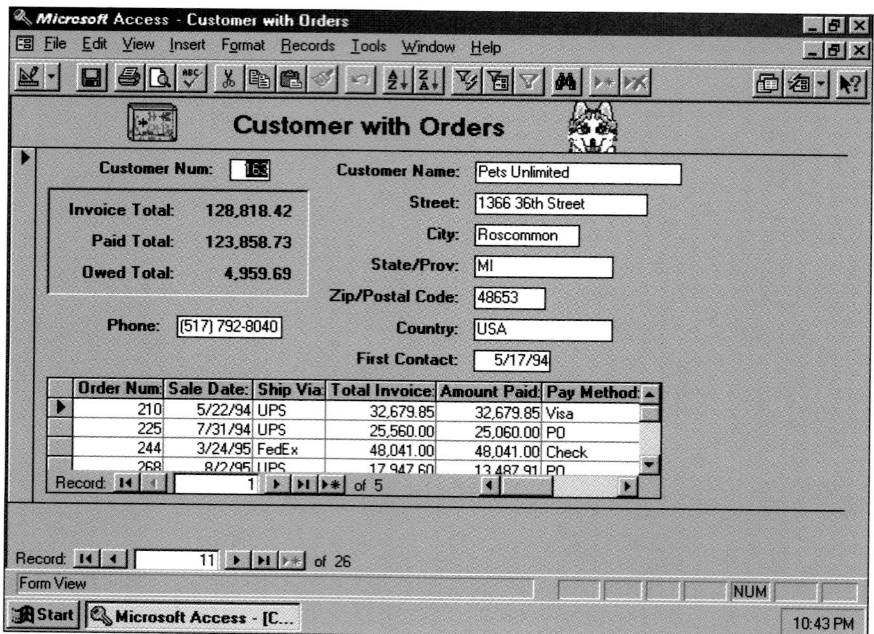

Figure 11 Custom rptCustomer-Statement report

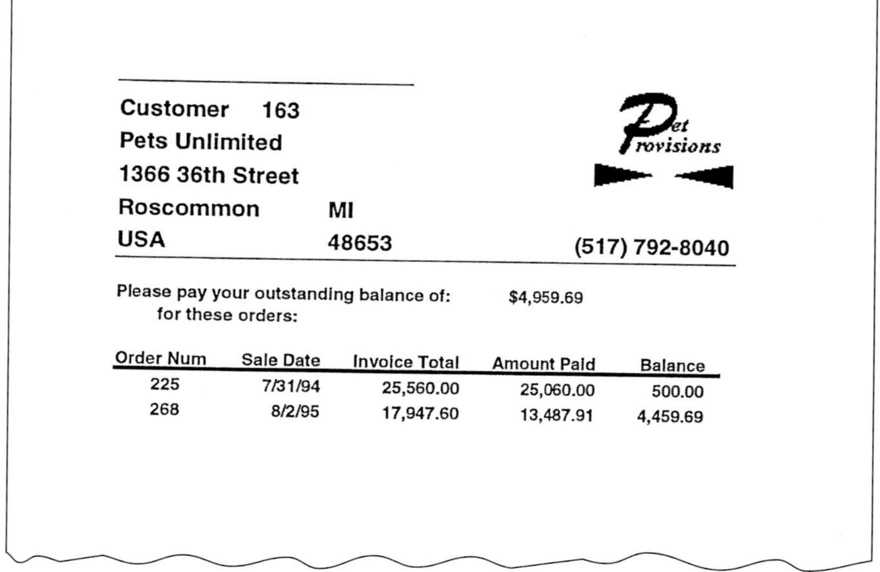

Customer 163
Pets Unlimited
1366 36th Street
Roscommon MI
USA 48653 (517) 792-8040

Pet Provisions

Please pay your outstanding balance of: $4,959.69
for these orders:

Order Num	Sale Date	Invoice Total	Amount Paid	Balance
225	7/31/94	25,560.00	25,060.00	500.00
268	8/2/95	17,947.60	13,487.91	4,459.69

Complete the following to analyze profits at Pet Provisions:

1. Place your Student Disk in the appropriate drive, start Access, and open the Pet database in the AddCases folder on your Student Disk.
2. Review the tblCustomer and tblOrder tables to become familiar with their structures and datasheet contents. If you are unfamiliar with any property settings, use the Access Help system for an explanation of that property.
3. Create and save a query with the name qryOrderTotals that displays the grand total number of orders and grand totals for the Total Invoice, Amount Paid, and Amount Owed fields. Amount Owed, a calculated field, is the difference between the Total Invoice and Amount Paid fields. Print the query results.
4. For all orders that have not been paid in full, display the Customer Name, Phone, Sale Date, Total Invoice, Amount Paid, and Amount Owed. Print the query results in descending order by Amount Owed and save the query with the name qryOpenOrders.
5. For all orders that have not been paid in full, create and save a query with the name qryOwedByCustomer that displays the total number of orders and totals for the Total Invoice, Amount Paid, and Amount Owed fields, grouped by Customer Name. Print the query results. (*Hint:* Use the qryOpenOrders query as the basis for this query. The query contains five columns, including one for the Customer Name field.)
6. Use the Form Wizard to create a form to maintain all fields in the tblCustomer table and a second form to maintain all fields in the tblOrder table. Save the forms with the names frmCustomer and frmOrder, respectively. Use the forms to print the first record from each table.
7. Create and save two special queries that will be used with the special form shown in Figure 10. For the first query, use the tblOrder table to display totals for the Total Invoice, Amount Paid, and Amount Owed fields, grouping by Customer Num and using the column names Invoice Total, Paid Total, and Owed Total, respectively. Save the query with the name qryCustomerOrderTotals and print the query results. For the second query, use the qryCustomerOrderTotals query and the tblCustomer table; display the Customer Num, Invoice Total, Paid Total, Owed Total, Customer Name, Street, City, State/Prov, Zip/Postal Code, Country, Phone, and First Contact fields; and sort in ascending order by Customer Num. Save the query with the name qryCustomerWithTotals and print the query results.

8. Create the custom form shown in Figure 10 and save it with the name frmCustomerWithOrders. Create an initial approximation of the form using the qryCustomerWithTotals query for the main form. Using the Subform/subreport tool in the toolbox, place a subform based on the tblOrder table. Select all the fields from the tblOrder table. Save the subform with the name frmSubOrder. Then change the form so that it looks similar to the form shown in Figure 10. Use the Border Style property to remove the boxes from the three text boxes between the Customer Num and Phone boxes. Print the first record of the custom form. (*Note:* The bitmaps that appear on the top of the form are stored as petfish.bmp and petdog.bmp on your Student Disk.)

9. Create and save a query with the name qryForSpecialReport that selects customers who owe money to Pet Provisions and unpaid orders for these customers. Refer to Figure 11 to determine which fields to include in the query. (*Hint:* Use the qryCustomerWithTotals query and the tblOrder table to create this query, create a join line between the Customer Num fields, and sort in ascending order by Customer Num as the primary sort key and Order Num as the secondary sort key.) Then create the custom report shown in Figure 11, using the qryForSpecialReport query as the basis for the report, using a Group

Header section based on Customer Num, and placing orders in the Detail section. Set the Force New Page property in the Group Header section to the value Before Section so that one customer statement is printed per page. Save the report with the name rptCustomerStatement and print pages six to eight of the report. (*Note:* The logo in the upper-right of the report is stored as petlogo.bmp on your Student Disk.)

10. Design and create a switchboard with frmSwitchboard as the saved form name. Place command buttons on the switchboard to coordinate the running of these three forms, three queries, and one report, that is, frmCustomer, frmOrder, frmCustomerWithOrders, qryOpenOrders, qryOrderTotals, qryOwedByCustomer, and rptCustomerStatement. Also provide a command button to close the switchboard and return to the Database window.

ADDITIONAL CASE 3

Internship Program for Pontiac College

OBJECTIVES

In this case you will:

- Design a database and draw its entity-relationship diagram
- Create the tables and relationships for the database
- Create forms to maintain the database
- Design and enter test data for the database
- Create queries and reports from the database
- Design and create a switchboard

CASE

Pontiac College

Pontiac College provides students with opportunities for professional development and field study through its internship program which is administered by the Office of Internships and Field Experience. Students complement their courses with a structured training experience provided by qualified professionals in selected fields. Internships are offered in many different areas, including law, counseling, government, administration, public relations, communications, health care, computer programming, and marketing.

Anjali Bhavnani has just been hired as Pontiac's new Internship Coordinator. She is eager to make information about the sponsoring agencies, potential internships, and current student interns more readily available to her office and to the students who qualify for the program. Anjali's most ambitious project is to develop a computerized database for the internship program to help meet these goals.

Instead of visually scanning all internship possibilities, Anjali, her staff, and interested students will be able to select internships of specific interest to them. The new database will allow potential interns to view only the internships that meet the criteria they specify. Anjali asks Roula Mendes, an information systems major working in the Office of Internships and Field Experience, to help the office develop a computerized database system for the internship system.

Anjali first outlines the steps in the internship program process for Roula:

- Identify and document the available internships
- Arrange for student intern placements
- Assign and track student interns

As the first step in the internship program process, Anjali receives a letter or phone call from a potential sponsoring agency. After some discussions, a sponsoring agency proposes an internship possibility and fills out the Agency/Internship Information form, shown in Figure 12 (Anjali's office currently maintains this form on a word processor).

Figure 12 The Agency/Internship Information form

AGENCY/INTERNSHIP INFORMATION

AGENCY INFORMATION

NAME OF AGENCY ______________________

DEPARTMENT ______________________

ADDRESS ______________________
Street

____
City State Zip

CONTACT ______________ PHONE ______________

INTERNSHIP INFORMATION

TITLE ______________________

DESCRIPTION OF DUTIES ______________________

ORIENTATION & TRAINING ______________________

ACADEMIC BACKGROUND REQUIRED ______________________

SUPERVISOR ______________ PHONE ______________

Office Use

Agency ID ________

Internship ID ________

Category ________

Many agencies offer more than one type of internship possibility. For each possible internship, the agency fills out a separate form and assigns one person as the contact for all internship questions and problems. In addition, each internship lists a supervisor who will work with the student intern. The internship remains active until the agency notifies the Internship Office that the internship is filled or no longer available.

Anjali assigns a three-digit Agency ID to each new agency and a four-digit Internship ID to each new internship. These are sequential numbers. She also classifies each internship into a category that helps students identify internships that are related to their major or interests. A student might be interested for example, in health care, accounting, social service, or advertising.

A copy of each Agency/Internship Information form is placed in reference books in the Office of Internships and Field Experience. Students browse through these books to find internships that are of interest to them. If an internship interests a student, the student copies the information about the internship and contacts the sponsoring agency directly to request an interview.

When a student gets an internship, the student and agency establish a Learning Contract, outlining the goals to be accomplished during the internship. The student then fills out the Student Internship form, shown in Figure 13, to provide basic information on the student for the office files.

Figure 13 The Student Internship form

STUDENT INTERNSHIP

NAME ______________________ SS# __________

ADDRESS ______________________________
Street
____
City State ZIP

PHONE __________

MAJOR __________ GPA ______ CLASS ___ Junior _____ Senior

Office Use
Internship ID __________
Internship Term ___ Fall ___ Spring ___ Summer
Internship Year __________

Anjali enters the Internship ID and year on the Student Internship form and checks the term for the internship. Next, a clerk enters information from the form into a word processor to prepare lists of current interns and internships and then places the form in a binder.

Anjali and Roula determine that getting these two forms into an on-line Access database is their first priority, and then they will work on creating several new reports. The first report, the design of which is shown in Figure 14, lists all student interns, alphabetically by last name, for a selected term. In order to identify the student interns who should be included in the report, the system prompts the user for the term and year.

Figure 14 Student Interns report design

<today's date> **Student Interns** Page x
As of <term><year>

Last Name	First Name	Agency Name	Internship Title
X_____________X	X_________X	X___________________X	X______________X
X_____________X	X_________X	X___________________X	X______________X
X_____________X	X_________X	X___________________X	X______________X
X_____________X	X_________X	X___________________X	X______________X

End of Report

A second new report, the design of which is shown in Figure 15, lists all agencies in the database alphabetically by agency name.

Figure 15 Internship Agencies report design

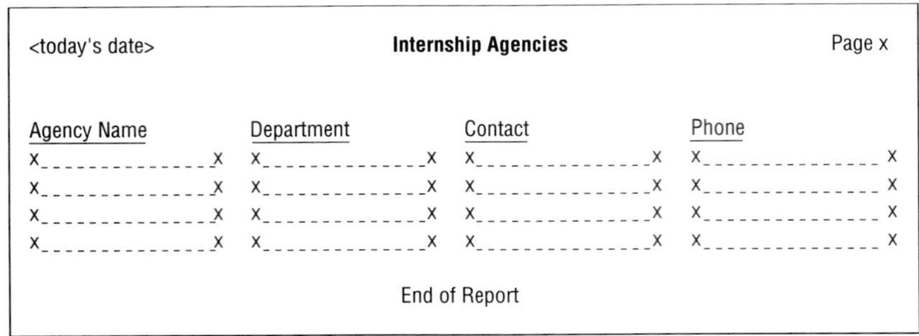

<today's date>
Internship Agencies
Page x
Agency Name
Department
Contact
Phone
End of Report

The Internship by Category report, the design of which is shown in Figure 16, lists internships grouped by category. The staff will use this report when talking with students about the internship program.

Figure 16 Internship by Category report design

<today's date> **Internship by Category** Page x

Category x__________x

Internship ID	Internship Title	Internship Description
xxxx	x_______________x	x________________________________x
		x________________________________x
		x________________________________x
xxxx	x_______________x	x________________________________x
xxxx	x_______________x	x________________________________x
		x________________________________x

Category x__________x

Internship ID	Internship Title	Internship Description
xxxx	x_______________x	x________________________________x
xxxx	x_______________x	x________________________________x
		x________________________________x
		x________________________________x

End of Report

At the end of an internship, the intern's supervisor evaluates the intern's work experience, using an evaluation form mailed from the Office of Internships and Field Experience. Anjali needs mailing labels addressed to the supervisor of each intern for the current term and year. The mailing labels should contain the supervisor name on the first line; the agency name on the second line; the agency's street on the third line; and the agency's city, state, and zip on the fourth line.

Complete the following to create the complete database system:

1. Identify each entity (relation) in the database for the internship system.
2. Draw an entity-relationship diagram showing the entities and the relationships between the entities.
3. Design the database for the internship system. For each relation, list the fields and their attributes, such as data types, field sizes, and validation rules. Place the set of relations in third normal form and identify all primary, alternate, and foreign keys.
4. Create the database structure using Access and the database name Intern. Be sure to add relationships between appropriate tables.
5. Create and save forms to maintain data on agencies, internships, student interns, and any other entity in your database structure. The forms should be used to view, add, edit, and delete records in the database.
6. Create test data for each table in the database, and add it, using the forms created in Step 5.
7. Create and save the Student Interns report, Internship Agencies report, Internship by Category report, and mailing labels report. The layouts shown in Figures 14 through 16 are guides—improve the formats as you see fit.
8. Design, create, and save a form that a student can use to view internships for a selected category. Display one internship at a time on the screen. For each internship, display the category, internship ID, title, description of duties, orientation and training, academic background, agency name, department, agency address, contact name, and contact phone. Provide an option to print the internship displayed on the screen.
9. Design, create, and save a switchboard to coordinate the running of the internship system. (*Note:* Two graphic images, intmatch.bmp and inttrack.bmp, are available on your Student Disk for use on the switchboard or the form created in Step 8.)
10. Test all features of the internship system.

REFERENCE 1

Microsoft Access 7 Menu Commands

Menus Without an Open Database

File Menu Commands (No Open Database)

New Database Creates a new database.
Open Database Opens an existing database.
Toolbars Shows, hides, or customizes the toolbars.
Unhide Shows a hidden window.
[File Name] Displays the four most recently opened files; select any one to open it.
Exit Exits the application.

Tools Menu Commands (No Open Database)

Database Utilities Converts, compacts, or repairs a database.
Security Adds or removes users from a group or makes a database readable only to Access.
Macro Runs the macro.
Custom Controls Registers or unregisters the custom controls.
Options Customizes the Microsoft Access environment.

Help Menu Commands (No Open Database)

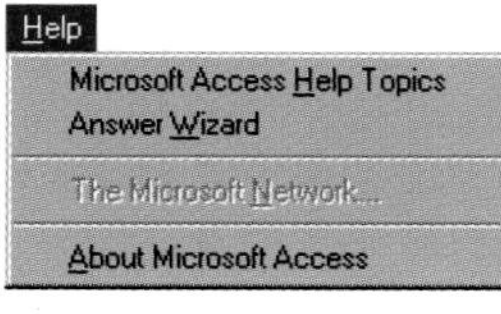

Microsoft Access Help Topics Displays Help topics.
Answer Wizard Locates Help topics based on an entered question or request.
The Microsoft Network Connects to a desired forum on The Microsoft Network.
About Microsoft Access Displays the version number and system information.

Database View Menu Commands

File Menu Commands (Database View)

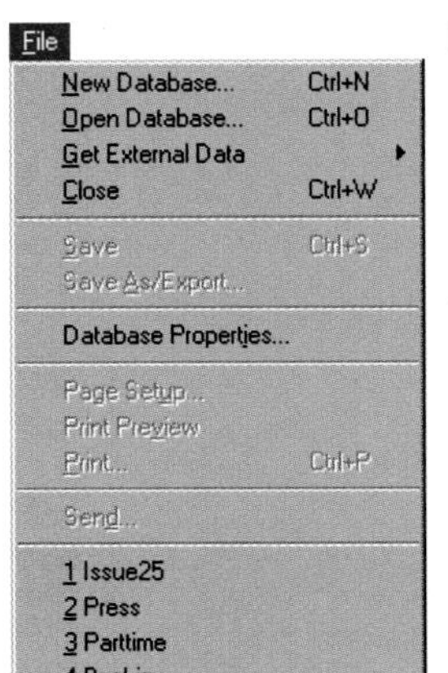

New Database Creates a new database.
Open Database Opens an existing database.
Get External Data Imports from or links to an external source.
Close Closes the current database.
Save Saves the active document.
Save As/Export Saves the active document with a new name or exports to another file.
Database Properties Views the properties of the database.
Page Setup Sets page properties and/or selects or changes printer settings.
Print Preview Displays the document as it will look when printed.
Print Prints the document.
Send Sends the output of the current object by mail.
[File Names] Displays the four most recently opened files; select any one to open it.
Exit Exits the application.

Edit Menu Commands (Database View)

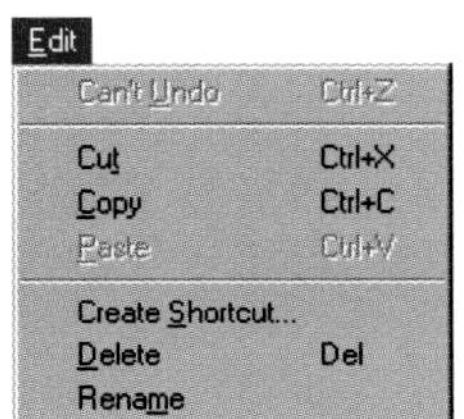

Undo/Can't Undo Undoes the most recent change.
Cut Deletes the selected item and copies it to the Clipboard.
Copy Copies the selected item to the Clipboard.
Paste Inserts item from the Clipboard.
Create Shortcut Creates a shortcut object.
Delete Deletes selection without copying onto the Clipboard.
Rename Renames the selected database object.

View Menu Commands (Database View)

Database Objects Views a list of tables, queries, forms, reports, macros, or modules.
Large Icons Views database objects using large icons.
Small Icons Views database objects using small icons.
List Displays database objects in a list.
Details Views database objects in detail.
Arrange Icons Sorts database objects by name, type, date created, last modified date, or automatically arranges the objects.
Line up Icons Arranges icons in a grid.
Properties Views the properties of the database objects.
Code Opens the module window.
Toolbars Shows, hides, or customizes the toolbars.

Insert Menu Commands (Database View)

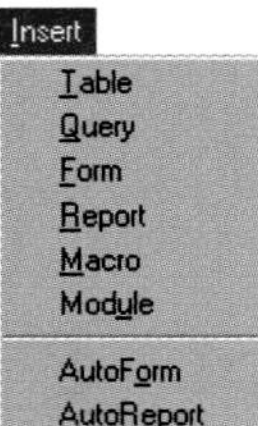

Table Creates a new table.
Query Creates a new query.
Form Creates a new form.
Report Creates a new report.
Macro Creates a new macro.
Module Creates a new module.
AutoForm Automatically creates a simple form based on the selected table or query.
AutoReport Automatically creates a simple report based on the selected table or query.

Tools Menu Commands (Database View)

Spelling Checks the spelling.
AutoCorrect Sets the AutoCorrect options.
OfficeLinks Merges or views the current object as a Microsoft Excel file or as a Microsoft Word file.
Relationships Creates and edits relationships between tables.
Analyze Splits your table into related tables or makes performance suggestions or documents the database objects.
Security Sets the password of the current database or assigns permissions to users/groups or adds/removes users from a group or sets up permission levels for each user.
Replication Synchronizes/creates replica of selected database or resolves conflicts or designates the current replica as the design master.
Startup Pops up a database property sheet.
Macro Runs the macro.
Custom Controls Registers or unregisters custom controls.
Add-ins Displays a list of additional options you can make available for use during a session.
Options Customizes the Microsoft Access environment.

Window Menu Commands (Database View)

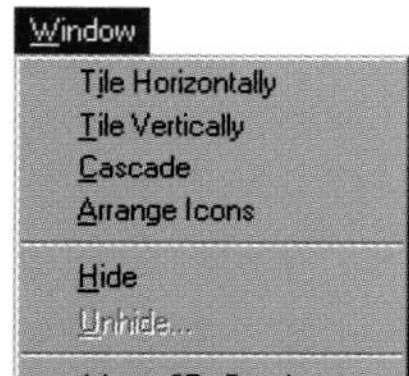

Tile Horizontally Arranges all open windows in a horizontal tile format.
Tile Vertically Arranges all open windows in a vertical tile format.
Cascade Arranges all open windows in a cascading format.
Arrange Icons Arranges minimized windows.
Hide Hides the active window.
Unhide Shows a hidden window.

Help Menu Commands (Database View)

Same as Help Menu Commands in No Open Database View

Datasheet View Menu Commands

File Menu Commands (Table Datasheet View)

Same as File Menu Commands in Database View

Edit Menu Commands (Table Datasheet View)

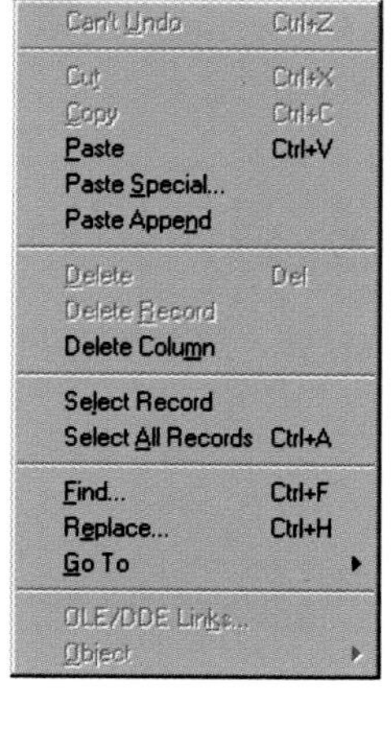

Undo/Can't Undo Undoes the most recent change.
Cut Deletes the selected item and copies it to the Clipboard.
Copy Copies the selected item to the Clipboard.
Paste Inserts item from the Clipboard.
Paste Special Inserts contents of Clipboard in a specific format.
Paste Append Appends contents of Clipboard.
Delete Deletes selection without copying onto the Clipboard.
Delete Record Deletes the current record.
Delete Column Deletes the selected column and all data it contains.
Select Record Selects the current record.
Select All Records Selects all records.
Find Finds the specified text.
Replace Finds and replaces the specified text.
Go To Goes to the first, last, next, previous, or new record at the end of the datasheet.
OLE/DDE Links Updates, modifies, or deletes links in selected object or field.
Object Edits the selected object.

View Menu Commands (Table Datasheet View)

Table Design Displays the table in Design view.
Datasheet Displays the document in Datasheet view.
Toolbars Shows, hides, or customizes the toolbars.

Insert Menu Commands (Table Datasheet View)

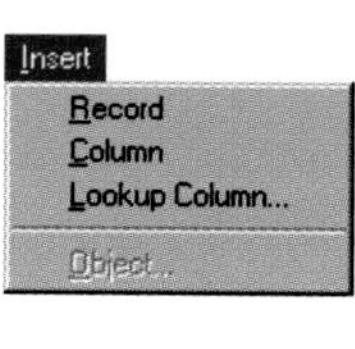

Record Moves to the new record at the end of the datasheet or form.
Column Inserts a new column.
Lookup Column Starts the lookup wizard.
Object Inserts a new embedded object.

Format Menu Commands (Table Datasheet View)

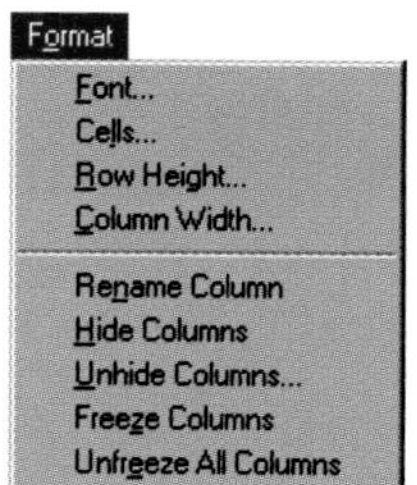

Font Sets the font for the datasheet.
Cells Formats the cells.
Row Height Sets the row height for the datasheet.
Column Width Sets the width of the current or selected column(s).
Rename Column Renames the selected column.
Hide Columns Hides current or selected column(s).
Unhide Columns Specifies columns to show or hide.
Freeze Columns Freezes current or selected column(s).
Unfreeze All Columns Unfreezes all columns.

Records Menu Commands (Table Datasheet View)

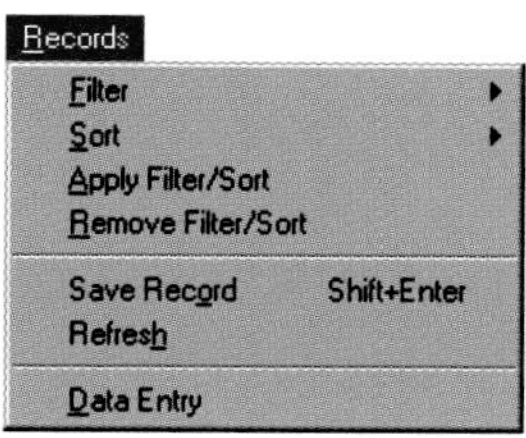

Filter Filters the data by using your form, selected criteria, or specific filter.
Sort Sorts the data in ascending or descending order.
Apply Filter/Sort Applies the filter and sort criteria.
Remove Filter/Sort Removes the filter and requeries the underlying records.
Save Record Saves the current record to the database.
Refresh Updates the data on the screen to show other users' changes.
Data Entry Hides current records and adds new ones.

Tools Menu Commands (Table Datasheet View)

Same as Tools Menu Commands in Database View

Window Menu Commands (Table Datasheet View)

Same as Window Menu Commands in Database View

Help Menu Commands (Table Datasheet View)

Same as Help Menu Commands in No Open Database View

Table Design View Menu Commands

File Menu Commands (Table Design View)

Same as File Menu Commands in Database View

Edit Menu Commands (Table Design View)

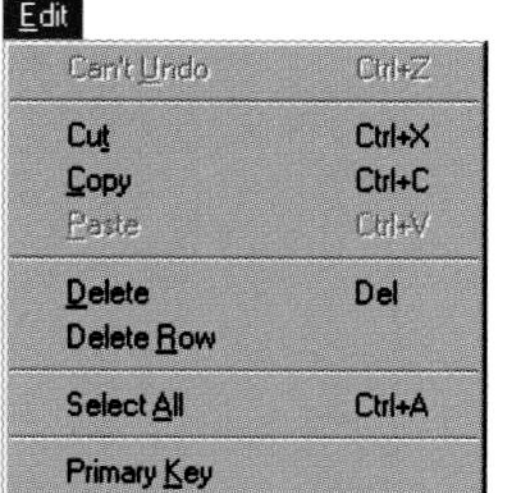

Undo/Can't Undo Undoes the most recent change.
Cut Deletes the selected item and copies it to the Clipboard.
Copy Copies the selected item to the Clipboard.
Paste Inserts item from the Clipboard.
Delete Deletes selection without copying onto the Clipboard.
Delete Row Deletes the current row.
Select All Selects all fields.
Primary Key Designates the selected column(s) as the primary key.
Test Validation Rules Tests existing data against the validation rules.

View Menu Commands (Table Design View)

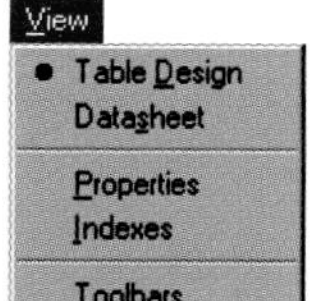

Table Design Displays the table in Design view.
Datasheet Displays the document in Datasheet view.
Properties Opens or closes the property sheet for the selected item.
Indexes Views and edits indexes.
Toolbars Shows, hides, or customizes the toolbars.

Insert Menu Commands (Table Design View)

Field Inserts a row above the current row.
Lookup Field Starts the Lookup Wizard.

Tools Menu Commands (Table Design View)

Same as Tools Menu Commands in Database View

Window Menu Commands (Table Design View)

Same as Window Menu Commands in Database View

Help Menu Commands (Table Design View)

Same as Help Menu Commands in No Open Database View

Query Datasheet View Menu Commands

File Menu Commands (Query Datasheet View)

Same as File Menu Commands in Database View

Edit Menu Commands (Query Datasheet View)

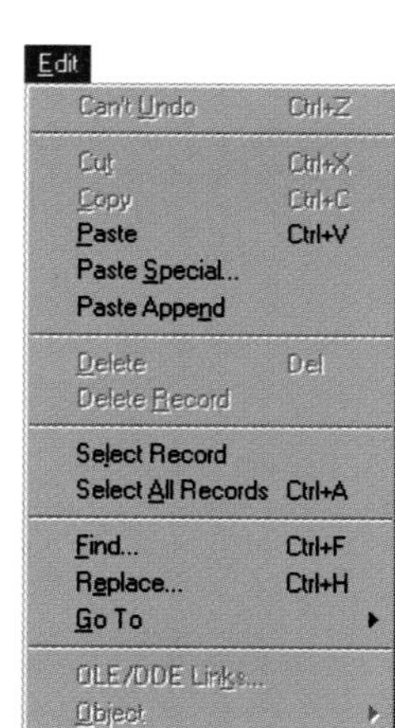

Undo/Can't Undo Undoes the most recent change.
Cut Deletes the selected item and copies it to the Clipboard.
Copy Copies the selected item to the Clipboard.
Paste Inserts item from the Clipboard.
Paste Special Inserts contents of Clipboard in specific format.
Paste Append Appends contents of the Clipboard.
Delete Deletes selection without copying onto the Clipboard.
Delete Record Deletes the current record.
Select Record Selects the current record.
Select All Records Selects all records.
Find Finds the specified text.
Replace Finds and replaces the specified text.
Go To Goes to the first, last, next, previous, or new record at the end of the datasheet.
OLE/DDE Links Updates, modifies, or deletes links in selected object or field.
Object Edits the selected object.

View Menu Commands (Query Datasheet View)

Query Design Displays the query in Design view.
SQL Displays the query in SQL view.
Datasheet Displays the document in Datasheet view.
Toolbars Shows, hides, or customizes the toolbars.

Insert Menu Commands (Query Datasheet View)

Record Moves to the new record at the end of the datasheet or form.
Object Edits the selected objects.

Format Menu Commands (Query Datasheet View)

Font Sets the font for the datasheet.
Cells Formats the cells.
Row Height Sets the row height for the datasheet.
Column Width Sets the width of the current or selected column(s).
Hide Columns Hides the current or selected column(s).
Unhide Columns Specifies the columns to show or hide.
Freeze Columns Freezes the current or selected column(s).
Unfreeze All Columns Unfreezes all columns.

Records Menu Commands (Query Datasheet View)

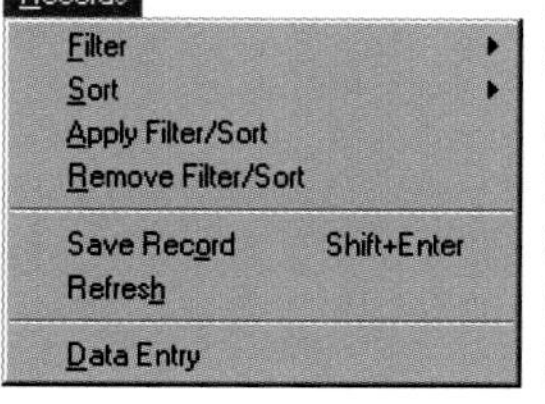

Filter Filters the data by using your form, selected criteria, or specific filter.
Sort Sorts the data in ascending or descending order.
Apply Filter/Sort Applies the filter and sort criteria.
Remove Filter/Sort Removes the filter and requeries the underlying records.
Save Record Saves the current record to the database.
Refresh Updates the data on the screen to show other users' changes.
Data Entry Hides the current records and adds new ones.

Tools Menu Commands (Query Datasheet View)

Same as Tools Menu Commands in Database View

Window Menu Commands (Query Datasheet View)

Same as Window Menu Commands in Database View

Help Menu Commands (Query Datasheet View)

Same as Help Menu Commands in No Open Database View

Query Design or SQL View Menu Commands

File Menu Commands (Query Design or SQL View)

Same as File Menu Commands in Database View

Edit Menu Commands (Query Design or SQL View)

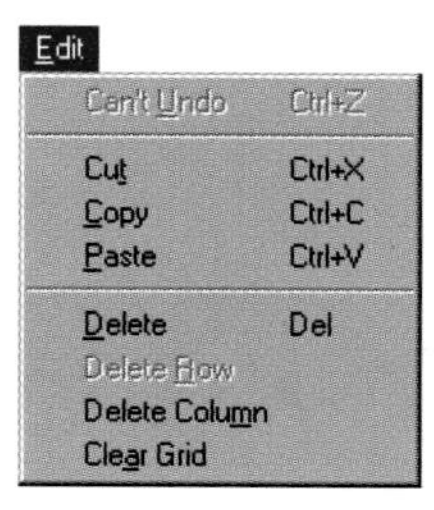

Undo/Can't Undo Undoes the most recent change.
Cut Deletes the selected item and copies it to the Clipboard.
Copy Copies the selected item to the Clipboard.
Paste Inserts the item from the Clipboard.
Delete Deletes the selection without copying onto the Clipboard.
Delete Row Deletes the current row.
Delete Column Permanently deletes the selected column and all its data.
Clear Grid Clears the contents of query design grid.

View Menu Commands (Query Design or SQL View)

Query Design Displays the query in Design view.
SQL Displays the query in SQL view.
Datasheet Displays the query in Datasheet view.
Totals Shows or hides the totals section of the query.
Table Names Shows or hides the table names section of the query.
Properties Sets the query properties.
Join Properties Sets the type of join.
Toolbars Shows, hides, or customizes the toolbars.

Insert Menu Commands (Query Design or SQL View)

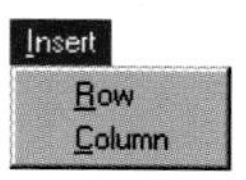

Row Inserts a row before the current or selected row in the query design grid.
Column Inserts a new column.

Query Menu Commands (Query Design or SQL View)

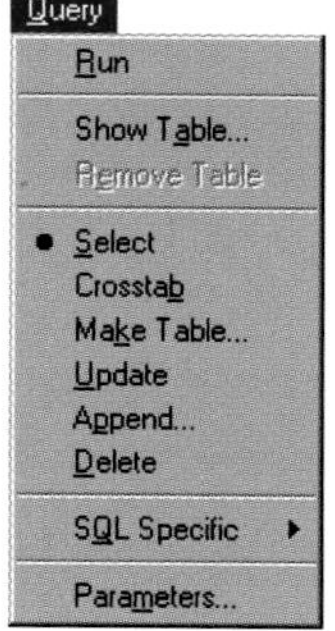

Run Runs the query.
Show Table Includes another table in the query.
Remove Table Removes the selected table from the query.
Select Makes the query a select query.
Crosstab Makes the query a crosstab query.
Make Table Makes the query a make-table query.
Update Makes the query an update query.
Append Makes the query an append query.
Delete Makes the query a delete query.
SQL Specific Makes the query a union, SQL pass-through, or data definition query.
Parameters Makes the query a parameter query.

Tools Menu Commands (Query Design or SQL View)

Same as Tools Menu Commands in Database View

Window Menu Commands (Query Design or SQL View)

Same as Window Menu Commands in Database View

Help Menu Commands (Query Design or SQL View)

Same as Help Menu Commands in No Open Database View

Form Datasheet or Form View Menus

File Menu Commands (Form Datasheet or Form View)

Same as File Menu Commands in Database View

Edit Menu Commands (Form Datasheet or Form View)

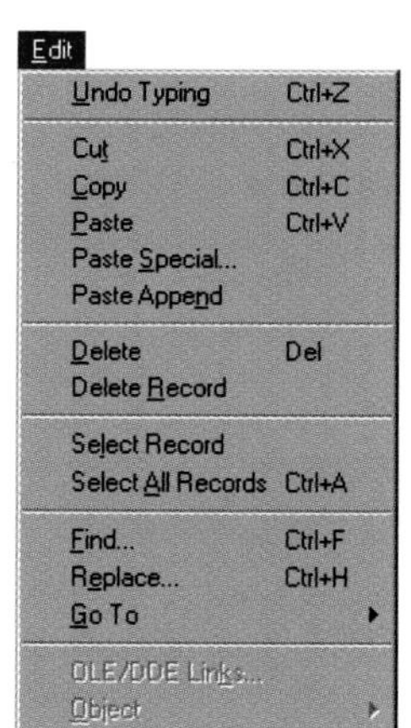

Undo/Can't Undo Undoes the most recent change.
Cut Deletes the selected item and copies it to the Clipboard.
Copy Copies the selected item to the Clipboard.
Paste Inserts an item from the Clipboard.
Paste Special Inserts contents of Clipboard in specific format.
Paste Append Appends contents of the Clipboard.
Delete Deletes selection without copying onto the Clipboard.
Delete Record Deletes the current record.
Select Record Selects the current record.
Select All Records Selects all records.
Find Finds the specified text.
Replace Finds and replaces the specified text.
Go To Goes to the first, last, next, previous, or new record at the end of the datasheet.
OLE/DDE Links Updates, modifies, or deletes links in selected object or field.
Object Edits the selected object.

View Menu Commands (Form Datasheet or Form View)

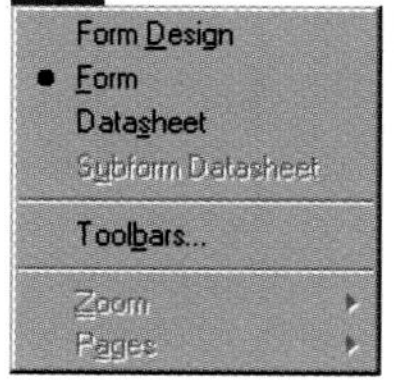

Form Design Displays the form in Design view.
Form Displays the form in Form view.
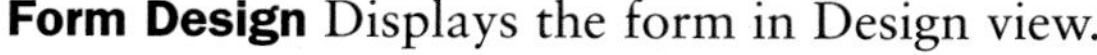
Datasheet Displays the document in Datasheet view.
Subform Datasheet Displays the subform in Datasheet view.
Toolbars Shows, hides, or customizes the toolbars.

Insert Menu Commands (Form Datasheet or Form View)

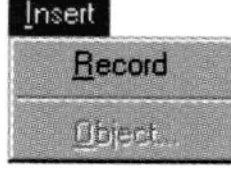

Record Moves to the new record at the end of the datasheet or form.
Object Inserts a new embedded object.

Format Menu Commands (Form Datasheet or Form View)

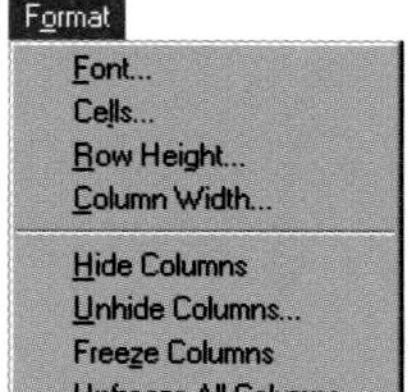

Font Sets the font for the datasheet.
Cells Formats the cells.
Row Height Sets the row height for the datasheet.
Column Width Sets the width of the current or selected column(s).
Hide Columns Hides current or selected column(s).
Unhide Columns Specifies the columns to show or hide.
Freeze Columns Freezes the current or selected column(s).
Unfreeze All Columns Unfreezes all columns.

Records Menu Commands (Form Datasheet or Form View)

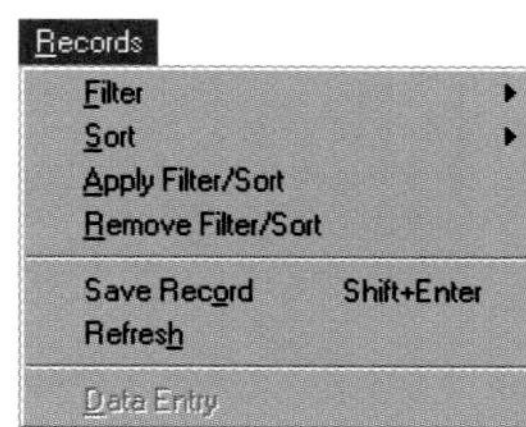

Filter Filters the data by using your form, selected criteria, or specific filter.
Sort Sorts the data in ascending or descending order.
Apply Filter/Sort Applies the filter and sort criteria.
Remove Filter/Sort Removes the filter and requeries the underlying records.
Save Record Saves the current record to the database.
Refresh Updates the data on the screen to show other users' changes.
Data Entry Hides the current records and adds new ones.

Tools Menu Commands (Form Datasheet or Form View)

Same as Tools Menu Commands in Database View

Window Menu Commands (Form Datasheet or Form View)

Same as Window Menu Commands in Database View with this exception:
Size to fit form In form view, sizes the window to fit the form.

Help Menu Commands (Form Datasheet or Form View)

Same as Help Menu Commands in No Open Database View

Form Design View Menus

File Menu Commands (Form Design View)

Same as File Menu Commands in Database View

Edit Menu Commands (Form Design View)

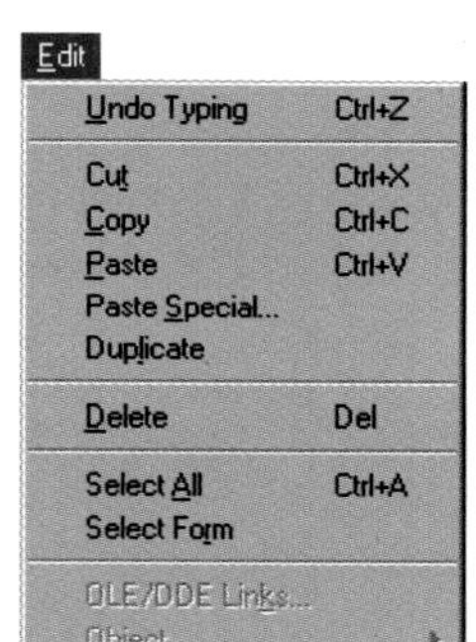

Undo/Can't Undo Undoes the most recent change.
Cut Deletes the selected item and copies it to the Clipboard.
Copy Copies the selected item to the Clipboard.
Paste Inserts an item from the Clipboard.
Paste Special Inserts the contents of the Clipboard in a specific format.
Duplicate Duplicates the selected control.
Delete Deletes selection without copying onto the Clipboard.
Select All Selects all Controls on form or report.
Select Form Selects form or report.

View Menu Commands (Form Design View)

Form Design Displays the form in Design view.
Form Displays the form in Form view.
Datasheet Displays the document in Datasheet view.
Properties Opens or closes the property sheet for the selected item.
Field List Opens or closes a list of fields you can drag to your form or report.
Tab Order Changes the tab order of the controls.
Code Opens the Module window.
Ruler Shows or hides the ruler.
Grid Shows or hides the grid.
Toolbox Opens or closes the toolbox used to create the controls.
Page Header/Footer Adds or removes the page header and footer.
Form Header/Footer Adds or removes the form header and footer.
Toolbars Shows, hides, or customizes the toolbars.

Insert Menu Commands (Form Design View)

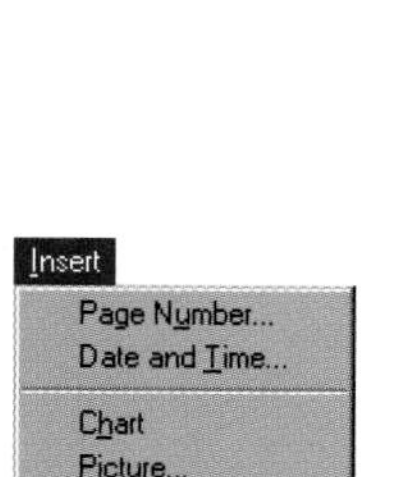

Page Number Inserts a page number control.
Date and Time Inserts a date/time field.
Chart Inserts a new chart.
Picture Inserts a new picture.
Object Inserts a new embedded object.
Custom Control Inserts a new OLE custom control.

Format Menu Commands (Form Design View)

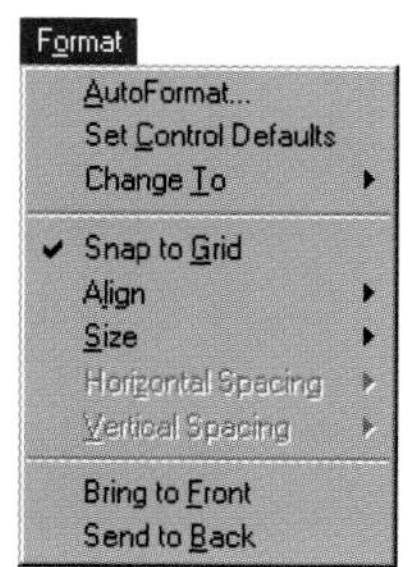

AutoFormat Applies a predefined form style.
Set Control Defaults Saves the property settings of the current selection as the defaults.
Change To Changes the control to a text box, label, list box, combo box, check box, toggle button, option button, or image.
Snap to Grid Turns the snap to grid behavior on or off.
Align Aligns the controls.
Size Resizes the controls.
Horizontal Spacing Equalizes and increases or decreases the horizontal spacing between selected controls.
Vertical Spacing Equalizes and increases or decreases the vertical spacing between selected controls.
Bring to Front Brings the selected control(s) to the front.
Send to Back Sends the selected control(s) to the back.

Tools Menu Commands (Form Design View)

Same as Tools Menu Commands in Database View

Window Menu Commands (Form Design View)

Same as Window Menu Commands in Database View

Help Menu Commands (Form Design View)

Same as Help Menu Commands in No Open Database View

Report Print Preview or Layout Preview View Menus

File Menu Commands (Report Print Preview or Layout Preview View)

Same as File Menu Commands in Database View

View Menu Commands (Report Print Preview or Layout Preview View)

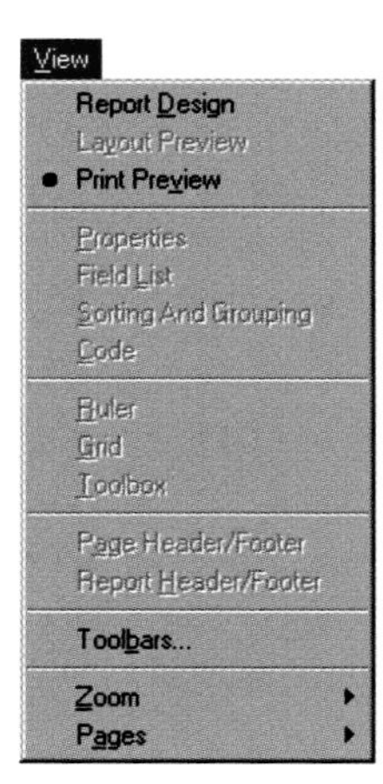

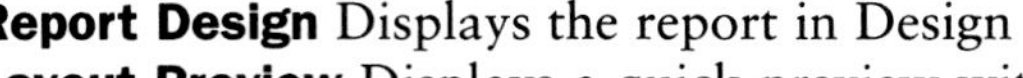

Report Design Displays the report in Design view.
Layout Preview Displays a quick preview with sample data.
Print Preview Displays the report as it will look when printed.
Properties Opens or closes the property sheet for the selected item.
Field List Opens or closes a list of fields you can drag to your form or report.
Sorting And Grouping Adds, deletes, or changes group levels.
Code Opens the Module window.
Ruler Shows or hides the ruler.
Grid Shows or hides the grid.
Toolbox Opens or closes the toolbox used to create the controls.
Page Header/Footer Adds or removes the page header and footer.
Report Header/Footer Adds or removes the report header and footer.
Toolbars Shows, hides, or customizes the toolbars.
Zoom Zooms in or out.
Pages Changes the number of previewed pages.

Tools Menu Commands (Report Print Preview or Layout Preview View)

Same as Tools Menu Commands in Database View

Window Menu Commands (Report Print Preview or Layout Preview View)

Same as Window Menu Commands in Database View

Help Menu Commands (Report Print Preview or Layout Preview View)

Same as Help Menu Commands in No Open Database View

Report Design View Menus

File Menu Commands (Report Design View)

Same as File Menu Commands in Database View

Edit Menu Commands (Report Design View)

Edit
Undo Typing Ctrl+Z
Cut Ctrl+X
Copy Ctrl+C
Paste Ctrl+V
Paste Special...
Duplicate
Delete Del
Select All Ctrl+A
Select Report
OLE/DDE Links...
Object

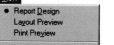

Undo/Can't Undo Undoes the most recent change.
Cut Deletes the selected item and copies it to the Clipboard.
Copy Copies the selected item to the Clipboard.
Paste Inserts item from the Clipboard.
Paste Special Inserts contents of Clipboard in specific format.
Duplicate Duplicates the selected control.
Delete Deletes selection without copying onto the Clipboard.
Select All Selects all controls on form or report.
Select Report Selects form or report.

View Menu Commands (Report Design View)

View
Report Design
Layout Preview
Print Preview
Properties
Field List
Sorting And Grouping
Code
Ruler
Grid
Toolbox
Page Header/Footer
Report Header/Footer
Toolbars...
Zoom
Pages

Report Design Displays the report in Design view.
Layout Preview Displays a quick preview with sample data.
Print Preview Displays the report as it will look when printed.
Properties Opens or closes the property sheet for the selected item.
Field List Opens or closes a list of fields you can drag to your form or report.
Sorting And Grouping Adds, deletes, or changes group levels.
Code Opens the module window.
Ruler Shows or hides the ruler.
Grid Shows or hides the grid.
Toolbox Opens or closes the toolbox used to create the controls.
Page Header/Footer Adds or removes the page header and footer.
Report Header/Footer Adds or removes the report header and footer.
Toolbars Shows, hides, or customizes the toolbars.
Zoom Zooms in or out.
Pages Changes the number of previewed pages.

Insert Menu Commands (Report Design View)

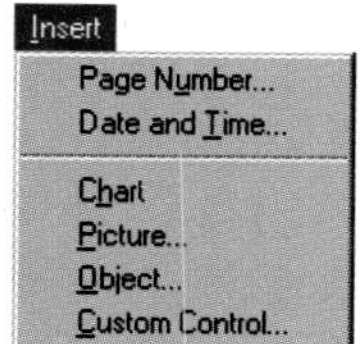

Page Number Inserts a page number control.
Date and Time Inserts a date/time field.
Chart Inserts a new chart.
Picture Inserts a new picture.
Object Inserts a new embedded object.
Custom Control Inserts a new OLE custom control.

Format Menu Commands (Report Design View)

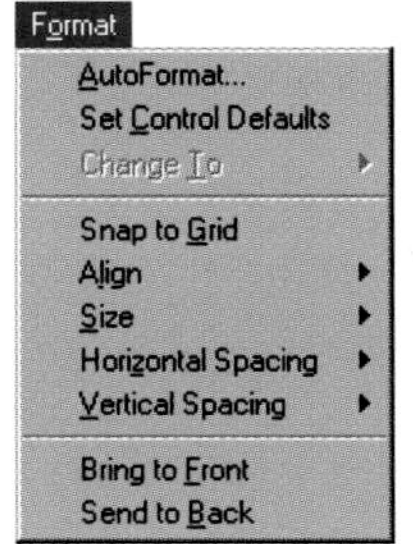

AutoFormat Applies a predefined form style.
Set Control Defaults Saves the property settings of the current selection as the defaults.
Change To Changes the control to a text box, label, list box, combo box, check box, toggle button, option button, or image.
Snap to Grid Turns the snap to grid behavior on or off.
Align Aligns the controls.
Size Resizes the controls.
Horizontal Spacing Equalizes and increases or decreases the horizontal spacing between selected controls.
Vertical Spacing Equalizes and increases or decreases the vertical spacing between selected controls.
Bring to Front Brings the selected control(s) to the front.
Send to Back Sends the selected control(s) to the back.

Tools Menu Commands (Report Design View)

Same as Tools Menu Commands in Database View

Window Menu Commands (Report Design View)

Same as Window Menu Commands in Database View

Help Menu Commands (Report Design View)

Same as Help Menu Commands in No Open Database View

Macro Design View Menu Commands

File Menu Commands (Macro Design View)

Same as File Menu Commands in Database View

Edit Menu Commands (Macro Design View)

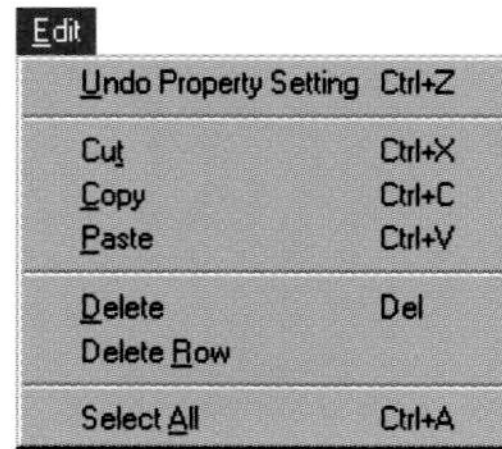

Undo/Can't Undo Undoes the most recent change.
Cut Deletes the selected item and copies it to the Clipboard.
Copy Copies the selected item to the Clipboard.
Paste Inserts item from the Clipboard.
Delete Deletes selection without copying onto the Clipboard.
Delete Row Deletes the current row.
Select All Selects all fields.

View Menu Commands (Macro Design View)

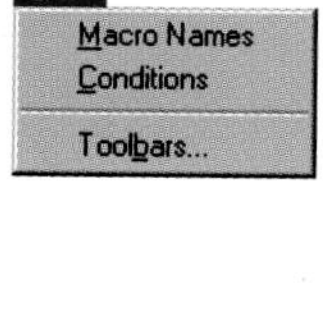

Macro Names Shows or hides the Macro Name column.
Conditions Shows or hides the Condition column.
Toolbars Shows, hides, or customizes the toolbars.

Insert Menu Commands (Macro Design View)

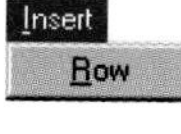

Row Inserts a row above the current row.

Run Menu Commands (Macro Design View)

Start Runs a specified macro.
Single Step Single steps through a macro when it runs.

Tools Menu Commands (Macro Design View)

Same as Tools Menu Commands in Database View

Window Menu Commands (Macro Design View)

Same as Window Menu Commands in Database View

Help Menu Commands (Macro Design View)

Same as Help Menu Commands in No Open Database View

Module Design View Menus

File Menu Commands (Module Design View)

Same as File Menu Commands in Database View

Edit Menu Commands (Module Design View)

Undo/Can't Undo Undoes the most recent change.
Redo/Can't Redo Redoes the last change to the text.
Cut Deletes the selected item and copies it to the Clipboard.
Copy Copies the selected item to the Clipboard.
Paste Inserts an item from the Clipboard.
Clear Deletes the selected text without copying it to the Clipboard.
Find Finds the specified text.
Replace Finds and replaces the specified text.
Indent Indents the currently highlighted command.
Outdent Outdents the currently highlighted command.

View Commands (Module Design View)

Procedure Definition Views the defined procedure.
Last Position Goes to the last position.
Object Browser Views members of an application's type library.
Debug Window Shows the Debug window.
Toolbars Shows, hides, or customizes the toolbars.

Insert Menu Commands (Module Design View)

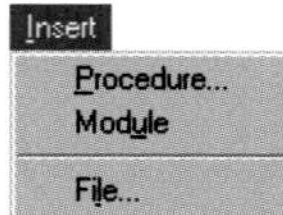

Procedure Inserts a procedure in the current module.
Module Creates a new module.
File Loads a file into the Module window.

Run Menu Commands (Module Design View)

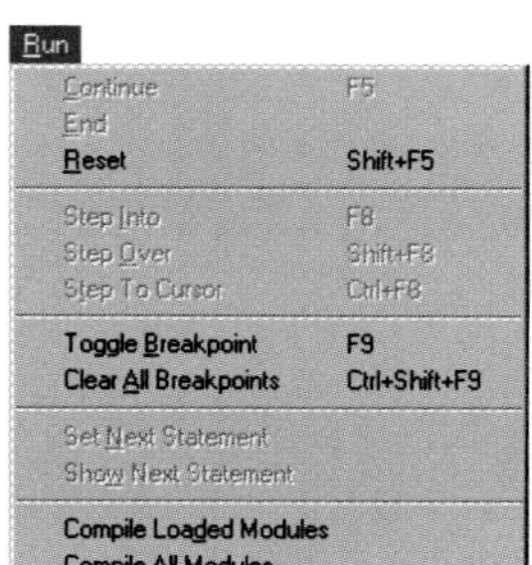

Continue Continues the execution.
End Terminates the Visual Basic execution state.
Reset Terminates the Visual Basic execution and clears all variables.
Step Into Single steps, steps into procedures.
Step Over Single steps, steps over procedures.
Step To Cursor Steps to the cursor.
Toggle Breakpoint sets the breakpoint on the current line.
Clear All Breakpoints Clears all breakpoints in all the modules.
Set Next Statement Sets the next statement to be executed.
Show Next Statement Shows the next statement to be executed.
Compile Loaded Modules Compiles all the loaded modules.
Compile All Modules Compiles all the modules in the database.

Tools Menu Commands (Module Design View)

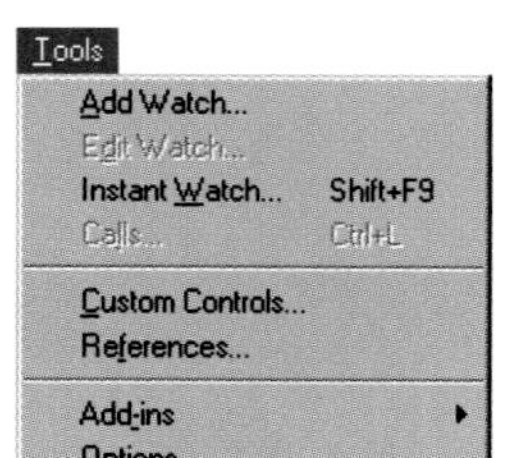

Add Watch Selects an expression to be monitored in the Debug window.
Edit Watch Edits an expression to be monitored in the Debug window.
Instant Watch Displays the Instant Watch dialog box, where the value of the expression is viewed.
Calls Views the procedure calls.
Custom Controls Registers or unregisters the custom controls.
References Adds references to the current project.
Add-ins Displays a list of additional options you can make available for use during a session.
Options Customizes the Microsoft Access environment.

Window Menu Commands (Module Design View)

Same as Window Menu Commands in Database View with this exception:
Split Window Splits the window to see two different parts of a module.

Help Menu Commands (Macro Design View)

Same as Help Menu Commands in No Open Database View with this exception:
Help on Keyword Displays help on the keyword selected.

R E F E R E N C E   2

Microsoft Access 7 Toolbar Buttons

This section contains descriptions of toolbar buttons that appear in this text, categorized by type. Some buttons may appear on more than one Access toolbar, but are only listed once here.

Edit Buttons

Removes selected object and places it on the Clipboard.
Creates a copy of the selection and places it on the Clipboard.
Inserts data from the Clipboard to the current location.
Creates and edits relationships between the database tables and queries.
Locates specified text.
Adds a new, empty row above the current row.
Removes the highlighted row from the database.
Reverses newest change.

File Buttons

Creates a new database.
Opens an existing database.
Creates a link to a table in an external source.
Prints the current document.
Shows how the document will look when printed.
Takes data from another Access database or a non-Access source into the current database.
Transfers data from an Access database to an external application.
Merges data with a Microsoft Word document.
Creates output and view of the current object as a Microsoft Excel file.
Makes a new query.
Makes a new form.
Makes a new report.
Generates a simple form based on the parameters of the current database table or query.
Generates a simple report based on the data of the current database table or query.
Saves the data and setup of the current database object to the database.
Selects and modifies the printer and print options.
Creates output and view of the current object as a Microsoft Word RTF file.
Creates a new table, query, form, report, macro, or module. Also can be used to generate a simple report or form.
Checks for spelling errors.

Analyzes table to split into related tables, if necessary.
Views the database objects using large icons.
Views the database objects using small icons.
Views the database objects in detail.
Views the database objects in a list format.

Form or Report Design Buttons

Displays the form in Datasheet view.
Opens the module window to create, edit, or view procedures.
Font Presents fonts available for text.
Pts Modifies the size of the text.
Selected Obje Selects the object.
Makes (removes) boldface from the selected text.
Makes (removes) italics from the selected text.
Makes (removes) underlines from the selected text.
Changes the text to be aligned along the left side.
Centers the text.
Changes the text to be aligned along the right side.
Opens or closes a list of fields you can drag to your form or report.
Shows how the report looks in a preview sample.
Modifies the sorting and grouping of the report.
Copies the appearance of one control or selection to another.
Formats a document automatically.
Opens a module window to create a Visual Basic module.
Changes the background color.
Chooses the color of the foreground or text.
Chooses the color of the border.
Selects the width of the border.
Utilizes special effects such as sunken, raised, etched, chiseled, shadowed, and flat.

Macro Design Buttons

Shows (hides) the Macro Name column.
Shows (hides) the Condition column of the macro.
Toggles single-stepping.

Module Design Buttons

Adds a new procedure to the module.
Stops procedures and clears all variables.
Creates (deletes) a line that will stop a procedure at that point to allow debugging.
Displays the Immediate window, which allows for the debugging and testing of Access procedures.
Compiles all loaded procedures in the current database.
Steps through Access Basic code one line at a time.
Steps through Access Basic code one procedure at a time.

Traces all active procedures called by Access Basic code.
Creates a new module.
Inserts a procedure in the current module.
Views members of an application's type library.
Continues the execution of the module.
Terminates the execution state of a module.
Displays the value of a selected expression or adds it to the Debug window's Watch pane.
Indents selected lines of code.
Outdents selected lines of code.

Query Design Buttons

SQL Shows the Structured Query Language version of a query.
Includes an additional table.
Σ Shows (hides) the Totals row for the query.
Shows (hides) the tables list.
Selects the type of query such as select, crosstab, make table, update, append, or delete.
100% Lets you choose whether to return a specified number of records, a percentage of records, or all values.

Records Buttons

Moves the cursor to a blank record at the end of the current database object.
Arranges the data in ascending order in the current datasheet or form.
Arranges the data in descending order in the current datasheet or form.
Modifies the filter that determines how the records are sorted or which records are selected.
Uses the criteria of the filter to sort the records into groups and to select records.
Removes any existing filter.
Begins the active database object.

Table Design Buttons

Modifies indexes.
Modifies which fields provide identification for each record in the table.
Begins an Access Builder Wizard.

Datasheet or Query View Buttons

Shows only records that have matching values in the selected field(s).
A fill-in-the-blank method to design your filter.
Moves to a new blank record.
Deletes the selected record.

Toolbox Buttons

Shows (hides) the toolbox.
Highlights an item.
Creates descriptive text.
Creates a group that can contain other controls.
Adds a single option control.
Adds a list of options.
Adds an image.
Creates a control that displays a picture, graph, or OLE object that isn't stored in the underlying table or query.
Draws a straight line.
Inserts a page break.
Toggles the Control Wizards.
Inserts an area for text.
Adds a toggle button.
Adds a check-box control.
Embeds a form or report.
Creates a control that displays an OLE object that is stored in the underlying table or query.
Draws a rectangle.
Adds a command button.
Lets you select controls in the Design window.
Adds a list of values.

View Buttons

Shows the design characteristics of the current database object.
Shows the current database object in a spreadsheet format.
Modifies the display attributes of the current database object, control, or section.
Shows the form in its standard format.
Closes the active window.
Toggle to magnify the report on the screen.
Previews one page at a time.
Previews two pages at a time.
100% Zooms the preview in or out.
Close Closes the Preview window.

Window and Help Buttons

Returns to the Database window.
Adds a question mark icon to the cursor; while it is active, clicking on any item will open the Help file on the topic related to the item.

REFERENCE 3

Microsoft Access 7 Functions

The function name appears in boldface. Arguments are italicized and appear in parentheses. Optional arguments are enclosed in brackets.

Abs Abs(number) returns the absolute value of number.

Array Array(*arglist*) returns a Variant containing an array. The *arglist* consists of a comma-delimited list of an arbitrary number of values that are assigned to the elements of the array contained within the Variant. If no arguments are specified, an array of zero-length is created.

Asc Asc(*stringexpression*) returns the ANSI code for the first character of *stringexpression*.

AscB AscB(*stringexpression*) is provided for use with byte data contained in a *stringexpression*. Instead of returning the character code for the first character, AscB returns the first byte.

Atn Atn(*number*) returns the inverse tangent of *number*.

Avg Avg(*expr*) returns the average (arithmetic mean) of the values in the field specified by *expr*.

Choose Choose(*indexnum, varexpr [, varexpr] . . .*) returns the value of the *varexpr* specified by *indexnum*, a numeric expression from 1 to the number of *varexpr* expressions (up to 13).

Chr Chr[$](*charcode*) returns the character specified by the ANSI code *charcode*. Chr returns a Variant data type, and Chr$ returns a String.

Cos Cos(*number*) returns the cosine of an angle. The *number* argument can be any valid numeric expression that expresses an angle in radians.

CodeDB CodeDB() returns a database object that specifies the database in which the code is running.

Command Command[$][()] returns the argument portion (anything following /cmd) of the command line that started Access. Command returns a Variant data type, and Command$ returns a String.

Count Count(*expr*) returns the number of selected records in the field specified by *expr*.

CreateControl CreateControl(*formname* As String, *controltype* As Integer [, *section* As Integer [, *parent* As String [, *fieldname* As String [, *left* As Integer [, *top* As Integer [, *width* As Integer [, *height* As Integer]]]]]]]) creates a control on the open form.

CreateForm CreateForm([*database* [, *form template*]]) creates a *form*, returning a Form object.

CreateGroupLevel CreateGroupLevel(*report, expression, header, footer*) creates a new group level on the specified *report*, sorting or grouping by *expression*, giving the group a *header* or *footer* if True (!1).

CreateObject CreateObject(*class*) creates an OLE Automation object, specified by *class*, an argument with two parts (separated by a period), the name of the application used to create the object and the type of object created.

CreateReport CreateReport([*database* [,*reporttemplate*]]) creates a report, returning a Report object.

CreateReportControl CreateReportControl (*reportname* As String, *controltype* As Integer [, *section* As Integer [, *parent* As String [, *fieldname* As String [, *left* As Integer [, *top* As Integer [, *width* As Integer [, *height* As Integer]]]]]]]) creates a control on the open report.

CurDir CurDir[$][(*drive*)] returns the directory in the Open Database dialog box, as Variant data type, or as a String if $ is included.

CurrentUser CurrentUser() returns the current user's name.

CVDate CVDate(*expression*) converts an *expression* that can be interpreted as a date to the Variant data type VarType 7.

Data Type Conversion Functions CBool, CByte CCur, Cdate, CDbl, CInt, CLng, CSng, CStr, and CVar (all with the argument *expression*) convert *expression* to the data types Boolean, Byte, Currency, Date, Double, Integer, Long, Single, String, and Variant, respectively.

Date Date[$][()] returns the current system date, as Variant data type (VarType 7) if $ is omitted, or as a String, if $ is included.

DateAdd DateAdd(*interval, number, date*) returns a date (as Variant data type VarType 7) after or before *date*, the length of time being *number* times *interval*, which is *yyyy* (years), *q* (quarters), *m* (months), *y* (day of year), *d* (days), *w* (weekdays), *ww* (week), *h* (hours), *n* (minutes), or *s* (seconds).

DateDiff DateDiff(*interval, date1, date2*[, *firstweekday*][, *firstweek*]) returns a Variant data type that contains the number of time intervals between *date1* and *date2*; *interval* is as in DateAdd.

DatePart DatePart(*interval, date*[, *firstweekday*] [, *firstweek*]) returns the part of *date* specified by *interval*, as in DateAdd.

DateSerial DateSerial(*year, month, day*) returns the date for the specified *year, month*, and *day* as Variant date type VarType 7.

DateValue DateValue(*stringexpression*) returns the date specified by *stringexpression* as Variant data type VarType 7.

DAvg DAvg(*expr, domain*[, *criteria*]) calculates and returns the arithmetic mean of the values in the records specified by *domain*, in the field *expr*.

Day Day(*number*) returns the day of the month (an integer from 1 to 31) of the date represented by *number*.

DCount DCount(*expr, domain*[, *criteria*]) returns the number of selected records in the *domain* of the field *expr*.

DDB DDB(*cost, salvage, life, period*) returns the depreciation of an item with initial price *cost*, salvage value *salvage*, and useful lifetime *life*, using the double-declining balance method.

DDE DDE(*application, topic, item*) initiates dynamic data exchange with *application*, and returns the *item* of information in *topic* (two arguments recognizable by the application).

DDEInitiate DDEInitiate(*application, topic*) initiates dynamic data exchange with *application*, and returns a Variant data type containing a channel number, which is used by other DDE functions and statements to refer to this link.

DDERequest DDERequest(*channum, item*) requests information via the DDE link *channum*.

DDESend DDESend(*application, topic, item, data*) initiates dynamic data exchange with *application*, and sends *data* to the *item* in the *topic* of the other application.

Derived Math Functions Here is a list of derived mathematical functions available in Access Basic:

Arccos(*x*)	Inverse cosine
Arccosec(*x*)	Inverse cosecant
Arccotan(*x*)	Inverse cotangent
Arcsec(*x*)	Inverse secant
Arcsin(*x*)	Inverse sine
Cosec(*x*)	Cosecant
Cotan(*x*)	Cotangent
HArccos(*x*)	Inverse hyperbolic cosine
HArccosec(*x*)	Inverse hyperbolic cosecant
HArccotan(*x*)	Inverse hyperbolic cotangent
HArcsec(*x*)	Inverse hyperbolic secant
HArcsin(*x*)	Inverse hyperbolic sine
HArctan(*x*)	Inverse hyperbolic tangent
HCos(*x*)	Hyperbolic cosine
HCosec(*x*)	Hyperbolic cosecant
HCotan(*x*)	Hyperbolic cotangent
HSec(*x*)	Hyperbolic secant
HSin(*x*)	Hyperbolic sine
HTan(*x*)	Hyperbolic tangent
LogN(*x*)	Logarithm
Sec(*x*)	Secant

Dir Dir[$][(*filespec*)] returns a file name matching the path or file name *filespec*, as a Variant, or a String if $ is included.

DLookup DLookup(*expr, domain*[, *criteria*]) returns a field value from the set of records *domain*; *expr* identifies the field or performs calculations using data in a field.

DMax DMax(*expr, domain*[, *criteria*]) returns the maximum value of the values in the field specified by *expr*, in the records of *domain*.

DMin DMin(*expr, domain*[, *criteria*]) returns the minimum value of the values in the field specified by *expr*, in the records of *domain*.

DoEvents DoEvents() yields execution so that the operating system can process other events. The DoEvents function returns the number of open forms in standalone versions of Visual Basic, such as Visual Basic, Standard Edition. DoEvents returns 0 in all other applications.

DStDev DStDev(*expr, domain*[, *criteria*]) returns an estimate of the sample standard deviation of the values in the field specified by *expr*, in the records of *domain*.

DStDevP DStDevP(*expr, domain*[, *criteria*]) returns an estimate of the population standard deviation of the values in the field specified by *expr*, in the records of *domain*.

DSum DSum(*expr, domain*[, *criteria*]) returns the sum of the values in the field specified by *expr*, in the records of *domain*.

DVar DVar(*expr, domain*[, *criteria*]) returns an estimate of the sample variation of the values in the field specified by *expr*, in the records of *domain*.

DVarP DVarP(*expr, domain*[, *criteria*]) returns an estimate of the population variation of the values in the field specified by *expr*, in the records of *domain*.

Environ Environ[$](*environmentstring*) returns the string associated with the operating system environment variable *environmentstring*, as Variant data type if $ is omitted, or as a String if $ is included. Environ[$](*n*) returns the nth string of the environment string table.

EOF EOF(*filenumber*) returns True if the end of a file has been reached and False if not.

Error Error[$][(*errorcode*)] returns the error message corresponding to *errorcode*, or the message corresponding to the most recent run-time error, as Variant data type if $ is omitted, or as a String if $ is included.

Eval Eval(*stringexpr*) returns the value of *stringexpr* evaluated.

Exp Exp(*number*) returns e raised to the power *number*.

FileAttr FileAttr(*filenumber, attribute*) returns file handle information about the open file specified by *filenumber*, the number used in the Open statement that opened the file. If *attribute* is 2, the operating system handle for the file is returned; if *attribute* is 1, the return indicates the file's mode: 1 for Input, 2 for Output, 4 for Random, 8 for Append, and 32 for Binary.

First First(*expr*) returns the field value of the field specified by *expr*, from the first record.

Fix Fix(*number*) returns the integer portion of a positive number, or the first negative integer greater than or equal to *number*, if it is negative.

Format Format[$](*expression*[, *fmt*][, *firstweekday*][, *firstweek*]) formats *expression* to the format specified by *fmt*. If *fmt* is omitted and *expression* is numeric, Format[$] converts *expression* to the appropriate data type, as the Str[$] function.

FreeFile FreeFile[()] returns the next unused file number.

FV FV(*rate, nper, pmt, pv, due*) returns the future value of an annuity with *rate* interest rate per period, *nper* payments of size *pmt*, and present value *pv*; *due* is 0 if payments are due at the end of each period, and 1 if at the beginning.

GetObject GetObject(*filename*[, *class*]) returns an OLE object from the specified file; *class* represents the object class, and is a two-part argument, *appname.objecttype*.

Hex Hex[$](*number*) converts *number* from decimal to hexadecimal, and returns the result as Variant data type if $ is omitted, or as a String if $ is included.

Hour Hour(*number*) returns an integer between 0 and 23, the hour of the day of the time *number*.

IIf IIf(*expr, truepart, falsepart*) returns *truepart* if *expr* is true, and *falsepart* if expr is false.

Input Input[$](*n*, [#]*filenumber*) returns the first n characters read from the file specified by *filenumber*, the number used in the open statement that opened the file, as Variant data type if [$] is omitted, or as a String if $ is included.

InputBox InputBox[$](*prompt*[, [*title*] [, [*default*][, *xpos, ypos*]]]) displays a prompt in the dialog box, allowing input or a button choice, and returns the contents of the text box; *prompt* is the message displayed in the dialog box, title appears in the title bar, *default* is the default return, *xpos* is the distance in twips from the left edge of the screen to the left edge of the box, and *ypos* is the distance in twips from the top of the screen to the top of the box.

InStr InStr([*start*,] *strexpr1, strexpr2*) returns the position of the first occurrence of *strexpr2* within *strexpr1*, starting the search from character number *start*. InStr(*start, strexpr1, strexpr2, compare*) performs a case-sensitive search if *compare* is 0; if *compare* is 1, the search is not case sensitive; if *compare* is 2, the string comparison method is Database, using the New Database Sort Order.

Int Int(*number*) returns the integer portion of *number* if it is positive; if it is negative, the first negative integer less than or equal to *number* is returned.

IPmt IPmt(*rate, per, nper, pv, fv, due*) returns the interest payment for the payment period *per*, on an annuity with *rate* interest rate per period, *nper* total periods, *pv* present value, *fv* future value; *due* is 0 if payments are due at the end of the periods, and 1 if payments are due at the beginning.

IRR IRR(*valuearray*(), *guess*) returns the internal rate of return for periodic cash flows contained in *valuearray*; *guess* is a guess at the return (usually 0.1).

IsDate IsDate(*variant*) returns True if *variant* can be converted to a date and False if not.

IsEmpty IsEmpty(*variant*) returns True if *variant* contains the Empty value (has not been initialized) and False if not.

IsMissing IsMissing(*argname*) returns a Boolean value indicating whether an optional argument has been passed to a procedure. The *argname* argument is the name of an optional procedure argument.

IsNull IsNull(*variant*) returns True if *variant* contains Null and False if not.

IsNumeric IsNumeric(*variant*) returns True if *variant* can be converted to a number, and False if not.

IsObject IsObject(*expression*) returns a Boolean value indicating whether an expression references a valid OLE Automation object. The *expression* argument can be any expression.

Last Last(*expr*) returns the field value of the field specified by *expr* from the last record.

LBound LBound(*array*[, *dimension*]) returns the smallest available subscript for *array*; *dimension* determines which dimension of the array is examined; if omitted, the default is 1, for the first dimension.

LCase LCase[$](*strexpr*) converts *strexpr* to lowercase, and returns as Variant data type if $ is omitted, or as a String if $ is included.

Left Left[$](*strexpr, n*) returns the *n* left characters of *strexpr*, as Variant data type if $ is omitted, and as a String if $ is included.

Len Len(*strexpr*) returns the number of characters (length) of *strexpr.* Len(*variablename*) returns the number of bytes used to store *variablename*.

Loc Loc(*filenumber*) returns the current position within the file specified by *filenumber*, the number used in the Open statement that opened the file.

LOF LOF(*filenumber*) returns the size (in bytes) of the file specified by *filenumber*, the number used in the Open statement that opened the file.

Log Log(*number*) returns the natural logarithm of *number*.

LTrim LTrim[$](*stringexpr*) returns *stringexpr* with the leftmost spaces removed, as Variant data type if $ is omitted, and as a String if $ is included.

Max Max(*expr*) returns the largest of a set of values in the field specified by *expr*.

Mid Mid[$](*stringexpr, start*[, *length*]) returns the portion of *stringexpr* starting from character number start, of length *length*, or to the end of *stringexpr* if *length* is omitted. Returns Variant data type if $ is omitted, and a String if $ is included.

Min Min(*expr*) returns the smallest of a set of values in the field specified by *expr*.

Minute Minute(*number*) returns a number between 0 and 59, the minutes after the hour of the time *number*.

MIRR MIRR(*valuearray*(), *financerate*, *reinvestrate*) calculates and returns the modified internal rate of return for the cash flows in *valuearray*, where *financerate* is the rate paid on payments, and *reinvestrate* is the rate earned on receipts.

Month Month(*number*) returns a number between 1 and 12, the month of the year of the date *number*.

MsgBox MsgBox(*prompt*[, *buttons*][, *title*][, *helpfile*, *context*]) displays a message in a dialog box, waits for the user to choose a button, and returns a value indicating which button the user has chosen.

Now Now[()] returns the current system date and time as Variant data type VarType 7.

NPer NPer(*rate, pmt, pv, fv, due*) returns the number of payment periods for an annuity with *rate* interest rate per period, payment size *pmt*, present value *pv*, and future value *fv*; *due* is 0 if payments are due at the end of the payment period, and 1 if they are due at the beginning.

NPV NPV(*rate, valuearray*()) returns the net present value of cash flows in *valuearray*, with discount rate *rate*.

Oct Oct[$](*number*) returns the decimal number *number* in octal form, as Variant data type if $ is omitted, and as a String if $ is included.

Partition Partition(*number, start, stop, interval*) returns a range of numbers that includes *number*. The ranges are calculated from *start* to *stop* (nonnegative integers) with length *interval*, and the one that contains *number* is returned.

Pmt Pmt(*rate, nper, pv, fv, due*) returns the payment for an annuity with *rate* interest rate per period, *nper* payment periods, present value *pv*, and future value *fv*; due is 0 if payments are due at the end of each period, and 1 if they are due at the beginning.

PPmt PPmt(*rate, per, nper, pv, fv, due*) returns the principal payment for payment period *per*, for an annuity with *rate* interest rate per period, *nper* payment periods, present value *pv*, and future value *fv*; *due* is 0 if payments are due at the end of each period, and 1 if they are due at the beginning.

PV PV(*rate, nper, pmt, fv, due*) returns the present value of an annuity with *rate* interest rate per period, *nper* payment periods, payment size *pmt*, and future value *fv*; *due* is 0 if payments are due at the end of each period, and 1 if they are due at the beginning.

QBColor QBColor(*qbcolor*) returns the red-green-blue color value corresponding to color number *qbcolor*.

Rate Rate(*nper, pmt, pv, fv, due, guess*) returns the interest rate per period of an annuity with *nper* payment periods, payment size *pmt*, present value *pv*, and future value *fv*; *due* is 0 if payments are due at the end of each period, and 1 if they are due at the beginning; *guess* is your guess for the rate (usually .1).

RGB RGB(*red, green, blue*) returns a number of Long data type that represents the color with components *red, green*, and *blue*.

Right Right[$](*stringexpr, n*) returns the *n* rightmost characters of *stringexpr*, as Variant data type if $ is omitted, and as a String if $ is included.

Rnd Rnd[(*number*)] returns a random number less than 1 and greater than or equal to 0. If *number* is positive or omitted, the next random number in the sequence is generated; if *number* is negative, the same random number is returned every time; if *number* is 0, the most recently generated random number is returned.

RTrim RTrim[$](*stringexpr*) returns *stringexpr* with the rightmost spaces removed, as Variant data type if $ is omitted, and as a String if $ is included.

Second Second(*number*) returns a number between 0 and 59, the seconds of the time *number*.

Seek Seek(*filenumber*) returns the current file position of the file specified by *filenumber*, the number used in the Open statement used to open the file.

Sgn Sgn(*number*) returns 1 if *number* is positive, 0 if *number* is 0, and !1 if *number* is negative.

Shell Shell(*commandstring*[, *windowstyle*]) runs the program specified by *commandstring*.

Sin Sin(number) returns the sine of an angle. The *number* argument can be any valid numeric expression that expresses an angle in radians.

SLN SLN(*cost, salvage, life*) returns the straight-line depreciation of an asset with initial price *cost*, salvage value *salvage*, and useful life *life*.

Space Space[$](*number*) returns *number* of spaces, as Variant data type if $ is omitted, and as a String if $ is included.

Spc Spc(*number*) prints *number* of blank spaces, in a Print # statement or Print method.

Sqr Sqr(*number*) returns the positive square root of *number*.

StDev StDev(*expr*) returns an estimate of the sample standard deviation of the values in the field specified by *expr*.

StDevP StDevP(*expr*) returns an estimate of the population standard deviation of the values in the field specified by *expr*.

Str Str[$](*number*) returns *number* as Variant data type if $ is omitted, and as a String if $ is included.

StrComp StrComp(*stringexpr1, stringexpr2*[, *compare*]) converts *stringexpr1* and *stringexpr2* to Variant data types and compares them; if *compare* is 0, the comparison is case sensitive; 1, the comparison is not case sensitive; 2, the comparison uses the New Database Sort Order; if *compare* is omitted, the comparison method is that set by the Option Compare statement. The return is !1 if *stringexpr1* is less than *stringexpr2*, 0 if they are equal, and 1 if *stringexpr1* is greater than *stringexpr2*.

String String[$](*number, charcode*) returns a string of the character with ANSI code *charcode*, repeated *number* times. String[$](*number, string*) returns a *string* of the first character of string, repeated *number* times.

Sum Sum(*expr*) returns the sum of the values in the field specified by *expr*.

Switch Switch(*varexpr1, var1*[, *varexpr2, var2. . .* [, *varexpr7, var7*]]) returns the *var* expression corresponding to the first *varexpr* expression that is True (!1).

SYD SYD(*cost, salvage, life, period*) returns the sum-of-years' digits depreciation for an asset with initial price *cost*, salvage value *salvage*, useful lifetime *life*, and period of depreciation *period*.

SysCmd ReturnValue = SysCmd(*action*[, *text*][, *value*]) is used to display a progress meter, return the version number of Access, information about .INI and .EXE files, or the state of the active database object.

Tab Tab(*column*) is used with the Print # statement and the Print method, and causes the next character to be printed starting at column number *column*.

Tan Tan(*number*) returns the tangent of an angle. The *number* argument can be any valid numeric expression that expresses an angle in radians.

Time Time[$][()] returns the current system time, as Variant data type if $ is omitted, and as a String if $ is included.

Timer Timer[()] returns the number of seconds elapsed since midnight.

TimeSerial TimeSerial(*hour, minute, second*) returns the specified time as Variant data type of VarType 7, a number between 0 and 0.99999.

TimeValue TimeValue(*stringexpression*) returns the time represented by the string argument *stringexpression*, as Variant data type of VarType 7, a number between 0 and 0.99999.

Trim Trim[$](*stringexpr*) returns *stringexpr* with leading and trailing spaces removed.

UBound UBound(*array*[, *dimension*]) returns the largest available subscript for *array*; *dimension* determines which dimension of the array is examined; if omitted, the default is 1, for the first dimension.

UCase UCase[$](*stringexpr*) returns *stringexpr* with all letters converted to uppercase, as Variant data type if $ is omitted, and as a String if $ is included.

Val Val(*stringexpression*) returns the numeric value of *stringexpression*, ignoring blanks and stopping at any character that is not part of a number.

Var Var(*expr*) returns an estimate of the sample variation of the values in the field specified by *expr*.

VarP VarP(*expr*) returns an estimate of the population variance of the values in the field specified by *expr*.

VarType VarType(*variant*) returns a number from 0 to 8, corresponding to the VarType of *variant* (Empty, Null, Integer, Long, Single, Double, Currency, Date, and String, respectively).

Weekday Weekday(*dateexpression* [, *firstweekday*]) returns a number between 1 (Sunday) and 7 (Saturday), the day of the week of the date *number*.

Year Year(*dateexpression* [, *firstweekday*] [, *firstweek*]) returns a number between 100 and 9999, the year of the date *number*.

Answers to Quick Check Questions

SESSION 1.1

1 What is a replica set?
A replica set consists of a Design Master and all of its replicas.

2 How does a Design Master differ from a replica?
A Design Master has extra tables and fields (added by Access) to keep track of changes made to the data and objects in the database. Users may change data in a replica or a Design Master. Users can change the design of database objects only in the Design Master.

3 What does Access do when you synchronize a Design Master and a replica?
Access updates the Design Master with any changes that have been made to the data in the replica. Access updates the replica with any changes that have been made to the data in the Design Master. Access updates the replica with any changes to the design of Design Master database objects (tables, forms, etc.) as long as those objects are specified as replicable.

4 What is the purpose of a crosstab query?
A crosstab query uses aggregate functions to summarize table data. The summary takes the form of a crosstabulation.

5 What is a find duplicates query?
The find duplicates query finds all records in a table that have matching values in a given field or group of fields.

6 What does a find unmatched query do?
The find unmatched query finds records in one table for which there are no matching records in another table.

SESSION 1.2

1 What is an action query?
An action query is a query that modifies data in a database.

2 What precautions should you take before running an action query?
You should always run the query as a select query before changing it to an action query. That way, you get to see the effect before it is permanent. It is also a good idea to create a backup of a database before running an action query.

3 How does the Query Design grid change when you create an update query?
The Sort and Show lines in the Query Design grid are replaced with the Update to line.

4 What is the Expression Builder?
The Expression Builder assists you in creating an expression for use in query selection criteria or calculated fields.

5 What does an update query do?
An update query updates the selected records in a table with new field values.

6 Why is it advisable not to save an update query?
Typically, an update query is run only once. If the query is saved, it might accidentally be run again, changing the data twice.

7 What does a delete query do?
A delete query deletes records in a table that match given criteria.

SESSION 1.3

1 What happens if you enter 23 for the Top Values property for a table that has only 20 records? Give an example of an alternative entry for this property.
The Top Values query will select all records. An alternative entry in the Top Values property is All.

2 What is the difference between an inner join and an outer join?
An inner join selects records from two tables when they have matching values in the common field(s). An outer join selects all records from one table and records from a second table which have common field values that match records in the first table.

3 In what form does Access save a query?
Access saves a query in its SQL form.

4 What is the basic form of an SQL statement?
An SQL statement has the basic form: SELECT - FROM - WHERE - ORDER BY. The SELECT clause identifies the fields selected, the FROM clause specifies the table from which the records are selected, the WHERE clause specifies the selection criteria, the ORDER BY clause specifies the ordering.

5 Figure 1-38 lists the field names from two tables: Telephones and Phone Calls.
  a. What is the primary key for each table?
     Primary key for Telephones table: Telephone Number
     There is no single field that serves as a primary key for the Phone Calls table. A primary key can be constructed using the Calling Telephone Number, Call Date, and Call Start Time fields.
  b. What type of relationship exists between the two tables?
     There is a one-to-many relationship from Telephones to Phone Calls.
  c. Is an inner join possible between the two tables? If so, give one example of an inner join.
     Yes an inner join is possible. Examples use these common fields: Telephone Number and Calling Telephone Number; Telephone Number and Called Telephone Number; Telephone Number and Billed Telephone Number.
  d. Is either type of outer join possible between the two tables? If so, give one example of an outer join.
     Yes, assume the primary keys defined as in a above, and that Telephones is the left table. Examples of a left outer-join use these common fields: Telephone Number and Calling Telephone Number; Telephone Number and Called Telephone Number; Telephone Number and Billed Telephone Number.
  e. Is a self-join possible for one of the tables? If so, give one example of a self-join.
     No, a self-join is not possible for either of these tables.

SESSION 2.1

1 Give a definition of a switchboard, describe its significant features, and provide two reasons for using one.
A switchboard is a user-created form that appears when you open a database and that provides controlled access to the database's tables, queries, forms, and reports. A switchboard can contain command buttons, a custom menu bar, a custom toolbar, hot keys, text boxes, and graphic images. Use a switchboard to give an attractive look to the user interface, to organize the user interface, and to prevent users from changing the design of the database's tables, queries, forms, and reports.

2 What is a macro and what is the relationship between a macro and an action?
A macro is a command or a series of commands that Access can perform automatically. Each command in a macro is called an action, so a macro consists of one or more actions.

3 What is an action argument? Give an example of an action argument.
If an action has available options, these options are called action arguments. An example can be any of the arguments for any of the 47 actions. For example, the OpenQuery action has an argument that is the name of the query that is to be opened.

4 What are you trying to accomplish when you single-step through a macro?
Single-stepping through a macro lets you execute one action at a time to locate errors in the macro and to verify the macro's correctness.

5 What are two different ways to cause a macro to be executed when Access is started?
You can specify the name of the macro in the Startup dialog box or you can designate the macro as an AutoExec macro.

SESSION 2.2

1 What is a hot key and how do you define one for a command button?
A hot key is a key that can be pressed after the Alt key to select a menu option, command button, or other action. Insert an ampersand (&) in the option or button name before the letter to define the hot key.

2 What is the effect of setting a form's Border Style property to Dialog?
When a form's Border Style is set to Dialog, the size of the form cannot be changed by the user.

3 How do you copy an object in the same database?
Right-click the object to open the shortcut menu, then click Copy. Right-click in the database window, then click Paste. Enter the name of the new object copy.

4 What is an event property?
An event property is a named attribute of a control, section, form, or report to which the control, section, form, or report can respond.

5 What form components do not appear on a dialog box? What additional component does not appear on a switchboard?
Dialog boxes do not contain scroll bars, navigation buttons, record selectors, or sizing buttons. In addition, a switchboard does not contain a Close box.

6 What are two reasons for using macro groups?
A macro group is a macro that contains more than one macro. Use a macro group to consolidate related macros and to manage large numbers of macros better.

7 What are two special effects you can use for a control?
Two special effects are Raised and Shadowed to give a control a three-dimensional appearance.

SESSION 3.1

1 What is the difference between a menu bar macro and a menu macro group?
A menu bar macro displays a custom menu bar and uses AddMenu actions, one action for each menu name. A menu macro group uses macros to define the commands for a drop-down menu.

2 What is a global custom menu bar?
If an application has a global custom menu bar, Access displays it for all windows of an application.

3 When you use the Menu Builder, how do you distinguish between a menu name and a menu-item name?
Place menu names flush left in the Menu Builder list box and indent menu-item names one level.

4 What is the function of the text in the Status Bar Text text box in the Menu Builder?
The Status Bar Text text box determines the text that will appear in the status bar when the menu item is selected.

5 What are the rules for determining hot keys in a menu?
A hot key must be unique for each active control (menu item, command buttons, etc.) on the screen.

6 What can you do if the menu you create using Menu Builder is missing a menu item?
You can add missing menu items in the Macro window.

SESSION 3.2

1 What two Access "tools" can you float anywhere on the screen?
You can float toolbars and toolboxes anywhere on the screen.

2 When does the Deactivate event occur?
The Deactivate event occurs when a form loses the focus or is closed.

3 What are the three options for the Show Toolbar action?
The three options are Yes (show), No (hide), and Where Appropriate.

4 What is a startup option?
A startup option specifies settings or actions, such as opening a form or executing a macro, that Access should perform when a database is opened.

5 How can you change the image on a toolbar button?
Right-click the toolbar button, then click Choose Button Image. Select a button image from the Choose Button Image dialog box, then click the OK button.

6 How do you resize and dock a toolbar?
Resize a toolbar by holding the Shift key down and moving the rightmost toolbar button right or left. Dock a toolbar by clicking on the toolbar (but not on a toolbar button) and dragging the toolbar to its new position.

SESSION 4.1

1 Why is Visual Basic called an event-driven, object-oriented language?
Visual Basic is called an event-driven and an object-oriented language because Visual Basic code is composed of statements that are executed in response to events that occur with the objects in a database.

2 What are the differences between a function and a sub procedure?
A function is a procedure that performs operations, returns a value, can accept arguments, and can be used in expressions (recall that an expression is a calculation resulting in a single value).
A sub procedure, or subroutine, performs operations and can accept arguments but does not return a value and cannot be used in expressions.

3 What are the two different types of modules?
A standard module is a separate database object that is stored in memory with other database objects when you open the database.
Form and report modules are automatically created by Access when the form or report is created. Each form or report module contains event procedures that respond to an event that occurs for that specific form or report.

4 What is an event procedure?
An event procedure is a procedure that is coded to respond to an event that occurs for a specific database object.

5 What can you accomplish in the Debug window?
In the Debug window, you can test a Visual Basic function or procedure.

6 What does Access do when you compile a procedure?
When you compile a procedure, Access checks the Visual Basic code to make sure that it follows the rules of the Visual Basic language. If the code is correct, Access translates it into an executable form.

SESSION 4.2

1 What is the difference between a variable and a constant?
A constant is a named memory location the value of which cannot change. Its value is fixed at the time the code is compiled. A variable is a named memory location the value of which can change as the code is executed.

2 How many times would the following loop be executed?

```
For MyCounter = 2 To 11 Step 3
```

The loop will be executed four times. The variable MyCounter takes on the values 2, 5, 8, and 11.

3 What is a method?
A method is an action that operates on specific objects or controls.

4 What is the Boolean data type?
The Boolean data type can take on one of two possible values: True or False.

5 What is the variant data type?
The variant data type is the default data type for Visual Basic variables. A variable of the variant data type can store a value of any data type.

Relational Databases and Database Design

APPENDIX

APPENDIX

Relational Databases and Database Design

OBJECTIVES

In this section you will:

- Learn the characteristics of a relation
- Learn about primary, candidate, alternate, foreign, and composite keys
- Study one-to-one, one-to-many, and many-to-many relationships
- Learn to describe relations and relationships with entity-relationship diagrams and with a shorthand method
- Study database integrity constraints for primary keys, referential integrity, and domains
- Learn about determinants, functional dependencies, anomalies, and normalization

This appendix introduces you to the basics of database design. Before trying to master this material, be sure you have an understanding of the following concepts: data, information, field, field value, record, table, relational database, common fields, database management system (DBMS), and relational database management system.

Relations

A relational database stores its data in tables. A **table** is a two-dimensional structure made up of rows and columns. The terms table, row, and column are the popular names for the more formal terms **relation** (table), **tuple** (row), and **attribute** (column), as shown in Figure AP-1.

Figure AP-1 A relation consisting of tuples and attributes

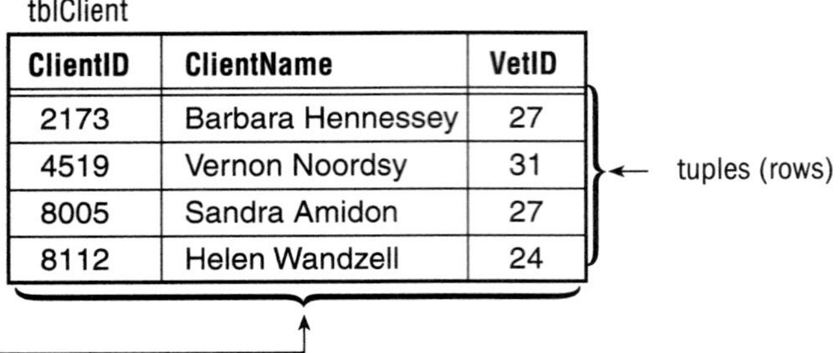
tblClient

ClientID	ClientName	VetID
2173	Barbara Hennessey	27
4519	Vernon Noordsy	31
8005	Sandra Amidon	27
8112	Helen Wandzell	24

The tblClient table shown in Figure AP-1 is an example of a relation, a two-dimensional structure with the following characteristics:

- Each row is unique. Because no two rows are the same, you can easily locate and update specific data. For example, you can locate the row for Client ID 8005 and change the Client Name value, Sandra Amidon, or the Vet ID value, 27.
- The order of the rows is unimportant. You can add or view rows in any order. For example, you can view the rows in Client Name order instead of Client ID order.
- Each table entry contains a single value. At the intersection of each row and column, you cannot have more than one value. For example, each row in Figure AP-1 contains one Client ID, one Client Name, and one Vet ID.
- The order of the columns is unimportant. You can add or view columns in any order.
- Each column has a unique name called the **attribute name**. The attribute name allows you to access a specific column without needing to know its position within the relation.
- The entries in a column are from the same domain. A **domain** is a set of values from which one or more columns draw their actual values. A domain can be broad, such as "all legitimate names of people" for the Client Name column, or narrow, such as "24, 27, or 31" for the Vet ID column. The domain of "all legitimate dates" could be shared by the Birth Date, Start Date, and Last Pay Date columns in a company's employee relation.
- The columns in a relation describe, or are characteristics of, an entity. An **entity** is a person, place, object, event, or idea for which you want to store and process data. For example, Client ID, Client Name, and Vet ID are characteristics of the clients of a pet-sitting company. The tblClient relation represents the client entity and its characteristics. That is, the sets of values in the rows of the tblClient relation describe the different clients of the company. The tblClient relation includes only characteristics of a client. Other relations would exist for the company's other entities. For example, a tblPet relation might describe the clients' pets and a tblEmployee relation might describe the company's employees.

Knowing the characteristics of a relation leads directly to a definition of a relational database. A **relational database** is a collection of relations.

Keys

Primary keys ensure that each row in a relation is unique. A **primary key** is an attribute, or a collection of attributes, whose values uniquely identify each row in a relation. In addition to being *unique*, a primary key must be *minimal* (that is, contain no unnecessary extra attributes) and must not change in value. For example, in Figure AP-2 the tblState relation contains one record per state and uses State Abbrev as its primary key.

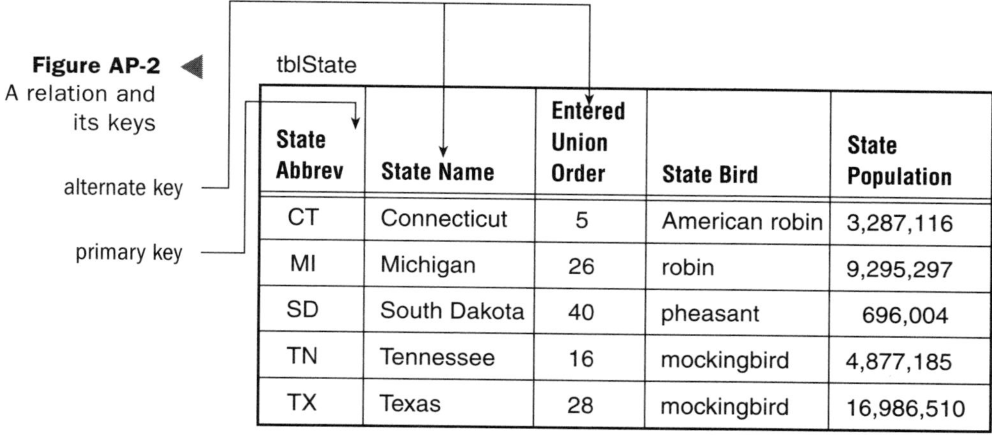

State Abbrev	State Name	Entered Union Order	State Bird	State Population
CT	Connecticut	5	American robin	3,287,116
MI	Michigan	26	robin	9,295,297
SD	South Dakota	40	pheasant	696,004
TN	Tennessee	16	mockingbird	4,877,185
TX	Texas	28	mockingbird	16,986,510

Figure AP-2 A relation and its keys

Could any other attribute, or collection of attributes, be the primary key of the tblState relation?

- Could State Bird serve as the primary key? No, because the column does not have unique values (for example, the mockingbird is the state bird of more than one state).
- Could State Population serve as the primary key? No, because the column values change periodically and are not guaranteed to be unique.
- Could State Abbrev and State Name together serve as the primary key? No, because the combination is not minimal. Something less, State Abbrev by itself, can serve as the primary key.
- Could State Name serve as the primary key? Yes, because the column has unique values. In a similar way, you could select Entered Union Order as the primary key for the tblState relation. One attribute, or collection of attributes, that can serve as a primary key is called a **candidate key**. The candidate keys for the tblState relation are State Abbrev, State Name, and Entered Union Order. You choose one of the candidate keys to be the primary key, and the remaining candidate keys are called alternate keys.

Figure AP-3 shows a tblCity relation containing the attributes State Abbrev, City Name, and City Population.

Figure AP-3 A relation with a composite key

tblCity

primary key

State Abbrev	City Name	City Population
CT	Hartford	139,739
CT	Madison	14,031
CT	Portland	8,418
MI	Lansing	127,321
SD	Madison	6,257
SD	Pierre	12,906
TN	Nashville	488,374
TX	Austin	465,622
TX	Portland	12,224

What is the primary key for the tblCity relation? The values for City Population periodically change and are not guaranteed to be unique, so City Population cannot be the primary key. Because the values for each of the other two columns are not unique, State Abbrev alone cannot be the primary key and neither can City Name (for example, there are two Madisons and two Portlands). The primary key is the combination of State Abbrev and City Name. Both attributes together are needed to identify, uniquely and minimally, each row in the tblCity relation. A multiple-attribute primary key is also called a **composite key** or a **concatenated key**.

The State Abbrev attribute in the tblCity relation is also a foreign key. A **foreign key** is an attribute, or a collection of attributes, in one relation whose values must match the values of the primary key of some relation. As shown in Figure AP-4, the values in the tblCity relation's State Abbrev column match the values in the tblState relation's State Abbrev column. Thus, State Abbrev, the primary key of the tblState relation, is a foreign key in the tblCity relation. Although the attribute name State Abbrev is the same in both relations, the names could be different. Most people give the same name to an attribute stored in two or more tables to broadcast clearly they are really the same attribute.

Figure AP-4 State Abbrev as a primary key (tbleState relation) and a foreign key (tblCity relation)

primary key

tblState

State Abbrev	StateName	Entered Union Order	StateBird	State Population
CT	Connecticut	5	American robin	3,287,116
MI	Michigan	26	robin	9,295,297
SD	South Dakota	40	pheasant	696,004
TN	Tennessee	16	mockingbird	4,877,185
TX	Texas	28	mockingbird	16,986,510

primary key

foreign key

tblCity

State Abbrev	CityName	City Population
CT	Hartford	139,739
CT	Madison	14,031
CT	Portland	8,418
MI	Lansing	127,321
SD	Madison	6,257
SD	Pierre	12,906
TN	Nashville	488,374
TX	Austin	465,622
TX	Portland	12,224

A **nonkey attribute** is an attribute that is not part of the primary key. In the two relations shown in Figure AP-4, all attributes are nonkey attributes except State Abbrev in the tblState and tblCity relations and City Name in the tblCity relation. *Key* is an ambiguous word because it can refer to a primary, candidate, alternate, or foreign key. When the word key appears alone, however, it means primary key and the definition for a nonkey attribute consequently makes sense.

Relationships

The tblCapital relation, shown in Figure AP-5, has one row for each state capital. The Capital Name and State Abbrev attributes are candidate keys; selecting Capital Name as the primary key makes State Abbrev an alternate key. The State Abbrev attribute in the tblCapital relation is also a foreign key, because its values match the values in the tblState relation's State Abbrev column.

Figure AP-5 A one-to-one relationship

primary key

tblState

State Abbrev	StateName	Entered Union Order	StateBird	State Population
CT	Connecticut	5	American robin	3,287,116
MI	Michigan	26	robin	9,295,297
SD	South Dakota	40	pheasant	696,004
TN	Tennessee	16	mockingbird	4,877,185
TX	Texas	28	mockingbird	16,986,510

foreign key

primary key

tblCaptial

Capital Name	State Abbrev	Year Designated	Phone Area Code	Capital Population
Austin	TX	1845	512	465,622
Hartford	CT	1662	203	139,739
Lansing	MI	1847	517	127,321
Nashville	TN	1843	615	488,374
Pierre	SD	1889	605	12,906

One-to-One

The tblState and tblCapital relations, shown in Figure AP-5, have a one-to-one relationship. A **one-to-one relationship** (abbreviated 1:1) exists between two relations when each row in one relation has at most one matching row in the other relation. State Abbrev, which is a foreign key in the tblCapital relation and the primary key in the tblState relation, is the common field that ties together the rows of each relation.

Should the tblState and tblCapital relations be combined into one relation? Although the two relations in any 1:1 relationship can be combined into one relation, each relation describes different entities and should usually be kept separate.

One-to-Many

The tblState and tblCity relations, shown once again in Figure AP-6, have a one-to-many relationship. A **one-to-many relationship** (abbreviated 1:M) exists between two relations when one row in the first relation matches many rows in the second relation and one row in the second relation matches only one row in the first relation. Many can mean zero rows, one row, or two or more rows. State Abbrev, which is a foreign key in the tblCity relation and the primary key in the tblState relation, is the common field that ties together the rows of each relation.

Figure AP-6 A one-to-many relationship

primary key

tblState

State Abbrev	StateName	Entered Union Order	StateBird	State Population
CT	Connecticut	5	American robin	3,287,116
MI	Michigan	26	robin	9,295,297
SD	South Dakota	40	pheasant	696,004
TN	Tennessee	16	mockingbird	4,877,185
TX	Texas	28	mockingbird	16,986,510

primary key

foreign key

tblCity

State Abbrev	CityName	City Population
CT	Hartford	139,739
CT	Madison	14,031
CT	Portland	8,418
MI	Lansing	127,321
SD	Madison	6,257
SD	Pierre	12,906
TN	Nashville	488,374
TX	Austin	465,622
TX	Portland	12,224

Many-to-Many

In Figure AP-7, the tblState relation with a primary key of State Abbrev and the tblCrop relation with a primary key of Crop Name have a many-to-many relationship. A **many-to-many relationship** (abbreviated as M:N) exists between two relations when one row in the first relation matches many rows in the second relation and one row in the second relation matches many rows in the first relation. You form a many-to-many relationship between two relations indirectly by adding a third relation that has the primary keys of the M:N relations as its primary key. The original relations now each have a 1:M relationship with the new relation. The State Abbrev and Crop Name attributes represent the primary key of the tblProduction relation that is shown in Figure AP-7. State Abbrev, which is a foreign key in the tblProduction relation and the primary key in the tblState relation, is the common field that ties together the rows of the tblState and tblProduction relations. Likewise, Crop Name is the common field for the tblCrop and tblProduction relations.

Figure AP-7
A many-to-many relationship

primary key

tblState

State Abbrev	State Name	Entered Union Order	State Bird	State Population
CT	Connecticut	5	American robin	3,287,116
MI	Michigan	26	robin	9,295,297
SD	South Dakota	40	pheasant	696,004
TN	Tennessee	16	mockingbird	4,877,185
TX	Texas	28	mockingbird	16,986,510

tblCrop

Crop Name	Exports	Imports
Corn	$4,965.8	$68.5
Cotton	$2,014.6	$11.4
Soybeans	$4,462.8	$15.8
Wheat	$4,503.2	$191.1

primary key

foreign key

tblProduction

State Abbrev	Crop Name	Quantity
MI	Corn	241,500
MI	Soybeans	47,520
MI	Wheat	35,280
SD	Corn	377,200
SD	Soybeans	63,000
SD	Wheat	119,590
TN	Corn	79,360
TN	Soybeans	33,250
TN	Wheat	13,440
TX	Corn	202,500
TX	Cotton	3,322
TX	Soybeans	12,870
TX	Wheat	129,200

Entity Subtype

Figure AP-8 shows a special type of one-to-one relationship. The tblShipping relation's primary key is State Abbrev and contains one row for each state having an ocean shoreline. Because not all states have an ocean shoreline, the tblShipping relation has fewer rows than the tblState relation. However, each row in the tblShipping relation has a matching row in the tblState relation with State Abbrev serving as the common field; State Abbrev is the primary key in the tblState relation and is a foreign key in the tblShipping relation.

Figure AP-8 An entity subtype

tblStat

primary key → State Abbrev

State Abbrev	State Name	Entered Union Order	State Bird	State Population
CT	Connecticut	5	American robin	3,287,116
MI	Michigan	26	robin	9,295,297
SD	South Dakota	40	pheasant	696,004
TN	Tennessee	16	mockingbird	4,877,185
TX	Texas	28	mockingbird	16,986,510

tblShipping

primary key → State Abbrev
foreign key → State Abbrev

State Abbrev	Ocean Shoreline	Export Tonnage	Import Tonnage
CT	618	3,377,466	2,118,494
TX	3,359	45,980,912	109,400,314

The tblShipping relation, in this situation, is called an **entity subtype**, a relation whose primary key is a foreign key to a second relation and whose attributes are additional attributes for the second relation. You can create an entity subtype when a relation has attributes that could have null values. A **null value** is the absence of a value. A null value is not blank, nor zero, nor any other value. You give a null value to an attribute when you do not know its value or when a value does not apply. For example, instead of using the tblShipping relation, you could store the Ocean Shoreline, Export Tonnage, and Import Tonnage attributes in the tblState relation and allow them to be null for states not having an ocean shoreline. You should be aware that database experts are currently debating the validity of the use of nulls in relational databases and many experts insist that you should never use nulls. Part of this warning against nulls is based on the inconsistent way different relational DBMSs treat nulls and part is due to the lack of a firm theoretical foundation for how to use nulls. In any case, entity subtypes are an alternative to the use of nulls.

Entity-Relationship Diagrams

A common shorthand method for describing relations is to write the relation name followed by its attributes in parentheses, underlining the attributes that represent the primary key and identifying the foreign keys for a relation immediately after the relation. Using this method, the relations that appear in Figures AP-5 through AP-8 are described in the following way:

tblState (State Abbrev, State Name, Entered Union Order, State Bird, State Population)
tblCapital (Capital Name, State Abbrev, Year Designated, Phone Area Code, Capital Population)
    Foreign key: State Abbrev to tblState relation
tblCity (State Abbrev, City Name, City Population)
    Foreign key: State Abbrev to tblState relation
tblCrop (Crop Name, Exports, Imports)
tblProduction (StateAbbrev, Crop Name, Quantity)
    Foreign key: State Abbrev to tblState relation
    Foreign key: Crop Name to tblCrop relation
tblShipping (State Abbrev, Ocean Shoreline, Export Tonnage, Import Tonnage)
    Foreign key: State Abbrev to tblState relation

Another popular way to describe relations *and their relationships* is with entity-relationship diagrams. An **entity-relationship diagram (ERD)** graphically shows a database's entities and the relationships among the entities. In an entity-relationship diagram, an entity and a relation are equivalent. Figure AP-9 shows an entity-relationship diagram for the relations that appear in Figures AP-5 through AP-8.

Figure AP-9
An entity-relationship diagram

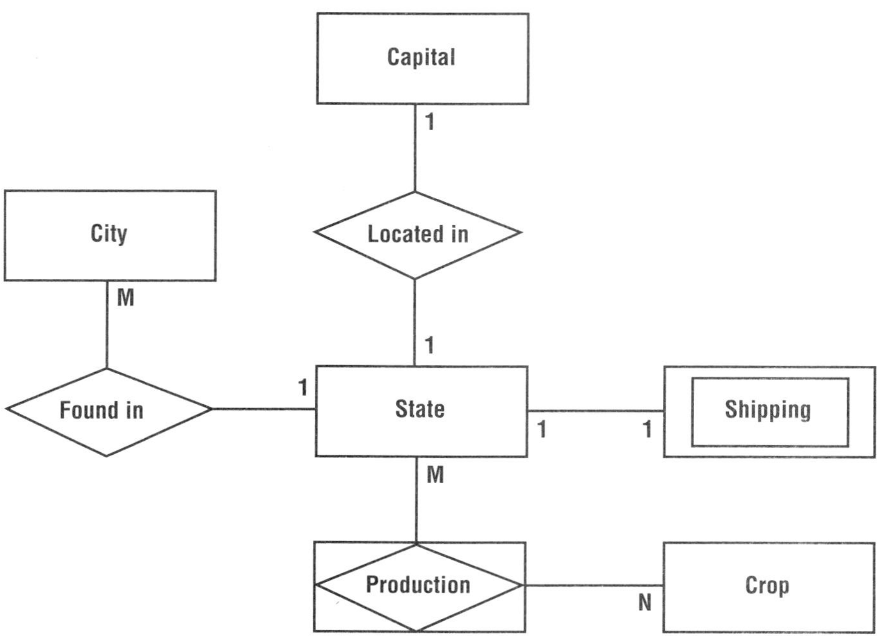

Entity-relationship diagrams have the following characteristics:

- Entities, or relations, appear in rectangles and relationships appear in diamonds. The entity name appears inside the rectangle and a verb describing the relationship appears inside the diamond. For example, the City rectangle is connected to the State rectangle by the FOUND IN diamond and is read: "a city is found in a state."
- The 1 by the State entity and the M by the City entity identify a 1:M relationship between these two entities. In a similar manner, an M:N relationship exists between the State and Crop entities and 1:1 relationships exist between the State and Capital entities and between the State and Shipping entities.
- A diamond inside a rectangle defines a composite entity. A **composite entity** is a relationship that has the characteristics of an entity. For example, Production connects the State and Crop entities in an M:N relationship and acts as an entity by containing the Quantity attribute, along with the composite key of the State Abbrev and Crop Name attributes.
- An entity subtype appears in a double rectangle and is connected without an intervening diamond directly to its related entity, State.

You can also show attributes in an ERD by placing each individual attribute in a bubble connected to its entity or relationship. However, typical ERDs have large numbers of entities and relationships, so including the attributes might confuse rather than clarify the ERD.

Integrity Constraints

A database has **integrity** if its data follows certain rules, known as **integrity constraints**. The ideal is to have the DBMS enforce all integrity constraints. If a DBMS can enforce some integrity constraints but not others, the other integrity constraints must be enforced by other programs or by the people who use the DBMS. Integrity constraints can be divided into three groups: primary key constraints, referential integrity, and domain integrity constraints.

- One primary key constraint is inherent in the definition of a primary key, which says that the primary key must be unique. The **entity integrity constraint** says that the primary key cannot be null. For a composite key, none of the individual attributes can be null. The uniqueness and nonnull properties of a primary key ensure that you can reference any data value in a database by supplying its table name, attribute name, and primary key value.
- Foreign keys provide the mechanism for forming a relationship between two tables, and referential integrity ensures that only valid relationships exist. **Referential integrity** is the constraint specifying that each nonnull foreign key must match a primary key value in the related relation. Specifically, referential integrity means that you cannot add a row with an unmatched foreign key value. Referential integrity also means that you cannot change or delete the related primary key value and leave the foreign key orphaned. In some relational DBMSs, if you try to change or delete a primary key value, you can specify one of these options: restricted, cascades, or nullifies. If you specify **restricted**, the DBMS updates or deletes the value only if there are no matching foreign key values. If you choose **cascades** and then change a primary key value, the DBMS changes the matching foreign keys to the new primary key value, or, if you delete a primary key value, the DBMS also deletes the matching foreign-key rows. If you choose **nullifies** and then change or delete a primary key value, the DBMS sets all matching foreign keys to null.
- A domain is a set of values from which one or more columns draw their actual values. **Domain integrity constraints** are the rules you specify for an attribute. By choosing a data type for an attribute, you impose a constraint on the set of values allowed for the attribute. You can create specific validation rules for an attribute to limit its domain further. As you make an attribute's domain definition more precise, you exclude more and more unacceptable values for an attribute. For example, in the tblState relation you could define the domain for the Entered Union Order attribute to be a unique integer between 1 and 50 and the domain for the State Bird attribute to be any name containing 25 or fewer characters.

Dependencies and Determinants

Relations are related to other relations. Attributes are also related to other attributes. Consider the tblStateCrop relation shown in Figure AP-10. Its description is:

tblStateCrop (<u>State Abbrev</u>, <u>Crop Name</u>, State Bird, Bird Scientific Name, State Population, Exports, Quantity)

Figure AP-10 A relation combining several attributes from the tblState, tblCrop, and tblProduction relations

null value

primary key

tblStateCrop

State Abbrev	Crop Name	State Bird	Bird Scientific Name	State Population	Exports	Quantity
CT	Corn	American robin	Planesticus migratorius	3,287,116	$4,965.8	
MI	Corn	robin	Planesticus migratorius	9,295,297	$4,965.8	241,500
MI	Soybeans	robin	Planesticus migratorius	9,295,297	$4,462.8	47,520
MI	Wheat	robin	Planesticus migratorius	9,295,297	$4,503.2	35,280
SD	Corn	pheasant	Phasianus colchicus	696,004	$4,965.8	277,200
SD	Soybeans	pheasant	Phasianus colchicus	696,004	$4,462.8	63,000
SD	Wheat	pheasant	Phasianus colchicus	696,004	$4,503.2	119,590
TN	Corn	mockingbird	Mimus polyglottos	4,977,185	$4,965.8	79,360
TN	Soybeans	mockingbird	Mimus polyglottos	4,977,185	$4,462.8	33,250
TN	Wheat	mockingbird	Mimus polyglottos	4,977,185	$4,503.2	13,440
TX	Corn	mockingbird	Mimus polyglottos	16,986,510	$4,965.8	202,500
TX	Cotton	mockingbird	Mimus polyglottos	16,986,510	$2,014.6	3,322
TX	Soybeans	mockingbird	Mimus polyglottos	16,986,510	$4,462.8	12,870
TX	Wheat	mockingbird	Mimus polyglottos	16,986,510	$4,503.2	129,200

The tblStateCrop relation combines several attributes from the tblState, tblCrop, and tblProduction relations that appeared in Figure AP-7. The State Abbrev, State Bird, and State Population attributes are from the tblState relation. The Crop Name and Exports attributes are from the tblCrop relation. The State Abbrev, Crop Name, and Quantity attributes are from the tblProduction relation. The Bird Scientific Name attribute is a new attribute for the tblStateCrop relation, whose primary key is the combination of the State Abbrev and Crop Name attributes.

Notice the null value in the Quantity attribute for the state of Connecticut (State Abbrev CT). If you look back to Figure AP-7, you can see that there were no entries for Quantity for the state of Connecticut, which is why Quantity is null in the tblStateCrop table. However, note that Crop Name requires an entry because it is part of the composite key for the relation. If you want the state of CT to be in the relation, you need to assign a dummy Crop Name for the CT entry, in this case, Corn.

In the tblStateCrop relation, each attribute is related to other attributes. For example, a value for State Abbrev determines the value of State Population, and a value for State Population depends on the value of State Abbrev. In database discussions, the word functionally is used, as in: "State Abbrev functionally determines State Population" and "State Population is functionally dependent on State Abbrev." In this case, State Abbrev is called a determinant. A **determinant** is an attribute, or a collection of attributes, whose values determine the values of another attribute. We also state that an attribute is functionally dependent on another attribute (or collection of attributes) if that other attribute is a determinant for it.

You can graphically show a relation's functional dependencies and determinants in a bubble diagram. Bubble diagrams are also called data model diagrams and functional dependency diagrams. Figure AP-11 shows the bubble diagram for the tblStateCrop relation.

Figure AP-11 A bubble diagram for the tblStateCrop relation

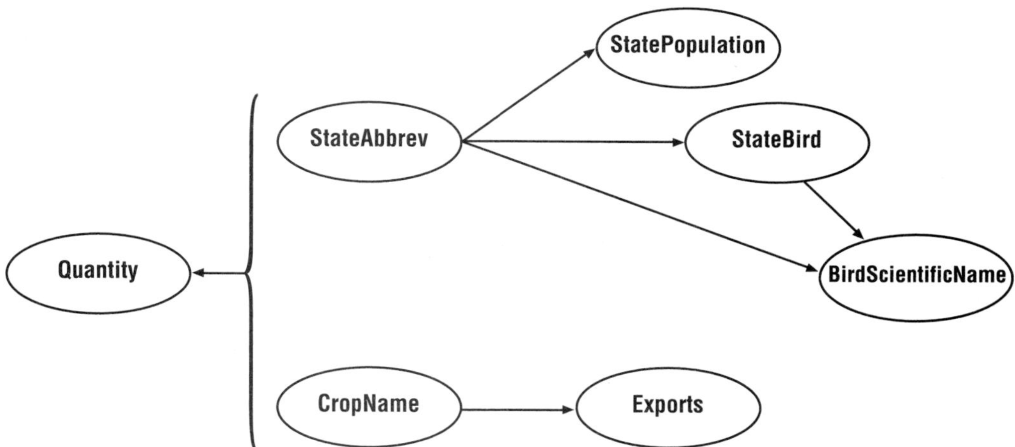

- State Abbrev is a determinant for State Population, State Bird, and Bird Scientific Name.
- Crop Name is a determinant for Exports.
- Quantity is functionally dependent on State Abbrev and Crop Name together.
- State Bird is a determinant for Bird Scientific Name.

Only Quantity is functionally dependent on the relation's full primary key, State Abbrev and Crop Name. State Population, State Bird, and Bird Scientific Name have partial dependencies, because they are functionally dependent on State Abbrev, which is part of the primary key. A **partial dependency** is a functional dependency on part of the primary key, instead of the entire primary key. Does another partial dependency exist in the tblStateCrop relation? Yes, Exports has a partial dependency on Crop Name.

Because State Abbrev is a determinant of both State Bird and Bird Scientific Name, and State Bird is a determinant of Bird Scientific Name, State Bird and Bird Scientific Name have a transitive dependency. A **transitive dependency** is a functional dependency between two nonkey attributes, which are both dependent on a third attribute.

How do you know which functional dependencies exist among a collection of attributes, and how do you recognize partial and transitive dependencies? The answers lie with the questions you ask as you gather the requirements for a database application. For each attribute and entity, you must gain an accurate understanding of its meaning and relationships in the context of the application. **Semantic object modeling** is an entire area of study within the database field devoted to the meanings and relationships of data.

Anomalies

When you use a DBMS, you are more likely to get results you can trust if you create your relations carefully. For example, problems might occur with relations that have partial and transitive dependencies, whereas you won't have as much trouble if you ensure that your relations include only attributes that are directly related to each other. Also, when you remove data redundancy from a relation, you improve that relation. **Data redundancy** occurs when you store the same data in more than one place.

The problems caused by data redundancy and by partial and transitive dependencies are called **anomalies**, because they are undesirable irregularities of relations. Anomalies are of three types: insertion, deletion, and update.

To examine the effects of these anomalies, consider the tblClient relation that is shown in Figure AP-12. The tblClient relation represents part of the database for Pet Sitters Unlimited, which is a company providing pet-sitting services for homeowners while they are on vacation. Pet Sitters Unlimited keeps track of the data about its clients and the clients' children, pets, and vets. The attributes for the tblClient relation include the composite key Client ID and Child Name, along with Client Name, Vet ID, and Vet Name.

Figure AP-12 The tblClient relation with insertion, deletion, and update anomalies

tblClient

primary key

ClientID	ChildName	ClientName	VetID	VetName
2173	Ryan	Barbara Hennessey	27	Pet Vet
4519	Pat	Vernon Noordsy	31	Pet Care
4519	Dana	Vernon Noordsy	31	Pet Care
8005	Dana	Sandra Amidon	27	Pet Vet
8005	Dani	Sandra Amidon	27	Pet Vet
8112	Pat	Helen Wandzell	24	Pets R Us

- An **insertion anomaly** occurs when you cannot add a row to a relation because you do not know the entire primary key value. For example, you cannot add the new client Cathy Corbett with a Client ID of 3322 to the tblClient relation when you do not know her children's names. Entity integrity prevents you from leaving any part of a primary key null. Because Child Name is part of the primary key, you cannot leave it null. To add the new client, your only option is to make up a Child Name, even if the client does not have children. This solution misrepresents the facts and is unacceptable, if a better approach is available.
- A **deletion anomaly** occurs when you delete data from a relation and unintentionally lose other critical data. For example, if you delete Client ID 8112 because Helen Wandzell is no longer a client, you also lose the only instance of Vet ID 24 in the database. Thus, you no longer know that Vet ID 24 is Pets R Us.
- An **update anomaly** occurs when you change one attribute value and either the DBMS must make more than one change to the database or else the database ends up containing inconsistent data. For example, if you change the Client Name, Vet ID, or Vet Name for Client ID 4519, the DBMS must change multiple rows of the tblClient relation. If the DBMS fails to change all the rows, the Client Name, Vet ID, or Vet Name now has two different values in the database and is inconsistent.

Normalization

Database design is the process of determining the precise relations needed for a given collection of attributes and placing those attributes into the correct relations. Crucial to good database design is understanding the functional dependencies of all attributes; recognizing the anomalies caused by data redundancy, partial dependencies, and transitive dependencies when they exist; and knowing how to eliminate the anomalies.

The process of identifying and eliminating anomalies is called **normalization**. Using normalization, you start with a collection of relations, apply sets of rules to eliminate anomalies, and produce a new collection of problem-free relations. The sets of rules are called **normal forms**. Of special interest for our purposes are the first three normal forms: first normal form, second normal form, and third normal form. First normal form improves the design of your relations, second normal form improves the first normal form design, and third normal form applies even more stringent rules to produce an even better design.

First Normal Form

Consider the tblClient relation shown in Figure AP-13. For each client, the relation contains Client ID, which is the primary key; the client's name and children's names; the ID and name of the client's vet; and the ID, name, and type of each client's pets. For example, Barbara Hennessey has no children and three pets, Vernon Noordsy has two children and one pet, Sandra Amidon has two children and two pets, and Helen Wandzell has one child and one pet. Because each entry in a relation must contain a single value, the structure shown in Figure AP-13 does not meet the requirements for a relation, therefore it is called an **unnormalized relation.** Child Name, which can have more than one value, is called a **repeating group.** The set of attributes that includes Pet ID, Pet Name, and Pet Type is a second repeating group in the structure.

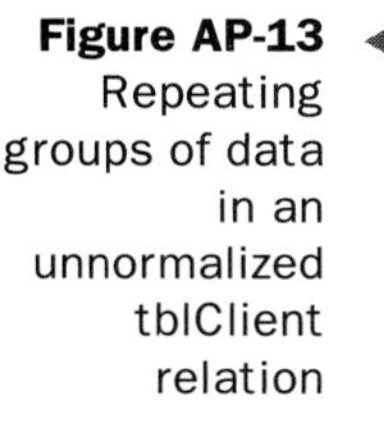

Figure AP-13 Repeating groups of data in an unnormalized tblClient relation

repeating group

tblClient

ClientID	ClientName	ChildName	VetID	VetName	PetID	PetName	PetType
2173	Barabara Hennessey		27	Pet Vet	1 2 4	Sam Hoober Sam	Bird Dog Hamster
4519	Vernon Noordsy	Pat Dana	31	Pet Care	2	Charlie	Cat
8005	Sandra Amidon	Dana Dani	27	Pet Vet	1 2	Beefer Kirby	Dog Cat
8112	Helen Wandzell	Pat	24	Pets R Us	3	Kirby	Dog

First normal form addresses this repeating-group situation. A relation is in **first normal form (1NF)** if it does not contain repeating groups. To remove a repeating group and convert to first normal form, you expand the primary key to include the primary key of the repeating group. You must perform this step carefully, however. If the unnormalized relation has independent repeating groups, you must perform the conversion step separately for each.

The repeating group of Child Name is independent from the repeating group of Pet ID, Pet Name, and Pet Type. That is, the number and names of a client's children are independent of the number, names, and types of a client's pets. Performing the conversion step to each independent repeating group produces the two 1NF relations shown in Figure AP-14.

Figure AP-14 After conversion to 1NF

primary key

tblChild

ClientID	ChildName	ClientName	VetID	VetName
4519	Pat	Vernon Noordsy	31	Pet Care
4519	Dana	Vernon Noordsy	31	Pet Care
8005	Dana	Sandra Amidon	27	Pet Vet
8005	Dani	Sandra Amidon	27	Pet Vet
8112	Pat	Helen Wandzell	24	Pets R Us

primary key

tblClient

ClientID	PetID	ClientName	VetID	VetName	PetName	PetType
2173	1	Barbara Hennessey	27	Pet Vet	Sam	Bird
2173	2	Barbara Hennessey	27	Pet Vet	Hoober	Dog
2173	4	Barbara Hennessey	27	Pet Vet	Sam	Hamster
4519	2	Vernon Noordsy	31	Pet Care	Charlie	Cat
8005	1	Sandra Amidon	27	Pet Vet	Beefer	Dog
8005	2	Sandra Amidon	27	Pet Vet	Kirby	Cat
8112	3	Helen Wandzell	24	Pets R Us	Kirby	Dog

The alternative way to describe the 1NF relations is:
tblChild (<u>Client ID</u>, <u>Child Name</u>, Client Name, Vet ID, Vet Name)
tblClient (<u>Client ID</u>, <u>Pet ID</u>, Client Name, Vet ID, Vet Name, Pet Name, Pet Type)

tblChild and tblClient are now true relations and both have composite keys. Both relations, however, suffer from insertion, deletion, and update anomalies. (Find examples of the three anomalies in both relations.) In the tblChild and tblClient relations, Client ID is a determinant for Client Name, Vet ID, and Vet Name, so partial dependencies exist in both relations. It is these partial dependencies that cause the anomalies in the two relations, and second normal form addresses the partial-dependency problem.

Second Normal Form

A relation in 1NF is in **second normal form (2NF)** if it does not contain any partial dependencies. To remove partial dependencies from a relation and convert it to second normal form, you perform two steps. First, identify the functional dependencies for every attribute in the relation. Second, if necessary, create new relations and place each attribute in a relation, so that the attribute is functionally dependent on the entire primary key. If you need to create new relations, restrict them to ones with a primary key that is a subset of the original composite key. Note that partial dependencies occur only when you have a composite key; a relation in first normal form with a single-attribute primary key is automatically in second normal form.

Figure AP-15 shows the functional dependencies for the 1NF tblChild and tblClient relations.

Figure AP-15 A bubble diagram for the 1NF tblChild and the tblClient relations

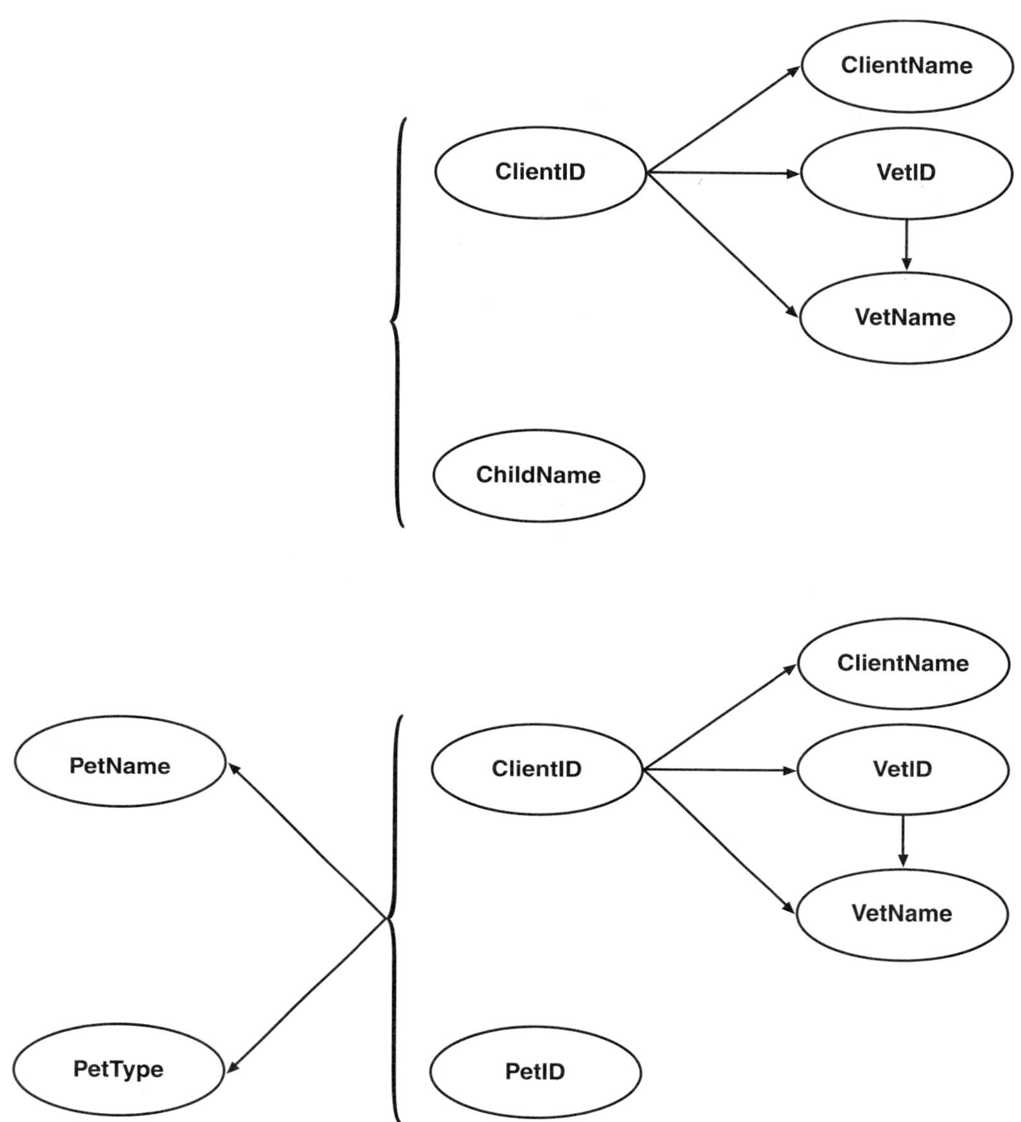

Client ID is a determinant for Client Name, Vet ID, and Vet Name in both relations. The composite key Client ID and Pet ID is a determinant for Pet Name and Pet Type. Child Name is not a determinant, nor is Pet ID. Is the composite key of Client ID and Child Name a determinant? No, it is not a determinant. What happens, however, if you do not have a relation with this composite key? You lose the names of the children of each client. You need to retain this composite key in a relation to preserve the important 1:M attribute relationship between Client ID and Child Name. Performing the second conversion step produces the three 2NF relations shown in Figure AP-16.

Figure AP-16 After conversion to 2NF

tblClient

primary key

ClientID	ClientName	VetID	VetName
2173	Barbara Hennessey	27	Pet Vet
4519	Vernon Noordsy	31	Pet Care
8005	Sandra Amidon	27	Pet Vet
8112	Helen Wandzell	24	Pets R Us

primary key

tblChild

ClientID	ChildName
4519	Pat
4519	Dana
8005	Dana
8005	Dani
8112	Pat

primary key

tblPet

ClientID	PetID	PetName	PetType
2173	1	Sam	Bird
2173	2	Hoober	Dog
2173	4	Sam	Hamster
4519	2	Charlie	Cat
8005	1	Beefer	Dog
8005	2	Kirby	Cat
8112	3	Kirby	Dog

The alternative way to describe the 2NF relations is:
tblClient (<u>Client ID</u>, Client Name, Vet ID, Vet Name)
tblChild (<u>Client ID</u>, <u>Child Name</u>)
    Foreign key: Client ID to tblClient relation
tblPet (<u>Client ID</u>, <u>Pet ID</u>, Pet Name, Pet Type)
    Foreign key: Client ID to tblClient relation

All three relations are in second normal form. Do anomalies still exist? The tblChild and tblPet relations show no anomalies, but tblClient suffers from anomalies caused by the transitive dependency between Vet ID and Vet Name. (Find examples of the three anomalies caused by the transitive dependency.) You can see the transitive dependency in the bubble diagram shown in Figure AP-15; Vet ID is a determinant for Vet Name and Client ID is a determinant for Vet ID and Vet Name. Third normal form addresses the transitive-dependency problem.

Third Normal Form

A relation in 2NF is in **third normal form (3NF)** if every determinant is a candidate key. This definition for 3NF is referred to as **Boyce-Codd normal form (BCNF)** and is an improvement over the original version of 3NF.

To convert a relation to third normal form, remove the attributes that depend on the non-candidate-key determinant and place them into a new relation with the determinant as the primary key. For the tblClient relation, you remove Vet Name from the relation, create a new tblVet relation, place Vet Name in the tblVet relation, and then make Vet ID the primary key of the tblVet relation. Note that only Vet Name is removed from the tblClient relation; Vet ID remains as a foreign key in the tblClient relation. Figure AP-17 shows the database design for the four 3NF relations.

Figure AP-17 After conversion to 3NF

tblVet (primary key: VetID)

VetID	VetName
24	Pets R Us
27	Pet Vet
31	Pet Care

tblClient (primary key: ClientID)

ClientID	ClientName	VetID
2173	Barbara Hennessey	27
4519	Vernon Noordsy	31
8005	Sandra Amidon	27
8112	Helen Wandzell	24

tblChild (primary key: ClientID + ChildName)

ClientID	ChildName
4519	Pat
4519	Dana
8005	Dana
8005	Dani
8112	Pat

tblPet (primary key: ClientID + PetID)

ClientID	PetID	PetName	PetType
2173	1	Sam	Bird
2173	2	Hoober	Dog
2173	4	Sam	Hamster
4519	2	Charlie	Cat
8005	1	Beefer	Dog
8005	2	Kirby	Cat
8112	3	Kirby	Dog

The alternative way to describe the 3NF relations is:
tblVet (Vet ID, Vet Name)
tblClient (Client ID, Client Name, Vet ID)
  Foreign key: Vet ID to tblVet relation
tblChild (Client ID, Child Name)
  Foreign key: Client ID to tblClient relation
tblPet (Client ID, Pet ID, Pet Name, Pet Type)
  Foreign key: Client ID to tblClient relation

The four relations have no anomalies, because you have eliminated all the data redundancy, partial dependencies, and transitive dependencies. Normalization provides the framework for eliminating anomalies and delivering an optimal database design, which you should always strive to achieve. You should be aware, however, that experts often denormalize relations to improve database performance—specifically, to decrease the time it takes the database to respond to a user's commands and requests. When you denormalize a relation, you reintroduce redundancy to the relation. At the same time, you reintroduce anomalies. Thus, improving performance exposes a database to potential integrity problems. Only database experts should denormalize relations, but even experts first complete the normalization of their relations.

Questions

1. What are the formal names for a table, for a row, and for a column?
2. What is a domain?
3. What is an entity?
4. What is the relationship between a primary key and a candidate key?
5. What is a composite key?
6. What is a foreign key?
7. EXPLORE Look for an example of a one-to-one relationship, an example of a one-to-many relationship, and an example of a many-to-many relationship in a newspaper, magazine, book, or everyday situation you encounter. For each one, name the entities and select the primary and foreign keys.
8. When do you use an entity subtype?
9. What is a composite entity in an entity-relationship diagram?
10. What is the entity integrity constraint?
11. What is referential integrity?
12. What does the cascades option, which is used with referential integrity, accomplish?
13. What are partial and transitive dependencies?
14. What three types of anomalies can be exhibited by a relation, and what problems do they cause?
15. Figure AP-18 shows the tblVet, tblClient, and tblChild relations with primary keys Vet ID, Client ID, and both Client ID and Child Name, respectively. Which two integrity constraints do these relations violate and why?

Figure AP-18

tblVet

VetID	VetName
24	Pets R Us
27	Pet Vet
31	Pet Care

tblClient

ClientID	ClientName	VetID
2173	Barbara Hennessey	27
4519	Vernon Noordsy	31
8005	Sandra Amidon	37
8112	Helen Wandzell	24

tblChild

ClientID	ChildName
4519	Pat
4519	Dana
8005	
8005	Dani
8112	Pat

16. The tblState and tblCapital relations, shown in Figure AP-5, are described as follows:
    tblState (State Abbrev, State Name, Entered Union Order, State Bird, State Population)
    tblCapital (Capital Name, State Abbrev, Year Designated, Phone Area Code, Capital Population)
    Foreign key: State Abbrev to tblState relation
    Add the attribute County Name for the county or counties containing the state capital to this database, justify where you placed it (that is, in an existing relation or in a new one), and draw the entity–relationship diagram for all the entities. The counties for the state capitals shown in Figure AP-5 are Travis and Williamson counties for Austin TX; Hartford county for Hartford CT; Clinton, Eaton, and Ingham counties for Lansing MI; Davidson county for Nashville TN; Hughes county for Pierre SD.
17. Suppose you have a relation for a dance studio. The attributes are dancer's identification number, dancer's name, dancer's address, dancer's telephone number, class identification number, day that the class meets, time that the class meets, instructor name, and instructor identification number. Assume that each dancer takes one class, each class meets only once a week and has one instructor, and each instructor can teach more than one class. In what normal form is the relation currently, given the following shorthand description?
    tblDancer (<u>Dancer ID</u>, Dancer Name, Dancer Addr, Dancer Phone, Class ID, Class Day, Class Time, Instr Name, Instr ID)
    Convert this relation to 3NF and then draw an entity–relationship diagram for this database.
18. Store the following attributes for a library database: Author Code, Author Name, Book Title, Borrower Address, Borrower Name, Borrower Card Number, Copies Of Book, ISBN (International Standard Book Number), Loan Date, Publisher Code, Publisher Name, and Publisher Address. A one-to-many relationship exists between publishers and books. Many-to-many relationships exist between authors and books and between borrowers and books.
    a. Name the entities for the library database.
    b. Create the relations for the library database and describe them using the shorthand method. Be sure the relations are in third normal form.
    c. Draw an entity–relationship diagram for the library database.

Relational Databases and Database Design Index

Index

D

N

T

Task Reference

TASK	PAGE #	RECOMMENDED METHOD
Access, exiting	AC 10	Click the Access window Close button
Access, starting	AC 9	Click Start, point to Programs, then click Microsoft Access
Action Arguments, setting by dragging	IAC 67	Drag the appropriate object from the Database window list to the appropriate argument text box in the Macro window
Action, adding by dragging	IAC 63	See Reference Window: Creating an Action by Dragging
Action, adding by selecting	IAC 60	In the Macro window, click the Action list arrow, then select the action
Aggregate function, adding to a query	AC 141	See Reference Window: Using Aggregate Function in the Query Design Grid
Answer Wizard, accessing	AC 24	Click Help, then click Answer Wizard
Append query, creating	IAC 25	See Reference Window: Creating an Append Query
AutoForm form, creating	AC 163	See Reference Window: Creating a Form with AutoForm
AutoReport report, creating	AC 217	See Reference Window: Creating a Report with AutoReport
Blank report, creating	AC 223	See Reference Window: Creating a Blank Report in the Report Design Window
Briefcase replica, creating	IAC 4	See Reference Window: Creating a Briefcase Replica of a Database
Briefcase replica, synchronizing	IAC 8	See Reference Window: Synchronizing the Design Master and a Replica
Button image, choosing for custom toolbar button	IAC 117	Right-click the toolbar button, click Choose Button Image, select button image, then click OK
Calculated field, adding to a query	AC 139	See Reference Window: Adding a Calculated Field to the Query Design Grid
Caption, entering for a field	AC 49	Type caption in the Caption property text box in the Design View window
Caption, changing a label's	AC 188	See Reference Window: Changing a Label's Caption
Change, undoing		Click
Chart, embedding in a report	AC 248	See Reference Window: Using the Chart Wizard to Create a Report with an Embedded Chart
Colors, changing in a form	AC 199	See Reference Window: Adding Background Color to a Control on a Form
Column, resizing	AC 50	See Reference Window: Resizing Columns in a Datasheet

Task Reference

TASK	PAGE #	RECOMMENDED METHOD
Command button, adding to a form	IAC 81	See Reference Window: Adding a Command Button to a Form
Command button, adding to a form using Control Wizards	IAC 82	See Reference Window: Adding a Command Button to a Form Using Control Wizards
Control, deleting	AC 229	See Reference Window: Deleting Controls
Control, morphing	AC 202	Right click the control, point to Change to, then click the new type
Control, resizing	AC 189	Click the control to display sizing handles, then drag a sizing handle
Controls, aligning on a form	AC 191	See Reference Window: Aligning Objects in a Form
Controls, arranging on a form	AC 186	See Reference Window: Selecting, Moving and Deleting Controls
Controls, arranging on a report	AC 228	See Reference Window: Moving and Resizing Controls
Crosstab query, creating	IAC 13	See Reference Window: Using the Crosstab Query Wizard
Custom form, creating	AC 182	See Reference Window: Creating a Form in the Form Design Window
Custom menu bar, attaching to a form	IAC 112	See Reference Window: Attaching a Custom Menu Bar to a Form
Custom menu bar, creating	IAC 103	See Reference Window: Creating a Custom Menu Bar with Menu Builder
Custom toolbar, creating	IAC 116	See Reference Window: Creating a Custom Toolbar
Data, finding in a datasheet	AC 88	See Reference Window: Finding Data in a Table
Data, maintaining using a form	AC 170	See Reference Window: Maintaining Table Data Using a Form
Data, replacing in a datasheet	AC 91	See Reference Window: Replacing Data in a Table
Database, backing up	AC 103	See Reference Window: Backing Up an Access Database
Database, closing	AC 22	Click the Database window Close button
Database, compacting	AC 105	See Reference Window: Compacting a Database
Database, creating	AC 37	See Reference Window: Creating a Database
Database, opening	AC 11	Click [icon], then select the file from the Open dialog box
Datasheet View, switching to	AC 47	Click [icon]

Task Reference

TASK	PAGE #	RECOMMENDED METHOD
Datasheet, printing	AC 47	Click
Data type, assigning to field	AC 40	Select data type from the data type list in the Design View window
Date, adding to a report	AC 233	See Reference Window: Adding a Date to a Report
Decimal places, changing the number of in a field	AC 53	Select decimal places in Decimal Places property text box in the Design View window
Default value, defining for a field	AC 52	Type default value in Default Value property text box in the Design View window
Delete query, creating	IAC 31	See Reference Window: Creating a Delete Query
Design Master, creating	IAC 4	See Reference Window: Creating a Briefcase Replica of a Database
Design Master, synchronizing	IAC 8	See Reference Window: Synchronizing the Design Master and a Replica
Design View, switching to	AC 47	Click
Duplicate values, hiding in a report	AC 243	See Reference Window: Hiding Duplicate Values in a Report
Embedded object, editing	AC 246	Double-click the object to start the application that created it
Event procedure, adding	IAC 142	See Reference Window: Adding an Event Procedure
Field, adding to a form or report	AC 185	Click field name in the field list box, then drag the field to the form
Field, adding to a table structure	AC 59	See Reference Window: Adding a Field to a Table Structure
Field, deleting from a table structure	AC 58	See Reference Window: Deleting a Field from a Table Structure
Field, deleting from the Query Design grid	AC 139	Right click the field selector, then click Cut
Field, excluding from the query results	AC 123	Click the field's Show box in the Query Design grid to remove the check mark
Field, inserting in Query Design grid	AC 118	Drag the field name from the field list to the Query Design grid
Field description, assigning	AC 42	Type description in Description text box in Design View window
Field size, assigning	AC 43	Select or enter field size in Field Size text box in the Design View window
Field values, changing	AC 79	See Reference Window: Changing Field Values in a Record

Task Reference

TASK	PAGE #	RECOMMENDED METHOD
Fields, adding all to a Query Design grid	AC 118	Double-click field list box title bar, then drag the field list to the Query Design grid
Fields, naming	AC 40	Type name in the Field Name text box in the Design View window
Filter, applying	AC 179	Click
Filter by form, creating	AC 175	See Reference Window: Selecting Records with Filter by Form
Filter by selection, creating	AC 173	See Reference Window: Selecting Records with Filter by Selection
Filter saved as a query, applying	AC 179	See Reference Window: Applying a Filter that Was Saved as a Query
Filter, removing	AC 174	Click
Filter, saving as a query	AC 178	See Reference Window: Saving a Filter as a Query
Find Duplicates query, creating	IAC 18	See Reference Window: Using the Find Duplicates Query Wizard
Find Unmatched query, creating	IAC 20	See Reference Window: Using the Find Unmatched Query Wizard
First record, moving to	AC 17	Click
Font, changing a datasheet's	AC 86	See Reference Window: Changing a Datasheet's Font Properties
Foreground color, setting in a form	IAC 152	Right-click the object, click Properties, then set the Fore Color property value
Form Header and Footer, adding to a form	AC 185	Click View, then click Form Header/Footer
Form View, switching to	AC 192	Click
Form, creating using AutoForm	AC 163	See Reference Window: Creating a Form with AutoForm
Form, creating in the Form Design Window	AC 182	See Reference Window: Creating a Form in the Form Design Window
Form, creating using the Form Wizard	AC 166	See Reference Window: Creating a Main/Subform Form using the Form Wizard
Form, opening	AC 21	Select the form in the Database window, then click the Open button
Form, printing	AC 174	Click
Form, saving	AC 165	Click
Function, creating	IAC 135	Enter function code in the Module window
Graphic image, adding to a form	AC 194	See Reference Window: Adding a Graphic Image to a Form

Task Reference

TASK	PAGE #	RECOMMENDED METHOD
Graphic image, linking in a report	AC 254	See Reference Window: Inserting a Linked Object in a Report
Grouping fields, adding to a report	AC 224	Click [icon], then either double-click the field list title bar to highlight all the fields and drag to the report, or place pointer on field names and drag to the report
Help, accessing	AC 23	Click Help on the menu bar
Index, creating	AC 67	Type Yes in the Indexed property text box in the Design View window
Indexes, displaying a table's	AC 67	Click [icon]
Input mask, defining for a field	AC 54	See Reference Window: Creating an Input Mask with the Input Mask Wizard
Label, adding to a form or report	AC 231	See Reference Window: Adding a Label to a Report
Last record, moving to	AC 17	Click [icon]
Lines, adding to a form or report	AC 236	See Reference Window: Adding a Line to a Report
Linked object, editing	AC 250	Start the application that created the object, open the object and edit it
Links, updating	AC 257	Click Edit, then click OLE/DDE Links, select the object, then click the Update Now button
List box, adding to a form or report	AC 196	See Reference Window: Adding a List Box to a Form with the Control Wizard
List box control, adding to a form	IAC 79	See Reference Window: Adding a List Box to a Form with the Control Wizard
Lookup Wizard field, defining	AC 98	See Reference Window: Defining a Lookup Wizard Field
Macro group, creating	IAC 88	See Reference Window: Creating a Macro Group
Macro window, opening	IAC 57	In the Database window, click the Macros tab, then click Open
Macro, running	IAC 59	In the Database window, click the Macros tab, select the macro, then click Run
Macro, saving	IAC 58	Click [icon]
Macro, single stepping	IAC 67	See Reference Window: Single-Stepping a Macro
Macros, creating	IAC 57	See Reference Window: Creating a New Macro
Make table query	IAC 23	See Reference Window: Creating a Make Table Query
Module, saving	IAC 138	Click [icon], enter module name, then click OK

Task Reference

TASK	PAGE #	RECOMMENDED METHOD
Multiple selection criteria, defining in Query Design grid	AC 135	See Reference Window: Defining Multiple Selection Criteria
Next record, moving to	AC 17	Click
Object, copying in the same database	IAC 84	See Reference Window: Copying an Object in the Same Database
On Load property, setting in a form	IAC 154	Right-click the form selector, click Properties, then set the On Load property value
Page numbers, adding to a report	AC 234	See Reference Window: Adding Page Numbers to a Report
Parameter query, creating	AC 154	See Reference Window: Creating a Parameter Query
Previous record, moving to	AC 17	Click
Primary key, defining	AC 42	Click
Procedure, adding to a standard module	IAC 148	See Reference Window: Adding a New Procedure to a Standard Module
Procedure, testing in the Debug Window	IAC 139	See Reference Window: Testing a Procedure in the Debug Window
Procedures, compiling	IAC 143	See Reference Window: Compiling Procedures in Modules
Query results, printing	AC 133	Click
Query results, sorting a single field	AC 130	See Reference Window: Selecting a Sort Key in the Query Design Window
Query results, viewing	AC 115	Click
Query, creating with the Simple Query Wizard	AC 113	See Reference Window: Creating a Query with the Simple Query Wizard
Query, opening	AC 120	Click the query name, then click the Open button
Query, running	AC 117	Click
Query, saving	AC 120	Click
Query, saving under a new name	AC 120	Click File, click Save As/Export, type new name in the New Name text box, then click the OK button
Record, creating a new blank	AC 77	Click
Record group calculations, adding to a query	AC 144	See Reference Window: Using Record Group Calculations
Record, adding to a table	AC 77	See Reference Window: Adding a Record to a Table

Task Reference

TASK	PAGE #	RECOMMENDED METHOD
Record, deleting from a table	AC 80	Right click record selector, then click Cut
Records, printing selected	AC 132	Select records in Datasheet View, then click
Records, quick sorting on a single field	AC 95	See Reference Window: Sorting Records on a Single Field in Datasheet View with Quick-Sort
Records, grouping in a report	AC 238	See Reference Window: Sorting and Grouping Data in a Report
Records, sorting in a report	AC 238	See Reference Window: Sorting and Grouping Data in a Report
Records, quick sorting on multiple fields	AC 95	See Reference Window: Sorting Records on Multiple Fields in Datasheet View with Quick-Sort
Records, sorting in a query	AC 130	See Reference Window: Selecting a Sort Key in the Query Design Window
Relationship, defining between tables	AC 152	See Reference Window: Adding a Relationship Between Two Tables
Relationship, establishing	AC 151	See Reference Window: Adding a Relationship Between Two Tables
Replica, creating	IAC 4	See Reference Window: Creating a Briefcase Replica of a Database
Replica, synchronizing	IAC 8	See Reference Window: Synchronizing the Design Master and a Replica
Report Header and Footer, adding to a report	AC 239	Click View, then click Report Header and Footer
Report, creating using AutoReport	AC 217	See Reference Window: Creating a Report with AutoReport
Report, creating using the Report Wizard	AC 219	See Reference Window: Creating a Report with the Report Wizard
Report, printing	AC 221	Click
Report, saving	AC 218	Click
Self Join, creating	IAC 41	See Reference Window: Creating a Self-Join
Selection criteria, defining in Query Design grid	AC 121	See Reference Window: Defining Record Selection Criteria
Selection criteria, deleting in Query Design grid	AC 127	Click in criterion text box, press the [F2] key, then press the [Delete] key
Shortcut menu, displaying an object's	AC 29	Right click on object
Sort keys, adding to a report	AC 238	See Reference Window: Sorting and Grouping Data in the Report

Task Reference

TASK	PAGE #	RECOMMENDED METHOD
Special effects, adding to an object	AC 200	See Reference Window: Changing the Special Effects Property for a Control
Spelling, checking in records	AC 97	See Reference Window: Using Access's Spelling Feature to Check Spelling of Field Values
SQL window, viewing	IAC 45	See Reference Window: Viewing the SQL Window
Standard module, creating	IAC 134	See Reference Window: Creating a New Standard Module
Startup options, setting	IAC 126	See Reference Window: Setting the Database Startup Options
Switchboard, creating	IAC 92	See Reference Window: Creating a Switchboard with the Switchboard Manager
Table structure, saving	AC 46	Click
Table, creating in Design View	AC 39	See Reference Window: Creating a Table in Design View
Table, creating using Table Wizard	AC 63	See Reference Window: Creating a Table with the Table Wizard
Table, deleting	AC 85	See Reference Window: Deleting a Table
Table, importing	AC 82	See Reference Window: Importing an Access Table
Table, opening	AC 15	Click the table name, then click the Open button
Table, renaming	AC 85	Right click table name, then click Rename
Table Analyzer Wizard, using	AC 83	See Reference Window: Using the Table Analyzer Wizard
Text box, adding to a form or report	AC 231	Click the Text Box button in the toolbox, move the pointer to the form or report, then click the mouse button to place the text box
Top-Value query, creating	IAC 34	See Reference Window: Creating a Top-Value Query
Totals, calculating in a report	AC 240	See Reference Window: Calculating Totals in a Report
Update query, creating	IAC 28	See Reference Window: Creating an Update Query